S0-BAK-284

Sixth Edition

World Civilizations

The Global Experience

AP* Edition

Peter N. Stearns
George Mason University

Michael Adas
Rutgers University

Stuart B. Schwartz
Yale University

Marc Jason Gilbert
Hawaii Pacific University

Longman

Boston Columbus Indianapolis New York San Francisco Upper Saddle River
Amsterdam Cape Town Dubai London Madrid Milan Munich Paris Montréal Toronto
Delhi Mexico City São Paulo Sydney Hong Kong Seoul Singapore Taipei Tokyo

Editorial Director: Craig Campanella
Publisher: Charlyce Jones Owen
Editorial Assistant: Maureen Diana
Director of Marketing: Brandy Dawson
Senior Marketing Manager: Maureen E. Prado Roberts
Senior Managing Editor: Ann Marie McCarthy
Marketing Assistant: Marissa C. O'Brien
Senior Project Manager: Denise Forlow
Senior Manufacturing and Operations Manager for Arts & Sciences: Nick Sklitsis
Operations Specialist: Christina Amato
Senior Art Director: Maria Lange
Interior Design: Jill Little
Cover Designer: Jill Lehan
Cover Art: Babur (r.1526–30) Reading, Mughal (w/c on paper), Das, Bishn (fl.1613–19) / British Library, London, UK / The Bridgeman Art Library

Photo Researchers: Beth Brenzel and Francelle Carapetyan
Manager, Rights and Permissions: Zina Arabia
Manager, Visual Research: Beth Brenzel
Manager, Cover Visual Research and Permissions: Karen Sanatar
Image Permissions Coordinator: Debbie Hewitson
Director of Media and Assessment: Brian Hyland
Media Editor: Sarah Kinney
Supplements Editor: Emsal Hasan
Full-Service Project Management and Composition: Bruce Hobart/Laserwords Maine
Printer/Binder: Courier/Kendallville
Cover Printer: Lehigh-Phoenix Color/Hagerstown
Text Type Face: Minion

Credits and acknowledgements borrowed from other sources and reproduced, with permission, in this textbook appear on appropriate page within text (or on page C-1).

Copyright © 2011, 2007, 2004, 2001 Pearson Education, Inc., publishing as Longman, One Lake St., Upper Saddle River, NJ 07458. All rights reserved. Manufactured in the United States of America. This publication is protected by Copyright, and permission should be obtained from the publisher prior to any prohibited reproduction, storage in a retrieval system, or transmission in any form or by any means, electronic, mechanical, photocopying, recording, or likewise. To obtain permission(s) to use material from this work, please submit a written request to Pearson Education, Inc., Permissions Department, One Lake St., Upper Saddle River, NJ 07458.

Many of the designations used by manufacturers and sellers to distinguish their products are claimed as trademarks. Where those designations appear in this book, and the publisher was aware of the trademark claim, the designations have been printed in initial or all caps.

AP* and Advanced Placement Programs are registered trademarks of The College Board, which was not involved in the production of, and does not endorse, this book.

Library of Congress Cataloging-in-Publication Data

World civilizations : the global experience / Peter N. Stearns . . . [et al.].—6th ed.
   p. cm.
Includes bibliographical references and index.
ISBN 0-205-65956-X (combined)—ISBN 0-205-65958-6 (vol. 1)—
  ISBN 0-205-65959-4 (vol. 2)—ISBN 0-13-136020-5 (AP edition)
  1. Civilization—History. 2. Civilization—History—Sources. I. Stearns, Peter N.
CB69.W666 2011
909—dc22
    2009038635

10 9 8 7 6 5 4 3 2

Longman
is an imprint of

www.pearsonhighered.com

High School Binding ISBN 10: 0-13-136020-5
High School Binding ISBN 13: 978-0-13-136020-4

Brief Contents

PART I

FROM HUNTING AND GATHERING TO CIVILIZATIONS, 2.5 MILLION–1000 B.C.E.: ORIGINS 2

1 From Human Prehistory to the Early Civilizations 8

PART II

THE CLASSICAL PERIOD, 1000 B.C.E.–500 C.E.: UNITING LARGE REGIONS 34

2 Classical Civilization: China 40
3 Classical Civilization: India 60
4 Classical Civilizations in the Mediterranean and Middle East 80
5 The Classical Period: Directions, Diversities, and Declines by 500 C.E. 104

PART III

THE POSTCLASSICAL PERIOD, 500–1450: NEW FAITH AND NEW COMMERCE 130

6 The First Global Civilization: The Rise and Spread of Islam 136
7 Abbasid Decline and the Spread of Islamic Civilization to South and Southeast Asia 162
8 African Civilizations and the Spread of Islam 184
9 Civilization in Eastern Europe: Byzantium and Orthodox Europe 204
10 A New Civilization Emerges in Western Europe 220
11 The Americas on the Eve of Invasion 244
12 Reunification and Renaissance in Chinese Civilization: The Era of the Tang and Song Dynasties 266
13 The Spread of Chinese Civilization: Japan, Korea, and Vietnam 290
14 The Last Great Nomadic Challenges: From Chinggis Khan to Timur 314
15 The World in 1450: Changing Balance of World Power 336

PART IV

THE EARLY MODERN PERIOD, 1450–1750: THE WORLD SHRINKS 354

16 The World Economy 360
17 The Transformation of the West, 1450–1750 380
18 The Rise of Russia 400
19 Early Latin America 416
20 Africa and the Africans in the Age of the Atlantic Slave Trade 444
21 The Muslim Empires 468
22 Asian Transitions in an Age of Global Change 494

PART V

THE DAWN OF THE INDUSTRIAL AGE, 1750–1914 520

23 The Emergence of Industrial Society in the West, 1750–1914 526
24 Industrialization and Imperialism: The Making of the European Global Order 550
25 The Consolidation of Latin America, 1830–1920 574
26 Civilizations in Crisis: The Ottoman Empire, the Islamic Heartlands, and Qing China 602
27 Russia and Japan: Industrialization Outside the West 626

PART VI

THE NEWEST STAGE OF WORLD HISTORY: 1914–PRESENT 650

28 Descent into the Abyss: World War I and the Crisis of the European Global Order 658
29 The World between the Wars: Revolutions, Depression, and Authoritarian Response 686
30 A Second Global Conflict and the End of the European World Order 724
31 Western Society and Eastern Europe in the Decades of the Cold War 752
32 Latin America: Revolution and Reaction into the 21st Century 782
33 Africa, the Middle East, and Asia in the Era of Independence 804
34 Rebirth and Revolution: Nation-Building in East Asia and the Pacific Rim 830
35 Power, Politics, and Conflict in World History, 1990–2010 860
36 Globalization and Resistance 882

Contents

Maps   xi

Teacher to Teacher   xiii

AP* Course Topic Correlation   xiv

Preface   xviii

Supplements   xxiii

About the Authors   xxv

Prologue   xxvii

PART I

FROM HUNTING AND GATHERING TO CIVILIZATIONS, 2.5 MILLION–1000 B.C.E.: ORIGINS   2

CHAPTER 1 From Human Prehistory to the Early Civilizations   8
Human Life in the Era of Hunters and Gatherers   9
The Neolithic Revolution   12
Civilization   15
VISUALIZING THE PAST: Mesopotamia in Maps   20
DOCUMENT: Aryan Poetry in Praise of a War Horse   23
The Heritage of the River Valley Civilizations   25
THINKING HISTORICALLY: The Idea of Civilization in World Historical Perspective   26
GLOBAL CONNECTIONS: The Early Civilizations and the World   29
Further Readings   29
On the Web   30
AP* Test Prep   31

PART II

THE CLASSICAL PERIOD, 1000 B.C.E.–500 C.E.: UNITING LARGE REGIONS   34

CHAPTER 2 Classical Civilization: China   40
Establishment of Political Order   41
Patterns in Classical China   42
Political Institutions   46
VISUALIZING THE PAST: Capital Designs and Patterns of Political Power   47
Religion and Culture   48
DOCUMENT: Teachings of the Rival Chinese Schools   50
Economy and Society   52
THINKING HISTORICALLY: Women in Patriarchal Societies   52
How Chinese Civilization Fits Together   55
GLOBAL CONNECTIONS: Classical China and the World   57
Further Readings   57

On the Web   57
AP* Test Prep   59

CHAPTER 3 Classical Civilization: India   60
The Framework for Indian History: Geography and a Formative Period   62
Patterns in Classical India   64
Political Institutions   66
Religion and Culture   67
DOCUMENT: A Guardian's Farewell Speech to a Young Woman About to Be Married   69
Economy and Society   72
Indian Influence and Comparative Features   73
THINKING HISTORICALLY: Inequality as the Social Norm   74
VISUALIZING THE PAST: The Pattern of Trade in the Ancient Eurasian World   76
GLOBAL CONNECTIONS: India and the Wider World   76
Further Readings   77
On the Web   78
AP* Test Prep   79

CHAPTER 4 Classical Civilizations in the Mediterranean and Middle East   80
The Persian Empire: A New Perspective in the Middle East   82
Patterns of Greek and Roman History   84
Greek and Roman Political Institutions   88
THINKING HISTORICALLY: The Classical Mediterranean in Comparative Perspective   89
Religion and Culture   92
VISUALIZING THE PAST: Political Rituals in Persia   95
Economy and Society in the Mediterranean   95
DOCUMENT: Rome and a Values Crisis   97
Toward the Fall of Rome   98
GLOBAL CONNECTIONS: Persia, Greece, Rome, and the World   99
Further Readings   100
On the Web   101
AP* Test Prep   103

CHAPTER 5 The Classical Period: Directions, Diversities, and Declines by 500 C.E.   104
Expansion and Integration   106
Beyond the Classical Civilizations   107
THINKING HISTORICALLY: Nomads and Cross-Civilization Contacts and Exchanges   108
Decline in China and India   112
Decline and Fall in Rome   113
The New Religious Map   118
DOCUMENT: The Popularization of Buddhism   119
VISUALIZING THE PAST: Religious Geography   123
GLOBAL CONNECTIONS: The Late Classical Period and the World   124

Further Readings   125
On the Web   125
AP* Test Prep   127

PART III

THE POSTCLASSICAL PERIOD, 500–1450:
NEW FAITH AND NEW COMMERCE   130

CHAPTER 6 **The First Global Civilization:**
The Rise and Spread of Islam   136
Desert and Town: The Pre-Islamic Arabian World   137
The Life of Muhammad and the Genesis of Islam   142
The Arab Empire of the Umayyads   145
THINKING HISTORICALLY: Civilization and Gender
    Relationships   152
From Arab to Islamic Empire: The Early Abbasid Era   154
VISUALIZING THE PAST: The Mosque as a Symbol of Islamic
    Civilization   156
DOCUMENT: *The Thousand and One Nights* as a Mirror
    of Elite Society in the Abbasid Era   158
GLOBAL CONNECTIONS: Early Islam and the World   159
Further Readings   160
On the Web   160
AP* Test Prep   161

CHAPTER 7 **Abbasid Decline and the Spread**
of Islamic Civilization to South and Southeast
Asia   162
The Islamic Heartlands in the Middle
    and Late Abbasid Eras   163
DOCUMENT: Ibn Khaldun on the Rise and Decline
    of Empires   168
An Age of Learning and Artistic Refinements   168
The Coming of Islam to South Asia   172
VISUALIZING THE PAST: The Patterns of Islam's
    Global Expansions   173
THINKING HISTORICALLY: Conversion and Accommodation
    in the Spread of World Religions   178
The Spread of Islam to Southeast Asia   180
GLOBAL CONNECTIONS: Islam: A Bridge Between
    Worlds   182
Further Readings   182
On the Web   182
AP* Test Prep   183

CHAPTER 8 **African Civilizations and the Spread**
of Islam   184
African Societies: Diversity and Similarities   185
Kingdoms of the Grasslands   189
DOCUMENT: The Great Oral Tradition and the Epic
    of Sundiata   192

VISUALIZING THE PAST: The Architecture of Faith   195
The Swahili Coast of East Africa   195
Peoples of the Forest and Plains   197
THINKING HISTORICALLY: Two Transitions in the History
    of World Population   198
GLOBAL CONNECTIONS: Internal Development
    and Global Contacts   202
Further Readings   202
On the Web   203
AP* Test Prep   203

CHAPTER 9 **Civilization in Eastern Europe:**
Byzantium and Orthodox Europe   204
Civilization in Eastern Europe   204
The Byzantine Empire   206
VISUALIZING THE PAST: Women and Power
    in Byzantium   209
The Split Between Eastern and Western Christianity   210
THINKING HISTORICALLY: Eastern and Western Europe:
    The Problem of Boundaries   213
The Spread of Civilization in Eastern Europe   213
The Emergence of Kievan Rus'   215
DOCUMENT: Russia Turns to Christianity   216
GLOBAL CONNECTIONS: Eastern Europe and the World   218
Further Readings   218
On the Web   218
AP* Test Prep   219

CHAPTER 10 **A New Civilization Emerges in Western**
Europe   220
Stages of Postclassical Development   221
VISUALIZING THE PAST: Peasant Labor   223
DOCUMENT: European Travel: A Monk Visits Jerusalem   229
THINKING HISTORICALLY: Western Civilization   231
Western Culture in the Postclassical Era   232
Changing Economic and Social Forms in the Postclassical
    Centuries   234
The Decline of the Medieval Synthesis   238
GLOBAL CONNECTIONS: Medieval Europe
    and the World   240
Further Readings   241
On the Web   241
AP* Test Prep   242

CHAPTER 11 **The Americas on the Eve of Invasion   244**
Postclassic Mesoamerica, 1000–1500 C.E.   245
Aztec Society in Transition   251
DOCUMENT: Aztec Women and Men   253
Twantinsuyu: World of the Incas   254
VISUALIZING THE PAST: Archeological Evidence of Political
    Practices   256
THINKING HISTORICALLY: The "Troubling" Civilizations
    of the Americas   258

The Other Peoples of the Americas   261
GLOBAL CONNECTIONS: The Americas and the World   264
Further Readings   264
On the Web   264
AP* Test Prep   265

CHAPTER 12 Reunification and Renaissance
in Chinese Civilization: The Era of the Tang
and Song Dynasties   266
Rebuilding the Imperial Edifice in the Sui-Tang Era   267
DOCUMENT: Ties That Bind: Paths to Power   272
Tang Decline and the Rise of the Song   274
Tang and Song Prosperity: The Basis of a Golden Age   278
VISUALIZING THE PAST: Footbinding as a Marker of Male
    Dominance   282
THINKING HISTORICALLY: Artistic Expression
    and Social Values   284
GLOBAL CONNECTIONS: China's World Role   286
Further Readings   286
On the Web   287
AP* Test Prep   288

CHAPTER 13 The Spread of Chinese Civilization:
Japan, Korea, and Vietnam   290
Japan: The Imperial Age   291
The Era of Warrior Dominance   296
THINKING HISTORICALLY: Comparing Feudalisms   298
Korea: Between China and Japan   302
Between China and Southeast Asia: The Making
    of Vietnam   305
VISUALIZING THE PAST: What Their Portraits Tell Us:
    Gatekeeper Elites and the Persistence of Civilizations   308
DOCUMENT: Literature as a Mirror of the Exchanges
    Between Civilized Centers   311
GLOBAL CONNECTIONS: In the Orbit of China: The East
    Asian Corner of the Global System   311
Further Readings   312
On the Web   312
AP* Test Prep   313

CHAPTER 14 The Last Great Nomadic Challenges:
From Chinggis Khan to Timur   314
The Transcontinental Empire of Chinggis Khan   316
DOCUMENT: A European Assessment of the Virtues
    and Vices of the Mongols   320
The Mongol Drive to the West   322
VISUALIZING THE PAST: The Mongol Empire as a Bridge
    Between Civilizations   325
The Mongol Interlude in Chinese History   326
THINKING HISTORICALLY: The Global Eclipse
    of the Nomadic Warrior Culture   330
GLOBAL CONNECTIONS: The Mongol Linkages   332
Further Readings   333
On the Web   334
AP* Test Prep   335

CHAPTER 15 The World in 1450: Changing Balance
of World Power   336
Key Changes in the Middle East   337
The Rise of the West   340
VISUALIZING THE PAST: Population Trends   341
DOCUMENT: Bubonic Plague   342
Western Expansion: The Experimental Phase   345
Outside the World Network   346
THINKING HISTORICALLY: The Problem
    of Ethnocentrism   348
GLOBAL CONNECTIONS: 1450 and the World   349
Further Readings   349
On the Web   350
AP* Test Prep   351

PART IV

THE EARLY MODERN PERIOD, 1450–1750:
THE WORLD SHRINKS   354

CHAPTER 16 The World Economy   360
The West's First Outreach: Maritime Power   360
THINKING HISTORICALLY: Causation and the West's
    Expansion   365
Toward a World Economy   366
VISUALIZING THE PAST: West Indian Slaveholding   369
Colonial Expansion   371
DOCUMENT: Western Conquerors: Tactics
    and Motives   372
GLOBAL CONNECTIONS: The World Economy—
    And the World   377
Further Readings   378
On the Web   378
AP* Test Prep   379

CHAPTER 17 The Transformation of the West,
1450–1750   380
The First Big Changes: Culture and Commerce,
    1450–1650   381
The Commercial Revolution   386
The Scientific Revolution: The Next Phase
    of Change   389
VISUALIZING THE PAST: Versailles   391
Political Change   391
THINKING HISTORICALLY: Elites and Masses   392
The West by 1750   394
DOCUMENT: Controversies About Women   395
GLOBAL CONNECTIONS: Europe and the World   398
Further Readings   398
On the Web   398
AP* Test Prep   399

CHAPTER 18 The Rise of Russia   400
Russia's Expansionist Politics Under the Tsars   400
THINKING HISTORICALLY: Multinational Empires   404
Russia's First Westernization, 1690–1790   405

DOCUMENT: The Nature of Westernization 407
Themes in Early Modern Russian History 410
VISUALIZING THE PAST: Oppressed Peasants 411
GLOBAL CONNECTIONS: Russia and the World 413
Further Readings 413
On the Web 414
AP* Test Prep 415

CHAPTER 19 Early Latin America 416
Spaniards and Portuguese: From Reconquest
to Conquest 418
DOCUMENT: A Vision from the Vanquished 423
The Destruction and Transformation
of Indigenous Societies 426
Colonial Economies and Governments 427
THINKING HISTORICALLY: An Atlantic History? 428
Brazil: The First Plantation Colony 431
Multiracial Societies 434
VISUALIZING THE PAST: Race or Culture? A Changing
Society 435
The 18th-Century Reforms 436
GLOBAL CONNECTIONS: Latin American Civilization
and the World Context 441
Further Readings 441
On the Web 442
AP* Test Prep 443

CHAPTER 20 Africa and the Africans in the Age
of the Atlantic Slave Trade 444
Africa and the Creation of an Atlantic System 445
The Atlantic Slave Trade 446
African Societies, Slavery, and the Slave Trade 451
THINKING HISTORICALLY: Slavery and Human
Society 452
White Settlers and Africans in Southern Africa 457
The African Diaspora 460
DOCUMENT: An African's Description of the Middle
Passage 461
VISUALIZING THE PAST: The Cloth of Kings in an Atlantic
Perspective 463
GLOBAL CONNECTIONS: Africa and the African Diaspora
in World Context 465
Further Readings 465
On the Web 466
AP* Test Prep 467

CHAPTER 21 The Muslim Empires 468
The Ottomans: From Frontier Warriors
to Empire Builders 469
DOCUMENT: An Islamic Traveler Laments the Muslims'
Indifference to Europe 477
The Shi'a Challenge of the Safavids 477
THINKING HISTORICALLY: The Gunpowder Empires
and the Shifting Balance of Global Power 480
The Mughals and the Apex of Muslim Civilization
in India 484

VISUALIZING THE PAST: Art as A Window into the Past:
Paintings and History in Mughal India 488
GLOBAL CONNECTIONS: Gunpowder Empires
and the Restoration of the Islamic Bridge
Between Civilizations 491
Further Readings 492
On the Web 492
AP* Test Prep 493

CHAPTER 22 Asian Transitions in an Age
of Global Change 494
The Asian Trading World and the Coming
of the Europeans 496
Ming China: A Global Mission Refused 503
DOCUMENT: Exam Questions as a Mirror
of Chinese Values 505
VISUALIZING THE PAST: The Great Ships of the Ming
Expeditions that Crossed the Indian Ocean 509
THINKING HISTORICALLY: Means and Motives for Overseas
Expansion: Europe and China Compared 510
Fending Off the West: Japan's Reunification
and the First Challenge 511
GLOBAL CONNECTIONS: An Age of Eurasian
Protoglobalization 515
Further Readings 515
On the Web 516
AP* Test Prep 517

PART V

THE DAWN OF THE INDUSTRIAL AGE, 1750–1914 520

CHAPTER 23 The Emergence of Industrial Society
in the West, 1750–1914 526
The Age of Revolution 527
VISUALIZING THE PAST: The French Revolution
in Cartoons 530
The Consolidation of the Industrial Order,
1850–1914 534
DOCUMENT: Protesting the Industrial Revolution 536
Cultural Transformations 539
Western Settler Societies 542
THINKING HISTORICALLY: Two Revolutions: Industrial
and Atlantic 543
Diplomatic Tensions and World War I 546
GLOBAL CONNECTIONS: Industrial Europe
and the World 547
Further Readings 548
On the Web 548
AP* Test Prep 549

CHAPTER 24 Industrialization and Imperialism:
The Making of the European Global Order 550
The Shift to Land Empires in Asia 552
THINKING HISTORICALLY: Western Education and the Rise
of an African and Asian Middle Class 558

Industrial Rivalries and the Partition of the World,
    1870–1914 560
Patterns of Dominance: Continuity and Change 563
DOCUMENT: Contrary Images: The Colonizer Versus
    the Colonized on the "Civilizing Mission" 564
VISUALIZING THE PAST: Capitalism and Colonialism 567
GLOBAL CONNECTIONS: A European-Dominated Early
    Phase of Globalization 572
Further Readings 572
On the Web 572
AP* Test Prep 573

**CHAPTER 25 The Consolidation of Latin America,
    1830–1920 574**
From Colonies to Nations 575
New Nations Confront Old and New Problems 579
Latin American Economies and World Markets,
    1820–1870 582
DOCUMENT: Confronting the Hispanic Heritage:
    From Independence to Consolidation 588
Societies in Search of Themselves 591
THINKING HISTORICALLY: Explaining
    Underdevelopment 594
VISUALIZING THE PAST: Images of the Spanish-American
    War 596
GLOBAL CONNECTIONS: New Latin American Nations
    and the World 598
Further Readings 600
On the Web 600
AP* Test Prep 601

**CHAPTER 26 Civilizations in Crisis: The Ottoman
    Empire, the Islamic Heartlands, and Qing China 602**
From Empire to Nation: Ottoman Retreat and the Birth
    of Turkey 603
Western Intrusions and the Crisis in the Arab Islamic
    Heartlands 607
THINKING HISTORICALLY: Western Dominance
    and the Decline of Civilizations 608
The Last Dynasty: The Rise and Fall of the Qing Empire
    in China 613
VISUALIZING THE PAST: Mapping the Decline
    of Civilizations 614
DOCUMENT: Transforming Imperial China
    into a Nation 622
GLOBAL CONNECTIONS: Muslim and Chinese Decline
    and a Shifting Global Balance 623
Further Readings 624
On the Web 624
AP* Test Prep 625

**CHAPTER 27 Russia and Japan: Industrialization
    Outside the West 626**
Russia's Reforms and Industrial Advance 627

DOCUMENT: Conditions for Factory Workers in Russia's
    Industrialization 632
Protest and Revolution in Russia 633
Japan: Transformation Without Revolution 636
THINKING HISTORICALLY: The Separate Paths of Japan
    and China 638
VISUALIZING THE PAST: Two Faces of Western Influence 641
GLOBAL CONNECTIONS: Russia and Japan in the World 644
Further Readings 644
On the Web 645
AP* Test Prep 646

PART VI

THE NEWEST STAGE OF WORLD HISTORY:
1914–PRESENT 650

**CHAPTER 28 Descent into the Abyss: World War I
    and the Crisis of the European Global Order 658**
The Coming of the Great War 660
A World at War 663
VISUALIZING THE PAST: Trench Warfare 664
Failed Peace and Global Turmoil 670
The Nationalist Assault on the European
    Colonial Order 671
DOCUMENT: Lessons for the Colonized from the Slaughter
    in the Trenches 672
THINKING HISTORICALLY: Women in Asian and African
    Nationalist Movements 680
GLOBAL CONNECTIONS: World War and Global
    Upheavals 683
Further Readings 683
On the Web 684
AP* Test Prep 685

**CHAPTER 29 The World between the Wars: Revolutions,
    Depression, and Authoritarian Response 686**
The Roaring Twenties 687
Revolution: The First Waves 692
THINKING HISTORICALLY: A Century of Revolutions 698
The Global Great Depression 705
The Authoritarian Response 708
VISUALIZING THE PAST: *Guernica* and the Images
    of War 711
DOCUMENT: Socialist Realism 716
GLOBAL CONNECTIONS: Economic Depression, Authoritarian
    Response, and Democratic Retreat 718
Further Readings 719
On the Web 720
AP* Test Prep 722

**CHAPTER 30 A Second Global Conflict and the End
    of the European World Order 724**
Old and New Causes of a Second World War 725

THINKING HISTORICALLY: Total War, Global
    Devastation   727
Unchecked Aggression and the Coming of War in Europe
    and the Pacific   728
The Conduct of a Second Global War   730
DOCUMENT: Japan's Defeat in a Global War   737
War's End and the Emergence of the Superpower
    Standoff   738
Nationalism and Decolonization in South and Southeast
    Asia and Africa   739
VISUALIZING THE PAST: National Leaders for a New Global
    Order   742
GLOBAL CONNECTIONS: Persisting Trends in a World
    Transformed by War   747
Further Readings   747
On the Web   748
AP* Test Prep   750

CHAPTER 31 Western Society and Eastern Europe
in the Decades of the Cold War   752
After World War II: A New International Setting
    for the West   752
The Resurgence of Western Europe   756
THINKING HISTORICALLY: The United States and Western
    Europe: Convergence and Complexity   760
Cold War Allies: The United States, Canada, Australia,
    and New Zealand   762
Culture and Society in the West   764
VISUALIZING THE PAST: Women at Work in France
    and the United States   766
Eastern Europe After World War II: A Soviet Empire   770
Soviet Culture: Promoting New Beliefs and Institutions   773
DOCUMENT: A Cold War Speech   778
GLOBAL CONNECTIONS: The Cold War and the World   779
Further Readings   779
On the Web   780
AP* Test Prep   781

CHAPTER 32 Latin America: Revolution and Reaction
into the 21st Century   782
Latin America After World War II   784
Radical Options in the 1950s   786
VISUALIZING THE PAST: Murals and Posters: Art
    and Revolution   787
DOCUMENT: The People Speak   790
The Search for Reform and the Military Option   790
THINKING HISTORICALLY: Human Rights
    in the 20th Century   794
Societies in Search of Change   797
GLOBAL CONNECTIONS: Struggling Toward the Future
    in a Global Economy   801
Further Readings   802
On the Web   802
AP* Test Prep   803

CHAPTER 33 Africa, the Middle East, and Asia
in the Era of Independence   804
The Challenges of Independence   805
DOCUMENT: Cultural Creativity in the Emerging Nations:
    Some Literary Samples   813
THINKING HISTORICALLY: Artificial Nations and the Rising
    Tide of Communal Strife   814
Post-Colonial Options for Achieving Economic Growth
    and Social Justice   816
Delayed Revolutions: Religious Revivalism and Liberation
    Movements in Settler Societies   822
VISUALIZING THE PAST: Globalization and Postcolonial
    Societies   827
GLOBAL CONNECTIONS: Postcolonial Nations in the Cold
    War World Order   827
Further Readings   828
On the Web   828
AP* Test Prep   829

CHAPTER 34 Rebirth and Revolution: Nation-Building
in East Asia and the Pacific Rim   830
East Asia in the Postwar Settlements   831
The Pacific Rim: More Japans?   838
VISUALIZING THE PAST: Pacific Rim Growth   840
THINKING HISTORICALLY: The Pacific Rim
    as a U.S. Policy Issue   842
Mao's China: Vanguard of World Revolution?   843
DOCUMENT: Women in the Revolutionary Struggles
    for Social Justice   848
Colonialism and Revolution in Vietnam   850
GLOBAL CONNECTIONS: East Asia and the Pacific Rim
    in the Contemporary World   855
Further Readings   856
On the Web   856
AP* Test Prep   858

CHAPTER 35 Power, Politics, and Conflict in World
History, 1990–2010   860
The End of the Cold War   861
VISUALIZING THE PAST: Symbolism in the Breakdown
    of the Soviet Bloc   868
The Spread of Democracy   869
DOCUMENT: Democratic Protest and Repression
    in China   870
The Great Powers and New Disputes   871
The United States as Sole Superpower   874
THINKING HISTORICALLY: Terrorism, Then
    and Now   876
GLOBAL CONNECTIONS: New Global Standards,
    New Divisions   878
Further Readings   878
On the Web   880
AP* Test Prep   881

CHAPTER 36 Globalization and Resistance   882
Globalization: Causes and Processes   883
DOCUMENT: Protests Against Globalization   890
Resistance and Alternatives   892
THINKING HISTORICALLY: How Much Historical
    Change?   893
The Global Environment   894
VISUALIZING THE PAST: Two Faces of Globalization   897

Toward the Future   899
GLOBAL CONNECTIONS: Civilizations and Global Forces   900
Further Readings   900
On the Web   901
AP* Test Prep   903

Credits   C-1

Index   I-1

Maps

PART I Initial Centers and Spread of Agriculture 3

PART I Early Centers of Civilization 3

1.1 The Spread of Human Populations, c. 10,000 B.C.E. 12
1.2 The Spread of Agriculture 14
1.3 Early Sumer 19
1.4 Mesopotamia and the Middle East 20
1.5 Egypt, Kush, and Axum, Successive Dynasties 21

PART II Political Units of the World, c. 800–750 B.C.E. 35

PART II Political Units of the World, c. 1–100 C.E. 35

2.1 China from the Later Zhou Era to the Han Era 43
2.2 Ancient Capitals 47
3.1 India at the Time of Ashoka 65
3.2 The Gupta Empire 66
3.3 Eurasian and African Trading Goods Routes, c. 300 B.C.E. to 300 C.E. 77
4.1 Persia in Its Main Stages 83
4.2 Greece and Greek Colonies, c. 431 B.C.E. 85
4.3 Alexander's Empire, c. 323 B.C.E., and the Hellenistic World 86
4.4 The Roman Empire from Augustus to 180 C.E. 87
5.1 Trade Routes at the End of the Classical Era 109
5.2 Civilizations of Central and South America 111
5.3 Germanic Kingdoms after the Invasions 116
5.4 The Mediterranean, Middle East, Europe, and North Africa, c. 500 C.E. 117
5.5 Major Religions of the Modern World 123

PART III Spread of Buddhism, Christianity, and Islam to c. 1450 131

PART III Main Routes of Afro-Eurasian Trade, c. 1250 131

6.1 Arabia and Surrounding Areas Before and During the Time of Muhammad 139
6.2 The Expansion of the Islamic Empire in the 7th and 8th Centuries 148
6.3 Emergence of the Abbasid Dynasty 154
7.1 The Abbasid Empire at Its Peak 164
7.2 The Spread of Islam, 10th–16th Centuries 170
7.3 Early Islam in India 174
7.4 The Spread of Islam in Southeast Asia 181
8.1 Empires of the Western Sudan 190
8.2 The Swahili Coast; African Monsoon Routes and Major Trade Routes 196
9.1 The Byzantine Empire Under Justinian 208
9.2 The Byzantine Empire, 1000–1100 212

9.3 East European Kingdoms and Slavic Expansion, c. 1000 214
10.1 Charlemagne's Empire and Successor States 224
10.2 Western Europe Toward the End of the Middle Ages, c. 1360 C.E. 228
10.3 Leading Trade Routes Within Europe and to the Mediterranean 235
11.1 Central Mexico and Lake Texcoco 248
11.2 Inca Expansion 255
11.3 The Ancient Cities of Peru 257
12.1 China During the Age of Division 268
12.2 The Sui Dynasty and the Tang Dynasty 269
12.3 China in the Song and Southern Song Dynastic Periods 276
13.1 Key Centers of Civilization in East Asia in the First Millennium C.E. 292
13.2 Japan in the Imperial and Warlord Periods 293
13.3 The Korean Peninsula During the Three Kingdoms Era 302
13.4 South China and Vietnam on the Eve of the Han Conquest 305
14.1 The Transcontinental Empire of Chinggis Khan 315
14.2 The Four Khanates of the Divided Mongol Empire 322
14.3 The Mongol Empire and the Global Exchange Network 325
15.1 Polynesian Expansion 347

PART IV Major Political Units of the World, c. 1450 355

PART IV Major Political Units of the World, c. 1750 355

16.1 Spain and Portugal: Explorations and Colonies 363
16.2 French, British, and Dutch Holdings, c. 1700 366
17.1 Western Europe During the Renaissance and Reformation 384
17.2 Europe Under Absolute Monarchy, 1715 387
17.3 European Population Density, c. 1600 388
18.1 Russian Expansion Under the Early Tsars, 1462–1598 403
18.2 Russia Under Peter the Great 406
18.3 Russia's Holdings by 1800 410
19.1 Major Spanish Expeditions of Conquest in and from the Caribbean Region 419
19.2 Colonial Brazil 421
19.3 Latin America around 1800 437
20.1 Portuguese Contact and Penetration of Africa 446
21.1 The Ottoman, Safavid, and Mughal Empires 470
21.2 The Expansion of the Ottoman Empire 471
21.3 The Safavid Empire 478
21.4 The Growth of the Mughal Empire, from Akbar to Aurangzeb 485
22.1 Routes and Major Products Exchanged in the Asian Trading Network, c. 1500 497
22.2 The Pattern of Early European Expansion in Asia 499
22.3 Ming China and the Zheng He Expeditions, 1405–1433 507
22.4 Japan During the Rise of the Tokugawa Shogunate 512

PART V Major World Empires, c. 1910 521

PART V World Centers of Industrialization, c. 1910 521

23.1 Napoleon's Empire in 1812 532
23.2 Industrialization in Europe, c. 1850 535
23.3 The Unification of Italy 537
23.4 The Unification of Germany, 1815–1871 538
23.5 Early 19th-Century Settlement in the United States, Canada, Australia, and New Zealand 545
23.6 The Balkans After the Regional Wars, 1913 547
24.1 European Colonial Territories, Before and After 1800 553
24.2 The Stages of Dutch Expansion in Java 554
24.3 The Growth of the British Empire in India, from the 1750s to 1858 556
24.4 The Partition of Africa Between c. 1870 and 1914 562
24.5 The Partition of Southeast Asia and the Pacific to 1914 563
25.1 Independent States of Latin America in 1830 580
26.1 British Egypt and the Anglo-Egyptian Sudan 612
26.2 Ottoman Empire from Late 18th Century to World War I 614
26.3 Qing Empire from Opium War of 1839–1841 to World War I 615
26.4 Coastal China and Its Hinterland in the 19th Century 618
27.1 Russian Expansion, 1815–1914 630
27.2 The Russo-Japanese War 635
27.3 Japanese Colonial Expansion to 1914 643

PART VI Political Map of the World in 1914 651

PART VI Political Map of the Present-Day World 651

28.1 World War I Fronts in Europe and the Middle East 661
28.2 Africa During World War I 667

28.3 The Middle East After World War I 676
29.1 From Dominions to Nationhood: Formation of Canada, Australia, and New Zealand 691
29.2 Eastern Europe and the Soviet Union, 1919–1939 692
29.3 China in the Era of Revolution and Civil War 703
29.4 The Expansion of Japan to the Outbreak of World War II 714
30.1 World War II in Europe and the Middle East 731
30.2 Asia and the Pacific in World War II 735
30.3 The Partition of Palestine After World War II 746
31.1 Soviet and Eastern European Boundaries by 1948 754
31.2 Germany After World War II 755
31.3 The European Union 759
32.1 U.S. Military Interventions, 1898–2000 796
33.1 The Emergence of New Nations in Africa after World War II 808
33.2 The Partition of South Asia: The Formation of India, Pakistan, Bangladesh, and Sri Lanka 809
33.3 The New West African Nations 816
33.4 The Middle East in the Cold War Era 819
34.1 The Pacific Rim Area by 1960 832
34.2 China in the Years of Japanese Occupation and Civil War, 1931–1949 843
34.3 Vietnam: Divisions in the Nguyen and French Periods 850
34.4 North and South Vietnam 853
40.1 Post–Soviet Union Russia, Eastern Europe, and Central Asia by 1991 867
40.2 The Implosion of Yugoslavia, 1991–2008 872
35.3 Main U.S. Overseas Military Installations by 2007 879
36.1 Multinational Corporations in 2000 886

Teacher to Teacher

The AP* World History survey encourages students to grasp concepts and patterns across a huge breadth of time and space. *World Civilizations: The Global Experience, AP* Edition* provides students with a text that helps to facilitate these global understandings and connections in the classroom. Of particular note is the emphasis on social history, allowing for greater insight and analysis into an underrepresented part of the course. The conscious attention to a broad spectrum of world history beyond political and military events is essential to the teaching of world history in the 21st century. Since, as the authors note, the book is based on "comparative work and focuses on global processes," students are able to see the history of the world as one based on multiple disciplines. The book is not regionally compartmentalized but requires an understanding of interaction and comparison through time.

Throughout the book, students are encouraged to think analytically and comparatively through the inclusion of primary sources, as well as additional special features. The Visualizing the Past sections bring out suggestions for analysis of visual images and make connections between chapters and places. Within the In-Depth analysis pages, the authors take a broad topic and stretch it out across time or place without the constraints of the chapter's parameters. Really interesting comparisons, connections, and long-term causes and consequences come up within this section on a wide array of topics. This is also where some of the best sociohistorical analysis finds its place. The AP* course description asks students to reflect on diverse interpretations in history, and this is often done within these sections with topics such as civilization, race, population, gender, the rise of the West, nomadic peoples, and slavery. In addition, students are often able to draw contemporary comparisons with the subjects covered. The Global Connections sections are new and allow for a broadening of context that might otherwise be lost in the detail of the chapter. This is essential for student understanding of global historical context. These sections are most effective when they are specific, mentioning specific movements of people, ideas, or goods between specific places.

The book also offers a particularly rich companion Web site organized according to the book's table of contents. Students find the Web links within the chapters as well as the Web site with online material useful. Teachers and students benefit from the site being an additional resource for content enhancement and reinforcement.

No matter how good a textbook is, the AP* course description, not the textbook layout, should drive the pace of the course. This textbook allows a teacher to make the decisions about pacing and selection. The three major strengths of this text are its attention to issues of social history, including class and social structure, the modeling of good analysis, and a rich Web site with many resources and student activities. Students experience success with this text not only as they become familiar with the new scholarship and language that are part of a dynamic research field, but also as they see modeled the analytical and comparative skills necessary to apply this new knowledge.

DEBORAH SMITH JOHNSTON

Lexington High School, Lexington, Mass.

AP* World History Topics Correlated to *World Civilizations: The Global Experience*, AP* Edition 6/e

Upon publication, this text was correlated to the College Board's World History Course Description dated May 2010, May 2011. We continually monitor the College Board's AP* Course Description for updates to exam topics. For the most current AP* Exam Topic correlation for this textbook, visit PearsonSchool.com/AdvancedCorrelations.

The following chart is an excellent resource in preparation for topics that will be a part of the AP* World History examination. The numbered entries in the left-hand column show one way to break down the material into historical eras and overarching themes studied in AP* World History courses. The right column includes a detailed breakdown of chapters in your *World Civilizations: The Global Experience* AP* Edition textbook where you can learn more about those historical topics.

AP* Topics	World Civilizations: The Global Experience, 5/e
1. Foundations:	
c. 8000 B.C.E.–600 C.E.	**Chapters 1–5**
a. Locating world history	pp. xvi–xxi
i. Environment	pp. 3, 11–14
ii. Time	pp. 2, 4–5, 11
iii. Diverse interpretations	pp. xxiv–xxv
b. Developing agriculture and technology	pp. 2–33
i. Types of early societies	pp. 2–16
ii. Emergence of agriculture and technology	pp. 12–33
iii. Nature of village settlements	pp. 12–33
iv. Impact of agriculture	pp. 12–33
v. Introduction of metal use	pp. 12–33
c. Basic features of early civilizations	pp. 17–33
i. Mesopotamia	pp. 19–21
ii. Egypt	pp. 21–22
iii. Indus valley civilization	pp. 22–23
iv. Shang dynasty	pp. 23–25
v. Mesoamerica and Andean South America	pp. 110–111
d. Classical civilizations	pp. 34–129
i. Major political developments	pp. 34–129
ii. Social and gender structures	pp. 34–129
iii. Major trading patterns	pp. 34–129
iv. Arts, sciences, and technology	pp. 34–129
e. Major belief systems	p. 118
i. Polytheism	pp. 2–33
ii. Hinduism	pp. 60–79
iii. Judaism	pp. 28, 121
iv. Confucianism	pp. 38–59
v. Daoism	pp. 38–59
vi. Buddhism	pp. 60–79, 118–120
vii. Christianity	pp. 120–123, 204–218
f. Late Classical period (200 C.E. to 600 C.E.)	pp. 104–129
i. Collapse of empires	pp. 112–118
ii. Movements of peoples	pp. 104–118
iii. Interregional networks by 600 C.E.	pp. 108–109, 112–125
2. The Postclassical Era:	
600 C.E.–1450 C.E.	**Chapters 6–15**
a. Questions of periodization	pp. 112–135
i. Nature and causes of changes	pp. 112–135
ii. Emergence of new empires	pp. 112–135
iii. Continuities and breaks with the period	pp. 112–353
b. The Islamic world	pp. 136–203
i. The rise and role of Islam	pp. 136–183
ii. Islamic political structures	pp. 136–183, 194–197
iii. Arts, sciences, and technologies	pp. 136–161, 168–171, 191–195
c. Interregional networks and contacts	pp. 130–135, 170–173, 180–181, 184, 187–189, 196, 214, 224, 257, 290–293, 305, 311–312, 314–316, 325, 347

   i. Trade, technology, and cultural
      exchange   pp. 144–353
      1. Trans-Sahara trade   pp. 130–135,
                                       184–195
      2. Indian Ocean trade   pp. 130–135,
                                       162–163,
                                     180–181,
                                     195–197,
                                     336–340,
                                     345–346
      3. Silk routes   pp. 130–135,
                                     278–279,
                                     325
  ii. Missionary outreach of major
      religions   pp. 130–135,
                                     162–189,
                                   205–214,
                                   220–222
 iii. Contacts between major religions   pp. 130–135,
                                   162–189,
                                   207–208,
                                   228–230,
                                   271–277,
                                   290–313
 iv. Impact of Mongol empires   pp. 314–335
d. China's internal and external expansion pp. 266–313,
                                   336–340
   i. Tang and Song economic revolutions pp. 266–289
  ii. Chinese influence on surrounding
      areas   pp. 282–340
 iii. Arts, sciences, and technologies   pp. 266–340
e. Developments in Europe   pp. 204–243,
                                   336–346
   i. Restructuring of European
      institutions   pp. 204–243,
                                   336–346
  ii. The division of Christendom   pp. 244–265
f. Patterns in the Amerindian world   pp. 244–265
                                   346–347
   i. Maya   pp. 245–248,
                                   254,
                                   346–347
  ii. Aztec   pp. 245–254,
                                   258–261,
                                   346–347
 iii. Inca   pp. 254–261,
                                   346–347
g. Demographic and environmental
   changes   pp. 104–114,
                                   198–199,
                                   220–228,
                                   252,
                                   278–280,
                                   340–353

   i. Impact of nomadic migrations   pp. 104–114,
                                   137–147,
                                   195–196,
                                   217–218,
                                   244–248,
                                   290,
                                   307–311,
                                   314–335,
                                   340–353
  ii. Consequences of plague pandemics
      in 14th century   pp. 220–225,
                                   321, 333,
                                   340–342
 iii. Growth and role of cities   pp. 155–159,
                                   180–181,
                                   191–195,
                                   200–207,
                                   225–226,
                                   244–248,
                                   255–257,
                                   266–269,
                                   278–280,
                                   293–295

**3. The Interaction of World
   Cultures: 1450–1750**   **Chapters 16–22**
  a. Questions of periodization   pp. 354–359
     i. Continuities and breaks   pp. 354–359,
                                   518–519
  b. Changes in trade, technology,
     and global interactions   pp. 354–379
     i. The Columbian Exchange   pp. 354–379
    ii. Impact of guns   pp. 354–379
   iii. Changes in shipbuilding   pp. 354–379
   iv. New navigational devices   pp. 354–379
  c. Major empires, other political units,
     and social systems   pp. 354–519
     i. Ottoman   pp. 354–360,
                                   368,
                                   468–484
    ii. China   pp. 354–360,
                                   368–370,
                                   376–377,
                                   494–515
   iii. Portugal   pp. 354–364,
                                   416–443,
                                   494–502
   iv. Spain   pp. 354–364,
                                   416–443,
                                   494–502
    v. Russia   pp. 354–360,
                                   368–370,
                                   400–415
   vi. France   pp. 354–379,
                                   380–399

vii. England — pp. 354–379, 380–399

viii. Tokugawa — pp. 354–360, 494, 511–515

ix. Mughal — pp. 354–360, 368–371, 376–377, 468–469, 484–493

x. Benin — pp. 354–360, 369, 375, 444–467

xi. Songhay — pp. 354–360, 369, 375, 444–467

xii. Oyo — pp. 354–360, 369, 375, 444–467

xiii. Kongo — pp. 354–360, 369, 375, 444–467

d. Gender and empire — pp. 358, 375, 395, 436, 482–490, 506

e. Slave systems and slave trade — pp. 354–360, 369, 377, 410–411, 416–467, 472–473, 499

f. Demographic and environmental changes — pp. 367, 382, 389, 396–398, 411–412, 416–467, 506–507

g. Cultural and intellectual developments — pp. 380–399, 510–515

i. Scientific Revolution and Enlightenment — pp. 389–391, 394–396

ii. Causes and impacts of cultural change — pp. 394–396, 401–410, 416–479, 490–502, 510–515

iii. Changes and continuities in Confucianism — pp. 503–515

iv. Major developments in the arts — pp. 381–383, 391, 431 456, 463, 473–475, 481–482, 484–490, 507

4. Western Global Hegemony: 1750–1914 — **Chapters 23–27**

a. Questions of periodization — pp. 520–524

i. Continuities and breaks — pp. 520–524

b. Global commerce, communications, and technology — pp. 520–549, 582–584, 593–597, 610–612, 635–641

i. Changes in world trade — pp. 550–573, 598, 648–649

ii. Industrial Revolution — pp. 520–549, 626–649

c. Demographic and environmental changes — pp. 520–529, 567–579, 648–649

d. Changes in social and gender structure — pp. 520–549, 556–566, 579, 587–592, 633–647

e. Political revolutions and independence movements — pp. 520–534, 574–601, 613–621, 633–640

i. Latin American independence movements — pp. 574–601

ii. Revolutions — pp. 521–531, 575–576, 584–587, 613–625

iii. Rise of nationalism and nation-states — pp. 536–537, 574–582, 619–625

iv. Overlaps between nations and empires — pp. 602–625

v. Rise of democracy and its limitations — pp. 527–539, 575–582, 595–597, 635–640

f. Rise of Western dominance — pp. 520–579, 598, 602–613, 641

i. Patterns of expansion   pp. 550–573

ii. Imperialism and Colonialism   pp. 550–573, 618–619

iii. Cultural and political reactions   pp. 554–579, 595–613, 618–625, 637–649

iv. Impact of European ideologies in the colonies   pp. 557–560, 598–600

g. Patterns of cultural interactions among societies   pp. 556–557, 590–591

5. **The 20th Century in World History: 1914–Present**   **Chapters 28–36**

a. Questions of Periodization   pp. 650–657

i. Continuities and breaks   pp. 650–657,

b. The World Wars, the Holocaust, nuclear weaponry, and the cold war   pp. 658–685, 724–781

c. International organizations and their impact   pp. 755–762, 816, 842, 874–875, 890–892

d. New patterns of nationalism   pp. 671–692, 708–720, 739–753, 770–781, 804–829, 871–874

e. Impact of major global economic developments   pp. 718–719, 882–903

i. Great Depression   pp. 705–723

ii. Technology   pp. 882–885

iii. Pacific Rim   pp. 713–715, 830–859

iv. Multinational corporations   pp. 886–888

f. New forces of revolution and other political innovations   pp. 693–704, 782–793, 875–881

g. Social reform and social revolution   pp. 756–767, 793–803, 860–870

h. Globalization of science, technology, and culture   pp. 768–770, 882–903

i. Global cultures and regional reactions   pp. 888–890

ii. Elite, popular culture and art   pp. 716, 768–770, 787, 800–801, 813

iii. Patterns of resistance   pp. 892–893

iv. Demographic and environmental changes   pp. 894–903

Preface

World history explores the human past, around the globe, to help us understand the world we live in today. It seeks to identify how major forces have developed over time, like patterns of migration or world trade. It explores the cultures and political institutions of different regions, to help explain commonalities and differences. World history builds on a growing amount of historical scholarship, some of which has truly altered the picture of the past. It involves a rich array of stories and examples of human variety, intriguing in themselves. It helps develop skills that are vital not just to the history classroom, but to effective operation in a global society—skills like comparing different societies, appreciating various viewpoints, identifying big changes and continuities in the human experience. Always, however, it uses the past as a prologue to the present. World historians argue that no one society, past or present, can be understood without reference to other societies and to larger global forces. They argue, even more vigorously, that the present—which clearly involves relationships that embrace the whole world—cannot be grasped without a sense of the global historical record.

From its first edition, *World Civilizations: The Global Experience,* AP* Edition has aimed at capturing a truly global approach by discussing and comparing major societies and focusing on their interactions. The goal is to present a clear factual framework while stimulating analysis about global contacts, regional patterns, and the whole process of change and continuity on a world stage. This kind of world history, focused on the development over time of the forces that shape the world today, helps students make sense of the present and prepare to meet the challenges of the future. It is hard to imagine a more important topic.

Embracing the whole world's history obviously requires selectivity and explicit points of emphasis. This text gains coherence through decisions about time, about place and about topic. In all three cases, the book encourages analysis, relating facts to vital issues of interpretation. Through analysis and interpretation students become active, engaged learners, rather than serving as passive vessels for torrents of historical facts. Underpinning analysis, the issues of time, place, and topic are the three keys to an intelligible global past.

Decisions about Time: Periodization

This text pays a great deal of attention to periodization, or the identification of major points of change in the global experience. This is an essential requirement for coherent presentation—going well beyond the one-thing-after-another type of chronology—and ultimately a precondition of relating the past to the present.

World Civilizations: The Global Experience, AP* Edition identifies six periods in world history. Each period is determined by three basic criteria: a geographical rebalancing among major civilizational areas, an increase in the intensity and extent of contact across civilizations (or, in the case of the earliest period, cross-regional contact), and the emergence of new and roughly parallel developments in many major civilizations. The book is divided into six parts corresponding to these six major periods of world history. In each part, basic characteristics of each period are referred to in chapters that discuss the major societies in the Middle East, Africa, Asia, Europe and the Americas, and in several cross-cutting chapters that address larger world trends. Each period offers a distinctive set of themes, or Big Concepts, that are defined in general terms and then explored in terms of particular regions. Part introductions identify the fundamental new characteristics and new levels of interaction that define each period.

Part I, *Early Human Societies, 2.5 Million–1000 B.C.E.: Origins and Development,* sketches the hunting-and-gathering phase of human existence, then focuses on the rise of agriculture and the emergence of civilization in parts of Asia, Africa, Central America, and southeastern Europe—the sequence of developments that set world history in motion from the origin of the human species until about 3000 years ago.

Part II, *The Classical Period, 1000 B.C.E.–500 C.E.: Uniting Large Regions,* deals with the growing complexity of major civilizations in several areas of the world. During the classical period, civilizations developed a new capacity to integrate large regions and diverse groups of people through overarching cultural and political systems. Yet many regions and societies remained unconnected to the increasingly complex centers of civilization. Coverage of the classical period of world history, then, must consider both types of societies.

The period covered in Part III, *The Postclassical Period, 500–1450: New Faith and New Commerce,* saw the emergence of new commercial and cultural linkages that brought most civilizations into contact with one another and with nomadic groups. The decline of the great classical empires, the rise of new civilizational centers, and the emergence of a network of world contacts, including the spread of major religions, are characteristics of the postclassical era.

Developments in world history over the three centuries from 1450 to 1750 mark a fourth period in world history, which is covered in Part IV, *The Early Modern Period, 1450–1750: The World Shrinks.* The rise of the West, the intensification of global contacts, the growth of trade, and the formation of new empires define this period and separate it from the preceding postclassical period.

Part V, *The Dawn of the Industrial Age, 1750–1914,* covers the period of world history dominated by the advent of industrialization in western Europe and growing European imperialism. The increase and intensification of commercial interchange, technological innovations, and cultural contacts all reflected the growth of Western power and the spread of Western influence.

The Newest Stage of World History: 1914–Present, the focus of Part VI, defines the characteristics of this period as the retreat of Western imperialism, the rise of new political systems such as communism, the surge of the United States and the Soviet Union, and a variety of economic innovations, including the achievements of Japan, China, Korea, and the Pacific Rim. Part VI deals with this most recent period of world history and some of its portents for the future.

Underlying Issues

Two related themes and one standard historical complexity rise above the six-stage world history periodization. The first involves the interaction between tradition and change—and in recent periods, modern change. Many societies established key ideas and institutions early on, at least by the classical period. These traditions would then condition responses to change and modernity. Elements of this interplay become visible from the post-classical period onward; the tradition-change encounter remains vivid in the 21st century, though in forms very different from a thousand years ago. Each world history period involves important shifts in the interaction between change and tradition.

Theme two involves divergence and convergence. Societies emerged separately in many parts of the world, though the process was almost always affected by some wider contacts. This is part of the first phase of the human experience. Separation, or divergence, did not always mean difference, for many societies solved key problems in similar ways; but it did tend to produce separate identities. With growing contacts over time, opportunities and pressures produced various forms of imitation and convergence. The interplay between divergence and convergence is lively in the 21st century, but its shape has changed greatly over time. Here, too, each period involves a different statement of the balance between divergence and convergence.

Periodization emphasizes change, including changes in the basic frameworks in which traditions interacted with new forces and in which separate identities confronted new levels of convergence. Always, however, change must be complicated by recognition of key continuities from the past. At various points in human history, including recently, huge new forces prompt some people to claim that "everything has changed." In fact, strong traces of the past always linger. The challenge is to figure out how the balance works.

Place: Regions and Civilizations

Usable world history requires decisions about coherence in place as well as time. Even in the present day, and certainly in the past, key developments did not occur evenly across the whole globe: regional conditions always come into play. At the same time, not every definable society can be encompassed—early hunting-and-gathering bands of humans, after all, could number no more than sixty people. No world history survey can even approach that level of detail. World history seeks legitimate ways to define larger regions and societies that serve as the basis for meaningful contacts and reactions to global forces.

Major regions of the world depend on a combination of geography and historical developments in the form of shared institutions and beliefs. This book uses several regions as frameworks for discussing patterns of activity and larger interactions: East Asia; South and Southeast Asia; the Middle East, ultimately with the addition of North Africa; sub-Saharan Africa; Europe, often with some division between eastern and western; and the Americas. Australia and key island groups, and also patterns in central Asia, must be added in as well.

In several regions, beginning in key cases several thousand years ago, major civilizations helped organize and define regional characteristics. East Asia, to take one example, would be profoundly shaped by emerging features of Chinese civilization. Civilizations used economic surpluses, beyond basic survival needs, to generate relatively elaborate political institutions, cities, and trading networks. They also emphasized particular kinds of institutional arrangements and value systems that would provide a recognizable identity, differentiating their civilization from other societies. Using, but also debating, the concept of civilization helps organize the geographical foundation of world history, by introducing not only key regions, but regional characteristics and identities. Civilizations provide the basis for key comparisons, with each other and in terms of regional reactions to larger forces for change. The internal developments in major civilizations, along with mutual interaction and responses to broader factors like migration or missionary religions form much of the stuff of world history for the past 5000 years. At the same time, other types of societies, including nomadic groups played a vital role throughout world history, particularly as they long dominated strategically vital regions like central Asia. Most of these other societies were smaller than civilizations, in terms of population, but they played crucial functions in world history and developed successful cultural and institutional forms.

Attention to the major regions of the world does more than set the stage for comparative analysis, in each of the chronological periods in world history. It also promotes a sense of geographic balance that is vital to the field. Many earlier historical efforts understandably focused on developments in one's own society, assuming that the rest of the world was unimportant or somehow revolved around what was happening nearer home. Until recently, many Americans were urged to pay primary attention to the history of Western Europe and the expansion of Western civilization across the Atlantic. These remain valid themes, but in the world history context they become only a part of a larger and more complicated civilizational pattern. The transition from Western to world history is still under discussion, but the global context gains ground steadily because it more accurately mirrors the world around us today. This book, paying attention to Western developments as part of the larger world story, and showing their interaction with other societies and other influences, strives to distribute appropriate attention to all the major regions and to their changing roles in the larger global story.

Topics and Themes

A final way to focus world history, intersecting with decisions about time and place, involves the kinds of human and social activities that are highlighted. The first theme follows obviously from the uses of periodization and the need to deal coherently with world history over time: *World Civilizations: The Global Experience,* AP* Edition deals consistently with change and continuity and with the causes of basic changes in global dynamics from one period to the next.

Interactions among the major regions and societies, the second theme, focus attention on the ways individual regions and civilizations were shaped by contacts with other areas. Contacts include trade, of course, but also war, diplomacy, and international organizations from religious entities to the multinational companies and global agencies of more modern times.

A cluster of factors deal with economic activities and population patterns as they affect people, societies and the environment. Technology has a key role here, but also population structures and disease, labor systems, migrations, plus manufacturing and agriculture. Each civilization must be discussed with these patterns in mind, as well as the broader diffusion of trade, technologies and population exchange as they formed core parts of the larger patterns of interaction.

Each society featured characteristic social and gender structures that organized and tried to justify various systems of inequality. Dealing with how social systems changed over time and comparing them from one region to the next are core features of world history; social systems could also be affected by changing patterns of contact.

The fifth thematic area clusters around culture—belief systems, values, and artistic styles—as these emerged in religions, intellectual systems, and science. Here too, change over time and the results of interactions among societies form key elements in the cultural dynamics of world history.

Finally, politics demands emphasis: the functions and structures of states, as they formed and changed, along with ideas about politics and political identity (political culture). In modern centuries, this topic embraces the emergence of nation states and also their limitations in global context.

The topical themes of this book help organize discussions of change over time but also the possibility of developing comparisons from one society to the next. Interactions among the themes—how new trading patterns affected, and were affected by, cultural systems, for example—help structure more challenging analytical efforts.

What's New in This Edition?

New! The most consistently novel feature of this sixth edition involves the enhanced focus on the evolution of interregional and ultimately global contacts. Each Part Opener clearly discusses the nature of contacts in the time period involved, and from the post-classical period onward this involves also the assessment of basic systems of interaction and exchange. This theme is recaptured in chapters on individual societies but also in the Part Retrospective.

New! Each Part Opener clearly identifies leading themes and Big Concepts, and chapters on the major regions allow the concepts to be explored more fully and compared across regional lines.

New! Chapter Updates 20th century materials have been substantially revised, with particular attention to greater clarity and emphasis on the end of the Cold War and ensuing developments. The emergence of globalization, and resistance to globalization, have also been reexamined. All of the other chapters have been reviewed and updated as necessary.

New! In-text Pronunciation Guide New to the sixth edition is a pronunciation guide, which is intended to help familiarize students with new terminology by providing in-text pronunciations of key words and phrases that will help students become comfortable when discussing text passages. Pronunciations are also included in the glossary at the end of the text.

New! Marginal Glossary A new marginal glossary positions the definition of conceptual terms, frequently used foreign terms, and names of important geographic regions and key characters on the world stage on the page for students to review and study when preparing for a test. Much of world history will be new to most students, and marginal glossary will help them develop a global vocabulary.

New! AP*Test Prep Practice tests have been added to the end of each chapter to help students review content in preparation for the AP* World History exam.

Key Features

Part Introductions

Part introductions, reviewed for this edition, discuss the conditions that set the stage for the developments that define each new period in world history. They identify the characteristics of the period of world history covered in the part, and recap the continuities that exist from one period to the next. Two world maps at the beginning of each part introduction provide a graphic reference for the major changes of the period. Part timelines list the major events of the chronological period covered.

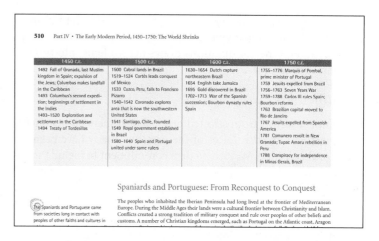

Part Retrospectives

Following the final chapter in each part is a retrospective essay that recaps the dominant cross-civilizational (or cross-regional) contacts and divisions that occurred during the era under examination. These sections encourage analysis of the dominant contact patterns in the period as well as the relationship to them of major individual societies.

Section-Opening Focal Points

Focal points listed below each main chapter heading identify for the student the principal points to be explored in the section.

Chapter Introductions

Each chapter introduction tells a compelling story about a particular pattern, individual, or incident to spark students' interest and introduce chapter material in an engaging and dramatic way. The opening story concludes with an explanation of how the story relates to the chapter content and the key themes and analytical issues that will be examined in the chapter.

Timelines

In addition to the timeline in each part introduction, each chapter includes a timeline that orients the student to the period, countries, and key events of the chapter.

Visualizing the Past

The Visualizing the Past feature of each chapter supports visual literacy by showing students how to read and analyze visual material such as maps, charts, graphs, tables or photos to interpret historical patterns. Text accompanying the illustrations provides a level of analysis, and a series of questions draws the students into providing their own analyses.

Documents

Substantial excerpts from selected original documents put students in contact with diverse voices of the past, and many have been revised for this edition. We share a firm commitment to include social history involving women, the non-elite, and experiences and events outside the spheres of politics and high culture. Each document is preceded by a brief scene-setting narration and followed by probing questions to guide the reader through an understanding of the document and to encourage interpretive reflections and analysis.

Thinking Historically

Each chapter contains an analytical essay on a topic of broad application related to the chapter's focus but extending across chronological and geographical boundaries. Critical thinking questions at

the end of each essay prompt the reader to think beyond the "who, what, where, and when" of historical events and consider instead the far-reaching implications of historical developments.

Global Connections

Each chapter ends with a Global Connections section that reinforces the key themes and issues raised in the chapter and makes clear their importance not only to the areas of civilization discussed in the chapter but also to the world as a whole.

Further Readings

Each chapter includes several annotated paragraphs of suggested readings, substantially updated for this edition. Students receive reliable guidance on a variety of books: source materials, standards in the field, encyclopedia coverage, more readable general interest titles, and the like.

On the Web

Each chapter ends with a list of Web sites with annotations to give students the key words necessary to search for similar sites.

Icons

Throughout the text are icons that lead students to additional resources—documents, images, maps, and case studies—found on the MyHistoryLab website that relate to the text they are reading.

Supplements

Note to Teachers

Most of the teacher supplements and resources for this text are available electronically to qualified adopters on the online Instructor Resource Center (IRC). Upon adoption or to preview, please go to PearsonSchool.com/Advanced and select "Online Teacher Supplements." You will be required to complete a one-time registration subject to verification before being emailed access information to download materials.

For Teachers

AP* Instructor's Resource Manual

This helpful manual includes DBQ rubrics and lesson plans in addition to lesson and discussion suggestions and activities for the world history AP* classroom. Additionally, there are chapter summaries, vocabulary, various types of review and skills activities, and reproducible worksheets. The manual also contains pacing and assignment guides as well as review questions to promote needed history and world history skills.

AP* Test Item File

Over 2000 test items are referenced by topic, type, and text page number. Specifically for the AP* Edition of *World Civilizations: The Global Experience*, this supplement contains AP* style multiple-choice and essay questions.

AP* Test Generator CD-ROM

This easy-to-use test generation software program provides the wealth of multiple-choice and essay questions from the printed test item file and allows users to add, delete, and print tests.

AP* Instructor's Resource CD-ROM

This CD-ROM contains files of the instructor's manual, lesson plans, test item file, and PowerPoint® slides that are available with the text.

AP* Transparency Set

This set of full-color transparency acetates reproduces all of the maps and charts from the text.

For Students

The following supplements are available for purchase:

AP* Test Prep Workbook

Created specifically for the AP* Edition of *World Civilizations: The Global Experience*, this student guide contains an overview of the AP* program and the AP* World History exam. It also provides test-taking strategies, correlations between key AP* test topics and the textbook, practice study questions, guidelines for mastering multiple-choice and free-response questions, DBQs, and two practice tests.

AP* Reading and Note Taking Study Guide

This supplement provides a chapter-by-chapter guide to help students read their textbook effectively, using various reading and study skills and strategies for an organized approach to reading and studying.

Primary Sources in World History

Over 300 primary source documents with head notes and critical thinking questions help students strengthen their analytical skills. Available in two volumes.

Visual Sources in World History

Over 200 hundred visual resources are provided with head notes and critical thinking questions to engage students in analyzing visual documents.

Prentice Hall Atlas of World History, 2/E

Produced in collaboration with Dorling Kindersley, the leader in cartographic publishing, the updated second edition of *The Prentice Hall Atlas of World History* applies the most innovative cartographic techniques to present world history in all of its complexity and diversity.

Primary Source: Documents in Global History DVD

This DVD-ROM offers a rich collection of textual and visual—many never before available to a wide audience—and serves as an indispensable tool for working with sources. Extensively developed with the guidance of historians and teachers, *Primary Source: Documents in Global History* includes over 800 sources in World History—from cave art, to text documents, to satellite images of Earth from space. All sources are accompanied by head notes and focus questions and are searchable by topic, region, or theme. In addition, a built-in tutorial guides students through the process of working with documents.

MyHistoryLab™ is a state-of-the-art, comprehensive Web resource, organized according to the contents of *World Civilizations, The Global Experience, AP* Edition*, offering a unique interactive experience that brings history to life. Students are able to self-study, take pre-loaded sample tests, and receive personalized study plans. **MyHistoryLab™** offers numerous study aids, chapter review material, several hundred primary sources, video clips, maps, map activities with quizzes, **AP* test prep practice and DBQ activities**. All student work can be tracked in the teacher's online gradebook. This comprehensive resource also includes a History Bookshelf with fifty of the most commonly assigned books and a History Toolkit with tutorials and helpful links. Upon textbook purchase, students and teachers are granted access to **MyHistoryLab™** as described above. Or, teachers can choose purchase the textbook with **MyHistoryLab™ with Pearson eText.**

High school teachers can obtain teacher and student preview or adoption access for **MyHistoryLab™** as described above (no eText).

Preview Access
- Ask your sales representative for a Preview Access Code Card (ISBN 0-13-111589-8).

Adoption Access
- Register online at www.PearsonSchool.com/Access_Request, using Option 2.
  OR
- Ask your sales representative for an Adoption Access Code Card (ISBN 0-13-034391-9).

Supplementary Reading Materials

Library of World Biography Series

Available for purchase, this series of biographies focuses on figures whose actions and ideas significantly influenced the course of world history. Pocket-sized and brief, each book relates the life of its subject to the broader themes and developments of the times. For more information about these titles, contact your local Pearson sales representative.

Titles include:

- *Ahmad al-Mansur: Islamic Visionary*, Richard L. Smith
- *Alexander the Great: Legacy of a Conqueror*, Winthrop Lindsay Admas
- *Benito Mussolini: The First Fascist*, Anthony L. Cardoza
- *Fukusawa Yûkichi: From Samurai to Capitalist*, Helen M. Hopper
- *Ignatius of Loyola: Founder of the Jesuits*, Patrick Donnelly
- *Jacques Coeur: Entrepreneur and King's Bursar*, Kathryn L. Reyerson
- *Kató Shidzue: A Japanese Feminist*, Helen M. Hopper
- *Simón Bolivar: Liberaton and Disappointment*, David Bushnell
- *Vasco da Gama: Renaissance Crusader*, Glenn J. Ames
- *Zheng He: China and the Oceans in the Early Ming Dynasty, 1405-1433*, Edward. L. Dreyer
- *Wu Zhao: China's Only Female Emperor*, N. Harry Rothschild
- *Chinggis Khan*, Ruth Dunnell
- *Emperor Qianlong: Son of Heaven, Man of the World*, Mark Elliott
- *Sun Yatsen: Seeking a Newer China*, David B. Gordon
- *Martin Luther: A Life Reformed*, Paul W. Robinson

Connections: Key Themes in World History

- *The Globe Encompassed: The Age of European Discovery (1500 to 1700)*, Glenn J. Ames
- *Captives as Commodities: The Transatlantic Slave Trade*, Lisa A. Lindsay
- *First Horseman, The: Disease in Human History*, John Aberth
- *Trading Tastes: Commodity and Cultural Exchange to 1750*, Erik Gilbert and Jonathan T. Reynolds

About the Authors

Peter N. Stearns

Peter N. Stearns is provost and professor of history at George Mason University. He received his Ph.D. from Harvard University. Before moving to George Mason University, he taught at Rutgers University, the University of Chicago, and Carnegie Mellon, where he won the Robert Doherty Educational Leadership Award and the Elliott Dunlap Smith Teaching Award. He has taught world history for more than 15 years. He currently serves as chair of the Advanced Placement World History Committee and also founded and is the editor of the *Journal of Social History*. In addition to textbooks and readers, he has written studies of gender and consumerism in a world history context. Other books address modern social and cultural history and include studies on gender, old age, work, dieting, and emotion. His most recent book in this area is *American Fear: Causes and Consequences of High Anxiety*.

Michael Adas

Michael Adas is the Abraham Voorhees Professor of History and a board of governor's chair at Rutgers University in New Brunswick, New Jersey. Over the past couple of decades his teaching has focused on patterns and processes of global and comparative history. His courses on race and empire in the early modern and industrial eras and on world history in the 20th century have earned him a number of teaching prizes. In addition to texts on world history, Adas has written mainly on the comparative history of colonialism and its impact on the peoples and societies of Asia and Africa. His books include *Machines as the Measure of Men: Science, Technology, and Ideologies of Western Dominance*, which won the Dexter Prize, and the recently published *Dominance by Design: Technological Imperatives and America's Civilizing Mission*. He is currently writing a global history of the First World War.

Stuart B. Schwartz

Stuart B. Schwartz was born and educated in Springfield, Massachusetts, and then attended Middlebury College and the Universidad Autonoma de Mexico. He has an M.A. and Ph.D. from Columbia University in Latin American history. He taught for many years at the University of Minnesota and joined the faculty at Yale University in 1996. He has also taught in Brazil, Puerto Rico, Spain, France, and Portugal. He is a specialist on the history of colonial Latin America, especially Brazil, and is the author of numerous books, notably *Sugar Plantations in the Formation of Brazilian Society* (1985), which won the Bolton Prize for the best book in Latin American History. He is also the author of *Slaves, Peasants, and Rebels* (1992), *Early Latin America* (1983), and *Victors and Vanquished* (1999). He has held fellowships from the Guggenheim Foundation and the Institute for Advanced Study (Princeton). For his work on Brazil he was decorated by the Brazilian government. His recent book *All Can Be Saved* (2008) won the Bolton Prize as well as three awards from the American Historical Association.

Marc Jason Gilbert

Marc Jason Gilbert is the holder of the National Endowment for the Humanities Endowed Chair in World History at Hawaii Pacific University in Honolulu, Hawaii. He is a former University System of Georgia Distinguished Professor of Teaching and Learning. He was a founding member of the World History Association and one of its initial elected officers. He also founded two currently active WHA regional affiliates (Southeast and Hawaii) and is editor of the WHA-affiliated journal, *World History Connected*. He frequently conducts institutes for teachers of world history and serves as an Advanced Placement World History Reader. He has attempted to bring a global dimension to Asian history in numerous articles and in books, such as *Why the North Won the Vietnam War*.

Prologue

The study of history is the study of the past. Knowledge of the past gives us perspective on our societies today. It shows different ways in which people have identified problems and tried to resolve them, as well as important common impulses in the human experience. History can inform through its variety, remind us of some human constants, and provide a common vocabulary and examples that aid in mutual communication.

The study of history is also the study of change. Historians analyze major changes in the human experience over time and examine the ways in which those changes connect the past to the present. They try to distinguish between superficial and fundamental change, as well as between sudden and gradual change. They explain why change occurs and what impact it has. Finally, they pinpoint continuities from the past along with innovations. History, in other words, is a study of human society in motion.

World history has become a subject in its own right. It involves the study of historical events in a global context. It does not attempt to sum up everything that has happened in the past. World history focuses on two principal subjects: the evolution of leading societies and the interaction among different peoples around the globe.

The Emergence of World History

Serious attempts to deal with world history are relatively recent. Many historians have attempted to locate the evolution of their own societies in the context of developments in a larger "known world": Herodotus, though particularly interested in the origins of Greek culture, wrote also of developments around the Mediterranean; Ibn Khaldun wrote of what he knew about developments in Africa and Europe as well as in the Muslim world. But not until the 20th century, with an increase in international contacts and a vastly expanded knowledge of the historical patterns of major societies, did a full world history become possible. In the West, world history depended on a growing realization that the world could not be understood simply as a mirror reflecting the West's greater glory or as a stage for Western-dominated power politics. This hard-won realization continues to meet some resistance. Nevertheless, historians in several societies have attempted to develop an international approach to the subject that includes, but goes beyond, merely establishing a context for the emergence of their own civilizations.

Our understanding of world history has been increasingly shaped by two processes that define historical inquiry: detective work and debate. Historians are steadily uncovering new data not just about particular societies but about lesser-known contacts. Looking at a variety of records and artifacts, for example, they learn how an 8th-century battle between Arab and Chinese forces in central Asia brought Chinese prisoners who knew how to make paper to the Middle East, where their talents were quickly put to work. And they argue about world history frameworks: how central European actions should be in the world history of the past 500 years, and whether a standard process of modernization is useful or distorting in measuring developments in modern Turkey or China. Through debate come advances in how world history is understood and conceptualized, just as the detective work advances the factual base.

What Civilization Means

Humans have always shown a tendency to operate in groups that provide a framework for economic activities, governance, and cultural forms such as beliefs and artistic styles. These groups, or societies, may be quite small; hunting-and-gathering bands often numbered no more than 60 people. World history usually focuses on somewhat larger societies, with more extensive economic relationships (at least for trade) and cultures.

One vital kind of grouping is called civilization. The idea of civilization as a type of human society is central to most world history, though it also generates debate and though historians are now agreed that it is not the only kind of grouping that warrants attention. Civilizations, unlike some other societies, generate surpluses beyond basic survival needs. This in turn promotes a variety of specialized occupations and heightened social differentiation, as well as regional and long-distance trading networks. Surplus production also spurs the growth of cities and the development of formal states, with some bureaucracy, in contrast to more informal methods of governing. Most civilizations have also developed systems of writing.

Civilizations are not necessarily better than other kinds of societies. Nomadic groups have often demonstrated great creativity in technology and social relationships, and some were more vigorous than settled civilizations in promoting global contacts. Moreover, there is disagreement about exactly what defines a civilization—for example, what about cases like the Incas where there was no writing?

Used carefully, however, the idea of civilization as a form of human social organization, and an unusually extensive one, has merit. Along with agriculture (which developed earlier), civilizations have given human groups the capacity to fundamentally reshape their environments and to dominate most other living creatures. The history of civilizations embraces most of the people who have ever lived; their literature, formal scientific discoveries, art, music, architecture, and inventions; their most elaborate social, political, and economic systems; their brutality and destruction caused by conflicts; their exploitation of other species; and their degradation of the environment—a result of changes in technology and the organization of work.

The study of civilizations always involves more, however, than case-by-case detail. World history makes sense only if civilizations are compared, rather than treated separately. Equally important, civilizations (and other societies) developed important mutual contacts, which could have wide impact in reshaping several societies at the same time. And civilizations responded to still wider forces, like migration, disease, or missionary activity, that could reshape the frameworks within which they operated. Civilizations in these wider contexts—as they changed through internal dynamics, mutual interactions, and responses to broader forces—form the basic patterns of world history for the past 5000 years.

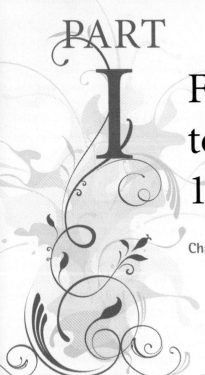

From Hunting and Gathering to Civilizations, 2.5 million–1000 B.C.E.: Origins

Chapter 1   From Human Prehistory to the Early Civilizations

OVERVIEW

The earliest known, fully human species lived in east Africa about 2.5 million years ago. Gradually humans developed a more erect stance and greater brain capacity. Early humans lived by hunting and gathering. Because hunting-and-gathering economies require a great deal of space—on average about 2.5 square miles per person—populations remained small, and people lived in small groups. Even a modest population increase in a hunting-and-gathering group required part of the group to migrate in search of new game. Tens of thousands of years ago, the most advanced of the human species, *Homo sapiens sapiens*, migrated from Africa into the Middle East, then into Europe, Asia, Australia, and the Americas. Early humans developed tools, first using stones, sticks, and other natural objects. Gradually, people learned to fashion tools and weapons from stone, bone, and wood.

Agriculture began at different times in different places, from about 10,000 years ago onward. It developed independently in at least three regions and perhaps more. The map shows the early centers of food production. Gradually, agriculture spread widely, though not universally, from these initial centers.

The development of agriculture was a radical change in humans' way of life. By providing a dependable source of food, it allowed people to live in larger groups. Later on, toolmaking technology advanced with the discovery of metalworking, which in turn fur-

ther increased agricultural production. Increased production freed some members of the society to perform other kinds of work. This in turn encouraged a further series of organizational changes we call civilization.

Early civilizations arose in five different sites, four of them along the fertile shores of great rivers. At least three and possibly all five of these early civilizations arose entirely independently of each other. The map of early civilizations makes another point clear: large parts of the world were not involved in these developments. Early world history focuses on agricultural civilizations, but it must also pay attention to regions that developed different kinds of economies and different organizational structures.

Hunting-and-gathering societies offered an intriguing mixture of features. Not surprisingly, material life could be meager. The food supply could be precarious, which was one reason for frequent movement and migration, as when the supply of game ran low. On the other hand, average workdays were short, leaving a good bit of time for rest, ritual, and play. Warfare was limited. Hunting bands might confront one another, but conflict involved more bluster than bloodshed—more serious wars developed only when societies become more advanced. Men and women both had important though separate economic tasks, and overall formal inequality was usually limited. Here too, more complex societies would bring changes that were not necessarily improvements.

Initial Centers and Spread of Agriculture

Early Centers of Civilization

Big Concepts

Each of the key phases of the long period of early human history (2.5 million B.C.E.–1000 B.C.E.) can be characterized by a central topic or Big Concept. The first of these is the development of human hunting skills, the adaptation of those skills to the shifting geography and climate of the Ice Age, and the patterns of human migration. The second Big Concept is the rise of agriculture and the changes in technology associated with the Neolithic revolution (9000 and 4000 B.C.E.). These changes set in motion the agricultural phase of the human experience that lasted until just a few centuries ago. The final Big Concept is the appearance of increasingly distinctive human societies through agriculture or nomadic pastoralism and the earlier contacts among these early societies, particularly after 3500 B.C.E. when larger and more formally organized societies, often with early cities as well, emerged and began to develop more consistent patterns of interregional trade.

TRIGGERS FOR CHANGE

The key story in the long early phases of human history focuses on adaptation to environments, and particularly the search for adequate food supplies. Humans still react to their environment, but the process was more visible in earlier periods, when human ability to control aspects of the environment was less well developed. The early changes in human history—evolutionary development, more advanced toolmaking, and the extensive migrations—all occurred within the context of a hunting-and-gathering economy.

About ten thousand years ago, in the Black Sea region, hunting became less productive. With the end of the Ice Age, climate changes may have reduced big game animals in the region. Perhaps a human population increase led to excessive hunting, depleting the supply of animals. Hunting groups sometimes deliberately kill off too much game, far more than needed, with the unintended consequence of producing a food crisis. Whatever the causes of the shortage, people were forced to look for new sources of food. Women, as gatherers, had undoubtedly become aware of the possibility of deliberately planting seeds and harvesting grain. Thus the rise of agriculture was under way.

Even the advent of new social organizations associated with civilization involved efforts at greater environmental control. Early civilizations provided social structures that could coordinate projects like irrigation. The early civilizations also emerged after the invention of new kinds of tools. The wheel and metal hand tools, initially of bronze, could increase agricultural production and transport. But they also depended on some new manufacturing skills. Greater specialization and greater productivity alike encouraged the kind of organization that early civilization involved. New technology helped shape another new stage in world history.

THE BIG CHANGES

Agriculture offered a very different set of opportunities and problems than hunting-and-gathering, and these had far-reaching consequences. Agriculture al-

INITIAL CENTERS AND SPREAD OF AGRICULTURE
EARLY CENTERS OF CIVILIZATION

2.5 million B.C.E.	1.25 million B.C.E.	150,000 B.C.E.	30,000 B.C.E.	10,000 B.C.E.
2.5 million Emergence of *Homo sapiens* in eastern Africa	1 million Emergence of *Homo erectus*, an upright, tool-using human 600,000 Wide spread of human species across Asia, Europe, Africa; control of fire	120,000 Emergence of *Homo sapiens sapiens*, which displaces other human species	30,000–25,000 Passage of first people to Americas 15,000–12,000 Domestication of dogs	8500–6500 Domestication of sheep, pigs, goats, cattle 8500–3500 Neolithic Age; development of farming in Middle East

tered family forms, for example, by encouraging higher birth rates. It reduced migration, for in most agricultural regions, permanent settlements arose fairly quickly. By creating a surplus of food in most years, agriculture permitted a portion of the population to engage in occupations other than food production. This led to the development of unprecedented levels of social inequality, including heightened inequality between men and women. Agriculture altered the environment, sometimes resulting in overcultivation that depleted the soil. Surplus food allowed humans to live in larger groups, and by doing so it created new vulnerability to communicable diseases. While agriculture clearly generated a mixture of advantages and disadvantages, its greater food production helps explain why it tended to spread and why many people were willing to change basic aspects of their lives to create this economic shift.

As agriculture produced surplus food, the population grew rapidly. In the most fertile areas, agricultural centers developed the organizational forms associated with civilization, most notably formal political structures and cities. Not all did so: stateless, loosely organized agricultural societies persisted in a few places until relatively modern times. But more formal political structures—states—plus larger urban centers—cities—as places to exchange goods and ideas could further the direction of agricultural economies. It was no accident that the first four centers of civilization developed along river valleys, with their opportunities for irrigation: civilization resulted from the prosperity of this kind of agriculture but also responded to its or-

ganizational needs. Civilizations also helped direct many of the surpluses of agricultural economies to upper-class groups—rulers, landlords, and sometimes priests. As with agriculture, though to a lesser extent, the arrival of civilizations had wider consequences. Most early civilizations, for example, developed monumental buildings—often associated with religion—and more formal art and culture were standard features of this final great innovation in early human history.

CONTINUITY

While the development of agriculture brought enormous changes, it is important to remember that important continuities persisted as well. Changes took place very slowly. It took thousands of years for humans to develop New Stone Age technologies such as fashioning tools rather than simply picking up suitably shaped objects.

The slow pace of change had two causes. First, inventing fundamental new devices took time. In some cases, it never occurred at all: impressive agricultural societies flourished without ever developing the wheel or metal tools. In addition, many people remained attached to old ways. Because the food supply was so precarious, taking the risk of innovation probably seemed dangerous. This was one reason that agriculture, though it did fan out from its initial centers, took so long to spread widely. People cherished the habits long associated with migration. Many men valued the challenge of hunting. Some groups held out against agriculture, even when they knew of it.

8000 B.C.E.	6000 B.C.E.	5000 B.C.E.	4000 B.C.E.	2000 B.C.E.
7000 First town at Jericho	5600 Beans domesticated in Western Hemisphere	5000 Domestication of maize (corn) 5000–2000 Yangshao culture in north China	4000–3000 Development of writing, bronze metal-working, wheel, plow in Middle East 3500–1800 Sumerian civilization 3100–1087 Founding and flowering of Egyptian civilization 2500–1500 Indus civilization in south Asia	1850 Origins of Shang kingdom in China 1800 Formation of Babylonian Empire in Middle East 1700–1300 Rise of village culture in Mesoamerica 1600 Beginning of Indo-European invasions of India and parts of the Mediterranean and Middle East 1600 Spread of civilization to Crete (Minoan) 1250 Moses and Jewish exodus from Egypt (according to Jewish belief)

Change could produce efforts to preserve older values in new ways. In hunting-and-gathering societies, men and women both had key productive roles; the roles were very different but they generated some mutual respect. With agriculture, men took on functions that probably seemed rather feminine, because they were linked to food gathering. They had far less time to hunt or to enjoy the masculine rituals associated with hunting. So men looked for ways within agriculture to emphasize manhood. One common response was to claim new levels of superiority over women. This was a key change in gender relations, but it can also be seen as a kind of compensation. To this extent, men could feel that not all traditions were being lost.

Once established, agriculture generated its own impulses toward continuity. Many peasant farmers clung fervently to traditional techniques and village structures, regarding further change with great suspicion. Thus, a tension between change and continuity was built into early human experience.

IMPACT ON DAILY LIFE: CHILDREN

Children are an important part of any human society. Some aspects of children's lives are doubtless natural, part of human experience at any time, in any place. But the arrival of agriculture had huge implications for children. Hunting-and-gathering societies depended on a relatively low birth rate, with few children per family. Too many children would overwhelm resources; and no family could easily transport more than one young child during migrations. So hunters and gatherers limited births, mainly by breast feeding each child for up to four or five years, thus reducing the chances of new conception.

With agriculture, however, more children could be supported, and indeed children became a vital part of the family labor force. Infants began to be weaned at about 18 months on average, a huge change from earlier human patterns. Birth rates shot up—agricultural families usually averaged five to seven children, though some would die, as infant mortality rates were high. Childhood began to be defined in terms of work. Even young children had obligations. And by the time they were teenagers, their families depended on their labor. This was a dramatic redefinition of childhood, even as children became more numerous in the population at large.

Civilization, as an organizational form, had less impact on children, but it added its own changes. Most civilizations developed written language, though only a minority could afford the time to learn to write. As a result, the vast majority of children worked, but an elite minority were sent to school. Also, civilizations used codes of law and other prescriptions to emphasize the duties of children to their families. All agricultural civilizations emphasized the authority of parents over children and children's obligation to obey their parents. In this way, civilizations tried to instill in children a willingness to work for the benefit of their families. Some law codes, as in early Judaism, allowed parents to kill disobedient children. An early Chinese saying stated simply:

"No parent is ever wrong." Children could be loved and could flourish, but there was a distinctive tone of strict discipline and obedience in agricultural civilizations that bolstered the necessity of children's labor.

Small wonder that some hunting-and-gathering or herding groups, when they encountered civilizations, were shocked at how rigorously children were handled. Many American Indians were appalled by the harsh physical discipline European immigrants dealt out to their children. Here was an example of agriculture's profound impact on daily life.

Chapter 1 describes the development of agriculture and the ways in which it changed the lives of early humans. It then describes how farming led, in fertile river valleys, to the development of civilization. It also notes the limits of these developments—the many regions that continued living by hunting and gathering as well as the different trajectory that was followed by societies whose people lived by herding animals rather than by farming. ■

From Human Prehistory to the Early Civilizations

Human Life in the Era of Hunters and Gatherers

The Neolithic Revolution

Civilization

VISUALIZING THE PAST: Mesopotamia in Maps

DOCUMENT: Aryan Poetry in Praise of a War Horse

The Heritage of the River Valley Civilizations

THINKING HISTORICALLY: The Idea of Civilization in World Historical Perspective

GLOBAL CONNECTIONS: The Early Civilizations and the World

One day about 10,000 years ago, in a rock shelter near the Pecos River, an early human inhabitant of what is today West Texas inserted the bloom stalk of a yucca plant into one of several holes worn into a fire-starting stick and, holding the stalk upright, twirled it between her hands, as depicted in the artist's recreation on the next page. After much effort on the part of the young woman, as shown here, the friction between the spinning stalk and the stick produced wisps of smoke, then sparks, then glowing embers. The woman used the embers to set fire to a small pile of dried yucca leaves that she had gathered nearby. Yucca leaves have thin tendrils which, when dry, catch fire readily. Carefully tended, the leaves could be used to kindle a steady fire that provided not only warmth, but the means for cooking a meal. And, importantly, stalks, fire-sticks, and leaves could easily be carried by migratory groups of early humans.

Several yucca-based fire-starter kits, some including bows used in the place of hands to turn the yucca stalk, have been found across the American Southwest. These Neolithic (New Stone Age) kits send us a number of messages about early world history. Most obviously, early men and women were tool users. They not only deliberately selected branches, stones, and other natural objects from the environment, they crafted them into weapons, utensils, and tools that could be used to ward off animal and human enemies, hunt, trap, fish, prepare food, and construct shelters. This capacity to fashion tools distinguishes human beings from all other animals. Although a number of other animals, including apes, are tool users, only human beings construct their tools. By this time, humans had known how to make and use fire for thousands of years—another discovery unique to humans. The use of fire for cooking allowed early humans to eat a wider variety of foods, particularly animal protein.

The toolmakers of the American Southwest lived far from eastern Africa, where human beings first evolved. Just decades ago, it was believed that the first humans migrated from northeast Asia into what is now Alaska only 12,000 years ago. Vastly improved archeological techniques have recently revealed that the crossing had been made at least as early as 25,000 B.C.E. and that the migrants spread out quickly, probably traveling both overland and by boat along the Pacific Coast, from Alaska to Chile.

Finally, we know our early ancestors could talk. Human beings had developed what some call the "speech gene" about 70,000 years earlier, vastly improving the species' capacity to communicate, beyond the sounds and gestures common to a number of animal groups. Neolithic humans were what we sometimes call "primitive," but they had already experienced a number of fundamental changes and, in some places, they were poised to introduce some more. ■

The creation of fire-starters and other tools, including weapons, proved critical to the survival of early humans and to the development of ever larger communities and eventually whole societies. In the chapter that follows we will trace the successive stages of the early material and social development of the human species. We will explore the technological and organizational innovations that made it possible for what became the great majority of humans to move from tiny bands of wandering hunters and gatherers to sedentary village dwellers and then the builders of walled cities with populations in the thousands. More than any other factor, these transformations were made possible by the development of agriculture that increased and made more secure the supply of food by which more and more humans could be sustained.

The domestication of animals and the shift to agriculture was accompanied by major changes in the roles and relationships between men and women and patterns of childrearing. They also led

Figure 1.1 Crouching against a wall to shelter the first sparks from wind, a Neolithic woman spins a dried yucca stalk against a much-used fire-starter to generate heat that will kindle a fire on the dried plant material she has placed under the fire-starting stick.

to increasing social stratification, new forms of political organization, increasingly elaborate means of artistic expression, and more lethal ways of waging war, During these millennia of transition farming communities occupied only small pockets of the earth's land area and only rarely ventured out on the sea or large rivers. Pastoral peoples who depended on herds of domesticated animals for their livelihood occupied a far greater share of the space where there was a human presence. An uneasy balance between the peoples who followed these two main adaptations to the diverse ecosystems in which humans proved able to survive was a dominant feature of the history of the species and the planet until five or six centuries.

Human Life in the Era of Hunters and Gatherers

The human species has accomplished a great deal in a relatively short period of time. There are significant disagreements over how long an essentially human species, as distinct from other primates, has existed. However, a figure of 2 or 2.5 million years seems acceptable. This is approximately 1/4000 of the time the earth has existed. That is, if one thinks of the whole history of the earth to date as a 24-hour day, the human species began at about 5 minutes before midnight. Human beings have existed for less than 5 percent of the time mammals of any sort have lived. Yet in this brief span of time—by earth-history standards—humankind has spread to every landmass (with the exception of the polar regions) and, for better or worse, has taken control of the destinies of countless other species.

Hunting and gathering economies dominated human history until 9000 B.C.E. These economies helped propel migration over most of the lands on earth.

To be sure, human beings have some drawbacks as a species, compared to other existing models. They are unusually aggressive against their own kind: While some of the great apes, notably chimpanzees, engage in periodic wars, these conflicts can hardly rival human violence. Human babies are dependent for a long period, which requires some special child-care arrangements and often has limited the activities of many adult women. Certain ailments, such as back problems resulting from an upright stature, also burden the species. And, insofar as we know, the human species is alone in its awareness of the inevitability of death—a knowledge that imparts some unique fears and tensions.

	Transition Phase	
2.5 Million B.C.E.	**30,000 B.C.E.**	**10,000 B.C.E.**
2.5 million Emergence of more humanlike species, initially in eastern Africa 750,000 Further development of human species into *Homo erectus* 600,000 Wide spread of human species across Asia, Europe, Africa; development of fire use 240,000–100,000 Apparent completion of basic human evolution; migrations from Africa begin; *Homo sapiens sapiens* displaces other human species	25,000 Migration of people from Siberia to tip of South America 14,000 End of great ice age 12,000 Fashioning of stone tools; end of Paleolithic (Old Stone) Age	10,000–8000 Development of farming in the Middle East 9000 Domestication of sheep, pigs, goats, cattle 8000 Transition of agriculture; introduction of silk weaving in China

Distinctive features of the human species account for considerable achievement as well. Like other primates, but unlike most other mammals, people can manipulate objects fairly readily because of the grip provided by an opposable thumb on each hand. Compared to other primates, human beings have a relatively high and regular sexual drive, which aids reproduction. Being omnivores, they are not dependent exclusively on plants or animals for food, which helps explain why they can live in so many different climates and settings. The unusual variety of their facial expressions aids communication and enhances social life. The distinctive human brain and a facility for elaborate speech are even more important: much of human history depends on the knowledge, inventions, and social contracts that resulted from these assets. Features of this sort explain why many human cultures, including the Western culture that many Americans share, promote a firm separation between human and animal, seeing in our own species a power and rationality, and possibly a spark of the divine, that "lower" creatures lack.

Although the rise of humankind has been impressively rapid, its early stages can also be viewed as painfully long and slow. Most of the two million plus years during which our species has existed are described by the term **Paleolithic (Old Stone) Age.** Throughout this long time span, which runs until about 14,000 years ago, human beings learned only simple tool use, mainly through employing suitably shaped rocks and sticks for hunting and warfare. Fire was tamed about 750,000 years ago. The nature of the species also gradually changed during the Paleolithic, with emphasis on more erect stature and growing brain capacity. Archeological evidence, remnants of tools from early settlements, also indicates some increases in average size. A less apelike species, whose larger brain and erect stance allowed better tool use, emerged between 500,000 and 750,000 years ago; it is called, appropriately enough, *Homo erectus*. Several species of *Homo erectus* developed and spread in Africa, then to Asia and Europe, reaching a population size of perhaps 1.5 million 100,000 years ago.

Paleolithic Age The Old Stone Age ending in 12,000 B.C.E.; typified by use of crude stone tools and hunting and gathering for subsistence.

Late Paleolithic Developments

Considerable evidence suggests that more advanced types of humans killed off or displaced many competitors over time, which explains why there is only one basic human type throughout the world today, rather than a number of rather similar human species, as among monkeys and apes. There was also a certain amount of intermarriage. The newest human breed, **Homo sapiens sapiens,** of which all humans in the world today are descendants, originated about 240,000 years ago, also in Africa. The success of this subspecies means that no major changes in the basic human physique or brain size have occurred since its advent.

Homo sapiens The humanoid species that emerged as most successful at the end of the Paleolithic period.

Even after the appearance of *Homo sapiens sapiens,* human life faced important constraints. People who hunted food and gathered nuts and berries could not support large numbers or elaborate societies. Most hunting groups were small, and they had to roam widely for food. Two people required at least one square mile for survival. Population growth was slow, partly because women breast-fed infants for several years to limit their own fertility. On the other hand, people did not have to work very hard—hunting took about seven hours every three days on average. Women, who gathered fruits and

The Toolmaker

Neolithic Age			Metal Age	
6000 B.C.E.	**4000** B.C.E.	**3000** B.C.E.	**2000** B.C.E.	
6000 First potter's wheel 5500 Çatal Hüyük at its peak 5000 Domestication of maize (corn) in Mesoamerica	4000 Yangshao culture in China 4000–3000 Age of innovation in the Middle East: introduction of writing, bronze metalwork, wheel, plow 3500–1800 Civilization of Sumer; cuneiform alphabet 3100 Rise of Egyptian civilization	2500 Emergence of Harappan (Indus) civilization	2000 Kotosh culture in Peru 2000 Conversion to agriculture in northern Europe, southern Africa 1500 Emergence of Shang kingdom in China; writing develops 1500 First ironwork in the Middle East 1200 Jews settle near the Mediterranean; first monotheistic religion 1122 Western Zhou kings	

vegetables, worked harder, but there was significant equality between the sexes based on common economic contributions.

Paleolithic people gradually improved their tool use, beginning with the crude shaping of stone and wooden implements. Speech developed with *Homo erectus* 100,000 years ago, allowing more group cooperation and the transmission of technical knowledge. By the later Paleolithic period, people had developed rituals to lessen the fear of death and created cave paintings to express a sense of nature's beauty and power (Figure 1.2). Goddesses often played a prominent role in the religious pantheon. Thus, the human species came to develop cultures—that is, systems of belief that helped explain the environment and set up rules for various kinds of social behavior. The development of speech provided rich language and symbols for the transmission of culture and its growing sophistication. At the same time, different groups of humans, in different locations, developed quite varied belief systems and corresponding languages.

The greatest achievement of Paleolithic people was the sheer spread of the human species over much of the earth's surface. The species originated in eastern Africa; most of the earliest types of human remains come from this region, in the present-day countries of Tanzania, Kenya, and Uganda. But gradual migration, doubtless caused by the need to find scarce food, steadily pushed the human reach to other areas. Key discoveries, notably fire and the use of animal skins for clothing—both of which enabled people to live in colder climates—facilitated the spread of Paleolithic groups. The first people moved out of Africa about 750,000 years ago. Human remains (Peking man, Java man) dating from 600,000 and 350,000 years ago have been found in China and southeast Asia, respectively. Humans inhabited Britain 250,000 years ago. They first crossed to Australia 60,000 years ago, followed by another group 20,000 years later; these combined to form the continent's aboriginal population. Dates of the migration from Asia to the Americas are under debate. Most scholars now believe that humans crossed what was then a land bridge from Siberia to Alaska about 30,000 years ago, with several subsequent migration waves until warmer climates and rising ocean levels eliminated the land bridge by 8000 B.C.E.*

Figure 1.2 In Lascaux, France, in 1940, four boys happened upon a long-hidden cave filled with thousands of complex and beautiful Stone Age paintings like this one. Most of the paintings are of animals, some of which were extinct by the time they were painted. No one knows for sure why Stone Age artists painted these pictures, but they remain a powerful reminder of the sophistication of so-called primitive peoples.

 The Spread of Human Populations

* In Christian societies, historical dating divides between years "before the birth of Christ" (B.C.) and after (A.D., *anno Domini*, or "year of our Lord"). This system came into wide acceptance in Europe in the 18th century, as formal historical consciousness increased (although ironically, 1 A.D. is a few years late for Jesus' actual birth). China, Islam, Judaism, and many other societies use different dating systems, referring to their own history. This text, like many recent world history materials, uses the Christian chronology (one has to choose some system) but changes the terms to B.C.E. ("before the common era") and C.E. ("of the common era") as a gesture to less Christian-centric labeling.

Map 1.1 The Spread of Human Populations, c. 10,000 B.C.E.   As the map indicates, *Homo sapiens sapiens* first emerged in a single core area in east Africa and then migrated over long periods of time north to the Mediterranean and Europe, east to Asia, and then ultimately across the seas to the Americas and Oceania.

Many of the new arrivals quickly spread out, reaching the tip of the South American continent possibly within a mere thousand years. Settlers from China reached Taiwan, the Philippines, and Indonesia 4500 to 3500 years ago.

In addition, soon after this time—roughly 14,000 years ago—the last great ice age ended, which did wonders for living conditions over much of the Northern Hemisphere. Human development began to accelerate. In the Mesolithic (Middle Stone) Age, a span of several thousand years, from about 12,000 to 8000 B.C.E., human ability to fashion stone tools and other implements improved greatly. People learned to sharpen and shape stone, to make better weapons and cutting edges. Animal bones were used to make needles and other precise tools. People built log rafts and dugouts, which improved fishing, and manufactured pots and baskets for food storage. Mesolithic people domesticated more animals, such as cows, which again improved food supply. Population growth accelerated, which also resulted in more conflicts and wars. Skeletons from this period show frequent bone breaks and skull fractures caused by weapons.

Neolithic Age The New Stone Age between 8000 and 5000 B.C.E.; period in which adaptation of sedentary agriculture occurred; domestication of plants and animals accomplished.

In time, better tool use, somewhat more elaborate social organization, and still more population pressure led people in many parts of the world to the final Stone Age—the **Neolithic (New Stone) Age** (Map 1.1). From Neolithic people, in turn, came several more dramatic developments that changed the nature of human existence—the invention of agriculture, the creation of cities, and other foreshadowings of civilization, which ended the Stone Age altogether throughout much of the world.

The Neolithic Revolution

The Neolithic revolution centered on the development of agriculture.

Agriculture generated a variety of important changes in human cultures. Human achievements during the various ages of stone are both fascinating and fundamental, and some points are hotly debated. Our knowledge of Stone Age society is of course limited, although archeologists have been creative in their interpretations of tool remains and other evidence, such as cave paintings and burial sites, that Stone Age people produced in various parts of the world. What people accomplished during this long period of prehistory remains essential to human life today; our ability to make and manipulate tools thus depends directly on what our Stone Age ancestors learned about physical matter.

However, it was the invention of agriculture that most clearly moved the human species toward more elaborate social and cultural patterns of the sort that people today would find recognizable. With agriculture, human beings were able to settle in one spot and focus on particular economic, political, and religious goals and activities. Agriculture also spawned a great increase in the sheer number of people in the world—from about 6 to 8 million across the earth's surface during early Neolithic times, to about 100 million some 3000 years later.

The initial development of agriculture—that is, the deliberate planting of grains for later harvest—was probably triggered by two results of the ice age's end. First, population increases, stemming from improved climate, prompted people to search for new and more reliable sources of food. Second, the end of the ice age saw the retreat of certain big game animals, such as mastodons. Human hunters had to turn to smaller game, such as deer and wild boar, in many forested areas. Hunting's overall yield declined. Here was the basis for new interest in other sources of food. There is evidence that by 9000 B.C.E., in certain parts of the world, people were becoming increasingly dependent on regular harvests of wild grains, berries, and nuts. This undoubtedly set the stage for the deliberate planting of seeds (probably accidental to begin with) and the improvement of key grains through the selection of seeds from the best plants.

As farming evolved, new animals were also domesticated. Particularly in the Middle East and parts of Asia, by 9000 B.C.E. pigs, sheep, goats, and cattle were being raised. Farmers used these animals for meat and skins and soon discovered dairying as well. These results not only contributed to the development of agriculture but also served as the basis for nomadic herding societies.

 The Spread of Agriculture

The Geography of Early Agriculture

Farming was initially developed in the Middle East, in an arc of territory running from present-day Turkey to Iraq and Israel. This was a very fertile area, more fertile in those days than at present. Grains such as barley and wild wheat were abundant. At the same time, this area was not heavily forested, and animals were in short supply, presenting a challenge to hunters. In the Middle East, the development of agriculture may have begun as early as 10,000 B.C.E., and it gained ground rapidly after 8000 B.C.E. Gradually during the Neolithic centuries, knowledge of agriculture spread to other centers, including parts of India, north Africa, and Europe. Agriculture also developed independently; for example, with the rise of rice cultivation in southeast Asia, from which it spread to China. Thus, within a few thousand years agriculture had spread to the parts of the world that would produce the first human civilizations (Map 1.2). We will see that agriculture spread later to much of Africa south of the Mediterranean coast, reaching west Africa by 2000 B.C.E., although here too there were additional developments with an emphasis on local grains and also root crops such as yams. Agriculture had to be invented separately in the Americas, based on corn cultivation, where it was also a slightly later development (about 5000 B.C.E.).

Many scholars have termed the development of agriculture a **Neolithic revolution.** The term is obviously misleading in one sense: agriculture was no sudden transformation, even in the Middle East where the new system had its roots. Learning the new agricultural methods was difficult, and many peoples long combined a bit of agriculture with considerable reliance on the older systems of **hunting and gathering.** A "revolution" that took over a thousand years, and then several thousand more to spread to key population centers in Asia, Europe, and Africa, is hardly dramatic by modern standards.

Neolithic revolution The succession of technological innovations and changes in human organization that led to the development of agriculture, 8500–3500 B.C.E.

hunting and gathering The original human economy, ultimately eclipsed by agriculture; groups hunt for meat and forage for grains, nuts, and berries.

Patterns of Change

The concept of revolution is, however, appropriate in demonstrating the magnitude of change involved. Early agriculture could support far more people per square mile than hunting ever could; it also allowed people to settle more permanently in one area. The system was nonetheless not easy. Agriculture required more regular work, at least of men, than hunting did. Hunting groups today, such as the pygmies of the Kalahari Desert in southwest Africa, work an average of 2.5 hours a day, alternating long, intense hunts with periods of idleness. As much as agriculture was demanding, it

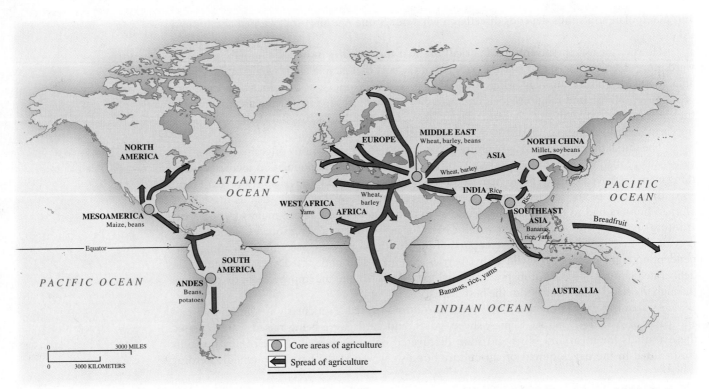

Map 1.2 The Spread of Agriculture Agriculture appears to have spread in ways similar to human populations, but from a Middle Eastern rather than African epicenter. And in important cases, particularly in the Americas, a wide range of staple crops were known in only some parts of the world until Columbus's voyage in the late-15th century brought together the civilizations of the Americas and Afro-Euroasia.

was also rewarding. Agriculture supported larger populations, and with better food supplies and a more settled existence, agricultural peoples could afford to build houses and villages. Domesticated animals provided not only hides but also wool for more varied clothing.

We know next to nothing of the debates that must have raged when people were first confronted with agriculture, but it is not hard to imagine that many would have found the new life too complicated, too difficult, or too unexciting. Most evidence suggests that gathering-and-hunting peoples resisted agriculture as long as they could. Gradually, of course, agriculture did gain ground. Its success was hard to deny. And as farmers cleared new land from forests, they automatically drove out or converted many hunters. Disease played a role: settled agricultural societies suffered from more contagious diseases because of denser population concentrations. Hunting-and-gathering peoples lacked resistance and often died when agriculturists who had developed immunity to these diseases carried them into their areas.

Not all the peoples of the world came to embrace the slowly spreading wave of agriculture, at least not until very recently. Important small societies in southern Africa, Australia, the islands of southeast Asia, and even northern Japan were isolated for so long that news of this economic system simply did not reach them. The light-skinned hunting tribes of northern Japan flourished until about a hundred years ago. Northern Europeans and southern Africans converted to agriculture earlier, about 2000 years ago, but well after the Neolithic revolution had transformed other parts of their continents. Agriculture was initiated in the Americas as early as 5000 B.C.E. and developed vigorously in Central America and the northern part of South America. However, most Indian tribes in North America continued a hunting-and-gathering existence, sometimes combined with limited agriculture, until recent centuries. Finally, the peoples of the vast plains of central Asia long resisted a complete conversion to agriculture, in part because of a harsh climate; herding, rather than grain-growing, became the basic socioeconomic system of this part of the world. From this area would come waves of tough, nomadic invaders whose role in linking major civilizations was a vital force in world history until a few centuries ago.

Further Technological Change

Development possibilities among people who became agriculturists were more obvious than those among smaller populations who resisted or simply did not know of the system. Agriculture set the basis for more rapid change in human societies. Greater wealth and larger populations freed some people for other specializations, from which new ideas or techniques might spring. Agriculture itself depended on control over nature that could be facilitated by newly developed techniques and objects. For example, during the Neolithic period, farming people needed storage facilities for grains and seeds, which promoted the development of basket-making and pottery. The first potter's wheel came into existence around 6000 B.C.E., and this, in turn, encouraged faster and higher-quality pottery production. Agricultural needs also encouraged certain kinds of science, supporting the human inclination to learn more about weather or flooding.

Much of what we think of as human history involves the doings of agricultural societies—societies, that is, in which most people are farmers and in which the production of food is the central economic activity. Nonagricultural groups, like the nomadic herders in central Asia, made their own mark, but their greatest influence usually occurred in interactions with agricultural peoples. Many societies remain largely agricultural today. The huge time span we have thus far considered, including the Neolithic revolution itself, is all technically "prehistorical"—involved with human patterns before the invention of writing allowed the kinds of recordkeeping historians prefer. In fact, since we now know how to use surviving tools and burial sites as records, the prehistoric–historic distinction means less than it once did. The preagricultural–agricultural distinction is more central. Fairly soon after the development of agriculture—although not, admittedly, right away—significant human change began to occur in decades and centuries, rather than in the sizeable blocks of time, several thousand years or more, that describe preagricultural peoples.

Indeed, one basic change took place fairly soon after the introduction of agriculture, and, again, societies in the Middle East served as its birthplace. The discovery of metal tools dates back to about 4000 B.C.E. Copper was the first metal with which people learned how to work, although a more resilient metal, bronze, soon entered the picture. In fact, the next basic age of human existence was the **Bronze Age.** By about 3000 B.C.E., metalworking had become so commonplace in the Middle East that the use of stone tools dissipated, and the long stone ages were over at last—although, of course, an essentially Neolithic technology persisted in many parts of the world, even among some agricultural peoples.

Bronze Age From about 4000 B.C.E., when bronze tools were first introduced in the Middle East, to about 1500 B.C.E., when iron began to replace it.

Metalworking was extremely useful to agricultural or herding societies. Metal hoes and other tools allowed farmers to work the ground more efficiently. Metal weapons were obviously superior to those made from stone and wood. Agricultural peoples had the resources to free up a small number of individuals as toolmakers, who would specialize in this activity and exchange their products with farmers for food. Specialization of this sort did not, however, guarantee rapid rates of invention; indeed, many specialized artisans seemed very conservative, eager to preserve methods that had been inherited. But specialization did improve the conditions or climate for discovery, and the invention of metalworking was a key result. Like agriculture, knowledge of metals gradually fanned out to other parts of Asia and to Africa and Europe.

Gradually, the knowledge of metal tools created further change, for not only farmers but also manufacturing artisans benefited from better tools. Woodworking, for example, became steadily more elaborate as metal replaced stone, bone, and fire in the cutting and connecting of wood. We are still living in the metal ages today, although we rely primarily on iron—whose working was introduced around 1500 B.C.E. by herding peoples who invaded the Middle East—rather than copper and bronze.

Civilization

The emergence of civilization occurred in many though not all agricultural societies.

Agriculture encouraged the formation of larger as well as more stable human communities than had existed before Neolithic times. A few Mesolithic groups had formed villages, particularly where opportunities for fishing were good, as around some of the lakes in Switzerland. However, most

Early civilizations formed in Mesopotamia, Egypt, the Indus River basin, and China.

hunting peoples moved in relatively small groups, or tribes, each containing anywhere from 40 to 60 individuals, and they could not settle in a single spot without the game running out. With agriculture, these constraints changed. To be sure, some agricultural peoples did move around. A system called **slash and burn agriculture** existed in many parts of the world, including portions of the American South, until about 150 years ago. Here, people would burn off trees in an area, farm intensively for a few years until the soil was depleted, and then move on—often returning to earlier sites every 20–30 years. Herding peoples also moved in tribal **bands,** with strong kinship ties. The rise of nomadic herding economies was a vital development in Central Asia, the Middle East, the Sudan and elsewhere.

slash and burn agriculture   A system of cultivation typical of shifting cultivators; forest floors cleared by fire are then planted.

band   A level of social organization normally consisting of 20 to 30 people; nomadic hunters and gatherers; labor divided on a gender basis.

Settled Societies

The Neolithic
Village

The major agricultural regions, however, involved more permanent settlements. There were advantages to staying put: houses could be built to last, wells built to bring up water, and other "expensive" improvements afforded because they would serve many generations. In the Middle East, China, and parts of Africa and India, a key incentive to stability was the need for irrigation devices to channel river water to the fields. This same need helps explain why agriculture generated communities and not a series of isolated farms. Small groups simply could not regulate a river's flow or build and maintain irrigation ditches and sluices. Irrigation and defense encouraged villages—groupings of several hundred people—as the characteristic pattern of residence in almost all agricultural societies from Neolithic days until our own century. Neolithic settlements spread widely in agricultural societies. New ones continued to be founded as agriculture spread to regions such as northern Europe, as late as 1500 B.C.E. (Figure 1.3).

Çatal Hüyük   [kah-THAL HOHY-uhk] Early urban culture based on sedentary agriculture; located in modern southern Turkey; was larger in population than Jericho, had greater degree of social stratification.

One Neolithic village, **Çatal Hüyük** (kah-THAL HOHY-uhk) in southern Turkey, has been elaborately studied by archeologists. It was founded about 7000 B.C.E. and was unusually large, covering about 32 acres. Houses were made of mud bricks set in timber frameworks, crowded together, with few windows. People seem to have spent a good bit of time on their rooftops in order to experience daylight and make social contacts—many broken bones attest to frequent falls. Some houses were lavishly decorated, mainly with hunting scenes. Religious images, both of powerful male hunters and "mother goddesses" devoted to agricultural fertility, were common, and some people in the village seem to have had special religious responsibilities. The village produced almost all the goods it consumed. Some trade was conducted with hunting peoples who lived in the hills surrounding the village, but apparently it was initiated more to keep the peace than to produce economic gain (Figure 1.4). By 5500 B.C.E., important production activities developed in the village, including those of skilled toolmakers and jewelers. With time also came links with other communities. Large villages like Çatal Hüyük ruled over smaller communities. This meant that some families began to specialize in politics, and military forces were organized. Some villages became small cities, ruled by kings who were typically given divine status.

By 3000 B.C.E., Çatal Hüyük had become part of a civilization. Although many of the characteristics of civilization had existed by 6000 or 5000 B.C.E. in this Middle Eastern region, the origins of civilization, strictly speaking, approximately date to only 3500 B.C.E. The first civilization arose in the Middle East along the banks of the Tigris and Euphrates rivers. Another center of civilization started soon thereafter in northeast Africa (Egypt), and a third by around 2500 B.C.E. along the banks of the Indus River in northwestern India. These three early centers of civilization had some interaction. The fourth and fifth early civilization centers, a bit later and considerably more separate, arose in China and Central America.

Figure 1.3 Skara Brae, located in the Orkney Islands off the coast of Scotland, is an excellent example of a late Neolithic settlement. It dates from 1500 B.C.E. Houses included special storage areas for grain, water, and other essentials. Most were centered on clay or stone hearths that were ventilated through a hole in the roof or built into the wall. More dependable and varied food supplies and sturdy houses greatly enhanced the security and comfort of the people who lived in these settlements. Better conditions spurred higher birth rates and lowered mortality rates, at least in times when crop yields were high.

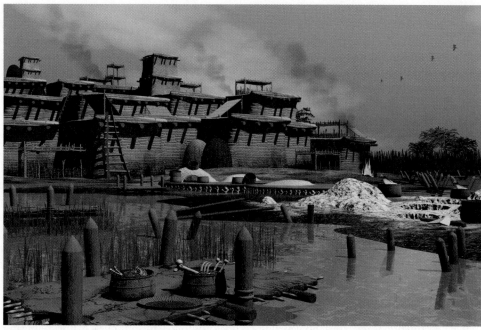

Figure 1.4 This artist's rendering depicts the ancient settlement at Çatal Hüyük, in what is now southern Turkey. Movement within the settlement was mainly across the roofs and terraces of the houses. Because each dwelling had a substantial storeroom for food, the settlement was often the target of attacks by outsiders. As the painting shows, the houses were joined together to provide protection from such attacks; when the outside entrances were barricaded, the complex was transformed into a fortress.

Defining Civilization

Unlike an agricultural society, which can be rather precisely defined, **civilization** is a more subjective construct. Some scholars prefer to define civilizations only as societies with enough economic surpluses to form divisions of labor and a social hierarchy involving significant inequalities. This is a very inclusive definition, and under it most agricultural societies and even some groups like North American Indians who combined farming with hunting would be drawn in. Others, however, press the concepts of civilization further, arguing, for example, that a chief difference between civilizations and other societies (whether hunting or agricultural) involves the emergence of formal political organizations, or states, as opposed to dependence on family or tribal ties. Most civilizations produce political units capable of ruling large regions, and some characteristically produce huge kingdoms or empires.

The word *civilization* itself comes from the Latin term for *city,* and in truth most civilizations do depend on the existence of significant cities. In agricultural civilizations, most people do not live in cities. But cities are crucial because they amass wealth and power, and they allow the rapid exchange of ideas among relatively large numbers of people, thereby encouraging intellectual thought and artistic expression. Cities also promote specialization in manufacturing and trade and encourage the emergence of centers of political power.

Most civilizations developed writing, starting with the emergence of **cuneiform** (kyoo-NAY-uh-form) (writing based on wedgelike characters) in the Middle East around 3500 B.C.E. Societies that employ writing can organize more elaborate political structures because of their ability to send messages and keep records. They can tax more efficiently and make contracts and treaties. Societies with writing also generate a more explicit intellectual climate because of their ability to record data and build on past, written wisdom. (One of the early written records from the Middle East is a recipe for making beer—a science of a sort.) Some experts argue that the very fact of becoming literate changes the way people think, encouraging them to consider the world as a place that can be understood by organized human inquiry, or "rationally," and less by a host of spiritual beliefs. In all agricultural civilizations—that is, in all human history until less than 200 years ago—only a minority

civilization Societies distinguished by reliance on sedentary agriculture, ability to produce food surpluses, and existence of nonfarming elites, as well as merchant and manufacturing groups.

cuneiform [kyoo-NAY-uh-form] A form of writing developed by the Sumerians using a wedge-shaped stylus and clay tablets.

of people was literate, and usually that was a small minority. Nonetheless, the existence of writing did make a difference in such societies.

Since civilizations employ writing and are by definition unusually well organized, it is not surprising that almost all recorded history is about what has happened to civilized societies. We simply know the most about such societies, and we often are particularly impressed by what they produce in the way of great art or powerful rulers. It is also true that civilizations tend to be far more populous than nomadic or hunting-and-gathering societies. Therefore, the history of civilization generally covers the history of most people.

But the history of civilization does not include everybody. Few hunting or nomadic peoples could generate a civilization—they lacked the stability and resources, and, with the exception of a limited number of signs and symbols, they never developed writing, unless it came from the outside. Furthermore, some agricultural peoples did not develop a full civilization, *if* our definition of civilization goes beyond the simple acquisition of economic surplus to formal states, cities, and writing. Portions of west Africa, fully agricultural and capable of impressive art, have long lacked writing, major cities, or more than loose regional government.

People in civilizations, particularly during the long centuries when they were surrounded by nomadic peoples, characteristically looked down on any society lacking in civilization. The ancient Greeks coined the word *barbarian* to describe such cases—indeed, they were prone to regard all non-Greeks as barbarians. As a result of labels like this, it is easy to think of much human history as divided between civilizations and primitive **nomads.**

Such a distinction is incorrect, however, and it does not follow from the real historical meaning of civilization. In the first place, like agriculture, civilization brings losses as well as gains. As Çatal Hüyük moved toward civilization, distinctions based on social class and wealth increased. Civilizations often have firmer class or caste divisions, including slavery, than do "simpler" societies. They also often promote greater separation between the rulers and ruled, monarchs and subjects. Frequently, they are quite warlike, and there is greater inequality between men and women than in hunter-gatherer societies. With civilization, more fully patriarchal structures emerged. In cities, male superiority was even clearer than in agriculture, as men did most of the manufacturing and assumed political and religious leadership, thus relegating women to subordinate roles. "Civilization," then, is not a synonym for "good."

By the same token, nomadic or hunter-gatherer societies may be exceptionally well regulated, with complex and imaginative cultures. Many such societies, in fact, have more regulations—in part, because they depend on rules transmitted by word of mouth—than civilized societies. Some of the societies most eager to repress anger and aggression in human dealings, such as Zuni Indians in the American Southwest, are based at least in part on hunting and gathering. Although some hunting-gathering societies treat old people cruelly, others display more respect and veneration toward elders than most civilizations do. Many nomadic societies may be shocked by the doings of civilized peoples. For example, American Indians were appalled at the insistence of European settlers on spanking their children, a behavior they regarded as vicious and unnecessary. A fascinating, although probably unanswerable, question involves determining whether or not the civilization form has left more or less good in its wake.

It is also important to note that many nomadic peoples contributed greatly to world history. While many remaining hunting-and-gathering peoples became increasingly isolated, except in parts of the Americas, nomadic herding economies continued to flourish in many places. They depended on the domestication of animals and on key technological improvements, for example in riding equipment and weaponry. Precisely because they traveled widely, nomadic peoples could play vital roles in world trade and in developing contacts among more settled areas. Nomadic groups in central Asia would play a particularly great role in world history, but groups in the Middle East and Africa were significant as well.

Despite the importance of alternatives, it remains true that the development of civilization most obviously continued the process of technological change and political organization. Civilizations also generated the largest populations and the most elaborate artistic and intellectual forms. It is in this context that the term has real meaning and in which it legitimately commands the attention of most historians.

Civilizations also increased human impact on the environment. For example, the first center of copper production in Europe, along the Danube valley, led to such deforestation that the fuel supply was destroyed, and the industry collapsed after about 3000 B.C.E. The extensive agriculture

nomads   Cattle- and sheep-herding societies normally found on the fringes of civilized societies; commonly referred to as "barbarian" by civilized societies.

needed to support Indus River cities opened the land to erosion and flooding because of overuse of the soil and removal of trees.

Having started in 3500 B.C.E., civilization developed in its four initial centers—the Middle East, Egypt, northwestern India, and northern China—over the following 2500 years. (An early civilization would also emerge in Central America, though slightly later in time.) These areas covered only a tiny portion of the inhabited parts of the world, although they were the most densely populated. Such early civilizations, all clustered in key river valleys, were in a way pilot tests of the new form of social organization. Only after about 1000 B.C.E. did a more consistent process of development and spread of civilization begin—and with it came the main threads of world history. However, the great civilizations unquestionably built on the achievements of the river valley pioneers, and so some understanding of this contribution to the list of early human accomplishments is essential.

Tigris–Euphrates Civilization

The most noteworthy achievements of the earliest civilizations were early versions of organizational and cultural forms that most of us now take for granted: writing, formal codes of law, city planning and architecture, and institutions for trade, including the use of money. Once developed, most of these building blocks of human organization did not have to be reinvented, although in some cases they spread only slowly to other parts of the world.

It is not surprising then, given its lead in agriculture, metalworking, and village structure, that the Middle East generated the first example of human civilization. Indeed, the first civilization, founded in the valley of the Tigris and Euphrates rivers in a part of the Middle East long called **Mesopotamia** (Map 1.3), forms one of only a few cases of a civilization developed absolutely from scratch—and with no examples from anyplace else to imitate. (Chinese civilization and civilization in Central America also developed independently.) By 4000 B.C.E., the farmers of Mesopotamia were familiar with bronze and copper and had already invented the wheel for transportation. They had a well established pottery industry and interesting artistic forms. Farming in this area, because of the need for irrigation, required considerable coordination among communities, and this in turn served as the basis for complex political structures.

Mesopotamia   Literally "between the rivers"; the civilizations that arose in the alluvial plain of the Tigris and Euphrates river valleys.

By about 3500 B.C.E., a people who had recently invaded this region, the **Sumerians**, developed a cuneiform alphabet, the first known case of human writing. Their alphabet at first used different pictures to represent various objects but soon shifted to the use of geometric shapes to symbolize spoken sounds. The early Sumerian alphabet may have had as many as 2000 such symbols, but this number was later reduced to about 300. Even so, writing and reading remained complex skills, which only a few had time to master. Scribes wrote on clay tablets, using styluses shaped quite like the modern ballpoint pen.

Sumerians   People who migrated into Mesopotamia c. 4000 B.C.E.; created first civilization within region; organized area into city-states.

Sumerian art developed steadily, as statues and painted frescoes were used to adorn the temples of the gods. Statues of the gods also decorated individual homes. Sumerian science aided a complex agricultural society, as people sought to learn more about the movement of the sun and stars—thus founding the science of astronomy—and improved their mathematical knowledge. (Astronomy defined the calendar and provided the astrological forecasts widely used in politics and religion.) The Sumerians employed a system of numbers based on units of 10, 60, and 360 that we still use in calculating circles and hours. In other words, Sumerians and their successors in Mesopotamia created patterns of observation and abstract thought about nature that a number of civilizations, including our own, still rely on, and they also introduced specific systems, such as charts of major constellations, that have been current at least among educated people for 5000 years, not only in the Middle East, but by later imitation in India and Europe as well.

ziggurats   [ZIG-uh-rat] Massive towers usually associated with Mesopotamian temple complexes.

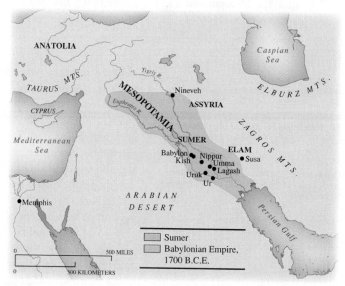

Sumerians developed complex religious rituals. Each city had a patron god and erected impressive shrines to please and honor this and other deities. Massive towers, called **ziggurats** (ZIG-uh-rat), formed the first monumental architecture in this civilization. Professional priests operated these temples and conducted the rituals within. Sumerians

Map 1.3 Early Sumer

Mesopotamia in Maps

Throughout their centuries of existence, the Mesopotamian civilizations steadily expanded from their roots in the fertile valley between the Tigris and Euphrates Rivers. Reading the maps can help explain the nature of the civilizations in the region.

QUESTIONS What do these maps suggest about the relationship between Mesopotamian civilizations and the topography of the Middle East? Does geography suggest reasons for invasion and political instability in this civilization center? Did later empires in the region have the same relationship to river valleys as did the earlier states? What were the potential contacts between Mesopotamia and other river valley civilization centers? Why has the Middle East been so significant in European, African, and Asian history?

Map 1.4 Mesopotamia and the Middle East   This map shows the location of Sumer and two later empires in the Middle East and eastern Mediterranean.

---

city-state   A form of political organization typical of Mesopotamian civilizations; consisted of agricultural hinterlands ruled by an urban-based king.

Babylonian Empire   Unified all of Mesopotamia c. 1800 B.C.E.; collapsed due to foreign invasion c. 1600 B.C.E.

Hammurabi   (r. 1792–1750 B.C.E.) The most important ruler of the Babylonian empire; responsible for codification of law.

pharaoh   Title of kings of ancient Egypt.

pyramids   Monumental architecture typical of Old Kingdom Egypt; used as burial sites for pharaohs.

believed in many powerful gods, for the nature on which their agriculture depended often seemed swift and unpredictable. Prayers and offerings to prevent floods as well as to protect good health were a vital part of Sumerian life. Sumerian ideas about the divine force in natural objects—in rivers, trees, and mountains—were common among early agricultural peoples. A religion of this sort, which sees gods in many aspects of nature, is known as polytheism. More specifically, Sumerian religious notions, notably their ideas about the gods' creation of the earth from water and about the divine punishment of humans through floods, later influenced the writers of the Old Testament and thus continue to play a role in Jewish, Christian, and Muslim cultures. Sumerian religious ideas, which had a decidedly gloomy cast, also included a belief in an afterlife of punishment—an original version of the concept of hell.

Sumerian political structures stressed tightly organized **city-states,** ruled by a king who claimed divine authority. The Sumerian state had carefully defined boundaries, unlike the less formal territories of precivilized villages in the region. Here is a key early example of how civilization and a more formal political structure came together. The government helped regulate religion and enforce its duties; it also provided a court system in the interests of justice. Kings were originally military leaders during times of war, and the function of defense and war, including leadership of a trained army, remained vital in Sumerian politics. Kings and the noble class, along with the priesthood, controlled considerable land, which was worked by slaves. Thus began a tradition of slavery that would long mark Middle Eastern societies. Warfare remained vital to ensure supplies of slaves taken as prisoners during combat. At the same time, slavery was a variable state of existence, and many slaves were able to earn money and even buy their freedom.

The Sumerians added to their region's agricultural prosperity not only by using wheeled carts but also by learning about fertilizers and by adopting silver as a means of exchange for buying and selling—an early form of money. However, the region was also hard to defend and proved a constant temptation to outside invaders from Sumerian times to the present. The Sumerians themselves fell to a people called the Akkadians, who continued much of Sumerian culture. Another period of decline was followed by conquest by the **Babylonians,** who extended their own empire and thus helped bring civilization to other parts of the Middle East. It was under Babylonian rule that the king **Hammurabi** introduced the most famous early code of law, boasting of his purpose: "to promote the welfare of the people, I, Hammurabi, the devout, god-fearing prince, cause justice to prevail in the land by destroying the wicked and the evil, that the strong might not oppress the weak." Hammurabi's code established rules of procedure for courts of law and regulated property rights and the duties of family members, setting harsh punishments for crimes.

For many centuries during and after the heyday of Babylon, peace and civilization in the Middle East were troubled by the invasions of hunting and herding groups. Indo-European peoples pressed in from the north, starting about 2100 B.C.E. In the Middle East itself, invasions by Semitic peoples from the south were more important, and Semitic peoples and languages increasingly dominated the region. The new arrivals adopted the culture of the conquered peoples as their own, so the key features of the civilization persisted. But large political units declined in favor of smaller city-states or regional kingdoms, particularly during the centuries of greatest turmoil, between 1200 and 900 B.C.E. Thereafter, new invaders, first the Assyrians and then the Persians, created large new empires in the Middle East.

Egyptian Civilization

A second center of civilization sprang up in northern Africa, along the Nile River. Egyptian civilization, formed by 3000 B.C.E., benefited from the trade and technological influence of Mesopotamia, but it produced a quite different society and culture. Less open to invasion, Egypt retained a unified state throughout most of its history. The king, or **pharaoh,** possessed immense power. The Egyptian economy was more fully government-directed than its Mesopotamian counterpart, which had a more independent business class. Government control may have been necessary because of the complexity of coordinating irrigation along the Nile. It nonetheless resulted in godlike status for the pharaohs, who built splendid tombs for themselves—the **pyramids**—from 2700 B.C.E. onward. During periods of weak rule and occasional invasions, Egyptian society suffered a decline, but revivals kept the framework of Egyptian civilization intact until after 1000 B.C.E. (Map 1.5). At key points, Egyptian influence spread up the Nile to the area now known as the Sudan, with an impact on the later development of African culture. The kingdom of **Kush** interacted with Egypt and invaded it at some point.

Neither Egyptian science nor the Egyptian alphabet was as elaborate as its Mesopotamian equal, although mathematics was more advanced in this civilization. Egyptian art was exceptionally lively; cheerful and colorful

Kush An African state that developed along the upper reaches of the Nile c. 1000 B.C.E.; conquered Egypt and ruled it for several centuries.

Hammurabi's Law Code

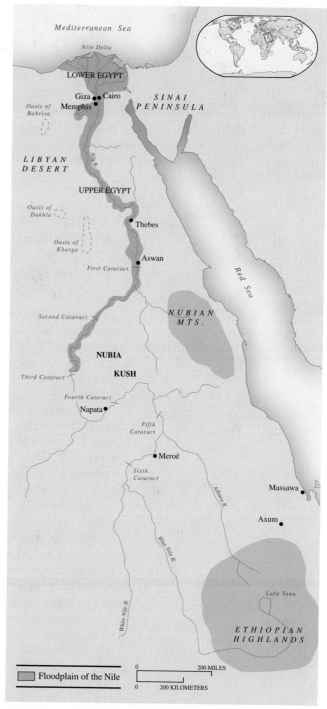

Map 1.5 Egypt, Kush, and Axum, Successive Dynasties. As Egypt weakened, kingdoms farther up the Nile and deeper into Africa rose in importance.

Figure 1.5 This detail from Egyptian tomb art shows a husband and wife harvesting grain. As dictated by patriarchal values, the husband takes the lead in the work and the wife follows, but in Egypt, unlike Mesopotamia, men and women were depicted working together.

Early Civilization in India MAP

Indus River valley   River sources in Himalayas to mouth in Arabian Sea; location of Harappan civilization.

Harappa   Along with Mohenjodaro, major urban complex of the Harappan civilization; laid out on planned grid pattern.

Mohenjo Daro   [moh-HEN-joh-DA-roh] Along with Harappa, major urban complex of the Harappan civilization; laid out on planned grid pattern.

pictures decorated not only the tombs—where the belief in an afterlife made people want to be surrounded by objects of beauty—but also palaces and furnishings. Egyptian architectural forms were also quite influential, not only in Egypt but in other parts of the Mediterranean as well. Egyptian mathematics produced the idea of a day divided into 24 hours, and here too Egypt influenced the development of later Mediterranean cultures (Figure 1.5).

Indian and Chinese River Valley Civilizations

River valley civilizations developed in two other centers. A prosperous urban civilization emerged along the **Indus River** by 2500 B.C.E., supporting several large cities, including **Harappa** and **Mohenjo Daro** (moh-HEN-joh-DA-roh), whose houses even had running water. Indus River peoples had trading contacts with Mesopotamia, but they developed their own distinctive alphabet and artistic forms. Infiltrations by Indo-Europeans, however, plus natural calamities, resulted in such destruction that it makes it hard to speak with confidence about either the nature of this culture or its subsequent influence on India. Harappan writing, for example, has yet to be deciphered. It remains true that civilization never had to be fully reinvented in India. The Indo-European migrants combined their religious and political ideas with those that had taken root in the early cities. In recent times, Indians' pride in their early civilized history has become an important part of their national identity.

The Great Cities of the Indus Valley

Though hundreds of miles apart, Harappa, Mohenjo Daro, and other urban centers were remarkably similar in layout and construction. Both were built on a square grid pattern that was divided by main roads into 12 precisely measured segments. Each city was surrounded by walls, which extended a mile from east to west and one-half mile from north to south. The buildings and the city walls were usually made of standardized kiln-dried bricks. Coordinated construction on such a massive scale might have meant an effective central government that could organize and supervise the daily tasks of large numbers of laborers.

The existence of a strong ruling class is also indicated by the presence of large, well fortified citadels in each capital city. These citadels may have served as sanctuaries for the cities' populations in times of attack and as community centers in times of peace. The citadel at Mohenjo Daro included a very large building that may have been a palace. Both citadels contained what are believed to have been audience and assembly halls or places of worship as well as public bathing tanks. The elaborately decorated bath at Mohenjo Daro was surrounded by a cloister, which opened onto many small rooms that may have housed priests. Large granaries near each of the citadels suggest that the state stored grain for ceremonial purposes, times of shortage, and possibly the regulation of grain production and sale.

The great cities and many towns of the Harappan complex were supported by a rather advanced agricultural system based on the cultivation of wheat, rye, peas, and possibly rice. Cotton was widely cultivated, and numerous domesticated animals were reared. It is likely that irrigation systems were built to catch and control waters from the monsoon and the rivers, and that fish caught in the rivers were a dietary staple. Local goods were carried by riverboats and ox carts, reproduced in clay models.

The cities of Harappa were major trading centers. Jade from China and precious jewels from what later became Burma have been unearthed at various Indus sites. Stone seals produced in the Indus region, such as those shown in Figure 3.5, have been found in the urban ruins of other ancient civilizations such as Sumer in Mesopotamia. In addition to realistic depictions of animals and human figures, the seals contain a complex writing system that no one has ever deciphered. The fact that Harappan merchants used large numbers of the seals to ensure that crates and urns were not opened during transport suggests that trade was highly developed in the Indus valley civilization.

Despite these overseas contacts, Harappan peoples appear to have been conservative and highly resistant to innovations introduced from the outside. They cast tools and weapons in bronze,

Aryan Poetry in Praise of a War Horse

The following early Vedic hymn exults in the power of a great Aryan war horse.

> Rushing to glory, to the capture of herds,
> Swooping down as a hungry falcon,
> Eager to be first, he darts amid the ranks of the chariots
> Happy as a bridegroom making a garland,
> Spurning the dust and champing at the bit.
> And the victorious steed and faithful,
> His body obedient to his driver in battle,
> Speeding on through the melee,
> Stirs up the dust to fall on his brows.

> And at his deep neigh, like the thunder of heaven,
> The foemen tremble in fear,
> For he fights against thousands, and none can resist him,
> So terrible is his charge.

QUESTIONS In what ways does this poem convey the Aryans' delight in warfare? What does it tell us about the way they fought their battles and their attitudes toward the herd animals that were so central to their culture? How does it convey the Aryans' ideals of manliness, heroism, and loyalty, and what does it say about their attitudes toward death?

---

but most of their implements were inferior to those of Mesopotamian peoples, with whom they had contact. Their weapons were even more primitive and would have left them vulnerable to invasions by peoples more adept at warfare.

Harappan society appears to have been dominated by a powerful priestly class, which ruled from the citadel of each capital. The priests would have derived this control from their role as intermediaries between the Harappan populace and a number of gods and goddesses, who controlled fertility. Representations of mother goddesses appear to have been objects of worship for the common people, whereas a horned god was apparently favored by the priests and upper classes. The presence of these figures in Sumer and other urban sites in the Persian Gulf region suggests that large quantities of various commodities were traded in the region spanning Mesopotamia and the Indus River valley.

It is likely that a combination of factors led to Harappa's demise. There is evidence of severe flooding at Mohenjo Daro and other sites. Short-term natural disasters, including severe earthquakes, may have compounded the adverse effects of long-term climatic changes. Shifts in the monsoon pattern and changes in temperature may have begun the process of desertification that eventually transformed the region into the arid steppe that it has been for most of recorded history. Rapid changes in pottery types suggest sudden waves of migrants into the region. It is possible that the Harappans were too weak militarily to prevent these incoming peoples from settling down or taking over their towns and cities. In many cases these centers of urban life had already been abandoned in response to natural calamities, particularly flooding. A marked decline in the quality of building and town planning suggests that the priestly elite may have lost control over the artisans and laborers.

Some of the migrants were bands of Aryan herders who entered the Indus region over an extended period of time rather than in militant waves. But the Aryan pastoralists may have consciously destroyed or neglected the dikes and canals on which the agrarian life of the Harappan peoples had once depended. Cattle raising would then have replaced crop cultivation, further undermining the economic basis of the civilization. That there was a good deal of violent conflict in this transition cannot be ruled out. Groups of skeletons with smashed skulls or in postures of flight from floods or foreign invaders have been found on the stairways at some sites. Thus, environmental changes and related administrative decline may have combined with the effects of nomadic migrations to undermine south Asia's first civilization.

Early Civilization in China

Civilization along the **Yellow River** in China developed in considerable isolation, although some overland trading contact with India and the Middle East did develop. Huang he civilization was the subject of much later Chinese legend, which praised the godlike kings of early civilization, starting with the mythic ancestor of the Chinese, P'an Ku. The Chinese had an unusually elaborate concept of their remote origins, and they began early to record a part-fact, part-fiction history of their early kings. What is clear is the following: First, an organized state existed that carefully regulated irrigation in the fertile but flood-prone river valley. Second, by about 2000 B.C.E. the Chinese had produced an advanced technology and developed an elaborate intellectual life. They had learned how

 Ancient China MAP

Yellow River Also known as the Huanghe; site of development of sedentary agriculture in china.

23

Figure 1.6 This elaborately decorated vessel from the Shang era, with its whimsical elephant figure, shows the sophisticated artistic expression achieved very early in Chinese history. It also demonstrates a high level of metalworking ability, which carried over into Shang weapons and tools. Although the design of these ritual vessels often was abstract, mythical creatures such as dragons and sacred birds were deftly cast in bronzes that remain some of the great treasures of Chinese art.

The Shang
Kingdom

MAP

Shang   First Chinese dynasty for which archeological evidence exists; capital located in Ordos bulge of the Huanghe; flourished 1600 to 1046 B.C.E.

oracles   Shamans or priests in Chinese society who foretold the future through interpretations of animal bones cracked by heat; inscriptions on bones led to Chinese writing.

to ride horses and were skilled in pottery; they used bronze well and by 1000 B.C.E. had introduced iron, which they soon learned to work with coal. Their writing progressed from scratches of lines on bone to the invention of **ideographic** symbols. Science, particularly astronomy, arose early. Chinese art emphasized delicate designs, and the Chinese claim an early interest in music (Figure 1.6).

By 1500 B.C.E., one of the tribes in the north China, the Shang, conquered most of the other tribes and established a kingdom that would lay the foundations of Chinese civilization. Until recent decades we knew little more about the **Shang** than about their Xia predecessors. But extensive excavation of Shang sites at Anyang (ahn-yahng), Zhengzhou (jehng-joh), and elsewhere have given us insights into many aspects of Shang culture and society. In some respects they were very much like the Aryans, who were conquering northern India during this same period. Like the Aryans, the Shang were warlike nomads. They fought on horseback and from chariots with deadly bronze weapons. Non-Shang subject peoples provided the foot soldiers that made up the bulk of their armies. Like those of Aryan India and Homeric Greece, Shang battles were wild clashes between massed soldiers that hinged on hand-to-hand combat between a few champions on each side. But unlike the Aryans and ancient Greeks, the Shang warriors were ruled by strong kings, who drew on their vassals' energies and military prowess to build an extensive empire.

The Shang monarch was seen as the intermediary between the supreme being, Shangdi (shahng-dee), and ordinary mortals. His kingdom was viewed as the center of the world, and he claimed dominion over all humankind. Shang rulers directed the affairs of state and bore ritual responsibilities for the fertility of their kingdom and the well-being of their subjects. In the springtime, they participated in special ceremonies that included a symbolic mating with female fertility spirits. In times of drought and famine, Shang rulers, or perhaps designated surrogates, were obliged to perform ritual dances in the nude. The dancer—presumably the surrogate—was later burned alive to placate the spirits whose anger had caused the natural calamities.

Shang monarchs were served by a sizeable bureaucracy in the capital city at Anyang and the surrounding areas. But most of the peasant and artisan populations of the kingdom were governed by vassal retainers: subordinate leaders serving the king and great lords and usually bound to them by personal ties. These officials were recruited from the former ruling families and the aristocratic classes of the many subordinate states. The vassals depended on the produce and labor of the commoners in these areas to support their families and military forces. In return for grants of control over varying numbers of peasants, warrior aristocrats collected tribute (usually in the form of agricultural produce), which went to support the monarch and his court. They supplied soldiers for the king's armies in times of war, and they kept the peace and administered justice among the peasants and townspeople.

Like the elites of many early civilizations, the Shang rulers and nobility were preoccupied with rituals, oracles, and sacrifices. In addition to the fertility functions of the ruler, the entire elite was involved in persuading spirits to provide good crops and large families. Shang artistic expression reached its peak in the ornately carved and expertly cast bronze vessels that were used to make these offerings. Offerings included fine grain, incense, wine, and animals, but Shang records also tell of water festivals at which ritual contests were waged between rival boats, each attempting to sink the other. Those aboard the losing craft drowned when it capsized, and they were offered up to the deities responsible for fertility and good harvests.

Concern for abundant harvests and victory in war led the Shang elite to put great stock in the predictions of shamans, or priests, who served as **oracles**—sacred people who could prophesy the future. Much of Shang artistic expression went into producing the ritual objects used by the oracles. Warriors about to go into battle, officials embarking on long journeys, or families negotiating marriage alliances routinely consulted these oracles to ensure that their efforts would turn out well. This reliance on the shamans strongly influenced beliefs and behavior in the Shang era.

The actual procedures followed by the shamans who presided over these rituals gave rise to perhaps the single most important element in Chinese culture—writing. Since pre-Shang times, Chinese oracles had based their predictions on readings taken from animal bones or tortoise shells. A bone or shell was drilled with a hole and seared with a red-hot iron poker. The bone or shell cracked, and the patterns of the cracks were interpreted by a shaman or priest. Over time the practice evolved of inscribing the bones and shells with painted designs that became part of the patterns the shamans read. These designs gradually were standardized and came to form the basis of a written Chinese language.

Like the hieroglyphics of the ancient Egyptians, early Chinese characters were pictographic. Thus, they readily conveyed the ideas they were intended to express. The original character for the sun, for example, was a circle with a dot in the center, the character for a tree was a single tree, and a forest was a set of three trees. Combinations of characters made it possible for the Chinese elite to convey increasingly complex ideas. The character for emperor, for example, combined elements of the **ideographs** for king, heaven, earth, and harmony.

ideographs Pictographic characters grouped together to create new concepts; typical of Chinese writing.

Over time the number of characters increased substantially. By the end of the Shang period, there were an estimated 3000 characters. A well educated scholar in the modern era would need to master some 8000 characters. The way they are written also changed significantly. Many characters were simplified, and most were stylized so that they are less pictographic. The bones or bronze vessels on which the characters were originally carved gradually gave way to bamboo slips, silk scrolls, and wooden plates, and they in turn were supplanted in the 1st century C.E. by paper (a critical Chinese invention). Assorted fine brushes and inks were developed to paint the characters, which themselves became a major mode of artistic expression in later periods.

Writing became the key to Chinese identity and the growth of civilization in China. The peoples of the loess region and the north China plain spoke a bewildering variety of languages, often unintelligible from one group to the next. They were surrounded by nomadic herders to the north and shifting cultivators to the south, whose contacts with and movements into the loess zone further complicated the linguistic muddle. But the use of increasingly standardized and sophisticated written characters provided the bond that gave growing numbers of these loess zone peoples a common identity. This sense of identity was felt most keenly by the elite groups, who monopolized the use of the characters, but eventually it filtered down to the cultivating and artisan classes. With the persistence and growth of this identity, the Chinese people entered history for the first time.

The Heritage of the River Valley Civilizations

Many accomplishments of the river valley civilizations had a lasting impact. Monuments such as the Egyptian pyramids have long been regarded as one of the wonders of the world. Other achievements, although more prosaic, are fundamental to world history even today: the invention of the wheel, the taming of the horse, the creation of usable alphabets and writing implements, the production of key mathematical concepts such as square roots, the development of well organized monarchies and bureaucracies, and the invention of functional calendars and other divisions of time. These basic achievements, along with the awe that the early civilizations continue to inspire, are vital legacies to the whole of human history. Almost all the major alphabets in the world today are derived from the writing forms pioneered in the river valleys, apart from the even more durable concept of writing itself. For this reason, almost all later civilizations are built on the massive foundations first constructed in the river valleys.

Most river valley civilizations declined after about 1200 B.C.E.

A number of small centers emerged in the Middle East that introduced further innovations, including the religion of Judaism.

Despite these accomplishments, most of the river valley civilizations were in decline by 1000 B.C.E. The civilizations had flourished for as many as 2500 years, although of course with periodic disruptions and revivals. But, particularly in India, the new waves of invasion did produce something of a break in the history of civilization, a dividing line between the river valley pioneers and later cultures.

Heritage of Early Civilizations

This break raises one final question: besides the vital achievements—the fascinating monuments and the indispensable advances in technology, science, and art—what legacies did the river valley civilizations impart for later ages? The question is particularly important for the Middle East and Egypt. In India, there is still much ignorance about possible links between Indus River accomplishments and what came later. In China, there is a definite connection between the first civilization and subsequent forms. Indeed, the new dynasty in China, the Zhou, took over from the Shang about 1000 B.C.E., ruling a loose coalition of regional lords; recorded Chinese history flowed smoothly at this point. But what was the legacy of Mesopotamia and Egypt for later civilizations in or near their centers?

Europeans, even North Americans, are sometimes prone to claim these cultures as the "origins" of the Western civilization in which we live. These claims should not be taken too literally. It is

The Idea of Civilization in World Historical Perspective

The belief that there are fundamental differences between civilized and "barbaric" or "savage" peoples is very ancient and widespread. For thousands of years the Chinese set themselves off from cattle- and sheep-herding peoples of the vast plains to the north and west of China proper, whom they saw as barbarians. To the Chinese, being civilized was cultural, not biological or racial. If barbarians learned the Chinese language and adopted Chinese ways—from the clothes they wore to the food they ate—they were regarded as civilized.

A similar pattern of demarcation and cultural absorption was found among the American Indian peoples of present-day Mexico. Those who settled in the valleys of the mountainous interior, where they built great civilizations, lived in fear of invasions by peoples they regarded as barbarous and called **Chichimecs,** meaning "sons of the dog." The latter were nomadic hunters and gatherers who periodically moved down from the desert regions of north Mexico into the fertile central valleys in search of game and settlements to pillage. The Aztecs were simply the last, and perhaps the fiercest, of a long line of Chichimec peoples who entered the valleys and conquered the urban-based empires that had developed there. But after the conquerors settled down, they adopted many of the religious beliefs and institutional patterns and much of the material culture of defeated peoples.

The word *civilization* is derived from the Latin word *civilis,* meaning "of the citizens." The term was coined by the Romans. They used it to distinguish between themselves as citizens of a cosmopolitan, urban-based civilization and the "inferior" peoples who lived in

> The word *civilization* is derived from the Latin word *civilis,* meaning "of the citizens."

the forests and deserts on the fringes of their Mediterranean empire. Centuries earlier, the Greeks, who had contributed much to the rise of Roman civilization, made a similar distinction between themselves and outsiders. Because the languages of the non-Greek peoples to the north of the Greek heartlands sounded like senseless babble to the Greeks, they lumped all the outsiders together as *barbarians,* which meant "those who cannot speak Greek." As in the case of the Chinese and Aztecs, the boundaries between civilized and barbarian for the Greeks and Romans were cultural, not biological.

Until the 17th and 18th centuries C.E., the priority given to cultural attributes (e.g., language, dress, manners) as the means by which civilized peoples set themselves off from barbaric ones was rarely challenged. But in those centuries, a major change occurred among thinkers in western Europe. Efforts were made not only to define the differences between civilized and barbarian but to identify a series of stages in human development that ranged from the lowest savagery to the highest civilization. Depending on the writer in question, candidates for civilization ranged from Greece and Rome to (not surprisingly) Europe of the 17th and 18th centuries. Most of the other peoples of the globe, whose "discovery" since the 15th century had prompted the efforts to classify them in the first place, were ranked in increasingly complex hierarchies. Nomadic cattle- and sheep-herding peoples, such as the Mongols of central Asia, usually were classified as barbarians. In the 19th century, racial differences were added to the hierarchy, with white people seen as having evolved the most advanced civilizations.

The second major shift in Western ideas about civilization began at the end of the 18th century but did not really take hold until a century later. In keeping with a growing emphasis in European thinking and social interaction on racial or biological differences, modes of human social organization and cultural expression

not altogether clear that either Egypt or Mesopotamia contributed much to later political traditions, although the Roman Empire emulated the concept of a godlike king, as evidenced in the trappings of the office, and the existence of strong city-state governments in the Middle East itself continued to be significant. Ideas about slavery may also have been passed on from these early civilizations. Specific scientific achievements are vital, as the Greeks, for example, carefully studied Egyptian mathematics. Scholars argue, however, over how much of a connection exists between Mesopotamian and Egyptian science and later Greek thinking, aside from certain techniques of measuring time or charting the stars.

Some historians of philosophy have asserted a basic division between a Mesopotamian and Chinese understanding of nature, which they claim affected later civilizations around the Mediterranean in contrast to China. Mesopotamians were prone to stress a gap between humankind and nature, whereas Chinese thinking developed along ideas of basic harmony. It is possible, then, that some fundamental thinking helped shape later outlooks, but the continuities here are not easy to assess. Mesopotamian art and Egyptian architecture had a more measurable influence on Greek styles, and through these, in turn, later European and Muslim cultures. The Greeks thus learned much about temple building from the Egyptians, whose culture had influenced island civilizations, such as Crete, which then affected later Greek styles.

were increasingly linked to what were alleged to be the innate capacities of each human race. Although no one could agree on what a race was or how many races there were, most European writers argued that some races were more inventive, moral, courageous, and artistic—thus more capable of building civilizations—than others. Of course, white (or Caucasian) Europeans were considered by white European authors to be the most capable of all. The hierarchy from savage to civilized took on a color dimension, with white at the top, where the civilized peoples clustered, to yellow, red, brown, and black in descending order.

Some authors sought to reserve all the attainments of civilization for whites, or peoples of European stock. As the evolutionary theories of thinkers such as Charles Darwin came into vogue in the late 1800s, race and level of cultural development were seen in the perspective of thousands of years of human change and adaptation rather than as being fixed in time. Nevertheless, this new perspective had little effect on the rankings of different human groups. Civilized whites were simply seen as having evolved much further than backward and barbaric peoples.

The perceived correspondence between race and level of development and the hardening of the boundaries between civilized and "inferior" peoples affected much more than intellectual discourse about the nature and history of human society. These beliefs were used to justify European imperialist expansion, which was seen as a "civilizing mission" aimed at uplifting barbaric and savage peoples across the globe. In the last half of the 19th century, virtually all non-Western peoples came to be dominated by the Europeans, who were confident that they, as representatives of the highest civilization ever created, were best equipped to govern lesser breeds of humans.

In the 20th century, much of the intellectual baggage that once gave credibility to the racially embedded hierarchies of civilized and savage peoples was discarded. Racist thinking was discredited by 20th-century developments, including the revolt of the colonized peoples and the crimes committed by the Nazis before and during World War II in the name of racial purification. In addition, these ideas have failed because racial supremacists cannot provide convincing proof of innate differences in mental and physical aptitude between various human groups. These trends, as well as research that has resulted in a much more sophisticated understanding of evolution, have led to the abandonment of rigid and self-serving 19th-century ideas about civilization. Yet even though non-European peoples such as the Indians and Chinese are increasingly given credit for their civilized attainments, much ethnocentrism remains in the ways social theorists determine who is civilized and who is not.

Perhaps the best way to avoid the tendency to define the term with reference to one's own society is to view civilization as one of several human approaches to social organization rather than attempting to identify specific kinds of cultural achievement (e.g., writing, cities, monumental architecture). All peoples, from small bands of hunters and gatherers to farmers and factory workers, live in societies. All societies produce cultures: combinations of the ideas, objects, and patterns of behavior that result from human social interaction. But not all societies and cultures generate the surplus production that permits the levels of specialization, scale, and complexity that distinguish civilizations from other modes of social organization. All peoples are intrinsically capable of building civilizations, but many have lacked the resource base, historical circumstances, or desire to do so.

QUESTIONS Identify a society you consider civilized. What criteria did you use to determine that it was civilized? Can you apply those criteria to other societies? Can you think of societies that might not fit your criteria and yet be civilizations? Do the standards that you and others use reflect your own society's norms and achievements rather than neutral, more universal criteria?

New Societies in the Middle East

There was a final connection between early and later civilizations in the form of regional cultures that sprang up under the influence of Mesopotamia and Egypt, along the eastern shores of the Mediterranean mainly after 1200 B.C.E. Although the great empires from Sumer through Babylon were disrupted and the Egyptian state finally declined, civilization in the Middle East had spread widely enough to encourage a set of smaller cultures capable of surviving and even flourishing after the great empires became weak. These cultures produced important innovations that would affect later civilizations in the Middle East and throughout the Mediterranean. They also created a diverse array of regional identities that would continue to mark the Middle East even as other forces, like the Roman Empire or the later religion of Islam, took center stage. Several of these small cultures proved immensely durable, and in their complexity and capacity to survive, they would influence other parts of the world as well.

A people called the **Phoenicians,** for example, devised a greatly simplified alphabet with 22 letters around 1300 B.C.E.; this alphabet, in turn, became the predecessor of Greek and Latin alphabets. The Phoenicians also improved the Egyptian numbering system and, as great traders, set up colony cities in north Africa and on the coasts of Europe. Another regional group, the Lydians, first introduced coined money.

Phoenicians Seafaring civilization located on the shores of the eastern Mediterranean; established colonies throughout the Mediterranean.

Judaism

The most influential of the smaller Middle Eastern groups, however, were the Jews, who gave the world the first clearly developed monotheistic religion. We have seen that early religions, both before and after the beginnings of civilization, were polytheistic, claiming that many gods and goddesses worked to control nature and human destiny. The Jews, a Semitic people influenced by Babylonian civilization, settled near the Mediterranean around 1200 B.C.E. The Jewish state was small and relatively weak, retaining independence only when other parts of the Middle East were in political turmoil. What was distinctive about this culture was its firm belief that a single God guided the destinies of the Jewish people. Priests and prophets defined and emphasized this belief, and their history of God's guidance of the Jews formed the basis for the Hebrew Bible. The Jewish religion and moral code persisted even as the Jewish state suffered domination by a series of foreign rulers, from 772 B.C.E. until the Romans seized the state outright in 63 B.C.E. Jewish **monotheism** has sustained a distinctive Jewish culture to our own day; it would also serve as a key basis for the development of both Christianity and Islam as major world religions.

monotheism The exclusive worship of a single god; introduced by the Jews into Western civilization.

Because Judaism stressed God's special compact with the chosen Jewish people, there was no premium placed on converting non-Jews. This belief helps explain the durability of the Jewish faith itself; it also kept the Jewish people in a minority position in the Middle East as a whole. However, the elaboration of monotheism had a wide, if not immediate, significance. In Jewish hands, the concept of God became less humanlike, more abstract. This represented a basic change in not only religion but also humankind's overall outlook. God had not only a power but also a rationality far different from what the traditional gods of the Middle East or Egypt possessed. These gods were whimsical and capricious; the Jewish God was orderly and just, and individuals would know what to expect if they obeyed God's rules. God was also linked to ethical conduct, to proper moral behavior. Religion for the Jews was a way of life, not merely a set of rituals and ceremonies. The full impact of this religious transformation on Middle Eastern civilization would be realized only later, when Jewish beliefs were embraced by other, proselytizing faiths. However, the basic concept of monotheistic religion was one of the legacies of the end of the first great civilization period to the new cultures that would soon arise.

Assessing the Early Civilization Period

Overall, the river valley civilizations, flourishing for many centuries, created a basic set of tools, intellectual concepts such as writing and mathematics, and political forms that would persist and spread to other parts of Europe, Asia, and Africa. Invasion and natural calamities in India, and invasion and political decline in Egypt, marked a fairly firm break between the institutions of these river valley civilizations and those that would later develop. Huang he civilization, in contrast, flowed more fully into the more extensive Chinese civilization that would follow. The Middle East, where civilization had first been born, provided the most complex heritage of all. Here too there was a break between the initial series of riverine empires and the civilizations of Greece and Persia that would later dominate the region. However, the development of smaller cultures, such as that of the Jews, provided a bridge between the river valley period and later Middle Eastern society, producing vital new inventions and ideas. The smaller cultures also generated a deeply entrenched network of regional or minority values and institutions that would continue to make the Middle East a complex, vibrant, and sometimes troubled part of the world.

One final result of the first, long period of human civilization is certainly clear: a pattern of division among the world's peoples. The diffusion of *Homo sapiens sapiens* set the initial stage. Small groups of people spread to almost every corner of the world but maintained little contact with each other thereafter. Separate languages and cultures developed widely. The rise of agriculture stimulated new links, and the spread of farming and new technologies began to cut into local isolation. Trade soon entered the picture. Although most commerce centered within a region, linking a city to its hinterland, a few routes traveled greater distances. By 1000 B.C.E., Phoenicians traded with Britain for metals (they bought lead to make bronze), while Chinese silk was reaching Egypt. Here we have one of the basic themes of world history: steadily proliferating contacts against a background of often fierce local identity.

The rise of civilization further reduced local autonomy, as kings and priests tried to spread trade contacts and cultural forms and warred to gain new territory. Civilization itself was an integrating force at a larger regional level, although, as we have seen in the Middle East, smaller identities persisted. However, individual civilizations had only sporadic contacts with each other. They, and their leading institutions and cultural forms, developed separately. Thus, four distinct centers of civilization developed (five, if the emerging Olmec culture in Mexico is included), each with widely varied patterns, from style of writing to beliefs about nature.

The early civilizations shared important features, including cities, trade, and writing, that helped them meet the common basic definition of civilization in the first place. They also frequently developed some mutual relationships, although the Huang he culture in China is one example of a civilization that flourished in relative isolation. Egypt and Mesopotamia, in particular, had recurrent contacts through trade and war. But the values or belief systems of each civilization, and their manifestation in political and business styles, were not so easily disseminated. Even relatively close neighbors, such as Egypt and Mesopotamia, developed radically different political attitudes, beliefs about death, and artistic styles. Civilization and considerable diversity thus coexisted hand in hand.

Global Connections

The Early Civilizations and the World

Mesopotamia and Egypt presented two different approaches to relationships outside the home region. Mesopotamia was flat, with few natural barriers to recurrent invasion from the north. Perhaps for this reason, Mesopotamian leaders thought in terms of expansion. Many conquering emperors expanded their territory, though within the Middle East. Many traders pushed outward, dealing either with merchants to the east or sending expeditions into the Mediterranean and beyond, and also to India. The Middle East's role as active agent in wider contact was clearly being established.

Egypt, though not isolated, was more self-contained. There was important trade and interaction along the Nile to the south, which brought mutual influences with the peoples of Kush and Ethiopia. Trade and influence also linked Egypt to Mediterranean islands like Crete, south of Greece. A few interactions, finally, occurred with Mesopotamia. But most Egyptians, including the leaders, thought of Egypt as its own world. There was less need or desire to learn of wider horizons. Correspondingly, ancient Egypt played less of a role as intermediary among regions than did Mesopotamia.

River valley civilization in China had fewer far-reaching contacts than its counterpart in Mesopotamia. Ultimately, however, contacts with China would shape developments in Japan, Korea, and Vietnam. Already in the river valley period, the Chinese were advancing new technologies, for example in the manufacture of silk, which would have wide influence on later interregional trade. Chinese irrigation systems became increasingly sophisticated, involving engineering principles that would gain wider scope later on.

Harappan society traded widely with Mesopotamia, but there is little evidence of significant influence. The decline of Harappan civilization also limited the civilization's impact on later developments in world history. Harappan civilization proved much more vulnerable to natural disasters and climate change, particularly in contrast to China. Comparison of the early civilizations thus emphasizes quite different patterns of scope and legacy.

Further Readings

World historians have been drawn to Ronald Wright's *A Short History of Progress* (2004), which attempts to show how even the most recent of humanity's struggles can be better understood by examining its origins and early history. Perhaps the fullest account of human prehistory available is Brian Fagan's *People of the Earth* (1998), which includes an extensive bibliography on prehistoric developments in virtually all regions of the world. A considerable literature has developed in recent years on early humans and the critical Neolithic transformations. John Mears's pamphlet on *Agricultural Origins in Global Perspective* (American Historical Association, 2000) provides a concise and authoritative survey of this process in key regions over much of the globe. For other broad overviews that trace the archeological and historical discoveries that made it possible for us to understand these critical processes in the shaping of human history, see Robert J. Wenke's *Patterns in Prehistory* (1984) and C. Wesley Cowan and Patty Jo Watson, eds., *The Origins of Agriculture: An International Perspective* (1992).

For a clear discussion of debates on the Neolithic revolution and references to major authors and works, see Stephen K. Sanderson, *Social Transformations* (1995). Several of these works are of special relevance, despite their sometimes technical language and details, especially Donald O. Henry's *From Foraging to Agriculture* (1989), Douglas Price and James A. Brown, eds., *Prehistoric Hunter-Gatherers: The Emergence of Cultural Complexity* (1986), and Allen W. Johnson and Timothy Earle, *The Evolution of Human Societies: From Foraging to Agriculture* (1987).

Two excellent studies can guide additional work on early civilization in Mesopotamia: C. L. Redman's *The Rise of Civilization: From Early Farmers to Urban Society in the Ancient Near East* (1988) and Marc Van de Mieroop, *King Hammurabi of Babylon: A Biography* (2005). See also Trevor Bryce, *The Trojans and Their Neighbors* (2006); Sarah Iles Johnston, *Ancient Religions* (2007); C. B. F. Walker, *Cuneiform* (1987); G. W. Bowersock, *Mosaics as History: The Near East from Late Antiquity to Islam* (2006); and

H. W. F. Saggs, *Babylonians* (1995). Important studies of Egypt include T. G. H. James, *Ancient Egypt: The Land and Its Legacy* (1988); N. C. Grimal, *A History of Ancient Egypt* (1992); Christiance Cesroches Noblecourt, *Gifts from the Pharaohs: How Egyptian Civilization Shaped the Modern World* (2007); Zahi Hawass, and *Mountains of the Pharaohs: The Untold Story of the Pyramid Builders* (2006). See also Donald B. Redford's *From Slave to Pharaoh: The Black Experience of Ancient Egypt* (2004).

For an excellent study of non-Western science beginning with the Egyptians and Mesopotamians, see Dick Teresi, *Lost Discoveries: The Ancient Roots of Modern Science—From the Babylonians to the Maya* (2002).

For the most authoritative, up-to-date and detailed coverage of all aspects of Harappan civilization, see Gregory L. Possehl, *Indus Age: The Beginnings* (1999); and Mark Kenoyer, *Ancient Cities of the Indus Valley Civilization* (1998). For a sense of the state of archeological research and recent discoveries, see the sometimes technical essays in Possehl, ed., *Harappan Civilization: A Contemporary Perspective* (1982); and N. N. Bhattacharyya, *Ancient Indian History and Civilization: Trends and Perspectives* (1988). On ancient Indian political systems, see A. C. Pandey, *Government in Ancient India* (2000).

For ancient China, the most current interpretations can be found in the superb essays in Michael Loewe and Edward L. Shaughnessy, eds., *The Cambridge History of Ancient China: From the Origins of Civilization to 221 B.C.* (1999). The nomadic impact on the formation of China is treated mainly from the Chinese perspective by Nicola Di Cosmo, *Ancient China and Its Enemies* (2002).

On the Web

A virtual tour of the social life of early humans in the Americas, including weaving and toolmaking can be taken at http://pecosrio.com/. The dramatic findings at Olduvai Gorge made by the Leakey family that revolutionized knowledge about human prehistory can be viewed at http://www.talkorigins.org/. Views of Chauvet, rich in cave paintings, can be found at http://www.culture.gouv.fr/culture/arcnat/chauvet/en/. A virtual walk through an exhibit on human prehistory is offered at http://users.hol.gr/~dilos/prehis/prerm5.htm includes a gallery of art and artifacts, and an artist's reconstruction of Çatal Hüyük. Çatal Hüyük is served by an exciting interactive site at http://okapi.dreamhosters.com/remixing/mainpage.html.

It is possible to make a virtual visit to the Mesopotamian city of Ur at http://www.mnsu.edu/emuseum/archaeology/sites/middle_east/ur.html and also the city of Nippur at http://oi.uchicago.edu/research/projects/nip/nsc.html.

It is also possible to take virtual tours of key sites of Egyptian (http://www.ancientegypt.co.uk/menu.html) and Nubian/Kushite civilizations (http://www.nubianet.org/about/about_history6.html and http://oi.uchicago.edu/OI/PROJ/NUB/NUBX92/NUBX92_brochure.html). A head-turning virtual three-dimensional walk through an Egyptian pyramid is offered at http://www.pbs.org/wgbh/nova/pyramid/explore/khufu.html. The daily life of ancient Egyptians is addressed at http://homepage.powerup.com.au/~ancient/life1.htm and http://www.touregypt.net/historicalessays/lifeinEgypt11.htm. How the Egyptian goddess Isis may have influenced the women of ancient Nubia is explored at http://wysinger.homestead.com/nubianwomen.html. The ancient civilizations of Persia can be viewed at http://members.ozemail.com.au/~ancientpersia/intro_frm.html, while the Persian capital of Persepolis receives close treatment at http://oi.uchicago.edu/museum/collections/pa/persepolis/ and http://www.crystalinks.com/iran.html.

Ancient mathematical and writing systems are examined at http://www.math.wichita.edu/history/topics/ancient.html, http://www-groups.dcs.st-andrews.ac.uk/~history/Indexes/Egyptians.html, http://oi.uchicago.edu/museum/virtual/eg/d.html, and at the amazingly colorful http://www.eyelid.co.uk/hiromenu.htm.

The history of early Judaism and its traditions can be studied at http://www.dinur.org/1.html?rsID=219, http://www.pbs.org/wnet/heritage/index.html, http://score.rims.k12.ca.us/activity/ancient_hebrews/, and http://www.jewishvirtuallibrary.org/jsource/Archaeology/archtoc.html (accessed also via http://www.jewishvirtuallibrary.org/). For Judaism's place among other Abrahamic religions (Christianity and Islam), see http://en.wikipedia.org/wiki/Abrahamic_religions.

The Yellow River as the cradle of Chinese civilization is analyzed at http://www.cis.umassd.edu/~gleung/ and http://wsu.edu/~dee/ANCCHINA/YELLOW.HTM. Early Chinese oracle bones and their place in the evolution of writing are explored at http://en.wikipedia.org/wiki/Oracle_bone. Images drawn from early Chinese history and culture can be viewed at http://www.chaos.umd.edu/history/ancient1.html and http://www.chinapage.com/content.html . Early Chinese ethical systems are discussed at http://www.san.beck.org/EC13-Chou.html.

An overview of early Indian history and culture may be found at http://www.mnsu.edu/emuseum/prehistory/india/indus/geography.html, http://pubweb.cc.u-tokai.ac.jp/indus/english/index.html, and http://library.thinkquest.org/11372/data/history.htm. Two principal cities of the Indus Valley, Harappa and Mohenjo Daro, can be visited virtually at http://www.harappa.com/index.html and http://www.harappa.com/indus/slideindex.html.

The art of the Indus Valley is explored at http://www.art-and-archaeology.com/timelines/india/early.html and http://www.accd.edu/sac/vat/arthistory/arts1303/India1.htm. The cultures of ancient Sumer and India are compared at http://www.hyperhistory.net/apwh/essays/comp/cw02summeriansharappans34100118.htm. Early daily life among Indo-European speaking people in Greece and India is compared at http://www.oldandsold.com/articles32n/history-outline-94.shtml.

The influence of India and China on early trade patterns in Southeast Asia is discussed at http://www.seasite.niu.edu/Tagalog/Tagalog_Default_files/Philippine_Culture/trade_and_early_empires.htm and http://findarticles.com/p/articles/mi_m1310/is_1984_June/ai_3289705. Early trade between India and China is briefly surveyed at http://www.historyforkids.org/learn/india/economy/ and http://depts.washington.edu/silkroad/exhibit/trade/trade.html.

AP* | Test Prep

1. The transformation that was most responsible for initially moving humans toward civilization was the

   (A)   the introduction of the use of iron.

   (B)   growth of towns and cities.

   (C)   rise of agriculture.

   (D)   rise of specialized classes.

2. The emergence of sedentary agriculture

   (A)   occurred simultaneously in various places and spread around the world.

   (B)   began only in the savannas of West Africa.

   (C)   started in the Middle East first but developed independently in other areas.

   (D)   arose in the river valleys of the Huang he and Yangtze.

3. Cuneiform and other types of writing are important in part because they

   (A)   help organize elaborate political structures.

   (B)   normally reduce social stratification.

   (C)   can compel leaders to follow written guidelines of behavior.

   (D)   hinder economic development in certain circumstances.

4. Which of the following is NOT a feature of Sumerian civilization?

   (A)   a simplified alphabet of 22 letters.

   (B)   ziggurats.

   (C)   cuneiform.

   (D)   a numeric system based on 10, 60, and 360.

5. Unlike Sumer and Egypt, the Indus Valley or Harappan civilization

   (A)   became a geographic center for a unified, continuous culture lasting millennia.

   (B)   is particularly difficult to study because its writing has not been deciphered.

   (C)   was secure from nomadic incursions and invasions.

   (D)   never developed a military social class.

6. Compared to river valley cultures in Egypt and Mesopotamia, Chinese civilization

   (A)   probably developed after civilizations in the Nile Valley and Mesopotamia.

   (B)   predates the rise of civilization in both Egypt and Mesopotamia.

   (C)   developed simultaneously with Egypt and Mesopotamia.

   (D)   did not rely on heavy irrigation as year round water was plentiful.

7. Stone tools, hunting and gathering, and an increasing number of *Homo sapiens sapiens* are features of the

   (A)   Late Paleolithic Age.

   (B)   Bronze Age.

   (C)   Early Copper Age.

   (D)   River valley civilizations.

Free-Response Question

To what extent was the Neolithic revolution responsible for the development of early civilizations? What are the problems in positing a direct connection?

Retrospective

From Hunting and Gathering to Civilizations, 2.5 million–1000 B.C.E.: Origins

Contacts and Their Limits

No regular pattern of contacts among the major population centers developed during the long early phases of human history. Even at the end of the period of the river valley civilizations, no such pattern existed. To be sure, separate developments did not prevent many similar features. In broad outline, early civilizations developed many of the same functions, as they introduced formal governments, writing systems, and significant cities. Agriculture generated similar tendencies to establish patriarchal family structures, but these similarities occurred spontaneously, the result of similar needs, not because they learned extensively from one another. And of course the specifics varied considerably—the system of government and the gender relations in Egypt, for example, differed from those in Mesopotamia.

Three kinds of contacts did exist during the early phases of human history. Their results were significant, though they were somewhat sporadic. First, local or long-distance trade could bring knowledge of new developments or products. People in one region could learn about innovations in the region next door. Local exchanges of products or symbolic gifts—the latter designed to help keep the peace—served as conduits. Through this kind of interaction, diffusion occurred. This was the mechanism through which knowledge of agriculture gradually spread from the areas where it was first developed to neighboring regions, and ultimately over whole subcontinents. Knowledge of new technologies, like metalwork, spread the same way. So did knowledge

of new foodstuffs: some crops original to southeast Asia, for example, reached Africa by 1000 C.E. and became staples.

This kind of diffusion was the most important contact in early human history. We do not always know the precise processes involved. For example, an Indian Ocean trade system existed by 1000 C.E., involving timber and perfumes; this led to a southeast Asian migration to the island of Madagascar. But we know almost nothing about the specifics of the system. It is also true that some trade contacts, like the Phoenician voyages to southern England to get tin, did not seem to produce wider diffusion of products or technologies.

A second kind of contact resulted from migration and invasion. We have seen that this combination occurred frequently in the Middle East, leading to changes in language but also the spread of new technologies. The wheel was almost certainly invented in central Asia, then brought by a migrant group to the Middle East. Migrations and invasions could be extremely disruptive, as when the Indo-Europeans moved into India, doing great violence to local populations. But they could also bring new knowledge to immigrants and local populations alike.

A third kind of contact involved direct trade, diplomatic relations, and military activity between two major early civilization centers. While Mesopotamia and Egypt developed separately for the most part, there were periods of invasion from one direction or another, some trade, and some cultural exchange. Tablets have been found, for example, whose text was written in both cuneiform and hieroglyphics, showing a need for direct translations. Egyptians and Mesopotamians both interacted with parts of Greece, including the island of Crete, which was therefore able to borrow from both societies. Some trade (though no military contact) probably occurred between Mesopotamia and the Indus valley. Early civilizations in China and the Americas were more fully isolated.

Contacts brought fundamental changes to the people involved, even in these early periods. Diffusion, particularly, was responsible for basic shifts in economic and therefore social systems. Most contact was sporadic, however, and did not lead to elaborate exchanges of religious or scientific ideas or political institutions. Here, the emphasis on separate patterns of development remains valid. ■

PART II

The Classical Period, 1000 B.C.E.–500 C.E.: Uniting Large Regions

Chapter 2   Classical Civilization: China

Chapter 3   Classical Civilization: India

Chapter 4   Classical Civilization in the Mediterranean: Greece and Rome

Chapter 5   The Classical Period: Directions, Diversities, and Declines by 500 C.E.

The major development during the classical period of world history was the formation of large regional civilizations in China, India, the Mediterranean, the Middle East, East Africa, and Mesoamerica. These developments can be seen in the accompanying maps. The map on the top depicts the Eastern Hemisphere early in the classical period (around 800 B.C.E.); the map on the bottom shows the same area around 100 C.E. In China and the Mediterranean, what had been a set of small states—or no states at all—had been replaced by two giant empires. India also developed substantial empires at several key points in the classical centuries.

Although much of the world remained outside the main areas of civilization, these areas had by far the largest concentration of population. Furthermore, the influence of these civilizations extended into surrounding regions outside their direct control. Classical civilizations also had important relationships with nomadic groups, mostly from central Asia, who traded with them and periodically attempted invasion. Nevertheless, regions outside the world's main civilizational areas require some separate attention during this long period.

Except for brief interludes, the main civilizations did not share direct borders. Much of the development of each civilization was separate, and the establishment of distinctive cultural and institutional patterns was a key legacy of this period. Nevertheless, trade offered some contacts, as products like silk were carried from east Asia to the Mediterranean. Occasionally interaction was more direct. The conquests of the Greek-trained warrior Alexander the Great resulted in the creation of a short-lived empire that stretched from the Mediterranean into northwestern India. This empire brought into direct contact Mediterranean, cultural Asian, Middle-Eastern, and Indian societies, an encounter that yielded interesting results, some of which are clearly evident in art of the period. For example, a statue sculpted by an Indian artist depicts the beloved Buddha clothed in Greek fashions. This combination of cultural elements, called syncretism, is a common result of significant contact between cultures. It can have lasting implications. Syncretism was not the most common feature of the classical period, but its occurrence hinted at what would develop more fully later.

Political Units of the World, c. 800–750 B.C.E.

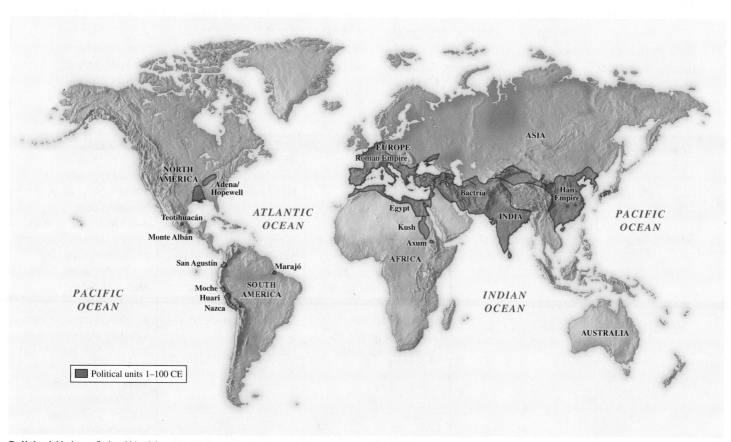

Political Units of the World, c. 1–100 C.E.

BIG CONCEPTS

The formation of the classical societies involved two striking features. First was the emergence and standardization (within each society) of key cultural and religious traditions and second, in the political real, was the development of state and empires—again, with each society producing some characteristic political forms within this category. Finally, as the period's third overarching feature, the contacts that did develop among different regions spurred trade and, to some degree, communication. All three of these features would affect world history long after the classical period had itself ended.

TRIGGERS FOR CHANGE

Despite the lack of a clear transition, the classical civilizations that began to emerge about 1000 B.C.E. were measurably different from their river valley predecessors. While they built on the earlier achievements, they grew noticeably larger in their geographic, cultural, economic, and political reach.

What allowed this greater reach was military conquest, made possible by the introduction of iron tools and weapons, beginning about 1500 B.C.E.

As larger empires developed, leaders worked to tie their territories together both commercially and culturally. New trade links emerged, sometimes encouraged by new infrastructure such as canals (China) or postal service (Persia). Religion and philosophy were formalized and disseminated as part of training a cohesive elite. New conquests, possible in part because of technological change, led to further developments intended to integrate larger regions.

Each of the classical societies ultimately declined, and great empires like the Han dynasty in China, the Gupta in India, and the western Roman Empire collapsed altogether. Though these developments did not happen at exactly the same time, together they brought the classical period to a close by 500 C.E.

THE BIG CHANGES

Each of the classical civilizations had its own social structure, religion, political system, system of science, and styles of art. Comparisons of these differences, which have continued to the present day, form a vital part of studying the classical period. To take one example: in the late 20th century the Chinese government proved reasonably effective in mandating drastic changes in birth rates. The Indian government tried and failed to enforce somewhat similar regulations. Many factors accounted for China's success and India's failure in enforcing a population policy, but an important one was the extent to which people in each country accepted as legitimate government monitoring of personal behavior. These differences in attitude can be traced back to the classical period. The civilization styles

5000 B.C.E	2000 B.C.E.	1000 B.C.E.	750 B.C.E.	500 B.C.E.
5000 Early Japanese Settlement	2000 Germans settle in Denmark 1200–700 Vedas composed 1500–500 Polynesian migrations 1122–770 Initial Zhou kingdom	1000 Germans expand southward 900 Maya begins 850–250 Chavin culture (Andes) 800 Rise of Greek city-states 800 B.C.E.–1000 C.E. Bantu migration, sub-Saharan Africa 770–403 Later Zhou kingdom; beginning of China's classical period	750–600 Meroë (Kush) rules Egypt 600 Zoroastrian religion in Iran 600 Legendary ruler in Japan 551–c. 233 Periods of the great Chinese philosophers: Confucius, Laozi, Mencius, Legalists 550 Formation of Persian Empire C. 542–483 Buddha	500–449 Greek wars with Persia; Persia defeated 500–450 Beginnings of Roman republic 470–430 Height of Athenian culture; Socrates and Greek philisophical style 431 ff. Peloponnesian Wars; decline of Greece 330 Alexander the Great 327–325 Alexander's invasion 322–185 Mauryan Empire 300–100 Hellenistic Period 300 B.C.E.–900 C.E. Heights of Maya 264–140 Roman expansion in North Africa (Punic Wars) and eastern Mediterranean

set in the classical period hardly predetermined the future, but they had, and have, undeniable influence.

The first major change, then, was the establishment of cultures that developed over time during the classical period and left durable legacies. All of the major civilizations set up vigorous internal trade that allowed considerable regional specialization—each region within a civilization produced the crops most suitable to its ecology and traded for other necessities.

Each major civilization promoted a common cultural system that would legitimate characteristic social and family customs, integrate elites, and provide bonds between ordinary people and leadership groups. This system might involve more than one component. For example, there was outright, though usually peaceful, competition between Buddhism and Hinduism in India. But the generation of powerful beliefs and their spread within each civilization was an important development in the classical period, and one that had lasting impact.

Each major civilization, at least periodically, conquered other peoples and areas and created large empires. Although empires were not new in world history, those of the classical period in world history were more powerful and widespread than any precedent.

The growth of the classical civilizations, with their impressive achievements and monuments, clearly had an impact on surrounding peoples. Some trade with neighboring regions was common. India had the widest commercial reach, extending all the way into southeast Asia, but Rome also traded with parts of Africa and Asia outside its own empire. Even more widely, nomadic peoples were often attracted toward the centers of civilization as immigrants, soldiers, or invaders. Some nomadic peoples facilitated trade between civilizations. These developments were important at the time and had implications for later patterns in world history. For example, cultural and trade contacts often prepared the way for later nomadic migrations into the classical societies.

The achievements of the major classical civilizations inspired awe, at the time and later. Great developments in philosophy, politics, and art in classical civilizations provided the foundations for subsequent civilizations. Confucianism, for example, would influence other Asian societies besides China, and a number of societies would build on the achievements of Greek science. It is for this reason that the term *classical* is commonly used to refer to this period.

CONTINUITY

While the introduction of iron helped usher in the classical period, the period itself did not witness sweeping technological developments. Most peasants continued to use traditional agricultural tools and methods. Similarly, except for the improved road systems introduced by more powerful governments,

250 B.C.E.	1 C.E.	250 C.E.	500 C.E.	750 C.E.
221 Shi Huangdi proclaimed first emperor of China	23–220 Later Han dynasty; invention of paper and compass	300 Decline of Meroë	451 First Han invasion	800–1300 Mississippian culture
202 B.C.E.–9 C.E. Initial Han dynasty; key technical developments of horse collar and water mill	27 Augustus founds Roman Empire	300 Spread of Buddhism	476 Last Roman emperor in West	900 Polynesians to New Zealand
200 B.C.E.–200 C.E. Greater Buddhist influence	30 Crucifixion of Jesus	300–400 Yamato claim imperial control of Japan	527–565 Justinian Eastern emperor	900–1200 Toltecs
133 ff. Decline of Roman republic	88 Beginning of Han decline	300–700 Rise of Axum; conversion to Chistianity	580 ff. Spread of Buddhism in Japan	1000 Height of kingdom of Ghana, Africa
100 Germans begin contact with Rome; Slavs migrate into eastern Europe	106 Height of Roman territory	300–900 Intermediate Horizon period (Andes)	589–618 Sui dynasty	
	180 Beginning of decline of Rome	300–1000 Second wave of Polynesian migrations to Hawaii	600–647 Harsha's Empire	
	200–500 Nasca culture (Andes)	312–337 Constantine; formation of Eastern Empire; adoption of Christianity	618 Tang dynasty	
	200–700 Mochica culture (Andes)	319–540 Gupta Empire	700 ff. Spread of Islam; trans-Sahara trade in Africa	
	200–1300 Anasazi in North America	400 Chinese script imported		
	220 Last Han emperor deposed	401 ff. Large-scale Germanic invasions in Roman Empire		

there were no great advances in transportation during this period. Rural culture remained somewhat apart from classical culture, particularly in China and the Mediterranean. Many rural people retained their traditional festivals and polytheistic religious beliefs alongside official religions and philosophies.

Patriarchal culture prevailed in each of the major civilizations of the classical period. Each culture had particular ways of defining women's roles and obligations. Comparisons among the classical civilizations are important in this area, for different styles of patriarchy would affect family life and even art, but the basic idea of patriarchal superiority had already been established. The civilizations simply related a patriarchal system to the particular cultures they developed and emphasized.

Finally, though the classical civilizations all introduced significant innovations beyond their river valley predecessors, they also retained and built on key achievements of the earlier societies. They did not have to reinvent money, the idea of codes of law, or scientific interests such as astronomy. While the classical civilizations left a heritage that shaped future developments, they also drew upon a heritage established in earlier periods.

IMPACT ON DAILY LIFE: OLD AGE

In all the classical civilizations, the achievement of old age won respect. It was seen, legitimately enough, as a sign of good habits and wisdom. Furthermore, in groups where literacy was uncommon, the elderly could be vital sources of information and cultural memory—the kinds of stories that help shape the identity of families and cultures. Respect for the elderly was a sign of good manners in all the classical societies.

But the classical civilizations also differed in their attitudes toward the elderly. Chinese Confucianism placed particular emphasis on venerating the elderly. Even older women, if they were mothers (and especially if they were widows and mothers of sons) had clear status, although officially their sons ran the household.

In Mediterranean cultures, there was greater ambivalence concerning older people. The themes of wisdom and respect were visible (though they applied much more clearly to men than to women). But the elderly also were depicted as both greedy and laughable as their capacities declined. Stories made fun of old misers or men who lusted after younger women. In the Mediterranean, more attention was paid to the physical and mental deterioration of older people, and while this sometimes produced sympathy, it could also generate scorn. The Greek dramatist Aeschylus wrote about people "old in their bones, dishonored, cut off," and the Bible offered many accounts of enfeebled, foolish elders. Societies that placed great emphasis on military prowess and youthful beauty could be harsh to people past their prime, and in the Mediterranean, there was no systematic set of beliefs, like Confucianism, to cut through these contradictions.

Did these cultural differences matter in the actual way older people were treated? Here, the evidence is sketchier; we know much more about classical value systems than about the details of daily life. What is clear is that this ambivalence to-ward the elderly had staying power. Even today, many argue, ambivalence about older people that goes back to Greeks, Romans, and Hebrews affects policy and outlook in the West, while in contrast, some east Asian systems write respect for the elderly into their constitutions.

TRENDS AND SOCIETIES

Initial chapters in this section describe developments in each of the major civilizations during the classical period, starting with China in Chapter 2 and India in Chapter 3. Chapter 4 returns to the Mediterranean, to take up the history of Greece and Rome. Chapter 5 returns to the main classical centers, dealing with patterns of decline and with concurrent religious innovations, including the rise of Christianity. The story of the decline of each civilization was distinct, but the overall pattern of change had some important common features.

Classical Civilization: China

Establishment of Political Order

Patterns in Classical China

Political Institutions

VISUALIZING THE PAST: Capital Designs and Patterns
of Political Power

Religion and Culture

DOCUMENT: Teachings of the Rival Chinese Schools

Economy and Society

THINKING HISTORICALLY: Women in Patriarchal Societies

How Chinese Civilization Fits Together

GLOBAL CONNECTIONS: Classical China and the World

Late in the 6th century B.C.E., a brilliant middle-aged scholar-philosopher applied for a high post in the bureaucracy of the small kingdom of Lu in northeast China. Perhaps because Kong Fuzi—or Confucius as he came to be known centuries later in the West—was widely reputed to be an opinionated and outspoken person, he was denied the position for which he was confident he was well qualified. Angered by this rebuff, Confucius left Lu and took to the road in search of the ideal ruler, who presumably would recognize his talents and offer him employment at a suitable level of distinction at his court.

The China of Confucius's day offered abundant options for a talented political advisor. The declining power of the Zhou kingdom, which had for centuries dominated early Chinese civilization along the Yellow River, opened the way for the rise of a patchwork of rival states. Many of these competing states were ruled by nomadic peoples who had migrated from the north or west. Wars between these upstart forces and the lords of long-established households with imperial pretensions were frequent, banditry was widespread, commerce was threatened, and displaced peasants and warrior bands wandered throughout the countryside. The monarchs of some nomad kingdoms had extensively adopted the distinct culture that had been developing in the Huanghe region since the age of the Shang warrior kings. Nonetheless, Confucius and others in the emerging scholar-gentry—or shi—social strata continued to regard most of the nomads as uncouth, warlike barbarians. Convinced that he was a man with a mission, Confucius undertook a lifelong quest to become the chief advisor to a ruler who possessed the vision and skills to restore centralized control, peace, and order.

One among many wandering scholars in the late Zhou era, Confucius attracted numerous disciples, some of whom became distinguished philosophers in their own right. The master's students preserved, spread, and debated his teachings, and after his death in the early 5th century B.C.E., they compiled his wisdom in what would come to be known as the *Analects,* or collected sayings: hence, "Confucius says."

Over time, Confucius's political and social philosophy became foundational for one of humanity's greatest and most enduring civilizations. In view of the turmoil in China when Confucian teachings were formulated, it is not surprising that they idealized strong rulers and the consolidation of political power. Confucius advocated rule by a highly educated, exclusively male elite, but one that was deemed responsible for the well-being of all of the subjects of the state. Primarily an ethical rather than a religious system, Confucianism sought to establish norms for all aspects of Chinese life, from relationships within the family that stressed respect for one's elders to manners for rulers and subjects. Confucianism also highlighted the importance of art, music, and elegant calligraphy in the cultivation of the scholar-bureaucrats.

Measured in terms of the acquisition of wealth and power, Confucius was a failure. He never found his ideal monarch, or even a suitable post at any of the numerous royal households that jostled for dominance across China. In fact, in the centuries following his death—often appropriately designated as the era of the warring states—political and social disintegration intensified. But the students and disciples of Confucius found a large and enthusiastic audience for his teachings in these troubled times. ■

Figure 2.1 This painting, *The First Emperor of the Han Dynasty Entering Guandang* by Zhao Bozhu seeks to capture the pomp and splendor associated with the founder of the Han dynasty, one of the most powerful and long-lived in Chinese history. By the last centuries B.C.E., large, richly attired entourages, which often moved about among several palaces and walled cities, were deemed essential for the emperors and regional lords who had become the dominant force in Chinese political life.

This chapter focuses on the conditions that gave rise to Confucianism as well as the teachings of rival philosophical systems, such as Legalism, Daoism, and Buddhism. As we shall see, even as late as the end of the 3rd century B.C.E., when Chinese political unity was again restored by the warrior strongman Shi Huangdi's kingdom of Qin, Confucian social norms and political prescriptions were eclipsed by more authoritarian alternatives. But with the rise of the Han dynasty after 207 B.C.E., the teachings of Confucius and several of his more prominent followers came to provide the ideological underpinnings of both the Chinese state and society. In subsequent dynasties, the influence of Confucianism waxed and waned, but even after its alleged extinction in the crisis-ridden decades of the 20th century, it has persisted as a major cultural force to the present day. Confucianism has also exerted a pervasive and enduring influence on other societies throughout Asia, from Japan and Korea through central Asia and southward into present-day Vietnam. China's Confucian ideals, scholar-gentry bureaucracy, technological advancements, and prosperous agrarian state captivated major thinkers in Europe and the United States—from Jesuit missionaries to Thomas Jefferson.

Establishment of Political Order

The Zhou dynasty's ability to control its vassals broke down in the 8th century B.C.E. and led to a long period of political conflict and social turmoil throughout China. Political structures developed in key phases, with cultural traditions contributing as well. In both the Yellow and the Yangzi river basins, many states rose and fell, each seeking to replace the Zhou as the paramount power in east Asia. Chinese expansions to the south and west created periodic instability as local peoples tried to defend themselves. Internal conflicts left China vulnerable to outside invaders, and between the 8th and 3rd centuries B.C.E., nomadic peoples often raided the farming areas of the north China plain. Many of the nomads settled down and eventually assimilated the distinct culture that had been developing in the region since the age of the Shang warrior kings. Some of these invaders captured existing states; others established new dynasties that further intensified the already complex political maneuvers and wars for supremacy.

A period of political disorganization led to concerted efforts to promote political order, with cultural emphases to match.

1200 B.C.E.	500 B.C.E.	250 B.C.E.
1029–258 Zhou dynasty; introduction of a standard spoken language 551–478 Life of Confucius	c. 500 Laozi and Daoism c. 500 Editing of the Five Classics c. 450 Development of Chinese calendar 402–201 Era of the Warring States	221–202 Qin dynasty: the First Emperor, the Great Wall begun, a single basic language 202 B.C.E.–220 C.E. Han dynasty c. 200 Introduction of ox-drawn plow, horse collar, water mill 141–87 Reign of Han Wu Ti, increased bureaucracy; examinations, spread of Confucianism

Shi Huangdi   [shiuh-hwahng-dee] Founder of the brief Qin dynasty in 221 B.C.E.

Qin dynasty   [chin] Established in 221 B.C.E. at the end of the Warring States period following the decline of the Zhou dynasty; fell in 207 B.C.E.

Han dynasty   Chinese dynasty that succeeded the Qin in 202 B.C.E.; ruled for next 400 years.

The yearning for unity and an end to civil strife appeared to be answered in the 3rd century B.C.E. by the emergence of the warrior strongman **Shi Huangdi** (shiuh-hwahng-dee). By 221 B.C.E., Shi Huangdi's state of **Qin** (chin) had vanquished all its rivals, and he founded a new imperial dynasty that promised to bring an end to the centuries of strife. But Shi Huangdi proved to be a tyrant. His death in 210 B.C.E. was the signal for resistance throughout the empire to the rule of his less despotic and less capable son and his inner circle of advisors. A rapidly spreading revolt, led by two peasants, toppled the Qin dynasty in 207 B.C.E. and gave rise to its much longer-lived successor, the **Han.**

The Han era, which lasted, with a brief interruption, for more than 400 years, saw the consolidation of Chinese civilization. Unity was established in the old core regions, and Chinese political control was greatly extended in all directions. Perhaps more critically, the Han rulers founded the largest, most effective, and most enduring bureaucracy in the preindustrial world. They oversaw the development of the first civil service examinations and the professionalization of Chinese administration. These institutions helped build a sense of Chinese distinctiveness and identity that was reflected in later centuries by Chinese references to themselves as the "sons of Han." This identity proved critical to the survival of Chinese civilization in the centuries of war, foreign invasion, and internal division that returned when the Han dynasty collapsed in the early 3rd century C.E.

Cultural Traditions

China generated the first of the great classical societies. The region's isolation limited its ability to learn from other cultures but also spared it frequent invasion and encouraged an intense, and distinctive, Chinese identity. The decline of the Shang dynasty did not result in as much internal chaos as did invasions of parts of the Middle East and particularly India. Hence, the Chinese could build more strongly on Huang he precedents, including technological advancements. Particularly important was a general, if somewhat vague, worldview developed by thinkers in the Shang and Zhou dynasties and accepted as a standard approach in later Chinese thinking. This intellectual heritage stressed the basic harmony of nature: every feature is balanced by an opposite, every *yin* by a *yang*. Thus for hot there is cold, for male, female. According to this philosophy, an individual should seek a way to relate to this harmony, avoiding excess and appreciating the balance of opposites. Individuals and human institutions existed within this world of balanced nature not, as in later Mediterranean philosophy, on the outside. Chinese traditions about balance, Dao, and yin/yang were intrinsic to diverse philosophies and religions established in the classical period, and they provided some unity among various schools of thought in China.

Despite important cultural continuity, classical China did not simply maintain earlier traditions. The formative centuries of classical Chinese history were witness to a great many changes. The religious and particularly the political habits of the Shang kingdom were substantially modified as China built the world's largest classical empire. These new developments led to much diversity, but also to often painful conflict. From them, the Chinese emerged with an unusually well integrated system in which government, philosophy, economic incentives, the family, and the individual were intended to blend into a harmonious whole.

Patterns in Classical China

The Zhou dynasty featured decentralized politics but important cultural innovations, while later dynasties emphasized order and centralization.

Of all the societies in the world today, it is China that has maintained the clearest links to its classical past—a past that has been a source of pride but also the cause of some problems of adaptation. Already in the period of classical Chinese history, a pattern was set in motion that lasted until the early part of the 20th century. A family of kings, called a *dynasty,* would start its rule of China with great vigor, developing strong political institutions and encouraging an active economy. Subsequently, the dynasty grew weaker and tax revenues declined, while social divisions increased in the larger society. Internal rebellions and sometimes invasions from the outside hastened the dynasty's decline. As the ruling dynasty declined, another dynasty emerged, usually from the family of a successful general, invader, or peasant rebel, and the pattern would start anew. Small wonder that many Chinese conceive of history in terms of cycles, in contrast to the Western tendency to think of steady progress from past to present.

The Zhou Dynasty

Three dynastic cycles cover the many centuries of classical China: the Zhou, the Qin, and the Han (Map 2.1). The **Zhou** (joh) dynasty lasted from 1029 to 258 B.C.E. Although lengthy, this dynasty flourished only until about 700 B.C.E.; it was then beset by a decline in the political infrastructure and frequent invasions by nomadic peoples from border regions. Even during its strong centuries, the Zhou did not establish a powerful government, ruling instead through alliances with regional princes and noble families. The dynasty initially came into China from the north, displacing its predecessor, the Shang rulers. The alliance systems the Zhou used as the basis for their rule were standard in agricultural kingdoms. (We will see similar forms later emerge in Japan, India, Europe, and Africa.) Rulers lacked the means to control their territories directly and so gave large regional estates to members of their families and other supporters, hoping that their loyalties would remain intact. The supporters, in exchange for land, were supposed to provide the central government with troops and tax revenues. This was China's feudal period, with rulers depending on a network of loyalties and obligations to and from their landlord-vassals. Such a

China in the Shang and Zhou Eras

Zhou [joh] Originally a vassal family of Shang China; possibly Turkic in origin; overthrew the Shang and established second historical Chinese dynasty that flourished 1122 to 256 B.C.E.

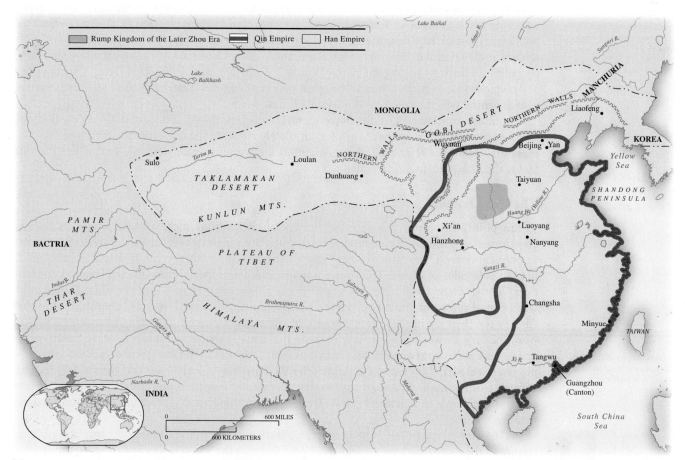

Map 2.1 China from the Later Zhou Era to the Han Era   As this map showing the boundaries of successive Chinese dynasties illustrates the extent of the early Han empire greatly exceeded even that of the Qin dynasty, which was the first to effectively unify the core regions of Chinese civilization.

system was, of course, vulnerable to regional disloyalties, and the ultimate decline of the Zhou dynasty occurred when regional land-owning aristocrats solidified their own power base and disregarded the central government.

The Zhou did, however, contribute in several ways to the development of Chinese politics and culture in their active early centuries. First, they extended the territory of China by encouraging settlers to move into the Yangzi River valley. While the Zhou were too weak to take this territory over directly, the expanded settlement, from the Huang he to the Yangzi, became China's core—often called the "Middle Kingdom." It provided rich agricultural lands plus the benefits of two different agricultures—wheat-growing in the north, rice-growing in the south—a diversity that encouraged population growth. The territorial expansion obviously complicated the problems of central rule, for communication and transport from the capital to the outlying regions were difficult.

Despite limited control over key regions, the Zhou did actually heighten the focus on the central government. Zhou rulers claimed direct links to the Shang rulers. They also asserted that heaven had transferred its mandate to rule China to the Zhou emperors. This political concept of a Mandate of Heaven remained a key justification for Chinese imperial rule from the Zhou onward. Known as Sons of Heaven, the emperors lived in a world of awe-inspiring pomp and ceremony.

The Zhou worked to provide greater cultural unity in their empire. They discouraged some of the primitive religious practices of the Huang he civilization, banning human sacrifice and urging more restrained ceremonies to worship the gods. They also promoted linguistic unity, beginning the process by which a standard spoken language, ultimately called Mandarin Chinese, would prevail over the entire Middle Kingdom. This resulted in the largest single group of people speaking the same language in the world at this time. Regional dialects and languages remained, but educated officials began to rely on the single Mandarin form. Oral epics and stories in Chinese, many gradually recorded in written form, aided in the development of a common cultural currency.

Increasing cultural unity helps explain why, when the Zhou empire began to fail, scholars were able to use philosophical ideas to lessen the impact of growing political confusion. Indeed, the political crisis spurred efforts to define and articulate Chinese culture. During the late 6th and early 5th centuries B.C.E., the philosopher known in the West as **Confucius** wrote an elaborate statement on political ethics, providing the core of China's distinctive philosophical heritage. Other writers and religious leaders participated in this great period of cultural creativity, which later reemerged as a set of central beliefs throughout the Middle Kingdom.

Cultural innovation did not, however, reverse the prolonged and painful Zhou downfall. Regional rulers formed independent armies, ultimately reducing the emperors to little more than figureheads. Between 402 and 201 B.C.E., a period known aptly enough as the Era of the Warring States, the Zhou system disintegrated.

The Qin Dynasty

At this point, China might have gone the way of civilizations such as India, where centralized government was more the exception than the rule. But a new dynasty arose to reverse the process of political decay. One regional ruler deposed the last Zhou emperor and within 35 years made himself sole ruler of China. The young warrior took the imperial title Qin Shi Huangdi, or "the tiger." The dynastic name, Qin, conferred on the whole country its name of China. Shi Huangdi was a brutal ruler, but effective given the circumstances of internal disorder. He understood that China's problem lay in the regional power of the aristocrats, and like many later centralizers in world history, he worked vigorously to undo this force. He ordered nobles to leave their regions and appear at his court, assuming control of their feudal estates. China was organized into large provinces ruled by bureaucrats appointed by the emperor. Shi Huangdi was careful to select his officials from nonaristocratic groups, so that they would owe their power to him and not dare to develop their own independent bases. Under Shi Huangdi's rule, powerful armies crushed regional resistance.

The First Emperor followed up on centralization by extending Chinese territory and political control to the south, reaching present-day Hong Kong on the South China Sea and even influencing northern Vietnam. In the north, to guard against outside invasions and to protect his own expansionist drives. Shi Huangdi built the **Great Wall,** extending over 3000 miles, wide enough for chari-

Confucius Also known as Kung Fuzi; major Chinese philosopher born in 6th century B.C.E.; author of *Analects*; philosophy based on need for restoration of order through advice of superior men to be found among the shi.

Great Wall Chinese defensive fortification intended to keep out the nomadic invaders from the north; initiated during Qin dynasty and reign of Shi Huangdi.

The Great Wall

IMAGE

ots to move along its crest. This wall, probably the largest construction project in human history, was built by forced labor, conscripted by the central bureaucracy from among the peasantry.

The Qin dynasty was responsible for a number of innovations in Chinese politics and culture. To determine the empire's resources, Shi Huangdi ordered a national census, which provided data for the calculation of tax revenues and labor service. The government standardized coinage, weights, and measures through the entire realm. Even the length of axles on carts was regulated to promote coherent road planning. The government also made Chinese written script uniform, completing the process of creating a single basic language in which all educated Chinese could communicate. The government furthered agriculture, sponsoring new irrigation projects, and promoted manufacturing, particularly that of silk cloth. The activist government also attacked formal culture, burning many books. Thinking, according to Shi Huangdi, was likely to be subversive to his autocratic rule.

Although it created many durable features of Chinese government, the Qin dynasty was short-lived. Shi Huangdi's attacks on intellectuals and particularly the high taxes needed to support military expansion and the construction of the Great Wall made him fiercely unpopular. One opponent described the First Emperor as a monster who "had the heart of a tiger and a wolf. He killed men as though he thought he could never finish, he punished men as though he were afraid he would never get around to them all." On the emperor's death, in 210 B.C.E., massive revolts organized by aggrieved peasants broke out. One peasant leader defeated other opponents and in 202 B.C.E. established the third dynasty of classical China, the Han.

The Han Dynasty

The Han dynasty, which lasted over 400 years, to 220 C.E., rounded out China's basic political and intellectual structure. Han rulers retained the centralized administration of the Qin but sought to reduce the brutal repression of that period. Like many dynasties during the first flush of power, early Han rulers expanded Chinese territory, pushing into Korea, Indochina, and central Asia. This expansion gave rise to direct contact with India and also allowed the Chinese to develop contact with the Parthian Empire in the Middle East, through which trade with the Roman Empire around the Mediterranean was conducted. The most famous Han ruler, Wu Ti (140–87 B.C.E.), enforced peace throughout much of the continent of Asia, rather like the peace the Roman Empire would bring to the Mediterranean region a hundred years later, but embracing even more territory and a far larger population. Peace brought great prosperity to China itself. A Han historian conveys the self-satisfied, confident tone of the dynasty:

> The nation had met with no major disturbances so that, except in times of flood or drought, every person was well supplied and every family had enough to get along on. The granaries in the cities and the countryside were full and the government treasures were running over with wealth. In the capital the strings of cash had stacked up by the hundreds of millions until they could no longer be counted. In the central granary of the government, new grain was heaped on top of the old until the building was full and the grain overflowed and piled up outside, where it spoiled and became unfit to eat. Even the keepers of the community gates ate fine grain and meat.

Under the Han dynasty, the workings of the state bureaucracy also improved and the government was linked to formal training that emphasized the values of Confucian philosophy. Reversing the Qin dynasty's policies, Wu Ti urged support for Confucianism, seeing it as a vital supplement to formal measures on the government's part. Shrines were established to promote the worship of the ancient philosopher as a god.

The quality of Han rule declined after about two centuries. Central control weakened, and invasions from central Asia, spearheaded by a nomadic people called the Huns, who had long threatened China's northern borders, overturned the dynasty entirely. Between 220 and 589 C.E., China was in a state of chaos. Order and stability were finally restored, but by then the classical or formative period of Chinese civilization had ended. Well before the Han collapse, however, China had established distinctive political structures and cultural values of unusual clarity, capable, as it turned out, of surviving even three centuries of renewed confusion.

Political Institutions

The power of the emperor, the development of a bureaucracy, and the expansion of state functions became the hallmarks of classical Chinese politics.

The Qin and Han dynasties of classical China established a distinctive, and remarkably successful, kind of government. The Qin stressed central authority, whereas the Han expanded the powers of the bureaucracy. More than any other factor, it was the structure of this government that explained how such a vast territory could be effectively ruled—for the Chinese empire was indeed the largest political system in the classical world. This structure would change after the classical period, particularly in terms of streamlining and expanding bureaucratic systems and procedures, but it never required fundamental overhaul.

The political framework that emerged as a result of the long centuries of China's classical period had several key elements. Strong local units never disappeared. Like most successful agricultural societies, China relied heavily on tightly knit patriarchal families. Individual families were linked to other relatives in extended family networks that included brothers, uncles, and any living grandparents. Among the wealthy land-owning groups, family authority was enhanced by the practice of ancestor worship, which joined family members through rituals devoted to important forebears who had passed into the spirit world. For ordinary people, among whom ancestor worship was less common, village authority surmounted family rule. Village leaders helped farming families regulate property and coordinate planting and harvest work. During the Zhou dynasty, and also in later periods when dynasties weakened, the regional power of great landlords also played an important role at the village level. Landed nobles provided courts of justice and organized military troops.

Strong local rule was not the most significant or distinctive feature of Chinese government under the Qin and Han dynasties, however. Shi Huangdi not only attacked local rulers but also provided a single law code for the whole empire and established a uniform tax system. He appointed governors to each district of his domain, who exercised military and legal powers in the name of the emperor. They, in turn, named officials responsible for smaller regions. Here indeed was a classic model of centralized government that other societies would replicate in later times: the establishment of centralized codes and appointment of officials directly by a central authority, rather than reliance on arrangements with numerous existing local governments. The effectiveness of a central government was further enhanced by the delegation of special areas and decisions to the emperor's ministers. Some dealt with matters of finance, others with justice, others with military affairs, and so on.

Strong Bureaucracy

Able rulers of the Han dynasty resumed the attack on local warrior-landlords. In addition, they realized the importance of creating a large, highly skilled bureaucracy, one capable of carrying out the duties of a complex state. By the end of the Han period, China had about 130,000 bureaucrats, representing 0.2 percent of the population. The emperor Wu Ti established examinations for his bureaucrats—the first example of civil service tests of the sort that many governments have instituted in modern times. These examinations covered classics of Chinese literature as well as law, suggesting a model of the scholar-bureaucrat that would later become an important element of China's political tradition. Wu Ti also established a school to train men of exceptional talent and ability for the national examinations. Although most bureaucrats were drawn from the landed upper classes, who alone had the time to learn the complex system of Chinese characters, individuals from lower ranks of society were occasionally recruited under this system. China's bureaucracy thus provided a slight check on complete upper-class rule. It also tended to limit the exercise of arbitrary power by the emperor himself. Trained and experienced bureaucrats, confident in their own traditions, could often control the whims of a single ruler, even one who, in the Chinese tradition, regarded himself as divinely appointed—the "Son of Heaven." It was no accident then that the Chinese bureaucracy lasted from the Han period until the 20th century, outliving the empire itself.

Small wonder that from the classical period at least until modern times, and possibly still today, the Chinese were the most tightly governed people in any large society in the world. When it worked well—and it is important to recall that the system periodically broke down—Chinese politics represented a remarkable integration of all levels of authority. The edicts of an all-powerful emperor were administered by trained scholar-bureaucrats, widely respected for their learning and,

Capital Designs and Patterns of Political Power

The design and physical layout of the capital cities of early civilizations can tell us a great deal about the distribution of political power and social status in different centers of the ancient world. In addition, the configurations of these pivotal cities usually manifest religious beliefs and conceptions of the cosmic order in the ways they are oriented and physically constructed. Therefore, plans of the capital centers of ancient civilizations can be read like written texts to help us understand the early history of some of humankind's greatest civilizations. Reproduced here are schematic diagrams of some of the key features of the capital cities of three of the great early civilizations of Eurasia: from Xi'an in Han China, Athens in Greece, and Harappa in India. Study and compare these diagrams for what they tell us about the kinds of elite groups that exercised political power, social stratification, and thinking about the relationship between the supernatural and human rulers in each civilization for which they served as capitals. In thinking about these issues, you may want to refer to relevant sections in Chapters 3, 4, and 5.

QUESTIONS Which social groups were the most powerful politically in each society? How prominent was military force in the exercise of power by the elites in each civilization? To what extent was political power legitimized by religious figures, ideas, and conceptions of the workings of the cosmos? To what degree did the rulers and political elites seek to separate themselves from the subject population, and what evidence could you use to determine this?

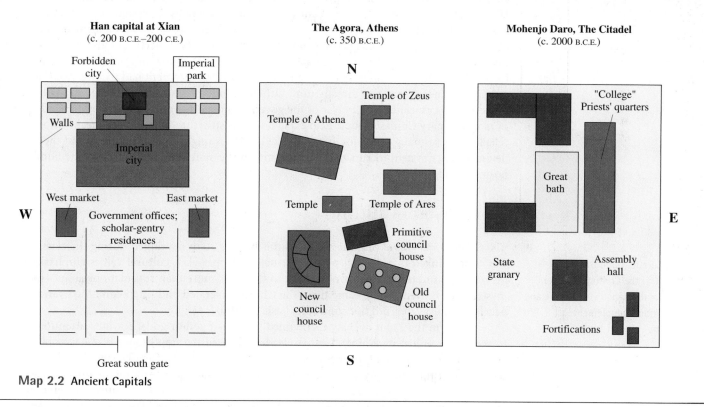

Map 2.2 Ancient Capitals

often, their noble birth. Individual families also emphasized this strong principle of authority, with the father in charge, presumably carrying on the wishes of a long line of ancestors to which the family paid reverence. The Chinese were capable of periodic rebellions, and gangs of criminals regularly came to disrupt the social scene—indeed, frequently harsh punishments reflected the need of the government to eradicate such deviant forces. Nevertheless, whether within the family or the central state, most Chinese in ordinary times believed in the importance of respect for those in power.

Roles of the State

Government traditions established during the classical period included an impressive list of state functions. Like all organized states, the Chinese government operated military and judicial systems. Military activity fluctuated, as China did not depend on steady expansion. Although classical China produced some enduring examples of the art of war, the state was not highly militaristic by the Han period. Judicial matters—crime and legal disputes—commanded more attention by local government authorities.

The government also sponsored much intellectual life, organizing research in astronomy and the maintenance of historical records. Under the Han rulers, the government played a major role in promoting Confucian philosophy as an official statement of Chinese values and in encouraging the worship of Confucius himself. The government developed a durable sense of mission as the primary keeper of Chinese beliefs.

The imperial government was also active in the economy. It directly organized the production of iron and salt. Its standardization of currency, weights, and measures facilitated trade throughout the vast empire. The government additionally sponsored public works, including complex irrigation and canal systems. Han rulers even tried to regulate agricultural supplies by storing grain and rice in good times to control price increases—and potential popular unrest—when harvests were bad.

China's ambitious rulers in no sense directed the daily lives of their subjects; the technology of an agricultural society did not permit this. Even under the Han, it took over a month for a directive from the capital city to reach the outlying districts of the empire—an obvious limit on imperial authority. A revealing Chinese proverb held that "heaven is high, and the emperor is far away." However, the power of the Chinese state did extend considerably. Its system of courts was backed by a strict code of law; torture and execution were widely employed to supplement the preaching of obedience and civic virtue. The central government taxed its subjects and also required some annual labor on the part of every male peasant—this was the source of the incredible physical work involved in building canals, roads, and palaces. No other government had the organization and staff to reach ordinary people so directly until virtually modern times, except in much smaller political units such as city-states. The power of the government and the authority it commanded in the eyes of most ordinary Chinese people help explain why its structure survived decline, invasion, and even rebellion for so many centuries. Invaders like the Huns might topple a dynasty, but they could not devise a better system to run the country, and so the system and its bureaucratic administrators normally endured.

Religion and Culture

Chinese culture featured the development of the Confucian system, but Daoism and distinctive scientific and artistic traditions complemented Confucianism.

The Chinese way of viewing the world, as this belief system developed during the classical period, was closely linked to a distinct political structure. Upper-class cultural values emphasized a good life on earth and the virtues of obedience to the state, more than speculations about God and the mysteries of heaven. At the same time, the Chinese tolerated and often combined various specific beliefs, so long as they did not contradict basic political loyalties.

Rulers in the Zhou dynasty maintained belief in a god or gods, but little attention was given to the nature of a deity. Rather, Chinese leaders stressed the importance of a harmonious earthly life, which would maintain proper balance between earth and heaven. Harmony included carefully constructed rituals to unify society and prevent individual excess. Among the upper classes, people were trained in elaborate exercises and military skills such as archery. Commonly, ceremonies venerating ancestors and even marking special meals were conducted. The use of chopsticks began at the end of the Zhou dynasty; it encouraged a code of politeness at meals. Soon after this, tea was introduced, although the most elaborate tea-drinking rituals developed later on.

Even before these specific ceremonies arose, however, the basic definition of a carefully ordered existence was given more formal philosophical backing. Amid the long collapse of the Zhou dynasty, many thinkers and religious prophets began to challenge Chinese traditions. From this ferment came a restatement of the traditions that ultimately reduced intellectual conflict and established a long-lasting tone for Chinese cultural and social life.

Confucianism

Confucius, or Kong Fuzi (which means Kung the philosopher), lived from roughly 551 to 478 B.C.E. His life was devoted to teaching, and he traveled through many parts of China preaching his ideas of political virtue and good government. Confucius was not a religious leader; he believed in a divine order but refused to speculate about it. Chinese civilization was unusual, in the classical period and well beyond, in that its dominant values were secular rather than religious.

Confucius saw himself as a spokesman for Chinese tradition and for what he believed were the great days of the Chinese state before the Zhou declined. He maintained that if people could be taught to emphasize personal virtue, which included a reverence for tradition, a solid political life would naturally result. The Confucian list of virtues stressed respect for one's social superiors—including fathers and husbands as leaders of the family. However, this emphasis on a proper hierarchy was balanced by an insistence that society's leaders behave modestly and without excess, shunning abusive power and treating courteously those people who were in their charge. According to Confucius, moderation in behavior, veneration of custom and ritual, and a love of wisdom should characterize the leaders of society at all levels. With virtuous leaders, a sound political life would inevitably follow: "In an age of good government, men in high stations give preference to men of ability and give opportunity to those who are below them, and lesser people labor vigorously at their husbandry to serve their superiors."

Confucianism was primarily a system of ethics—do unto others as your status and theirs dictate—and a plea for loyalty to the community. It confirmed the distaste that many educated Chinese had developed for religious mysteries, as well as their delight in learning and good manners. Confucian doctrine, carefully recorded in a book called the *Analects,* was revived under the Han emperors, who saw the usefulness of Confucian emphasis on political virtue and social order. Confucian learning was also incorporated, along with traditional literary works, into the training of aspiring bureaucrats.

The problems Confucius set out to rectify, notably political disorder, were approached through an emphasis on individual virtuous behavior, both by the ruler and the ruled. "When the ruler does right, all men will imitate his self-control. What the ruler does, the people will follow." According to Confucius, only a man who demonstrated proper family virtues, including respect for parents and compassion for children and other inferiors, should be considered for political service. "When the ruler excels as a father, a son, and a brother, then the people imitate him." Confucius thus built into his own system the links among many levels of authority that came to characterize larger Chinese politics at its best. His system also emphasized personal restraint and the careful socialization of children.

For subordinates, Confucius largely recommended obedience and respect; people should know their place, even under bad rulers. However, he urged a political system that would not base rank simply on birth but would make education accessible to all talented and intelligent members of society. The primary emphasis still rested nonetheless on the obligations and desirable characteristics of the ruling class. According to Confucius, force alone cannot permanently conquer unrest, but kindness toward the people and protection of their vital interests will. Rulers should also be humble and sincere, for people will grow rebellious under hypocrisy or arrogance. Nor should rulers be greedy; Confucius warned against a profit motive in leadership, stressing that true happiness rested in doing good for all, not individual gain. Confucius projected the ideal of a gentleman, best described by his benevolence and self-control, a man always courteous and eager for service and anxious to learn.

Legalism

During the Qin and early Han periods, an alternate system of political thought, called "Legalism," sprang up in China. Legalist writers prided themselves on their pragmatism. They disdained Confucian virtues in favor of an authoritarian state that ruled by force. Human nature for the Legalists was evil and required restraint and discipline. In a proper state, the army would control and the people would labor; the idea of pleasures in educated discourse or courtesy was dismissed as frivolity. Although Legalism never captured the widespread approval that Confucianism did, it too entered the political traditions of China, where a Confucian veneer was often combined with strong-arm tactics.

 Legalism: The Way of the State

Confucianists did not explicitly seek popular loyalty. Like many early civilizations, China did not produce a single system of beliefs, as different groups embraced different values, with the same individual even turning to contrasting systems depending on his or her mood. Confucianism had some obvious limits in its appeal to the masses and indeed to many educated Chinese. Its reluctance to explore the mysteries of life or nature deprived it of a spiritual side. The creed was most easily accepted by the upper classes, who had the time and resources to pursue an education and participate in ceremony. However, elements of Confucianism, including a taste for ritual, self-control, and polite manners, did spread beyond the upper classes. But most peasants needed more than civic virtue

Teachings of the Rival Chinese Schools

The brief passages quoted here are taken from the writings of Confucius, Mencius, Xunzi, and Laozi. Identify whether each passage is Confucian or Daoist and explain why you made each choice.

> I take no action and the people are reformed.
> I enjoy peace and people become honest.
> I do nothing and people become rich.
> I have no desires and people return to the good and simple life.
> The gentleman cherishes virtue; the inferior man cherishes possessions.
> The gentleman thinks of sanctions; the inferior man thinks of personal favors.
> The nature of man is evil; his goodness is acquired.
> His nature being what it is, man is born, first, with a desire for gain.
> If this desire is followed, strife will result and courtesy will disappear.
> Keep your mouth closed.
> Guard your senses.
> Temper your sharpness.
> Simplify your problems.
> Mask your brightness.
> Be at one with the dust of the earth.
> This is primal union.
> Personal cultivation begins with poetry, is made firm with rules of decorum, and is perfected by music.
> When it is left to follow its natural feelings, human nature will do good. That's why I say it is good. If it becomes evil, it is not the fault of man's original capability.

QUESTIONS Which of these ideas are most compatible with each other? Which of them could be called religious? Which are secular? Which philosophers propose ideas that are best suited to people who want to build a strong and unified political order?

to understand and survive their harsh life, where in constant toil they eked out only a precarious and meager existence. During most of the classical period, polytheistic beliefs, focusing on the spirits of nature, persisted among much of the peasant class. Many peasants strove to attract the blessing of conciliatory spirits by creating statues, emblems, and household decorations honoring the spirits, and by holding parades and family ceremonies for the same purpose. A belief in the symbolic power of dragons stemmed from one such popular religion, which combined fear of these creatures with a more playful sense of their activities in its courtship of the divine forces of nature. Gradually, ongoing rites among the ordinary masses integrated the Confucian values urged by the upper classes.

Daoism

Daoism: The Classic of the Way and Virtue

Classical China also produced a more religious philosophy—Daoism—which arose at roughly the same time as Confucianism, during the waning centuries of the Zhou dynasty. Daoism first appealed to many in the upper classes, who had an interest in a more elaborate spirituality. Daoism embraced traditional Chinese beliefs in nature's harmony and added a sense of nature's mystery. As a spiritual alternative to Confucianism, Daoism produced a durable division in China's religious and philosophical culture. This new religion, vital for Chinese civilization although never widely exported, was furthered by Laozi (low-dzuh), who probably lived during the 5th century B.C.E. Laozi stressed that nature contains a divine impulse that directs all life. True human understanding comes in withdrawing from the world and contemplating this life force. Dao, which means "the way of nature," refers to this same basic, indescribable force:

> There is a thing confusedly formed,
> Born before heaven and earth.
> Silent and void
> It stands alone and does not change,
> Goes round and does not weary.
> It is capable of being the mother of the world.
> I know not its name,
> So I style it "the way."

Along with secret rituals, Daoism promoted its own set of ethics. Daoist harmony with nature best resulted through humility and frugal living. According to this movement, political activity and learning were irrelevant to a good life, and general conditions in the world were of little importance.

Daoism, which would join with a strong Buddhist influence from India during the chaos that followed the collapse of the Han dynasty, guaranteed that China's people would not be united by a single religious or philosophical system. Individuals did come to embrace some elements from both Daoism and Confucianism, and indeed many emperors favored Daoism. They accepted its spread with little anxiety, partly because some of them found solace in Daoist belief but also because the religion, with its otherworldly emphasis, posed no real political threat. Confucian scholars disagreed vigorously with Daoist thinking, particularly its emphasis on mysteries and magic, but they saw little reason to challenge its influence. As Daoism became an increasingly formal religion, from the later Han dynasty onward, it provided many Chinese with a host of ceremonies designed to promote harmony with the mysterious life force. Finally, the Chinese government from the Han dynasty onward was able to persuade Daoist priests to include expressions of loyalty to the emperor in their temple services. This heightened Daoism's political compatibility with Confucianism.

Literature, Art, and Science

Confucianism and Daoism were not the only intellectual products of China's classical period, but they were the most important. Confucianism blended easily with the high value of literature and art among the upper classes. In literature, a set of Five Classics, written during the early part of the Zhou dynasty and then edited during the time of Confucius, provided an important tradition. They were used, among other things, as a basis for civil service examinations. The works provided in the Five Classics included some historical treatises, speeches, and other political materials; a discussion of etiquette and ceremonies; and in the Classic of Songs, over 300 poems dealing with love, joy, politics, and family life. The Chinese literary tradition developed on the basis of mastering these early works, plus Confucian writing; each generation of writers found new meanings in the classical literature, which allowed them to express new ideas within a familiar framework. Several thinkers during the Han dynasty elaborated Confucian philosophy. In literature, poetry commanded particular attention because the Chinese language featured melodic speech and variant pronunciations of the same basic sound, a characteristic that promoted an outpouring of poetry. From the classical period onward, the ability to learn and recite poetry became the mark of an educated Chinese. Finally, the literary tradition established in classical China reinforced the Confucian emphasis on human life, although the subjects included romance and sorrow as well as political values.

Chinese art during the classical period was largely decorative, stressing careful detail and craftsmanship (Figure 2.2). Artistic styles often reflected the precision and geometric qualities of the many symbols of Chinese writing. Calligraphy itself became an important art form. In addition, Chinese artists painted, worked in bronze and pottery, carved jade and ivory, and wove silk screens. Classical China did not produce monumental buildings, aside from the awe-inspiring Great Wall and some imperial palaces and tombs, in part

Figure 2.2 A Han relief on a funeral tile found in the Chengdu region in Sichuan (eastern Han dynasty, 25 C.E.–221 C.E.). The hunting scene in a luxuriant landscape (upper panel) is linked with a scene (lower panel) of peasants working in the fields. Such illustrations enable historians to track the development of toolmaking and weaponmaking in ancient civilizations such as China. They also make it possible to study patterns of organization in agrarian and artisan production (for which direct evidence is sparse) as well as the leisure activities of officials and the landed elites.

Women in Patriarchal Societies

Most agricultural civilizations, including China, downgraded the status and potential of women, at least according to modern Western standards and to the implicit standards of hunting-and-gathering societies. Agricultural civilizations were characteristically patriarchal; that is, they were run by men and based on the assumption that men directed political, economic, and cultural life. Furthermore, as agricultural civilizations developed over time and became more prosperous and more elaborately organized, the status of women deteriorated from its initial level. Individual families were normally set up on a patriarchal basis. The husband and father determined fundamental conditions and made the key decisions, and the woman gave humble obedience to this male authority at least in principle. Patriarchal family structure rested on men's control of most or all property, starting with land itself. Marriage was based on property relationships, and it was assumed that marriage, and therefore subordination to men, was the normal condition for the vast majority of women. A revealing symptom of patriarchy in family life was the fact that after marrying, a woman usually moved to the orbit (and often the residence) of her husband's family.

Characteristic patriarchal conditions had developed in Mesopotamian civilization. Marriages were arranged for women by their parents, and a formal contract was drawn up. The husband served as authority over his wife and children just as he did over his slaves. Early Sumerian society may have given women greater latitude than they enjoyed later on. The Sumerian religion attributed considerable power to female sexuality, and their law gave women important rights, so that they could not be treated as outright property. Still, even in Sumerian law, the adultery of a wife was punishable by death, while a husband's adultery was treated far more lightly—a double standard characteristic of patriarchalism. Mesopotamian societies after Sumerian times began to emphasize the importance of a woman's virginity at marriage and to impose the veil on respectable women when they were in public to emphasize their modesty. These changes showed a progressive cramping of women's social position and daily freedom. At all points a good portion of Mesopotamian law (such as the Hammurabic code) was given over to prescriptions for women, assuring certain basic protections but clearly emphasizing limits and inferiority.

Specific patriarchal conditions varied from one agricultural civilization to another. This means that comparisons are important, and sometimes subtle. Egyptian civilization gave upper-class women more credit than Mesopotamia did, and there were several powerful queens. Jewish law traced descent from mothers rather than fathers, though it held women to be separate and inferior even in worship. Confucianism, in China, had important implications for women, recommending their good treatment, but in the context

> A good portion of Mesopotamian law (such as the Hammurabic code) was devoted to prescriptions for women, ensuring certain basic protections but clearly emphasizing limits and inferiority.

because of the absence of a single religion; indeed, the entire tone of upper-class Confucianism was such that it discouraged the notion of temples soaring to the heavens.

In science, important practical work was encouraged, rather than imaginative theorizing. Chinese astronomers had developed an accurate calendar by 444 B.C.E., based on a year of 365.5 days. Later astronomers calculated the movement of the planets Saturn and Jupiter and observed sunspots—more than 1500 years before comparable knowledge developed in Europe. The purpose of Chinese astronomy was to make celestial phenomena predictable, as part of the wider interest in ensuring harmony between heaven and earth. Chinese scientists steadily improved their instrumentation, inventing a kind of seismograph to register earthquakes during the Han dynasty. The Chinese were also active in medical research, developing precise anatomical knowledge and studying principles of hygiene that could promote longer life.

Chinese mathematics also stressed the practical. Daoism encouraged some exploration of the orderly processes of nature, but far more research focused on how things actually worked. For example, Chinese scholars studied the mathematics of music in ways that led to advances in acoustics. This focus for science and mathematics contrasted notably with the more abstract definition of science developed in classical Greece.

Economy and Society

Although the most distinctive features of classical China centered on politics and culture, developments in the economy, social structure, and family life also shaped Chinese civilization and continued to have an impact on the empire's history for a significant period of time.

China's economy featured extensive internal trade and important technological innovations.

China's family system stressed a rigid patriarchy.

of their deference and subservience to men. Variety, in other words, operated within a clearly patriarchal framework.

Why was patriarchalism so pervasive? As agriculture improved with the use of better techniques, women's labor, though still absolutely vital, became less important than it had been in hunting-and-gathering societies. This was particularly true in the upper classes and in cities where men frequently took over the most productive work—craft production, for example—and political leadership. The inferior position of women was less marked in peasant families, where their work was essential. More generally, agricultural societies were based on concepts of property. It seemed essential for men to know who their heirs were, in order to pass along land; this meant attention to regulating women's sexuality, to try to assure faithfulness. All this helps explain why women became seen as both inferior and ornamental, really as part of men's property. Patriarchalism, in sum, responded to economic and legal conditions in agricultural civilizations and often deepened over time.

Patriarchalism raises important questions about women themselves. Many women internalized patriarchal culture, believing that they should obey and please men and agreeing that they were inferior. But patriarchalism did not preclude some important options for women. In many societies a minority of women could gain some relief through religious functions, which could provide them a chance to operate independently of family structures. Patriarchal laws defined some rights for women even within marriage, protecting them at least in theory from the worst abuses. Confucian theorists argued that women must obey men but urged men to treat them decently in return. Women could also wield informal power in patriarchal societies by their emotional hold over husbands or sons. Such power was indirect, behind the scenes, but a forceful woman might use these means to figure prominently in a society's history. Women could also form networks within a large household. Older women, who commanded the obedience of many daughters-in-law as well as unmarried daughters and servant women, could powerfully shape the activities of a family.

The fact remains that patriarchalism was a commanding theme in most agricultural civilizations. Enforcement of patriarchalism, through law and culture, provided one means by which these societies regulated their members and tried to achieve order. While women were not reduced to literal servitude by most patriarchal systems, they might have come close. Their options were severely constrained. Girls were reared to accept patriarchal conditions, and boys were fully conscious of their own superiority. In many agricultural civilizations, patriarchalism dictated that boys, because of their importance in carrying on the family name and chief economic activities, were more likely to survive. When population excess threatened a family's well-being, patriarchal assumptions often determined that female infants be killed as a means of population control.

QUESTIONS How do you think most women reared in a patriarchal society would react to their conditions? What might cause differences in women's conditions in patriarchal societies, or from one society to another? Why were upper-class women often considered more inferior to men than lower-class women were?

As in many agricultural societies, considerable gaps developed between China's upper class, which controlled large landed estates, and the masses, farmer-peasants who produced little more than what was needed for their own subsistence. The difficulty of becoming literate symbolized these gaps, for landlords enjoyed not only wealth but also a culture denied to most common people. Prior to the Zhou dynasty, slaveholding may have been common in China, but by the time of the Zhou the main social division existed between the land-owning gentry—about 2 percent of the total population—and peasants, who provided dues and service to these lords while also controlling some of their own land. The Chinese peasantry depended on intensive cooperation, particularly in the southern rice region; in this group, property was characteristically owned and regulated by the village or the extended family, rather than by individuals. Beneath the peasantry, Chinese social structure included a group of "mean" people who performed rough transport and other unskilled jobs and suffered from the lowest possible status. In general, social status was passed from one generation to the next through inheritance, although unusually talented individuals from a peasant background might be given access to an education and rise within the bureaucracy.

The Confucian Social System

Officially then, and to a large extent in fact, classical China consisted of three main social groups. The landowning aristocracy plus the educated bureaucrats, or mandarins, formed the top group. Next came the laboring masses: peasants and also urban artisans who manufactured goods. These people, far poorer than the top group and also condemned to a life of hard manual labor, sometimes worked directly on large estates but in other cases had some economic independence. Finally, came the mean people, the general category we already identified as applying to those without meaningful skills. Interestingly, performing artists were ranked in this group, despite the fact that the upper classes enjoyed plays and other entertainments provided by this group. Mean people were punished for crime more harshly than other groups and were required to wear identifying green scarves. Household slaves also existed within this class structure, but their number was relatively few, and China did not depend on slaves for actual production.

Trade and Technology

Trade became increasingly important during the Zhou and particularly the Han dynasties. Much trade focused on luxury items for the upper class, produced by skilled artisans in the cities—silks, jewelry, leather goods, and furniture. There was also food exchange between the wheat- and rice-growing regions. Copper coins began to circulate, which facilitated trade, with merchants even sponsoring commercial visits to India. Although significant, trade and its attendant merchant class did not become the focal points of Chinese society, and the Confucian emphasis on learning and political service led to considerable scorn for lives devoted to moneymaking. The gap between the real importance and wealth of merchants and their officially low prestige was an enduring legacy in Confucian China.

If trade fit somewhat uncomfortably into the dominant view of society, there was no question about the importance of technological advance; here, the Chinese excelled. Agricultural implements improved steadily. Ox-drawn plows were introduced around 300 B.C.E., which greatly increased productivity. Under the Han, a new collar was invented for draft animals, allowing them to pull plows or wagons without choking—this was a major improvement that became available to other parts of the world only many centuries later. Chinese iron mining was also well advanced, as pulleys and winding gear were devised to bring material to the surface. Iron tools and other implements such as lamps were widely used. Production methods in textiles and pottery were also highly developed by world standards. Under the Han, the first water-powered mills were introduced, allowing further gains in manufacturing. Finally, during the Han, paper was invented, which was a major boon to a system of government that emphasized the bureaucracy. In sum, classical China reached far higher levels of technical expertise than Europe or western Asia in the same period, a lead that it would long maintain.

The relatively advanced technology of classical China did not, however, steer Chinese society away from its primary reliance on agriculture. Farming technology helped increase the size of the population in the countryside; with better tools and seeds, smaller amounts of land could support more families. But China's solid agricultural base, backed by some trade in foodstuffs among key regions, did permit the expansion of cities and of manufacturing. Nonagricultural goods were mainly produced by artisans, working in small shops or in their homes. Even though only a minority of the workforce was involved in such tasks that used manual methods for the most part, the output of tools, porcelain, and textiles increased considerably, aided in this case as well by the interest in improving techniques.

Gender and Family Life

In all major social groups, tight family organization helped solidify economic and social views as well as political life. The structure of the Chinese family resembled that of families in other agricultural civilizations in emphasizing the importance of unity and the power of husbands and fathers. Within this context, however, the Chinese stressed authority to unusual extremes. Confucius said, "There are no wrongdoing parents"—and in practice, parents could punish disobedient children freely. Law courts did not prosecute parents who injured or even killed a disobedient son, but they would severely punish a child who scolded or attacked a parent. In most families, the emphasis on obedience to parents, and a corresponding emphasis on wives' obedience to husbands, did not produce great friction. Chinese popular culture stressed strict control of one's emotions, and the family was seen as the center of such an orderly, serene hierarchy. Indeed, the family served as a great training ground for the principles of authority and restraint that applied to the larger social and political world.

Women, although subordinate, had their own clearly defined roles and could sometimes gain power through their sons and as mothers-in-law of younger women brought into the household. The mother of a famous Confucian philosopher, Mencius, continually claimed how humble she was, but during the course of his life she managed to exert considerable influence over him. There was even a clear hierarchical order for children, with boys superior to girls and the oldest son having the most enviable position of all. Chinese rules of inheritance, from the humblest peasant to the emperor himself, followed strict primogeniture, which meant that the oldest male child would inherit property and position alike.

How Chinese Civilization Fits Together

China's politics and culture meshed readily, especially around the emergence of a Confucian bureaucracy. Economic innovation did not disrupt the emphasis on order and stability, and family structures were closely linked to political and cultural goals.

Classical Chinese technology, religion, philosophy, and political structure evolved with very little outside contact. Although important trade routes led to India and the Middle East, most Chinese saw the world in terms of a large island of civilization surrounded by barbarian peoples with nothing to offer save the periodic threat of invasion. Proud of their culture and of its durability, the Chinese had neither the need nor the desire to learn from other societies. Nor, except to protect their central territory by exercising some control over the mountainous or desert regions that surrounded the Middle Kingdom, did Chinese leaders have any particular desire to teach the rest of the world. A missionary spirit was foreign to Chinese culture and politics. China displayed some patterns that were similar to those of the other agricultural civilizations, and it occasionally embraced the concepts of these cultures. Indeed, the spread of Buddhism from India, during and after the Han decline, was a notable instance of a cultural diffusion that altered China's religious map and also its artistic styles. Nevertheless, the theme of unusual isolation, developed during the formative period of Chinese civilization, was to prove persistent in later world history—in fact, it has not entirely disappeared to this day.

Chinese civilization coordinated many aspects of politics, culture, and even family life, a key reason that emperors ultimately encouraged Confucianism.

Social and Cultural Links to Politics

Chinese civilization was also noteworthy for the relative harmony among its various major features. We have, in this chapter, examined the pattern of leading historical events in classical China and then the systems of government, belief, economy, and social structure. All these facets were closely meshed. Although the centralized government, with its elaborate functions and far-reaching bureaucracy, gave the clearest unity and focus to Chinese society, it did not do so alone. Confucianism provided a vital supplement, making the bureaucracy more than a collection of people with similar political objectives, but rather a trained corps with some common ideals. An appreciation of distinctive artistic styles, poetry, and the literary tradition added to this common culture. Cohesive government and related beliefs about human ideals and aesthetics were linked, in turn, to the economy. Political stability over a large and fertile land aided economic growth, and the government took a direct role in encouraging both agriculture and industry. A strong economy, in turn, provided the government with vital tax revenues. Economic interests were also related to the pragmatic Chinese view of science, whose aim was to determine how nature worked. Finally, social relationships reinforced all these systems. The vision of a stable hierarchy and tight family structures meshed with the strong impulse toward orderly politics and helped instill the virtues of obedience and respect that were important to the larger political system.

Not surprisingly, given the close links among the various facets of their civilization, the Chinese tended to think of their society as a whole. They did not distinguish clearly between private and public sectors of activity. They did not see government and society as two separate entities. In other words, these Western concepts that we have used to define classical China and to facilitate comparisons with other societies do not really fit the Chinese view of their own world. Confucius himself, in seeing government as basically a vast extension of family relationships, similarly suggested that the pieces of the Chinese puzzle were intimately joined.

Complexities in Classical China

A grasp of Chinese civilization as a whole, however, should not distract us from recognizing some endemic tensions and disparities. The division in belief systems, between Confucianism and Daoism, modifies the perception of an ultimately tidy classical China. Confucianists and Daoists tolerated each other. Sometimes, their beliefs coincided in such a way that a single individual who behaved politically as a Confucianist might explore deeper mysteries through Daoist rituals. However, between both groups there was considerable hostility and mutual disdain, as many Confucianists found Daoists superstitious and overexcited. Daoism did not inherently disrupt the political unity of Chinese culture, but at times the religion inspired attacks on established politics in the name of a mysterious divine will.

Tension in Chinese society showed in the way Confucian beliefs were combined with strict policing. Chinese officials did believe in fundamental human goodness and the importance of ceremony and mutual respect. However, they also believed in stern punishment, not only against criminals but also as warnings to the larger, potentially restless population. People arrested were presumed guilty and often subjected to torture before trial. The Chinese, in fact, early discovered the usefulness of alternating torture with benevolence, to make accused individuals confess. In the late Han period, a thief who refused to confess even under severe torture was then freed from chains, bathed, and fed, "so as to bring him in a happy mood"—whereupon he usually confessed and named his whole gang. In sum, both Confucianism and the Chinese penal system supported tight control, and the combination of the two was typically effective; however, they involved quite different approaches and quite different moral assumptions.

All of this suggests that classical China, like any vigorous, successful society, embraced a diversity of features that could not be fully united by any single formula. Elites and masses were divided by both economic interests and culture. Some shared the same values, particularly as Confucianism spread, and upper-class concern for careful etiquette and the general welfare of the population mitigated the tension. But such calm was a precarious balance, and when overpopulation or some other factor tipped the scale, recurrent and often violent protest could be the result.

Despite any divisions, the symbiosis among the various institutions and activities of many people in classical China does deserve strong emphasis. It helps account for the durability of Chinese values. Even in times of political turmoil, families would transfer beliefs and political ideals by the ways in which they instructed their children. The overall wholeness of Chinese society also helps account for its relative immunity to outside influence and for its creativity despite considerable isolation.

Chinese wholeness, finally, provides an interesting contrast to the other great Asian civilization that developed in the classical period. India, as fully dynamic as China in many ways, produced different emphases, but also a more disparate society in which links among politics and beliefs and economic life were less well defined. Many would argue that this contrast between the two Asian giants persists to our own time.

Global Connections

Classical China and the World

The short-lived Qin dynasty and four centuries of Han rule established the basic components of a civilization that would last for thousands of years, making it the longest-lived in world history. As the achievements of the classical age demonstrate, China had also become one of the most creative and influential civilizations of all human history. The strength of its agrarian base has allowed China to carry about one-fifth of the total human population from the last centuries B.C.E. to the present day. The productivity of its peasants has made it possible for some of the world's largest cities to flourish in China, and nurtured one of history's largest and most creative elites. In China's classical age, the world's largest and for much of history its best-run bureaucracy was established, and civil service exams were invented. The Chinese also pioneered in the development of a whole range of basic technologies that were later disseminated over much of Eurasia and northern Africa. These ranged from paper and compasses, which created new possibilities for human communication and cross-cultural interaction, and water mills, which provided new sources of power and food processing, to porcelain, which elevated dining to unparalleled levels of elegance and opened up exciting possibilities for artistic expression. Over the centuries, beginning in this classical period itself, Chinese merchants and central Asian nomads disseminated these inventions over much of the globe. Chinese innovations consequently contributed to technological transformations in societies as diverse as those found in Japan, Rome, the Middle East, and England.

Chinese influence was directly involved in the patterns of world trade that began to emerge during the classical centuries. China's silk was unusually high quality, and the product began to be valued elsewhere, in India, the Middle East, and even the distant Mediterranean during the Roman Empire. Trade in silk and other luxury products generated a network of roads through central Asia known collectively as the **Silk Road.** Under the Han, the Chinese government actively encouraged this trade with regions to the west. Improved roads, both in China and in the Middle East, encouraged trade as well. One Chinese emissary, Zhang Qian, actually traveled to western India. Most trade along the Silk Road was carried by nomadic merchants, and until well after the classical period no one seems to have traveled all the way from China to the Mediterranean or vice versa. But the trade was lively, spurring attention also to sea routes in the Indian Ocean. While we do not know the volume of goods involved, Silk Road trade was important enough to win considerable attention in upper-class and government circles, and it provided an initial framework on which global trading patterns would later elaborate. China's role was greater still in the huge swath of territory from central Asia to the Pacific.

Over much of central and east Asia, Chinese influence in political thought and organization, approaches to warfare, art and architecture, religion, and social norms was pervasive. For nearly 2000 years, China would serve as the "Middle Kingdom" for the diverse peoples of this vast area—the focus of their trade and the model for their often successful efforts to fashion their own variants of empire, prosperity, and sophisticated lifestyles.

Further Readings

Several sources offer original materials on classical Chinese thought and politics: John Fairbank, ed., *Chinese Thought and Institutions* (1973); Wing-stit Chan, *A Source Book in Chinese Philosophy* (1963); and P. Ebrey, *Chinese Civilization and Society: A Sourcebook* (1981). An excellent general survey for this period and later ones is J.K. Fairbank, et. al., *East Asia: Tradition and Transformation* (1989); see also Arthur Cotterell, *The First Emperor of China* (1981). Briefer but useful are M. J. Coye and J. Livingston, eds., *China, Yesterday and Today* (1975); Wolfram Eberhard, *A History of China* (1977); and X. Z. Liu, *Ancient India and Ancient China* (1988). See also D. Twitchett and M. Loewe, eds., *The Cambridge History of China,* Vol. 1 (1986). On more specialized topics, see E. Balazs, *Chinese Civilization and Bureaucracy* (1964); J. Needham, *Science and Civilization in China,* 4 vols. (1970); Richard J. Smith, *Traditional Chinese Culture: An Interpretive Introduction* (1978); Benjamin Schwartz, *The World of Thought in Ancient China* (1983); Michael Loewe, *Everyday Life in Early Imperial China* (1968); Cho-yun Hsu and K. M. Linduff, *Western Chou Civilization* (1988); Michele Pirazzoli-t'Sersteven, *The Han Civilization of China* (1982); R. Wilke and M. Wolf, *Women in Chinese Society* (1975); and Bella Vivante, ed., *Women's Roles in Ancient Civilizations: A Reference Guide* (1999).

On the Web

The Yellow River as the cradle of Chinese civilization is analyzed at http://www.cis.umassd.edu/~gleung/. Early Chinese oracle bones and their place in the evolution of writing are explored at http://acc6.its.brooklyn.cuny.edu/~phalsall/images/shnagbon.jpg. Images drawn from early Chinese history and culture can be viewed at http://www.chaos.umd.edu/history/ancient1.html and http://www.chinapage.com/chinese.html. Early Chinese ethical systems are discussed at http://www.san.beck.org/EC13-Chou.html. An introduction to Chinese history prior to the Chin dynasty (221 B.C.E.) is provided at http://asterius.com/china/ and http://www.chaos.umd.edu/history/ancient1.html.

The life of Confucius is addressed at http://www.confucius .org/intro/edbio.htm. A useful comparison between Confucius and Socrates is made at http://www.san.beck.org/C&S-Contents .html. Connections between Confucianism, Daoism, and Western philosophy are made at http://www.friesian.com/confuci.htm. These sites also offer extensive examinations of Confucian philosophy. Mencius' life is reviewed at http://www.san.beck.org/EC14 -Confucian.html#4. The life of Laozi and philosophy of Daoism is explored in an enjoyable, informal, and therefore Daoist way at http://plato.stanford.edu/entries/laozi/ and http://www.synaptic.bc .ca/ejournal/laotse.htm. The place of Legalist ruler Shi Huangdi's Qin dynasty and its impact on Chinese history is debated at http://emuseum.mnsu.edu/prehistory/china/early_imperial_chin a/qin.html. An analysis of his famous tomb can be found at http://www.utexas.edu/courses/wilson/ant304/biography/arybios98/ smithbio.html. This site features a diagram of the layout of the buried army of terra-cotta warriors.

Take a virtual tour of later versions of the Great Wall at http://www.thechinaguide.com/great_wall_of_china/index.html, which offers panoramic views and music to tour by. Another virtual tour of the Great Wall is conducted at http://www.chinavista .com/travel/greatwall/greatwall.html. Visit the Imperial Forbidden City at http://www.chinavista.com/beijing/gugong/!start.html (enter by clicking on the red dragon). The value of such marvels, or lack of same, is analyzed in Sunzi's *Art of War*, the text of which is offered at http://www.chinapage.com/sunzi-e.html and http://www .swan.ac.uk/poli/texts/index.html; it is also presented indexed by topic at http://acc6.its.brooklyn.cuny.edu/~phalsall/texts/artofwar .html. Daily life in ancient China is colorfully explored at http://ancienthistory.mrdonn.org/Chinalife.html and http://www .kidsnewsroom.org/elmer/infoCentral/frameset/civilizations/china/ daily/index.html. Join others in an exploration of "Women and Confucianism" at http://www.womeninworldhistory.com/lesson3 .html. A comparison of the role of women in ancient China and in Rome is offered at http://adam.burnetta.com/Writings/ancient -rome-china-women-comparison.html.

Links for the study of Chinese art are offered at http://witcombe.sbc.edu/ARTHchina.html. Further links for the study of ancient Chinese cultural traditions are supplied at http://www.chinapage.com/china-rm.html.

AP* Test Prep

1. Confucianism and Daoism

    (A) were officially sanctioned doctrines of the Qin and Han emperors.

    (B) emphasized the needs of the individual over the welfare of the state.

    (C) had little influence upon China and Chinese society until the late 900s C.E.

    (D) offered answers to societal problems during times of disruption.

2. Confucian social relationships

    (A) established a hierarchy and insisted upon reciprocal duties between people.

    (B) taught its practitioners to seek inner harmony with the natural way.

    (C) promoted the use of material rewards for correct behavior and punishments for transgressions.

    (D) were based on universal love and forgiveness.

3. The policy sponsored by the Qin Dynasty to support its state

    (A) encouraged education, new ideas, and tolerated criticism of the state.

    (B) broke the power of vassals in order to enhance the power of the emperor.

    (C) paid the northern nomadic groups tribute to prevent invasions.

    (D) tolerated local lords performing functions for the central government.

4. During the Han Dynasty, scholar officials

    (A) came increasingly from the merchant and peasant classes.

    (B) utilized Legalism as a ruling doctrine.

    (C) insisted on harsh law codes to maintain control.

    (D) instituted a system of examinations to prepare professional civil servants.

5. Although they varied greatly in wealth and social status in China,

    (A) the commoners, especially the peasants, remained the largest group.

    (B) the scholar bureaucrats cooperated to limit the influence of the ruler.

    (C) aristocrats owned all of the land.

    (D) women had many legal rights and protections.

6. Chinese women in the Classical Age

    (A) were free to choose the men they would marry.

    (B) could become scholar-gentry provided they passed the state exams.

    (C) were legally subordinated to fathers and husbands at all class levels.

    (D) dominated the intellectual and artistic activities of China.

7. Despite their material success and increased wealth,

    (A) foreigners were prohibited from settling in China.

    (B) Chinese rulers were isolated from the masses and did not intervene in government.

    (C) Chinese aristocrats had no influence within the government.

    (D) merchants in China ranked below peasants and had little political influence.

Free-Response Question

In what ways did the three philosophical movements of classical China shape its civilization?

3 Classical Civilization: India

The Framework for Indian History: Geography
and a Formative Period

Patterns in Classical India

Political Institutions

Religion and Culture

DOCUMENT: A Guardian's Farewell Speech to a Young Woman
About to Be Married

Economy and Society

Indian Influence and Comparative Features

THINKING HISTORICALLY: Inequality as the Social Norm

VISUALIZING THE PAST: The Pattern of Trade in the Ancient
Eurasian World

GLOBAL CONNECTIONS: India and the Wider World

Of the many enduring expressions of religious devotion in human history, few can match the splendid complexes of temples and monasteries carved from stone into the cliffs at Ajanta and Ellora in the western reaches of the Deccan plateau, which stretches across central India. More than sixty religious structures were carved into or out of solid rock at the two sites, which are approximately thirty miles apart. These monumental religious edifices were constructed in successive stages from the last centuries B.C.E. through the 8th century C.E. This millennium of history spans an era of momentous change and creativity that in many ways culminated in the Gupta Empire, which ruled most of north India from early in the 4th until the mid-6th century C.E.

The art and architecture of Ajanta and Ellora provide dramatic evidence of the intensity of the religious ferment that shaped all aspects of Indian life as a result of the challenges to the existing brahmanical order posed by the emergence of Buddhism and other popular religious alternatives in the 6th and 5th centuries B.C.E. But these monumental buildings, and particularly the exquisite sculptures and paintings they contain, also tell us a great deal about the nature of society, everyday life, and popular culture, as well as the worldview and aspirations of those who lived in what many historians consider India's golden age. The mixture, for example, of Buddhist shrines and monastic quarters and Hindu and Jain cave temples exemplifies the overwhelmingly nonviolent nature of the rivalry between these major religious systems. The blend of religions at Ajanta and Ellora also mirrored the common adoption of rituals, objects of worship, and basic beliefs by the adherents of different Indian religions in this era.

Beyond religious thought and practice, the wall paintings and stone-carved sculptures provide some of the best illustrations we have of everything from Indian ships and styles of dress at differ-

ent social levels to musical instruments, weapons, and tools for farming and construction. Stone friezes decorating the walls of the shrines and temples illustrate in remarkable detail popular legends of the Buddha's life and path to enlightenment and the rich mythology that developed around the gods and goddesses propitiated by the brahman priests. One of the most celebrated temples, carved out of solid rock to be a free-standing structure, relates in stone carvings numerous episodes from the *Ramayana,* which had become one of the two great epics of Indian civilization by the last centuries B.C.E.

The kings and their consorts, brahman priests and Buddhist monks, workers and temple dancers portrayed in the Ajanta and Ellora cave temples help us to visualize more than a millennium of history that is covered in this chapter. Lasting from roughly 700 B.C.E. to 650 C.E., this era saw the rise and fall of some of India's most powerful dynasties. The brahman-dominated society which emerged in the kingdoms Aryan migrants established in the Gangetic plains, was challenged in fundamental ways by the rise of Buddhism in the 6th century B.C.E. Buddhism also played a major role in the rise of the powerful Maurya dynasty and was in turn weakened by the decline of their empire. The political fragmentation in the centuries after the demise of the Mauryas was mirrored in the intense, though largely peaceful, competition among different schools of Buddhism, Brahmanism, and a wide variety of other religious sects. The patronage of the rulers of the Gupta empire that controlled much of north India from the 4th to the mid-6th centuries C.E. sparked a revival of Brahmanism, which made for an age of remarkable religious effervescence, artistic creativity, and scientific breakthroughs that secured India's enduring stature as one of the core civilizations of the preindustrial world. ■

Figure 3.1 The cave temples carved out of solid stone at Ajanta in central India provide dramatic evidence of the religious fervor that swept through south Asia in the age of the Buddha and the Hindu revival.

(© David Gurr/Eye Ubiquitous/Corbis. All Rights Reserved.)

After the long period of disruption following Harappa's fall—around 1500 B.C.E.—a new civilization arose in India. India became the third great center of classical civilization, along with the Mediterranean and Middle East (Greece, Persia, and Rome) and China. India also served as a key hub of the trans-regional trading patterns that emerged in the classical period. The new foundations for Indian civilization were laid between 1500 and 500 B.C.E. by nomadic Aryans who moved into India during the centuries after Harappa's collapse. By the end of this period, fairly large states, ruled by kings who claimed divine descent, controlled much of the fertile farmland of the Ganges River plains. The settlement of this vast area came at the cost of clearing the great forests that once covered it. As in northwest India and the Mediterranean, cultivation and forest-clearing on the Ganges plains contributed to significant climate change.

Ritual divisions and restrictions on intermarriage between different social groups grew more rigid as an increasingly complex social hierarchy became a pervasive force in Indian life. Vedic priests, or brahmans, emerged as the dominant force in Indian society and culture. As the brahmans' power peaked, however, forces were building in Indian society that threatened to alter the

1600 B.C.E.	1200 B.C.E.	750 B.C.E.	500 B.C.E.	250 B.C.E.	1 C.E.
1600–1000 Aryan invasions of India 1500–1000 Vedic Age	1200–700 Sacred Vedas composed 1000–600 Epic Age: *Mahabharata*, *Ramayana*, and *Upanishads* composed	700–c. 550 Era of unrivaled brahman dominance 563–483 Life of the Buddha	327–325 Alexander the Great invades India 322–298 Chandragupta Maurya rules 269–232 Reign of Ashoka	200 B.C.E.–200 C.E. Period of greatest Buddhist influence	319 Gupta Empire founded; one of the world's first universities established 535 Gupta Empire overturned by the Huns

Buddha   Creator of a major Indian and Asian religion; born in 6th century B.C.E. as son of local ruler among Aryan tribes located near Himalayas; became an ascetic; found enlightenment under bo tree; taught that enlightenment could be achieved only by abandoning desires for all earthly things.

course of civilized development in south Asia. By the 6th century B.C.E., many religious seers and dissenting philosophers wanted to move beyond the rituals associated with sacrifices to the gods and were weary of the power seeking and materialism of the priestly class. One of these thinkers, now known as the **Buddha,** founded one of the great world religions—a religion that provided a powerful challenge to the brahmans and many of the ancient Vedic beliefs and practices.

The Framework for Indian History: Geography and a Formative Period

Indian civilization was deeply influenced by geography and climate.

Centuries of Aryan invasion and consolidation laid the foundation of classical Indian civilization.

In the centuries that followed the Aryan incursions, the rivalry between Buddhists and brahmans played a major role in shaping gender relationships and the nature of social hierarchies as a whole in south Asia. The Buddha's teachings also contributed to the establishment of India's first genuine empire. Beginning in the late 4th century B.C.E., the rulers of a local dynasty in eastern India, the Mauryas, built what would become the largest empire in premodern India, but the Mauryan Empire was short-lived. When it collapsed, it was followed by another round of nomadic invasions through the Himalayan passes in the northwest, and the subcontinent was again fragmented politically. But in the early 4th century C.E., there arose in north India a powerful new dynasty, the Gupta, that was committed to reasserting brahmans' dominance. The Gupta rulers' patronage of the religion we now know as Hinduism reaffirmed the position of the brahmans as high priests and political advisors. It also led to an age of splendid achievement in architecture, painting, sculpture, philosophy, literature, and the sciences.

The classical period of Indian history includes a number of contrasts to that of China—and many of these contrasts have proved enduring. Whereas the focus in classical China was on politics and on social structures that would support the Confucian order, the focus in classical India was on religion and social structures that would support a Hindu way of life. A political culture existed in India, of course, but it was less cohesive and less important to the larger culture than its Chinese counterpart. In religion, science, economics, and family life, the classical period generated a culture that continues to make India unique among the world's major civilizations.

While India's distinctiveness was considerable, the fact that it was an agricultural society dictated that it would be similar in many ways to China. Most people were peasant farmers, whose lives were shaped around the production of food for their family's survival. In both India and China, peasant families clustered together in villages for mutual aid and protection. This village structure gave a strong localist flavor to many aspects of life in both cultures. In addition, agriculture influenced family life. Patriarchy dictated that women seldom owned property other than their personal possessions. Although they were primarily agricultural, both China and India built great cities and engaged in extensive trade. These added to social and economic complexity and created the basis for most formal intellectual life, including schools and academies.

Formative Influences

India's distinctive culture was born of its geography and early historical experience. India was much closer to the orbit of other civilizations than China. Trading contacts with China developed late in the classical period and had little impact—China was more affected. But India was frequently open to influences from the Middle East and even the Mediterranean world. Persian empires spilled over into India at several points, bringing new artistic styles and political concepts. **Alexander the Great** invaded India, and while he did not establish a durable empire, he made possible important Indian contacts with Hellenistic culture. Periodic influences from the Middle East continued after the classical age, forcing India to react and adapt in ways that China largely avoided because it was more isolated.

In addition to links with other cultures, India's topography shaped a number of vital features of its civilization. The vast Indian subcontinent is partially separated from the rest of Asia, and particularly from east Asia, by northern mountain ranges, notably the **Himalayas.** However, important passes through the mountains, especially in the northwest, linked India to other civilizations in the Middle East. At the same time, divisions within the subcontinent made full political unity difficult. India was thus marked by greater diversity than China's Middle Kingdom. The most important agricultural regions are those along the two great rivers, the Indus and the Ganges. However, India also has mountainous northern regions, where a herding economy took root, and a southern coastal rim, separated by mountains and the Deccan plateau, where an active trading and seafaring economy arose. India's separate regions help explain not only economic diversity but also the racial and language differences that, from early times, have marked the subcontinent's populations.

Much of India is semitropical in climate. In the river valley plains, heat can rise to 120° F during the early summer. Summer also brings torrential **monsoon** rains, crucial for farming. But the monsoons vary from year to year, sometimes bringing too little rain or coming too late and causing famine-producing drought, or sometimes bringing catastrophic floods. Certain features of Indian civilization may have resulted from a need to come to terms with a climate that could produce abundance one year and grim starvation the next. In a year with favorable monsoons, Indian farmers could plant and harvest two crops and thus support a sizeable population.

The Great Epics

Indian civilization was shaped not only by its physical environment but also by a formative period, lasting several centuries, between the destruction of the Indus River civilization and the revival of full civilization elsewhere on the subcontinent. During this formative period, called the Vedic and Epic ages, the **Aryan** (Indo-European) migrants—hunting and herding peoples originally from central Asia—gradually came to terms with agriculture but had their own impact on the culture and social structure of their new home. During the Vedic Age, from about 1500 to 1000 B.C.E., Indian agriculture extended from the Indus River valley to the more fertile Ganges valley, as the Aryans used iron tools to clear away the dense vegetation.

Most of what we know about this preclassical period in Indian history comes from literary epics developed by the Aryans, initially passed on orally. They were later written down in **Sanskrit,** which became the first literary language of the new culture. These sacred books were called the **Vedas.** The initial part of this formative period, the Vedic Age, takes its name from the Sanskrit word *Veda,* or "knowledge." The first epic, the *Rig-Veda,* consists of 1028 hymns dedicated to the Aryan gods and composed by various priests. New stories, developed during the Epic Age between 1000 and 600 B.C.E., include the *Mahabharata* (muh-hah-BUH-uh-tuh), India's greatest epic poem, and the *Ramayana* (ruh-MEYE-ehn), both of which deal with real and mythical battles; these epics reflect a more settled agricultural society and better-organized political units than the *Rig-Veda.* The Epic Age also saw the creation of the *Upanishads* (oo-PAHN-uh-shadz), epic poems with a more mystical religious flavor.

Aryan ideas and social and family forms also became increasingly influential. As the Aryans settled down to agriculture, they encouraged tight levels of village organization that came to be characteristic of Indian society and politics. Village chiefs, initially drawn from the leadership of one of the Aryan tribes, helped organize village defenses and regulate property relationships among families. Family structure emphasized patriarchal controls, and extended family relationships among grandparents, parents, and children were close.

The characteristic Indian caste system also began to take shape during the Vedic and Epic ages, perhaps initially as a means of establishing relationships between the Aryan invaders and the indigenous people, whom the Aryans regarded as inferior. Aryan social classes (**varnas**) partly

Alexander the Great   Successor of Philip II; successfully conquered Persian Empire prior to his death in 323 B.C.E.; attempted to combine Greek and Persian cultures.

Himalayas   Mountain region marking the northern border of the Indian subcontinent; site of the Aryan settlements that formed small kingdoms or warrior republics.

monsoons   Seasonal winds crossing Indian subcontinent and southeast Asia; during summer bring rains.

Excerpts from the *Ramayana* and *Mahabharata*

DOCUMENT

Aryans   Indo-European nomadic pastoralists who replaced Harappan civilization; militarized society.

Sanskrit   The sacred and classical Indian language.

Vedas   Aryan hymns originally transmitted orally but written down in sacred books from the 6th century B.C.E.

Mahabharata   [muh-hah-BUH-uh-tuh] Indian epic of war, princely honor, love, and social duty; written down in the last centuries B.C.E.; previously handed down in oral form.

Ramayana   [ruh-MEYE-ehn] One of the great epic tales from classical India; traces adventures of King Rama and his wife, Sita; written 4th to 2nd centuries B.C.E.

Upanishads   [oo-PAHN-uh-shadz] Later books of the Vedas; contained sophisticated and sublime philosophical ideas; utilized by Brahmans to restore religious authority.

varnas   Clusters of caste groups in Aryan society; four social castes- Brahmans (priests), warriors, merchants, and peasants; beneath four Aryan castes was group of socially untouchable Dasas.

enforced divisions familiar in agricultural societies. Thus, a warrior or governing class, the Kshatriyas (kuh-shuh-TREE-uhs), and the priestly class, or brahmans, stood at the top of the social pyramid, followed by Vaisyas, the traders and farmers, and Sudras, or common laborers. Many of the Sudras worked on the estates of large landowners. A fifth group gradually evolved, later called the **untouchables,** who were confined to a few jobs, such as transporting the bodies of the dead or hauling refuse. It was widely believed that touching these people would defile anyone from a superior class. Initially, the warrior group ranked highest, but during the Epic Age the brahmans replaced them, signaling the importance of religious links in Indian life. Thus, a law book stated, "When a brahman springs to light he is born above the world, the chief of all creatures, assigned to guard the treasury of duties, religious and civil." Gradually, the five social groups became hereditary, with marriage between castes forbidden and punishable by death; the basic castes divided into smaller subgroups, called *jati,* each with distinctive occupations and each tied to its social station by birth.

The *Rig-Veda,* the first Aryan epic, attributed the rise of the caste system to the gods:

> When they divided the original Man
> into how many parts did they divide him?
> What was his mouth, what were his arms,
> what were his thighs and his feet called?
> The brahman was his mouth, of his
> arms was made the warrior.
> His thighs became the vaisya, of
> his feet the sudra was born.

The Aryans brought to India a religion of many gods and goddesses, who regulated natural forces and possessed human qualities. Thus, **Indra,** the god of thunder, was also the god of strength. Gods presided over fire, the sun, death, and so on. This system bore some resemblances to the gods and goddesses of Greek myth or Scandinavian mythology, for the very good reason that they were derived from a common Indo-European oral heritage. However, India was to give this common tradition an important twist, ultimately constructing a vigorous, complex religion that, in contrast to the Indo-European polytheistic faiths, endures to this day.

During the epic periods, the Aryans offered hymns and sacrifices to the gods. Certain animals were regarded as particularly sacred, embodying the divine spirit. Gradually, this religion became more elaborate. The epic poems reflect an idea of life after death and a religious approach to the world of nature. Nature was seen as informed not only by specific gods but also by a more basic divine force. These ideas, expressed in the mystical *Upanishads,* added greatly to the spiritual power of this early religion and served as the basis for later Hindu beliefs. By the end of the Epic Age, the dominant Indian belief system included a variety of convictions. Many people continued to emphasize rituals and sacrifices to the gods of nature; specific beliefs, as in the sacredness of monkeys and cattle, illustrated this ritualistic approach. The brahman priestly class specified and enforced prayers, ceremonies, and rituals. However, the religion also produced a more mystical strand through its belief in a unifying divine force and the desirability of seeking union with this force. Toward the end of the Epic period one religious leader, Gautama Buddha, built on this mysticism to create what became Buddhism, another major world religion.

Patterns in Classical India

By 600 B.C.E., India had passed through its formative phase. Regional political units grew in size, cities and trade expanded, and the development of the Sanskrit language, although dominated by the priestly brahman class, furthered an elaborate literary culture. A full, classical civilization could now build on the social and cultural themes first launched during the Vedic and Epic ages.

Indian development during the classical era and beyond did not take on the convenient structure of rising and falling dynasties characteristic of Chinese history. Political eras were even less clear than in classical Greece. The rhythm of Indian history was irregular and often consisted of landmark invasions that poured in through the mountain passes of the subcontinent's northwestern border.

Toward the end of the Epic Age and until the 4th century B.C.E., the Indian plains were divided among powerful regional states. Sixteen major states existed by 600 B.C.E. in the plains of northern

untouchables Low social caste in Hindu culture; performed tasks that were considered polluting—street sweeping, removal of human waste, and tanning.

Indra Chief deity of the Aryans; depicted as a colossal, hard-drinking warrior.

Two major empires united large parts of India at crucial periods in classical Indian history.

India, some of them monarchies, others republics dominated by assemblies of priests and warriors. Warfare was not uncommon. One regional state, Magadha, established dominance over a considerable empire. In 327 B.C.E., Alexander the Great, having conquered Greece and much of the Middle East, pushed into northwestern India, establishing a small border state called Bactria.

The Mauryan Dynasty

Political reactions to this incursion produced the next major step in Indian political history, in 322 B.C.E., when a young soldier named **Chandragupta Maurya** (chuhn-druh-GOOP-duh MAHR-yeh) seized power along the Ganges River. He became the first of the **Mauryan** (MAHR-yuhn) dynasty of Indian rulers, who in turn were the first rulers to unify much of the entire subcontinent. While it is difficult to know what, if anything, the Mauryan dynasty borrowed directly from Persian political models or the example of Alexander the Great, Chandragupta and his successors maintained large armies, with thousands of chariots and elephant-borne troops. The Mauryan rulers also developed a substantial bureaucracy, even sponsoring a postal service.

Chandragupta's style of government was highly autocratic, relying on the ruler's personal and military power. This style would surface periodically in Indian history, just as it did in the Middle East, a region with which India had important contacts. A Greek ambassador from one of the Hellenistic kingdoms described Chandragupta's life:

> Attendance on the king's person is the duty of women, who indeed are bought from their fathers. Outside the gates [of the palace] stand the bodyguards and the rest of the soldiers. . . . Nor does the king sleep during the day, and at night he is forced at various hours to change his bed because of those plotting against him. Of his nonmilitary departures [from the palace] one is to the courts, in which he passed the day hearing cases to the end . . . [When he leaves to hunt,] he is thickly surrounded by a circle of women, and on the outside by spear-carrying bodyguards. The road is fenced off with ropes, and to anyone who passes within the ropes as far as the women, death is the penalty.

Such drastic precautions paid off. Chandragupta finally designated his rule to a son and became a religious ascetic (a person who renounces the pleasures of the material world), dying peacefully at an advanced age.

Chandragupta's grandson, **Ashoka** (269–232 B.C.E.), was an even greater figure in India's history. First serving as a governor of two provinces, Ashoka enjoyed a lavish lifestyle, with frequent horseback riding and feasting. However, he also engaged in a study of nature and was strongly influenced by the intense spiritualism not only of the brahman religion but also of Buddhism. Ashoka extended Mauryan conquests, gaining control of all but the southern tip of India through fierce fighting (Map 3.1). His methods were bloodthirsty; in taking over one coastal area, Ashoka admitted that "one hundred and fifty thousand were killed (or maimed) and many times that number later died." But Ashoka could also be compassionate. He ultimately converted to Buddhism, seeing in the belief in **dharma,** or the law of moral consequences, a kind of ethical guide that might unite and discipline the diverse people under his rule. Ashoka vigorously propagated Buddhism throughout India while also honoring Hinduism, sponsoring shrines for its worshippers. Ashoka sent Buddhist missionaries to the Hellenistic kingdoms in the Middle East, and also to Sri Lanka to the south. The "new" Ashoka urged humane behavior on the part of his officials and insisted that they oversee the moral welfare of his empire. Like Chandragupta, Ashoka also worked to improve trade and communication, sponsoring an extensive road network dotted with wells and rest stops for travelers. Stability and the sheer expansion of the empire's territory encouraged growing commerce.

The Mauryan dynasty did not, however, succeed in establishing durable roots, and Ashoka's particular style of government did not have much later impact, although a strong Buddhist current persisted in India for some time. After Ashoka, the empire began to fall apart, and regional kingdoms surfaced once again. New invaders, the **Kushans,** pushed into central India from the northwest. The greatest Kushan king, Kanishka, converted to Buddhism but actually hurt this religion's popularity in India by associating it with foreign rule.

Chandragupta Maurya [chuhn-druh-GOOP-duh MAHR-yeh] (r. 322–298 B.C.E.) Founder of Maurya dynasty; established first empire in Indian subcontinent; first centralized government since Harappan civilization.

Classical India

Mauryan [MAHR-yuhn] Dynasty established in Indian subcontinent in 4th century B.C.E. following invasion by Alexander the Great.

Ashoka (r. 273–232 B.C.E.) Grandson of Chandragupta Maurya; completed conquests of Indian subcontinent; converted to Buddhism and sponsored spread of new religion throughout his empire.

dharma The caste position and career determined by a person's birth; Hindu culture required that one accept one's social position and perform occupation to the best of one's ability in order to have a better situation in the next life.

Kushans See Kush, p. 21.

Map 3.1 India at the Time of Ashoka.
Though, as the map shows, the Mauryan monarchs claimed to rule most of present-day South Asia, much of the subcontinent was only loosely controlled.

Map 3.2 The Gupta Empire. Not only was the territory claimed by the Gupta dynasty a good deal smaller than the empire of their Mauryan predecessors, even the area controlled was ruled to a far greater extent by local lords than the Gupta emperors.

Local and regional governments dominated in India, which placed less emphasis on politics than other early civilizations.

Guptas Dynasty that succeeded the Kushans in the 3rd century C.E.; built empire that extended to all but the southern regions of Indian sub-continent; less centralized than Mauryan Empire.

Kautilya [kah-TIHL-yeh] (350–275 B.C.E.) Political advisor to Chandragupta Maurya; one of the authors of *Arthashastra*; believed in scientific application of warfare.

The Guptas

The collapse of the Kushan state, by 220 C.E., ushered in another hundred years of political instability. Then a new line of kings, the **Guptas,** established a large empire, beginning in 320 C.E. (Map 3.2). The Guptas produced no individual rulers as influential as the two great Mauryan rulers, but they had perhaps greater impact. One Gupta emperor proclaimed his virtues in an inscription on a ceremonial stone pillar:

> His far-reaching fame, deep-rooted in peace, emanated from the restoration of the sovereignty of many fallen royal families. . . . He, who had no equal in power in the world, eclipsed the fame of the other kings by the radiance of his versatile virtues, adorned by innumerable good actions.

Bombast aside, Gupta rulers often preferred to negotiate with local princes and intermarry with their families, which expanded influence without constant fighting. Two centuries of Gupta rule gave classical India its greatest period of political stability, although the Guptas did not administer as large a territory as the Mauryan kings had. The Gupta empire was overturned in 535 C.E. by a new invasion of nomadic warriors, the Huns.

Classical India thus alternated between widespread empires and a network of smaller kingdoms. Periods of regional rule did not necessarily suggest great instability, and both economic and cultural life advanced in these periods as well as under the Mauryas and Guptas.

Political Institutions

Classical India did not develop the solid political traditions and institutions of Chinese civilization, or the high level of political interest that would characterize classical Greece and Rome. The most persistent political features of India, in the classical period and beyond, involved regionalism, plus considerable diversity in political forms. Autocratic kings and emperors dotted the history of classical India, but there were also aristocratic assemblies in some regional states with the power to consult and decide on major issues.

As a result of India's diversity and regionalism, even some of the great empires had a rather shaky base. Early Mauryan rulers depended heavily on the power of their large armies, and, as we have seen, often feared betrayal and attack. Early rulers in the Gupta dynasty used various devices to consolidate support. They claimed that they had been appointed by the gods to rule, and they favored the Hindu religion over Buddhism because the Hindus believed in such gods. The Guptas managed to create a demanding taxation system, seeking up to a sixth of all agricultural produce. However, they did not create an extensive bureaucracy, rather allowing local rulers whom they had defeated to maintain regional control so long as they deferred to Gupta dominance. The Guptas stationed a personal representative at each ruler's court to ensure loyalty. A final sign of the great empire's loose structure was the fact that no single language was imposed. The Guptas promoted Sanskrit, which became the language of educated people, but this made no dent in the diversity of popular, regional languages.

The Guptas did spread uniform law codes. Like the Mauryan rulers, they sponsored some general services, such as road building. They also served as patrons of much cultural activity, including university life as well as art and literature. These achievements were more than enough to qualify the Gupta period as a golden age in Indian history.

The fact remains, however, that the political culture of India was not very elaborate. There was little formal political theory and few institutions or values other than regionalism that carried through from one period to the next. Chandragupta's chief minister, **Kautilya** (kah-TIHL-yeh), wrote an important treatise on politics, but it was devoted to telling rulers what methods would work to maintain power—somewhat like the Legalists in China. Thinking of this sort encouraged efficient authority, but it did not spread political values or a sense of the importance of political service very widely, in contrast to Confucianism in China and also to the intense interest in political ethics in Greece and Rome. Ashoka saw in Buddhism a kind of ethic for good behavior, as well as a spiritual beacon, but Buddhist leaders in the long run were not greatly interested in affairs of state. Indeed, Indian religion generally did not stress the importance of politics, even for religious purposes, but rather the preeminence of priests as sources of authority.

The limitations on the political traditions developed during this period of Indian history can be explained partly by the importance of local units of government—the tightly organized villages—and particularly by the essentially political qualities of social relationships under the caste system. Caste rules, interpreted by priests, regulated many social relationships and work roles. To a great extent, the caste system and religious encouragement in the faithful performance of caste duties did for Indian life what more conventional government structures did in many other cultures, in promoting public order.

India's caste system became steadily more complex after the Epic Age, as the five initial classes subdivided into ultimately almost 300 jati (or livings), which became further divided into a multitude of subcastes—the true basis of the caste system—which defined the groups that a person could eat with or marry within. Hereditary principles grew ever stronger, so that it became virtually impossible to rise above the caste in which a person was born or to marry someone from a higher caste. It was possible to fall to a lower caste by marrying outside one's caste or by taking on work deemed inappropriate for one's caste. Upward mobility could occur within castes, as individuals might gain greater wealth through success in the economic activities appropriate to the caste. Rulers, like the Mauryans, might spring from the merchant castes, although most princes were warrior-born. It is important not to characterize the caste system in an oversimplified way, for it did offer some flexibility. Nevertheless, the system gave India the most rigid overall framework for a social structure of any of the classical civilizations.

In its origins, the caste system provided a way for India's various races, the conquerors and the conquered, to live together without perpetual conflict and without full integration of cultures and values. Quite different kinds of people could live side by side in village or city, separated by caste. In an odd way, castes promoted tolerance, and this was useful, given India's varied peoples and beliefs. The caste system also meant that extensive outright slavery was avoided. The lowest, untouchable castes were scorned, confined to poverty and degrading work, but their members were not directly owned by others.

The political consequences of the caste system derived from the detailed rules for each caste. These rules governed marriages and permissible jobs, but also social habits such as eating and drinking. For example, a person could not eat or drink with a lower-caste individual or perform any service for that person. This kind of regulation of behavior made detailed political administration less necessary. Indeed, no state could command full loyalty from subjects, for their first loyalty was to caste.

Religion and Culture

More of the qualities of Indian civilization rested on widely shared cultural values than was the case in China. Religion, and particularly the evolving Hindu religion as it gained ground on Buddhism under the Guptas, was the clearest cultural cement of this society, cutting across political and language barriers and across the castes. Hinduism itself embraced considerable variety, and it gave rise to important religious dissent. Nor did it ever displace important minority religions. However, Hinduism has shown a remarkable capacity to survive and is the major system of belief in India even today. It also promotes other features in Indian culture. Thus, contemporary Indian children are encouraged to indulge their imaginations longer than Western children, with less urging to test flights of fancy against external reality. It is this kind of tradition that illustrates how classical India, although not the source of enduring political institutions beyond the local level, produced a civilization that would retain clear continuity and cultural cohesiveness from this point onward—even though the subcontinent was rarely politically united, at least under indigenous rulers.

Hinduism and Buddhism were the religions of classical India, helping also to shape distinctively Indian arts and sciences.

The culture of classic India was not just religious, however. Along with religion, an important tradition of rational scientific inquiry emerged. This helped sustain major initiative in higher education. It is also important to note that the Indian religions themselves were tolerant—both of other religious and of other aspects of culture. Indian governments might support religious missionaries, but they also established an openness to religious diversity. This, too, was a legacy to Indian cultures in later periods.

The Formation of Hinduism

Hinduism, the religion of India's majority, developed gradually over a period of many centuries. Its origins lie in the Vedic and Epic ages, as the Aryan religion gained greater sophistication, with concerns about an overarching divinity supplementing the rituals and polytheistic beliefs supervised by the brahman caste of priests. The *Rig-Veda* expressed the growing interest in a higher divine principle in its Creation Hymn:

> Then even nothingness was not, nor existence. There was no air then, nor the heavens beyond it. Who covered it? Where was it? In whose keeping . . . ? The gods themselves are later than creation, so who knows truly whence it has arisen?

Unlike all other world religions, Hinduism had no single founder, no central holy figure from whom the basic religious beliefs stemmed. This fact helps explain why the religion unfolded so gradually, sometimes in reaction to competing religions such as Buddhism or Islam. Moreover, Hinduism pursued a number of religious approaches, from the strictly ritualistic and ceremonial approach many brahmans preferred, to the high-soaring mysticism that sought to unite individual humans with an all-embracing divine principle. Unlike Western religions or Daoism (which it resembled in part), Hinduism could also encourage political and economic goals (called artha) and worldly pleasures (called karma)—and important textbooks of the time spelled out these pursuits. Part of Hinduism's success, indeed, was the result of its fluidity, its ability to adapt to the different needs of various groups and to change with circumstance. With a belief that there are many suitable paths of worship, Hinduism was also characteristically tolerant, coexisting with several offshoot religions that garnered minority acceptance in India.

Under brahman leadership, Indian ideas about the gods gradually became more elaborate (scholars call early Hinduism *brahmanism* for this reason, though Hindus always called their religion *dharma,* or moral path). Original gods of nature were altered to represent more abstract concepts. Thus, Varuna changed from a god of the sky to the guardian of ideas of right and wrong. The great poems of the Epic Age increasingly emphasized the importance of gentle and generous behavior, and the validity of a life devoted to concentration on the Supreme Spirit. The *Upanishads* particularly stressed the shallowness of worldly concerns—riches and even health were not the main point of human existence—in favor of contemplation of the divine spirit. It was in the *Upanishads* that the Hindu idea of a divine force informing the whole universe, of which each individual creature's soul is thought to be part, first surfaced clearly, in passages such as the following:

> "Fetch me a fruit of the banyan tree."
> "Here is one, sir."
> "Break it."
> "I have broken it, sir."
> "What do you see?"
> "Very tiny seeds, sir."
> "Break one."
> "I have broken it, sir."
> "What do you see now?"
> "Nothing, sir."
> "My son, . . . what you do not perceive is the essence, and in that essence the mighty banyan tree exists. Believe me, my son, in that essence is the self of all that is. That is the True, that is the Self."

However, the *Upanishads* did more than advance the idea of a mystical contact with a divine essence. They also attacked the conventional brahman view of what religion should be, a set of proper ceremonies that would lead to good things in this life or rewards after death. From the Epic Age onward, Hinduism embraced this clear tension between a religion of rituals, with fixed ceremonies and rules of conduct, and the religion of mystical holy men, seeking communion with the divine soul.

gurus Originally referred to as Brahmans who served as teachers for the princes of the imperial court of the Guptas.

Vishnu The Brahman, later Hindu, god of sacrifice; widely worshipped.

Shiva Hindu, god of destruction and reproduction; worshipped as the personification of cosmic forces of change.

Transmigration of Souls in the *Upanishads* DOCUMENT

A Guardian's Farewell Speech to a Young Woman About to Be Married

One of the great plays written during the Hindu revival of the early centuries C.E. was *Shakuntala*, by Kalidasa. The play is a Cinderella-style tale about a beautiful young woman, Shakuntala, who is loved by a king, and the travails she must endure before they are happily united. In the following exchange, as Shakuntala sets out to join her husband at his palace, she is instructed by her guardians (the hermits Kashyapa and Gautami) on the proper behavior for a young wife, in a manner that recalls the famous speech by Polonius to his son, Laertes, in Shakespeare's *Hamlet*.

Kashyapa: Now you Shakuntala. Respect your superiors,
Be friendly toward the ladies of the palace.
Never be angry with your husband, no matter what happens.
Be polite with the maids;
In everything be humble.
These qualities make a woman; those without them are black sheep in their families.

What is your opinion, Gautami?
Gautami: A bride needs nothing more. Remember his advice, Shakuntala.
Shakuntala: How will I ever manage in the palace? I feel so lost. I belong here, Father.
Kashyapa: Don't worry, my child; you are privileged.
You will be his great wife;
He is noble and great.
You will give him a son, as the East gives us light.
The pain of separation will then pass.

QUESTIONS What does this conversation tell you about gender relationships and marriage in classical India? What does it say about attitudes toward women? How do these relationships and attitudes compare with those found in China and Greece in this era? How do they compare with those in our own society?

The mystics, often called **gurus** as they gathered disciples around them, and the brahman priests agreed on certain doctrines, as Hinduism became an increasingly formal religion by the first centuries of the common era. The basic holy essence, called *brahma*, formed part of everything in this world. Every living creature participates in this divine principle. The divine aspects of brahma are manifested in the forms of several gods, including **Vishnu,** the preserver, and **Shiva,** the destroyer, who could be worshipped or placated as expressions of the holy essence. The world of our senses is far less important than the world of the divine soul, and a proper life is one devoted to seeking union with this soul. However, this quest may take many lifetimes, and Hindus stressed the principle of **reincarnation,** in which souls do not die when bodies do but pass into other beings, either human or animal. Where the soul goes, whether it rises to a higher-caste person or falls perhaps to an animal, depends on how good a life the person has led. Ultimately, after many good lives, the soul reaches full union with the soul of brahma, and worldly suffering ceases.

Hinduism provided several channels for the good life. For people who renounced this world in search of salvation, there was the meditation and self-discipline of *yoga*, which means "union," allowing the mind to be freed to concentrate on the divine spirit. For others, there were the rituals and rules of the brahmans. These included proper ceremonies in the cremation of bodies at death, appropriate prayers, and obedience to injunctions such as treating cows as sacred animals and refraining from the consumption of beef. Many Hindus also continued the idea of lesser gods represented in the spirits of nature, or purely local divinities, which could be seen as expressions of Shiva or Vishnu (Figure 3.2). Personal devotion to these divinities through prayer could aid the process of reincarnation to a higher state. Thus, many ordinary Hindus placed a lot of importance on prayers. Symbolic sacrifices or gifts to the gods might also bring them salvation or entry, through reincarnation, into a higher caste.

Hinduism also provided a basic, if complex, ethic that helped supply some unity amid the various forms of worship. The epic poems, richly symbolic, formed the key texts. They illustrated a central emphasis on the moral law of dharma as a guide to living in this world and simultaneously pursuing higher, spiritual goals. The concept of dharma directed attention to the moral consequences of action and at the same time the need to act. Each person must meet the obligations of life, serving the family, producing a livelihood

reincarnation The successive attachment of the soul to some animate form according to merits earned in previous lives.

Figure 3.2 Perhaps the most frequently depicted Indian religious image is of god in the form of Shiva as the celestial dancer, here portrayed in a South Indian bronze. His dance represents the patterns of creation and destruction that are inescapable elements of the cosmos. The drum in his far left hand keeps the time between cycles of birth and death. The left hand below the drum is open as a gesture of reassurance to the righteous of their ultimate salvation. His foot crushes the demon of ignorance, shown as small compared with divine truth and welcoming of its own inevitable conquest by divine knowledge.
("Nataraja: Shiva as King of Dance." © The Cleveland Museum of Art, 2001, Purchase from the J.H. Wade Fund. 1930.331.)

The Song of Songs, from *Bhagavad Gita* DOCUMENT

and even earning money, and serving in the army when the need arises. These actions cannot damage, certainly cannot destroy, the eternal divine essence that underlies all creation. In the *Bhagavad Gita*, a classic sacred hymn, a warrior is sent to do battle against his own relatives. Fearful of killing them, he is advised by an incarnation of Brahma (Krishna) that he must carry out his duties. He will not really be killing his victims because their divine spirit will live on. This ethic urged that honorable behavior, even pleasure seeking, is compatible with spirituality and can lead to a final release from the life cycle and to unity with the divine essence. The Hindu ethic explains how devout Hindus could also be aggressive merchants or eager warriors. In encouraging honorable action, it could legitimize government and the caste system as providing the frameworks in which the duties of the world might be carried out, without distracting from the ultimate spiritual goals common to all people.

The ethical concept of dharma was far less detailed and prescriptive than the ethical codes associated with most other world religions, including Christianity and Islam. Dharma stresses inner study and meditation, building from the divine essence within each creature, rather than adherence to a fixed set of moral rules.

The spread of Hinduism through India, and at least briefly to some other parts of Asia, had many sources. The religion accommodated extreme spirituality. It also provided satisfying rules of conduct for ordinary life, including rituals and a firm emphasis on the distinction between good and evil behavior. The religion allowed many people to retain older beliefs and ceremonies, which they may have derived from a more purely polytheistic religion. It reinforced the caste system, giving people in lower castes hope for a better time in lives to come and giving upper-caste people, including the brahmans, the satisfaction that if they behaved well, they might be rewarded by communion with the divine soul. Even though Hindu beliefs took shape only gradually and contained many ambiguities, the religion was sustained by a strong cadre of priests and through the efforts of individual gurus and mystics.

Buddhism

At times, however, the tensions within Hinduism broke down for some individuals, producing rebellions against the dominant religion. One such rebellion, which occurred right after the Epic Age, led to a new religion closely related to Hinduism. Around 563 B.C.E. an Indian prince, Siddhartha Gautama, was born who came to question the fairness of earthly life in which so much poverty and misery abounded. Gautama, later called **Buddha** or "enlightened one," lived as a Hindu mystic, fasting and torturing his body. After six years, he felt that he had found truth, then spent his life traveling and gathering disciples to spread his ideas. Buddha accepted the spiritual truth behind many Hindu beliefs, such as reincarnation, but he denied the validity of others, such as caste. He held the material world to be a snare that warped human relations and caused pain via the frustrations inherent in it: all worldly things decay, but men and women suffer and harm others as they struggle to hold onto youth, health, and life itself, though all are destined to pass away.

Buddha did not reject the possibility of rewards after life, but he saw salvation as arising from the destruction of the self, whose annihilation opens the door to a realm where suffering and decay are no more, literally a world beyond existence itself: **nirvana.** Individuals could regulate their lives and aspirations toward this goal without elaborate ceremonies. Great stress was placed on self-control: "Let a man overcome anger by love, let him overcome evil by good, let him overcome the greedy by liberalness, the liar with the truth." By arguing that a holy life could be achieved through individual effort by people at every level of society, Buddhism denied the spiritual value not only of caste and the performance of rituals, but also of priests. This was another sign of the complexity of Indian social life in practice.

Buddhism spread and retained coherence through the example and teachings of groups of monks, organized in monasteries but preaching throughout the world (Figure 3.3). Buddhism attracted many followers in India itself, and its growth was greatly spurred by the conversion of the Mauryan emperor Ashoka. Increasingly, Buddha himself was seen as divine. Prayer and contemplation at Buddhist holy places and works of charity and piety

Figure 3.3 This beautifully detailed sandstone statue of the Buddha meditating in a standing position was carved in the 5th century C.E. Note the nimbus, or halo, which was common in later Buddhist iconography. The calm radiated by the Buddha's facial expression suggests that he has already achieved Enlightenment. As Buddhism spread throughout India and overseas, a wide variety of artistic styles developed to depict the Buddha himself and key incidents of his legendary life. The realism and stylized robes of the sculpture shown here indicate that it was carved by artists following the conventions of the Indo-Greek school of northwestern India.

(© The Trustees of the British Museum/Art Resource, NY)

gave substance to the idea of a holy life on earth. Ironically, however, Buddhism did not witness a permanent following in India. Brahman opposition was strong, and it was ultimately aided by the influence of the Gupta emperors. Furthermore, Hinduism showed its adaptability by emphasizing its mystical side, thus retaining the loyalties of many Indians. Buddhism's greatest successes, aided by the missionary encouragement of Ashoka and later the Kushan emperors, came in other parts of southeast Asia, including the island of Sri Lanka, off the south coast of India, and in China, Korea, and Japan. Still, pockets of Buddhists remained in India, particularly in the northeast. They were joined by other dissident groups who rejected aspects of Hinduism. Thus, Hinduism, although dominant, had to come to terms with the existence of other religions early on.

If Hinduism, along with the caste system, formed the most distinctive and durable products of the classical period of Indian history, they were certainly not the only ones. Even aside from dissident religions, Indian culture during this period was vibrant and diverse, and religion encompassed only part of its interests. Hinduism itself encouraged many wider pursuits.

Indian thinkers wrote actively about various aspects of human life. Although political theory was sparse, a great deal of legal writing occurred. The theme of love was important also. A manual of the "laws of love," the **Kamasutra** (kah-muh-SOO-truh), written in the 4th century C.E., discusses relationships between men and women.

Arts and Sciences

Indian literature, taking many themes from the great epic poems and their tales of military adventure, stressed lively story lines. The epics were recorded in final written form during the Gupta period, and other story collections, like the *Panchatantra,* which includes Sinbad the Sailor, Jack the Giant Killer, and the Seven League Boots, produced adventurous yarns now known all over the world. Classical stories were often secular, but they sometimes included the gods and also shared with Hinduism an emphasis on imagination and excitement. Indian drama flourished also, again particularly under the Guptas, and stressed themes of romantic adventure in which lovers separated and then reunited after many perils. This literary tradition created a cultural framework that still survives in India. Even contemporary Indian movies reflect the tradition of swashbuckling romance and heroic action.

Classical India also produced important work in science and mathematics. The Guptas supported a vast university center—one of the world's first—in the town of Nalanda that attracted students from other parts of Asia as well as Indian brahmans. Nalanda had over a hundred lecture halls, three large libraries, an astronomical observatory, and even a model dairy. Its curriculum included religion, philosophy, medicine, architecture, and agriculture.

At the research level, Indian scientists, borrowing a bit from Greek learning after the conquests of Alexander the Great, made important strides in astronomy and medicine. The great astronomer Aryabhatta calculated the length of the solar year and improved mathematical measurements. He also calculated the circumference of the earth with remarkable accuracy—which also indicates that he believed it to be round. Indian astronomers understood and calculated the daily rotation of the earth on its axis, predicted and explained eclipses, and developed a theory of gravity, and through telescopic observation they identified seven planets. Medical research was hampered by religious prohibitions on dissection, but Indian surgeons nevertheless made advances in bone setting and plastic surgery. Inoculation against smallpox was introduced, using cowpox serum. Indian hospitals stressed cleanliness, including sterilization of wounds, while leading doctors promoted high ethical standards. As was the case with Indian discoveries in astronomy, many medical findings reached the Western world only in modern times.

Indian mathematics produced still more important discoveries. The Indian numbering system is the one we use today, although we call it Arabic because Europeans imported it secondhand from the Arabs. Indians invented the concept of zero, and through it they were able to develop the decimal system. Indian advances in numbering rank with writing itself as key human inventions. Indian mathematicians also developed the concept of negative numbers, calculated square roots and a table of sines, and computed the value of pi more accurately than the Greeks did.

Finally, classical India produced lively art, although much of it perished under later invasions. Ashoka sponsored many spherical shrines to Buddha, called **stupas,** and statues honoring Buddha were also common. Under the Guptas, sculpture and painting moved away from realistic portrayals

Buddha's Sermon at Benares and the Edicts of Ashoka

Buddha   Creator of a major Indian and Asian religion; born in 6th century B.C.E. as son of local ruler among Aryan tribes located near Himalayas; became an ascetic; found enlightenment under bo tree; taught that enlightenment could be achieved only by abandoning desires for all earthly things.

nirvana   The Buddhist state of enlightenment, a state of tranquility.

Kamasutra   [kah-muh-SOO-truh] Written by Vatsayana during Gupta era; offered instructions on all aspects of life for higher-caste males, including grooming, hygiene, etiquette, selection of wives, and lovemaking.

stupas   Stone shrines built to house pieces of bone or hair and personal possessions said to be relics of the Buddha; preserved Buddhist architectural forms.

Buddhist Religious Site

of the human form toward more stylized representation. Indian painters, working on the walls of buildings and caves, filled their work with forms of people and animals, captured in lively color. Indian art showed a keen appreciation of nature. It could pay homage to religious values, particularly during the period in which Buddhism briefly spread, but could also celebrate the joys of life.

There was, clearly, no full unity to this cultural outpouring. Religion, legalism, abstract mathematics, and art and literature coexisted. The result, however, was a somewhat distinctive overall tone, different from the more rational approaches of the West or the Chinese concentration on political ethics. In various cultural expressions, Indians developed an interest in spontaneity and imagination, whether in fleshly pleasures or a mystical union with the divine essence.

Economy and Society

The caste system described many key features of Indian social and economic life, as it assigned people to occupations and regulated marriages. Low-caste individuals had few legal rights, and servants were often abused by their masters, who were restrained only by the ethical promptings of religion toward kindly treatment. A brahman who killed a servant for misbehavior faced a penalty no more severe than if he had killed an animal. This extreme level of abuse was uncommon, but the caste system did unquestionably make its mark on daily life as well as on the formal structure of society. The majority of Indians living in peasant villages had less frequent contact with people of higher social castes, and village leaders were charged with trying to protect peasants from too much interference by landlords and rulers.

Family life also emphasized the theme of hierarchy and tight organization, as it evolved from the Vedic and Epic ages. The dominance of husbands and fathers remained strong. One Indian code of law recommended that a wife worship her husband as a god. Indeed, the rights of women became increasingly limited as Indian civilization took clearer shape. Although the great epics stressed the control of husband and father, they also recognized women's independent contributions. As agriculture became better organized and improved technology reduced (without eliminating) women's economic contributions, the stress on male authority expanded. Here India followed a common pattern in agricultural societies, as women's sphere of action was gradually circumscribed. Hindu thinkers debated whether a woman could advance spiritually without first being reincarnated as a man, and there was no consensus. The limits imposed on women were reflected in laws and literary references. A system of arranged marriage evolved in which parents contracted unions for children, particularly daughters, at quite early ages, to spouses they had never even met. The goal of these arrangements was to ensure solid economic links, with child brides contributing dowries of land or domestic animals to the ultimate family estates, but the result of such arrangements was that young people, especially girls, were drawn into a new family structure in which they had no voice.

However, the rigidities of family life and male dominance over women were often greater in theory than they usually turned out to be in practice. The emphasis on loving relations and sexual pleasure in Indian culture modified family life, since husband and wife were supposed to provide mutual emotional support as a marriage developed. The *Mahabharata* epic called a man's wife his truest friend: "Even a man in the grip of rage will not be harsh to a woman, remembering that on her depend the joys of love, happiness, and virtue." Small children were often pampered. "With their teeth half shown in causeless laughter, their efforts at talking so sweetly uncertain, when children ask to sit on his lap, a man is blessed." Families thus served an important and explicit emotional function as well as a role in supporting the structure of society and its institutions. They also, as in all agricultural societies, formed economic units. Children, after early years of indulgence, were expected to work hard. Adults were obligated to assist older relatives. The purpose of arranged marriages was to promote a family's economic well-being, and almost everyone lived in a family setting.

The Indian version of the patriarchal family was thus subtly different from that in China, although women were officially just as subordinate and later trends—as in many patriarchal societies over time—would bring new burdens. But Indian culture often featured clever and strong-willed women and goddesses, and this contributed to women's status as wives and mothers. Stories also celebrated women's emotions and beauty.

The caste system structured India's social framework, but a strong emphasis on trade was also important.

Family life combined patriarchy with an emphasis on affection.

Cast(e)aways? Women in Classical India   DOCUMENT

The economy of India in the classical period became extremely vigorous, certainly rivaling China in technological sophistication and probably briefly surpassing China in the prosperity of its upper classes. In manufacturing, Indians invented new uses for chemistry, and their steel was the best in the world. Indian capacity in ironmaking outdistanced European levels until a few centuries ago. Indian techniques in textiles were also advanced, as the subcontinent became the first to manufacture cotton cloth, calico, and cashmere. Most manufacturing was done by artisans who formed guilds and sold their goods from shops.

Indian emphasis on trade and merchant activity was far greater than in China, and indeed greater than that of the classical Mediterranean world. Indian merchants enjoyed relatively high caste status and the flexibility of the Hindu ethic. They also traveled widely, not only over the subcontinent but by sea to the Middle East and east Asia. The seafaring peoples along the southern coast, usually outside the large empires of northern India, were particularly active. These southern Indians, the Tamils, traded cotton and silks, dyes, drugs, gold, and ivory, often earning great fortunes. From the Middle East and the Roman Empire, they brought back pottery, wine, metals, some slaves, and above all gold. Their trade with southeast Asia was even more active, as Indian merchants transported not only sophisticated manufactured goods but also the trappings of India's active culture to places like Malaysia and the larger islands of Indonesia. In addition, caravan trade developed with China.

The Indian economy remained firmly agricultural at its base. The wealth of the upper classes and the splendor of cities like Nalanda were confined to a small group, as most people lived near the margins of subsistence. But India was justly known by the time of the Guptas for its wealth as well as for its religion and intellectual life—always understanding that wealth was relative in the classical world and very unevenly divided. A Chinese Buddhist on a pilgrimage to India wrote:

> The people are many and happy. They do not have to register their households with the police. There is no death penalty. Religious sects have houses of charity where rooms, couches, beds, food, and drink are supplied to travelers.

Indian Influence and Comparative Features

Classical India, from the Mauryan period onward, had a considerable influence on other parts of the world. In many ways, the Indian Ocean, dominated at this point by Indian merchants and missionaries, was the most active linkage point among cultures, although admittedly, the Mediterranean, which channeled contact from the Middle East to north Africa and Europe, was a close second. Indian dominance of the waters of southern Asia, and the impressive creativity of Indian civilization itself, resulted in goods and influence traveling well beyond the subcontinent's borders. No previous civilization had developed in southeast Asia to compete with Indian influence. And while India did not attempt political domination, dealing instead with the regional kingdoms of Burma, Thailand, parts of Indonesia, and Vietnam, Indian travelers or settlers did bring to these locales a persuasive way of life. Many Indian merchants married into local royal families. Indian-style temples were constructed and other forms of Indian art traveled widely. Buddhism spread from India to many parts of southeast Asia, and Hinduism converted many upper-class people, particularly in several of the Indonesian kingdoms. India thus serves as an early example of a major civilization expanding its influence well beyond its own regions.

Indian influence had affected China, through Buddhism and art, by the end of the classical period. Earlier, Buddhist emissaries to the Middle East stimulated new ethical thinking that informed Greek and Roman groups like the Stoics and through them aspects of Christianity later on.

Within India itself, the classical period, starting a bit late after the Aryan invasions, lasted somewhat longer than that of China or Rome. Even when the period ended with the fall of the Guptas, an identifiable civilization remained in India, building on several key factors first established in the classical period: the religion, to be sure, but also the artistic and literary tradition and the complex social and family network. The ability of this civilization to survive, even under long periods of foreign domination, was testimony to the meaning and variety it offered to many Indians themselves.

Because of its extensive trade, India's artistic and cultural influence reached many parts of the ancient world, even as India shaped a distinctive version of classical civilization.

Inequality as the Social Norm

The Indian caste system is perhaps the most extreme expression of a type of social organization that violates the most revered principles on which modern Western societies are based. Like the Egyptian division between a noble and a commoner and the Greek division between a freeperson and a slave, the caste system rests on the assumption that humans are inherently unequal and that their lot in life is determined by the families and social strata into which they are born. The caste system, like the social systems of all other classical civilizations, presumed that social divisions were fixed and stable and that people ought to be content with the station they had been allotted at birth.

Furthermore, all classical social systems (with the partial exception of the Greeks, at least in Athens) played down the importance of the individual and stressed collective obligations and loyalties that were centered in the family, extended kin groups, or broader occupational or social groups. Family or caste affiliation, not individual ambition, determined a person's career goals and activities.

All of these assumptions directly contradict some of the West's most cherished current beliefs. They run counter to one of the most basic organizing principles of modern Western culture, rooted in a commitment to equality of opportunity. This principle is enshrined in European and American constitutions and legal systems, taught in Western schools and churches, and proclaimed in Western media. The belief in human equality, or at least equality of opportunity, is one of the most important ideas that modern Western civilization has exported to the peoples of Africa, Asia, and Latin America.

> In nearly all societies . . . fixed social hierarchies were upheld by creation myths and religious beliefs that proclaimed their divine origins and the danger of punishment if they were challenged.

The modern concept of equality rests on two assumptions. The first is that a person's place in society should be determined not by the class or family into which he or she is born but by personal actions and qualities. The second is that the opportunity to rise—or fall—in social status should be open to everyone and protected by law. Some of our most cherished myths reflect these assumptions: that anyone can aspire to be president of the United States, for example, or that an ordinary person has the right to challenge the actions of the politically and economically powerful.

Of course, equality is a social ideal rather than something any human society has achieved. No one pretends that all humans are equal in intelligence or talent, and there are important barriers to equality of opportunity. But the belief persists that all humans should have an equal chance to better themselves by using the brains and skills they have. In the real world, race, class, and gender differences often favor some individuals over others, and laws and government agencies often do not correct these inequities. But the citizens of modern Western societies, and increasingly the rest of the world, champion the principles of equality of opportunity and the potential for social mobility as the just and natural bases for social organization and interaction.

China and India Compared

The thrusts of classical civilization in China and India reveal the diversity generated during the classical age. The restraint of Chinese art and poetry contrasted with the more dynamic sensual styles of India. India ultimately settled on a primary religion, though with important minority expressions, that embodied diverse impulses within it. China opted for separate religious and philosophical systems that would serve different needs. China's political structures and values found little echo in India, whereas the Indian caste system involved a social rigidity considerably greater than that of China. India's cultural emphasis was, on balance, considerably more otherworldly than that of China, despite the impact of Daoism. Quite obviously, classical India and classical China created vastly different cultures. Even in science, where there was similar interest in pragmatic discoveries about how the world works, the Chinese placed greater stress on purely practical findings, whereas the Indians ventured further into the mathematical arena.

Beyond the realm of formal culture and the institutions of government, India and China may seem more similar. As agricultural societies, both civilizations relied on a large peasant class, organized in close-knit villages with much mutual cooperation. Cities and merchant activity, although vital, played a secondary role. Political power rested primarily with those who controlled the land, through ownership of large estates and the ability to tax the peasant class. On a more personal level, the power of husbands and fathers in the family—the basic fact of patriarchy—encompassed Indian and Chinese families alike.

However, what is just and natural for modern societies would have been incomprehensible in the classical age. In fact, most human societies through most of human history have been organized on assumptions that are much closer to those underlying the Indian caste system than to those underlying modern Western norms. Ancient Egyptians and Greeks, medieval Europeans, and early modern Chinese believed that career possibilities, political power, and social privileges should be set by law according to the position of one's family in the social hierarchy. The Indian caste structure was the most rigid and complex of the systems by which occupations, resources, and status were allotted. But all classical civilizations had similar social mechanisms that determined the obligations and privileges of members of each social stratum.

In some ways, classical Chinese and Greek societies provided exceptions to these general patterns. In China, people from lowly social origins could rise to positions of great status and power, and well placed families could fall on hard times and lose their gentry status. But "rags to riches" success stories were the exception rather than the rule, and mobility between social strata was limited. In fact, Chinese thinkers made much of the distinctions between the **scholar-gentry** elite and the common people.

Although some of the Greeks, particularly the Athenians, developed the idea of equality for all citizens in a particular city-state, most of the people of these societies were not citizens, and many were slaves. By virtue of their birth the latter were assigned lives of servitude and often drudgery. Democratic participation and the chance to make full use of their talents were limited to the free males of the city-states.

In nearly all societies, these fixed social hierarchies were upheld by creation myths and religious beliefs that proclaimed their divine origins and the danger of punishment if they were challenged. Elite thinkers stressed the importance of the established social order to human peace and well-being; rulers were duty bound to defend it. Few challenged the naturalness of the hierarchy itself; fewer still proposed alternatives to it. Each person was expected to accept his or her place and to concentrate on the duties and obligations of that place rather than worry about rights or personal desires. Males and females alike were required to subordinate their individual yearnings and talents to the needs of their families, clans, communities, or social superiors. In return for a person's acceptance of his or her allotted place in the hierarchy, he or she received material sustenance and a social slot. Of course, these benefits were denied to people who fought the system. They might be outcast or exiled, physically punished, or even killed.

QUESTIONS What arguments did the thinkers of the classical civilizations of Greece, China, and India use to explain and justify the great differences in social status and material wealth? How did those who belonged to elite groups justify their much greater status, wealth, and power compared to the peasants, artisans, and servants who made up most of the population? Comparing these modes of social organization with the ideals of your own society, what do you see as the advantages and drawbacks of each?

However, Indian and Chinese societies differed in more than their religion, philosophy, art, and politics. Ordinary people had cultures along with elites. Hindu peasants saw their world differently from their Chinese counterparts. They placed less emphasis on personal emotional restraint and detailed etiquette; they expected different emotional interactions with family members. Indian peasants were less constrained than were the Chinese by recurrent efforts by large landlords to gain control of their land. Although there were wealthy landlords in India, the system of village control of most land was more firmly entrenched than in China. Indian merchants played a greater role than their Chinese counterparts. There was more sea trade, more commercial vitality. Revealingly, India's expanding cultural influence was due to merchant activity above all else, whereas Chinese expansion involved government initiatives in gaining new territory and sending proud emissaries to satellite states. These differences were less dramatic, certainly less easy to document, than those generated by elite thinkers and politicians, but they contributed to the shape of a civilization and to its particular vitality, its areas of stability and instability.

Because each classical civilization developed its own unique style, in social relationships as well as in formal politics and intellectual life, exchanges between two societies like China and India involved specific borrowings, not wholesale imitation. India and China, the two giants of classical Asia, remain subjects of comparison to our own time, because they have continued to build distinctively on their particular traditions, established before 500 C.E. These characteristics, in turn, differed from those of yet another center of civilization, the societies that sprang up on the shores of the Mediterranean during this same classical age.

scholar-gentry Chinese class created by the marital linkage of the local land-holding aristocracy with the office-holding shi; superseded shi as governors of China.

The Pattern of Trade in the Ancient Eurasian World

The period of Maurya rule in India coincided with a great expansion in trade between the main centers of civilization in Eurasia and Africa. In the centuries that followed, a permanent system of exchange developed that extended from Rome and the Mediterranean Sea to China and Japan. The trading networks that made up this system included both those established between ports connected by ships and sea routes and those consisting of overland exchanges transmitted along the chain of trading centers that crossed central Asia and the Sudanic region of Africa. By the last centuries B.C.E., this far-flung trading system included much of the world as it was known to the peoples of the Eastern Hemisphere.

Some products produced at one end of the system, such as Chinese silks and porcelains, were carried the entire length of the network to be sold in markets at the other edge—in Rome, for example. As a general rule, products carried over these great distances tended to be high-priced luxury goods such as spices and precious jewels. But most of the exchanges, particularly in bulk goods such as metal ores or foodstuffs, were between adjoining regions. The ports of western India, for example, carried on a brisk trade with those in the Red Sea and Persian Gulf, while trading centers in southeast Asia supplied China with forest products and other raw materials in exchange for the many items manufactured by China's highly skilled artisans. Although some merchants and sailors, particularly the Chinese and Arabs, could be found in ports far from their homelands, most confined their activities within regional orbits, such as the Arabian Sea, the Persian Gulf, or the South China Sea.

Map 3.3 provides an overview of this great trading network in the age of the classical civilizations, roughly the 3rd century B.C.E. to the 3rd century C.E. It shows the main centers of production, the goods exported overland and overseas, and the main directions of trade in these products. Key ports, inland trading centers, and products are shown for each of the main sectors participating in the system.

QUESTIONS Which civilizations or areas in the global trading network were the main centers for the production of finished products, such as cloth and pottery? What major centers supplied raw materials, such as forest products or foods? Why were luxury goods likely to be transported the greatest distances? Why were bulk goods, especially foods, usually shipped only short distances, if at all? Besides trade goods, what other things might be transmitted through the trading networks?

Global Connections

India and the Wider World

No classical civilization was more open to outside influences than those of the Indian subcontinent. None were more central to cross-cultural exchanges in the centuries that ushered what we have come to label the common era (C.E.) of world history. The brahman-dominated, caste-ordered civilization that flourished at the end of the Vedic era and later under the Guptas produced some of humanity's most sublime art and philosophy; important breakthroughs in mathematics, the sciences, and technology; prosperous urban centers; and a population that has been second only to that of China through much of human history.

The period dominated by the Mauryas in between saw the rise of Buddhism, one of a handful of truly world religions. In this era and the age of the Guptas that followed, Buddhism was but one of numerous components of Indian civilization that were exported to China and east Asia, across the steppes of central Asia, throughout most of southeast Asia, and as far west as the Mediterranean.

In mainland and island southeast Asia, the impact of Indian civilization was especially critical. Indian merchants played a key role in trade with these regions, and other influences followed. Indian religions and epics, art and architecture, and concepts of kingship sparked the rise of centralized states and complex societies that culminated in great civilizations, such as those centered at Angkor Wat in Cambodia and the kingdom of Majapahit in central Java. In the Mediterranean, Indian influences were felt in areas as diverse as artistic techniques, philosophies such as Stoicism, and religious ideas that significantly affected Christianity. Central to all of these developments was the fact that in the centuries that witnessed the flowering of Indian civilization under the Mauryas and Guptas, the coastal areas of the Indian subcontinent became, and would remain for millennia, one of the core areas of an ever expanding trading network that would eventually encompass most of the Eastern Hemisphere. Indian manufactured goods, such as cotton textiles and bronze statuary, soon became some of the most coveted commodities in this system of exchange. Indian merchants and sailors would carry them throughout the Indian Ocean and to the emporiums of the Silk Road that dominated overland trade beyond the Himalaya Mountains. Indian religions, artwork, scientific discoveries, and epic literature came to enrich, and at times spur major transformations in, civilizations over much of the known world.

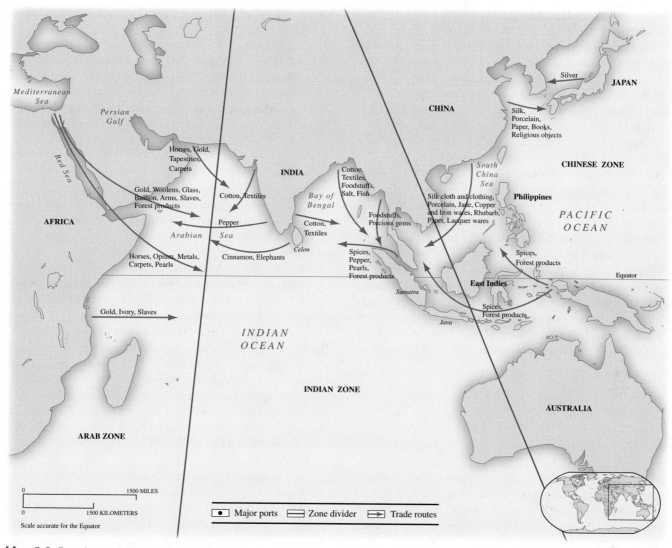

Map 3.3 **Eurasian and African Trading Goods Routes, c. 300 B.C.E. to 300 C.E.**   As the map above illustrates, a vibrant oceanic trading system was in place across the AfroEurasian continents by the last centuries B.C.E., and the Indian subcontinent was central as a producer and consumer in this vast network of contact and exchange.

Further Readings

Perhaps the most readable introductions to life and society in India's classical age can be found in A. L. Basham's *The Wonder That Was India* (1963) and Jeannine Auboyer's *Daily Life in Ancient India* (2002 reprint ed.). The works of Romilla Thapar, especially *Ashoka and the Decline of the Mauryas* (1997) and *Early India: From the Origins to AD 1300* (2003), are the best on the political history of the era. Her more general *A History of India,* Vol. 1 (1991 reprint), and more recent *Cultural Pasts: Essays in Early Indian History* (2000) are very detailed and quite technical—certainly a challenge for the beginner. On the Guptas the most comprehensive recent work is Ashvini Agrawal's *Rise and Fall of the Imperial Guptas* (1989). Fine narrative histories of all aspects of Indian civilization in this period can be found in the appropriate chapters of *The*

History and Culture of the Indian People (1964), edited by R. C. Majumdar, A. K. Majumdar, and D. K. Ghose. Some of the best works on the position of women and social life more generally include Pandharinath Prabhu's *Hindu Social Organization* (1940), L.K. Tripathi, *Position and Status of Women in Ancient India* (1988), and S. Tharu & K. Lalita, eds., Women Writing in India 600 to the Present (1991). On the development of the caste system, see B. R. Kamble, *Caste and Philosophy in Pre-Buddhist India* (1979). A wide range of other aspects of ancient Indian culture is covered in the fine essays in A. L. Basham's *A Cultural History of India* (1975).

Superb introductions to various branches of Indian religious and philosophical thinking, with well selected portions of the appropriate texts, can be found in S. Radhakrishnan and Charles Moore, eds., *A Source Book in Indian Philosophy* (1967); and Ainslee Embree, ed., *Sources of Indian Tradition,* Vol. 1, *From the Beginning to 1800* (2nd ed., 1988). Of the many books on Buddhism, Trevor Ling's *The Buddha* (1973) is one of the more accessible, but needs to be supplemented with recent research, many of the findings of which are explored in Jonathan S. Walters, *Finding Buddhists in Global History* (1998). The spread of Indian culture to SE Asia in this period is covered in the classic work by G. Coedés, *The Indianized States of Southeast Asia* (1964), and more recently in G. C. Pande's *India's Interaction with Southeast Asia* (2006).

S. Radhakrishnan's *Hindu View of Life* (1927) provides a useful insider's view of Hindu religious beliefs and social organization. Heinrich Zimmer's *Philosophies of India* (1956), though somewhat dated, remains a good place to begin exploring the riches and diversity of Indian mythology and religious thinking. Susan Huntington's *The Art of Ancient India* (1985) offers a stimulating and very accessible discussion of the art of this period. Benjamin Rowland's *The Art and Architecture of India* (1970), which includes Southeast Asia, remains the most comprehensive work available in English on Indian art overall; J. C. Harle's *Gupta Sculpture* (1974) provides an introduction to some of the glories of the Gupta age. For a taste of Indian literature in the classical period, there are English translations of the *Ramayana* and the *Mahabharata* and P. Lal's fine translations of *Great Sanskrit Plays* (1957).

On the Web

An introduction to early Indian history and culture may be found at http://www.mnsu.edu/emuseum/prehistory/india/indus/geography.html and http://pubweb.cc.u-tokai.ac.jp/indus/english/index.html. Hindu values and ethics are analyzed at http://www.bbc.co.uk/religion/religions/hinduism/index.shtml. Daily life in ancient India is explored at http://ancienthistory.mrdonn.org/Indialife.html and http://www.my-ecoach.com/online/webresourcelist.php?rlid=709.

The life of Buddha is examined at http://www.as.miami.edu/phi/bio/Buddha/bud-life.htm, http://www.bbc.co.uk/religion/religions/buddhism/index.shtmlabud-life.htm, http://www.buddhanet.net/ and viewed through Buddhist art and architecture at http://www.buddhanet.net/gallery.htm, http://media.graniteschools.org/curriculum/korea/bud_arch.htm and http://www.sscnet.ucla.edu/southasia/Culture/Archit/BudhArch.html. Buddhist values and ethics are explored at http://www.bbc.co.uk/religion/religions/buddhism/index.shtml. The roughly parallel life of Mahavira and the development of Jainism are examined at http://www.pujas.com/Jainism-History.html, http://www.san.beck.org/EC8-Mahavira.html, and http://www.cs.colostate.edu/~malaiya/jainhout1.html.

Alexander the Great's life and campaigns can be explored via the links provided at http://www.socialstudiesforkids.com/subjects/alexanderthegreat.htm and http://www.historyofmacedonia.org/AncientMacedonia/AlexandertheGreat.html. However, Alexander's sojourn in India exposed him as "Alexander the Ordinary,"

according to an essay at http://sify.com/itihaas/fullstory.php?id=13225593.

The man who is considered India's first imperial ruler, Chandragupta Maurya, is the subject of study at http://en.wikipedia.org/wiki/Chandragupta_Maurya and http://www.indhistory.com/chandragupta-maurya.html. His grandson, Ashoka, is arguably one of the world's greatest monarchs. Several sites explore his achievements, including http://www.csuchico.edu/~cheinz/syllabi/asst001/spring98/Ashoka.htm. The texts of his famous edicts are illuminated at http://www.cs.colostate.edu/~malaiya/ashoka.html and http://www.indiaprofile.com/monuments-temples/ashokainscriptions.htm.

The work of one of the ancient world's finest philosophers of government, Chanakya (Kautilya), is discussed at http://www.sscnet.ucla.edu/southasia/History/Ancient/Kautilya.html, http://www.hinduism.co.za/chanakya.htm, and http://www.philosophy.ru/library/asiatica/indica/authors/kautilya/canakya_niti_sastra.html. The text of his political manual, the *Arthashastra,* is offered at http://www.fordham.edu/halsall/india/kautilya1.html, and http://www.wsu.edu:8080/~wldciv/world_civ_reader/world_civ_reader_1/arthashastra.html. Democracy as practiced in ancient India is analyzed at http://www.nipissingu.ca/department/history/muhlberger/histdem/indiadem.htm. Links and other resources for the study of "caste" in South Asia are offered at http://www.hawaii.edu/csas/caste_index.html. aspects of "caste" and the manner in which that subject is poorly represented in textbooks is discussed at http://jan.ucc.nau.edu/~sj6/elderunderstandingcaste.pdf. Social hierarchy in South Asia is placed in a global context at http://www.friesian.com/caste.htm.

The artistry of the Ajanta and Ellora religious centers is revealed at http://www.indiamonuments.org/Ajanta.htm, http://www.sscnet.ucla.edu/southasia/Culture/Archit/Ajanta.html, http://www.cs.unm.edu/~shapiro/INDIA/MIDSIZE/ellora.html, and http://www.columbia.edu/itc/mealac/pritchett/00routesdata/0600_0699/ellora/ellora.html.

The artistic global reach of the *Ramayana* can be explored in depth through text and maps at http://www.maxwell.syr.edu/moynihan/programs/sac/Outreach/ramayana/index.asp and at http://www.sscnet.ucla.edu/southasia/Religions/texts/Ramaya.html, while the grandeur of the *Mahabharata* is examined at http://web.utk.edu/~jftzgrld/MBh1Home.html. Hinduism's tents, rituals and prayers are illuminated at http://www.asia.si.edu/education/pujaonline/puja/homes.html, while a related user-friendly glimpse into the form and practice of Hindu worship is provided in exhibition form at http://www.asia.si.edu/education/pujaonline/puja/exhibit.html.

The art and politics of the imperial Guptas is explored at http://www.indhistory.com/samudragupta.html, http://www.webindia123.com/history/ANCIENT/gupta_period.htm, http://www.infoplease.com/ce6/ent/A0858793.html, and http://www.indianartcircle.com/arteducation/page_7_gupta.shtml.

AP* | Test Prep

1. The highest Hindu social class members in India after the Epic Age were usually the
   (A) Shudras (workers).
   (B) Vaisayas (merchants, herders).
   (C) Kshatriya (warriors, rulers).
   (D) Brahmans (priests, scholars).
   (E) Dasas or the Dravidian peoples.

2. A central message of the Bhagavad Gita is that
   (A) the only pathway to salvation is meditation.
   (B) a soul can be destroyed by human action.
   (C) upward mobility into higher castes was a vital social goal.
   (D) one must carry out the duties that come with one's caste.

3. A major difference between Buddhism and Hinduism was that
   (A) Buddhism denied the need for caste, rites, and sacrifice to achieve nirvana.
   (B) Buddhism monks married in splendor, most Hindu priests remained unmarried.
   (C) Buddhism denied the possibility of human rebirth or reincarnation.
   (D) Hinduism taught respect for all living things to the point of rejecting the killing of all animals.

4. Buddhism spread primarily as a result of
   (A) the appeal of its flawless performance of intricate rites.
   (B) its monastic community and related missionary activity.
   (C) the support of Gupta rulers.
   (D) successful wars against Brahman-backed political opponents.

5. Buddhism lost its appeal and influence in Guptan India in part because
   (A) Hinduism showed its adaptability by emphasizing its mystical side, thus retaining the loyalties of many Indians.
   (B) unpopular Guptas supported Buddhism, which led to Buddhism's decline.
   (C) Islam was introduced and replaced both Hinduism and Buddhism.
   (D) Hindus abandoned the caste system, making Hinduism more attractive.

6. During the classical era in India, all of the following occurred EXCEPT
   (A) the invasion of Alexander the Great prevented contacts with the Mediterranean world.
   (B) spherical shrines to Buddha, called *stupas*, were erected.
   (C) the concept of zero was invented.
   (D) sculpture and painting emphasized religious themes.

7. Over time in classical India, the caste system
   (A) died out as Buddhism spread throughout India.
   (B) intensified in complexity and began to differ from region to region.
   (C) lost its religious significance.
   (D) removed restrictions on gender

Free-Response Question

Compare and contrast the classical civilizations of India and China.

4

Classical Civilizations in the Mediterranean and Middle East

The Persian Empire: A New Perspective in the Middle East

Patterns of Greek and Roman History

Greek and Roman Political Institutions

THINKING HISTORICALLY: The Classical Mediterranean in Comparative Perspective

Religion and Culture

VISUALIZING THE PAST: Political Rituals in Persia

Economy and Society in the Mediterranean

DOCUMENT: Rome and a Values Crisis

Toward the Fall of Rome

GLOBAL CONNECTIONS: Persia, Greece, Rome, and the World

It is one of the most famous stories in history: In 490 B.C.E., the Greeks, under Athenian leaders, defeated a huge Persian army at Marathon. Fear of the Persians had run strong, and news of victory was accordingly sweet. According to legend, a Greek soldier named Pheidippides ran 26 miles to bring the word to Athens and, having delivered the message, collapsed and died. The first modern Olympic Games, in 1896, featured a long-distance endurance race called the "marathon" in memory of that great feat. Pheidippides' run reminds us not only of a great military victory and strong emotion, but of the Greeks' powerful devotion to the public good of the cities they loved.

The Persian invasion of Greece began as a punishment for the revolt of several Greek city-states against Persian rule—a revolt the Persians easily put down. Immediately following the Greek victory at the Battle of Marathon, the Persians tried to attack Athens by sea, but the Athenian soldiers had hurried back to defend their city. Vowing revenge, the Persians returned to Asia.

A new Persian king, Xerxes, took personal charge of the plan to conquer the Greeks. By 480 B.C.E. he had amassed an army and fleet that outnumbered Greek forces by two to one. Many Greek states held back, assuming the Persians would win this time. Even the Greek priests, trying to foretell the future, urged surrender. To make matters worse, a Greek traitor showed the Persians a pass that would lead them to Athens, which was indefensible. Most Athenians were evacuated to an island, where they watched the Persians set fire to their temples on the hill of the Acropolis. But Themistocles, the Athenian leader, realized that the huge Persian navy could not move fast. If it could be led into a narrow strait, where its numbers did not count, it could be defeated. Themistocles sent a slave to trick Xerxes, telling him that the Greeks were quarreling among themselves. Thinking that this was their chance to finish off the Greeks, the Persians rowed into the narrow strait of Thermopylae. There, instead of the divided and weakened opponent they were expecting, they found a united force ready to fight them. Xerxes watched the battle from a hill overlooking the strait, where he had thought he would be able to see and reward the bravest of his warriors. Instead he saw his navy virtually destroyed, and he fled.

History is full of might-have-beens. It is important to consider what would have happened if the normal advantage in military strength had prevailed and the Persians had won; and what difference this would have made to world history.

One point is sure. The battle highlighted the developments of not one but two major civilizations in the eastern Mediterranean and Middle East. A massive Persian empire developed, spurred initially by the kind of outside invasion that had earlier produced various Mesopotamian empires. But the Persian Empire grew far larger, illustrating the new capacities of the classical period. Durable political and cultural traditions were established that persisted in and around present-day Iran well beyond the classical period.

At the same time, Greek city-states established a presence along the eastern Mediterranean and into parts of southern Europe. Like China and Persia, the Greeks built on earlier civilizations, but they established a strong and independent culture of their own. Greeks thought foreigners' speech sounded like "bar, bar, bar"—so they called them barbarians, establishing Greek identity by contrast. Greek society generated less tidy political structures than China or Persia, but their expansion and outreach affected a large portion of western Asia and the eastern half of the Mediterranean basin. As Greek states faded, Alexander the Great—the young Macedonian king who had been tutored by the Greek philosopher Aristotle—forged a military empire that briefly embraced Persia as well. Through his military conquests, Greek cultural influence was spread so widely that the years that followed are known as the Hellenistic ("from the Greek") period of history. ■

Figure 4.1 Sarcophagus cover: Battle of Marathon.

The classical civilizations that sprang up on the shores of the Mediterranean Sea from about 800 B.C.E. until the fall of the Roman Empire in 476 C.E. rivaled their counterparts in India and China in richness and impact. Centered first in the peninsula of Greece, then in Rome, the new Mediterranean culture did not embrace all of the civilized lands of the ancient Middle East. Greece rebuffed the advance of the mighty Persian Empire and established some colonies on the eastern shore of the Mediterranean, in what is now Turkey, but it only briefly conquered more than a fraction of the civilized Middle East. Rome conquered a vast empire, but even it had to contend with strong kingdoms to the east. Nevertheless, Greece and Rome do not merely constitute a westward push of civilization from its earlier bases in the Middle East and along the Nile—although this is a part of their story. They also represent the formation of new institutions and values that would reverberate in the later history of the Middle East and Europe alike.

For most Americans, and not only those who are descendants of European immigrants, classical Mediterranean culture constitutes "our own" classical past, or at least a goodly part of it. The framers of the U.S. Constitution were extremely conscious of Greek and Roman precedents. Designers of public buildings in the United States, from the early days of the American republic to the present, have dutifully copied Greek and Roman models, as in the Lincoln Memorial and most state capitols. Plato and Aristotle continue to be thought of as the founders of our philosophical tradition, and skillful teachers

2000 B.C.E.	1000 B.C.E.	500 B.C.E.	250 B.C.E.	1 C.E.	250 C.E.
1700 IndoEuropean invasions of Greek peninsula 1400 Kingdom of Mycenae; Trojan War	800–600 Rise of Greek city-states; Athens and Sparta become dominant c. 700 Homerian epics *Iliad, Odyssey*; flowering of Greek architecture 550 Cyrus the Great forms Persian Empire 509 Beginnings of Roman Republic	470–430 Athens at its height: Pericles, Phidias, Sophocles, Socrates 450 Twelve Tables of Law 431–404 Peloponnesian Wars 359–336 Philip II of Macedonia 338–323 Macedonian Empire, Alexander the Great 300–100 Hellenistic period 264–146 Punic Wars	49 Julius Caesar becomes dictator in Rome; assassinated in 44 27 Augustus Caesar seizes power; rise of Roman Empire c. 4 Birth of Jesus	c. 30 Crucifixion of Jesus 63 Forced dissolution of independent Jewish state by Romans 101–106 Greatest spread of Roman territory 180 Death of Marcus Aurelius; beginning of decline of Roman Empire	313 Constantine adopts Christianity 476 Fall of Rome

still rely on some imitation of the Socratic method. Our sense of debt to Greece and Rome may inspire us to find in their history special meaning or links to our own world; the Western educational experience has long included elaborate explorations of the Greco-Roman past as part of the standard academic education. But from the standpoint of world history, greater balance is obviously necessary. Greco-Roman history is one of the three major classical civilizations, more dynamic than its Chinese and Indian counterparts in some respects but noticeably less successful in others. The challenge is to discern the leading features of Greek and Roman civilization and to compare them with those of their counterparts elsewhere. We can then clearly recognize the connections and our own debt without adhering to the notion that the Mediterranean world somehow dominated the classical period.

Classical Mediterranean civilization is complicated by the fact that it passed through two centers during its centuries of vigor, as Greek political institutions rose and then declined and the legions of Rome assumed leadership. Roman interests were not identical to those of Greece, although the Romans carefully preserved most Greek achievements. Rome mastered engineering; Greece specialized in scientific thought. Rome created a mighty empire, whereas the Greek city-states proved rather inept at forming an empire. It is possible, certainly, to see more than a change in emphases from Greece to Rome, and to talk about separate civilizations instead of a single basic pattern. And it is true that Greek influence was always stronger than Roman in the eastern Mediterranean, whereas western Europe would encounter a fuller Greco-Roman mixture, with Roman influence predominating in language and law. However, Greek and Roman societies shared many political ideas; they had a common religion and artistic styles; they developed similar economic structures. Certainly, their classical heritage would be used by successive civilizations without fine distinctions drawn between what was Greek and what was Roman.

For several centuries, the Persian Empire far surpassed Greece in significance, certainly in the Middle East but also in the eastern Mediterranean more generally. The Empire also established significant traditions that shaped a strong Persian political and cultural presence, still visible in present day Iran. And the Empire generated one of the significant religions in the world history, in Zoroastrianism. The Greek tradition was largely separate, but Greek and Persian influences interacted not only in mutual warfare, but as a result of Alexander the Great's conquests and his efforts to merge cultural strands in the vast territory that briefly came under his control.

Cyrus the Great   Established massive Persian Empire by 550 B.C.E.; successor state to Mesopotamian empires.

The Persian Empire: A New Perspective in the Middle East

The Persians worked quickly to unify their vast empire. Persia established durable political and cultural traditions.

After the fall of the great Egyptian and Hittite empires in the Middle East by 1200 B.C.E., much smaller states predominated. Then new powers stepped in, first the Assyrians and then an influx of Persians. A great conqueror, **Cyrus the Great,** emerged by 550 B.C.E. and established the massive

Persian Empire, which ran across the northern Middle East and into northwestern India. The new empire was the clearest successor to the great Mesopotamian states of the past, but it was far larger. Cyrus allowed some parts of the empire to preserve older traditions, such as the use of cuneiform writing, but he introduced important changes as well. In addition to their territorial expansion, the Persians significantly advanced iron technology in the Middle East.

For several centuries, the Persian Empire far surpassed Greece in significance, certainly in the Middle East but also in the eastern Mediterranean more generally. The Empire also established significant traditions that shaped a strong Persian political and cultural presence, still visible in present day Iran (Map 4.1).

The Persian Empire at Its Greatest Extent

Political Styles and Innovations

Persian politics featured several emphases. The first was wide tolerance. The Persian Empire embraced a host of languages and cultures, and the early Persian rulers were careful to grant considerable latitude for this diversity. Second, however, was a strong authoritarian streak. Darius, successor to Cyrus, worked hard to centralize laws and tax collection. The idea of wide participation in politics was rejected. Third, and related to the centralization process, Persian rulers developed a vital infrastructure for the whole empire. A major system of roads reduced travel time, though it still took 90 days to go from one end of the empire to the other. An east–west highway, largely paved, simplified commerce and troop movement from the Indian border to the Mediterranean, and another highway reached Egypt. Regularly spaced inns provided rest stops and fresh horses for travelers. The Persians established the first regular postal service, and they built a network of inns along their roads to accommodate travelers. These achievements would help connect the Middle East to trade routes coming from central and eastern Asia, a vital step in the growth of new trans-regional commercial connections.

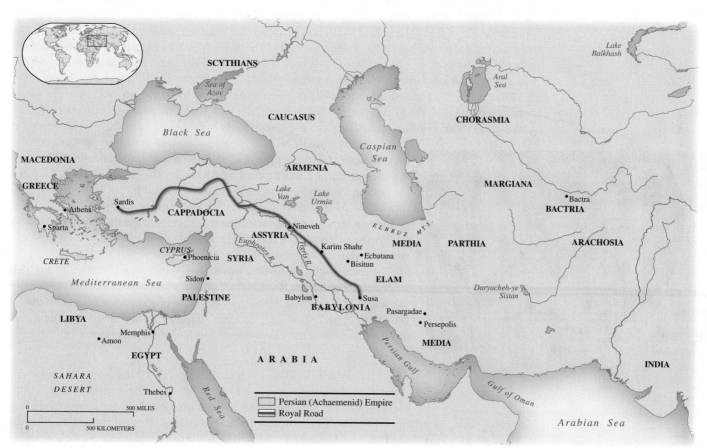

Map 4.1 Persia in Its Main Stages

Figure 4.2 Persians established a distinct artistic tradition including fine craftwork, as shown in this chariot.

Zoroastrianism [zohr-oh-AS-tree-uh-NIH-zuhm] Animist religion that saw material existence as battle between forces of good and evil; stressed the importance of moral choice; righteous lived on after death in "House of Song"; chief religion of Persian Empire.

Persian emperors, particularly Darius, who worked hard not only to expand but to integrate his vast territories, developed a substantial bureaucracy. This existed alongside an earlier, military nobility. The central government introduced several measures to control the activities of officials assigned to distant provinces. Tax collection was carefully regulated, and spies were sent out to make sure regional officials remained loyal to the central government, rather than allying with local political forces.

Persia was also the center of a major new religion. A Zoroastrianian religious leader, Zoroaster (c. 630–550 B.C.E.), revised the polytheistic religious tradition of the Sumerians through the introduction of monotheism. He banned animal sacrifice and the use of intoxicants. He introduced the idea of individual salvation through the free choice of God over the spirit of evil. Zoroaster, and the growing group of Zoroastrian priests (the *Magi*) saw life as a battle between two divine forces: good and evil. **Zoroastrianism** (zohr-oh-AS-tree-uh-NIH-zuhm) emphasized the importance of personal moral choice in picking one side or the other, with a Last Judgment ultimately deciding the eternal fate of each person. The righteous would live on in a heaven, the "House of Song," while the evil would be condemned to eternal pain. Zoroastrianism influenced Persia's later emperors and spread widely in the population as a whole. A Greek traveler, Herodotus, noted that the Persian religion was much more spiritual than that of the Greeks, for they did not believe in humanlike gods.

Indeed, the Persian religious influence would prove far greater than that of the Greeks, through Greek culture had wide impact in other respects. Only small groups of Zoroastrians survive in the world today, in Iran and through immigration in a few other places including the United States. But the religion retained a wide hold for a considerable period of time and its ideas and beliefs strongly affected Judaism, Christianity and Islam. Religion did not consume all of Persian cultural energies. An important artistic tradition also emerged with distinctive styles of painting and architecture (See Figure 4.3).

Later kings expanded Persian holdings. They were unable to conquer Greece, but they long dominated much of the Middle East, providing an extensive period of peace and prosperity. Conquests also extended into North Africa and the Indian River valley. At its height, Persia embraced at least fourteen million people. The population of Persia proper (present-day Iran), at four million people, had doubled under imperial rule. Ultimately, the Persian Empire was toppled by Alexander the Great, a Greek-educated conqueror. Persian language and culture survived in the northeastern portion of the Middle East, periodically affecting developments in the region as a whole. After the Hellenistic period, a series of Persian empires arose in the northeastern part of the Middle East, competing with Roman holdings and later states.

Persian political institutions strongly impressed Alexander and his successors. Persian art would affect not only the region, but also India and the wider Middle East. Zoroastrianism, one of the major belief systems of the classical period, would ultimately fade in its competition with Islam, but its hold and influences continued well beyond the classical centuries.

Patterns of Greek and Roman History

Even as Persia developed, a new civilization took shape to the west, building on a number of earlier precedents. The river valley civilizations of the Middle East and Africa had spread to some of the islands near the Greek peninsula, although less to the peninsula itself. The island of Crete, in particular,

Figure 4.3 Using ceremonial styles similar to those of earlier Mesopotamia, the Persian Empire celebrated its powerful kings. This wall relief is on the great ceremonial stairway leading to the royal audience hall of Darius and Xerxes.

showed the results of Egyptian influence by 2000 B.C.E., and from this the Greeks were later able to develop a taste for monumental architecture. The Greeks were an Indo-European people, like the Aryan conquerors of India, who took over the peninsula by 1700 B.C.E. An early kingdom in southern Greece, strongly influenced by Crete, developed by 1400 B.C.E. around the city of Mycenae. This was the kingdom later memorialized in Homer's epics about the Trojan War. Mycenae was then toppled by a subsequent wave of Indo-European invaders, whose incursions destroyed civilization on the peninsula until about 800 B.C.E.

Stages in Greek Development

The rapid rise of civilization in Greece between 800 and 600 B.C.E. was based on the creation of strong city-states, rather than a single political unit. Each city-state had its own government, typically either a tyranny of one ruler or an aristocratic council. The city-state served Greece well, for the peninsula was so divided by mountains that a unified government would have been difficult to establish. Trade developed rapidly under city-state sponsorship, and common cultural forms, including a rich written language with letters derived from the Phoenician alphabet, spread throughout the peninsula. The Greek city-states also joined in regular celebrations such as the athletic competitions of the **Olympic Games.** Sparta and Athens came to be the two leading city-states. The first represented a strong military aristocracy dominating a slave population; the other was a more diverse commercial state, also including the extensive use of slaves, justly proud of its artistic and intellectual leadership. Between 500 and 449 B.C.E., the two states cooperated, along with smaller states, to defeat the huge Persian invasion. It was during and immediately after this period that Greek and particularly Athenian culture reached its highest point. Also during this period several city-states, and again particularly Athens, developed more colonies in the eastern Mediterranean and southern Italy, as Greek culture fanned out to create a larger zone of civilization (Map 4.2).

Greek culture reached its height during the 5th century B.C.E.; its influence spread through the empire of Alexander the Great.

Rome was deeply influenced by Greek tradition as it developed its Republic and its Empire.

 Greece in the Archaic and Classical Ages

Olympic games   One of the pan-Hellenic rituals observed by all Greek city-states; involved athletic competitions and ritual celebrations.

Map 4.2 Greece and Greek Colonies, c. 431 B.C.E.   On the eve of the Peloponnesian Wars, Greek civilization had succeeded in spreading to key points around the Mediterranean world.

Pericles [PEHR-uh-kleez] Athenian political leader during 5th century B.C.E.; guided development of Athenian Empire; died during early stages of Peloponnesian War.

Peloponnesian Wars [PEL-uh-poh-nee-zhun] Wars from 431 to 404 B.C.E. between Athens and Sparta for dominance in southern Greece; resulted in Spartan victory but failure to achieve political unification of Greece.

The Peloponnesian War

The Conquests of Alexander the Great

Philip II   Ruled Macedon from 359 to 336 B.C.E.; founder of centralized kingdom; later conquered rest of Greece, which was subjected to Macedonian authority.

Hellenistic period   That culture associated with the spread of Greek influence as a result of Macedonian conquests; often seen as the combination of Greek culture with eastern political forms.

Alexandria, Egypt   One of the cities founded by and named for Alexander the Great; site of ancient Mediterranean's greatest library; center of literary studies.

It was during the 5th century B.C.E. that the most famous Greek political figure, **Pericles** (PEHR-uh-kleez), dominated Athenian politics. Pericles was an aristocrat, but he was part of a democratic political structure in which each citizen could participate in city-state assemblies to select officials and pass laws. Pericles ruled not through official position but by wise influence and negotiation. He helped restrain some of the more aggressive views of the Athenian democrats, who urged even further expansion of the empire to garner more wealth and build the economy. Ultimately, however, Pericles' guidance could not prevent the tragic war between Athens and Sparta that would deplete both sides.

Political decline soon set in, as Athens and Sparta vied for control of Greece during the bitter **Peloponnesian** (PEL-uh-poh-nee-zhun) **Wars** (431–404 B.C.E.). Ambitious kings from Macedonia, in the northern part of the peninsula, soon conquered the cities. **Philip II of Macedon** won the crucial battle in 338 B.C.E., and then his son Alexander extended the Macedonian Empire through the Middle East, across Persia to the border of India, and southward through Egypt (Map 4.3). Alexander the Great's empire was short-lived, for its creator died at the age of 33 after a mere 13 years of breathtaking conquests. However, successor regional kingdoms continued to rule much of the eastern Mediterranean for several centuries. Under their aegis, Greek art and culture merged with other Middle Eastern forms during the **Hellenistic period,** the name derived because of the influence of the Hellenes, as the Greeks were known. Although there was little political activity under the autocratic Hellenistic kings, trade flourished and important scientific centers were established in such cities as **Alexandria** in Egypt. In sum, the Hellenistic period saw the consolidation of Greek civilization even after the political decline of the peninsula itself, as well as some important new cultural developments.

Rome

The rise of Rome formed the final phase of classical Mediterranean civilization, for by the first century B.C.E. Rome had subjugated Greece and the Hellenistic kingdoms alike. The Roman state began humbly enough, as a local monarchy in central Italy around 800 B.C.E. Roman aristocrats succeeded in driving

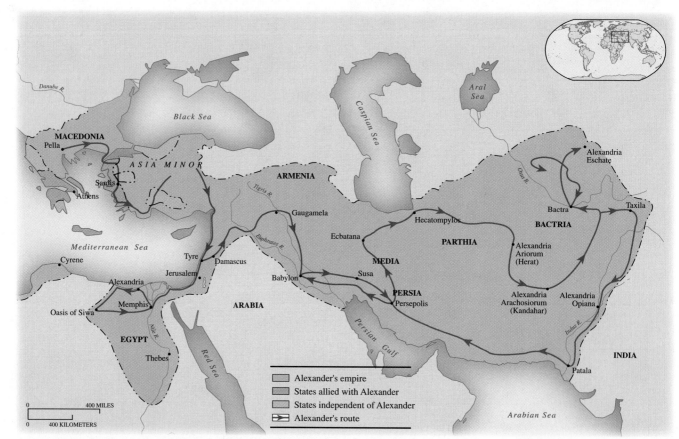

Map 4.3 Alexander's Empire, c. 323 B.C.E., and the Hellenistic World   Note the movement through Persia and other parts of the northern Middle East, and into the Indian subcontinent and North Africa.

out the monarchy around 509 B.C.E. and established more elaborate political institutions for their city-state. The new **Roman republic** gradually extended its influence over the rest of the Italian peninsula, among other things conquering the Greek colonies in the south. Thus, the Romans early acquired a strong military orientation, although initially they may have been driven simply by a desire to protect their own territory from possible rivals. Roman conquest spread more widely during the three **Punic Wars,** from 264 to 146 B.C.E., during which Rome fought the armies of the Phoenician city of **Carthage,** situated on the northern coast of Africa. These wars included a bloody defeat of the invading forces of the brilliant Carthaginian general **Hannibal,** whose troops were accompanied by pack-laden elephants. The war was so bitter that the Romans in a final act of destruction spread salt around Carthage to prevent agriculture from surviving there. Following the final destruction of Carthage, the Romans proceeded to seize the entire western Mediterranean along with Greece and Egypt.

The politics of the Roman republic grew increasingly unstable, however, as victorious generals sought even greater power while the poor of the city rebelled. Civil wars between two generals led to a victory by **Julius Caesar,** in 45 B.C.E., and the effective end of the traditional institutions of the Roman state. Caesar's grandnephew, ultimately called **Augustus Caesar,** seized power in 27 B.C.E., following another period of rivalry after Julius Caesar's assassination, and established the basic structures of the Roman Empire. For 200 years, through the reign of the emperor Marcus Aurelius in 180 C.E., the empire maintained great vigor, bringing peace and prosperity to virtually the entire Mediterranean world, from Spain and north Africa in the west to the eastern shores of the great sea. The emperors also moved northward, conquering France and southern Britain and pushing into Germany. Here was a major, if somewhat tenuous, extension of the sway of Mediterranean civilization to western Europe (Map 4.4).

Then the empire suffered a slow but decisive fall that lasted over 250 years, until invading peoples from the north finally overturned the government in Rome in 476 C.E. The decline manifested itself in terms of both economic deterioration and population loss: trade levels and the birth rate both fell. Government also became generally less effective, although some strong later emperors, particularly **Diocletian** and **Constantine,** attempted to reverse the tide. It was the emperor Constantine who, in 313, adopted the then somewhat obscure religion called Christianity in an attempt to unite the empire in new ways. However, particularly in the western half of the empire, most effective government became local, as the imperial administration could no longer guarantee order or provide a system of justice. The Roman armies depended increasingly on non-Roman recruits, whose loyalty was suspect. Then, in this deepening mire, the invasion of nomadic peoples from the north marked the end of the classical period of Mediterranean civilization—a civilization that, like its counterparts in Gupta India and Han China during the same approximate period, could no longer defend itself.

Roman republic The balanced constitution of Rome from c. 510 to 47 B.C.E.; featured an aristocratic Senate, a panel of magistrates, and several popular assemblies.

Punic Wars Fought between Rome and Carthage to establish dominance in the western Mediterranean; won by Rome after three separate conflicts.

Carthage Originally a Phoenician colony in northern Africa; became a major port and commercial power in the western Mediterranean; fought the Punic Wars with Rome for dominance of the western Mediterranean.

The Career of Julius Caesar

Hannibal Great Carthaginian general during Second Punic War; successfully invaded Italy but failed to conquer Rome; finally defeated at Battle of Zama.

Caesar, Julius Roman general responsible for conquest of Gaul; brought army back to Rome and overthrew republic; assassinated in 44 B.C.E. by conservative senators.

The Roman Empire at Its Greatest Extent

Augustus Caesar (63 B.C.E.–14 C.E.) Name given to Octavian following his defeat of Mark Anthony and Cleopatra; first emperor of Rome.

Diocletian Roman emperor from 284 to 305 C.E.; restored later empire by improved administration and tax collection.

Constantine Roman emperor from 312 to 337 C.E.; established second capital at Constantinople; attempted to use religious force of Christianity to unify empire spiritually.

Map 4.4 The Roman Empire from Augustus to 180 C.E.   The empire expanded greatly in its first centuries, but such far-flung colonies proved impossible to maintain, both militarily and economically.

In sum, the Mediterranean civilization was built on earlier cultures along the eastern Mediterranean and within the Greek islands, taking firm shape with the rise of the Greek city-states after 800 B.C.E. These states began as monarchies but then evolved into more complex and diverse political forms. They also developed a more varied commercial economy, moving away from a purely grain-growing agriculture; this spurred the formation of a number of colonial outposts around the eastern Mediterranean and in Italy. The decline of the city-states ushered in the Macedonian conquest and the formation of a wider Hellenistic culture that established deep roots in the Middle East and Egypt. Then Rome, initially a minor regional state distinguished by political virtue and stability, embarked on its great conquests, which would bring it control of the Mediterranean with important extensions into western and southeastern Europe plus the whole of north Africa. Rome's expansion ultimately overwhelmed its own republic, but the successor empire developed important political institutions of its own and resulted in two centuries of peace and glory.

Greek and Roman Political Institutions

Greece and Rome were ruled by aristocrats but also introduced some democratic elements.

The Roman Empire encompassed a huge territory and population.

polis   City-state form of government; typical of Greek political organization from 800 to 400 B.C.E. (pl. poleis).

Politics were very important in classical Mediterranean civilization, from the Greek city-states through the early part of the Roman Empire. Indeed, our word *politics* comes from the Greek word for city-state, **polis,** which correctly suggests that intense political interests were part of life in a city-state in both Greece and Rome. The "good life" for an upper-class Athenian or Roman included active participation in politics and frequent discussions about the affairs of state. The local character of Mediterranean politics, whereby the typical city-state governed a surrounding territory of several hundred square miles, contributed to this intense preoccupation with politics. Citizens felt that the state was theirs, that they had certain rights and obligations without which their government could not survive. In the Greek city-states and also under the Roman republic, citizens actively participated in the military, which further contributed to this sense of political interest and responsibility. Under the Roman Empire, of course, political concerns were restricted by the sheer power of the emperor and his officers. Even then, however, local city-states retained considerable autonomy in Italy, Greece, and the eastern Mediterranean—the empire did not try to administer most local regions in great detail. The minority of people throughout the empire who were Roman citizens were intensely proud of this privilege.

Strong political ideals and interests created some similarities between Greco-Roman society and the Confucian values of classical China, although the concept of active citizenship was distinctive in the Mediterranean cultures. However, Greece and Rome did not develop a single or cohesive set of political institutions to rival China's divinely sanctioned emperor or its elaborate bureaucracy. So in addition to political intensity and localism as characteristics of Mediterranean civilization, we must note great diversity in political forms. Here the comparison extends to India, where various political forms—including participation in governing councils—ran strong. Later societies, in reflecting on classical Mediterranean civilization, selected from a number of political precedents. Monarchy was not a preferred form; the Roman republic and most Greek city-states had abolished early monarchies as part of their prehistory. Rule by individual strongmen was more common, and our word *tyranny* comes from this experience in classical Greece. Many tyrants were effective rulers, particularly in promoting public works and protecting the common people against the abuses of the aristocracy. Some of the Roman generals who seized power in the later days of the republic had similar characteristics, as did the Hellenistic kings who succeeded Alexander in ruling regions of his empire.

Greece

direct democracy   Where people participate directly in assemblies that make laws and select leaders, rather than electing representatives.

Democracy (the word is derived from the Greek *demos,* "the people") was another important political alternative in classical Mediterranean society. The Athenian city-state traveled furthest in this direction, before and during the Peloponnesian Wars, after earlier experiences with aristocratic rule and with several tyrants. In 5th-century Athens, the major decisions of state were made by general assemblies in which all citizens could participate—although usually only a minority attended. This was **direct democracy,** not rule through elected representatives. The assembly met every 10 days. Executive officers, including judges, were chosen for brief terms to control their power, and they

The Classical Mediterranean in Comparative Perspective

The three great classical civilizations lend themselves to a variety of comparisons. The general tone of each differed from the others, ranging from India's otherworldly strain to China's emphasis on government centralization, although it is important to note the varieties of activities and interests and the changes that occurred in each of the three societies. Basic comparisons include several striking similarities. Each classical society developed empires. Each relied primarily on an agricultural economy. Greco-Roman interest in secular culture bears some resemblance to Confucian emphasis in China, although in each case religious currents remained as well. But Greco-Roman political values and institutions differed from the Confucian emphasis on deference and bureaucratic training. Greek definitions of science contrasted with those of India and China, particularly in the emphasis on theory. Several focal points can be used for comparison.

> Each classical civilization emphasized a clear social hierarchy, with substantial distance between elites and the majority of people who did the manual and menial work.

Each classical civilization emphasized a clear social hierarchy, with substantial distance between elites and the majority of people who did the manual and menial work. This vital similarity between the civilizations reflected common tensions between complex leadership demands and lifestyles and the limited economic resources of the agricultural economy. Groups at the top of the social hierarchy judged that they had to control lower groups carefully to ensure their own prosperity. Each classical society generated ideologies that explained and justified the great social divisions. Philosophers and religious leaders devoted great attention to this subject.

Within this common framework, however, there were obvious differences. Groups at the top of the social pyramid reflected different value systems. The priests in India, the bureaucrats in China, and the aristocrats in Greece and the Roman republic predominated. The status of merchants varied despite the vital role commerce played in all three civilizations.

Opportunities for mobility varied also. India's caste system allowed movement within castes, if wealth was acquired, but little overall mobility. This was the most rigid classical social structure because it tied people to their basic social and occupational position by birth. China's bureaucratic system allowed a very small number of talented people from below to rise on the basis of education, but most bureaucrats continued to come from the landed aristocracy. Mediterranean society, with its aristocratic emphasis, limited opportunities to rise to the top, but the importance of acquired wealth (particularly in Rome) gave some nonaristocrats important economic and political opportunities. Cicero, for example, came from a merchant family. Various classes also shared some political power in city-state assemblies; the idea of citizens holding basic political rights across class lines was unusual in classical civilizations.

Each classical civilization distinctively defined the position of the lowest orders. India's untouchables performed duties culturally evaluated as demeaning but often vital. So did China's "mean people," who included actors. As Greece and then Rome expanded, they relied heavily on the legal and physical compulsions of slavery to provide menial service and demanding labor. Greece and Rome gave unusual voice to farmers when they maintained their own property but tended to scorn manual labor itself, a view that helped justify and was perpetuated by slavery. Confucianism urged deference but offered praise for peasant work.

Finally, each classical civilization developed a different cultural glue to help hold its social hierarchy together. Greece and Rome left much of the task of managing the social hierarchy to local authorities; community bonds, as in the city-states, were meant to pull different groups into a sense of common purpose. They also relied on military force and clear legal statements that defined rights according to station. Force and legal inequalities played important roles in China and India as well, but there were additional inducements. India's Hinduism helped justify and sustain the hierarchy by promising rewards through reincarnation for those who submitted to their place in any given existence. Chinese Confucianism urged general cultural values of obedience and self-restraint, creating some agreement—despite varied religions and philosophies—on the legitimacy of social ranks by defining how gentlemen and commoners should behave.

In no case did the social cement work perfectly; social unrest surfaced in all the classical civilizations, as in major slave rebellions in the Roman countryside or peasant uprisings in China. At the same time, the rigidity of classical social structures gave many common people some leeway. Elites viewed the masses as being so different from themselves that they did not try to revamp all their beliefs or community institutions.

Differences in approach to social inequality nevertheless had important results. China and particularly India generated value systems that might convince people in the lower classes and the upper ranks that there was some legitimacy in the social hierarchy. Greece and Rome attempted a more difficult task in emphasizing the importance of aristocracy while offering some other elements a share in the political system. This combination could work well, although some groups, including slaves and women, were always excluded. It tended to deteriorate, however, when poorer citizens lost property. Yet no sweeping new social theory emerged to offer a different kind of solace to the masses until Christianity began to spread. It is no accident, then, that Indian and Chinese social structures survived better than Mediterranean structures did, lasting well beyond the classical period into the modern era.

QUESTIONS Why did the classical civilizations seem to need radical social inequalities? What was the relationship between wealth and social position in each classical civilization? If India used religion to compensate for social inequalities, what did China and the Mediterranean cultures use?

were subject to review by the assembly. Furthermore, they were chosen by lot, not elected—on the principle that any citizen could and should be able to serve. To be sure, only a minority of the Athenian population were active citizens. Women had no rights of political participation. And half of all adult males were not citizens at all, being slaves or foreigners. This, then, was not exactly the kind of democracy we envision today. But it did elicit widespread popular participation and devotion, and certainly embodied principles that we would recognize as truly democratic. Pericles, who led Athens during its decades of greatest glory between the final defeat of the Persians and the agony of war with Sparta, described the system this way:

> The administration is in the hands of the many and not of the few. But while the law secures equal justice to all alike in their private disputes, the claim of excellence is also recognized; and when a citizen is in any way distinguished he is preferred to the public service, not as a matter of privilege but as the reward of merit. Neither is poverty a bar, but a man may benefit his country whatever be the obscurity of his condition.

During the Peloponnesian Wars, Athens even demonstrated some of the potential drawbacks of democracy. Lower-class citizens, eager for government jobs and the spoils of war, often encouraged reckless military actions that weakened the state in its central dispute with Sparta.

Neither tyranny nor democracy, however, was the most characteristic political form in the classical Mediterranean world. The most widely preferred political framework centered on the existence of aristocratic assemblies, whose deliberations established guidelines for state policy and served as a check on executive power. Thus, Sparta was governed by a singularly militaristic aristocracy, intent on retaining power over a large slave population. Other Greek city-states, although less bent on disciplining their elites for rigorous military service, also featured aristocratic assemblies. Even Athens during much of its democratic phase found leadership in many aristocrats, including Pericles himself. The word *aristocracy,* which comes from Greek terms meaning "rule of the best," suggests where many Greeks—particularly, of course, aristocrats themselves—thought real political virtue lay.

Comparing Athens and Sparta   CASE STUDY

Rome

The constitution of the Roman republic tried to reconcile the various elements suggested by the Greek political experience, with primary reliance on the principle of aristocracy. All Roman citizens in the republic could gather in periodic assemblies, the function of which was not to pass basic laws but rather to elect various magistrates, some of whom were specifically entrusted with the task of representing the interests of the common people. The most important legislative body was the **Senate,** composed mainly of aristocrats, whose members held virtually all executive offices in the Roman state. Two **consuls** shared primary executive power, but in times of crisis the Senate could choose a dictator to hold emergency authority until the crisis had passed. In the Roman Senate, as in the aristocratic assemblies of the Greek city-states, the ideal of public service, featuring eloquent public speaking and arguments that sought to identify the general good, came closest to realization.

The diversity of Greek and Roman political forms, as well as the importance ascribed to political participation, helped generate a significant body of political theory in classical Mediterranean civilization. True to the aristocratic tradition, much of this theory dealt with appropriate political ethics, the duties of citizens, the importance of incorruptible service, and key political skills such as oratory. Roman writers like **Cicero,** himself an active senator, expounded eloquently on these subjects. Some of this political writing resembled Confucianism, although there was less emphasis on hierarchy and obedience or bureaucratic virtues, and more on participation in deliberative bodies that would make laws and judge the actions of executive officers. Classical Mediterranean writers also paid great attention to the structure of the state itself, debating the virtues and vices of the various political forms. This kind of theory both expressed the political interests and diversity of the Mediterranean world and served as a key heritage to later societies.

The Roman Empire was a different sort of political system from the earlier city-states, although it preserved some older institutions, such as the Senate, which became a rather meaningless forum for debates. Of necessity, the empire developed organizational capacities on a far larger scale than the city-states; it is important to remember, however, that considerable local autonomy prevailed in many regions. Only in rare cases, such as the forced dissolution of the independent Jewish

Senate Assembly of Roman aristocrats; advised on policy within the republic; one of the early elements of the Roman constitution.

consuls Two chief executives or magistrates of the Roman republic; elected by an annual assembly dominated by aristocracy.

Cicero (106–43 B.C.E.) Conservative Roman senator; Stoic philosopher; one of great orators of his day; killed in reaction to assassination of Julius Caesar.

state in 63 C.E. after a major local rebellion, did the Romans take over distant areas completely. Careful organization was particularly evident in the vast hierarchy of the Roman army, whose officers wielded great political power even over the emperors themselves.

In addition to considerable tolerance for local customs and religions, plus strong military organization, the Romans emphasized carefully crafted laws as the one factor that would hold their vast territories together. Greek and Roman republican leaders had already developed an understanding of the importance of codified, equitable law. Aristocratic leaders in 8th-century Athens, for example, sponsored clear legal codes designed to balance the defense of private property with the protection of poor citizens, including access to courts of law administered by fellow citizens. The early Roman republic introduced its first code of law, the Twelve Tables, by 450 B.C.E. These early Roman laws were intended, among other things, to restrain the upper classes from arbitrary action and to subject them, as well as ordinary people, to some common legal principles. The Roman Empire carried these legal interests still further, in the belief that law should evolve to meet changing conditions without, however, fluctuating wildly.

The idea of Roman law was that rules, objectively judged, rather than personal whim should govern social relationships; thus, the law steadily took over matters of judgment earlier reserved for fathers of families or for landlords. Roman law also promoted the importance of common-sense fairness. In one case cited in the law texts of the empire, a slave was being shaved by a barber in a public square; two men were playing ball nearby, and one accidentally hit the barber with the ball, causing him to cut the slave's throat. Who was responsible for the tragedy: the barber, catcher, or pitcher? According to Roman law, the slave—for anyone so foolish as to be shaved in a public place was asking for trouble and bore the responsibility himself.

Slaves in Roman Law

Roman law codes spread widely through the empire, and with them came the notion of law as the regulator of social life. Many non-Romans were given the right of citizenship—although most ordinary people outside Rome preferred to maintain their local allegiances. With citizenship, however, came full access to Rome-appointed judges and uniform laws. Imperial law codes also regulated property rights and commerce, thus creating some economic unity in the vast empire. The idea of fair and reasoned law, to which officers of the state should themselves be subject, was a key political achievement of the Roman Empire, comparable in importance, although quite different in nature, to the Chinese elaboration of a complex bureaucratic structure.

The Greeks and Romans were less innovative in the functions they ascribed to government than in the political forms and theories they developed. Most governments concentrated on maintaining systems of law courts and military forces. Athens and, more durably and successfully, Rome placed great premium on the importance of military conquest. Mediterranean governments regulated some branches of commerce, particularly in the interest of securing vital supplies of grain. Rome, indeed, undertook vast public works in the form of roads and harbors to facilitate military transport as well as commerce. And the Roman state, especially under the empire, built countless stadiums and public baths to entertain and distract its subjects. The city of Rome, which at its peak contained over a million inhabitants, provided cheap food as well as gladiator contests and other entertainment for the masses—the famous "bread and circuses" that were designed to prevent popular disorder. Colonies of Romans elsewhere were also given theaters and stadiums. This provided solace in otherwise strange lands like England or Palestine.

Governments also supported an official religion, sponsoring public ceremonies to honor the gods and goddesses; civic religious festivals were important events that both expressed and encouraged widespread loyalty to the state. However, there was little attempt to impose this religion on everyone, and other religious practices were tolerated so long as they did not conflict with loyalty to the state. Even the later Roman emperors, who advanced the idea that the emperor was a god as a means of strengthening authority, were normally tolerant of other religions. They only attacked Christianity, and then irregularly, because of the Christians' refusal to place the state first in their devotion.

Localism and fervent political interests, including a sense of intense loyalty to the state; a diversity of political systems together with the preference for aristocratic rule; the importance of law and the development of an unusually elaborate and uniform set of legal principles—these were the chief political legacies of the classical Mediterranean world. The sheer accomplishment of the Roman Empire, which united a region never before or since brought together, still stands as one of the great political monuments of world history. This was a distinctive political mix. Although there was attention to careful legal procedures, no clear definition of individuals' rights existed. Indeed, the emphasis on duties to the state could lead, as in Sparta, to an essentially totalitarian framework in which the state controlled even the raising of children. Nor, until the peaceful centuries of the early Roman Empire, was it an entirely successful political structure, as wars and instability were common. Nonetheless, there can be no question of the richness of this political culture or of its central importance to the Greeks and Romans themselves.

Religion and Culture

Greece and Rome did not generate a major religion.

The Greeks and Romans did not create a significant, world-class religion; in this they differed from India and Persia and to some extent from China. Christianity, which was to become one of the major world religions, did of course arise during the Roman Empire. It owed some of its rapid geographical spread to the ease of movement within the huge Roman Empire. However, Christianity was not really a product of Greek or Roman culture, although it would ultimately be influenced by this culture. It took on serious historical importance only as the Roman Empire began its decline. The characteristic Greco-Roman religion was a much more primitive affair, derived from a belief in the spirits of nature elevated into a complex set of gods and goddesses who were seen as regulating human life. Greeks and Romans had different names for their pantheon, but the objects of worship were essentially the same: a creator or father god, Zeus or Jupiter, presided over an unruly assemblage of gods and goddesses whose functions ranged from regulating the daily passage of the sun (Apollo) or the oceans (Neptune) to inspiring war (Mars) or human love and beauty (Venus). Specific gods were the patrons of other human activities such as metalworking, the hunt, even literature and history. Regular ceremonies to the gods had real political importance, and many individuals sought the gods' aid in foretelling the future or in ensuring a good harvest or good health.

Philosophy, science, and art were the most durable elements of classical Mediterranean culture.

Religious Values

In addition to its political functions, Greco-Roman religion had certain other features. It tended to be rather human, of-this-world in its approach. The doings of the gods made for good storytelling; they read like soap operas on a superhuman scale. Thus, the classical Mediterranean religion early engendered an important literary tradition, as was also the case in India. (Indeed, Greco-Roman and Indian religious lore reflected the common heritage of Indo-European invaders.) The gods were often used to illustrate human passions and foibles, thus serving as symbols of a serious inquiry into human nature. Unlike the Indians, however, the Greeks and Romans became interested in their gods more in terms of what they could do for and reveal about humankind on this earth than the principles that could elevate people toward higher planes of spirituality (Figure 4.4).

Aristotle (384–322 B.C.E.) Greek philosopher; teacher of Alexander the Great; knowledge based on observation of phenomena in material world.

Stoics Hellenistic group of philosophers; emphasized inner moral independence cultivated by strict discipline of the body and personal bravery.

This dominant religion also had a number of limitations. Its lack of spiritual passion failed to satisfy many ordinary workers and peasants, particularly in times of political chaos or economic distress. "Mystery" religions, often imported from the Middle East, periodically swept through Greece and Rome, providing secret rituals and fellowship and a greater sense of contact with unfathomable divine powers. Even more than in China, a considerable division arose between upper-class and popular belief.

The gods and goddesses of Greco-Roman religion left many upper-class people dissatisfied also. They provided stories about how the world came to be, but little basis for a systematic inquiry into nature or human society. And while the dominant religion promoted political loyalty, it did not provide a basis for ethical thought. Hence, many thinkers, both in Greece and Rome, sought a separate model for ethical behavior. Greek and Roman moral philosophy, as issued by philosophers like **Aristotle** and Cicero, typically stressed the importance of moderation and balance in human behavior as opposed to the instability of much political life and the excesses of the gods themselves. Other ethical systems were devised, particularly during the Hellenistic period. Thus, **Stoics** emphasized an inner moral independence, to be cultivated by strict discipline of the body and by personal bravery. These ethical systems, established largely apart from religious considerations, were major contributions in their own right; they would also be blended with later religious thought, under Christianity.

Figure 4.4 After murdering his wife and children Hercules, who became the Greeks' greatest mythical hero, was sentenced to perform 12 tasks that would have been impossible for most mortals. This vase depicts the fourth labor of Hercules, in which he was ordered to capture the Erymanthian boar and bring it to his master, Eurystheus. The frightened Eurystheus has hidden in a wine jar.
(Copyright The British Museum)

Philosophy and Science

The need for a philosophy separate from the official religion helped generate classical Mediterranean political theory, which made little reference to religious principles. Mediterranean philosophy also considerably emphasized the powers of human thought. In Athens, **Socrates** (born in 469 B.C.E.) encouraged his pupils to question conventional wisdom, on the grounds that the chief human duty was "the improvement of the soul." Socrates ran afoul of the Athenian government, which thought that he was undermining political loyalty; given the choice of suicide or exile, Socrates chose the former. However, the Socratic principle of rational inquiry by means of skeptical questioning became a recurrent strand in classical Greek thinking and in its heritage to later societies. Thus, a philosophical tradition arose in Greece, although in very diverse individual expressions, which tended to deemphasize the importance of human spirituality in favor of a celebration of the human ability to think. The result bore some similarities to Chinese Confucianism, although with greater emphasis on skeptical questioning and abstract speculations about the basic nature of humanity and the universe.

Socrates Athenian philosopher of later 5th century B.C.E.; tutor of Plato; urged rational reflection of moral decisions; condemned to death for corrupting minds of Athenian young.

Greek interest in rationality carried over to an inquiry into the underlying order of physical nature. The Greeks were not outstanding empirical scientists. Relatively few new scientific findings emanated from Athens, or later from Rome, although philosophers like Aristotle did collect large amounts of biological data. The Greek interest lay in speculations about nature's order, and many non-Westerners believe that this tradition continues to inform what they see as an excessive Western passion for seeking basic rationality in the universe. In practice, the Greek concern translated into a host of theories, some of which were wrong, about the motions of the planets and the organization of the elemental principles of earth, fire, air, and water, and into a considerable interest in mathematics as a means of rendering nature's patterns comprehensible. Greek and later Hellenistic work in geometry was particularly impressive, featuring among other achievements the basic theorems of Pythagoras. Scientists during the Hellenistic period, working mainly in Egypt or the Middle East, made some important empirical contributions, especially in studies of anatomy; medical treatises by Galen were not improved on, in the Western world, for many centuries. The mathematician Euclid produced what was long the world's most widely used compendium of geometry. Less fortunately, the Hellenistic astronomer Ptolemy produced an elaborate theory of the sun's motion around a stationary earth. This new Hellenistic theory contradicted much earlier Middle Eastern astronomy, which had recognized the earth's rotation; nonetheless, it was Ptolemy's theory that was long taken as fixed wisdom in Western thought.

Roman intellectuals, actively examining ethical and political theory, had nothing to add to Greek and Hellenistic science. They did help to preserve this tradition in the form of textbooks that were administered to upper-class schoolchildren. The Roman genius was more practical than the Greek and included engineering achievements such as the great roads and aqueducts that carried water to cities large and small. Roman ability to construct elaborate arches so that buildings could carry great structural weight was unsurpassed anywhere in the world. These feats, too, would leave their mark, as Rome's huge edifices long served as a reminder of ancient glories. But ultimately, it was the Greek and Hellenistic impulse to extend human reason to nature's principles that would result in the most impressive legacy.

In classical Mediterranean civilization, however, science and mathematics loomed far less large than art and literature in conveying key cultural values. The official religion inspired themes for artistic expression and the justification for temples, statues, and plays devoted to the glories of the gods. Nonetheless, the human-centered qualities of the Greeks and Romans also registered, as artists emphasized the beauty of realistic portrayals of the human form and poets and playwrights used the gods as foils for inquiries into the human condition. Early Greek poets included a woman author, Sappho (around 600 B.C.E.).

All the arts received some attention in classical Mediterranean civilization. Performances of music and dance were vital parts of religious festivals, but their precise styles have unfortunately not been preserved. Far more durable was the Greek interest in drama, for plays, more than poetry, took a central role in this culture. Greek dramatists produced both comedy and tragedy, indeed making a formal division between the two approaches that is still part of the Western tradition, as in the labeling of current television shows as either form. On the whole, in contrast to Indian writers, the Greeks placed the greatest emphasis on tragedy. Their belief in human reason and balance

Sophocles, *Antigone*

Sophocles (496–406 B.C.E.) Greek writer of tragedies; author of *Oedipus Rex*.

Homer, *The Iliad*

Iliad Greek epic poem attributed to Homer but possibly the work of many authors; defined gods and human nature that shaped Greek mythos.

Odyssey Greek epic poem attributed to Homer but possibly the work of many authors; defined gods and human nature that shaped Greek mythos.

Doric Along with Ionian and Corinthian, distinct style of Hellenistic architecture; the least ornate of the three styles.

Ionic Along with Doric and Corinthian, distinct style of Hellenistic architecture; more ornate than Doric but less than Corinthian.

The Athenian Acropolis

Corinthian Along with Doric and Ionian, distinct style of Hellenistic architecture; the most ornate of the three styles.

Roman Coliseum

also involved a sense that these virtues were precarious, so a person could easily become ensnared in situations of powerful emotion and uncontrollable consequences. The Athenian dramatist **Sophocles,** for example, so insightfully portrayed the psychological flaws of his hero Oedipus that modern psychology long used the term *Oedipus complex* to refer to a potentially unhealthy relationship between a man and his mother.

Greek literature contained a strong epic tradition as well, starting with the beautifully crafted tales of the **Iliad** and **Odyssey,** attributed to the poet Homer, who lived in the 8th century B.C.E. Roman authors, particularly the poet Vergil, also worked in the epic form, seeking to link Roman history and mythology with the Greek forerunner. Roman writers made significant contributions to poetry and to definitions of the poetic form that would long be used in Western literature. The overall Roman literary contribution was less impressive than the Greek, but it was substantial enough both to provide important examples of how poetry should be written and to furnish abundant illustrations of the literary richness of the Latin language.

In the visual arts, the emphasis of classical Mediterranean civilization was sculpture and architecture. Greek artists also excelled in ceramic work, whereas Roman painters produced realistic (and sometimes pornographic) decorations for the homes of the wealthy. In Athens's brilliant 5th century—the age of Pericles, Socrates, Sophocles, and so many other intensely creative figures—sculptors like Phidias developed unprecedented skill rendering simultaneously realistic yet beautiful images of the human form, from lovely goddesses to muscled warriors and athletes. Roman sculptors, less innovative, continued this heroic-realistic tradition. They molded scenes of Roman conquests on triumphal columns and captured the power but also the human qualities of Augustus Caesar and his successors on busts and full-figure statues alike.

Greek architecture, from the 8th century B.C.E. onward, emphasized monumental construction, square or rectangular in shape, with columned porticoes. The Greeks devised three embellishments for the tops of columns supporting their massive buildings, each more ornate than the next: the **Doric,** the **Ionic,** and the **Corinthian.** The Greeks, in short, invented what Westerners and others in the world today still regard as "classical" architecture, although the Greeks themselves were influenced by Egyptian models in their preferences. Greece, and later Italy, provided abundant stone for ambitious temples, markets, and other public buildings. Many of these same structures were filled with products of the sculptors' workshops. They were brightly painted, although over the centuries the paint would fade so that later imitators came to think of the classical style as involving unadorned (some might say drab) stone.

Roman architects adopted the Greek themes quite readily. Their engineering skill allowed them to construct buildings of even greater size, as well as new forms such as the free-standing stadium. Under the empire, the Romans learned how to add domes to rectangular buildings, which resulted in some welcome architectural diversity. At the same time, the empire's taste for massive, heavily adorned monuments and public buildings, while a clear demonstration of Rome's sense of power and achievement, moved increasingly away from the simple lines of the early Greek temples (Figure 4.5).

Classical Mediterranean art and architecture were intimately linked with the society that produced them. There is a temptation, because of the formal role of classical styles in later societies, including our own, to attribute a stiffness to Greek and Roman art that was not present in the original. Greek and Roman structures were built to be used. Temples and marketplaces and the public baths that so delighted the Roman upper classes were part of daily urban life. Classical art was also flexible, according to need. Villas or small palaces—built for the Roman upper classes and typically constructed around an open courtyard—had a light, even simple quality rather different from that of temple architecture. Classical dramas were not merely examples of high art, performed in front of a cultural elite. Indeed, Athens lives in the memory of many humanists today as much because of the large audiences that trooped to performances of plays by authors like Sophocles as for the creativity of

Figure 4.5 This is an artist's recreation of the Roman Forum in imperial times. The use of decorative styles that originated in classical Greece was a central feature of Roman architecture, but as the empire grew, buildings became steadily more massive. Larger columns and greater heights reflected the Roman taste for the monumental. Ultimately, Roman architects also developed the capacity to build domed structures—a feat of engineering.

(Hypothetical reconstruction of the Roman Forum in Imperial Times. Southern part. Watercolor. Soprintendenza alle Antichita, Rome, Italy/Scala/Art Resource, NY.)

Political Rituals in Persia

This is a relief from the Audience Hall of the Persian royal Palace in Persepolis, built by Darius I (522–486 B.C.E.). The scene shows court rituals in Persia. Later, when Alexander conquered Persia, he was in-clined to install the same rituals, but many of his soldiers objected vigorously, and the whole issue caused great furor in the ranks. It has been speculated, however, that some of these rituals later passed to Europe, where they helped define appropriate behavior in the presence of kings.

QUESTIONS: What kinds of rituals does this scene suggest, and what kinds of relationships between subjects and the emperor? Why, and on what basis, might Greeks object to this kind of behavior toward a ruler? Why was Alexander tempted to transfer these rituals to his own court?

the writers and philosophers themselves. Literally thousands of people gathered in the large hillside theaters of Athens and other cities for the performance of new plays and for associated music and poetry competitions. Popular taste in Rome, to be sure, seemed less elevated. Republican Rome was not an important cultural center, and many Roman leaders feared the more emotional qualities of Greek art. The Roman Empire is known more for monumental athletic performances—chariot races and gladiators—than for high-quality popular theater. However, elements of classical art—the great monuments if nothing more—were part of daily urban life and the pursuit of pleasure. Roman styles were also blended with Christianity during the later empire (Figure 4.6) providing another lasting expression.

Economy and Society in the Mediterranean

Politics and formal culture in Greece and Rome were mainly affairs of the cities—meaning that they were of intense concern only to a minority of the population. Most Greeks and Romans were farmers, tied to the soil and often to local rituals and festivals that were different from urban forms. Many Greek farmers, for example, annually gathered for a spring passion play to celebrate the recovery of the goddess of fertility from the lower world, an event that was seen as a vital preparation for planting and that also suggested the possibility of an afterlife—a prospect important to many people who endured a life of hard labor and poverty. A substantial population of free farmers, who owned their own land, flourished in the early days of the Greek city-states and later around Rome. However, there was a constant tendency, most pronounced in Rome, for large land-lords to squeeze these farmers, forcing them to become tenants or laborers or to join the swelling crowds of the urban lower class. Tensions between tyrants and aristocrats or democrats and aristocrats in Athens often revolved around free farmers'

Figure 4.6 This mosaic from the city of Ravenna, Italy, depicts the Last Supper, which took place on the night before Jesus was crucified. According to Christian belief, at this supper Jesus broke bread and drank wine with his disciples, teaching them the ritual of the Eucharist, and predicted that one of them would betray him. Mosaic designs like this one were common in Roman buildings, often inlaid into floors and depicting both secular and religious scenes. The mosaic tradition continued in the Eastern Empire, mainly used there to depict Christian figures, becoming ever more elegant and richly detailed.

Greek and Roman economies were based on commercial agriculture, trade, and slavery.

 The two societies developed somewhat different versions of the patriarchal family.

attempts to preserve their independence and shake off the heavy debts they had incurred. The Roman republic declined in part because too many farmers became dependent on the protection of large landlords, even when they did not work their estates outright, and so no longer could vote freely.

Agriculture and Trade

Farming in Greece and in much of Italy was complicated by the fact that soil conditions were not ideal for grain growing, and yet grain was the staple of life. First in Greece, then in central Italy, farmers were increasingly tempted to shift to the production of olives and grapes, which were used primarily for cooking and winemaking. These products were well suited to the soil conditions, but they required an unusually extensive conversion of agriculture to a market basis. That is, farmers who produced grapes and olives had to buy some of the food they needed, and they had to sell most of their own product in order to do this. Furthermore, planting olive trees or grape vines required substantial capital, for they would not bear fruit for at least five years after planting. This was one reason so many farmers went into debt. It was also one of the reasons that large landlords gained increasing advantage over independent farmers, for they could enter into market production on a much larger scale if only because of their greater access to capital.

The rise of commercial agriculture in Greece and then around Rome was one of the prime forces leading to efforts to establish an empire. Greek city-states, with Athens usually in the lead, developed colonies in the Middle East and then in Sicily mainly to gain access to grain production; for this, they traded not only olive oil and wine but also manufactured products and silver. Rome pushed south, in part to acquire the Sicilian grain fields, and later used much of north Africa as its granary. Indeed, the heavy cultivation in north Africa resulted in a soil depletion that helps account for the region's reduced agricultural fertility in later centuries.

The importance of commercial farming obviously dictated extensive concern with trade. Private merchants operated most of the ships that carried agricultural products and other goods. Greek city-states and ultimately the Roman state supervised the grain trade, promoting public works and storage facilities and carefully regulating the vital supplies. Other kinds of trade were vital also. Luxury products from the shops of urban artists or craftsworkers played a major role in the lifestyle of the upper classes. There was some trade also beyond the borders of Mediterranean civilization itself, for goods from India and China. In this trade, the Mediterranean peoples found themselves at some disadvantage, for their manufactured products were less sophisticated than those of eastern Asia; thus, they typically exported animal skins, precious metals, and even exotic African animals for Asian zoos in return for the spices and artistic products of the east.

For all the importance of trade, merchants enjoyed a somewhat ambiguous status in classical Mediterranean civilization. Leading Athenian merchants were usually foreigners, mostly from the trading peoples of the Middle East—the descendants of Lydians and Phoenicians. Merchants had a somewhat higher status in Rome, clearly forming the second most prestigious social class under the landed patricians, but here, too, the aristocracy frequently disputed the merchants' rights. Overall, merchants fared better in the Mediterranean than in China in terms of official recognition, but worse than in India; classical Mediterranean society certainly did not set in motion a culture that distinctly valued capitalist moneymaking.

Slavery

Slavery was another key ingredient of the classical economy. Philosophers such as Aristotle produced elaborate justifications for the necessity of slavery in a proper society. Athenians used slaves as household servants and also as workers in their vital silver mines; slaves provided the labor force for Athens's empire and commercial operations alike. Sparta used slaves extensively for agricultural work. Slavery spread steadily in Rome from the final centuries of the republic. Since most slaves came from conquered territories, the need for slaves was another key element in military expansion. Here was a theme visible in earlier civilizations in the eastern Mediterranean, and within later societies in this region as well. The need for slaves helps explain the greater importance of military forces and expansion in these areas than in India or China. Roman slaves performed household tasks—including the tutoring of upper-class children, for which cultured Greek slaves were highly

Greek and Phoenician Colonies and Trade MAP

Greek and Roman Slavery CASE STUDY

Rome and a Values Crisis

Rome's increasing contact with the eastern Mediterranean, particularly Greece, brought important debates about culture. Many conservatives deplored Greek learning and argued that it would corrupt Roman virtue. Cicero, a leading politician in the Senate and a major Latin writer, here defends Greek literature, using Hellenistic justifications of beauty and utility. Cicero played a major role in popularizing Greek culture during the 1st century B.C.E. His comments also reflect the concerns that Greek culture inspired a source of change.

Do you think that I could find inspiration for my daily speeches on so manifold a variety of topics, did I not cultivate my mind with study, or that my mind could endure so great a strain, did not study provide it with relaxation? I am a votary of literature, and make the confession unashamed; shame belongs rather to the bookish recluse, who knows not how to apply his reading to the good of his fellows, or to manifest its fruits to the eyes of all. But what shame should be mine, gentlemen, who have made it a rule of my life for all these years never to allow the sweets of a cloistered ease or the seductions of pleasure or the enticements of repose to prevent me from aiding any man in the hour of his need? How then can I justly be blamed or censured, if it shall be found that I have devoted to literature a portion of my leisure hours no longer than others without blame devote to the pursuit of material gain, to the celebration of festivals or games, to pleasure and the repose of mind and body, to protracted banqueting, or perhaps to the gaming-board or to ballplaying? I have the better right to indulgence herein, because my devotion to letters strengthens my oratorical powers, and these, such as they are, have never failed my friends in their hour of peril. Yet insignificant though these powers may seem to be, I fully realize from what source I draw all that is highest in them. Had I not persuaded myself from my youth up, thanks to the moral lessons derived from a wide reading, that nothing is to be greatly sought after in this life save glory and honour, and that in their quest all bodily pains and all dangers of death or exile should be lightly accounted, I should never have borne for the safety of you all the brunt of many a bitter encounter, or bared my breast to the daily onsets of abandoned persons. All literature, all philosophy, all history, abounds with incentives to noble action, incentives which would be buried in black darkness were the light of the written word not flashed upon them. How many pictures of high endeavor the great authors of Greece and Rome have drawn for our use, and bequeathed to us, not only for our contemplation, but for our emulation! These I have held ever before my vision throughout my public career, and have guided the workings of my brain and my soul by meditating upon patterns of excellence.

But let us for the moment waive these solid advantages; let us assume that entertainment is the sole end of reading; even so, I think you would hold that no mental employment is so broadening to the sympathies or so enlightening to the understanding. Other pursuits belong not to all times, all ages, all conditions; but this gives stimulus to our youth and diversion to our old age; this adds a charm to success, and offers a haven of consolation to failure. In the home it delights, in the world it hampers not. Through the night watches, on all our journeying, and in our hours of country ease, it is an unfailing companion.

If anyone thinks that the glory won by the writing of Greek verse is naturally less than that accorded to the poet who writes in Latin, he is entirely in the wrong. Greek literature is read in nearly every nation under heaven, while the vogue of Latin is confined to its own boundaries, and they are, we must grant, narrow. Seeing, therefore, that the activities of our race know no barrier save the limits of the round earth, we ought to be ambitious that whithersoever our arms have penetrated there also our fame and glory should extend; for the reason that literature exalts the nation whose high deeds it sings, and at the same time there can be no doubt that those who stake their lives to fight in honour's cause find therein a lofty incentive to peril and endeavor. We read that Alexander the Great carried in his train numbers of epic poets and historians. And yet, standing before the tomb of Achilles at Sigeum, he exclaimed, "Fortunate youth, to have found in Homer an herald of thy valor!" Well might he so exclaim, for had the *Iliad* never existed, the same mound which covered Achilles' bones would also have overwhelmed his memory.

QUESTIONS What kind of objections to Greek learning is Cicero arguing against? Which of his arguments had the most lasting appeal to those who were reshaping Roman culture? Can you think of similar debates about foreign culture in other times and places in history? How would you use this document to reconstruct the debate Cicero was participating in and why it seemed important?

Source: Cicero, *Pro Archia Poeta*. Translated by N. H. Watts. Loeb Classical Library. Cicero, *Pro Archia* (Harvard University Press, 1965), 12–14, 16, 23–24.

valued. This kind of slavery was sometimes preferable to "free" life as a poor peasant. But slaves also worked the mines, for precious metals and for iron; as in Greece, slave labor in the mines was particularly brutal, and few slaves survived more than a few years of such an existence. Roman estate owners used large numbers of slaves for agricultural work, along with paid laborers and tenant farmers. This practice was another source of the steady pressure placed on free farmers who could not easily compete with unpaid forced labor.

Partly because of slavery, partly because of the overall orientation of upper-class culture, neither Greece nor Rome was especially interested in technological innovations applicable to agriculture or manufacturing. The Greeks made important advances in shipbuilding and navigation, which were vital for their trading economy. Romans, less adept on the water, developed their skill in engineering to provide greater urban amenities and good roads for the swift and easy movement of troops. But a technology designed to improve the production of food or manufactured goods did not figure largely in this civilization, which mainly relied on the earlier achievements of previous Mediterranean societies. Abundant slave labor probably discouraged concern for more efficient production methods. So did a sense that the true goals of humankind were artistic and political. One Hellenistic scholar, for example, refused to write a handbook on engineering because "the work of an engineer and everything that ministers to the needs of life is ignoble and vulgar." As a consequence of this outlook, Mediterranean society lagged behind both India and China in production technology, which was one reason for its resulting unfavorable balance of trade with eastern Asia.

Both Greek and Roman society emphasized the importance of a tight family structure, with a husband and father firmly in control. Women had vital economic functions, particularly in farming and artisan families. In the upper classes, especially in Rome, women often commanded great influence and power within a household. In law and culture, however, women were held inferior. Families burdened with too many children sometimes put female infants to death because of their low status and their potential drain on the family economy. Pericles stated common beliefs about women when he noted, "For a woman not to show more weakness than is natural to her sex is a great glory, and not to be talked about for good or for evil among men." Early Roman law stipulated that "the husband is the judge of his wife. If she commits a fault, he punishes her; if she has drunk wine, he condemns her; if she has been guilty of adultery, he kills her." Later, however, such customs were held in check by family courts composed of members of both families. Here was a case where Roman legal ideas modified traditional family controls. If divorced because of adultery, a Roman woman lost a third of her property and had to wear a special garment that set her apart like a prostitute. On the other hand, the oppression of women was probably less severe in this civilization than in China. Many Greek and Roman women were active in business and controlled a portion, even if only the minority, of all urban property.

Because of the divisions within classical Mediterranean society, no easy generalizations about culture or achievement can be made. An 18th-century English historian called the high point of the Roman Empire, before 180 C.E., the period in human history "during which the condition of the human race was most happy or prosperous." This is doubtful, given the technological accomplishments of China and India. And certainly, many slaves, women, and ordinary farmers in the Mediterranean world might have disagreed with this viewpoint. Few farmers, for example, actively participated in the political structures or cultural opportunities that were the most obvious mark of this civilization. Many continued to work largely as their ancestors had done, with quite similar tools and in very similar poverty, untouched by the doings of the great or the bustle of the cities except when wars engulfed their lands.

We are tempted, of course, exclusively to remember the urban achievements, for they exerted the greatest influence on later ages that recalled the glories of Greece and Rome. The distinctive features of classical Mediterranean social and family structures had a less enduring impact, although ideas about slavery or women were revived in subsequent periods. However, the relatively unchanging face of ordinary life had an important influence as well, as many farmers and artisans long maintained the habits and outlook they developed during the great days of the Greek and Roman empires, and because their separation from much of the official culture posed both a challenge and opportunity for new cultural movements such as Christianity.

Toward the Fall of Rome

Rome began to decline after about 180 C.E., losing territory and suffering economic reversals. The legacy of the classical civilizations in the Mediterranean and Middle East was important even after this decline.

Classical Mediterranean society had one final impact on world history through its rather fragmentary collapse. Unlike China, classical civilization in the Mediterranean region was not simply disrupted only to revive. Unlike India, there was no central religion, derived from the civilization itself, to serve as link between the classical period and what followed. Furthermore, the fall of Rome was not uniform: Rome fell more in some parts of the Mediterranean than it did in others. The result, among other things, was that no single civilization ultimately rose to claim the mantle of Greece and Rome. At the same time, there was no across-the-board maintenance of the classical Mediterranean institutions and values in any of the civilizations that later claimed a relationship to the Greek and Roman past. Greece and Rome would live on, in more than idle memory, but their heritage was unquestionably more complex and more selective than proved to be the case for India or China.

A Complex Legacy

Classical Greece, Persia and their Hellenistic successors lasted for about 600 years, and Rome another 600 years beyond this. Although major political and social changes took place during this span, some durable characteristics also developed.

Greece's political legacy obviously lay more in the realm of ideas than in enduring political institutions such as China's emperor and bureaucracy, although Rome copied some Greek structures. On the whole, Greek art and philosophy formed the most lasting heritage of this classical civilization. But, partly because they did not generate a major religion, Greek and Roman contributions to a durable popular culture were more limited than was true in China or India.

There are two final complexities in dealing with the classical civilizations of the eastern Mediterranean and the Middle East. The first involves the relationship of Greek and Roman achievements to contemporary North Americans. Classical Greece is often presented as the first phase of North Americans' own classical past. The framers of the Constitution of the United States were very conscious of Greek and Roman precedents. Designers of public buildings in the United States have copied classical Mediterranean models. The Western educational tradition has long invited elaborate explorations of the Greco-Roman past as part of the standard intellectual equipment for the educated person.

Yet this important legacy should not obscure the actual Greek and Roman record as a classical civilization. Classical ideas did not flow smoothly into a Western tradition (indeed, they had far more initial impact on the Middle East, which was where Greeks and even Romans tended to look when they thought of spreading their key achievements). Important revivals and modifications had to occur before the Greek approach to science had a fruitful impact on western Europe many centuries later. And democracy did not spread directly from Greece or Rome to other societies, although the Greek example was cited by later advocates whose passions had very different sources.

The second complexity involves Persia, an important civilization in its own right. Hellenistic conquests brought Greek cultural influence into Persia. Influences were mutual, however. Hellenistic kings imitated Persian centralization and bureaucracy. Cultural exchange also gave Zoroastrian influences a wider range. This furthered the influence these religious ideas would have on Mediterranean religions, including Judaism, and later, Christianity and Islam. The Jewish book of Daniel, for example, picked up the Zoroastrian idea that humans would be rewarded for good or bad behavior in a future life.

At the same time, there was no tidy homogenization. Persians continued to see themselves as partially distinct, and viewed Alexander's successors as foreigners. Later, more purely Persian kingdoms arose as the Hellenistic states declined. Parthians and then Sasanids revived Persian political institutions and culture in their realms to the east of the Roman Empire's Middle Eastern holdings. Under Hellenism and Persia alike, the Middle East enhanced its role as a point of exchange among many different merchants and cultures.

Global Connections

Persia, Greece, Rome, and the World

The Persian Empire fostered trade with both Asia and with the eastern Mediterranean. Persian roads and institutions facilitated commerce from Asia to the Mediterranean. Cultural influences spread widely as well. Greeks developed wide contacts, also, but more gradually and with some definite prejudices.

Like other classical civilizations, notably China, Greeks had a definite sense of the inferiority of other peoples. Classical Greeks indiscriminately called non-Greeks "barbarians," and some Greek city-states, like Sparta, were quite closed to outside influences. But overall, the Greeks were also a trading and expansionist people. They set up Greek colonies in various parts of the Mediterranean. They traded even more widely, and relied heavily on foreigners for part of this trade. Greek scholars went to Egypt to further their training in science and mathematics. Some

Greeks were immensely curious about other peoples and their habits. The historian and traveler Herodotus (484–425 B.C.E.) talked enthusiastically about customs very different from his own, though he was also capable of believing wild exaggerations about how some people lived.

Greek outreach was extended by Alexander the Great, who did not have such a keen belief in Greek superiority. Alexander forged important new contacts between the eastern Mediterranean, the rest of the Middle East including Persia, and western India. He even hoped to extend his system into China, but obviously this did not occur. The system did not last, but the interest in setting up stronger links between the eastern Mediterranean and Asia remained an important concern.

Rome's world connections were in some ways more varied. The empire obviously influenced Europeans beyond the actual Roman borders, acquainting various Germanic and Celtic peoples with some Roman styles. Trade with Africa, also beyond the borders, particularly involved the northeast. Roman expeditions to India constituted an important commercial outreach. Most Roman attention, in trade as well as politics, focused on creating ties within the vast territories of the empire, but significant influence extended to other parts of the world. Some of these connections would affect trading patterns and missionary religious outreach even as the empire began to decline.

Further Readings

The archeology, arts, and culture of ancient Persia are addressed in J. Curtis, *Ancient Persia* (1989). On the Persian Empire, see J. M. Cook, *The Persian Empire* (1983). Important recent works on Persia include Bruce Lincoln, *Religion, Empire, and Torture: The Case of Achaemenian Persia, with a Postscript on Abu Ghraib* (2007); Oded Lipschits, Oded and Manfred Oeming, eds., *Judah and the Judeans in the Persian Period* (2006); Peter Green, *The Greco-Persian Wars* (1996); Donald Kagan, *The Peloponnesian War* (2003); and John Curtis and Nigel Tallis, eds., *Forgotten Empire: The World of Ancient Persia* (2005). Two good surveys on classical Greece are Stephanie Lynn Budin, *The Ancient Greeks: New Perspectives* (2004) and Nancy Demand's *A History of Ancient Greece* (1996); both have bibliographies. An older study on Greek culture is extremely solid: H. D. F. Kitto's *The Greeks* (1957). Recent works on Hellenism include Kathryn Gutzwiller, *A Guide to Hellenistic Literature*. Malden (2007); Glenn R. Bugh, editor, *The Cambridge Companion to the Hellenistic World* (2006); Christian Habicht, *The Hellenistic Monarchies: Selected Papers* (2006); Waldemar Heckel, *Crossroads of History: The Age of Alexander* (2003); and A. B. Bosworth, *The Legacy of Alexander: Politics, Warfare, and Propaganda under the Successors* (2002). Works on key special topics are R. Zelnick-Abramovitz, *Not Wholly Free: The Concept of Manumission and the Status of Manumitted Slaves in the Ancient Greek World* (2005); Oswyn Murray, *Early Greece* (1993); and Frank Frost, *Greek Society* (3rd ed., 1987). On Greek intellectual life, see Silvia Montiglio, *Wandering*

in Ancient Greek Culture (2005); W. Burkert, *Greek Religions* (1985); and G. E. R. Lloyd, *The Revolutions of Wisdom: Studies in the Claims and Practices of Ancient Greek Science* (1987). Particular features of Greek society are treated in Moses Finley, *Slavery in the Ancient World* (1972), an exciting study; Sarah Pomeroy, *Goddesses, Whores, Wives, and Slaves: Women in Classical Antiquity* (1975); R. Just, *Women in Athenian Law and Life* (1988); Yvon Garlan, *Slavery in Ancient Greece* (1988); and Victor Hanson, *The Western Way of War: Infantry Battle in Classical Greece* (1989). On politics, Donald Kagan's *Western Heritage* (1991) deals with a key issue.

An excellent way to approach Greek history is through documents from the period. See Herodotus, *The Histories* (trans. de Selincourt, 1972); M. Crawford, ed., *Sources for Ancient History* (1983); M. R. Lefkowitz and M. B. Fant, eds., *Women's Life in Greece and Rome: A Source Book in Translation* (1982); and Eric W. Robinson, ed., *Ancient Greek Democracy: Readings and Sources* (2004).

Though it deals with a later period, key social features of the region are explored in F. Braudel's classic *The Mediterranean and the Mediterranean World* (2 vols., 1972).

Two solid surveys with bibliographies are K. Christ, *The Romans: An Introduction to Their History and Civilization* (1984); and M. Grant, *The World of Rome* (1990). On Rome's early history, see H. H. Sculard, *A History of the Roman World 753–146 B.C.* (1961). Excellent analyses of the basic features of Roman cultural and social life are M. Grant, *A Social History of Greece and Rome* (1992); and P. Garnsey and R. Saller, *The Roman Empire: Economy, Society and Culture* (1987). See also R. MacMullen, *Roman Social Relations 50 B.C. to A.D. 284* (1981). A bold quantitative study is R. Duncan-Jones, *The Economy of the Roman Empire* (1982). J. Andreau offers close study of *Banking and Business in the Roman World* (1999). On slavery, the best recent works are K. Hopkins, *Conquerors and Slaves: Slaves and Masters in the Roman Empire* (1987); and K. R. Bradley and W. Philips Jr., *Slavery from Roman Times to the Early Transatlantic Trade* (1985). On women, see S. Dixon, *The Roman Mother* (1989); J. F. Gardner, *Women in Roman Law and Society* (1986); and Elaine Fanthum and others, *Women in the Classical World: Image and Text* (1994). Florence DuPont's *Daily Life in Ancient Rome* (1999 ed.) examines Roman ideas of space and time and of honor as well as family relations and social divisions. See also L. Casson, *Everyday Life in Ancient Rome* (1998).

For war and diplomacy, see Y. Garlan, *War in the Ancient World* (1975); E. N. Luttwak, *The Grand Strategy of the Roman Empire* (1976); Susan Raven, *Rome in Africa* (1993); and Stephen Dyson, *The Creation of the Roman Frontier* (1985).

Collections of source materials include M. Crawford, ed., *Sources for Ancient History* (1983); and C. Fornara, *Translated Documents of Greece and Rome* (1977). J. Boardman, J. Griffin, and O. Murray, *The Oxford History of the Roman World* (1990); and T. Cornell and J. Mathews, *Atlas of the Roman World* (1982) are useful reference guides to Roman civilization.

The rise and spread of Christianity are treated in two outstanding studies: R. MacMullen's *Christianizing the Roman Empire*

(1984) and Peter Brown's *The World of Late Antiquity,* A.D. *150–750* (1971). Brown has also written several more specialized studies on early Christianity in the West.

On the Web

Accounts, documents and analyses of the course of the Persian Empire are offered at http://www.fordham.edu/halsall/ancient/asbook05.html. Persian art and architecture is illuminated at http://www.ancientpersia.com/. A virtual tour of Persian emperor Darius' capital at Persepolis can be taken at http://www.ancientpersia.com/art_f.htm. An inspired reconstruction of Persepolis can be viewed at http://www.ancientpersia.com/art_f.htm. The life of Zoroaster and the Zoroastrianism of the Persian Empire is examined at http://www.bbc.co.uk/religion/religions/zoroastrian/, http://www.zoroaster.net/indexe.htm, http://www.sacred-texts.com/zor/, and http://www.avesta.org/avesta.html.

A fine site linking Greek texts, geography, and art is http://www.perseus.tufts.edu/. A massive links page to Greek life is offered at http://www.kchanson.com/LINKS/ancweb.html#9. Daily life in ancient Greece is explored at http://www.museum.upenn.edu/Greek_World/greek_house.html and http://ancienthistory.mrdonn.org/Greeklife.html. Greek religion is analyzed at http://www.museum.upenn.edu/Greek_World/religion.html, while Greek medicine receives treatment at http://www.nlm.nih.gov/hmd/greek/index.html.

The world of Greco-Roman women, from their private life to legal status, is examined at http://www.bbc.co.uk/schools/landmarks/ancientgreece/athens/women.shtml and http://dmoz.org/Society/People/Women/History/Ancient/Greece/. A free on-line text of Thucydides' *History of the Peloponnesian War,* written in 431 B.C.E., is provided at http://classics.mit.edu/Thucydides/pelopwar.html. The life and work of the Greek historian Herodotus is examined at http://www.losttrails.com/pages/Hproject.html.

Some of the leading personalities of classical Greek and Hellenistic times are illuminated at Web sites, including those devoted to Aristophanes (http://www.imagi-nation.com/moonstruck/clsc13.htm), Sophocles (http://www.imagi-nation.com/moonstruck/clsc1.htm), Socrates (http://www.san.beck.org/SOCRATES1-Life.html), Philip II (http://www.historyofmacedonia.org/AncientMacedonia/PhilipofMacedon.html), Alexander the Great (http://www.historyofmacedonia.org/AncientMacedonia/AlexandertheGreat.html), and Cleopatra (http://womenshistory.about.com/cs/cleopatrabios/). Plato's life and times are illustrated at http://plato-dialogues.org/life.htm and at http://www.philosophypages.com/ph/plat.htm, which also offers many links to the works of this famous philosopher.

The monumental architecture and the art of Greece are introduced at http://www.ancient-greece.org/art.html, http://www.ancientgreece.com/s/Main_Page/ and http://witcombe.sbc.edu/ARTHgreece.html. For a virtual tour of the acropolis of Athens and the Parthenon, go to http://www.dkv.columbia.edu/vmc/learning/, http://www.stoa.org/athens/, and http://www.greatbuildings.com/ types/styles/greek.html (click on itemized list for detailed photographs and discussion). To understand the lasting influence of these ancient buildings, see the study of classical Greek themes in the architecture of Buffalo, New York, at http://ah.bfn.org/a/archsty/grk/index.html.

The world of ancient Crete, a predecessor of classical Greek civilization, is the subject of a picture gallery at http://dilos.com/region/crete/minoan_pictures.html and a lecture at http://projectsx.dartmouth.edu/history/bronze_age/lessons/les/12.html. A 3-D tour of the Minoan palace at Knossos in Crete is conducted at http://www.bsa.ac.uk/knosos/index.htm?vrtour.

For trade contacts between Greece and other parts of the ancient world, see http://www.museum.upenn.edu/Greek_World/trade.html and http://www.ucalgary.ca/applied_history/tutor/oldwrld/overview/first.html. The historic amber trade route began at this time and can be toured at http://www.cichw.net/amber.html and http://www.american.edu/ted/AMBER.HTM.

It is possible to experience the Roman world through its dramatic history and daily life at http://members.aol.com/Donnclass/Romelife.html, http://depthome.brooklyn.cuny.edu/classics/dunkle/romnlife/index.htm, or through links at http://duke.usask.ca/~porterj/CourseNotes/life.html, http://www.perseus.tufts.edu/hopper/, and especially at http://www.capitolium.org/eng/virtuale/vita.htm, which offers views of ancient Rome as it was then and what remains today.

Enter into the world of Rome in the First Century C.E. at http://www.pbs.org/empires/romans/index.html or explore the entire Roman world at http://www.forumromanum.org/index2.html. Glimpses of Roman life can also be seen through Roman architecture (http://harpy.uccs.edu/roman/html/romarch.html and http://www.greatbuildings.com/types/styles/roman.html) and technology (http://www.romanconcrete.com/, http://www.bbc.co.uk/schools/romans/tech.shtml, and http://www.bbc.co.uk/history/ancient/romans/tech_01.shtml).

The place of gladiator games in Roman society is explored at http://depthome.brooklyn.cuny.edu/classics/gladiatr/index.htm. The organization of the Roman army is discussed at http://www.roman-empire.net/army/army.html and http://members.tripod.com/~S_van_Dorst/reparmy.html.

Views of the ancient city of Rome based on computer-generated reconstructions, including an aerial image provided by a model, a simulated flyover and tours of the city can be found at http://earth.google.com/rome/index.html, http://www.capitolium.org/eng/virtuale/virtuale.htm, and http://depthome.brooklyn.cuny.edu/classics/gladiatr/colmodel.htm. Real-time images of Rome can be viewed at http://www.capitolium.org/eng/virtuale/webview.htm. The Roman city of Pompeii can be visited virtually at http://www.iath.virginia.edu/pompeii/forummap.html. The role of the volcano Vesuvius in Roman history is explored at http://volcano.und.nodak.edu/vwdocs/volc_images/img_vesuvius.html and through its link to http://www.westnet.com/~dobran/publ.html, which examines such disasters as a force in world history. Eyewitness accounts of the city's destruction are offered at http://pompeii.virginia.edu/pliny.html and http://www.eyewitnesstohistory.com/pompeii.htm.

A web-based video documentary on the destruction of Pompeii is provided by the Discovery Channel at http://dsc.discovery.com/convergence/pompeii/pliny/video.html.

The daily life of Romans is traced at http://library.thinkquest.org/22866/English/Romday/RomDag.html, http://carlos.emory.edu/ODYSSEY/ROME/daily.html, and http://rome.mrdonn.org/dailylife.html.

The women of the Roman Empire are the focus of http://dominae.fws1.com/ and http://www.stoa.org/diotima/. The men of Rome have their day at Web sites devoted to Julius Caesar (http://www.livius.org/caa-can/caesar/caesar01.html and http://www.vroma.org/~bmcmanus/caesar.html, which includes a link to historians' judgments of his career), Pompeii (http://www.hadrians.com/rome/romans/emperors/emperor_hadrian.html), and Tiberius Gracchus (http://www.gracchus.esmartweb.com/). The home of the quintessential Roman poet Horace, his life, art, and the world in which he lived is beautifully presented at http://www.humnet.ucla.edu/horaces-villa/. Links to the homepage of a well known, if somewhat controversial, group of scholars who study Jesus of Nazareth as a historical figure can be found at http://www.valpo.edu/home/faculty/fniedner/Jesuspage.html. Visit hadrian's Wall in Britain at http://www.bbc.co.uk/history/ancient/romans/hadrian_gallery.shtml.

Roman trade with India is discussed at http://en.wikipedia.org/wiki/Roman_trade_with_India. Rome's role in the Silk Road is described at http://www.metmuseum.org/toah/hd/silk/hd_silk.htm. Rome's relations with China are explored at http://en.wikipedia.org/wiki/Sino-Roman_relations. Roman mines in Britain are explored at http://www.bbc.co.uk/dna/h2g2/A3240037. Rome's north African possessions are examined at http://www.utexas.edu/research/isac/light/map.html and http://www.usd.edu/~clehmann/pir/how_gain.htm, while Roman Egypt is surveyed at http://www.metmuseum.org/toah/hd/regy/hd_regy.htm.

AP* Test Prep

1. The major impact of Alexander the Great's conquests was the
   (A) establishment of a unified government for the eastern Mediterranean.
   (B) the elimination of foreign influences from Greek culture.
   (C) spread of Greek culture throughout the eastern Mediterranean.
   (D) destruction of regional trade and commerce.

2. Greco-Roman philosophers attempted to understand human nature through
   (A) emotion, especially the desire for love and brotherhood.
   (B) its rigid adherence to societal norms with rewards and punishments.
   (C) human sin, salvation, and redemption.
   (D) rational observation and deduction.

3. Roman culture
   (A) developed in relative isolation.
   (B) borrowed heavily, especially from the Greek and Hellenistic states.
   (C) influenced heavily the cultures of Africa and southwest Asia.
   (D) was highly innovative in the arts and sciences.

4. Rome successfully expanded for all of these reasons EXCEPT:
   (A) it possessed a disciplined, trained military.
   (B) it had a rich agricultural economy, with local and imported products, which supported a large population.
   (C) Roman leaders made citizens out of conquered elites.
   (D) it had no organized and powerful rivals to oppose expansion in the area.

5. What sentence best describes both Roman and Chinese gender relations?
   (A) Roman and Chinese women had numerous political rights.
   (B) Roman women had more nearly equal legal and property rights and were more active in commerce than their Chinese counterparts.
   (C) Both cultures were matrilocal—husbands resided with their wives' families.
   (D) Rome and China were both patriarchal societies where elite women had considerable influence.

6. With regard to merchants, classical civilizations in Rome, Greece, and China
   (A) accorded them high social status.
   (B) saw little use for their talents in otherwise largely agricultural societies.
   (C) eagerly made them state bureaucrats.
   (D) were ambivalent or negative in their views of merchants despite their vital roles in commerce.

Free-Response Question

Compare and contrast the Greek, Confucian, and Hindu ethical systems.

The Classical Period: Directions, Diversities, and Declines by 500 C.E.

Expansion and Integration

Beyond the Classical Civilizations

THINKING HISTORICALLY: Nomads and Cross-Civilization Contacts and Exchanges

Decline in China and India

Decline and Fall in Rome

The New Religious Map

DOCUMENT: The Popularization of Buddhism

VISUALIZING THE PAST: Religious Geography

GLOBAL CONNECTIONS: The Late Classical Period and the World

At the highpoint of the classical period, with the Han and Roman empires in full swing, the Indian Ocean provided a network of important contacts. The major civilizations did not depend on long-distance trade: Rome, China, and India were economically and culturally self-sufficient. But Roman fleets and Chinese ships regularly sailed the ocean, along with more local Persian, Arab, and Indonesian merchants. The Roman government arranged for archers on their convoys to beat back local pirates. Rome wanted spices and textiles from the region. The Chinese wanted exotic goods as well—one Han emperor sent a mission to India to acquire a rhinoceros.

All this raises two questions concerning the period in which the classical empires declined. First, how much cultural exchange occurred? How much did Greeks and Middle Eastern intermediaries pick up from Buddhism, the best-established religion in the Indian Ocean region? Buddhism had established a number of institutions, rituals, and symbols prior to the rise of Christianity. These included the halo (technically, the nimbus) used in artistic representations of saints, the very idea of saints, monasteries, holy water, the five-chained censer to burn incense, and the hand blessing. Christianity would later develop versions of these same practices. Had these elements of Buddhism become familiar to early Christians as a result of trade (and some Buddhist missions to Persia)? We simply do not know, but the similarities between Buddhist and Christian elements are striking. There was also movement in the other direction. Early Christians from the Middle East established at least one temple for their community in India, and later Christian missionaries traveled to India as well. According to legend, the apostle Thomas went to India, and there is a tomb designated for Saint Thomas in southern India.

The second question is more obvious, and answerable: what would happen when the decline of Rome and Han China opened the region to other initiatives? Trading opportunities still existed, but they now invited other participants. India was the first beneficiary. The Gupta Empire ran strong for a century or more after Rome foundered. Indian merchants fanned out from the Persian Gulf to southeast Asia, as the Guptas encouraged free enterprise. Indian elites valued gold highly, which motivated much of their trade with southeast Asia; in return, they could offer fine cotton cloth. Indian prosperity reached new levels, and many new temples were built as one result. Indian influence helped expand Hinduism and, to a greater degree, Buddhism, into southeast Asia.

The Gupta dynasty finally fell. Indian trading activity continued for a time, but there were new opportunities for Persians and Greeks (from the eastern Roman Empire) to rekindle competition for trade in the Indian Ocean. China would begin to reassert itself as well, and new competition from Arab traders proved even more important. When the dust settled from the long crisis of the classical world, the Indian Ocean was open to new claimants for trade supremacy. It would be the Arabs, previously confined to lesser commercial roles, including piracy, who would meet this postclassical challenge first. ■

This chapter continues to focus on the centers of classical civilization in Eurasia and North Africa. The end of the classical era is defined by changes in Asia, North Africa, and the Mediterranean, not the whole world. Nevertheless, the fading of the great classical empires had consequences beyond their borders, for example in spurring new missionary activities. The resulting change in civilization boundaries unleashed new forces that affected sub-Saharan Africa, northern Europe, and other parts of Asia.

Three issues predominate. First, why did these civilizations decline? Invasions were an important cause. Nomadic forces accustomed to fighting on horseback had an advantage over the armies

Figure 5.1 This twelfth-century Sicilian mosaic, Christ as Pantocrator (ruler of all), depicts him as many Christian artists have, his head surrounded by a halo, representing his holiness.

of the classical civilizations. But in their prime, the empires would have been able to turn the invaders back—so what else was going on? Second, why did different regions see different patterns of decline, with different results? And third, what was the significance of these developments—not just for the end of one period but for the beginning of another? The rapid spread of world religions, as the empires faded, provides a vital part of the answer.

The basic themes of the three great classical civilizations involved expansion and integration. From localized beginnings in northern China, the Ganges region, or the Aegean Sea, commercial, political, and cultural outreach pushed civilization through the Middle Kingdom and beyond, through the Indian subcontinent, and into the western Mediterranean. The growth set in motion deliberate but also implicit attempts to pull the new civilizations together in more than name. Correspondingly, the most telling comparisons among the three classical civilizations—identifying similarities as well as differences—involve this same process of integration and some of the problems it encountered.

1000 B.C.E.	1 C.E.	250 C.E.	500 C.E.
c. 1000 Polynesians reach Fiji, Samoa 1000 Independent kingdom of Kush 800–400 Spread of Olmec civilization: cultivation of maize (corn), potatoes; domestication of turkeys, dogs c. 300 Rise of Axum	c. 30 Crucifixion of Jesus c. 100 Root crops introduced to southern Africa through trade 100 Beginning of decline of Han dynasty 180 Rome begins to decline c. 200 Extensive agriculture practiced in Japan 227 Beginning of Sassanid Empire in Persia	284–305 Reign of Diocletian c. 300 Ethiopia adopts Christianity c. 312–337 Reign of Constantine 370–480 Nomadic invasions of western Europe c. 400 Growth of Mayan civilization c. 400 Polynesians reach Hawaii 450 Huns begin to invade India 476 Collapse of Rome	c. 500 Buddhism takes root in east and southeast Asia c. 500 Formation of Ghana c. 600 Beginning of Islam 618 Tang dynasty in China: glorious cultural period 700 Shintoism unified into single national religion in Japan

Throughout the classical world, integration and expansion faltered between 200 and 500 C.E. Decline, even collapse, began to afflict civilization—first in China, then in the Mediterranean, and finally in India. These developments signaled the end of the classical era and ushered in important new themes in world history that would define the next major period. The response of major religions to political decline shaped world history for centuries to come.

Classical civilizations (including Persia) had never embraced the majority of the territory around the globe, although they did include the majority of the world's population. Developments outside the classical orbit had rhythms of their own during the classical period, and they would gain new prominence as the great civilizations faltered. This describes the third historical theme—along with basic comparisons and the process of decline and attendant religious responses—that must be addressed in moving from the classical period to world history's next phase.

Expansion and Integration

All the classical civilizations involved territorial expansion and related efforts to integrate the new territories.

The heritage of the classical civilizations features a host of new ideas, styles, technologies, and institutions. Many of these arose as part of the broad process of adjusting to the expansion of civilization. Thus, it was not entirely accidental that in scarcely more than a century, between about 550 and 400 B.C.E., seminal thinkers arose in all three civilizations—Confucius and Laozi, Buddha, and Socrates. The thinkers had no contact with each other, and their specific ideas varied widely. However, all three were inspired by the common need to articulate central values in their respective societies, as part of a larger process of generating a shared culture on the basis of which their expanding societies might operate.

The civilizations of China, India, and the Mediterranean set about the tasks of uniting their expanding territories in different ways. China emphasized greater centralization, particularly in politics, generating a political culture to match. India and the Mediterranean remained more localized and diverse. India, however, used key religious values, and particularly the spread of Hinduism, to cement its civilization even across political boundaries. Mediterranean cultural achievements spread widely also, but involved less of the population—one reason the region proved more vulnerable to fragmentation after its political unity collapsed under Rome.

Integration involved two basic issues, the most obvious of which was territorial. China had to rein in its new southern regions, and the government devoted considerable attention to settling some northerners in the south, promoting a common language for the elite, and other techniques. The southward spread of the caste system and ultimately Hinduism in India addressed territorial issues. Rome combined considerable local autonomy and tolerance with common laws, the expansion of citizenship to elites across the empire, and a tight commercial network that created interdependencies between grain-growing regions and the olive and grape regions.

The second challenge to integration was social. All three classical civilizations fostered great inequalities between men and women and between upper and lower classes. The nature of the inequalities varied, from Mediterranean slavery to the Indian caste system to the Confucian sense of hierarchy; these differences were significant. Nevertheless, the assumption of inequality as normal was common to all three societies. Most leading thinkers—Buddha was an exception—did not oppose inequalities, writing openly of the need for deference and even (in the case of the Mediterranean) for slavery.

All the classical civilizations made some efforts to maintain a basic social cohesion while acknowledging inequality. None took the modern, Western-inspired route of arguing for opportunities of upward mobility. Confucianism stressed mutual respect between upper and lower classes, along with special deference on the part of the lower social orders. Shared values about family and self-restraint provided some further links across the social hierarchy. Mediterranean aristocrats treated some locals as clients, offering them protection; they also supported civic rituals intended to foster loyalty. India offered a religion that was shared by all social classes and gave hope to the lower castes of future incarnation into a higher caste. None of these approaches consistently united the society. Lower-class risings, even slave rebellions, were part of the classical experience. On balance, however, some techniques may have worked better than others. And as the Roman Empire fell, many elements of the lower classes quickly turned their attention to other interests. This suggests that here, too, the integration of Mediterranean society was slightly more tenuous than that of the classical civilizations of Asia.

Beyond the Classical Civilizations

Although the development of the three great civilizations is the central thread in world history during the classical period, significant changes also occurred in other parts of the world. On the borders of the major civilizations, as in northeastern Africa, Japan, and northern Europe, these changes bore some relationship to the classical world, although they were partly autonomous. Elsewhere, most notably in the Americas, new cultures evolved in an entirely independent way. In all cases, changes during the classical period set the stage for more important links in world history later on. Southeast Asia gained access to civilization during the classical period mainly through its contacts with India. Regional kingdoms had already been established, and agricultural economies were familiar on the principal islands of Indonesia as well as on the mainland. Participation in wider trade patterns developed through the efforts of Indian merchants. Hindu and particularly Buddhist religion and art also spread from India. Here was a case of the outright expansion of civilization without the creation of a fully distinctive or unified culture.

Significant civilizations developed in the Americas and Africa outside the immediate classical orbit.

Developments in Africa's Kush and its Heritage

A similar case of expansion from an established civilization affected parts of sub-Saharan Africa; indeed, in this case the interaction had begun well before the rise of Greece and Rome. By the year 1000 B.C.E., the independent kingdom of Kush was flourishing along the upper Nile. It possessed a form of writing derived from Egyptian hieroglyphics (and which has not yet been fully deciphered) and mastered the use of iron. Briefly, around 750 B.C.E., armies from Kush conquered Egypt (Figure 5.2). Major cities were built. The Kushites seem to have established a strong monarchy, with elaborate ceremonies illustrating a belief that the king was divine. The kingdom of Kush was defeated by a rival kingdom called **Axum** by about 300 B.C.E.; Axum ultimately fell to another regional kingdom, **Ethiopia.** Axum and Ethiopia had active contacts with the eastern Mediterranean world until after the fall of Rome. They traded with this region for several centuries. The activities of Jewish merchants brought some conversions to Judaism, and a small minority of Ethiopians has remained Jewish to the present day. Greek-speaking merchants also had considerable influence, and it was through them that Christianity was brought to Ethiopia by the 4th century C.E. The Ethiopian Christian church, however, was cut off from mainstream Christianity thereafter, flourishing in isolation to modern times. And Ethiopia had the world's oldest continuous monarchy, which lasted until it was abolished in the late 20th century.

It is not clear how much influence, if any, the kingdoms of the upper Nile had on the later history of sub-Saharan Africa. Knowledge of ironworking certainly spread, facilitating the expansion of agriculture in other parts of the continent. Patterns of strong, ceremonial kingship—sometimes called divine kingship—would surface in other parts of Africa later, but whether this occurred

Axum   Kingdom located in Ethiopian highlands; replaced Meroë in first century C.E.; received strong influence from Arabian peninsula; eventually converted to Christianity.

Ethiopia   A Christian kingdom that developed in the highlands of eastern Africa under the dynasty of King Lalaibela; retained Christianity in the face of Muslim expansion elsewhere in Africa.

Nomads and Cross-Civilization Contacts and Exchanges

Through much of recorded human history, nomadic peoples have been key agents of contact between sedentary, farming peoples and town dwellers in centers of civilization across the globe. Nomadic peoples pioneered all the great overland routes that linked the civilized cores of Eurasia in ancient times and the Middle Ages. The most famous was the fabled **Silk Road** that ran from western China across the mountains and steppes of central Asia to the civilized centers of Mesopotamia in the last millennium B.C.E., and to Rome, the Islamic heartlands, and western Europe in the first millennium and a half C.E.

> Pastoral peoples played critical roles in establishing and expanding trading links.

Chinese rulers at one end of these trading networks, and Roman emperors and later Islamic sultans at the other end, often had to send their armies to do battle with hostile nomads whose raids threatened to cut off the flow of trade. But perhaps more often, pastoral peoples played critical roles in establishing and expanding trading links. For periodic payments by merchants and imperial bureaucrats, they provided protection from bandits and raiding parties for caravans passing through their grazing lands. For further payments, nomadic peoples supplied animals to transport both the merchants' goods and the food and drink needed by those in the caravan parties. At times, pastoralists themselves took charge of transport and trading, but it was more common for the trading operations to be controlled by specialized merchants. These merchants were based either in the urban centers of the civilized cores or in the trading towns that grew up along the Silk Road in central Asia, the oases of Arabia, and the savanna zones that bordered on the north and south the vast Sahara desert in Africa.

Until they were supplanted by the railroads and steamships of the Industrial Revolution, the overland trading routes of Eurasia and the Americas, along with comparable networks established for sailing vessels, were the most important channels for contacts between civilizations. Religions such as Buddhism and Islam spread peacefully along the trading routes throughout central Asia, Persia, and Africa. Artistic motifs and styles, such as those developed in the cosmopolitan Hellenistic world created by Alexander the Great's conquests, were spread by trading contacts in northern Africa, northern India, and western China.

Inventions that were vital to the continued growth and expansion of the civilized cores were carried in war and peace by traders or nomadic peoples from one center to another. For example, central Asian steppe nomads who had converted to Islam clashed with the armies of China in the 8th century C.E. The victorious Muslims found craftspeople among their prisoners who knew the secrets of making paper, which had been invented many centuries earlier by the Chinese. The combination of nomadic mobility and established trading links resulted in the rapid diffusion of papermaking techniques to Mesopotamia and Egypt in the 8th and 9th centuries and across northern Africa to Europe in the centuries that followed.

Nomadic warriors also contributed to the spread of new military technologies and modes of warfare, particularly across the great Eurasian land mass. Sedentary peoples often adopted the nomads' reliance on heavy cavalry and hit-and-run tactics. Saddles, bits, and bow and arrow designs developed by nomadic herders were avidly imitated by farming societies. And defense against nomadic assaults inspired some of the great engineering feats of the preindustrial world, most notably the Great Wall of China (discussed in Chapter 2). It also spurred the development of gunpowder and cannons in China, where the threat of nomadic incursions persisted well into the 19th century.

In addition, nomadic peoples have served as agents for the transfer of food crops between distant civilized cores, even if they

Figure 5.2 This tomb painting from about 1300 B.C.E. highlights black-skinned people from the rising kingdom of Kush, who interacted increasingly with Egyptian society and at one point controlled Egypt directly.

did not usually themselves cultivate the plants being exchanged. In a less constructive vein, nomadic warriors have played a key role in transmitting diseases. In the best-documented instance of this pattern, Mongol cavalry carried the bacterium that causes the strain of the plague that came to be known as the Black Death from central Asia to China in the 14th century. They may also have transmitted it to the West, where it devastated the port cities of the Black Sea region and was later carried by merchant ships to the Middle East and southern Europe.

QUESTIONS What other groups played roles as intermediaries between civilizations in early global history? What features of the nomads' culture and society rendered them ideal agents for transmitting technology, trade goods, crops, and diseases between different cultural zones? Why have the avenues of exchange they provided been open only for limited time spans and then blocked for years or decades at a time? What agents of transmission have taken the place of nomadic peoples in recent centuries?

Map 5.1 Trade Routes at the End of the Classical Era

through some contact with the Kushite tradition or independently is not known. Knowledge of Kushite writing did not spread, which suggests that the impact of this first case of civilization below the Sahara was somewhat limited.

For most of Africa below the Sahara but north of the great tropical jungles, the major development up to 500 C.E. was the further extension of agriculture. Well organized villages arose, often very similar in form and structure to those that still exist. Farming took earliest root on the southern fringes of the **Sahara,** which was less arid than it is today. Toward the end of the classical era, important regional kingdoms were forming in western Africa, leading to the first great state in the region: Ghana. Because of the barriers of dense vegetation and the impact of African diseases on domesticated animals, agriculture spread only slowly southward. However, the creation of a strong agricultural economy prepared the way for the next, more long-lasting and influential wave of African kingdoms, far to the west of the Nile. New crops, including root crops and plantains introduced through trade with southeast Asia about 100 C.E., helped African farmers push into new areas.

Sahara Desert running across northern Africa; separates the Mediterranean coast from southern Africa.

Japan and Northern Europe

Advances in agriculture and manufacturing also occurred in other parts of the world besides sub-Saharan Africa. In northern Europe and Japan, there was no question, as yet, of elaborate contacts with the great civilizations, no counterpart to the influences that affected parts of southeast Asia and the upper Nile valley. Japan, by the year 200 C.E., had established extensive agriculture. The population of the islands had been formed mainly by migrations from the peninsula of Korea, over a 200,000-year span. These migrations had ceased by the year 200. In Japan, a regional political organization based on tribal chiefs evolved; each tribal group had its own god, thought of as an ancestor. A Chinese visitor in 297 described the Japanese as law-abiding, fond of drink, expert at agriculture and fishing; they observed strict social differences, indicated by tattoos or other body markings. Japan had also developed considerable ironworking; the Japanese seem to have skipped the stage of using bronze and copper tools, moving directly from stone tools to iron. Finally, regional states in Japan became increasingly sophisticated, each controlling somewhat larger territories. In 400 C.E., one such state brought in scribes from Korea to keep records—this represented the introduction of writing in the islands.

Japan's religion, **Shintoism,** provided for the worship of political rulers and the spirits of nature, including the all-important god of rice. Many local shrines and rituals revolved around Shinto beliefs, which became unified into a single national religion by 700 C.E. However, this was a simple religion, rather different in ritual and doctrine from the great world religions and philosophies developing in the classical civilizations. Something like national politics arose only around 400 C.E., when one regional ruler began to win the loyalty and trust of other local leaders. This was the basis for Japan's imperial house, with the emperor worshipped as a religious figure. Such growing political sophistication and national cultural unity were just emerging by 600 C.E., however. It was at this point that Japan was ready for more elaborate contacts with China—a process that would move Japan squarely into the orbit of major civilizations.

Much of northern Europe lagged behind Japan's pace. Teutonic or Celtic peoples in what today is Germany, England, and Scandinavia, as well as Slavic peoples in much of eastern Europe, were loosely organized into regional kingdoms. Some, in Germany and England, had succumbed to the advances of the distant Roman Empire, but after Rome's decline the patterns of regional politics resumed. There was no written language, except in cases where Latin had been imported. Agriculture, often still combined with hunting, was rather primitive. Scandinavians were developing increasing skill as sailors, which would lead them into wider trade and pillage in the centuries after 600 C.E. Religious beliefs featured a host of gods and rituals designed to placate the forces of nature. This region would change, particularly through the spread of the religious and intellectual influences of Christianity. However, these shifts still lay in the future, and even conversions to Christianity did not bring northern and eastern Europe into the orbit of a single civilization. Until about 1000 C.E., northern Europe remained one of the most backward areas in the world.

Central America

Yet another portion of the world was developing civilization by 600 C.E.—indeed, its progress was greater than that of much of Europe and Africa. In Central America, an Indian group called the Olmecs developed and spread an early form of civilization from about 800 until 400 B.C.E. The Olmecs seem to have lacked writing, but they produced massive, pyramid-shaped religious monuments.

The first American civilization was based on many centuries of advancing agriculture, expanding from the early cultivation of corn. Initially, in the wild state, corn ears were scarcely larger than strawberries, but patient breeding gradually converted this grain into a staple food crop. In the Andes areas of South America, root crops were also grown, particularly the potato. The development of American agriculture was limited by the few domesticated animals available—turkeys, dogs, and guinea pigs in Central America. Nevertheless, **Olmec culture** displayed many impressive achievements. It explored artistic forms in precious stones such as jade. Religious statues and icons blended human images with those of animals. Scientific research produced accurate and impressive calendars. Olmec culture, in its religious and artistic emphases, powerfully influenced later Indian civilizations in Central America. The Olmecs disappeared without a clear trace around 400 B.C.E., but their successors soon developed a hieroglyphic alphabet and built the first great city—

Shinto   Religion of early Japanese culture; devotees worshipped numerous gods and spirits associated with the natural world; offers of food and prayers made to gods and nature spirits.

Celtic Expansion, Fifth to Third Century BCE   MAP

A Mayan Town   IMAGE

Olmec culture   Cultural tradition that arose at San Lorenzo and La Venta in Mexico c. 1200 B.C.E.; featured irrigated agriculture, urbanism, elaborate religion, beginnings of calendrical and writing systems.

Teotihuacan (tay-oh-tee-wah-KAHN)—in the Americas, as a center for trade and worship. This culture, in turn, suffered setbacks from migrations and regional wars, but from its base developed a still fuller American civilization, starting with the **Maya,** from about 400 C.E. onward.

In essence, the Olmecs and their successors had provided for the Central American region the equivalent of the river valley civilizations in Asia and the Middle East, although many centuries later (Map 5.2). A similar early civilization arose in the Andes region in present-day Peru and Bolivia, where careful agriculture allowed the construction of elaborate cities and religious monuments. This culture would lead, later, to the civilization of the **Inca.** The two centers of early civilization in the Americas developed in total isolation from developments elsewhere in the world. As a result, they lacked certain advantages that come from the ability to copy and react to other societies, including such basic technologies as the wheel or the capacity to work iron. However, the early American Indian cultures were considerably ahead of most of those in Europe during the same period. And they demonstrate the common, although not invariable, tendency of humans to move from the establishment of agriculture to the creation of the more elaborate trappings of a civilized society.

Teotihuacan [tay-oh-tee-wah-KAHN] Site of classic culture in central Mexico; urban center with important religious functions; supported by intensive agriculture in surrounding regions; population of as much as 200,000.

Maya Classic culture emerging in southern Mexico and Central America contemporary with Teotihuacan; extended over broad region; featured monumental architecture, written language, calendrical and mathematical systems, highly developed religion.

Inca Group of clans centered at Cuzco that were able to create empire incorporating various Andean cultures; term also used for leader of empire.

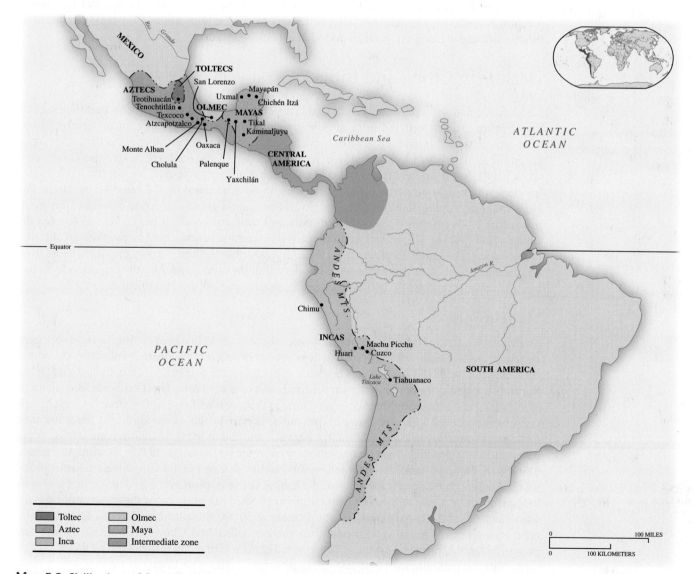

Map 5.2 Civilizations of Central and South America Three cultural "hearths" are represented: Mesoamerica, extending from north-central Mexico to Nicaragua; the Andean region in South America, and the Intermediate zone of modern-day Colombia and Panama which shared many characteristics with the other zones but did not build in stone.

Polynesia

Another case of isolated development featured the migration of agricultural peoples to new island territories in the Pacific. **Polynesian** peoples had reached islands such as Fiji and Samoa by 1000 B.C.E. Further explorations in giant outrigger canoes led to the first settlement of island complexes such as Hawaii by 400 C.E., where the new settlers adapted local plants, brought in new animals (notably pigs), and imported a highly stratified caste system under powerful local kings.

Agriculture, in sum, expanded into new areas during the classical period; early civilizations, or early contacts, were also forming. These developments were not central to world history during the classical period itself, but they folded into the larger human experience thereafter.

The herding peoples of central Asia also contributed to world history, particularly toward the end of the classical period. Some nomadic groups gained new contacts with established civilizations, like China, which brought changes in political organization as well as some new goals for conquest. Central Asian herders played a vital role in trade routes between east Asia and the Middle East, transporting goods like silk across long distances. Other herding groups produced important technological innovations, such as the stirrup, which allowed riders to aim weapons better. The herding groups thus enjoyed an important history of their own, and they provided important contacts among the civilizations that they bordered. Finally, perhaps because of internal population pressure as well as new appetites and opportunities, herding groups invaded the major civilizations directly, helping to bring the classical period as a whole to an end.

Polynesia Islands contained in a rough triangle whose points lie in Hawaii, New Zealand, and Easter Island.

Nomad Empires MAP

A combination of internal weakness and invasion led to important changes, first in China, then in India.

Decline in China and India

Between 200 and 600 C.E., all three classical civilizations collapsed entirely or in part. During this four-century span, all suffered from outside invasions, the result of growing incursions by groups from central Asia. This renewed wave of nomadic expansion was not as sweeping as the earlier Indo-European growth, which had spread over India and much of the Mediterranean region many centuries before, but it severely tested the civilized regimes. Rome, of course, fell directly to Germanic invaders, who fought on partly because they were, in turn, harassed by the fierce Asiatic Huns. The Huns swept once across Italy, invading the city of Rome amid great destruction. Another Hun group from central Asia overthrew the Guptas in India, and similar nomadic tribes had earlier toppled the Chinese Han dynasty. The central Asian nomads were certainly encouraged by a growing realization of the weakness of the classical regimes. Han China as well as the later Roman Empire suffered from serious internal problems long before the invaders dealt the final blows. And the Guptas in India had not permanently resolved that area's tendency to dissolve into political fragmentation.

The Han Collapse

By about 100 C.E., the Han dynasty in China entered a serious decline, and its deteriorations operated on several levels. Confucian intellectual activity gradually became less creative. Politically, the central government's control diminished, and bureaucrats became more corrupt. Assassinations of and by bureaucrats competing for power at the top occurred on several occasions. Local landlords took up much of the slack, ruling their neighborhoods according to their own wishes. The free peasants, long heavily taxed, were burdened with new taxes and demands of service by these same landlords. Many lost their farms and became day laborers on the large estates. Some had to sell their children into service. Social unrest increased, producing a great revolutionary effort led by Daoists in 184 C.E. Daoism now gained new appeal, shifting toward a popular religion and adding healing practices and magic to earlier philosophical beliefs. The Daoist leaders, called the **Yellow Turbans,** promised a golden age that was to be brought about by divine magic. The Yellow Turbans attacked the weakness of the emperor but also the self-indulgence of the current bureaucracy. As many as 30,000 students demonstrated against the decline of government morality. However, their protests failed, and Chinese population growth and prosperity spiraled further downward. The imperial court was mired in intrigue and civil war.

This dramatic decline paralleled the slightly later collapse of Rome, as we shall see. It obviously explained China's inability to push back invasions from borderland nomads, who finally overthrew the Han dynasty outright. As in Rome, growing political ineffectiveness formed part of the decline. Another important factor was the spread of devastating new epidemics, which may have

Yellow Turbans Chinese Daoists who launched a revolt in 184 C.E. in China promising a golden age to be brought about by divine magic.

killed up to half of the population. These combined blows not only toppled the Han but led to almost three centuries of chaos—an unusually long span of unrest in Chinese history. Regional rulers and weak dynasties rose and fell during this period. Even China's cultural unity was threatened as the wave of Buddhism spread—one of the only cases in which China imported a major idea from outside its borders, until the 20th century. Northern China, particularly, seemed near collapse.

Nonetheless, China did revive itself near the end of the 6th century. Strong native rulers in the north drove out the nomadic invaders. The **Sui** (sway) dynasty briefly ruled, and then in 618 C.E. it was followed by the **Tang,** who sponsored one of the most glorious periods in Chinese history. Confucianism and the bureaucratic system were revived, and indeed the bureaucratic tradition became more elaborate. The period of chaos left its mark somewhat in the continued presence of a Buddhist minority and new styles in art and literature. But, unlike the case of Rome, there was no permanent disruption.

The structures of classical China were simply too strong to be overturned. The bureaucracy declined in scope and quality, but it did not disappear during the troubled centuries. Confucian values and styles of life remained current among the upper class. Many of the nomadic invaders, seeing that they had nothing better to offer by way of government or culture, simply tried to assimilate the Chinese traditions. China thus had to recover from a serious setback but did not have to reinvent its civilization.

The End of the Gupta Empire

The decline of classical civilization in India was less drastic than the collapse of Han China. The ability of the Gupta emperors to control local princes was declining by the 5th century. Invasions by nomadic peoples, probably Hun tribes similar to those who were pressing into Europe, affected some northern portions of India as early as 500 C.E. During the next century, the invaders penetrated much deeper, destroying the Gupta Empire in central India. Many of the invaders were integrated into the warrior caste of India, forming a new ruling group of regional princes. For several centuries, no native ruler attempted to build a large Indian state. The regional princes, collectively called **Rajput** (RAHJ-poot), controlled the small states and emphasized military prowess. Few political events of more than local significance occurred.

Within this framework, Indian culture continued to evolve. Buddhism declined further in India proper. Hindu beliefs gained ground, among other things converting the Hun princes, who had originally worshipped gods of battle and had no sympathy for the Buddhist principles of calm and contemplation. Within Hinduism, the worship of a mother goddess, **Devi** (DAY-vee), spread widely, encouraging a new popular emotionalism in religious ritual. Indian economic prosperity also continued at high levels.

Although Indian civilization substantially maintained its position, another threat was to come, after 600 C.E., from the new Middle Eastern religion of **Islam.** Arab armies, fighting under the banners of **Allah,** reached India's porous northwestern frontier during the 7th century, and while there was initially little outright conquest on the subcontinent, Islam did win some converts in the northwest. Hindu leaders reacted to the arrival of this new faith by strengthening their emphasis on religious devotion, at the expense of some other intellectual interests. Hinduism also underwent further popularization; Hindu texts were written in vernacular languages such as Hindi, and use of the old classical language, Sanskrit, declined. These reactions were largely successful in preventing more than a minority of Indians from abandoning Hinduism, but they distracted from further achievements in science and mathematics. Islam also hit hard at India's international economic position and affected its larger impact throughout Asia. Arab traders soon wrested control of the Indian Ocean from Tamil merchants, and India, though still prosperous and productive, saw its commercial dynamism reduced. In politics, regionalism continued to prevail. Clearly, the glory days of the Guptas were long past, although classical traditions survived particularly in Hinduism and the caste system.

Decline and Fall in Rome

The Roman Empire exhibited a great many symptoms of decay after about 180 C.E. The population was declining, and the empire faced growing difficulties in recruiting effective armies. There were also political manifestations in the greater brutality and arbitrariness of many Roman emperors

Sui [sway] Dynasty that succeeded the Han in China; emerged from strong rulers in northern China; united all of northern China and reconquered southern China.

Tang Dynasty that succeeded the Sui in 618 C.E.; more stable than previous dynasty.

 Political Regionalism and Cultural Unity in the Gupta-Harsha Eras

Rajput [RAHJ-poot] Regional princes in western India; emphasized military control of their regions.

Devi [DAY-vee] Mother goddess within Hinduism; widely spread following collapse of Guptas; encouraged new emotionalism in religious ritual.

Islam Major world religion having its origins in 610 C.E. in the Arabian peninsula; meaning literally submission; based on prophecy of Muhammad.

Allah Supreme God in strictly monotheistic Islam.

Decline in Rome was complex, involving a mix of internal and external factors.

The eastern and western portions of the empire developed differently after the fall of Rome.

who, according to one commentator at the time, were given to "lustful and cruel habits." Tax collection became increasingly difficult, as residents of the empire fell on hard times. The governor of Egypt complained that "the once numerous inhabitants of the aforesaid villages have now been reduced to a few, because some have fled in poverty and others have died and for this reason we are in danger owing to impoverishment of having to abandon the tax-collectorship."

Above all, there were human symptoms. Inscriptions on Roman tombstones increasingly ended with the slogan, "I was not, I was, I am not, I have no more desires," suggesting a pervasive despondency over the futility of this life and despair at the absence of an afterlife.

Symptoms of Decline

The decline of Rome was more disruptive than the collapse of the classical dynasties in Asia. For this reason, and because memories of the collapse of this great empire became part of the Western tradition, the process of deterioration deserves particular attention. Every so often, Americans or western Europeans concerned about changes in their own society wonder if there might be lessons in Rome's fall that apply to the uncertain future of Western civilization today.

We have seen that the quality of political and economic life in the Roman Empire began to shift after about 180 C.E. Political confusion produced a series of weak emperors and many disputes over succession to the throne. Intervention by the army in the selection of emperors complicated political life and contributed to the deterioration of rule from the top. More important in initiating the process of decline was a series of plagues that swept over the empire. As in China, the plagues' source was growing international trade, which brought diseases endemic in southern Asia to new areas like the Mediterranean, where no resistance had been established even to contagions such as the measles. The resulting diseases decimated the population. The population of Rome decreased from a million people to 250,000. Economic life worsened in consequence. Recruitment of troops became more difficult, so the empire was increasingly reduced to hiring Germanic soldiers to guard its frontiers. The need to pay troops added to the demands on the state's budget, just as declining production cut into tax revenues.

The Rise and Fall of Rome

CASE STUDY

Here, perhaps, is the key to the process of decline: a set of general problems, triggered by a cycle of plagues that could not be prevented, resulting in a rather mechanistic spiral that steadily worsened. However, it is hard to say whether another side to Rome's downfall is either a cause or result of the initial difficulties. Rome's upper classes became steadily more pleasure-seeking, turning away from the political devotion and economic vigor that had characterized the republic and early empire. Cultural life decayed. Aside from some truly creative Christian writers—the fathers of Western theology—there was very little sparkle to the art or literature of the later empire. Many Roman scholars contented themselves with writing textbooks that rather mechanically summarized earlier achievements in science, mathematics, and literary style. Writing textbooks is not, of course, proof of absolute intellectual incompetence—at least, not in all cases—but the point was that new knowledge or artistic styles were not being generated, and even the levels of previous accomplishment began to slip. The later Romans wrote textbooks about rhetoric instead of displaying rhetorical talent in actual political life. And they wrote simple compendiums, for example, about animals or geometry, that barely captured the essentials of what earlier intellectuals had known, and often added superstitious beliefs that previous generations would have scorned.

This cultural decline, finally, was not clearly due to disease or economic collapse, for it began in some ways before these larger problems surfaced. Something was happening to the Roman elite, perhaps because of the deadening effect of authoritarian political rule, perhaps because of a new interest in luxuries and sensual indulgence. Revealingly, the upper classes no longer produced many offspring, for bearing and raising children seemed incompatible with a life of pleasure-seeking.

Rome's fall, in other words, can be blamed on large, impersonal forces that would have been hard for any society to control or a moral and political decay that reflected growing corruption among society's leaders. Probably elements of both were involved. Thus, the plagues would have weakened even a vigorous society, but they would not necessarily have produced an irreversible downward spiral had not the morale of the ruling classes already been sapped by an unproductive lifestyle and superficial values.

Effort at Revival: An East/West Split

Regardless of precise causes, the course of Roman decay is quite clear. As the quality of imperial rule declined, as life became more dangerous and economic survival more precarious, many farmers clustered around the protection of large landlords, surrendering full control over their plots of land in the hope of military and judicial protection. The decentralization of political and economic authority, which was greatest in the western, or European, portions of the empire, foreshadowed the manorial system of Europe in the Middle Ages. The system of estates gave great political power to landlords and provided some local stability. But, in the long run, it weakened the power of the emperor and also tended to move the economy away from the elaborate and successful trade patterns of Mediterranean civilization in its heyday. Many estates tried to be self-sufficient. Trade and production declined further as a result, and cities shrank in size. The empire was locked in a vicious circle, in which responses to the initial deterioration merely lessened the chances of recovery.

Some later emperors tried vigorously to reverse the tide. Diocletian, who ruled from 284 to 305 C.E., tightened up the administration of the empire and tried to improve tax collection. Regulation of the dwindling economy increased. Diocletian also attempted to direct political loyalties to his own person, exerting pressure to worship the emperor as god. This was what prompted him to persecute Christians with particular viciousness, for they would not give Caesar preference over their god. The emperor Constantine, who ruled from 312 to 337 C.E., experimented with other methods of control. He set up a second capital city, Constantinople, to regulate the eastern half of the empire more efficiently. He tried to use the religious force of Christianity to unify the empire spiritually, extending its toleration and adopting it as his own faith. These measures were not without result. The Eastern empire, ruled from Constantinople (now the Turkish city of Istanbul), remained an effective political and economic unit. Christianity spread under his official sponsorship, although there were some new problems linked to its success.

None of these measures, however, revived the empire as a whole. Division merely made the weakness of the western half worse. Attempts to regulate the economy reduced economic initiative and lowered production; ultimately tax revenues declined once again. The army deteriorated further. And, when the Germanic invasions began in earnest in the 400s, there was scant basis to resist. Many peasants, burdened by the social and economic pressures of the decaying empire, actually welcomed the barbarians. A priest noted that "in all districts taken over by the Germans, there is one desire among all the Romans, that they should never again find it necessary to pass under Roman jurisdiction." German kingdoms were established in many parts of the empire by 425 C.E., and the last Roman emperor in the West was displaced in 476 C.E. The Germanic invaders numbered at most 5 percent of the population of the empire, but so great was the earlier Roman decline that this small, poorly organized force was able to put an end to one of the world's great political structures (Map 5.3).

 Germanic Kingdoms, c. 525

The collapse of Rome echoed mightily through the later history of Europe and the Middle East. Rome's fall split the unity of the Mediterranean lands that had been so arduously won through Hellenistic culture and then by the Roman Empire. This was one sign that the end of the Roman Empire was a more serious affair than the displacement of the last classical dynasties in India and China, for Greece and Rome had not produced the shared political culture and bureaucratic traditions of China that could allow revival after a period of chaos. Nor had Mediterranean civilization, for all its vitality, generated a common religion that appealed deeply enough, or satisfied enough needs, to maintain unity amid political fragmentation, as in India. Such religions would reach the Mediterranean world as Rome fell, but they came too late to save the empire and produced a deep rift in this world—between Christian and Muslim—that has not been healed to this day.

However, Rome's collapse, although profound, was uneven. In effect, the fall of Rome divided the Mediterranean world into three zones, which formed the starting points of three distinct civilizations that would develop in later centuries (Map 5.4).

The Early Byzantine Empire

In the eastern part of the empire, centered now on Constantinople, the empire in a sense did not fall. Civilization was more deeply entrenched here than in some of the western European portions of the empire, and there were fewer pressures from invaders. Emperors continued to rule Greece

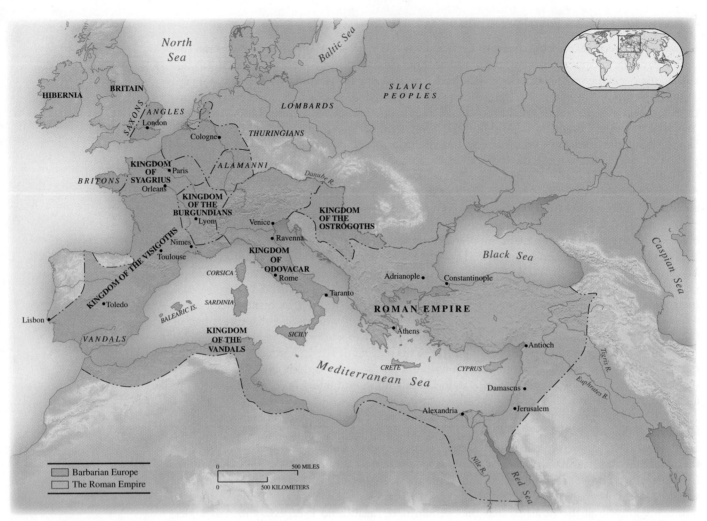

Map 5.3 Germanic Kingdoms after the Invasions. Nomadic tribes converged mainly on the western part of the Roman Empire, invading Rome itself and its European outposts.

Byzantine Empire Eastern half of Roman Empire following collapse of western half of old empire; retained Mediterranean culture, particularly Greek; later lost Palestine, Syria, and Egypt to Islam; capital at Constantinople.

Justinian (c. 482–565) Early Byzantine emperor, responsible for major building in Constantinople and a codification of Roman law; his efforts to recapture some additional previously Roman territory ended in failure.

and other parts of southeast Europe, plus the northern Middle East. This Eastern empire—later to be known as the **Byzantine Empire**—was a product of late imperial Rome, rather than a balanced result of the entire span of classical Mediterranean civilization. Thus, although its language was Greek, it maintained the authoritarian tone of the late Roman rulers. But the Eastern empire was vibrant, artistically creative, and active in trade. Briefly, especially under the emperor **Justinian** (who ruled from 527 to 565 C.E.), the eastern emperors tried to recapture the whole heritage of Rome. However, Justinian was unable to maintain a hold in Italy and even lost the provinces of north Africa. He did issue one of the most famous compilations of Roman law, in the code that bore his name. But his was the last effort to restore Mediterranean unity.

The Byzantine Empire did not control the whole of the northern Middle East, even in its greatest days. During the late Hellenistic periods and into the early centuries of the Roman Empire, a Parthian empire had flourished, centered in the Tigris–Euphrates region but spreading into northwestern India and to the borders of Rome's holdings along the Mediterranean. Parthian conquerors had taken over this portion of Alexander the Great's empire. They produced little culture of their own, being content to rely on Persian styles, but they long maintained an effective military and bureaucratic apparatus. Then, around 227 C.E., a Persian rebellion displaced the Parthians and created a new Sassanid Empire that more directly revived the glories of the earlier Persian Empire. Persian religious ideas, including the religion of Zoroastrianism, revived although there was some conversion to Christianity as well. Persian styles in art and manufacturing experienced a brilliant resurgence.

Map 5.4 The Mediterranean, Middle East, Europe, and North Africa, c. 500 C.E.   Soon after the fall of Rome, the former empire split into three distinct zones.

Both the Parthian and the Sassanid empires served as bridges between the Mediterranean and the East, transmitting goods and some artistic and literary styles between the Greek-speaking world and India and China. As the Roman Empire weakened, the Sassanids joined the attack, at times pushing into parts of southeastern Europe. Ultimately, however, the Byzantine Empire managed to create a stable frontier. The Sassanid Empire preserved the important strain of Persian culture in the eastern part of the Middle East, and this continued to influence this region as well as India. The Sassanids themselves, however, were finally overthrown by the surge of Arab conquest that followed the rise of Islam, in the 7th century C.E.

Rome's fall, then, did not disrupt the northern Middle East—the original cradle of civilization—as much as might have been expected. Persian rule simply continued in one part of the region, until the Arab onslaught, which itself did not destroy Persian culture. Byzantium maintained many of the traditions of the later Roman Empire, plus Christianity, in the western part of the Middle East and in Greece and other parts of southeastern Europe.

Western Europe and North Africa

The second zone that devolved from Rome's fall consisted of North Africa and the southeastern shores of the Mediterranean. Here, a number of regional kingdoms briefly succeeded the empire. While Christianity spread into the area—indeed, one of the greatest Christian theologians, **Augustine,** was a bishop in North Africa—its appearance was not so uniformly triumphant as in the Byzantine Empire or western Europe. Furthermore, separate beliefs and doctrines soon split north African Christianity from the larger branches, producing most notably the **Coptic** church in Egypt, which still survives as a Christian minority in that country. Soon this region would be filled with the still newer doctrines of Islam and a new Arab empire.

Finally, there was the western part of the empire—Italy, Spain, and points north. Here is where Rome's fall not only shattered unities but also reduced the level of civilization itself. Crude, regional Germanic kingdoms developed in parts of Italy, France, and elsewhere. Cities shrank still further, and, especially outside Italy, trade almost disappeared. The only clearly vital forces in this region emanated not from Roman traditions but from the spread of Christianity. Even Christianity

Augustine (Saint)   Influential church father and theologian (354–430 C.E.); born in Africa and ultimately bishop of Hippo in Africa; champion of Christian doctrine against various heresies and very important in the long-term development of Christian thought on such issues as predestination.

Coptic   Christian sect in Egypt, later tolerated after Islamic takeover.

could not sustain a sophisticated culture of literature or art, however. In the mire of Rome's collapse, this part of the world forgot for several centuries what it had previously known.

In this western domain, what we call the fall of Rome was scarcely noted at the time, for decay had been progressing for so many decades that the failure to name a new emperor meant little. There was some comprehension of loss, some realization that the present could not rival the past. Thus, Christian scholars were soon apologizing for their inability to write well or to understand some of the doctrines of the earlier theologians like Augustine. This sense of inferiority to classical achievements would long mark the culture of this western zone, even as times improved.

The New Religious Map

The end of the classical period is not simply the story of decay and collapse. This same period, from 200 to 600 C.E., saw the effective rise of many of the world's major religions. The devastating plagues caused new interest in belief systems that could provide solace amid rising death rates. From Spain to China, growing political instability clearly prompted many people to seek solace in joys of the spirit, and while the religious surge was not entirely new, the resulting changes in the religious map of Europe and Asia and the nature and intensity of religious interests were significant new forces. Christianity, born two centuries before Rome's collapse began, became a widespread religion throughout the Mediterranean region as the empire's political strength weakened. Buddhism, although launched still earlier, saw its surge into eastern Asia furthered by the growing problems of classical China. Thus, two major faiths, different in many ways but similar in their emphasis on spiritual life and the importance of divine power, reshaped major portions of Europe and Asia precisely as the structures of the classical period declined or disappeared. Finally, shortly after 600 C.E., an entirely new religion, Islam, surfaced and became the most dynamic force in world history during the next several centuries. In sum, the religious map of the world, although by no means completed by 500 C.E., was beginning to take on dramatic new contours. This means that while civilization in many ways declined, it was also being altered, taking new directions as well as losing some older strengths. Never before had single religions spread so widely, crossing so many cultural and political boundaries.

The newly expanding religions shared some general features. Christianity, Buddhism, and Hinduism (as well as Islam later on) all emphasized intense devotion and piety, stressing the importance of spiritual concerns beyond the daily cares of earthly life. All three offered the hope of a better existence after this life ended, and each one responded to new political instability and to the growing poverty of people in various parts of the civilized world.

The spread of the major religions meant that hundreds of thousands of people, in Asia, Europe, and Africa, underwent a conversion process as the classical period drew to a close. Radically changing beliefs is an unusual human experience, symptomatic in this case of the new pressures on established political structures and on ordinary life. At the same time, many people blended new beliefs with the old, in a process called *syncretism*. This meant that the religions changed too, sometimes taking on the features of individual civilizations even while maintaining larger religious claims.

Hinduism, Buddhism, and Daoism

Despite important common features, the major religions were very different. Hinduism, as we have seen, retained its belief in reincarnation and its combination of spiritual interest in union with the divine essence and extensive rituals and ceremonies. The religion did experience greater popular appeal after the fall of the Guptas, associated with the expanded use of popular languages and with the worship of the mother goddess Devi.

Buddhism was altered more substantially than Hinduism as it traveled mainly beyond India's borders, becoming only a small minority faith in India itself. The chief agents of Buddhist expansion and leadership were monks, for Buddhism tended to divide the faithful among a minority who abandoned earthly life in favor of spiritual dedication and the larger number who continued to work in the world while doing the best they could to meet their spiritual obligations. Some centuries after

The period of classical decline saw the rapid expansion of Buddhism and Christianity.

Religious change had wider cultural, social, and political implications.

The Popularization of Buddhism

Chinese Buddhism, unlike most Chinese beliefs, spread among all regions and social groups. Although it divided into many sects that disagreed over details of theology and rituals by commenting on earlier Buddhist scriptures (the Sutras), many ordinary Chinese believers cared little for such details and were more concerned with direct spiritual benefits. Often they arranged to have Buddhist sermons copied, as a means of obtaining merit, while adding a note of their own. The following passages come from such notes, written mainly in the 6th century. They suggest the various reasons people might go through the challenging process of converting to a new religion.

Recorded on the 15th day of the fourth month of 531.
The Buddhist lay disciple Yuan Rong—having lived in this degenerate era for many years, fearful for his life, and yearning for home—now makes a donation of a thousand silver coins to the Three Jewels [the Buddha, the Law, and the Monastic Order]. This donation is made in the name of the Celestial King Vaisravana. In addition, he makes a donation of a thousand to ransom himself and his wife and children [from their earthly existence], a thousand more to ransom his servants, and a thousand more to ransom his domestic animals. This money is to be used for copying sutras. It is accompanied by the prayer that the Celestial King may attain Buddhahood; that the disciple's family, servants, and animals may be blessed with long life, may attain enlightenment, and may all be permitted to return to the capital.

Dated the 29th day of the fourth month of 550.
Happiness is not fortuitous: Pray for it and it will respond. Results are not born of thin air: Pay heed to causes and results will follow. This explains how the Buddhist disciple and nun Daorong—because her conduct in her previous life was not correct—came to be born in her present form, a woman, vile and unclean.

Now if she does not honor the awesome decree of Buddha, how can future consequences be favorable for her? Therefore, having cut down her expenditures on food and clothing, she reverently has had the Nirvana Sutra copied once. She prays that those who read it carefully will be exalted in mind to the highest realms and that those who communicate its meaning will cause others to be so enlightened.

She also prays that in her present existence she will have no further sickness or suffering, that her parents in seven other incarnations (who have already died or will die in the future) and her present family and close relatives may experience joy in the four realms [earth, water, fire, and air], and that whatever they seek may indeed come to pass. Finally, she prays that all those endowed with knowledge may be included within this prayer.

Recorded on the 28th day of the fifth month of 583.
The Army Superintendent, Sung Shao, having suffered the heavy sorrow of losing both his father and mother, made a vow on their behalf to read one section each of [many] sutras. He prays that the spirits of his parents will someday reach the Pure Land [paradise] and will thus be forever freed from the three unhappy states of existence and the eight calamities and that they may eternally listen to the Buddha's teachings.

He also prays that the members of his family, both great and small, may find happiness at will, that blessings may daily rain down upon them while hardships disperse like clouds. He prays that the imperial highways may be open and free of bandits, that the state may be preserved from pestilence, that wind and rain may obey their proper seasons, and that all suffering creatures may quickly find release. May all these prayers be granted!

The preceding incantation has been translated and circulated.

If this incantation is recited 7, 14, or 21 times daily (after having cleansed the mouth in the morning with a willow twig, having scattered flowers and incense before the image of Buddha, having knelt and joined the palms of the hands), the four grave sins, the five wicked acts, and all other transgressions will be wiped away. The present body will not be afflicted by untimely calamities; one will at last be born into the realm of immeasurably long life; and reincarnation in the female form will be escaped forever.

Now, the Sanskrit text has been reexamined and the Indian Vinaya monk Buddhasangha and other monks have been consulted; thus we know that the awesome power of this incantation is beyond comprehension. If it is recited 100 times in the evening and again at noon, it will destroy the four grave sins and five wicked acts. It will pluck out the very roots of sin and will ensure rebirth in the Western Regions. If, with sincerity of spirit, one is able to complete 200,000 recitations, perfect intelligence will be born and there will be no relapses. If 300,000 recitations are completed, one will see Amita Buddha face to face and will certainly be reborn into the Pure Land of tranquility and bliss.

Copied by the disciple of pure faith Sun Szu-chung on the 8th day of the fourth month of 720.

> **QUESTIONS** Why did Buddhism spread widely in China by the 6th century? How did popular Buddhism compare with original Buddhist teachings (see Chapter 2)? How did Chinese Buddhists define holy life? How do these documents suggest some of the troubles China faced after the collapse of the Han dynasty?

Buddha's death, a doctrine of **bodhisattvas** (boh-dih-SAHT-vuh) developed, which held that some people could attain nirvana through their own meditation while choosing to remain in the world as saints and to aid others by prayer and example. Buddhism increasingly shifted from an original emphasis on ethics to become a more emotional cult stressing the possibility of popular salvation. The role of the bodhisattvas, in broadening the prospects of salvation for ordinary people by leading them in prayer and advising on spiritual matters, was crucial in this transformation.

Buddhism evolved further as the religion spread seriously to China after the fall of the Han dynasty, when the idea of a celestial afterlife proved almost irresistible. Monasteries in India and the Himalaya Mountains continued to serve as spiritual centers for Chinese Buddhism, but the religion developed strong roots in east Asia directly, spreading through China and from there to

bodhisattvas [boh-dih-SAHT-vuh] Buddhist holy men; built up spiritual merits during their lifetimes; prayers even after death could aid people to achieve reflected holiness.

Mahayana   Chinese version of Buddhism; placed considerable emphasis on Buddha as god or savior.

Korea and Japan. The east Asian form of Buddhism, called **Mahayana**, or the Greater Vehicle, retained basic Buddhist beliefs. However, the emphasis on Buddha as a divine savior increased in the Mahayana version. Statues devoted to Buddha as god countered the earlier Buddhist hostility to religious images. And the religion improved its organization, with priests, temples, creeds, and rituals. Buddhist holy men, the bodhisattvas, remained important. Their souls after death resided in a kind of superheaven, where they could receive prayers and aid people. Intense spirituality continued to inform Buddhist faith as well. But prayers and rituals could now help ordinary people to become holy. Buddha became a god to whom one could appeal for solace, "the great physician for a sick and impure world." East Asian Buddhism also spurred new artistic interests in China and, later, in Japan, including the pagoda style of temple design and the statues devoted to Buddha.

Buddhism had a fascinating impact on women in China, largely among families who converted. On the face of things, Buddhism should have disrupted China's firm belief in patriarchal power, because Buddhists believed that women, like men, had souls. Indeed, some individual women in China captured great attention because of their spiritual accomplishments. But Chinese culture generated changes in Buddhism within the empire. Buddhist phrases like "husband supports wife" were changed to "husband controls his wife," whereas "the wife comforts the husband"—another Buddhist phrase from India—became "the wife reveres her husband." Here was a vital case of cultural blending, or syncretism. Finally, many men valued pious Buddhist wives, because they might benefit the family's salvation and because Buddhist activity would keep their wives busy, calm, and out of mischief. Buddhism was perhaps appealing to Chinese women because it led to a more meaningful life, but it did not really challenge patriarchy. A biography of one Buddhist wife put it this way: "At times of crisis she could be tranquil and satisfied with her fate, not letting outside things agitate her mind."

Buddhism was not popular with all Chinese. Confucian leaders, particularly, found in Buddhist beliefs in an afterlife a diversion from appropriate political interests. They disliked the notion of such intense spirituality and also found ideas of the holy life incompatible with proper family obligations. More important, Buddhism was seen as a threat that might distract ordinary people from loyalty to the emperor. When imperial dynasties revived in China, they showed some interest in Buddhist piety for a time, but ultimately they attacked the Buddhist faith, driving out many missionaries. Buddhism remained a minority current in China, and many villages worshiped in Buddhist shrines. Thus, China's religious composition became increasingly complex, but without overturning earlier cultural directions.

Daoism reacted to Buddhism as well, by improving its organization and emphasizing practical benefits obtainable through magic. It was at this point that Daoism developed a clear hold on many peasants, incorporating many of their beliefs in the process.

Buddhism had a greater lasting influence in the religious experience of other parts of east Asia, notably Japan, Korea, and Vietnam, than in China itself. Buddhism had also spread to significant parts of southeast Asia, where it remained somewhat truer to earlier Buddhist concepts of individual meditation and ethics.

In the world today, some 500 million people count themselves as Buddhists. Most live in the areas of east and southeast Asia, where the religion had taken root by 500 C.E. Buddhism did not, by itself, dominate any whole civilization; rather, it lived alongside other faiths. However, it provided major additions to Asia's religious map and an important response to changing conditions in the troubled centuries after the classical period had ended.

Christianity and Islam

The Spread of Christianity
MAP

Christianity moved westward, from its original center in the Middle East, as Buddhism was spreading east from India. Although initially less significant than Buddhism in terms of the number of converts, Christianity would ultimately prove to be one of the two largest faiths worldwide. And it would play a direct role in the formation of two postclassical civilizations, those of eastern and western Europe. Despite important similarities to Buddhism in its emphasis on salvation and the guidance of saints, Christianity differed in crucial ways. It came to place more emphasis on church organization and structure, copying from the example of the Roman Empire. Even more than Buddhism, it placed a premium on missionary activity and widespread conversions. Christianity also stressed the exclusive nature of its truth and was intolerant of competing beliefs. Such fierce confidence was not the least of the reasons for the new religion's success.

Christianity began in reaction to rigidities that had developed in the Jewish priesthood during the two centuries before the birth of Jesus Christ. A host of reform movements sprang up, some of them preaching the coming of a Messiah, or savior, who would bring about a Last Judgment on humankind. Many of these movements also stressed the possibility of life after death for the virtuous, which was a new element in Judaism. **Jesus of Nazareth,** believed by Christians to be the son of God sent to earth to redeem human sin, crystallized this radical reform movement. Combining extraordinary gentleness of spirit and great charisma, Jesus preached widely in Israel and gathered a group of loyal disciples around him. Initially, there seems to have been no intent on his or his followers' part to found a new religion. After Jesus' crucifixion, the disciples expected his imminent return and with it the end of the world. Only gradually, when the Second Coming did not transpire, did the disciples begin to fan out and, through their preaching, attract growing numbers of supporters in various parts of the Roman Empire.

The message of Jesus and his disciples seemed clear: There was a single supreme being, God, who loved humankind despite earthly sin. A virtuous life was one dedicated to the worship of God and fellowship among other believers; worldly concerns were secondary, and a life of poverty might be most conducive to holiness. God sent Jesus (called "Christ" from the Greek word for "God's anointed") to preach his holy word and through his sacrifice to prepare his followers for the widespread possibility of an afterlife and heavenly communion with God. Belief, good works, and the discipline of fleshly concerns would lead to heaven; rituals, such as commemorating Christ's Last Supper with wine and bread, would promote the same goal.

Christianity's message spread at an opportune time. The official religion of the Greeks and Romans had long seemed rather sterile, particularly to many of the poor. The Christian emphasis on the beauty of a simple life and the spiritual equality of all people, plus the fervor of the early Christians and the satisfying rituals they created, captured growing attention. The great reach of the Roman Empire made it relatively easy for Christian missionaries to travel widely in Europe and the Middle East, to spread the new word, although as we have seen, they also reached beyond, to Persia, Axum, and Ethiopia. Then, when conditions began to deteriorate in the empire, the solace this otherworldly religion provided resulted in its even wider appeal. Early Christian leaders made several important adjustments to maximize their conversions. Under the guidance of **Paul,** not one of the original disciples but an early convert, Christians began to see themselves as part of a new religion, rather than part of a Jewish reform movement, and they welcomed non-Jews. Paul also encouraged more formal organization within the new church, with local groups selecting elders to govern them; soon, a leader, or bishop, was appointed for each city. This structure paralleled the provincial government of the empire. Finally, Christian doctrine became increasingly organized, as the writings of several disciples and others were collected into what became known as the New Testament of the Christian Bible.

During the first three centuries after Christ, Christianity did not advance entirely smoothly. The new religion faced, as we have seen, periodic persecution from the normally tolerant imperial government. Even so, by the time Constantine converted to Christianity and accepted it as the one true legitimate faith, perhaps 10 percent of the empire's population had accepted the new religion. Constantine's conversion brought new troubles to Christianity, particularly some interference by the state in matters of doctrine. However, it became much easier to spread Christianity with official favor, and the continued deterioration of the empire added to the impetus to join this amazingly successful new church. In the eastern Mediterranean, where imperial rule remained strong from its center in Constantinople, state control of the church became a way of life. But in the West, where conditions were far more chaotic, bishops had a freer hand. A centralized church organization under the leadership of the bishop of Rome, called **pope** from the word *papa,* or "father," gave the Western church unusual strength and independence.

By the time Rome collapsed, Christianity had thus demonstrated immense spiritual power and developed a solid organization, although one that differed from East to West. The new church faced a number of controversies over doctrine but managed to promote certain standard beliefs against several heresies. A key tenet involved a complex doctrine of the Trinity, which held that the

Jesus of Nazareth   Prophet and teacher among the Jews; believed by Christians to be the Messiah; executed c. 30 C.E.

Paul   (3–67) One of the first Christian missionaries; moved away from insistence that adherents of the new religion follow Jewish law; use of Greek as language of Church.

pope   Bishop of Rome; head of the Christian Church in western Europe.

Early Christian Symbols

one God had three persons—the Father, the Son (Christ), and the Holy Ghost. Experience in fighting heresies promoted Christian interest in defending a single belief and strengthened its resistance to any competing doctrine or faith. Early Christianity also produced an important formal theology, through formative writers such as Augustine. This theology incorporated many elements of classical philosophy with Christian belief and aided the church in its attempts to gain respectability among intellectuals. Theologians like Augustine grappled with such problems as freedom of the will. If God is all-powerful, can mere human beings have free will? And if not, how can human beings be justly punished for sin? By working out these issues in elaborate doctrine, the early theologians, or church fathers, provided an important role for formal, rational thought in a religion that continued to emphasize the primary importance of faith.

Finally, Christianity was willing to accommodate some earlier polytheistic traditions among the common people. The celebration of Christ's birth was thus moved to coincide with the winter solstice, a classic example of syncretism, which allowed the new faith to benefit from the power of selective older rituals.

Like all successful religions, Christianity combined a number of appeals. It offered deep devotion to an all-powerful God. Christianity also developed its own complex intellectual system. Mystical holy men and women flourished under Christian banners, particularly in the Middle East. In the West, soon after the empire's collapse, this impulse was partially disciplined through the institution of monasticism, first developed in Italy under **Benedict,** who started a monastery among Italian peasants whom he lured away from the worship of the sun god Apollo. The Benedictine Rule, which soon spread to many other monasteries and convents, urged a disciplined life, with prayer and spiritual fulfillment alternating with hard work in agriculture and study. Thus, Christianity attempted to encourage but also to discipline intense piety, and to avoid a complete gulf between the lives of saintly men and women and the spiritual concerns of ordinary people.

Christianity's success and organizational strength obviously appealed to political leaders. But the new religion never became the creature of the upper classes alone. Its popular message of salvation and satisfying rituals continued to draw the poor, more than most of the great classical belief systems; in this regard, it was somewhat like Hinduism in India. Christianity also provided some religious unity among different social groups. It even held special appeal for women. Christianity did not create equality among men and women, but it did preach the equal importance of male and female souls. And it encouraged men and women to worship together, unlike many other faiths.

Christianity promoted a new culture among its followers. The rituals, the otherworldly emphasis, the interest in spiritual equality—these central themes were far different from those of classical Mediterranean civilizations. Christianity modified classical beliefs in the central importance of the state and of political loyalties. Although Christians accepted the state, they did not put it first. Christianity also worked against other classical institutions, such as slavery, in the name of brotherhood (although later Christians would accept slavery in other contexts). Christianity may have fostered greater respectability for disciplined work than had been the case in the Mediterranean civilization, where an aristocratic ethic dominated. Western monasteries, for example, set forth rigid work routines for monks. Certainly, Christianity sought some changes in classical culture beyond its central religious message, including greater emphasis on sexual restraint. But Christianity preserved important classical values as well, in addition to an interest in solid organization and some of the themes of classical philosophy. Church buildings retained Roman architectural styles, although often with greater simplicity if only because of the poverty of the later empire and subsequent states. Latin remained the language of the church in the West, Greek the language of most Christians in the eastern Mediterranean. Through the patient librarianship of monks, monasticism played an immensely valuable role in preserving classical as well as Christian learning.

When the Roman Empire fell, Christian history was still in its infancy. The Western church would soon spread its missionary zeal to northern Europe, and the Eastern church would reach into the Slavic lands of the Balkans and Russia. By then, Christianity was already established as a significant world religion—one of the few ever generated. A world religion is defined as a faith of unusual durability and drawing power, one whose complexity wins the devotion of many different kinds of people. Major world religions, like Christianity and Buddhism, do indeed show some

Benedict of Nursia   Founder of monasticism in what had been the western half of the Roman Empire; established Benedictine Rule in the 6th century; paralleled development of Basil's rules in Byzantine Empire.

The Roman and Christian Views of the Good Life   CASE STUDY

Religious Geography

The distribution of the world's major religions calls for knowledge both of numerical data and geography. Map 5.5 and this table, using contemporary data, also suggest which aspects of the world's religious distribution were beginning to solidify at the end of the late classical period and which aspects depended on developments yet to come.

QUESTIONS Where are the greatest concentrations of the four major religions today? Which aspects of modern religious geography follow from the patterns of religious dissemination underway by the end of the classical period? Which cannot be explained by these late-classical developments?

Religions and Their Distribution in the World Today

Religion	Distribution*
Christianity	1.9 billion
Roman Catholic	(1 billion)
Protestant	(458 million)
Eastern Orthodox	(173 million)
Other	(195 million)
Islam	1 billion
Hinduism	751 million
Buddhism	334 million
Shintoism	3 million
Daoism	31 million
Judaism	18 million

*Figures for several religions have been reduced over the past 50 years by the impact of communism in eastern Europe and parts of Asia.

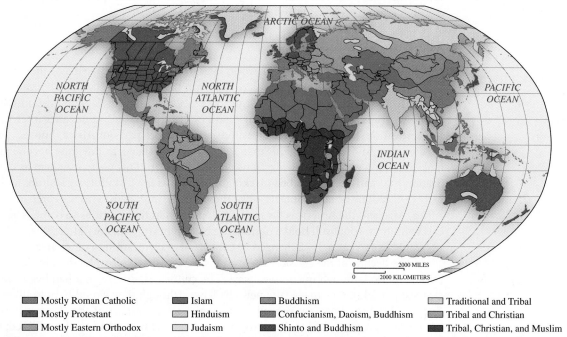

Map 5.5 Major Religions of the Modern World. This map shows the contemporary geography of the major religions, including areas of considerable mixture, like Africa.

Legend:
- Mostly Roman Catholic
- Mostly Protestant
- Mostly Eastern Orthodox
- Islam
- Hinduism
- Judaism
- Buddhism
- Confucianism, Daoism, Buddhism
- Shinto and Buddhism
- Traditional and Tribal
- Tribal and Christian
- Tribal, Christian, and Muslim

---

ability to cut across different cultures, to win converts in a wide geographic area and amid considerable diversity.

Islam, launched early in the 7th century, would initially surpass Christianity as a world faith and has remained Christianity's most tenacious rival (see Chapter 6). With Islam, the roster of world religions was essentially completed. Changes would follow, but no totally new religion of major significance arose—unless one counts some of the secular faiths, like communism, that appeared in the last century. The centuries after Christianity's rise, the spread of Buddhism, and the inception of Islam would see the conversion of most of the civilized world to one or another of the great faiths. This produced a religious map that, in Europe and Asia and even parts of Africa, would not alter greatly until our own time. (The table in the Visualizing the Past feature shows the distribution of religions in the world today.)

The Spread of the Major Religions

The spread of major religions—Hinduism in India, Buddhism in east and southeast Asia, a more popular Daoism in China, Christianity in Europe and parts of the Mediterranean world, and ultimately Islam—was a vital result of the changes in classical civilizations brought on by attack and decay. Despite the important diversity among these great religions, which included fierce hatreds, particularly between Christians and Muslims, their overall development suggests the way important currents could run through the civilized world, crossing political and cultural borders—thanks in part to the integrations and contacts built by the classical civilizations. Common difficulties, including invading forces that journeyed from central Asia and contagious epidemics that knew no boundaries, help explain parallel changes in separate civilizations. Trade and travel also provided common bonds. Chinese travelers learned of Buddhism through trading expeditions to India, whereas Ethiopians learned about Christianity from Middle Eastern traders. The new religions spurred a greater interest in spiritual matters and resulted in a greater tendency to focus on a single basic divinity instead of a multitude of gods. Polytheistic beliefs and practices continued to flourish as part of popular Hinduism and popular Daoism, and they were not entirely displaced among ordinary people who converted to Christianity, Buddhism, or Islam. But the new religious surge reduced the hold of literal **animism** in much of Asia and Europe, and this too was an important development across boundaries.

animism A religious outlook that sees gods in many aspects of nature and propitiates them to help control and explain nature; typical of Mesopotamian religions.

The World Around 500 C.E.

Developments in many parts of the world by 500 C.E. produced three major themes for world history in subsequent centuries. First, and particularly in the centers of classical civilization, there was a response to the collapse of classical forms. Societies in China, India, and around the Mediterranean faced the task of reviving or reworking their key institutions and values after internal decline and external invasion. Second, in these areas, but also in other parts of Africa, Europe, and Asia, was the need to react to the new religious map that was taking shape, to integrate new religious institutions and values into established civilizations or, as in northern Europe, to use them as the basis for a civilization that had previously been lacking. Finally, increased skill in agriculture and the creation of early civilizations or new contacts—like the Japanese import of writing—prepared parts of Europe, Africa, Asia, and the Americas for new developments in the centuries to come. The centers of classical civilization would still hold a dominant position in world history after 500 C.E., but their monopoly would be increasingly challenged by the spread of civilization to other areas.

The decline of the classical civilizations obviously transformed the Big Concepts of the whole classical period, though in complex ways. The cultural traditions that had been codified during the classical period might survive the new challenges, though they would have to interact with new influences. Empires, however, proved more fragile, so this aspect of the classical heritage underwent even more extensive change. Patterns of trans-regional contact were also affected, but the motivation of trade, and some of the routes that had been established during the classical period, particularly in the Indian Ocean, proved to be quite resilient.

Global Connections

The Late Classical Period and the World

During most of the classical period, key developments often focused within civilizations. We have seen that there were wider contacts. Each civilization radiated trade and other influences to a larger region; thus India had contacts with other parts of south and southeast Asia, and China with Korea and Vietnam. Trade

along the Silk Road through central Asia, conducted mainly by nomadic merchants, was another key connection.

As the classical civilizations began to fail, contacts in some ways accelerated—but they also encountered new difficulties. Overland travel between China and Rome became more dangerous, because government protection faltered in both empires. This placed a new premium on using shipping connections, particularly in the Indian Ocean. On the other hand, traders, missionaries, and of course nomadic invaders began to reach out in new ways as borders became more porous. The end of the classical period thus witnessed important new cultural exchanges across regions. These included the spread of Buddhism from India to China and to other parts of east Asia, and the spread of Christianity beyond the Roman Empire into parts of northeast Africa and into Armenia. These developments set new bases for connections among various societies in Afro-Eurasia.

Further Readings

The fall of the Roman Empire has generated rich and interesting debate. For recent works, see Simon Swain and Mark Edwards, eds., *Approaching Late Antiquity: The Transformation from Early to Late Empire* (2004); James W. Ermatinger, *The Decline and Fall of the Roman Empire* (2004); Bryan Ward-Perkins, *The Fall of Rome and the End of Civilization* (2005). On barbarian attacks, J.H.G.W. Liebeschuetz, *Decline and Change in Late Antiquity: Religion, Barbarians and their Historiography* (2006); Simon MacDowall, *Adrianopole, AD 378: The Goths Crush Rome's Legions* (2005); Peter Heather, *The Fall of the Roman Empire: A New History of Rome and the Barbarians* (2007); and Stephen Mitchell, *A History of the Later Roman Empire, AD 284-641* (2007).

For interpretation and discussion of earlier views, see A. H. M. Jones, *The Decline of the Ancient World* (1966); J. Vogt, *The Decline of Rome* (1965); and F. W. Walbank, *The Awful Revolution: The Decline of the Roman Empire in the West* (1960). On India and China in decline, worthwhile sources include R. Tharpar, *Early History of India* (2004); R. C. Majumdar, ed., *The Classical Age* (1966); Raymond Dawson, *Imperial China* (1972); and J. A. Harrison, *The Chinese Empire* (1972). See also J. R. Fairbank and E. O. Reischauer, *China: Tradition and Transformation* (1989), a fine survey with good postclassical coverage.

On the role of disease in imperial decline, W. McNeill's *Plagues and Peoples* (1977) is provocative and useful. Speculations on the causes of the rise and fall of civilizations, including those of the classical world, are addressed in Jared Diamond, *Guns, Germs, and Steel: The Fate of Human Societies* (1997); Christopher Chase-Dunn and Thomas D. Hall, *Rise and Demise: Comparing World Systems* (1997); Walter Goffart, *Barbarian Tides: The Migration Age and the Later Roman Empire* (2006); Michael Whitby, *Rome at War, AD 293–696* (2003); Joseph A. Tainter, *The Collapse of Complex Societies* (1988); and Norman Yoffee and George L. Cowgill, eds., *The Collapse of Ancient States and Civilizations* (1991).

For the rise and spread of world faiths, see Ann Heirman and Stephan Peter Bumbacher, eds., *The Spread of Buddhism* (2007); and Frederick Denny, *Atlas of the World's Religions* (2007). A good overview is Geoffrey Parinder, ed., *World Religions* (1971); see also Lewis M. Hopfe, *Religions of the World* (1997); and Jamail Ragi al Farugi, ed., *Historical Atlas of the Religions of the World* (1974). On Hinduism, see N. C. Chandhuri's *Hinduism: A Religion to Live By* (1979). Two good studies of Buddhism are N. Ross Reat, *Buddhism: A History* (1994); and A. F. Wright, *Buddhism in Chinese History* (1959). Christianity's spread is the subject of S. Renko, *Pagan Rome and the Early Christians* (1986); and M. Hengel, *Acts and the History of Earliest Christianity* (1986). Important

special topics are covered in J. Bowker, *Problems of Suffering in Religions of the World* (1975), a fascinating comparative effort; A. Sharma, ed., *Women in World Religions* (1987); and on Christianity, B. Witherington, *Women in the Earliest Churches* (1988). An important study of civilization contacts in this period and later is Jerry Bentley's *Old World Encounters: Cross-Cultural Exchanges and Contacts in Pre-Modern Times* (1993).

On the Web

Bantu language migration and the multiethnic character of Africa can be explored at http://www.wsu.edu/~dee/CIVAFRCA/IRONAGE .HTM and http://emuseum.mnsu.edu/cultural/oldworld/africa/ bantu.html. The Web offers a brief history of Axum (http://www .wsu.edu:8080/~dee/CIVAFRCA/AXUM.HTM), accounts of this and other Nubian kingdoms (http://www.fordham.edu/halsall/ ancient/nubia1.html), and images of their cities and monuments (http://www.hp.uab.edu/image_archive/um/umn.html). How the trans-Saharan trade was captured by the state of Ghana and how it flourished before its conquest by the Almoravids is discussed at http://www.mrdowling.com/609-trade.html.

Many Web sites offer insights and/or virtual visits to Teotihuacan (http://archaeology.asu.edu/teo/index.php, http://www.wsu .edu/~dee/CIVAMRCA/TEO.HTM), Tenochtitlan (http://www .mnsu.edu/emuseum/archaeology/sites/meso_america/tenochtitlan .html), Monte Alban (http://www.latinamericanstudies.org/monte- alban.htm), the Incan center of Machu Picchu (http://en.wikipedia .org/wiki/Machu_Picch), the Hopewell Amerindian site (including a study guide, at http://www.michigan.pic.org/historythemes/ resources/hopewell_why.html), cliff dwellings of the Anasazi (http:// www.mnsu.edu/emuseum/archaeology/sites/northamerica/chaco .html, http://www.exploratorium.edu/chaco/, and http://www .learner.org/exhibits/collapse/chacocanyon.html (see the Chaco Digital Archive at http://www.chacoarchive.org/resources.html).

A virtual visit can also be made to the Chavin culture of the Andes at http://www.globalheritagefund.org/where/chavin.html, http://www.mnsu.edu/emuseum/prehistory/latinamerica/south/ cultures/chavin.html, http://chavin.perucultural.org.pe/vvirtual .shtml. The intriguing flat-topped temples, burial practices and agriculture of the Moche people of northwestern Peru are addressed at http://www.latinamericanstudies.org/moche.htm, http://www .mc.maricopa.edu/dept/d10/asb/anthro2003/legacy/moche/el_nino _2.html, http://www.archaeology.org/0203/abstracts/moche.html, and http://www.doaks.org/moche.pdf. Moche art is discussed at http://www.museum.upenn.edu/Moche/mocheculture.html and http://www.ancientworlds.net/aw/Post/254792. The magnificent tomb of the Moche Lord of Sipan, compared in terms of golden splendor to the tomb of ancient Egypt's Tutankhamen, is discussed at http://agutie.homestead.com/files/Sipan.htm (see also the Power-Point presentation at http://employees.oneonta.edu/walkerr/ Mesoamerica/Andean%20Civilizations.ppt.).

The Maya are the subject of several excellent Web sites that offer a detailed look at that civilization. Take a virtual visit to their capital at Chichén Itzá at (http://www.mysteriousplaces.com/mayan/ TourEntrance.html), and other principal sites (http://www.smm.org/

sln/ma/sites.html and http://www.civilization.ca/civil/maya/mmintery.html), illuminate their astronomical and social calendars (http://www.webexhibits.org/calendars/calendar-mayan.html and http://www.sacred-texts.com/time/cal/mayacal.htm). An animated look at a Mayan ball player and the continuing controversy over the nature and purpose of this Mayan sport receives attention at http://www.ballgame.org, http://www.library.umaine.edu/hudson/palmer/Maya/ballgame.asp, http://www.greatdreams.com/mayan/mayan-games.htm and http://www.ancientworlds.net/aw/Article/726643. The course of Mayan society and the collapse of classical Mayan cities prior to the arrival of Europeans are examined at http://earthobservatory.nasa.gov/Study/Maya/, http://www.mnsu.edu/emuseum/prehistory/latinamerica/meso/cultures/maya.html, http://www.american.edu/ted/ice/maya.htm, and http://en.wikipedia.org/wiki/Maya_collapse. For an extensive list of Maya-related online sources, go to http://www.angelfire.com/ca/humanorigins/index.html. For early Mexican culture, see http://www.indians.org/welker/aztec.htm.

Mound builder culture worldwide reveals both unique and common elements of early civilizations. Virtual visits can be made to mound-building sites in North America (http://www.cahokiamounds.com/cahokia.html, http://www.adena.com/adena/ad/ad01.htm, and http://www.mississippian-artifacts.com/), Tonga (http://www.science-frontiers.com/sf120/sf120p14.htm), Japan (http:www.hgeo.h.Kyoto-u.ac.jp/soramitsu/kofun.html, http://www.hgeo.h.kyoto-u.ac.jp/soramitsu/kofun.html, and http://www.t-net.ne.jp/~keally/kofun.html), and in northern Europe (http://www.mythicalireland.com/ancientsites/knowth/index.html, http://www.travelsinireland.com/ireland/knowth.htm, and http://www.nedu/~ikuijt/Ireland/sites/mdonnel2/tombdetail.htm.htm).

Exceptional coverage of Eurasian nomads can be found at http://www.heritagenet.unesco.kz/kz/content/history/monument/berel/berel_text1.htm. The past and future of Tibetan nomads is examined at http://uvalde.tamu.edu/rangel/apr99/miller.pdf. The possible end to nomadic society in Arabia is discussed at http://www.hartford-hwp.com/archives/51/083.html. The nomads of Iran are described at http://destinationiran.com/Nomads.htm. Links to the art of nomadic peoples are provided at http://www.utexas.edu/students/husa/origins/nomadart.html. The textiles of the nomadic as well as settled peoples of Central Asia are exhibited at http://www.powerhousemuseum.com/hsc/textiles/textiles.htm.

African and other horse and camel nomads are the subject of analysis at http://depts.washington.edu/silkroad/exhibit/trade/horcamae.html, http://en.wikipedia.org/wiki/Eurasian_nomads, and http://history-world.org/nomads.htm. However, nomads were not always dependent on animal transport, as is suggested by the "sea nomads" of southeast Asia (http://www.unesco.org/csi/act/thailand/moken_e.htm).

Nomadic and pastoral peoples played a major role in the functioning of major conduits of long distance trade and cultural exchange in the ancient world, such as the Silk Road, which is examined at http://www.ciolek.com/owtrad.html. Further historical treatments and virtual tours of the Silk Road (including the Silk Road Center at Dunhuang) are available at http://www.ess.uci.edu/~oliver/silk.html, http://www.silk-road.com/, http://www.chinapage.com/silkroad.html, and http://www.metmuseum.org/toah/hd/ince/

hd_ince.htm. Though designed as a study guide, http://www.isop.ucla.edu/eas/sum-inst/links/silkunit.htm#background is very useful for identifying the factors that led to cultural exchange along the Silk Road. The "Spice Road" across southwest Asia to Petra and beyond can be traveled at http://www.metmuseum.org/toah/hd/silk/hd_silk.htm, http://www.textilesociety.org/abstracts_2002/Shamir.htm, and http://whc.unesco.org/archive/advisory_body_evaluation/1107rev.pdf.

The view of the society and culture of early Japan offered at http://www.japan-guide.com/e/e2131.html features a narrative loaded with links that further illuminate virtually all the subjects addressed in this chapter, including Jomon culture, the Yamato, and the coming of Buddhism to Japan. Other links to ancient Japanese culture are offered at http://www.wsu.edu:8080/~dee/ANCJAPAN/GALLERY.HTM and http://www.archaeolink.com/ancient_japan.htm. One of these links to Shinto at http://www.religioustolerance.org/shinto.htm, provides clear illustrations of Shinto practice and tradition.

Comprehensive guides to Internet sources on the peoples and peopling of the Pacific are provided at http://www.archaeolink.com/polynesian_studies_people_of_the.htm, http://www.cwis.org/wwwvl/indig-vl.html#pacific, http://www.abc.net.au/ra/pacific/people/, and http://www.otagomuseum.govt.nz/pacific_cultures.html. The early settlement of Polynesia is discussed at http://pvs.kcc.hawaii.edu/migrationspart1.html and http://pvs.kcc.hawaii.edu/migrationspart2.html. Insight into the life of one of the best-known leaders of a Pacific people, the Hawaiian King Kamehameha, and the Hawaiian monarchy may be found at http://en.wikipedia.org/wiki/Kamehameha_I, http://www.americaslibrary.gov/cgi-bin/page.cgi/aa/kamehameh, http://www.janesoceania.com/hawaii_monarchy/index.htm, http://www.hawaiian-roots.com/monarchy.htm, and also http://coe-dmha.org/Liaison/Vol_2No_3/Lia03.htm, which offers an account of the "The Law of the Splintered Paddle," the Hawaiian contribution to international humanitarian law. Hawaiian canoe-building and voyaging is explored at http://pvs.kcc.hawaii.edu/L2canoebuild.html and http://pvs.kcc.hawaii.edu/L2life.html.

The Web provides easy access to the lives of the political and church leaders of the early Byzantine world, such as Diocletian (http://latter-rain.com/eccle/diocle.htm), Justinian (http://www.roman-emperors.org/justinia.htm), Benedict of Nursia (http://www.worth.org.uk/guides/m6.htm), Saint Basil (http://www.orthodox.net/saints/st_basil.html). Notable among the non-religio-political figures of the era is Hypatia of Alexandria, an important philosopher and mathematician (http://www.cosmopolis.com/people/hypatia.html). The fall of the Roman West is analyzed at http://ancienthistory.about.com/library/weekly/aa061599.htm, http://www.fordham.edu/halsall/source/gibbon-fall.html, and http://en.wikipedia.org/wiki/Roman_Empire. The Council of Nicea is examined at http://www.columbia.edu/cu/augustine/arch/sbrandt/nicea.htm.

A comparative essay on the spread of Christianity and Islam is offered at http://www.hyperhistory.net/apwh/essays/comp/cw11christislamexpand.htm. The tenets of Islam are addressed at http://islamicity.com/mosque/Intro_Islam.htm. There are many web pages offering online sources for the study of early Islam, including http://www.islamic-world.net/links/islamic_history_sites.htm, http://www.pbs.org/wgbh/globalconnections/mideast/index.html, and http://www.fordham.edu/halsall/islam/islamsbook.html.

The Vikings, who had contacts with both the Muslim World and Byzantium, receive treatment at http://www.bbc.co.uk/schools/vikings/ and http://www.pbs.org/wgbh/nova/vikings/who.htm. Arab accounts of Viking traders can be found at http://www.nordicway.com/search/Vikings%20in%20the%20East.htm. The place of Vikings in British history is analyzed at http://www.bbc.co.uk/schools/vikings/. The story of the Vikings in North America is traced at http://www.mnh.si.edu/vikings/.

The decline of the Gupta Empire is addressed at http://en.wikipedia.org/wiki/Gupta_Empire. The Hindu concept of the female aspect of the divine is examined at http://www.asia.si.edu/devi/interpretingdevi.htm. The development of Mahayana Buddhism is discussed at http://www.geocities.com/Athens/8916/index2.html. The spread of Buddhism from its place of origin in India is charted at http://www.thebuddhistsociety.org/resources/Spread.html. The role of the Silk Road in the spread of Buddhism to China is traced at http://www.silk-road.com/artl/buddhism.shtml, while the development of Buddhism in Southeast Asia is described at http://www.buddhanet.net/e-learning/buddhistworld/southeast.htm.

AP* Test Prep

1. The core or mother civilization for other civilizations in Mesoamerica was the
   - (A) Olmecs.
   - (B) Toltecs.
   - (C) Aztecs.
   - (D) Chavin peoples.

2. In Ethiopia, trade and contacts
   - (A) insulated the culture from Muslim influences.
   - (B) led to the kingdom's conversion to Christianity.
   - (C) brought the state into contact with China.
   - (D) led to its conquest by Arabs.

3. Shinto
   - (A) is, in Western terms, an extremely well-developed local form of animism or nature worship.
   - (B) arrived in Japan with the first official embassy from China.
   - (C) is a branch of Buddhism.
   - (D) is a branch of Hinduism.

4. At the end of the Classical Age
   - (A) major belief systems failed to survive the collapse of classical civilizations.
   - (B) only the Mediterranean Greco-Roman civilization experienced upheavals.
   - (C) there was a religious upsurge as a result of social and economic problems.
   - (D) trade ceased to be important.

5. As the Han Empire collapsed
   - (A) Daoists established political control of the various Chinese states.
   - (B) nomads replaced the Han with a powerful "barbarian" dynasty.
   - (C) landowners and warlords dominated the successor governments.
   - (D) Christianity was introduced to China and began to spread.

6. In India during the period after the Guptan collapse,
   - (A) Buddhism reasserted its influence, replacing Hinduism.
   - (B) the caste system lost its influence.
   - (C) Hinduism helped secure India's cultural cohesion when the central state collapsed.
   - (D) invaders rarely assimilated into Hindu culture.

7. All of these contributed to the decline and fall of Rome EXCEPT
   - (A) the spread of Christianity.
   - (B) nomadic invasions.
   - (C) the collapse of effective government.
   - (D) plagues which decimated populations.

Free-Response Question

Compare and contrast the collapses of the Roman Empire and Han China.

PART II

Retrospective

The Classical Period, 1000 B.C.E.–500 C.E.: Uniting Large Regions

Contacts and Their Limits

In contrast to the early river valley civilizations, which had no regular interregional exchange system (save possibly in the Indian Ocean), reasonably systematic contacts developed during the classical period linking China to India, the Middle East, and the Mediterranean. Some goods were shipped along sea routes in the Indian Ocean, reaching as far as Egypt via the Red Sea. Important overland routes—the routes historians have labeled collectively as the Silk Road—brought goods from western China through central Asia to the Middle East and Mediterranean. Important systems connected south Indian merchants and some Hindu and Buddhist missionaries to various parts of southeast Asia. Ethiopians in northeastern Africa traded actively with both the Mediterranean and the Middle East.

In 70 C.E. in southern Italy, Mount Vesuvius erupted, burying neighboring Roman cities, including Pompeii. Almost 2000 years later archaeologists, excavating the ruins of Pompeii, found an ivory carving of a woman made at Taxila in what is now northwestern Pakistan. This find confirmed the importance of trade links between Rome and south Asia. Taxila had been part of the Hellenistic orbit established by Alexander the Great, and exchanges with the Mediterranean continued thereafter. Roman merchants visited India directly, seeking trading opportunities. Taxila was also a major center along the Silk Road, serving as a link not only to the Mediterranean but also to east and southeast Asia. The activity along trade routes gave many elites an active taste for goods, like silk, produced in distant places.

Besides the trade routes, two major episodes occurred that involved direct contact between different civilizations. Alexander the Great's conquests brought Greek culture into interaction with those of Persia and India, as well as with Egypt. We have seen that Indian artists imitated Greek styles in their own work. Greeks and Indians both gained new mathematical knowledge (though it is intriguing that the Greeks did not adopt Indian numbering which, later transmitted to Europe by the Arabs, proved much superior to Greek and Roman numbering systems). Indian missionaries to the Middle East, though failing to establish Buddhism, may have influenced ethical thought in the later Roman Empire and, through this, Christianity.

Interest in Asian goods also motivated Rome, though with less wide-ranging results. Once they controlled Egypt, the Romans established regular Indian Ocean expeditions from the Red Sea. A desire for more direct access to Indian spices and Chinese silks also helped motivate frequent wars with empires in Persia, though the Romans often fared badly and were unable to break through to the sources of the goods they valued. China, for its part, had established regular diplomatic relations with empires in Persia, largely to further direct trade. None of these interesting interactions, however, seems to have had significant results in terms of institutional or cultural exchange.

The second major contact, toward the end of the classical period, involved China's fascination with Indian Buddhism. Chinese knowledge of Buddhism initially spread as a result of Chinese merchant ventures into India; later, religious students were sent directly. This was the only major case of successful outside influence on Chinese culture until very recent times.

These developments were exceedingly important. They also had serious limits. Interregional trade was certainly vital to some of the trading hubs in central Asia, such as Samarkand, but it had relatively little economic importance to societies like China. It was nothing compared to the growth of production in China's internal trade. There is no uncontested evidence that anyone traveled all the way from Rome to China, and Roman knowledge of China (as well as Chinese knowledge of Rome) was extremely hazy. There was trade, but no interaction between Chinese and Roman culture or technology. The two cases of direct exchange between civilizations described above are fascinating but they also stand out as unusual. And the lasting effects of the Hellenistic experience in northwestern India are questionable. Even in art, after about two centuries, this influence seems to have disappeared, and stylistic differences once again became apparent.

So, while contacts advanced significantly in this period, the primary framework for the major societies remained internal. The classical civilizations developed largely separately. The most important kinds of contacts occurred *within* the civilizations, not among them: the careful, sometimes tense mixing of the northern Chinese with the people of the newer territories in the south; the partial extension of Greek culture to the western Mediterranean and portions of the Middle East and north Africa; the spread of Hinduism and the caste system southward on the Indian subcontinent. These contacts were vital to the formation of larger civilizational areas, which was a fundamental feature of the classical period. Clearly, far more energy went into this process than into interregional linkages at this stage in world history. ∎

PART III

The Postclassical Period, 500–1450: New Faith and New Commerce

Chapter 6   The First Global Civilization: The Rise and Spread of Islam

Chapter 7   Abbasid Decline and the Spread of Islamic Civilization to South and Southeast Asia

Chapter 8   African Civilizations and the Spread of Islam

Chapter 9   Civilization in Eastern Europe: Byzantium and Orthodox Europe

Chapter 10   A New Civilization Emerges in Western Europe

Chapter 11   The Americas on the Eve of Invasion

Chapter 12   Reunification and Renaissance in Chinese Civilization: The Era of the Tang and Song Dynasties

Chapter 13   The Spread of Chinese Civilization: Japan, Korea, and Vietnam

Chapter 14   The Last Great Nomadic Challenges: From Chinggis Khan to Timur

Chapter 15   The West and the Changing World Balance

THE OVERVIEW: THE WORLD MAP CHANGES

The big changes in the period 500–1450 did not involve political boundaries. They involved the spread of the major world religions—Buddhism, Christianity, and Islam—across political and cultural borders and the development of new, more regular systems of trade that connected much of Asia, Africa, and Europe.

In some ways, an age characterized by faith and trade may seem contradictory. Indeed, many religious leaders looked down on merchants as likely to be seduced from a life of piety by the lure of wealth. But in fact the spread of trade often helped disseminate religion, and confidence in a divine order helped merchants to take risks.

The maps included here show the surge of Buddhism, Christianity, and Islam from their initial centers and the expansion of Afro-Eurasian trade around the same period. While Buddhism and Christianity started well before this period, they gained new vigor as the classical empires collapsed. Islam, which spread most rapidly, was entirely new. All three religions involved active missionary efforts. All periodically benefited from government sponsorship and sometimes from military pressure as well. For example, conquerors might impose higher taxes on those they conquered who did not convert to the conquerors' religion, or they might forcibly expel "nonbelievers" from the territory. Through a combination of persuasion and pressure, many millions of people changed their beliefs about the world around them and about the goals of life. The religious beliefs they adopted during the postclassical period established the dominant religious frameworks that still prevail in Asia, Europe, and parts of Africa today.

During the postclassical period, systematic international trade developed that went far beyond the

■ Christian in 750	■ Islamic in 750	■ Buddhism in 750	▦ China 750-1450: Buddhism, Confucianism, Taoism
■ Spread of Christianity to 1450	■ Spread of Islam to 1450	■ Spread of Buddhism to 1450	▦ Korea 750-1450: Buddhism, Confucianism

Spread of Buddhism, Christianity, and Islam to c. 1450

⬜ The Silk Road
⬜ Roman Trade Routes
⬜ African Trade Routes
⬜ The Vikings
⬜ Indian Ocean Trade Routes

Main Routes of Afro-Eurasian Trade, c. 1250

carrying capacity of the old Silk Road. The Indian Ocean and the Mediterranean Sea were the hubs of this trade, which brought northwestern Europe, west Africa, Japan, and other regions into the existing east–west trade routes between China and Egypt. Gradually and tentatively, these connections among societies (rather than separate developments within societies) began to shape world history in important ways.

Big Concepts

Along with, and partly because of, religious change, three Big Concepts help organize the understanding of the postclassical period. First, trans-regional communication and exchange networks expanded with important new routes added. Missionary activity and new seafaring technologies both contributed to this. Second, forms of state organization diversified, with centralized empires now juxtaposed to a variety of looser political structures. Third, several societies—headed by China—increased their productive capacity, with social consequences extending to the emergence of new urban centers and the experimentation with different forms of labor.

TRIGGERS FOR CHANGE

As its name indicates, the postclassical period followed the decline of the great classical empires. As areas that had previously been under the control of these empires experienced economic decline and increasing disorder, people turned toward religious faith for security, reassurance, and guidance.

A second effect of the decline of the classical empires was the collapse of established boundaries, which caused ambitious people to turn their attention to new areas. The fall of the Roman Empire, for example, opened up new opportunities in the eastern Mediterranean, most notably for the Arabs. When the Eastern Roman Empire (the Byzantine Empire) could not regain lost territories in the Mediterranean, it turned its attention to opportunities in Russia and eastern Europe. These reorientations encouraged missionary activity and trade alike.

Expanding trade encouraged the development of better ships and new navigational devices. This was another trigger for change as the postclassical period moved along. The Chinese invented the compass, and from the Middle East came better ship designs. Maps also improved as a result of wider trade. They in turn encouraged further travel. The same held true for new banking and commercial practices: long-distance credit arrangements, for example, facilitated international exchange.

THE BIG CHANGES

Religion and commerce were the engines of change in the postclassical period. Changes in their own right, they were the causes of many other changes. Buddhism, Christianity, and Islam were the religions that showed the greatest capacity to spread beyond the cultures in which they arose. Their spread created larger groups of people with broadly shared beliefs and religious institutions than ever before. This gener-

500 C.E.	600 C.E.	700 C.E.	800 C.E.	900 C.E.
527–565 Justinian, Eastern Roman (Byzantine) Emperor	610–613 Origins of Islam	711 First Islamic incursions into India	800–814 Charlemagne's Empire in western Europe	960–1127 Song dynasty (China)
570–632 Muhammad	618–907 Tang dynasty (China)	718 Byzantines defeat Arab attack on Constantinople	c. 855 Russian kingdom around Kiev	968 Tula established by Toltecs (Mesoamerica)
589–618 Sui dynasty (China)	634–750 Arab Invasions in Middle East; spread of Islam in North Africa	750 Abbasid caliphate founded	864 Cyril and Methodius missionaries in eastern Europe	980–1015 Christian Conversion of Vladimir I of Russia
	661–750 Ummayad Caliphate	777 Independent Islamic kingdoms begin in North Africa	878 Last Japanese embassy to China	
	668 Korea becomes independent from China			

ated new opportunities for mutual intolerance—many Christians and Muslims, particularly, developed disdain for each other—but also examples of constructive tolerance. Under Islamic rule, Iberia or what is present day Spain and Portugal became a center of creative interaction among Muslims, Christians, and Jews. Religion also created new loyalties that could compete with other values, including political values, and political issues on the whole received less attention during this period than in the classical era.

While the spread of otherworldly religion generally was a major theme, it was obvious that during these centuries Islam developed a particular dynamism that affected more different cultures and peoples than the other religions. All major societies in Asia, Europe, and Africa reacted to the spread of missionary religions in this period, and all reacted to some extent to the power of Islam.

Religion, however, meant different things to different people, even within the same faith. The number of devoted religious communities and leaders increased, for example, with monastic movements in Buddhism and Christianity. Economic contributions to religious institutions sometimes outstripped tax payments to governments. But many people combined religion with other interests, including commercial life. And most peoples combined new religions with older values and artistic forms.

The development of regular trade created a coherent world network joining key parts of Asia, Africa, and Europe. The most sophisticated exchanges linked the more prosperous and urbanized societies of the era. China, India, the Middle East and north Africa, and the Byzantine Empire traded manufactured goods of various sorts, mainly for elite customers interested in silks and porcelains. North–south trade routes linked sub-Saharan Africa, southeast Asia, Japan, northwestern Europe, and Russia to this commercial network. These areas provided less-processed goods, including gold and slaves.

Trade facilitated the spread of technologies. A number of Chinese inventions, first paper (when Islamic troops captured some papermakers in western China), then printing and explosives spread to the Middle East and on to Europe. Early in the postclassical period, this exchange was very slow (though faster than in previous centuries), but it became more rapid as time went on. At the end of the postclassical period, key Chinese inventions like printing and explosives moved westward more swiftly. Ideas spread as well. Thanks to trade, Indian mathematics, including the numbering system, spread to the Middle East. Then Arab mathematics, blending earlier Greek and Indian achievements with Arab innovations, reached western Europe. The spread of disease accelerated as well. In the 14th century a new epidemic of bubonic plague—the "Black Death"—moved from China through the Middle East to Europe, killing up to a third of the population in many areas.

The international trade of the postclassical era was not what we think of as a world economy today. Fewer societies were involved, and the volume and range of trade were far lower. However, despite downsides like disease, the international exchange of the

1000 C.E.	1100 C.E.	1200 C.E.	1300 C.E.	1400 C.E.
1000 Ghana Empire at its height (West Africa)	c. 1100 Invention of explosive powder (China)	1200 Rise of empire of Mali (West Africa)	1320s Europeans first use cannon in war	1400 End of Polynesian expeditions
1054 Schism between Eastern and Western Christianity	1150 Disintegration of Toltec Empire	1206 Delhi sultanate in India	1320–1340 Bubonic plague breaks out in Gobi desert and spreads to other parts of Asia	1405–1433 Chinese trading expeditions
1055 Seljuk Turks control Abbasid caliphate	1150–1350 Spread of Gothic style; scholasticism in western Europe	1231–1392 Mongols rule Korea	1325 Rise of Aztec Empire (MesoAmerica)	1439 Portugal captures Azores Islands
1066 Norman conquest of England; rise of feudal monarchy in western Europe	1185–1333 Kamakura Shogunate (Japan)	1236 Capture of Baghdad by Mongols; end of Abbasid caliphate	1338–1453 Hundred Years' War in Europe	1453 Turks capture Constantinople; end of Byzantine Empire
1096–1099 First Christian Crusade to Palestine		1260 Death of Sundiata	1350 Rise of Incas (Andes)	1471–1493 Peak of Inca Empire
		1265 First English parliament	1392–1910 Yi dynasty (Korea)	
		1279–1368 Mongol Empire in China		
		1290s Islam begins to spread to southeast Asia		

postclassical era had major effects. Along with religion, trade opportunities and merchants' interests became themes that had to be dealt with by each major society in Afro-Eurasia.

THE TRANSCONTINENTAL NETWORK

We live today in a period of rapidly intensifying contacts among all the world's major societies, and the process is increasingly referred to as globalization. Globalization has many new features, starting with dramatic communications technologies like the Internet. We increasingly realize, however, that contemporary globalization was prepared by previous periods in which interactions among major regions expanded. The postclassical period marked a major separation between earlier eras, in which contacts among different regions were slow or occasional, into a situation in which trade, travel and exchange created significant new, often routinized, influences on the ways individual societies developed.

The key process involved a series of routes for trade and travel that formed a new transcontinental network. The term network sums up the real innovations in contacts among the societies of Africa, Asia, and Europe—accurately suggesting the seeds of the high level of interaction we experience today. Defining the relationship between the systems of interaction in the postclassical period and later patterns provides a key way to map the process of change in world history.

The transcontinental network itself compelled many societies in Afro-Eurasia to decide on how to organize their participation in trade and exchange, and how to take advantage of the opportunities involved. No society responded in exactly the same way—comparing responses is an obvious assignment in analyzing the postclassical period—and some societies changed their responses over time. The spread of world religions, which created huge new areas of shared faith, but also new divisions among the religions themselves, contributed to but also complicated the evolution of the transcontinental network.

CONTINUITY

Change, including the formation of the transcontinental network, inevitably affected different societies to different degrees. Continuities combined with change. Even though the classical empires had collapsed, the successes of classical civilization encouraged many people to maintain or revive classical forms. China eagerly revived the structures of its clas-

sical age, including the empire, the bureaucracy, and Confucianism. It was touched by Islam and Buddhism, but ultimately it limited the influence of outside religions. China was not a changeless society—its growing participation in interregional trade proved its capacity to take advantage of new opportunities—but continuity remained extremely important.

The Middle East underwent great change as a result of the rise of Islam, but it also maintained continuities. Hellenistic science interacted with Islam, leading to important philosophical discussions of the relationship between science and faith. Earlier practices, such as the veiling of women in the cities, were revived. Although Islam opposed the enslavement of fellow Muslims, slavery continued to be a major component of social and labor systems over much of Afro-Eurasia. This marked a revival of traditions of the Greek and Roman world.

Continuities also showed in the blending of traditional forms with the missionary religions. Christian architecture had long used Greco-Roman styles. Buddhism adapted to Chinese values, for example, by placing more emphasis on the family loyalties of women. But no systematic changes in social structures or even political forms occurred during the postclassical centuries. The expansion of a merchant class affected social structure, but landlords remained dominant in most societies and peasants made up the bulk of the population. In key areas slavery or (in India) the caste system also maintained or revived older social institutions. Large political units developed in a few places, but outside of China polities were mainly loosely organized.

Finally, major areas were not part of the system shaped by world religions and interregional trade. Most notably, the Americas and Pacific Oceania, though scenes of significant developments, operated on separate dynamics and had few if any contacts with the rest of the world.

IMPACT ON DAILY LIFE: WOMEN

The postclassical period saw an intriguing tension that affected conditions for women in many parts of Afro-Eurasia. On the one hand, the major religions all insisted that women were spiritually equal to men—that they had souls or shared in the divine essence. This was a huge innovation. And religious change was not a matter of ideals alone. Buddhist leaders in Japan argued for women's importance. Islam established new rights for women, including property ownership. Buddhism and Christianity both established religious communities for women, giving them not only new forms of expression but also new leadership roles. As these religions spread, many women gained new positions and modes of expression through religious life. On the other hand, the condition of women also deteriorated during this period. Many scholars have argued that growing trade and urban prosperity reduced women's role in political and economic life and created conditions in which upper-class women were treated as ornaments. So, although religion helped women, it may also have distracted them from other issues: as they found spiritual solace, trade may have contributed to new gender inequalities.

Other changes were less favorable to women. Foot-binding—the clearest attempt to make women more purely ornamental—spread in China. In India the practice of sati, in which some widows threw themselves on their husbands' funeral pyres to demonstrate their grief, developed during this period. As Islamic society matured in the Middle East, women were increasingly secluded, and excluded from active roles in public life. But in other Islamic societies, especially in Africa, this was less true. At the same time, most historians conclude that the condition of women in western Europe had deteriorated by the later postclassical period, as judged, for example, by their greater exclusion from most skilled urban crafts. Thus, the postclassical period was an important one in women's history. New religions were important to many women, but new customs also limited opportunities for women to a greater degree than in the classical era. In much of the world, at least the vestiges of these limitations survive to the present day.

TRENDS AND SOCIETIES IN THE EARLY MODERN PERIOD

Chapters 6 and 7 examine the surge of Islam, first in the Middle East and then in other parts of Asia. Chapter 8 describes the expansion of trade and civilization in sub-Saharan Africa, which had various facets, but the link to Islam and the Islamic trading system was crucial. Two dynamics developed in Europe; each had contacts (both creative and hostile) with Islam and certainly with interregional trade. In eastern Europe, as detailed in Chapter 9, Byzantine culture took root, while a newer society emerged in western Europe, as described in Chapter 10. Chapter 11 describes the major cultures that developed in the Americas and the contacts among them. Chapters 12 and 13 address developments in China and the expansion of Chinese influence in Japan, Korea, and Vietnam—key parts of the network of interregional trade.

The last two centuries of the postclassical period, as Arab power declined, saw important new developments. Chapter 14 describes the Mongol conquests in the 13th and 14th centuries that, for a time, revolutionized the political map of Asia and parts of Europe, accelerating and redefining interregional trade and other exchanges. The decline of the Mongols, and the end of a brief Chinese experiment in leading world trade, left the world poised for further innovation. Chapter 15 describes a transitional moment and the complex factors that would alter world balance yet again. ■

6

The First Global Civilization: The Rise and Spread of Islam

Desert and Town: The Pre-Islamic Arabian World

The Life of Muhammad and the Genesis of Islam

The Arab Empire of the Umayyads

THINKING HISTORICALLY: Civilization and Gender Relationships

From Arab to Islamic Empire: The Early Abbasid Era

VISUALIZING THE PAST: The Mosque as a Symbol of Islamic Civilization

DOCUMENT: *The Thousand and One Nights* as a Mirror of Elite Society in the Abbasid Era

GLOBAL CONNECTIONS: Early Islam and the World

I n any ranking of the greatest survivors in world history, 'Abd al-Rahman I would have to be near or at the top of the list. The grandson of the last distinguished caliph (leader of the Muslim faithful) of the Umayyad dynasty, he had barely survived the vengeful slaughter of the many male descendants of that first house of Muslim rulers by the warriors of the 'Abbasid coalition that had seized power in 749. After narrowly escaping capture and beheading on his estate on the upper Euphrates River, 'Abd al-Rahman, dodging 'Abbasid pursuers and bounty hunters alike, fled through Syria and Palestine and across north Africa. After a half decade as fugitive, he finally found uneasy sanctuary in Morocco at the western end of the lands to which Islam had spread to that point in time. In 755, the twenty-four-year-old crossed the narrow Straits of Gibraltar that separated north Africa from the Iberian peninsula. Rallying to his cause several hundred Syrians, whose homelands had been the mainstay of the vanquished Umayyad dynasty and who had joined in earlier Arab-Berber campaigns to conquer the peninsula, 'Abd al-Rahman began his quest to become master of Iberia.

Despite continuing resistance by rivals and rebels from within and invasions plotted by Abbasid rulers in distant Baghdad, 'Abd al-Rahman steadily consolidated his control over Iberia. His early victories, particularly the capture of Córdoba in 756, secured his position as the paramount lord on the peninsula within years of his arrival. In the following decades as the capital of a flourishing Muslim kingdom, Córdoba grew rapidly into one of the most cosmopolitan and celebrated cities in the Mediterranean world. Córdoba boasted well paved and well lit streets, houses with running water, one of the world's finest universities, and a library with over 400,000 volumes at a time when the largest collections in Christian Europe contained a thousand at best. But Córdoba's crowning glory was its great mosque. It was famed for its hundreds of splendid marble columns topped by ornate horseshoe arches and its elaborately decorated vaulted ceilings, shown here (Figure 6.1). But even more remarkable than its distinctive architecture and decoration were the ways in which the mosque encapsulated the exceptional synergy generated by cooperation among and the blending of the diverse peoples and cultures that came together in Islamic Spain.

Like the development of Muslim civilization more generally, the construction of the great mosque of Córdoba owed much to earlier and even contemporary rival civilizations. It was built on the ruins of a Christian church, and many of the pillars that supported the signature horseshoe arches were taken from Roman ruins. And though the influence of Syrian-style Islamic architecture is apparent, the mosque's bell tower and thick walls decorated with geometric stone carvings shared key features with the Romanesque churches then found throughout Latin Christendom. Much of the mosque's stonework, and especially its intricate mosaics, were crafted by Christian Orthodox artisans from Constantinople, and its architects, laborers, and overseers were drawn from Arab and Berber Muslim migrants as well as the majority Christian population of Iberia.

The cross-cultural influences and interethnic and religious cooperation that played such vital roles in the construction of the grand mosque of Cordoba were also prominent features of Muslim Iberian society as a whole. Under the Muslims the peninsula became a key locus for the transmission of ideas, technology, and material culture between the Middle East, north Africa, and Europe. Arab and Berber migrants brought paper (originally invented, as we have seen, in China) and refined steel working to al-Andalus, and their descendants carried leather working skills back to Morocco and the broader Muslim world. Muslim migrants to Iberia also introduced sophisticated irrigation systems and a wide variety of staple foods and plants, including oranges, sugar cane, and cotton.

Jews and Christians, as "people of the book" were allowed in Iberia as in the rest of the Muslim world to worship openly, to regulate their everyday lives according to their own laws, and to collaborate with Muslims in trade, scholarship, and the arts. Arab and Jewish scholars in Córdoba, Seville, and other urban centers, for example, were renowned throughout the Mediterranean for their translations of classic Greek texts. By the tenth and eleventh centuries, their collaboration had become pivotal for the recovery in Latin Christendom of the writings of the great Greek philosopher and scientist Aristotle in such critical areas as astronomy, mathematics, geography and meteorology. Muslim Spain was also a key source of the tradition of wandering minstrels or troubadours, who carried music, fables, and the notion of romantic love northward into Christian Europe. And upper-class, educated women—Muslim, Christian and Jewish—flourished as poets, musicians, scribes and university students. ■

In the chapter that follows we shall see that in many ways Muslim Iberia was a microcosm—albeit a very forward looking one—of much of the Islamic world in its early centuries. Though spread initially mainly by nomadic camel-herding peoples of Arabia, Islam was from its inception a religion of the towns and trade. Muhammad himself was a successful caravan leader before he began to receive the divine revelations that transformed him into the founder of one of the great world religions. As in Iberia, conversion to Islam as it spread from Arabia was generally peaceful and voluntary, and in the early decades the faithful were, if anything, reluctant to recruit new believers. Even after the new faith came to undergird vast and expansive empires, such as those fashioned by the Umayyads and Abbasids, adherents of other religions based on divinely-inspired scriptures—from the Jews and Christians to the Hindus—prayed and practiced their rituals openly, and their communities very often flourished economically. As had been the case in Iberia, many of the most brilliant contributions of early Islamic civilization came from the openness of Arabs to borrowing from the ancient and rich civilizations that surrounded the Arab heartlands. Their absorption and then innovations on the sciences, arts, and technologies of Greece, Rome, Byzantium, Persia, Egypt, India, and China were essential to the rise of the first genuinely global civilization in human history.

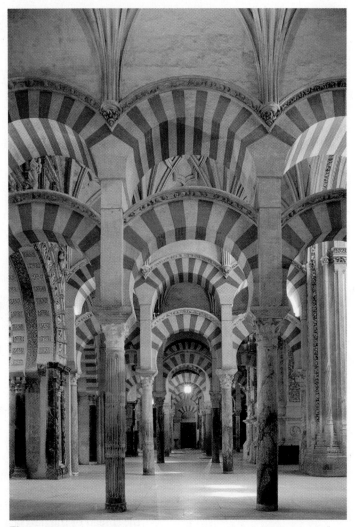

Figure 6.1 The graceful "horseshoe" arches of the Great Mosque at Córdoba in southern Spain provide a striking example of the sophistication and beauty of the arts and architecture produced by the fusion of Muslim, Jewish and Christian cultural traditions in Islamic Iberia from the 8th to the 15th centuries.

Desert and Town: The Pre-Islamic Arabian World

The Arabian Peninsula (Map 6.1) was a very unlikely birthplace for the first global civilization. Much of the area is covered by some of the most inhospitable desert in the world. An early traveler wrote of the region,

> All about us is an iron wilderness; a bare and black shining beach of heated volcanic stones . . . a vast bed and banks of rusty and basaltic bluish rocks . . . stubborn as heavy matter, as iron and sounding like bell metal; lying out eternally under the sand-driving desert wind.

In the scrub zones on the edges of the empty quarters, or uninhabitable desert zones, a wide variety of **Bedouin** (BEHD-oo-ihn), or nomadic, cultures had developed over the centuries, based on camel and goat herding. In oases like that pictured in Figure 6.2, which dotted the dry landscape, towns and agriculture flourished on a limited scale. Only in the coastal regions of the far south had extensive agriculture, sizeable cities, and regional kingdoms developed in ancient times. Over much of the rest of the peninsula, the camel nomads, organized in tribes and clans, were dominant. Yet in the rocky regions adjacent to the Red Sea, several trading towns had developed that played pivotal roles in the emergence of Islam.

Before the rise of Islam, Arabia was a peripheral desert wasteland whose once great trading cities had fallen on hard times. The sparse population of the Arabian peninsula was divided into rival tribes and clans that worshiped local gods.

bedouin [BEHD-oo-ihn] Nomadic pastoralists of the Arabian peninsula; culture based on camel and goat nomadism; early converts to Islam.

600 C.E.	620 C.E.	640 C.E.	660 C.E.	680 C.E.
c. 570 Birth of the prophet Muhammad	622 Muhammad's flight (hijra) from Mecca to Medina	644–656 Rule of Caliph Uthman	661–680 Mu'awiya	680 Death of Ali's son Husayn at Karbala
597–626 Wars between the Byzantine and Sasanian (Persian) empires	624–627 Wars between the followers of Muhammad and the Quraysh of Mecca	656–661 Rule of Caliph Ali; first civil war	661–750 Umayyad caliphate	680–692 Second civil war
610 Muhammad's first revelations	628 Muslim–Meccan Truce			744–750 Third civil war; Abbasid revolt
613 Muhammad begins to preach the new faith	630 Muhammad enters Mecca in triumph			750 Abbasid caliphate begins
	632 Death of Muhammad			
	632–634 Rule of Caliph Abu Bakr			
	633–634 Ridda Wars in Arabia			
	634–643 Early Muslim conquests in the Byzantine Empire			
	634–644 Rule of Caliph Umar			
	637 Arab invasion and destruction of Sasanian Empire			

Although the urban roots of Islam have often been stressed by writers on Muslim civilization, the bedouin world in which the religion arose shaped the career of its prophet, his teachings, and the spread of the new beliefs. In fact, key towns such as Mecca and Medina were largely extensions of the tribal culture of the camel nomads. Their populations were linked by kinship to bedouin peoples. For example, Mecca had been founded by bedouins and at the time of Muhammad was ruled by former bedouin clans. The safety of the trade routes on which the towns depended was in the hands of the nomadic tribes that lived along the vulnerable caravan routes to the north and south. In addition, the town dwellers' social organization, which focused on clan and family, and their culture, including language and religion, were much like those of the nomads.

Clan Identity, Clan Rivalries, and the Cycle of Vengeance

The harsh desert and scrub environment of Arabia gave rise to forms of social organization and a lifestyle that were similar to those of other nomadic peoples. Bedouin herders lived in kin-related clan groups in highly mobile tent encampments. Clans, in turn, were clustered in larger tribal groupings, but these were rarely congregated together and then only in times of war or severe crisis. The struggle for subsistence in the unforgiving Arabian environment resulted in a strong dependence on and loyalty to one's family and clan. Survival depended on cooperation with and support from kin. To be cut off from them or expelled from the clan encampment was in most cases fatal. The use of watering places and grazing lands, which were essential to maintaining the herds on which bedouin life depended, was regulated by clan councils. But there could be wide disparities of wealth and status within clan groups and between clans of the same tribe. Though normally elected by councils of elder advisors, the **shaykhs** (shayks), or leaders of the tribes and clans, were almost always men with large herds, several wives, many children, and numerous retainers. The shaykhs' dictates were enforced by bands of free warriors whose families made up a majority of a given clan group. Beneath the warriors were slave families, often the remnants of rival clans defeated in war, who served the shaykhs or the clan as a whole.

Clan cohesion was reinforced by fierce interclan rivalries and struggles to control vital pasturelands and watering places. If the warriors from one clan found those from another clan drawing

shaykhs [shayks] Leaders of tribes and clans within bedouin society; usually men with large herds, several wives, and many children.

Map 6.1 Arabia and Surrounding Areas Before and During the Time of Muhammad   Though much of Arabia was separated by vast deserts from surrounding classical civilizations, as the map shows it maintained contact by sea in the west and south and through camel caravans into Palestine and Syria.

water from one of their wells, they were likely to kill them. Wars often broke out as a result of one clan encroaching on the pasture areas of another clan. In a culture in which one's honor depended on respect for one's clan, the flimsiest pretexts could lead to interclan violence. For instance, an insult to a warrior in a market town, the theft of a prize stallion, or one clan's defeat in a horse race by another clan could end in battles between clan groups. All the men of a given clan joined in these fights, which normally were won by the side that could field several champions who were famed for their strength and skill with spears or bows and arrows.

These battles were fought according to a code of chivalry that was quite common in early cultures. Although battles usually were small in terms of the numbers involved, they were hard-fought

Figure 6.2 With their supply of water, shade, and date palms, oases like this one in Egypt have long been key centers of permanent settlement and trade in the desert. Major towns usually grew around the underground springs and wells or small rivers that fed the oases. Travelers' and traders' caravans stopped at the oases to water their camels and horses and to rest and eat after their arduous treks through the desert. As points of concentration of wealth, food, and precious water, oases were tempting targets for raids by bedouin bands.

and often bloody affairs. Almost invariably the battles either initiated or perpetuated clan feuds, which could continue for hundreds of years. The deaths of the warriors of one clan required that revenge be taken on the clan that had killed them. Their deaths led in turn to reprisals. This constant infighting weakened the bedouins in relation to the neighboring peoples and empires and allowed them to be manipulated and set against each other.

Towns and Long-Distance Trade

Mecca City located in mountainous region along Red Sea in Arabian peninsula; founded by Umayyad clan of Quraysh; site of Ka'ba; original home of Muhammad; location of chief religious pilgrimage point in Islam.

Umayyad [oo-MY-yad] Clan of Quraysh that dominated politics and commercial economy of Mecca; clan established dynasty as rulers of Islam, 661 to 750.

Quraysh [koo-RAYSH] Tribe of bedouins that controlled Mecca in 7th century C.E.

Ka'ba Most revered religious shrine in pre-Islamic Arabia; located in Mecca; focus of obligatory annual truce among bedouin tribes; later incorporated as important shrine in Islam.

Although bedouin herders occupied most of the habitable portions of Arabia, farmers and town dwellers carved out small communities in the western and southern parts of the peninsula in the classical era. Foreign invasions and the inroads of bedouin peoples had all but destroyed these civilizations centuries before the birth of Muhammad. But a number of cities had developed farther north as links in the transcontinental trading system that stretched from the Mediterranean to east Asia. The most important of these cities was **Mecca,** located in the mountainous region along the Red Sea on the western coast of Arabia (Map 6.1). The town had been founded by the **Umayyad** (oo-MY-yad) clan of the **Quraysh** (koo-RAYSH) bedouin tribe, and members of the clan dominated its politics and commercial economy.

The wealth and status of Mecca and its merchant elite were enhanced by the fact that the city was the site of the **Ka'ba,** one of the most revered religious shrines in pre-Islamic Arabia. Not only did the shrine attract pilgrims and customers for Mecca's bazaars, but at certain times of the year it was the focus of an obligatory truce in the interclan feuds. Freed from fears of assault by rival groups, merchants and bedouins flocked to the town to trade, exchange gossip, and taste the delights of city life.

Northeast of Mecca was a town named Yathrib (Map 6.1) that later came to be known as **Medina,** or the city of the prophet Muhammad. Like most of the other towns in the peninsula, Medina was established in an oasis. Wells and springs made sedentary agriculture possible. In addition to wheat and other staples, Medina's inhabitants grew date palms, whose fruit and seeds (which were fed to camels) they traded to the bedouins. Medina was also engaged, though on a much smaller scale than Mecca, in the long-distance caravan trade that passed through Arabia. In contrast to Umayyad-dominated Mecca, control in Medina was contested by two bedouin and three Jewish clans. Their quarrels left the city a poor second to Mecca as a center of trade, and these divisions proved critical to the survival of the prophet Muhammad and the Islamic faith.

Medina Also known as Yathrib; town located northeast of Mecca; grew date palms whose fruit was sold to bedouins; became refuge for Muhammad following flight from Mecca (hijra).

Marriage and Family in Pre-Islamic Arabia

Although the evidence is scant, there are several indications that women in pre-Islamic Arabian bedouin culture enjoyed greater freedom and higher status than those who lived in neighboring civilized centers, such as the Byzantine and Sasanian empires that then dominated the Middle East (Map 6.1). Women played key economic roles, from milking camels and weaving cloth to raising children. Because the men of the clan were often on the move, many tribes traced descent through the mother rather than the father. In some tribes, both men and women were allowed multiple marriage partners. To seal a marriage contract, the man was required to pay a bride-price to his prospective wife's family, rather than the woman's father sending a dowry or gift to the prospective husband. Unlike the women (especially those of elite status) in neighboring Syria and Persia, women in pre-Islamic Arabia were not secluded and did not wear veils. Their advice was highly regarded in clan and tribal councils, and they often composed poems that were the focus of bedouin cultural life in the pre-Islamic era.

Despite these career outlets, women were not by any means considered equal to men. They could not gain glory as warriors, the most prized occupation of the bedouins, and often they were little more than drudge laborers. Their status depended on the custom of individual clans and tribes rather than on legal codes. As a result, it varied widely from one clan or family to the next. Customary practices of property control, inheritance, and divorce heavily favored men. In the urban environment of trading centers such as Mecca, the rise of a mercantile elite and social stratification appear to have set back the position of women on the whole. The more stable family life of the towns led to the practice of tracing descent through the male line, and while men continued to practice polygamy, women were expected to be monogamous.

Poets and Neglected Gods

Because of the isolation of Arabia in the pre-Islamic age and the harshness and poverty of the natural environment, Arab material culture was not highly developed. Except in the far south, there was little art or architecture of worth. Even Mecca made little impression on the cosmopolitan merchants who passed through the city in caravans from the fabled cities of the ancient civilizations farther north. The main focus of bedouin cultural creativity in the pre-Islamic era was poetry, which was composed and transmitted orally because there was as yet no written language. Clan and tribal bards narrated poems that told of their kinsmen's heroics in war and the clan's great deeds. Some poets were said to have magical powers or to be possessed by demons. More than any other source, poems provide a vision of life and society in pre-Islamic Arabia. They tell of lovers spurned and passion consummated, war and vendettas, loyalty, and generosity.

Bedouin religion was for most clans a blend of animism and polytheism, or the worship of many gods and goddesses. Some tribes, such as the Quraysh (koo-RAYSH), recognized a supreme god named Allah. But they seldom prayed or sacrificed to Allah, concentrating instead on less abstract spirits who seemed more relevant to their daily lives. Both spirits and gods (for example, the moon god, Hubal) tended to be associated with night, a cool period when dew covered the earth, which had been parched by the blaze of the desert sun. Likewise, the worship of nature spirits focused on sacred caves, pure springs, and groves of trees—places where the bedouins could take shelter from the heat and wind. Religion appears to have had little to do with ethics. Rather, standards of morality and proper behavior were rooted in tribal customs and unwritten codes of honor.

How seriously the bedouins took their gods is also a matter of some doubt. Their lukewarm adherence is illustrated by the famous tale of a bedouin warrior who had set out to avenge his father's death at the hands of a rival clan. He stopped at an oracle along the way to seek advice by drawing arrows that indicated various courses of action he might take. Three times he drew arrows that advised him to abandon his quest for revenge. Infuriated by this counsel, he hurled the arrows at the idol of the oracle and exclaimed, "Accursed one! Had it been thy father who was murdered, thou would not have forbidden my avenging him."

The Life of Muhammad and the Genesis of Islam

In the 7th century the revelations of the prophet Muhammad provided the basis for the emergence of a new religion—Islam—in the Arabian peninsula. Though initially an Arab religion, in both beliefs and practices, Islam contained a powerful appeal that eventually made it one of the great world religions.

Muhammad Prophet of Islam; born c. 570 to Banu Hashim clan of Quraysh tribe in Mecca; raised by father's family; received revelations from Allah in 610 C.E. and thereafter; died in 632.

By the 6th century C.E., camel nomads were dominant throughout much of Arabia. The civilized centers to the south were in ruins, and trading centers such as Mecca and Medina depended on alliances with neighboring bedouin tribes to keep the caravan routes open. The constricted world of clan and kin, nomadic camp, blood feud, and local gods persisted despite the lure of the empires and cosmopolitan urban centers that stretched in a great arc to the north and east of the Arabian peninsula (see Map 6.1).

But pressures for change were mounting. Both the Byzantine and Sasanian empires struggled to assert greater control over the nomadic tribes of the peninsula. In addition, Arab peoples migrated into Mesopotamia and other areas to the north, where they came increasingly under foreign influence. From these regions, the influence of established monotheistic religions, especially Judaism and Christianity, entered Arabia. These new currents gave rise to a number of Arab prophets who urged the bedouin tribes to renounce idol worship and rely on a single, almighty god. The prophet **Muhammad** and the new religion that his revelations inspired in the early decades of the 7th century responded both to these influences flowing into Arabia and to related social dislocations that were disrupting Arab life.

The hardships of Muhammad's early life underscore the importance of clan ties in the Arabian world. He was born around 570 C.E. into a prominent clan of the Quraysh tribe, the Banu Hashim, in a bedouin encampment where he spent the first six years of his life. Because his father died before he was born, Muhammad was raised by his father's relatives. The loss of his father was compounded by the death of Muhammad's mother shortly after he went to live with her some years later. Despite these early losses, Muhammad had the good fortune to be born into a respected clan and powerful tribe. His paternal uncle, Abu Talib, was particularly fond of the boy and served as his protector and supporter through much of his early life. Muhammad's grandfather, who like other leading members of the clan was engaged in commerce, educated the young man in the ways of the merchant. With Abu Talib, Muhammad made his first caravan journey to Syria, where on this and later trips he met adherents of the Christian and Jewish faiths, whose beliefs and practices had a great impact on his teachings.

Khadijah [kah-DEE-juh] (595–619) First wife of the prophet Muhammad, who had worked for her as a trader.

In his adolescence, Muhammad took up residence in Mecca. By his early 20s he was working as a trader for **Khadijah** (kah-DEE-juh) (the widow of a wealthy merchant), whom he married some years later. His life as a merchant in Mecca and on the caravan routes exposed Muhammad to the world beyond Arabia and probably made him acutely aware of the clan rivalries that had divided the peoples of the region for millennia. He would also have become increasingly concerned about new forces undermining solidarity within the clans. The growth of the towns and trade had enriched some clan families and left others behind, often in poverty. It had also introduced a new source of tension between clan and tribal groupings because some clans, such as the Umayyads, grew rich on the profits from commerce, whereas others maintained their herding lifestyle.

As a trader and traveler, Muhammad would almost certainly have been aware of the new religious currents that were sweeping Arabia and surrounding areas in the early 7th century. Particularly notable among these was the spread of monotheistic ideas and a growing dissatisfaction with the old gods that had been venerated by the bedouin peoples. In Muhammad's time, several prophets had arisen, proclaiming a new faith for the Arabs.

Figure 6.3 Over much of Eurasia, and across the vast Andes Mountain range of South America, pack animals, including the camels in this photo, have been the major means of moving trading goods over land through most of human history. Framed by a cluster of Egypt's renown pyramids, caravans similar to this one connected the cities and nomadic people of the Arab world and with the spread of Islam provided critical linkages for the first world civilization from Morocco in the west to the outer regions of China in the east

Though socially prominent, economically well off, and widely admired for his trading skills and trustworthiness, Muhammad grew increasingly distracted and dissatisfied with a life focused on material gain. He spent increasing amounts of time in meditation in the hills and wilderness that surrounded Mecca. In 610 or earlier, he received the first of many revelations, which his followers believe Allah transmitted to him through the angel Gabriel. These revelations were later written in Arabic and collected in the **Qur'an** (kuh-RAHN). The teachings and injunctions of the Qur'an formed the basis of the new religion that Muhammad began to preach to his clan and the people of Mecca.

Persecution, Flight, and Victory

At first Muhammad's following was small, consisting mainly of his wife, several clanspeople, and some servants and slaves. As his message was clarified with successive revelations, the circle of the faithful grew so that the Umayyad notables who dominated Meccan life saw him as a threat to their own wealth and power. Above all, the new faith threatened to supplant the gods of the Ka'ba, whose shrines had done so much to establish the city as a center of commerce and bedouin interchange. Although he was protected for a time by his own clan, Muhammad was increasingly threatened by the Umayyads, who plotted with other clans to murder him. It was clear that Muhammad must flee Mecca, but where was he to find refuge? Muhammad's reputation as a skillful and fair negotiator prepared the way for his successful flight from Umayyad persecution. The quarrels between the clans in the nearby city of Medina had set off increasingly violent clashes, and the oasis community was on the verge of civil war. Leaders of the bedouin clans in Medina sent a delegation to invite Muhammad, who was related to them on his mother's side, to mediate their disputes and put an end to the strife that had plagued the town.

Clever ruses and the courage of his clansman **Ali,** who at one point took Muhammad's place and thus risked becoming the target of assassins, secured in 622 the safe passage of Muhammad and a small band of followers from Mecca to Medina. His *hijra* (HIH-jruh), or flight to Medina marks the first year of the Islamic calendar. In Medina he was given a hero's welcome. He soon justified this warm reception by deftly settling the quarrels between the bedouin clans of the town. His wisdom and skill as a political leader won him new followers, who joined those who had accompanied him from Mecca as the core believers of the new faith.

The Holy Qur'an

The Qur'an

Qur'an [kuh-RAHN] Recitations of revelations received by Muhammad; holy book of Islam.

Ali (c. 599–661) Cousin and son-in-law of Muhammad; one of orthodox caliphs; focus for Shi'a.

In the eyes of the Umayyad notables, Muhammad's successes made him a greater threat than ever. Not only was he preaching a faith that rivaled their own, but his leadership was strengthening Mecca's competitor, Medina. Muslim raids on Meccan caravans provided yet another source of danger. Determined to put an end to these threats, the Quraysh launched a series of attacks in the mid-620s on Muhammad and his followers in Medina. These attacks led to several battles. In these clashes, Muhammad proved an able leader and courageous fighter.

The ultimate victory for Muhammad and his followers was signaled by a treaty with the Quraysh in 628, which included a provision granting the Muslims permission to visit the shrine at Ka'ba in Mecca during the season of truce. By then Muhammad's community had won many bedouin allies, and more than 10,000 converts accompanied him on his triumphal return to his hometown in 629. After proving the power of Allah, the single god he proclaimed, by smashing the idols of the shrine, Muhammad gradually won over the Umayyads and most of the other inhabitants of Mecca to the new faith.

Arabs and Islam

Although Islam was soon to become one of the great world religions, the beliefs and practices of the prophet Muhammad were initially adopted only by the Arab town dwellers and bedouins among whom he had grown up. There is a striking parallel here with early Christianity, which focused on Jewish converts. The new religion preached by Muhammad had much to offer the divided peoples of Arabia. It gave them a form of monotheism that belonged to no single tribe and transcended clan and class divisions. It provided a religion that was distinctly Arab in origin and yet the equal of the monotheistic faiths held by the Christians and Jews, who lived in the midst of the bedouin tribes. If anything, the monotheism preached by Muhammad was even more uncompromising than that of the Christians because it allowed no intermediaries between the individual and God. God was one; there were no saints, and angels were nothing more than messengers. In addition, there were no priests in the Christian or Jewish sense of the term.

umma   Community of the faithful within Islam; transcended old tribal boundaries to create degree of political unity.

Islam offered the possibility of an end to the vendettas and feuds that had so long divided the peoples of Arabia and had undermined their attempts to throw off the domination of neighboring empires. The **umma,** or community of the faithful, transcended old tribal boundaries, and it made possible a degree of political unity undreamed of before Muhammad's time. The new religion provided a single and supernaturally sanctioned source of authority and discipline. With unity, the skills and energies that the bedouins had once channeled toward warring with each other were turned outward in a burst of conquest that is perhaps unmatched in human history in its speed and extent. From vassals, march warriors, or contemptible "savages" of the desert waste, the Arab bedouins were transformed into the conquerors and rulers of much of the Middle Eastern world.

zakat   Tax for charity; obligatory for all Muslims.

The new religion also provided an ethical system that did much to heal the deep social rifts within Arabian society. Islam stressed the dignity of all believers and their equality in the eyes of Allah. It promoted a moral code that stressed the responsibility of the well-to-do and strong for the poor and weak, the aged and infirm. Payment of the **zakat,** a tax for charity, was obligatory in the new faith. In both his revelations and his personal behavior, Muhammad enjoined his followers to be kind and generous to their dependents, including slaves. He forbade the rich to exploit the poor through exorbitant rents or rates of interest for loans.

The prophet's teachings and the revelations of the Qur'an soon were incorporated into an extensive body of law that regulated all aspects of the lives of the Muslim faithful. Held accountable before Islamic law on earth, they lived in a manner that would prepare them for the Last Judgment, which in Islam, as in Christianity, would determine their fate in eternity. A stern but compassionate God and a strict but socially minded body of law set impressive standards for the social interaction between adherents of the new faith.

Universal Elements in Islam

Although only Arabs embraced the religion of Islam in its early years, from the outset it contained beliefs and practices that would give it a strong appeal to peoples at virtually all stages of social development and in widely varying cultural settings. Some of these beliefs—Islam's uncompromising

Figure 6.4 The Ka'ba in Mecca, with masses of pilgrims. Each year tens of millions of the Muslim faithful from all around the world make the journey to the holy sites of Arabia. The rituals performed by pilgrims at Mecca and Medina are key religious duties for all who can afford to travel to the holy cities.

monotheism, highly developed legal codes, egalitarianism, and strong sense of community—were the same as the attributes that had won it support among the peoples of Arabia. Its potential as a world religion was enhanced by the fact that most of the attributes of Islam were to some degree anticipated by the other Semitic religions, particularly Judaism and Christianity, with which Muhammad had contact for much of his life. He accepted the validity of the earlier divine revelations that had given rise to the Jewish and Christian faiths. He taught that the revelations he had received were a refinement of these earlier ones and that they were the last divine instructions for human behavior and worship.

In addition to the beliefs and practices that have given Islam a universal appeal, its **five pillars,** principles that must be accepted and followed by all believers, provided the basis for an underlying religious unity. (1) The confession of faith was simple and powerful: "There is no God but Allah, and Muhammad is his Prophet." The injunctions (2) to pray, facing the holy city of Mecca, five times a day and (3) to fast during the month of **Ramadan,** enhanced community solidarity and allowed the faithful to demonstrate their fervor. (4) The zakat, or tithe for charity, also strengthened community cohesion and won converts from those seeking an ethical code that stressed social responsibility and the unity of all believers. (5) The **hajj,** or pilgrimage to the holy city of Mecca, to worship Allah at the Ka'ba, shown in Figure 6.4, drew together the faithful from Morocco to China. No injunction did more to give Islam a universal character.

The Arab Empire of the Umayyads

Many of the bedouin tribes that had converted to Islam renounced the new faith in the months after Muhammad's death, and his remaining followers quarreled over who should succeed him. Although these quarrels were never fully resolved, the community managed to find new leaders who directed a series of campaigns to force those who had abandoned Islam to return to the fold. Having

five pillars The obligatory religious duties of all Muslims; confession of faith, prayer, fasting during Ramadan, zakat, and hajj.

The Sea of Precious Virtues

Ramadan Islamic month of religious observance requiring fasting from dawn to sunset.

hajj A Muslim's pilgrimage to the holy city of Mecca, to worship Allah at the Ka'ba.

Despite a time of crisis after the death of the prophet Muhammad in 632 C.E., the Muslim community held together. Eventually, Muhammad's old adversaries, the Umayya clan, seized leadership of the Muslim faithful and began a sequence of stunning conquests throughout the Middle East and north Africa.

united most of Arabia under the Islamic banner by 633, Muslim military commanders began to mount serious expeditions beyond the peninsula, where only probing attacks had occurred during the lifetime of the prophet and in the period of tribal warfare after his death. The courage, military prowess, and religious zeal of the warriors of Islam, and the weaknesses of the empires that bordered on Arabia, resulted in stunning conquests in Mesopotamia, north Africa, and Persia, which dominated the next two decades of Islamic history. The empire built from these conquests was Arab rather than Islamic. Most of it was ruled by a small Arab warrior elite, led by the Umayyads and other prominent clans. These groups had little desire to convert the subject populations, either Arab or otherwise, to the new religion.

The Spread of Islam **MAP**

Consolidation and Division in the Islamic Community

The leadership crisis brought on by Muhammad's death in 632 was compounded by the fact that he had not appointed a successor or even established a procedure by which a new leader would be chosen. Opinion within the Muslim community was deeply divided as to who should succeed him. In this moment of extreme danger, a strong leader who could hold the Islamic community together was urgently needed. On the afternoon Muhammad died, one of the clans that remained committed to the new faith called a meeting to select a leader who would be designated as the **caliph, the political and religious successor to Muhammad.** Several choices were possible, and a deadlock between the clans appeared likely—a deadlock that would almost certainly have been fatal to a community threatened by enemies on all sides.

caliph   The political and religious successor to Muhammad.

One of the main candidates, Ali, the cousin and son-in-law of Muhammad, was passed over because he was considered too young to assume a position of such great responsibility. This decision later proved to be a major source of division in the Islamic community. But in 632, it appeared that a difficult reconciliation had been won by the choice of one of Muhammad's earliest followers and closest friends, **Abu Bakr** (ah-BOO BA-kuhr) (caliph from 632 to 634). In addition to his courage, warmth, and wisdom, Abu Bakr was well versed in the genealogical histories of the bedouin tribes, which meant that he knew which tribes could be turned against each other and which ones could be enticed into alliances. Initially, at least, his mandate was very limited. He received no financial support from the Muslim community. Thus, he had to continue his previous occupation as a merchant on a part-time basis, and he only loosely controlled the military commanders.

Bakr, Abu   [ah-BOO BA-kuhr] (c. 573–634) One of Muhammad's earliest converts; succeeded Muhammad as first caliph of Islamic community.

These commanders turned out to be very able. After turning back attacks on Mecca, the Islamic faithful routed one after another of the bedouin tribes. The defeat of rival prophets and some of the larger clans in what were known as the **Ridda Wars** soon brought about the return of the Arabian tribes to the Islamic fold. Emboldened by the proven skills of his generals and the swelling ranks of the Muslim faithful, Abu Bakr oversaw raids to the north of Arabia into the sedentary zones in present-day Iraq and Syria and westward into Egypt (Map 6.1).

Ridda Wars   Wars that followed Muhammad's death in 632; resulted in defeat of rival prophets and some of larger clans; restored unity of Islam.

The unified bedouin forces had originally intended to raid for booty and then retreat back into the desert. But their initial probes revealed the vulnerability of the Byzantine and Persian empires, which dominated or ruled the territories into which the Muslim warriors rode. The invaders were also encouraged by the growing support of the Arab bedouin peoples who had been migrating into the Fertile Crescent for centuries. These peoples had long served as the vassals and frontier guardians of the Byzantine and Persian empires. Now they joined their brethren in a combined assault on both of them.

Motives for Arab Conquests

The Arab warriors were driven by many forces. The unity provided by the Islamic faith gave them a new sense of common cause and strength. United, they could stand up to the non-Arab rulers who had so long played them against each other and despised them as unwashed and backward barbarians from the desert wastelands. It is also probable that the early leaders of the community saw the wars of conquest as a good way to release the pent-up energies of the martial bedouin tribes they now sought to lead (see Figure 6.5). Above all, the bedouin warriors were drawn to the campaigns of expansion by the promise of a share in the booty to be won in the rich farmlands raided and the tribute that could be exacted from towns that came under Arab rule. As an early Arab writer observed, the bedouins forsook their life as desert nomads not out of a promise of religious rewards, but because of a "yearning after bread and dates."

The chance to glorify their new religion may have been a motive for the Arab conquests, but they were not driven by a desire to win converts to it. In fact, other than fellow bedouin tribes of Arab descent, the invaders had good reason to avoid mass conversions. Not only would Arab warriors have to share the booty of their military expeditions with ever larger numbers if converts were made, but Muslims were exempted from some of the more lucrative taxes levied on Christian, Jewish, and other non-Muslim groups. Thus, the vision of **jihads** (jih-HAHDs), or holy wars launched to forcibly spread the Muslim faith, which has long been associated with Islam in the Christian West, misrepresents the forces behind the early Arab expansion.

jihad [jih-HAHD] Struggle; often used for wars in defense of the faith.

Weaknesses of the Adversary Empires

Of the two great empires that had once fought for dominance in the Fertile Crescent transit zone, the Sasanian Empire of Persia proved the more vulnerable. Power in the extensive Sasanian domains was formally concentrated in the hands of an autocratic emperor. By the time of the Arab explosion, the emperor was manipulated by a landed, aristocratic class that harshly exploited the farmers who made up most of the population of the empire. Zoroastrianism, the official religion of the emperor, lacked popular roots. By contrast, the religion of a visionary reformer named Mazdak, which had won considerable support among the peasants, had been brutally suppressed by the Sasanian rulers in the period before the rise of Islam.

At first, the Sasanian commanders had contempt for the Arab invaders and set out against them with poorly prepared forces. By the time the seriousness of the Islamic threat was made clear by decisive Arab victories in the Fertile Crescent region and the defection of the Arab tribes on the frontier, Muslim warriors had broken into the Sasanian heartland. Further Muslim victories brought about the rapid collapse of the vast empire. The Sasanian rulers and their forces retreated eastward in the face of the Muslim advance. The capital was taken, armies were destroyed, and generals were slain. When in 651 the last of the Sasanian rulers was assassinated, Muslim victory and the destruction of the empire were ensured.

The Persian Empire Under the Sasanian Dynasty **MAP**

Figure 6.5 This illustration from an account of the Muslim conquest of Sicily in the 9th century C.E. is one of the earliest known artistic renderings of an Arab army at war. The camp, the armored warriors, and the siege in progress help us to envision the Muslim forces that built the first great Arab empire under the early caliphs in the 7th century C.E.

Despite an equally impressive string of Muslim victories in the provinces of their empire, the Byzantines proved a stronger adversary (see Chapter 9). However, their ability to resist the Muslim onslaught was impeded by both the defection of their own frontier Arabs and the support the Muslim invaders received from the Christians of Syria and Egypt. Members of the Christian sects dominant in these areas, such as the **Copts** and **Nestorians,** had long resented the rule of the Orthodox Byzantines, who taxed them heavily and openly persecuted them as heretics. When it became clear that the Muslims would not only tolerate the Christians but tax them less heavily than the Byzantines did, these Christian groups rallied to the Arabs.

Weakened from within and exhausted by the long wars fought with Persia in the decades before the Arab explosion, the Byzantines reeled from the Arab assaults. Syria, western Iraq, and Palestine were quickly taken by the Arab invaders, and by 640 a series of probes had been made into Egypt, one of the richest provinces of the empire (Map 6.2). In the early 640s, the ancient center of learning and commerce, Alexandria, was taken, most of Egypt was occupied, and Arab armies extended their conquests into Libya to the west. Perhaps even more astounding from the point of view of the Byzantines, by the mid-640s the desert bedouins were putting together war fleets that increasingly challenged the long-standing Byzantine mastery of the Mediterranean. The rise of Muslim naval supremacy in the eastern end of the Mediterranean sealed the loss of Byzantium's rich provinces in Syria and Egypt. It also opened the way to further Muslim conquests in north Africa, the Mediterranean islands, and even southern Italy (Map 6.2 & Figure 6.5). For a time the Byzantines managed to rally their forces and stave off further inroads into their Balkan and Asia Minor heartlands. But the early triumphs of the Arab invaders had greatly reduced the strength of the Byzantine Empire. Although it survived for centuries, it was henceforth a kingdom under siege.

Copts   Christian sect of Egypt; tended to support Islamic invasions of this area in preference to Byzantine rule.

Nestorians   A Christian sect found in Asia; tended to support Islamic invasions of this area in preference to Byzantine rule; cut off from Europe by Muslim invasions.

Map 6.2 The Expansion of the Islamic Empire in the 7th and 8th Centuries   Whether by land or sea, Islamic civilization expanded by both conquest and trade, while the Muslim faith was spread mainly peacefully along ancient trading routes, often by sufi holymen.

The Problem of Succession and the Sunni–Shi'a Split

The stunning successes of Muslim armies and the sudden rise of an Arab empire diverted attention, for a time at least, from continuing divisions within the community. Although these divisions were often generations old and the result of personal animosities, resentments had also begun to build over how the booty from the conquests should be divided among the tribal groups that made up the Islamic community. In 656, just over two decades after the death of the prophet, the growing tensions broke into open violence. The spark that began the conflict was the murder of the third caliph, **Uthman,** by mutinous warriors returning from Egypt. His death was the signal for the supporters of Ali to proclaim him as caliph. Uthman's unpopularity among many of the tribes, particularly those from Medina and the prophet's earliest followers, arose in part from the fact that he was the first caliph to be chosen from Muhammad's early enemies, the Umayyad clan. Already angered by Uthman's murder, the Umayyads rejected Ali's claims and swore revenge when he failed to punish Uthman's assassins. Warfare erupted between the two factions.

Ali was a renowned warrior and experienced commander, and his deeply committed supporters soon gained the upper hand. After his victory at the Battle of the Camel in late 656, most of the Arab garrisons shifted to his side against the Umayyads, whose supporters were concentrated in the province of Syria and the holy city of Mecca. Just as Ali was on the verge of defeating the Umayyad forces at the **Battle of Siffin** in 657, he was won over by a plea for mediation. His decision to accept mediation was fatal to his cause. Some of his most fervent supporters renounced his leadership and had to be suppressed violently. While representatives of both parties tried unsuccessfully to work out a compromise, the Umayyads regrouped their forces and added Egypt to the provinces backing their claims. In 660, **Mu'awiya** (moo-UH-wee-uh), the new leader of the Umayyads, was proclaimed caliph in Jerusalem, directly challenging Ali's position. A year later, Ali was assassinated, and his son Hasan was pressured by the Umayyads into renouncing his claims to the caliphate.

In the decades after the prophet's death, the question of succession generated deep divisions in the Muslim community. The split between the **Sunnis,** who backed the Umayyads, and the **Shi'a,** or supporters of Ali, remains to this day the most fundamental in the Islamic world. Hostility between these two branches of the Islamic faithful was heightened in the years after Ali's death by the continuing struggle between the Umayyads and Ali's second son, Husayn. After being abandoned by the clans in southern Iraq, who had promised to rise in a revolt supporting his claims against the Umayyads, Husayn and a small party were overwhelmed and killed at **Karbala** in 680. From that point on, the Shi'a mounted sustained resistance to the Umayyad caliphate.

Over the centuries, factional disputes about who had the right to succeed Muhammad, with the Shi'a recognizing none of the early caliphs except Ali, have been compounded by differences in belief, ritual, and law that have steadily widened the gap between Sunnis and Shi'a. These divisions have been further complicated by the formation of splinter sects within the Shi'a community in particular, beginning with those who defected from Ali when he agreed to arbitration.

The Umayyad Imperium

After a pause to settle internal disputes over succession, the remarkable sequence of Arab conquest was renewed in the last half of the 7th century. Muslim armies broke into central Asia, inaugurating a rivalry with Buddhism in the region that continues to the present day (Map 6.2). By the early 8th century, the southern prong of this advance had reached into northwest India. Far to the west, Arab armies swept across north Africa and crossed the Straits of Gibraltar to conquer Spain and threaten France. Although the Muslim advance into western Europe was blocked by the hard-fought victory of Charles Martel and the Franks at Poitiers in 732, the Arabs did not fully retreat beyond the Pyrenees into Spain until decades later. Muslim warriors and sailors dominated much of the Mediterranean, a position that was solidified by the conquest of key islands such as Crete, Sicily, and Sardinia in the early decades of the 9th century. By the early 700s, the Umayyads ruled an empire that extended from Spain in the west to the steppes of central Asia in the east. Not since the Romans had there been an empire to match it; never had an empire of its size been built so rapidly.

Although Mecca remained the holy city of Islam, under the Umayyads the political center of community shifted to **Damascus** in Syria, where the Umayyads chose to live after the murder of

Uthman Third caliph and member of Umayyad clan; murdered by mutinous warriors returning from Egypt; death set off civil war in Islam between followers of Ali and the Umayyad clan.

Battle of Siffin Fought in 657 between forces of Ali and Umayyads; settled by negotiation that led to fragmentation of Ali's party.

Mu'awiya [moo-UH-wee-uh] (602–680) Leader of Umayyad clan; first Umayyad caliph following civil war with Ali.

Sunnis Political and theological division within Islam; supported the Umayyads.

Shi'a Also known as Shi'ites; political and theological division within Islam; followers of Ali.

Karbala Site of defeat and death of Husayn, son of Ali; marked beginning of Shi'a resistance to Umayyad caliphate.

The Expansion of Islam: The Umayyad Caliphate, c. 750

Damascus Syrian city that was capital of Umayyad caliphate.

Uthman. From Damascus a succession of Umayyad caliphs strove to build a bureaucracy that would bind together the vast domains they claimed to rule. The empire was very much an Arab conquest state. Except in the Arabian peninsula and in parts of the Fertile Crescent, a small Arab and Muslim aristocracy ruled over peoples who were neither Arab nor Muslim. Only Muslim Arabs were first-class citizens of this great empire. They made up the core of the army and imperial administration, and only they received a share of the booty derived from the ongoing conquests. They could be taxed only for charity. The Umayyads sought to keep the Muslim warrior elite concentrated in garrison towns and separated from the local population. It was hoped that isolation would keep them from assimilating to the subjugated cultures, because intermarriage meant conversion and the loss of taxable subjects.

Converts and "People of the Book"

mawali   Non-Arab converts to Islam.

jizya   [JIHZ-yuh] Head tax paid by all non-believers in Islamic territories.

dhimmi   [DIH-mee] Literally "people of the book"; applied as inclusive term to Jews and Christians in Islamic territories; later extended to Zoroastrians and even Hindus.

Umayyad attempts to block extensive interaction between the Muslim warrior elite and their non-Muslim subjects had little chance of succeeding. The citified bedouin tribes were soon interacting intensively with the local populations of the conquered areas and intermarrying with them. Equally critical, increasing numbers of these peoples were voluntarily converting to Islam, despite the fact that conversion did little to advance them socially or politically in the Umayyad period. In this era Muslim converts, **mawali,** still had to pay property taxes and in some cases the **jizya** (JIHZ-yuh), or head tax, levied on nonbelievers. They received no share of the booty and found it difficult, if not impossible, to get important positions in the army or bureaucracy. They were not even considered full members of the umma but were accepted only as clients of the powerful Arab clans.

As a result, the number of conversions in the Umayyad era was low. By far the greater portion of the population of the empire were the **dhimmi** (DIH-mee), or "people of the book." As the name suggests, it was originally applied to Christians and Jews who shared the Bible with the Muslims. As Islamic conquests spread to other peoples, such as the Zoroastrians of Persia and the Hindus of India, the designation dhimmi was necessarily stretched to accommodate the majority groups within these areas of the empire. As the early illustration of Jewish worship in Muslim Spain in Figure 6.6 shows, the Muslim overlords generally tolerated the religions of dhimmi. Although they had to pay the jizya and both commercial and property taxes, their communities and legal systems were left intact, and they were allowed to worship as they pleased. This approach made it a good deal easier for these peoples to accept Arab rule, particularly because many had been oppressed by their pre-Muslim overlords.

Figure 6.6 Jews worshiping in a synagogue. As dhimmi, or "people of the book," Jews were allowed to build impressive synagogues and worship freely throughout the Muslim world. Jewish merchant families amassed great wealth, often in partnership with Muslims, and Jewish scholars were revered from Spain to Baghdad for their many contributions to learning.

Family and Gender Roles in the Umayyad Age

Broader social changes within the Arab and widening Islamic community were accompanied by significant shifts in the position of women, both within the family and in society at large. In the first centuries of Arab expansion, the greatly strengthened position of women under Islam prevailed over the seclusion and subordination that were characteristic features of women's lives through much of the rest of the pre-Islamic Middle East. Muhammad's teachings and the dictates of the Qur'an stressed the moral and ethical dimensions of marriage. The kindness and concern the prophet displayed for his own wives and daughters did much to strengthen the bonds between husband and wife and the nuclear family in the Islamic community.

Muhammad encouraged marriage as a replacement for the casual and often commercial sexual liaisons that had been widespread in pre-Islamic Arabia. He vehemently denounced adultery on the part of both husbands and wives, and he forbade female infanticide, which apparently had been widely practiced in Arabia in pre-Islamic times. Men were allowed to marry up to four wives. But the Qur'an forbade multiple marriages if the husband could not support more than one wife or treat all of his wives equally. Women could not take more than one husband. But Muhammad gave his own daughters a say as to whom they would marry and greatly strengthened the legal rights of women in inheritance and divorce. He insisted that the bride-price paid by the husband's family be given to his future wife rather than to her father.

The prophet's teachings proclaimed the equality of men and women before God and in Islamic worship. Women, most notably his wife Khadijah, were some of Muhammad's earliest and bravest followers. In the battle with the Meccans, women accompanied the forces on both sides, and a woman was the first martyr for the new faith. Many of the **hadiths** (huh-DEETHs), or traditions of the prophet, which have played such a critical role in Islamic law and ritual, were recorded by women. In addition, Muhammad's wives and daughters played an important role in compiling the Qur'an.

> **hadiths** [huh-DEETHs] Traditions of the prophet

Although women were not allowed to lead prayers, they played an active role in the politics of the early community. Muhammad's widow, Aisha, actively promoted the claims of the Umayyad party against Ali, while Zainab, Ali's daughter, went into battle with the ill-fated Husayn. Through much of the Umayyad period, little is heard of veiled Arab women, and women appear to have pursued a wide range of occupations, including scholarship, law, and commerce. Perhaps one of Zainab's nieces best epitomizes the independent-mindedness of Muslim women in the early Islamic era. When chided for going about without a veil, she replied that Allah in his wisdom had chosen to give her a beautiful face and that she intended to make sure that it was seen in public so that all might appreciate his grace.

Umayyad Decline and Fall

The ever-increasing size of the royal harem was just one manifestation of the Umayyad caliphs' growing addiction to luxury and soft living. Their legitimacy had been disputed by various Muslim factions since their seizure of the caliphate. But the Umayyads further alienated the Muslim faithful as they became more aloof in the early 8th century and retreated from the dirty business of war into their pleasure gardens and marble palaces. Their abandonment of the frugal, simple lifestyle followed by Muhammad and the earliest caliphs—including Abu Bakr, who made a trip to the market the day after he was selected to succeed the prophet—enraged the dissenting sects and sparked revolts throughout the empire. The uprising that proved fatal to the short-lived dynasty began among the frontier warriors who had fought and settled in distant Iran.

By the mid-8th century, more than 50,000 warriors had settled near the oasis town of Merv in the eastern Iranian borderlands of the empire. Many of them had married local women, and over time they had come to identify with the region and to resent the dictates of governors sent from distant Damascus. The warrior settlers were also angered by the fact that they were rarely given the share of the booty, now officially tallied in the account books of the royal treasury, that they had earned by fighting the wars of expansion and defending the frontiers. They were contemptuous of the Umayyads and the

Figure 6.7 Muslim worshippers in modern Pakistan. Whether in a nearby mosque or in their homes and shops, Muslims are required to pray five times a day, facing the holy city of Mecca. Those congregating in a mosque, as in this photo, are oriented to Mecca by the qibla wall, which is marked by a highly ornamented inset that indicates the direction of the holy city. Men congregate in the open spaces in the center of and outside the mosque, while women pray in areas on the sides or in the back or, sometimes, in balconies above that are screened off by pillars or carved panels from the areas where the men worship.

Civilization and Gender Relationships

Within a century of Muhammad's death, the strong position women had enjoyed as a result of the teachings and example of the prophet had begun to erode. We do not fully understand all the forces that account for this decline. Ambiguities in the Qur'an and other early sources—especially the hadith, or traditions of the prophet—provide part of the answer. These sources indicate that, in both his domestic and public life, Muhammad was concerned about good treatment for women and defined certain rights, for example to property. But early records also stipulate women's inferiority to men in key legal rights (differential punishments for adultery were a case in point). And, like their Christian counterparts, Islamic thinkers argued that women were more likely than men to be sinners. But more critical were the beliefs and practices of the urbanized, sedentary peoples in the areas the Arabs conquered and where many of them settled from the mid-7th century onward.

The example of these ancient and long-civilized peoples increasingly influenced the Arab bearers of Islam. They developed a taste for city life and the superior material and artistic culture of the peoples they ruled. In terms of gender roles, most of these influences weakened the position of women. We have seen this apparent connection between increasing political centralization and urbanization and the declining position of women in many of the ancient and classical civilizations treated thus far. In China, India, Greece, and the Middle East, women enjoyed broader occupational options and a stronger voice within the family, and in society as a whole, before the emergence of centralized polities and highly stratified social systems. In each case, the rise of what we have called civilizations strengthened paternal control within the family, inheritance through the male line, and male domination of positions of power and the most lucrative occupations. Women in these societies became more and more subjected to men—their fathers and brothers, husbands and sons—and more and more confined to the roles of homemakers and bearers of children. Women's legal rights were reduced, often sharply. In many civilizations, various ways were devised to shut women off from the world.

> "Islamic law preserved for women property, inheritance, divorce, and remarriage rights that were often denied in other civilizations."

As we have seen, women played active and highly valued roles in the bedouin tribes of pre-Islamic Arabia. Particularly in towns such as Mecca, they experienced considerable freedom in terms of sexual and marriage partners, occupational choices (within the limited range available in an isolated pastoral society), and opportunities to influence clan decisions. The position of Muhammad's first wife, Khadijah, is instructive. Her position as a wealthy widow in charge of a thriving trading enterprise reveals that women were able to remarry and to own and inherit property. They could also pursue careers, even after their husbands died. Khadijah employed Muhammad. After he had successfully worked for her for some time, she asked him to marry her, which apparently neither surprised nor scandalized her family or Meccan society. It is also noteworthy that Khadijah was 10 to 15 years older than Muhammad, who was 25 at the time of their betrothal.

The impact of the bedouin pattern of gender roles and relationships is also clear in the teachings and personal behavior of Muhammad. Islam did much to legalize the strong but by no means equal status of women. In addition, it gave greater uniformity to their position from one tribe, town, or region to the next. For a century or two after the prophet's death, women in the Islamic world enjoyed unprecedented opportunities for education, religious expression, and social fulfillment.

Then the influences of the cultures into which the Arabs had expanded began to take hold. The practices of veiling and female seclusion that were long followed by the non-Arab dwellers of Syria and Persia were increasingly adopted by or imposed upon Muslim women. Confined more and more to the home, women saw their occupational options decrease, and men served as their go-betweens in legal and commercial matters.

Ironically, given the earlier status of women such as Khadijah, the erosion of the position of women was especially pronounced

---

Damascus elite, whom they saw as corrupt and decadent. In the early 740s, an attempt by Umayyad palace officials to introduce new troops into the Merv area touched off a revolt that soon spread over much of the eastern portions of the empire (Map 6.2).

Abbasid Dynasty that succeeded the Umayyads as caliphs within Islam; came to power in 750 C.E.

Marching under the black banners of the **Abbasid** party, which traced its descent from Muhammad's uncle, al-Abbas, the frontier warriors openly challenged Umayyad armies by 747. Deftly forging alliances with dissident groups that resisted the Umayyads throughout the empire, their leader, Abu al-Abbas, the great-great-grandson of the prophet's uncle, led his forces from victory to victory. Among his most important allies were the Shi'a, who, as we have seen, had rejected Umayyad authority from the time of Ali. Also critical were the mawali, or non-Arab converts to Islam. The mawali felt that under Umayyad rule they had never been recognized as fully Muslim. In supporting the Abbasids, the mawali hoped to attain full acceptance in the community of believers.

among those who lived in the cities that became the focus of Islamic civilization. Upper-class women, in particular, felt growing restrictions on their movement and activities. In the great residences that sprang up in the wealthy administrative centers and trading towns of the Middle East, the women's quarters were separate from the rest of the household and set off by high walls and gardens. In the palaces of Islamic rulers and provincial governors, this separation was marked by the development of the *harem*, or forbidden area. In the harem, the notables' wives and concubines lived in seclusion. They were constantly guarded by the watchful eyes and sharp swords of corps of eunuchs, men castrated specifically to qualify them for the task.

When upper-class women went into the city, they were veiled from head to toe and often were carried in covered sedan chairs by servants who guarded them from the glances of the townsmen and travelers. In their homes, upper-class women were spared the drudgery of domestic chores by large numbers of female slaves. If we are to judge from stories such as those related in the *Arabian Nights* (from which excerpts are included in the Document feature on page 158), female slaves and servants were largely at the mercy of their male masters. Although veiling, seclusion, and other practices that limited the physical and occupational mobility of women also spread to the lower urban classes and rural areas, they were never as strictly observed there as in urban, upper-class households. Women from poorer families had to work to survive. Thus, they had to go out, "veiled but often unchaperoned," to the market or to work as domestic servants. Lower-class women also worked hard at home, not just at housekeeping but at weaving, rugmaking, and other crafts that supplemented the family income. In rural areas and in towns distant from the main urban centers, veiling and confinement were observed less strictly. Peasant women worked the family or local landlord's fields, planted their own gardens, and tended the livestock.

Because of Islamic religion and law, in all locales and at all class levels the position of women in the Middle East never deteriorated to the same extent as in India, China, and many other civilized centers. Because of the need to read the Qur'an, women continued to be educated, family resources permitting, even if they rarely were able to use their learning for scholarship or artistic expression. Islamic law preserved for women property, inheritance, divorce, and remarriage rights that often were denied in other civilized societies. Thus, the strong position women had enjoyed in bedouin cultures, and that in many respects had been built into Islam, was never entirely undone by the customs and practices Muslims encountered as they came to rule the civilized centers in the rest of the Middle East.

The fact that the position of women has also been strong in other cultural areas where authority is decentralized and social organization not highly stratified, such as those in west Africa (see Chapter 8), suggests that at least in certain stages of its development, civilization works against the interests of women. Women in decentralized societies have often been able to own their own property, to engage in key economic activities, and to play important roles in religious ceremonies. The positions and status they have achieved in decentralized societies, such as those in early Arabia or much of sub-Saharan Africa and southeast Asia, suggest factors that may help explain the greater balance in gender roles and power in less centralized societies. The very immediate connection between women and agriculture and stock-raising, which are central to survival in these societies, may also account for the greater respect accorded them and for their often prominent roles in fertility rituals and religious cults. Whatever the explanation, until the present era, higher degrees of centralization and social stratification—both characteristic features of civilized societies—have almost always favored men in the allotment of power and career opportunities.

QUESTIONS Compare the position of upper-class women in classical Indian, Chinese, Greek, and Roman societies with regard to their ability to hold property, opportunity to pursue careers outside the home, rights in marriage and divorce, and level of education. In which of these societies were women better off, and why? Were differences in the position of women at lower-class levels similar between these societies? In what ways were women better off in decentralized pastoral or forest-farming societies? What advantages have they enjoyed in highly urbanized and more centralized civilizations?

This diverse collection of Muslim rebels made short work of what remained of the Umayyad imperium. Persia and then Iraq fell to the rebels. In 750, the Abbasid forces met an army led by the Umayyad caliph himself in the massive **Battle of the River Zab** near the Tigris. The Abbasid victory opened the way for the conquest of Syria and the capture of the Umayyad capital.

Wanting to eliminate the Umayyad family altogether to prevent recurring challenges to his rule, Abu al-Abbas invited many members of the clan to what was styled as a reconciliation banquet. As the Umayyads were enjoying the feast, guards covered them with carpets and they were slaughtered by Abbas's troops. An effort was then made to hunt down and kill all the remaining members of the family throughout the empire. Most were slain, but, as we have seen, the grandson of a former caliph fled to Spain and founded there what later became the Umayyad caliphate of Córdoba, which lived on for centuries after the rest of the Umayyads' empire had disappeared (See Map 6.3 and Figure 6.1).

Battle of the River Zab Victory of Abbasids over Umayyads; resulted in conquest of Syria and capture of Umayyad capital.

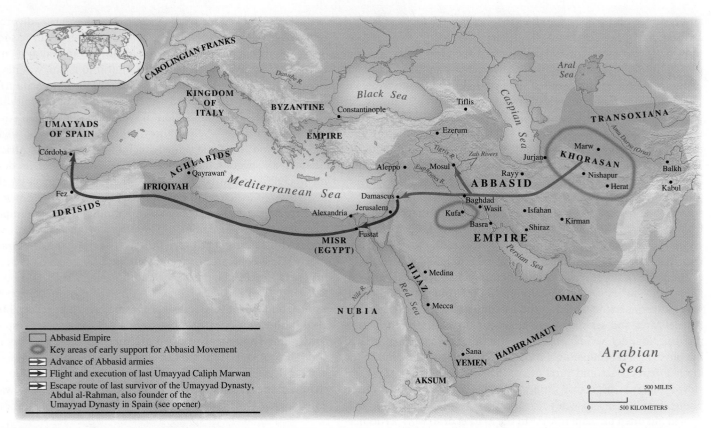

Map 6.3 Emergence of the Abbasid Dynasty Frontier warriors from Khorasan far from the Umayyad capital at Damascus built a military force that overthrew the Umayyads between 747 and 750 C.E.

From Arab to Islamic Empire: The Early Abbasid Era

Under the Abbasids, who succeeded the Umayyads, Islam became a universal religion that spread across of much of north Africa and Euro-Asia. With their capital at Baghdad, Islamic civilization flourished under the Abbasids, even as their empire began to fragment into regional power centers.

Baghdad Capital of Abbasid dynasty located in Iraq near ancient Persian capital of Ctesiphon.

wazir [wuh-ZEER] Chief administrative official under the Abbasid caliphate; initially recruited from Persian provinces of empire.

The rough treatment the Umayyad clan had received at the hands of the victorious Abbasids should have forewarned their Shi'a and mawali allies of what was to come. But the Shi'a and other dissenting groups continued the support that allowed the Abbasids to level all other centers of political rivalry. Gradually, the Abbasids rejected many of their old allies, becoming more and more righteous in their defense of Sunni Islam and increasingly less tolerant of what they called the heretical views of the various sects of Shi'ism. With the Umayyads all but eliminated and their allies brutally suppressed, the way was clear for the Abbasids to build a centralized, absolutist imperial order.

The fact that they chose to build their new capital, **Baghdad,** in Iraq near the ancient Persian capital of Ctesiphon was a clear sign of things to come. Soon the Abbasid caliphs were perched on jewel-encrusted thrones, reminiscent of those of the ancient Persian emperors, gazing down on the great gatherings of courtiers and petitioners who bowed before them in their gilt and marble audience halls. The caliphs' palaces and harems expanded to keep pace with their claims to absolute power over the Islamic faithful as well as the non-Muslim subjects of their vast empire.

The ever expanding corps of bureaucrats, servants, and slaves who strove to translate Abbasid political claims into reality lived and worked within the circular walls of the new capital at Baghdad. The bureaucratization of the Islamic Empire was reflected above all in the growing power of the **wazir** (wuh-ZEER), or chief administrator and head of the caliph's inner councils. It was also embodied in a more sinister way in the fearful guise of the royal executioner, who stood close to the throne in the public audiences of the Abbasid rulers. The wazirs oversaw the building of an administrative infrastructure that allowed the Abbasids to project their demands for tribute to the most distant provinces of the empire. Sheer size, poor communication, and collusion between Abbasid officials and local notables meant that the farther the town or village was from the capital, the less effectively royal commands were carried out. But for more than a century, the Abbasid regime was fairly effective at collecting revenue from its subject peoples and preserving law and order over much of the empire.

Islamic Conversion and Mawali Acceptance

The Abbasid era saw the full integration of new converts, both Arab and non-Arab, into the Islamic community. In the last decades of the Umayyad period, there was a growing acceptance of the mawali, or non-Arab Muslims, as equals. There were also efforts to win new converts to the faith, particularly among Arab peoples outside the Arabian peninsula. In the Abbasid era, when the practice of dividing booty between the believers had long been discarded, mass conversions to Islam were encouraged for all peoples of the empire, from the Berbers of north Africa to the Persians and Turkic peoples of central Asia. Converts were admitted on an equal footing with the first generations of believers, and over time the distinction between mawali and the earlier converts all but disappeared.

Most converts were won over peacefully through the great appeal of Islamic beliefs and the advantages they enjoyed over non-Muslim peoples in the empire. Not only were converts exempt from paying the head tax, but they had greater opportunities to get advanced schooling and launch careers as administrators, traders, or judges. No group demonstrated the new opportunities open to converts as dramatically as the Persians, who, in part through their bureaucratic skills, soon came to dominate the upper levels of imperial administration. In fact, as the Abbasid rulers became more dissolute and less interested in affairs of state, several powerful Persian families close to the throne became the real locus of power in the imperial system.

dhows   Arab sailing vessels with triangular or lateen sails; strongly influenced European ship design.

Town and Country: Commercial Boom and Agrarian Expansion

The rise of the mawali was paralleled in the Abbasid era by the growth in wealth and social status of the merchant and landlord classes of the empire. The Abbasid age was a time of great urban expansion that was linked to a revival of the Afro-Eurasian trading network, which had declined with the fall of the Han dynasty in China in the early 3rd century C.E. and the slow collapse of the Roman Empire in the 4th and 5th centuries. The Abbasid domains in the west and the great Tang and Song empires in the east became the pivots of the revived commercial system.

From the western Mediterranean to the South China Sea, Arab **dhows,** or sailing vessels with lateen (triangular) sails, which later influenced European ship design, carried the goods of one civilized core to be exchanged with those of another. Muslim merchants often formed joint ventures with Christians and Jews. Because each merchant had a different Sabbath, the firm could do business all week. Merchants grew rich by supplying the cities of the empire with provisions. Mercantile concerns also took charge of the long-distance trade that specialized in luxury products for the elite classes. The great profits from trade were reinvested in new commercial enterprises, the purchase of land, and the construction of the great mansions that dominated the central quarters of the political and commercial hubs of the empire. Some wealth also went to charity, as required by the Qur'an. A good deal of the wealth was spent on building and running mosques and religious schools, baths, and rest houses for weary travelers (Figure 6.8). Large donations were also made to hospitals, which in the numbers of their patients and the quality of their medical care surpassed those of any other civilization of that time.

The growth of Abbasid cities was also fed by a great increase in handicraft production. Both government-run and privately owned

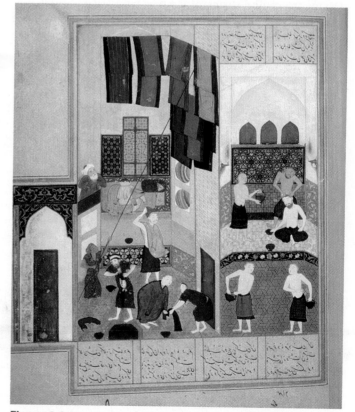

Figure 6.8 The rulers and nobility of the Abbasid capital in Baghdad frequented baths like that shown in this Persian miniature painting. Here the caliph, Haroun al-Rashid, receives a haircut while servants prepare the steam rooms. At the baths, the Abbasid elite could relax, exchange gossip, and enjoy expert massages.

(British Library, London.)

The Mosque as a Symbol of Islamic Civilization

From one end of the Islamic world to the other, Muslim towns and cities can be readily identified by the domes and minarets of the mosques where the faithful are called to prayer five times daily. The illustrations included here trace the development of the mosque and the refinement of mosque architecture, the crowning glory of Islamic material culture, during the early centuries of Muslim expansion. As you look at these pictures and follow the development of the mosque, consider what the functions of the mosque and the evolving style of mosque architecture can tell us about Muslim beliefs and values and the impact of earlier religions, such as Judaism and Christianity, on Islam.

Given the low level of material culture in pre-Islamic Arabia, it is not surprising that the earliest prayer houses were simple in design and construction. In fact, these first mosques were laid out along the lines suggested by Muhammad's own house. They were square enclosures with a shaded porch on one side, a columned shelter on the other, and an open courtyard in between. The outer perimeter of the earliest mosques was made of reed mats, but soon more permanent stone walls surrounded the courtyard and prayer areas. After Mecca was taken and the Ka'ba became the central shrine of the new faith, each mosque was oriented to the qibla, or Mecca wall, which always faced in the direction of the holy city.

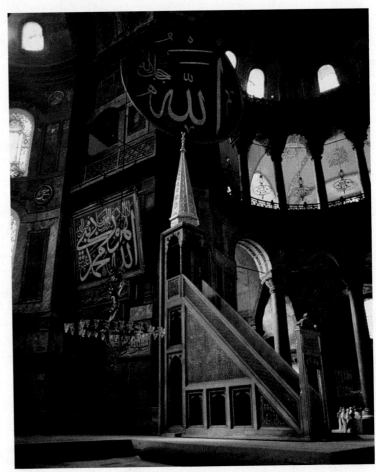

Pulpit (minbar) from which the Friday sermons are delivered throughout the Muslim world.

Domes and minarets of the Shah Mosque at Isfahan, Iran.

In the last years of the prophet, his chair was located so that the faithful could see and hear him during prayer sessions. During the time of the first caliphs, the raised area became the place from which sermons were delivered. From the mid-8th century, this space evolved into a genuine pulpit (*minbar* in Arabic). Somewhat earlier, the practice of building a special and often elaborately decorated niche in the qibla had developed.

Over time, mosques became more elaborate. Very often the remains of Greek or Roman temples or abandoned Christian churches formed the core of major mosques, or the ruins of these structures were mined for stone for mosque construction. In the larger cities, the courtyards of the great mosques were surrounded by columns and arches, and eventually they were enclosed by great domes such as that at the Dome of the Rock in Jerusalem.

Drawing of the early mosque design.

Al-Aqsa Mosque (or Dome of the Rock) in Jerusalem, the third holiest site in Islam.

The first minarets, or towers from which the faithful were called to prayer, were added in the early 8th century and soon became a key feature of the mosque complex. As mosques grew larger and more architecturally refined, elaborate decoration in brightly colored ceramic tiles, semiprecious stones, and gold and silver filigree adorned their sides and domes. Because human and animal images were forbidden, geometric designs, passages from the Qur'an in swirling Arabic, and flower and plant motifs were favored. Nowhere were these decorations more splendid than in the great mosques of Persia. Thus, in the early centuries of Islam, these great houses of worship became the focal points of Islamic cities, key places of community worship and socialization, and, with the schools that were often attached, vital intellectual and educational centers of the Islamic world.

QUESTIONS What do the design and decoration of Muslim mosques tell us about the Islamic view of a supreme being and the relationship between Allah and humans? Discuss the Christian and Jewish influences you detect in mosque design and the pattern of religious worship conducted there. What do you think is the significance of the lavish application of color and the frequent use of floral and plant motifs and Arabic verses from the Qur'an in the decoration of mosques through much of the Muslim world?

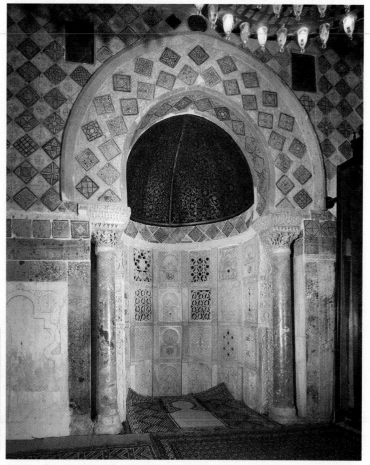

Qibla wall with decorated section facing Mecca.

157

The Thousand and One Nights as a Mirror of Elite Society in the Abbasid Era

The luxurious lifestyle of the Abbasid rulers and their courtiers reflected the new wealth of the political and commercial elites of the Islamic Empire. At the same time, it intensified sectarian and social divisions in the Islamic community. As the compilation of folktales from many parts of the empire titled *The Thousand and One Nights* testifies, life for much of the elite in Baghdad and other major urban centers was luxurious and oriented to the delights of the flesh. Caliphs and wealthy merchants lived in palatial residences of stone and marble, complete with gurgling fountains and elaborate gardens, which served as retreats from the glare and heat of the southern Mediterranean climate. In the Abbasid palaces, luxurious living and ostentation soared to fantastic heights. In the Hall of the Tree, for example, there was a huge artificial tree, made entirely of gold and silver and filled with gold mechanical birds that chirped to keep the caliph in good cheer.

Because the tales were just that—tall tales—there is some exaggeration of the wealth, romantic exploits, and sexual excesses of the world depicted. But for some members of the elite classes, the luxuries, frivolities, and vices of the Abbasid age were very real. The following passages are taken from an English translation of *The Thousand and One Nights*. Each is selected to reveal a different facet of high society in the Abbasid era. The first, which describes the sumptuous interior of a mansion in Baghdad, indicates that conspicuous material consumption existed far beyond the palace.

> They reached a spacious ground-floor hall, built with admirable skill and beautified with all manner of colors and carvings, with upper balconies and groined [sharply curved] arches and galleries and cupboards and recesses whose curtains hung before them. In the midst stood a great basin full of water surrounding a fine fountain, and at the upper end on the raised dais was a couch of juniper wood set with gems and pearls, with a canopy-like mosquito curtain of red satin-silk looped up with pearls as big as filberts [hazelnuts] and bigger.

In another tale, a fallen prince details the proper upbringing and education for a person of substance:

> I am a king, son of a king, and was brought up like a prince. I learned intoning the Koran [Qur'an] according [to] the seven schools and I read all manner [of] books, and held disputations on their contents with the doctors and men of science. Moreover, I studied star lore and the fair sayings of poets, and I exercised myself in all branches of learning until I surpassed the people of my time. My skill in calligraphy [writing, in this case Arabic and perhaps Persian] exceeded that of all of the scribes, and my fame was bruited abroad over all climes and cities, and all the kings learned to know my name.

In the following passage, a stylishly dressed woman from the elite classes is described in great detail:

> There stood before him an honorable woman in a mantilla [veil] of Mosul silk broidered with gold and bordered with brocade [a rich cloth with a raised design, often of gold or silver]. Her walking shoes were also [broidered] with gold, and her hair floated in long plaits. She raised her face veil . . . showing two black eyes fringed with jetty lashes, whose glances were soft and languishing and whose perfect beauty was ever blandishing.

The woman leads a porter to a marketplace, which again reflects the opulence accessible to the rich and powerful of Abbasid society:

> She stopped at the fruiter's shop and bought from him Shami apples and Osmani quinces and Omani peaches, and cucumbers of Nile growth, and Egyptian limes and Sultani oranges and citrons, besides Aleppine jasmine, scented myrtle berries, Damascene nenuphars [water lilies], flower of privit and camomile, blood-red anemones, violets, and pomegranate bloom, eglantine [wild rose], and narcissus, and set the whole in the porter's crate.

QUESTIONS What objects are key symbols of wealth in Abbasid society? What attainments are highly valued for upper-class men? What do they tell us about occupations and talents that brought high status in Abbasid society, and how do they compare with career aspirations in our own? In comparison, what attributes of women are stressed in these passages?

 Trade Routes in the Medieval Islamic World **MAP**

workshops expanded or were established to produce a wide range of products, from necessities such as furniture and carpets to luxury items such as glassware, jewelry, and tapestries. Although the artisans often were poorly paid and some worked in great workshops, they were not slaves or drudge laborers. They owned their own tools and were often highly valued for their skills. The most accomplished of the artisans formed guildlike organizations, which negotiated wages and working conditions with the merchants and supported their members in times of financial difficulty or personal crisis.

In towns and the countryside, much of the unskilled labor was left to slaves, often attached to prominent families as domestic servants. Large numbers of slaves also served the caliphs and their highest advisors. It was possible for the more clever and ambitious slaves to rise to positions of great power, and many eventually were granted their freedom or were able to buy it. Less fortunate were the slaves forced into lives of hard labor under the overseer's whip on rural estates and government projects, such as those devoted to draining marshlands, or into a lifetime of labor in the nightmare conditions of the great salt mines in southern Iraq. Most of these drudge laborers were non-Muslims captured on slaving raids in east Africa.

In the countryside, a wealthy and deeply entrenched landed elite called the **ayan** emerged in the early decades of Abbasid rule. Many of these landlords had been long established. Others were newcomers: Arab soldiers who invested their share of the booty in land, or merchants and administrators who funneled their profits and kickbacks into sizeable estates. In many regions, most peasants did not own the land they worked. They occupied it as tenants, sharecroppers, or migrant laborers who were required to give the greater portion of the crops they harvested to the estate owners.

ayan   The wealthy landed elite that emerged in the early decades of Abbasid rule.

The First Flowering of Islamic Learning

In the first phase of Abbasid rule, the Islamic contribution to human artistic expression focused on the great mosques, such as those featured in the Visualizing the Past box, and great palaces. In addition to advances in religious, legal, and philosophical discourse, the Islamic contribution to learning focused on the sciences and mathematics. In the early Abbasid period, the main tasks were recovering and preserving the learning of the ancient civilizations of the Mediterranean and Middle East. Beyond the works of Plato, for example, much of Greek learning had been lost to the peoples of western Europe. Thanks to Muslim and Jewish scholars, the priceless writings of the Greeks on key subjects such as medicine, algebra, geometry, astronomy, anatomy, and ethics were saved, recopied in Arabic, and dispersed throughout the empire. From Spain, Greek writings found their way into Christendom. Among the authors rescued in this manner were Aristotle, Galen, Hippocrates, Ptolemy, and Euclid.

In addition, scholars working in Arabic transmitted ideas that paralleled the rise of Arab traders and merchants as the carriers of goods and inventions. For example, Muslim invaders of south Asia soon learned of the Indian system of numbers. From India they were carried by Muslim scholars and merchants to the Middle Eastern centers of Islamic civilization. Eventually the Indian numerical system was transmitted across the Mediterranean to Italy and from there to northern Europe. Along with Greek and Arab mathematics, Indian numbers later proved critical to the early modern Scientific Revolution in western Europe.

Excerpt from
1001 Nights

Global Connections

Early Islam and the World

The rise of Islamic civilization from the 7th to 9th centuries C.E. was a stunning development without precedent in human history. Not only had the largely nomadic peoples from an Arabian backwater built one of the greatest empires of the preindustrial world, but they had laid the basis for the first truly global civilization if one excludes the Americas, which were unknown to the peoples of the Eastern Hemisphere. Building on earlier religious traditions, especially Christianity and Judaism, Arab culture had nurtured Islam, one of the great universal religions of humankind. The mosques, the prayer rituals and pilgrimages of the faithful, and the influence of Islamic law proclaimed the pervasive effects of this new creed on societies from Spain to eastern Indonesia and from central Asia to the savannas of west Africa.

Islamic and Arab commitment to trade and merchant activity was crucial in setting up wider connections among Asia, Africa, and Europe, with the Middle East as hub. The region's earlier functions in commerce, in and between the Indian Ocean and Mediterranean Sea, expanded greatly.

In the arts and sciences, the Muslims initially relied heavily on the achievements of the classical civilizations of Greece and Mesopotamia. But the work of preserving and combining the discoveries of earlier peoples soon led to reformulation and innovation. As in religion and politics, Muslim peoples were soon making important contributions to learning, invention, and artistic creativity, which were carried by their armies and religious teachers to other civilizations in Europe, Africa, and Asia.

Never before had a civilization spanned so many different cultures and combined such a patchwork of linguistic groups, religions, and ethnic types. Never before had a single civilization mediated so successfully between the other centers of civilized life. Never had a civilized lifestyle so deeply affected so many of the nomadic cultures that surrounded the pools of sedentary agriculture and urban life. Ironically, the contacts Islamic mediation made possible between the civilized cores of the Eastern Hemisphere contributed much to the transformations in technology and organization that increasingly tilted the balance of power against the Muslim peoples. But those reversals were still far in the future. In the short run, Islamic conversion and contact ushered in an age of unparalleled nomadic intervention in and dominance over global history.

Further Readings

There are many accounts of Muhammad's life and the rise of Islam. The most readable is Karen Armstrong's *Muhammad: A Biography of the Prophet* (1992). A sense of the very different interpretations that have been offered to explain these pivotal developments in global history can be gained by comparing W. Montgomery Watt, *Muhammad: Prophet and Statesman* (1961); Tor Andrae, *Muhammad: The Man and His Faith* (1960); Maxime Rodinson, *Mohammad* (1971); and the more recent revisionist (and somewhat less accessible) writings of Elizabeth Crone and Michael Cook.

Despite its title, H. A. R. Gibb's *Mohammedism* (1962) remains a useful introduction to Islam as a religion. John Esposito's *Islam: The Straight Path* (1991) and Karen Armstrong's *Islam: A Short History* (2000) also provide good and updated overviews of the faith. On early Islamic expansion and civilization through the first centuries of the Abbasid caliphate, see G. E. von Grunebaum's *Classical Islam* (1970) and M. A. Shaban's *Islamic History: An Interpretation* (1971) and *The Abbasid Revolution* (1970). On nearly all of these topics, it is difficult to surpass Marshall G. S. Hodgson's brilliant analysis, *The Venture of Islam*, vol. 1 (1974), but some grounding in the history and beliefs of the Muslims is recommended before one attempts this sweeping and provocative work. More accessible, dated in some respects, but still authoritative and highly interpretive is Philip Hitti's *History of the Arabs* (1967 ed.), which can be supplemented by his very engaging *Makers of Arab History* (1968). More encyclopedic and benefiting from recent research the surveys of Ira M. Lapidus, *A History of Islamic Societies* (1988); and Albert Hourani, *A History of the Arab Peoples* (1991) provide useful overviews.

On early Islamic society generally, see M. M. Ahsan, *Social Life Under the Abbasids* (1979). On women in Islam specifically, there is a superb essay by Guity Nashat, "Women in the Middle East, 8000 B.C.–A.D. 1800," in the collection titled *Restoring Women to History* (1988), published by the Organization of American Historians. See also the relevant portions of the essays in Lois Beck and Nikki Keddi, eds., *Women in the Muslim World* (1978); and the early chapters of Leila Ahmed, *Women and Gender in Islam* (1992). For a broad treatment of the roles and position of women in ancient civilizations more generally, see Sarah and Brady Hughes, *Women in Ancient Global History* (1998). For insights into Islamic culture and civilization from a literary perspective, a good place to begin is Eric Schroeder's delightful *Muhammad's People: A Tale by Anthology* (1955) and N. J. Dawood's translation of *Tales from the Thousand and One Nights* (1954). Of the many works on Muslim art and architecture Robert Hillenbrand's recent *Islamic Art and Architecture* (1999) is engaging, well researched and lavishly illustrated. K. A. Creswell's *Early Muslim Architecture,* 2 vols. (1932–1940), and the more recent Markus Hattstein and Peter Delius, eds., *Islam: Art and Architecture* (2000), provide even greater detail and ample illustrations.

On the Web

The religion and society of Islam (http://islamicity.com/mosque/Intro_Islam.htm and http://www.pbs.org/empires/islam/), Islam's revealed text, the Qu'ran (http://www.usc.edu/dept/MSA/quran), and its arts (http://www.colostate.edu/orgs/MSA/find_more/islart.html and the links page at http://witcombe.sbc.edu/ARTHislamic.html) set new standards for civilization for much of the world. A monotheistic religion, Islam seeks to promote the submission (Islam) of humankind to the will of God, Allah (http://www.usc.edu/dept/MSA/fundamentals/tawheed/abutaw/abutaw_1.html) through the message vouchsafed to the prophet Muhammad (http://www.bbc.co.uk//religion/religions/islam/ and http://www.pbs.org/muhammad/timeline_html.shtml). The immediate successor as leader of the fledgling Muslim community, Abu Bakr (http://i-cias.com/e.o/abubakr.htm), proved equal to the task of ensuring its survival. An annotated list of links to early Islamic history from Abu Bakr to rise of the Ottoman Empire is provided at http://www.uga.edu/islam/history.html. Links to sites exploring the story of Islam from the Ottomans to the 1990s are provided at http://www.fordham.edu/halsall/islam/islamsbook.html.

The evolution of Islamic art from its Arab roots, its capacity to influence non-Islamic art, and its capacity for synthesis of non-Arab themes can be traced at http://www.islamicart.com/main/architecture/impact.html and http://www.lacma.org/islamic_art/intro.htm. The golden age of Islamic science, literature, and scholarship, as well as religious philosophy, can be studied at http://islamicity.com/mosque/IGC/knowledge.htm and http://regentsprep.org/Regents/global/themes/goldenages/islam.cfm. The advances in medical science made by Islamic scholars are illustrated at http://www.nlm.nih.gov/hmd/arabic/med_islam.html (or http://www.nlm.nih.gov/hmd/arabic/arabichome.html).

Muslim mathematics can be studied via resources at http://www-groups.dcs.st-and.ac.uk/~history/Indexes/Arabs.html, http://mtcs.truman.edu/~thammond/history/IslamicWorld.html, http://www.math.tamu.edu/~dallen/masters/islamic/index.htm, and http://www.math.uu.nl/people/hogend/Islamath.html. Sites exploring Mecca and the Muslim pilgrimage to Mecca can be found at http://www.channel4.com/culture/microsites/H/hajj/ and http://www.sacredsites.com/middle_east/saudi_arabia/mecca.html.

Images of medieval Muslim life, from art production to women and the family can be found at http://www.sfusd.k12.ca.us/schwww/sch618/Islam_New_Main.html. A rich site for documents and accounts of early Islam is located at http://www.fordham.edu/halsall/sbook1d.html. A virtual pilgrimage can be taken via the Public Broadcasting System's Web site at http://www.pbs.org/muhammad/virtualhajj.shtml. An account of a recent experience of the hajj is provided at http://www.islamonline.net/english/hajj/2002/01/Experience/article6.shtml. Muslim interaction with, and attitudes towards the West is examined at http://www.pbs.org/wgbh/pages/frontline/shows/muslims/, http://www.forpeoplewhothink.org/Editorials/Islam-and-Western-Civilization.html, http://news.bbc.co.uk/2/hi/in_depth/world/2002/islamic_world/2188307.stm.

The contributions of Islam to Western Civilization are as numerous as they are complex. Muslim science was shaped by Greek thought, which they improved upon; Western science would largely emerge as a result of explorations of Greek/Muslim scientific thought. This exchange is traced at sites exploring the development of science generally (http://www.cyberistan.org/islamic/index.htm), medicine (http://www.levity.com/alchemy/islam19.html, http://www.nlm.nih.gov/exhibition/islamic_medical/islamic_02.html), and the global roots of algebra (http://www.ucs.louisiana.edu/~sxw8045/history.htm).

AP* Test Prep

1. In pre-Islamic times, the status of the city of Mecca was enhanced by
   - (A) the presence in the city of a Christian bishop.
   - (B) the Ka'aba, a religious shrine which attracted pilgrims.
   - (C) its merchants' direct control over the trade of Africa.
   - (D) its close political alliance with the Byzantine empire.

2. Both Islam and Christianity were successful in universalizing religion because of their:
   - (A) insistence that all of humanity were brothers under one God.
   - (B) support of commercial interests over spiritual concerns.
   - (C) insistence that the state take measures to reduce economic inequality.
   - (D) democratic political values.

3. The issue which eventually split Muslims into Shi'a and Sunni sects involved
   - (A) the toleration or persecution of Christians and Jews.
   - (B) who was the rightful leader of the Islamic community following the death of the Prophet Muhammad.
   - (C) the legitimacy of the holy war (jihad) against enemies of the faith.
   - (D) whether or not to accept the conversion of non-Arabs to Islam.

4. The primary reason for the Arabs' successful conquest of the Middle East and north Africa was most likely attributable to:
   - (A) the promise of profits to be won and tribute to be exacted.
   - (B) overpopulation in the Arabian peninsula.
   - (C) the desire to force others to convert to Islam.
   - (D) the weakness of the Persian and the Byzantine Empires.

5. Women's status in Islamic societies began to decline during the caliphate because:
   - (A) Muslim leaders' insistence putting the practices of conquered peoples before their own to lessen the chance of rebellion.
   - (B) the necessities of war tended to overemphasize the importance of males.
   - (C) there was a high death rate of males which decreased the "relative" value of women.
   - (D) Pre-Islamic traditions remained very strong within the caliphate families and advisors.

6. Islamic societies were most similar to Rome in that they
   - (A) granted married women extensive legal and familial rights.
   - (B) denied merchants equivalent social status to landed elites.
   - (C) discouraged toleration of foreigners and conversion to the official religion.
   - (D) used slave labor extensively.

7. When scholars write of an "Islamic flowering" during the age of the caliphate, to what are they referring?
   - (A) the culmination of centuries of indigenous Arabian and Bedouin traditions.
   - (B) cross-cultural borrowing exclusively from the Chinese.
   - (C) Muslims' advances along the lines laid down by many classical Eurasian civilizations, while making significant contributions that were new.
   - (D) the emergence and growth of Sufi poetry.

Free-Response Question

Explain the reasons for the rapid rise and spread of Islam and its status as a near-global religion by 850?

7 Abbasid Decline and the Spread of Islamic Civilization to South and Southeast Asia

The Islamic Heartlands in the Middle and Late Abbasid Eras
DOCUMENT: Ibn Khaldun on the Rise and Decline of Empires
An Age of Learning and Artistic Refinement
The Coming of Islam to South Asia
VISUALIZING THE PAST: The Patterns of Islam's Global Expansions

THINKING HISTORICALLY: Conversion and Accommodation in the Spread of World Religions
The Spread of Islam to Southeast Asia
GLOBAL CONNECTIONS: Islam: A Bridge Between Worlds

Of all of the factors that contributed to the spread of Islamic civilization in the millennium after the prophet Muhammad received his divine revelations in the early 7th century C.E., perhaps none was as crucial—yet neglected—as the rather modest sailing vessels that plied the waters of the Red Sea and Persian Gulf. Most commonly known as *dhows* (see Chapter 6, p. 253), but appearing in numerous variations with different names and found from the Mediterranean Sea to the Indian Ocean, these ships were probably first developed along the Nile River. Compared to the great junks of China, or even many of the less imposing trading ships in the Indian Ocean in the classical age, dhows were rather small vessels. They normally had one or two masts and planked, wooden hulls that resembled modern yachts in shape, with pointed bows and square sterns (Figure 7.1). The dhows' hull design contributed to their swiftness and maneuverability, but it was the configuration of their sails that have made them one of the most popular and enduring of the world's ships for two millennia. Dhows were propelled by one or two large, triangular **lateen** sails that attached to the masts by long booms or yard arms, which extended diagonally high across both the fore and aft portions of the ship.

Although their relatively shallow hulls meant that dhows could not match junks or bulkier merchant ships in cargo capacity, their slender shape gave them a considerable advantage over most other ships in speed, and their triangular sails meant that they could tack against the wind, which square-rigged ships could not. Most often, however, those who sailed them followed a seasonal pattern set by the direction of the monsoon winds that alternated between flows to the sea or land according to the time of the year in the India Ocean and adjacent waterways. Though galleys like those of classical Greece and Rome were widely used by Arabs in the Mediterranean, from Spain to China tens of thou-

sands of dhows were the main carriers of Muslim commerce. And along with merchants and their trade goods, many of the same ships conveyed Sufis or Muslim holy men to regions as far-flung as India, Java and Malaya, and the Philippine Islands.

Seaworthy ships like the dhows were essential to the remarkable spread of the Islamic faith and the civilization it gave rise to in this era. In contrast to the expansion of Muslim empires, which was largely carried out by Arab armies traveling over land, lasting mass conversions of conquered peoples to the religion of Islam were mainly due to the efforts of Sufis and other spiritual leaders who traveled by caravan into central Asia and across the Sahara or traversed the seas in sturdy dhows. In either case, those who went out to win converts to Islam also disseminated broader products of Muslim culture. These included the Arabic language; advanced technologies, such as water pumps and windmills; Muslim science, law, and philosophy; and Islamic art and architecture.

Despite their speed and dexterity, dhows did not make great warships, either before or after gunpowder was introduced into sea warfare. They were too small to provide a suitable firing platform for regular cannon, and they could not carry enough soldiers to grapple, board, and overwhelm the crews of enemy ships. Like most of the ships that sailed the seas of the Middle East, east Africa, and Asia, dhows were built for trade and not war. Designs for that purpose served the peoples of the Indian Ocean and adjoining seas well until the last years of the 15th century. But with the arrival of well armed Portuguese fleets after 1498, neither the dhows nor any of the ships in Asia west of the South China Sea could hold back expansionist Christian warriors and seafarers eager to tap into the wealth, knowledge, and technological acumen of Islamic and Chinese culture zones far more advanced in most areas of human endeavor than their own. ■

Figure 7.1 Arab traders made the most of seasonal winds, sailing dhows like this one to Africa and Asia in winter and returning home during the summer months. Dhows were small but sturdy, graceful, and highly maneuverable sailing vessels that carried Arab traders, Sufi holy men, and warriors from the Middle East across the Mediterranean, the Red Sea and Persian Gulf, and throughout the vast Indian Ocean trading system.

Even as Muslim traders and Sufi holymen spread Islam across a great swath of Afroeuroasia from north Africa in the west to the Philippines in the east, the Abbasid empire was crumbling from within. In many of the areas newly won to the faith, rival dynasties arose to challenge Abbasid power. These new polities and the Abbasids themselves were in turn threatened by the invasions of nomadic peoples launched by successive waves of Turkish-speakers and the Mongols from central Asia as well as berber jihadists from Saharan Africa. Ironically, as the political hold of various Muslim rulers weakened, Islamic civilization reached new heights of creativity.

As we shall see in the chapter that follows, the Abbasid age was a time of remarkable achievements in architecture and the fine arts, in literature and philosophy, and in mathematics and the sciences. Many of these developments were enriched by the wealth, knowledge and products exchanged among the many regions of an ever expanding Muslim world and the non-Muslim peoples contacted in border regions from Europe to China. From the 10th to the 14th centuries, Muslim mystics, traders and at times warriors carried the faith of Muhammad across much of the known world. In this chapter we will focus on this process in south and southeast Asia. In those that follow, north and west Africa and central Asia will be the focus of our inquiry.

The Islamic Heartlands in the Middle and Late Abbasid Eras

As early as the reign of the third Abbasid caliph, **al-Mahdi** (775–785), the courtly excesses and political divisions that eventually contributed to the decline of the empire were apparent. Al-Mahdi's efforts to reconcile the moderates among the Shi'a opposition to Abbasid rule ended in failure. This meant that Shi'a revolts and assassination attempts against Abbasid officials would plague the dynasty to the end of its days. Al-Mahdi also abandoned the frugal ways of his predecessor. In the brief

The Indian Ocean Dhow Sailing Vessel

lateen Triangular sails attached to the masts of dhows by long booms, or yard arms, which extended diagonally high across the fore and aft of the ship.

al-Mahdi (r. 775–785) Third of the Abbasid caliphs; attempted but failed to reconcile moderates among Shi'a to Abbasid dynasty; failed to resolve problem of succession.

The vast Abbasid empire (Map 7.1) gradually disintegrated between the 9th and 13th centuries C.E. Political decline and recurring social turmoil were fed both by the emergence of rival centers of power and the inroads of nomadic peoples attracted to the rich and fertile regions where Muslim urban life and power were centered.

163

700 C.E.	800 C.E.	900 C.E.	1000 C.E.	1200 C.E.
661–750 Umayyad caliphate (Damascus)	**800** Independent dynasty established in Tunisia	**945** Persian Buyids capture Baghdad; caliphs become puppet rulers	**c. 1020** Death of Firdawsi, author of the *Shah-Nama*	**1206** Establishment of the Delhi sultanate in India
711–713 First Muslim raids into India	**809** First war of succession between Abbasid princes	**973–1050** Life of al-Biruni, scientist	**1055** Seljuk Turks overthrow Buyids, control caliphate	**1258** Fall of Baghdad to Mongols; end of Abbasid caliphate
750 Establishment of the Abbasid caliphate (Baghdad)	**813–833** Reign of al-Ma'mun; first mercenary forces recruited	**998** Beginning of Ghanzi raids into western India	**1096–1099** First Christian Crusade in Palestine	**1290s** Beginning of the spread of Islam in southeast Asia
775–785 Reign of al-Mahdi	**865–925** Life of al-Razi, physician and scientist		**1058–1111** Life of al-Ghazali, philosopher and scientist	**1291** Fall of Acre; last crusader stronghold in Middle East
777 Independent dynasty established in Algeria			**1038–1123** Life of Omar Khayyam, scientist and poet	
786–809 Reign of al-Rashid				
788 Independent dynasty established in Morocco				

span of his reign, he established a taste for luxury and monumental building and surrounded himself with a multitude of dependent wives, concubines, and courtiers. These habits would prove to be an ever greater financial drain in the reigns of later caliphs.

Perhaps most critically, al-Mahdi failed to solve the vexing problem of succession. Not only did he waver between which of his older sons would succeed him, but he allowed his wives and concubines, the mothers of different candidates, to become involved in the palace intrigues that became a standard feature of the transfer of power from one caliph to the next. Although a full-scale civil war was avoided after al-Mahdi's death, within a year his eldest son and successor was poisoned. That act cleared the way for one of the most famous and enduring of the Abbasid caliphs, **Harun al-Rashid** (786–809), to ascend the throne.

Harun al-Rashid   One of the great Islamic rulers of the Abbasid era.

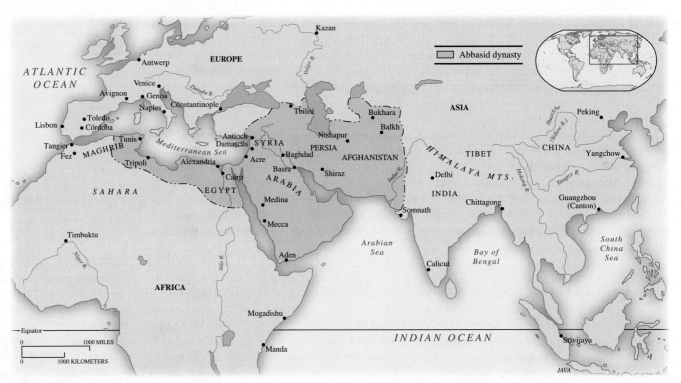

Map 7.1 The Abbasid Empire at Its Peak

Imperial Extravagance and Succession Disputes

Emissaries sent in the early 9th century to Baghdad from Charlemagne, then the most powerful monarch in Christian Europe, provide ample evidence that Harun al-Rashid shared his father's taste for sumptuous living. Harun al-Rashid dazzled the Christians with the splendor of Baghdad's mosques, palaces, and treasure troves, which is reflected in the painting of nightlife in a palace in Figure 7.2. He also sent them back to Charlemagne with presents, including an intricate water clock and an elephant, which were literally worth a king's ransom.

The luxury and intrigue of Harun's court have also been immortalized by the tales of *The Thousand and One Nights* (see the Document in Chapter 6), set in the Baghdad of his day. The plots and maneuvers of the courtesans, eunuchs, and royal ministers related in the tales suggest yet another source of dynastic weakness. Partly because he was only 23 at the time of his accession to the throne, Harun became heavily dependent, particularly in the early years of his reign, on a family of Persian advisors. Although he eventually resisted their influence, the growth of the power of royal advisors at the expense of the caliphs became a clear trend in succeeding reigns. In fact, from the mid-9th century onward, most caliphs were pawns in the power struggles between different factions at the court.

Harun al-Rashid's death prompted the first of several full-scale civil wars over succession. In itself, the precedent set by the struggle for the throne was deeply damaging. But it had an additional consequence that would all but end the real power of the caliphs. The first civil war convinced the sons of al-Ma'mun (813–833), the winner, to build personal armies in anticipation of the fight for the throne that would break out when their father died. One of the sons, the victor in the next round of succession struggles, recruited a "bodyguard" of some 4000 slaves, mostly Turkic-speaking nomads from central Asia. On becoming caliph, he increased this mercenary force to more than 70,000.

Not surprisingly, this impressive army soon became a power center in its own right. In 846 slave mercenaries murdered the reigning caliph and placed one of his sons on the throne. In the next decade, four more caliphs were assassinated or poisoned by the mercenary forces. From this time onward, the leaders of the slave mercenary armies were often the real power behind the Abbasid throne and were major players in the struggles for control of the capital and empire. The mercenaries also became a major force for violent social unrest. They were often the catalyst for the food riots that broke out periodically when the price of everyday staples rose too sharply because of shortages or price gouging in Baghdad and other urban centers.

Figure 7.2 The richness and vitality of urban life in the Islamic world in the Abbasid age and later eras are wonderfully captured in this 16th-century Persian illustration from the *Khamsah* (Five Poems) of Nizami. The miniature painting gives us a bird's-eye view of a typical night in one of the great palaces of Baghdad. The multiple scenes vividly capture the bustle and high artistry of the splendidly decorated rooms and gardens, from a group of musicians serenading a man who is presumably the lord of the mansion, to kitchen servants buying food and preparing to serve it to the lord and his guests. (Attributed to Mir Sayyid 'Ali "Nighttime in a Palace." Folio from a Manuscript, c. 1539–1543. Harvard Art Museum, Arthur M. Sackler Museum, Gift of John Goelet, formerly in the collection of Louis J. Cartier, 1958.76. Katya Kallsen © President and Fellows of Harvard College.)

Imperial Breakdown and Agrarian Disorder

In the last decades of the 9th century, the dynasty brought the slave armies under control for a time, but at a great cost. Constant civil violence drained the treasury and alienated the subjects of the Abbasids. A further strain was placed on the empire's dwindling revenues by some caliphs' attempts to escape the turmoil of Baghdad by establishing new capitals near the original one. The construction of palaces, mosques, and public works for each of these new imperial centers added to the already exorbitant costs of maintaining the court and imperial administration. Of course, the expense fell heavily on the already hard-pressed peasantry of the central provinces of the empire, where some imperial control remained. The need to support growing numbers of mercenary troops also increased the revenue demands on the peasantry.

Spiraling taxation and outright pillaging led to the destruction or abandonment of many villages in the richest provinces of the empire. The great irrigation works that had for centuries been essential to agricultural production in the fertile Tigris–Euphrates basin fell into disrepair, and in some areas they collapsed entirely. Some peasants perished through flood, famine, or violent assault; others fled to wilderness areas beyond the reach of the Abbasid tax collectors or to neighboring kingdoms. Some formed bandit gangs or joined the crowds of vagabonds that trudged the highways and camped in the towns of the imperial heartland. In many cases, dissident religious groups, such as the various Shi'a sects, instigated peasant uprisings. Shi'a participation meant that these movements sought not only to correct the official abuses that had occurred under the Abbasid regime but to destroy the dynasty itself.

The Declining Position of Women in the Family and Society

The harem and the veil became the twin emblems of women's increasing subjugation to men and confinement to the home in the Abbasid era. Although the seclusion of women had been practiced by some Middle Eastern peoples since ancient times, the harem was a creation of the Abbasid court. The wives and the concubines of the Abbasid caliphs were restricted to the forbidden quarters of the imperial palace. Many of the concubines were slaves, who could win their freedom and gain power by bearing healthy sons for the rulers. The growing wealth of the Abbasid elite created a great demand for female and male slaves, who were found by the tens of thousands in Baghdad and other large cities. Most of these urban slaves continued to perform domestic services in the homes of the wealthy. One of the 10th-century caliphs is said to have had 11,000 eunuchs among his slave corps; another is said to have kept 4000 slave concubines.

Most of the slaves had been captured or purchased in the non-Muslim regions surrounding the empire, including the Balkans, central Asia, and Sudanic Africa. They were sold in the slave markets found in all of the larger towns of the Abbasid realm. Female and male slaves were prized for both their beauty and their intelligence. Some of the best-educated men and women in the empire were slaves. Consequently, caliphs and high officials often spent more time with their clever and talented slave concubines than with their less-educated wives. Slave concubines and servants often had more personal liberty than freeborn wives. Slave women could go to the market, and they did not have to wear the veils and robes that were required for free women in public places.

Although women from the lower classes farmed, wove clothing and rugs, or raised silkworms to help support their families, rich women were allowed almost no career outlets beyond the home. Often married at puberty (legally set at age 9), women were raised to devote their lives to running a household and serving their husbands. But at the highest levels of society, wives and concubines cajoled their husbands and plotted with eunuchs and royal advisors to advance the interests of their sons and win for them the ruler's backing for succession to the throne. Despite these brief incursions into power politics, by the end of the Abbasid era, the freedom and influence—both within the family and in the wider world—that women had enjoyed in the first centuries of Islamic expansion had been severely curtailed.

Nomadic Incursions and the Eclipse of Caliphal Power

Buyids [BOO-yihds] Regional splinter dynasty of the mid-10th century; invaded and captured Baghdad; ruled Abbasid Empire under title of sultan; retained Abbasids as figureheads.

Preoccupied by struggles in the capital and central provinces, the caliphs and their advisors were powerless to prevent further losses of territory in the outer reaches of the empire. In addition, areas as close to the capital as Egypt and Syria broke away from Abbasid rule (Map 7.1). More alarmingly, by the mid-10th century, independent kingdoms that had formed in areas that were once provinces of the empire were moving to supplant the Abbasids as lords of the Islamic world. In 945, the armies of one of these regional splinter dynasties, the **Buyids** (BOO-yihds) of Persia, invaded the heartlands of the Abbasid Empire and captured Baghdad. From this point onward, the caliphs were little more than puppets controlled by families such as the Buyids. Buyid leaders took the title of *sultan* ("victorious" in Arabic), which came to designate Muslim rulers, especially in the West.

The Buyids controlled the caliph and the court, but they could not prevent the further disintegration of the empire. In just over a century, the Buyids' control over the caliphate was broken, and they were supplanted in 1055 by another group of nomadic invaders from central Asia via Persia, the **Seljuk Turks** (SEHL-jook Turks). For the next two centuries, Turkic military leaders ruled the remaining portions of the Abbasid Empire in the name of caliphs, who were usually of Arab or Persian extraction. The Seljuks were staunch Sunnis, and they moved quickly to purge the Shi'a officials who had risen to power under the Buyids and to rid the caliph's domains of the Shi'a influences the Buyids had tried to promote. For a time, the Seljuk military machine was also able to restore political initiative to the much reduced caliphate. Seljuk victories ended the threat of conquest by a rival Shi'a dynasty centered in Egypt. They also humbled the Byzantines, who had hoped to take advantage of Muslim divisions to regain some of their long-lost lands. The Byzantines' crushing defeat also opened the way to the settlement of Asia Minor, or Anatolia, by nomadic peoples of Turkic origins, some of whom would soon begin to lay the foundations of the Ottoman Empire.

Seljuk Turks [SEHL-jook Turks] Nomadic invaders from central Asia via Persia; staunch Sunnis; ruled in name of Abbasid caliphs from mid-11th century.

The Impact of the Christian Crusades

Soon after seizing power, the Seljuks faced a very different challenge to Islamic civilization. It came from Christian crusaders, knights from western Europe (see Chapter 10) who were determined to capture the portions of the Islamic world that made up the Holy Land of biblical times. Muslim political divisions and the element of surprise made the first of the crusaders' assaults, between 1096 and 1099, by far the most successful. Much of the Holy Land was captured and divided into Christian kingdoms. In June 1099, the main objective of the Crusade, Jerusalem, was taken, and its Muslim and Jewish inhabitants were massacred by the rampaging Christian knights.

 The Crusades

For nearly two centuries, the Europeans, who eventually mounted eight **Crusades** that varied widely in strength and success, maintained their precarious hold on the eastern Mediterranean region. But they posed little threat to the more powerful Muslim princes, whose disregard for the Christians was demonstrated by the fact that they continued to quarrel among themselves despite the intruders' aggressions. When united under a strong leader, as they were under Salah-ud-Din (known as **Saladin** in Christian Europe) in the last decades of the 12th century, the Muslims rapidly reconquered most of the crusader outposts. Saladin's death in 1193 and the subsequent breakup of his kingdom gave the remaining Christian citadels some respite. But the last of the crusader kingdoms was lost with the fall of Acre in 1291.

Crusades Series of military adventures initially launched by western Christians to free Holy Land from Muslims; temporarily succeeded in capturing Jerusalem and establishing Christian kingdoms; later used for other purposes such as commercial wars and extermination of heresy.

Saladin Muslim leader in the last decades of the 12th century; reconquered most of the crusader outposts for Islam.

Undoubtedly, the impact of the Crusades was much greater on the Christians who launched them than on the Muslim peoples who had to fend them off. Because there had long been so much contact between western Europe and the Islamic world through trade and through the Muslim kingdoms in Spain and southern Italy, it is difficult to be sure which influences to attribute specifically to the Crusades. But the crusaders' firsthand experiences in the eastern Mediterranean certainly intensified European borrowing from the Muslim world that had been going on for centuries. Muslim weapons, such as the famous damascene swords (named after the city of Damascus), were highly prized and sometimes copied by the Europeans, who were always eager to improve on their methods of making war. Muslim techniques of building fortifications were adopted by many Christian rulers, as can be seen in the castles built in Normandy and coastal England by William the Conqueror and his successors in the 11th and 12th centuries. Richard the Lionhearted's legendary preference for Muslim over Christian physicians was but one sign of the Europeans' avid centuries-old interest in the superior scientific learning of Muslim peoples.

From Muslims and Jews in Spain, Sicily, Egypt, and the Middle East, the Europeans recovered much of the Greek learning that had been lost to northern Europe during the waves of nomadic invasions after the fall of Rome. They also mastered Arabic (properly Indian) numerals and the decimal system, and they benefited from the great advances Arab and Persian thinkers had made in mathematics and many of the sciences. The European demand for Middle Eastern rugs and textiles is demonstrated by the Oriental rugs and tapestries that adorned the homes of the European upper classes in Renaissance and early modern paintings. It is also reflected in European (and our own) names for different kinds of cloth, such as *fustian, taffeta, muslin,* and *damask,* which are derived from Persian terms or the names of Muslim cities where the cloth was produced and sold.

Muslim influences affected both the elite and popular cultures of much of western Europe in this period. These included Persian and Arabic words, games such as chess, chivalric ideals and troubadour ballads, as well as foods such as dates, coffee, and yogurt. Some of these imports,

Ibn Khaldun on the Rise and Decline of Empires

Although he lived in the century after the Abbasid caliphate was destroyed in 1258, **Ibn Khaldun** was very much a product of the far-flung Islamic civilization that the Abbasids had consolidated and expanded. He was also one of the greatest historians and social commentators of all time. After extensive travels in the Islamic world, he served as a political advisor at several of the courts of Muslim rulers in north Africa. With the support of a royal patron, Ibn Khaldun wrote a universal history that began with a very long philosophical preface called *The Muqaddimah*. Among the subjects he treated at length were the causes of the rise and fall of dynasties. The shifting fortunes of the dynasties he knew well in his native north Africa, as well as the fate of the Abbasids and earlier Muslim regimes, informed his attempts to find persistent patterns in the complex political history of the Islamic world. The following passages are from one of the most celebrated sections of *The Muqaddimah* on the natural life span of political regimes.

> We have stated that the duration of the life of a dynasty does not as a rule extend beyond three generations. The first generation retains the desert qualities, desert toughness, and desert savagery. [Its members are used to] privation and to sharing their glory [with each other]; they are brave and rapacious. Therefore, the strength of group feeling continues to be preserved among them. They are sharp and greatly feared. People submit to them.
>
> Under the influence of royal authority and a life of ease, the second generation changes from the desert attitude to sedentary culture, from privation to luxury and plenty, from a state in which everybody shared in the glory to one in which one man claims all the glory for himself while the others are too lazy to strive for [glory], and from proud superiority to humble subservience. Thus, the vigor of group feeling is broken to some extent. People become used to lowliness and obedience. But many of [the old virtues] remain in them, because they had direct personal contact with the first generation and its conditions.
>
> The third generation, then, has [completely] forgotten the period of desert life and toughness, as if it had never existed. They have lost [the taste for] group feeling, because they are dominated by force. Luxury reaches its peak among them, because they are so much given to a life of prosperity and ease. They become dependent on the dynasty and are like women and children who need to be defended [by someone else]. Group feeling disappears completely. People forget to protect and defend themselves and to press their claims. With their emblems, apparel, horseback riding, and [fighting] skill, they deceive people and give them the wrong impression. For the most part, they are more cowardly than women upon their backs. When someone comes and demands something from them, they cannot repel him. The ruler, then, has need of other, brave people for his support. He takes many clients and followers. They help the dynasty to some degree, until God permits it to be destroyed, and it goes with everything it stands for.
>
> Three generations last one hundred and twenty years. As a rule, dynasties do not last longer than that many years, a few more, a few less, save when, by chance, no one appears to attack [the dynasty]. When senility becomes preponderant [in a dynasty], there may be no claimant [for its power, and then nothing will happen] but if there should be one, he will encounter no one capable of repelling him. If the time is up [the end of the dynasty] cannot be postponed for a single hour, no more than it can be accelerated.

QUESTIONS What does this passage reveal about Ibn Khaldun's views of the contrasts between nomads and urban dwellers? Why does he see the former as a source of military power and political strength? What forces undermine dynasties in later generations? How well do these patterns correspond to the history of the Umayyad and Abbasid dynasties we have been studying?

Ibn Khaldun (1332–1406) A Muslim historian; developed concept that dynasties of nomadic conquerors had a cycle of three generations—strong, weak, dissolute.

namely the songs of the troubadours, can be traced directly to the contacts the crusaders made in the Holy Land. But most were part of a process of exchange that extended over centuries, and was largely a one-way process. Though Arab traders imported some manufactures, such as glass and cloth, and raw materials from Europe, Muslim peoples in this era showed little interest in the learning or institutions of the West. Nevertheless, the Italian merchant communities, which remained after the political and military power of the crusaders had been extinguished in the Middle East, contributed a good deal more to these ongoing interchanges than all the forays of Christian knights.

An Age of Learning and Artistic Refinements

Paradoxically, even as the political power of the Abbasids declined, Islamic civilization reached new heights of achievement and entered into a phase of renewed expansion.

Although town life became more dangerous, the rapid growth and increasing prosperity that characterized the first centuries of Muslim expansion continued until late in the Abbasid era. Despite the declining revenue base of the caliphate and deteriorating conditions in the countryside, there was a great expansion of the professional classes, particularly doctors, scholars, and legal and religious experts (Figure 7.3). Muslim, Jewish, and in some areas Christian entrepreneurs amassed great fortunes supplying the cities of the empire with staples such as grain and barley, essentials such as cotton and woolen textiles for clothing, and luxury items such as precious gems, citrus fruits, and sugar cane. Long-distance trade between the Middle East and Mediterranean Europe and between coastal India and southeast Asia, in addition to the overland caravan trade with China, flourished through much of the Abbasid era (Map 7.2).

Among the chief beneficiaries of the sustained urban prosperity were artists and artisans, who continued the formidable achievements in architecture and the crafts that had begun in the Umayyad period. Mosques and palaces grew larger and more ornate in most parts of the empire. Even in outlying areas, such as Córdoban Spain, Muslim engineers and architects created some of the great architectural treasures of all time. The tapestries and rugs of Muslim peoples, such as the Persians, were in great demand from Europe to China. To this day, Muslim rugs have rarely been matched for their exquisite designs, their vivid colors, and the skill with which they are woven. Muslim artisans also produced fine bronzes and superb ceramics.

The Full Flowering of Persian Literature

As Persian wives, concubines, advisors, bureaucrats, and (after the mid-10th century) Persian caliphs came to play central roles in imperial politics, Persian gradually replaced Arabic as the primary written language at the Abbasid court. Arabic remained the language of religion, law, and the natural sciences. Persian was favored by Arabs, Turks, and Muslims of Persian descent as the language of literary expression, administration, and scholarship. In Baghdad and major cities throughout the Abbasid Empire and in neighboring kingdoms, Persian was the chief language of "high culture," the language of polite exchanges between courtiers as well as of history, poetic musings, and mystical revelations.

Written in a modified Arabic script and drawing selectively on Arabic vocabulary, the Persian of the Abbasid age was a supple language as beautiful to look at when drafted by a skilled calligrapher as it was to read aloud (Figure 7.4). Catch phrases ("A jug of wine, a loaf of bread, and Thou") from the *Rubaiyat* (ROO-bee-AHT) of Omar Khayyam (OH-mahr keye-YAHM) are certainly the pieces of Persian literature best known in the West. But other writers from this period surpassed Khayyam in profundity of thought and elegance of style. Perhaps the single most important work was the lengthy epic poem **Shah-Nama** (Book of Kings), written by Firdawsi in the late 10th and early 11th centuries. The work relates the history of Persia from the beginnings of time to the Islamic conquests, and it abounds in dramatic details of battles, intrigues, and illicit love affairs. Firdawsi's Persian has been extolled for its grand, musical virtuosity, and portions of the *Shah-Nama* and other Persian works were read aloud to musical accompaniment. Brilliantly illustrated manuscripts of Firdawsi's epic history are among the most exquisite works of Islamic art.

In addition to historical epics, Persian writers in the Abbasid era wrote on many subjects, from doomed love affairs and statecraft to incidents from everyday life and mystical striving for communion with the divine. One of the great poets of the age, Sa'di, fuses an everyday message with a religious one in the following relation of a single moment in his own life:

> Often I am minded, from the days of my childhood,
> How once I went out with my father on a festival;
> In fun I grew preoccupied with all the folk about,
> Losing touch with my father in the popular confusion;
> In terror and bewilderment I raised up a cry,
> Then suddenly my father boxed my ears:
> "You bold-eyed child, how many times, now,

Figure 7.3 The subtlety and depth attained by Muslim civilizations in the far-flung regions in which they were found is illustrated by this 17th-century miniature painting of a scholar-poet in an imagined nighttime garden in Kashmir in northern India. The meditative figure with book in hand and framed by the flowering tree in the background captures the commitment to learning and refined aesthetic sense that was cultivated by members of the elite classes throughout the Islamic world.

Indian Poetry

DOCUMENT

Shah-Nama Written by Firdawsi in late 10th and early 11th centuries; relates history of Persia from creation to the Islamic conquests.

The Language of Love

CASE STUDY

Map 7.2 The Spread of Islam, 10th–16th Centuries Arrows indicate the routes by which Islam spread to south and southeast Asia.

Have I told you not to lose hold of my skirt?"
A tiny child cannot walk out alone,
For it is difficult to take a way not seen;
You too, poor friend, are but a child upon endeavour's way:
Go, seize the skirts of those who know the way!

The *Rubaiyat* of Omar Khayyam

This blend of the mystical and commonplace was widely adopted in the literature of this period. It is epitomized in the *Rubaiyat,* whose author is much more concerned with finding meaning in life and a path to union with the divine than with extolling the delights of picnics in the garden with beautiful women.

Achievements in the Sciences

From preserving and compiling the learning of the ancient civilizations they had conquered in the early centuries of expansion, Muslim peoples—and the Jewish scholars who lived peacefully in Muslim lands—increasingly became creators and inventors in their own right. For several centuries, which spanned much of the period of Abbasid rule, Islamic civilization outstripped all others in scientific discoveries, new techniques of investigation, and new technologies. The many Muslim accomplishments in these areas include major corrections to the algebraic and geometric theories of the ancient Greeks and great advances in the use of basic concepts of trigonometry: the sine, cosine, and tangent.

Two discoveries in chemistry that were fundamental to all later investigation were the creation of the objective experiment and al-Razi's scheme of classifying all material substances into three categories: animal, vegetable, and mineral. The sophistication of Muslim scientific techniques is indicated by the fact that in the 11th century, al-Biruni was able to calculate the specific weight of 18 major minerals. This sophistication was also manifested in astronomical instruments such as those in Figure 7.5, developed through cooperation between Muslim scholars and skilled artisans. Their astronomical tables and maps of the stars were in great demand among scholars of other civilizations, including those of Europe and China.

As these breakthroughs suggest, much of the Muslims' work in scientific investigation had very practical applications. This practical bent was even greater in other fields. For example, Muslim cities such as Cairo boasted some of the best hospitals in the world. Doctors and pharmacists had to follow a regular course of study and pass a formal examination before they were allowed to practice. Muslim scientists did important work on optics and bladder ailments. Muslim traders introduced into the Islamic world and Europe many basic machines and techniques—namely, papermaking, silk-weaving, and ceramic firing—that had been devised earlier in China. In addition, Muslim scholars made some of the world's best maps, which were copied by geographers from Portugal to Poland.

Religious Trends and the New Push for Expansion

The contradictory trends in Islamic civilization—social strife and political divisions versus expanded trading links and intellectual creativity—were strongly reflected in patterns of religious development in the later centuries of the caliphate. On one hand, a resurgence of mysticism injected Islam with a new vibrancy. On the other, orthodox religious scholars, such as the **ulama,** grew increasingly suspicious of and hostile to non-Islamic ideas and scientific thinking. The Crusades had promoted the latter trend. This was particularly true regarding Muslim borrowing from ancient Greek learning, which the ulama associated with the aggressive civilizations of Christian Europe. Many orthodox scholars suspected that the questioning that characterized the Greek tradition would undermine the absolute authority of the Qur'an. They insisted that the Qur'an was the final, perfect, and complete revelation of an all-knowing divinity. Brilliant thinkers such as **al-Ghazali** (al Gaz-AHL-ee), perhaps the greatest Islamic theologian, struggled to fuse the Greek and Qur'anic traditions. Their ideas were often rejected by orthodox scholars.

Much of the religious vitality in Islam in the later Abbasid period was centered on the Sufist movement. In its various guises, including both Sunni and Shi'a manifestations, Sufism was a reaction against the impersonal and abstract divinity that many ulama scholars argued was the true god of the Qur'an. Like the Indian mystics, the Sufis—whose title was derived from the woolen robes they wore—and their followers tried to see beyond what they believed to be the illusory existence of everyday life and to delight in the presence of Allah in the world. True to the strict monotheism of Islam, most Sufis insisted on a clear distinction between Allah and humans. But in some Sufist teachings, Allah permeated the universe in ways that appeared to compromise his transcendent status.

Some Sufis gained reputations as great healers and workers of miracles; others led militant bands that tried to spread Islam to nonbelievers. Some Sufis used asceticism or bodily denial to find Allah; others used meditation, songs, drugs, or ecstatic dancing, which gave the famous whirling dervishes their name. Most Sufis built up a sizeable following, and the movement as a whole was a central factor in the continuing expansion of the Muslim religion and Islamic civilization in the later centuries of the Abbasid caliphate.

Figure 7.4 As the intricate details of this vividly illuminated book of tales of the prophet Muhammad illustrate, Muslim scripts, whether Arabic, Persian, or Turkish, were viewed as works of art in themselves. Artists were expected to be masters of writing and pictorial representation, and books such as this were usually produced in workshops, at times employing several master painters and hundreds of artisans. Verses from the Qur'an, exquisitely rendered in porcelain tiles, were frequently used to decorate mosques and other public buildings.

ulama Orthodox religious scholars within Islam; pressed for a more conservative and restrictive theology; increasingly opposed to non-Islamic ideas and scientific thinking.

al-Ghazali [al Gaz-AHL-ee] (1058–1111) Brilliant Islamic theologian; struggled to fuse Greek and Qur'anic traditions; not entirely accepted by ulama.

Figure 7.5 This 15th-century Persian miniature of a group of Arab scientists testing and working with a wide variety of navigational instruments conveys a strong sense of the premium placed on scientific investigation in the Muslim world in the Abbasid age and the centuries thereafter. Muslim prototypes inspired European artisans, cartographers, and scientists to develop instruments and maps, which were essential to European overseas expansion from the 14th century onward.

From the 7th century onward, Muslim invaders, traders, and migrants carried the Islamic faith and Islamic civilization to the vast south Asian subcontinent. Muslim conquests and conversions provoked a variety of Hindu responses and attempts by some followers of both religions to reconcile their differences.

Mongols   Central Asian nomadic peoples; smashed Turko-Persian kingdoms; captured Baghdad in 1258 and killed last Abbasid caliph.

Chinggis Khan   [JEHNG-gihs KAHN] Born in 1170s in decades following death of Kabul Khan; elected khagan of all Mongol tribes in 1206; responsible for conquest of northern kingdoms of China, territories as far west as the Abbasid regions; died in 1227, prior to conquest of most of Islamic world.

New Waves of Nomadic Invasions and the End of the Caliphate

As we have seen, in the 10th and 11th centuries the Abbasid domains were divided by ever growing numbers of rival successor states. In the early 13th century, a new threat arose at the eastern edge of the original Abbasid domains. Another central Asian nomadic people, the **Mongols,** united by their great commander, **Chinggis Khan** (JEHNG-gihs KAHN), first raided in the 1220s and then smashed the Turko-Persian kingdoms that had developed in the regions to the east of Baghdad. Chinggis Khan died before the heartlands of the Muslim world were invaded, but his grandson, **Hulegu** (hoo-LAY-goo), renewed the Mongol assault on the rich centers of Islamic civilization in the 1250s. In 1258, the Abbasid capital at Baghdad was taken by the Mongols, and much of it was sacked. The 37th and last Abbasid caliph was put to death by the Mongols. They then continued westward until they were finally defeated by the **Mamluks,** or Turkic slaves, who then ruled Egypt.

Baghdad never recovered from the Mongol attacks. In 1401, it suffered a second capture and another round of pillaging by the even fiercer forces of Timur or Tamerlane, another Turkic conqueror from Central Asia. Baghdad shrank from the status of one of the great cities of the world to a provincial backwater. It was gradually supplanted by Cairo to the west and then Istanbul to the north.

The Coming of Islam to South Asia

All through the millennia when a succession of civilizations from Harappa to the brahmanic empire of the Guptas developed in south Asia, foreigners had entered India in waves of nomadic invaders or as small bands of displaced peoples seeking refuge. Invariably, those who chose to remain were assimilated into the civilizations they encountered in the lowland areas. They converted to the Hindu or Buddhist religion, found a place in the caste hierarchy, and adopted the dress, foods, and lifestyles of the farming and city-dwelling peoples of the many regions of the subcontinent. This capacity to absorb peoples moving into the area resulted from the strength and flexibility of India's civilizations and from the fact that India's peoples usually enjoyed a higher level of material culture than migrant groups entering the subcontinent. As a result, the persistent failure of Indian rulers to unite against aggressors meant periodic disruptions and localized destruction but not fundamental challenges to the existing order. All of this changed with the arrival of the Muslims in the last years of the 7th century C.E. (Map 7.2).

With the coming of the Muslims, the peoples of India encountered for the first time a large-scale influx of bearers of a civilization as sophisticated, if not as ancient, as their own. They were also confronted by a religious system that was in many ways the very opposite of the ones they had nurtured. Hinduism, the predominant Indian religion at that time, was open, tolerant, and inclusive of widely varying forms of religious devotion, from idol worship to meditation in search of union with the spiritual source of all creation. Islam was doctrinaire, proselytizing, and committed to the exclusive worship of a single, transcendent god.

Socially, Islam was highly egalitarian, proclaiming all believers equal in the sight of God. In sharp contrast, Hindu beliefs validated the caste hierarchy. The latter rested on the acceptance of inborn differences between individuals and groups and the widely varying levels of material wealth, status, and religious purity these differences were believed to produce. Thus, the faith of the invad-

The Patterns of Islam's Global Expansions

The table shows the present-day distribution of Muslims in key countries from Africa to Asia. It indicates the total number of Muslims in each of the countries represented, the percentage of Muslims in the total population of that area, and the numbers and percentages of other religious groups. The table also indicates the manner in which Islam was spread to each of these areas and the key agents of that diffusion. After using the table to compare the patterns of Islamization in different areas, answer the questions that follow.

QUESTIONS Which areas have the highest absolute numbers of Muslims in the present day? Is this distribution what you would have expected, or is it surprising? What were the main ways that Islam was transmitted to most areas? What does this say about the popular notion that Islam was historically a militant religion spread primarily by forcible conversion? Does Islam appear to be able to coexist with other faiths?

Comparative Statistics of Modern States with a Sizeable Muslim Population

	Total Population (2000 est.)	Total Number of Muslims	Percentage of Muslims	Total Number of Non-Muslims	Percentages of Other Religious Groups	Principle Agents/Modes of Conversion
Nigeria	114 million	57 million	50	57 million	40–Christian; 10–Other (African religions)	Trading Contacts Sufi Missionaries
Egypt	67 million	63 million	94	4 million	4–Christian 2–Other	Arab Migration Voluntary Mass Conversion
Iraq	22.5 million	21.8 million	97: Shi'a: 60–65; Sunni: 32–37	700,000	3–Other (Zoroastrian, Christian, Jewish)	Arab Migration Voluntary Mass Conversion
Iran	65 million	64.35 million	99: Shi'a: 89; Sunni: 10	650,000	1—Other (Zoroastrian, Bahai, Christian, Jewish)	Arab Migration Voluntary Mass Conversion
Pakistan	138 million	133.85 million	97: Shi'a 20; Sunni: 77	4.15 million	3–Other (Hindu, Christian, Buddhist)	Sufi Missionaries Voluntary Mass Conversion
India	1.001 billion	140.1 million	14	860.9 million	80–Hindu; 6–Other (Buddhist, Sikh, Christian, Jain)	Sufi Missionaries Trading Contacts Voluntary Mass Conversion
Indonesia	216 million	188 million	87	28 million	6–Protestant; 7–Other (Catholic Buddhist, etc.)	Sufi Missionaries Trading Contacts
The Phillipines	79.5 million	4 million	5	75.5 million	83–Catholic; 9–Protestant; 3–Other	Trading contacts Sufi Missionaries
Morocco	30 million	29.7 million	99	300,000	1–Other	Voluntary Mass Conversion Sufi Missionaries

Note: Numbers based on information from Wiesenfeld and Famighetti et al., eds., *The World Almanac and Book of Facts 2000* (Mahwah, NJ: World Almanac Books).

ing Muslims was religiously more rigid than that of the absorptive and adaptive Hindus. But the caste-based social system of India was much more compartmentalized and closed than the society of the Muslim invaders, with their emphasis on mobility and the community of believers. Because growing numbers of Muslim warriors, traders, Sufi mystics, and ordinary farmers and herders entered south Asia and settled there, extensive interaction between invaders and the indigenous peoples was inevitable. In the early centuries of the Muslim influx, conflict, often violent, predominated. But there was also a good deal of trade and even religious interchange between them. As time passed, peaceful (if wary) interaction became the norm. Muslim rulers employed large numbers of Hindus to govern the largely non-Muslim populations they conquered, mosques and temples dominated different quarters within Indian cities, and Hindu and Muslim mystics strove to find areas of agreement between their two faiths. Nonetheless, tensions remained, and periodically they erupted into communal rioting or warfare between Hindu and Muslim lords.

Hulegu [hoo-LAY-goo] (1217–1265) Ruler of the Ilkhan khanate; grandson of Chinggis Khan; responsible for capture and destruction of Baghdad in 1257.

Mamluks Muslim slave warriors; established a dynasty in Egypt; defeated the Mongols at Ain Jalut in 1260 and halted Mongol advance.

Map 7.3 Early Islam in India Beginning with raids into the Indus Valley in the 8th century C.E., Muslim armies invaded and established a succession of dynasties centered on Delhi in north-central India.

Muhammad ibn Qasim [moh-HAM-ihd ihbn KAH-sihm] (661–750) Arab general; conquered Sind in India; declared the region and the Indus valley to be part of Umayyad Empire.

Political Divisions and the First Muslim Invasions

The first and least enduring Muslim intrusion, which came in 711, resulted indirectly from the peaceful trading contacts that had initially brought Muslims into contact with Indian civilization. Since ancient times, Arab seafarers and traders had been major carriers in the vast trading network that stretched from Italy in the Mediterranean to the South China Sea. After converting to Islam, these traders continued to visit the ports of India, particularly those on the western coast. An attack by pirates sailing from Sind in western India (Map 7.3) on ships owned by some of these Arab traders prompted the viceroy of the eastern provinces of the Umayyad Empire to launch a punitive expedition against the king of Sind. An able Arab general, **Muhammad ibn Qasim** (moh-HAM-ihd ihbn KAH-sihm), who was only 17 years old when the campaign began, led more than 10,000 horse- and camel-mounted warriors into Sind to avenge the assault on Arab shipping. After victories in several fiercely fought battles, Muhammad ibn Qasim declared the region, as well as the Indus valley to the northeast, provinces of the Umayyad Empire.

In these early centuries, the coming of Islam brought little change for most inhabitants of the Indian subcontinent. In fact, in many areas, local leaders and the populace surrendered towns and districts willingly to the conquerors because they promised lighter taxation and greater religious tolerance. The Arab overlords decided to treat both Hindus and Buddhists as protected "people of the book," despite the fact that their faiths had no connection to the Bible, the book in question. This meant that although they were obliged to pay special taxes, non-Muslims, like Jews and Christians, enjoyed the freedom to worship as they pleased.

As in other areas conquered by the Arabs, most of the local officials and notables retained their positions, which did much to reconcile them to Muslim rule. The status and privileges of the brahman castes were respected. Nearly all Arabs, who made up only a tiny minority of the population, lived in cities or special garrison towns. Because little effort was expended in converting the peoples of the conquered areas, they remained overwhelmingly Hindu or Buddhist.

Indian Influences on Islamic Civilization

Although the impact of Islam on the Indian subcontinent in this period was limited, the Arab foothold in Sind provided contacts by which Indian learning was transmitted to the Muslim heartlands in the Middle East. As a result, Islamic civilization was enriched by the skills and discoveries of yet another great civilization. Of particular importance was Indian scientific learning, which rivaled that of the Greeks as the most advanced of the ancient world. Hindu mathematicians and astronomers traveled to Baghdad after the Abbasids came to power in the mid-8th century. Their works on algebra and geometry were translated into Arabic, and their instruments for celestial observation were copied and improved by Arab astronomers.

Most critically, Arab thinkers in all fields began to use the numerals that Hindu scholars had devised centuries earlier. Because these numbers were passed on to the Europeans through contacts with the Arabs in the early Middle Ages, we call them Arabic numerals today, but they originated in India. Because of the linkages between civilized centers established by the spread of Islam, this system of numerical notation has proved central to two scientific revolutions. The first in the Middle East was discussed earlier in this chapter. The second, discussed in Chapter 17, occurred in Europe some centuries later. From the 16th century to the present, it has brought fundamental transformations to Europe and much of the rest of the world.

In addition to science and mathematics, Indian treatises on subjects ranging from medicine to music were translated and studied by Arab scholars. Indian physicians were brought to Baghdad to run the well endowed hospitals that the Christian crusaders found a source of wonderment and a cause for envy. On several occasions, Indian doctors were able to cure Arab rulers and officials whom Greek physicians had pronounced beyond help. Indian works on statecraft, alchemy, and palmistry were translated into Arabic, and it is believed that some of the tales in the *Arabian Nights* were based on ancient Indian stories. Indian musical instruments and melodies made their way into the repertoires of Arab performers, and the Indian game of chess became a favorite of both royalty and ordinary townspeople.

Arabs who emigrated to Sind and other Muslim-ruled areas often adopted Indian dress and hairstyles, ate Indian foods, and rode on elephants as the Hindu *rajas* (kings) did. As Figure 7.6 illustrates, the conquerors also adopted Indian building styles and artistic motifs. In this era, additional Arab colonies were established in other coastal areas, such as Malabar to the south and Bengal in the east (Map 7.3). These trading enclaves later provided the staging areas from which Islam was transmitted to island and mainland southeast Asia.

Figure 7.6 The Shahi mosque, surrounded by the Hindu Kush mountains in northwestern Pakistan, is a superb example of the blending of Islamic and Hindu architectural forms, building materials, and artistic motifs.

From Booty to Empire: The Second Wave of Muslim Invasions

After the initial conquests by Muhammad ibn Qasim's armies, little territory was added to the Muslim foothold on the subcontinent. In fact, disputes between the Arabs occupying Sind and their quarrels with first the Umayyad and later the Abbasid caliphs gradually weakened the Muslim hold on the area. This was reflected in the reconquest of parts of the lower Indus valley by Hindu rulers. But the gradual Muslim retreat was dramatically reversed by a new series of military invasions, this time launched by a Turkish slave dynasty that in 962 had seized power in Afghanistan to the north of the Indus valley. The third ruler of this dynasty, **Mahmud of Ghazni** (ma-MOOD of GAHZ-nee), led a series of expeditions that began nearly two centuries of Muslim raiding and conquest in northern India. Drawn by the legendary wealth of the subcontinent and a zeal to spread the Muslim faith, Mahmud repeatedly raided northwest India in the first decades of the 11th century. He defeated one confederation of Hindu princes after another, and he drove deeper and deeper into the subcontinent in the quest of ever richer temples to loot.

The raids mounted by Mahmud of Ghazni and his successors gave way in the last decades of the 12th century to sustained campaigns aimed at seizing political control in north India. The key figure in this transition was a tenacious military commander of Persian extraction, **Muhammad of Ghur.** After barely surviving several severe defeats at the hands of Hindu rulers, Muhammad put together a string of military victories that brought the Indus valley and much of north central India under his control. In the following years, Muhammad's conquests were extended along the Gangetic plain as far as Bengal, and into west and central India, by several of his most gifted subordinate commanders. After Muhammad was assassinated in 1206, **Qutb-ud-din Aibak** (KUHTH-uhd-dihn ay-BAHK), one of his slave lieutenants, seized power.

Mahmud of Ghazni [ma-MOOD of GAHZ-nee] (971–1030) Third ruler of Turkish slave dynasty in Afghanistan; led invasions of northern India; credited with sacking one of wealthiest of Hindu temples in northern India; gave Muslims reputation for intolerance and aggression.

Muhammad of Ghur (1173–1206) Military commander of Persian extraction who ruled small mountain kingdom in Afghanistan; began process of conquest to establish Muslim political control of northern India; brought much of Indus valley, Sind, and northwestern India under his control.

Qutb-ud-din Aibak [KUHTH-uhd-dihn ay-BAHK] Lieutenant of Muhammad of Ghur; established kingdom in India with capital at Delphi; proclaimed himself Sultan of India (r. 1206–1210).

A World
Traveler in
India

Significantly, the capital of the new Muslim empire was at Delhi along the Jumna River on the Gangetic plain. Delhi's location in the very center of northern India graphically proclaimed that a Muslim dynasty rooted in the subcontinent itself, not an extension of a Middle Eastern central Asian empire, had been founded. For the next 300 years, a succession of dynasties ruled much of north and central India. Alternately of Persian, Afghan, Turkic, and mixed descent, the rulers of these imperial houses proclaimed themselves the *sultans of Delhi* (literally, princes of the heartland). They fought each other, Mongol and Turkic invaders, and the indigenous Hindu princes for control of the Indus and Gangetic heartlands of Indian civilization.

Patterns of Conversion

Al-Biruni on
India's Hindus

Although the Muslims fought their way into India, their interaction with the indigenous peoples soon came to be dominated by accommodation and peaceful exchanges. Over the centuries when much of the north was ruled by dynasties centered at Delhi, sizeable Muslim communities developed in different areas of the subcontinent. The largest of these were in Bengal to the east and in the northwestern areas of the Indus valley that were the points of entry for most of the Muslim peoples who migrated into India.

Few of these converts were won forcibly. The main carriers of the new faith often were merchants, who played a growing role in both coastal and inland trade, but were most especially Sufi mystics. The latter shared much with Indian gurus and wandering ascetics in both style and message. Belief in their magical and healing powers enhanced the Sufis' stature and increased their following. Their mosques and schools often became centers of regional political power. Sufis organized their devotees in militias to fend off bandits or rival princes, oversaw the clearing of forests for farming and settlement, and welcomed low-caste and outcaste Hindu groups into Islam. After their deaths, the tombs of Sufi mystics became objects of veneration for Indian Muslims as well as Hindu and Buddhist pilgrims.

Most of the indigenous converts, who came to form a majority of the Muslims living in India, were drawn from specific regions and social groups. Surprisingly small numbers of converts were found in the Indo-Gangetic centers of Muslim political power, a fact that suggests the very limited importance of forced conversions. Most Indians who converted to Islam were from Buddhist or low-caste groups. In areas such as western India and Bengal, where Buddhism had survived as a popular religion until the era of the Muslim invasions, esoteric rituals and corrupt practices had debased Buddhist teachings and undermined the morale of the monastic orders.

This decline was accelerated by Muslim raids on Buddhist temples and monasteries, which provided vulnerable and lucrative targets for the early invaders. Without monastic supervision, local congregations sank further into orgies and experiments with magic. All of these trends opposed the Buddha's social concerns and religious message. Disorganized and misdirected, Indian Buddhism was no match for the confident and vigorous new religion the Muslim invaders carried into the subcontinent. This was particularly true when those who were spreading the new faith had the charisma and organizing skills of the Sufi mystics.

Buddhists probably made up the majority of Indians who converted to Islam. But untouchables and low-caste Hindus, as well as tribal peoples who were animists worshiping spirits found in the natural world, were also attracted to the more egalitarian social arrangements promoted by the new faith. As was the case in earlier centuries with the Buddhists, group conversions were essential because those who remained in the Hindu caste system would have little to do with those who converted. Some conversions resulted from the desire of Hindus or Buddhists to escape the head tax the Muslim rulers levied on unbelievers. It was also prompted by intermarriage between local peoples and Muslim migrants. In addition, Muslim migrants swelled the size of the Islamic community in the subcontinent. This was particularly true in periods of crisis in central Asia. In the 13th and 14th centuries, for example, Turkic, Persian, and Afghan peoples retreated to the comparative safety of India in the face of the Mongol and Timurid conquests that are examined in detail in Chapter 14.

Patterns of Accommodation

Although Islam won many converts in certain areas and communities, it initially made little impression on the Hindu population as a whole. Despite military reverses and the imposition of Muslim political rule over large areas of the subcontinent, high-caste Hindus in particular saw the invaders as the bearers of an upstart religion and as polluting outcastes. Al-Biruni, one of the chief chroniclers of the Muslim conquests, complained openly about the prevailing Indian disdain for the newcomers:

> The Hindus believe that there is no country but theirs, no nation like theirs, no kings like theirs, no religion like theirs, no science like theirs. They are haughty, foolishly vain, self-conceited and stolid.

Many Hindus were willing to take positions as administrators in the bureaucracies of Muslim overlords or as soldiers in their armies and to trade with Muslim merchants. But they remained socially aloof from their conquerors. Separate living quarters were established everywhere Muslim communities developed. Genuine friendships between members of high-caste groups and Muslims were rare, and sexual liaisons between them were severely restricted.

During the early centuries of the Muslim influx, the Hindus were convinced that like so many of the peoples who had entered the subcontinent in the preceding millennia, the Muslims would soon be absorbed by the superior religions and more sophisticated cultures of India. Many signs pointed to that outcome. Hindus staffed the bureaucracies and made up a good portion of the armies of Muslim rulers. In addition, Muslim princes adopted regal styles and practices that were Hindu-inspired and contrary to the Qur'an. Some Muslim rulers proclaimed themselves to be of divine descent, and others minted coins decorated with Hindu images such as Nandi, the bull associated with a major Hindu god, Shiva.

More broadly, Muslim communities became socially divided along caste lines. Recently arrived Muslims generally were on top of the hierarchies that developed, and even they were divided depending on whether they were Arab, Turk, or Persian. High-caste Hindu converts came next, followed by "clean" artisan and merchant groups. Lower-caste and untouchable converts remained at the bottom of the social hierarchy. This may help to explain why conversions in these groups were not as numerous as one would expect given the original egalitarian thrust of Islam. Muslims also adopted Indian foods and styles of dress and took to chewing *pan,* or limestone wrapped with betel leaves.

The Muslim influx had unfortunate consequences for women in both Muslim and Hindu communities. The invaders increasingly adopted the practice of marrying women at the earlier ages favored by the Hindus and the prohibitions against the remarriage of widows found especially at the high-caste levels of Indian society. Some high-caste Muslim groups even performed the ritual of *sati,* the burning of widows on the same funeral pyres as their deceased husbands, which was found among some high-caste Hindu groups.

Islamic Challenge and Hindu Revival

Despite a significant degree of acculturation to Hindu lifestyles and social organization, Muslim migrants to the subcontinent held to their own distinctive religious beliefs and rituals. The Hindus found Islam impossible to absorb and soon realized that they were confronted by an actively proselytizing religion with great appeal to large segments of the Indian population. Partly in response to this challenge, the Hindus placed greater emphasis on the devotional cults of gods and goddesses that earlier had proved so effective in neutralizing the challenge of Buddhism.

Membership in these **bhaktic** (BAHK-teek) **cults** was open to all, including women and untouchables. In fact, some of the most celebrated writers of religious poetry and songs of worship were women, such as **Mira Bai** (MIHR-uh BAY). Saints from low-caste origins were revered by warriors and brahmans as well as by farmers, merchants, and outcastes. One of the most remarkable of these mystics was a Muslim weaver named **Kabir.** In plain and direct verse, Kabir played down the significance of religious differences and proclaimed that all faiths could provide a path to spiritual fulfillment. He asked,

> O servant, where do thou seek Me?
> Lo! I am beside thee.
> I am neither in temple nor in mosque:
> Neither am I in rites and ceremonies, nor in Yoga and renunciation.

Because many songs and poems, such as those by Mira Bai and Kabir, were composed in regional languages, such as Bengali, Marathi, and Tamil, they were more accessible to the common people and became prominent expressions of popular culture in many areas.

bhaktic cults   [BAHK-teek] Hindu groups dedicated to gods and goddesses; stressed the importance of strong emotional bonds between devotees and the god or goddess who was the object of their veneration; most widely worshipped gods were Shiva and Vishnu.

Mira Bai   [MIHR-uh BAY] (1498–1547) Celebrated Hindu writer of religious poetry; reflected openness of bhaktic cults to women.

Kabir   (1440–1518) Muslim mystic; played down the importance of ritual differences between Hinduism and Islam.

Conversion and Accommodation in the Spread of World Religions

Although not all great civilizations have produced world religions, the two tend to be closely associated throughout human history. World religions are those that spread across many cultures and societies, forge links between civilized centers, and bring civilized lifestyles to nomadic pastoral or shifting cultivating peoples. Religions with these characteristics appeared before the rise of Islam. As we have seen, India alone produced two of these faiths in ancient times: Hinduism, which spread to parts of southeast and central Asia, and Buddhism, which spread even more widely in the Asian world. At the other end of the Eastern Hemisphere, Christianity spread throughout the Mediterranean region before claiming northern and western Europe as its core area. Judaism spread not because it won converts in non-Jewish cultures but because the Jewish people were driven from their homeland by Roman persecution and scattered throughout the Middle East, north Africa, and Europe.

Because religious conversion affects all aspects of life, from the way one looks at the universe to more mundane decisions about whom to marry or how to treat others, a world religion must be broad and flexible enough to accommodate the existing culture of potential converts. At the same time, its core beliefs and practices must be well enough defined to allow its followers to maintain a clear sense of common identity despite their great differences in culture and society. These beliefs and practices must be sufficiently profound and sophisti-

> "The fact that Islam won converts overwhelmingly through peaceful contacts between long-distance traders and the preaching and organizational skills of Sufis exemplifies its capacity for accommodation."

cated to convince potential converts that their own cultures can be enriched and their lives improved by adopting the new religion.

In most instances, until the 16th century, when Christianity spread through the Western Hemisphere, no world religion could match Islam in the extent to which it spread across the globe and in the diversity of peoples and cultures that identified themselves as Muslims. Given its uncompromising monotheism, very definite doctrines, and elaborate rituals and principles of social organization, Islam's success at winning converts from very different cultural backgrounds is surprising at first glance. This is particularly true if it is compared with the much more flexible beliefs and ceremonial patterns of earlier world religions such as Buddhism and Hinduism. However, closer examination reveals that Islamic beliefs and social practices, as written in the Qur'an and interpreted by the ulama, proved quite flexible and adaptable when the religion was introduced into new, non-Islamic cultures.

The fact that Islam won converts overwhelmingly through peaceful contacts between long-distance traders and the preaching and organizational skills of Sufis exemplifies this capacity for accommodation. Those adopting the new religion did not do so because they were pressured or forced to convert but because they saw Islam as a way to enhance their understanding of the supernatural, enrich their ceremonial expression, improve the quality of their social interaction, and establish ongoing links to a transcultural community beyond their local world.

Because Islam was adopted rather than imposed, those who converted had a good deal to say about how much of their own

Bhakti mystics and gurus stressed the importance of a strong emotional bond between the devotee and the god or goddess who was the object of veneration. Chants, dances, and in some instances drugs were used to reach the state of spiritual intoxication that was the key to individual salvation. Once one had achieved the state of ecstasy that came through intense emotional attachment to a god or goddess, all past sins were removed and caste distinctions were rendered meaningless. The most widely worshiped deities were the gods Shiva and Vishnu, the latter particularly in the guise of Krishna the goat herder depicted in the folk painting in Figure 7.7. The goddess Kali was also venerated in a number of different manifestations. By increasing popular involvement in Hindu worship and by enriching and extending the modes of prayer and ritual, the bhakti movement may have done much to stem the flow of converts to Islam, particularly among low-caste groups.

Stand-Off: The Muslim Presence in India at the End of the Sultanate Period

The attempts of mystics such as Kabir to minimize the differences between Hindu and Islamic beliefs and worship won over only small numbers of the followers of either faith. They were also strongly repudiated by the guardians of orthodoxy in each religious community. Sensing the long-term threat to Hinduism posed by Muslim political dominance and conversion efforts, the cultures they would change and which aspects of Islam they would emphasize or accept. Certain beliefs and practices were obligatory for all true believers: the worship of a single god, adherence to the prophet Muhammad and the divine revelations he received as recorded in the Qur'an, and the observance of the five pillars of the faith. But even these were subject to reinterpretation. In virtually all cultures to which it spread, Islamic monotheism supplanted but did not eradicate the animistic veneration of nature spirits or person and place deities. Allah was acknowledged as the most powerful supernatural force, but people continued to make offerings to spirits that could heal, bring fertility, protect their homes, or punish their enemies. In such areas as Africa and western China, where the veneration of ancestral spirits was a key aspect of religious life, the spirits were retained not as powers in themselves but as emissaries to Allah. In cultures such as those found in India and southeast Asia, Islamic doctrines were recast in a heavily mystical, even magical mode.

The flexibility of Islam was exhibited in the social as well as the religious sphere. In Islamic southeast Asia and in sub-Saharan Africa, the position of women remained a good deal stronger in critical areas, such as occupation and family law, than it had become in the Middle East and India. In both regions, the male-centric features of Islam that had grown more pronounced through centuries of accommodation in ancient Middle Eastern and Persian cultures were played down as Islam adapted to societies where women had traditionally enjoyed more influence, both within the extended family and in occupations such as farming, marketing, and craft production. Even the caste system of India, which in principle is opposed to the strong egalitarian strain in Islam, developed among Muslim groups that migrated into the subcontinent and survived in indigenous south Asian communities that converted to Islam.

Beyond basic forms of social organization and interaction, Islam accommodated diverse aspects of the societies into which it spread. For example, the African solar calendar, which was essential for coordinating the planting cycle, was retained along with the Muslim lunar calendar. In India, Hindu-Buddhist symbols of kingship were appropriated by Muslim rulers and acknowledged by both their Hindu and Muslim subjects. In island southeast Asia, exquisitely forged knives, called *krises,* which were believed to have magical powers, were among the most treasured possessions of local rulers both before and after they converted to Islam.

There was always the danger that accommodation could go too far: that in winning converts, Islamic principles would be so watered down and remolded that they no longer resembled or actually contradicted the teachings of the Qur'an. Sects that came to worship Muhammad or his nephew Ali as godlike, for example, clearly violated fundamental Muslim principles. This danger was a key source of the periodic movements for purification and revival that have been a notable feature of nearly all Islamic societies, particularly those on the fringes of the Islamic world. But even these movements, which were built around the insistence that the Muslim faith had been corrupted by alien ideas and practices and that a return to Islamic fundamentals was needed, were invariably cast in the modes of cultural expression of the peoples who rallied to them.

QUESTIONS Can you think of ways in which world religions, such as Christianity, Hinduism, and Buddhism, changed to accommodate the cultures and societies to which they spread? Do these religions strike you as more or less flexible than Islam? Why?

---

brahmans denounced the Muslims as infidel destroyers of Hindu temples and polluted meat-eaters. Later Hindu mystics, such as the 15th-century holy man Chaitanya, composed songs that focused on love for Hindu deities and set out to convince Indian Muslims to renounce Islam in favor of Hinduism.

For their part, Muslim ulama, or religious experts, grew increasingly aware of the dangers Hinduism posed for Islam. Attempts to fuse the two faiths were rejected on the grounds that although Hindus might argue that specific rituals and beliefs were not essential, they were fundamental for Islam. If one played down the teachings of the Qur'an, prayer, and the pilgrimage, one was no longer a true Muslim. Thus, contrary to the teachings of Kabir and like-minded mystics, the ulama and even some Sufi saints stressed the teachings of Islam that separated it from Hinduism. They worked to promote unity within the Indian Muslim community and to strengthen its contacts with Muslims in neighboring lands and the Middle Eastern centers of the faith.

After centuries of invasion and migration, a large Muslim community had been established in the Indian subcontinent. Converts had been won, political control had been established throughout much of the area, and strong links had been forged with Muslims in other lands such as Persia and Afghanistan. But non-Muslims, particularly Hindus, remained the overwhelming majority of the population of the vast and diverse lands south of the Himalayas. Unlike the Zoroastrians in Persia or the animistic peoples of north Africa and the Sudan, most Indians showed little inclination to

Figure 7.7 This Indian miniature painting of milkmaids serving the Hindu god Krishna reflects the highly personalized devotional worship that was characteristic of the bhakti movement. The eroticism in the milkmaids' songs, in praise of Krishna's great beauty, reveals a blending of sacred and secular, carnal and spiritual that is a recurring motif in Hindu worship and art.

From the 13th century, traders and Sufi mystics spread Islam to island southeast Asia. As was the case in India, conversion was generally peaceful, and Islamic teachings and rituals were mixed with the animist, Hindu, and Buddhist religions long established in Malaya, Java, and other areas.

Shrivijaya [SHREE-vih-JAY-uh] Trading empire centered on Malacca Straits between Malaya and Sumatra; controlled trade of empire; Buddhist government resistant to Muslim missionaries; fall opened up southeastern Asia to Muslim conversion.

Malacca Portuguese factory or fortified trade town located on the tip of the Malayan peninsula; traditionally a center for trade among the southeastern Asian islands.

Demak Most powerful of the trading states on north coast of Java; converted to Islam and served as point of dissemination to other ports.

convert to the religion of the Muslim conquerors. After centuries of Muslim political dominance and missionary activity, south Asia remained one of the least converted and integrated of all the areas Muhammad's message had reached.

The Spread of Islam to Southeast Asia

From a world history perspective, island southeast Asia had long been mainly a middle ground. It was the zone where the Chinese segment of the great Euro-Asian trading complex met the Indian Ocean trading zone to the west. At ports on the coast of the Malayan peninsula, east Sumatra, and somewhat later north Java, goods from China were transferred from east Asian vessels to Arab or Indian ships. In these same ports, products from as far west as Rome were loaded into the emptied Chinese ships to be carried to east Asia. By the 7th and 8th centuries C.E., sailors and ships from areas of southeast Asia, particularly Sumatra and Malaya, had become active in the seaborne trade of the region. Southeast Asian products had also become important exports to China, India, and the Mediterranean region. Many of these products were luxury items, such as aromatic woods from the rain forests of Borneo and Sumatra and spices such as cloves, nutmeg, and mace from the far end of the Indonesian archipelago. These trading links were to prove even more critical to the expansion of Islam in southeast Asia than they had earlier been to the spread of Buddhism and Hinduism.

From the 8th century onward, the coastal trade of India came increasingly to be controlled by Muslims from such regions as Gujarat in western India and various parts of south India. As a result, elements of Islamic culture began to filter into island southeast Asia. But only in the 13th century, after the collapse of the far-flung trading empire of **Shrivijaya** (SHREE-vih-JAY-uh), centered on the Strait of Malacca between Malaya and the northeast of Sumatra (Map 7.4), was the way open for the widespread introduction of Islam. Indian traders, Muslim or otherwise, were welcome to trade in the chain of ports controlled by Shrivijaya. But because the rulers and officials of Shrivijaya were devout Buddhists, there was little incentive for the traders and sailors of southeast Asian ports to convert to Islam, the religion of growing numbers of the merchants and sailors from India. With the fall of Shrivijaya, incentives increased for the establishment of Muslim trading centers and efforts to preach the faith to the coastal peoples.

Trading Contacts and Conversion

As in most of the areas to which Islam spread, peaceful contacts and voluntary conversion were far more important than conquest and force in spreading the faith in southeast Asia. Throughout the islands of the region, trading contacts paved the way for conversion. Muslim merchants and sailors introduced local peoples to the ideas and rituals of the new faith and impressed on them how much of the known world had already been converted. Muslim ships also carried Sufis to various parts of southeast Asia, where they played as vital a role in conversion as they had in India. The first areas to be won to Islam in the late 13th century were several small port centers on the northern coast of Sumatra. From these ports, the religion spread in the centuries that followed across the Strait of Malacca to Malaya.

On the mainland, the key to widespread conversion was the powerful trading city of **Malacca,** whose smaller trading empire had replaced the fallen Shrivijaya. From Malacca, Islam spread along the coasts of Malaya to east Sumatra and to the trading center of **Demak** on the north coast of Java. From Demak, the most powerful of the trading states on north Java, the Muslim faith spread to other Javanese ports. After a long struggle with a Hindu-Buddhist kingdom in the interior, the rest of the

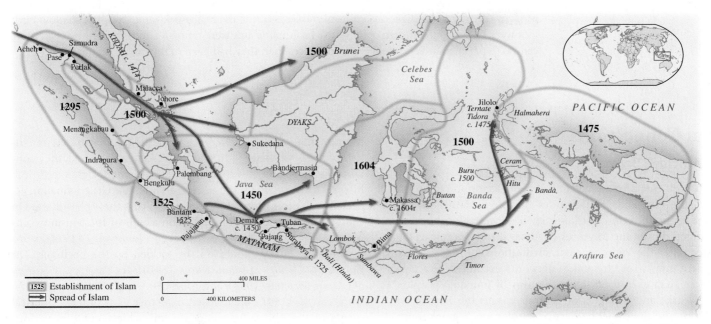

Map 7.4 The Spread of Islam in Southeast Asia   Traders and Islamic mystics were the main agents responsible for the rapid spread of Islam throughout island southeast Asia.

island was eventually converted. From Demak, Islam was also carried to the Celebes and the Spice Is-lands in the eastern archipelago, and from the latter to Mindanao in the southern Philippines. This progress of Islamic conversion shows that port cities in coastal areas were particularly re-ceptive to the new faith. Here trading links were critical. Once one of the key cities in a trading clus-ter converted, it was in the best interest of others to follow suit to enhance personal ties and provide a common basis in Muslim law to regulate business deals. Conversion to Islam also linked these centers, culturally as well as economically, to the merchants and ports of India, the Middle East, and the Mediterranean.

Islam made slow progress in areas such as central Java, where Hindu-Buddhist dynasties con-tested its spread. But the fact that the earlier conversion to these Indian religions had been confined mainly to the ruling elites in Java and other island areas left openings for mass conversions to Islam that the Sufis eventually exploited. The island of Bali, where Hinduism had taken deep root at the popular level, remained largely impervious to the spread of Islam. The same was true of most of mainland southeast Asia, where centuries before the coming of Islam, Buddhism had spread from India and Ceylon and won the fervent adherence of both the ruling elites and the peasant masses.

Sufi Mystics and the Nature of Southeast Asian Islam

Because Islam was spread in many areas by Sufis from South Asia, it was often infused with mystical strains and incorporated animist, Hindu, and Buddhist elements. Just as they had in the Middle East and India, the Sufis who spread Islam in southeast Asia varied widely in personality and approach. Most were believed by those who followed them to have magical powers, and nearly all Sufis estab-lished mosque and school centers from which they traveled in neighboring regions to preach the faith.

In winning converts, the Sufis were willing to allow the inhabitants of island southeast Asia to retain pre-Islamic beliefs and practices that orthodox scholars would have found contrary to Islamic doctrine. Pre-Islamic customary law remained important in regulating social interaction, whereas Is-lamic law was confined to specific sorts of agreements and exchanges. Women retained a much stronger position, both within the family and in society, than they had in the Middle East and India. For example, trading in local and regional markets continued to be dominated by small-scale female buyers and sellers. In such areas as western Sumatra, lineage and inheritance continued to be traced through the female line after the coming of Islam, despite its tendency to promote male dominance and descent. Perhaps most tellingly, pre-Muslim religious beliefs and rituals were incorporated into

Muslim ceremonies. Indigenous cultural staples, such as the brilliant Javanese puppet shadow plays that were based on the Indian epics of the brahmanic age, were refined, and they became even more central to popular and elite beliefs and practices than they had been in the pre-Muslim era.

Global Connections

Islam: A Bridge Between Worlds

Although problems of political control and succession continued to plague the kingdoms and empires that divided the Muslim world, the central position of Islamic civilization in global history was solidified during the centuries of Abbasid rule. Its role as the go-between for the more ancient civilizations of the Eastern Hemisphere grew as Arab trading networks expanded into new areas. More than ever, it enriched the lives of nomadic peoples, from the Turks and Mongols of central Asia to the Berbers of north Africa and the camel herders of the savanna regions south of the Sahara. Equally critically, Islam's original contributions to the growth and refinement of civilized life greatly increased. From its great cities and universities and the accomplishments they generated in the fine arts, sciences, and literature to its vibrant religious and philosophical life, Islam pioneered patterns of organization and thinking that would affect the development of human societies in major ways for centuries to come.

For more than five centuries, the spread of Islam played a central role in the rise, extension, or transformation of civilization in much of the Afro-Asian world. The Islamic world also became a great conduit for the exchange of ideas, plants and medicines, commercial goods, and inventions both between centers of urban and agrarian life and between these core regions of civilization and the areas dominated by nomadic peoples that still encompassed much of the globe.

In the midst of all this achievement, however, there were tendencies that would put the Muslim peoples at a growing disadvantage, particularly in relation to their long-standing European rivals. Muslim divisions would leave openings for political expansion that the Europeans would eagerly exploit, beginning with the island southeast Asian extremities of the Islamic world and then moving across India. The growing orthodoxy and intolerance of many of the ulama, as well as the Muslim belief that the vast Islamic world contained all requirements for civilized life, caused Muslim peoples to grow less receptive to outside influences and innovations. These tendencies became increasingly pronounced at precisely the time when their Christian rivals were entering a period of unprecedented curiosity, experimentation, and exploration of the world beyond their own heartlands.

Further Readings

M. A. Shaban's *Islamic History: An Interpretation*, 2 vols. (1971), contains the most readable and thematic survey of early Islam, concentrating on the Abbasid period. Although Philip Hitti's monumental *History of the Arabs* (1967) and J. J. Saunders' *A History of Medieval Islam* (1965) are now somewhat dated, they contain much valuable information and some fine insights into Arab history. Also useful are the works of G. E. von Gruenenbaum, especially *Classical Islam* (1970), which covers the Abbasid era. On changes in Islamic religion and the makeup of the Muslim community, Marshall Hodgson's *Venture of Islam*, vol. 2 (1974), is indispensable, but it should not be tackled by the beginner. *The Cambridge History of Islam*, 2 vols. (1970); Ira Lapidus, *A History of Islamic Societies* (1988); and Albert Hourani, *A History of the Islamic Peoples* (1991), are excellent reference works for the political events of the Abbasid era and Muslim achievements in various fields. D. M. Dunlop's *Arab Civilization to A.D. 1500* (1971) also contains detailed essays on Islamic culture as well as an article on the accomplishments of Muslim women in this era.

On social history, B. F. Musallam's *Sex and Society in Islam* (1983) has material on the Abbasid period, and some of the more prominent works on urban life include Ira Lapidus's *Muslim Cities in the Later Middle Ages* (1984 ed.), Nezar al-Sayyid's *Cities and Caliphs* (1991), and Albert Hourani and S. M. Stern, eds., *The Islamic City* (1970). Two essential works on the spread of Islam to India are S. M. Ikram, *Muslim Civilization in India* (1964); and Aziz Ahmad, *Studies in Islamic Culture in the Indian Environment* (1964). For the role of the Sufis in Islamic conversion, Richard Eaton's *Sufis of Bijapur* (1978) and *The Rise of Islam and the Bengal Frontier* (1993) are particularly revealing. The best introduction to the pattern of Islamic conversion in southeast Asia is H. J. de Graaf's essay in *The Cambridge History of Islam*, vol. 2 (1976). Toby Huff's *The Rise of Early Modern Science: Islam, China, and the West* (1993) is a stimulating account of the ways in which science and technology were transmitted between these key centers of the Eastern Hemisphere and the effects of these exchanges on global history. On the exchanges among Islamic and other Eurasian civilizations more generally, see R.M. Savory, ed., *Introduction to Islamic Civilization* (1976).

On the Web

The glories of Abbasid Baghdad are illuminated at http://www.fordham.edu/halsall/source/1000baghdad.html. Omar Khayyam was no mere writer of verses, but also a leading scientist as were many other Abbasid intellectuals, whose place of origin, lives, and attainments are described at http://www.cyberistan.org/islamic/ (scroll down for links).

Turkish art, architecture, and music are explored at http://www.columbia.edu/~sss31/Turkiye/art.html. The Seljuk Turks had to confront both the Christian Crusades (http://en.wikipedia

.org/wiki/Crusade) and the Mongol warriors of Chinggis Khan (http://www.pma.edmonton.ab.ca/vexhibit/genghis/intro.htm), but they succeeded in helping to preserve the Islamic heartland. Despite these challenges, Islam spread even further into Africa and south and southeast Asia and China. That process is described at a variety of sites which indicate the importance of two factors in the expansion of Islam to those and other regions: trade and Sufism. A case study in the role of the spice trade in the spread of Islam can be found at http://www.american.edu/TED/SPICE.HTM. The specific role of merchants is examined at http://www.islamweb.net/ver2/archive/article.php?lang=E&id=137272.

A short introduction to Sufism is offered at http://philtar.ucsm.ac.uk/encyclopedia/islam/sufi/geness.html. The place of Sufism in the development of Islam in the West and in Asia is exam-ined at http://www.uga.edu/islam/sufismwest.html, a website that demonstrates that, while Islam could arrive via the sword, it was more often than not spread by Muslim mystics whose practice led to the building of bridges between peoples and cultures.

The encounter between pre-Islamic indigenous traditions and the teachings of Islam led to cultural synthesis in Africa (http://www.metmuseum.org/TOAH/HD/tsis/hd_tsis.htm) and also in southeast Asia (http://www.islamonline.net/English/ArtCulture/2005/10/article01.shtml). This process is further illuminated by the life and work of the Indian *bhakti* poet Kabir (http://www.upanishad.org/kabir/index.htm, http://www.cs.colostate.edu/~malaiya/kabir.html, and http://www.boloji.com/kabir/), whose message is sufficiently universal that he is claimed by the adherents of many religions as one of their own.

AP* | Test Prep

1. The slow decline of Abbasid power was due to all of these reasons EXCEPT
   (A) succession disputes.
   (B) attacks by European crusaders.
   (C) the growing political power of Turkish "slave" officers and men.
   (D) breakaway provinces and internal rebellions.

2. Why were the Sufis increasing popular throughout the Islamic world in the later Abbasid dynasty?
   (A) they advocated a less academic, more personal or devotional form of worship.
   (B) they led religious wars against Christian "crusaders" in Europe and the Middle East.
   (C) they attempted to blend Islam with Judaism and Christianity.
   (D) they sought a return to a more dogmatic and less tolerant version of Islam.

3. The Abbasid Caliphate in Iraq ended when:
   (A) Mongol soldiers crushed Baghdad.
   (B) the Seljuk Turks overran the empire.
   (C) Christian crusaders took Jerusalem.
   (D) Shi'a troops assassinated the last caliph.

4. Which of the following was a major literary figure during the Abbasid period?
   (A) Mahmud of Ghazna.
   (B) Muhammad ibn Qasim.
   (C) al-Ghazali.
   (D) Omar Khyayyam

5. Why might have some Buddhists and low-caste Hindus of the Indian subcontinent been attracted to Islam in the 7th century?
   (A) They were attracted by the egalitarian beliefs and social organization of Islam.
   (B) They saw conversion as a way to overthrow oppressive Hindu monarchs.
   (C) They would not have to pay Hindu religious taxes to Islamic rulers.
   (D) They feared they would be killed by Arab invaders if they did not convert.

6. Increasingly contacts between Hindus and Muslims in South Asia led to
   (A) the end of the seclusion of Hindu women.
   (B) the absorption of many Hindu social practices by Muslims in South Asia.
   (C) conversion of the majority of Hindus to Islam.
   (D) decreased trade opportunities for Hindu merchant converts to Islam.

7. What city proved to be the key to the conversion to Islam of parts of mainland Southeast Asia?
   (A) Malacca.
   (B) Shrivajaya.
   (C) Demak.
   (D) Bombay.

Free-Response Question

What role did the spread of Islam play in the rise, extension, or transfer of civilization and/or cultural ideas throughout much of the Afro-Asian world.

8 African Civilizations and the Spread of Islam

African Societies: Diversity and Similarities

Kingdoms of the Grasslands

DOCUMENT: The Great Oral Tradition and the Epic of Sundiata

VISUALIZING THE PAST: The Architecture of Faith

The Swahili Coast of East Africa

Peoples of the Forest and Plains

THINKING HISTORICALLY: Two Transitions in the History of World Population

GLOBAL CONNECTIONS: Internal Development and Global Contacts

In 1324, a great caravan of more than a hundred camels, many slaves, and a multitude of retainers crossed the arid Sahara desert and wended its way into Cairo, on the banks of the Nile. Mansa Musa, lord of the African empire of Mali, was making the *hajj*, the pilgrimage to Mecca, distributing gold with an open hand. The wealth and prodigality of the young king dazzled all who witnessed it, his polished manners and command of Arabic impressed those who met him, and his fame spread throughout the Islamic world and beyond. The chronicler al-Omari, who visited Cairo a dozen years later, reported that people still spoke of the entourage of the young king that had spent so much gold in the markets and had given so much as gifts and alms that the price of gold actually declined due to its ample supply. Other great caravans had made the trek from Mali across the desert before and some came after but none had been so magnificent. Mansa Musa's caravan symbolized the wealthy potential of Africa, but even by the time he made his trip, west African gold was already well known in the world economy and Africa was already involved in contacts of various kinds with other areas of the world.

Mali, the kingdom of this great lord, fascinated the Muslim observers in Cairo, Damascus, and Fez. Like the earlier kingdom of Ghana, Mali was another state of the savannah country, between the desert and the forests of west Africa. Formed by the Malinke peoples, its access to gold and control of the caravan routes had promoted its rise, and its powerful army had created an empire that extended over much of the savannah from the Niger to the Senegal River. Its ruling families had converted to Islam, but the famous and cosmopolitan Moroccan traveler Abdallah Ibn Batuta, who visited Mali not long after Mansa Musa's pilgrimage, found the local customs and food less refined than those of the elegant courts to which he was accustomed and some of the practices shocking. Yet much was recognizable to him as well. Mali was an African kingdom that had become an extension of the Islamic world, and its success was tied to the trade routes that linked it to the Mediterranean and the Middle East. ■

The history of Mali underlines the fact that Africa below the Sahara was never totally isolated from the centers of civilization in Egypt, west Asia, or the Mediterranean, but for long periods the contacts were difficult and intermittent. This chapter will examine the increasing impact of a growing international network on Africa roughly in the period between 800 and 1600 C.E. Chief among those influences was the arrival of Islam which transformed many aspects of life in some African societies and brought them through trade, politics and cultural exchange into increasing contact. But, we must also recognize the African societies influenced by Islam often maintained their own traditions that other African societies remained little touched by Islam and continued to develop along their own trajectories.

African civilizations built somewhat less clearly on prior societies than did other postclassical civilizations. Some earlier themes, such as the Bantu migration and the formation of large states in the western Sudan, persisted. Overall, sub-Saharan Africa remained a varied and distinctive setting; parts of it like the port cities of the East African coast were drawn into new contacts with the growing world network, but much of it retained a certain isolation or cultural autonomy. The spread of universal faiths like Islam and Christianity was an important aspect of African history in this period, but much of central and southern Africa still flourished relatively unaffected by these outside influences.

Figure 8.1 In 1324, Mansa Musa, King of Mali, made a pilgrimage to Mecca that brought the attention of the Muslim world to the wealth of his kingdom. A Jewish cartographer in Spain, Abraham Cresques, depicted the trip more than fifty years later in the map shown above. Mansa Musa is depicted at the bottom right with a golden sceptre and crown, symbolizing his royal power, and an enormous gold nugget, symbolizing his country's wealth.

African Societies: Diversity and Similarities

Like most continents, Africa is so vast and its societies so diverse that it is almost impossible to generalize about them. Differences in geography, language, religion, politics, and other aspects of life contributed to Africa's lack of political unity over long periods of time. Unlike in many parts of Asia, Europe, and north Africa, neither universal states nor universal religions characterized the history of sub-Saharan Africa. Yet universal religions, first Christianity and later Islam, did find adherents in Africa and sometimes contributed to the formation of large states and empires.

Societies With and Without States

Some African societies had rulers who exercised control through a hierarchy of officials in what can be called states, but others were **stateless societies,** organized around kinship or other forms of obligation and lacking the concentration of political power and authority we normally associate with the state. Sometimes the stateless societies were larger and more extensive than the neighboring states. Stateless societies had forms of government, but the authority and power normally exercised by a ruler and his court in a kingdom could be held instead by a council of families or by the community, with no need to tax the population to support the ruler, the bureaucrats, the army, or the nobles, as was usually the case in state-building societies. Stateless societies had little concentration of authority, and that authority affected only a small part of the peoples' lives. In these societies, government was rarely a full-time occupation.

Other alternatives to formal government were possible. Among peoples of the west African forest, secret societies of men and women controlled customs and beliefs and were able to limit the authority of rulers. Especially among peoples who had sharp rivalries between lineages or family groupings, secret societies developed that cut across the lineage divisions. Members' allegiance to these groups transcended their lineage ties. The secret societies settled village disputes. They acted to maintain stability within the community, and they served as an alternative to the authority of state institutions.

African societies developed diverse forms, from stateless societies organized around kinship or age sets to large centralized states, and within this diversity were many shared aspects of language and beliefs. Universalistic faiths penetrated the continent and served as the basis for important cultural developments in Nubia and Ethiopia.

stateless societies African societies organized around kinship or other forms of obligation and lacking the concentration of political power and authority associated with states.

185

100 C.E.	600 C.E.	1000 C.E.	1200 C.E.	1400 C.E.
100–200 Camels introduced for trade in the Sahara 300 Origins of the kingdom of Ghana	600–700 Islam spreads across North Africa	1000 Ghana at height of its power 1100 Almoravid movement in the Sahara	1200 Rise of the empire of Mali 1260 Death of Sundiata; earliest stone buildings at Zimbabwe; Lalibela rules in Ethiopia; Yoruba culture flourishes at Ile-Ife 1300 Mali at its height; Kanem Empire is a rival 1324 Pilgrimage of Mansa Musa	1400 Flourishing of cities of Timbuktu and Jenne; Ethiopian Christian kingdom; Swahili cities flourish on east African coast 1417, 1431 Last Chinese trade voyages to east Africa 1500 Songhay Empire flourishes; Benin at height of power

Throughout Africa many stateless societies thrived, perhaps aided by the fact that internal social pressures or disputes often could be resolved by allowing dissidents to leave and establish a new village in the sparsely populated continent. Still, stateless societies found it difficult to resist external pressures, mobilize for warfare, organize large building projects, or create stable conditions for continuous long-distance trade with other peoples. All these needs or goals contributed to the formation of states in sub-Saharan Africa.

State-building took place under a variety of conditions. For example west Africa experienced both the cultural influence of Islam and its own internal developments. The formation of some powerful states, such as Mali and Songhay, depended more on military power and dynastic alliances than on ethnic or cultural unity. In this development and in the process of state formation itself, Africa paralleled the roughly contemporaneous developments of western Europe. The growth of city-states with strong merchant communities in west Africa and on the Indian Ocean coast bore certain similarities to the urban developments of Italy and Germany in this period. However, disparities between the technologies and ideologies of Europeans and Africans also created differences in the ways these societies developed. That was made clear with the arrival of Europeans—the Portuguese—in the 15th century whose contact drew Africans increasingly into the world economy in ways that transformed African development in the following centuries.

Common Elements in African Societies

Even amid the diversity of African cultures, certain similarities in language, thought, and religion provided some underlying unities. The spread of the Bantu-speaking peoples provided a linguistic base across much of Africa, so that even though specific languages differed, structure and vocabulary allowed some mutual understanding between neighboring Bantu speakers.

The same might be said of the animistic religion that characterized much of Africa. From its earliest beginnings it was a belief that a soul or spirit existed in every object, even if it was inanimate. In a future state this soul or spirit would exist as part of an immaterial soul. The spirit, therefore, was thought to be universal. Africans, like Europeans, believed that some evil, disasters, and illnesses were produced by witchcraft. Specialists were needed to combat the power of evil and eliminate the witches. This led in many societies to the existence of a class of diviners or priests who guided religious practice and helped protect the community. Above all, African religion provided a cosmology—a view of how the universe worked—and a guide to ethics and behavior.

Many African peoples shared an underlying belief in a creator deity whose power and action were expressed through spirits or lesser gods and through the founding ancestors of the group. The ancestors often were viewed as the first settlers and thus the "owners" of the land or the local resources. Through them, the fertility of the land, game, people, and herds could be ensured. Among some groups, working the land took on religious significance, so the land itself had a meaning beyond its economic usefulness.

Religion, economics, and history were thus closely intertwined. The family, lineage, or clan around which many African societies were organized also had an important role in dealing with the gods. Deceased ancestors often were a direct link between their living relatives and the spirit world.

Veneration of the ancestors and gods was part of the same system of belief. Such a system was strongly linked to specific places and people. It showed remarkable resiliency even in the face of contact with monotheistic religions such as Islam and Christianity.

The economies of Africa are harder to describe in general terms than some basic aspects of politics and culture. North Africa, fully involved in the Mediterranean and Arab economic world, stands clearly apart. Sub-Saharan Africa varied greatly from one region to the next. In many areas, settled agriculture and skilled ironwork had been established before or advanced rapidly during the postclassical period. Specialization encouraged active local and regional trade, the basis for many lively markets and the many large cities that grew in both the structured states and the decentralized areas. The bustle and gaiety of market life were important ingredients of African society, and women as well as men participated actively. Professional merchants, in many cases in hereditary kinship groupings, often controlled trade. Participation in international trade increased in many regions in this period, mainly with the Islamic world and often through Arab traders.

Finally, one of the least known aspects of early African societies is the size and dynamics of their populations. This is true not only of Africa but of much of the world. Archeological evidence, travelers' reports, and educated guesses are used to estimate the population of early African societies, but in truth, our knowledge of how Africa fits into the general trends of the world population is very slight. By 1500, Africa may have had 30 to 60 million inhabitants.

The Arrival of Islam in North Africa

Africa north of the Sahara had long been part of the world of classical antiquity, where Phoenicians, Greeks, Romans, and Vandals traded, settled, built, battled, and destroyed. The Greek city of Cyrene (c. 600 B.C.E.) in modern Libya and the great Phoenician outpost at Carthage (founded c. 814 B.C.E.) in Tunisia attest to the part north Africa played in the classical world. After the age of the pharaohs, Egypt (conquered by Alexander in 331 B.C.E.) had become an important part of the Greek world and then later a key province in the Roman Empire, valued especially for its grain. Toward the end of the Roman Empire, Christianity had taken a firm hold in Mediterranean Africa, but in the warring between the Vandals and the Byzantines in north Africa in the 5th and 6th centuries C.E., great disruption had taken place. During that period, the Berber peoples of the Sahara had raided the coastal cities. As we have seen with Egypt, north Africa was linked across the Sahara to the rest of Africa in many ways. With the rise of Islam, those ties became even closer.

Between 640 and 700 C.E., the followers of Muhammad swept across north Africa from Suez to Morocco's Atlantic shore. By 670 C.E., Muslims ruled Tunisia, or **Ifriqiya** (IHF-rih-kee-uh)— what the Romans had called Africa. (The Arabs originally used this word as the name for eastern north Africa and **Maghrib** (MAH-grihb) for lands to the west.) By 711, Arab and Berber armies had crossed into Spain. Only their defeat in France by Charles Martel at Poitiers in 732 brought the Muslim advance in the West to a halt. The message of Islam found fertile ground among the populations of north Africa. Conversion took place rapidly within a certain political unity provided by the Abbasid dynasty. This unity eventually broke down, and north Africa divided into several separate states and competing groups.

In opposition to the states dominated by the Arabic rulers, the peoples of the desert, the Berbers, formed states of their own at places such as Fez in Morocco and at Sijilimasa, the old city of the trans-Saharan caravan trade. By the 11th century, under pressure from new Muslim invaders, a great puritanical reformist movement, whose followers were called the Almoravids (ahl-MOHR-uh-vihdz), grew among the desert Berbers of the western Sahara. Launched on the course of a *jihad*—a holy war waged to purify, spread, or protect the faith—the Almoravids moved south against the African kingdoms of the savanna and west into Spain. In 1130 another reformist group, the **Almohadis** (AHL-moh-HAH-dees), followed the same pattern. These north African and Spanish developments were an essential background to the penetration of Islam into sub-Saharan Africa.

Islam offered many attractions within Africa. Its fundamental teaching that all Muslims are equal within the community of believers made the acceptance of conquerors and new rulers easier. The Islamic tradition of uniting the powers of the state and religion in the person of the ruler or caliph appealed to some African kings as a way of reinforcing their authority. The concept that all members of the umma, or community of believers, were equal put the newly converted Berbers and

The Spread of Islam

Ifriqiya [IHF-rih-kee-uh] The Arabic term for eastern north Africa.

Maghrib [MAH-grihb] The Arabic word for western north Africa.

Almohadis [AHL-moh-HAH-dees] A reformist movement among the Islamic Berbers of northern Africa; later than the Almoravids; penetrated into sub-Saharan Africa.

later Africans on an equal footing with the Arabs, at least in law. Despite these egalitarian and somewhat utopian ideas within Islam, practices differed considerably at local levels. Social stratification remained important in Islamicized societies, and ethnic distinctions also divided the believers. Despite certain teachings on the equality between men and women, the fine for killing a man was twice that for killing a woman. The disparity between law and practice—between equality before God and inequality within the world—sometimes led to utopian reform movements. Groups such as the Almohadis are characteristic within Islamic history, often developing in peripheral areas and dedicated to purifying society by returning to the original teachings of Muhammad.

The Christian Kingdoms: Nubia and Ethiopia

Islam was not the first universalistic religion to take root in Africa, and the wave of Arab conquests across northern Africa had left behind it islands of Christianity. Christian converts had been made in Egypt and Ethiopia even before the conversion of the Roman Empire in the 4th century C.E. In addition to the Christian kingdom of Axum, Christian communities thrived in Egypt and Nubia, farther up the Nile. The Christians of Egypt, the Copts, developed a rich tradition in contact with Byzantium, translating the gospels and other religious literature from Greek to Coptic, their own tongue, which was based on the language of ancient Egypt. On doctrinal and political issues, they eventually split from the Byzantine connection. When Egypt was conquered by Arab armies and then converted to Islam, the Copts were able to maintain their faith; Muslim rulers recognized them as followers of a revealed religion and thus entitled to a certain tolerance. The Coptic influence had already spread up the Nile into Nubia, the ancient land of Kush. Muslim attempts to penetrate

Figure 8.2 This extraordinary 13th-century church, *Bet Giorgis,* represents the power of early Christianity in Ethiopia. It was one of a great complex of eleven churches that King Lalibela believed God had commanded him to build. Dedicated to St. George, the patron saint of Ethiopia, it was cut out of the bedrock of the earth. Its roof, in the shape of an enormous cross, lies at ground level. Though it is surrounded by impassable walls and can be reached only by way of an underground tunnel carved in stone, it is still used for worship today.

Nubia were met with such stiff resistance in the 9th century that the Christian descendants of ancient Kush were left as independent Christian kingdoms until the 13th century.

The Ethiopian kingdom that grew from Axum was perhaps the most important African Christian outpost. Cut off from Christian Byzantium by the Muslim conquest of Egypt and the Red Sea coast, surrounded by pagan neighbors, and probably influenced by pagan and Jewish immigrants from Yemen, the Christian kingdom turned inward. Its people occupied the Ethiopian highlands, living in fortified towns and supporting themselves with agriculture on terraced hillsides. Eventually, through a process of warfare, conversion, and compromise with non-Christian neighbors, a new dynasty emerged, which under King Lalibela (d. 1221) sponsored a remarkable building project in which 11 great churches were sculpted from the rock in the town that bore his name (Figure 8.2).

In the 13th and 14th centuries, an Ethiopian Christian state emerged under a dynasty that traced its origins back to the biblical marriage of Solomon and Sheba. Using the Ge'ez language of Axum as a religious language and Amharic as the common speech, this state maintained its brand of Christianity in isolation while facing constant pressure from its increasingly Muslim neighbors.

The struggle between the Christian state in the Ethiopian highlands and the Muslim peoples in Somalia and on the Red Sea coast shaped much of the history of the region and continues to do so today. When one of these Muslim states, with help from the Ottoman Turks, threatened the Ethiopian kingdom, a Portuguese expedition arrived in 1542 at Massawa on the Red Sea and turned the tide in favor of its Christian allies. Portuguese attempts thereafter to bring Ethiopian Christianity into the Roman Catholic church failed, and Ethiopia remained isolated, Christian, and fiercely independent.

Kingdoms of the Grasslands

As the Islamic wave spread across north Africa, it sent ripples across the Sahara, not in the form of invading armies but at first in the merchants and travelers who trod the dusty and ancient caravan routes toward the savanna. Africa had three important "coasts" of contact: the Atlantic, the Indian Ocean, and the savanna on the southern rim of the Sahara.

On the edge of the desert, where several resource zones came together, African states such as Ghana had already formed by the 8th century by exchanging gold from the forests of west Africa for salt or dates from the Sahara or for goods from Mediterranean north Africa. Camels, which had been introduced from Asia to the Sahara between the 1st and 5th centuries C.E., had greatly improved the possibilities of trade, but these animals, which thrived in arid and semiarid environments, could not live in the humid forest zones because of disease. Thus, the Sahel, the extensive grassland belt at the southern edge of the Sahara, became a point of exchange between the forests to the south and north Africa—an active border area where ideas, trade, and people from the Sahara and beyond arrived in increasing numbers. Along the Sahel, several African states developed between the trading cities, taking advantage of their position as intermediaries in the trade. But their location on the open plains of the dry Sahel also meant that these states were subject to attack and periodic droughts.

Founded probably in the 3rd century C.E., Ghana rose to power by taxing the salt and gold exchanged within its borders. By the 10th century, its rulers had converted to Islam, and Ghana was at the height of its power. At a time when William the Conqueror could muster perhaps 5000 troops for his invasion of England, Muslim accounts reported that the king of Ghana could field an army many times that size. Eventually, however, Almoravid armies invaded Ghana from north Africa in 1076. The kingdom survived, but its power declined. By the beginning of the 13th century, new states had risen in the savanna to take Ghana's place of leadership.

Sudanic States

There were several Sudanic kingdoms, and even during the height of Ghana's power, neighboring and competing states persisted, such as Takrur on the Senegal River to the west and Gao (on the Niger River) to the east. Before we deal with the most important kingdoms that followed Ghana, it is useful to review some of the elements these states had in common.

In the Sahel grasslands, several powerful states emerged that combined Islamic religion and culture with local practices. The kingdoms of Mali and Songhay and the Hausa states were African adaptations of Islam and its fusion with African traditions.

Trade Routes in Africa

African Empires in the Western Sudan

Map 8.1 Empires of the Western Sudan

The Sudanic states often had a patriarch or council of elders of a particular family or group of lineages as leaders. Usually these states had a territorial core area in which the people were of the same linguistic or ethnic background, but their power extended over subordinate communities. These were conquest states, which drew on the taxes, tribute, and military support of the subordinate areas, lineages, and villages. The effective control of subordinate societies and the legal or informal control of their sovereignty are the usual definition of empires. The Sudanic states of Ghana, Mali, and Songhay fit that definition (Map 8.1).

The rulers of these states were considered sacred and were surrounded by rituals that separated them from their subjects. With the conversion of the rulers of Ghana and Takrur after the 10th century, Islam was used to reinforce indigenous ideas of kingship, so that Islam became something of a royal cult. Much of the population never converted, and the Islamicized ruling families also drew on their traditional powers to fortify their rule.

Several savanna states rose among the various peoples in the Sudan. We can trace the development and culture of two of the most important, Mali and Songhay, as examples of the fusion of Islamic and indigenous African cultures within the context of trade and military expansion.

The Empire of Mali and Sundiata, the "Lion Prince"

Travel Accounts vs. Oral History
CASE STUDY

The empire of Mali, centered between the Senegal and Niger rivers, was the creation of the Malinke peoples, who in the 13th century broke away from the control of Ghana, which was by then in decline. In Mali the old forms of kingship were reinforced by Islam. As in many of the Sudanic states, the rulers supported Islam by building mosques, attending public prayers, and supporting preachers. In return, sermons to the faithful emphasized obedience and support of the king. Mali became a model of these Islamicized Sudanic kingdoms. The economic basis of society in the Mali Empire was agriculture. This was combined with an active tradition of trade in many products, although like Ghana, Mali also depended on its access to gold-producing areas to the south. Malinke merchants, or **juula** (JOO-luh), formed small partnerships and groups to carry out trade throughout the area. They spread beyond the borders of the empire and throughout much of west Africa.

The beginning of Malinke expansion is attributed to **Sundiata** (sometimes written Sunjata), a brilliant leader whose exploits were celebrated in a great oral tradition. The **griots,** professional oral historians who also served as keepers of traditions and advisors to kings, began their epic histories of Mali with Sundiata, the "Lion Prince."

> Listen then sons of Mali, children of the black people, listen to my word, for I am going to tell you of Sundiata, the father of the Bright Country, of the savanna land, the ancestor of those who draw the bow, the master of a hundred vanquished kings. . . . He was great among kings, he was peerless among men; he was beloved of God because he was the last of the great conquerors.

After a difficult childhood, Sundiata emerged from a period of interfamily and regional fighting to create a unified state. Oral histories ascribed to him the creation of the basic rules and relationships of Malinke society and the outline of the government of the empire of Mali. He became the mansa, or emperor. It was said that Sundiata "divided up the world," which meant that he was considered the originator of social arrangements. Sixteen clans of free people were entitled to bear arms and carry the bow and quiver of arrows as the symbol of their status, five clans were devoted to religious duties, and four clans were specialists such as blacksmiths and griots. Such clan arrangements were traditional among the peoples of the savanna and had existed in ancient Ghana, but now Sundiata was credited with their origins. Although he created the political institutions of rule that allowed for great regional and ethnic differences in the federated provinces, he also stationed garrisons to maintain loyalty and security. Travel was secure and crime was severely punished, as **Ibn Batuta,** the Arab traveler, reported: "Of all peoples," he said, "the Blacks are those who most hate injustice, and their emperor pardons none who is guilty of

juula [JOO-luh] Malinke merchants; formed small partnerships to carry out trade throughout Mali Empire; eventually spread throughout much of west Africa.

Sundiata The "Lion Prince"; a member of the Keita clan; created a unified state that became the Mali Empire; died about 1260.

griots Professional oral historians who served as keepers of traditions and advisors to kings within the Mali Empire.

Ibn Batuta (b. 1304) Arab traveler who described African societies and cultures in his travel records.

it." The security of travelers and their goods was an essential element in a state where commerce played so important a role.

Sundiata died about 1260, but his successors expanded the borders of Mali until it controlled most of the Niger valley almost to the Atlantic coast. A sumptuous court was established and hosted a large number of traders. Mali grew wealthy from the trade. Perhaps the most famous of Sundiata's successors was Mansa Kankan Musa (c. 1312–1337), whose pilgrimage to Mecca in 1324 brought the attention of the Muslim world to Mali, as was described in the beginning of this chapter. Mansa Musa's trip had other consequences as well. From Mecca he brought back poet and architect Ishak al-Sahili, who came from Muslim Spain. The architect directed the building of several important mosques, and eventually a distinctive form of Sudanic architecture developed that made use of beaten clay. This can still be seen in the great mosque of Jenne (Figure 8.3). Mali's contact with the outer world brought change and innovation.

The Catalan Map

City Dwellers and Villagers

The cities of the western Sudan began to resemble those of north Africa, but with a distinctive local architectural style. The towns were commercial and often included craft specialists and a resident foreign merchant community. The military expansion of states such as Ghana, Mali, and later Songhay contributed to their commercial success because the power of the state protected traders. A cosmopolitan court life developed as merchants and scholars were attracted by the power and protection of Mali. Mandinka traders ranged across the Sudan and exploited their position as intermediaries. Cities of commercial exchange flourished, such as Jenne and **Timbuktu,** which lay just off the flood plain on the great bend in the Niger River. Timbuktu was reported to have a population of 50,000, and by the 14th century, its great Sankore mosque contained a library and an associated university where scholars, jurists, and Muslim theologians studied. The book was the symbol of civilization in the Islamic world, and it was said that the book trade in Timbuktu was the most lucrative business.

Timbuktu Port city of Mali; located just off the flood plain on the great bend in the Niger River; population of 50,000; contained a library and university.

For most people in the empire of Mali and the other Sudanic states, life was not centered on the royal court, the great mosque, or long-distance trade but rather on the agricultural cycle and the village. Making a living from the land was the preoccupation of most people, and about 80 percent

The Maghrib and West Africa

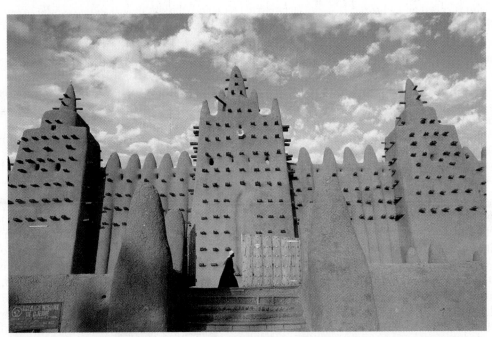

Figure 8.3 The spread of Islam in Africa is represented by the great mosque at Jenne on the Niger River in what is now the Republic of Mali. Jenne was a major center of iron working and trade. Along with Timbuktu, 200 miles to the north, it was also a center of Islamic learning and scholarship.

The Great Oral Tradition and the Epic of Sundiata

Oral traditions take various forms. Some are simply the shared stories of a family or people, but in many west African societies, the mastery of oral traditions is a skill practiced by *griots*. Although today's griots are professional musicians and bards, historically they held important places at the courts of west African kingdoms. The epic of Sundiata, the great ruler of Mali, has been passed down orally for centuries. In the following excerpts from a version collected among the Mandingo (Malinke) people of Guinea by the African scholar D. T. Niane, the role of the griot and the advantages of oral traditions are outlined.

We are now coming to the great moments in the life of Sundiata. The exile will end and another sun will rise. It is the sun of Sundiata. Griots know the history of kings and kingdoms and that is why they are the best counsellors of kings. Every king wants to have a singer to perpetuate his memory, for it is the griot who rescues the memories of kings from oblivion, as men have short memories. Kings have prescribed destinies just like men, and seers who probe the future know it. They have knowledge of the future, whereas we griots are depositories of the knowledge of the past. But whoever knows the history of a country can read its future.

Other peoples use writing to record the past, but this invention has killed the faculty of memory among them. They do not feel the past any more, for writing lacks the warmth of the human voice. With them everybody thinks he knows, whereas learning should be a secret. The prophets did not write and their words have been all the more vivid as a result. What paltry learning is that which is concealed in dumb books!

The following excerpt describes the preparation for a major battle fought by Sundiata against the forces of Soumaoro, king of the Sossos, who had taken control of Mali and who is called an evil sorcerer in the epic. Note the interweaving of proverbs, the presence of aspects of Muslim and animist religion, the celebration of Sundiata's prowess, the recurring references to iron, and the high value placed on the cavalry, the key to military power in the savanna. Note how the story of Alexander the Great inspires this "African Alexander."

Every man to his own land! If it is foretold that your destiny should be fulfilled in such and such a land, men can do nothing against it. Mansa Tounkara could not keep Sundiata back because the destiny of Songolon's son was bound up with that of Mali. Neither the jealousy of a cruel stepmother, nor her wickedness could alter for a moment the course of great destiny.

The snake, man's enemy, is not long-lived, yet the serpent that lives hidden will surely die old. Djata (Sundiata) was strong enough now to face his enemies. At the age of eighteen he had the stateliness of the lion and the strength of the buffalo. His voice carried authority, his eyes were live coals, his arm was iron, he was the husband of power.

Moussa Tounkara, king of Mema, gave Sundiata half of his army. The most valiant came forward of their own free will to follow Sundiata in the great adventure. The cavalry of Mema, which he had fashioned himself, formed his iron squadron. Sundiata, dressed in the Muslim fashion of Mema, left the town at the head of his small but redoubtable army. The whole population sent their best wishes with him. He was surrounded by five messengers from Mali, and Manding Bory [Sundiata's brother] rode proudly at his side. The horsemen of Mema formed behind Djata a bristling iron squadron. The troop took the direction of Wagadou, for Djata did not have enough troops to confront Soumaoro directly, and so the king of Mema advised him to go to Wagadou and take half the men of the king, Soumaba Cissé. A swift messenger had been sent there and so the king of Wagadou came out in person to meet Sundiata and his troops. He gave Sundiata half of his cavalry and blessed the weapons. Then Manding Bory said to his brother, "Djata, do you think yourself able to face Soumaoro now?"

"No matter how small a forest may be, you can always find there sufficient fibers to tie up a man. Numbers mean nothing; it is worth that counts. With my cavalry I shall clear myself a path to Mali."

Djata gave out his orders. They would head south, skirting Soumaoro's kingdom. The first objective to be reached was Tabon, the iron-gated town in the midst of the mountains, for Sundiata had promised Fran Kamara that he would pass Tabon before returning to Mali. He hoped to find that his childhood companion had become king. It was a forced march and during the halts the divines, Singbin Mara Cissé and Mandjan Bérété, related to Sundiata the history of Alexander the Great and several other heroes, but of all of them Sundiata preferred Alexander, the king of gold and silver, who crossed the world from west to east. He wanted to outdo his prototype both in the extent of his territory and in the wealth of his treasury.

QUESTIONS Can oral traditions be used like other sources? Even if they are not entirely true, do they have historical value? Judging from this epic, how did people of the Sudan define the qualities of a king? What aspects of the epic reveal contacts between this part of Africa and the wider world?

of the villagers lived by farming. This was a difficult life. The soils of the savanna were sandy and shallow. Plows were rarely used. The villagers were people of the hoe who looked to the skies in the spring for the first rains to start their planting. Rice in the river valleys, millet, sorghums, some wheat, fruits, and vegetables provided the basis of daily life in the village and supplied the caravan trade. Even a large farm rarely exceeded 10 acres, and most were much smaller. Clearing land often was done communally, accompanied by feasts and competition, but the farms belonged to families and were worked by them. A man with two wives and several unmarried sons could work more land than a man with one wife and a smaller family. Polygamy, the practice of having multiple wives, was common in the region, and it remains so today.

Given the difficulties of the soil, the periodic droughts, insect pests, storage problems, and the limitations of technology, the farmers of the Sudanic states—by the methods of careful cultivation, crop rotation, and in places such as Timbuktu, the use of irrigation—were able to provide for their people the basic foods that supported them and the imperial states on which they were based. The hoe and the bow became symbols of the common people of the savanna states.

The Songhay Kingdom

As the power of Mali began to wane, a successor state from within the old empire was already beginning to emerge. The people of **Songhay** (sohng-HEYE) dominated the middle areas of the Niger valley. Traditionally, the society of Songhay was made up of "masters of the soil," that is, farmers, herders, and "masters of the waters," or fishers. Songhay had begun to form in the 7th century as an independent kingdom, perhaps under a Berber dynasty. By 1010, a capital was established at Gao on the Niger River, and the rulers had become Muslims, although the majority of the population remained pagan. Dominated by Mali for a while, by the 1370s Songhay had established its independence again and began to thrive as new sources of gold from the west African forests began to pass through its territory. Gao became a large city with a resident foreign merchant community and several mosques. Under a dynamic leader, Sunni Ali (1464–1492), the empire of Songhay was forged.

Sunni Ali was a great tactical commander and a ruthless leader. His cavalry expanded the borders and seized the traditional trading cities of Timbuktu and Jenne. The middle Niger valley fell under his control, and he developed a system of provincial administration to mobilize recruits for the army and rule the far-flung conquests. Although apparently a Muslim, he met any challenge to his authority even when it came from the Muslim scholars of Timbuktu, whom he persecuted. A line of Muslim rulers who took the military title *askia* succeeded him. These rulers, especially **Muhammad the Great,** extended the boundaries of the empire so that by the mid-16th century Songhay dominated the central Sudan.

Life in the Songhay Empire followed many of the patterns established in the previous savanna states. The fusion of Islamic and pagan populations and traditions continued. Muslim clerics and jurists sometimes were upset by the pagan beliefs and practices that continued among the population, and even more by the local interpretation of Islamic law. They wanted to impose a strict interpretation of the law of Islam and were shocked that men and women mixed freely in the markets and streets, that women went unveiled.

Songhay remained the dominant power in the region until the end of the 16th century. In 1591, a Muslim army from Morocco, equipped with muskets, crossed the Sahara and defeated the vastly larger forces of Songhay. This sign of weakness stimulated internal revolts against the ruling family, and eventually the parts of the old empire broke away.

The demise of the Songhay imperial structure did not mean the end of the political and cultural tradition of the western Sudan. Other states that combined Muslim and pagan traditions rose among the **Hausa** peoples of northern Nigeria, based on cities such as Kano and Katsina. The earliest Muslim ruler of Kano took control in the late 14th century and turned the city into a center of Muslim learning. In Kano and other Hausa cities of the region, an urbanized royal court in a fortified capital ruled over the animistic villages, where the majority of the population lived. With powerful cavalry forces these states extended their rule and protected their active trade in salt, grains, and cloth. Although these later Islamicized African states tended to be small and their goals were local, they reproduced many of the social, political, and religious forms of the great empires of the grasslands.

Beyond the Sudan, Muslim penetration came in various forms. Merchants became established in most of the major trading cities, and religious communities developed in each of these, often associated with particular families. Networks of trade and contact were established widely over the region as merchants and groups of pastoralists established their outposts in the area of Guinea. Muslim traders, herders, warriors, and religious leaders became important minorities in these segmented African societies, composed of elite families, occupational groups, free people, and slaves. Intermarriage often took place, but Muslim influence varied widely from region to region.

Leo Africanus's Description of West Africa

Songhay   [sohng-HEYE] Successor state to Mali; dominated middle reaches of Niger valley; formed as independent kingdom under a Berber dynasty; capital at Gao; reached imperial status under Sunni Ali (1464–1492).

Muhammad the Great   Extended the boundaries of the Songhay Empire; Islamic ruler of the mid-16th century.

Hausa   Peoples of northern Nigeria; formed states following the demise of Songhay Empire that combined Muslim and pagan traditions.

Nevertheless, families of traders and lineages that became known as specialists in Muslim law spread widely through the region, so that by the 18th century Muslim minorities were scattered widely throughout west Africa, even in areas where no Islamicized state had emerged.

Political and Social Life in the Sudanic States

We can generalize from these brief descriptions of Mali and Songhay about the nature of the Sudanic states. The village communities, clans, and various ethnic groups continued to organize many aspects of life in the savanna. The development of unified states provided an overarching structure that allowed the various groups and communities to coexist. The large states usually represented the political aims and power of a particular group and often of a dominant family. Many states pointed to the immigrant origins of the ruling families, and in reality the movement and fusion of populations were constant features in the Sudan. Islam provided a universalistic faith that served the interests of many groups. Common religion and law provided solidarity and trust to the merchants who lived in the cities and whose caravans brought goods to and from the savanna. The ruling families used Islamic titles, such as *emir* or *caliph,* to reinforce their authority, and they surrounded themselves with literate Muslim advisors and scribes, who aided in government administration. The Muslim concept of a ruler who united civil and religious authority reinforced traditional ideas of kingship. It is also important to note that in Africa, as elsewhere in the world, the formation of states heightened social differences and made these societies more hierarchical.

In all the Sudanic states, Islam was fused with the existing traditions and beliefs. Rulership and authority were still based on the ability to intercede with local spirits, and although Sundiata and Sunni Ali were nominally Muslim, they did not ignore the traditional basis of their rule. For this reason, Islam in these early stages in the Sudan tended to accommodate pagan practice and belief. Large proportions of the populations of Mali and Songhay never converted to Islam, and those who did convert often maintained many of the old beliefs as well.

We can see this fusion of traditions clearly in the position of women. Several Sudanic societies were matrilineal, and some recognized the role of women within the lines of kinship, contrary to the normal patrilineal customs inscribed in the **Sharia,** or Islamic law. As in the case of Songhay, north African visitors to the Sudan were shocked by the easy familiarity between men and women and the freedom enjoyed by women.

Finally, slavery and the slave trade between black Africa and the rest of the Islamic world had a major impact on women and children in these societies. Various forms of slavery and dependent labor had existed in Africa before Islam was introduced. Although we know little about slavery in central Africa in this period, slavery had been a marginal aspect of the Sudanic states. Africans had been enslaved by others before, and Nubian (African) slaves had been known in the classical world, but with the Muslim conquests of north Africa and commercial penetration to the south, slavery became a more widely diffused phenomenon, and a slave trade in Africans developed on a new scale.

In theory, Muslims viewed slavery as a stage in the process of conversion—a way of preparing pagans to become Muslims—but in reality, conversion did not guarantee freedom. Slaves in the Islamic world were used in a variety of occupations, as domestic servants and laborers, but they were also used as soldiers and administrators who, having no local ties and affiliations, were considered to be dependent on and thus trustworthy by their masters. Slaves were also used as eunuchs and concubines, hence the emphasis on enslaving women and children. The trade caravans from the Sahel across the Sahara often transported slaves as well as gold, and as we shall see, other slave trade routes developed from the African interior to the east African coast.

Frequently the children of slave mothers were freed and integrated into Muslim society. Although this custom was positive in one sense, it also meant a constant demand for more slaves to replace those freed. Estimates of the volume of the trans-Saharan slave trade vary widely. One scholar places the total at 4.8 million, with another 2.4 million sent to the Muslim ports on the Indian Ocean coast. Actual figures may have been considerably lower, but the trade extended over 700 years and affected a large area. It was one more way in which Islamic civilization changed sub-Saharan Africa.

Sharia Islamic law; defined among other things the patrilineal nature of Islamic inheritance.

The Architecture of Faith

The spread of Islam eventually created spiritual, commercial, and cultural bonds between west Africa and the Middle East and especially north Africa and Spain. The process of Islam's expansion and its local adaptation is apparent in the distinctive architectural style of west African mosques. Built usually of clay, incorporating wood beams for support and decoration, with a *mirab* tower and an open courtyard, these places of worship created spaces of simple elegance with local materials that reflect ethnic and regional differences. West African mosques vary considerably from the traditional patterns of the Middle East and south Asia. Mosques like the simple buildings among the Dogon people, or the elabo-rate Sankoré mosque at Timbuktu begun in 1324 by Mansa Musa and later the center of a university, reflect the integration of Islam into African life.

QUESTIONS The architectural styles of west African mosques differ from the classic models of the Middle East. In what way does that suggest that Islam's entry to the region was gradual and transmitted by merchants and traders? In what ways do the mosques of West Africa reflect local conditions and practices? What functions beside prayer did mosques play and how did their construction tie west Africa to a wider world?

Dogon Village mosque in Kani-Kombole, Mali, west Africa.

Domed Middle Eastern mosques shown in the skyline of Yazd, Iran.

The Swahili Coast of East Africa

While the kingdoms of west Africa came under the influence of Islam from across the Sahara, another center of Islamic civilization was developing on the seaboard and offshore islands of Africa's Indian Ocean coast (Map 8.2). Along that coast, extending south from the horn of Africa to modern-day Mozambique, a string of Islamicized trading cities developed that reflected their cosmopolitan contacts with trading partners from Arabia, Persia, India, and China. Islam provided the residents of these towns a universal set of ethics and beliefs that made their maritime contacts easier, but in east Africa, as in the savanna kingdoms of west Africa, Islamization was slow to reach the general population. When it did, the result often was a compromise between indigenous ways and the new faith.

A string of Islamicized African ports tied to the trade across the Indian Ocean dotted the east African coast. Although these cities were Islamicized, African customs and the Bantu Swahili language remained so strong that they represented a cultural fusion, mostly limited to the coast.

The Coastal Trading Ports

A 1st-century Greek account of the Indian Ocean, *The Periplus of the Erythraean Sea,* mentioned some ports in east Africa but was vague about whether the inhabitants were Africans or immigrants from the Arabian peninsula. From that century to the 10th century, the wave of Bantu migration had clearly reached the east African interior. Bantu-speaking herders in the north and farmers in the south mixed with older populations in the region. Other peoples were also moving to the African coast. Contact across the Indian Ocean dated back to at least the 2nd century B.C.E. From Indonesia or Malaya, seaborne immigrants settled on the large island of Madagascar and from there introduced foods such as bananas and coconuts to the African coast. These were widely adopted

Excerpts from the Travels of Ibn Batuta in East Africa

195

Map 8.2 The Swahili Coast; African Monsoon Routes and Major Trade Routes

Zenj [zehnj] Arabic term for the east African coast.

and spread rapidly along the coast and into central Africa. Small coastal villages of fishers and farmers, making rough pottery and working iron, dotted this coast. By the 8th and 9th centuries, visitors and refugees from Oman and the Persian Gulf had established themselves at some of these villages, attracted by the possibilities of trade with the land of **Zenj** (zehnj), the Arabic term for the east African coast.

By the 13th century, a string of urbanized east African trading ports had developed along the coast. These towns shared the common Bantu-based and Arabic-influenced Swahili (which means "coastal") language and other cultural traits, although they were governed by separate Muslim ruling families. Towns such as Mogadishu, Mombasa, Malindi, Kilwa, Pate, and Zanzibar eventually contained mosques, tombs, and palaces of cut stone and coral. Ivory, gold, iron, slaves, and exotic animals were exported from these ports in exchange for silks from Persia and porcelain from China for the ruling Muslim families. The Arab traveler Ibn Batuta was impressed with the beauty and refinement of these towns. He described Kilwa as "one of the most beautiful and well constructed towns in the world" and was also impressed by the pomp and luxury of its ruler. Kilwa's advantage was its access to the gold coming from the interior and the fact that it was the furthest point south from which the ships sailing from India could hope to return in a single monsoon season.

From the 13th to the 15th centuries, Kilwa flourished in the context of international trade, but it was not alone; about 30 of these port towns eventually dotted the coast. They were tied to each other by an active coastal commerce and, in a few places, to the interior by a caravan trade, although it was usually Africans who brought the goods to the coast. Some Chinese ports sent goods directly to Africa in the 13th century, and as late as 1417 and 1431, large, state-sponsored expeditions sailing directly from China stopped at the east African coast to load ivory, gold, and rare woods. The Chinese discontinued such contact after 1431, and goods from China came to the coast thereafter in the ships of Arab or Indian traders.

The Mixture of Cultures on the Swahili Coast

The Islamic influence in these towns promoted long-distance commerce. The 13th century was a period of great Islamic expansion, and as that faith spread eastward to India and Indonesia, it provided a religious bond of trust and law that facilitated trade throughout ports of the Indian Ocean. The ruling families in the east African trading ports built mosques and palaces; the mosque at Mogadishu was begun in 1231. Many of these ruling families claimed to be descendants of immigrants from Shiraz in Persia—a claim intended to legitimize their position and orthodoxy. In fact, some evidence indicates that the original Muslim families had emigrated to the Somali coast and from there to other towns farther south. The institutions and forms of the Muslim world operated in these cities. Whereas the rulers and merchants tended to be Muslim, the majority of the population on the east African coast, and perhaps even in the towns themselves, retained their previous beliefs and culture.

African culture remained strong throughout the area. The Swahili language was essentially a Bantu language containing a large number of Arabic words, although many of these words were not incorporated until the 16th century. The language was written in an Arabic script some time before the 13th century; the ruling families could also converse in Arabic. Islam itself penetrated very little into the interior among the hunters, pastoralists, and farmers. Even the areas of the coast near the trading towns remained largely unaffected. In the towns, the mud and thatch houses of the non-Muslim common peoples surrounded the stone and coral buildings of the Muslim elite. Islamization was to some extent class-based. Still, a culture developed that fused Islamic and traditional elements. For example, family lineage was traced both through the maternal line, which controlled property (the traditional African practice), and through the paternal line, as was the Muslim custom. Swahili culture was a dynamic hybrid, and the Swahili people spread their language and culture along the coast of east Africa.

By the time the Portuguese arrived on this coast around 1500, the Swahili culture was widely diffused. Kilwa was no longer the predominant city, and the focus of trade had shifted to Malindi and Mombasa on the Kenya coast, but the commerce across the Indian Ocean continued. Eventually, the Portuguese raided Kilwa and Mombasa in an attempt to take control of trade. Their outpost on Mozambique and their control of Sofala put much of the gold trade in their hands. Although the Portuguese built a major outpost at Fort Jesus in Mombasa in 1592, they were never able to control the trade on the northern Swahili coast. The east African patterns, as established by 1500, persisted even more than those of the Sudanic kingdoms. In some areas like the Swahili coast and the West African savanna, Islam became a dominant cultural force. In other areas such as the forest region of West Africa, Muslims remained a minority, and in other areas like the central African forests Islam hardly penetrated at all.

A Description of the Coasts of East Africa and Malabar

Peoples of the Forest and Plains

As important as the Islamic impact was on the societies of the savanna and the east African coast, other African peoples in the continent's interior and in the forests of west Africa were following their own trajectories of development. We must emphasize that African societies were diverse. By 1000 C.E., most of these societies were based on a varied agriculture, sometimes combined with herding, and most societies used iron tools and weapons. Many were still organized in small village communities. In various places, however, states had formed. Some of them began to resolve the problems of integrating large territories under a single government and ruling subject peoples. Whereas Egypt, Kush, and Ethiopia had developed writing and other areas borrowed the Arabic script, many sub-Saharan African societies were preliterate and transmitted their knowledge, skills, and traditions by oral methods and direct instruction. The presence or absence of writing has often been used as a measure of civilization by Western observers, but as in pre-Columbian Peru, various African societies made great strides in the arts, building, and statecraft, sometimes in the context of highly urbanized settings, without a system of writing.

Across central Africa, kingdoms developed that were supported by complex agrarian societies capable of great artistic achievements. At Benin, in the Kongo, in the Yoruba city-states, and at Great Zimbabwe, royal authority—often considered divinely inspired—led to the creation of powerful states.

Artists and Kings: Yoruba and Benin

In the forests of central Nigeria, terra-cotta objects of a realistic and highly stylized form have been discovered near the village of Nok. These objects, most of which date from about 500 B.C.E. to 200 C.E., reveal considerable artistic skill. The inhabitants of ancient Nok and its region practiced agriculture and used iron tools. They remain something of a mystery, but it appears that their artistic traditions spread widely through the forest areas and influenced other peoples. Nevertheless, there is a long gap in the historical and archeological record between the Nok sculptures and the renewed flourishing of artistic traditions in the region after about 1000 C.E.

Among the Yoruba-speaking peoples of Nigeria, at the city of Ile-Ife (eel-EE-fuh), remarkable terra-cotta and bronze portrait heads of past rulers were produced in the period after 1200 C.E. The lifelike quality of these portraits and the skill of their execution place them among the greatest achievements of African art (Figure 8.4). The artists of Ile-Ife also worked in wood and ivory. Much of the art seems to be associated with kings and the authority of kingship. Ile-Ife, like other Yoruba states, seems to have been an agricultural society supported by a peasantry and dominated by a ruling family and an aristocracy. Ile-Ife was considered by many peoples in the region to be the original cultural center, and many of them traced their own beginnings to it.

Yoruba origins are obscure. Ile-Ife was seen as the holiest city of the Yoruba, their place of birth. Another legend maintained by the royal historians was that Oduduwa, a son of the king of

Figure 8.4 In the 13th and 14th centuries, Ile-Ife artists worked in terracotta as well as bronze and produced skilled individual portraits like this one.

(The Brooklyn Museum of Art.)

Two Transitions in the History of World Population

Africa and the ancient Americas are two regions that make clear the difficulty of establishing the past size and structure of populations. Estimates based on fragmentary sources, the amount of available resources, and analysis of agricultural or hunting techniques have been used as rough guesses about population size. The results often are inadequate or controversial, but historians believe that the question is important. **Demography,** the study of population, has increasingly become a valued tool of historical inquiry. Clearly, unless we know the size, density, age structure, health, and reproductive capacity of a population, it is difficult to understand many aspects of its society, politics, and economy. In the contemporary world, most nations conduct periodic censuses to assess the present situation of their populations and to plan for the future. Before the mid-18th century, when census-taking became a regular procedure, population estimates and counts were sporadic and usually inaccurate. Estimating populations in the past, especially in nonliterate societies, is a highly speculative exercise in which archeological evidence and estimates of productive capacity of agricultural practices and technology are used. The earliest date for a population estimate with a margin of error less than 20 percent is probably 1750.

The history of human population can be divided into two basic periods: a long era—almost all of human history—of very slow growth and a very short period—about 250 years from 1750 to the present—of very rapid growth. For most of this history, the human population was very small and grew very slowly. Before agriculture was developed, the hunting-and-gathering economies of the world's populations supported 5 to 10 million people, if modern studies of such populations can be used as a guide. After about 8000 B.C.E., when plants and animals were domesticated, population began to increase more rapidly but still at a modest level. Agriculture pro-

> "At present, the world's population is growing because of a moderate rate of growth in the industrialized nations and a high rate in the developing countries."

vided a more secure and larger food supply, but population concentration in villages and towns may have made people more susceptible to disease and thus reduced their numbers. Other historians believe that the settled agricultural life also led to intensified warfare (because of the struggle for land and water) and increasing social stratification within societies.

Still, the Neolithic revolution and the development of agriculture stimulated population growth. It was the first major transition in the history of world population. One estimate, based on Roman and Chinese population counts and some informed guesses about the rest of the world, is an annual growth rate of about 0.36 per million. By 1 C.E., the world population may have been about 300 million people. It increased between 1 C.E. and 1750 C.E. to about 500 million people. We should bear in mind that during this period of general increase, there were always areas that suffered decline, sometimes drastic, because of wars, epidemics, or natural catastrophes. The disastrous decline of American Indian populations after contact with Europeans, caused by disease, conquest, and social disruption, is a case in point. The effect of the slave trade on Africa, though still debated, is another. Sharp population changes usually resulted in profound social and cultural adjustments. Some scholars argue that the slave trade had just such an impact on social and political patterns in Africa.

A second and extremely important transition took place between the mid-17th and the mid-18th centuries. Initially based on new food resources, this transition often is associated with the Industrial Revolution, when new sources of energy were harnessed. The growth rate greatly increased during this period in the countries most affected. Between 1750 and 1800, the world population grew at a rate of more than 4 percent a year to more than a billion people. By the mid-20th century, the world growth rate had tripled, and by 1990 world population had risen to more than 5 billion.

This **demographic transition** took place first in Europe and is still more characteristic of the developed world. Most premodern agrarian economies were characterized by a balance between the

demography The study of population.

demographic transition Shift to low birth rate, low infant death rate, stable population; first emerged in western Europe and United States in late 19th century.

Mecca, migrated from the east and settled in Yoruba. Modern historians have suggested that the real origins were perhaps Meroë and Nubia, or at least in the savanna south of the Sahara. In any case, the Yoruba spoke a non-Bantu language of the west African Kwa family and recognized a certain affinity between themselves and neighboring peoples, such as the Hausa, who spoke Afro-Asian languages.

The Yoruba were organized in small city-states, each controlling a radius of perhaps 50 miles. The Yoruba were highly urbanized, although many of the town inhabitants farmed in the surrounding countryside. These city-states developed under the strong authority of regional kings, who were considered divine. A vast royal court that included secondary wives, musicians, magicians, and bodyguards of soldier-slaves surrounded the king. His rule was not absolute, however. We can use the example of the Yoruba state of Oyo, which had emerged by the 14th century. Its king, the alafin, controlled subject peoples through "princes" in the provinces, drawn from local lineages, who were allowed to exercise traditional rule as long as they continued to pay tribute to Oyo. In the capital, a council of state, made up of nobles from the seven city districts, advised the annual number of births and deaths; both were high. Life expectancy usually was less than 35 years, and the high mortality was compensated by high fertility; that is, women had many children. Improvements in medicine, hygiene, diet, and the general standard of living contributed to a decrease in mortality in the 18th century. This allowed populations to begin to grow at a faster rate. By the 19th century in most of western Europe, the decline in mortality was followed by a decline in fertility brought about by contraception. In some countries such as France, these two transitions took place at about the same time, so population growth was limited. In much of Europe, however, the decline in fertility lagged behind the decrease in mortality, so there was a period of rapid population growth. Until the 1920s, population growth in western Europe and the United States was higher than in the rest of the world, especially in the less industrialized countries. In recent times, that situation has been reversed.

Some demographers believe that demographic transition is part of the process of shifting from a basically agrarian society to an industrial, urbanized one and that the improvements in medicine, technology, and higher standards of living will necessarily result in a change to a modern demographic structure. They believe that a decreasing need for children as part of the family economic unit, laws against child labor, and state intervention in family planning will eventually lower the world birth rate and decrease the pressure of population on economic growth. This assumption remains to be proved, and responses may vary greatly from one region of the world to another because of economic conditions and cultural attitudes about proper family size.

Finally, we should also note that responses to demographic transition can vary greatly according to historical conditions. In the 18th and 19th centuries, Europe resolved the problem of population growth with an enormous wave of emigration to the Americas, Australia, and various colonies around the globe. Present-day political circumstances make this solution less possible, although the new waves of migration in the global economy may indicate that the process is continuing.

Still, it is clear that a demographic transition has begun to take place in the developing world of Latin America, Africa, and Asia. Mortality has dropped very rapidly since 1950 because of modern medical technology, and life expectancy has doubled. To cite a single example, in Sri Lanka the mortality rate was almost cut in half between 1945 and 1952 simply by eliminating malarial mosquitoes. Fertility has declined in many places in Asia and Latin America, but in Africa, where children continue to have an important economic and social role in the extended family, it remains high. It is difficult to project what demographic transitions will take place in these areas of the world. However, all countries are faced with the problem of balancing their population's growth against the ability of the society to feed and provide an adequate standard of living to the people.

At present, the world's population is growing because of a moderate rate of growth in the industrialized nations and a high rate in the developing countries. In the 1970s, demographer Ansley Coale pointed out that the rate of growth, about 2 percent a year, is 100 times greater than it had been for most of human history. At this rate the world's population would be multiplied by 1000 every 350 years. The results of such growth would be disastrous. Coale concluded that the present period of growth is transitory. Some people who are concerned with rapid population growth believe that the solution is to limit population growth in the developing nations by state intervention, through incentives to have smaller families and education about birth control. Others believe that a redistribution of resources from rich nations to poor nations would alleviate the human misery created by population pressure and eventually lead to political and social conditions that would contribute to a gradual lowering of the birth rates. Clearly, demographic questions must always be set in political, economic, and social contexts.

QUESTIONS Why do nations differ in their need to control population growth? Why has the rate of population growth varied in different areas of the world? Is overpopulation essentially a biological, social, or political problem?

---

ruler and limited his power, and the Ogboni, or secret society of religious and political leaders, reviewed decisions of the king and the council. The union of civil and supernatural powers in the person of the ruler was the basis of power. The highly urbanized nature of Yoruba society and the flourishing of artisan traditions within these towns bear some similarity to those of the city-states of medieval Italy or Germany.

Patterns similar to those in the Yoruba city-states could be found among Edo peoples to the east of Yoruba. A large city-state called **Benin** was formed sometime in the 14th century. Under Ewuare the Great (r. 1440–1473), Benin's control extended from the Niger River to the coast near modern Lagos. Benin City was described by early European visitors in the 16th century as a city of great population and broad avenues. The oba, or ruler, lived in a large royal compound surrounded by a great entourage, and his authority was buttressed by ritual and ceremony.

That authority was also the theme of the magnificent artistic output in ivory and cast bronze that became characteristic of Benin. Tradition had it that Iguegha (eh-GUAY-gah), an artisan in

Benin Powerful city-state (in present-day Nigeria) which came into contact with the Portuguese in 1485 but remained relatively free of European influence; important commercial and political entity until the 19th century.

bronze casting, was sent from Ile-Ife to introduce the techniques of making bronze sculptures. Benin then developed its own distinctive style, less naturalistic than that of Ile-Ife but no less impressive. Celebration of the powers and majesty of the royal lineage as well as objects for the rituals surrounding kingship were the subjects of much of this art. When the first Europeans, the Portuguese, visited Benin in the 1480s, they were impressed by the power of the ruler and the extent of his territory. Similarly, the artists of Benin were impressed with the Portuguese, and Benin bronzes and ivories began to include representations of Portuguese soldiers and other themes that reflected the contact with outsiders (Figure 8.5).

Central African Kingdoms

South of the rain forest that stretched across Africa almost to Lake Victoria lay a broad expanse of savanna and plain, cut by several large rivers such as the Kwango and the Zambezi. From their original home in Nigeria, the Bantu peoples had spread into the southern reaches of the rain forest along the Congo River, then southward onto the southern savannas, and eventually to the east coast. By the 5th century C.E., Bantu farmers and fishers had reached beyond the Zambezi, and by the 13th century they were approaching the southern end of the continent. Mostly beyond the influence of Islam, many of these central African peoples had begun their own process of state formation by about 1000 C.E., replacing the pattern of kinship-based societies with forms of political authority based on kingship. Whether the idea of kingship developed in one place and was diffused

Kongo Kingdom, based on agriculture, formed on lower Congo River by late 15th century; capital at Mbanza Kongo; ruled by hereditary monarchy.

elsewhere or had multiple origins is unknown, but the older system based on seniority within the kinship group was replaced with rule based on the control of territory and the parallel development of rituals that reinforced the ruler's power. Several important kingdoms developed. In Katanga, the Luba peoples modified the older system of village headmen to a form of divine kinship in which the ruler and his relatives were thought to have a special power that ensured fertility of people and crops; thus, only the royal lineage was fit to rule. A sort of bureaucracy grew to administer the state, but it was hereditary, so that brothers or male children succeeded to the position. In a way, this system was a half step toward more modern concepts of bureaucracy, but it provided a way to integrate large numbers of people in a large political unit.

The Kingdoms of Kongo and Mwene Mutapa

Beginning about the 13th century, another kingdom was forming on the lower Congo River. By the late 15th century this kingdom, **Kongo,** was flourishing. On a firm agricultural base, its people also developed the skills of weaving, pottery, blacksmithing, and carving. Individual artisans, skilled in the working of wood, copper, and iron, were highly esteemed. There was a sharp division of labor between men and women. Men took responsibility for clearing the forest and scrub, producing palm oil and palm wine, building houses, hunting, and long-distance trade. Women took charge of cultivation in all its aspects, the care of domestic animals, and household duties. On the seacoast, women made salt from seawater, and they also collected the seashells that served as currency in the Kongo kingdom. The population was distributed in small family-based villages and in towns. The area around the capital, Mbanza Kongo, had a population of 60,000 to 100,000 by the early 16th century.

The kingship of the Kongo was hereditary but local chieftainships were not, and this gave the central authority power to control subordinates. In a way, the Kongo kingdom was a confederation of smaller states brought under the control of the manikongo, or king,

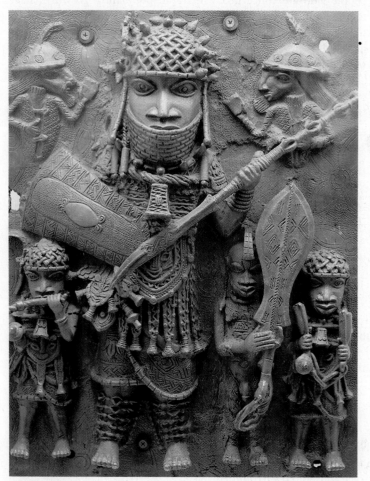

Figure 8.5 Copper plaque of Oba and retainers. African rulers often negotiated with the Portuguese on equal terms and incorporated them into local political and commercial networks. In this plaque, the presence of Portuguese retainers—the helmeted figures armed with muskets on each side of the main figure's head— were marks of the Oba's power.

and by the 15th century it was divided into eight major provinces. The word *mani* means "black-smith," and it demonstrated the importance of iron and the art of working it in its association with political and ritual power.

Farther to the east, another large Bantu confederation developed among the farming and cattle-herding Shona-speaking peoples in the region between the Zambezi and Limpopo rivers. Beginning in the 9th century C.E., migrants from the west began to build royal courts in stone, to which later immigrants added more polished constructions. There were many of these zimbabwe, or stone house, sites (about 200 have been found) that housed local rulers and subchiefs, but the largest site, called **Great Zimbabwe,** was truly impressive (Figure 8.6). It was the center of the kingdom and had a religious importance, associated with the bird of God, an eagle that served as a link between the world and the spirits. The symbol of the bird of God is found at the ruins of Great Zimbabwe and throughout the area of its control. Great Zimbabwe (not to be confused with the modern nation of Zimbabwe) included several structures, some with strong stone walls 15 feet thick and 30 feet high, a large conical tower, and extensive cut-stone architecture made without the use of mortar to join the bricks together. Observers in the 19th century suspected that Phoenicians or Arabs had built these structures, mostly because their prejudices prevented them from believing that Africans were capable of erecting such buildings, but archeologists have established that a Bantu kingdom had begun construction in stone by the 11th century C.E. and had done its most sophisticated building in the 14th and 15th centuries.

By the 15th century, a centralized state ruled from Great Zimbabwe had begun to form. It controlled a large portion of the interior of southeast Africa all the way to the Indian Ocean. Under

Great Zimbabwe Bantu confederation of Shona-speaking peoples located between Zambezi and Limpopo rivers; developed after 9th century; featured royal courts built of stone; created centralized state by 15th century; king took title of Mwene Mutapa.

Figure 8.6 Great Zimbabwe was one of several stone settlement complexes in southeastern Africa. Added to at different times, it served as the royal court of the kingdom. In their search for traces of the non-African people they believed "must" have built these massive stone structures, European explorers and treasure-seekers stripped the site of layers of artifacts that might have told more of the story of Great Zimbabwe.

a king who took the title *Mwene Mutapa* (which the Portuguese later pronounced "Monomotapa"), this kingdom experienced a short period of rapid expansion in the late 15th and 16th centuries. Its dominance over the sources of gold in the interior eventually gave it great advantages in commerce, which it developed with the Arab port of Sofala on the coast. Evidence of this trade is found in the glass beads and porcelain unearthed by archeologists at Great Zimbabwe. By the 16th century, internal divisions and rebellion had split the kingdom apart, and perhaps an emphasis on cattle as a symbol of wealth led to soil exhaustion. Control of the gold fields still provided a source of power and trade. Representatives of the Mwene Mutapa called at the east-coast ports to buy Indian textiles, and their regal bearing and fine iron weapons impressed the first Europeans who saw them. As late as the 19th century, a much smaller kingdom of Mwene Mutapa survived in the interior and provided some leadership against European encroachment, but pastoralism had come to play a central role in the lives of the Shona people who descended from the great tradition.

Global Connections

Internal Development and Global Contacts

This chapter has concentrated on the Sudanic states and the Swahili coast, where the impact of Islam was the most profound and where, because of the existence of written sources, it is somewhat easier to reconstruct the region's history. Sub-Saharan Africa had never been totally isolated from the Mediterranean world or other outside contacts, but the spread of Islam obviously brought large areas of Africa into more intensive contact with the global community, even though Africa remained something of an Islamic frontier. Still, the fusion of Islamic and indigenous African cultures created a synthesis that restructured the life of many Africans. Sudanic kingdoms and the Swahili coast participated in extensive borrowing and interactions with north Africa and the Middle East, similar to imitation efforts by several other societies in the postclassical period. Islamic contacts were also heavily involved in the growing integration of several parts of sub-Saharan Africa with global trade.

Although the arrival of Islam in Africa in the period from 800 to 1500 was clearly a major event, it would be wrong to see Africa's history in this period exclusively in terms of the Islamic impact. Great Zimbabwe and the Kongo kingdom, to cite only two examples, represented the development of Bantu concepts of kingship and state-building independently of trends taking place elsewhere on the continent. Similar processes and accomplishments could also be seen in Benin and among the Yoruba of west Africa. Meanwhile in Ethiopia, east Africa, and the eastern Sudan, the impact of Christianity and the pre-Islamic Mediterranean world had been long felt. The dynamic relationship between the impact of the civilizations and peoples external to Africa and the processes of development within the continent itself was a major theme in Africa's history.

By the late 15th century, when the first Europeans, the Portuguese, began to arrive on the west and east coasts of Africa, in many places they found well developed, powerful kingdoms that were able to deal with the Portuguese as equals. This was even truer in the parts of Africa that had come under the influence of Islam and through it had established links with other areas of Muslim civilization. In this period, Africa had increasingly become part of the general cultural trends of the wider world. Moreover, the intensified export trade in ivory, slaves, and especially gold from Africa drew Africans, even those far from the centers of trade, into a widening network of global relations. With the arrival of Europeans in sub-Saharan Africa in the late 15th century, the pace and intensity of the cultural and commercial contacts became even greater, and many African societies faced new and profound challenges.

Further Readings

Robert O. Collins and James M. Burns' *A History of Sub-Saharan Africa* (2007) is a useful introduction to this period in African history. Essential reading on central Africa is Jan Vansina, *Paths in the Rainforests* (1990) and his *How Societies Are Born: Governance in West Central Africa (2004)*. On the Swahili coast, see *The World of the Swahili* (1992) and Mark Horton and John Middleton *The Swahili: The Social Landscape of a Mercantile Society* (2000). On Ethiopia see Harold Marcus, *A History of Ethiopia* (1994). Stuart Munro-Hay, *The Quest for the Ark of the Covenant* (2005) delves into the Judaic and Christian origins of Ethiopia. N. Levtzion's *Ancient Ghana and Mali* (1973) is still the best short introduction to these kingdoms of the sahel. On Islam, David Robinson, *Muslim Societies in African History* (2004) is an excellent starting point.

Two good books on the Kongo kingdom are Anne Hilton's *The Kingdom of the Kongo* (1985), which shows how African systems of thought accommodated the arrival of Europeans and their culture, and Georges Balandier's older *Daily Life in the Kingdom of the Kongo* (1969), which makes good use of travelers' reports and other documents to give a rounded picture of Kongo society. The most recent account of Great Zimbabwe is Joseph Vogel, *Great Zimbabwe: The Iron Age in South Central Africa* (2004).

Some important source materials on African history for this period include three translations of the Mande epic *Sundiata*: David C. Conrad and Djanta Tassey Conde's *Sunjata: A West African Epic of the Mande Peoples* (2004); D. T. Niane's *Sundiata: An Epic of Old Mali* (1986); and Bamba Suso and Banna Kanute, *Sunjata: Gambian Versions of the Mande Epic* (2000). Other sources include G. R. Crone, ed., *The Voyages of Cadamosto*, 2nd series, vol. 80 (1937), which deals with Mali, Cape Verde, Senegal, and Benin; and Ross Dunn's indispensable edition of *The Adventures of Ibn*

Batuta: A Muslim Traveler of the 14th Century (1990). Arab sources are translated in Nehemia Levtzion and Jay Spaulding, *Medieval West Africa: Views from Arab Scholars and Merchants (2003).*

On the Web

Excellent brief descriptions of various African civilizations are provided on the Internet at http://www.bbc.co.uk/worldservice/africa/features/storyofafrica/index.shtml. Virtual visits and overviews of Great Zimbabwe are provided at http://www.mc.maricopa.edu/dept/d10/asb/anthro2003/legacy/africa/zimbabwe/ and http://www.manuampim.com/ZIMBABWE.html.

Web sites devoted to the trans-Saharan empires such as Mali and Songhay include http://www.learner.org/exhibits/collapse/mali.html and http://www.ucalgary.ca/applied_history/tutor/islam/fractured/westAfrica.html.

The lives of the of the empire of Mali, Sundiata, and Mansa Musa are explored at http://www.mrdowling.com/609-sundiata.html and http://www.mrdowling.com/609-mansamusa.html.

Many Saharan communities, including Timbuktu, are explored through travelers' accounts at http://www.manntaylor.com/shabeni.html and http://www.pbs.org/wonders/fr_e5.htm.

The art of the sub-Saharan empire of Benin can be explored at http://www.nmafa.si.edu/pubaccess/acrobat/benin.pdf and http://www.dia.org/collections/aonwc/africanart/beninkings.html. The role that Western racism played in the interpretation of Black African kingdoms of the Sudan history is explored at http://www.pbs.org/wonders/Episodes/Epi1/1_retel1.htm.

AP* Test Prep

1. Unlike in the Americas, the peoples of sub-Saharan Africa
   (A) never developed a classical civilization.
   (B) were never totally isolated from other civilizations.
   (C) had no large river systems to exploit.
   (D) developed its indigenous civilizations much later.

2. A common concern for west African Muslim jurists and clerics like Ibn Battuta was
   (A) the persistence of non-Islamic or "pagan" beliefs and practices among its population.
   (B) the growing influence of Christianity among west Africans.
   (C) the puritanical nature of west African Muslim society.
   (D) the practice of polygamy by many African families.

3. The grassland belt at the southern edge of the Sahara that served as a point of exchange between the forests to the south and the Mediterranean regions of Africa was called the
   (A) Sahel.
   (B) griot.
   (C) qadi.
   (D) Zanj.

4. The slave trade from Africa to the Muslim world
   (A) ended with the spread of Islam south of the Sahara.
   (B) existed before the arrival of Islam but the export of slaves to the Middle East expanded over the centuries.
   (C) was first introduced by Muslim Indian merchants.
   (D) far exceeded Central Asia as the primary source of Abbasid recruitment for high status administrative and military occupations.

5. The first black African states and civilizations developed
   (A) in the Sahel, the grassland belt south of the Sahara.
   (B) in the tropical forests along the coasts of the Atlantic Ocean.
   (C) in the Ahaggar and Atlas Mountains around and in the Sahara.
   (D) along the coasts of east Africa.

6. The "Lion Prince" of Mali was
   (A) Sunni Ali.
   (B) Sundiata.
   (C) Askia Muhmmad.
   (D) Mansa Kankhan Musa.

7. A common concern for west African Muslim jurists and clerics was
   (A) the persistence of pagan beliefs and practices among its population.
   (B) control of the trans-Saharan trade.
   (C) influence of Christianity on west Africans.
   (D) the practice of polygamy by many African families.

Free-Response Question

In what ways did Islam influence sub-Saharan African culture? Evaluate the changes and continuities in 2 regions in Africa after the introduction of Islam. (North, West, Central, Sudanic, Swahili States)

9 Civilization in Eastern Europe: Byzantium and Orthodox Europe

Civilization in Eastern Europe

The Byzantine Empire

VISUALIZING THE PAST: Women and Power in Byzantium

The Split Between Eastern and Western Christianity

The Spread of Civilization in Eastern Europe

The Emergence of Kievan Rus

DOCUMENT: Russia Turns to Christianity

THINKING HISTORICALLY: Eastern and Western Europe: The Problem of Boundaries

GLOBAL CONNECTIONS: Eastern Europe and the World

Late in the 10th century, Vladimir, king of a Russian state centered in the city of Kiev, faced an important decision. What major religion should he choose—not only for himself, but for his people. Some Christian activity had been brought in from the Byzantine Empire to the south, and Vladimir's grandmother had converted, but the majority of Russians were traditional polytheists.

Vladimir's decision raised two issues. First, why decide? Why not adhere to tradition? Most of the societies around Russia were part of the growing surge of world religions—religions that appealed to people of many cultures. Vladimir likely thought that his kingdom's growing trade and military activity would be complemented by a religion that had wider appeal than that of the traditional Russian gods. Vladimir was also defending his rule against internal strife and external attack: a successful move to impose a new religion would bolster his authority.

Second, decide on what? Placed as Russia was, Vladimir had knowledge of Islam, Judaism, Western Catholicism, and Byzantine, or Orthodox, Christianity. Legend has it that he rejected Judaism because it was not associated with a strong state. He rejected Catholicism (gaining ground in neighboring Poland) because he wanted no interference from the pope. He rejected Islam because of its prohibition of alcohol: "for drink is the joy of the Russian."

In truth, the decision was probably easy. The Byzantine Empire was Russia's prosperous neighbor, a leading trading partner and sometime military ally. Vladimir was eager to marry the sister of the Byzantine emperor—according to another legend, the emperor was reluctant to give his sister in marriage to what he considered a backward warrior, but Vladimir captured a major Byzantine city and refused to give it back until the emperor relented. Choosing Orthodox Christianity would be a part of this larger relationship with Byzantium. ∎

Constantine I, Vladimir, and the Selection of Christianity | CASE STUDY

Vladimir's decision was unquestionably important. Additional Byzantine influences, from art and literature to manners, began to shape Russian history. Christianity was extended eastward, changing the boundaries between Christianity and Islam. The Russian state did gain new prestige, and used religion to help unify its far-flung populace. At the same time, Vladimir's choice separated the kingdom from Roman Catholic western Europe, helping to create what would become a long-standing cultural division between eastern and western Europe. The implications of this separation continue to affect world affairs, even as other parts of eastern and western Europe are uniting.

Civilization in Eastern Europe

The power of the Byzantine Empire and the spread of Orthodox Christianity long surpassed the global influence of Christian Western Europe.

During the postclassical period two major Christian civilizations took shape in Europe. Both developed close relations with the Islamic world and both played major roles in world trade. One, centered on the papacy in Rome, encompassed Western Europe, but the other radiated out from Constantinople. Both civilizations had distinctive features of their own with desirable implications for the regions involved. Eastern Europe certainly came to illustrate the diversification of state forms that was characteristic of the post-classical period.

Figure 9.1 This 15th-century miniature shows Russia's King Vladimir I being baptized in Cherson in the year 988.

The Power of the Byzantine Empire

The Byzantine Empire maintained high levels of political, economic, and cultural activity during much of the period from 500 to 1450 C.E. It controlled an important but fluctuating swath of territory in the Balkans, the northern Middle East, and the eastern Mediterranean. Its leaders saw themselves as Roman emperors, and their government was in many ways a direct continuation of the eastern portion of the late Roman Empire.

The real significance of the Byzantine Empire goes well beyond its ability to keep Rome's memory alive. The empire lasted for almost a thousand years, between Rome's collapse in the West and the final overthrow of the regime by Turkish invaders. The empire's capital, Constantinople, was one of the truly great cities of the world, certainly the most opulent and important city in Europe in this period. From Constantinople radiated one of the two major branches of Christianity: the Orthodox Christian churches that became dominant throughout most of eastern Europe.

Like the other great civilizations of the period, the Byzantine Empire spread its cultural and political influence to parts of the world that had not previously been controlled by any major civilization. Just as Muslim influence helped shape civilization in parts of Africa south of the Sahara, the Byzantines began to create a new civilization in the Balkans and western Russia (present-day Ukraine and Belarus as well as western Russia proper).

The Empire also served as a major agent in interregional trade. It had active exchanges with the Arab world and with other parts of Asia. The Empire even imported techniques of silk production from China, which reduced its dependence on foreign trade for this commodity but showed its connection to larger fashion standards. Constantinople served as a hub for goods brought in from east central Europe and Russia, to be exchanged for Arab and Byzantine products. In various ways, the Empire played a key role in extending the range of contacts as part of the formation of the transcontinental network. There were many commonalities between developments in eastern and in western Europe. In both cases, civilization spread northward partly because of the missionary appeal of the Christian religion. In both cases, polytheism gave way to monotheism, although important compromises were made, particularly at the popular level. In both cases, more northerly political units, such as Russia, Poland, Germany, and France, struggled for political definition without being able to rival the political sophistication of the more advanced societies in Asia and north Africa or in Byzantium itself. In both cases, new trading activities brought northern regions into contact with the major centers of world commerce, including Constantinople. In both cases, newly civilized areas looked back to the Greco-Roman past, as well as to Christianity, for cultural inspiration, using some of the same political ideas and artistic styles.

100 C.E.	600 C.E.	800 C.E.	1000 C.E.	1200 C.E.	1400 C.E.
330s Constantinople becomes capital of eastern Roman Empire 527–565 Reign of Justinian	650s Slavic migrations into eastern Europe 718 Arab attack on Constantinople defeated	855 Rurik king of Kievan Russia (according to legend) 864 Beginning of Christian missionary work of Cyril and Methodius in Slavic lands 870 First kingdom in what is now Czech and Slovak republics 896 Magyars settle in Hungary c. 960 Emergence of Polish state 980–1015 Conversion of Russia to Christianity	1018 Byzantine defeat of Bulgarian kingdom 1019–1054 Reign of Yaroslav, king of Rus' 1054 Schism between Eastern and Western Christianity 1100–1453 Byzantine decline; under growing attack by Ottomans	1203–1204 Fourth Crusade, Westerners sack Constantinople 1237–1241 Mongols (Tatars) capture Russia	1453 Ottoman Turks capture Constantinople; end of Byzantine Empire 1480 Expulsion of Tatars from Russia

Yet with all these shared ingredients, the civilizations that expanded in the east and developed in the west operated largely on separate tracks. They produced different versions of Christianity that were culturally as well as organizationally separate, even hostile. The civilizations had little mutual contact. Until late in this period, commercial patterns in both cases ran south to north rather than east to west. During most of the postclassical millennium, major portions of eastern Europe were significantly more advanced than western Europe in political sophistication, cultural range, and economic vitality. Byzantium long surpassed the West in its involvement with interregional trade. When the two civilizations did meet, in this period and later, they met as distant cousins, related but not close kin.

The Byzantine Empire

The Byzantine Empire was shaped by the decline of the Roman Empire and the rise of the Arabs. The empire weathered many attacks and flourished for several centuries, playing a major role in Asian and European trade.

The Byzantine Empire in some senses began in the 4th century C.E., when the Romans set up their eastern capital in Constantinople. This city quickly became the most vigorous center of the otherwise fading imperial structure. Emperor Constantine constructed a host of elegant buildings, including Christian churches, in his new city, which was built on the foundations of a previously modest town called Byzantium. Soon, separate eastern emperors ruled from the new metropolis, even before the western portion of the empire fell to the Germanic invaders. They warded off invading Huns and other intruders while enjoying a solid tax base in the peasant agriculture of the eastern Mediterranean. Constantinople was responsible for the Balkan peninsula, the northern Middle East, the Mediterranean coast, and north Africa. Although for several centuries Latin was the court language of the eastern empire, Greek was the common tongue, and after Emperor Justinian in the 6th century, it became the official language as well. Indeed, in the eyes of the easterners, Latin became an inferior, barbaric means of communication. Knowledge of Greek enabled the scholars of the eastern empire to read freely in the ancient Athenian philosophical and literary classics and in the Hellenistic writings and scientific treatises.

The new empire benefited from the high levels of commerce long present in the eastern Mediterranean. New blood was drawn into administration and trade as Hellenized Egyptians and Syrians, long excluded from Roman administration, moved to Constantinople and entered the expanding bureaucracy of the Byzantine rulers. The empire faced many foreign enemies, although the pressure was less severe than that provided by the Germanic tribes in the West. It responded by recruiting armies in the Middle East itself, not by relying on barbarian troops. Complex administration around a remote emperor, who was surrounded by elaborate ceremonies, increasingly defined the empire's political style.

Justinian's Achievements

The early history of the Byzantine Empire was marked by a recurrent threat of invasion. Eastern emperors, relying on their local military base plus able generalship by upper-class Greeks, beat off attacks by the Sassanian Empire in Persia and by Germanic invaders. Then, in 533 C.E., with the empire's borders reasonably secure, a new emperor, Justinian, tried to reconquer western territory in a last futile effort to restore an empire like that of Rome (see Map 9.1). He was somber, autocratic, and prone to grandiose ideas. A contemporary historian named Procopius described him as "at once villainous and amenable; as people say colloquially, a moron. He was never truthful with anyone, but always guileful in what he said and did, yet easily hoodwinked by any who wanted to deceive him." The emperor was also heavily influenced by his power-hungry wife Theodora, a courtesan connected with Constantinople's horse-racing world. Theodora stiffened Justinian's resolve in response to popular unrest and pushed the plans for expansion.

Emperor Justinian

Justinian's positive contributions to the Byzantine Empire lay in rebuilding Constantinople, ravaged by earlier riots against high taxes, and systematizing the Roman legal code. Extending later Roman architecture, with its addition of domes to earlier classical styles, Justinian's builders created many new structures, the most inspiring of which was the huge new church, the **Hagia Sophia** (EYE-uh so-FEYE-uh), long one of the wonders of the Christian world. (The great church would later become a mosque, and is now a museum.) This was an achievement in engineering as well as architecture, for no one had previously been able to build the supports needed for a dome of its size. Justinian's codification of Roman law reached a goal that earlier emperors had sought but not achieved, summing up and reconciling many prior edicts and decisions. Unified law not only reduced confusion but also united and organized the new empire, paralleling the state's bureaucracy. Updated by later emperors, the code ultimately helped spread Roman legal principles in various parts of Europe.

Hagia Sophia [EYE-uh so-FEYE-uh] New church constructed in Constantinople during reign of Justinian.

Justinian's military exploits had more ambiguous results. The emperor wanted to recapture the old Roman Empire itself. With the aid of a brilliant general, **Belisarius,** new gains were made in north Africa and Italy. Justinian's forces made their temporary capital, Ravenna, a key artistic center, embellished by some of the most beautiful Christian mosaics known anywhere in the world (Figure 9.2). But the major Italian holdings were short-lived, unable to withstand Germanic pressure, and north African territory was soon besieged as well.

Belisarius (c. 505–565) One of Justinian's most important military commanders during period of reconquest of western Europe; commanded in north Africa and Italy.

Furthermore, Justinian's westward ambitions had weakened the empire in its own sphere. Persian forces attacked in the northern Middle East, while new Slavic groups, moving into the Balkans, pressed on another front (Map 9.1). Justinian finally managed to create a new line of defense and even pushed Persian forces back again, but some Middle Eastern territory was lost. Furthermore, all these wars, offensive and defensive alike, created new tax pressures on the government and forced Justinian to exertions that contributed to his death in 565 C.E.

The Byzantine Empire Under Justinian

Arab Pressure and the Empire's Defenses

After some setbacks, Justinian's successors began to concentrate on defending the eastern empire itself. Persian advances in the northern Middle East were reversed in the 7th century, and the population was forcibly reconverted to Christianity. The resultant empire, centered in the southern Balkans and the western and central portions of present-day Turkey, was a far cry from Rome's greatness. However, it was sufficient to amplify a rich Hellenistic culture and blend it more fully with Christianity while advancing Roman achievements in engineering and military tactics as well as law.

The Byzantine Empire was also strong enough to withstand the great new threat of the 7th century, the surge of the Arab Muslims, though not without massive losses. By the mid-7th century, the Arabs had built a fleet that challenged Byzantine naval supremacy in the eastern Mediterranean

Figure 9.2 Dazzling mosaics from the early period of the Byzantine Empire illustrate some of the highest achievements of Byzantine religious art. This mosaic features a rather militant Christ the Redeemer.

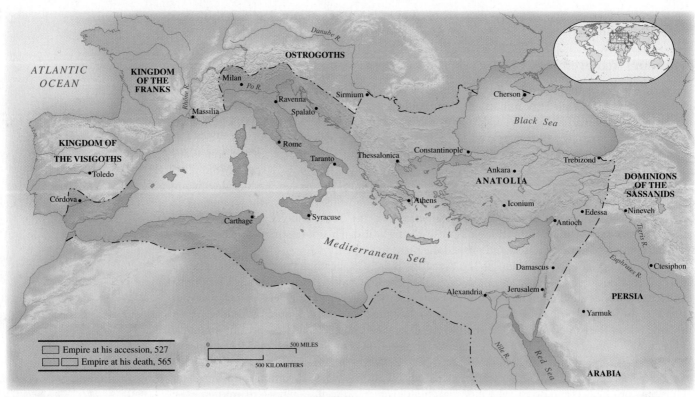

Map 9.1 The Byzantine Empire Under Justinian   Justinian's ambitious expansion exhausted his treasury, and the empire had lost all its holdings outside the northeastern Mediterranean within 50 years after his death.

Greek fire Byzantine weapon consisting of mixture of chemicals that ignited when exposed to water; utilized to drive back the Arab fleets that attacked Constantinople.

Bulgaria Slavic kingdom established in northern portions of Balkan peninsula; constant source of pressure on Byzantine Empire; defeated by Emperor Basil II in 1014.

while repeatedly attacking Constantinople. They quickly swallowed the empire's remaining provinces along the eastern seaboard of the Mediterranean and soon cut into the northern Middle Eastern heartland as well. Arab cultural and commercial influence also affected patterns of life in Constantinople. Byzantine territory was cut back to about half the size of the earlier eastern Roman Empire.

The Byzantine Empire held out nevertheless. A major siege of the capital in 717–718 C.E. was beaten back, partly because of a new weapon, a kind of napalm called **Greek fire** (a petroleum, quicklime, and sulfur mixture) that devastated Arab ships. The Arab threat was never removed entirely. Furthermore, wars with the Muslims had added new economic burdens to the empire. Invasions and taxation weakened the position of small farmers and resulted in greater aristocratic estates plus new power for aristocratic generals. The free rural population that had served the empire during its early centuries—providing military recruits and paying the bulk of the taxes—was forced into greater dependence. Greater emphasis was given to organizing the army and navy.

After the greatest Arab onslaughts had been faced, the empire was run by a dizzying series of weak and strong emperors. Periods of vigor alternated with seeming decay. Arab pressure continued. Conquest of the island of Crete in the 9th century allowed the Muslims to harass Byzantine shipping in the Mediterranean for several centuries. Slavic kingdoms, especially **Bulgaria,** periodically pressed Byzantine territory in the Balkans, although at times military success and marriage alliances brought Byzantine control over the feisty Bulgarian kingdom. Thus, while a Bulgarian king in the 10th century took the title of *tsar*, a Slavic version of the word *Caesar*, steady Byzantine pressure through war eroded the regional kingdom. In the 11th century, the Byzantine emperor Basil II, known as *Bulgaroktonos*, or slayer of the Bulgarians, used the empire's wealth to bribe many Bulgarian nobles and generals. He defeated the Bulgarian army in 1014, blinding as many as 15,000 captive soldiers. The sight of this tragedy brought on the Bulgarian king's death. Bulgaria became part of the empire, its aristocracy settling in Constantinople and merging with the leading Greek families.

Briefly, at the end of the 10th century, the Byzantine emperor may have been the most powerful monarch on earth, with a capital city whose rich buildings and abundant popular entertainments awed visitors from western Europe and elsewhere.

Women and Power in Byzantium

This mosaic, developed between 1034–1042, portrays the Empress Zoë, her consort, and Christ (in the center). Zoë would later rule jointly with her sister Theodora, despite their earlier struggle for power.

QUESTIONS What evidence does this mosaic provide about the political relationship between Zoë and her husband? What does it suggest about the relationship between church and state in Byzantium and about ways religion might be used to bolster political power? (Interpreting the haloes is a good start in answering this question.) What sense of history and religion made it reasonable to show Christ between two 11th-century people?

Istanbul, St. Sophia, Mosaic in the South Tribune: Christ with the Empress Zoë, who is presenting him with a scroll listing her donations to the church, and her consort, Monomachus, who is offering him a purse containing gold coins.

(Dagli Orti/Picture Desk, Inc./Kobal Collection.)

Byzantine Society and Politics

The Byzantine political system had remarkable similarities to the earlier patterns in China. The emperor was held to be ordained by God, head of church as well as state. He appointed church bishops and passed religious as well as secular laws. The power of the state over the church was a key feature of Orthodox Christianity, in contrast to patterns in Western Europe. Elaborate court rituals symbolized the ideals of a divinely inspired, all-powerful ruler, although they often immobilized rulers and inhibited innovative policy.

At key points, women held the imperial throne while maintaining the ceremonial power of the office. The experiences of Empress Theodora (981–1056), namesake of Justinian's powerful wife, illustrate the complex nature of Byzantine politics and the whims of fate that affected women rulers. Daughter of an emperor, Theodora was strong and austere; she refused to marry the imperial heir, who then wed her sister Zoë. Zoë was afraid of Theodora's influence and had her confined to a convent. A popular rebellion against the new emperor installed Theodora and Zoë jointly (and one assumes uneasily) as empresses. Later, Theodora managed to check unruly nobles and limit bureaucratic corruption, although her severe retaliation against personal enemies brought criticism.

Supplementing the centralized imperial authority was one of history's most elaborate bureaucracies. Trained in Greek classics, philosophy, and science in a secular school system that paralleled church education for the priesthood, Byzantine bureaucrats could be recruited from all social classes. As in China, aristocrats predominated, but talent also counted among this elite of highly educated scholars. Bureaucrats were specialized into various offices, and officials close to the emperor were mainly eunuchs. Provincial governors were appointed from the center and were charged with keeping tabs on military authorities. An elaborate system of spies helped preserve loyalty while creating intense distrust even among friends. It is small wonder that the word *Byzantine* came to refer to complex institutional arrangements. Careful military organization arose as well. Byzantine rulers adapted the later Roman system by recruiting troops locally and rewarding them with grants of land in return for their military service. The land could not be sold, but sons inherited its administration in return for continued military responsibility. Many outsiders, particularly Slavs and Armenian Christians, were recruited for the army in this way. Increasingly, hereditary military leaders assumed regional power,

Figure 9.3 A view of the interior of the Hagia Sophia, or St. Sophia—the Church of Holy Wisdom—in what is today the city of Istanbul. This magnificent church was built 532–537 C.E. under the reign of the Emperor Justinian.

Icon An icon is an artistic representation, usually of a religious figure.

Growing divisions opened up between the two main branches of Christianity. The impact of these divisions increased when the Byzantine Empire began to decline.

Twelfth-Century Image of Christ IMAGE

displacing more traditional and better-educated aristocrats. One emperor, Michael II, was a product of this system and was notorious for his hatred of Greek education and his overall personal ignorance. On the other hand, the military system had obvious advantages in protecting a state recurrently under attack from Muslims of various sorts—Persians, Arabs, and later Turks—as well as nomadic intruders from central Asia. Until the 15th century, the Byzantine Empire effectively blocked the path to Europe for most of these groups.

Socially and economically, the empire depended on Constantinople's control over the countryside, with the bureaucracy regulating trade and controlling food prices. The large peasant class was vital in supplying goods and providing the bulk of tax revenues. Food prices were kept artificially low, to content the numerous urban lower classes, in a system supported largely by taxes on the hard-pressed peasantry. Other cities were modest in size—for example, Athens dwindled—because the focus was on the capital city and its food needs. The empire developed a far-flung trading network with Asia to the east and Russia and Scandinavia to the north. Silk production expanded in the empire, and various luxury products, including cloth, carpets, and spices, were sent north. This gave the empire a favorable trading position with less sophisticated lands. Only China produced luxury goods of comparable quality. The empire also traded actively with India, the Arabs, and east Asia while receiving simpler products from western Europe and Africa. At the same time, the large merchant class never gained significant political power, in part because of the elaborate network of government controls. In this, Byzantium again resembled China and differed notably from the looser social and political networks of the West, where merchants were gaining greater voice.

Byzantine cultural life centered on the secular traditions of Hellenism, so important in the education of bureaucrats, and on the evolving traditions of Eastern, or Orthodox, Christianity. The Byzantine strength lay in preserving and commenting on past forms more than in developing new ones. Art and architecture were exceptions; a distinct Byzantine style developed fairly early. The adaptation of Roman domed buildings, the elaboration of powerful and richly colored religious mosaics, and a tradition of **icon** paintings—paintings of saints and other religious figures, often richly ornamented—expressed this artistic impulse and its marriage with Christianity. The icons' blue and gold backgrounds set with richly dressed religious figures were meant to represent the unchanging brilliance of heaven.

The Split Between Eastern and Western Christianity

Byzantine culture and politics, as well as the empire's economic orientation toward Asia and northeastern Europe, helped explain the growing break between its eastern version of Christianity and the western version headed by the pope in Rome. There were many milestones in this rift. Different rituals developed as the Western church translated the Greek Bible into Latin in the 4th century. Later, Byzantine emperors deeply resented papal attempts to loosen state control over the Eastern church to make it conform more fully to their own idea of church–state relations. Contact between the two branches of Christianity trailed off, though neither the Eastern nor Western church cared to make a definitive break. The Eastern church acknowledged the pope as first among equals, but papal directives had no hold in the Byzantine church, where state control loomed larger. Religious art conveyed different styles and beliefs, as Figures 9.4 and 9.5 suggest. Even monastic movements operated according to different rules.

The Schism

Then, in 1054, an ambitious church patriarch in Constantinople raised a host of issues, including a quarrel over what kind of bread to use for the celebration of Christ's last supper in the church liturgy. The bread quarrel was an old one, relating to ritual use of bread in Christ's day, and whether communion bread must be baked without yeast. The patriarch also attacked the Roman Catholic practice, developed some centuries earlier, of insisting on celibacy for its priests; Eastern Orthodox priests could marry. Delegations of the two churches discussed these disputes, but this led only to new bitterness. The Roman pope finally excommunicated the patriarch and his followers, banishing them from Christian fellowship and the sacraments. The patriarch responded by excommunicating all Roman Catholics. Thus, the split, or schism, between the Roman Catholic church and Eastern Orthodoxy—the Byzantine or Greek, as well as the Russian Orthodox, Serbian Orthodox, and others—became formal and has endured to this day. A late-12th-century church patriarch in Constantinople even argued that Muslim rule would be preferable to that of the pope: "For if I am subject to the Muslim, at least he will not force me to share his faith. But if I have to be under the Frankish rule and united with the Roman Church, I may have to separate myself from God."

The split between the Eastern and Western churches fell short of complete divorce. A common Christianity with many shared or revived classical traditions and frequent commercial and cultural contacts continued to enliven the relationship between the two European civilizations. The division did reflect the different patterns of development the two civilizations followed during the postclassical millennium. Not only separate artistic forms and rituals, but also different ideas about the role of scholarship separated the two regions—with eastern Europe developing a less elaborate philosophical tradition in relation to religion. Differences in the role of the state in religious affairs may have contributed not just to divisions at this time, but to later distinctions in governments' claims to power between the two main European regions.

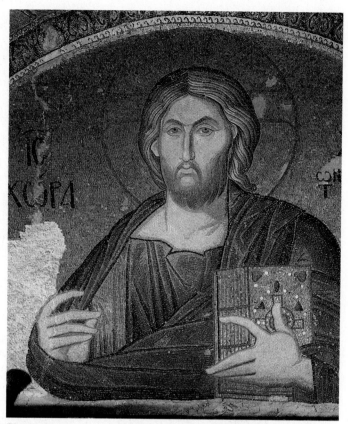

Figure 9.4 Just as theologians through the centuries have worked to understand Christ's message, so too have artists struggled to capture his image. This powerful mosaic of Christ at the Church of Chora in Istanbul was created in the first part of the 14th century. Notice the difference between this image and the images of Christ common in Western Christianity, which place more emphasis on suffering and less on divine majesty.

Figure 9.5 The Byzantine Empire developed a distinctively stylized religious art, adapted from earlier Roman painting styles and conveying the solemnity of the holy figures of the faith. This 11th-century miniature features the holy women at the sepulchre of Christ.

Map 9.2 The Byzantine Empire, 1000–1100   The Byzantine Empire went from a major to a minor power in the period portrayed on this map. After the Turkish defeat at Manzikert in 1071, the Byzantines maintained effective control of only a small fringe of Anatolia. In the Balkans, new Serbian, Bulgarian, and Hungarian states grew powerful, despite the Byzantines' claim to control of the region.

The Empire's Decline

Shortly after the split between the Eastern and Western churches, the Byzantine Empire entered a long period of decline (Map 9.2). Turkish invaders who had converted to Islam in central Asia began to press on its eastern borders, having already gained increasing influence in the Muslim caliphate. In the late 11th century, Turkish troops, the Seljuks, seized almost all the Asiatic provinces of the empire, thus cutting off the most prosperous sources of tax revenue and the territories that had supplied most of the empire's food. The Byzantine emperor lost the battle of Manzikert in 1071, his larger army was annihilated, and the empire never recovered. It staggered along for another four centuries, but its doom, at least as a significant power, was sealed. The creation of new, independent Slavic kingdoms in the Balkans, such as Serbia, showed the empire's diminished power.

A Byzantine View of the Crusades

Eastern emperors appealed to Western leaders for help against the Turks, but their requests were largely ignored. Although the appeals helped motivate Western Crusades to the Holy Land, this did not help the Byzantines. At the same time, Italian cities, blessed with powerful navies, gained increasing advantages in Constantinople, such as special trading privileges—a sign of the shift in power between East and West. Byzantium's role in world trade now attracted Western—particularly, Italian—appetites. One Crusade, in 1204, ostensibly set up to conquer the Holy Land from the Muslims, actually turned against Byzantium. Led by greedy Venetian merchants, the Crusade attacked and conquered Constantinople, briefly unseating the emperor and weakening the whole imperial structure. But the West was not yet powerful enough to hold this ground, and a small Byzantine Empire was restored, able through careful diplomacy to survive for another two centuries.

Turkish settlements pressed ever closer to Constantinople in the northern Middle East—in the area that is now Turkey—and finally, in 1453, a Turkish sultan brought a powerful army, equipped with artillery purchased from Hungary, against the city, which fell after two months. By 1461, the

Eastern and Western Europe: The Problem of Boundaries

The problem of boundaries between civilizations and even between states has long attracted the attention of scholars. The continuing evolution of nation states and their often self-serving desire to define themselves within larger civilizational boundaries greatly complicates the task of deciding where one civilization ends and another begins.

Defining the territory of the two related civilizations that developed in Europe is particularly difficult. A number of states sat, and still sit, on the borders of the two civilizations, sharing some characteristics of each. Furthermore, political disputes and nationalist attachments, fierce in this border territory of east central Europe during the past two centuries, make territorial definitions an emotional issue. So the question of defining Europe's civilizations is a particularly thorny case of a larger problem.

If a civilization is defined simply by its mainstream culture, then eastern and western Europe in the postclassical period divide logically according to Orthodox and Catholic territories (and use of the Cyrillic and Greek or of the Latin alphabet). By this reckoning, Poland, the Czech areas, and the Baltic states (these latter did not convert to Catholicism until the 14th century) are western, and Hungary is largely so. South Slavs are mainly but not entirely Orthodox, a regional division that can provoke recurrent violence. Russia and Ukraine are decidedly Orthodox in tradition. Religion matters. Poland and other Catholic regions have long maintained much more active ties with western Europe than Russia has. At the end of the postclassical period, a Czech religious dissenter, Jan Hus, even foreshadowed the later Protestant Reformation in his attacks on the Catholic church.

Politically, the case is more complicated. Poland, Hungary, and Lithuania formed large regional kingdoms at various times

> *"Russian expansion later pulled parts of eastern Europe, including Poland, into its orbit, although it never eliminated their strong cultural identities."*

during and after the postclassical period. But these kingdoms were very loosely organized, much more so than the feudal monarchies that were developing in western Europe. Exceptionally large aristocracies in Poland and Hungary (by western or by Russian standards) helped limit these states.

Trade patterns also did not closely unite Poland or Hungary with western Europe until much later, when the two regions were clearly different in economic structure. Also, Polish and Hungarian societies often shared more features with Russia than with western Europe.

Russian expansion later pulled parts of eastern Europe, including Poland, into its orbit, although it never eliminated strong cultural identities. It is also important to remember that borders can change. The Mongol invasions that swept through Russia also conquered Poland and Hungary, but the armies did not stay there. Part of the Ukraine was also free from direct Mongol control, which helped differentiate it from Russia proper. For two centuries, at the end of the postclassical period, the divisions within eastern Europe intensified. Since 1989, many eastern European countries have again achieved full independence from Russia, and they want to claim their distinctive pasts. Not an easy border area to characterize in terms of a single civilization, east central Europe has also been a victim of many conquests interspersed with periods of proud independence.

QUESTIONS What were the main characteristics of Russian civilization as it first emerged in the postclassical period? In what ways did Poland, Hungary, and the Czech lands differ from these characteristics? Are there other civilization border areas, in the postclassical period or later, that are similarly difficult to define because of their position between two other areas?

Turks had conquered remaining pockets of Byzantine control, including most of the Balkans, bringing Islamic power farther into eastern Europe than ever before. The great eastern empire was no more.

The fall of Byzantium was one of the great events in world history, and we will deal with its impact in several later chapters. It was a great event because the Byzantine Empire had been so durable and important, anchoring a vital corner of the Mediterranean and an important segment of world trade even amid the rapid surge of Islam. The empire's commercial contacts and its ability to preserve and spread classical and Christian learning made it a vital unit throughout the postclassical period. After its demise, its influence continued to affect other societies, including the new Ottoman Empire.

Kritovoulos on the Fall of Constantinople: Nestor-Iskander on the Fall of Constantinople

The Spread of Civilization in Eastern Europe

Long before the Byzantine decline after the 11th century, the empire had been the source of a new northward surge of Christianity. Orthodox missionaries sent from Constantinople busily converted most people in the Balkans to their version of Christianity, and some other trappings of Byzantine culture came in their wake. In 864, the Byzantine government sent the missionaries **Cyril** and **Methodius** to the territory that is now the Czech and Slovak republics. Here the venture failed, in

Christian missionaries, new trade routes, and Byzantine military activity affected much of eastern Europe. Within this context, the Kievan Rus' formed the core of Russian culture and politics.

213

Cyril (827–869) Along with Methodius, missionary sent by Byzantine government to eastern Europe and the Balkans; converted southern Russia and Balkans to Orthodox Christianity; responsible for creation of written script for Slavic known as Cyrillic.

Methodius (826–885) Along with Cyril, missionary sent by Byzantine government to eastern Europe and the Balkans; converted southern Russia and Balkans to Orthodox Christianity; responsible for creation of written script for Slavic known as Cyrillic.

that Roman Catholic missionaries were more successful. But Cyril and Methodius continued their efforts in the Balkans and in southern Russia, where their ability to speak the Slavic language greatly aided their efforts. The two missionaries devised a written script for this language, derived from Greek letters; to this day, the Slavic alphabet is known as Cyrillic. Thus, the possibility of literature and some literacy developed in eastern Europe along with Christianity, well beyond the political borders of Byzantium. Byzantine missionaries were quite willing to have local languages used in church services—another contrast with Western Catholicism, which insisted on church Latin.

The East Central Borderlands

Eastern missionaries did not monopolize the borderlands of eastern Europe. Roman Catholicism and the Latin alphabet prevailed not only in the Czech area but also in most of Hungary (which was taken over in the 9th century by a Turkic people, the Magyars) and in Poland. Much of this region would long be an area of competition between Eastern and Western political and intellectual mod-

Map 9.3 East European Kingdoms and Slavic Expansion c. 1000 Beginning around the 5th century C.E., the Slavs moved in all directions from their lands around the Pripet River in what is today Ukraine and Belarus. Their migrations took them from the Baltic Sea to the Oder River and down to the Adriatic and Aegean seas. The arrival of the Hungarians in the 9th and 10th centuries prevented the Slavs from unifying. The arrival of the Hungarians in the 9th and 10th centuries complicated the Slavic holdings, tending to separate Russians and Slavs in the Balkans. Still, the various Salvic peoples dominated a vast territory in eastern Europe.

els. During the centuries after the conversion to Christianity, this stretch of eastern Europe north of the Balkans was organized in a series of regional monarchies, loosely governed amid a powerful, land-owning aristocracy. The kingdoms of Poland, Bohemia, and Lithuania easily surpassed most western kingdoms in territory. This was also a moderately active area for trade and industry. For example, ironworking was more developed than in the West until the 12th century.

Eastern Europe during these centuries also received an important influx of Jews, who were migrating away from the Middle East but also fleeing intolerance in western Europe. Poland gained the largest single concentration of Jews. Eastern Europe's Jews, largely barred from agriculture and often resented by the Christian majority, gained strength in local commerce while maintaining their own religious and cultural traditions. A strong emphasis on extensive education and literacy, though primarily for males, distinguished Jewish culture not only from the rest of eastern Europe but also from most other societies in the world at this time.

The Emergence of Kievan Rus'

Russia shared many features with the rest of northeastern Europe before the 15th century. As in much of eastern Europe, the centuries of Byzantine influence were an important formative period that would influence later developments, even as Russia became more important. Slavic peoples had moved into the sweeping plains of Russia and eastern Europe from an Asian homeland during the time of the Roman Empire (Map 9.3). They mixed with and incorporated some earlier inhabitants and some additional invaders, such as the Bulgarians, who adopted Slavic language and customs. The Slavs already used iron, and they extended agriculture in the rich soils of what is now Ukraine and western Russia. The Slavs maintained an animist religion with gods for the sun, thunder, wind, and fire. The early Russians also had a rich tradition of folk music and oral legends, and they developed some very loose regional kingdoms.

Russia gradually emerged through its role in trade, growing political claims, and the decision to participate in Christianity.

Kiev   Trade city in southern Russia established by Scandinavian traders in 9th century; became focal point for kingdom of Russia that flourished to 12th century.

New Patterns of Trade

During the 6th and 7th centuries, traders from Scandinavia began to work through the Slavic lands, moving along the great rivers of western Russia, which run south to north, particularly the Dnieper (DNEE-puhr). Map 9.3 shows the route that led from Scandinavia to Byzantium, and the Russian territory that began to coalesce around it. Through this route the Norse traders were able to reach the Byzantine Empire, and a regular, flourishing trade developed between Scandinavia and Constantinople. Luxury products from Byzantium and the Arab world traveled north in return for furs and other crude products. The Scandinavian traders, militarily superior to the Slavs, gradually set up some governments along their trade route, particularly in the city of **Kiev**. A monarchy emerged, and according to legend a man named **Rurik**, a native of Denmark, became the first prince of what came to be called **Kievan Rus'** (KEE-eh-vehn ROOS) about 855 C.E. This principality, though still loosely organized through alliances with regional, landed aristocrats, flourished until the 12th century. It was at this time that the word *Russia* was coined, possibly from a Greek word for "red," for the hair color of many of the Norse traders.

The Expanding States of Eastern and Northern Europe

Rurik   Legendary Scandinavian, regarded as founder of the first kingdom of Russia based in Kiev in 855 C.E.

Kievan Rus'   [KEE-eh-vehn ROOS] The predecessor to modern Russia, Kievan Rus' was a medieval state which existed from the end of the 9th to the middle of the 13th century. Its territory spanned parts of modern Belarus, Ukraine, and Russia.

Vladimir of Kiev's Acceptance of Christianity

Contacts between Kievan Rus' and Byzantium extended steadily. Kiev, centrally located, became a prosperous trading center, and from there many Russians visited Constantinople. This was the context in which Prince **Vladimir I**, a Rurik descendant who ruled from 980 to 1015, took the step of converting to Christianity, not only in his own name but on behalf of all his people. Having made his decision, Vladimir organized mass baptisms for his subjects, forcing conversions by military pressure. Early church leaders were imported from Byzantium, and they helped train a literate Russian priesthood. As in Byzantium, the king characteristically controlled major appointments, and a separate **Russian Orthodox** church soon developed.

Vladimir I   Ruler of Russian kingdom of Kiev from 980 to 1015; converted kingdom to Christianity.

As Kievan Rus' became Christian, it was the largest single state in Europe, though highly decentralized. Rurik's descendants managed for some time to avoid damaging battles over succession to the throne. Following Byzantine example, they issued a formal law code that reduced the severity of traditional punishments and replaced community vendettas with state-run courts, at least in principle. The last of the great Kievan princes, **Yaroslav**, issued the legal codification while building many churches and arranging the translation of religious literature from Greek to Slavic.

Russian Orthodoxy   Russian form of Christianity imported from Byzantine Empire and combined with local religion; king characteristically controlled major appointments.

Yaroslav   (978–1054) Last of great Kievan monarchs; issued legal codification based on formal codes developed in Byzantium.

Russia Turns to Christianity

This document from a monk's chronicle, describing King Vladimir's conversion policy, indicates what was officially believed about the power of Russian princes, Russian social structure, and the relationship between Christianity and earlier animism. These official claims are important, but they may not reflect the whole reality of this important transition in Russia history. Here is a classic case of the need to understand a particular mindset and genre of writing, to understand why particular explanations are offered without accepting their reality.

> For at this time the Russes were ignorant pagans. The devil rejoiced threat, for he did not know that his ruin was approaching. He was so eager to destroy the Christian people, yet he was expelled by the true cross even from these very lands. . . . Vladimir was visited by Bulgars of the Mohammedan faith. . . . [He] listened to them for he was fond of women and indulgence, regarding which he heard with pleasure. But . . . abstinence from pork and wine were disagreeable to him. "Drinking," said he, "is the joy of the Russes. We cannot exist without that pleasure." [Russian envoys sent to Constantinople were astonished by the beauty of the churches and the chanting], and in their wonder praised the Greek ceremonial. . . .
>
> [Later, Vladimir was suffering from blindness; a Byzantine bishop baptized him] and as the bishop laid his hand upon him, he straightway recovered his sight. Upon experiencing this miraculous cure, Vladimir glorified God, saying, "I have now perceived the one true God." When his followers beheld this miracle, many of them were also baptized. . . . Thereafter Vladimir sent heralds throughout the whole city to proclaim that if any inhabitant, rich or poor, did not betake himself to the river [for mass baptism] he would risk the Prince's displeasure. When the people heard these words, they wept for joy and exclaimed in their enthusiasm, "If this were not good, the Prince and his nobles would not have accepted it." . . . There was joy in heaven and upon earth to behold so many souls saved. But the devil groaned, lamenting, "Woe is me. How am I driven out hence . . . my reign in these regions is at an end." . . .
>
> He [Vladimir] ordered that wooden churches should be built and established where [pagan] idols have previously stood. He founded the Church of Saint Basil on the hill where the idol of Perun and the other images had been set, and where the prince and the people had offered their sacrifices. He began to found churches, to assign priests throughout the cities and towns, and to bring people in for baptism from all towns and villages. He began to take the children of the best families and send them for instruction from books.

QUESTIONS In what ways might the account be simplistic in describing royal powers and popular response? What explanations does this religious chronicler offer for the conversion of Russians to Christianity? Which of the explanations are most likely, and which are the results of some kind of bias? What kind of church–state relationship did this kind of conversion predict?

Institutions and Culture in Kievan Rus'

Kievan Rus' borrowed much from Byzantium, but it was in no position to replicate major institutions such as the bureaucracy or an elaborate educational system. Major princes were attracted to Byzantine ceremonials and luxury and to the concept (if not yet the reality) that a central ruler should have wide powers. Many characteristics of Orthodox Christianity gradually penetrated Russian culture. Fervent devotion to the power of God and to many Eastern saints helped organize worship. Churches were ornate, filled with icons and the sweet smell of incense. A monastic movement developed that stressed prayer and charity. Traditional practices, such as polygamy, gradually yielded to the Christian practice of monogamy. The emphasis on almsgiving long described the sense of obligation felt by wealthy Russians toward the poor.

The Russian literature that developed, which used the Cyrillic alphabet, featured chronicles that described a mixture of religious and royal events and showered praises on the saints and the power of God. Disasters were seen as expressions of the just wrath of God against human wickedness, and success in war followed from the aid of God and the saints in the name of Russia and the Orthodox faith. This tone also was common in Western Christian writing during these centuries, but in Kievan Rus' it monopolized formal culture; a distinct philosophical or scientific current did not emerge in the postclassical period.

Russian and Ukrainian art focused on the religious also, with icon painting and illuminated religious manuscripts becoming a Kievan specialty. Orthodox churches, built in the form of a cross surmounted by a dome, similarly aped Byzantine models, although the building materials often were wood rather than stone. Domed structures, as Figure 9.6 shows, adapted Byzantine themes to Russian conditions, in what proved to be a durable regional style. Religious art and music were rivaled by popular entertainments in the oral tradition, which combined music, street performances, and some theater. The Russian church unsuccessfully tried to suppress these forms, regarding them as pagan.

St. Basil's Cathedral, Moscow IMAGE

Chapter 9 • Civilization in Eastern Europe: Byzantium and Orthodox Europe

Just as Russia's religious culture developed separately from western Europe's, Russian social and economic patterns took distinctive shape. Russian peasants were fairly free farmers, although an aristocratic landlord class existed. Russian aristocrats, called **boyars**, had less political power than their counterparts in western Europe, although the Kievan princes had to negotiate with them.

For all its distinctiveness, Russia was not unaware of other parts of Europe. The greatest ruler of the period, Yaroslav the Wise (1019–1054), used marriages to create ties. He arranged over 30 marriages with central European royalty, including 11 with Germany, pressing six Russian princes to take German wives while inducing five German nobles to accept Russian brides. Even here, however, Yaroslav kept his main focus on Byzantium, promoting Byzantine styles in the great cathedral of Kiev and using Byzantine example as the basis for Russia's first law code.

Kievan Decline

The Kievan principality began to fade in the 12th century. Rival princes set up regional governments, and the royal family often squabbled over succession to the throne. Invaders from Asia whittled at Russian territory. The rapid decline of Byzantium reduced Russian trade and wealth, for the kingdom had always depended heavily on the greater prosperity and sophisticated manufacturing of its southern neighbor. The final blow in this first chapter of Russian history came in 1237–1238 and 1240–1241, when two invasions by Mongols from central Asia moved through Russia and into other parts of eastern Europe. The initial Mongol intent was to add the whole of Europe to their growing empire. The Mongols easily captured the major Russian cities, but they did not penetrate much farther west because of political difficulties in their Asian homeland. Called **Tatars** in the Russian tradition (from a Turkish word), the invaders were quickly despised but also feared—"the accursed raw-eating Tatars," as one chronicle put it.

For over two centuries much of Russia remained under Tatar control. This control further separated the dynamic of Russian history from that of western Europe. Russian literature languished under Tatar supervision. Trade lapsed in western Russia, and the vigorous north–south commerce of the Kievan period never returned. At the same time, loose Tatar supervision did not destroy Russian Christianity or a native Russian aristocratic class. As long as tribute was paid, Tatar overlords left day-to-day Russian affairs alone. Thus, when Tatar control was finally forced out in the second half of the 15th century, a Russian cultural and political tradition could reemerge, serving as a partial basis for the further, fuller development of Russian society.

Russian leaders retained an active memory of the glories of Byzantium. When Constantinople fell to the Turks in 1453, just as Russia was beginning to assert its independence from the Tatars, it was logical to claim that the mantle of east European leadership had fallen on Russia. A monk, currying favor, wrote the Russian king in 1511 that whereas heresy had destroyed the first Roman Empire and the Turks had cut down the second, Byzantium—a "third, new Rome" under the king's "mighty rule"—"sends out the Orthodox Christian faith to the ends of the earth and shines more brightly than the sun." According to the monk, "Two Romes have fallen, but the third stands, and there will be no fourth." This sense of an Eastern Christian mission, inspiring a Russian resurgence, was just one result of this complicated formative period in the emergence of a separate European civilization in the Slavic lands.

The End of an Era in Eastern Europe

With Byzantium and Russia both under siege, east European civilization fell on hard times at the end of the postclassical era. These difficulties confirmed the largely separate trajectories of western and eastern Europe. Western Europe remained free from outside control and, despite some new

Figure 9.6 The Cathedral of St. Dimitry was built from 1194–1197, during the reign of Prince Vsevolod III. Its famous white stone carvings celebrate the myths and heroes of many cultures as well as the beauty of the biblical God's creation through the portrayal of numerous plants and animals.

The Rise of Moscow

Filofei's Concept of the "Third Rome"

boyars Russian aristocrats; possessed less political power than did their counterparts in western Europe.

Tatars Mongols; captured Russian cities and largely destroyed Kievan state in 1236; left Russian Orthodoxy and aristocracy intact.

problems, maintained a clearer vigor in politics, economy, and culture. When eastern Europe did reemerge, it was at some disadvantage to western Europe in terms of power and economic and cultural sophistication—a very different balance from that of the glory days of Byzantium and the vigor of Kievan Russia.

Tatar invasion and Byzantine collapse were profoundly disruptive. Key features of Kievan social structure disappeared in the later development of imperial Russia. Yet continuity was not entirely lost. Not only Christianity but also eastern European assumptions about political rulers and church–state relations and the pride in a lively artistic culture served as organizing threads when Russia and other Slavic societies turned to rebuilding.

Global Connections

Eastern Europe and the World

The Byzantine Empire participated actively in interregional trade. Constantinople had become one of the world's great trading cities, a connecting point between Europe and Asia. The Byzantine import of a silk industry from China was a sign of their active awareness of the world beyond their borders. The empire also served as a crucial link in the postclassical global system between northern Europe and the Mediterranean.

The situation was somewhat different for Russia. Russia's geographical position inevitably encouraged awareness both of Europe and of western Asia. Vladimir I reflected this when he pondered his religious choices, among Judaism, Western Christianity, Orthodox Christianity, or Islam. But Russia became dependent on Byzantium as its main trading contact with the wider world. When Byzantium declined, and when the Mongols conquered Russia, this led to a period of unusual isolation. Russia was not able to benefit from wider relationships during the Mongol centuries, though the Mongol influence itself left a mark. When, by the 15th century, Russia began to regain independence, it faced decisions about what kind of broader contacts to foster, and how.

Further Readings

Recent overviews include John Rosser, *The A to Z of Byzantium* (2006); Averil Cameron, *The Byzantines* (2006); and Cyril Mango, ed., *The Oxford History of Byzantium* (2002). On early Byzantium, see Peter Sarris, *Economy and Society in the Age of Justinian* (2006); and James Allan Evans, *The Emperor Justinian and the Byzantine Empire* (2005). Byzantine Christianity is studied in G. Every, *The Byzantine Patriarchate, 451–1204* (1978); Derek Krueger, ed., *Byzantine Christianity* (2006); and S. Runciman, *The Byzantine Theocracy* (1977). On culture, see William Brumfield, ed., *Christianity and the Arts in Russia* (1991); Helen Evans and William Wixom, *The Glory of Byzantium: Art and Culture of the Middle Byzantine Era A.D. 843–1261* (1997); and E. Kitzinger, *Byzantine Art in the Making* (1977). For Byzantine external relations see H. J. Magoulias, *Byzantine Christianity: Emperor, Church and the West* (1982) and D. Obolensky, *The Byzantine Commonwealth: Eastern Europe, 500–1453* (1971). See also Lynda Garland, ed., *Byzantine Women: Varieties of Experience 800–1200* (2006).

On Russian history, the best survey is Nicholas Riasanovsky, *A History of Russia* (1992), which has a good bibliography. See also Alfred Rambaud, *The History of Russia: From the Earliest Times to 1877* (2006); Serhii Plokhy, *The Origins of the Slavic Nations: Premodern Identities in Russia, Ukraine, and Belarus* (2006), and Natalia Pushkareva and Eve Levin's survey *Women in Russian History: From the Tenth to the Twentieth Century* (1997). Books dealing with early Russian culture include Mary Charmot, *Russian Painting and Sculpture* (1963); J. H. Billington, *The Icon and the Axe: An Interpretive History of Russian Culture* (1966). Vladimir Volkoff, *Vladimir the Russian Viking, 960–1015* (1985), offers a unique glimpse of early Russia. The impact of the Mongols on the shaping of Russian history is examined in Robert Marshall, *Storm from the East: From Genghis Khan to Khubilai Khan* (1993).

On the Web

Useful overviews and assessments of Byzantine Civilization and links to related sites are provided at http://www.fordham.edu/halsall/byzantium/. A virtual visit to one of the oldest cities of Kievan Rus', Novgorod http://emuseum.mnsu.edu/history/russia/kievanrus.html or http://www.neva.ru/EXPO96/book/chap1-1.html; sample its ancient chronicle is offered at http://www.fordham.edu/halsall/source/novgorod1.html.

The lives of the Russian women who rose to positions of authority or respect, particularly within the church, are explored at http://www.macedonian-heritage.gr/HellenicMacedonia/en/D2.5.html and http://byzantium.seashell.net.nz/articlemain.php?artid=mtp_women.

The great schism that came to separate and define Western Catholicism and Eastern Orthodoxy is examined from the Orthodox perspective at http://orthodoxphotos.com/readings/Orthodox_Church/schism.shtml. The Catholic perspective is offered at http://www.newadvent.org/cathen/13535a.htm.

The Emperor Justinian (http://www.historyguide.org/ancient/justinian.html and http://www.newadvent.org/cathen/08578b.htm)

influenced much of the history of the Mediterranean world with Theodora as co-ruler (http://en.wikipedia.org/wiki/Theodora_(6th_century), http://www.roman-emperors.org/dora.htm). Information about Anna Comnena, a politically ambitious daughter of a Byzantine emperor and also a historian, can be found at http://womeninworldhistory.com/heroine5.html and http://www.wsu.edu:8080/~wldciv/world_civ_reader/world_civ_reader_1/comnena.html.

AP* Test Prep

1. Justinian's Code was similar to Hammurabi's Law Codes in that it
    (A) dealt primarily with religious issues.
    (B) became the basic law code for his state, and influenced future law codes.
    (C) led to internal disruptions and faced harsh opposition.
    (E) deviated sharply from previous legal precedents when it sought to create a new tradition.

2. The schism within the Christian church was due to all of these issues EXCEPT
    (A) clerical celibacy; Orthodox priests could marry, but Catholic priest could not.
    (B) papal interference in Byzantine political and religious affairs.
    (C) the Byzantine state control of the church in the eastern lands.
    (D) Muslim influence on the Orthodox branch of Christianity.

3. The spread of Christianity was accelerated in the Balkans and Russia through
    (A) the mass migration of Greeks into these regions.
    (B) forced conversions of the Slavs by the victorious Byzantine armies.
    (C) Christian merchants who intermarried and settled amongst non-Christians.
    (D) the missionary activities of Cyril and Methodius directed from the Byzantine Empire.

4. The first organized state in Russia arose when
    (A) nomadic pastoralists established a sedentary Jewish state.
    (B) Byzantine missionaries converted Russian farmers.

    (C) after Scandinavian traders set up a government along their southern trade routes.
    (D) Arabs who conquered the area established a province of the Abbasid Caliphate.

5. Byzantine trade flourished with all of the following EXCEPT
    (A) sub-Saharan Africa.
    (B) Asia.
    (C) the Mediterranean.
    (D) northern Europe.

6. All of the following were factors in the decline of Byzantium EXCEPT
    (A) Russian invaders.
    (B) Slejuk Turks.
    (C) Western crusaders.
    (D) Italian trading city-states such as Venice and Genoa.

7. How did the Tatar (Mongol) conquest of Russia shape Russian history?
    (A) It destroyed Christianity.
    (B) It further separated Russia from the cultures of Western Europe.
    (C) It lead to the destruction of the Russian nobility.
    (D) Arabs who conquered the area established a province of the Abbasid Caliphate.

Free-Response Question

Compare the political, religious, and economic structures of the Arab and Byzantine empires in the post-classical period.

10 A New Civilization Emerges in Western Europe

Stages of Postclassical Development

Western Culture in the Postclassical Era

Changing Economic and Social Forms in the Postclassical Centuries

VISUALIZING THE PAST: Peasant Labor

DOCUMENT: European Travel: A Monk Visits Jerusalem

The Decline of the Medieval Synthesis

THINKING HISTORICALLY: Western Civilization

GLOBAL CONNECTIONS: Medieval Europe and the World

Sometimes an individual life displays the complexities of a larger society. Godric—ultimately, Saint Godric—was a 12th-century Englishman (Figure 10.1). His father was an ordinary farmer, but he early developed greater ambition. Godric started as a peddler and, according to his biographer, quickly learned how to turn a profit on cheap items. He was physically strong, and a hard worker—necessary qualities for a life of trade and travel. He soon turned to urban commerce, which was beginning to increase rapidly during the 1100s. He participated in seagoing trade with other parts of Britain and with the European continent, and clearly made a good living, acquiring a number of ships.

But he was not entirely at peace with himself. His biographer, a clergyman named Reginald of Durham, is eager to emphasize Godric's consistent Christianity. So he portrays him as content with a simple life even amid his riches, and quickly attracted to the saints and a life of God. He argues that Godric's sea voyages, undoubtedly risky, helped the future saint realize the importance of divine aid—and surely religion did often provide a sense of security to venturesome merchants. Finally, however, a purely material life did not seem sufficient.

Godric began visiting saints' shrines with increasing frequency. He began to be disturbed by the high living—feasting and drinking—of some of his merchant colleagues. He also found that some of them stole outright. He attempted to correct them but was rebuffed. Ashamed of his own materialism (and possibly of some misdeeds of his own), he went on a pilgrimage to Rome. After that, with his parents' blessing, he decided to give himself entirely to a religious life. He sold all of his goods, gave the proceeds to the poor, and spent the rest of his life wandering as a religious hermit.

Few Europeans lived lives as polarized as that of Godric, but many, particularly in growing cities, felt some tension between commercial change and religious commitment. Could someone interested in making money keep a primary devotion to God? Some, as Godric discovered, would choose commerce. Others opted for religion. Still others worked for some combination. While few made Godric's dramatic ultimate choice, many merchants gave abundantly to the splendid churches of the cities, and not a few made deathbed renunciations of their commercial pasts. ■

Middle Ages The period in western European history from the decline and fall of the Roman Empire until the 15th century.

Vikings Seagoing Scandinavian raiders from Sweden, Denmark, and Norway who disrupted coastal areas of western Europe from the 8th to the 11th centuries.

manorialism System that described economic and political relations between landlords and their peasant laborers during the Middle Ages; involved a hierarchy of reciprocal obligations that exchanged labor or rents for access to land.

The postclassical period was a great age of faith in western Europe, and Christianity provided the most obvious unifying factor in the new geography of western European civilization. Christian missionary efforts led most western Europeans to convert from polytheistic faiths in the initial postclassical centuries. But there were other key developments as well, including Europe's growing participation in trade and in wider interregional contacts. Not surprisingly, it was not always easy, even for individuals, to put the pieces together.

The postclassical period in western Europe began with the fall of the Roman Empire and lasted until the 15th century. The period is known as the **Middle Ages** in European history (the adjective form is *medieval*). The period featured gradual recovery from the shock of Rome's collapse. At the same time, the forms of civilization spread northward, beyond the Roman orbit, covering the whole of western Europe. Key characteristics of western European civilization emerged from these dynamic processes.

Medieval western Europe participated in the network of expanding contacts among major societies in Asia, Europe, and parts of Africa. New tools introduced by invaders from Asia, including a new kind of plow, helped spur medieval agriculture from the 10th century onward. New crops from

Africa, including new varieties of wheat, increased food production. The revival of trade in the Mediterranean, bringing contacts with the Arabs, yielded other technological gains, such as the first European paper factory. Medieval culture was at least as powerfully shaped by connections with the wider world. By the 11th and 12th centuries, contact with the Byzantines and the Arabs had taught Western scholars new lessons in mathematics, science, and philosophy. The medieval West unquestionably took more from the emerging world network than it contributed, but it was also challenged by its international position to seek new world roles.

 Europe, c. 750

serfs Peasant agricultural laborers within the manorial system of the Middle Ages.

Stages of Postclassical Development

From about 550 C.E. until about 900, western Europe suffered from a number of problems. Rome continued to serve as the center of the growing Catholic church, in turn the most powerful institution in the West. But Italy was divided politically. Spain, another key region of the Roman Empire in the West, lay in the hands of the Muslims through much of the Middle Ages. A vibrant intellectual and economic life was focused there, and it would have an important influence on Western developments later on, but it was for the time being out of the Western mainstream. The center of the postclassical West lay in France, the Low Countries, and southern and western Germany, with England increasingly drawn in—areas where civilization, as a form of human organization, was new.

Postclassical western Europe was hard hit by the Roman collapse. However, after about 900, agriculture and trade revived, while political development advanced under the influence of feudalism and the Catholic church.

Frequent invasions reflected and prolonged the West's weakness, making it difficult to develop durable government or economic forms. Raids by the seagoing **Vikings** from Scandinavia periodically disrupted life from Ireland to Sicily. With weak states and little more than subsistence agriculture, it was small wonder that intellectual activity declined. The few who could read and write were concentrated in the hierarchy and the monasteries of the Catholic church, where they kept learning alive. But they could do little more than copy older manuscripts, including those of the great Christian thinkers of the later Roman Empire. By their own admission, they could not understand much of the philosophy involved, and they often apologized for their inability to write good Latin. Western Europe was still shaped by elements of the Roman heritage, but the connection was disrupted.

The Manorial System: Obligations and Allegiances

Between Rome's fall and the 10th century, effective political organization was largely local, although Germanic kings ruled some territories, such as a portion of what is France today. **Manorialism** was the system of economic and political relations between landlords and their peasant laborers. Most people were **serfs,** living on self-sufficient agricultural estates called manors. Serfs were agricultural workers who received some protection, including the administration of justice, from the landlords; in return, they were obligated to turn over part of their goods and to remain on the land. The manorial system had originated in the later Roman Empire. It was strengthened by the decline of trade and the lack of larger political structures. Serfs needed the military forces the landlords could muster for their security. Without much market economy to stimulate production and specialization, these same landlords used the serfs' produce and labor to support their own modest establishments.

Life for most serfs was difficult. Agricultural equipment was limited, and production was low. The available plows, copied

Figure 10.1 Having experienced many close calls with the weather during his years at sea, St. Godric was troubled on stormy nights for the rest of his life, thinking of the peril of sailors. He is best remembered for his extraordinary affinity for wild animals. He protected hunted animals and is said to have allowed snakes to warm themselves at his fire.

500 C.E.	800 C.E.	1000 C.E.	1150 C.E.	1300 C.E.	1450 C.E.
500–900 Recovery period after Rome's fall; Christian missionaries work in northern Europe 732 Franks defeat Muslims in France	800–814 Charlemagne's empire 900–1000 Spread of new plows; use of horses in agriculture and transport 962 Germanic kings revive Roman Empire	1018 Beginning of Christian reconquest of Spain 1066 Norman conquest of England, strong feudal monarchy 1070–1141 Peter Abelard 1073–1085 Gregory VII, reform pope 1096–1270 Crusades	1150–1300 Gothic style spreads 1180 University of Paris 1200–1274 Thomas Aquinas and flowering of scholasticism 1215 Magna Carta 1226–1270 Louis IX of France 1265 First English parliament	1303 Seizure of papacy by French king 1338–1453 Hundred Years War 1348–1380 Black Death (bubonic plague)	1469 Formation of single Spanish monarchy

Social Conditions in the Ninth Century 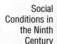 DOCUMENT

from Mediterranean models, were too light to work the heavy soils of France and Germany effectively. In the 9th century a better plow, the **moldboard** (a curved iron plate), was introduced that allowed deeper turning of the soil. Most Western peasants early in the postclassical period also left half their land uncultivated each year to restore nutrients. This again limited productivity, although by the 9th century a new **three-field system** improved the situation. Here, only a third of the land was left unplanted each year, to regain fertility.

moldboard   Heavy plow introduced in northern Europe during the Middle Ages; permitted deeper cultivation of heavier soils; a technological innovation of the medieval agricultural system.

The obligations of the manorial system bore as heavily on most serfs as did the technological limitations. Serfs had to give their lord part of their crops in return for grazing their animals on his land or milling their grain. They also provided many days of labor repairing the lord's castle or working the lands under his control. Serfs were not slaves: they could not be bought or sold, and they retained essential ownership of their houses and lands as long as they kept up with their obligations. They could also pass their property rights on through inheritance. Nevertheless, life remained hard, particularly in the early postclassical centuries. Some serfs escaped landlord control, creating a host of wanderers who added to the disorder of the early Middle Ages.

The Church: Political and Spiritual Power

During the centuries of recovery after the Roman Empire's collapse in the 6th century, the Catholic church was the only extensive example of solid organization. Here was a crucial contrast with the state's dominance over religion in the Byzantine Empire. In theory, and to an extent in fact, the church copied the government of the Roman Empire to administer Christendom. The pope in Rome was the top authority. Regional churches were headed by bishops, who were supposed to owe allegiance to the church's central authority; bishops, in turn, appointed and to some degree supervised local priests. The popes did not always appoint the bishops, for monarchs and local lords often claimed this right, but they did send directives and receive information. The popes also regulated doctrine, beating back several heresies that threatened a unified Christian faith. Moreover, they sponsored extensive missionary activity. Papal missionaries converted the English to Christianity. They brought the religion to northern and eastern Germany, beyond the borders of the previous Roman Empire, and, by the 10th century, to Scandinavia. They were active in the border regions of eastern Europe, sometimes competing directly with Orthodox missionaries.

The interest of early Germanic kings in Christianity was a sign of the political as well as spiritual power of the church. A warrior chieftain, Clovis, converted to Christianity about 496 C.E. to gain greater prestige over local rivals, who were still pagan. This authority, in turn, gave him a

Figure 10.2 *Anxiety for Salvation: The Resurrection.* This picture was part of materials to be read in religious services in the 11th century in Germany. The dead are rising from their tombs for the Last Judgment, summoned by angels escorted by the winds. The picture illustrates the goals Christians were urged to make paramount, focusing on life after death.

Peasant Labor

This scene, from an illuminated (illustrated) manuscript of the 15th century, shows peasant labor and tools in France, near a stylized great palace.

QUESTIONS What kind of social and gender structure does the picture suggest? What kinds of tools were used in farming, and how productive would they be? The picture should be compared to earlier medieval representations, such as the representation of Charlemagne's coronation: What were the trends in medieval artistic styles, in terms of dealing with human figures and nature?

Peasants at labor.

vague dominion over the Franks, a Germanic tribe located in much of what is France today. Conversion of this sort also strengthened beliefs by Western religious leaders, particularly the popes, that they had a legitimate authority separate from and superior to the political sphere. As Figure 10.2 suggests, religious commitments continued to expand to many people.

The church also developed an important chain of monasteries during the centuries immediately after Rome's fall. Western monasteries helped discipline the intense spirituality felt by some individual Christians, people who wanted to devote themselves to prayer and religious discipline and escape the limits of ordinary material life. The most important set of monastic rules was developed by Benedict of Nursia (in Italy) in the 6th century; the spread of Benedictine monasteries promoted Christian unity in western Europe. Monasteries also served ordinary people as examples of a holy life, adding to the spiritual focus that formed part of the fabric of medieval society. Many monasteries helped improve the cultivation of the land at a time when agricultural techniques were at a low ebb. Monasteries also provided some education and promoted literacy.

Charlemagne and His Successors

One significant development occurred during the early postclassical centuries in the more strictly political sphere. The royal house of the Franks grew in strength during the 8th century. A new family, the **Carolingians,** took over this monarchy, which was based in northern France, Belgium, and western Germany. One founder of the Carolingian line, **Charles Martel,** or "Charles the Hammer," was responsible for defeating the Muslims in the battle of Tours in 732, although his victory had more to do with Arab exhaustion and an overextended invasion force than Carolingian strength. This defeat helped confine the Muslims to Spain and, along with the Byzantine defeat of the Arabs in the same period, preserved Europe for Christianity.

Gregory of Tours
DOCUMENT

Rule of St. Benedict
DOCUMENT

three-field system System of agricultural cultivation by 9th century in western Europe; included one-third in spring grains, one-third fallow.

Clovis Early Frankish king; converted Franks to Christianity c. 496; allowed establishment of Frankish kingdom.

Carolingians Royal house of Franks after 8th century until their replacement in 10th century.

Martel, Charles (686–741) Carolingian monarch of Franks; responsible for defeating Muslims in battle of Tours in 732; ended Muslim threat to western Europe.

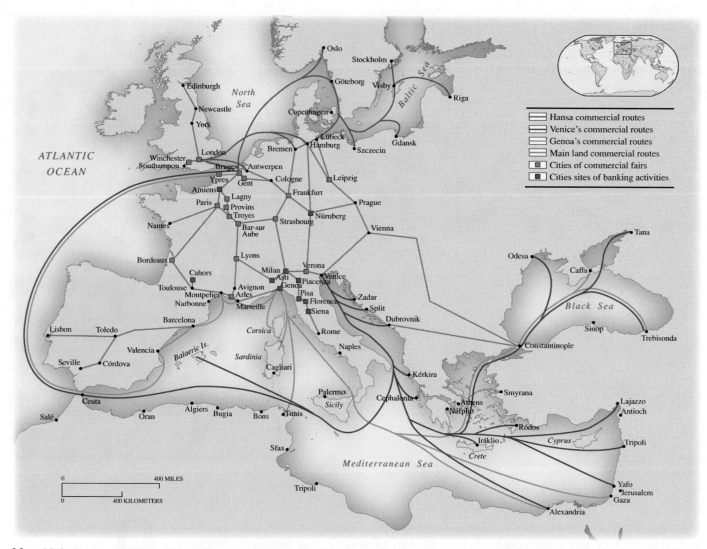

Map 10.1 Charlemagne's Empire and Successor States Charlemagne gathered a wide section of western Europe under his sway, but the empire was divided among his three grandsons after his death.

Einhard,
Life of
Charlemagne

Charlemagne [SHAR-luh-mayn] Charles the Great; Carolingian monarch who established substantial empire in France and Germany c. 800.

Carolingian
Empire

A later Carolingian ruler in this same royal line, Charles the Great, or **Charlemagne** (SHAR-luh-mayn), established a substantial empire in France and Germany around the year 800 (see Map 10.1). Briefly, it looked as if a new Roman Empire might revive in the West; indeed, Charlemagne's successors in Germany continued to use the title of emperor (see Figure 10.3). Charlemagne helped to restore some church-based education in western Europe, and the level of intellectual activity began a slow recovery, in part because of these efforts. When Charlemagne died in 814, however, this empire did not long survive him. Rather, it was split into three portions as inheritance for his three grandsons: the outlines of modern France, Germany, and a middle strip consisting of the Low Countries, Switzerland, and northern Italy (Map 10.1). Several of Charlemagne's successors, with nicknames such as "the Bald" and "the Fat," were not great leaders even in their regional kingdoms.

From this point onward, the essential political history of western Europe consisted of the gradual emergence of regional monarchies; a durable empire proved impossible, given competing loyalties and the absence of a strong bureaucracy. Western Europe proved to have strong cultural unity, initially centered in Catholic Christianity, but with pronounced political divisions. No single language united this civilization, any more than did a single government. Intellectuals and the church officials used Latin, but during the Middle Ages separate spoken languages evolved, usually merging Germanic and Latin elements. These separate languages, such as French and English, in turn helped form the basis of halting national identities when political and cultural boundaries roughly coincided, which is what began to happen in key cases after the 9th century.

The royal houses of several lands gained new visibility soon after Charlemagne's empire split. At first, the rulers who reigned over Germany and northern Italy were in the strongest position. It was they who claimed the title *emperor,* beginning around the 10th century. Later they called themselves **Holy Roman emperors,** merging Christian and classical claims. By this time, however, their rule had become increasingly hollow, precisely because they relied too much on their imperial claims and did not build a solid monarchy from regional foundations. Local lords often went their own way in Germany, and city-states showed independence in northern Italy. The future lay elsewhere, with the rise of monarchies in individual states—states that ultimately would become nations.

New Economic and Urban Vigor

By 900, a series of developments began to introduce new sources of strength into Western society that ultimately had clear political and cultural repercussions. New agricultural techniques developed from contacts with eastern Europe and with Asian raiders into central Europe. The new moldboard plow and the three-field system were crucial gains; so was a new horse collar that allowed horses to be yoked without choking. The use of horse collars and stirrups also confirmed the military dominance of the lords, who monopolized fighting on horseback. The European nobility became defined by land ownership and military power. But better plows helped the ordinary people by allowing deeper

Figure 10.3 The pope's coronation of the emperor Charlemagne was a vital precedent for the idea that church approval was essential for a legitimate state in western Europe. In fact, however, Charlemagne's power greatly exceeded the pope's.

(Coronation of Charlemagne at St. Peter's by Pope Leo III. Grandes Chroniques de France, fol. 106r. Musee Goya, Castres, France. Giraudon/Art Resource, NY.)

Holy Roman emperors   Emperors in northern Italy and Germany following split of Charlemagne's empire; claimed title of emperor c. 10th century; failed to develop centralized monarchy in Germany.

working of heavy soil and the opening of new land. Monasteries also promoted better agricultural methods (in contrast to the less worldly orientation of monks in eastern Europe). During the 10th century, Viking raids began to taper off, partly because regional governments became stronger (sometimes when the Vikings themselves took over, as in the French province of Normandy) and partly because the Vikings, now Christianized, began to settle down. Greater regional political stability and improved agriculture promoted population growth, an important fact of Western history from the 10th through the 13th centuries.

Population growth encouraged further economic innovation. More people created new markets. There was a wedge here for growing trade, which in turn encouraged towns to expand, another source of demand. Landlords and serfs alike began to look to lands that had not previously been converted to agriculture. Whole regions, such as northeastern Germany, became colonized by eager farmers, and new centers sprang up throughout settled regions such as France. To woo labor to the new farms, landlords typically had to loosen the bonds of serfdom and require less outright labor service, sometimes simply charging a money rent. Harsh serfdom still existed, but most serfs gained greater independence, and some free peasants emerged. Contacts with other countries brought knowledge of new crops, such as durum wheat (from north Africa), the vital ingredient for pasta, and alfalfa (from Persia). The pace of economic life created a less rigid social structure, and more commercial, market-oriented economic motives began to coexist with earlier military and Christian ideals.

The growth of towns reflected the new vigor of western Europe's agriculture. In parts of Italy and the Low Countries, where trade and urban manufacturing were especially brisk, urban populations soared to almost 20 percent of the total by the 13th century. Overall, the townspeople made up about 5 percent of the West's population—a significant figure, though still below the often 15 percent

Medieval Town: Customs of the Town of Chester, England

levels of the advanced Asian civilizations. Few European cities approached a population level of 100,000 people (in contrast, China had 52 larger cities), but the rise of modest regional centers was an important development. Literacy spread in the urban atmosphere, spurring the popular languages; professional entertainers introduced new songs as well as dazzling tricks such as fire-eating and bear-baiting; urban interests spurred new forms of religious life, including city-based monastic orders dedicated to teaching or hospital work. Merchant activity and craft production expanded.

Europe's economic and urban surge helped feed formal cultural life, which had already gained somewhat under Charlemagne's encouragement. By the 9th and 10th centuries, schools began to form around important cathedrals, training children who were destined for church careers. By the 11th century, there was enough demand for educated personnel to sustain the first universities. Italy offered universities to train students in medicine and law; the legal faculties profited from a growing revival in knowledge of Roman law, and medicine benefited from new learning imported from the Arabs and from revived Greek and Hellenistic science. By the 12th century, a more characteristic university was forming in Paris. It specialized in training clergy, with theology as the culminating subject but with faculties in other subjects as well. The Parisian example inspired universities in England (Oxford and Cambridge), Germany, and elsewhere. Solid educational institutions, though destined for only a small minority of Europe's population, supported increasingly diverse and sophisticated efforts in philosophy and theology. At the same time, medieval art and architecture reached a new high point, spurred by the same prosperity.

Feudal Monarchies and Political Advances

Prosperity also promoted political change, influenced by structures established in more unstable times. From the 6th century onward, the key political and military relationships in western Europe had evolved in a system called feudalism. Feudal relationships linked military elites, mostly landlords, who could afford the horses and iron weaponry necessary to fight. Greater lords provided protection and aid to lesser lords, called **vassals;** vassals in turn owed their lords military service, some goods or payments, and advice. Early feudalism after Rome's fall was very local; many landlords had armed bands of five or ten local vassals, easily converted into raiding parties. But feudal relationships could be extended to cover larger regions and even whole kingdoms. Charlemagne's empire boosted this more stable version of feudalism. He could not afford to pay his own bureaucracy, so he rewarded most of his military leaders with estates, which they quickly converted into family property in return for pledges of loyalty and service. Many German duchies were created by powerful lords with their own armies of vassals, ostensibly deferring to the Holy Roman emperor. On the whole, European feudalism inhibited the development of strong central states, but it also gradually reduced purely local warfare.

Furthermore, kings could use feudalism to build their own power. Kings of France began to win growing authority, from the 10th century onward, under the Capetian royal family. At first they mainly exploited their position as regional feudal lords in the area around Paris. They controlled many serf-stocked manors directly, and they held most other local landlords as vassals. More attentive administration of this regional base produced better revenues and armies. The kings also formed feudal links with great lords in other parts of France, often through marriage alliances, gradually bringing more territory under their control. They experimented with the beginnings of bureaucratic administration by separating their personal accounts from government accounts, thus developing a small degree of specialization among the officials who served them. Later Capetian kings sent out officials to aid in regional administration.

The growth of a strong feudal monarchy in France took several centuries. By the early 14th century, the process of cautious centralization had gone so far in France that a king could claim rights to make the church pay taxes (an issue that caused great conflict). The king could mint money and employ some professional soldiers apart from the feudal armies that still did most of the fighting.

Feudal monarchy in England was introduced more abruptly. The Duke of Normandy, of Viking descent, who had already built a strong feudal domain in his French province, invaded England in 1066. The duke, now known as **William the Conqueror,** extended his tight feudal system to his new kingdom. He tied the great lords of England to his royal court by bonds of loyalty, giving them estates in return for their military service. But he also used some royal officials, called sheriffs,

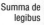

Summa de
legibus

vassals   Members of the military elite who received land or a benefice from a feudal lord in return for military service and loyalty.

William the Conqueror   Invaded England from Normandy in 1066; extended tight feudal system to England; established administrative system based on sheriffs; established centralized monarchy.

The Battle of
Hastings
(1066)

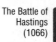

to help supervise the administration of justice throughout the kingdom. In essence, he and his successors merged feudal principles with a slightly more centralized approach, including more standardized national law codes issued by the royal court.

The growth of feudal monarchy unknowingly duplicated measures taken earlier in other centralizing societies, such as China. Developing an explicit bureaucracy, with some specialized functions, and sending emissaries to outlying provinces are examples. In Europe, kings often chose urban business or professional people to staff their fledgling bureaucracies, because unlike the feudal nobles, they would be loyal to the ruler who appointed them. Government functions expanded modestly, as kings tried to tax subjects directly and hire a small professional army to supplement feudal forces.

Limited Government

Western European Kingdoms in the Late Twelfth Century

Stronger monarchies did not develop evenly throughout Europe. The West remained politically divided and diverse. Germany and Italy, though nominally controlled by the Holy Roman emperor, were actually split into regional states run by feudal lords and city-states. The pope directly ruled the territory of central Italy. The Low Countries, a vigorous trade and manufacturing region, remained divided into regional units. Equally important were the limitations over the most successful feudal monarchies. The power of the church continued to limit political claims, for the state was not supposed to intrude on matters of faith except in carrying out decisions of the popes or bishops.

Feudalism created a second limitation, for aristocrats still had a powerful independent voice and often their own military forces. The growth of the monarchy cut into aristocratic power, but this led to new statements of the limits of kings. In 1215, the unpopular English King John faced opposition to his taxation measures from an alliance of nobles, townspeople, and church officials. Defeated in his war with France and then forced down by the leading English lords, John was compelled to sign the Great Charter, or **Magna Carta,** which confirmed feudal rights against monarchical claims. John promised to observe restraint in his dealings with the nobles and the church, agreeing, for example, not to institute new taxes without the lords' permission or to appoint bishops without the church's permission. The Magna Carta showed how feudalism could generate claims of rights against the power of a king.

Magna Carta   Great Charter issued by King John of England in 1215; confirmed feudal rights against monarchical claims; represented principle of mutual limits and obligations between rulers and feudal aristocracy.

Late in the 13th century, this same feudal balance led to the creation of **parliaments** as bodies representing not individual voters but privileged groups such as the nobles and the church. (Even earlier, in 1000, the regional kingdom of Catalonia created a parliament.) The first full English parliament convened in 1265, with the House of Lords representing the nobles and the church hierarchy, and the Commons made up of elected representatives from wealthy citizens of the towns. As with the Magna Carta, the parliament institutionalized the feudal principle that monarchs should consult with their vassals. In particular, parliaments gained the right to rule on any proposed changes in taxation; through this power, they could also advise the crown on other policy issues. Although the parliamentary tradition became strongest in England, similar institutions arose in France, Spain, Scandinavia, and several of the regional governments in Germany. Here too, parliaments represented the key **three estates:** church, nobles, and urban leaders. They were not widely elected.

parliaments   Bodies representing privileged groups; institutionalized feudal principle that rulers should consult with their vassals; found in England, Spain, Germany, and France.

three estates   The three social groups considered most powerful in Western countries: church, nobles, and urban leaders.

Feudal limited government was not modern limited government. People had rights according to the estate into which they were born; nobles transmitted membership in their estate to their children. There was no general concept of citizenship and certainly no democracy. Still, by creating the medieval version of representative institutions, Western feudal monarchy produced the beginnings of a distinctive political tradition. This tradition differed from the political results of Japanese feudalism, which emphasized group loyalty more than checks on central power.

Even with feudal checks, European monarchs developed more capacity for central administration during the later Middle Ages (see Map 10.2). The results clearly were uneven and by Asian standards still woefully limited. European rulers also continued to see war as a key purpose. Local battles gave way to larger wars, such as the conflicts between the proud rulers of France and England. In the 14th century, a long battle began—the **Hundred Years War,** between the national monarchies of France and England—over territories the English king controlled in France and over feudal rights versus the emerging claims of national states.

Hundred Years War   Conflict between England and France from 1337 to 1453; fought over lands England possessed in France and feudal rights versus the emerging claims of national states.

Map 10.2 Western Europe Toward the End of the Middle Ages, c. 1360 C.E. Near the end of the postclassical period, strong monarchies had consolidated their holdings, and boundaries between states were coming into sharper focus.

The West's Expansionist Impulse

Christian Reconquest of Muslim Spain

During the period of political development and economic advance, western Europe began to show its muscle beyond its initial postclassical borders (Map 10.2). Population growth spurred the expansionist impulse, as did the memory of Rome's lost greatness and the righteous zeal provided by Christianity. Germanic knights and agricultural settlers poured into sparsely settled areas in what is now eastern Germany and Poland, changing the population balance and clearing large areas of forest. A different kind of expansionist surge occurred in Spain. Small Christian states remained in northern Spain by the 10th century, and they gradually began to attack the Muslim government that held most of the peninsula. The "reconquest" escalated by the 11th century, as Christian forces, swelled by feudal warriors from various areas, pushed into central Spain, conquering the great Muslim center of Toledo. Full expulsion of Muslim rulers occurred only at the end of the Middle Ages in 1492, but the trend of the Christian offensive was clear even earlier. During the 15th century, regional Spanish monarchies fused through the marriage of Ferdinand and Isabella, which provided the political muscle to complete the Christian "reconquesta."

At Europe's other extreme, Viking voyagers had pushed out into the northern Atlantic, establishing settlements in Iceland. By the 11th century, other voyages had pushed to Greenland and the Hudson Bay area in what is now Canada, where short-lived outposts were created. By the 13th century, Spanish and Italian seafarers entered the Atlantic from the Mediterranean, though without much initial result except several lost expeditions.

European Travel: A Monk Visits Jerusalem

Willibald, an English monk, journeyed to Jerusalem between 721 and 727 C.E. His account was written down by a German nun.

In Syria

Willibald's party had now grown to eight in number, and they became an object of suspicion to the Muslims, who, seeing that they were strangers, seized them and threw them into prison, because they knew not of what country they were, and supposed them to be spies. They carried them as prisoners before a certain rich old man, that he might examine them; and he inquired whence they came and the object of their mission; whereupon they related to him the true cause of their journey. The old man replied, "I have often seen men of the parts of the earth whence these come, traveling hither; they seek no harm, but desire to fulfil their law." And upon that they went to the palace, to obtain leave to proceed to Jerusalem.

While they were in prison it happened, by a manifest intervention of Devine Providence, that a merchant residing there was desirous, as an act of charity, and for the salvation of his soul, to purchase their deliverance, that they might pursue their way, but he was not allowed to carry his generous design into effect; nevertheless he sent them daily their meals, and on Wednesdays and Saturdays sent his son to them in prison, who took them out to the bath, and brought them back again. And on Sunday he took them to church through the market, that they might see the shops, and whatever they seemed to take a liking to he afterwards bought for them at his own expense. The townsmen used then to come there to look at them, because they were young and handsome, and clad in good garments.

Then, while they were still remaining in prison, a man, who was a native of Spain, came and spoke with them, and inquired earnestly who they were and from whence they came, and they told him the object of their pilgrimage. This Spaniard had a brother in the kind's palace, who was chamberlain to the king of the Muslims. . . . When [Willibald and the Spaniard] came before the king, and told him the case, he asked whence the prisoners came. And they said, "These men come from the west country, where the sun sets; and we know of no land beyond them, but water only." And the king replied, "Why ought we to punish them? they have not sinned against us: – give them leave, and let them go." And even the fine of four deniers, which the other prisoners had to pay, was remitted to them. . . .

Jerusalem and Bethlehem

On their arrival at Jerusalem, they first visited the spot where the holy cross was found, where there is now a church which is called the Place of Calvary, and which was formerly outside of Jerusalem; but when St. Helena found the cross, the place was taken into the circuit of the city. Three wooden crosses stand in this place, on the outside of the wall of the church, in memory of our Lord's cross and of those of the other persons crucified at the same time.

He next came to the place where the angel appeared to the shepherds, and thence to Bethlehem, where our Lord was born, distant seven miles from Jerusalem.

[Later, heading home they] reached Constantinople. Here repose in one altar the three saints, Andres, Timothy, and Luke the evangelist; and the sepulcher of John Chrysostome is before the altar where the priest stands when he performs mass. Willibald remained there two years, and was lodged in the church, so that he might behold daily where the saints reposed.

QUESTIONS What relationships between Christians and Muslims does this passage suggest, for the post-classical period? Why would a Spaniard play a special role in Willibald's Middle Eastern Experience? What were Willibald's motives for travel? What kind of larger results did this sort of travel have, in post-classical world history?

The most dramatic expansionist move involved the great Crusades against the Muslim control of the Holy Land. Pope **Urban II** called for the First Crusade in 1095, appealing to the piety of the West's rulers and common people. Crusaders were promised full forgiveness of sins if they died in battle, ensuring their entry to heaven, which obviously enhanced the religious motivations involved. The idea of attacking Islam had great appeal, as Figure 10.4 suggests. The attraction of winning spoils from the rich Arab lands added to the inducement, as did the thirst for excitement among the West's feudal warriors. Internal wars were declining in Europe, and the military values of feudalism sought outlets elsewhere. Three great armies, with tens of thousands of crusaders from various parts of the West, assembled in Constantinople in 1097, much to the distress of the Byzantine government. The Western crusaders moved toward Jerusalem, winning it from the Turkish armies that held the area by that time. For almost a century, Western knights ruled the "kingdom of Jerusalem," losing it to a great Muslim general, Saladin, during the 12th century.

Several later Crusades attempted to win back the Holy Land, but many later efforts turned toward other goals or toward pure farce. The Third Crusade at the end of the 12th century led to the death of the German emperor and the imprisonment of the English king, although it did produce a brief truce with Saladin that facilitated Christian pilgrims' visits to Jerusalem. The Fourth Crusade was manipulated by merchants in Venice, who turned it into an attack on their commercial rivals in Constantinople.

The Crusades did not demonstrate a new Western superiority in the wider world, despite brief successes. In the Middle East, they generated only a passing episode. But in expressing a

The Crusades
MAP

Dueling Crusaders
IMAGE

Urban II Called First Crusade in 1095; appealed to Christians to mount military assault to free the Holy Land from the Muslims.

Fulcher of Chartres, Chronicle of the First Crusade: Geoffrey of Vilhardouin on the 4th Crusade

Figure 10.4 This imaginary duel between the noble Christian champion King Richard of England and the Muslim leader Saladin clearly shows the difference between "good guys" and "bad guys." Though many actual crusaders respected Saladin as a skilled military leader, in Europe he was condemned as an infidel.

Gregory VII Pope during the 11th century who attempted to free church from interference of feudal lords; quarreled with Holy Roman Emperor Henry IV over practice of lay investiture.

combination of religious zeal and growing commercial and military vigor on the part of the knights and merchants who organized the largest efforts, the Crusades unquestionably showed the aggressive spirit of the Western Middle Ages at their height. They also helped expose the West to new cultural and economic influences from the Middle East. This was a major spur to further change, including a greater thirst for goods, like spices, available only through international trade. Simply visiting the thriving urban center of Constantinople during the Crusades could open European eyes to new possibilities. One crusader exclaimed, "Oh, what a great and beautiful city is Constantinople! How many churches and palaces it contains, fashioned with wonderful skill! Their tradesmen at all times bring by boat all the necessities of man."

Religious Reform and Evolution

As medieval society developed, the Catholic church went through several periods of decline and renewal. At times, church officials and the leading monastic groups became preoccupied with their land holdings and their political interests. The church was a wealthy institution; it was tempting for many priests and monks to behave like ordinary feudal lords in pursuit of greater worldly power. Several reform movements fought this secularism, such as the 13th-century flowering that created orders such as the Franciscans, devoted to poverty and service in Europe's bustling cities. Saint Clare of Assisi (1194–1253) exemplified this new spirit of purity and dedication to the church (Figure 10.5). She was deeply influenced by Saint Francis, also from Assisi, who had converted to a life of piety and preaching in 1205 and who founded a new monastic order around him. Clare refused to marry, as her parents wanted, but rather founded a women's Franciscan order (later known as the Order of Saint Clare, or the Poor Clares) with Francis's backing. Like many women in Europe, Clare found in monasticism a vital means of personal expression. In 1958 Pope Pius XII declared her the patron saint of television, for during her last illness she miraculously heard and saw on the wall of her room a Christmas mass being performed on the other side of Assisi.

In addition to monastic leaders, reform-minded popes, such as **Gregory VII** (1073–1085), tried to purify the church and free it from interference by feudal lords. One technique was insistence on the particularly holy character of the priesthood. Reformers stipulated that all priests remain unmarried, to separate the priesthood from the ordinary

Figure 10.5 On the night of March 20, 1212, the Count of Sasso-Rosso's 18-year-old daughter, Clare, stole away from her father's house to dedicate herself to a life of poverty and holiness. She resisted all attempts by her father to bring her home and by the church to persuade her to accept some income as a guarantee against starvation for her order, which depended entirely on the begging of local friars for its daily bread. Clare was named abbess of a convent just three years later, and she never again left its grounds. Her sisters, her mother, and an aunt followed her into the order. She was canonized Saint Clare of Assisi in 1255.

Western Civilization

In recent years, historians have been critically examining the term "Western civilization," which is sometimes (wrongly) taken as self-evident.

The concept of "the West" or "Western civilization" was actively used in the 20th-century cold war with the Soviet Union, yet it is hard to define. We have seen that the classical Mediterranean world did not directly identify a "Western" civilization, and this classical heritage was used most selectively by postclassical western Europe. Further, the consistent absence of political unity in western Europe complicates any definition of common structures.

Western Europeans could not have identified Western civilization in the postclassical period, but they would have recognized the concept of Christendom, along with some difference between their version of this religion and that of eastern Europe. The first definition of this civilization was primarily religious, although artistic forms associated with religion also figured in this definition. Regional cultures varied, of course, and there was no linguistic unity, but cultural developments in one area—for example, the creation of universities, which started in Italy—surfaced elsewhere fairly quickly. Supplementing culture were some reasonably common social structures—like manors and guilds—and trade patterns that increasingly joined northern and much of southern Europe. The resulting civilization was by no means as coherent as Chinese civilization; many of its members detested each other, like the English and French, who were often in conflict and sometimes engaged in name-calling (the English were "les goddams," because

> "Defining Western civilization is also complicated . . . because Western leaders copied so much from other societies."

they swore so much, and the French were "frogs" because of what they ate). Until very recently, Europeans thought in terms of distinctive national histories, not European ones. But it is possible to define some common features that differed from those of neighboring civilizations. Even as the civilization began to change, late in the postclassical period, it preserved some common directions. Debate continues about the balance between the Western and more purely national features.

Defining Western civilization is also complicated in the postclassical period because Western leaders copied so much from other societies. They eagerly learned of new technologies from Asia. They benefited from Arab mathematics and philosophy, and they imitated Muslim commercial law on how to treat tradespeople from outside the locality. But even in imitating, most Europeans were keenly conscious of their distinctiveness as Christians. They sometimes resented the societies they copied from. Toward the end of the Middle Ages, as Europeans began to seek a new role in the world at large, the openness to imitation also began to decline, as part of the further definition of a Western or European identity.

QUESTIONS Was there a Western civilization before the postclassical period? What were the defining features of Western civilization by the end of the postclassical period? How does the definition of Western civilization today compare to that of the postclassical period?

---

world of the flesh. Gregory also tried to free the church from any trace of state control. He quarreled vigorously with Holy Roman Emperor Henry IV over the practice of state appointment, or **investiture,** of bishops in Germany. Ultimately, by excommunicating the emperor from the church, Gregory won his point. The emperor appealed to the pope for forgiveness on his knees in the snow of a northern Italian winter, and the investiture controversy ended, apparently in the church's favor. Gregory and several later popes made clear their beliefs that the church not only was to be free from state interference but was superior to the state in its function as a direct channel of God's word. While governments still influenced religious affairs, a network of church courts developed to rule on matters of religious law and to bring heretics to trial and occasionally to execution. This was the origin of recurrent Western beliefs in church–state separation.

 Spread of Latin Christianity in Western Europe

investiture Practice of state appointment of bishops; Pope Gregory VII attempted to ban the practice of lay investiture, leading to war with Holy Roman Emperor Henry IV.

The High Middle Ages

The postclassical version of Western civilization reached its high mark in the 12th and 13th centuries. Fed by the growing dynamism of western Europe's population, agriculture, and cities, the High Middle Ages were characterized by a series of creative tensions. Feudal political structures, derived from local and personal allegiances, were balanced by emerging central monarchies. The unquestionable authority of the church and the cultural dominance of Christianity jostled with the intellectual vitality and diversity that formed part of university life. A social order and economy, based primarily on agriculture and the labor of serfs, now had to come to terms with important cities, merchants, and some new opportunities even for ordinary farmers.

231

Western Culture in the Postclassical Era

Christian culture dominated European philosophy and art, but it generated both change and some conflict.

During the centuries before about 1000, a small number of clergy continued the efforts of preserving and interpreting past wisdom, particularly the writings of church fathers such as Augustine, but also the work of some non-Christian Latin authors. During Charlemagne's time, a favorite practice was to gather quotations from ancient writers around key subjects. Interest in classical principles of rhetoric, particularly logic, reflected the concern for coherent organization; Aristotle, known to the Middle Ages as *the* philosopher, was valued because of his clear exposition of rational thought.

Theology: Assimilating Faith and Reason

From 1000 onward, a series of outstanding clerics advanced the logical exposition of philosophy and theology to new levels. They stressed the importance of absolute faith in God's word, but they believed that human reason could move toward an understanding of some aspects of religion and the natural order as well. Thus, according to several theologians, it was possible to prove the existence of God. Fascination with logic led some intellectuals to a certain zeal in pointing out inconsistencies in past wisdom, even in the writings of the church fathers. In the 12th century, **Peter Abelard** in Paris wrote a treatise called *Yes and No* in which he showed several logical contradictions in established interpretations of doctrine. Although Abelard protested his faith, saying, "I would not be an Aristotle if this were to part me from Christ," he clearly took an impish delight in suggesting skepticism. Here was a fascinating case of an individual's role in history. Abelard was clearly working in an established logical tradition, but his personality helped move the tradition to a new critical level. At the same time, his defiant attitudes may have drawn more attack than a softer approach would have done, which had consequences too.

The logical-rationalist current in Western philosophy was hardly unopposed. A powerful monk, **Bernard of Clairvaux** (klehr-VOH), successfully challenged Abelard. Bernard, an intellectual of a different sort, stressed the importance of mystical union with God, attainable even on this earth in brief blissful glimpses, rather than rationalist endeavor. Bernard believed that reason was dangerous and that God's truth must be received through faith alone.

The debates over how and whether to combine the classical Mediterranean philosophical and scientific tradition with revealed religious faith reflected the earlier debates among Arab intellectuals during the 10th and 11th centuries. Both Christianity and Islam relied heavily on faith in a revealed word, through the Bible or Qur'an, respectively, but some intellectuals in both cultures strained to include other approaches.

Combining rational philosophy and Christian faith was the dominant intellectual theme in the postclassical West, showing the need to come to terms with both Christian and classical heritages, and with Middle Eastern learning as well. This combination of rational philosophy and Christian faith also posed formidable and fascinating problems. By the 12th century, the zeal for this kind of knowledge produced several distinctive results. It explained the intellectual vitality of most of the emerging universities, where students flocked to hear the latest debates by leading theologians. Higher education certainly benefited students through resulting job opportunities; for example, trained lawyers could hope for advancement in the growing bureaucracies of church or state. In contrast to China's institutions, however, the new universities were not directly tied into a single bureaucratic system, and the excitement they engendered during the Middle Ages was not just opportunistic. A large number of students, from the whole of western Europe, sought out the mixture of spiritual and rational understanding that leading thinkers were trying to work out.

The postclassical intellectual drive also motivated a growing interest in knowledge newly imported from the classical past and from the Arab world, and this knowledge fed the highest achievements of medieval learning. By the 12th century, Western scholars were reading vast amounts of material translated from Greek in centers in the Byzantine Empire, Italy, and Muslim Spain. They gained familiarity with the bulk of ancient Greek and Hellenistic philosophy and science. They also read translations of Arab and Jewish learning, particularly the works in which Middle Eastern scholars had wrestled with the problems of mixing human reasoning with truths gained by faith.

With much fuller knowledge of Aristotelian and Hellenistic science, plus the work of Arab rationalists such as Ibn-Rushd (IH-buhn RUSHT) (known in the West as Averroës (uh-VEHR-oh-eez), Western philosopher-theologians in the 13th century proceeded to the final great synthesis of

Abelard, Peter (1079–1142) Author of *Yes and No;* university scholar who applied logic to problems of theology; demonstrated logical contradictions within established doctrine.

Bernard of Clairvaux [klehr-VOH] (1090–1153) Emphasized role of faith in preference to logic; stressed importance of mystical union with God; successfully challenged Abelard and had him driven from the universities.

medieval learning. The leading figure was **Thomas Aquinas** (Thomas ah-KWY-nuhs), the Italian-born monk who taught at the University of Paris. Aquinas maintained the basic belief that faith came first, but he greatly expanded the scope given to reason. Through reason alone, humans could know much of the natural order, moral law, and the nature of God. Aquinas had complete confidence that all essential knowledge could be organized coherently, and he produced a host of *Summas,* or highest works, that used careful logic to eliminate all possible objections to truth as revealed by reason and faith. Essentially, this work restated in Christian terms the Greek efforts to seek a rationality in nature that would correspond to the rational capacities of the human mind. To be sure, a few philosophers carried the interest in logic to absurd degrees. After the 13th century, **scholasticism**—as the dominant medieval philosophical approach was called because of its base in the schools—sometimes degenerated into silly debates such as the one about how many angels could dance on the head of a pin. But at its height, and particularly with Aquinas, scholasticism demonstrated an unusual confidence in the logical orderliness of knowledge and in human ability to know.

Medieval philosophy did not encourage a great deal of new scientific work. The emphasis on mastering past learning and organizing it logically could lead to overemphasis on previous discoveries rather than empirical research. Thus, university-trained doctors stressed memorization of Galen, the Hellenistic authority, rather than systematic practical experience. Toward the end of the 13th century, a current of practical science developed. In Oxford, members of the clergy, such as Roger Bacon, did experimental work with optics, pursuing research done earlier by Muslim scholars. An important by-product of this interest was the invention of eyeglasses. During the 14th and 15th centuries, experimenters also advanced knowledge in chemistry and astronomy. This early work set the stage for the flourishing of Western science.

Popular Religion

Far less is known about popular beliefs than about formal intellectual life in the Middle Ages. Christian devotion undoubtedly ran deep and may well have increased with time among many ordinary people. At least in the early medieval centuries, many people diligently followed Christian rituals yet seemed unaware of how many of their actions might contradict Christian morality. For example, Raoul de Cambrai, hero of a French epic written down in the late 12th century but orally transmitted earlier, sets fire to a convent filled with nuns, then asks a servant to bring him some food. The servant berates him for burning the convent, then reminds him that it is Lent, a time of fasting and repentance before Easter. Raoul denies that his deed was unjust, for the nuns deserved it for insulting his knights, but admits that he had forgotten Lent and goes off to distract himself from his hunger by playing chess.

Whether day-to-day morality improved or not, popular means of expressing religious devotion expanded over time. The rise of cities saw the formation of lay groups to develop spirituality and express their love of God. The content of popular belief evolved as well. Enthusiasm for the veneration of Mary, the mother of Jesus, expanded by the 12th century, showing a desire to stress the merciful side of Christianity, rather than the supposed sternness of God the Father, and new hopes for assistance in gaining salvation. The worship of various saints showed a similar desire for intermediaries between humanity and God. At the same time, ordinary people continued to believe in various magical rituals, and they celebrated essentially pagan festivals, which often involved much dancing and merriment. They blended their version of Christianity with great earthiness and spontaneity, some of which was conveyed by late medieval authors such as English writer Geoffrey Chaucer.

Religious Themes in Art and Literature

Religious art was another cultural area in which the medieval West came to excel, as was the case in other societies where religious enthusiasm ran strong, such as the Islamic Middle East or Hindu India. Like philosophy, medieval art and architecture were intended to serve the glory of God. Western painters used religious subjects almost exclusively. Painting mainly on wooden panels, artists in most parts of western Europe depicted Christ's birth and suffering and the lives of the saints, using stiff, stylized figures. By the 14th and 15th centuries, artists improved their ability to render natural scenes realistically and portrayed a host of images of medieval life as backdrops to their religious subjects. Stained-glass designs and scenes for churches were another important artistic expression.

Medieval architecture initially followed Roman models, particularly in church building, using a rectangular, or Romanesque, style sometimes surmounted by domes. During the 11th century,

Aquinas, Thomas [Thomas ah-KWY-nuhs] (1225–1274) Creator of one of the great syntheses of medieval learning; taught at University of Paris; author of several *Summas;* believed that through reason it was possible to know much about natural order, moral law, and nature of God.

scholasticism Dominant medieval philosophical approach; so-called because of its base in the schools or universities; based on use of logic to resolve theological problems.

Notre-Dame, Paris

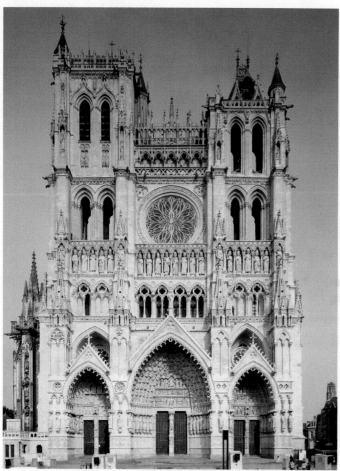

Figure 10.6 The cathedral of Notre-Dame (Our Lady) at Amiens, France, is a grand example of gothic architecture, which flourished during the later Middle Ages in western Europe. The cathedral, which dwarfs the surrounding buildings, was built between 1220 and 1402 and was the tallest building in Europe at the time of its completion.

Song of Roland
DOCUMENT

Gothic   An architectural style developed during the Middle Ages in western Europe; featured pointed arches and flying buttresses as external supports on main walls.

While merchant capitalism gained ground in western Europe, other economic values predominated.

however, a new style took hold that was far more original, though it benefited from knowledge of Muslim design plus advances in structural engineering in the West itself. **Gothic** architects built soaring church spires and tall arched windows, as Figure 10.6 illustrates. Although their work focused on creating churches and great cathedrals, some civic buildings and palaces also picked up the Gothic motif. It is not far-fetched to see the Gothic style as representative of Western postclassical culture more generally. Its spiritual orientation showed in the towers cast up to the heavens. It built also on growing technical skills and deep popular devotion, expressed in the money collected to build the huge monuments and the patient labor needed for construction that often lasted many decades. The originality of Gothic styles reflected the growing Western ability to find suitable new means of expression, just as use of Gothic styles in the later Western world showed the ongoing power of medieval models.

Medieval literature and music reflected strong religious interests. Most Latin writing dealt with points of philosophy, law, or political theory. However, alongside writing in Latin came the development of a growing literature in the spoken languages, or vernaculars, of western Europe. The pattern was not unlike that of India a few centuries earlier after the fall of the Gupta empire, when Sanskrit served as a scholarly language but increasing power was given to popular languages such as Hindi. Vernacular literature helped develop separate European languages and focused largely on secular themes. Several oral sagas, dealing with the deeds of great knights and mythic figures in the past, were written down. From this tradition came the first known writing in early English, *Beowulf,* and in French, *The Song of Roland.* Late in the Middle Ages, a number of writers created adventure stories, comic tales, and poetry in the vernacular tongues, such as Chaucer's *Canterbury Tales.* Much of their work, and also plays written for performance in the growing cities, reflected the tension between Christian values and a desire to portray the richness and coarseness of life on earth. Chaucer's narrative shows a fascination with bawdy behavior, a willingness to poke fun at the hypocrisy of many Christians, and an ability to capture some of the tragedies of human existence. In France, a long poem called *The Romance of the Rose* used vivid sexual imagery, and the poet Villon wrote, in largely secular terms, of the terror and poignancy of death.

Also using vernacular language, a series of courtly poets, or troubadours, based particularly in southern France in the 14th century, wrote hymns to the love that could flourish between men and women. Although their verses stressed platonic devotion rather than sexual love and paid homage to courtly ceremonies and polite behavior, their concern with love was the first sign of a new valuation of this emotional experience in the Western tradition.

In sum, medieval intellectual and artistic life created a host of important themes. Religion was the centerpiece, but it did not preclude a growing range of interests, from science to romantic poetry. Medieval culture was a rich intellectual achievement in its own right. It also set in motion a series of developments—in rationalist philosophy, science, artistic representations of nature, and vernacular literature—that would be building blocks for later Western thought and art.

Changing Economic and Social Forms in the Postclassical Centuries

Although culture provided the most obvious cement for Western society during the Middle Ages, economic activity and social structure also developed common features. Here too, the postclassical West demonstrated impressive powers of innovation, for classical patterns had little hold. As trade revived by the 10th century, the West became a common commercial zone. Most regions produced primarily for local consumption, as was true in agricultural societies generally. But Italian merchants actively sought cloth manufactured in the Low Countries (present-day Belgium and the Netherlands), and merchants in many areas traded for wool produced in England or timber supplies and furs brought from Scandinavia and the Baltic lands. Great ports and trading fairs, particularly in the Low Countries and northern France, served as centers for Western exchange as well as markets for a few exotic products such as spices brought in from other civilizations (Map 10.3).

Western Europe also saw a clear expansion in productive capacity during much of the post-classical period, with gains in agriculture supporting some growth in urban manufacturing. Their achievements here did not rival those of East Asia, where the production gains and social consequences were more substantial, but they did contribute to this larger theme in the period as a whole.

New Strains in Rural Life

The improvements in agriculture after 900 C.E. brought important new ingredients to rural life. Some peasants were able to shake off the most severe constraints of manorialism, becoming almost free farmers with only a few obligations to their landlords, although rigid manorialism remained in place in many areas. Noble landlords still served mainly military functions, for ownership of a horse and armor were prerequisites for fighting until the end of the medieval period. Although most nobles shunned the taint of commerce—like aristocrats in many societies, they found too much money-grubbing demeaning—they did use trade to improve their standard of living and adopt more polished habits. The courtly literature of the late Middle Ages reflected this new style of life.

Map 10.3 Leading Trade Routes Within Europe and to the Mediterranean

As many lords sought improved conditions they were often tempted to press their serfs to pay higher rents and taxes, even as serfs were gaining a new sense of freedom and control over their own land. From the late Middle Ages until the 19th century, this tension produced a recurrent series of peasant–landlord battles in Western society. Peasants sought what they viewed as their natural and traditional right to the land, free and clear. They talked of Christian equality, turning such phrases as "When Adam delved and Eve span, Who was then a gentleman?" A more complex economy clearly brought new social strains, similar to the recurrent wave of popular unrest in China or the rural uprisings in the Middle East, where religion helped prompt egalitarian sentiments as well. The gap between lord and peasant was the crucial social inequality in Europe, but it was open to change and it generated some egalitarian ideas in response.

On the whole, the lives of Western peasants improved between 900 and 1300. Landlord controls were less tight than they had become in other societies, such as the Middle East. Western agriculture was not yet particularly advanced technologically (compared with east Asia, for example), but it had improved notably over early medieval levels.

Growth of Trade and Banking

Gains in agriculture promoted larger changes in medieval economic life. Urban growth allowed more specialized manufacturing and commercial activities, which in turn promoted still greater trade. Spearheaded by Italian businesspeople, banking was introduced to the West to facilitate the

Figure 10.7 This 14th-century miniature shows views of a banking house. People might keep money in banks, seek loans, or arrange transactions with merchants in faraway centers of trade.

Medieval Trade Routes and Trade Fairs

Hanseatic League   An organization of cities in northern Germany and southern Scandinavia for the purpose of establishing a commercial alliance.

European Fairs and Trade Routes

long-distance exchange of money and goods (Figure 10.7). The use of money spread steadily, to the dismay of many Christian moralists and many ordinary people who preferred the more direct, personal ways of traditional society. The largest trading and banking operations, not only in Italy but in southern Germany, the Low Countries, France, and Britain, were clearly capitalistic. Big merchants invested funds in trading ships and the goods they carried, hoping to make large profits on this capital. Profitmaking was not judged kindly by Christian thinkers such as Thomas Aquinas, who urged that all prices should be "just," reflecting only the labor put into the goods.

Rising trade took several forms. There were exchanges between western Europe and other parts of the known world. Wealthy Europeans developed a taste for some of the luxury goods and spices of Asia. The latter were not used merely to flavor food but were vital in preserving perishable items such as meat. Spice extracts also had great medicinal value. The Crusades played a role in bringing these products to wider attention. A Mediterranean trade redeveloped, mainly in the hands of Italian merchants, in which European cloth and some other products were exchanged for the more polished goods of the East. Commerce within Europe involved exchanges of timber and grain from the north for cloth and metal products manufactured in Italy and the Low Countries. At first an exporter of raw wool, England developed some manufactured goods for exchange by the later Middle Ages. Commercial alliances developed. Cities in northern Germany and southern Scandinavia grouped together in the **Hanseatic League** to encourage trade. With growing banking facilities, it became possible to organize commercial transactions throughout much of western Europe. Bankers, including many Jewish businesspeople, were valued for their service in lending money to monarchs and the papacy.

The growth of trade and banking in the Middle Ages served as the origin of capitalism in Western civilization. The greater Italian and German bankers, the long-distance merchants of the Hanseatic cities, were clearly capitalistic in their willingness to invest in trading ventures with the expectation of profit. Given the dangers of trade by land and sea, the risks in these investments were substantial, but profits of 100 percent or more were possible. In many cities, such as London, groups of powerful merchants banded together to invest in international trade, each buying shares in the venture and profiting or losing accordingly.

Individual merchants could amass—and lose—great fortunes. Jacques Coeur (JAHK KUR) (c. 1395–1456), one of Europe's most extraordinary merchants, demonstrated the opportunities and risks of new forms of trade (Figure 10.8). Son of a furrier, he married the daughter of a royal official and served as a tax official until he was caught minting coins with less valuable metals.

He then founded a trading company that competed with Italians and Spaniards in dealing with the Middle East. He visited Damascus to buy spices, setting up a regular trade in rugs, Chinese silk, and Indonesian spices and sugar. He also became financial advisor and supplier to the French king and was ennobled. With the largest fleet ever owned by a French subject, Coeur surrounded himself with splendor, even arranging with the pope for his 16-year-old son to become an archbishop. But he had enemies, many of them nobles in debt to him, and they turned the king against him. Tortured, he admitted to various crimes, including supplying weapons to Muslims. His property was confiscated, but adventurer to the last, he died on a Greek island while serving in a papal fleet against the Turks.

By world standards this was not a totally unprecedented merchant spirit. European traders were still less venturesome and less wealthy than some of their Muslim counterparts. Nor was Western society as tolerant of merchants as Muslim or Indian societies were. Yet Western commercial endeavors clearly were growing. Because Western governments were weak, with few economic functions, merchants had a freer hand than in many other civilizations. Many of the growing cities were ruled by commercial leagues. Monarchs liked to encourage the cities as a counterbalance to the power of the landed aristocracy, and in the later Middle Ages and beyond, traders and kings typically were allied. However, aside from taxing merchants and using them as sources of loans, royal governments did not interfere much with trading activities. Merchants even developed their own codes of commercial law, administered by city courts. Thus, the rising merchant class was staking out an unusually powerful and independent role in European society.

Capitalism was not yet typical of the Western economy, even aside from the moral qualms fostered by the Christian tradition. Most peasants and landlords had not become enmeshed in the market system. In the cities, the dominant economic ethic stressed group protection, not profitmaking. The characteristic institution was not the international trading firm but the merchant or artisan guild. **Guilds** grouped people in the same business or trade in a single city, sometimes with loose links to similar guilds in other cities. These organizations were new in western Europe, although they resembled guilds in various parts of Asia but with greater independence from the state. They stressed security and mutual control. Merchant guilds thus attempted to give all members a share in any endeavor. If a ship pulled in loaded with wool, the clothiers' guild of the city insisted that all members participate in the purchase so that no one member would monopolize the profits.

Artisan guilds were made up of the people in the cities who actually made cloth, bread, jewelry, or furniture. These guilds tried to limit their membership so that all members would have work. They regulated apprenticeships to guarantee good training but also to ensure that no member would employ too many apprentices and so gain undue wealth. They discouraged new methods because security and a rough equality, not maximum individual profit, were the goals; here was their alternative to the capitalistic approach. Guilds also tried to guarantee quality so that consumers would not have to worry about shoddy quality on the part of some unscrupulous profit-seeker. Guilds played an important political and social role in the cities, giving their members recognized status and often a voice in city government. Their statutes were in turn upheld by municipal law and often backed by the royal government as well.

Despite the traditionalism of the guilds, manufacturing and commercial methods improved in medieval Europe. Western Europe was not yet as advanced as Asia in ironmaking and textile manufacture, but it was beginning to catch up. In a few areas, such as clockmaking—which involved both sophisticated technology and a concern for precise time initially linked to the schedule of church services—European artisans led the world. Furthermore, some manufacturing spilled beyond the bounds of guild control. Particularly in the Low Countries and parts of Italy, groups of manufacturing workers were employed by capitalists to produce for a wide market. Their techniques were simple, and they worked in their own homes, often alternating manufacturing labor with agriculture. Their work was guided not by the motives of the guilds but by the inducements of merchant capitalists, who provided them with raw materials and then paid them for their production.

Thus, by the later Middle Ages, western Europe's economy and society embraced many contradictory groups and principles. Commercial and capitalist elements jostled against the slower pace of economic life in the countryside and even against the dominant group protectionism of most urban guilds. Most people remained peasants, but a minority had escaped to the cities, where they found more excitement, along with increased danger and higher rates of disease. Medieval tradition held that a serf who managed to live in the city for a year and a day became a free person. A few prosperous capitalists flourished, but most people operated according to very different economic values, directed toward group welfare rather than individual profit. This was neither a static society nor an early model of a modern commercial society. It had its own flavor and its own tensions—the fruit of several centuries of economic and social change.

Limited Sphere for Women

The increasing complexity of medieval social and economic life may have had one final effect, which is familiar from patterns in other agricultural societies: new limits on the conditions of women. Women's work remained vital in most families. The Christian emphasis on the equality of

Figure 10.8 In the late Middle Ages, Jacques Coeur was one of a small but increasingly important class of wealthy merchants—men whose wealth came not from landed estates, but from ships and trading companies. His fabulous fortune financed the wars that drove the English from French soil, but he had many enemies. He was forced to flee France in 1454, when his enemies falsely accused him of a number of crimes, including poisoning the king's mistress.

guilds Sworn associations of people in the same business or craft in a single city; stressed security and mutual control; limited membership, regulated apprenticeship, guaranteed good workmanship; often established franchise within cities.

all souls and the practical importance of women's monastic groups in providing an alternative to marriage continued to have distinctive effects on women's lives in Western society. The veneration of Mary and other female religious figures gave women real cultural prestige, counterbalancing the biblical emphasis on Eve as the source of human sin. In some respects, women in the West had higher status than their sisters under Islam: they were less segregated in religious services (although they could not lead them) and were less confined to the household. Still, women's voice in the family may have declined in the Middle Ages.

Urban women often played important roles in local commerce and even operated some craft guilds, but they found themselves increasingly hemmed in by male-dominated organizations. In contrast to Islam, women were not assured of property rights. By the late Middle Ages, a literature arose that stressed women's roles as the assistants and comforters to men, listing supplemental household tasks and docile virtues as women's distinctive sphere. Patriarchal structures seemed to be taking deeper root.

Black Death Plague that struck Europe in 14th century; significantly reduced Europe's population; affected social structure.

The Decline of the Medieval Synthesis

Key characteristics of western Europe began to shift after 1300, with new problems of overpopulation and disease.

Spread of the Black Death
MAP

A major war engulfed France and England during the 14th and 15th centuries, and this proved to be both symptom and cause of larger difficulties. The Hundred Years War, which sputtered into the mid-15th century, lasted even longer than its name and initially went very badly for France—a sign of new weakness in the French monarchy. As the war dragged on, kings reduced their reliance on the prancing forces of the nobility in favor of paid armies of their own. New military methods challenged the key monopoly of the feudal lords, as ordinary paid archers learned how to unseat armored knights with powerful bows and arrows and with crossbows (Figure 10.9). The war ended with a French victory, sparked in part by the heroic leadership of the inspired peasant woman Joan of Arc, but both its devastation and the antifeudal innovations it encouraged suggested a time of change.

Concurrently, from about 1300 onward, key sources of Western vitality threatened to disappear. Medieval agriculture could no longer keep pace with population growth: The readily available new lands had been used up, and there were no major new technological gains to compensate. The result included severe famines and a decline in population levels until the end of the century. A devastating series of plagues that persisted for several centuries, beginning with the **Black Death** in 1348, further challenged Europe's population and social structure (Figure 10.10). New social disputes arose, heightening some of the tensions noted earlier between peasants and landlords, artisans and their employees. Not until the 16th century would the West begin to work out a new social structure.

The West's economy did not go into a tailspin. In some respects, as in manufacturing and mining technology, progress may even have accelerated. The 150 to 200 years after 1300 form in Western history a transition period in which the features of the Middle Ages began to blur while new problems and developments began to take center stage. Western civilization was not in a spiral of decline, but the postclassical version of this civilization was.

Signs of Strain

The decline of medieval society involved increasing challenges to several typical medieval institutions. During the 14th century, the ruling class of medieval society, the land-owning aristocracy, began to show signs of confusion. It had long staked its claim to power on its control of land and its military prowess, but its skill in warfare was now open to question. The growth of professional armies and new weaponry such as cannon and gunpowder made traditional fighting methods, including fortified castles, increasingly irrelevant. The aristocracy did not simply disappear, however. Rather, the nobility chose to emphasize a rich cere-

Figure 10.9 The Siege of Paris, pictured here, took place in 1465, after the French nobility rose up against King Louis XI, whose treatment of them had left them angry and ambitious to reestablish their independence from the Crown. Calling themselves the League of Public Good, they marched on Paris, but the fighting there was indecisive and gave Louis the chance to regroup. The uprising was ended by treaty two months later. This incident was a revealing clash between feudal values and new royal ambition.

Figure 10.10 This painting shows survivors at Tournai placing plague victims in coffins before mass burial became the only way to keep up with the deaths. The Black Death, which killed up to a quarter of the population of Europe in just twenty years, devastated medieval society.

monial style of life, featuring tournaments in which military expertise could be turned into competitive games. The idea of chivalry—carefully controlled, polite behavior, including behavior toward women—gained ground. The upper class became more cultivated. We have seen similar transformations in the earlier Chinese and Muslim aristocracy. Yet at this transitional point in Europe, some of the elaborate ceremonies of chivalry seemed rather hollow, even a bit silly—a sign that medieval values were losing hold without being replaced by a new set of purposes.

Another key area involved decisive shifts in the balance between church and state that had characterized medieval life. For several decades in the aftermath of the taxation disputes in the early 14th century, French kings wielded great influence on the papacy, which they relocated from Rome to Avignon, a town surrounded by French territory. Then rival claimants to the papacy confused the issue further. Ultimately a single pope was returned to Rome, but the church was clearly weakened. Moreover, the church began to lose some of its grip on Western religious life. Church leaders were so preoccupied with their political involvement that they tended to neglect the spiritual side. Religion was not declining; indeed, signs of intense popular piety continued to blossom, and new religious groups formed in the towns. But devotion became partially separated from the institution of the church. One result, again beginning in the 14th century, was a series of popular heresies, with leaders in places such as England and Bohemia (the present-day Czech Republic) preaching against the hierarchical apparatus of the church in favor of direct popular experience of God. Another result was an important new series of mystics, many of them women, who claimed direct, highly emotional contacts with God.

A third area in which medievalism faded was the breakdown of the intellectual and even artistic synthesis. After the work of Aquinas, church officials became less tolerant of intellectual daring, and they even declared some of Aquinas's writings heretical. The earlier blend of rationalism and religion no longer seemed feasible. Ultimately, this turned some thinkers away from religion, but this daring development took time. In art, growing interest in realistic portrayals of nature, though fruitful, suggested the beginnings of a shift away from medieval artistic standards. Religious figures became less stylized as painters grew more interested in human features for their own sake. The various constraints on forms of postclassical culture prompted many Western intellectuals to look for different emphases. In Italy most clearly, new kinds of literature and art took shape that differed from the styles and subjects of the postclassical centuries.

The Postclassical West and Its Heritage

Medieval Europe had several faces. The term *Middle Ages* implies a lull, between the glories of Rome and the glitter of more modern Europe. There is some truth to this, for medieval Europe did grapple with backwardness and vulnerability.

But the Middle Ages were also a period of growing dynamism. Particularly after 900 C.E., gains in population, trade and cities, and intellectual activity created a vigorous period in European history. Key developments set a tone that would last even after the specifically medieval centuries had ended. Universities and Gothic art (often intertwined, as in the many American campuses that revived the Gothic style for their buildings) were an enduring legacy to Western society. Distinctive ideas about government, building on Christian and feudal traditions, constituted another medieval contribution.

The medieval period was also a special moment in the relationship between Europe and the regions around it. Opportunities to advance by imitation were particularly striking, from technology to science to trade and consumption. Even the medieval university may have had Arab origins, in the higher schools of the Muslim world.

Medieval Europe warrants a particular comparison with other areas in which civilization was partially new during the postclassical period and where change and imitation proceeded rapidly. Divided political rule in Europe resembled conditions in west Africa and Japan (the only other feudal society in the period). The imitation process can be compared among Europe, Africa, Japan, and Russia. But the Crusades revealed a distinctive expansionist spirit in Europe that also warrants attention, suggesting a more aggressive interest in the wider world than the other emerging societies were demonstrating.

Global Connections

Medieval Europe and the World

During the Middle Ages, western Europe developed something of a love-hate relationship with the world around it. In the early Middle Ages, Europe seemed at the mercy of invasions, from the Vikings in the north or various nomadic groups pushing in from central Asia. European leaders were also keenly aware of the power of Islam, which controlled most of the Mediterranean, including Spain. Most Europeans saw Islam as a dangerously false religion and an obvious threat.

At the same time, there was much to be learned from this wider world. During the Middle Ages, Europeans actively copied a host of features from Islam, from law to science and art. They imported products and technologies from Asia. This process of imitation accelerated during the centuries of Mongol control, when European traders and travelers eagerly pushed into eastern Asia. A key question for Europe at the end of the Middle Ages involved how to gain greater control over the benefits that came from world contacts, while reducing the sense of threat. Partly through weakness, partly because of the advantages that Europeans learned from contact, the new civilization developed an active sense of global awareness.

Western Europe's role in the transcontinental network during the post-classical centuries changed during the period itself. Appetite for trade grew, and European merchants and travelers began to reach out more actively to other areas, particularly in the Middle East but sometimes beyond. Europe itself did not, however, become a major attraction for people in other societies, except for some of the raiders who helped keep the region off balance during the early part of the period. Neither European manufacturing nor culture was widely appealing, outside the region itself. This limitation must be factored into the analysis of change over time, for it would help shape European motivations and actions in the wider world not only toward the end of the post-classical period, but even beyond.

Further Readings

For the Middle Ages generally, Joseph Strayer's *Western Europe in the Middle Ages* (1982) is a fine survey. More recent works include Charles H. Parker and Jerry H. Bentley, eds., *Between the Middle Ages and Modernity: Individual and Community in the Early Modern World* (2007); Eric H. Mielants, *The Origins of Capitalism and the "Rise of the West."* (2007); and David Power, ed., *The Central Middle Ages: Europe 950 – 1320* (2006). Key topics are covered in Peter Reid, *Medieval Warfare: Triumph and Domination in the Wars of the Middle Ages* (2007); Huw Pryce and John Watts, eds., *Power and Identity in the Middle Ages* (2007); Isabel Davis, *Writing Masculinity in the Later Middle Ages* (2007); R. S. Lopez, *The Commercial Revolution of the Middle Ages, 950–1350* (1976); and C. H. Lawrence, *Medieval Monasticism: Forms of Religious Life in Western Europe in the Middle Ages* (1984). National histories are important for the period, particularly on political life; see J. W. Baldwin, *The Government of Philip Augustus: Foundations of French Royal Power in the Middle Ages* (1986); G. Barraclough, *The Origins of Modern Germany* (1984); Michael Alexander, *Medievalism: The Middle Ages in Modern England* (2007); and Christopher Dyer, *An Age of Transition?: Economy and Society in England in the Later Middle Ages* (2005). R. Barlett, *The Making of Medieval Europe* (1992), suggests that Western civilization was the product of cross-cultural fertilization.

Social history has dominated much recent research on the period. See P. Ariès and G. Duby, eds., *A History of Private Life*, vol. 2 (1984); and Barbara Hanawalt, *The Ties That Bound: Peasant Families in Medieval England* (1986), for important orientation in this area. David Herlihy's *Medieval Households* (1985) is a vital contribution, as is J. Chapelot and R. Fossier's *The Village and House in the Middle Ages* (1985). J. Kirshner and S. F. Wemple, eds., *Women of the Medieval World* (1985), is a good collection. On tensions in popular religion, see C. Bynum, *Jesus as Mother: Studies in the Spirituality of the High Middle Ages* (1982); and L. Little, *Religious Poverty and the Profit Economy in Medieval Europe* (1978). A highly readable account of medieval life is E. Leroy Ladurie, *Montaillou: The Promised Land of Error* (1979).

Several excellent studies take up the theme of technological change: J. Gimpel, *The Medieval Machine: The Industrial Revolution of the Middle Ages* (1977); Lynn White Jr., *Medieval Technology and Social Change* (1962); and David Landes, *Revolution in Time: Clocks and the Making of the Modern World* (1985). On environmental impact, see Roland Bechmann, *Trees and Man: The Forest in the Middle Ages* (1990).

On intellectual and artistic life, E. Gilson's *History of Christian Philosophy in the Middle Ages* (1954) is a brilliant sketch, and his *Reason and Revelation* (1956) focuses on key intellectual issues of the age. S. C. Ferruolo's *The Origins of the University* (1985) and N. Pevsner's *An Outline of European Architecture* (1963) deal with other important features; see also H. Berman's *Law and Revolution:*

The Formation of the Western Legal Tradition (1983). On contacts, see Khalil Semaan, *Islam and the Medieval West: Aspects of Intercultural Relations* (1980). An intriguing classic, focused primarily on culture, is J. Huizinga, *The Waning of the Middle Ages* (1973).

On the Web

The postclassical period of the West witnessed the beginning of a new world order as well as the decline and collapse of the old one. This is visible in the patterns of daily life examined at http://www.medieval-life.net/life_main.htm, http://www.middle-ages.org.uk/life-in-middle-ages.htm, http://www.mnsu.edu/emuseum/history/middleages/pdailylife.html.

New political systems were emerging to meet new conditions, as exemplified by the career of Charlemagne (http://www.humnet.ucla.edu/santiago/histchrl.html), and by the writing of the later English Magna Carta (http://www.archives.gov/exhibits/featured_documents/magna_carta/ and http://www.yale.edu/lawweb/avalon/medieval/magframe.htm.)

Resources for the study of manorial life are identified at http://www.medievalgenealogy.org.uk/guide/man.shtml. How manorial life underwent changes and how new economic relations, such as the monetization of labor, undermined the tradition of serfdom in western Europe are suggested by a document manumitting a serf at http://www.fordham.edu/halsall/source/manumission.html.

The value, nature, and sources of human knowledge were being reevaluated in the works of men such as Peter Abelard (http://www.fordham.edu/halsall/source/abelard-sel.html and http://justus.anglican.org/resources/bio/142.html), Thomas Aquinas (http://www.utm.edu/research/iep/a/aquinas.htm), and those pursuing new avenues in both European and Islamic medicine and science (http://www.medieval-spell.com/Medieval-Medicine.html, and http://en.wikipedia.org/wiki/Medieval_medicine).

This was not a period that witnessed the advancement of the position of women, but insight into the lives of medieval women, ordinary and extraordinary, including Joan of Arc and the role of women in the Crusades, can be found at http://www.womeninworldhistory.com/heroine3.html, http://faculty.smu.edu/bwheeler/Joan_of_Arc/indexx.html, and http://www2.sunysuffolk.edu/westn/essaymedieval.html (click on Women in Childbirth from menu on left).

The Black Death had an impact on all facets of life in the Middle Ages. It can be explored at http://www.iath.virginia.edu/osheim/intro.html, http://www.brown.edu/Departments/Italian_Studies/dweb/plague/origins/spread.shtml, http://www.themiddleages.net/plague.html, and http://www.fidnet.com/~weid/plague.htm. The effect of the plague on one English land holding is illuminated at http://www.bbc.co.uk/history/british/middle_ages/plague_countryside_04.shtml. The impact of the plague on the economy of Europe is discussed as part of an excellent short introduction to economy and trade in the later Middle Ages at http://www.ucalgary.ca/applied_history/tutor/endmiddle/economy.html. This site includes a colorful map of contemporary trade routes.

AP* | Test Prep

1. During the Middle Ages, primary political and military power in Europe was

   (A) wielded by the Roman Catholic church.

   (B) monopolized by strong national monarchs like the King of France, and backed professional bureaucracies.

   (C) maintained by the feudal nobility and their vassals.

   (D) furnished by mercenary armies supported by the rich towns and cities.

2. In medieval Europe, serfs differed from slaves in that

   (A) serfs were largely commercialized artisans while slaves were agricultural.

   (B) serfs were ethnically Europeans while slaves were Africans.

   (C) serfs could not be bought or sold, and they had some rights of ownership over the land.

   (D) serfs could serve in the military, while slaves could not.

3. After the collapse of Charlemagne's empire, the pattern of political life in western Europe

   (A) was dominated by his sons and heirs.

   (B) was dominated by the Byzantine Empire.

   (C) was dominated by elites of the Roman Catholic Church.

   (D) was dominated by regional states with strong aristocracies.

4. Scholars in Medieval universities and schools in Western Europe

   (A) were eager to study the classical Greek literature and art.

   (B) trained students mainly in theology, medicine, and law.

   (C) arose in rural settings around the larger, more famous monasteries.

   (D) welcomed members of all classes, including women.

AP* Test Prep

5. The overwhelming significance of the Crusades for Western Europe was the

   (A) reunification of the Roman Catholic and Eastern Orthodox churches.

   (B) expansion of cultural and economic contacts between western Europe and the Middle East.

   (C) lasting conquest by European crusaders of the Holy Land and Jerusalem.

   (D) destruction of the European nobility and military class.

6. All of the following were examples of the rising importance of trade in the late medieval European economy EXCEPT

   (A) artisanal guilds.

   (B) the Hanseatic League.

   (C) international bankers and banking facilities.

   (D) the growth of professional armies.

7. Although western European society was not as tolerant of merchants as were Muslim and Indian societies,

   (A) weak governments allowed merchants to assert considerable power in semi-independent trading cities.

   (B) the Roman Catholic Church encouraged profits.

   (C) Christian merchants amassed greater wealth than their Muslim and Hindu counterparts.

   (D) western European rulers rarely interfered in or regulated trade or commerce.

Free-Response Question

To what extent did medieval Western Europe participate in the political, religious, and intellectual trends of the post-classical world?

11 The Americas on the Eve of Invasion

Postclassic Mesoamerica, 1000–1500 C.E.

Aztec Society in Transition

DOCUMENT: Aztec Women and Men

Twantinsuyu: World of the Incas

VISUALIZING THE PAST: Archeological Evidence of Political Practices

THINKING HISTORICALLY: The "Troubling" Civilizations of the Americas

The Other Peoples of the Americas

GLOBAL CONNECTIONS: The Americas and the World

I f you climbed the steep stairway to the temple at its summit and looked out from atop the great pyramid at its center, you could see that the splendid city of Tenochtitlan, capital of the Aztec Empire, rose from two islands in a large lake (Figure 11.1). All around its shores were densely settled towns and cities surrounded by cultivated fields. Canoes constantly traversed the lake and entered the city through a maze of canals, large crowds trod across the causeways that linked the city and its markets to the shores, and in some marshy areas, complex farming on "floating gardens" kept thousands of peasants at work. The Mexica or Tenocha people (sometimes called the Aztecs) who built the city considered it the "foundation of Heaven." For them it was a sacred space as well as a thriving metropolis and the heart of their empire.

When the first Europeans saw Tenochtitlan in 1520, the city had a population of over 150,000 and covered about 5 square miles, making it as large as contemporary Seville or Paris. The first Europeans who saw it were amazed. Some of them compared the city and its canals to Venice. Hernán Cortés, the Spanish captain who first entered the city, reported "the stone masonry and the woodwork are equally good; they could not be bettered anywhere." His companion, the foot soldier Bernal Díaz del Castillo, a man usually given to plain speech, could not hide his admiration:

Gazing on such wonderful sights, we did not know what to say, or whether what appeared before us was real, for on one side, on the land, there were great cities, and in the lake ever many more, and the lake was crowded with canoes, and in the causeway were many bridges at intervals, and in front of us stood the great city of Mexico.

Díaz del Castillo went on to describe the palaces and temples, the two-storied homes of the nobles, the stuccoed buildings hung with garlands of flowers, the smell of the cedar wood beams, the zoo, the aviary, the rooftop gardens, and the bustling markets filled with everything from chocolate to elaborate textiles and from parrot feathers to precious stones and slaves. The hum of the crowd in the great market, he said, could be heard miles away. Of course, there was much about the city that he did not understand, such as the fact that each city ward was controlled by a kin group that cared for its temples, shrines, and palaces. Later, he came to understand that the purpose of temples was for ceremonies of human sacrifice, which he found appalling, but his overall impression was one of admiration and wonder.

Tenochtitlan, clearly a great urban center, was the largest of about 50 such city-states that dotted central and southern Mexico. They were the heirs of the long development of civilization in the Americas, a process that seems to have taken place in relative isolation from the other centers of world history. ■

Indian Misnomer created by Columbus referring to indigenous peoples of New World; implies social and ethnic commonality among Native Americans that did not exist; still used to apply to Native Americans.

By 1500, the Americas were densely populated in many places by peoples long indigenous to the New World. These peoples were later called **Indians.** That term of course, is derived from a mistake Columbus made when he thought he had reached the Indies, what Europeans called India and the lands beyond, but the label is also misleading because it implies a common identity among the peoples of the Americas that did not exist until after the arrival of Europeans. *Indian* as a term to describe all the peoples of the Americas could have a meaning only when there were non-Indians from which to distinguish them. Still, the term has been used for so long—and is still in use by many Native Americans today—that we will continue to use it along with the term *Native Americans* to describe the early peoples of the Americas.

Figure 11.1 The great Aztec city-state of Tenochtitlan was established on an island in the midst of a large lake. Connected to the shores by causeways, supplied with fresh water by an aqueduct, it housed a population estimated to be over 150,000. Early Spanish observers compared its canals to Venice and were fascinated by its markets and gardens. To the Aztecs it was the center of political and spiritual power, or as they called it, "the foundation of heaven."

As should already be clear, there were many different peoples with a vast array of cultural achievements. The variety of cultural patterns and ways of life of pre-Columbian civilizations makes it impossible to discuss each in detail here, but we can focus on a few areas where major civilizations developed, based on earlier achievements. By concentrating on these regions, we can demonstrate the continuity of civilization in the Americas. This chapter examines in some detail Mesoamerica, especially central Mexico, and the Andean heartland. In both these areas great imperial states were in place when European expansion brought them into direct contact with the Old World. Discussed in less detail are a few areas influenced by the centers of civilization—and some whose development seems to have been independent of them—to provide an overview of the Americas on the eve of invasion.

Postclassic Mesoamerica, 1000–1500 C.E.

With the collapse of Teotihuacan (tay-oh-tee-wah-KAHN) in central Mexico and the abandonment of the classical Maya cities in the 8th century C.E., Mesoamerica experienced significant political and cultural change. In central Mexico, nomadic peoples from the north took advantage of the political vacuum to move into the richer lands. Among these peoples were the Toltecs, who established a capital at Tula about 968. **Toltec culture** adopted many features from the sedentary peoples and added a strongly militaristic ethic. This included the cult of sacrifice and war that is often portrayed in Toltec art. Later Mesoamerican peoples, such as the Aztecs, had some historical memory of the Toltecs and thought of them as the givers of civilization. However, the archeological record indicates that Toltec accomplishments often were fused or confused with those of Teotihuacan in the memory of the Toltecs' successors.

The Toltec Heritage

Among the legends that survived about the Toltecs were those of **Topiltzin** (toh-PEYEL-tzihn), a Toltec leader and apparently a priest dedicated to the god **Quetzalcoatl** (keht-zahl-KOH-ah-tuhl) (the Feathered Serpent) who later became confused with the god himself in the legends. Apparently, Topiltzin, a religious reformer, was involved in a struggle for priestly or political power with another faction. When he lost, Topiltzin and his followers went into exile, promising to return in the future to claim his throne on the same date, within the cyclical calendar system. Supposedly, Topiltzin and

The Toltecs and later the Aztecs were the chief civilizations that followed the fall of Teotihuacan and the abandonment of the classic Maya cities in the 8th century C.E. These new civilizations built on the accomplishments of their predecessors but rarely surpassed them except in political and military organization.

Toltec culture Succeeded Teotihuacan culture in central Mexico; strongly militaristic ethic including human sacrifice; influenced large territory after 1000 C.E.; declined after 1200 C.E.

Topiltzin [toh-PEYEL-tzihn] Religious leader and reformer of the Toltecs in 10th century; dedicated to god Quetzalcoatl; after losing struggle for power, went into exile in the Yucatan peninsula.

Quetzalcoatl [keht-zahl-KOH-ah-tuhl] Toltec deity; Feathered Serpent; adopted by Aztecs as a major god.

245

900 C.E.	1150 C.E.	1300 C.E.	1450 C.E.
900 End of intermediate horizon and decline of Tihuanaco and Huari **900–1465** Chimor Empire based on Chan-Chan on north coast of Peru **968** Tula established by Toltecs **1000** Toltec conquest of Chichén Itzá and influence in Yucatan	**1150** Fall of Tula, disintegration of Toltec Empire **1200–1500** Mississippian culture flourishes	**1325** Aztecs established in central Mexico; Tenochtitlan founded **1350** Incas established in Cuzco area **1434** Creation of triple alliance **1434–1471** Great expansion under Inca Pachacuti **1434–1472** Rule of Nezhualcoyotl at Texcoco **1438** Incas dominate Cuzco and southern highlands **1440–1469** Reign of Moctezuma I	**1471–1493** Inca Topac Yupanqui increases areas under control **1493–1527** Huayna Capac expands into Ecuador; his death results in civil war **1502–1520** Reign of Moctezuma II

his followers sailed for Yucatan; there is much evidence of Toltec influence in that region. The legend of Topiltzin/Quetzalcoatl was well known to the Aztecs and may have influenced their response when the Europeans arrived.

Chichén Itzá, Mexico

The Toltecs created an empire that extended over much of central Mexico, and their influence spread from their capital, Tula, to areas as far away as Guatemala (Figure 11.2). About 1000 C.E., Chichén Itzá (chee-CHEHN-eet-she) in Yucatan was conquered by Toltec warriors, and it and several other cities were ruled for a long time by central Mexican dynasties or by Maya rulers under Toltec influence.

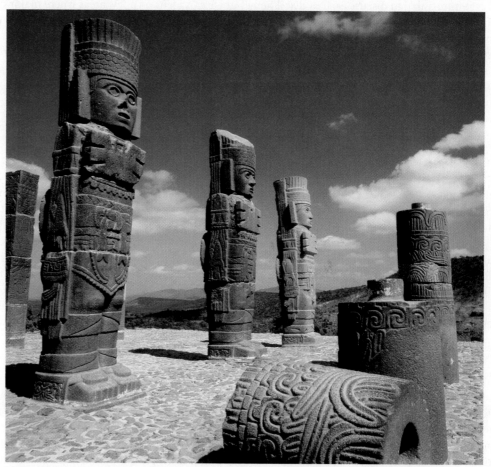

Figure 11.2 Toltec political and cultural influence spread from its capital at Tula in northern Mexico to places as far south as Chichén Itzá in Yucatan. The colossal statues of warriors shown here served as columns that supported the roof of a great temple.

Toltec influence spread northward as well. Obsidian was mined in northern Mexico, and the Toltecs may have traded for turquoise in the American Southwest. It has been suggested that the great Anasazi adobe town at Chaco Canyon in New Mexico was abandoned when the Toltec Empire fell and the trade in local turquoise ended.

How far eastward Toltec influence spread is a matter of dispute. Was there contact between Mesoamerica and the elaborate culture and concentrated towns of the Hopewell peoples of the Ohio and Mississippi valleys? Scholars disagree. Eventually, in the lower Mississippi valley from about 700 C.E., elements of Hopewell culture seem to have been enriched by external contact, perhaps with Mexico. This Mississippian culture, which flourished between 1200 and 1500 C.E., was based on maize and bean agriculture that probably spread from Mexico. Towns, usually located along rivers, had stepped temples made of earth, and sometimes large burial mounds. Some of the burial sites include well produced pottery and other goods, and some burials seem to have been accompanied by ritual executions or sacrifices of servants or wives. This indicates social stratification in the society. Cahokia, near East St. Louis, Illinois, covered 5 square miles and may have had more than 30,000 people in and around its center. Its largest earthen pyramid, now called Monk's Mound, covers 15 acres and is comparable in size to the largest pyramids of the classic period in Mexico. Many of these cultural features seem to suggest contact with Mesoamerica.

The Aztec Rise to Power

The Toltec Empire lasted until about 1150, when it apparently was destroyed by nomadic invaders from the north, who also seem to have sacked Tula about that time. The center of population and political power in central Mexico shifted to the valley of Mexico and especially to the shores of the large chain of lakes in that basin. These provided a rich aquatic environment. The shores of the lakes were dotted with settlements and towns and supported a dense population. Of the approximately 3000 square miles in the basin of the valley, about 400 square miles were under water. The lakes became the cultural heartland and population center of Mexico in the postclassic period. In the unstable world of post-Toltec Mesoamerica, various peoples and cities jockeyed for control of the lakes. The winners of this struggle, the Aztecs—or, as they called themselves, the *Mexica*—eventually built a great empire, but when they first emerged on the historical scene, they were the most unlikely candidates for power.

The Aztec rise to power and formation of an imperial state was as spectacular as it was rapid. According to some of their legends, the Mexica had once inhabited the central valley and had known agriculture and the "civilized" life but had lived in exile to the north in a place called Aztlan (AZT-lahn) (from whence we get the name *Aztec*). This may be an exaggeration by people who wanted to lay claim to a distinguished heritage. Other sources indicate that the Aztecs were simply one of the nomadic tribes that used the political anarchy, after the fall of the Toltecs, to penetrate the area of sedentary agricultural peoples. Like the ancient Egyptians, the Aztecs rewrote history to suit their purposes.

What seems clear is that the Aztecs were a group of about 10,000 people who migrated to the shores of Lake Texcoco (Map 11.1) in the central valley of Mexico around 1325. After the fall of the Toltec Empire, the central valley was inhabited by a mixture of peoples: Chichimec migrants from the northwest and various groups of sedentary farmers. In this period, the area around the lake was dominated by several tribes or peoples organized into city-states. Much like medieval Europe, this was a world of political maneuvers and state marriages, competing powers and shifting alliances. These political units claimed authority on the basis of their military power and their connections to Toltec culture. Many of these peoples spoke Nahuatl (NAH-wahtl), the language the Toltecs had spoken. The Aztecs also spoke this language, a fact that made their rise to power and their eventual claims to legitimacy more acceptable.

An intrusive and militant group, the Aztecs were distrusted and disliked by the dominant powers of the area, but their fighting skills could be put to use, and this made them attractive as mercenaries or allies. For about a century the Aztecs wandered around the shores of the lake, being allowed to settle for a while and then driven out by more powerful neighbors.

In a period of warfare, the Aztecs had a reputation as tough warriors and fanatical followers of their gods, to whom they offered human sacrifices. This reputation made them both valued and feared. Their own legends held that their wanderings would end when they saw an eagle perched on

Tlaltecatzin of Cuauhchinan-co, "Song of Tlaltecatzin"

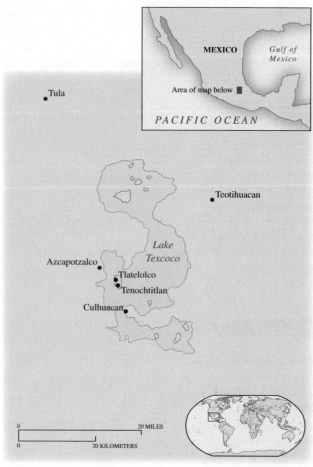

Map 11.1 Central Mexico and Lake Texcoco An aquatic environment at the heart of the Aztec Empire.

Xicohtencatl, the Elder, "I Say This"

Tenochtitlan [teh-nahk-teet-LAHN] Founded c. 1325 on marshy island in Lake Texcoco; became center of Aztec power; joined with Tlacopan and Texcoco in 1434 to form a triple alliance that controlled most of central plateau of Mesoamerica.

Tlaloc [tlah-LOHK] Major god of Aztecs; associated with fertility and the agricultural cycle; god of rain.

Polytheistic

The Importance of War in Ancient American Culture

a cactus with a serpent in its beak. Supposedly, this sign was seen on a marshy island in Lake Texcoco, and there, on that island and one nearby, the Mexica settled. The city of **Tenochtitlan** (teh-nahk-teet-LAHN) was founded about 1325.

From this secure base the Aztecs began to take a more active role in regional politics. Serving as mercenaries and then as allies brought prosperity to the Aztecs, especially to their ruler and the warrior nobles, who took lands and tribute from conquered towns. By 1428, the Aztecs had emerged as an independent power. In 1434, Tenochtitlan created an alliance with two other city-states that controlled much of the central plateau. In reality, Tenochtitlan and the Aztecs dominated their allies and controlled the major share of the tribute and lands taken.

The Aztec Social Contract

Aztec domination extended from the Tarascan frontier about a hundred miles north of present-day Mexico City southward to the Maya area. Subject peoples were forced to pay tribute, surrender lands, and sometimes do military service for the growing Aztec Empire.

Aztec society had changed in the process of expansion and conquest. From a loose association of clans, the Mexica had become a stratified society under the authority of a supreme ruler. The histories were rewritten and the Mexica were described as a people chosen to serve the gods. Human sacrifice, long a part of Mesoamerican religion, greatly expanded into an enormous cult in which the military class played a central role as suppliers of war captives to be used as sacrificial victims. A few territories were left unconquered so that periodic "flower wars" could be staged in which both sides could obtain captives for sacrifice. Whatever the religious motivations of this cult, the Aztec rulers manipulated it as an effective means of political terror. By the time of Moctezuma II, (1502–1520) the Aztec state was dominated by a king who represented civil power and served as a representative of the gods on earth. The cult of human sacrifice and conquest was united with the political power of the ruler and the nobility.

Religion and the Ideology of Conquest

Aztec religion incorporated many features that had long been part of the Mesoamerican belief system. Religion was a vast, uniting, and sometimes oppressive force in which little distinction was made between the world of the gods and the natural world. The traditional deities of Mesoamerica—the gods of rain, fire, water, corn, the sky, and the sun, many of whom had been worshiped as far back as the time of Teotihuacan—were venerated among the Aztecs. There were at least 128 major deities, but there seemed to be many more: as in popular Hinduism each deity had a male and female form, because a basic duality was recognized in all things. Moreover, gods might have different manifestations, somewhat like the avatars of the Hindu deities. Each god had at least five aspects, each associated with one of the cardinal directions and the center. Certain gods were thought to be the patrons of specific cities, ethnic groups, or occupations.

The gods were supported by a round of yearly festivals and ceremonies that involved feasting and dancing along with penance and sacrifice. This complex array of deities can be organized into three major themes or cults. The first were the gods of fertility and the agricultural cycle, such as **Tlaloc** (tlah-LOHK), the god of rain (called *Chac* by the Maya), and the gods and goddesses of water, maize, and fertility. A second group centered on the creator deities, the great gods and goddesses who had brought the universe into being. The story of their actions played a central role in Aztec cosmography. Much Aztec abstract and philosophical thought was devoted to the theme of creation. Finally, the cult of warfare and sacrifice built on the preexisting Mesoamerican traditions that had been expanding since Toltec times and, under the militaristic Aztec state, became the cult of the state. **Huitzilopochtli** (WEE-tsuh-loh-POHKT-lee), the Aztec tribal patron, became the central figure of this cult.

The Aztecs revered the great traditional deities—such as Tlaloc and Quetzalcoatl, the ancient god of civilization—so holy to the Toltecs, but their own tribal deity, Huitzilopochtli, was paramount. The Aztecs identified him with the old sun god, and they saw him as a warrior in the daytime sky fighting to give life and warmth to the world against the forces of the night. To carry out that struggle, the sun needed strength, and just as the gods had sacrificed themselves for humankind, the nourishment the gods needed most was that which was most precious: human life in the form of hearts and blood. The great temple of Tenochtitlan was dedicated to both Huitzilopochtli and Tlaloc. The tribal deity of the Aztecs and the ancient agricultural god of the sedentary peoples of Mesoamerica were thus united.

In fact, although human sacrifice had long been a part of Mesoamerican religion, it expanded considerably in the postclassic period of militarism. Warrior cults and the militaristic images of jaguars and eagles devouring human hearts were characteristic of Toltec art. The Aztecs simply took an existing tendency and carried it further. Both the types and frequency of sacrifice increased, and a whole symbolism and ritual, which included ritual cannibalism, developed as part of the cult (Figure 11.3). How much of Aztec sacrifice was the result of religious conviction and how much was a tactic of terror and political control by the rulers and priests is still open to debate.

Beneath the surface of this polytheism, there was also a sense of spiritual unity. **Nezhualcoyotl** (nehz-uh-WAHL-koh-YOH-tihl), the king of Texcoco, wrote hymns to the "lord of the close vicinity," an invisible creative force that supported all the gods. Yet his conception of a kind of monotheism, much like that of Pharaoh Akhenaton in Egypt, appears to have been too abstract and never gained great popularity.

Although the bloody aspects of Aztec religion have gained much attention, we must also realize that the Aztecs concerned themselves with many of the same great religious and spiritual questions that have preoccupied other civilizations: Is there life after death? What is the meaning of life? What does it mean to live a good life? Do the gods really exist?

Huitzilopochtli [WEE-tsuh-loh-POHKT-lee] Aztec tribal patron god; central figure of cult of human sacrifice and warfare; identified with old sun god.

Nezhualcoyotl [nehz-uh-WAHL-koh-YOH-tihl] Leading Aztec king of the 15th century.

Figure 11.3 Human sacrifice was practiced by many Mesoamerican peoples, but the Aztecs apparently expanded its practice for political and religious reasons. This image shows Aztec priests cutting out their victims' hearts and then rolling the bodies down the steps of the pyramid.

(Ms. Magliabechiano: sacrificio umano azteco. Biblioteca Nazionale Firenze. Scala/Art Resource, NY.)

Song for
Admonishing
Those Who
Seek No
Honor in War

DOCUMENT

chinampas   Beds of aquatic weeds, mud, and earth placed in frames made of cane and rooted in lakes to create "floating islands"; system of irrigated agriculture utilized by Aztecs.

pochteca   [pahk-TEHK-uh] Special merchant class in Aztec society; specialized in long-distance trade in luxury items.

Figure 11.4 Agriculture was the basis of Aztec society, and a diet centered on maize sustained the dense populations of the valley of Mexico. The plow was unknown, and planting was done with a digging stick.

Nezhualcoyotl, whose poetry survived in oral form and was written down in the 16th century, wondered about life after death:

Do flowers go to the land of the dead?
In the Beyond, are we dead or do we still live?
Where is the source of light, since that which gives life hides itself?

As in the Vedas of ancient India, he also wondered about the existence of the gods:

Are you real, are you fixed?
Only You dominate all things
The Giver of Life.
Is this true?
Perhaps, as they say, it is not true.

Aztec religious art and poetry are filled with images of flowers, birds, and song, all of which the Aztecs greatly admired, as well as human hearts and blood, the "precious water" needed to sustain the gods. This mixture of images makes the symbolism of Aztec religion difficult for modern observers to appreciate.

Aztec religion depended on a complex mythology that explained the birth and history of the gods and their relationship to peoples, and on a religious symbolism that infused all aspects of life. As we have seen, the Mesoamerican calendar system was religious, and many ceremonies coincided with particular points in the calendar cycle. Moreover, the Aztecs also believed in a cyclical view of history, and that the world had been destroyed four times before and would be destroyed again. Thus, there was a certain fatalism in Aztec thought and a premonition that eventually the sacrifices would be insufficient and the gods would again bring catastrophe.

Feeding the People: The Economy of the Empire

Feeding the great population of Tenochtitlan and the Aztec confederation in general depended on traditional forms of agriculture and on innovations developed by the Aztecs. Lands of conquered peoples often were appropriated, and food sometimes was demanded as tribute. In and around the lake, however, the Aztecs adopted an ingenious system of irrigated agriculture by building **chinampas** for agriculture. These were beds of aquatic weeds, mud, and earth that had been placed in frames made of cane and rooted to the lake floor. They formed artificial floating islands about 17 feet long and 100 to 330 feet wide. This narrow construction allowed the water to reach all the plants, and willow trees were also planted at intervals to give shade and help fix the roots. Much of the land of Tenochtitlan itself was chinampa in origin, and in the southern end of the lake, more than 20,000 acres of chinampas were constructed. The yield from chinampa agriculture was high: four corn crops a year were possible. Apparently, this system of irrigated agriculture had been used in preclassic days, but a rise in the level of the lakes had made it impossible to continue. After 1200, however, lowering water levels once again stimulated chinampa construction, which the Aztecs carried out on a grand scale.

Production by the Aztec peasantry, whom we see at work in Figure 11.4, and tribute provided the basic foods. In each Aztec community, the local clan apportioned the lands, some of which were also set aside for support of the temples and the state. In addition, individual nobles might have private estates, which were worked by servants or slaves from conquered peoples. Each community had periodic markets—according to various cycles in the calendar system, such as every 5 and 13 days—in which a wide variety of goods were exchanged. Cacao beans and gold dust sometimes were used as currency, but much trade was done as barter. The great market at Tlatelolco (TLAT-ehl-UHL-koh) operated daily and was controlled by the special merchant class, or **pochteca** (pahk-TEHK-uh), which specialized in long-distance trade in luxury items such as plumes of tropical birds and cacao. The markets were highly regulated and under the control of inspectors and special judges. Despite the importance of markets, this was not a market economy as we usually understand it.

The state controlled the use and distribution of many commodities and redistributed the vast amounts of tribute received from subordinate peoples. Tribute levels were assigned according to whether the subject peoples had accepted Aztec rule or had fought against it. Those who surrendered paid less. Tribute payments, such as food, slaves, and sacrificial victims, served political and economic ends. More than 120,000 mantles of cotton cloth alone were collected as tribute each year and sent to Tenochtitlan. The Aztec state redistributed these goods. After the original conquests, it rewarded its nobility richly, and the commoners received far less.

Aztec Society in Transition

Like all societies, Aztec society experienced changes over time. The Mexica were one of a number of peoples who spoke the Nahuatl language and occupied the region of central Mexico. From their humble origins as hunters and gatherers they emerged as a dominant power, and their rise created opportunities for some groups and a loss of status for others within their society. Eventually, they held sway over the fifty or so political units of the central valley of Mexico. Expansion by warfare privileged the warriors, and the religious basis for expansion made the priests and the cults of the temples a force in society. No ruler could govern without the support of these sectors of society, a support obtained and preserved by giving out rewards and benefits. But such policies transformed the nature of Aztec society.

A Widening Social Gulf

During their wanderings, the Aztecs had been divided into seven **calpulli** (kal-PUHL-lee), or clans, a form of organization that they later expanded and adapted to their imperial position. The calpulli were no longer only kinship groups but also residential groupings, which might include neighbors, allies, and dependants. Much of Aztec local life was based on the calpulli, which performed important functions such as distributing land to heads of households, organizing labor gangs and military units in times of war, and maintaining a temple and school. Calpulli were governed by councils of family heads, but not all families were equal, nor were all calpulli of equal status.

The calpulli obviously had been the ancient and basic building block of Aztec society. In the origins of Aztec society every person, noble, and commoner had belonged to a calpulli but as Aztec power increased, the calpulli had been transformed, and other forms of social stratification had emerged. As the empire expanded, a class of nobility emerged, based on certain privileged families in the most distinguished calpulli. Originating from the lineages that headed calpulli and from marriages, military achievements, or service to the state, this group of nobles accumulated high offices, private lands, and other advantages. The most prominent families in the calpulli, those who had dominated leadership roles and formed a kind of local nobility, eventually were overshadowed by the military and administrative nobility of the Aztec state.

Although some commoners might be promoted to noble status, most nobles were born into the class. Nobles controlled the priesthood and the military leadership. In fact, the military was organized into various ranks based on experience and success in taking captives (Figure 11.5). Military virtues were linked to the cult of sacrifice and infused the whole society; they became the justification for the nobility's status. The "flowery death," or death while taking prisoners for the sacrificial knife, was the fitting end to a noble life and ensured eternity in the highest heaven—a reward also promised to women who died in childbirth. The military was highly ritualized. There were orders of warriors: the Jaguar and Eagle "Knights" and other groups each had a distinctive uniform and ritual and fought together as units. Banners, cloaks, and other insignia marked off the military ranks.

The social gulf that separated the nobility from the commoners was widening as the empire grew. Egalitarian principles that may have existed in Aztec life disappeared, as happened among the warring Germanic tribes of early medieval Europe. Social distinctions were made apparent by the use of and restrictions on clothing, hairstyles, uniforms, and other symbols of rank. The imperial family became the most distinguished of the pipiltin families.

As the nobility broke free from their old calpulli and acquired private lands, a new class of workers almost like serfs was created to serve as laborers on these lands. Unlike the commoners attached to the land-controlling calpulli, these workers did not control land and worked at the will of others. Their status was low, but it was still above that of the slaves, who might have been war captives,

Aztec society became more hierarchical as the empire grew and social classes with different functions developed, although the older organization based on clans and kinship groups never disappeared. Tribute was drawn from subject peoples, but Aztec society confronted technological barriers that made it difficult to maintain the large population of central Mexico.

calpulli   [kal-PUHL-lee] Clans in Aztec society, later expanded to include residential groups that distributed land and provided labor and warriors.

CASE STUDY   Death in War and Childbirth in the Americas

IMAGE   Aztec Warriors

Figure 11.5 In the militarized society of the Aztec Empire, warriors were organized into regiments and groups distinguished by their uniforms. They gained rank and respect by capturing enemies for sacrifice. Note the symbolic gripping of the defeated captives' hair as a sign of military success.

criminals, or people who had sold themselves into bondage to escape hunger. Finally, there were other social groups. The scribes, artisans, and healers all were part of an intermediate group that was especially important in the larger cities. The long-distance merchants formed a sort of calpulli with their own patron gods, privileges, and internal divisions. They sometimes served as spies or agents for the Aztec military, but they were subject to restrictions that hindered their entry into or rivalry with the nobility.

It is possible to see an emerging conflict between the nobility and the commoners and to interpret this as a class struggle, but some specialists emphasize that to interpret Aztec society on that basis is to impose Western concepts on a different reality. Corporate bodies such as the calpulli, temple maintenance associations, and occupational groups cut across class and remained important in Aztec life. Competition between corporate groups often was more apparent and more violent than competition between social classes.

Overcoming Technological Constraints

Membership in society was thus defined by participation in various wider groups, such as the calpulli or a specific social class. It was also defined by gender roles. Aztec women assumed a variety of roles. Peasant women helped in the fields, but their primary domain was the household, where child-rearing and cooking took up much time. Above all, weaving skill was highly regarded. The responsibility for training young girls fell on the older women. Marriages often were arranged between lineages, and virginity at marriage was highly regarded for young women. Polygamy existed among the nobility, but the peasants were monogamous. Aztec women could inherit property and pass it to their heirs. The rights of Aztec women seem to have been fully recognized, but in political and social life their role, though complementary to that of men, remained subordinate.

The technology of the Americas limited social development in a variety of ways. Here we can see a significant difference between the lives of women in Mesoamerica and in the Mediterranean world. In the maize-based economies of Mesoamerica, women spent six hours a day grinding corn by hand on stone boards, or *metates,* to prepare the household's food. Although similar hand techniques were used in ancient Egypt, they were eventually replaced by animal- or water-powered mills that turned wheat into flour. The miller or baker of Rome or medieval Europe could do the work of hundreds of women. Maize was among the simplest and most productive cereals to grow but among the most time-consuming to prepare. Without the wheel or suitable animals for power, the Indian civilizations were unable to free women from the 30 to 40 hours a week that went into preparing the basic food.

Finally, we must consider the size of the population of the Aztec state. Estimates have varied widely, from as little as 1.5 million to more than 25 million, but there is considerable evidence that population density was high, resulting in a total population that was far greater than previously suspected. Some historical demographers estimate that the population of central Mexico under Aztec control reached over 20 million, excluding the Maya areas. This underlines the extraordinary ability of the Aztec state to intimidate and control such vast numbers of people.

Aztec Women and Men

In the mid-16th century, Bernardino de Sahagún, a Spanish missionary, prepared an extraordinary encyclopedia of Aztec culture. His purpose was to gather this information to learn the customs and beliefs of the Indians and their language in order to better convert them. Although Sahagún hated the Indian religion, he came to admire many aspects of their culture. His *Florentine Codex: The General History of the Things of New Spain* is one of the first ethnographies and a remarkable compendium of Aztec culture. Sahagún used many Indian informants to tell him about the days before the European arrival, and even though this work dates from the postconquest era, it contains much useful information about earlier Aztec life.

In the following excerpts, the proper behavior for people in different roles in Aztec society are described by the Aztecs themselves.

Father

One's father is the source of lineage. He is the sincere one. One's father is diligent, solicitous, compassionate, sympathetic, a careful administrator of his household. He rears, he teaches others, he advises, he admonishes one. He is exemplary; he leads a model life. He stores up for himself; he stores up for others. He cares for his assets; he saves for others. He is thrifty; he saves for the future, teaches thrift. He regulates, distributes with care, establishes order.

The bad father is incompassionate, negligent, unreliable. He is unfeeling … a shirker, a loafer, a sullen worker.

Mother

One's mother has children; she suckles them. Sincere, vigilant, agile, she is an energetic worker—diligent, watchful, solicitous, full of anxiety. She teaches people; she is attentive to them. She caresses, she serves others; she is apprehensive for their welfare; she is careful, thrifty—constantly at work.

The bad mother is evil, dull, stupid, sleepy, lazy. She is a squanderer, a petty thief, a deceiver, a fraud. Unreliable, she is one who loses things through neglect or anger, who heeds no one. She is disrespectful, inconsiderate, disregarding, careless. She shows the way to disobedience; she expounds nonconformity.

The Rulers

The ruler is a shelter—fierce, revered, famous, esteemed, well-reputed, renowned.

The good ruler is a protector: one who carries his subjects in his arms, who unites them, who brings them together. He rules, he takes responsibilities, assumes burdens. He carries his subjects in his cape; he bears them in his arms. He governs; he is obeyed. To him as a shelter, as refuge, there is recourse….

The bad ruler is a wild beast, a demon of the air, an ocelot, a wolf—infamous, avoided, detested as a respecter of nothing. He terrifies with his gaze; he makes the earth rumble; he implants; he spreads fear. He is wished dead.

The Noble

The noble has a mother, a father. He resembles his parents. The good noble is obedient, cooperative, a follower of his parents' ways, a discreet worker; attentive, willing. He follows the ways of his parents; he resembles his father; he becomes his father's successor; he assumes his lot.

One of noble lineage is a follower of the exemplary life, a taker of the good example of others, a seeker, a follower of the exemplary life. He speaks eloquently; he is soft-spoken, virtuous, deserving of gratitude. He is noble of heart, gentle of word, discreet, well-reared, well-taught. He is moderate, energetic, inquiring, inquisitive. He scratches the earth with a thorn. He is one who fasts, who starves his entrails, who parches his lips. He provides nourishment to others. He sustains one, he serves food, he provides comfort. He is a concealer [of himself], a belittler of himself. He magnifies and praises others. He is a mourner for the dead, a doer of penances, a gracious speaker, devout, godly, desirable, wanted, memorable.

The bad noble is ungrateful and forgetful, a debaser, a disparager of things, contemptuous of others, arrogant, bragging. He creates disorder, glories over his lineage, extols his own virtues.

The Mature Common Woman

The good mature woman is candid. She is resolute, firm of heart, constant—not to be dismayed; brave like a man; vigorous, resolute, persevering—not one to falter. She is long-suffering; she accepts reprimands calmly—endures things like a man. She becomes firm—takes courage. She is intent. She gives of herself. She goes in humility. She exerts herself.

The bad woman is thin, tottering, weak—an inconstant companion, unfriendly. She annoys others, chagrins them, shames, oppresses one. She becomes impatient; she loses hope, becomes embarrassed—chagrined. Evil is her life; she lives in shame.

The Weaver of Designs

She concerns herself with using thread, works with thread. The good weaver of designs is skilled—a maker of varicolored capes, an outliner of designs, a blender of colors, a joiner of pieces, a matcher of pieces, a person of good memory. She does things dexterously. She weaves designs. She selects. She weaves tightly. She forms borders. She forms the neck….

The bad weaver of designs is untrained—silly, foolish, unobservant, unskilled of hand, ignorant, stupid. She tangles the thread, she harms her work—she spoils it.

The Physician

The physician is a knower of herbs, of roots, of trees, of stones; she is experienced in these. She is one who conducts examinations; she is a woman of experience, of trust, of professional skill: a counselor.

The good physician is a restorer, a provider of health, a relaxer—one who makes people feel well, who envelops one in ashes. She cures people; she provides them health; she lances them; she bleeds them … pierces them with an obsidian lancet.

QUESTIONS In what ways do the expectations for men and women differ in Aztec society? To what extent do the roles for men and women in Aztec society differ from our own? Did the Aztecs value the same characteristics as our own and other historical societies?

A Tribute Empire

Each city-state was ruled by a speaker chosen from the nobility. The Great Speaker, the ruler of Tenochtitlan, was first among supposed equals. He was in effect the emperor, with great private wealth and public power, and was increasingly considered a living god. His court was magnificent and surrounded with elaborate rituals. Those who approached him could not look him in the eye and were required to throw dirt upon their heads as a sign of humility. In theory he was elected, but his election was really a choice between siblings of the same royal family. The prime minister held a position of tremendous power and usually was a close relative of the ruler. There was a governing council; in theory, the rulers of the other cities in the alliance also had a say in government, but in reality most power was in the hands of the Aztec ruler and his chief advisor.

During the century of greatest Aztec expansion after 1426, a social and political transformation had taken place. The position and nature of the old calpulli clans had changed radically, and a newly powerful nobility with a deified and nearly absolute ruler had emerged. The ancient cult of military virtues had been elevated to a supreme position as the religion of the state, and the double purpose of securing tribute for the state and obtaining victims for Huitzilopochtli drove further Aztec conquests.

The empire was never integrated, and local rulers often stayed in place to act as tribute collectors for the Aztec overlords. In many ways the Aztec Empire was simply an expansion of long-existing Mesoamerican concepts and institutions of government, and it was not unlike the subject city-states over which it gained control. These city-states, in turn, were often left unchanged if they recognized Aztec supremacy and met their obligations of labor and tribute. Tribute payments served both an economic and a political function, concentrating power and wealth in the Aztec capital. Archeologists at the recent excavations of the Great Temple beneath the center of Mexico City have been impressed by the large number of offerings and objects that came from the farthest ends of the empire and beyond. At the frontiers, neighboring states such as that of the Tarascans of Michoacan in West Central Mexico preserved their freedom, while within the empire enclaves of independent kingdoms such as Tlaxcala (tlaks-KAHL-uh) maintained a fierce opposition to the Aztecs. There were many revolts against Aztec rule or a particular tribute burden, which the Aztecs often put down ruthlessly.

In general, the Aztec system was a success because it aimed at exerting political domination and not necessarily direct administrative or territorial control. In the long run, however, the increasing social stresses created by the rise of the nobles and the system of terror and tribute imposed on subject peoples were internal weaknesses that contributed to the Aztec Empire's collapse.

The Aztecs were a continuation of the long process of civilization in Mesoamerica. The civilizations of the classic era did not simply disappear in central Mexico or among the Maya in Yucatan and Central America, but they were reinterpreted and adapted to new political and social realities. When Europeans arrived in Mexico, they assumed that what they found was the culmination of Indian civilization, when in fact it was the militarized afterglow of earlier achievements.

Twantinsuyu: World of the Incas

After about 1300 C.E. ,the Inca empire emerged in the highlands of Peru and eventually spread its control over the whole region by integrating many ethnic groups into an extensive imperial state.

Almost at the same time that the Aztecs extended their control over much of Mesoamerica, a great imperial state was rising in the Andean highlands, and it eventually became an empire some 3000 miles in extent (Map 11.2). The Inca Empire incorporated many aspects of previous Andean cultures but fused them together in new ways. With a genius for state organization and bureaucratic control over peoples of different cultures and languages, it achieved a level of integration and domination previously unknown in the Americas.

Throughout the Andean cultural hearth, after the breakup of the large "intermediate horizon" states of Tihuanaco and Huari (c. 550–1000 C.E.), several smaller regional states continued to exercise some power. Unlike the breakdown of power that took place in postclassic Mesoamerica, in the Andean zone many large states continued to be important. Some states in the Andean highlands on the broad open areas near Lake Titicaca and the states along rivers on the north coast, such as those in the Moche valley, remained centers of agricultural activity and population density. This was a period of war between rival local chiefdoms and small states and in some ways was an Andean parallel to the post-Toltec militaristic era in Mesoamerica. Of these states, the coastal kingdom of Chimor, centered on its capital of Chan-Chan, emerged as the most powerful. Between 900 and its conquest by the Incas in 1465, it gained control of most of the north coast of Peru.

The Inca Rise to Power

While Chimor spread its control over 600 miles of the coast, in the southern Andean highlands, where there were few large urban areas, ethnic groups and politics struggled over the legacy of Tihuanaco. Among these groups were several related Quechua-speaking clans, or **ayllus** (EYEL-lehs), living near Cuzco, an area that had been under the influence of Huari but had not been particularly important. Their own legends stated that 10 related clans emerged from caves in the region and were taken to Cuzco by a mythical leader. Wherever their origins, by about 1350 c.e. they lived in and around Cuzco, and by 1438 they had defeated their hostile neighbors in the area. At this point under their ruler, or *inca*, **Pachacuti** (PACH-uh-KOO-tee) (r. 1438–1471), they launched a series of military alliances and campaigns that brought them control of the whole area from Cuzco to the shores of Lake Titicaca.

Over the next 60 years, Inca armies were constantly on the march, extending control over a vast territory. Pachacuti's son and successor, Topac Yupanqui (TOH-pak YUH-pan-KEE), conquered the northern coastal kingdom of Chimor by seizing its irrigation system, and he extended Inca control into the southern area of what is now Ecuador. At the other end of the empire, Inca armies reached the Maule River in Chile against stiff resistance from the Araucanian Indians. The next ruler, Huayna Capac (WEYE-nah kah-PAHK) (r. 1493–1527), consolidated these conquests and suppressed rebellions on the frontiers. By the time of his death, the Inca Empire—or, as they called it, **Twantinsuyu** (twahn-tihn-SOO-yoo)—stretched from what is now Colombia to Chile and eastward across Lake Titicaca and Bolivia to northern Argentina. Between 9 and 13 million people of different ethnic backgrounds and languages came under Inca rule, a remarkable feat, given the extent of the empire and the technology available for transportation and communication.

Conquest and Religion

What impelled the Inca conquest and expansion? The usual desire for economic gain and political power that we have seen in other empires is one possible explanation, but there may be others more in keeping with Inca culture and ideology. The cult of the ancestors was extremely important in Inca belief. Deceased rulers were mummified and then treated as intermediaries with the gods, paraded in public during festivals, offered food and gifts, and consulted on important matters by special oracles. From the Chimor kingdom the Incas adopted the practice of royal **split inheritance,** whereby all the political power and titles of the ruler went to his successor but all his palaces, wealth, land, and possessions remained in the hands of his male descendants, who used them to support the cult of the dead Inca's mummy for eternity. To ensure his own cult and place for eternity, each new Inca needed to secure land and wealth, and these normally came as part of new conquests. In effect, the greater the number of past rulers, the greater the number of royal courts to support, and the greater the demand for labor, lands, and tribute. This system created a self-perpetuating need for expansion, tied directly to ancestor worship and the cult of the royal mummies, as well as tensions between the various royal lineages. The cult of the dead weighed heavily on the living.

Map 11.2 Inca Expansion   Each ruler expanded the empire in a series of campaigns to increase wealth and political control.

Inca Expansion

ayllus [EYEL-lehs] Households in Andean societies that recognized some form of kinship; traced descent from some common, sometimes mythical ancestor.

Pachacuti [PACH-uh-KOO-tee] Ruler of Inca society from 1438 to 1471; launched a series of military campaigns that gave Incas control of the region from Cuzco to the shores of Lake Titicaca.

Twantinsuyu [twahn-tihn-SOO-yoo] Word for Inca Empire; region from present-day Colombia to Chile and eastward to northern Argentina.

split inheritance Inca practice of descent; all titles and political power went to successor, but wealth and land remained in hands of male descendants for support of cult of dead inca's mummy.

Archeological Evidence of Political Practices

The Inca system of split inheritance probably originated in the Chimu kingdom. Chimu king lists recorded 10 rulers' names. Excavations at Chan-Chan, the Chimu capital, have revealed 10 large walled structures. Archeologists believe that each of these palatial compounds was a different king's residence and that each became a mausoleum for his mummy upon his death.

QUESTIONS To what extent does such evidence indicate the composite nature of Inca culture? What are some of the possible problems of archeological interpretation? To what extent can material remains be used to explain or illustrate social phenomena?

Chan-Chan covered more than 2 square miles. It contained palace compounds, storehouses, residences, markets, and other structures.

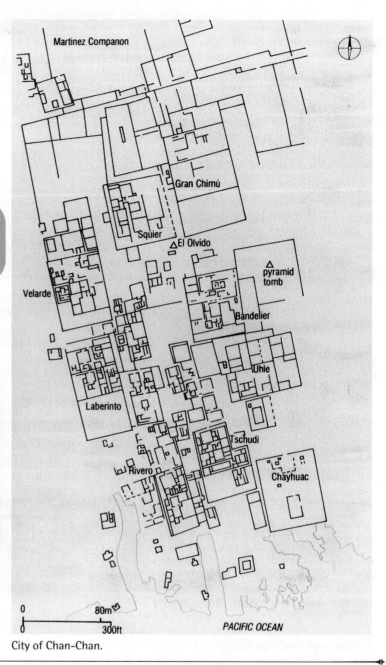

City of Chan-Chan.

Temple of the Sun Inca religious center located at Cuzco; center of state religion; held mummies of past Incas.

Inca political and social life was infused with religious meaning. Like the Aztecs, the Incas held the sun to be the highest deity and considered the Inca to be the sun's representative on earth. The magnificent **Temple of the Sun** in Cuzco was the center of the state religion, and in its confines the mummies of the past Incas were kept. The cult of the sun was spread throughout the empire, but the Incas did not prohibit the worship of local gods.

Other deities were also worshiped as part of the state religion. Viracocha (vee-reh-KOH-chuh), a creator god, was a favorite of Inca Pachacuti and remained important. Popular belief was based on a profound animism that endowed many natural phenomena with spiritual power. Mountains, stones, rivers, caves, tombs, and temples were considered *huacas*, or holy shrines. At these places, prayers were offered and animals, goods, and humans were sacrificed. In the Cuzco area, imaginary lines running from the Temple of the Sun organized the huacas into groups for which certain ayllus took responsibility. The temples were served by many priests and women dedicated to preparing cloth and food for sacrifice. The temple priests were responsible mainly for the great festivals and celebrations and for the divinations on which state actions often depended.

The Techniques of Inca Imperial Rule

The Inca were able to control their vast empire by using techniques and practices that ensured cooperation or subordination. The empire was ruled by the Inca, who was considered almost a god. He ruled from his court at Cuzco, which was also the site of the major temple; the high priest usually was a close relative. Twantinsuyu was divided into four great provinces, each under a governor, and then divided again. The Incas developed a state bureaucracy in which almost all nobles played a role. Although some chroniclers spoke of a state organization based on decimal units of 10,000, 1000, 100, and smaller numbers of households to mobilize taxes and labor, recent research reveals that many local practices and variations were allowed to continue under Inca rule. Local rulers, or *curacas,* were allowed to maintain their positions and were given privileges by the Inca in return for their loyalty. The curacas were exempt from tribute obligations and usually received labor or produce from those under their control. For insurance, the sons of conquered chieftains were taken to Cuzco for their education.

The Incas intentionally spread the Quechua (KEHCH-uh-wah) language as a means of integrating the empire. The Incas also made extensive use of colonists. Sometimes Quechua-speakers from Cuzco were settled in a newly won area to provide an example and a garrison. On other occasions, the Incas moved a conquered population to a new home. Throughout the empire, a complex system of roads was built, with bridges and causeways when needed (Map 11.3). Along these roads, way stations, or **tambos,** were placed about a day's walk apart to serve as inns, storehouses, and supply centers for Inca armies on the move. Tambos also served as relay points for the system of runners who carried messages throughout the empire. The Inca probably maintained more than 10,000 tambos.

The Inca Empire extracted land and labor from subject populations. Conquered peoples were enlisted in the Inca armies under Inca officers and were rewarded with goods from new conquests. Subject peoples received access to goods not previously available to them, and the Inca state undertook large building and irrigation projects that formerly would have been impossible. In return, the Incas demanded loyalty and tribute. The state claimed all resources and redistributed them. The Incas divided conquered areas into lands for the people, lands for the state, and lands for the sun—that is, for religion and the support of priests. Also, some nobles held private estates.

With few exceptions the Incas, unlike the Aztecs, did not demand tribute in kind but rather exacted labor on the lands assigned to the state and the religion. Communities were expected to take turns working on state and church lands and sometimes on building projects or in mining. These labor turns, or **mita,** were an essential aspect of Inca control. In addition, the Inca required women to weave high-quality cloth for the court and for religious purposes. The Incas provided the wool, but each household was required to produce cloth. Woven cloth, a great Andean art form, had political and religious significance. Some women were taken as concubines for the Inca; others were selected as servants at the temples, the so-called Virgins of the Sun. In all this, the Inca had an overall imperial system but remained sensitive to local variations, so that its application accommodated regional and ethnic differences.

In theory, each community aimed at self-sufficiency and depended on the state for goods it could not acquire easily. The ayllus of each community controlled the land, and the vast majority of the men were peasants and herders. Women worked in the fields, wove cloth, and cared for the

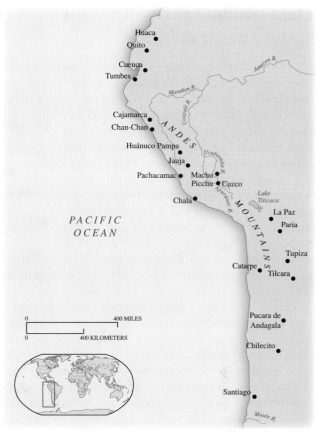

Map 11.3 The Ancient Cities of Peru   The Inca system of roads, with its series of tambos, linked major towns and cities and allowed rapid communication and troop movement.

tambos   Way stations used by Incas as inns and storehouses; supply centers for Inca armies on move; relay points for system of runners used to carry messages.

mita   Labor extracted for lands assigned to the state and the religion; all communities were expected to contribute; an essential aspect of Inca imperial control.

The "Troubling" Civilizations of the Americas

From the first encounter with the peoples of the Americas, European concepts and judgments about civilization, barbarism, morality, power, politics, and justice were constantly called into question. The American Indian societies had many religious ideas and practices that shocked Christian observers, and aspects of their social and familial arrangements clashed with European sensibilities. Those sensibilities often were influenced by religious and political considerations. Many of those who most condemned human sacrifice, polygamy, or the despotism of Indian rulers were also those who tried to justify European conquest and control, mass violence, and theft on a continental scale. Other European voices also were heard. Not long after the Spanish conquests in the 16th century, defenders of Indian rights came forward to argue that despite certain "unfortunate" habits, Indian civilization was no less to be admired than that of the ancient (and pagan) Romans and Greeks.

For Western civilization, evaluating and judging non-Western or past societies has always been a complex business that has mixed elements of morality, politics, religion, and self-perception along with the record of what is observed or considered to be reality. That complexity is probably just as true for Chinese, Persian, or any culture trying to understand another. Still, Western society seems to have been particularly troubled by the American civilizations, with their peculiar combination of Neolithic technology and imperial organization. At times this has led to abhorrence and rejection—as of Aztec sacri-

> "Perhaps nothing challenges our appreciation of the American civilizations more than the extensive evidence of ritual torture and human sacrifice."

fice—but at other times it has led to a kind of utopian romanticism in which the accomplishments of the Indian past are used as a critique of the present and a political program for the future.

The existence of **Inca socialism** is a case in point. Some early Spanish authors portrayed Inca rule as despotic, but others saw it as a kind of utopia. Shortly after the conquest of Peru, Garcilaso de la Vega, the son of a Spaniard and an Indian noblewoman, wrote a glowing history of his mother's people in which he presented an image of the Inca Empire as a carefully organized system in which every community contributed to the whole, and the state regulated the distribution of resources on the basis of need and reciprocity. There was some truth in this view, but it ignored some aspects of exploitation as well. In the 20th century, Peruvian socialists, faced with underdevelopment and social inequality in their country, used this utopian view of Inca society as a possible model for their own future. Their interpretation and that of historians who later wrote of Inca socialism tended to ignore the hierarchy in the Inca Empire and the fact that the state extracted labor and goods from the subject communities to support the nobles, who held extensive power. The utopian view of the Incas was no less political than the despotic view. Perhaps the lesson here is that what we see in the past often depends on what we think about the present or what we want for the future.

But if Inca socialism and despotism have fascinated students of the past, Aztec religion has caught the imagination of historians and the general public. It causes us to ask how a civilization as advanced as this could engage in a practice so cruel and, to us, so morally reprehensible. Perhaps nothing challenges our appreciation

---

Inca socialism A view created by Spanish authors to describe Inca society as a type of utopia; image of the Inca Empire as a carefully organized system in which every community collectively contributed to the whole.

household (Figure 11.6). Roles and obligations were gender-specific and, at least in theory, equal and interdependent. Andean peoples recognized parallel descent, so that property rights within the ayllus and among the nobility passed in both the male and female lines. Women passed rights and property to daughters, men to sons. Whether in pre-Inca times women may have served as leaders of ayllus is open to question, but under the Incas this seems to have been uncommon. The Inca emphasis on military virtues reinforced the inequality of men and women.

The concept of close cooperation between men and women was also reflected in the Inca view of the cosmos. Gods and goddesses were worshiped by men and women, but women felt a particular affinity for the moon and the goddesses of the earth and corn: the fertility deities. The Inca queen, the Inca's senior wife (usually also a sister of the Inca), was seen as a link to the moon. Queen and sister of the sun, she represented imperial authority to all women. But despite an ideology of gender equality, Inca practice created a gender hierarchy that paralleled the dominance of the Inca state over subject peoples. This fact is supported, and the power of the empire over local ethnic groups is demonstrated, by the Incas' ability to select the most beautiful young women to serve the temples or be given to the Inca.

The integration of imperial policy with regional and ethnic diversity was a political achievement. Ethnic headmen were left in place, but over them were administrators drawn from the Inca nobility in Cuzco. Reciprocity and hierarchy continued to characterize Andean groups as they came under Inca rule; reciprocity between the state and the local community was simply an added level.

of the American civilizations more than the extensive evidence of ritual torture and human sacrifice, which among the Aztecs reached staggering proportions. On some occasions thousands of people were slain, usually by having their hearts ripped out.

First, we must put these practices in perspective. Cruelty and violence can be found in many cultures, and to a world that has seen genocide, mass killings, and atomic warfare, the Aztec practices are not so different from what our own age has seen. Certain customs in many past civilizations and present cultures seem to us strange, cruel, and immoral. We find Aztec human sacrifice particularly abhorrent, but such practices also were found among the ancient Canaanites and the Celtic peoples, and the Old Testament story of Abraham and Isaac, though its message is against such sacrifice, reflects a practice known in the ancient Near East. Human sacrifice was practiced in pre-Christian Scandinavia and ancient India. Although by the time of Confucius human sacrifice of wives and retainers at the burial of a ruler was no longer practiced in China, the custom had been known. Sati, the Hindu ritual suicide of the widow on the funeral pyre of her husband, existed in India in the 19th century, although admittedly it may have been exaggerated by the British colonial authorities. The Aztecs certainly were not alone in taking human life as a religious rite. Whatever our moral judgments about such customs, it remains the historian's responsibility to understand them in the context of their own culture and time.

How have historians tried to explain or understand Aztec human sacrifice? Some defenders of Aztec culture have seen it as a limited phenomenon, greatly exaggerated by the Spanish for political purposes. Many scholars have seen it as a religious act central to the Aztec belief that humans must sacrifice that which was most precious to them—life—to receive the sun, rain, and other blessings of the gods that make life possible. Others have viewed Aztec practice as the intentional manipulation and expansion of a widespread phenomenon that had long existed among many American peoples. In other words, the Aztec rulers, priests, and nobility used the cult of war and large-scale human sacrifice for political purposes, to terrorize their neighbors and subdue the lower classes. Another possible explanation is demographic. If central Mexico was as densely populated as we believe, then the sacrifices may have been a kind of population control.

Other interpretations have been even more startling. Anthropologist Marvin Harris has suggested that Aztec sacrifice, accompanied by ritual cannibalism, was a response to a lack of protein. He argued that in the Old World, human sacrifice was replaced by animal sacrifice, but in Mesoamerica, which lacked cattle and sheep, that transformation never took place. Harris called the Aztec Empire a "cannibal kingdom." Other scholars have strongly objected to Harris's interpretation of the evidence, which gave little attention to the ritual aspects of these acts. Still, human sacrifice shades all assessments of Aztec civilization.

These debates ultimately raise important questions about the role of moral judgments in historical analysis and the way in which our vision of the past is influenced by our own political, moral, ethical, and social programs. We cannot and perhaps should not abandon those programs, but we must always try to understand other times and other peoples in their own terms.

QUESTIONS What special features of Aztec civilization must be explained? Are they really distinctive? What explanations are most persuasive in terms of historical sensitivity and contemporary standards? What features of 21st-century society are similar to those of Aztec civilization and will later need to be explained?

The Inca state could provide roads, irrigation projects, and hard-to-get goods. For example, maize usually was grown on irrigated land and was particularly important as a ritual crop. State-sponsored irrigation added to its cultivation. The Inca state manipulated the idea of reciprocity to extract labor power, and it dealt harshly with resistance and revolt. In addition to the ayllu peasantry, there was also a class of people, the **yanas,** who were removed from their ayllus and served permanently as servants, artisans, or workers for the Inca or the nobility.

Members of the Inca nobility were greatly privileged, and those related to the Inca himself held the highest positions. The nobility were all drawn from the 10 royal ayllus. In addition, the residents of Cuzco were given noble status to enable them to serve in high bureaucratic posts. The nobles were distinguished by dress and custom. Only they were entitled to wear the large ear spools that enlarged the ears and caused the Spaniards to later call them *orejones,* or "big ears." Noticeably absent in most of the Inca Empire was a distinct merchant class. Unlike in Mesoamerica, where long-distance trade was so important, the Incas' emphasis on self-sufficiency and state regulation of production and surplus limited trade. Only in the northern areas of the empire, in the chiefdoms of Ecuador, the last region brought under Inca control, did a specialized class of traders exist.

The Inca imperial system, which controlled an area of almost 3000 miles, was a stunning achievement of statecraft, but like all other empires it lasted only as long as it could control its subject populations and its own mechanisms of government. A system of royal multiple marriages as a way of forging alliances created rival claimants for power and the possibility of civil war. That is

yanas A class of people within Inca society removed from their ayllus to serve permanently as servants, artisans, or workers for the inca or the Inca nobility.

Figure 11.6 This Inca sculpture, made of gold, portrays one of the mamaconas, or "chosen women," who served as concubines to the Inca emperors. The wool of her cloak is woven in a classic Inca design.

quipu   [KEE-poo] System of knotted strings utilized by the Incas in place of a writing system; could contain numerical and other types of information for censuses and financial records.

exactly what happened in the 1520s, just before the Europeans arrived. When the Spanish first arrived in Peru, they saw an empire weakened by civil strife.

Inca Cultural Achievements

The Incas drew on the artistic traditions of their Andean predecessors and the skills of subject peoples. Beautiful pottery and cloth were produced in specialized workshops. Inca metalworking was among the most advanced in the Americas, and Inca artisans worked gold and silver with great skill. The Incas also used copper and some bronze for weapons and tools. Like the Mesoamerican peoples, the Incas made no practical use of the wheel, but unlike them, they had no system of writing. However, the Incas did use a system of knotted strings, or **quipu** (KEE-poo), to record numerical and perhaps other information. It worked like an abacus, and with it the Incas took censuses and kept financial records. The Incas had a passion for numerical order, and the population was divided into decimal units from which population, military enlistment, and work details could be calculated. The existence of so many traits associated with civilization in the Old World combined with the absence of a system of writing among the Incas illustrates the variations of human development and the dangers of becoming too attached to certain cultural characteristics or features in defining civilizations.

The Incas' genius was best displayed in their land and water management, extensive road system, statecraft, and architecture and public buildings. They developed ingenious agricultural terraces on the steep slopes of the Andes, using a complex technology of irrigation to water their crops. The empire was linked together by almost 2500 miles of roads, many of which included rope suspension bridges over mountain gorges and rivers. Inca stonecutting was remarkably accurate; the best buildings were built of large fitted stones without the use of masonry. Some of these buildings were immense. These structures, the large agricultural terraces and irrigation projects, and the extensive system of roads were among the Incas' greatest achievements, displaying their technical ability as well as their ability to mobilize large amounts of labor.

Comparing Incas and Aztecs

The Inca and the Aztec cultures were based on a long development of civilization that preceded them. Although in some areas of artistic and intellectual achievement earlier peoples had surpassed their accomplishments, both cultures represented the success of imperial and military organization. Both empires were based on intensive agriculture organized by a state that accumulated surplus production and then controlled the circulation of goods and their redistribution to groups or social classes. In both states, older kinship-based institutions, the ayllu and the calpulli, were transformed by the emergence of a social hierarchy in which the nobility was increasingly predominant. In both areas, these nobles also were the personnel of the state, so that the state organization was almost an image of society.

Although the Incas tried to create an overarching political state and to integrate their empire as a unit (the Aztecs did less in this regard), both empires recognized local ethnic groups and political leaders and allowed variation from one group or region to another as long as Inca or Aztec sovereignty was recognized and tribute paid. Both the Aztecs and the Incas, like the Spaniards who followed them, found that their military power was less effective against nomadic peoples who lived on their frontiers. Essentially, the empires were created by the conquest of sedentary agricultural peoples and the extraction of tribute and labor from them.

We cannot overlook the great differences between Mesoamerica and the Andean region in terms of climate and geography or the differences between the Inca and Aztec civilizations. Trade and markets were far more developed in the Aztec Empire and earlier in Mesoamerica in general than in the Andean world. There were differences in metallurgy, writing systems, and social definition and hierarchy. But within the context of world civilizations, it is probably best to view these two empires and the cultural areas they represent as variations of similar patterns and processes, of which sedentary agriculture is the most important. Basic similarities underlying the variations can also be seen in systems of belief and cosmology and in social structure. Whether similar origins, direct or indirect contact between the areas, or parallel development in Mesoamerica and the Andean area explains the similarity is unknown. But the American Indian civilizations shared much with each other; that factor and their isolation from external cultural and biological influences gave them their peculiar character and their vulnerability. At the same time, their ability to survive the shock of conquest and contribute to the formation of societies after conquest demonstrates much of their strength. Long after the Aztec and Inca empires had ceased to exist, the peoples of the Andes and Mexico continued to draw on these cultural traditions.

The Other Peoples of the Americas

Rather than seeing a division between "primitive" and "civilized" peoples in the Americas, it is more useful to consider gradations of material culture and social complexity. Groups such as the Incas had many things in common with the tribal peoples of the Amazon basin, such as the division into clans or halves—that is, a division of villages or communities into two major groupings with mutually agreed-upon roles and obligations. Moreover, as we have seen, the diversity of ancient America forces us to reconsider ideas of human development based on Old World examples. Social complexity, for example, was not necessarily dependent on agriculture. In the Americas, some groups of fishers and hunters and gatherers, such as the peoples of the northwest coast of the United States and British Columbia, developed complex hierarchical societies. For those who see control of water for agriculture as the starting point for political authority and the state, such societies as the Pimas of Colorado and some of the chiefdoms of South America, who practiced irrigated agriculture but did not develop states, also provide exceptions to theories based on Old World evidence. Finally, archaeological finds in the Amazon now suggest that pottery and agriculture may have developed there even before it did in the Andean region.

The civilizations of Mesoamerica and the Andes, were high points of a Native American cultural achievement. However, the Americas continued to be occupied by a variety of peoples who lived in different ways, ranging from highly complex sedentary agricultural empires to simple kin-based bands of hunters and gatherers.

How Many People?

A major issue that has fascinated students of the Americas for centuries is the question of population size. For years after the European conquests, many observers discounted the early descriptions of large and dense Indian populations as the exaggeration of conquerors and missionaries who wanted to make their own exploits seem more impressive. In the early 20th century, the most repeated estimate of Native American population about 1492 was 8.4 million (4 million in Mexico, 2 million in Peru, and 2.4 million in the rest of the hemisphere). Since that time, new archeological discoveries, a better understanding of the impact of disease on indigenous populations, new historical and demographic studies, and improved estimates of agricultural techniques and productivity have led to major revisions. Estimates still vary widely, and some have gone as high as 112 million at the time of contact. Most scholars agree that Mesoamerica and the Andes supported the largest populations. Table 11.1 summarizes one of the most careful estimates, which places the total figure at more than 67 million, although a Native American demographer has increased this figure to 72 million. Other scholars are still unconvinced by these estimates.

These figures should be considered in a global context. In 1500, the population of the rest of the world was probably about 500 million, of which China and India each had 75 to 150 million

TABLE 11.1 Population Estimate for the Western Hemisphere, 1492	
Area	**Population (thousands)**
North America	4,400
Mexico	21,400
Central America	5,650
Caribbean	5,850
Andes	11,500
Lowland South America	18,500
Total	67,300

Sources: William M. Deneven, *The Native Population of the Americas in 1492* (1976), 289–292; John D. Durand, "Historical Estimates of World Population," *Population and Development Review 3* (1957): 253–296; Russell Thornton, *American Indian Holocaust and Survival* (1987).

TABLE 11.2 World Population, c. 1500	
Area	**Population (thousands)**
China	100,000–150,000
Indian subcontinent	75,000–150,000
Southwest Asia	20,000–30,000
Japan	15,000–20,000
Rest of Asia (except Russia)	15,000–30,000
Europe (except Russia)	60,000–70,000
Russia (USSR)	10,000–18,000
Northern Africa	6,000–12,000
Rest of Africa	30,000–60,000
Oceania	1,000–2,000
Americas	57,000–72,000
Total	389,000–614,000

Sources: William M. Deneven, *The Native Population of the Americas in 1492* (1976), 289–292; John D. Durand, "Historical Estimates of World Population," *Population and Development Review* 3 (1957): 253–296; Russell Thornton, *American Indian Holocaust and Survival* (1987).

people and Europe had 60 to 70 million, a figure roughly equivalent to the population of the Americas (Table 11.2). If the modern estimates are valid, the peoples of the Americas clearly made up a major segment of humanity.

Differing Cultural Patterns

Although it is impossible to summarize the variety of cultural patterns and lifeways that existed in the Americas on the eve of contact with Europeans, we can describe the major patterns outside the main civilization areas. Northern South America and part of Central America were an intermediate area that shared many features with the Andes and some with Mesoamerica and perhaps served as a point of cultural and material exchange between the two regions. In fact, with the exception of monumental architecture, the intermediate zone chieftainships resembled the sedentary agriculture states in many ways.

Similar kinds of chieftainships based on sedentary agriculture were found elsewhere in the Americas. There is strong evidence of large chieftainships along the Amazon, where the rich aquatic environment supported complex and perhaps hierarchical societies. The island Arawaks or Tainos encountered by Columbus on the Caribbean island of Hispaniola, were farmers organized in a hierarchical society and divided into chiefdoms. These Indian chiefdom-level societies strongly resemble the societies of Polynesia. On the bigger Caribbean islands, such as Hispaniola and Puerto Rico, chieftainships ruled over dense populations, which lived primarily on the root crop called manioc.

Agriculture was spread widely throughout the Americas by 1500. Some peoples, such as those of the eastern North American woodlands and the coast of Brazil, combined agriculture with hunting and fishing. Techniques such as slash and burn farming led to the periodic movement of villages when production declined. Social organization in these societies often remained without strong class divisions, craft specializations, or the demographic density of people who practiced permanent, intensive agriculture. Unlike Europe, Asia, and Africa, the Americas lacked nomadic herders. However, throughout the Americas, from Tierra del Fuego to the Canadian forests, some people lived in small, mobile, kin-based groups of hunters and gatherers. Their material culture was simple and their societies were more egalitarian.

Nowhere is Native American diversity more apparent than in North America. In that vast continent, by 1500, perhaps as many as 200 languages were spoken, and a variety of cultures reflected Indian adaptation to different ecological situations. By that time, most concentrated towns of the Mississippian mound-builder cultures had been abandoned, and only a few groups in southeastern North America still maintained the social hierarchy and religious ideas of those earlier cultures. In the Southwest, descendants of the Anasazi and other cliff dwellers had taken up residence in the adobe pueblos mostly along the Rio Grande (Figure 11.7), where they practiced terracing and irrigation to support their agriculture. Their rich religious life, their artistic ceramic and weaving traditions, and their agricultural base reflected their own historical traditions.

Figure 11.7 Taos, in the foothills of what is now New Mexico. The pueblos of the Rio Grande Valley were based on agriculture and the concentration of population in urban areas. This reflected a number of the traditions of the older Native American cultures of the southwestern United States.

Elsewhere in North America, most groups were hunters and gatherers or like the Iroquois of the northeast or the Natchez of the southeast combined those activities with some agriculture. Sometimes an environment was so rich that complex social organization and artistic specialization could develop without an agricultural base. This was the case among the Indians of the northwest coast, who depended on the rich resources of the sea. In other cases, technology was a limiting factor. The tough prairie grasses could not be farmed easily without metal plows, nor could the buffalo be hunted effectively before Europeans introduced the horse. Thus, the Great Plains were only sparsely occupied.

Finally, we should note that although there was great variation among the Indian cultures, some aspects stood in contrast to contemporary societies in Europe and Asia. With the exception of the state systems of Mesoamerica and the Andes, most Indian societies were strongly kin-based. Communal action and ownership of resources, such as land and hunting grounds, were emphasized, and material wealth often was disregarded or placed in a ritual or religious context. It was not that these societies were necessarily egalitarian but rather that ranking usually was not based on wealth. Although often subordinate, women in some societies held important political and social roles and usually played a central role in crop production. Indians tended to view themselves as part of the ecological system and not in control of it, balancing their hunting or farming with existing resources. These attitudes stood in marked contrast to those of many contemporary European and Asian civilizations.

American Diversity in World Context

By the end of the 15th century, two great imperial systems had risen to dominate the two major centers of civilization in Mesoamerica and the Andes. Both empires were built on the achievements of their predecessors, and both reflected a militaristic phase in their area's development. These empires proved to be fragile, weakened by internal strains and the conflicts that any imperial system creates but also limited by their technological inferiority.

Central and South American Civilizations

The Aztec and Inca empires were one end of a continuum of cultures that went from the most simple to the most complex. The Americas contained a broad range of societies, from great civilizations with millions of people to small bands of hunters. In many of these societies, religion played a dominant role in defining the relationship between people and their environment and between the individual and society. How these societies would have developed and what course the American civilizations might have taken in continued isolation remain interesting and unanswerable questions. The first European observers were simultaneously shocked by the "primitive" tribespeople and astounded by the wealth and accomplishments of civilizations such as that of the Aztecs. Europeans generally saw the Indians as curiously backward. In comparison with Europe and Asia, the Americas did seem strange—more like ancient Babylon or Egypt than contemporary China or Europe—except that without the wheel, large domesticated animals, the plow, and to a large extent metal tools and written languages, even that comparison is misleading. The isolation of the Americas had remained important in physical and cultural terms, but that isolation came to an end in 1492, with disastrous results.

Global Connections

The Americas and the World

Conditions in the Americas before 1492 reveal the importance of global connections in Afro-Eurasia and the absence of such connections in the Americas. American isolation from effective global connections is exhibited by the absence of key technologies, like ironworking and the wheel, that would have been easily transmitted had contacts been available. American isolation shows in the absence of the standard range of domesticated animals. It would show, tragically, in the absence of any immunity to some of the common contagious diseases of Afro-Eurasia.

The absence of several features that had become normal in Afro-Eurasia must be stated carefully. It should not detract from the impressive economic, cultural, and political achievements of the key American Indian civilizations, including their ability (particularly in Mesoamerica) to sustain dense populations. It should not obscure the heritage of these societies to later patterns in the Americas. The comparative distinctions that resulted from lack of wider contact would count only when the Americas were forced into new global connections after 1492—but then they mattered greatly.

Further Readings

Charles c. Mann, *1491* (2005) provides a well written overview of many aspects of Native American cultures and accomplishments. Mary Miller, *Art of Mesoamerica: From Olmec to Aztec* (2006) surveys evidence from archaeology and art history. Friedrich Katz's *The Ancient Civilizations of the Americas,* 2nd revised ed. (1997), provides the best overall survey that compares Mesoamerica and Peru. It traces the rise of civilization in both areas. Michael Coe et al., *Atlas of Ancient America* (1986), includes excellent maps, illustrations, and an intelligent and comprehensive text.

The literature on the Aztecs continues to grow rapidly. Bernardino de Sahagún's *Florentine Codex: The General History of the Things of New Spain,* ed. and trans. Charles Dibble and Arthur J. O. Anderson, 12 vols. (1950–1968), is a fundamental source that most scholars still use as a starting point. Good overviews are provided by Frances Berdan's *The Aztecs of Central Mexico: An Imperial Society* 2nd ed. (2005) and Inga Clendinnin's *Aztecs: An Interpretation* (1995). Miguel Leon-Portilla's *Fifteen Aztec Poets* (1992) deals with religion and philosophy in a sympathetic way while David Carrasco, *Religions of Mesoamerica: Cosmovision and Ceremonial Centers* (1990) tries to integrate archaeology into an understanding of the Mesoamerican cosmology. Elizabeth Boone, *Stories in Red and Black: Pictorial Histories of the Aztecs and Mixtecs* (2000) deals with writing systems while Ross Hassig *Aztec Warfare* (1988) examines their military organization. Susan D. Gillespie, *The Aztec Kings* (1989), views Aztec history in terms of myth. Manuel Aguilar-Moreno, *Handbook to Life in the Aztec World* (2006) is a useful encyclopedia on many aspects of Aztec culture.

On Peru, a good overview through solid scholarly articles is provided in Richard W. Keatinge, ed., *Peruvian Prehistory* (1988). The article on Inca archeology by Craig Morris is especially helpful. Also useful is Michael Moseley, *The Incas and their Ancestors* (1992). Art and archeology are the focus of Rebecca Stone Miller, *Art of the Andes from Chavín to Inca* (1995). María Rostoworowski de Diez Canseco, *History of the Inca Realm* (1996), integrates historical and archeological sources, while Juan de Betanzos, *Narrative of the Incas* (1996), makes a classic available to modern readers. Terence D'altroy, *The Incas* (2002) integrates anthropology and archaeology. John Murra's *The Economic Organization of the Inca State* (1980) has influenced much thinking about the Incas. J. Hyslop's *The Inca Road System* (1984) examines the building and function of the road network. The work of Gary Urton, *The History of a Myth: Pacariqtambo and the Origin of the Inka* (1990), and Frank Salomon, *The Code Keepers* (2004), on the quipus show how ethnohistory is deepening our understanding of Inca society. Interesting social history is now being done. Irene Silverblatt's *Moon, Sun, and Witches: Gender Ideologies and Class in Inca and Colonial Peru* (1987) is a controversial book on the position of women before, during, and after the Inca rise to power. Brian S. Bauer, *The Development of the Inca State* (1996), offers a new interpretation of the state.

In Geoffrey W. Conrad and Arthur A. Demerest's *Religion and Empire: The Dynamics of Aztec and Inca Expansionism* (1984), two archeologists compare the political systems of the two empires and the motivations for expansion. The authors find more similarities than differences. On the native peoples who lived north of Mesoamerica there is an extensive literature. Colin G. Calloway, *One Vast Winter Count* (2003) provides an excellent and up to date overview while Linda Cordell, *Ancient Pueblo Peoples* (1994) and George Miner, *The Moundbuilders: Ancient Peoples of Eastern North America* (2004) provide more detail. Carroll L. Riley, *Becoming Aztlan: Mesoamerican Influence in the Greater Southwest, AD 1200-1500* (2005) weighs the evidence on the possible ties between Mesoamerica and the Anasazi and other groups. Claudia G. Mink, *Cahokia: City of the Sun* (1992) is a good starting point on Mississippian cultures. Finally, on the question of the populations of the Americas see Noble D. Cook, *Born to Die* (1998) which tries to establish the populations when post-1492 contact took place.

On the Web

Several sites exist on the still vibrant, but soon to perish, worlds of the Aztecs (http://www.mnsu.edu/emuseum/cultural/mesoamerica/aztec.html), Toltecs (http://www.mnsu.edu/emuseum/prehistory/latinamerica/meso/cultures/toltec.html), Incas (http://loki.stockton.edu/~gilmorew/consorti/1fcenso.htm), and Maya (http://mayaruins.com/, http://www.mnsu.edu/emuseum/prehistory/latinamerica/meso/cultures/maya.html) and others (http://www.mnsu.edu/emuseum/prehistory/latinamerica/meso/mesotable.html). Precolumbian art is introduced at http://www.artic.edu/artaccess/AA_Amerindian/index.html and http://www.peru-explorer.com/preco.htm.

The development of the Mayan calendar and its link to corn harvesting is examined at http://mayacalendar.com/mayacalendar .html. Mesoamerican writing is discussed at http://pages.prodigy .com/GBonline/ancwrite.html. The science of the Aztec calendar and its use in the present day is discussed at http://www .azteccalendar.com/. Tlaloc, the Aztec rain god "Who Makes Things Sprout," is examined at http://www.azteccalendar.com/ god/Tlaloc.html. The practice and underlying motives of human sacrifice practiced in Mesoamerica is explored at http://www .wynja.com/arch/aztec.html and http://en.wikipedia.org/wiki/ Human_sacrifice_in_Aztec_culture.

One of the last Mayan cities, Tulum, can be visited at http://www.d.umn.edu/cla/faculty/troufs/anth3618/matulum.html and http://en.wikipedia.org/wiki/Tulum. A virtual tour of the Mayan port of Xel Ha and resources for the study of Mayan seaborne trade is supplied at http://www.historycooperative.org/ journals/whc/3.2/gilbert.html. The role of commerce in Mayan society, and its indicator of the health of that society are discussed at http://www.mexconnect.com/mex_/travel/dconrad/dcmayatrade .html. Incan civil engineering is discussed alongside a moving panorama of the Incan city of Cuzco. This site also offers brilliant photographs and good text on things Incan from agriculture to weaving.

Child marriage and the complex family structure of the ancient Aztecs (Nahua) can be explored at http://www.hist.umn.edu/ ~rmccaa/index.html (scroll down to "Nahua Calli" and to "child marriage").

AP* Test Prep

1. During the postclassical period, societies in the Americas
   - (A) had a strong sense of common heritage and identity.
   - (B) did not have a sense of common identity.
   - (C) did not develop large urban centers.
   - (D) never formed imperial forms of government.

2. The Aztecs rose to power through all of the following means EXCEPT
   - (A) control of water and irrigation.
   - (B) political alliances with neighboring cities.
   - (C) warfare.
   - (D) a parliamentary system.

3. The religious justification for human sacrifice was that
   - (A) the gods of rain, maize, and fertility needed to be "fed" human blood in order to produce their own bounties.
   - (B) prisoners of war were too numerous, and needed to be removed because they were dangerous influences on the society.
   - (C) the sun god Huitzilopochtli needed constant nourishment to fight against the forces of the night.
   - (D) without human blood, the great city of Tenochtitlan would collapse.

4. Because of their level of technological development, Aztec work and production
   - (A) relied heavily on tools and machines.
   - (B) utilized domesticated beasts of burden extensively.
   - (C) richly rewarded intellectual invention and innovation.
   - (D) relied heavily on the physical labor of humans.

5. All land in the Inca state
   - (A) belonged to the priests and religious institutions.
   - (B) was owned by merchants and traders for investment purposes.
   - (C) belonged to the oldest woman of the family or clan.
   - (D) was owned by the state, but assigned to others for their use.

6. Which of the following is NOT true?
   - (A) While the Maya developed glyphs, the Inca never developed a writing system.
   - (B) Both the Aztecs and Inca forced other societies to recognize their supremacy.
   - (C) The Inca far exceeded the Aztecs in terms of trade.
   - (D) Both the Aztecs and Inca practiced extensive agriculture.

7. Incan state administration and resource distribution system was based on the concept of
   - (A) individualism.
   - (B) first come, first serve.
   - (C) age.
   - (D) reciprocity.

Free-Response Question

Choose three of the following catagories and compare the Aztec and Inca civilizations: Political, Religious, Economic, Social Structures

12 Reunification and Renaissance in Chinese Civilization: The Era of the Tang and Song Dynasties

Rebuilding the Imperial Edifice in the Sui-Tang Era
DOCUMENT: Ties That Bind: Paths to Power
Tang Decline and the Rise of the Song
Tang and Song Prosperity: The Basis of a Golden Age

VISUALIZING THE PAST: Foot Binding as a Marker of Male Dominance
THINKING HISTORICALLY: Artistic Expression and Social Values
GLOBAL CONNECTIONS: China's World Role

Under the aegis of two of its most celebrated dynasties, the Tang and the Song, which ruled from the early 7th century to the late 13th century C.E., Chinese society advanced in virtually all areas of human endeavor as far as any to that time. It was the largest empire on earth, both in population and territory. Nowhere during these centuries were China's remarkable achievements so obvious as in the great cities found throughout the empire (see Figure 12.1), several of which exceeded a million people, surpassing those of any other civilization of the age. Though it was not the largest city, Hangzhou (hohng-joh), the capital of the Song rulers, was renowned for its beauty and sophistication.

Located between a large lake and a river in the Yangzi delta (Map 12.1), Hangzhou was crisscrossed by canals and bridges. The city's location near the Yangzi and the coast of the East China Sea allowed its traders and artisans to prosper through the sale of goods and the manufacture of products from materials drawn from throughout China as well as overseas. By late Song times, Hangzhou had more than a million and a half residents and was famed for its wealth, cleanliness, and the number and variety of diversions it offered.

A visitor to Hangzhou could wander through its ten great marketplaces, each stocked with products from much of the known world. The less consumption-minded visitor could enjoy the city's many parks and delightful gardens or go boating on the Western Lake. There the pleasure craft of the rich mingled with special barges for gaming, dining, or listening to Hangzhou's famous "singing-girls." In the late afternoon, one could visit the bath houses that were found throughout the city. At these establishments, one could also get a massage and sip a cup of tea or rice wine.

In the evening, one might dine at one of the city's many fine restaurants, which specialized in the varied and delicious cuisines of the different regions of China. After dinner, there were a variety of entertainments from which to choose. One could take in the pleasure parks, where acrobats, jugglers, and actors performed for the passing crowds. Other options included the city's ornate tea houses, an opera performance by the lake, or a viewing of landscape paintings by artists from the city's famed academy. Having spent such a day, it would be hard for a visitor to disagree with Marco Polo (who hailed from another beautiful city of canals, Venice) that Hangzhou was "the most noble city and the best that is in the world." ■

Though enjoyed mainly by elite social groups, the good life in cities like Hangzhou was made possible by the large, well educated bureaucracy that had governed China for centuries. As we'll see in this chapter, centralized control and a strong military brought long periods of peace, during which the ruling elites promoted technological innovation, agrarian expansion, and commercial enterprise at both home and overseas. Despite increasing pressure from nomadic invaders from west and north from the 11th century onward, these trends persisted. Well into the modern era, China went on to produce some of the great art of humankind and remained one of the world's most prosperous societies.

Figure 12.1 This cityscape of the Song city of Bian Liang (Kaifeng) painted by Zhang Zeduan conveys the energy and prosperity that characterized Chinese urban life in the Tang-Song eras. Like Hangzhou, Bian Liang's graceful bridges, bustling river markets, and spacious parks attracted many visitors, especially at times of festival celebrations like that depicted here.

Rebuilding the Imperial Edifice in the Sui-Tang Era

The initial rise of the Sui dynasty in the early 580s appeared to be just another factional struggle of the sort that had occurred repeatedly in the splinter states fighting for control of China in the centuries after the fall of the Han. Yang Jian a member of a prominent north Chinese noble family that had long been active in these contests, struck a marriage alliance between his daughter and the ruler of the northern Zhou empire (Map 12.1). The Zhou monarch had recently defeated several rival rulers and united much of the north China plain. After much intrigue, Yang Jian seized the throne of his son-in-law and proclaimed himself emperor. Although Yang Jian was Chinese, he secured his power base by winning the support of neighboring nomadic military commanders. He did this by reconfirming their titles and showing little desire to favor the Confucian scholar-gentry class at their expense. With their support Yang Jian, who took the title Wendi (or Literary Emperor) extended his rule across north China. In 589 Wendi's armies attacked and conquered the weak and divided Chen kingdom, which had long ruled much of the south. With his victory over the Chen, Wendi reunited the traditional core areas of Chinese civilization for the first time in over three and a half centuries (Map 12.2).

Wendi won widespread support by lowering taxes and establishing granaries throughout his domains. Bins for storing grain were built in all of the large cities and in each village of the empire to ensure that there would be a reserve food supply in case floods or drought destroyed the peasants' crops and threatened the people with famine. Large landholders and poor peasants alike were taxed a portion of their crop to keep the granaries filled. Beyond warding off famine, the surplus grain was brought to market in times of food shortages to hold down the price of the people's staple food.

Sui Excesses and Collapse

The foundations Wendi laid for political unification and economic prosperity were at first strengthened even further by his son, the **Yangdi emperor,** who murdered his father to reach the throne. Yangdi extended his father's conquests and drove back the nomadic intruders who threatened the northern frontiers of the empire. He established a milder legal code and devoted resources to

The emergence of the Sui dynasty at the end of the 6th century C.E signaled a return to strong dynastic control in China. In the Tang era that followed, a Confucian revival enhanced the position of the scholar-gentry administrators and provided the ideological basis for a return to highly centralized rule under an imperial dynasty.

Yangdi Second member of Sui dynasty; murdered his father to gain throne; restored Confucian examination system; responsible for construction of Chinese canal system; assassinated in 618.

267

200 C.E.	600 C.E.	800 C.E.	950 C.E.	1100 C.E.	1250 C.E.
220 End of the Han dynasty 220–589 Era of the Six Dynasties; political discord in China; time of great Buddhist influence 589–618 Sui dynasty; building of the Grand Canal	618–626 Gaozu emperor 618–907 Tang dynasty 627–649 Tang Taizong emperor 688 Korean conquest; vassal state of Silla 690–705 Empress Wu; Buddhist influence in China peaks 712–756 Xuanzong emperor	840s Period of Buddhist persecution 907 End of the Tang dynasty	960–1279 Song dynasty; Neo-Confucian revival c. 1050 Invention of block printing with movable type 1067–1085 Shenzong emperor; reforms of Wang Anshi	c. 1100 Invention of gunpowder 1115 Jurchen (Jin) kingdom in north China 1119 First reference to use of compass for sea navigation 1127–1279 Southern Song dynasty	1279–1368 Mongol (Yuan) dynasty rules all China

Map 12.1 China During the Age of Division   After the collapse of the Han dynasty, China fragmented into warring kingdoms for nearly 400 years. The deep divisions of this period were captured by its designation in Chinese histories as the era of the Six Dynasties.

upgrading Confucian education. Yangdi also sought to restore the examination system for regulating entry into the bureaucracy. These legal and educational reforms were part of a broader policy of promoting the scholar-gentry in the imperial administration. But their advancement often worked to the detriment of the great aristocratic families and nomadic military commanders.

Yangdi was overly fond of luxury and extravagant construction projects. He forcibly conscripted hundreds of thousands of peasants to build palaces, a new capital city at Luoyang (lwoh-yahng) (Map 12.1), and a series of great canals to link the various parts of his empire. His demands on the people seemed limitless. In his new capital, Yangdi had an extensive game park laid out. Because there was not enough forest on the site chosen, tens of thousands of laborers were forced to

Map 12.2 The Sui Dynasty and the Tang Dynasty   The short-lived Sui dynasty laid the foundations for the expansive Tang. Under the latter the Chinese empire was restored on a scale not known since the Han era.

dig up huge trees in the nearby hills and cart them miles to be replanted in the artificial mounds that tens of thousands of other laborers had built.

Even before work on his many construction projects was completed, Yangdi led his exhausted and angry subjects into a series of unsuccessful wars to bring Korea back under Chinese rule. His failures in the Korean campaigns between 611 and 614 and the near-fatal reverse he suffered in central Asia at the hands of Turkic nomads in 615 set in motion widespread revolts throughout the empire. Provincial governors declared themselves independent rulers, bandit gangs raided at will, and nomadic peoples again seized large sections of the north China plain. Faced with a crumbling empire, the increasingly deranged emperor retreated to his pleasure palaces in the city of Hangzhou on the Yangzi River to the south. When Yangdi was assassinated by his own ministers in 618, it looked as if China would return to the state of political division and social turmoil it had endured in the preceding centuries.

The Emergence of the Tang and the Restoration of the Empire

The dissolution of the imperial order was averted by the military skills and political savvy of one of Yangdi's officials, **Li Yuan** (lee wahn), the Duke of Tang. Of noble and mixed Chinese-nomadic origins, Li Yuan was for many years a loyal supporter of the Sui ruler. In fact, on one occasion Li Yuan rescued Yangdi, whose forces had been trapped by a far larger force of Turkic cavalry in a small fort that was part of the Great Wall defenses. But as Yangdi grew more and more irrational and unrest spread from one end of the empire to another, Li Yuan was convinced by his sons and allies that only rebellion could save his family and the empire. From the many-sided struggle for the throne that followed Yangdi's death and continued until 623, Li Yuan emerged the victor. Together with his second son, Tang Taizong (tahng teye-zohng), in whose favor he abdicated in 626, Li Yuan laid the basis for the golden age of the Tang.

Li Yuan   [lee wahn] (566–635) Also known as Duke of Tang; minister for Yangdi; took over empire following assassination of Yangdi; first emperor of Tang dynasty; took imperial title of Gaozu.

Tang armies conquered deep into central Asia as far as present-day Afghanistan. These victories meant that many of the nomadic peoples who had dominated China in the Six Dynasties era had to submit to Tang rule. Tang emperors also completed the repairs begun by the Sui and earlier dynasties on the northern walls and created frontier armies. Partly recruited from Turkic nomadic peoples, these frontier forces gradually became the most potent military units in the empire. The sons of Turkic tribal leaders were sent to the capital as hostages to guarantee the good behavior of the tribe in question. At the Tang capital, they were also educated in Chinese ways in the hope of their eventual assimilation into Chinese culture.

Chinese Empires
MAP

The empire was also extended to parts of Tibet in the west, the Red River valley homeland of the Vietnamese in the south (see Chapter 8), and Manchuria in the north (Map 12.1). In the Tang period, the Yangzi River basin and much of the south were fully integrated with north China for the first time since the Han. In 668, under the emperor Gaozong, Korea was overrun by Chinese armies, and a vassal kingdom called Silla was established that long remained loyal to the Tang. In a matter of decades, the Tang had built an empire that was far larger than even that of the early Han empire whose boundaries in many directions extended beyond the borders of present-day China.

Rebuilding the World's Largest and Most Pervasive Bureaucracy

Crucial for the restoration of Chinese unity were the efforts of the early Tang monarchs to rebuild and expand the imperial bureaucracy. A revived scholar-gentry elite and reworked Confucian ideology played central roles in the process. From the time of the second Sui emperor, Yangdi, the fortunes of the scholar-gentry had begun to improve. This trend continued under the early Tang emperors, who desperately needed loyal and well educated officials to govern the vast empire they had put together in a matter of decades. The Tang rulers also used the scholar-gentry bureaucrats to offset the power of the aristocracy. As the aristocratic families' control over court life and administration declined, their role in Chinese history was reduced. From the Tang era onward, political power in China was shared by a succession of imperial families and the bureaucrats of the civil service system. Members of the hereditary aristocracy continued to occupy administrative positions, but the scholar-gentry class staffed most of the posts in the secretariats and executive ministries that oversaw a huge bureaucracy.

This bureaucracy reached from the imperial palace down to the subprefecture, or district level, which was roughly equivalent to an American county. One secretariat drafted imperial decrees; a second monitored the reports of regional and provincial officials and the petitions of local notables. The executive department, which was divided into six ministries—including war, justice, and public works—ran the empire on a day-to-day basis. In addition, there was a powerful Bureau of Censors whose chief task was to keep track of officials at all levels and report their misdeeds or failings. Finally, there was a very large staff to run the imperial household, including the palaces in the new capital at **Chang'an** (chahng-an) and the residences of the princes of the imperial line and other dignitaries.

Chang'an [chahng-an] Capital of Tang dynasty; population of 2 million, larger than any other city in the world at that time.

Institutionalizing Meritocracy: The Growing Importance of the Examination System

Like Yangdi, the Tang emperors patronized academies to train state officials and educate them in the Confucian classics, which were thought to teach moral and organizational principles essential to effective administrators. In the Tang era, and under the Song dynasty that followed, the numbers of the educated scholar-gentry rose far above those in the Han era. In the Tang and Song periods, the examination system was greatly expanded, and the pattern of advancement in the civil service was much more regularized. This meant that in the political realm more than any previous political system (and those yet to come for centuries), the Chinese connected merit as measured by tested skills with authority and status. Several different kinds of examinations were administered by the **Ministry of Rites** to students from government schools or to those recommended by distinguished scholars.

Ministry of Rites Administered examinations to students from Chinese government schools or those recommended by distinguished scholars.

The highest offices could be gained only by those who were able to pass exams on the philosophical or legal classics at the highest imperial or metropolitan level. Those who passed the latter earned the title of **jinshi.** Their names were announced throughout the empire, and their families'

jinshi Title granted to students who passed the most difficult Chinese examination on all of Chinese literature; became immediate dignitaries and eligible for high office.

positions were secured by the prospect of high office that was opened up by their success. Overnight they were transformed into dignitaries whom even their former friends and fellow students addressed formally and treated with deference. Success in exams at all levels won candidates special social status. This meant that they earned the right to wear certain types of clothing and were exempt from corporal punishment. They gained access to the higher level of material comfort and the refined pleasures that were enjoyed by members of the scholar-gentry elite, some of whom are shown at play in Figure 12.2.

Even though a much higher proportion of Tang bureaucrats won their positions through success in civil service examinations than had been the case in the Han era, birth and family connections continued to be important in securing high office. Some of these relationships are clearly illustrated by the petitioner's letter printed in the Document feature. Established bureaucrats not only ensured that their sons and cousins got into the imperial academies but could pull strings to see that even failed candidates from their families received government posts. Ethnic and regional ties also played a role in staffing bureaucratic departments. This meant that although bright commoners could rise to upper-level positions in the bureaucracy, the central administration was overwhelmingly dominated by a small number of established families. Sons followed fathers in positions of power and influence, and prominent households bought a disproportionate share of the places available in the imperial academies. Many positions were reserved for members of the old aristocracy and the low-ranking sons and grandsons of lesser wives and concubines belonging to the imperial household. Merit and ambition counted for something, but birth and family influence often counted for a good deal more.

State and Religion in the Tang and Song Eras

Increasing state patronage for Confucian learning threatened not only the old aristocratic families but also the Buddhist monastic orders, which had become a major force in Chinese life in the Six Dynasties era. These tensions represent a well documented instance of the longstanding (and still globally widespread) problem of delineating the boundaries between established religions and state systems. Many of the rulers in the pre-Tang era, particularly those from nomadic origins, were devout Buddhists and strong patrons of the Buddhist establishment. In the centuries after the fall of the Han, Buddhist sects proliferated in China. The most popular were those founded by Chinese monks, in part because they soon took on distinctively Chinese qualities. Among the masses, the salvationist **pure land** strain of Mahayana Buddhism won widespread conversions because it

Buddhist Stories I

pure land Buddhism   Emphasized salvationist aspects of Chinese Buddhism; popular among masses of Chinese society.

Figure 12.2 As shown in this ink drawing of Chinese philosophers of the Song dynasty, board games and musical recitals were highly esteemed leisure activities for the scholar-gentry class. Members of the scholar-gentry elite might also attend poetry reading or writing parties, travel to mountains to meditate amid scenic splendors, or paint the blossoming plum trees in their gardens. As in their work, members of this highly educated elite admired those who at leisure pursued a diverse array of activities.

(Handscroll "Gathering of Philosophers." The Metropolitan Museum of Art, New York, NY, U.S.A. Image copyright © The Metropolitan Museum of Art/Art Resource, NY.)

Ties That Bind: Paths to Power

The following letter was included in a short story by Tang author Niu Su. It was sent by a local functionary named Wu Bao to a high official to whom Wu hoped to attach himself and thus win advancement in the imperial bureaucracy. What can this letter tell us about the ways in which the Chinese bureaucracy worked in the Tang and Song eras?

To my great good fortune, we share the same native place, and your renown for wise counsel is well known to me. Although, through gross neglect, I have omitted to prostrate myself before you, my heart has always been filled with admiration and respect. You are the nephew of the Prime Minister, and have made use of your outstanding talents in his service. In consequence of this, your high ability has been rewarded with a commission. General Li is highly qualified both as a civil and a military official, and he has been put in full command of the expedition [to put down "barbarian" rebellions in the southern parts of the empire]. In his hands he unites mighty forces, and he cannot fail to bring these petty brigands to order. By the alliance of the General's heroic valor and your own talent and ability, your armies' task of subjugation will be the work of a day. I, in my youth, devoted myself to study.

Reaching manhood, I paid close attention to the [Confucian] classics. But in talent I do not compare with other men, and so far I have held office only as an officer of the guard. I languish in this out-of-the-way corner beyond the Jian[mountains], close to the haunts of the barbarians. My native place is thousands of miles away, and many passes and rivers lie between. What is more, my term of office here is completed, and I cannot tell when I shall receive my next appointment. So lacking in talent, I fear I am but poorly fitted to be selected for an official post; far less can I entertain the hope of some meager salary. I can only retire, when old age comes, to some rustic retreat, and "turn aside to die in a ditch." I have heard by devious ways of your readiness to help those in distress. If you will not overlook a man from your native place, be quick to bestow your special favour on me, so that I may render you service "as a humble groom." Grant me some small salary, and a share however slight in your deeds of merit. If by your boundless favor I could take part in this triumphal progress, even as a member of the rear-most company, the day would live engraved on my memory.

QUESTIONS What techniques does Wu use to win the high official's favor? How does Wu expect the official to help him? What does he promise in return? Does birth or merit appear to be more important in his appeals? What dangers to the imperial system are contained in the sorts of ties that Wu argues bind him to the high official?

Chan Buddhism Known as Zen in Japan; stressed meditation and appreciation of natural and artistic beauty; popular with members of elite Chinese society.

Zen Buddhism Known as Chan Buddhism in China; stressed meditation and the appreciation of natural and artistic beauty.

seemed to provide a refuge from an age of war and turmoil. Members of the elite classes, on the other hand, were more attracted to the **Chan** variant of Buddhism, or **Zen** as it is known in Japan and the West. With its stress on meditation and the appreciation of natural and artistic beauty, Zen had great appeal for the educated classes of China.

The goal of those who followed Chan was to come to know the ultimate wisdom, and thus find release from the cycle of rebirth, through introspective meditation. The nature of this level of consciousness often was expressed in poetic metaphors and riddles, such as those in the following lines from an 8th century C.E. treatise called the *Hymn to Wisdom*:

The power of wisdom is infinite.
It is like moonlight reflected in a thousand waves; it can see, hear, understand, and know.
It can do all these and yet is always empty and tranquil.
Being empty means having no appearance.
Being tranquil means not having been created.
One will then not be bound by good and evil, or be seized by quietness or disturbance.
One will not be wearied by birth and death or rejoice in Nirvana.

The combination of royal patronage and widespread conversion at both the elite and mass levels made Buddhism a strong social, economic, and political force by the time of the Tang unification. The early Tang rulers continued to patronize Buddhism while trying to promote education in the Confucian classics. Emperors such as Taizong endowed monasteries, built in the style of those pictured in Figure 12.3. They also sent emissaries to India to collect texts and relics and commissioned Buddhist paintings and statuary. However, no Tang ruler matched **Empress Wu** (r. 690–705) in supporting the Buddhist establishment. At one point she tried to elevate Buddhism to the status of a state religion.

Empress Wu also commissioned many Buddhist paintings and sculptures. The sculptures are noteworthy for their colossal size. She had statues of the Buddha, which were as much as two and three stories high, carved from stone or cast in bronze. Some of these statues, such as those pictured

Empress Wu Tang ruler 690–705 C.E. in China; supported Buddhist establishment; tried to elevate Buddhism to state religion; had multistory statues of Buddha created.

in Figure 12.4, were carved out of the rock in the great caves near her capital at Luoyang; for cast figures at other locations, Wu had huge pagodas built. With this sort of support, it is not surprising that Buddhism flourished in the early centuries of Tang rule. By the mid-9th century, there were nearly 50,000 monasteries and hundreds of thousands of Buddhist monks and nuns in China.

The Anti-Buddhist Backlash

Buddhist successes aroused the envy of Confucian and Daoist rivals. Some of these notables attacked the religion as alien, even though the faith followed by most of the Chinese was very different from that originally preached by the Buddha or that practiced in India or southeast Asia. Daoist monks tried to counter Buddhism's appeals to the masses by stressing their own magical and predictive powers. Most damaging to the fortunes of Buddhism was the growing campaign of Confucian scholar-administrators to convince the Tang rulers that the large Buddhist monastic establishment posed a fundamental economic challenge to the imperial order. Because monastic lands and resources were not taxed, the Tang regime lost huge amounts of revenue as

Figure 12.3 Tang era architecture at the Phoenix Pavilion in Japan. Some of the most characteristic features of this splendid style of construction are its steeply sloping tiled roofs with upturned corners, the extensive use of fine wood in the floors, walls, and ceilings, and the sliding panels that covered doors and windows in inclement weather and opened up the temples or monasteries to the natural world on pleasant days.

a result of imperial grants or the gifts of wealthy families to Buddhist monasteries. The state was also denied labor power because it could neither tax nor conscript peasants who worked on monastic estates.

Figure 12.4 At sites such as Longmen near the Tang capital of Luoyang on the Yellow River and Yunkang far to the north, massive statues of the Buddha were carved out of rocky cliffsides beginning in the 6th century C.E. Before the age of Buddhist predominance, sculpture had not been highly developed in China, and the art at these centers was strongly influenced by that of central and even west Asia. Known more for their sheer size than for artistic refinement, the huge Buddhas of sites such as Longmen attest to the high level of skill the Chinese had attained in stone- and metalworking.

Wuzong   Chinese emperor of Tang dynasty who openly persecuted Buddhism by destroying monasteries in 840s; reduced influence of Chinese Buddhism in favor of Confucian ideology.

By the mid-9th century, state fears of Buddhist wealth and power led to measures to limit the flow of land and resources to the monastic orders. Under Emperor **Wuzong** (r. 841–847), these restrictions grew into open persecution of Buddhism. Thousands of monasteries and Buddhist shrines were destroyed, and hundreds of thousands of monks and nuns were forced to abandon their monastic orders and return to civilian lives. They and the slaves and peasants who worked their lands were again subject to taxation, and monastery lands were parceled out to taxpaying landlords and peasant smallholders.

Although Chinese Buddhism survived this and other bouts of repression, it was weakened. Never again would the Buddhist monastic orders have the political influence and wealth they had enjoyed in the first centuries of Tang rule. The great age of Buddhist painting and cave sculptures gave way to art dominated by Daoist and Confucian subjects and styles in the late Tang and the Song dynastic era that followed. The Zen and pure land sects of Buddhism continued to attract adherents, with those of the latter numbering in the millions. But Confucianism emerged as the central ideology of Chinese civilization for most of the period from the 9th to the early 20th century. Buddhism left its mark on the arts, the Chinese language, and Chinese thinking about things such as heaven, charity, and law, but it ceased to be a dominant influence. Buddhism's fate in China contrasts sharply with its ongoing and pivotal impact on the civilizations of mainland southeast Asia, Tibet, and parts of central Asia, where it continued to spread in the centuries of Tang-Song rule.

Tang Decline and the Rise of the Song

Beset by internal rebellions and nomadic incursions, the Tang gave way to the Song in the early 10th century. Although the Song domains were smaller than those of the Tang, the Confucian revival flourished under the successor dynasty.

The motives behind the mid-9th-century Tang assault on the Buddhist monastic order were symptomatic of a general weakening of imperial control that had begun almost a century earlier. After the controversial but strong rule between 690 and 705 by Empress Wu, who actually tried to establish a new dynasty, a second attempt to control the throne was made by a highborn woman who had married into the imperial family. Backed by her powerful relatives and a group of prominent courtiers, Empress Wei poisoned her husband, the son of Empress Wu, and placed her own small child on the throne. But Empress Wei's attempt to seize power was thwarted by another prince, who led a palace revolt that ended with the destruction of Wei and her supporters. The early decades of the long reign of this prince, who became the **Xuanzong** (shwahn-dzong) emperor (r. 713–756), marked the peak of Tang power and the high point of Chinese civilization under the dynasty.

Xuanzong   [shwahn-dzong] Leading Chinese emperor of the Tang dynasty who reigned from 713 to 755 though he encouraged overexpansion.

Initially, Xuanzong took a strong interest in political and economic reforms, which were pushed by the very capable officials he appointed to high positions. But increasingly, his interest in running the vast empire waned. More and more he devoted himself to patronizing the arts and enjoying the pleasures available within the confines of the imperial city. These diversions included music, which he played himself and also had performed by the many musicians he patronized. Thousands of concubines vied in the imperial apartments for the attention of the monarch. After the death of his second wife, the aged and lonely emperor became infatuated with **Yang Guifei,** a beautiful young woman from the harem of one of the imperial princes (Figure 12.5).

Yang Guifei   (719–756) Royal concubine during reign of Xuanzong; introduction of relatives into royal administration led to revolt.

Court Lady Yang Guifei Ascending a Horse

Their relationship was one of the most famous and ill-fated romances in all of Chinese history. But it was only one of the more fateful of a multitude of interventions by powerful women at the courts of emperors and kings throughout Afro-Euroasia. Xuanzong promenaded in the imperial gardens and gave flute lessons to Yang. Soon she was raised to the status of royal concubine, and she used her new power to pack the upper levels of the government with her greedy relatives. They and Yang assumed an ever greater role in court politics. The arrogance and excessive ambition of Yang Guifei and her family angered members of the rival cliques at court, who took every opportunity to turn Yang's excesses into a cause for popular unrest. Xuanzong's long neglect of state affairs resulted in economic distress, which fed this discontent. It also led to chronic military weaknesses, which left the government unable to deal with the disorders effectively. The deepening crisis came to a head in 755 when one of the emperor's main military leaders, a general of nomadic origins named An Lushan, led a widely supported revolt with the aim of founding a new dynasty to supplant the Tang.

Although the revolt was crushed and the Tang dynasty preserved, victory was won at a very high cost. Early in the rebellion, Xuanzong's retreating and demoralized troops mutinied, first killing several members of the Yang family and then forcing the emperor to have Yang Guifei executed. Xuanzong lived on for a time, but his grief and disillusionment rendered him incapable of continuing as emperor. None of the Tang monarchs who followed him could compare with the able leaders that the dynasty had consistently produced in the first century and a half of its rule.

Equally critical, to defeat the rebels the Tang had sought alliances with nomadic peoples living on the northern borders of the empire. They had also delegated resources and political power to regional commanders who remained loyal to the dynasty. As had happened so often in the past, in the late 8th and 9th centuries the nomads used political divisions within China to gain entry into and eventually assert control over large areas of the north China plain. At the same time, many of the allied provincial governors became in effect independent rulers. They collected their own taxes, passing little or none on to the imperial treasury. These regional lords raised their own armies and bequeathed their titles to their sons without asking for permission from the Tang court. Worsening economic conditions led to a succession of revolts in the 9th century, some of which were popular uprisings led by peasants.

The Founding of the Song Dynasty

By the end of the 9th century, little remained of the once-glorious Tang Empire. By 907, when the last emperor of the Tang dynasty was forced to resign, China appeared to be entering another phase of nomadic dominance, political division, and social strife. In 960, however, a military commander emerged to reunite China under a single dynasty. **Zhao Kuangyin** (joh kwahng-zihng) had established a far-flung reputation as one of the most honest and able of the generals of the last of the Five Dynasties that had struggled to control north China after the fall of the Tang. Though a fearless warrior, Zhao was a scholarly man who collected books rather than booty while out campaigning. Amid the continuing struggles for control in the north, Zhao's subordinates and regular troops insisted that he proclaim himself emperor. In the next few years, Zhao, renamed Emperor Taizu, routed all his rivals except one, thus founding the Song dynasty that was to rule most of China for the next three centuries.

The one rival Taizu could not overcome was the northern **Liao** (lyow) **dynasty**, which had been founded in 907 by the nomadic **Khitan** (kiht-ahn) peoples from Manchuria. This failure set a precedent for weakness on the part of the Song rulers in dealing with the nomadic peoples of the north. This shortcoming plagued the dynasty from its earliest years to its eventual destruction by the Mongols in the late 13th century. Beginning in 1004, the Song were forced by military defeats at the hands of the Khitans to sign a series of humiliating treaties with their smaller but more militarily adept northern neighbors. These treaties committed the Song to paying a very heavy tribute to the Liao dynasty to keep it from raiding and possibly conquering the Song domains. The Khitans, who had been highly *Sinified,* or influenced by Chinese culture, during a century of rule in north China, seemed content with this arrangement. They clearly saw the Song empire as culturally superior—an area from which they could learn much in statecraft, the arts, and economic organization.

Song Politics: Settling for Partial Restoration

A comparison of the boundaries of the early Song Empire (Map 12.3) with that of the Tang domains (Map 12.2) reveals that the Song never matched its predecessor in political or military strength. The weakness of the Song resulted in part from imperial policies that were designed to ward off the conditions that had destroyed the Tang empire. From the outset, the military was sub-

Figure 12.5 This painting of Yang Guifei gives a vivid impression of the opulence and refinement of Chinese court life in the late Tang era. Here a very well dressed Yang Guifei is helped by some of her servants onto a well fed horse, presumably for a trot through the palace grounds. Two fan-bearers stand ready to accompany the now powerful concubine on her sedate ride while other attendants prepare to lead the horse through the confined space of the royal enclosure.

Zhao Kuangyin [joh kwahng-zihng] (r. 960–976) Founder of Song dynasty; originally a general following fall of Tang; took title of Taizu; failed to overcome northern Liao dynasty that remained independent.

Liao dynasty [lyow] Founded in 907 by nomadic Khitan peoples from Manchuria; maintained independence from Song dynasty in China.

Khitans [kiht-ahn] Nomadic peoples of Manchuria; militarily superior to Song dynasty China but influenced by Chinese culture; forced humiliating treaties on Song China in 11th century.

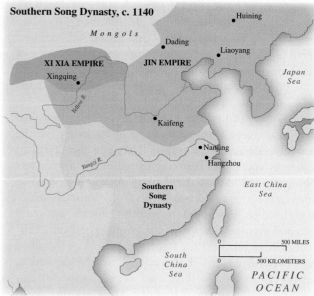

Map 12.3 China in the Song and Southern Song Dynastic Periods   A comparison of the territory controlled during the two phases of the Song dynasty clearly indicates both the growing power and pressure of nomadic peoples from the north and the weakened state of the Song rulers of China.

ordinated to the civilian administrators of the scholar-gentry class. Only civil officials were allowed to be governors, thereby removing the temptation of regional military commanders to seize power. In addition, military commanders were rotated to prevent them from building up a power base in the areas where they were stationed.

At the same time, the early Song rulers strongly promoted the interests of the Confucian scholar-gentry, who touted themselves as the key bulwark against the revival of warlordism. Officials' salaries were increased, and many perks—including additional servants and payments of luxury goods such as silk and wine—made government posts more lucrative. The civil service exams were fully routinized. They were given every three years at three levels: district, provincial, and imperial. Song examiners passed a far higher percentage of those taking the exams than the Tang examiners had, and these successful candidates were much more likely to receive an official post than their counterparts in the Tang era. As a result, the bureaucracy soon became bloated with well paid officials who often had little to do. In this way, the ascendancy of the scholar-gentry class over its aristocratic and Buddhist rivals was fully secured in the Song era.

The Revival of Confucian Thought

The great influence of the scholar-gentry in the Song era was mirrored in the revival of Confucian ideas and values that dominated intellectual life. Many scholars tried to recover long-neglected texts and decipher ancient inscriptions. New academies devoted to the study of the classical texts were founded, and impressive libraries were established. The new schools of philosophy propounded rival interpretations of the teachings of Confucius and other ancient thinkers. They also sought to prove the superiority of indigenous thought systems, such as Confucianism and Daoism, over imported ones, especially Buddhism.

The most prominent thinkers of the era, such as **Zhu Xi** (joo shee), stressed the importance of applying philosophical principles to everyday life and action. These **Neo-Confucians,** or revivers of ancient Confucian teachings, believed that cultivating personal morality was the highest goal for humans. They argued that virtue could be attained through knowledge gained by book learning and personal observation as well as through contact with men of wisdom and high morality. In these ways, the basically good nature of humans could be cultivated, and superior men, fit to govern

Zhu Xi   [joo shee] (1130–1200) Most prominent of neo-Confucian scholars during the Song dynasty in China; stressed importance of applying philosophical principles to everyday life and action.

neo-Confucians   Revived ancient Confucian teachings in Song era China; great impact on the dynasties that followed; their emphasis on tradition and hostility to foreign systems made Chinese rulers and bureaucrats less receptive to outside ideas and influences.

and teach others, could be developed. Neo-Confucian thinking had a great impact on Chinese intellectual life during the eras of all the dynasties that followed the Song. Its hostility to foreign philosophical systems, such as Buddhism, made Chinese rulers and bureaucrats less receptive to outside ideas and influences than they had been earlier. The Neo-Confucian emphasis on tradition and hostility to foreign influences was one of a number of forces that eventually stifled innovation and critical thinking among the Chinese elite.

The Neo-Confucian emphasis on rank, obligation, deference, and traditional rituals reinforced class, age, and gender distinctions, particularly as they were expressed in occupational roles. Great importance was given to upholding the authority of the patriarch of the Chinese household, who was compared to the male emperor of the Chinese people as a whole. If men and women kept to their place and performed the tasks of their age and social rank, the Neo-Confucians argued, there would be social harmony and prosperity. If problems arose, the best solutions could be found in examples drawn from the past. They believed that historical experience was the best guide for navigating the uncertain terrain of the future.

Roots of Decline: Attempts at Reform

The means by which the Song emperors had secured their control over China undermined their empire in the long run. The weakness they showed in the face of the Khitan challenge encouraged other nomadic peoples to carve out kingdoms on the northern borders of the Song domains. By the mid-11th century, **Tangut** tribes, originally from Tibet, had established a kingdom named **Xi Xia** (shee-shyah) to the southwest of the Khitan kingdom of Liao (Map 12.3). The tribute that the Song had to pay these peoples for protection of their northern borders was a great drain on the resources of the empire and a growing burden for the Chinese peasantry. Equally burdensome was the cost of the army—numbering nearly 1 million soldiers by the mid-11th century—that the Song had to maintain to guard against invasion from the north. But the very size of the army was a striking measure of the productivity and organizational ability of Chinese civilization. It dwarfed its counterparts in other civilizations from Japan to western Europe.

The emphasis on civil administration and the scholar-gentry and the growing disdain among the Song elite for the military also took their toll. Although Song armies were large, their commanders rarely were the most able men available. In addition, funds needed to upgrade weapons or repair fortifications often were diverted to the scholarly pursuits and entertainments of the court and gentry. At the court and among the ruling classes, painting and poetry were cultivated, while the horseback riding and hunting that had preoccupied earlier rulers and their courtiers went out of fashion.

In the 1070s and early 1080s, **Wang Anshi,** the chief minister of the Song Shenzong emperor, tried to ward off the impending collapse of the dynasty by introducing sweeping reforms. A celebrated Confucian scholar, Wang ran the government on the basis of the Legalist assumption that an energetic and interventionist state could greatly increase the resources and strength of the dynasty. For 20 years, in the face of strong opposition from the conservative ministers who controlled most of the administration, Wang tried to correct the grave defects in the imperial order. He introduced cheap loans and government-assisted irrigation projects to encourage agricultural expansion. He taxed the landlord and scholarly classes, who had regularly exempted themselves from military service. Wang used the increased revenue to establish well trained mercenary forces to replace armies that had formerly been conscripted from the untrained and unwilling peasantry. Wang even tried to reorganize university education and reorient the examination system. His reforms stressed analytical thinking rather than the rote memorization of the classics that had long been the key to success among the scholar-gentry.

Reaction and Disaster: The Flight to the South

Unfortunately, Wang's ability to propose and enact reforms depended on continuing support from the Shenzong emperor. In 1085 that emperor died, and his successor favored the conservative cliques that had long opposed Wang's changes. The Neo-Confucians came to power, ended reform,

Tangut   Rulers of Xi Xia kingdom of northwest China; one of regional kingdoms during period of southern Song; conquered by Mongols in 1226.

Xi Xia   [shee-shyah] Kingdom of Tangut people, north of Song kingdom, in mid-11th century; collected tribute that drained Song resources and burdened Chinese peasantry.

Wang Anshi   Confucian scholar and chief minister of a Song emperor in 1070s; introduced sweeping reforms based on Legalists; advocated greater state intervention in society.

Jurchens [YUHR-chehns] Founders of the Qin kingdom that succeeded the Liao in northern China; annexed most of the Yellow River basin and forced Song to flee to south.

Jin Kingdom north of the Song Empire; established by Jurchens in 1115 after overthrowing Liao dynasty; ended 1234.

Southern Song Rump state of Song dynasty from 1127 to 1279; carved out of much larger domains ruled by the Tang and northern Song; culturally one of the most glorious reigns in Chinese history.

The Tang and Song eras were a time of major shifts in the population balance within China, new patterns of trade and commerce, renewed urban expansion, novel forms of artistic and literary expression, and a series of technological innovations.

Grand Canal Built in 7th century during reign of Yangdi during Sui dynasty; designed to link the original centers of Chinese civilization on the north China plain with the Yangtze river basin to the south; nearly 1200 miles long.

and reversed many of Wang's initiatives. As a result, economic conditions continued to deteriorate, and peasant unrest grew throughout the empire. Facing banditry and rebellion from within, an unprepared military proved no match for the increasing threat from beyond the northern borders of the empire. In 1115, a new nomadic contender, the **Jurchens** (YUHR-chehns), overthrew the Liao dynasty of the Khitans and established the **Jin** kingdom north of the Song empire (Map 12.3). After successful invasions of Song territory, the Jurchens annexed most of the Yellow River basin to their Jin kingdom. These conquests forced the Song to flee to the south. With the Yangzi River basin as their anchor and their capital transferred to Hangzhou, the Song dynasty survived for another century and a half. Politically the **Southern Song** dynasty (1167–1279) was little more than a rump state carved out of the much larger domains ruled by the Tang and northern-based Song. Culturally, its brief reign was to be one of the most glorious in Chinese history—perhaps in the history of humankind.

Tang and Song Prosperity: The Basis of a Golden Age

The attention given to canal building by the Sui emperors and the Tang rulers who followed them was driven by a major shift in the population balance within Chinese civilization. The **Grand Canal**, which Yangdi risked his throne to have built, was designed to link the original centers of Chinese civilization on the north China plain with the Yangzi River basin more than 500 miles to the south (see Maps 12.1 and 12.2). Because the great river systems that were essential to China's agrarian base ran from west to east—from the mountains of central Asia to the sea—the movement of people and goods in that direction was much easier than from north to south.

Although no major geographic barriers separated the millet-growing areas of northern China from the rice-producing Yangzi basin, overland travel was slow and difficult. The transport of bulk goods such as millet and rice was prohibitively expensive. The great increase of the Chinese population in the southern regions in the later Han and Six Dynasties periods made it necessary to improve communications between north and south once the two regions were joined by the Sui conquests. Not only did more and more of the emperor's subjects live in the southern regions, but the Yangzi basin and other rice-growing areas in the south were fast becoming the major food-producing areas of the empire. By late Tang and early Song times, the south had surpassed the north in both crop production and population.

Yangdi's Grand Canal was intended to facilitate control over the southern regions by courts, bureaucracies, and armies centered in ancient imperial centers such as Chang'an and Luoyang in the north. The canal made it possible to transport to the capital revenue collected in the form of grain from the fertile southern regions and to transfer food from the south to districts threatened by drought and famine in the north. No wonder that Yangdi was obsessed with canal construction. By the time the Grand Canal was finished, more than a million forced laborers had worked, and many had died, on its locks and embankments. The completed canal system was an engineering achievement every bit as impressive as the northern wall. Most stretches of the canal, which was nearly 1200 miles long, were 40 paces wide, and imperial highways lined with willow trees ran along the banks on both sides.

A New Phase of Intercontinental Commercial Expansion by Land and Sea

Tang conquests in central Asia and the building of the canal system did much to promote commercial expansion in the Tang and Song eras. The extension of Tang control deep into central Asia meant that the overland silk routes between China and Persia were reopened and protected. This intensified international contacts in the postclassical period. Tang control promoted exchanges between China and Buddhist centers in the nomadic lands of central Asia as well as with the Islamic world farther west. Horses, Persian rugs, and tapestries passed to China along these routes, while fine silk textiles, porcelain, and paper were exported to the centers of Islamic civilization. As in the Han era, China exported mainly manufactured goods to overseas areas, such as southeast Asia, while importing mainly luxury products such as aromatic woods and spices.

In late Tang and Song times, Chinese merchants and sailors increasingly carried Chinese trade overseas instead of being content to let foreign seafarers come to them. Along with the dhows of the Arabs, Chinese **junks** were the best ships in the world in this period. They were equipped with watertight bulkheads, sternpost rudders, oars, sails, compasses, bamboo fenders, and gunpowder-propelled rockets for self-defense. With such vessels, Chinese sailors and merchants became the dominant force in the Asian seas east of the Malayan peninsula.

The heightened role of commerce and the money economy in Chinese life was readily apparent in the market quarters found in all cities and major towns (Figure 12.6). These were filled with shops and stalls that sold products drawn from local farms, regional centers of artisan production, and trade centers as distant as the Mediterranean. The Tang and Song governments supervised the hours and marketing methods in these centers, and merchants specializing in products of the same kind banded together in guilds to promote their interests with local officials and to regulate competition.

This expansion in scale was accompanied by a growing sophistication in commercial organization and forms of credit available in China. In the following millennium these innovations in instruments for economic exchange transformed domestic marketing and international commerce worldwide. The proportion of exchanges involved in the money economy expanded greatly, and deposit shops, an early form of the bank, were found in many parts of the empire. The first use of paper money also occurred in the Tang era. Merchants deposited their profits in their hometowns before setting out on trading caravans to distant cities. They were given credit vouchers, or what the Chinese called **flying money,** which they could then present for reimbursement at the appropriate office in the city of destination. This arrangement greatly reduced the danger of robbery on the often perilous journeys merchants made from one market center to another. In the early 11th century, the government began to issue paper money when an economic crisis made it clear that the private merchant banks could no longer handle the demand for the new currency.

junks Chinese ships equipped with watertight bulkheads, sternpost rudders, compasses, and bamboo fenders; dominant force in Asian seas east of the Malayan peninsula.

flying money Chinese credit instrument that provided credit vouchers to merchants to be redeemed at the end of the voyage; reduced danger of robbery; early form of currency.

Figure 12.6 One of the many urban scenes painted in the Song era provides a panoramic view of the bustling city of Kaifeng (once an imperial capital) on the Grand Canal. The broad-hulled riverboats pictured here were ideal for transporting bulk goods, such as rice or cloth, between north and south China. But they were no match for the great junks that ventured into the seas to trade with Japan and southeast Asia. The riverfront is dominated by markets and open-air restaurants that spread throughout China in this era of prosperity.
(A detail of a silk scroll painting called "Going Up the River at the Spring Festival." Werner Forman Archive. Peking Palace Museum. Art Resource, NY.)

The expansion of commerce and artisan production was complemented by a surge in urban growth in the Tang and Song eras. At nearly 2 million, the population of the Tang capital and its suburbs at Chang'an was far larger than that of any other city in the world at the time. The imperial city, an inner citadel within the walls of Chang'an, was divided into a highly restricted zone dominated by the palace and audience halls and a section crowded with the offices of the ministries and secretariats of the imperial government. Near the imperial city but outside Chang'an's walls, elaborate gardens and a hunting park were laid out for the amusement of the emperors and favored courtiers. The spread of commerce and the increasing population also fed urban growth in the rest of China. In the north and especially the south, old cities mushroomed as suburbs spread in all directions from the original city walls. Towns grew rapidly into cities, and the proportion of the empire's population living in urban centers grew steadily. The number of people living in large cities in China, which may have been as high as 10 percent, was also far greater than that found in any civilization until after the Industrial Revolution.

Expanding Agrarian Production and Life in the Country

The movement of the population southward to the fertile valleys of the Yangzi and other river systems was part of a larger process of agrarian expansion in the Tang and Song period. The expansion of Chinese settlement and agricultural production was promoted by the rulers of both dynasties. Their officials actively encouraged peasant groups to migrate to uncultivated areas or those occupied by shifting cultivators or peoples of non-Chinese descent. The state also supported military garrisons in these areas to protect the new settlements and to complete the task of subduing non-Chinese peoples. State-regulated irrigation and embankment systems advanced agrarian expansion. For example, the great canals made it possible for peasants who grew specialized crops, such as tea, or those who cultivated silkworms to market their produce over much of the empire.

The introduction of new seeds, such as the famed Champa rice from Vietnam; better use of human, animal, and silt manures; more thorough soil preparation and weeding; and multiple cropping and improved water control techniques increased the yields of peasant holdings. Inventions such as the wheelbarrow eased the plowing, planting, weeding, and harvesting tasks that occupied much of the time of most Chinese people. The engraving shown in Figure 12.7 gives us a glimpse of rural scenes that were reproduced hundreds of thousands of times across China all through the Tang and Song centuries and much of the millennium that followed.

The rulers of both the Sui and Tang dynasties had adopted policies aimed at breaking up the great estates of the old aristocracy and distributing land more equitably among the free peasant households of the empire. These policies were designed in part to reduce or eliminate the threat that the powerful aristocracy posed for the new dynasties. They were also intended to bolster the position of the ordinary peasants, whose labors and well-being had long been viewed by Confucian scholars as essential to a prosperous and stable social order. To a point, these agrarian measures succeeded. For a time the numbers of the free peasantry increased, and the average holding size in many areas rose. The fortunes of many of the old aristocratic families also declined, thus removing many of them as independent centers of power. They were supplanted gradually in the rural areas by the gentry side of the scholar-gentry combination that dominated the imperial bureaucracy.

Figure 12.7 The farming methods developed in the Song era are illustrated by this 17th-century engraving. Note the overseer, protected by an umbrella from the hot sun. Improved productivity, particularly of staple crops such as irrigated rice, meant that China's long-held advantages over other civilizations in terms of the population it could support increased in this era. By the early 14th century, as much as a quarter of humanity may have lived in the Chinese empire.

(©The Trustees of the British Museum/Art Resource, NY.)

The extended-family households of the gentry that were found in rural settlements in the Han era increased in size and elegance in the Tang and Song. The widespread use of the graceful curved roofs with upturned corners that one associates with Chinese civilization dates from the Tang period. By imperial decree, curved roofs were reserved for people of high rank, including the gentry families. With intricately carved and painted roof timbers topped with glazed tiles of yellow or green, the great dwellings of the gentry left no doubt about the status and power of the families who lived in them. At the same time, their muted colors, wood and bamboo construction, and simple lines blended beautifully with nearby gardens and groves of trees.

Family and Society in the Tang and Song Eras

Chinese family organization at various class levels in the Tang and Song centuries closely resembled that found in earlier periods. Nonetheless, the position of women showed signs of improving under the Tang and early Song eras, and then deteriorated steadily in the late Song. As in the classical age, extended-family households were preferred, but normally they could be afforded only by the upper classes. The male-dominated hierarchy promoted by Confucius and other early thinkers held sway at all class levels. In the Tang period, the authority of elders and males within the family was buttressed by laws that prescribed beheading as a punishment for children who struck their parents or grandparents in anger, and two and one-half years of hard labor for younger brothers or sisters who hit their older siblings.

Over the centuries, a very elaborate process of forging marriage alliances developed. Professional go-betweens, almost always women, helped both families to negotiate such prickly issues as matching young men and women and the amount of the dowry to be paid to the husband's family. Brides and grooms in China, in contrast to those in India, were generally about the same age, probably because of the Confucian reluctance to mix generations.

Both within the family and in society at large, women remained clearly subordinate to men. But some evidence suggests that at least for women of the upper classes in urban areas, the opportunities for personal expression increased in the Tang and early Song. As the example of the empresses Wu and Wei and the concubine Yang Guifei make clear, Tang women could wield considerable power at the highest levels of Chinese society. That they also enjoyed access to a broad range of activities, if not career possibilities, is indicated by a surviving pottery figure from the early Tang period of a young woman playing polo.

Tang and Song law allowed divorce by mutual consent of both husband and wife. There were also laws prohibiting a husband from setting aside his wife if her parents were dead or if he had been poor when they were married and later became rich. These suggest that Chinese wives had more defenses against capricious behavior by their husbands than was the case in India at this time. A remarkable degree of independence is also indicated by the practice, reported in late Song times, of wealthy women in large cities such as Hangzhou taking lovers (or what were politely called "complementary husbands") with the knowledge of their husbands.

The Neo-Confucian Assertion of Male Dominance

Evidence of the independence and legal rights enjoyed by a small minority of women in the Tang and Song eras is all but overwhelmed by the worsening condition of Chinese women in general. The assertion of male dominance was especially pronounced in the thinking of the Neo-Confucian philosophers, who, as we have seen, became a major force in the later Song period. The Neo-Confucians stressed the woman's role as homemaker and mother, particularly as the bearer of sons to continue the patrilineal family line. They advocated confining women and emphasized the importance of virginity for young brides, fidelity for wives, and chastity for widows. Like their counterparts in India, widows were discouraged from remarrying.

At the same time, men were permitted to have premarital sex without scandal, to take concubines if they could afford them, and to remarry if one or more of their wives died. The Neo-Confucians attacked the Buddhists for promoting career alternatives for women, such as scholarship and the monastic life, at the expense of marriage and raising a family. They drafted laws that favored men in inheritance, divorce, and familial interaction. They also excluded women from the sort of education

Footbinding as a Marker of Male Dominance

No aspect of gender relations exemplifies the degree to which women in the Tang-Song era were constricted in terms of career choices and subordinated to males as dramatically as **footbinding.** This counterpart of the veil and seclusion in Islam may have had its origins in the delight one of the Tang emperors took in the tiny feet of his favorite dancing girls or, as has been recently argued, the fashion preference of elite women for small feet. Whatever its rationales, by the later Song era, upper-class men had developed a preference for small feet for women. This preference gradually spread to some groups further down on the social scale, including the well-to-do peasantry.

In response to male demands, on which the successful negotiation of a young woman's marriage contract might hinge, mothers began to bind the feet of their daughters as early as age five or six. The young girl's toes were turned under and bound with silk, which was wound more tightly as she grew, as shown by the accompanying photo. By the time she reached marriageable age, a young woman's feet had been transformed into the "lotus petal" or "golden lily" shapes that were presumably preferred by prospective husbands.

Bound feet were a constant source of pain for the rest of a woman's life, and they greatly limited her mobility by making it very difficult to walk even short distances. Limited mobility made it easier for husbands to confine their wives to the family compound. It also meant that women could not engage in occupations except ones that could be pursued within the extended family household, such as textile production. For this reason, the lower classes, whose households often depended on women's labor in the fields, markets, or homes of the wealthy to make ends meet, were slow to adopt the practice. But once it was in fashion among the scholar-gentry and other elite classes, footbinding became vital to winning a husband. In part, because a good marriage for their daughters was the primary goal of Chinese mothers, the practice was usually unquestioningly passed from one generation of women to the next.

As this photograph vividly illustrates, mature women with bound feet needed special footware since they depended heavily on the very thick heel that resulted from footbinding for support when standing and walking. Little of the sole of the foot touched the ground, and toes were fused together to make a pointed foot.

QUESTIONS In what ways did the rise of the practice of footbinding reflect the level of prosperity achieved by China's upper classes in the Tang-Song eras and the Neo-Confucian conviction that women belonged in the domestic sphere? Why would it be much more difficult for the laboring classes of the towns and ordinary peasant families to adopt footbinding? How did the structure of the family, the nature of women's extra-family links, and the sorts of pressures that could be brought to bear make it nearly impossible for women in well-to-do households to resist the imposition of the footbinding procedures? Beyond their lack of military training, why might the practice of footbinding make them much more vulnerable than men, especially in times of social unrest and civil war?

footbinding Practice in Chinese society to mutilate women's feet in order to make them smaller; produced pain and restricted women's movement; made it easier to confine women to the household.

that would allow them to enter the civil service and rise to positions of political power. Footbinding epitomized the extent to which elite women's possibilities for self-fulfillment had been constricted by the later Song period.

Invention, Artistic Creativity, and China's Global Impact

Perhaps even more than for political and economic transformations, the Tang and Song eras are remembered as a time of remarkable Chinese accomplishments in science, technology, literature, and the fine arts. Major technological breakthroughs and scientific discoveries were made under each dynasty. Some of them, particularly those involving the invention of new tools, production techniques, and weapons, gradually spread to other civilizations and fundamentally changed the course of human development. Until recent centuries, the arts and literature of China were not well known beyond its borders. Their impact was confined mainly to areas such as central Asia, Japan, and Vietnam, where Chinese imports had long been a major impetus for cultural change. But the poetry and short stories of the Tang and the landscape paintings of the Song are some of the most splendid artistic creations of all human history.

As we have seen, new agricultural tools and innovations such as banks and paper money contributed a great deal to economic growth and social prosperity in the Tang and Song eras. In this respect, the engineering feats of the period are particularly noteworthy. In addition to building the Grand Canal, Tang and Song engineers made great advances in building dikes and dams and regulating the flow of water in complex irrigation systems. They also devised ingenious new ways to build bridges, long a major focus of engineering efforts in a land dominated by mountains and waterways. From arched and segmented to suspension and trussed, most of the basic bridge types known to humans were pioneered in China.

One of the most important of the many technological advances made in the Tang era, the invention of explosive powder, at first had little impact on warfare. For centuries, the Chinese used these potent chemical mixtures mainly for fireworks, which delighted emperors and the masses alike. By the late Song, however, explosive powder was widely used by the imperial armies in a variety of grenades and bombs that were hurled at the enemy by catapults. Song armies and warships also were equipped with naphtha flamethrowers, poisonous gases, and rocket launchers. These projectiles were perhaps the most effective weapons the dynasty used in its losing struggle to check nomadic incursions. On the domestic scene, chairs modeled on those found in India were introduced into the household, the habit of drinking tea swept the empire, coal was used for fuel for the first time, and the first kite soared into the heavens.

Although the number of major inventions in the Song era was lower than in the Tang, several were pivotal for the future of all civilizations. Compasses, which had been used since the last centuries B.C.E. by Chinese military commanders and magicians, were applied to sea navigation for the first time in the Song period. The abacus, the ancestor of the modern calculator, was introduced to help merchants count their profits and tax collectors keep track of revenues. In the mid-11th century, a remarkable artisan named Bi Sheng devised the technique of printing with movable type. Although block printing had been perfected in China in the preceding centuries, the use of movable type was a great advance in the production of written records and scholarly books. Combined with paper, which the Chinese had invented in the Han period, printing made it possible for them to attain a level of literacy that excelled that of any preindustrial civilization.

Scholarly Refinement and Artistic Accomplishment

The reinvigorated scholar-gentry elite was responsible for much of the artistic and literary creativity of the Tang and Song eras. Buddhist art and architecture had been heavily patronized by the court, prosperous merchants, and wealthy monasteries in the Tang period. But scholar-administrators and Confucian teachers wrote much of the literature for which the Tang is best remembered, and they painted the landscapes that were the most sublime cultural productions of the Song. Confucian thinkers valued skillful writing and painting, and educated people were expected to practice these arts. The Chinese educational establishment was geared to turning out generalists rather than the specialists who are so revered in our own society. A well educated man dabbled with varying degrees of success in many fields. After a hard day at the Ministry of Public Works, a truly accomplished official was expected to spend the evening composing songs on his lute, admiring a new painting or creating his own, or sipping rice wine while composing a poem to the harvest moon. Thus, talented and often well trained amateurs wrote most of the poems, composed much of the music, and painted the landscapes for which the Tang and Song eras are renowned (Figure 12.8).

As the Confucian scholar-gentry supplanted the Buddhists as the major producers of art and literature, devotional objects and religious homilies gave way to a growing fixation on everyday life and the delights of the natural world. Much of the short story literature was focused on the lives of the common people, popular beliefs in witchcraft and demons, ill-fated romances, and even detective stories

Literary Styles in China and Japan

Artistic Expression and Social Values

Studying artistic creativity is one of the most effective ways of probing the beliefs and values of a civilization. In some cases in which the civilization in question did not develop writing, or at least writing that we can now decipher, art and architecture provide much of the evidence by which we can learn about the attitudes and lifestyles of vanished peoples. Some of the most notable examples include the ancient Indus civilization of south Asia and many of the high civilizations of the Americas and sub-Saharan Africa. Even in civilizations for which written records have survived, we can learn a good deal about social structure by discovering who produced the art and for whom it was created, about technology by studying artistic techniques and materials, and about worldviews by exploring the messages the art was intended to convey. In comparing some of the major forms of artistic expression of the great civilizations, we can also identify underlying similarities and differences in the values by which the peoples who developed them organized their societies and responded to the natural and supernatural worlds.

> "The artistic creativity of China's political elite underscores the importance of the preference for civil over military leaders in Chinese society."

The fact that members of the ruling political elite produced most of the landscape paintings of the Song era is unusual in the history of civilization. The sculptures that adorned the temples of India and the statues, paintings, and stained glass that graced the cathedrals of medieval Europe were created mainly by specialized and highly trained artisans whose skills were passed down over many generations. By contrast, the Song artists were often amateurs who painted in their leisure time. Even the most talented, who won enough patronage to devote themselves to painting full time, began as Confucian scholars and very often administrators. It is not just the amateur and "master of all fields" ideals that are remarkable here but the fact that so much art was produced by the men who also ran the country. In most of the other civilizations we have studied, political life has been dominated by warrior and priestly classes, not artistic scholar-bureaucrats like those who governed China.

Even in civilizations such as those of medieval Europe and Islam, where priests and religious teachers produced fine art in the form of manuscript illuminations, the people involved seldom had political responsibilities or power. Thus, the artistic creativity of China's political elite underscores the importance of the preference for civil over military leaders in Chinese society. It also tells us a good deal about the qualities the Chinese associated with a truly civilized and superior person—a person who was deemed worthy to rule the Middle Kingdom.

Song landscapes expressed the reactions and ideals of individual people, whom we can identify by the distinctive seals with which they stamped their paintings. The paintings clearly were intended for the pleasure and edification of the Chinese educated classes, not for museum viewing or mass consumption. Landscape painting reinforced the identity and values of this scholarly elite across the vast spaces of the Chinese empire as well as across time. In a famous incident, the Confucian philosopher Zhu Xi remarked on the nobility and loyalty that he saw so clearly in the calligraphy of scholars from the Warring States era.

This individualism and elitism in Chinese art can be contrasted with the anonymous creation of sculptures and religious paintings in Hindu and Buddhist civilizations and medieval Europe or the mosaic decorations of the mosques of Islam. In each of these other civilizations, artistic works that adorned temples, cathedrals, and mosques were intended for a mass audience. The moral instruction for the scholarly few that was contained in the Song landscapes had a very different purpose than the religious sculptures or mosaics of other civilizations. The sculptures and mosaics were created to convey a religious message, to remind the viewers of a key event in the life of Christ or the Buddha, or to impress upon them the horrors of hell or the delights of heaven.

Thus, the highest art forms, linked to a common religion, bridged the gulf between elites and the masses in Hindu, Buddhist, Christian, and Muslim civilizations. Imported Buddhist art forms performed this function in some periods in Chinese history. But the more enduring Confucian-Daoist artistic creativity, best exemplified by landscape painting, accentuated the differences that separated the educated scholar-gentry and the common people.

QUESTIONS What do you think the small size of the people in Chinese landscape paintings can tell us about Chinese views on the relationship between humans and the natural world? Can you think of American or European politicians who have created great works of art? Do we expect this sort of creativity from our elected officials? If not, what does this tell us about the values of our own civilization?

Li Bo (701–762) Most famous poet of the Tang era; blended images of the mundane world with philosophical musings.

about brutal murders. Tang poetry moved from early verses that dwelt on the "pleasant breezes that envelope[d] the emperor's chair" to a seemingly endless variety of ways of celebrating the natural world. No one was better at the latter than the most famous poet of the Tang era, **Li Bo**. His poems, like those of the great Persian authors, blend images of the everyday world with philosophical musings:

> The rain was over, green covered the land.
> One last cloudlet melted away in the clear sky.
> The east wind came home with the spring
> Bearing blossoms to sprout on the branches.

Flowers are fading now and time will end.
All mortal men perceive it and their sighs are deep.
But I will turn to the sacred hills
And learn from Tao [Dao] and from magic how to fly.

This intense interest in nature came to full artistic fruition in the landscape paintings of the Song era. Most of them were produced by the cultivated men of the scholar-gentry class, and they pulled together diverse aspects of Chinese civilization. The brushes and techniques used were similar to those used in writing the Chinese language, which itself was regarded as a high art form. The paintings were symbolic, intended to teach moral lessons or explore philosophical ideas. The objects depicted were not only beautiful in themselves but stood for larger concepts: A crane and a pine tree, for example, represented longevity; bamboo shoots were associated with the scholar-gentry class; and a dragon could call to mind any number of things, including the emperor, the cosmos, or life-giving rain.

Figure 12.8 The simplicity of composition, the use of empty space, and the emphasis on nature are all characteristic of Chinese landscape painting at its height in the Song era. The colors used tended to be muted; often only brown or black ink was used. Most artists stamped their work with signature seals, like the red ones in this image, and poems describing scenes related to those in the painting floated in the empty space at the top or sides.

(Ma Yuan, Chinese, 1190–1235 "Bare Willows and Distant Mountains." Photograph © 2010 Museum of Fine Arts, Boston. Special Chinese and Japanese Fund, 14.61)

There was an abstract quality to the paintings that gives them a special appeal in the present day. The artists were not concerned with depicting nature accurately but rather with creating a highly personal vision of natural beauty. A premium was placed on subtlety and suggestion. For example, the winner of an imperial contest painted a lone monk drawing water from an icy stream to depict the subject announced by the emperor: a monastery hidden deep in the mountains during the winter. Song landscapes often were painted on scrolls that could be read as the viewer unfolded them bit by bit. Most were accompanied by a poem, sometimes composed by the painter, that complemented the subject matter and was aimed at explaining the artist's ideas.

Global Connections

China's World Role

The postclassical period in world history saw a vital consolidation of Chinese civilization. Although fewer fundamental changes occurred in China than those experienced in eastern and western Europe, the Americas, and certainly the Middle East, Chinese civilization developed in important new ways. Some of these innovations, especially the technological ones, soon affected the wider world. China also consolidated its own orbit of more intense influence in eastern Asia through ongoing exchanges with central Asia, Japan, Korea, Vietnam, and elsewhere in southeast Asia. Though more isolated than the Islamic empires and India, China nevertheless contributed vitally to other regions as it flourished under two vigorous dynasties, the Tang and the Song.

From the Tang era until the 18th century, the Chinese economy was one of the world's most advanced in terms of market networks, volume of overseas trade, productivity per land area, and the sophistication of its tools and techniques of craft production. Production of luxury goods, from silks to fine ceramics, attracted traders from abroad and delighted upper-class consumers in distant lands. As a key source of both manufactured goods and cultivated consumables, such as tea and rhubarb, China contributed in major ways to the expanding Afro-Eurasian commercial system. Chinese inventions such as paper, printing, and gunpowder were also widely disseminated and fundamentally changed the course of development in all other human civilizations. Until the 18th century, the imperial dynasties of China had political power and economic resources unmatched by those of any other civilization.

By retreating to the south, the Song rulers managed to survive the assaults of the nomads from the north. But as the dynasty weakened, enduring patterns of nomadic incursions resurfaced and built to the apex of pastoral military and political expansion under the Mongols. The Song emperors could not retreat far enough to escape the onslaught of the most brilliant nomadic commander of them all, Chinggis Khan, who directed perhaps the most powerful military machine the world had seen up to that time. The Song rulers bought time by paying tribute to the Mongol Khan and making alliances with him against their common enemies. But a later Mongol leader, Kubilai Khan, launched a sustained effort to conquer the southern refuge of the Song dynasty, which was completed by 1279.

Further Readings

In addition to the general histories of China suggested in Chapter 4, several important works cover the Tang and Song eras. The recent and magisterial history of *Imperial China, 900–1800* (1999) is a superb place to start, and the volume, edited by Denis Twitchett, devoted to the Tang and Song in the *Cambridge History of China* is an essential reference work. There are detailed works on the founding of the Tang dynasty by C. P. Fitzgerald (1970) and Woodbridge Bingham (1940), but these should be read in conjunction with the more recent *Mirror to the Son of Heaven* (1974), which provides valuable correctives to the interpretations of these earlier authors. Useful insights into political and cultural life in the Tang era can be gleaned from the specialized essays in the volume *Perspectives on the Tang* (1973), edited by Arthur Wright and Denis Twitchett. On social patterns in the Tang era, see Charles Benn, *Daily Life in Traditional China: The Tang Dynasty* (2002). Until recently, the most accessible work on society and politics in the Song era was Jacques Gernet, *Daily Life in China on the Eve of the Mongol Invasion, 1250–1276* (1962), which is highly entertaining and informative. On the great social and economic transitions of the Song era, Mark Elvin, *The Pattern of the Chinese Past* (1973), is insightful, provocative, and controversial. These standard accounts can now be supplemented by P. B. Ebry, *The Aristocratic Families of Early Imperial China* (1978); Heng Chye Kiang, *Cities of Aristocrats and Bureaucrats: The Development of Medieval Chinese Cities* (1999); and D. McMullen, *State and Scholars in T'ang China* (1988). Bret Hinsch, *Women in Early Imperial China* (2002), provides a useful introduction to this subject, which is closely examined in Kathryn Bernhardt, *Women and Property in China, 960–1949* (1999); and Bettine Birge, *Women, Property and Confucian Reaction in Sung and Yüan China, 960–1368* (2002).

Of the numerous works on Chinese art and painting, perhaps the best place to start is with the standard work by Mai-mai Sze, *The Way of Chinese Painting* (1956), which quotes extensively from Chinese manuals. Of more recent works, the general survey by Laurence Sickman and Alexander Soper, as well as James Cahill's study of landscape painting, stand out. And they can be supplemented by Alfreda Murch's recent study of *Poetry and Painting in Song China* (2000). A wonderful sampler of Li Bo's poetry can be found in a volume titled *Bright Moon, Perching Bird* (1987), edited by J. P. Seaton and James Cryer.

On the Web

The art of Six Dynasties, including calligraphy, is the subject of a virtual exhibit at http://www.artsmia.org/arts-of-asia/china/dynasties/six.cfm, http://cla.calpoly.edu/~jwetzel/Study/SECULA~1.HTM, and http://depts.washington.edu/chinaciv/callig/7calsixd.htm. Changan, the capital of the most culturally brilliant of these dynasties, the Tang, is presented in multimedia formats offering glimpses of daily life and/or set in the context of Chinese urban history at http://www.arch.nus.edu.sg/casa/projects/hck_changan/pages/content.htm, http://depts.washington.edu/silkroad/cities/china/xian/xian.html, and http://www.owlnet.rice.edu/~arch343/lecture8.html. The remarkable technological achievements of this period of Chinese history, which included the development of explosives and paper, are presented at http://www.mnsu.edu/emuseum/prehistory/china/classical_imperial_china/tang.html, and http://www.silkroadcn.com/chinainfo/fourinvention.htm. Examples of the poetry of the Tang Dynasty, considered the golden age of Chinese poetry, are offered at http://etext.virginia.edu/chinese/frame.htm. Mahayana and Chan (Zen) Buddhism, explored at http://www.ciolek.com (click on Buddhist Studies for links pages) survived the nativist revival that also characterized this era. Zen Buddhism's key concepts and relation to other Eastern and Western Philosophies is analyzed at http://arts.ucsc.edu/faculty/lieberman/zen.html. The Silk Road at its apex is illuminated at http://www.aasianst.org/EAA/silkroad.htm, http://www.saudiaramcoworld.com/issue/198804/default.htm, and http://www.ess.uci.edu/~oliver/silk.html. The Muslims who participated in that trade and in Chinese history are examined at http://www.saudiaramcoworld.com/issue/198504/muslims.in.china-the.country.htm. The prosperity of the times stimulated the spread of the practice of binding women's feet, the results of which are graphically shown at http://sfmuseum.org/chin/foot.html and http://academic.brooklyn.cuny.edu/core9/phalsall/studpages/vento.html.

AP* Test Prep

1. The era of Tang and Song rule is called the "golden age" of China because

    (A) it is the only period of Chinese rule in which foreign trade and ideas had little influence.

    (B) the Chinese abandoned naturalistic subjects like landscapes in favor for more "modern" abstract, non-representational art.

    (C) the Chinese government seized the wealth and land controlled by Buddhist monasteries.

    (D) this was the era of the discovery of explosive powder, the abacus, moveable type, and the first use of coal for energy.

2. The primary function of the scholar-gentry class in Tang and Song China was

    (A) to teach in the Confucian-based university system.

    (B) to spy on the land-based elites in the distant provinces.

    (C) to administer the imperial, provincial and local governments.

    (D) to create innovative scholarship, artwork and technological advances.

3. Why did Buddhism become a significant belief system in Tang China?

    (A) Confucian scholars preferred it to Islam, which was banned as a foreign religion.

    (B) The scholar-gentry class embraced it as a means of insuring their dominance over women.

    (C) It offered social opportunities to commoners, to women, easily mixed with Daoist and Confucian ideas, and had royal patronage.

    (D) It was brought into China by humble slaves whose behavior the Chinese admired.

4. Tang military expansion into central Asia

    (A) led to constant warfare between the Chinese and the Muslims.

    (B) promoted renewed commercial contacts between China and west Asia.

    (C) obtained land to settle large Chinese population surpluses.

    (D) was easily defeated by the Turks and other pastoral nomads.

AP* | Test Prep

5. What were the long-term consequences of new maritime technological advances such as the sea-going "junk" and the magnetic compass?

   (A)   A renewed focus on engineering and scientific work in the universities.

   (B)   Combined with the Grand Canal, they dramatically increased north-south trade within China.

   (C)   They facilitated dramatic increases in overseas trade in the eastern hemisphere.

   (D)   The scholar-gentry class became worried about the power of the rising merchant-class in the coastal urban areas.

6. The Tang rulers were able to control potential nomadic threats to China by

   (A)   bribery.

   (B)   playing one nomadic group against another.

   (C)   settling the nomads within the Chinese borders on land to farm.

   (D)   intermarriage between the nomadic and Chinese ruling families.

7. Which sect of Buddhism became popular in China for its focus on prayer and personal salvation?

   (A)   Pure Land

   (B)   Chan

   (C)   Tibetan

   (D)   Mahayana

Free-Response Question

Evaluate the extent to which the status of women changed over time from the beginning of the Tang dynasty to the end of the Song.

The Spread of Chinese Civilization: Japan, Korea, and Vietnam

Japan: The Imperial Age

The Era of Warrior Dominance

THINKING HISTORICALLY: Comparing Feudalisms

Korea: Between China and Japan

Between China and Southeast Asia: The Making of Vietnam

VISUALIZING THE PAST: What Their Portraits Tell Us: Gatekeeper Elites and the Persistence of Civilizations

DOCUMENT: Literature as a Mirror of the Exchanges Between Civilized Centers

GLOBAL CONNECTIONS: In the Orbit of China: The East Asian Corner of the Global System

Following a centuries-old protocol, a distinguished Vietnamese official named Ly Van Phúc entered the Chinese imperial capital at Beijing at the head of an embassy that had come to pay tribute to the Chinese ruler. Well versed in Confucian ways, Phúc was at home in the crowded streets of the great city. Because Chinese and other Asian potentates (often with good reason) regarded embassies as little more than spying parties, Phúc and his entourage were visiting rather than preparing to take up residence in the capital. The Vietnamese had been assigned a hostel near the Forbidden City, which housed the magnificent imperial palace where, in an elaborate ceremony, Phúc would pay homage to the Daoguang emperor (Figure 13.1).

As Phúc and his countrymen approached the quarters to which they had been officially assigned, they were confronted by a placard on the building that identified it as "The Vietnamese Barbarians' Hostel." Deeply humiliated and struggling to contain his anger, Phúc ordered his companions not to enter and to prepare an improvised campsite in the middle of the street. After commanding two of his companions to destroy the sign, he sat down and composed a strongly worded treatise entitled "On Distinguishing Barbarians." Demonstrating his admirable proficiency in Chinese calligraphy, he wrote to the Daoguang emperor, describing the insult that—whether out of ignorance or intent—the emperor's officials had directed toward the Vietnamese.

Phúc reminded the Chinese emperor (who was of Manchu descent, and thus just a few generations away from barbarian status in the Chinese view) that the Vietnamese had nurtured Chinese culture for millennia. Phúc pointed out that, like himself, the Vietnamese royal family and officials were fluent in Chinese, honored Confucian principles of governance and social organization, and organized their educational system around the classic works of Chinese civilization. As soon as it was composed, the essay was presented to Chinese officials to be delivered to the emperor. It is not certain that the very polite reprimand actually reached that exalted personage, but Vietnamese accounts of the incident expressed great satisfaction that the Chinese were most apologetic and even admitted their gratitude that the mistaken use of "barbarian" had been challenged and was corrected. ■

Both the reverence for Chinese civilization and the decided ambivalence regarding the extent of its influence illustrated by the Phúc incident capture key features of centuries of interaction between China and other societies across much of central and southeast Asia. In earlier chapters we dealt in some depth with the persisting and dynamic exchanges between the Chinese and the nomadic peoples of central and northeast Asia. A similar pattern of attraction and resistance runs through the centuries when Chinese influence contributed in vital ways to the rise of complex and sophisticated societies in Japan, Korea, and Vietnam. For two millennia, China has been the premier civilization of east Asia and surrounding areas—the seedbed of technological innovation; a model for social, military, and political organization; a persisting influence on philosophical and religious thinking; and a major locus of commercial exchange (see Map 13.1).

As Phúc's obvious pride in his mastery of the Chinese language, history, and manners strikingly reveals, these influences have been particularly pervasive in agrarian-based societies, such as those that developed in neighboring Japan, Korea, and Vietnam. But Phúc's sensitivity to insults to his people and culture and his vigorous response also reflect an underlying wariness of Chinese domination that was displayed by all three of these societies. Korea and Vietnam were ruled directly

Figure 13.1 At the height of the power and prosperity of the Qing dynasty, the emperor Qianlong, who ruled for more than sixty years, receives tribute from "the ten thousand countries" in one of his imposing palace complexes. Participation in the tribute ceremony, which had become essential for all countries—including Japan, Korea, and Vietnam—that wished to trade with China, had been established as early as the Tang dynasty in the 7th century C.E.

(The Art Archive/Picture Desk, Inc./Kobal Collection.)

by China for centuries and frequently rose in violent rebellions aimed at asserting their political independence. Japanese elites were often deeply divided about which and how much Chinese influence to introduce, and Japanese peasants and merchants often balked at integrating Chinese imports—whether ideas or new ways of growing rice or making war—into their daily lives.

 Japan in the Imperial and Warlord Periods

In all three cases, the tensions between the desire to emulate and borrow from China and the determination to preserve their distinctive languages, social customs, and other cultural forms profoundly shaped the nature of the highly civilized societies that developed in Japan, Korea, and Vietnam. As Phúc's confrontation with Chinese officialdom in the mid-19th century suggests, these tensions continued to shape social and political dynamics throughout east Asia well into the modern era.

Japan: The Imperial Age

By the late 600s C.E., the Japanese court at Nara (Map 13.2) was awash in imports from China, which had long been seen by Japan and China's other neighbors as the most advanced society in east Asia in pursuits as varied as politics, intellectual production, and material culture. Indigenous cultural influences, particularly those linked to Shinto views of the natural and supernatural world, remained central to Japanese cultural development. But in the Taika (645–710), Nara (710–784), and Heian (794–1185) periods, Japanese borrowing from China—though selective—peaked. This borrowing touched nearly all aspects of Japanese life, particularly at the level of the elites and among the people of the court towns.

In 646 the emperor and his advisors introduced the far-reaching **Taika** (teye-kuh) **reforms,** aimed at completely revamping the imperial administration along Chinese lines. Japanese court scholars struggled to master thousands of Chinese characters, which bore little relationship to the language they spoke. They wrote dynastic histories patterned after those commissioned by the emperors of China, and they followed an elaborate court etiquette that somewhat uneasily combined

Chinese influence on Japan peaked in the 7th and 8th centuries as Japanese rulers sought to build a Chinese-style bureaucracy and society. Over time the isolated court centers at Nara and later Heian lost political control to powerful aristocratic families and local warlords.

Taika reforms [teye-kuh] Attempt to remake Japanese monarch into an absolute Chinese-style emperor; included attempts to create professional bureaucracy and peasant conscript army.

291

200 B.C.E.	600 C.E.	800 C.E.	1000 C.E.	1200 C.E.	1400 C.E.
206 B.C.E.–220 C.E. Reign of Han dynasty in China	618–907 Tang dynasty in China	838 Last Japanese embassy to China	1160–1185 Taira clan dominant in Japan	1231–1392 Mongol rule in Korea	1467–1477 Onin War in Japan
111 Vietnam conquered by China	646 Taika reforms in Japan	857–1160 Period of Fujiwara dominance in Japan	1180–1185 Gempei Wars in Japan	1279–1368 Mongol rule in China	1500 Nguyen dynasty in central/south Vietnam founded
109 Choson (Korea) conquered by China	668 Korea wins independence from Tang conquerors	918–1392 Koryo dynasty in Korea	1185–1333 Kamakura Shogunate in Japan	1392–1910 Yi dynasty in Korea	1539–1787 Trinh dynasty in Red River area (Vietnam)
39 C.E. Trung sisters revolt in Vietnam	668–918 Silla kingdom in Korea	939 Vietnam wins independence from China			1600 Founding of the Tokugawa Shogunate in Japan
222–589 Era of Division in China	710–784 Imperial Japanese capital at Nara	960–1279 Song dynasty in China			
589–618 Sui dynasty in China	794 Japanese capital shifts to Heian (Kyoto)	980–1009 Le dynasty in Vietnam			

Chinese protocol with ancient Japanese ideas about politeness and decorum. The Japanese aristocracy struggled to master Confucian ways, worshiped in Chinese-style temples, and admired Buddhist art that was Chinese in subject matter and technique.

Even the common people were affected by the steady flow of influence from the mainland. In the towns, they stared in awe at the great Buddhist temples and bowed to passing aristocrats trying to present themselves as Confucian scholars. The peasants turned to Buddhist monks for cures when they were sick or to Buddhist magic when they needed a change of luck. They had begun to mesh the worship of Buddhist deities with that of the ancient *kami*, or nature spirits, of Japan.

Crisis at Nara and the Shift to Heian (Kyoto)

If they had succeeded, the Taika reforms of 646 would have represented the culmination of centuries of Japanese borrowing from China. The central objectives of the proposed changes were to remake the Japanese monarch into an absolutist Chinese-style emperor (even to the point of adding "Son of Heaven" to the Japanese ruler's many titles). The reforms also were intended to create a genuine professional bureaucracy and peasant conscript army in Japan to match those of Han and Tang China. But the changes necessary for these goals to be achieved were frustrated by the resistance of the aristocratic families and the Buddhist monastic orders, who dominated both the emperor and the capital as a whole.

A century after the reforms were introduced, the Buddhist monks in particular had grown so bold and powerful that the court and aristocracy lived in fear of street demonstrations by "rowdy monks" and of the escalating demands of the heads of the monastic orders. Their influence even threatened to engulf the throne in the 760s, when a clever Buddhist prelate worked his way into the inner circle of the empress Koken. His schemes to marry her and become emperor were uncovered and foiled. But it was clear to the emperor's advisors that measures had to be taken to ensure that women could never rule Japan and to check the growing influence of the monastic orders at court.

In 794 the emperor Kammu established a new capital city at Heian (hay-yan) (Map 13.2), which was later called Kyoto. Buddhists were forbidden to build monasteries in the new capital. But to get around this restriction, the monks established monasteries in the hills surrounding Heian, and they soon reemerged as a potent force at court as royal advisors.

Map 13.1 Key Centers of Civilization in East Asia in the First Millennium C.E.   Despite steady expansion over much of east Asia from the end of the last millennium B.C.E. through the first millennium C.E., the Chinese were not able to absorb three large areas on their periphery—Korea, Japan and Vietnam—into their civilization.

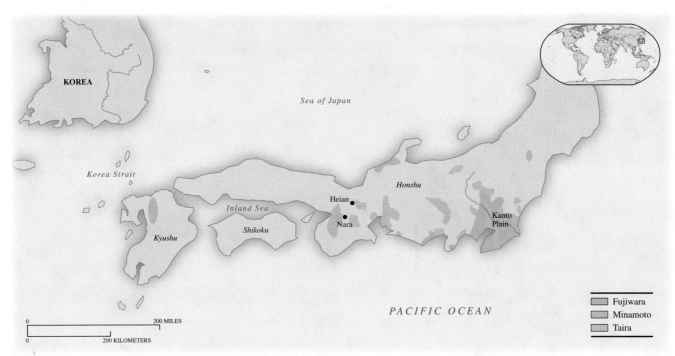

Map 13.2 Japan in the Imperial and Warlord Periods   Power in warlord era was concentrated in the region of the Kanto plain, which was the main rice granary of the islands and thus able to support a relatively dense population.

In addition to trying to control the Buddhist monks, the emperor abandoned all pretense of continuing the Taika reforms, which had long been stalled by aristocratic and popular opposition. He fully restored the great aristocratic families, whose power the reforms had been intended to curb. The elaborate system of ranks into which the aristocrats were divided (patterned after that in China) was maintained. But like the Koreans, the Japanese broke with Chinese precedent in determining rank solely by birth and by allowing little mobility between the various orders. The aristocrats had already taken over most of the positions in the central government. Now, their formal right to build up rural estates was restored as well. The emperor also gave up an ambitious scheme to build a peasant conscript army. In its place, local leaders were ordered to organize militia forces, which would soon play a critical role in further eroding the control of the imperial household.

Ultracivilized: Court Life in the Heian Era

Although the basis of imperial political power had been severely eroded within decades of the shift to Heian, court culture soared to new levels of refinement. For several centuries more, the Japanese emperors and their courtiers continued to inhabit a closed world of luxury and aesthetic delights. Men and women of the aristocratic classes followed strict codes of polite behavior, under the constant scrutiny of their peers and superiors. In this hothouse atmosphere, social status was everything, love affairs were a major preoccupation, and gossip was rampant. By our standards, life in this constricted and very artificial world was false and suffocating. Yet rarely in human history has so much energy been so focused on the pursuit of beauty or has social interaction—on the surface at least—been so gracious and well mannered.

At the Heian court, members of the imperial household and the leading aristocratic families lived in a complex of palaces and gardens, a section of which is depicted in the painting in Figure 13.2. The buildings were of unpainted wood, which the Japanese found the most appealing, with sliding panels, matted floors, and wooden walkways running between the separate residences where the many dignitaries lived. Fish ponds, artificial lakes with waterfalls, and fine gardens were scattered among the courtiers' living quarters. Writing verse was perhaps the most valued art at the court. The poems were often written on painted fans or scented paper, and sometimes they were sent in little boats down the streams that ran through the palace grounds. The verse was brief and

Figure 13.2 From this artist's impression of the elaborate dress and studied poses of Heian courtiers, as well as the carefully cultivated trees and the tasteful decor, one gains a vivid sense of the formality and attention to aesthetic pleasures that dominated the lives of the Japanese elite in this era. As the prominence of women in the painting suggests, the intense world of the Heian court provided a tiny minority of Japanese women with outlets for expressing emotion and creativity that have been denied to most women through much of civilized history.

full of allusions to Chinese and Japanese classical writings. In the following couplet, a young courtier expresses his disappointment at being denied access to a pretty young woman:

> Having come upon an evening blossom
> The mist is loath to go with the morning sun.

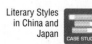

Literary Styles in China and Japan

Tale of Genji, The   Written by Lady Murasaki; first novel in any language; relates life history of prominent and amorous son of the Japanese emperor; evidence for mannered style of Japanese society.

Partly to accommodate the need for literary expression of this type, the written script the Japanese had borrowed from the Chinese was simplified, making it more compatible with spoken Japanese. One result of these changes was an outpouring of poetic and literary works that were more and more distinctively Japanese. The most celebrated of these was Lady Murasaki's ***The Tale of Genji***. None of the works on court life captured its charm and its underlying tensions and sadness as wonderfully as Lady Murasaki's classic, which was the first novel in any language (Figure 13.3). In the story, she relates the life history of a prominent and amorous son of the emperor and the fate of his descendants. As the story makes clear, Genji's life is almost wholly devoted to the pursuit of aesthetic enjoyment, whether in affairs with beautiful women or in musical entertainments in a garden scented with blooming flowers. Uncouth commoners and distasteful things, such as dirt, cheap pottery, and rough popular entertainments, are to be avoided at all costs. When her rivals at the court want to insult Genji's mother, for example, they leave spoiled fruit in the passages where she or her maidservants must pass. An encounter with a shriveled piece of fruit contributes to the illness that leads to her premature death.

Manyôshiu (Early Japanese Verse)

Everyone who matters in Genji's world is obsessed with the social conventions that govern everything, from which gown is proper for a given ceremony to the composition of a suitable poem to woo a potential lover or win the emperor's favor. Although women rivaled men as poets, artists, and musicians and in their pervasive cultivation of aesthetic pleasure, it was unseemly for them to openly pursue lovers. Nonetheless, as Lady Murasaki's poignant novel makes clear, some women did court prospective lovers with great guile and passion. It was not uncommon for a high-born woman to spurn a suitor and humiliate him in front of her maidservants.

In addition to novels such as Lady Murasaki's, some of the most elegant poetry in the Japanese language was written in this era. Again, it is sparing in words but rich in imagery and allusions to the natural world:

> This perfectly still
> Spring Day bathed in the soft light
> From the spread-out sky,
> Why do the cherry blossoms so restlessly scatter down?
> Although I am sure
> That he will not be coming
> In the evening light
> When the locusts shrilly call
> I go to the door and wait.

As the female authorship of this poem and *The Tale of Genji* clearly illustrate, women at the Heian court were expected to be as poised and cultured as men. Because they were less involved, however, with Chinese cultural imports (presumed to be a superior male preserve), they actually, for a time, played an unusually creative role in Japanese productions. They wrote poems, played flutes or stringed instruments in informal concerts, and participated in elaborate schemes to snub or disgrace rivals. Like their counterparts in China and the Islamic world, they also became involved in palace intrigues and power struggles.

The Decline of Imperial Power

While the emperor and his courtiers admired the plum blossoms and the newest fashions in court dress, some of the aristocratic families at court were busy running the rapidly shrinking imperial bureaucracy. By the mid-9th century, one of these families, the **Fujiwara**, exercised exceptional influence over imperial affairs. Not only did they pack the upper administration with family members and shape imperial policy, but they also increasingly married Fujiwaras into the imperial family. By the middle of the 10th century, one aged Fujiwara chief minister had seen four of his daughters married to emperors.

Families such as the Fujiwara used the wealth and influence of their high office to build up large estates that provided a stable financial base for their growing power. Especially in the vicinity of the capital, they had to compete in these purchases with the Buddhist monasteries. But both could work together in the steady campaign to whittle down imperial control and increase their own. As the lands under their control expanded, both the monks and the court nobility greatly increased the number of peasants and artisans they in effect ruled. Cooperation between monastic orders and court aristocrats was promoted by the introduction of the secret texts and ceremonies of esoteric Buddhism in this period. These teachings and techniques to achieve salvation through prayers and meditation, which were focused by mystical diagrams and special hand positions, were the rage among the Heian elite. As aristocrats and monks steadily built up their own power in the capital, however, they failed to reckon with the growing power of the local lords.

The Rise of the Provincial Warrior Elites

The pursuit of landed estates that increasingly preoccupied the court aristocracy was also taken up by elite families in the provinces. Some of these families had aristocratic origins, but most had risen to power as landowners, estate managers, or local state officials. These families came to control land and labor and to deny these resources to the court. They gradually carved out little kingdoms, ruled by "house" governments, in various parts of the islands. They dominated their mini-states within the larger Japanese realm from small fortresses surrounded by wooden or earthen walls and moat-like ditches. The local lord and his retainers were housed within the fortress, constantly on the alert for an attack by a neighboring lord or the forces of one of the powerful families at court. Granaries for storing the rice provided by local peasants, blacksmith forges and stables, wells for water, and even armories made the fortresses self-contained worlds.

Figure 13.3 This painting illustrating one of the episodes in Lady Murasaki's *The Tale of Genji* captures the inward-looking character of court life that gradually cut the emperor and his entourage off from the warriors, townspeople, and peasants they ruled. The growing isolation of the court provided opportunities for regional lords with a more military orientation and more effective links to the population as a whole to seize effective control of Japan.

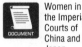 Women in the Imperial Courts of China and Japan

Fujiwara Japanese aristocratic family in mid-9th century; exercised exceptional influence over imperial affairs; aided in decline of imperial power.

Figure 13.4 The imposing presence of a fully armed samurai warrior is captured in this pen-and-ink drawing. The slats that make up the warrior's armor were crafted of fine steel braided together with leather, giving him protection against enemy arrows and sword thrusts as well as some freedom of movement. Note the two finely forged swords, his major weapons, and the flag attached to his armor, which identifies both the lord he serves and the unit to which he is attached.

(Woodcut, Masahiro Murai "Illustration from Tanki Yoryaku (A Single Horseman: Summary on How to Wear Armor)." The Metropolitan Museum of Art, New York, NY, U.S.A. Image copyright © The Metropolitan Museum of Art/Art Resource, NY.)

bushi Regional warrior leaders in Japan; ruled small kingdoms from fortresses; administered the law, supervised public works projects, and collected revenues; built up private armies.

From the 12th century onward, Japanese history was increasingly dominated by civil wars between shifting factions of the court aristocracy and local warlords, which ended only with the rise of the Tokugawa warlord family in the early 1600s. Chinese influence declined steadily in this era, but despite strife and social dislocation, the arts and literature flourished in Japan.

Within the mini-states ruled from the forts, the warrior leaders, or **bushi**, administered law, supervised public works projects, and collected revenue—mainly for themselves, not the court. The failure of the court's plans to build conscript armies also allowed the bushi to build up their own armies. These soon became the most effective military forces in the land. The troops who served the bushi came to be called **samurai**. They were loyal to the local lords, not to the court or high aristocratic officials, even though they were increasingly called in to protect the emperor and his retainers and to keep the peace in the capital. As the imperial government's control over the country weakened in the 11th and 12th centuries, bandits freely roamed the countryside and the streets of the capital. Buddhist monasteries employed armed toughs to protect them and attack rival sects. In this atmosphere of rampant crime and civil strife, the court and high officials hired provincial lords and their samurai retainers to serve as bodyguards and to protect their palaces and mansions from robbery and arson.

These trends proved critical to the emergence of a warrior class, a characteristically fierce member of which is depicted in Figure 13.4. Counting on peasant dependants to supply them with food and other necessities, the bushi and samurai devoted their lives to hunting, riding, archery practice, and other activities that sharpened their martial skills. Until the 12th century, the main weapons of the mounted warriors were powerful longbows and spears, although they also carried straight swords. From the 12th century on, they increasingly relied on the superbly forged, curved steel swords that we commonly associate with the Japanese samurai. The bushi and the samurai warriors who served them rode into battles that increasingly hinged on the duels of great champions. These combats represented heroic warfare in the extreme. The time and location of battles were elaborately negotiated beforehand, and each side tried to demonstrate the justice of its cause and the treachery of its enemies. Before charging into battle, Japanese warriors proudly proclaimed their family lineage and its notable military exploits to their adversaries, who often missed the details because they were shouting back their own.

A warrior code developed that stressed family honor and death rather than retreat or defeat. Beaten or disgraced warriors turned to ritual suicide to prove their courage and restore their family's honor. They called this practice **seppuku**, which meant disembowelment. But it has come to be known in the West by the more vulgar expression *hara-kiri*, or belly splitting. Battles were chaotic— lots of shouting and clashing but few fatalities—that were won or lost depending on the performance of the champions on each side. Although a full chivalric code did not develop until some centuries later, Japan was steadily moving toward a feudal order that was remarkably similar to that developing in western Europe in this same postclassical period.

The rise of the samurai frustrated all hopes of creating a free peasantry. In fact, Japanese peasants were reduced in the next centuries to the status of serfs, bound to the land they worked and treated as the property of the local lord. They were also separated by rigid class barriers from the warrior elite, which was physically set off by its different ways of dressing and by prohibitions against the peasants carrying swords or riding horses. In their growing poverty and powerlessness, the peasants turned to popular Buddhism in the form of the salvationist pure land sect. The teachings of the pure land offered the promise of bliss in heaven for those who lived upright lives on earth. Colorful figures, such as the dancing monk Kuya, were intended to make Buddhist teachings comprehensible and appealing to both the peasantry and the artisans, who were concentrated in the fortress towns. Buddhist shrines and images became popular destinations for pilgrimages and objects of veneration.

The Era of Warrior Dominance

As the power of the provincial lords grew, that of the imperial household and court aristocracy declined. Powerful families at the court, such as the Fujiwara, increasingly depended on alliances with regional lords to support them in disputes with their rivals. By the 11th and 12th centuries, the provincial families had begun to pack the court bureaucracy and compete for power. By the mid-12th century, competition turned to open feuding between the most powerful of these families, the **Taira** (teye-ruh) and the **Minamoto**. For a time, the Taira gained the upper hand by controlling the emperor and dominating at court. But when rivalry turned to open warfare in the early 1180s, the Minamoto commanders and their powerful network of alliances with provincial lords in various parts of the country proved superior to the leaders or allies the Taira could muster. More importantly, the Tairas' concentration of their power-grabbing efforts in the capital led to the breakdown of critical links with rural notables, who often sided with the Minamoto in the factional struggles.

The Declining Influence of China

As the power of the imperial house weakened, the relevance of Chinese precedents and institutions diminished for the Japanese. Pretensions to a heavenly mandate and centralized power became ludicrous; the emergence of a scholar-gentry elite was stifled by the reassertion of aristocratic power and prerogatives. Grand designs for an imperial bureaucracy never materialized. Buddhism was increasingly transformed by both aristocrats and peasants into a distinctively Japanese religion. With the decline of the Tang and a return to decades of political uncertainty and social turmoil in China, the Chinese model seemed even less relevant to the Japanese. As early as 838, the Japanese court decided to discontinue its embassies to the much-reduced Tang court. Japanese monks and traders still made the dangerous sea crossing to China, but the emperor's advisors no longer deemed official visits and groveling before the Son of Heaven to be worth all the bother.

For five years, the **Gempei** (gehm-pay) **Wars** raged in the heartland of the main island of Honshu (Map 13.2). This conflict brought great suffering to the peasantry, whose farmlands were ravaged. At the same time, they were compelled to fight against each other. Often large numbers of poorly trained peasants were cut down by the better-armed, professional samurai warriors, who met these hapless rivals in the course of their seemingly endless ritual combats. By 1185, the Taira house faction had been destroyed. The Minamoto then established the **bakufu** (which literally means "tent"), or military government. The Minamoto capital was located at Kamakura in their base area on the Kanto plain, far to the east of the old court center at Heian (Map 13.2). The emperor and his court were preserved, but real power now rested with the Minamoto and their samurai retainers. The feudal age in Japan had begun.

The Breakdown of Bakufu Dominance and the Age of the Warlords

Yoritomo, the leader of the victorious Minamoto, gravely weakened the Kamakura regime because of his obsessive fear of being overthrown by members of his own family. Close relatives, including his brother Yoshitsune, whose courage and military genius had much to do with the Minamoto triumph over the Taira, were murdered or driven into exile. Fear of spies lent an element of paranoia to elite life under the first of the Kamakura **shoguns**, or the military leaders of the bakufu. Although Yoritomo's rule went unchallenged, the measures he adopted to protect his throne left him without an able heir. His death and the weakness of those who succeeded him led to a scramble on the part of the bushi lords to build up their own power and enlarge their domains. The **Hojo**, one of the warrior families that had long been closely allied to the Minamoto, soon dominated the Kamakura regime, although they were content to leave the Minamoto as the formal rulers. Thus, a curious and confusing three-tiered system arose. Real power rested in the Hojo family, who manipulated the Minamoto shoguns, who in turn claimed to rule in the name of the emperor who lived at Kyoto.

In the early 14th century, the situation became even murkier when the head of one of the branches of the Minamoto family, **Ashikaga Takuaji** (ah-she-kah-gah tahk-oo-ah-jee), led a revolt of the bushi that overthrew the Kamakura regime and established the **Ashikaga Shogunate** (ah-she-kah-gah shoh-guh-nayt) (1336–1573) in its place. Because the emperor at the time of Ashikaga's seizure of power refused to recognize the usurper and tried to revive imperial power, he was driven from Kyoto to the mountain town of Yoshino. There, with the support of several warlords, the exiled emperor and his heirs fought against the Ashikaga faction and the puppet emperors they placed on the throne at Kyoto for much of the rest of the 14th century.

Although the Ashikaga were finally successful in destroying the rival Yoshino center of imperial authority, the long period of civil strife seriously undermined whatever authority the emperor had left as well as that of the shogunate. The bushi vassals of the warring factions were free to crush local rivals and to seize the lands of the peasantry, the old aristocracy, and competing warlords. As

samurai   Mounted troops of Japanese warrior leaders (bushi); loyal to local lords, not the emperor.

sepukku   Ritual suicide or disembowelment in Japan; commonly known in West as hara-kiri; demonstrated courage and a means to restore family honor.

Taira   [teye-ruh] Powerful Japanese family in 11th and 12th centuries; competed with Minamoto family; defeated after Gempei Wars.

Minamoto   Defeated the rival Taira family in Gempei Wars and established military government (bakufu) in 12th-century Japan.

Gempei Wars   [gehm-pay] Waged for five years from 1180, on Honshu between Taira and Minamoto families; resulted in destruction of Taira.

bakufu   Military government established by the Minamoto following the Gempei Wars; centered at Kamakura; retained emperor, but real power resided in military government and samurai.

shoguns   Military leaders of the bakufu (military governments in Japan).

Hojo   Warrior family closely allied with Minamoto; dominated Kamakura regime and manipulated Minamoto rulers who claimed to rule in name of Japanese emperor at Kyoto.

Ashikaga Takuaji   [ah-she-kah-gah tahk-oo-ah-jee] Member of the Minamoto family; overthrew the Kamakura regime and established the Ashikaga Shogunate from 1336–1573; drove emperor from Kyoto to Yoshino.

Ashikaga Shogunate   [ah-she-kah-gah shoh-guh-nayt] Replaced the Kamakura regime in Japan; ruled from 1336 to 1573; destroyed rival Yoshino center of imperial authority.

Comparing Feudalisms

In one sense, the existence of feudalism is easily explained. Many societies generated only weak central government structures simply because they lacked the resources, shared political values, and bureaucratic experience to develop alternatives. China under the Zhou dynasty is sometimes called feudal. The Russian kings from Rurik onward exercised only loose control over powerful landlords. Kings in the divine monarchy systems of sub-Saharan Africa, which flourished from about the 9th to the 19th century in various parts of the continent, similarly relied on deals and compromises with local and regional leaders. Indeed, African historians have often noted that kingdoms such as Ghana and Mali were ruled about as effectively as were Western monarchies during the Middle Ages.

A comparison of this sort reminds us that feudal systems were in many ways early, less sophisticated versions of political societies that were gradually moving from purely local toward more centralized organization. Indeed, almost all civilizations have experienced long periods of semicentralized rule. In all such cases, including feudal ones, the claims of central authorities are not matched by effective power. Regional leaders have armies of their own and do much of the effective administration of their localities. Kings have to make deals with such leaders, relying on personal negotiation and pledges of mutual respect, marriage alliances, negotiation, and a willingness to give the local princes free rein in practice.

The feudal systems that arose in the West and Japan differed in some respects from the many other decentralized systems they

> "The idea of personal ties between leaders or among elite groups as a foundation for political activity continued to affect political life and institutions, both in the West and in Japan, long after the feudal period ended."

resemble. These differences make it desirable not to call all such systems feudal, thus diluting an extremely useful term beyond recognition. For example, Russia was often decentralized and often saw its rulers, whatever their grandiose claims, make concessions to regional nobles because the tsars depended on the loyalty and service of these subordinate lords. But Russia never developed a genuinely feudal political hierarchy, which is one of the features that distinguished it from the West. The same holds true for Zhou China or even the Sudanic empires of Africa.

Japan and the medieval West developed feudal systems grounded in a set of political values that embraced, however imperfectly, most of the participants in the system. The most important of these participants were the aristocratic lords, who effectively controlled the mass of the peasants. The idea of mutual ties and obligations, and the rituals and institutions that expressed them, went beyond the more casual local deals and compromises characteristic of ancient China or medieval and early modern Russia.

In both western Europe and Japan, feudalism was highly militaristic. Both the medieval West and Japan went through long centuries of unusually frequent and bitter internal warfare, based in large part on feudal loyalties and rivalries. Although this warfare was more confined to the warrior-landlord class in Europe than in Japan, in both instances feudalism summed up a host of elite military virtues that long impeded the development of more stable, centralized government. These values included physical courage, personal or family alliances, loyalty, ritualized combat, and often contempt for nonwarrior groups such as peasants and merchants.

---

the power of the bushi warlords grew, the court aristocracy, which was impoverished by its inability to defend its estates, was nearly wiped out. The lands the warlords acquired were parceled out to their samurai retainers, who in turn pledged their loyalty and were expected to provide military support whenever their lord called on them.

The collapse of centralized authority was sharply accelerated by the outbreak of full-scale civil war, which raged from 1467 to 1477. Rival heirs to the Ashikaga Shogunate called on the warlord chiefs to support their claims. Samurai flocked to rival headquarters in different sections of Kyoto, where feuding soon broke into all-out warfare. Within a matter of years, the old imperial capital had been reduced to rubble and weed-choked fields. While the shogunate self-destructed in the capital, the provincial lords continued to amass power and plot new coalitions to destroy their enemies. Japan was divided into nearly 300 little kingdoms, whose warlord rulers were called **daimyo** (deye-mee-oh) rather than bushi.

daimyos [deye-mee-oh] Warlord rulers of 300 small states following civil war and disruption of Ashikaga Shogunate; holdings consolidated into unified and bounded mini-states.

Toward Barbarism? Military Division and Social Change

Although the rituals became more elaborate, the armor heavier, and the swords more superbly forged, the chivalrous qualities of the bushi era deteriorated noticeably in the 15th and 16th centuries. In the place of mud-walled forts, there arose the massive wood and stone castles, such as that at Himeji pictured in Figure 13.5. These imposing structures dominated the Japanese landscape in

The military aura of feudalism survived the feudal era in both cases. It left Japan with serious problems in controlling its samurai class after the worst periods of internal conflict had passed the early 17th century. In the West, the warrior ethic of feudalism persisted in the prominent belief that a central purpose of the state was to make war, thereby providing opportunities for military leaders to demonstrate their prowess. But the legacy of feudalism was not simply military. For example, the idea of personal ties between leaders or among elite groups as a foundation for political activity continued to affect political life and institutions, both in the West and in Japan, long after the feudal period ended.

The characteristics of feudalism in Japan and in the West were not identical. Western feudalism emphasized contractual ideas more strongly than did Japanese. Although mutual ties were acknowledged by members of the European warrior elite, feudal loyalties were sealed by negotiated contracts, in which the parties involved obtained explicit assurances of the advantages each would receive from the alliance. Japanese feudalism relied more heavily on group and individual loyalties, which were not confirmed by contractual agreements. Probably for this reason, the clearest ongoing legacy of feudalism in the West proved to be parliamentary institutions, where individual aristocrats (as well as townspeople and clergy) could join to defend their explicitly defined legal interests against the central monarch. (Western feudalism also helped encourage the emergence of lawyers, who have never played a comparable role in Japan.) In Japan, the legacy of feudalism involved a less institutionalized group consciousness. This approach encouraged individuals to function as part of collective decision-making teams that ultimately could be linked to the state.

Can the common fact of a feudal heritage be used to explain another similarity between the West and Japan that emerged clearly in the 20th century? Both societies have been unusually successful in industrial development. Both have also proven adept at running capitalist economies. It is certainly tempting to point to feudalism, the medieval feature the two societies uniquely shared, as a partial explanation for these otherwise unexpected 19th- and 20th-century resemblances. The feudal legacy may also help to account for less positive aspects of western European and Japanese development in these centuries, especially their propensity for imperialist expansion and the fact that they frequently resorted to war to solve conflicts with foreign powers. In the case of Japan and Germany, recent historians have established intriguing connections between the persistence of feudalism late into the early modern era and the rise of right-wing militarist regimes in the 1930s.

When the Japanese talent for group cohesion is identified so strikingly as an ingredient in 20th-century economic success, or when Western nations win political stability through use of parliamentary forms, it surely seems legitimate to point to some persistent threads that run through the experience of the two societies. Whether the common experience of feudalism is a basis for later economic dynamism is a matter for speculation. However, it need not be excluded from a list of provocative uses of comparative analysis simply because the links are challenging.

QUESTIONS Do you think the characteristics of feudalism help explain the later success of Western and Japanese societies? If so, in what ways? If not, why not? Which aspects of feudalism do you think had the greatest effect on these outcomes? What other factors should be taken into account if we want to fully analyze these trends?

the centuries that followed. Spying, sneak attacks, ruses, and timely betrayals became the order of the day. The pattern of warfare was fundamentally transformed as large numbers of peasants armed with pikes became a critical component of daimyo armies. Battles hinged less and less on the outcome of samurai combat. Victory depended on the size and organization of a warlord's forces and on how effectively his commanders used them in the field.

The badly trained and poorly fed peasant forces became a major source of the growing misery of the common people. As they marched about the countryside to fight the incessant wars of their overlords, they looted and pillaged. The peasantry in different areas sporadically rose up in hopeless but often ferocious revolts, which fed the trend toward brutality and destruction. It is no wonder that contemporary accounts of the era, as well as those written in later centuries, are dominated by a sense of pessimism and foreboding, a conviction that Japan was reverting from civilized life to barbarism.

Despite the chaos and suffering of the warlord period, there was much economic and cultural growth. Most of the daimyo clearly recognized the need to build up their petty states if they were to survive in the long run. The more able daimyo tried to stabilize village life within their domains by introducing regular tax collection, supporting the construction of irrigation systems and other public works, and building strong rural communities. Incentives were offered to encourage the settlement of unoccupied areas. New tools, the greater use of draft animals, and new crops—especially soybeans—contributed to the well-being of the peasantry in the better-run domains. Peasants were

Figure 13.5 Himeji Castle was one of the most formidable of the many fortresses that became focal points of much of the Japanese landscape in the era dominated by the samurai warriors. Although the inner buildings were often made of wood, these more vulnerable structures were defended by walls and long, fortified passageways made of stone. Like those of medieval Europe, each castle had wells and granaries for the storage of food that allowed its defenders to withstand long sieges by the forces of rival warlords.

also encouraged to produce items such as silk, hemp, paper, dyes, and vegetable oils, which were highly marketable and thus potential sources of household income. Daimyo vied with each other to attract merchants to their growing castle towns. Soon a new and wealthy commercial class emerged as purveyors of goods for the military elite and intermediaries in trade between Japan and overseas areas, especially China. As in medieval Europe, guild organizations for artisans and merchants were strong in this era. They helped provide social solidarity and group protection in a time of political breakdown and insecurity.

Evidence reveals that the growth of commerce and the handicraft industries gave some Japanese women opportunities to avoid the sharp drop in status that most experienced in the age of the warring daimyo. Women in merchant and artisan families apparently exercised a fair degree of independence. This was reflected in their participation in guild organizations and business management and by the fact that their positions were sometimes inherited by their daughters. But the status of women in the emerging commercial classes contrasted sharply with that of women in the warrior elites. In earlier centuries, the wives and daughters of the provincial bushi households learned to ride and to use a bow and arrow, and they often joined in the hunt. By the 14th and 15th centuries, however, the trend among the daimyo families toward primogeniture, or limiting inheritance to the eldest son, dealt a heavy blow to women of the elite classes. The wives and daughters of warrior households, who had hitherto shared in the division of the family estate, now received little or no land or income.

Disinheritance was part of a larger pattern that saw women increasingly treated as defenseless appendages of their warrior fathers or husbands. They were given in marriage to cement alliances between warrior households and reared to anticipate their warrior husband's every desire. They were also taught to slay themselves rather than dishonor the family line by being raped by illicit suitors or enemy soldiers. Japanese women of all classes lost the role of the celebrant in village religious ceremonies and were replaced in Japanese theatrical performances by men specially trained to impersonate women.

Figure 13.6 Patronage of landscape painting and the other fine arts in Japan allowed artistic expression to survive in the long centuries of political division and civil war. In paintings such as the one pictured here, Chinese aesthetic preferences and techniques were strong. In fact, Japanese artists consciously imitated the monochrome (one-colored) paintings of Song China, which they regarded as the apex of the genre. Japanese artists not only concentrated on the same themes, such as landscapes with tiny human figures, but imitated the brushstrokes that they believed had been used by the Song masters.

(Shen Zhou (Chinese 1427–1509), "Poet on a Mountain Top." The Nelson-Atkins Museum of Art, Kansas City, Missouri. Purchase: Nelson Trust, 46–51/2. Photo: Robert Newcombe.)

Artistic Solace for a Troubled Age

Fears that the constant wars between the swaggering samurai might drag Japan back to barbarism were somewhat mollified by continuing cultivation of the arts. Zen Buddhism, which because of its stress on simplicity and discipline had a special appeal to the warrior elite, played a critical role in securing the place of the arts in an era of strife and destruction. Zen monasteries provided key points of renewed diplomatic and trade contacts with China, which in turn led to a revival of Chinese influence in Japan, at least at the cultural level. Although much painting of the era imitated earlier Chinese work of the Song period, the monochrome ink sketches of Japanese artists were both brilliant and original. Also notable were screen and scroll paintings, such as the one in Figure 13.6, that capture the natural beauty of Japan; others provide us with invaluable glimpses into Japanese life in this period. Zen sensibilities are also prominent in some of the splendid architectural works of this period, including the Golden and Silver Pavilions that Ashikaga shoguns had built in Kyoto (Figure 13.7). Each pavilion was designed to blend into the natural setting in which it was placed to create a pleasing shelter that would foster contemplation and meditation.

This contemplative mood is also evident in the design of some of the more famous gardens of this era. One of these, at the Ryoanji Temple, consisted entirely of islands of volcanic rock set amid white pebbles, which were periodically raked into varying patterns. The influence of Shintoism and Zen Buddhism on such gardens, and the related Japanese ability to find great beauty in the rough and simple, were also present in the tea ceremony that developed in the era of warrior dominance. The graceful gestures, elaborate rituals, and subtly shaped and glazed pots and cups associated with the service of tea on special occasions all lent themselves to composure and introspection.

Figure 13.7 The Golden Pavilion (or Kinkakuji) is one of the great architectural treasures of the age of the warring houses in Japan. Built on a small lake near Kyoto in the 15th century, the wooden, tile-roofed structure reflects the Zen and Shinto stress on simplicity typical of almost all Japanese artistic production in the centuries of the warring states. Its gold-painted exterior and the reflecting pond enhance these sensibilities.

Choson [choh-suhn] Earliest Korean kingdom; conquered by Han emperor in 109 B.C.E.

These arts and aesthetic sensibilities were cultivated through centuries of warfare. They continued during the "long peace" of the Tokugawa shogunate which marked the last phase of the feudal period that persisted until the late-19th century.

Korea: Between China and Japan

Of all the areas to which the Chinese formula for civilized development spread, Korea was the most profoundly influenced for the longest period of time. Despite repeated Chinese interventions, the Korean people developed a separate identity that was expressed in distinctive forms of dress, cuisine, and a unique social class system.

Because the Korean peninsula is an extension of the Chinese mainland, and because, historically, Korean kingdoms were dwarfed by their giant neighbor to the west, most observers have treated Korea as little more than an appendage of China. But lumping Korea together with China overlooks the fact that the peninsula was ruled by indigenous dynasties through most of its history, even though these dynasties often paid tribute to the reigning Chinese emperor. At an even more basic level, the peoples who occupied the Korean peninsula represented a different ethnic blend than those who, centuries earlier, had come to identify themselves as Chinese. The Koreans descended from the hunting and herding peoples of eastern Siberia and Manchuria rather than the Mongolian- and Turkic-speaking tribes to the west. By the 4th century B.C.E., the peoples who moved into the Korean peninsula had begun to acquire sedentary farming and metalworking techniques from the Chinese.

From this point onward, the Koreans played a role in the dynastic struggles that preoccupied the peoples of the north China plain. In 109 B.C.E., the earliest Korean kingdom, **Choson** (choh-suhn), was conquered by the Han emperor Wudi. Thereafter, parts of Korea were colonized by Chinese settlers, who remained for nearly four centuries. These colonies soon became a channel by which Chinese influences began to filter into Korean culture in the critical centuries of its early development. A small Japanese enclave in the southeast of the peninsula provided contact with the islands as well, although cultural influences in this era ran overwhelmingly eastward, from China to Korea and then on to Japan.

Koguryo [koh-goor-yoo] Tribal people of northern Korea; established an independent kingdom in the northern half of the peninsula in 37 B.C.E.; adopted cultural Sinification.

The Korean Peninsula During the Three Kingdoms Era

Despite conquest and colonization under the Han, the tribal peoples of the peninsula, particularly the **Koguryo** (koh-goor-yoo) in the north, soon resisted Chinese rule. As Chinese control weakened, the Koguryo established an independent state in the northern half of the peninsula that was soon at war with two southern rivals, **Silla** and **Paekche** (pah-EHK-chee) (Map 13.3). Contacts between the splinter kingdoms that ruled north China after the fall of the Han and the Koguryo kingdom resulted in the first wave of **Sinification**—that is, the extensive adoption of Chinese culture—in Korea. As was the case in Japan, Buddhism supplied the key links between Korea and the successors of the Han dynasty in northeast China. Korean rulers patronized Buddhist artists and financed the building of monasteries and pagodas. Korean scholars traveled to China, and a select few went to the source of the Buddhist faith, India.

In addition to Sinified variants of Buddhism, Chinese writing was introduced, even though the spoken Korean language was as ill suited for adaptation to the Chinese characters as the Japanese language had been. The Koguryo monarch imposed a unified law code patterned after that of Han China. He established universities, where Korean youths struggled to master the Confucian classics and their teachers wrote histories of China rather than their own land. To expand his power and improve revenue collection, the Koguryo ruler also tried to put together a Chinese-style bureaucracy. But the noble families who supported him had little use for a project that posed such an obvious threat to their own power. Without their support, the monarch did not have the resources for such an ambitious undertaking. Thus, full implementation of these policies had to wait for a more powerful dynasty to emerge some centuries later.

Map 13.3 The Korean Peninsula During the Three Kingdoms Era The Chinese were often able to play off the rival kingdoms that dominated Korea's early history against each other and thereby exert great influence on the political and social development of the country.

Tang Alliances and the Conquest of Korea

Centuries of warfare between the three Korean kingdoms weakened each without giving paramount power in the peninsula to any. Internal strife also left Korea vulnerable to further attacks from the outside. In addition to the unsuccessful campaigns of the Sui (see Chapter 12), the founders of the more lasting Tang dynasty included Korea in the territories they staked out for their empire. But it was several decades before one of them could finally mount a successful invasion. The stubborn warriors of the Koguryo kingdom bore the brunt of the Tang assaults, just as they had borne those of the Sui rulers. Finally, Tang strategists hit on the idea of taking advantage of Korean divisions to bring the troublesome region into line. Striking an alliance with the rulers of the Silla kingdom to the southeast, they destroyed the Paekche kingdom and then defeated the Koguryo. Thus, the Chinese finally put an end to the long-lived dynasty that had played such a key role in Korea's early development.

The Chinese conquerors began to quarrel with their Silla allies over how to divide the spoils. When the Silla proved able to fight the larger Chinese forces in the peninsula to a standstill and revolts broke out in the former Paekche and Koguryo territories already conquered, the Tang decided it was time to strike a deal. In return for regular tribute payments and the Silla monarch's submission as a vassal of the Tang emperor, the Chinese withdrew their armies in 668. In so doing, they left the Silla the independent rulers of a united Korea. Despite brief lapses, the Koreans maintained this independence and roughly the same boundaries established by the Silla until the occupation of their land by the Japanese in the early 20th century.

Sinification: The Tributary Link

Under the Silla monarchs, who ruled from 668 until the late 9th century, and the Koryo dynasty (918–1392) that followed, Chinese influences peaked and Korean culture achieved its first full flowering. The Silla rulers consciously strove to turn their kingdom into a miniature of the Tang empire. They regularly sent embassies and tribute to the Tang court, where Korean scholars collected Chinese texts and noted the latest fashions in court dress and etiquette. The Koreans' regular attendance on the Chinese emperors was a key sign of their prominent and enduring participation in the Chinese tribute system. At various times, the participants in the system included nomads from central and north Asia, the Tibetans, many of the kingdoms of southeast Asia, and the emperors of Japan. None of these participants were more committed to the tributary arrangements than the Koreans. Rather than try to conquer the Koreans and other surrounding peoples, most Chinese emperors were content to receive their embassies. These emissaries offered tribute in the form of splendid gifts and acknowledged the superiority of the Son of Heaven by their willingness to kowtow to him (kowtowing involved a series of ritual bows in which the supplicant prostrated himself before the throne).

To most of the peoples involved, this seemed a small price to pay for the benefits they received from the Middle Kingdom. Not only did submission and tribute guarantee continuing peace with the Chinese, but it brought far richer gifts than the tribute bearers offered to the Chinese ruler. In addition, the tributary system provided privileged access to Chinese learning, art, and manufactured goods. Tribute missions normally included merchants, whose ability to buy up Chinese manufactures and sell their own goods in the lucrative Chinese market hinged on their country's participation in the Chinese system. Missions from heavily Sinified areas, such as Japan, Korea, and Vietnam, also included contingents of scholars. They studied at Chinese academies or Buddhist monasteries and busily purchased Chinese scrolls and works of art to fill the libraries and embellish the palaces back home. Thus, the tribute system became the major channel of trade and intercultural exchange between China and its neighbors.

The Sinification of Korean Elite Culture

The Silla rulers rebuilt their capital at Kumsong on the Kyongju plain to look like its Tang counterpart. The streets were laid out on a regular grid; there were central markets, parks, lakes, and a separate district to house the imperial family. Fleeing the tedium of the backward rural areas and provincial capitals, the aristocratic families who surrounded the throne and dominated imperial government crowded their mansions into the areas around the imperial palace. With their large extended families and hundreds of slaves and hangers-on, they made up a large portion of the capital's population. Some aristocrats studied in Chinese schools, and a minority even submitted to the rigors of the Confucian examination system introduced under the Silla rulers. Most of the aristocracy opted for the artistic pursuits and entertainments available in the capital. They could do so because most positions in the government continued to be occupied by members of the aristocratic

Silla   Independent Korean kingdom in southeastern part of peninsula; defeated Koguryo along with their Chinese Tang allies; submitted as a vassal of the Tang emperor and agreed to tribute payment; ruled united Korea by 668.

Paekche   [pah-EHK-chee] Independent Korean kingdom in southeastern part of peninsula; defeated by rival Silla kingdom and its Chinese Tang allies in 7th century.

Sinification   Extensive adaptation of Chinese culture in other regions; typical of Korea and Japan, less typical of Vietnam.

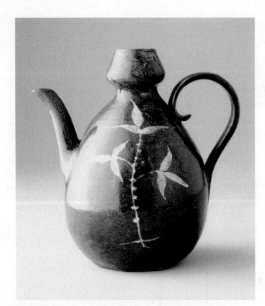

Figure 13.8 Although all of the major civilized centers of east Asia produced refined ceramics, perhaps nowhere was this art as highly developed as in Korea. As the simple, yet elegant, pitcher in this photo illustrates, Korean pottery was initially crafted for household use. That which has survived from earlier periods of Korean history has become sought after by collectors of fine arts and is prominently displayed in museums.

(The Bridgeman Art Library/Detroit Institute of Arts.)

families by virtue of their birth and family connections rather than their knowledge of the Confucian classics.

Partly out of self-interest, the Korean elite continued to favor Buddhism over Confucianism, which was much more strongly associated with Chinese culture. They and the Korean royal family lavishly endowed monasteries and patronized works of religious art, which became major forms of Korean cultural creativity. The capital at Kumsong soon became crowded with Buddhist temples, which usually were made of wood. Buddhist monks were constantly in attendance on the ruler as well as on members of the royal family and the more powerful aristocratic households. But the schools of Buddhism that caught on among the elite were Chinese. Korean artwork and monastic design reproduced, sometimes splendidly, Chinese prototypes. Even the location of monasteries and pagodas in high places followed Chinese ideas about the need to mollify local spirits and balance supernatural forces.

Sometimes the Koreans borrowed from the Chinese and then outdid their teachers. Most notable in this regard was the pottery produced in the Silla and Koryo eras. The Koreans first learned the techniques of porcelain manufacture from the Chinese. But in the pale green-glazed celadon bowls and vases of the late Silla and Koryo, they created masterworks that even Chinese connoisseurs admired and collected. They also pioneered in making oxide glazes that were used to make the black- and rust-colored stoneware of this era, which is pictured in Figure 13.8.

Another endeavor in which the Koreans improved on the Chinese was in the art of printing. As we have seen, the Chinese were the first to develop wood block and, later, moveable metal-type printing. But after the latter was introduced into Korea, local artisans came upon an ingenious way to hold the metal type in place in the long registers in which it was assembled for printing. Using honey as a sort of glue, they were able to fix the type temporarily and yet disassemble it when a particular task was finished. Until the Koreans devised this technique, the Chinese had found that the metal type wore down very fast and was difficult to stabilize in the registers.

Civilization for the Few

With the exception of Buddhist sects such as the pure land that had strong appeal for the ordinary people, imports from China in this and later eras were all but monopolized by the tiny elite. The aristocratic families were divided into several ranks that neither intermarried nor socialized with each other, much less the rest of the population. They not only filled most of the posts in the Korean bureaucracy but also dominated the social and economic life of the entire kingdom. Much of Korea's trade with the Chinese and Japanese was devoted to providing these aristocrats with the fancy clothing, special teas, scrolls, and artwork that occupied such an important place in their idle lives. In return, Korea exported mainly raw materials, such as forest products and metals such as copper, which was mined by near-slaves who lived in horrendous conditions.

Members of the royal family and the aristocratic households often financed artisan production for export or to supply the court. In addition, some backed mercantile expeditions and even engaged extensively in money lending. All of this limited the activities of artisans and traders. The former were usually considered low in status and were poorly paid for their talents and labor. The latter were so weak that they did not really form a distinct class.

The aristocrats were the only people who really counted for anything in Korean society. The classes beneath them were oriented to their service. These included government functionaries, who were recognized as a separate social category; commoners, who were mainly peasants; and near-slaves, who were known as the "low born" and ranged from miners and artisans to servants and entertainers. Buddhist festivals periodically relieved the drudgery and monotony of the lives of the common people, and Buddhist salvationist teachings gave them hope for bliss in the afterlife.

Koryo Collapse, Dynastic Renewal

Periodically, the common people and the low born found their lot too much to bear and rose up against a ruling class that was obviously much more devoted to pursuing its own pleasures than to their well-being. Most of these uprisings were local affairs and were ruthlessly repressed by armies of the ruling class. But collectively they weakened both the Silla and Koryo regimes, and in combination with quarrels between the aristocratic households and outside invasions, they contributed to the fall of both dynasties. In the absence of real alternatives, the aristocratic families managed to survive these crises and elevated one of their number to the royal throne. After nearly a century and a half of conflict and turmoil triggered by the Mongol invasion in 1231, the **Yi** dynasty was established in 1392. Remarkably, it ruled Korea until 1910. Although there were some modifications, the Yi quickly restored the aristocratic dominance and links to China that had predominated under their predecessors. Of all of the peoples who received higher civilization from China, none were as content to live in the shadow of the Middle Kingdom as the Koreans.

Yi Korean dynasty that succeeded Koryo dynasty following period of Mongol invasions; established in 1392; ruled Korea to 1910; restored aristocratic dominance and Chinese influence.

Khmers [kuh-MEHRs] Indianized rivals of the Vietnamese; moved into Mekong River delta region at time of Vietnamese drive to the south.

Between China and Southeast Asia: The Making of Vietnam

The preconquest culture of the Vietnamese gave them a strong sense of themselves as a distinct people with a common heritage that they did not want to see overwhelmed by an expanding China. The Viets were well aware of the benefits they derived from the superior technology, modes of political organization, and ideas they received from China. But their gratitude was tempered by their fear of losing their own identity and becoming just another part of China's massive civilization.

Ironically, the Viets first appear in recorded history as a group of "southern barbarians" mentioned by Chinese scholars in accounts of Qin raids in south China in the 220s B.C.E. At that time, their kingdom, which the Chinese called Nam Viet, meaning "people in the south," extended along the southern coastal area of what is now China (Map 13.4). The initial raids by Qin forces left little lasting Chinese presence. But they probably gave a boost to the lively trade that had been conducted between the Viets and the peoples of south China for centuries. In exchange for silk manufactured by the Chinese, the Viets traded ivory, tortoise shells, pearls, peacock feathers, aromatic woods, and other exotic products drawn from the sea and tropical forests. Some decades after the Qin raids, the Viet rulers defeated the feudal lords who controlled the Red River valley and brought their lands under the control of the Viet kingdom. In the centuries that followed, the Viets intermarried and blended with the Mon-Khmer- and Tai-speaking peoples who occupied the Red River area. This proved to be a crucial step in the formation of the Vietnamese as a distinct ethnic group.

As the Viets' willingness to intermarry with ethnic groups such as the **Khmers** (kuh-MEHRs) (today's Cambodians) and the Tais (teyes) suggests (Map 13.4), before their conquest by the Han their culture had many features characteristic of southeast Asia. Their spoken language was not related to Chinese. They enjoyed a strong tradition of village autonomy, physically symbolized by the bamboo hedges that surround northern Vietnamese villages to the present day. The Vietnamese favored the nuclear family to the extended household preferred by the Chinese, and they never developed the clan networks that have been such a prominent feature of south Chinese society. Vietnamese women have historically had greater freedom and more influence, both within the family and in society at large, than their Chinese counterparts. They were, for example, the dominant force in both local and large urban markets and the trading system more generally.

Vietnamese customs and cultural forms also differed very significantly from Chinese. The Vietnamese dressed very differently. For example, women preferred long skirts to the black pants that non-elite women wore in China. The Vietnamese delighted in the cockfight, a typical southeast Asian pastime; they chewed betel nut, which the Chinese found disgusting; and they blackened their teeth, which the Chinese also considered repulsive. In the centuries when they were dominated by the Chinese politically, the Vietnamese managed to preserve most of these features of their society. They also became much more fervently attached at the grassroots level to Buddhism, and they developed art and literature, especially poetry, that was refined and distinct from that of the Chinese.

At the end of the 2nd century B.C.E., the Han dynasty conquered the kingdom of the Nam Viet, thus beginning an effort to absorb the Vietnamese people into Chinese civilization that would span a thousand years. Though they benefited greatly from borrowings from China, the Vietnamese had a distinct identity that provided the basis for a series of rebellions and eventually produced an independent kingdom with expansionist designs against neighboring southeast Asian peoples.

Map 13.4 South China and Vietnam on the Eve of the Han Conquest As Map 13.4 illustrates, Nam Viet, which formed the original core of Vietnam, could be seen as a logical extension of China and was long ruled as the southern province of Chinese empires.

Conquest and Sinification

As the Han rulers who succeeded the Qin tried to incorporate south China into their empire, they came into conflict with the Viets. The Han emperor initially settled for the Viet ruler's admission of his vassal status and periodic payments of tribute. But by 111 B.C.E., the Han thought it best to conquer the feisty Viets outright and to govern them directly using Chinese officials. The Red River area was garrisoned by Chinese troops, and Chinese administrators set to work co-opting the local lords and encouraging them to adopt Chinese culture. Because the Viet elite realized that they had a great deal to learn from their powerful neighbors to the north, they cooperated with the agents of the new regime. Sensing that they had found another barbarian people ripe for assimilation, the Chinese eagerly introduced essential elements of their own culture into the southern lands.

In the centuries after the Chinese conquest, the Vietnamese elite was drawn into the bureaucratic machine that the Han emperors and the shi (bureaucrats) had developed to hold together the empire won by the Qin. They attended Chinese-style schools, where they wrote in the Chinese script and read and memorized the classical Chinese texts of Confucius and Mencius. They took exams to qualify for administrative posts, whose responsibilities and privileges were defined by Chinese precedents. They introduced Chinese cropping techniques and irrigation technology, which soon made Vietnamese agriculture the most productive in southeast Asia. This meant that Vietnamese society, like that of China, could support larger numbers of people. The result was the high population density characteristic of the Red River valley and the lowland coastal areas to the south.

The Vietnamese also found that Chinese political and military organization gave them a decisive edge over the peoples to the west and south, who had adopted Indian patterns of kingship and warfare, and with whom they increasingly clashed over the control of lands to settle and cultivate. Over time, the Vietnamese elite also adopted the extended family model and took to venerating their ancestors in the Confucian manner. Their Chinese overlords had every reason to assume that the Vietnamese "barbarians" were well on their way to becoming civilized—that is, like the Chinese themselves.

Roots of Resistance

Sporadic revolts led by members of the Vietnamese aristocracy, and the failure of Chinese cultural imports to make much of an impression on the Vietnamese peasantry, ultimately frustrated Chinese hopes for assimilating the Viets. Although they had learned much from the Chinese, the Vietnamese lords chafed under their rule, in part because the Chinese often found it difficult to conceal their disdain for local customs in what they considered a backward and unhealthy outpost of the empire. Vietnamese literature attests to the less than reverent attitudes felt by Vietnamese collaborators toward Chinese learning and culture. In the following poem, a teacher mocks himself and doubts his usefulness to the people he serves:

> I bear the title "Disciple of Confucius."
> Why bother with blockheads, wearing such a label?
> I dress like a museum piece:
> I speak only in learned quotations (poetry and prose);
> Long since dried out, I still strut like a peacock;
> Failed in my exams, I've been dropped like a shrivelled root.
> Doctorate, M.A.: all out of reach,
> So why not teach school, and beat the devil out of my students.

Elsewhere in Vietnamese writings, self-doubt and mockery turn to rage and a fierce determination to resist Chinese dominance, whatever the cost. The following sentiments of a Vietnamese caught up in resistance to the reimposition of rule from China by the Mongols in the 13th century provide a dramatic case in point:

> I myself often forget to eat at mealtime, and in the middle of the night I wake up and caress my pillow. My intestines hurt me incessantly, as if they had been cut off, and tears flow abundantly from my eyes. My only grief is that I have not yet succeeded in hacking apart the enemy's body, peeling off his skin, swallowing his liver, drinking his blood.

The intensity and ferocity of this passage give some sense of why the Chinese failed to assimilate the Vietnamese. They also failed because the peasantry rallied again and again to the call of their own lords to rise up and drive off the alien rulers. The fact that the most famous of these uprisings was led in 39 C.E. by the **Trung sisters,** who were children of a deposed local leader, points to the importance of the more favored position of women in Vietnamese society, in contrast to the Chinese, as a source of resistance.

Vietnamese women were understandably hostile to the Confucian codes and family system that would have confined them to the household and subjected them to male authority figures. We do not know whether this resentment figured in the Trung sisters' decision to revolt. But poetry written in later centuries by female authors leaves little doubt about the reactions of Vietnamese women to Confucian norms or male dominance. One of the most famous of these writers, Ho Xuan Huong (hoo shwahn wahng), flouts Confucian decorum in the following ribald verse and mocks her male suitors:

> Careful, careful where are you going:
> You group of know-nothings!
> Come here and let your older sister teach you to write poems.
> Young bees whose stingers itch rub them in wilted flowers.
> Young goats who have nothing to do with their horns butt them against sparse shrubbery.

In another poem, "Sharing a Husband," Huong ridicules those who advocate polygamy, a practice favored by any self-respecting Confucian:

> One wife is covered by a quilted blanket, while one wife is left in the cold.
> Cursed be this fate of sharing a common husband. Seldom do you have an occasion to possess
>   your husband,
> Not even twice in one month.
> You toil and endure hardships in order to earn your steamed rice, and then the rice is cold and
>   tasteless. It is like renting your services for hire, and then receiving no wages.
> How is it that I have turned out this way,
> I would rather suffer the fate of remaining unmarried and living alone by myself.

Winning Independence and Continuing Chinese Influences

In addition to a strong sense of identity and motives for resistance that crossed class and gender barriers, the Vietnamese struggle for independence was assisted by the fragility of the links that bound them to China. Great distances and mountain barriers created nightmare conditions for Chinese administrators responsible for supplying military expeditions to the far south. Only small numbers of Chinese—mostly bureaucrats, soldiers, and merchants—lived in the Red River area, and few of them did so permanently. Most critically, Chinese control over the distant Vietnamese depended on the strength of the ruling dynasties in China. The Vietnamese were quick to take advantage of political turmoil and nomadic incursions in northern China to assert their independence. After failing to completely free themselves on several occasions, they mounted a massive rebellion during the period of chaos in China after the fall of the Tang dynasty in 907.

By 939 the Vietnamese had won political independence from their northern neighbors. Although both the Mongol and Ming rulers of China later tried to reassert control, both efforts ended in humiliating retreats. From 939 until the conquests by the French in the 19th century, the Vietnamese were masters of their own land.

Although the Chinese political hold was broken, Chinese cultural exports continued to play central roles in Vietnamese society. A succession of Vietnamese dynasties beginning with the Le (980–1009), which became the source of legitimacy for the rest, built Chinese-style palaces, as in Figure 13.9, in the midst of forbidden cities patterned after those in Chang'an and Beijing. They ruled through a bureaucracy that was a much smaller copy of the Chinese administrative system, with secretariats, six main ministries, and a bureau of censors to keep graft and corruption in check. Civil service exams were reintroduced, and an administrative elite schooled in the Confucian classics sought the emperor's favor and commanded deference from the common people.

Trung sisters Leaders of one of the frequent peasant rebellions in Vietnam against Chinese rule; revolt broke out in 39 C.E.; demonstrates importance of Vietnamese women in indigenous society.

What Their Portraits Tell Us: Gatekeeper Elites and the Persistence of Civilizations

Some decades ago, a distinguished historian of ancient China called the scholar-gentry elite the gatekeepers of Chinese civilization. In his usage, gatekeepers are pivotal elite groups that have emerged in all civilizations and proved critical to their persistence over time. Although they usually shared power with other social groups and often did not rule in their own right, gatekeepers played vital roles in shaping the dominant social values and worldviews of the cultures in which they appeared. In everything from the positions they occupied to their manners and fashions in dress, gatekeepers defined the norms and served as role models for much of the rest of society. Some gatekeeper elites, such as the scholar-gentry in China and the brahmans in India, promoted norms and ideals in written treatises on good government or the proper social order. Other gatekeepers, such as the samurai of Japan and the Aztec warriors of Tenochtitlan, embodied these ideals in their public personas and

A Samurai Warrior.

(Woodcut, Masahiro Murai "Illustration from Tanki Yoryaku (A Single Horseman: Summary on How to Wear Armor)." The Metropolitan Museum of Art, New York, NY, U.S.A. Image copyright © The Metropolitan Museum of Art/Art Resource, NY.)

Warrior Ranks from the Aztec Empire.

Bankers and Merchants from Western Europe.

But the Vietnamese equivalent of the Chinese scholar-gentry never enjoyed as much power. For one thing, their control at the village level was much less secure than that of their Chinese counterparts. Much more than those in China, local Vietnamese officials tended to identify with the peasantry rather than with the court and higher administrators. To a much greater degree, they looked out for local interests and served as leaders in village uprisings against the ruling dynasty when its demands on the common people became too oppressive.

The power of the scholar-bureaucrats in Vietnam was also limited in the reign of many dynasties by competition from well educated Buddhist monks. The fact that the Buddhists had much stronger links with the Vietnamese peasantry than the monastic orders had in China strengthened the Buddhists in their struggles with the Confucian scholars. The high esteem in which women were held in Buddhist teachings and institutions also enhanced the popularity of the monks in Vietnam. Thus, competing centers of power and influence prevented most Vietnamese dynasties from enjoying the authority of their Chinese counterparts.

military enterprises, which at times were immortalized in songs, legends, and epics.

The illustrations shown here provide portraits of people belonging to gatekeeper elites from four of the civilizations we have considered in depth thus far. Because each of these portraits was produced by artists from the same society as the gatekeeper elite depicted here, we can assume that the portraits capture the values, symbols of legitimacy, and demeanor that these people intended to project to the viewer. Carefully examine each of these portraits, paying special attention to clothing, poses adopted, objects included in the portraits, backgrounds selected, and activities depicted.

For historical background of the civilizations that each exemplifies, see the relevant sections of Chapters 10, 11, 12, and 13. Compare each of the portraits to the others, and then answer the questions that follow.

QUESTIONS What do the dress, poses, and settings of each of these portraits tell you about the values, ideals, and worldviews that each gatekeeper elite group is intended to represent? With which elite groups did they share power? How did they legitimize their power and privileges and to what degree is this reflected in the portraits? What are comparable gatekeeper elite groups in the contemporary United States?

Chinese Scholars Enjoying Their Leisure Time.
(Handscroll "Gathering of Philosophers." The Metropolitan Museum of Art, New York, NY, U.S.A. Image copyright © The Metropolitan Museum of Art/Art Resource, NY.)

The Vietnamese Drive to the South

However watered down, the Chinese legacy gave the Vietnamese great advantages in the struggles within Indochina that became a major preoccupation of independent Vietnamese rulers. Because the Vietnamese refused to settle in the malarial highlands that fringed the Red River area and rose abruptly from the coastal plains farther south, their main adversaries were the **Chams** and Khmers, who occupied the lowland areas to the south that the Vietnamese sought to settle themselves (Map 13.4). The Vietnamese launched periodic expeditions to retaliate for raids on their villages by the hill peoples. They also regularly traded with the hill dwellers for forest products. But the Vietnamese tried to minimize cultural exchange with these hunters and shifting cultivators, whom they saw as "nude savages."

As they moved out in the only direction left to them—south along the narrow plain between the mountains and the sea—the Vietnamese made good use of the larger population and superior

Chams Indianized rivals of the Vietnamese; driven into the highlands by the successful Vietnamese drive to the south.

Figure 13.9 As this view of the moat and part of the palace of the Vietnamese emperors at Hue illustrates, Chinese taste and architectural styles strongly influenced the construction and decoration of the Vietnamese court. Not only were the upturned, tiled roofs and long galleries built in deliberate imitation of prototypes in Chang'an or Beijing, but they were set amid moats, ponds, and gardens patterned after those that Vietnamese envoys had seen in China. Despite this imitation, however, Vietnamese rulers were more accessible to their subjects, and their palaces and capital city made little impression on Chinese visitors, who disparaged the informality and lack of grandeur at the Hue court.

bureaucratic and military organization that the Chinese connection had fostered. From the 11th to the 18th century, they fought a long series of generally successful wars against the Chams, an Indianized people living in the lowland areas along the coast. Eventually most of the Chams were driven into the highlands, where their descendants, in much smaller numbers, live to the present day. Having beaten the Chams and settled on their former croplands, the Vietnamese next clashed with the Khmers, who had begun to move into the Mekong delta region during the centuries of the Vietnamese drive south. Again, Indianized armies proved no match for the Chinese-inspired military forces and weapons of the Vietnamese. By the time the French arrived in force in the Mekong area in the late 18th century, the Vietnamese had occupied much of the upper delta and were beginning to push into territory that today belongs to Cambodia.

Expansion and Division

As Vietnamese armies and peasant colonists moved farther and farther from the capital at Hanoi, the dynasties centered there found it increasingly difficult to control the commanders and peasants fighting and living in the frontier areas. As the southerners intermarried with and adopted some of the customs of the Chams and Khmers, differences in culture and attitude developed between them and the northerners. Although both continued to identify themselves as Vietnamese, the northerners (much like their counterparts in the United States) came to see the Vietnamese who settled in the frontier south as less energetic and slower in speech and movement. As the hold of the Hanoi-based dynasties over the southern regions weakened, regional military commanders grew less and less responsive to orders from the north and slower in sending taxes to the court. Bickering turned to violent clashes, and by the end of the 16th century a rival, the **Nguyen**, had emerged to challenge the claims of legitimacy of the **Trinh** family that ruled the north.

The territories of the Nguyen at this time were centered on the narrow plains that connected the two great rice bowls of present-day Vietnam along the Red and Mekong rivers. Their capital was

Nguyen   Rival Vietnamese dynasty that arose in southern Vietnam to challenge traditional dynasty of Trinh in north at Hanoi; kingdom centered on Red and Mekong rivers; capital at Hue.

Trinh   Dynasty that ruled in north Vietnam at Hanoi, 1533 to 1772; rivals of Nguyen family in south.

Literature as a Mirror of the Exchanges Between Civilized Centers

The following passages from Lady Murasaki's classic Japanese account of court life, *The Tale of Genji* (Vintage Press, 1985 edition), and from perhaps the most popular and beloved work of Vietnamese literature, Nguyen Du's *The Tale of Kieu* (Vintage Press, 1973 edition), are superb examples of the important and far-reaching exchanges between the civilizations of south and east Asia. Not surprisingly, Chinese influences, including many allusions to Chinese writings and historical events, are paramount, but Buddhist (hence originally Indian) themes are pervasive in both works. There is also evidence in one of these passages of significant exchanges between the satellite civilizations of China.

Dream

[Kieu] dreamed a girl appeared hard by her side and murmured: "Kieu! Your Karma's still undone. How can you shirk your debt of grief to fate? You yet have to play out your woman's role."

The moderator was a man of considerable learning. There was much of interest in his exchanges with the Korean. There were also exchanges of Chinese poetry, and in one of his poems the Korean succeeded most skillfully in conveying his joy at having been able to observe such a countenance on this the eve of his return to his own land. . . . Summoning an astrologer of the Indian school, the emperor was pleased to learn that the Indian view coincided with the Japanese and the Korean; and so he concluded that the boy should become a commoner with the name of Minamoto or Genji.

Looking at the keepsakes Myobu had brought back, [Genji] thought what a comfort it would be if some wizard were to bring him, like that Chinese emperor, a comb from the world where his lost love was dwelling. . . . There are limits to the powers of the most gifted artist. The Chinese lady in the paintings did not have the luster of life. Yang Kuei-fei was said to have resembled the lotus of the Sublime Pond, the willows of the Timeless Hall. No doubt she was very beautiful in her Chinese finery.

"You are well-famed as a lute-player," he said. "Like Chung Tzu-ch'i I've longed to hear you play." . . . Now [Kieu] began to play. A battle scene—oh how they clashed and clanged, Han and Chu swords! The Ssu-ma tune, A Phoenix Seeks His Mate—it sounded like an outburst of pure grief. Then Hsi K'ang's masterpiece, Kuang-ling, was heard: it rushed on like a stream or flew like clouds. Next came what Chao-chin played—she mourned her Prince and all her kinsfolk she must leave behind as she crossed the Great Wall to wed a Hun.

The [abbot] talked of this ephemeral world and of the world to come. His own burden of sin was heavy, thought Genji, that he had been lured into an illicit and profitless affair. He would regret it all his life and suffer even more terribly in the life to come. What a joy to withdraw to such a place [a mountain monastery] as this!

When one must weigh and choose between one's love and filial duty, which will turn the scale? Kieu brushed aside her solemn vows to [the young student] Kim—she'd pay a daughter's debt before all else. Resolved on what to do, she spoke her mind: "Hands off my father, please! I'll sell myself and ransom him."

QUESTIONS From these passages, can you identify Chinese precedents in terms of place names and historical personages, allusions to Chinese literary works, and attitudes toward gender or social organization that can be traced to Chinese models? Can you detect passages that convey Buddhist ideas about the nature of the world and human existence? Are additional Indian influences suggested? Are there ideas that are distinctively Japanese or Vietnamese, or are the authors totally caught up in Chinese precedents?

at Hue (Map 13.4), far north of the Mekong delta region that in this period had scarcely been settled by the Vietnamese. For the next two centuries, these rival houses fought for the right to rule Vietnam. Neither accepted the division of Vietnam as permanent; each sought to unite all of the Vietnamese people under a single monarch. This long struggle not only absorbed much of the Vietnamese energies but also prevented them from recognizing the growing external threat to their homeland. For the first time in history, the danger came not from the Chinese giant to the north but from a distant land and religion about which the Vietnamese knew and cared nothing—France and the conversion-minded Roman Catholic church.

Global Connections

In the Orbit of China: The East Asian Corner of the Global System

The first millennium C.E. was a pivotal epoch in the history of the peoples of east Asia. The spread of ideas, organizational models, and material culture from a common Chinese center spawned the rise of three distinct patterns of civilized development in Japan, Korea, and Vietnam. In contrast to the lands of the nomadic peoples who had long been in contact with China from the north and west, each of these regions contained fertile and well watered lowland areas that were suited to sedentary cultivation, which was essential to the spread of the Chinese pattern of civilized development. In fact, each provided an ideal environment for the cultivation of wet rice, which was increasingly replacing millet and other grains as the staple of China.

Common elements of Chinese culture, from modes of writing and bureaucratic organization to religious teachings and art, were transmitted to each of these three areas. In all three cases, Chinese imports, with the important exception of popular Buddhism, were all but monopolized by court and provincial elite groups, the former prominent in Japan and Korea, the latter in Vietnam. In all three cases, Chinese thought patterns and modes of social organization were actively and willingly cultivated by these local elites, who knew that they were the key to a higher level of development.

One of the great world religions, Buddhism, played key roles in the transmission of Chinese civilization and the development of all three of these "satellite" societies. Because Buddhism originated in India, the layers of cross-cultural interaction in these processes are all the more complex and profound. In each case, ideas and rituals originating in India were filtered through Chinese society and culture before being passed on to Japan, Korea, and Vietnam. Buddhism also provided a critical link between the civilizations developing in Korea and Japan.

In some phases of their borrowing from China, Japan, Korea, and Vietnam shared prominent aspects of political organization, social development, and intellectual creativity. But the differing ways in which Chinese influences were transmitted to each of these very different societies resulted in very different long-term outcomes. The various combinations of Chinese-derived and indigenous elements produced distinctive variations on a common pattern of civilized life. In Korea, the period of direct Chinese rule was brief, but China's physical presence and military power were all too apparent. Thus, the need for symbolic political submission was obvious and the desire for long-term cultural dependence firmly implanted. In Vietnam, where Chinese conquest and control lasted more than a thousand years, a hard-fought struggle for political independence gave way to a growing attachment to Chinese culture as a counterbalance to the Indian influences that had brought civilization to the southeast Asian rivals of the Vietnamese.

In Japan, where all attempts by Chinese dynasties to assert direct control had failed, Chinese culture was emulated by the courtly elite that first brought civilization to the islands. But the rise of a rival aristocratic class, which was based in the provinces and championed military values that were fundamentally opposed to Chinese Confucianism, led to the gradual limitation of Chinese influence in Japan and the reassertion of Japanese traditional ways. Japanese political patterns, in particular, formed a marked contrast with the predominance of rule by a centralized bureaucracy in China. Nonetheless, in Japan as in the rest of east Asia, China remained the epitome of civilized development; Chinese ways were the standard by which all peoples in this far-flung region were judged.

Despite different patterns, the power of the Chinese model had one other important result for Korea, Japan, and to a large extent Vietnam. Contacts with other parts of the world were slight to nonexistent, because there was no sense that any other place had examples worth emulating. The intensity of interactions within the east Asian region generated tendencies toward isolation from the world beyond.

Further Readings

The best short introduction to the history of Korea is C. J. Eckert, *Korea Old and New: A History* (1980), while L. Kendall, *Shahmans, Housewives, and Other Restless Spirits: Women in Korean Ritual Life* (1985) offers a fresh perspective on Korean social history. The best introductory works on Japanese history and culture are the writings of E. Reischauer especially his sections in J. K. Fairbank et al., *East Asia: The Modern Transformation* (1999). H. Paul Varley, *Japanese Culture: A Short History* (1973), has fine sections on the arts, religion, and literature of the warlord era.

For an understanding of the Chinese impact on Vietnam, there is no better place to begin than Alexander Woodside, *Vietnam and the Chinese Model* (1971). The best works on the earliest period in Vietnamese history are translations of the writings of French scholar Georges Coedes and the *Birth of Vietnam* (1983) by Keith Taylor. Troung Buu Lam's edited volume, *Patterns of Vietnamese Response to Foreign Intervention* (1967) provides a wonderful way to get inside Japanese and Vietnamese culture.

On the Web

A brief history of successive Japanese Shogunates, the art and literature of the period, and the lore, weapons, and code of the samurai (Bushido) can be examined at http://victorian.fortunecity .com/duchamp/410/main.html and http://www.samurai-archives .com/. The women warriors and leaders of Japan are discussed at http:// koryu.com/library/wwj1.html and http://www.womeninworldhistory .com/sample-08.html. The life of Lady Murasaki and her world is illuminated at http://mcel.pacificu.edu/as/students/genji/culture.html. *The Tale of Genji* is analyzed at http://www.taleofgenji.org/ and http://webworld.unesco.org/genji/en/index.shtml.

The successive independent Korean kingdoms of Koguryo, Packche, and Silla (http://www.asianinfo.org/asianinfo/korea/ history.htm) retained their identity while adapting facets of Chinese culture. The queens of Silla receive treatment at http:// www.womeninworldhistory.com/heroine7.html. The development of Chinese-influenced Korean court music can be examined at http://www.asiasound.com/content/Learn/Timelines/korea.

Korean family life, from family structure and values to the role of women is explored at http://www.pbs.org/hiddenkorea/ culture.htm, http://www.hcs.harvard.edu/~yisei/issues/spring_95/yisei _95_30.html, and http://asiasocietymuseum.org/ (scroll to small print at bottom of page and click on "Korea"). Examples of Korean technology, including the Korean development of the first movable metal type are examined at http://www.loc.gov/exhibits/ world/world-record.html.

A portal offering introductions to Vietnamese culture and the arts can be found at http://www.vietnam-culture.com/. The lands of present day Vietnam had a long history prior to the coming of the Chinese. An imperial kingdom, Champa, whose society had absorbed ancient Indian, rather than Chinese tradition (http://www.viettouch.com/champa/champa_history.html) had long ruled the southern portion of the country.

In the North, the Vietnamese development of and trade in bronze drums linked it to the wider world prior to the Chinese efforts to conquer them (http://www.viettouch.com/pre-hist/dongson_drums.html).

Vietnam absorbed much Chinese culture but also sought to retain its own values even within the Chinese model government they adopted. The Vietnamese admiration for Chinese culture and hostility to Chinese political domination and their equally ambivalent approach to other external forces is traced at http://www.mongabay.com/reference/country_studies/vietnam/all.html.

AP* Test Prep

1. One problem facing historians who study the Mongols is
   - (A) debate over whether Chinggis Khan really existed.
   - (B) the inability of scholars to translate the Mongolian language and its literature.
   - (C) all contemporary chroniclers used exaggeration and hyperbole to describe the Mongols.
   - (D) the Mongols never wrote anything down, leaving no direct records.

2. Although the Mongols were often brutal
   - (A) Chiggis Khan himself admired the peaceful pattern of urban life.
   - (B) they were tolerant of religious differences among the conquered peoples.
   - (C) they were careful to leave women and children unharmed, preferring to punish only males in the conquered areas.
   - (D) apt to leave some rebellious cities unpunished to spare their works of art and monumental buildings.

3. Pastoral nomads from the central Asian steppe who had threatened sedentary cultures throughout world history included all of these EXCEPT
   - (A) Indo-Europeans.
   - (B) Hsiung-nu (Huns).
   - (C) Scythians.
   - (D) Bantu.

4. The major concern of the Mongols upon conquering China was
   - (A) the integration of Chinese military forces into the Mongol military forces.
   - (B) the conversion of the Chinese to Islam.
   - (C) the reestablishment of the Confucian examination system.
   - (D) avoiding assimilation into Chinese culture.

5. Which of the following accurately illuminates the place of women in Mongol society?
   - (A) Hulagu's choice of a woman warrior to lead the attack on Baghdad
   - (B) the Mongol practice of binding the feet of their women to exclude them from full participation in Mongol life
   - (C) Kubilai Khan abiding by his wife Chabi's advice to drop his plans to harshly punish conquered Song dynasty officials and turn cultivated land near their capital into pastures to feed Mongol ponies
   - (D) the banning of Mongol women from fighting or hunting

6. The greatest impact of the Mongol unification of much of central Asia was
   - (A) the facilitation of trade, which also enabled the spread of the Black Death from China to Europe.
   - (B) the stoppage of trade and the exchange of ideas between China and Europe.
   - (C) the spread of new Mongol military technologies to China and Europe.
   - (D) the conversion of the Mongols to Islam.

7. The transformative power of pastoral nomads over sedentary states finally came to an end
   - (A) when nomadic populations grew too large to be supported by pastoralism.
   - (B) with the advances made by sedentary states in the centralization of their power and in the production of advanced military technology, such as mobile artillery, repeating rifles and railways.
   - (C) with the conversion of most nomadic peoples to Christianity.
   - (D) due to the steady advance of literacy and education in the nomadic heartlands.

Free-Response Question

Compare the Mongol impact on two major societies: China, Persia, Russia.

14 The Last Great Nomadic Challenges: From Chinggis Khan to Timur

The Transcontinental Empire of Chinggis Khan

DOCUMENT: A European Assessment of the Virtues and Vices of the Mongols

The Mongol Drive to the West

VISUALIZING THE PAST: The Mongol Empire as a Bridge Between Civilizations

The Mongol Interlude in Chinese History

THINKING HISTORICALLY: The Global Eclipse of the Nomadic War Culture

GLOBAL CONNECTIONS: The Mongol Linkages

The Mongol retribution came so swiftly and was so ferocious that it completely demoralized Muhammad Shah, the ruler of Khwarazm, whose arrogance brought death and destruction to his kingdom on an appalling scale. Muhammad Shah had scoffed at Chinggis Khan's demand for retribution for the plunder and slaughter of a Mongol caravan that had entered Khwarazm in 1218 (Map 14.1). Chinggis Khan had personally dispatched the caravan as a signal that he wished to establish political and commercial relations with Khwarazm. Having in effect declared war on the Mongols by ignoring their demands for just recompense, Muhammad Shah compounded his folly by quarreling with the caliph of Baghdad, who consequently had little inclination to come to his rescue.

Caught off guard by the Mongol assault that drove deep into his empire from several directions, Muhammad Shah was at first immobilized with fear, and then in full flight, leaving his hapless subjects to fend for themselves. Columns of battle-hardened Mongol cavalry besieged, then stormed, one after another of the legendary cities that were the glory of Khwarazm. Bukhara was taken in early 1220 after its Turkish garrison was eliminated; several months later, most of the inhabitants of Samarkand, who had initially attempted to resist the invaders, were massacred. The Mongols inundated Gurganj, the former capital of Khwarazm, which they won, after an extended siege, by opening the flood gates of a nearby river. And the ancient citadel of Bamian, where Chinggis Khan's much-loved grandson was killed by a defender's arrow, was obliterated and given the name "accursed city."

Over time the mass slaughters (often dramatized by references to pyramids of skulls) and the destruction of Khwarazm's ancient cities became defining features in accounts of the sudden emergence of the nomadic Mongols as conquerors of much of Eurasia. Until quite recently, most histories have depicted these and similar Mongol conquests as savage assaults by backward and barbaric peoples on ancient and highly developed centers of human civilization. But even the Khwarazm campaign, which was certainly one of the most violent launched by Mongol forces, provides ample illustration of another side to the Mongol imperium. Traditionally, the Mongols' contributions to cross-cultural exchange and human advance have been neglected by historians. But in many of the cities of Khwarazm, where the population resisted and was killed wholesale, skilled artisans were spared in the thousands. Some of these were sent to the Mongol capital at Karakorum. Others carried their skills throughout the empire, and both manufacturing and commerce soon thrived under the aegis of Mongol rule.

The century and a half of Mongol dominance also saw a revitalization of commerce and urban life in places like Bukara and Samarkand, along the Silk Road—the great trading network that had, for millennia, linked China and east Asia with the Middle East, India, and Europe (see the Visualizing the Past feature). Without question, the price of Muhammad Shah's treachery and resistance that opened the way to this renewal was high—perhaps intolerably so—but it is important to take fully into account the constructive aftermath of Mongol expansionism in Khwarazm and other regions. ■

As we shall see in this chapter, the Mongols very often exhibited great curiosity and openness towards the peoples and cultures that they conquered. And perhaps none of them exemplified these qualities more than the founder of the Mongol empire, Chinggis Khan himself, who sought to attract philosophers and religious scholars from throughout Eurasia to his capital at Karakorum. He delighted in questioning them and debating the merits and drawbacks of different belief systems. In Samarkand and other cities where Muslim scholars and mosque attendants refused to encourage resistance, they were usually left unharmed and permitted to attend to the spiritual and physical

Figure 14.1 A 14th-century miniature painting from Rashid al-Din's *History of the World* depicts Mongol cavalry charging into battle against retreating Persians. The speed and endurance of Mongol cavalry made it difficult for routed foes to retreat and live to fight another day. As the painting suggests, surrender or death were often the only options for those overrun by Mongol units.

(Bibliotheque Nationale de France.)

Map 14.1 The Transcontinental Empire of Chinggis Khan   Easily the largest empire built before the Industrial Revolution, the Mongol imperium linked most of the great Eurasian centers of civilization.

900 C.E.	1100 C.E.	1200 C.E.	1250 C.E.	1300 C.E.
907–1118 Khitan conquest of north China 1037–1194 Seljuk Turks dominate the Middle East	1115–1234 Jurchens (Jin dynasty) rule north China 1126 Song dynasty flees to south China 1130–c. 1250 Almohads rule north Africa and Spain	1206 Temujin takes the name of Chinggis Khan; Mongol state founded 1215 First Mongol attacks on north China; Beijing captured 1219–1223 First Mongol invasions of Russia and Islamic world 1227 Death of Chinggis Khan; Ogedei named successor 1234 Mongols take all of north China; end of Jin dynasty 1235–1279 Mongol conquest of south China; end of southern Song dynasty 1236–1240 Mongol conquest of Russia 1240–1241 Mongol invasion of western Europe	1253 Mongol victory over Seljuk Turks; rise of Ottoman Turks in Middle East 1258 Mongol destruction of Baghdad 1260 Mamluk (slave) rulers of Egypt defeat Mongols at Ain Jalut; end of drive west 1260–1294 Reign of Kubilai Khan in China 1271–1295 Journey of Marco Polo to central Asia, China, and southeast Asia 1271–1368 Reign of the Yuan (Mongol) dynasty in China 1274–1280 Failed Mongol invasions of Japan 1290s First true guns used in China	1336–1405 Life of Timur mid-14th century Spread of Black Death in Eurasia

needs of the survivors. In the aftermath of the Mongol invasions, this privileging of religious leaders was reflected in a broader tolerance on the part of these nomadic overlords for the diverse faiths and ethnic groups that had come under their rule

As we will argue in this chapter, though the Mongols were indeed fierce fighters and capable of terrible acts of retribution against those who dared to defy them, their conquests brought much more than death and devastation. At the peak of their power, the domains of the Mongol *khans* made up a vast realm in which once hostile peoples lived together in peace and most religions were tolerated. From the khanate of Persia in the west to the empire of the fabled Kubilai Khan in the east, the law code promulgated by Chinggis Khan gave order to human interaction. Like the Islamic expansion that preceded it, the Mongol explosion laid the foundations for human interaction on a global scale, extending and intensifying the world network that had been building since the classical age.

The Transcontinental Empire of Chinggis Khan

In most ways, the Mongols epitomized nomadic society and culture. Their survival depended on the well-being of the herds of goats and sheep they drove from one pasture area to another according to the cycle of the seasons. Their staple foods were the meat and milk products provided by their herds, supplemented in most cases by grain and vegetables gained through trade with sedentary farming peoples. They also traded hides and dairy products for jewelry, weapons, and cloth made in urban centers. They dressed in sheepskins, made boots from tanned sheep hides, and lived in round felt tents made of wool sheared from their animals (Figure 14.2). The tough little ponies they rode to round up their herds, hunt wild animals, and make war were equally essential to their way of life. Mongol boys and girls could ride as soon as they were able to walk. Mongol warriors could ride for days on end, sleeping and eating in the saddle.

Like the early Arabs and other nomadic peoples we have encountered, the basic unit of Mongol society was the tribe, which was divided into kin-related clans whose members camped and herded together on a regular basis. When threatened by external enemies or preparing for raids on other nomads or invasions of sedentary areas, clans and tribes could be combined in great confederations. Depending on the skills of their leaders, these confederations could be held together for

In the early 13th century, long-standing obstacles to Mongol expansion were overcome, primarily because of the leadership of Chinggis Khan. The Mongols and allied nomadic groups built an empire that stretched from the Middle East to the China Sea.

Figure 14.2 This sketch shows a Mongol household on the move. The Mongols depended on sheep for food, clothing, and shelter, and they rode both horses and camels. As the drawing shows, they also used oxen to transport their housing for seasonal or longer-term migrations. The Mongols mounted their tents and other goods on enormous wagons so heavy that large teams of oxen were required to pull them. This combination of animal transport and comfortable but moveable shelters made the Mongols one of the most mobile preindustrial societies.

months or even years. But when the threat had passed or the raiding was done, clans and tribes drifted back to their own pasturelands and campsites. At all organizational levels, leaders were elected by the free men of the group. Although women exercised influence within the family and had the right to be heard in tribal councils, men dominated leadership positions.

Courage in battle, usually evidenced by bravery in the hunt, and the ability to forge alliances and attract dependants were vital leadership skills. A strong leader could quickly build up a large following of chiefs from other clans and tribal groups. If the leader grew old and feeble or suffered severe reverses, his subordinates would quickly abandon him. He expected this to happen, and the subordinates felt no remorse. Their survival and that of their dependants hinged on attaching themselves to a strong tribal leader.

The Making of a Great Warrior: The Early Career of Chinggis Khan

Since the early millennia of recorded history, nomadic peoples speaking Mongolian languages had enjoyed moments of power and had actually carved out regional kingdoms in north China in the 4th and 10th centuries C.E. In the early 12th century, Chinggis Khan's (JEHNG-gihs kahn) great-grandfather, Kabul Khan, led a Mongol alliance that had won glory by defeating an army sent against them by the Jin kingdom of north China. Soon after this victory, Kabul Khan became ill and died. His successors could neither defeat their nomadic enemies nor hold the Mongol alliance together. Divided and beaten, the Mongols fell on hard times.

Chinggis Khan, who as a youth was named Temujin, was born in the 1170s into one of the splinter clans that fought for survival in the decades after the death of Kabul Khan. Temujin's father was an able leader who built up a decent following and negotiated a promise of marriage between his eldest son and the daughter of a stronger Mongol chief. According to Mongol accounts, just

Figure 14.3 In this miniature from a Persian history, Chinggis Khan is shown acknowledging the submission of a rival prince. Though he conquered a vast empire, Chinggis Khan did not live long enough to build a regular bureaucracy to govern it. His rule was dependent on vassal chieftains such as the one shown in the painting, whose loyalty in turn depended on the maintenance of Mongol military might. When the military strength of the Mongol Empire began to decline, subject princes soon rose up to establish the independence of their domains.

kuriltai [KURL-tuh] Meeting of all Mongol chieftains at which the supreme ruler of all tribes was selected.

khagan [KAH-gahn] Title of the supreme ruler of the Mongol tribes.

tumens Basic fighting units of the Mongol forces; consisted of 10,000 cavalrymen; each unit was further divided into units of 1000, 100, and 10.

when the family fortunes seemed to be on the upswing, Temujin's father was poisoned by the agents of a rival nomadic group. Suddenly, Temujin, who was still a teenager, was thrust into a position of leadership. But most of the chiefs who had attached themselves to his father refused to follow a mere boy, whose prospects of survival appeared to be slim.

In the months that followed, Temujin's much-reduced encampment was threatened and finally attacked by a rival tribe. He was taken prisoner in 1182, locked into a wooden collar, and led in humiliation to the camp of his enemies. After a daring midnight escape, Temujin rejoined his mother and brothers and found refuge for his tiny band of followers deep in the mountains. Facing extermination, Temujin did what any sensible nomad leader would have done: he and his people joined the camp of a more powerful Mongol chieftain who had once been aided by Temujin's father. With the support of this powerful leader, Temujin avenged the insults of the clan that had enslaved him and another that had taken advantage of his weakness to raid his camp for horses and women.

These successes and Temujin's growing reputation as a warrior and military commander soon won him allies and clan chiefs eager to attach themselves to a leader with a promising future (Figure 14.3). Within a decade, the youthful Temujin had defeated his Mongol rivals and routed the forces sent to crush him by other nomadic peoples. In 1206, at a **kuriltai** (KURL-tuh), or meeting of all of the Mongol chieftains, Temujin—renamed Chinggis Khan—was elected the **khagan** (KAH-gahn), or supreme ruler, of the Mongol tribes. United under a strong leader, the Mongols prepared to launch a massive assault on an unsuspecting world.

Building the Mongol War Machine

The men of the Mongol tribes that had elevated Chinggis Khan to leadership were natural warriors. Trained from youth not only to ride but also to hunt and fight, they were physically tough, mobile, and accustomed to killing and death. They wielded a variety of weapons, including lances, hatchets, and iron maces. None of their weapons was as devastating as their powerful short bows. A Mongol warrior could fire a quiver of arrows with stunning accuracy without breaking the stride of his horse. He could hit enemy soldiers as distant as 350 yards (the range for the roughly contemporary English longbow was 250 yards) while ducking under the belly of his pony, or leaning over the horse's rump. The fact that the Mongol armies were entirely cavalry meant that they moved so rapidly that their advances alone could be demoralizing to enemy forces.

To a people whose very lifestyle bred mobility, physical courage, and a love of combat, Chinggis Khan and his many able subordinate commanders brought organization, discipline, and unity of command. The old quarrels and vendettas between clans and tribes were overridden by loyalty to the khagan. Thus, energies once devoted to infighting were now directed toward conquest and the forcible exaction of tribute, both in areas controlled by other nomadic groups and in the civilized centers that fringed the steppes on all sides. The Mongol forces were divided into armies made up of basic fighting units called **tumens,** each consisting of 10,000 warriors. Each tumen was further divided into units of 1000, 100, and 10 warriors. Commanders at each level were responsible for training, arming, and disciplining the cavalrymen under their charge. The tumens were also divided into heavy cavalry, which carried lances and wore some metal armor, and light cavalry, which relied primarily on the bow and arrow and leather helmets and body covering. Even more lightly armed were the scouting parties that rode ahead of Mongol armies and, using flags and special signal fires, kept the main force informed of the enemy's movements.

Chinggis Khan also created a separate messenger force whose bodies were tightly bandaged to allow them to remain in the saddle for days, switching from horse to horse to carry urgent messages between the khagan and his commanders. Military discipline had long been secured by personal ties between commanders and ordinary soldiers. Mongol values, which made courage in battle a prerequisite for male self-esteem, were buttressed by a formal code that dictated the immediate execution of a warrior who deserted his unit. Chinggis Khan's swift executions left little doubt about the fate of traitors to his own cause or turncoats who abandoned enemy commanders in his favor. His generosity to brave foes was also legendary. The most famous of the latter, a man named Jebe, nicknamed the Arrow, won the khagan's affection and high posts in the Mongol armies by standing his ground after his troops had been routed and fearlessly shooting Chinggis Khan's horse out from under him.

A special unit supplied Mongol armies with excellent maps of the areas they were to invade. These were drawn largely according to the information supplied by Chinggis Khan's extensive network of spies and informers. New weapons, including a variety of flaming and exploding arrows, gunpowder projectiles, and later bronze cannons, were also devised for the Mongol forces. By the time Chinggis Khan's armies rode east and west in search of plunder and conquest in the second decade of the 13th century, they were among the best armed and trained and the most experienced, disciplined, and mobile soldiers in the world.

Conquest: The Mongol Empire Under Chinggis Khan

When he was proclaimed the khagan in 1206, Temujin probably was not yet 40 years old. At that point, he was the supreme ruler of nearly one-half million Mongols and the overlord of 1 to 2 million more nomads who had been defeated by his armies or had allied themselves with this promising young commander. But Chinggis Khan had much greater ambitions. He once said that his greatest pleasure in life was making war, defeating enemies, forcing "their beloved [to] weep, riding on their horses, embracing their wives and daughters." He came to see himself and his sons as men marked for a special destiny: warriors born to conquer the known world. In 1207, he set out to fulfill this ambition. His first campaigns humbled the Tangut (TANG-uht) kingdom of Xi Xia (shee-shyah) in northwest China (Map 14.1), whose ruler was forced to declare himself a vassal of the khagan and pay a hefty tribute. Next, the Mongol armies attacked the much more powerful Jin Empire, which the Manchu-related Jurchens (YUHR-chehns) had established a century earlier in north China.

In these campaigns, the Mongol armies were confronted for the first time with large, fortified cities whose inhabitants assumed that they could easily withstand the assaults of these uncouth nomads from the steppes. Indeed, the Mongol invaders were thwarted at first by the intricate defensive works that the Chinese had perfected over the centuries to deter nomadic incursions. But the adaptive Mongols, with the help of captured Chinese artisans and military commanders, soon devised a whole arsenal of siege weapons. These included battering rams, catapults that hurled rocks and explosive balls, and bamboo rockets that spread fire and fear in besieged towns.

Chinggis Khan and the early Mongol commanders had little regard for these towns, whose inhabitants they saw as soft. Therefore, when they met resistance, the Mongols adopted a policy of terrifying retribution. Although the Mongols often spared the lives of famous scholars, whom they employed as advisors, and artisans with particularly useful skills, towns that fought back were usually sacked once they had been taken. The townspeople were slaughtered or sold into slavery; their homes, palaces, mosques, and temples were reduced to rubble. Towns that surrendered without a fight were usually spared this fate, although they were required to pay tribute to their Mongol conquerors as the price of their deliverance.

The First Assault on the Islamic World

Once they had established a foothold in north China and solidified their empire in the steppes, the Mongol armies moved westward against the Kara Khitai (KAH-rah KIHT-uh) Empire, which had been established by a Mongolian-speaking people a century earlier (Map 14.1). Having overwhelmed and annexed the Kara Khitai by 1219, and, as we have seen, provoked by Muhammad

A European Assessment of the Virtues and Vices of the Mongols

As we have seen, much of what we know about the history of nomadic peoples is based on the records and reactions of observers from sedentary cultures that were often their mortal enemies. Some of the most famous observers were those, including Marco Polo, who visited the vast Mongol domains at the height of the khans' power in the 12th and 13th centuries. Many tried to assess the strengths and weaknesses of these people, who were suddenly having such a great impact on the history of much of the known world. One of the most insightful of these observers was a Franciscan friar named Giovanni de Piano Carpini. In 1245, Pope Innocent IV sent Piano Carpini as an envoy to the "Great Khan" to protest the recent assaults by his Mongol forces on Christian Europe. The pope's protest had little effect on the Mongol decision to strike elsewhere in the following years. But Piano Carpini's extensive travels produced one of the most detailed accounts of Mongol society and culture to be written in the mid-13th century. As the following passages suggest, like other visitors from sedentary areas, he gave the Mongols a very mixed review:

> In the whole world there are to be found no more obedient subjects than the Tartars [Mongols]. . . . They pay their lords more respect than any other people, and would hardly dare lie to them. Rarely do they revile each other, but if they should, the dispute hardly ever leads to blows. Wars, quarrels, the infliction of bodily harm, and manslaughter do not occur among them, and there are no large-scale thieves or robbers among them. . . .
>
> They treat one another with due respect; they regard each other almost as members of one family, and, although they do not have a lot of food, they like to share it with one another. . . . When riding

they can endure extreme cold and at times also fierce heat; they are neither soft, nor sensitive [to the weather]. They do not seem to feel in any way envious of one another, and no public trials occur among them. No one holds his fellow in contempt, but each helps and supports the other to the limits of his abilities.

> They are extremely arrogant toward other people and look down on all others with disdain. In fact, they regard them, both noble and humble people alike, as little better than nothing. . . . Toward other people the Tartars tend to anger and are easily roused. . . . They are the greatest liars in the world in dealing with other people [than the Tartars], and hardly a true word escapes from their mouths. Initially they flatter but in the end they sting like scorpions. They are crafty and sly, and wherever possible they try to get the better of everybody else by false pretenses. . . .
>
> They are messy in their eating and drinking and in their whole way of life. Drunkenness is honorable among them. . . . At the same time they are mean and greedy, and if they want something, they will not stop begging and asking for it, until they have got it. They cling fiercely to what they have, and in making gifts they are extremely miserly. They have no conscience about killing other people. In short, if one tried to enumerate all their bad characteristics there would be too many to put on paper.

QUESTIONS What might the qualities of the Mongols that Piano Carpini emphasizes tell us about his own society and its values or shortcomings? How are the Mongol virtues he extols linked to the achievements of Chinggis Khan and the stunning Mongol wars of conquest? To what extent would they be typical of nomadic societies more generally? In what ways might his account of Mongol vices be simply dismissed as sour grapes resulting from European defeats?

Shah, Chinggis Khan led his armies in the conquest of the Khwarazm (kwahr-ahzm) Empire further west. Again and again, the Mongols used their favorite battle tactic in these encounters. Cavalry were sent to attack the enemy's main force. Feigning defeat, the cavalry retreated, drawing the opposing forces out of formation in the hope of a chance to slaughter the fleeing Mongols. Once the enemy's pursuing horsemen had spread themselves over the countryside, the main force of Mongol heavy cavalry, until then concealed, attacked them in a devastating pincer formation. And the great cities of adversary powers fell to the new siege weapons and tactics the Mongols had perfected in their north China campaigns.

Within two years, his once flourishing cities in ruin and his kingdom in Mongol hands, Muhammad Shah, having retreated across his empire, died on a desolate island in the Caspian Sea. In addition to greatly enlarging his domains, Chinggis Khan's victories meant that he could bring tens of thousands of Turkic horsemen into his armies. By 1227, the year of his death, the Mongols ruled an empire that stretched from eastern Persia to the North China Sea.

The Mongol Empire in the Late Thirteenth Century
MAP

Long Distance Trade and Cross-Cultural Exchange: Life Under the Mongol Imperium

Despite their aggressiveness as warriors and the destruction they could unleash on those who resisted their demands for submission and tribute, the Mongols were remarkably astute and tolerant rulers. Chinggis Khan himself set the standard. He was a complex man, capable of gloating over the ruin of his enemies but also open to new ideas and committed to building a world where the diverse peoples of his empire could live together in peace. Though illiterate, Chinggis Khan was neither the ignorant savage nor the cultureless vandal often depicted in the accounts of civilized writers—usually those who had never met him. Once the conquered peoples had been subdued, he took a keen interest in their arts and learning, although he refused to live in their cities. Instead, he established a new capital at **Karakorum** on the steppes and summoned the wise and clever from all parts of the empire to the lavish palace of tents with gilded pillars where he lived with his wives and closest advisors.

Karakorum Capital of the Mongol Empire under Chinggis Khan, 1162 to 1227.

At Karakorum, Chinggis Khan consulted with Confucian scholars about how to rule China, with Muslim engineers about how to build siege weapons and improve trade with the lands farther west, and with Daoist holy men, whom he hoped could give him an elixir that would make him immortal. Although he himself followed the *shamanistic* (focused on nature spirits) beliefs of his ancestors, all religions were tolerated in his empire. An administrative framework that drew on the advice and talents of both Muslim and Chinese bureaucrats was created. A script was devised for the Mongolian language to facilitate recordkeeping and the standardization of laws. Chinggis Khan's legal code was enforced by specially designated policemen. Much of the code was aimed at ending the divisions and quarrels that had so long plagued the Mongols and other nomadic peoples. Grazing lands were allotted to specific tribes, and harsh penalties were established for rustling livestock or stealing horses.

The Mongol conquests brought a peace to much of Asia that in some areas persisted for generations. In the towns of the empire, handicraft production and scholarship flourished and artistic creativity was allowed free expression. Secure trade routes made for prosperous merchants and wealthy, cosmopolitan cities. One Muslim historian wrote of the peoples within the Mongol Empire that they "enjoyed such a peace that a man might have journeyed from the land of sunrise to the land of sunset with a golden platter upon his head without suffering the least violence from anyone." Paradoxically, Mongol expansion, which sedentary chroniclers condemned as a "barbarian" orgy of violence and destruction, also became a major force for economic and social development and the enhancement of civilized life. But there was also a downside, the movement of merchants and commercial goods also facilitated the spread of disease. In fact, some historians believe that the infamous intercontinental wave of bubonic plague that came to be known as the Black Death was carried from China by the fleas on rats nesting in the saddle bags of Mongol cavalrymen across central Asia to the Black Sea and from there by ships to the Mediterranean and Europe.

The Death of Chinggis Khan and the Division of the Empire

In 1226, his wars to the west won, Chinggis Khan turned east with an army of 180,000 warriors to complete the conquest of China that he regretted having left unfinished more than a decade earlier. After routing a much larger Tangut (TANG-uht) army in a battle fought on the frozen waters of the Yellow River, the Mongol armies overran the kingdom of Xi Xia, plundering, burning, and mercilessly hunting down Tangut survivors. As his forces closed in on the Tangut capital and last refuge, Chinggis Khan, who had been injured in a skirmish some months earlier, fell grievously ill. After lecturing his sons on the dangers of quarreling among themselves for the spoils of the empire, the khagan died in August 1227.

With one last outburst of wrath, this time directed against death itself, the Mongols carried his body back to Mongolia for burial. The Mongol forces escorting the funeral procession hunted down and killed every human and animal in its path. The vast pasturelands the Mongols now controlled were divided between Chinggis Khan's three remaining sons and **Batu** (BAH-too), a grandson and heir of the khagan's recently deceased son, Jochi. Towns and cultivated areas such as those in north China and parts of Persia were considered the common property of the Mongol ruling family. A kuriltai was convened at Karakorum, the Mongol capital, to select a successor to the great conqueror. In accordance with Chinggis Khan's preference, **Ogedei** (OHGD-dih), his third son, was elected grand khan. Though not as capable a military leader as his brothers or nephews, Ogedei was a crafty diplomat and deft manipulator. As it turned out, these skills were much needed to keep the ambitious heads of the vast provinces of the empire from each other's throats.

Batu [BAH-too] Ruler of Golden Horde; one of Chinggis Khan's grandsons; responsible for invasion of Russia beginning in 1236.

Ogedei [OHGD-dih] (1186–1241) Third son of Chinggis Khan; succeeded Chinggis Khan as khagan of the Mongols following his father's death.

Golden Horde One of the four subdivisions of the Mongol Empire after Chinggis Khan's death, originally ruled by his grandson Batu; territory covered much of what is today south central Russia.

Mongol commanders launched raids into Georgia and across the Russian steppe that set the stage for their conquest of the vulnerable Christian lands to the west.

khanates [KAHN-ayts] Four regional Mongol kingdoms that arose following the death of Chinggis Khan.

For nearly a decade, Ogedei directed Mongol energies into further campaigns and conquests. The areas targeted by this new round of Mongol expansion paid the price for peace within the Mongol Empire. The fate of the most important victims—Russia and eastern Europe, the Islamic heartlands, and China—will be the focus of much of the rest of this chapter.

The Mongol Drive to the West

Russia and Europe were added to the Mongols' agenda for world conquest. Subjugating these regions became the project of the armies of the **Golden Horde,** named after the golden tent of the early khans of the western sector of the Mongol Empire. The territories of the Golden Horde made up one of the four great **khanates** (KAHN-ayts) into which the Mongol Empire was divided at the time of Chinggis Khan's death (Map 14.2). Under the rule of Chinggis Khan's grandson Batu, Mongol armies began an invasion of Russia in 1236. In a very real sense, the assault on Russia was a side campaign, a chance to fine-tune the war machine and win a little booty on the way to the real prize: western Europe.

As we saw in Chapter 9, in the first half of the 13th century when the Mongol warriors first descended, Russia had been divided into numerous petty kingdoms, centered on trading cities such as Novgorod and Kiev (see Map 14.3). By this time, Kiev, which originally dominated much of cen-

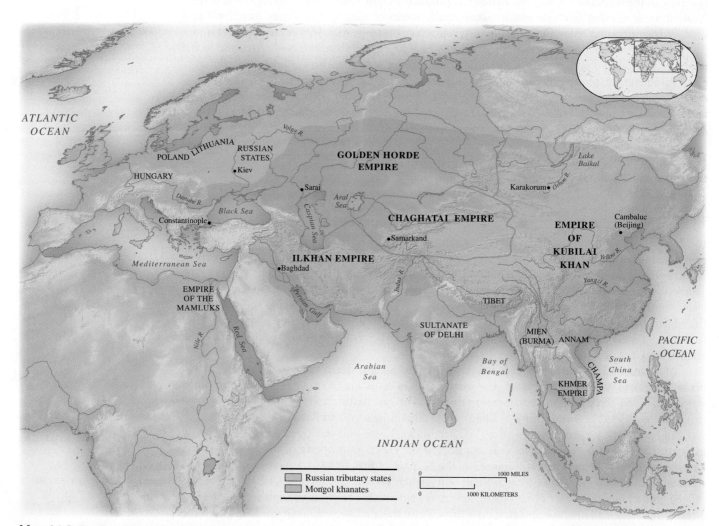

Map 14.2 The Four Khanates of the Divided Mongol Empire Sheer distances and slow-moving modes of transportation made it difficult to hold the vast domains conquered by Chinggis Khan and his immediate successors.

tral Russia, had been in decline for some time. As a result, there was no paramount power to rally Russian forces against the invaders. Despite the warnings of those who had witnessed the crushing defeats suffered by the Georgians in the early 1220s, the princes of Russia refused to cooperate. They preferred to fight alone, and they were routed individually.

In 1236, Batu led a Mongol force of more than 120,000 cavalrymen into the Russian heartlands. From 1237 to 1238 and later in 1240, these Tatars, or Tartars (meaning people from hell), as the Russians called them, carried out the only successful winter invasions in Russian history. In fact, the Mongols preferred to fight in the winter. The frozen earth provided good footing for their horses, and frozen rivers gave them access to their enemies. One after another, the Mongol armies defeated the often much larger forces of local nomadic groups and Russian princes. Cities such as Ryazan, Moscow, and Vladimir, which resisted the Mongol command to surrender, were destroyed; their inhabitants were slaughtered or led into slavery. As a contemporary Russian chronicler observed, "No eye remained to weep for the dead." Just as it seemed that all of Russia would be ravaged by the Mongols, whom the Russians compared to locusts, Batu's armies withdrew. The largest cities, Novgorod and Kiev, appeared to have been spared. Russian priests thanked God; the Mongol commanders blamed the spring thaw, which slowed the Mongol horsemen and raised the risk of defeat in the treacherous mud.

The Mongols returned in force in the winter of 1240. In this second campaign, even the great walled city of Kiev, which had reached a population of more than 100,000 by the end of the 12th century, fell. Enraged by Kievan resistance—its ruler had ordered the Mongol envoys thrown from the city walls—the Mongols reduced the greatest city in Russia to a smoldering ruin. The cathedral of Saint Sophia was spared, but the rest of the city was looted and destroyed, and its inhabitants were smoked out and slaughtered. Novgorod braced itself for the Mongol onslaught. Again, according to the Russian chroniclers, it was "miraculously" spared. In fact, it was saved largely because of the willingness of its prince, Alexander Nevskii, to submit, at least temporarily, to Mongol demands. In addition, the Mongol armies were eager to move on to the main event: the invasion of western Europe, which they perceived as a far richer but equally vulnerable region.

Russia in Bondage

The crushing victories of Batu's armies initiated nearly two and a half centuries of Mongol dominance in Russia. Russian princes were forced to submit as vassals of the khan of the Golden Horde and to pay tribute. Mongol demands fell particularly heavily on the Russian peasantry, who had to give their crops and labor to both their own princes and the Mongol overlords. Impoverished and ever fearful of the lightning raids of Mongol marauders, the peasants fled to remote areas or became, in effect, the serfs (see Chapter 9) of the Russian ruling class in return for protection. Some Russian towns made profits on the increased trade made possible by the Mongol links. Sometimes the gains exceeded the tribute they paid to the Golden Horde. No town benefited from the Mongol presence more than Moscow. Badly plundered and partially burned in the early Mongol assaults, the city was gradually rebuilt, and its ruling princes steadily swallowed up nearby towns and surrounding villages. After 1328, Moscow also profited from its status as the tribute collector for the Mongol khans. Its princes not only used their position to fill their own coffers but also annexed other towns as punishment for falling behind on tribute payments.

As Moscow grew in strength, the power of the Golden Horde declined. Mongol religious toleration benefited both the Orthodox Church and Moscow. The choice of Moscow as the seat of the Orthodox leaders brought new sources of wealth to its princes and buttressed its claims to be Russia's leading city. In 1380, those claims got an additional boost when the princes of Moscow shifted from being tribute collectors to being the defenders of Russia. In alliance with other Russian vassals, they raised an army that defeated the forces of the Golden Horde at the **Battle of Kulikova.** Their victory and the devastating blows Timur's attacks dealt the Golden Horde two decades later effectively broke the Mongol hold over Russia.

Battle of Kulikova Russian army victory over the forces of the Golden Horde; helped break Mongol hold over Russia.

Although much of the Mongols' impact was negative, their conquest was a turning point in Russian history in several ways. In addition to their importance to Moscow and the Orthodox Church, Mongol contacts led to changes in Russian military organization and tactics and in the political style of Russian rulers. Claims that the Tatars were responsible for Russian despotism, either tsarist or Stalinist, are clearly overstated. Still, the Mongol example may have influenced the desire of Russian princes to centralize their control and reduce the limitations placed on their power by the landed nobility, clergy, and wealthy merchants. By far the greatest effects of Mongol rule were those resulting from Russia's isolation from Christian lands farther west. On one hand, the Mongols protected a divided and weak Russia from the attacks of much more powerful kingdoms such as Poland, Lithuania, and Hungary (Map 14.2). On the other hand, in the period of Mongol rule, Russia was cut off from key transformations in western Europe that were inspired by the Renaissance and led ultimately to the Reformation.

Mongol Incursions and the Retreat from Europe

Francisco Alvarez, "The Land of Prester John," c. 1540 **DOCUMENT**

Prester, John In legends popular from 12th to 17th century, a mythical Christian monarch whose kingdom was cut off from Europe by Muslim conquests; Chinggis Khan was originally believed to be this mythical ruler.

Until news of the Mongol campaigns in Russia reached European peoples such as the Germans, Poles, and Hungarians farther west, Christian leaders had been quite pleased by the rise of a new military power in central Asia. Rumors and reports from Christians living in the area, chafing under what they saw as persecution by their Muslim overlords, convinced many in western Europe that the Mongol khan was none other than **Prester John.** Prester John was the name given to a mythical rich and powerful Christian monarch whose kingdom had supposedly been cut off from Europe by the Muslim conquests of the 7th and 8th centuries. Sometimes located in Africa, sometimes in central Asia, Prester John loomed large in the European imagination as a potential ally who could strike the Muslim enemy from the rear and join up with European Christians to destroy their common adversary. The Mongol assault on the Muslim Khwarazm Empire appeared to confirm the speculation that Chinggis Khan was indeed Prester John.

The assault on Christian, though Orthodox, Russia made it clear that the Mongol armies were neither the legions of Prester John nor more partial to Christians than to any other people who stood in their way. The rulers of Europe were nevertheless slow to realize the magnitude of the threat the Mongols posed to western Christendom. When Mongol envoys, one of whom was an Englishman, arrived at the court of King Bela of Hungary demanding that he surrender a group of nomads who had fled to his domains after being beaten by the Mongols in Russia, the king contemptuously dismissed them. King Bela also rebuffed Batu's demand that he submit to Mongol rule. The Hungarian monarch reasoned that he was the ruler of a powerful kingdom, whereas the Mongols were just another ragtag band of nomads in search of easy plunder. His refusal to negotiate provided the Mongols with a pretext to invade. Their ambition remained the conquest and pillage of all western Europe. That this goal was clearly attainable was demonstrated by the sound drubbing they gave to the Hungarians in 1240 and later to a mixed force of Christian knights led by the Polish ruler, King Henry of Silesia.

These victories left the Mongols free to raid and pillage from the Adriatic Sea region in the south to Poland and the German states of the north. It also left the rest of Europe open to Mongol conquest. Just as the kings and clergy of the western portions of Christendom were beginning to fear the worst, the Mongol forces disappeared. The death of the khagan Ogedei, in the distant Mongol capital at Karakorum, forced Batu to withdraw in preparation for the struggle for succession. The campaign for the conquest of Europe was never resumed. Perhaps Batu was satisfied with the huge empire of the Golden Horde that he ruled from his splendid new capital at Sarai on the Volga river in what is southern Russia today. Most certainly the Mongols had found richer lands to plunder in the following decades in the Muslim empires of the Middle East. Whatever the reason, Europe was spared the full fury of the Mongol assault. Of the civilizations that fringed the steppe homelands of the Mongols, only India was as fortunate.

The Mongol Assault on the Islamic Heartland

After the Mongol conquest of the Khwarazm Empire, it was only a matter of time before they struck westward against the far wealthier Muslim empires of Mesopotamia and north Africa (see Maps 7.2 and Map 14.2). The conquest of these areas became the main project of Hulegu, another grandson of Chinggis Khan and the ruler of the Ilkhan portions of the Mongol Empire. As we saw in Chapter 7, one of the key results of Hulegu's assaults on the Muslim heartlands was the capture

The Mongol Empire as a Bridge Between Civilizations

Chinggis Khan and his successors actively promoted the growth of trade and travelers by protecting the caravans that made their way across the ancient Asian silk routes. The Mongols also established rest stations for weary merchants and fortified outposts for those harassed by bandits. These measures transformed the Mongol imperium into a massive conduit between the civilizations of Europe, the Middle East, and the rest of Asia. The map illustrates a wide variety of marketable goods and inventions, as well as the agents and objects of several religions, between areas within the empire and along its lengthy borders. Study these patterns and then answer the questions that follow.

QUESTIONS Discuss some of the major ways in which the Mongol Empire facilitated exchanges and interaction between civilizations and culture areas. What were the main centers of different kinds of products? What were the main directions in which ideas, goods, and new inventions flowed? Based on the discussions in the preceding chapters, who were some of the key agents of these exchanges? Why were the networks of exchange established by the Mongols so short-lived?

Map 14.3 The Mongol Empire and the Global Exchange Network

and destruction of Baghdad in 1258 (Figure 14.4). The murder of the Abbasid caliph, one of some 800,000 people who were reported to have been killed in Mongol retribution for the city's resistance, ended the dynasty that had ruled the core regions of the Islamic world since the mid-8th century. A major Mongol victory over the Seljuk Turks in 1243 also proved critical to the subsequent history of the region. It opened up Asia Minor (present-day Turkey) to conquest by a different Turkic-speaking people, the Ottomans, who would eventually become the next great power in the Islamic heartlands.

Given the fate of Baghdad, it is understandable that Muslim historians treated the coming of the Mongols as one of the great catastrophes in the history of Islam. The murder of the caliph and his family left the faithful without a central authority. The sack of Baghdad and many other cities from central Asia to the shores of the Mediterranean devastated the focal points of Islamic civilization. One contemporary Muslim chronicler, Ibn al-Athir, found the violence the Mongols had done

The Mongol Empire, 1206–1405

Figure 14.4 The Abbasid capital at Baghdad had long been in decline when the Mongols besieged it in 1258. The Mongols' sack of the city put an end to all pretenses that Baghdad was still the center of the Muslim world. The Mongol assault on Baghdad also revealed how vulnerable even cities with high and extensive walls were to the artillery and other siege weapons that the Mongols and Chinese had pioneered. In the centuries that followed, major innovations in fortifications, many introduced first in Europe, were made to counter the introduction of gunpowder and the new siege cannons.

(The Mongols under their chief Hülegü conquering Baghdad in 1258. From Rashid al-Din's "Jami' al-Tawarikh" (Compendium of Chronicles). Illuminated manuscript page, 14th c.e. Inv. Diez A Fol.70, image 7. Bildarchiv Preussischer/Art Resource, NY. Photo: Ruth Schacht. Oriental Division.)

After decades of hard campaigning in the mid-13th century, the Mongols gained control of the greatest prize of all, China, which they ruled for a century. Although the Chinese capacity to assimilate nomadic conquerors was evident from the outset, the Mongols managed to retain a distinct culture and social separateness.

Baibars [BAY-bars] (1223–1277) Commander of Mamluk forces at Ain Jalut in 1260; originally enslaved by Mongols and sold to Egyptians.

to his people so horrific that he apologized to his readers for recounting it and wished that he had not been born to see it. He lamented,

> In just one year they seized the most populous, the most beautiful, and the best cultivated part of the earth whose inhabitants excelled in character and urbanity. In the countries that have not yet been overrun by them, everyone spends the night afraid that they may yet appear there, too. . . . Thus, Islam and the Muslims were struck, at that time by a disaster such as no people had experienced before.

Given these reverses, one can imagine the relief the peoples of the Muslim world felt when the Mongols were finally defeated in 1260 by the armies of the Mamluk, or slave, dynasty of Egypt. Ironically, **Baibars** (BAY-bars), the commander of the Egyptian forces, and many of his lieutenants had been enslaved by the Mongols some years earlier and sold in Egypt, where they rose to power through military service. The Muslim victory was won with the rare cooperation of the Christians, who allowed Baibars's forces to cross unopposed through their much diminished crusader territories in Palestine. Christian support demonstrated how far the former crusader states had gone in accommodating their more powerful Muslim neighbors.

Hulegu was in central Asia, engaged in yet another succession struggle, when the battle occurred. Upon his return, he was forced to reconsider his plans for conquest of the entire Muslim world. The Mamluks were deeply entrenched and growing stronger; Hulegu was threatened by his cousin **Berke,** the new khan of the Golden Horde to the north, who had converted to Islam. After openly clashing with Berke and learning of Baibars's overtures for an alliance with the Golden Horde, Hulegu decided to settle for the kingdom he already ruled, which stretched from the frontiers of Byzantium to the Amu Darya (Oxus) River in central Asia (14.2).

The Mongol Interlude in Chinese History

Soon after Ogedei was elected as the great khan, the Mongol advance into China was resumed. Having conquered the Xi Xia and Jin empires, the Mongol commanders turned to what remained of the Song Empire in south China (Maps 14.1 and 14.2). In the campaigns against the Song, the Mongol forces were directed by **Kubilai Khan** (KOO-bluh KAHN) (Figure 14.5). Kubilai was one of the grandsons of Chinggis Khan, and he would play a pivotal role in Chinese history for the next half century. Even under a decadent dynasty that had long neglected its defenses, south China was one of the toughest areas for the Mongols to conquer. From 1235 to 1279, the Mongols were constantly on the march; they fought battle after battle and besieged seemingly innumerable, well fortified Chinese cities. In 1260, Kubilai assumed the title of the great khan, much to the chagrin of his cousins who ruled other parts of the empire. A decade later, in 1271, on the recommendation of Chinese advisors, he changed the name of his Mongol regime to a Chinese-language dynastic title, the Yuan. Although he was still nearly a decade away from fully defeating the last-ditch efforts of Confucian bureaucrats and Chinese generals to save the Song dynasty, Kubilai ruled most of China. He now set about the task of establishing more permanent Mongol control.

As the different regions of China came under Mongol rule, Kubilai passed many laws to preserve the distinction between Mongol and Chinese. He forbade Chinese scholars to learn the Mongol script, which was used for records and correspondence at the upper levels of the imperial government. Mongols were forbidden to marry ethnic Chinese, and only women from nomadic families were selected for the imperial harem. Even friendships between the two peoples were discouraged, and Mongol military forces remained separate from the Chinese. Mongol religious ceremonies and customs were retained, and a tent encampment in the traditional Mongol style was set up in the imperial city even though Kubilai usually lived in a Chinese-style palace.

Despite his measures to ensure that the conquering Mongol minority was not completely absorbed by the culture of the defeated, Kubilai Khan had long been fascinated by Chinese civilization. Even before beginning the conquest of the Song Empire, he had surrounded himself with Chinese advisors, some Buddhist, others Daoist or Confucian. His capital at **Dadu** in the north (present-day Beijing) was built on the site occupied by earlier dynasties, and he introduced Chinese rituals and classical music into his own court. Kubilai also put the empire on the Chinese calendar and offered sacrifices to his ancestors at a special temple in the imperial city. But he rebuffed the pleas of his Confucian advisors to reestablish the civil service exams, which had been discontinued by the Jin rulers.

In the Yuan era, a new social structure was established in China, with the Mongols on top and their central Asian nomadic and Muslim allies right below them in the hierarchy. These two groups occupied most offices at the highest levels of the bureaucracy. Beneath them came the north Chinese; below them, the ethnic Chinese and the minority peoples of the south. Thus, ethnic Chinese from both north and south ran the Yuan bureaucracy at the regional and local levels, but they could exercise power at the top only as advisors to the Mongols or other nomadic officials. At all levels, their activities were scrutinized by Mongol functionaries from an enlarged and much strengthened censors' bureau.

Gender Roles and the Convergence of Mongol and Chinese Culture

Mongol women remained aloof from Chinese culture—at least Chinese culture in its Confucian guise. They refused to adopt the practice of footbinding, which so limited the activities of Chinese women. They retained their rights to property and control within the household as well as the freedom to move about the town and countryside. No more striking evidence of their independence can be found than contemporary accounts of Mongol women riding to the hunt, both with their husbands and at the head of their own hunting parties. The daughter of one of Kubilai's cousins went to war, and she refused to marry until one of her many suitors was able to throw her in a wrestling match.

Figure 14.5 This portrait of Kubilai Khan, by far the most important Mongol ruler of China, emphasizes his Mongol physical features, beard and hair styles, and dress. But Kubilai was determined to "civilize" his Mongol followers according to Chinese standards. Not only did he himself adopt a Chinese lifestyle, but he had his son educated by the best Confucian scholars to be a proper Chinese emperor. Kubilai also became a major patron of the Chinese arts and a promoter of Chinese culture.

The persisting influence of Mongol women after the Mongols settled down in China is exemplified by **Chabi** (CHAH-bee), the wife of Kubilai Khan (Figure 14.6). She was one of Kubilai's most important confidants on political and diplomatic matters, and she promoted Buddhist interests in the highest circles of government. Chabi played a critical role in fostering policies aimed at reconciling the majority ethnic Chinese population of the empire to Mongol rule. She convinced Kubilai that the harsh treatment of the survivors of the defeated Song imperial family would only anger the peoples of north China and make them more difficult to rule. On another occasion, she demonstrated that she shared Kubilai's respect for Chinese culture by frustrating a plan to turn cultivated lands near the capital into pasturelands for the Mongols' ponies. Thus, the imperial couple was a good match of astute political skills and cosmopolitanism, tempered by respect for their own traditions and a determination to preserve those they found the most valuable.

The Mongol era was too brief and the number of influential Mongol women far too small to reverse the trends that for centuries had been lowering the position of women in Chinese society. As Neo-Confucianism gained ground under Kubilai's successors, the arguments for confining women multiplied. Ultimately, even women of the Mongol ruling class saw their freedom and power reduced.

Berke (1257–1266) A ruler of the Golden Horde; converted to Islam; his threat to Hulegu combined with the growing power of Mamluks in Egypt forestalled further Mongol conquests in the Middle East.

Kubilai Khan [KOO-bluh KAHN] (1215-1294) Grandson of Chinggis Khan; commander of Mongol forces responsible for conquest of China; became khagan in 1260; established Sinicized Mongol Yuan dynasty in China in 1271.

Dadu Present-day Beijing; so-called when Kubilai Khan ruled China.

Chabi [CHAH-bee] Influential wife of Kubilai Khan; promoted interests of Buddhists in China; indicative of refusal of Mongol women to adopt restrictive social conventions of Chinese; died c. 1281.

Figure 14.6 A portrait of Chabi, the energetic and influential wife of Kubilai Khan. Kubilai's determination to adopt Chinese culture without being overwhelmed by it was bolstered by the advice and example of Chabi. Displaying the independent-mindedness and political savvy of many Mongol women, Chabi gave Kubilai critical advice on how to counter the schemes of his ambitious brother and how to handle the potentially hostile scholar-gentry elite and peasantry that came to be ruled by Mongol overlords.

Marco Polo
on Chinese
Society Under
Mongol Rule DOCUMENT

Mongol Tolerance and Foreign Cultural Influence

Like Chinggis Khan and other Mongol overlords, Kubilai and Chabi had unbounded curiosity and very cosmopolitan tastes. Their generous patronage drew scholars, artists, artisans, and office-seekers from many lands to the splendid Yuan court. Some of the most favored came from Muslim kingdoms to the east that had come under Mongol rule. Muslims were included in the second highest social grouping, just beneath the Mongols themselves. Persians and Turks were admitted to the inner circle of Kubilai's administrators and advisors. Muslims designed and supervised the building of his Chinese-style imperial city and proposed new systems for more efficient tax collection. Persian astronomers imported more advanced Middle Eastern instruments for celestial observations, corrected the Chinese calendar, and made some of the most accurate maps the Chinese had ever seen. Muslim doctors ran the imperial hospitals and added translations of 36 volumes on Muslim medicine to the imperial library.

In addition to the Muslims, Kubilai welcomed travelers and emissaries from many foreign lands to his court. Like his grandfather, Kubilai had a strong interest in all religions and insisted on toleration in his domains. Buddhists, Nestorian Christians, Daoists, and Latin Christians made their way to his court. The most renowned of the latter were members of the Polo family from Venice in northern Italy, who traveled extensively in the Mongol Empire in the middle of the 13th century. Marco Polo's account of Kubilai Khan's court and empire, where he lived and served as an administrator for 17 years, is perhaps the most famous travel account written by a European (Figure 14.7). Marco accepted fantastic tales of grotesque and strange customs, and he may have taken parts of his account from other sources. Still, his descriptions of the palaces, cities, and wealth of Kubilai's empire enhanced European interest in Asia and helped to inspire efforts by navigators such as Columbus to find a water route to these fabled lands.

Social Policies and Scholar-Gentry Resistance

Kubilai's efforts to promote Mongol adaptation to Chinese culture were overshadowed in the long run by measures to preserve Mongol separateness. The ethnic Chinese who made up the vast majority of his subjects, particularly in the south, were never really reconciled to Mongol rule. Despite Kubilai's cultivation of Confucian rituals and his extensive employment of Chinese bureaucrats, most of the scholar-gentry saw the Mongol overlord and his successors as uncouth barbarians whose policies endangered Chinese traditions. As it was intended to do, Kubilai's refusal to reinstate the examination route to administrative office prevented Confucian scholars from dominating politics. The favoritism he showed Mongol and other foreign officials further alienated the scholar-gentry.

To add insult to injury, Kubilai went to great lengths to bolster the position of the artisan classes, who had never enjoyed high standing, and the merchants, whom the Confucian thinkers had long dismissed as parasites. From the outset the Mongols had shown great regard for artisans and because of their useful skills had often spared them while killing their fellow city dwellers. During the Yuan period in China, merchants also prospered and commerce boomed, partly because of Mongol efforts to improve transportation and expand the supply of paper money. With amazing speed for a people who had no prior experience with seafaring, the Mongols developed a substantial navy, which played a major role in the conquest of the Song Empire. After the conquest of China was completed, the great Mongol war fleets were used to put down pirates, who threatened river and overseas commerce. Toward the end of Kubilai's reign, the navy also launched a number of

Figure 14.7 This 15th-century manuscript illumination depicts Marco Polo and his uncle offering homage to the Great Khan. The Polos were Venetian merchants, and Marco's elders had already traveled extensively in Asia in the decade before they set off with Marco. Marco had a great facility with languages, which served him well in his journeys through Asia by land and sea. On his way home in the mid-1290s, he related his many adventures to a writer of romances while both were prisoners of the Genoese, who were fierce rivals of the Venetians. Eventually published under the title *Description of the World*, Polo's account became one of a handful of definitive sources on the world beyond Europe for the explorers of the coming age of overseas expansion. (Paris, Bibliotheque Nationale, Ms. 2810.)

overseas expeditions of exploration and conquest, which led to attacks on Japan and a brief reoccupation of Vietnam.

Ironically, despite the Mongols' suspicion of cities and sedentary lifestyles, both flourished in the Yuan era. The urban expansion begun under the Tang and Song dynasties continued, and the Mongol elite soon became addicted to the diversions of urban life. Traditional Chinese artistic endeavors, such as poetry and essay writing, languished under the Mongols in comparison with their flowering in the Tang and Song eras. But popular entertainments, particularly musical dramas, flourished. Perhaps the most famous Chinese dramatic work, **The Romance of the West Chamber,** was written in the Yuan period. Dozens of major playwrights wrote for the court, the rising merchant classes, and the Mongol elite. Actors and actresses, who had long been relegated by the Confucian scholars to the despised status of "mean people," achieved celebrity and social esteem. All of this rankled the scholar-gentry, who waited for the chance to restore Confucian decorum and what they believed to be the proper social hierarchy for a civilized people.

Romance of the West Chamber Chinese novel written during the Yuan period; indicative of the continued literary vitality of China during Mongol rule.

Initially, at least, Kubilai Khan pursued policies toward one social group, the peasants, that the scholarly class would have heartily approved. He forbade Mongol cavalrymen from turning croplands into pasture and restored the granary system for famine relief that had been badly neglected in the late Song. Kubilai also sought to reduce peasant tax and forced-labor burdens, partly by redirecting peasant payments from local nonofficial tax farmers directly to government officials. He and his advisors also developed a revolutionary plan to establish elementary education in the villages. Although the level of learning they envisioned was rudimentary, such a project, if it had been enacted, would have been a major challenge to the educational system centered on the elite that long had dominated Chinese civilization.

The Fall of the House of Yuan

Historians often remark on the seeming contradiction between the military prowess of the Mongol conquerors and the short life of the dynasty they established in China. Kubilai Khan's long reign encompassed a good portion of the nine decades in which the Mongols ruled all of China. Already

The Global Eclipse of the Nomadic Warrior Culture

As the shock waves of the Mongol and Timurid explosions amply demonstrate, nomadic incursions into the civilized cores have had an impact on global history that far exceeds what one would expect, given the small numbers of nomadic peoples and the limited resources of the regions they inhabited. From the time of the great Indo-European migrations in the formative epoch of civilized development in the 3rd and 2nd millennia B.C.E. through the classical and postclassical eras, nomadic peoples periodically emerged from their steppe, prairie, and desert fringe homelands to invade, often build empires, and settle in the sedentary zones of Eurasia, Africa, and the Americas. Their intrusions have significantly changed political history by destroying existing polities and even, as in the case of Assyria, whole civilizations. They have also generated major population movements, sparked social upheavals, and facilitated critical cultural and economic exchanges across civilizations. As the Mongols' stunning successes in the 13th century illustrate, the ability of nomadic peoples to break through the defenses of the much more populous civilized zones and to establish control over much richer and more sophisticated peoples arose primarily from the nomads' advantages in waging war.

A reservoir of battle-ready warriors and mobility have proved to be the keys to success for expansion-minded nomads. Harsh environments and ongoing intertribal and interclan conflicts for survival within them produced tough, resourceful fighters who could live off the land on the march and who saw combat as an integral part of their lives. The horses and camels on which pastoral peoples in Eurasia and Sudanic Africa relied gave them a degree of mobility that

> "With the introduction early in the 17th century of light, mobile field artillery into the armies of the warring states of central and western Europe, the nomads' retreat began."

confounded the sedentary peoples who tried to ward off their incursions. The mounted warriors of nomadic armies had the advantages of speed, surprise, and superior intelligence, gathered by mounted patrols. The most successful nomadic invaders, such as the Mongols, also were willing to experiment with and adapt to technological innovations. Some of these, such as the stirrup and various sorts of harnesses, were devised by the nomads themselves. Others, such as gunpowder and the siege engine—both Muslim and Chinese—that the Mongols used to smash the defenses of walled towns were borrowed from sedentary peoples and adapted to the nomads' fighting styles.

Aside from the military advantages of the nomads' lifestyles and social organization, their successes in war owed much to the weaknesses of their adversaries in the sedentary, civilized zones. Even in the best circumstances, the great empires that provided the main defense for agricultural peoples against nomadic incursions were diverse and overextended polities. Imperial control and protection diminished steadily as one moved away from the capital and core provinces. Imperial boundaries were usually fluid, and the outer provinces were vulnerable to nomadic raids and conquest.

Classical and postclassical empires, such as the Egyptian and Han and the Abbasid, Byzantine, and Song, enjoyed great advantages over the nomads in terms of the populations and resources they controlled. But their armies, almost without exception, were too slow, too low on firepower, and too poorly trained to resist large and well organized forces of nomadic intruders. In times of dynastic strength in the sedentary zones, well defended fortress systems and ingenious weapons—such as the crossbow, which the peasant conscripts could master fairly easily—were quite effective against nomadic incursions. Nonetheless, even the strongest dynasties depended heavily on protection payments to nomad leaders and the

by the end of his reign, the dynasty was showing signs of weakening. Song loyalists raised revolts in the south, and popular hostility toward the foreign overlords was expressed more and more openly. The Mongol aura of military invincibility was badly tarnished by Kubilai's rebuffs at the hands of the military lords of Japan and the failure of the expeditions that he sent to punish them, first in 1274 and again in a much larger effort in 1280. The defeats suffered by Mongol forces engaged in similar expeditions to Vietnam and Java during this same period further undermined the Mongols' standing.

Kubilai's dissolute lifestyle in his later years, partly brought on by the death of his most beloved wife, Chabi, and five years later the death of his favorite son, led to a general softening of the Mongol ruling class as a whole. Kubilai's successors lacked his capacity for leadership and cared little for the tedium of day-to-day administrative tasks. Many of the Muslim and Chinese functionaries to whom they entrusted the imperial finances enriched themselves through graft and corruption. This greatly angered the hard-pressed peasantry, who bore the burden of rising taxes and divisions between the nomadic peoples on their borders for their security. Even the strongest sedentary empires were shaken periodically by nomadic raids into the outer provinces. When the empires weakened or when large numbers of nomads were united under able leaders, such as the prophet Muhammad and his successors or Chinggis Khan, nomadic assaults made a shambles of sedentary armies and fortifications.

In many ways, the Mongol and Timurid explosions represented the apex of nomadic power and influence on world history. After these remarkable interludes, age-old patterns of interaction between nomads and town-dwelling peoples were transformed. These transformations resulted in the growing ability of sedentary peoples to first resist and then dominate nomadic peoples, and they mark a watershed in the history of the human community. Some of the causes of the shift were immediate and specific. The most critical of these was the devastation wrought by the Black Death on the nomads of central Asia in the 14th century. Although the epidemic was catastrophic for large portions of the civilized zones as well, it dealt the sparse nomadic populations a blow from which they took centuries to recover.

In the centuries after the Mongol conquests, the rulers of sedentary states found increasingly effective ways to centralize their political power and mobilize the labor and resources of their domains for war. The rulers of China and the empires of the Islamic belt made some improvements, but the sovereigns of the emerging states of western Europe surpassed all others in this regard. Stronger control and better organization allowed a growing share of steadily increasing national wealth to be channeled toward military ends. The competing rulers of Europe also invested heavily in technological innovations with military applications, from improved metalworking techniques to more potent gunpowder and firearms. From the 15th and 16th centuries, the discipline and training of European armies also improved. With pikes, muskets, exacting drill in the use of firearms, and trained commanders, European armies were more

than a match for the massed nomad cavalry that had so long terrorized sedentary peoples.

With the introduction early in the 17th century of light, mobile field artillery into the armies of the warring states of central and western Europe, the nomads' retreat began. States such as Russia, which had centralized power on the western European model, as well as the Ottoman Empire in the eastern Mediterranean and the Qing in China, which had shared many of the armament advances of the Europeans, moved steadily into the steppe and desert heartlands of the horse and camel nomads. Each followed a conscious policy of settling part of its rapidly growing peasant population in the areas taken from the nomads. Thus, nomadic populations not only were brought under the direct rule of sedentary empires but saw their pasturelands plowed and planted wherever the soil and water supply permitted.

These trends suggest that the nomadic war machine had been in decline long before the new wave of innovation that ushered in the Industrial Revolution in the 18th century. But that process sealed its fate. Railways and repeating rifles allowed sedentary peoples to penetrate even the most wild and remote nomadic refuges and subdue even the most determined and fierce nomadic warriors, from the Plains Indians of North America to the bedouin of the Sahara and Arabia. The periodic nomadic incursions into the sedentary zones, which had recurred for millennia, had come to an end.

QUESTIONS What are some of the major ways in which nomadic peoples and their periodic expansions have affected global history? Which of their movements and conquests do you think were the most important? Why were the Mongols able to build a much greater empire than any previous nomadic contender? Why did the Mongol Empire collapse so rapidly, and what does its fall tell us about the underlying weaknesses of the nomadic war machine?

demands for forced labor. The scholar-gentry played on this discontent by calling on the people to rise up and overthrow the "barbarian" usurpers.

By the 1350s, the signs of dynastic decline were apparent. Banditry and piracy were widespread, and the government's forces were too weak to curb them. Famine hit many regions and spawned local uprisings, which engulfed large portions of the empire. Secret religious sects, such as the **White Lotus Society,** were dedicated to overthrowing the dynasty. Their leaders' claims that they had magical powers to heal their followers and confound their enemies helped encourage further peasant resistance against the Mongols. As in the past, rebel leaders quarreled and fought with each other. For a time, chaos reigned as the Yuan regime dissolved, and the Mongols who could escape the fury of the mob retreated into central Asia. The restoration of peace and order came from an unexpected quarter. Rather than a regional military commander or an aristocratic lord, a man from a poor peasant family, **Zhu Yuanzhang,** emerged to found the **Ming dynasty,** which ruled China for most of the next three centuries.

White Lotus Society Secret religious society dedicated to overthrow of Yuan dynasty in China; typical of peasant resistance to Mongol rule.

Yuanzhang, Zhu The given name of the Hongwu emperor, the founder of the Ming dynasty.

Ming dynasty Succeeded Mongol Yuan dynasty in China in 1368; lasted until 1644; initially mounted huge trade expeditions to southern Asia and elsewhere, but later concentrated efforts on internal development within China.

Timur-i Lang Also known as Tamerlane; leader of Turkic nomads; beginning in 1360s from base at Samarkand, launched series of attacks in Persia, the Fertile Crescent, India, and southern Russia; empire disintegrated after his death in 1405.

Aftershock: The Brief Ride of Timur, the Last of the Great Nomadic Conquerors

Just as the peoples of Europe and Asia had begun to recover from the upheavals caused by Mongol expansion, a second nomadic outburst from central Asia plunged them again into fear and despair. This time the nomads in question were Turks, not Mongols, and their leader, **Timur-i Lang** (Timur the Lame, or Tamerlane) was from a noble land-owning clan, not a tribal, herding background (Figure 14.8). Timur's personality was complex. On one hand, he was a highly cultured person who delighted in the fine arts, lush gardens, and splendid architecture and who could spend days conversing with great scholars such as Muslim historian Ibn Khaldun (see the Document feature in Chapter 7). On the other, he was a ruthless conqueror, apparently indifferent to human suffering and capable of commanding his troops to commit atrocities on a scale that would not be matched in the human experience until the 20th century. Beginning in the 1360s, his armies moved out from his base at Samarkand to conquests in Persia, the Fertile Crescent, India, and southern Russia.

Although his empire did not begin to compare with that of the Mongols in size, he outdid them in the ferocity of his campaigns. In fact, Timur is remembered for little more than barbaric destruction: his armies built pyramids of skulls with the heads of those they killed. Tens of thousands of people were slaughtered after they took the city of Aleppo in Asia Minor, and thousands of prisoners were massacred as a warning to the citizens of Delhi, in north India, not to resist his armies. In the face of this wanton slaughter, the fact that he spared artisans and scientists to embellish his capital city at Samarkand counts for little. Unlike that of the Mongols, his rule brought neither increased trade and cross-cultural exchanges nor internal peace. Fortunately, his reign was as brief as it was violent. After his death in 1405, his empire was pulled apart by his warring commanders and old enemies anxious for revenge. With his passing, the last great challenge of the steppe nomads to the civilizations of Eurasia came to an end.

Figure 14.8 In 1398, Timur-i Lang's central Asian armies left Delhi completely destroyed and India politically fragmented. Most of the rest of Timur's conquests were in central Asia, so they had much less of an effect on the Islamic heartlands, Europe, or China than Mongol expansion, which extended to these areas but ironically did not include India. Perhaps Timur's most lasting legacy was through his distant descendant Babur, who founded the last and most splendid Muslim dynasty in South Asia, the Mughals, who ruled much of India from the early 16th until the late 18th century.

Global Connections

The Mongol Linkages

From the first explosion of Mongol military might from the steppes of central Asia in the early 13th century to the death of Timur in 1405, the nomads of central Asia made a stunning return to center stage in world history. Mongol invasions ended or interrupted many of the great empires of the postclassical period and also extended the world network that had increasingly defined the period. Under Chinggis Khan, the Mongols and their many nomadic neighbors were forged into the mightiest war machine the world had ever seen. With stunning rapidity the Mongols conquered central Asia, northern China, and eastern Persia (Map 14.1). Under Chinggis Khan's sons and grandsons, the rest of China, Tibet, Persia, Iraq, much of Asia Minor, and all of southern Russia were added to the vast Mongol imperium.

Although much of what the Mongols did was destructive, their forays into Europe, China, and the Muslim heartlands brought some lasting changes that were often beneficial. They taught new ways of making war and impressed on their Turkic and European enemies the effectiveness of gunpowder. Mongol conquests facilitated trade between the civilizations at each end of Eurasia, making possible the exchange of foods, tools, and ideas on an unprecedented scale. The revived routes brought great wealth to traders, such as those from north Italy, who set up outposts in the eastern Mediterranean, along the Black Sea coast, and as far east as the Caspian Sea.

land-based travel more dangerous, which quickly turned attention toward sea routes. Again, the legacy of the Mongol period was both complex and durable.

Perhaps the greatest long-term impact of the Mongol drive to the west was indirect and unintended. In recent years, a growing number of historians have become convinced that the Mongol conquests played a key role in transmitting the fleas that carried bubonic plague from south China and central Asia to Europe and the Middle East. The fleas may have hitched a ride on the livestock the Mongols drove into the new pasturelands won by their conquests or on the rats that nibbled the grain transported by merchants along the trading routes the Mongol rulers fostered between east and west. Whatever the exact connection, the Mongol armies unknowingly paved the way for the spread of the dreaded Black Death across the steppes to much of China, to the Islamic heartlands, and from there to most of Europe in the mid-14th century. In so doing, they unleashed possibly the most fatal epidemic in all human history. From mortality rates higher than 50 percent in some areas of Europe and the Middle East to the economic and social adjustments that the plague forced wherever it spread, this accidental but devastating side effect of the Mongol conquests influenced the course of civilized development in Europe, Asia, and north Africa for centuries.

Further Readings

A substantial literature has developed on the Mongol interlude in global history. The most readable and reliable biography of Chinggis Khan is René Grousset, *Conqueror of the World* (1966). Grousset has also written a broader history of central Asia, *The Empire of the Steppes* (1970). Peter Brent's more recent *The Mongol Empire* (1976) provides an updated overview and wonderful illustrations. Berthold Spuler, *History of the Mongols* (1968), supplies a wide variety of firsthand accounts of the Mongols. Timothy May's *The Mongol Art of War: Chinggis Khan and the Mongol Military System* (2000) shows that the Mongol armies had much in common with modern forces.

For the Mongols' impact on global history, see David Morgan, *The Mongols* (2006), and Peter Jackson, *The Mongols and the West* (2005). Robert S. Marshall, *Storm From the East: From Genghis Khan to Khubilai Khan* (1993), and Charles J. Halperin, *Russia and the Golden Horde: The Mongol Impact on Medieval Russian History* (1985), examine the Mongol impact on Russia. While George Vernadsky, *The Mongols in Russia* (1953), remains the standard work on that subject, some of its views are now contested. Morris Rossabi, *Kubilai Khan: His Life and Times* (1988), is by far the best work on the Mongols in China. George James Chambers, *The Devil's Horsemen* (1979), and Denis Sinor, *History of Hungary* (1957), contain good accounts of the Mongol incursions into eastern and central Europe. T. Allsen, *Mongol Imperialism* (1987), is the best account of the rise and structure of the empires built by Chinggis Khan and his successors. The fullest and most accessible summary of the links between Mongol expansion and the spread of the Black Death can be found in William H. McNeill, *Plagues and Peoples* (1976).

Recent works examining the broader interactions between agricultural and pastoral societies in Eurasia include Thomas J. Barfield, *The Perilous Frontier* (1992); Donald Ostrowski, *Muscovy*

This beautiful Chinese scroll painting depicts the Mongol emperor of China, Kublai Khan, enjoying a traditional hunting expedition with his followers, while a caravan passes in the distant hills of an empire to which these nomadic conquerors have brought peace and security.

The Mongol framework for Asian-European interactions, though brief, also facilitated other exchanges. It opened China to influences from Arab and Persian lands, and even to contacts with Europe, which came to full fruition in the centuries of indigenous Chinese revival that followed under the Ming dynasty. Europeans, particularly, gained new knowledge of Chinese products and technologies that they would quickly adapt back home. Explosive powder and printing were the most important examples. Regions more remote from the Mongols, such as Africa, lacked this kind of stimulus. Even the collapse of the Mongol network had an impact. Many societies had an interest in maintaining contacts, though China grew more wary of outsiders. But the Mongol decline made *and the Mongols: Cross-Cultural Influences on the Steppe Fronier, 1304–1589* (1998); Andrew Bell-Fialkoff, *The Role of Migration in the History of the Eurasian Steppe* (2000); and Nicola Di Cosmo, *Ancient China and Its Enemies: The Rise of Nomadic Power in East Asian History* (2004).

On the Web

The last great empire of the steppe, the Mongol Empire, can be virtually toured at http://www.kiku.com/electric_samurai/virtual_mongol/index.html. A useful portal into all things Mongolian is maintained at http://www.isidore-of-seville.com/genghis/. The founder of the Mongol Empire, Chinggis Khan, receives close attention at http://en.wikipedia.org/wiki/Genghis_Khan. A useful summary of the strategic and tactical elements of Mongol warfare can be found at http://www.uwgb.edu/dutchs/WestTech/xmongol.htm. However, the definitive examination of Mongol arms and tactics can be found at http://www.accd.edu/sac/history/keller/Mongols/empsub2.html. The role of women in Mongol society is explored at http://www.coldsiberia.org/monwomen.htm. An in-troduction to Mongol art and examples of Mongol artistic tradition is offered at http://www.asianart.com/mongolia/.

The life of Chinggis Khan's grandson, Kubilai Khan, who continued his grandfather's unbroken string of victories with his conquest of China, is described at http://www.1upinfo.com/country-guide-study/mongolia/mongolia27.html.

Virtual exhibits at http://www.royalalbertamuseum.ca/vexhibit/genghis/intro.htm and http://www.nationalgeographic.com/features/97/genghis/index.html illuminate the world of inner Asia under Mongol control. Estimates of casualties attending the Mongol conquest are offered at http://users.erols.com/mwhite28/warstat0.htm#Mongol.

The place of the Mongol Empire in world history is analyzed at http://afe.easia.columbia.edu/mongols/pastoral/pastoral.htm. Two on-line essays are also useful. The first, at http://www.luc.edu/publications/medieval/vol2/2ch13.html, surveys the intercultural contact between Europe and Asia facilitated by the Mongols, while the second, at http://afe.easia.columbia.edu/mongols/china/china.htm, focuses on the literary legacy of Mongol writing on their conquests and the social and intellectual connections made through this literature with that of European society.

AP* Test Prep

1. The only indigenous aspect of Japanese culture during the Heian era was

   (A)   the imperial administration.

   (B)   written characters.

   (C)   Shinto.

   (D)   court etiquette and protocol.

2. The group which most directly challenged Chinese influences in Japan and Vietnam during the post classical era was

   (A)   Buddhist monks and priests.

   (B)   the emperor.

   (C)   the imperial bureaucracy.

   (D)   aristocrats, landowners, and local provincial administrators.

3. The influence of Chinese culture in Korea produced all of the following EXCEPT

   (A)   legal reform.

   (B)   Chinese forms of Buddhism.

   (C)   unified resistance from the three kingdoms.

   (D)   adoption of the Chinese writing system.

4. The typical pattern for relations between China and its neighbors during the postclassical period was

   (A)   military occupation by the Chinese armies.

   (B)   for these states to acknowledge Chinese superiority and pay tribute but remain independent.

   (C)   incorporation of these states as provinces in the Chinese empires.

   (D)   to form equal alliances as partners against nomadic invaders.

5. Local Vietnamese officials identified most with the interests of

   (A)   Confucian scholar officials.

   (B)   the imperial court and high administrators.

   (C)   the peasants and local village culture.

   (D)   merchants.

6. After independence, geography, environment, and movement in Vietnam

   (A)   successfully fostered the growth of a uniform Vietnamese culture.

   (B)   have increasingly isolated Vietnam from its neighbors.

   (C)   led to cultural divisions—one in the south along the Mekong River and the other in the north along the Red River.

   (D)   led to the spread of Christianity and Islam throughout the country.

7. In Japan, Korea, and Vietnam, the class that most welcomed Chinese influence and culture was

   (A)   the local aristocrats.

   (B)   the court bureaucracy (scholar-gentry).

   (C)   peasants.

   (D)   Buddhist.

Free-Response Question

Compare the role of the elites of Japan, Korea, and Vietnam in the process of Sinification. How did borrowing from China evolve along with their own political and cultural traditions?

15 The World in 1450: Changing Balance of World Power

Key Changes in the Middle East
The Rise of the West
VISUALIZING THE PAST: Population Trends
DOCUMENT: Bubonic Plague

Western Expansion: The Experimental Phase
Outside the World Network
THINKING HISTORICALLY: The Problem of Ethnocentrism
GLOBAL CONNECTIONS: 1450 and the World

The compass is a simple enough device—something you can make yourself with an iron needle and a magnet. Yet it was also a revolutionary device, allowing sailors (and now, airplane pilots) to maintain a sense of direction no matter how dark, stormy, foggy, or unfamiliar the environment.

Though there has been debate about the origins of the compass—the instrument was clearly developed first by the Chinese. Chinese scientists may have had some knowledge of magnetic principles as early as the 1st century. Actual compasses may have been developed during the Tang dynasty. They undoubtedly originated from the discovery of naturally magnetized iron, or lodestone, which could then be used to fashion a needle that would point north. Some believe that the Chinese first used compasses in the practice of *feng shui*, which was a set of design principles by which people could align their living quarters with the forces of nature.

Compasses for navigation had been introduced by 1100. They were part of a growing Chinese effort to make contact with sources of spices and teas in southeast Asia. Prior to that point,

Chinese seagoing had been confined to coastlines, but now it became much more venturesome. Wide-ranging Chinese expeditions introduced the compass to seafarers throughout the Indian Ocean, including Arab merchants, by the 12th century. Europeans are first known to have used the compass in 1187. Europeans may have invented the compass separately, but it is far more likely that they learned about its use as a result of contacts with Arabs or Asians.

The compass was fundamental to ambitious seagoing expeditions, like the great Chinese voyages through the Indian Ocean. Along with observation of the sun and stars, the compass provided the guidance for Columbus's travels to the Americas. It changed the shape of world history by facilitating dramatic new contacts and exchanges. By the 13th century, various seagoing peoples—Malaysians, for example, as well as Europeans—were introducing improvements in the compass, making it easier to read and more stable at sea. Italian navigators introduced the compass card, which involved placing the needle over a set of indicators. Knowledge of the compass reached Scandinavia by 1300, a further step in the long process of dissemination. ■

In 1400 the world was undergoing a profound transition. This chapter highlights the main features of that transition. The principal focus is the shifting balance of power among civilizations in Asia, Africa, and Europe and how these power shifts changed the nature of international contact.

This period of transition began with the decline of Arab strength—symbolized by the fall of the last Arab caliphate in 1258—and the disruptions that Mongol incursions caused elsewhere in Asia and eastern Europe. These developments created new opportunities in the Afro-Eurasian network that had been established during the postclassical centuries, initially under Arab sponsorship. Various candidates emerged to take a new international leadership role, including, for a short time, Ming China. The Chinese expeditions showed the importance trans-regional contacts had acquired. The end of the expeditions, however, opened the way for new alignments.

The most dynamic new contender for leadership in international trade ultimately proved to be western Europe; the conditions that propelled Western civilization into this new position around 1400 are the second key theme of this chapter. The West was not yet a major power; it did not replace the Arabs or Chinese as international leaders quickly or easily. The first stages of the rise of the West were accompanied by important changes in Western civilization itself, which were beginning to take shape by 1400. At this point, Italy, Spain, and Portugal took the lead in western European outreach, a lead that they would hold for about two centuries.

Figure 15.1 Chinese oceangoing ship from expeditions in the 16th century. This was a smaller ship than those used earlier in the great voyages of the early 15th century, whose end opened opportunities for other international traders. But the Chinese maintained active commerce even after this, particularly in maintaining contacts established in the postclassical period with the Philippines and with southeast Asia.

It is also vital to note changes in societies outside the international network, in the Americas and Polynesia. New difficulties in the great American empires, in particular, reduced their ability to respond to the challenge of contact with Europeans.

Focusing on new frameworks for international contacts, this chapter inevitably deals with the question of why individual civilizations reacted differently to key forces. This was a vital period of redefinition, comparable to the centuries that led from the classical to postclassical periods, but with developments that had even wider sweep.

Amid variations and great change, the transitions around 1450 highlighted one important continuity as well: the importance of the level of contacts that had developed through the formation of the transcontinental network. A variety of societies in Africa, Asia and Europe depended on far-flung trade relations, and when one exchange network collapsed – as with the decline in travel security overland when the Mongol empires faded – another system quickly moved into place. Not only trade, but continued exchanges of technology and ideas continued to mark Afro-Eurasian relationships during the 15th century.

Key Changes in the Middle East

In 1200, the Middle East was still dominated by two powerful empires, the Byzantine in the northwest and the Islamic caliphate through much of the Middle Eastern heartland. By 1400, this structure was in disarray. The Byzantine Empire still existed, but it was in rapid decline, pressed by invading Ottoman Turks. The imperial capital, Constantinople, fell to the Turks in 1453, effectively ending the empire. Two centuries earlier, the caliphate, long sapped by increasing reliance on foreign troops and advisors, including the Turks, had fallen to Mongol invasion. Division in the Middle East, and among Arab peoples, took new forms.

The new world order that was beginning to emerge by 1400 first involved major reshuffling in the Middle East and north Africa.

1250 C.E.	1300 C.E.	1350 C.E.	1400 C.E.	1450 C.E.
1258 Mongol conquest of Baghdad; fall of Abbasid caliphate c. 1266–1337 Life of Giotto 1275–1292 Marco Polo in China 1290–1317 Famines in Europe 1291 First Italian expedition seeks route to Indies	1304–1374 Life of Petrarch; development of Italian Renaissance 1320s Spread of bubonic plague (Black Death) in Gobi desert 1320s First European use of cannon in warfare 1330s Black Death reaches China 1347 Black Death reaches Sicily 1348 Peak of Black Death in Middle East 1348–1375 Black Death spreads in Europe and Russia	1368 Mongols expelled from China; Ming dynasty	1400 End of Polynesian migrations 1405–1433 Chinese trading expeditions 1439 Portugal takes over Azores; increasing expeditions into Atlantic and along northwest African coast	1453 Ottomans capture Constantinople, fall of Byzantine Empire 1469 Union of Aragon and Castile; rise of Spanish monarchy

Social and Cultural Change in the Middle East

Kritovoulos vs. Nestor-Iskandor on the Fall of Constantinople

Culture shifted, along with politics, in this crucial region. An earlier tension in philosophy and the arts yielded to the predominance of the Islamic faith. The new piety associated with the rising Sufi movement, discussed in Chapter 7, contributed to a new religious emphasis. In literature, attention to secular themes, such as the joys of feasting and hunting, gave way to more strictly religious ideas. In philosophy, the rationalistic current encountered new attack. In Muslim Spain, philosopher Ibn Rushd (IH-buhn RUSHT) (Averroës) (uh-VEHR-oh-eez), espoused Greek rationalism, but his efforts were largely ignored in the Middle East. In fact, European scholars were more heavily influenced by his work. In the Middle East proper, a more typical philosopher, Al-Ghazali, in a book revealingly titled *The Destruction of the Philosophers,* now claimed to use Aristotle's logic to show that it was impossible to discover religious truth by human reason. Many Sufi scholars wrote excitedly of their mystical contacts with God and the stages of their religious passion. Islamic science continued, but its role diminished.

Ibn Rushd (Averroës)

Changes in society and the economy were as telling as the shifts in politics and intellectual life. As the authority of the caliphate declined, landlords seized power over the peasantry. As a result, from about 1100 onward, Middle Eastern peasants increasingly lost their freedom, becoming serfs on large estates, providing the labor and produce landlords now sought. This loss was not the peasants' alone, for agricultural productivity suffered as a result. Landlords turned to sucking what they could from their estates rather than trying to develop a more vital agriculture. Tax revenues declined, and Arab and other Middle Eastern traders began to lose ground. Few Arab coins have been found in Europe dating from later than 1100. European merchants began to control their own turf and challenge the Arabs in other parts of the Mediterranean, gaining increasing initiative in this vital trading area.

The decline of the Islamic caliphate and its economy was gradual and incomplete. It cannot be compared with the dramatic fall of the Roman Empire many centuries before. A more subtle model is needed. The reduced dynamism in trade did not take the Arabs out of major world markets, for example. Indeed, Middle Eastern commerce rebounded somewhat by 1400.

The Ottoman Empire

Finally, the political fragmentation of the Arab world did not produce prolonged confusion in the Middle East. The emerging Ottoman Turkish state soon mastered most of the lands of the old caliphate as well as the Byzantine corner, expanding into southeastern Europe. (See Chapter 21 for the development of the new Ottoman Empire.) It is important to realize that the empire was far more powerful, politically and militarily, than the caliphate had been for many centuries. It was thus more frightening to observers in neighboring civilizations such as western Europe.

A Power Vacuum in International Leadership

Even the rise of the Ottoman Empire did not restore the full international vigor that the Islamic caliphate had at the height of its powers. The empire was not the sole hub of an international network, as the caliphate had been a few centuries before.

The Mongols developed the first alternative global framework, with their interlocking holdings that included central Asia, China, and Russia, with thrusts into the Middle East and south Asia. Here was a system that actively encouraged interregional travelers and provided unprecedented opportunities for exchanges of technology and ideas—exchanges that particularly benefited western Europe through contacts with Asia. The Mongol decline, first in China, then gradually elsewhere, raised again the question of domination of international contacts and trade. The end of the Mongol empires also turned attention to seaborne trade, as the overland Asian trade routes were disrupted. Two societies, China and Europe, successively stepped up to the challenge.

Chinese Outreach and Reconsideration

For a brief time China took full advantage of the new opportunities in international trade. Rebellions in China drove out the deeply resented Mongol overlords in 1368. A rebel leader from a peasant family, Zhu Yuanzhang (joo wan-jang), seized the Mongol capital of Beijing and proclaimed a new Ming—meaning "brilliant"—dynasty that was to last until 1644. This dynasty began with a burst of unusual expansionism. The initial Ming rulers pressed to secure the borders of the Middle Kingdom. This meant pushing the Mongols far to the north, to the plains of what is now Mongolia. It meant reestablishing influence over neighboring governments and winning tribute payments from states in Korea, Vietnam, and Tibet, reviving much of the east Asian regional structure set up by the Tang dynasty. Far more unusual was a new policy, adopted soon after 1400, of mounting huge, state-sponsored trading expeditions to southern Asia and beyond.

A first fleet sailed in 1405 to India, with 62 ships carrying 28,000 men. Later voyages reached the Middle East and the eastern coast of Africa, bringing chinaware and copper coinage in exchange for local goods. Chinese shipping at its height consisted of 2700 coastal vessels, 400 armed naval ships, and at least as many long-distance ships. Nine great treasure ships, the most sophisticated in the world at the time, explored the Indian Ocean, the Persian Gulf, and the Red Sea, establishing regular trade all along the way.

Between 1405 and their termination in 1433, these expeditions were commanded by the admiral **Zheng He,** (jehng huh). A Muslim from western China, Zheng He was well suited to deal with Muslims in southeast Asia on the Indian Ocean trade route. Zheng He was also a eunuch, castrated for service at the royal court. China's Ming emperors retained a large harem of wives to ensure succession, and eunuchs were needed to guard them without threat of sexual rivalry; many gained bureaucratic powers well beyond this service. Zheng He's expeditions usually hugged the coastline, but he had an improved compass and excellent maps as well as huge vessels that contained ample supplies—even gardens—as well as goods for trade. His fleets must have impressed, even terrified, the local rulers around the Indian Ocean, many of whom paid tribute to the emperor. For while Zheng He brought gifts, he also had well armed troops on his expeditions. Several missions visited China from the Middle East and Africa. From Africa also came ostriches, zebras, and giraffes for the imperial zoo; the latter became the unicorns of Chinese fable. But Zheng He was resented by the Confucian bureaucrats, who refused even to write much about him in their chronicles.

There is no question that the course of world history might have been changed dramatically had the Chinese thrust continued, for the tiny European expeditions that began to creep down the western coast of Africa at about the same time would have been no match for this combination of merchant and military organization. Indeed, historians wonder if one expedition might have rounded Africa to at least glimpse the Atlantic. But China's emperors called the expeditions to a halt in 1433. The bureaucrats had long opposed the new trade policy, out of rivalry with other officials such as Zheng He, but there were deeper reasons as well. The costs seemed unacceptable, given the continuing expenses of the campaigns against the Mongols and establishing a luxurious new capital city in Beijing. A new emperor also wanted to differentiate his policies from those of his predecessor.

 Voyages of Zheng He

Zheng He [jehng huh] Chinese Muslim admiral who commanded series of Indian Ocean, Persian Gulf, and Red Sea trade expeditions under third Ming emperor, Yunglo, between 1405 and 1433.

This was a crucial shift. It reflected a preference for traditional expenditures rather than distant foreign involvements. Chinese merchant activity continued to be extensive in southeast Asia. Chinese trading groups established permanent settlements in the Philippines, Malaysia, and Indonesia, where they added to the cultural diversity of the area and maintained a disproportionate role in local and regional trading activities into the 20th century. Nonetheless, China's chance to become a dominant world trading power was lost, at least for several centuries.

To Western eyes, accustomed to judging a society's dynamism by its ability to reach out and gain new territories or trade positions, China's decision may seem hard to understand—the precursor to decline. But to the Chinese, it was the ambitious expeditionary flurry that was unusual, not its end. Its leaders were suspicious of any policy that would unduly elevate commercial activity as opposed to rule by the scholar-gentry. Ming emperors consolidated their rule over the empire's vast territory. Internal economic development continued as well, with no need for foreign products save for goods from southeast Asia. Moreover, Chinese products continued to be highly valued in the world market. Industry expanded, with growth in the production of textiles and porcelain; ongoing trade with southeast Asia enriched the port cities; agricultural production and population increased.

The shift in Chinese policy unintentionally cleared the way for another, in most ways less organized civilization to work toward a new international position. With the Arabs in partial eclipse and with China retreating from its brief initiative, hesitant Western expansionism, ventured before 1400, began to take on new significance. Within a century, Western explorers and traders had launched an attempt to seize international trading dominance and had expanded the international network to include parts of the Americas for the first time.

The Rise of the West

Western expansion had many causes. It must be seen as the result of growing problems as well as new strengths.

The West's gradual emergence into larger world contacts during the 15th century was surprising in many respects. Westerners remained awed by the powerful bureaucracies and opulent treasuries of empires in the traditional civilization centers such as Constantinople. Furthermore, the West was changing in some painful ways. Key features of medieval culture and society were being questioned by 1400. The church, which had long been one of the organizing institutions of Western civilization, was under new attack. Medieval philosophy had passed its creative phase. Warrior aristocrats, long a key leadership group in feudal society, softened their style of life, preferring court rituals and jousting tournaments and adopting military armor so cumbersome that real fighting was difficult.

Even more strikingly, the lives and economic activities of ordinary Europeans were in disarray. This was a time of crisis, and Europe's expanding world role could not reverse the fundamental challenges to its internal economic and demographic structure. Europeans began to suffer from recurrent famine after 1300 because population outstripped the food supply and no new food production techniques were discovered. Famine reduced disease resistance, making Europe more vulnerable to the bubonic plagues that spread from Asia.

Spread of the Black Death

Bubonic plague, or Black Death, surfaced in various parts of Asia in the 14th century. In China it reduced the population by nearly 30 percent by 1400. Following trade routes, it then spread into India and the Middle East, causing thousands of deaths per day in the larger cities. The plague's worst European impact occurred between 1348 and 1375, by which time 30 million people, one-third of Europe's population, died. The resulting economic dislocation produced bitter strikes and peasant uprisings.

Sources of Dynamism: Medieval Vitality

The Hundred Years War

How, in this context, could the West be poised for a new global role? The answer to that question is complex. First, several key advances of medieval society were not really reversed by the troubles of the decades around 1400. For example, the strengthening of feudal monarchy provided more effective national or regional governments for much of the West. The Hundred Years War between Britain and France stimulated innovations in military organization, including nonaristocratic soldiers recruited and paid directly by the royal government, that enhanced central political power. Strong regional monarchies took hold in parts of Spain and in Portugal as Christian leaders drove

Population Trends

Percentages or Proportions of Total World Population

Continents	Years				
	1000	1700	1800	1900	1975
Europe	12.2	19.6	19.7	24.0	16.3
Asia	62.9	67.6	69.3	59.8	59.2
Africa	11.2	10.0	7.8	6.8	9.9
Americas	13.4	2.1	2.7	8.9	14.0
Oceania	0.4	0.4	0.3	0.3	0.6

Source: Adapted from Dennis H. Wrong, ed., *Population and Society* (1977).

QUESTIONS The following population charts show relationships in population size, and comparative trends in population size, among the major inhabited regions of the world. Population pressure did not drive European expansion in the 15th century, because population was falling temporarily, but there were longer-term trends, from the year 1000, that might have encouraged the expansionist effort. The chart allows comparison, showing what regions experienced the greatest changes in population levels between 1000 and 1800. What might have caused these changes? Finally, the chart extends comparisons into the later 20th century.

Reading population statistics provides vital information, but it also raises questions, including ones about causation, which numbers alone cannot answer. What other data would be most helpful to put these figures in appropriate world history contexts? Which figures are more revealing: absolute numbers or percentages? Why?

Population Levels (millions)

Continents	Years				
	1000	1700	1800	1900	1975
Europe	36	120	180	390	635
Asia (includes Middle East)	185	415	625	970	2300
Africa	33	61	70	110	385
Americas	39	13	24	145	545
Oceania (includes Australia)	1.5	2.25	2.5	6.75	23
Totals	294.5	611.25	901.5	1621.75	3888

Note: Earlier figures are only estimates; they are fairly accurate indicators of relative size.
Source: Adapted from Dennis H. Wrong, ed., *Population and Society* (1977).

back the Muslim rulers of this region. The growth of cities and urban economies continued to spur the commercial side of Western society. Even the church had made its peace with such key principles of capitalism as profit-seeking. Technology continued to advance, particularly in ironwork—used for bells and weapons—and timekeeping.

In short, explaining the new Western vigor involves an understanding that some of the gains the West achieved during the Middle Ages continued even as certain characteristic medieval forms wavered.

Imitation and Commercial Problems

Two additional factors involved western Europe's international position, one a clear plus, the other a growing problem. New opportunities for imitation were an obvious advantage. The Mongol Empire established in Asia and eastern Europe in the late 13th and early 14th centuries provided new access to Asian knowledge and technology. Political stability and an openness to foreign visitors by the great khans helped Westerners learn of Asian technologies, ranging from printing to the compass and explosive powder. Western Europe had ideal access in the Mongol period. It was not disrupted by the Mongols, as eastern Europe and so many parts of Asia were, but it was in active contact, unlike sub-Saharan Africa. Internal European warfare and merchant zeal made western Europe an eager learner, for the Asian technologies promised to meet existing military and commercial needs.

Bubonic Plague

The spread of the plague in the 14th century, affecting major parts of Asia, the Middle East and Egypt, and Europe, was one of the great devastations in world history. Muslim and Christian observers described the plague and reactions to it. Ibn al-Wardi was a Muslim scholar who died of the plague in 1349; Jean de Venette was a monk who died in 1368.

Ibn al-Wardi

God is my security in every adversity. My sufficiency is in God alone. Is not God sufficient protection for His servant? Oh God, pray for our master, Muhammad, and give him peace. Save us for his sake from the attacks of the plague and give us shelter.

The plague frightened and killed. It began in the land of darkness. Oh, what a visitor! It has been current for fifteen years. China was not preserved from it nor could the strongest fortress hinder it. The plague afflicted the Indians of India. It weighted upon the Sind. It seized with its hand and ensnared even the lands of the Uzbeks. The plague destroyed mankind in Cairo. Its eye was cast upon Egypt, and behold, the people were wide-awake. It stilled all movement in Alexandria. The plague did its work like a silkworm. . . .

Then, the plague turned to Upper Egypt. It, also, sent forth its storm to Barqah. The plague attacked Gaza, and it shook 'Asqalān severely. The plague oppressed Acre. The scourge came to Jerusalem and paid the *zakāt* [with the souls of men]. It overtook those people who fled to the al-'Aqsā Mosque, which stands beside the Dome of the Rock. If the door of mercy had not been opened, the end of the world would have occurred in a moment. It then hastened its pace and attacked the entire maritime plain. The plague trapped Sidon and descended unexpectedly upon Beirut, cunningly.

This plague is for the Muslims a martyrdom and a reward, and for the disbelievers a punishment and a rebuke. When the Muslim endures misfortune, then patience is his worship. It has been established by our Prophet: God bless him and give him peace, that the plague-stricken are martyrs. This noble tradition is true and assures martyrdom. And this secret should be pleasing to the true believer. If someone says it causes infection and destruction, say: God creates and recreates. If the liar disputes the matter of infection and tries to find an explanation, I say that the Prophet, on him be peace, said: who infected the first? If we acknowledge the plague's devastation of the people, it is the will of the Chosen Doer. So it happened again and again. . . .

Among the benefits . . . is the removal of one's hopes and the improvement of his earthly works. It awakens men from their indifference for the provisioning of their final journey.

Nothing prevented us from running away from the plague except our devotion to the noble tradition. Come then, seek the aid of God Almighty for raising the plague, for He is the best helper. Oh God, we call You better than anyone did before. We call You to raise from us the pestilence and plague. We do not take refuge in its removal other than with You. We do not depend on our good health against the Plague but on you. We seek your protection, oh Lord of creation, from the blows of this stick.

Jean de Venette

This sickness or pestilence was called an epidemic by the doctors. Nothing like the great numbers who died in the years 1348 and 1349 has been heard of or seen or read of in times past. This plague and disease came from *ymaginatione* or association and contagion, for if a well man visited the sick he only rarely avoided the risk of death. Wherefore in many towns timid priests withdrew, leaving the exercise of their ministry to such of the religious as were more daring. . . . A very great number of the saintly sisters of the Hôtel-Dieu who, not fearing to die, nursed the sick in all sweetness and humility, with no thought of honor, a number too often renewed by death, rest in peace with Christ, as we may piously believe.

Some said that this pestilence was caused by infection of the air and waters, since there was at this time no famine nor lack of food supplies, but on the contrary great abundance. As a result of this theory of infected water and air as the source of the plague the Jews were suddenly and violently charged with infecting wells and water and corrupting the air. The whole world rose up against them cruelly on this account. In Germany and other parts of the world where Jews lived, they were massacred and slaughtered by Christians, and many thousands were burned everywhere, indiscriminately. . . .

But woe is me! the world was not changed for the better but for the worse. . . . For men were more avaricious and grasping than before, even though they had far greater possessions. They were more covetous and disturbed each other more frequently with suits, brawls, disputes and pleas. Nor by the mortality resulting from this terrible plague inflicted by God was peace between kings and lords established. And this fact was very remarkable. Although there was an abundance of all goods, yet everything was twice as dear, whether it were utensils, victuals, or merchandise, hired helpers or peasants and serfs, except for some hereditary domains which remained abundantly stocked with everything. Charity began to cool, and iniquity with ignorance and sin to abound, for few could be found in the good towns and castles who knew how or were willing to instruct children in the rudiments of grammar. . . .

QUESTIONS: How did Christian and Muslim reactions compare? Did the reactions suggest that the plague might have different results in the Middle East and in Europe? How did the plague relate to other major developments toward the end of the postclassical period?

De Venette from Richard A. Newhall, ed., *The Chronicle of Jean de Venette*, pp. 51–2, *Records of Civilization, Sources and Studied*, No. 50. Copyright © 1953 Columbia University Press. Ibn al-Wardi from Michael Dols, "Ibn Al-Wardi's Risalha al-Naba, A translation of major sources for the history of the black death in the Middle East," in Dickran Kouymijian, ed., *Near Eastern Numismatics, Iconography, Epigraphy and History: Studies in Honor of George C. Miles*, Beirut, University of Beirut, 1974, pp. 443–55.

The second international factor was the intensification of European problems in the existing world market and international arena. From the Crusades onward, Western elites had become used to increasing consumption of Asian luxury products, including spices such as cinnamon and nutmeg, silks, sugar, perfumes, and jewels. In exchange for the luxury items, Europeans mainly had cruder goods to offer: wool, tin, copper, honey, and salt. The value of European exports almost never equaled the value of what was imported from Asia. The resulting unfavorable balance of trade had to be made up in gold, but western Europe had only a limited gold supply. By 1400, the constant drain to Asia was creating a gold famine that threatened the whole European economy with collapse.

Furthermore, there were legitimate fears of a new Muslim threat. The Ottoman Empire was taking shape, and Europeans began to fear a new Muslim surge. Even before this, the Muslim capture of the last crusader stronghold (the city of Acre in the Middle East) in 1291 gave Muslim traders, particularly Egyptians, new opportunities to act as intermediaries in the Asian trade, for there were no Western-controlled ports left in the eastern Mediterranean. One response to this was a series of conquests by the city-state of Venice along the eastern coast of the Adriatic. A more important response was to begin exploring alternative routes to Asia that would bypass the Middle East and the feared and hated Muslim realms.

Secular Directions in the Italian Renaissance

The final major ingredient of the West's surge involved changes within the West itself, starting with Italy, where medieval forms had never fully taken hold. In 1400, Italy was in the midst of a vital cultural and political movement known as the **Renaissance** (REHN-uh-sahns), or rebirth—referring to revival of styles and themes from classical Greece and Rome. The early phases of the Renaissance stressed more secular subjects in literature and art. Religious art remained dominant but used more realistic portrayals of people and nature, and some nonreligious themes surfaced outright (Figure 15.2). The doings of human beings deserved attention for their own sake, in the Renaissance view,

Renaissance [REHN-uh-sahns] Cultural and political movement in western Europe; began in Italy c. 1400; rested on urban vitality and expanding commerce; featured a literature and art with distinctly more secular priorities than those of the Middle Ages.

Figure 15.2 Europe's new spirit amid old values. Dante, Italian writer of the 14th century, holds a copy of his great work, the *Divine Comedy*, with both religious (souls tormented in hell) and Renaissance (the solid, classical-style urban buildings of the city of Florence) symbolism greeting him. The painting was designed by Domenico di Michelina for the cathedral of Florence in 1465.

not as they reflected a divine plan. Artists and writers became more openly ambitious for personal reputation and glory. Italy was the center of initial Renaissance culture because it had more contact with Roman tradition than did the rest of Europe and because by the 14th century it led the West in banking and trade.

Human Values and Renaissance Culture

Petrarch,
Letter to
Cicero
(14th c.)

Petrarch, Francesco [PEE-trahrk] (1304–1374) One of the major literary figures of the Western Renaissance; an Italian author and humanist.

Despite its political and commercial roots, the Renaissance was first and foremost a cultural movement, launched in Florence and manifesting itself in literature and various arts. The Renaissance focused on a new interest in stylistic grace and a concern for practical ethics and codes of behavior for urban gentlemen. One leading 14th-century writer, **Francesco Petrarch,** (PEE-trahrk) not only took pride in his city and his age but explored the glories of personal achievement with new confidence.

Innovation flourished in the visual arts and music as well. The subject matter of art moved toward nature and people, including cityscapes and portraits of the rich and powerful, whether the themes were religious or secular. Florentine painter Giotto (gee-YAW-toh), led the way, departing from medieval formalism and stiffness. While still a young apprentice to the painter Cimabue (chee-mah-BOO-eh), Giotto painted a fly on the nose of one of Cimabue's portrait subjects, and it was so realistic that Cimabue repeatedly tried to swat it off before going back to work on the canvas. Other painters, beginning later in the 14th century, started to introduce perspective while using new colors and other materials. In architecture, favor shifted away from the Gothic to a classicism derived from the styles of Greece and Rome. Vivid, realistic statues complemented the new palaces and public buildings.

The impact of the early Renaissance must not be exaggerated. It had little influence outside of Italy. Even in Italy, it focused on high culture, not popular culture, and on the arts; there was little initial interest in science. And although it built on distinctive political and economic forms, it was not a full break from medieval tendencies.

Nevertheless, these new cultural currents were an important innovation in Western history. The full ramifications of the Renaissance feed into the next period of both world and Western history (see Chapter 17). The movement was only getting started by 1400. However, the wide range of Italian commerce and shipping proved to be one of the building blocks of European outreach. By the 14th century, ships, particularly from the western Italian city of Genoa, which was less well placed than Venice for eastern Mediterranean trade and the resultant links to Asia, were ready for new roles. Ambitious city-state governments encouraged new ventures, eager to collect more tax money and promote commerce as one of their explicit functions. A general "Renaissance spirit" could also spur innovation. Whereas people such as Petrarch defined human ambition mainly in cultural terms, other urban and commercial leaders, including seafarers such as Genoa's Christopher Columbus, might apply some of the same confidence and desire for personal glory to different areas, such as exploration or conquest.

The Iberian Spirit of Religious Mission

Castile Along with Aragon, a regional kingdom of the Iberian peninsula; pressed reconquest of peninsula from Muslims; developed a vigorous military and religious agenda.

Aragon Along with Castile, a regional kingdom of the Iberian peninsula; pressed reconquest of peninsula from Muslims; developed a vigorous military and religious agenda.

Along with Italy, a key center for change by the 14th century was the Iberian peninsula, where Christian military leaders had for several centuries been pressing back the boundaries of the Muslim state in Spain. Soon after 1400, major regional monarchies had been established in the provinces of **Castile** and **Aragon,** which would be united through royal marriage in 1469.

Even before the marriage between Ferdinand and Isabella, Spanish and Portuguese rulers had developed a vigorous military and religious agenda. They supported effective armies, including infantry and feudal cavalry. And they believed that government had a mission to promote Christianity by converting or expelling Arabs and Jews and by maintaining doctrinal purity within the church. Close links between church and state, portrayed in art, provided revenues and officials for the royal government. In return, the government supported church courts in their efforts to enforce moral and doctrinal purity. Later in the 15th century, this interaction led to the reestablishment of the church-run courts of the Inquisition in Spain, designed to enforce religious orthodoxy. In other words, Spain and Portugal were developing effective new governments with a special sense of religious mission and religious support. These changes promoted the West's expansion into wider world contacts.

Western Expansion: The Experimental Phase

As early as 1291, two Italian brothers, the **Vivaldis** from Genoa, sailed with two galleys through the Straits of Gibraltar, seeking a western route to the "Indies," the spice-producing areas of south and southeast Asia. They were never heard from again. Although they were precursors of a major Western thrust into the southern Atlantic, it is not even entirely clear what they meant by the "Indies." Early in the 14th century, other explorers from Genoa rediscovered the Canary Islands, in the Atlantic, populated by a hunting-and-gathering people. These islands had been known vaguely since classical times but had never been explored by Europeans. Genoese sailors also visited the Madeiras and probably reached the more distant Azores by 1351. Soon after this, ships from northeastern Spain, based in the port of Barcelona, sailed along the African coast as far south as present-day Sierra Leone.

The Basis for Wider Exploration

Until 1430, technological barriers prevented further exploration for alternative routes. Without adequate navigation instruments, Europeans could not risk wider ventures into the Atlantic. They also needed better ships than the shallow-drafted, oar-propelled Mediterranean galleys. However, efforts were under way to develop an oceangoing sailing vessel. At the same time, the crucial navigational problems were met by the compass and the astrolabe, used to determine latitude at sea by reckoning from the stars. Contacts with Arab merchants and with the Chinese provided knowledge of these devices. European mapmaking, improving steadily during the 14th century, was another key innovation. Because of these advances, as well as mistaken geographic assumptions shown on the map in Figure 15.3, Europeans were ready in the decades after 1400 to undertake voyages impossible just a century before. In 1498, the Portuguese explorer **Vasco da Gama** was the

European ventures into the Atlantic led to experiments with a new colonial system.

Vivaldis Two Genoese brothers who attempted to find a Western route to the "Indies"; disappeared in 1291; precursors of thrust into southern Atlantic.

 Spanish and Portuguese Explorations, 1400–1600

da Gama, Vasco Portuguese captain who sailed for India in 1497; established early Portuguese dominance in Indian Ocean.

Figure 15.3 Columbus is supposed to have had a copy of this world map in Spain. The map, dating from about 1489, shows the Old World as Europeans were increasingly coming to know it. Note how reachable India looked to Europeans using this map—though, of course, they had to go around Africa.

Figure 15.4 This 18th-century engraving portrays Vasco da Gama's audience with the Indian ruler of Calicut in 1498. This picture was painted well after the fact. What kind of comparison does it suggest between European and Indian societies?

Henry the Navigator Portuguese prince responsible for direction of series of expeditions along the African coast in the 15th century; marked beginning of western European expansion.

Tensions in key societies in the Americas and Oceania made them vulnerable to conquest.

first European to reach India by sea, preparing Portuguese entry into the Indian Ocean (Figure 15.4).

Colonial Patterns

Even as these wider-ranging voyages began, Westerners, led by the Spanish and Portuguese, had begun to take advantage of the new lands they had already discovered. A driving force behind both the further expeditions and the efforts to make already discovered areas economically profitable was Prince Henry of Portugal, known as **Henry the Navigator.** A student of astronomy and nautical science, Henry sponsored about a third of Portuguese voyages of exploration before his death in 1460. His mixture of motivations—scientific and intellectual curiosity, desire to spread the name of Christ to unfamiliar lands, and financial interest—reflected some of the key forces in late postclassical Europe.

Portugal by 1439 had taken control of the Azores and had granted land to colonists. Soon Spaniards and Portuguese had conquered and colonized the Madeiras and Canaries, bringing in Western plants, animals, weapons, and diseases. The result was something of a laboratory for the larger European colonialism that would soon take shape, particularly in the Americas. European colonists quickly set up large agricultural estates designed to produce cash crops that could be sold on the European market. First they introduced sugar, an item once imported from Asia but now available in growing quantities from Western-controlled sources. Ultimately, other crops such as cotton and tobacco were also introduced to the Atlantic islands. To produce these market crops the new colonists brought in slaves from northwestern Africa, mainly in Portuguese ships—the first examples of a new, commercial version of slavery and the first sign that Western expansion could have serious impact on other societies as well.

These developments about 1400 remained modest, even in their consequences for Africa. They illustrate mainly how quickly Western conquerors decided what to do with lands and peoples newly in their grasp. The ventures were successful enough to motivate more extensive probes into the southern Atlantic as soon as technology permitted. Indeed, voyages of exploration down the coast of Africa and across the Atlantic began to occur as the island colonies were being fully settled. The ventures summed up the swirl of forces that were beginning to reshape the West's role in the world: inferiorities and fears, particularly with regard to the Muslims; economic pressure from an inferior but eager position in world trade; new energies of Renaissance merchants and Iberian rulers.

Outside the World Network

Developments in the Americas and Polynesia were not affected by the new international exchange. During the next period of world history, these regions all were pulled into a new level of international contact, but a world balance sheet in 1400 must emphasize their separateness.

At the same time, several of the societies outside the international network were experiencing some new problems during the 15th century that would leave them vulnerable to outside interference thereafter. Such problems included new political strains in the leading American civilizations and a fragmentation of the principal island groups in Polynesian culture.

Political Issues in the Americas

As we discussed in Chapter 11, the Aztec and Inca empires ran into increasing difficulties not long after 1400. Aztec exploitation of subject peoples for gold, slaves, and religious sacrifices roused great resentment. What would have happened to the Aztec Empire if the Spaniards had not intervened after 1500 is not clear, but it is obvious that disunity created opportunities for outside intervention that might not have existed otherwise. The Inca system, though far less brutal than that of the Aztecs, provided ongoing tension between central leadership and local initiative. This complicated effective control of the vast expanse of the Inca domains. Here too, overextension made change likely by the 1500s—indeed, the empire was already receding somewhat—even without European intervention. At the same time, other cultures were developing in parts of the Americas that might well have been candidates for new political leadership, if American history had proceeded in isolation or if European intervention had been less sweeping.

Expansion, Migration, and Conquest in Polynesia

A second culture that was later pulled into the expanding world network involved Polynesia. Here, as in the Americas, important changes took place during the postclassical era but with no relationship to developments in societies elsewhere in the world. The key Polynesian theme from the 7th century to 1400 was expansion, spurts of migration, and conquest that implanted Polynesian culture well beyond the initial base in islands such as Tahiti, Samoa, and Fiji (Map 15.1).

One channel of migration pointed northward to the islands of Hawaii. The first Polynesians reached these previously uninhabited islands before the 7th century, traveling in great war canoes. From the 7th century until about 1300 or 1400, recurrent contacts remained between the Hawaiian Islands and the larger Society Islands group, allowing periodic new migration. From about 1400 until the arrival of European explorers in 1778, Hawaiian society was cut off even from Polynesia.

Polynesians in Hawaii spread widely across the islands in agricultural clusters and fishing villages amid the volcanic mountains. Hawaiians were inventive in using local vegetation, weaving fabrics as well as making materials and fishing nets from grass. They also imported pigs from the Society Islands—a vital source of meat but a source of devastation to many plant species unique to Hawaii. Politically, Hawaii was organized into regional kingdoms, which were highly warlike. Society was structured into a caste system with priests and nobles at the top, who reserved many lands for their exclusive use. Commoners were viewed almost as a separate people, barred from certain activities.

Thus, with a Neolithic technology and no use of metals, the Hawaiians created a complex culture on their islands. Without a written language, their legends and oral histories, tracing the genealogies of chiefly families back to the original war canoes, provided a shared set of stories and values.

Isolated Achievements by the Maori

Another group of Polynesians migrated thousands of miles to the southwest of the Society Islands, perhaps as early as the 8th century, when canoe or raft crews discovered the two large islands that today make up New Zealand. The original numbers of people were small but were supplemented over the centuries that followed by additional migrations from the Polynesian home islands. The Polynesians in New Zealand, called the Maori, successfully adapted to an environment considerably colder and harsher than that of the home islands. They developed the most elaborate of all Polynesian art and produced an expanding population that may have reached 200,000 people by the 18th century, primarily on the northern of the two islands. As in Hawaii, tribal military leaders and priests held great power in Maori society; each tribe also included a group of slaves drawn from prisoners of war and their descendants.

All these achievements were accomplished in total isolation from the rest of the world and, particularly after 1400, substantial isolation of each major island grouping from the rest of the Polynesian complex. Polynesians would be the last of the major isolated cultures to encounter the larger world currents brought forcefully by European explorers in the 18th century. When this

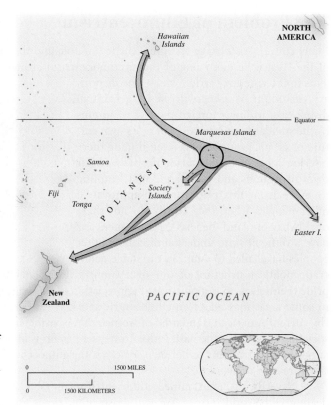

Map 15.1 Polynesian Expansion Starting in the 7th century, the Polynesians expanded north and south of their starting point in the Society Islands.

The Problem of Ethnocentrism

Many cultures encourage an ethnocentric outlook, and the culture of the West is certainly one of them. Ethnocentrism creates problems in interpreting world history. The dictionary definition of *ethnocentrism* is "a habitual disposition to judge foreign peoples or groups by the standards and practices of one's own culture or ethnic group"—and often finding them inferior. Most of us take pride in many of our own institutions and values, and it is tempting to move from this pride to a disapproval of other peoples when they clearly do not share our behaviors and beliefs. Many Americans have a difficult time understanding how other peoples have failed to establish the stable democratic political structure of our own country. Even liberals who pride themselves on a sophisticated appreciation of different habits in some areas may adopt an ethnocentric shock at the oppression (by current American standards) of women that is visible in certain societies today or in the past. Indeed, unless a person is almost totally alienated from his or her own society, some ethnocentric reactions are hard to avoid.

Nevertheless, unexamined ethnocentrism can be a barrier in dealing with world history. We will grasp other times and places better, and perhaps use our own values more intelligently, if we do not too readily dismiss cultures in which "objectionable" practices occur.

Ethnocentrism is not just an issue for modern Westerners. Civilized peoples in the past routinely accused outsiders of barbaric ways, as in the Islamic characterizations of the Mongols described in Chapter 14. But the current power of Western standards makes our own ethnocentric potential a real issue today in dealing with world history, as in the tendency to dismiss any people who did not exploit the latest available military technology as somehow inferior.

Controlling ethnocentrism does not mean abandoning all standards, as if any social behavior were as good as any other. It does involve a certain open-mindedness and sophistication. Reducing distracting levels of ethnocentrism can be aided by some spe-

> "Controlling ethnocentrism does not mean abandoning all standards, as if any social behavior were as good as any other."

cific procedures. It is important to realize that few cultures behave irrationally over long periods of time. They may differ from our taste, but their patterns respond to valid causes and problems. Our own values are not without complexity. We sometimes believe things about our own society that are not as true as we want, or in judging other societies, we forget about drawbacks in our own surroundings. Perspective on our own habits, including awareness of how other cultures might judge us, helps us restrain our ethnocentrism.

However, ethnocentrism may become a particularly strong impulse in dealing with some of the changes in world history taking shape about 1400. The West was gaining strength. Because many Americans identify with Western civilization, it is tempting to downplay some of the subtleties and disadvantages of this process or to exaggerate the extent to which the West began to organize world history more generally.

The balance of power among civilizations was beginning to shift about 1400, and it is legitimate—not simply ethnocentric—to note that the West's rise was one of the leading forces of this change. It is unnecessary to ignore the many other patterns continuing or emerging—including new vigor in several other societies—or to gloss over the motives and results that the West's rise entailed. The rise of the West was not just "good." It did not result simply from a triumph of progressive values. At the same time, avoiding ethnocentric impulses in evaluating this crucial transition period in world history does not require an anti-Western approach. Balance and perspective are essential—easy to say, not always easy to achieve.

QUESTIONS Why can ethnocentrism complicate interpretations of world history? How can one balance disapproval and understanding in dealing with practices such as female infanticide? What are some nonethnocentric ways to interpret initial European expansion?

---

encounter did come, it produced the same effects that it had in the Americas: vulnerability to disease, weakness in the face of superior weaponry and technology, and cultural disintegration.

Adding Up the Changes

It is tempting to see some sort of master plan in the various changes that began to occur around 1400. People who emphasize an ethnocentric approach to world history, stressing some inherent superiorities in Western values, might be tempted to simplify the factors involved. However, a series of complex coincidences provides a more accurate explanation, as in other cases in which the framework of world history changed substantially. Independent developments in the Americas and elsewhere figured in, as did crucial policy decisions in places such as China. Each of the separate steps can be explained, but their combination was partly accidental.

Several elements of the world history transition deserve particular attention. Technology played a role, as opportunities to copy Asian developments were supplemented by European initiative, particularly in gunnery and ship design. The role of individuals, such as Prince Henry, must be compared with the impact of more general forces, such as Europe's international trade woes.

The overall result of change affected even societies where existing patterns persisted. Sub-Saharan Africa, for example, was not experiencing great political or cultural shifts around 1400. Regional kingdoms fluctuated: the empire of Mali fell to regional rivals, but another Muslim kingdom, Songhay, soon arose in its stead, flourishing between 1464 and 1591. African political and religious themes persisted for several centuries, but the context for African history was shifting. The decline of the Arabs reduced the vitality of Africa's key traditional contact with the international network. In contrast to the Europeans, Africans had no exchange with the Mongols. Even as Africa enjoyed substantial continuity, its power relationship with western Europe was beginning to change, and this became a source of further change.

Global Connections

1450 and the World

The end of the postclassical period saw both change and continuity in the contacts that affected so many societies in Asia, Africa, and Europe. Change came in the procession of societies that served as active agents for contacts. Muslim traders and missionaries from the Middle East continued to be active, particularly in the Indian Ocean and in dealing with Africa. But the period of Mongol consolidation had introduced a new set of contacts, many of them land-based and involving Asia and Europe. Mongol overlords turned out to be delighted to encounter different ideas and to use officials from many different places and cultures. Mongol decline returned attention to sea-based contacts, particularly in the Indian Ocean. For a time, China took an unusually active role. The question of leadership in global contacts was a vital one, and by 1450 it was in flux.

The key continuity involved the interest and dependence of many societies on interregional trade and other contacts. African merchants and leaders continued to rely heavily on interactions with the Middle East. Western Europe's involvement in contacts was intensifying. Southeast Asia was increasingly drawn in, not only to trade but also to Muslim missionary efforts. The Middle East, India, and China continued to assume the availability of goods and merchant activities beyond their own borders. The diverse advantages of Afro-Eurasian contacts were widely realized, even amid changes in trade routes and regional initiatives.

The decades around the mid-15th century both reflected and intensified the transcontinental network. On the one hand, it was clear that the level of intercontinental connections developed in the post-classical period allowed increasingly rapid imitation, in areas like technology. This gave once-backward societies, like Western Europe, a chance to accelerate their economic and military development. The networks also brought sufficient advantages, in access to luxury consumer goods, that the decline of one trade system—for example, the overland Mongol routes—quickly brought forward other societies eager to develop an alternative framework—the Chinese, then the Europeans. This process, from the Mongols onward, quickened the pace of contact, from ambitious travelers like Ibn Battuta (IH-buhn BAH-too-tuh) and Marco Polo, to imaginative merchants and explorers. The stage was set for a next phase in the globalization process, in which the whole world would, for the first time, be directly involved.

Further Readings

On the world network, see Jerry Bentley, *Old World Encounters: Cross Cultural Contacts and Exchanges in Pre-Modern Times* (1993). Crucial changes in the Middle East are covered in F. Babinger, *Mehmed the Conqueror and His Times* (1978), on the Ottoman leader who captured Constantinople; and Bernard Lewis, *The Arabs in History* (1958), which offers a brisk interpretation of Arab decline. See also H. Islamoglu-Inan, ed., *The Ottoman Empire and the World Economy* (1987). On China under the early Ming dynasty, see Charles O. Hucker, *The Ming Dynasty: Its Origins and Evolving Institutions* (1978).

An important, highly readable interpretation of the West's rise in a world context is C. Cipolla, *Guns, Sails, and Empires: Technological Innovation and the Early Phases of European Expansion, 1400–1700* (1985). See also John M. Hobson, *The Eastern Origins of Western Civilization* (2004); and K. Ciggaar and M. Metcalf, eds., *East and West in the Medieval Eastern Mediterranean* (2006). An important interpretation of new Western interests is S. W. Mintz, *Sweetness and Power: The Place of Sugar in Modern History* (1985).

On the Black Death and economic dislocation, see M. W. Dols, *The Black Death in the Middle East* (1977); W. H. McNeill, *Plagues and Peoples* (1976); and the very readable B. Tuchman, *A Distant Mirror: The Calamitous 14th Century* (1979). A provocative study of relevant Western outlook is P. Ariès, *The Hour of Our Death* (1981).

J. Huizinga, *The Waning of the Middle Ages* (1973), deals with the decline of medieval forms in Europe. See also Gerald MacLean, ed., *Re-Orienting the Renaissance: Cultural Exchanges with the East* (2005). The early Renaissance is treated in D. Hay, *The Italian Renaissance* (1977); see also C. Hibbert, *Florence: The Biography of a City* (1993). For more cultural emphasis, see Guido Ruggiero, *Machiavelli in Love: Sex, Self, and Society in the Italian Renaissance* (2007); Manfredo Tafuri, *Interpreting the Renaissance: Princes, Cities, Architects* (2006); John Jeffries Martin, ed., *The Renaissance: Italy and Abroad* (2003); Richard Mackenney, *Renaissances: The Cultures of Italy c. 1300 – c. 1600* (2005); and C. Trinkhaus, *The Scope of Renaissance Humanism* (1983). On Spain, see F. Braudel, *The Mediterranean and the Mediterranean World*, 2 vols. (1978); and E. Paris, *The End of Days* (1995), on Spanish Jews and the Inquisition. On expansion in general, see Robert Bartlett, *The Making of Europe: Conquest, Colonization, and Cultural Change* (1993).

An excellent overview of the period is Janet L. Abu-Lughod's *Before European Hegemony: The World System A.D. 1250–1350* (1989).

On the Web

This transitional age in human history saw the decline of some empires, such as the Islamic Caliphate (http://www.jewishvirtuallibrary.org/jsource/History/Abassid.html), and the emergence of two great state systems, China's Ming Dynasty (http://www.wsu.edu:8080/~dee/MING/MING1.HTM) and the Ottoman Empire (http://www.friesian.com/turkia.htm and http://www.naqshbandi.org/ottomans/). It witnessed the rise of new navigational technologies, some arising in China (see the awesome animation of the Chinese naval expeditions of the early 15th century at http://www.pbs.org/wgbh/nova/sultan/media/expl_01q.html). Other naval advances were sponsored by Henry of Portugal (http://en.wikipedia.org/wiki/Henry_the_Navigator) that led up to the great European explorations (http://www.chenowith.k12.or.us/tech/subject/social/explore.html). The Web offers the means to examine the lives of some of the world's greatest explorers, including Zheng He (http://chinapage.com/zhenghe.html), Christopher Columbus (http://www.millersville.edu/~columbus/ and http://www.columbusnavigation.com/) and Vasco da Gama (http://www.fordham.edu/halsall/mod/1497degama.html), as well as the fabled travel literature of Marco Polo (http://www.silk-road.com/artl/marcopolo.shtml and http://www.korcula.net/mpolo/index.html).

Comprehensive guides to Internet sources on the peoples and peopling of the Pacific are provided at http://www.archaeolink.com/polynesian_studies_people_of_the.htm, http://www.cwis.org/wwwvl/indig-vl.html#pacific, http://www.abc.net.au/ra/pacific/people/, and http://www.otagomuseum.govt.nz/pacific_cultures.html. The early settlement of Polynesia is discussed at http://pvs.kcc.hawaii.edu/migrationspart1.html and http://pvs.kcc.hawaii.edu/migrationspart2.html. Insight into the life of one of the best-known leaders of a Pacific people, the Hawaiian King Kamehameha, and the Hawaiian monarchy may be found at http://en.wikipedia.org/wiki/Kamehameha_I, http://www.americaslibrary.gov/cgi-bin/page.cgi/aa/kamehameh, http://www.janesoceania.com/hawaii_monarchy/index.htm, http://www.hawaiian-roots.com/monarchy.htm, and http://pvs.kcc.hawaii.edu/L2life.html. The Maori of New Zealand receive treatment at http://history-nz.org/maori1.html.

This epoch also marked the climax of Muslim philosophy and science (http://www.muslimphilosophy.com/), as evidenced by the work of Ibn Rushd (www.muslimphilosophy.com/ir/default.htm, http://www.aljadid.com/classics/0320raslan.html, and http://www.fordham.edu/halsall/source/1190averroes.html). How Ibn Rushd's work and those of other Muslim scientists stimulated the Renaissance in Europe is an issue addressed at http://www.xmission.com/~dderhak/index/moors.htm and http://www.cyberistan.org/islamic/Intro13.html.

The art as well as daily activities of the period are reflected in the life and work of painters (see http://www.wga.hu/index.html), especially Giotto (http://www.ibiblio.org/wm/paint/auth/giotto/, and http://www.artchive.com/artchive/G/giotto.html), da Vinci, Raphael, and Michelangelo (http://www.artcyclopedia.com/artists/leonardo_da_vinci.html, http://www.kfki.hu/~arthp/bio/r/raphael/biograph.html, http://www.metmuseum.org/special/Leonardo_Master_Draftsman/draftsman_splash.htm, and http://www.michelangelo.com/buonarroti.html), in the work of writers such as Francesco Petrarch (http://latter-rain.com/eccle/petrarch.htm and http://history.hanover.edu/early/pet.html) and scientists such as Galileo (http://galileo.rice.edu/).

However, the period also witnessed the Hundred Years War (analyzed at http://www.vlib.us/medieval/lectures/hundred_years_war.html and as experienced at http://www.fordham.edu/halsall/source/froissart1.html), scientists struggling to deal with the Inquisition (http://es.rice.edu/ES/humsoc/Galileo/Things/inquisition.html), and the persistence of the Black Death, which can be explored at http://www.iath.virginia.edu/osheim/intro.html, http://www.brown.edu/Departments/Italian_Studies/dweb/plague/origins/spread.shtml, http://www.themiddleages.net/plague.html, and http://www.fidnet.com/~weid/plague.htm, and http://www.ucalgary.ca/applied_history/tutor/endmiddle/economy.html. War and disease, however, could not dim the civic pride, commercial zeal, and artistic achievements of the residents of Renaissance Florence, whose city can be virtually visited at the height of its glory at http://galileo.rice.edu/lib/student_work/florence96/index.html and http://mega.it/eng/egui/epo/refio.htm.

AP* Test Prep

1. What was the main purpose of the Ming maritime expeditions in the 15th century?

   (A) to create Chinese dominance on the Indian Ocean Basin trade network by defeating the Ottoman naval power

   (B) to map unknown realms of the Indian Ocean Basin and possibly the Atlantic Ocean

   (C) to demonstrate China's power so as to more easily maintain its tributary empire along the Indian Ocean Basin

   (D) to eliminate pirates from the eastern seas and the India Ocean

2. Why did the Ming maritime expeditions end?

   (A) The Chinese fleets were defeated by the Ottoman naval forces.

   (B) Confucian administrators decided that other investments were more important.

   (C) The emperor concluded that the imperial tributary system was outdated.

   (D) China decided to isolate itself from the outside world.

3. The long-term importance of the cultural and political movement known as the Renaissance in western Europe lies in its

   (A) influencing global trends in visual art, architecture, and literature.

   (B) emphasis on secularism and individual human capacities in the arts and politics.

   (C) close alliance with the Catholic church and Catholic monarchs such as Ferdinand and Isabella.

   (D) its combination of Greco-Roman, Indian, and Islamic knowledge to create new political theories of power.

4. The major barrier to west European maritime expansion prior to the 15th century was the

   (A) comparatively low level of European maritime technology.

   (B) lack of interest by western European rulers in acquiring territory that was not physically attached to their homeland.

   (C) the defensive alliances formed between Arab and Mongol states to prevent intruders in the Indian Ocean Basin.

   (D) preoccupation and expenses related to the religious civil wars that wracked western Europe.

5. The first western European nation to establish an overseas empire in the 15th century was

   (A) the Netherlands.

   (B) Portugal.

   (C) England.

   (D) Spain.

6. "A series of complex coincidences" in the 1400s would help a group of relatively weak Western European countries to be able to expand and conquer vast tracts of land. Which of the following is NOT one of those "complex coincidences"?

   (A) rapid population growth in Western Europe

   (B) integration and adaptation of technologies acquired from Asia in the Mongol period

   (C) political crises and weaknesses in the Aztec and Incan empires

   (D) a power vacuum in the Indian Ocean Basin trade network

Free-Response Question

Assess the changes and continuities in the economies of one of the regions below in the post-classical period, c. 600–c. 1450. Americas; East Asia; South Asia. Southwest Asia; Western Europe (to Russia/Balkans)

The Postclassical Period, 500–1450: New Faith and New Commerce

Contacts and Their Limits

New contacts form a key part of the postclassical period. Both trade and missionary exchanges brought about new connections among people in Asia, Africa, and Europe. Southeast Asia, for example, began to contribute spice production to world trade. In turn, by the end of the postclassical period, merchants and missionaries were importing Islam into the region.

Many world historians now argue that, because of the new patterns of contact, the basic dynamic of world history was reshaped around 1000 C.E. Before that point, most societies had separate patterns of activity, and contacts with other cultures were either superficial—a few luxury goods exchanged—or very gradual in their impact. After that point, contact became the name of the game, and a growing number of societies vigorously sought it.

A key aspect of the postclassical period involved explicit efforts at imitation. Trade and sometimes missionary connections brought outlying parts of the Afro-Eurasian world into interaction with regions that had complex cultural, manufacturing, and urban systems. Not surprisingly, many of these societies decided to copy—

selectively—in order to advance. Japan copied China; Russia copied the Byzantines; western Europe and parts of Africa borrowed widely (though differently) from Arab society. Mostly, societies imitated one another's technology and cultural forms (such as alphabets). It proved harder to copy political structures, and several ambitious efforts (particularly in Japan and western Europe) failed. Peoples in the Americas and in Pacific Oceania had contact with one another, but they remained isolated from Afro-Eurasia. Here were important exceptions to the patterns of exchange elsewhere.

While contacts increased, they hardly homogenized Afro-Eurasia. Societies on the peripheries, like western Europe or Russia, simply lacked the manufacturing sophistication or urban wealth required to imitate the leading centers of Asia. In other instances, explicit decisions were made to reject foreign influences. After a brief period of enthusiasm for Chinese political institutions, for example, Japanese leaders decided they did not want to imitate some aspects of Chinese society—for example, its bureaucracy. Despite ongoing trade and important new interactions with Islam, the majority of Indians remained Hindu and lived according to its distinctive caste system. And of course Europeans, while imitating some aspects of Islamic society, had no desire for religious change—unless it involved imposing their religion on Muslims. Religion, indeed, could create new barriers among people.

Long-distance travel increased in the postclassical centuries. Ibn Battuta, a north African, traveled almost 90,000 miles in his lifetime, visiting various parts of Africa and Asia as well as islands in the Indian Ocean. Toward the end of this period, several western Europeans traveled widely, as did some Chinese. Greater travel was a testimony to the power of world trade and the new religious map—Ibn Battuta, for example, journeyed mainly within the Islamic world, which gave him plenty of scope.

While travel reflected and encouraged contact, it also brought people to the limits of tolerance. While he praised the piety of his hosts in sub-Saharan Africa, Ibn Battuta was appalled by the freedom that women there enjoyed. This was not his view of a fully Muslim society. European travelers to China, at the end of the period, might hope to convert the Chinese or to imitate some of their achievements—in technology, for example—but they had a strong sense of the profound differences between European and Chinese culture. ■

PART IV

The Early Modern Period, 1450–1750: The World Shrinks

Chapter 16   The World Economy

Chapter 17   The Transformation of the West, 1450–1750

Chapter 18   The Rise of Russia

Chapter 19   Early Latin America

Chapter 20   Africa and the Africans in the Age of the Atlantic Slave Trade

Chapter 21   The Muslim Empires

Chapter 22   Asian Transitions in an Age of Global Change

THE OVERVIEW: THE WORLD MAP CHANGES

These maps depict two of the big changes in world history that occurred between 1450 and 1750. Over these centuries, a number of new empires came into being, replacing smaller political units characteristic of the preceding postclassical period. Several European countries acquired overseas empires the first time this option had ever been so dramatically developed, while new land-based empires arose in Asia and eastern Europe. The Russian and Ottoman empires extended over both European and Asian territory, while the new Mughal Empire ruled much of the Indian subcontinent.

The second big change involved trade routes. In 1450 international trade focused on exchanges among Asia, Africa, and Europe across some overland routes but also via seaways in the Indian Ocean and the Mediterranean Sea. By 1750, oceangoing routes across the Pacific and particularly the Atlantic had become increasingly important, although the Indian Ocean sea routes remained significant. For the first time, the Americas and, soon, Pacific Oceania were caught up in global exchanges, with results not only in these regions but for the rest of the world as well.

Change, of course, is never complete. Even as world geography shifted fundamentally, some political features persisted during the three early modern centuries. Trade routes also maintained some holdovers from the past.

Big Concepts

The contemporary period in world history organizes around global themes. A key concept involves the dissolution of global empires through decolonization. This was a major change, extending particularly from the 1920s through the 1970s that in some ways pushed back global forces in favor of new levels of nationalism and regional assertion. The contemporary era also, from 1914 onward, saw new global wars and conflict—including the recent global tensions associated with terrorism, another Big Concept for the period as a whole. New global institutions also emerged, at various points, in business, politics, finance, and even culture, a third organizing concept. Finally, particularly from the late 1940s onward and increasingly fueled by new technologies and explicit policies alike, new iterations of globalization form the final Big Concept for world history's newest period.

TRIGGERS FOR CHANGE

Several developments sparked the beginning of the early modern period, distinguishing it from the postclassical period that preceded it. The first was the revival of empire building. A striking example of this

Legend:
- Major Political Units, c.1450
- The Silk Road } routes opened during the "Mongol Peace" c. 1250–1350
- Other Route }
- Arab Trade Routes
- Chinese Trade Routes
- Genoese Trade Routes
- Main Hanseatic Trade Routes
- Venetian Trade Routes
- Other Trade Routes

Major Political Units of the World, c. 1450

Legend:
- Major Political Units, c.1750
- Portuguese Trade Routes
- Spanish Trade Routes
- Dutch Trade Routes
- Other Trade Routes

Major Political Units of the World, c. 1750

development involved the Ottoman Turks, who conquered Constantinople, the capital of the Byzantine Empire. Soon the Ottomans extended their rule over most Byzantine territories and beyond, putting a Muslim power in charge of one of the great Christian cities and territories of the past. Worried Christian leaders elsewhere in the world turned to new activities to compensate for the loss of influence and territory. The second development visible by 1450—the steady progression of explorations by Europeans along the Atlantic coast of Africa—was motivated in part by the desire to find ways to trade with east Asia that would circumvent the centers of Islamic power. New European outreach would soon have wider effects.

New military technologies constituted the third development that played a vital role in defining the new framework for this period. European mariners began to use compasses and other navigational devices, first introduced by the Chinese and Arabs. Europeans also learned how to design better sailing ships. The most important new military technology was the growing use of guns and gunpowder, another Chinese invention now adapted by Europeans and others. New guns played a vital role in the creation of new empires both on land and overseas. Guns also affected political patterns within Africa, Japan, and Europe, though with less sweeping results.

Larger, sturdier ships, armed with cannon and featuring greater shipping capacity, sailed the new trade routes across the Atlantic and Pacific oceans. Europeans exercised disproportionate dominance over these routes, and they employed the new military technologies in establishing their new overseas empires.

THE BIG CHANGES

The changes in world empires and trade routes depicted on the maps on page 355 and the effects of new naval and military technologies highlight the distinctive features of the early modern period. Every major society reacted differently, depending on world position and existing tradition. In general, however, these developments led to three broad changes: (a) the forging of a new global economy and through this the unfolding of an initial phase of globalization; (b) new biological exchanges of food, animals, and people; and (c) the new importance of large political units and their diplomatic and military interactions.

A New Global Economy and Proto-Globalization

International trade increased, for the first time including the Americas in the exchange. This was a major step in bringing the various regions of the world

1300 C.E.	1400 C.E.	1500 C.E.	1550 C.E.
1281 Founding of Ottoman dynasty	1405–1433 Chinese expedition period	1500–1600 Europe's commercial revolution	1552 Russia begins expansion in central Asia and western Siberia
1350s Ottoman invasion of southeastern Europe	1434–1498 Portuguese expeditions down west African coast	1501–1510 Safavid conquest of Iran	1570 Portuguese colony of Angola (Africa)
1368 Ming dynasty in China	1441 Beginning of European slave trade in Africa	1509 Spanish colonies on American mainland	1571 Ottoman naval defeat of Lepanto
1390 Ming restrictions in overseas trade	1453 Ottoman conquest of Constantinople	1510–1511 Portugal conquers Goa (India), Malacca (Malaysia)	1590 Hideyoshi unifies Japan
	1480 Moscow region free of Mongol control	1517–1541 Protestant Reformation (Europe)	1591 Fall of Songhay (Africa)
	1492 Columbus expeditions	1519–1521 Magellan circumnavigates globe	
	1498–1499 Vasco da Gama expedition opens seas to Asia	1519–1524 Cortes conquers Mexico	
		1520–1566 Suleiman the Magnificent (Ottoman)	
		1526 Babur conquest in northern India (Mughal)	
		1533 Pizarro wins Peru	
		1548 Portuguese government in Brazil	

closer together and exposing them more widely to international influences. The result was a process called proto-globalization—a foretaste of the fuller range of contacts now called globalization but (hence the term "proto") in a more preliminary sense.

Globalization involves intense and varied interactions among regions that help shape human lives; proto-globalization in this period helped set this process in motion. Several changes separated proto-globalization from the transcontinental network that had emerged in the postclassical period—though world trade still relied on some of the exchanges developed earlier, such as trade between East Africa and the Middle East. Most obviously, commerce was now global, including all major parts of the world and not just the three continents of Africa, Asia, and Europe. The intensity of contacts increased as well: trade, and production for trade, now involved more people, more effort, and it began to help shape political and social systems as well as commercial ones. Migration across oceans, some of it forced, was a new phenomenon as well. New consumer tastes developed in several societies that depended on goods imported from distant areas, going well beyond patterns in the earlier transcontinental network. Here, clearly, was an important step toward fuller globalization.

There was, however, still a gap between proto-globalization and the global patterns we see today.

The new technologies that would revolutionize global travel and communication were still in the future. Trade contacts were important, but they had not yet reached more contemporary levels. There were no internationally shared games or political standards, in contrast to the surge of cultural and political globalization that would emerge later on. Like contemporary globalization, proto-globalization brought both advantages and disadvantages, depending on the groups and regions involved. Those who profited form the new system would ultimately help prepare additional kinds of global connections.

Biological Exchange

The inclusion of the Americas global trade set in motion a number of biological exchanges of enormous consequence. Foods from the Americas, like corn and the potato, began to be grown in Asia and, later, Europe. Combined with local improvements in agriculture, these new foods resulted in population increases. Europeans introduced new diseases into the Americas and Pacific island territories, decimating the native populations. Population loss encouraged new migrations, particularly from Europe and Africa, into the Americas. The massive African slave trade was in part a response to a labor shortage in the Americas. New animals, like the horse, greatly altered life in the

1600 C.E.	1650 C.E.	1700 C.E.	1750 C.E.
1600 Dutch and British merchants begin activity in India	1652 Dutch colony South Africa	1713 New Bourbon dynasty, Spain	1756–1763 Seven Years War
1600–1690 Scientific Revolution (Europe)	1658–1707 Aurangzeb reign, beginning of Mughal decline	1722 Fall of Safavid dynasty (Iran)	1763 Britain acquires "New France"
1603 Tokugawa shogunate	1682–1699 Turks driven from Hungary	1759–1788 Reforms of Latin American colonial administration	1764 British East India Company controls Bengal (India)
1607 First British colonies in North America	1689–1725 Peter the Great (Russia)		1770s European–Bantu conflicts in southern Africa
1608 First French North American colonies			1772–1795 Partition of Poland
1637 Russian pioneers to Pacific			1775–1783 American Revolution
1640s Japan moves into isolation			1781 Indian revolts in New Grenada and Peru (Latin America)
1641 Dutch colonies in Indonesia			1792 Slave uprising in Haiti
1642–1727 Isaac Newton			
1644 Qing dynasty, China			

Americas. These biological exchanges, called the "Columbian exchange," altered many relationships among populations. New foods helped generate population increase worldwide, trumping the devastation wrought by new diseases. But new diseases and unprecedented levels of death were agonizing realities for many regions.

New Empires

The gunpowder empires formed large political units. Building and maintaining these new political structures required huge energies and huge expenses. New land-based empires in India, the Middle East, southeastern Europe, and Russia challenged political traditions in their imperial territories, while Spain, Portugal, France, England, and the Netherlands exerted pressure on their new overseas holdings.

The new empires also formed what would later be called "multinational" units, embracing different cultural and ethnic groups. The solidity of the multinational approach would be an important world history issue for the future.

The three main developments—the new global economy, the biological exchange, and the emergence of new empires—involved considerable shifts in world power. The world position of western Europe increased most obviously. Russia gained a new role as well. New masters ruled over many parts of the Americas, while portions of Africa found themselves immersed in novel orbits. Systematic patterns of inequality began to characterize some of the societies that supplied foods and raw materials to western Europe. Europe became wealthier and ever more powerful as it supplied processed goods and commercial services to these same regions, but several Asian societies headed by China also gained new wealth.

CONTINUITY

Change is never complete. Even as world geography shifted, some political features persisted during the three centuries of the early modern period. Some existing trade routes continued to be important avenues of global exchange.

Many societies reacted to the big changes of the early modern period by preserving key features of their past. No sweeping, global cultural change occurred during this era. Notable developments took place within individual societies, such as the new in-

fluence of science in western Europe or the rise of Japanese Confucianism. The spread of world religions continued, with Islam reaching southeast Asia and parts of southeastern Europe and, even more dramatically, with conversions to Christianity in the Americas. But cultural stability described much of the world, and global contacts did not overturn regional culture patterns.

No systematic changes occurred in gender relations in the early modern period. The new African slave trade affected gender balances on both sides of the Atlantic. More men than women were seized in Africa; as a result, the lack of adequate numbers of husbands encouraged African polygamy. New ideas sparked some debate over women's conditions in western Europe, though little real change. Relations between men and women in most other societies adhered to established patriarchal patterns.

Aside from the new developments in the military sphere, there were no technological breakthroughs until after 1750. Many societies participated only gradually in the use of guns and gunnery. Manufacturing techniques changed modestly, and little change took place in agriculture beyond the foodstuffs.

While political change, signaled by the rise of empires, was more general, several societies emphasized continuity in this realm as well. China prided itself on reviving and then maintaining its system of government. Many African societies preserved earlier traditions of divine kinship.

IMPACT ON DAILY LIFE: WORK

Changes of the early modern period profoundly affected ordinary people in many parts of the world. Indians in the Americas died by the thousands as European and African immigrants brought diseases like smallpox and measles. Europeans used silver to pay for desirable Chinese goods. Flush with new wealth, the Chinese government began to require that taxes be paid in silver, thus compelling ordinary Chinese to find new ways to obtain money. Often such efforts were unsuccessful, and as a result many Chinese fell ever deeper into poverty. Millions of Africans were seized from their homes and subjected to a terrifying and often deadly passage to the Americas. Those who managed to survive the voyage discovered that they were now compelled to live out their lives as slaves.

The most general social change during the early modern period was a growing pressure to work harder. The early modern world was increasingly commercial and crowded. Population increases in some regions demanded more from workers to help sustain larger families and villages. Many manufacturers and landowners tried to force their workers to increase their pace. The new forms of race-based slavery in the Americas placed greater emphasis on production. In western Europe, for example, Protestantism preached a work ethic that convinced many people that labor was a way to demonstrate God's grace.

People of all ages responded to the pressure to work harder. Child labor increased in many regions. Many European children were pressed into service as indentured laborers; for example, whole groups of orphans might be transported to work sites. By the 18th century, London orphans might be sent to work in new English factories or to North America as indentured servants. Even in old age, adults had to work if they wanted to survive. Master artisans, from makers of porcelain in China to gunsmiths in Europe, tried to compel their workers and apprentices to turn out more product. The pressure to work harder and longer was a personal side to the systemic changes that were reshaping the world.

The name commonly given to this period—early modern—captures complexity. The period is more recognizably modern than its predecessor. The renewed emphasis on political structures may strike a modern chord as well. But if modern, this was still early: many features, including the continued dominance of traditional agriculture even in the most advanced economies, make it clear that there were still many changes to come in world history after 1750.

TRENDS AND SOCIETIES IN THE EARLY MODERN PERIOD

The chapters that follow examine the differing reactions to the major developments and changes of the early modern period. Chapter 16 offers an overview of the new global trading patterns that followed from the changes in naval technology and warfare. New trading opportunities and colonial expansion were closely related to significant changes within western Europe, the subject of Chapter 17. European changes would ultimately affect other parts of the world as well. Russia, selecting aspects of Western society as a model for change, developed one of the most novel gunpowder empires, with major impact on the power balance in eastern Europe, east Asia, and part of the Muslim world. The story of Russia's rise is told in Chapter 18. Chapters 19 and 20 return to the Atlantic world. The early modern era was a formative period for a new society in Latin America, born of interactions among native populations, Europeans, and Africans. Chapter 21, on the new Muslim states in the Middle East and southern Asia, concentrates on the emergence of other gunpowder empires. East Asia responded in its own, largely successful way to the new world economy. In these areas internal dynamics had more to do with developments that occurred between 1450 and 1750.

Each of the chapters in this part deals with reactions to world trade, biological exchange, and new pressures on labor. Each also highlights the diversity of patterns emerging in different parts of the world, depending on cultural orientation and shifts in positions of world power. ■

16 The World Economy

The West's First Outreach: Maritime Power

THINKING HISTORICALLY: Causation and the West's Expansion

Toward a World Economy

VISUALIZING THE PAST: West Indian Slaveholding

Colonial Expansion

DOCUMENT: Western Conquerors: Tactics and Motives

GLOBAL CONNECTIONS: The World Economy—And the World

H ow did silver mined by conscripted South American Indians change China's tax system? Silver quickly became the global currency of the early modern period. Production and use of silver show the power of the new **world economy** emerging after 1500. Silver had long been valued, of course, but new sources of production made it a commonly traded commodity. Japanese mines raised their output, trading with Europe and China. But it was European discoveries of silver in the Americas that really turned the tide. Mexican silver mines were important, but the big find, in the mid-16th century, was at Potosi, in Bolivia, where there was an enormous vein of ore. (Figure 16.1) Desperate for labor, the Spanish revived *mita*—the Inca system of drafting workers for short stints. By 1600 there were 150,000 miners at Potosi, more than a third of them conscripted through the mita system.

Latin American silver was a godsend to Europeans. The Spanish crown kept a fifth of the silver its colonies produced, and this was its chief gain from the American colonies. Silver allowed Spain to build massive armies and grand new public buildings. But most of the silver sent to Europe passed through Spain to merchants elsewhere. They, in turn, used silver primarily to buy Asian goods that had long been sought, such as Indian spices and Chinese porcelain and silk. The Spanish also sent considerable silver to the Philippines, where it was traded for Chinese products sent to elites in the Americas and Europe. Silver greased the wheels of international commerce, allowing Europeans to buy Asian imports that could not otherwise have been afforded.

China and India were the largest recipients of New World silver—a clear sign of Asia's dynamism in the new world economy. Silver encouraged economic growth in Asia. It began to replace paper money. Merchants required silver even for purchases of common items like food. The Ming dynasty required periodic tax payments in silver. This reduced the number of tax collections (because each payment was now more valuable)—a reform known as "one whip of the lash." Silver imports helped sustain a standard of living in China that, into the early 19th century, was superior to that of western Europe.

But there were also worries. Many Chinese observers thought that silver was creating a wider gap between rich and poor, and they pointed out that the poor had to struggle to find the silver needed to pay their taxes. A few Europeans mused about expending so much effort to obtain silver that would only be swallowed up in Asia, but most agreed that the new consumer goods were well worth the trouble. A very few Europeans, but undoubtedly lots of ordinary Latin Americans, worried about the harsh working conditions in the mines. ■

This chapter deals with the consequences of some key developments long celebrated in American school texts: the voyages of Columbus and other explorers and the empires built by European conquerors and missionaries. The result was a power shift in world affairs, but another set of crucial developments in world history also resulted: the redefinition of interchanges among major societies in the world.

The story is not, however, simply the familiar one. European countries did play a disproportionate role in causing global change, particularly the huge shifts affecting the Americas and Africa. But African and Asian contributions were active as well.

European merchant fleets seized control of key international trading routes. Initial Spanish and Portuguese leadership was challenged by growing efforts from Britain, France, and Holland.

The West's First Outreach: Maritime Power

Various European leaders, particularly merchants but also some princes and clergy, had become increasingly aware of the larger world around them since 1100. The Crusades brought knowledge of the Islamic world's superior economy and the goods that could be imported from Asia. The Mongol

Figure 16.1 This engraving of the Potosi silver mine in 1590 shows a cut-away view of a mountain. Inside, Native American miners work by torchlight.

Empire, which sped up exchanges between the civilizations of Asia, also spurred European interest. The fall of the khans in China disrupted this interchange, as China became once again a land of mystery to Europeans. Europe's upper classes had by this time become accustomed to imported products from southeast Asia and India, particularly spices. These goods were transported to the Middle East in Arab ships, then brought overland, where they were loaded again onto vessels (mainly from Genoa and Venice, in Italy) for the Mediterranean trade.

Europeans entered into this era of growing contacts with several disadvantages. They remained ignorant of the wider world. Viking adventurers from Scandinavia had crossed the Atlantic in the 10th century, reaching Greenland and then North America, which they named Vinland. However, they quickly lost interest beyond establishing settlements on Greenland and Iceland, in part because they encountered indigenous warriors whose weaponry was good enough to cause them serious problems. Many Europeans were also fearful of distant voyages lest they fall off the world's edge.

As Europeans launched a more consistent effort at expansion from 1291 onward, they were pressed by new problems: fear of the strength of the emerging Ottoman Empire and the lack of gold to pay for Asian imports. Initial settlements in island groups in the south Atlantic fed their hopes for further gains. However, the first expeditions were limited by the small, oar-propelled ships used in the Mediterranean trade, which could not travel far into the oceans.

New Technology: A Key to Power

During the 15th century, a series of technological improvements began to change the equation. Europeans developed deep-draft, round-hulled sailing ships for the Atlantic, capable of carrying heavy armaments. They were using and improving the compass. Mapmaking and other navigational devices improved as well. Finally, European knowledge of explosives, another Chinese invention, was

1400 C.E.	1500 C.E.	1600 C.E.	1700 C.E.
1394–1460 Life of Prince Henry the Navigator	1509 First Spanish colonies on Latin American mainland	1607 First permanent British colony in Virginia	1744 French–British wars in India
1433 China ends its great expeditions	1514 Portuguese expedition to Indonesia	1608 First French colonies in Canada; England gains first trading concession in India	1756–1763 Seven Years War in Europe, India, and North America
1434 Portugal extends expeditions along west African coast	1519–1521 Magellan circumnavigates the globe	1641 Dutch begin conquests of Java (Indonesia)	1763 British acquire New France
1488 Portuguese round Cape of Good Hope	1534 First French explorations in Canada	1652 Dutch launch colony in southern Africa	1775–1783 American Revolution
1492 Columbus's first expedition	1542 Portuguese reach Japan		1756 "Black hole" of Calcutta
1497–1498 Vasco da Gama sails to India	1562 Britain begins its slave trade		1764 East India Company controls Bengal
	1571 Ottoman fleet defeated in Battle of Lepanto		
	1588 British defeat Spanish Armada		
	1597 Japan begins isolation policy		

adapted into gunnery. European metalwork, steadily advancing in sophistication, allowed Western metalsmiths to devise the first guns and cannons. Though not very accurate, these weapons were awesome by the standards of the time (and terrifying to many Europeans, who had reason to fear the new destructive power of their own armies and navies). The West began to forge a military advantage over all other civilizations of the world, at first primarily on the seas—an advantage it would retain into the 20th century. With an unprecedented ability to kill and intimidate from a distance, western Europe was ready for its big push.

Cape of Good Hope   Southern tip of Africa; first circumnavigated in 1488 by Portuguese in search of direct route to India.

Portugal and Spain Lead the Pack

The specific initiative came from the small kingdom of Portugal, whose Atlantic location made it well suited for new initiatives. Portugal's rulers were drawn by the excitement of discovery, the harm they might cause to the Muslim world, and a thirst for wealth—a potent mix. A Portuguese prince, Henry the Navigator (Figure 16.2), organized a series of expeditions along the African coast and also outward to islands such as the Azores. Beginning in 1434 the Portuguese began to press down the African coast, each expedition going a little farther than its predecessor. They brought back slaves, spices such as pepper, and many stories of gold hoards they had not yet been able to find.

Later in the 15th century, Portuguese sailors ventured around the **Cape of Good Hope** in an attempt to find India, where direct contact would give Europeans easier access to luxury cloths and spices. They rounded the cape in 1488, but weary sailors forced the expedition back before it could reach India. Then, after news of Columbus's discovery of America for Spain in 1492, Portugal redoubled its efforts, hoping to stave off the new Spanish competition. Vasco da Gama's fleet of four ships reached India in 1498, with the aid of a Hindu pilot picked up in east Africa. The Portuguese mistakenly believed that the Indians were Christians, for they thought the Hindu temples were churches. They faced the hostility of Muslim merchants, who had long dominated trade in this part of the world, and they brought only crude goods for sale, like iron pots. But fortunately they had some gold as well. They managed to return with a small load of spices. A later trip involved more violence, as Europeans substituted force for their lack of attractive items for world trade. Da Gama used ships' guns to intimidate, and his forces killed or tortured many Indian merchants to set an example.

Figure 16.2 Prince Henry the Navigator financed annual expeditions down the western coast of Africa in an effort to find a sea route to the Indies, establish trade with Africa, and find the fabled Christian kingdom of Prester John.

Map 16.1 Spain and Portugal: Explorations and Colonies   In the early years of exploration, Spanish and Portuguese voyagers surveyed much of the coast of South America and some choice ports in Africa and Asia.

Da Gama's success set in motion an annual series of Portuguese voyages to the Indian Ocean, outlined in Map 16.1. One expedition, blown off course, reached Brazil, where it proclaimed Portuguese sovereignty (Figure 16.3). Portugal began to set up forts on the African coast and also in India—the forerunners of such Portuguese colonies as Mozambique, in east Africa, and Goa, in India. By 1514 the Portuguese had reached the islands of Indonesia, the center of spice production, and China. In 1542 one Portuguese expedition arrived in Japan, where a missionary effort was launched that met with some success for several decades.

Meanwhile, only a short time after the Portuguese quest began, the Spanish reached out with even greater force. Here also was a country only reconquered from Muslim rule, full of missionary zeal and a desire for riches. The Spanish had traveled into the Atlantic during the 14th century. Then in 1492, the same year that the final Muslim fortress was captured in Spain, the Italian navigator **Christopher Columbus**, operating in the name of the newly united Spanish monarchy, set sail for a westward route to India, convinced that the round earth would make his quest possible. As is well known, he failed, reaching the Americas instead and mistakenly naming their inhabitants "Indians." Although Columbus believed to his death that he had sailed to India, later Spanish explorers realized that they had voyaged to a region where Europeans, Africans, and Asians had not traveled previously. One expedition, headed by Amerigo Vespucci, gave the New World its name. Spain, eager to claim this new land, won papal approval for Spanish dominion over most of what is now Latin America, although a later treaty awarded Brazil to Portugal.

Finally, a Spanish expedition under **Ferdinand Magellan** set sail westward in 1519, passing the southern tip of South America and sailing across the Pacific, reaching the Indonesian islands in 1521 after incredible hardships. It was on the basis of this voyage, the first trip around the world, that Spain claimed the Philippines, which it held until 1898.

Portugal emerged from this first round of exploration with coastal holdings in parts of Africa and in the Indian port of Goa, a lease on the Chinese port of Macao, short-lived interests in trade with Japan, and finally, the claim on Brazil. Spain asserted its hold on the Philippines, various Pacific islands, and the bulk of the Americas. During the 16th century, the Spanish backed up these

Portuguese Travelers in Africa

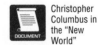

Christopher Columbus in the "New World"

Columbus, Christopher   Genoese captain in service of king and queen of Castile and Aragon; successfully sailed to New World and returned in 1492; initiated European discoveries in Americas.

Magellan, Ferdinand   (1480–1521) Spanish captain who in 1519 initiated first circumnavigation of the globe; died during the voyage; allowed Spain to claim Philippines.

Europeans in the World, Fifteenth and Sixteenth Centuries

Figure 16.3 This 1505 woodcut is the earliest known European portrayal of Native Americans. It was done by an unknown German artist who had never been to America but based his drawing on the testimony of those who had. The accompanying text reported: "The people are thus naked, handsome, brown. . . . They also eat each other . . . and hang the flesh of them in the smoke. They become a hundred and fifty years of age, and have no government."

claims by military expeditions to Mexico and South America. The Spanish also held Florida and sent expeditions northward from Mexico into California and other parts of what later became the southwestern United States.

Northern European Expeditions

Later in the 16th century, the lead in exploration passed to northern Europe, as newly strong monarchies, such as France and England, got into the act and zealous Protestants in Britain and Holland strove to rival Catholic gains (Map 16.2). In part this shift in dynamism occurred because Spain and Portugal were busy digesting the gains they had already made; in part it was because northern Europeans, particularly the Dutch and the British, improved the design of oceanic vessels, producing lighter, faster ships than those of their Catholic adversaries. Britain won a historic sea battle with Spain in 1588, routing the massive Spanish Armada. From this point onward, the British, the Dutch, and to some extent the French vied for dominance on the seas, although in the Americas they aimed mainly northward because they could not challenge the Spanish and Portuguese colonies. Only in the sugar-rich West Indies did northern Europe seize islands initially claimed by Spain.

The new adventurers, like their Spanish and Portuguese predecessors, appreciated the economic potential of such voyages. Britain and Holland, now Protestant countries, emphasized religious interests less than European Catholics did at this point. Two 16th-century English explorers, trying to find an Arctic route to China, were told to keep an eye out for any native populations en route, for such people would provide a perfect market for warm English woolens. And if the territory was unpopulated, it might be put to use as a source of fish for Britain. A quest for profit had become a dominant policy motive.

French explorers crossed the Atlantic first in 1534, reaching Canada, which they claimed. In the 17th century, various expeditions pressed down from Canada into the Great Lakes region and the Mississippi valley.

Causation and the West's Expansion

Because of their interest in social change, historians inevitably deal with causation. What prompted the fall of Rome? Why did Islam spread so widely? What factors explain why most agricultural civilizations developed patriarchal family structures?

Historical causation differs from the kinds of causation many scientists test. When experiments or observations can be repeated, scientists can gain a fairly precise understanding of the factors that produce a phenomenon: remove an ingredient, for example, and the product changes. Historical causation is more complex. Major developments may resemble each other, but they never happen the same way twice. Definitive proof that factor X explains 40 percent of the spread of Buddhism in east Asia is impossible. This is why historians often disagree about causation. But if precision is impossible, high probability is not. We can get a fairly good sense of why things happen, and sloppy causation claims can be disproved. Furthermore, probing causation helps us explore a phenomenon itself. We know more about the nature of Western expansion in the 15th and 16th centuries if we discuss what caused it.

Some historians and other social scientists look to a single kind of cause as the explanation of a variety of circumstances. Some anthropologists are cultural determinists. They judge that a basic set of cultural factors, usually assumed to be very durable, causes the ongoing differences between societies: Chinese and Greeks, on average, respond differently to emotional stimuli because of their different cultural conditioning. More common is a technological or economic determinism. Some historians see technological change as setting other changes in motion. Others, including Marxists, argue that economic arrangements—how the economy is structured and what groups control it—produce at least the basic framework for innovations. At another pole, some historians used to claim "great men" as the prime movers in history. The causes of change thus became Chinggis Khan or Ashoka, with no need to look much further.

Various approaches to causation have been applied to the West's explorations and colonial conquests in the early modern period. There is room for a "great man" analysis. Many descriptive accounts that dwell on explorers and conquerors (Vasco da Gama and Cortés, for example) and on leaders who sponsored them (such as Henry the Navigator) suggest that the key cause of the West's new role stemmed from the daring and vision of exceptional individuals.

> "[S]ome historians used to claim 'great men' as the prime movers in history."

Cultural causation can also be invoked. Somehow, Europe's expansion must relate to the wonders of innovation introduced by the Renaissance. The link with Christian culture is even easier to prove, for a missionary spirit quickly supplemented the efforts of early explorers, leading to more voyages and settlements in Asia and the Americas.

Political causation enters in, if not in causing the initial surge, at least in confirming it. Starting in the 16th century, rivalries between the nation-states motivated a continuing quest for new trade routes and colonies.

There is also room for a simpler, technologically determinist approach. In this view, Europe's gains came from a handful of new inventions. Benefiting from knowledge of advances in China and the Middle East, Europeans introduced naval cannons. Along with steady improvements in navigation and ship design, new techniques explain why Europe gained as it did. Except in the Americas, where they had larger technical and organizational advantages, Europeans advanced in areas they could reach by sea and dominate by ships' guns—port cities, islands, and trade routes—and not elsewhere. Put simply, Europe gained because of these few technological edges.

Like all determinisms, however, this technological approach raises as many questions as it answers. Why were Europeans so ready to adopt new inventions? (What caused the cause?) Why did other societies that were aware of Europe's innovations, such as China, deliberately scorn any adoption of Western naval techniques? Here a different culture determined a reaction different from that of the West. Technology and culture went hand in hand. Clearly, some combined causal framework is needed in this case.

We cannot expect uniform agreement on a precise ordering of causation. However, we can expect fruitful debate—the kind of debate that has already moved our understanding beyond surface causes, such as the powerful personalities of a few people, to a grasp of more underlying contexts.

QUESTIONS If you had to choose a single determinism (cultural, technological, or economic) as basic to social change, which one would you pick? Why? In what ways might the professed motives of Western explorers and colonists have differed from their real motives? Would they necessarily have been aware of the discrepancy?

The British also turned their attention to North America, starting with a brief expedition as early as 1497. The English hoped to discover a northwest passage to spice-rich India, but they accomplished little beyond exploration of the Hudson Bay area of Canada during the 16th century. England's serious work began in the 17th century, with the colonization of the east coast of North America. Holland also had holdings in North America and, for a time, in Brazil.

The Dutch entered the picture after winning independence from Spain, and Holland quickly became a major competitor with Portugal in southeast Asia. The Dutch sent many sailors and ships

Map 16.2 French, British, and Dutch Holdings, c. 1700   During the 17th century, northwestern Europe took the initiative in explorations, venturing into North America and seeking convenient trading stations elsewhere.

to the region, ousting the Portuguese from the Indonesian islands by the early 17th century. Voyagers from the Netherlands explored the coast of Australia, though without much immediate result. Finally, toward the mid-17th century, Holland established a settlement on the southern tip of Africa, mainly to provide a relay station for its ships bound for the East Indies.

Dutch East India Company   Joint stock company that obtained government monopoly over trade in Asia; acted as virtually independent government in regions it claimed.

British East India Company   Joint stock company that obtained government monopoly over trade in India; acted as virtually independent government in regions it claimed.

The Netherlands, Britain, and France all chartered great trading companies, such as the **Dutch East India Company.** These companies were given government monopolies of trade in the regions designated, but they were not rigorously supervised by their own states. They had rights to raise armies and coin money on their own. Thus, semiprivate companies, amassing great commercial fortunes, long acted almost like independent governments in the regions they claimed. For some time, a Dutch trading company effectively ruled the island of Taiwan off the coast of China. The **British East India Company** played a similar role in parts of India during much of the 18th century. The companies in North America traded actively in furs.

No matter where in Europe they came from, explorers and their crews faced many hardships at sea. The work was tiring and uncertain, with voyages lasting many months or years, and diseases such as scurvy were rampant. One expedition accepted only bachelors for its crew because married men would miss their families too much. A sailor on another trip complained that "he was tired of being always tired, that he would rather die once than many times, and that they might as well shut their eyes and let the ship go to the bottom."

Europe's new maritime strength and new trade patterns generated wider changes, developing from the 1490s onward. One was the Columbian exchange of foods, diseases, and people. New global economic inequalities and new overseas empires also emerged.

Toward a World Economy

Europe's new initiatives added to existing intercontinental trade patterns. The range and significance of exchange began to increase steadily—a key manifestation of proto-globalization. Simply including the Americas, making exchanges truly global, affected almost all major regions.

The Columbian Exchange of Disease and Food

The impact of wider exchange became visible quickly. The extension of international contacts spread disease (see Chapter 21). The greatest victims were millions of Native Americans who had not previously been exposed to Afro-Eurasian diseases such as smallpox and measles and who therefore had no natural immunities (Figure 16.4). During the 16th and 17th centuries, they died in huge numbers. Overall, in North and South America, more than half the native population would die; some estimates run as high as 80 percent. Whole island populations in the West Indies were wiped out. This was a major blow to earlier civilizations in the Americas as well as an opportunity for Europeans to forge a partially new population of their own citizens and slaves imported from Africa. The devastation occurred over a 150-year period, although in some areas it was more rapid. When Europeans made contact with Polynesians and Pacific Coast peoples in the 18th century, the same dreadful pattern played out, again undermining vibrant cultures.

Other exchanges were less dire. New World crops were spread rapidly via Western merchants. American corn and sweet potatoes were taken up widely in China (where merchants learned of them from Spaniards in the Philippines), the Mediterranean, and parts of Africa. In some cases these productive new crops, along with local agricultural improvements, triggered large population increases. For example, China began to experience long-term population pressure in the 17th century, and new crops played a key role. When Europeans introduced the potato around 1700, major population upheaval occurred there as well.

Indeed, food played a key role in the world system created during the early modern period. About 30 percent of the foods consumed in the world today come from plants of American origin. Corn became a staple in the African diet. Europeans, ironically, were more conservative. Rumors spread that American foods spread disease. It took more than a century for the potato to gain ground, but fried potatoes (French fries) were being sold on the streets of Paris by the 1680s.

Animal husbandry became more similar across the world as European and Asian animals, such as horses and cattle, were introduced to the New World. The spread of basic products and diseases formed an important backdrop to world history from the 16th century on, with varying effects on population structures in diverse regions.

Figure 16.4 This 16th-century print portrays Aztecs suffering from smallpox during the Cortés invasion (1518–1519).

The West's Commercial Outreach

Europeans did not displace all Asian shipping from the coastal waters of China and Japan, nor did they completely monopolize the Indian Ocean (see Chapter 22). Along the east African coast, while a few European bases were established, Muslim traders remained active, and commerce continued to move toward the Middle East. Generally, however, western Europe dominated a great deal of oceanic shipping, even muscling in on trade between other societies, as between India and southeast Asia. This greatly increased Europe's overall profits, and disproportionate control by the great merchant companies increased the European ability to determine the framework for international trade. In the eastern Mediterranean, for example, a Spanish-directed fleet defeated the navy of the Ottoman Empire in the battle of **Lepanto** in 1571. With this setback, any hope of successful Muslim rivalry against European naval power ended. The Turks rebuilt their fleet and continued their activity in the eastern Mediterranean, but they could not challenge the Europeans on the larger international routes.

Lepanto   Naval battle between the Spanish and the Ottoman Empire resulting in a Spanish victory in 1571.

Discovery and Exploration: Africa

Although western Europe did not conquer much inland territory in Africa or Asia, it did seek a limited network of secure harbors. Led by Spain and Portugal, then followed by the various northern powers, European ports spread along the west coast of Africa, several parts of the Indian subcontinent, and the islands of southeast Asia by the 17th century. Even in China, where unusually strong governments limited the Europeans' ability to seize harbors outright, the Portuguese won effective control over the island port of Macao. European-controlled ports served as areas for contact with overland traders (usually local merchants) and provided access to inland goods not directly within the reach of the West.

Where direct control was not feasible, European influence led to the formation of special Western enclaves in existing cities, where Western traders won special legal rights. This was the pattern in the Ottoman Empire, where Western merchants set up colonies within Constantinople, and in Russia, where Western factors (shipping agents) set up first in Moscow and then in St. Petersburg. Elements of this system even emerged in Japan after a firm isolationist policy was launched about 1600, as Dutch traders were given special access to the port of Nagasaki. The point was obvious: international trade gained growing importance in supplementing regional economies. Because western Europe now ran this trade, it won special rights of access.

Imbalances in World Trade

The most active competition in world trade emerged between European nations themselves. Spain briefly dominated, thanks to its imports of silver from the Americas. But it lacked a good banking system and could not support a full commercial surge. England, France, and Holland, where merchants had firmer status, soon pulled in the lion's share of profits from world trade. Western Europe quickly expanded its manufacturing operations, so that it could export expensive finished goods, such as guns and cloth, in return for unprocessed goods, such as silver and sugar, traded by other societies. Here was another margin for profit.

The dominant **core nations** in the new world system supplemented their growing economic prowess by self-serving political policies. The doctrines of **mercantilism**, which urged that a nation-state not import goods from outside its own empire but sell exports as widely as possible in its own ships, both reflected and encouraged the new world system. Tariff policies discouraged manufacturing in colonial areas and stimulated home-based manufacturing.

core nations   Nations, usually European, that enjoyed profit from world economy; controlled international banking and commercial services such as shipping; exported manufactured goods for raw materials.

mercantilism   Economic theory that stressed governments' promotion of limitation of imports from other nations and internal economies in order to improve tax revenues; popular during 17th and 18th centuries in Europe.

Beyond western Europe lay areas that were increasingly enmeshed in the world economy but as dependants to the core nations. These areas produced low-cost goods: precious metals and cash crops such as sugar, spice, tobacco, and later cotton. Human labor was a vital item of exchange. Parts of sub-Saharan Africa entered the new world economy mainly as suppliers of slaves. The earlier west African patterns of trade across the Sahara yielded to a dominant focus on the Atlantic and therefore to activities organized by Western shippers. In return for slaves and unprocessed goods, Europeans traded their manufactured items, including guns, while profiting from their control of commercial and shipping services.

West Indian Slaveholding

The following table describes the rise of the plantation system, and attendant slaveholding, on the British West Indian island of Antigua, where sugar growing for export gained increasing hold. Trends of the sort indicated in this table raise further analytical issues about cause and effect. What might have caused the main changes in Antigua's estate system? How might the changes have related to the larger framework of the world economy? What do the trends suggest about the European demand for sugar and about production methods used to meet this demand?

What impact would the trends have had on slaves themselves? Laws in the British Caribbean soon began to enforce the estate system, exempting masters from murder charges when slaves died from beatings administered as punishment and fining groups such as the Quakers for daring to bring slaves to religious meetings. How do the statistical trends help explain the imposition of new laws of this sort?

	1688	1706	1767
Taxables	53	36	65
Slaveholders	16	30	65
Planters with 20+ slaves	6	16	46
Planters with 100+ slaves	0	4	22
Slaves	332	1,150	5,610
Acreage	5,811	5,660	12,350

QUESTIONS What trends in the social and economic structure of this part of Antigua during the 18th century do these figures suggest? Did the estate economy become more or less labor intensive, given the acreage involved and the comparative growth rates of owner and slave populations? What do the trends suggest about the nature of the European-born or European-derived elite of Antigua?

A System of International Inequality

The new world economic relationships proved highly durable. Most of the areas established as dependent by the 17th century still carry some special burdens in world trade today. In dependent areas such as Latin America and the slave-supplying parts of Africa, not all people were mired in poverty. African slave traders and princes who taxed the trade might grow rich. In Latin America the silver mines and commercial estates required regional merchants and farmers to supply food. Furthermore, many peasants in Latin America and even more in Africa were not yet involved in a market economy at all—whether regional or international—but rather produced for local subsistence with traditional motives and methods. However, significant minorities were involved in production for the world market. Also, most African and Latin American merchants and landlords did not fully control their own terms of trade. They might prosper, but their wealth did not stimulate much local manufacturing or general economic advance. Rather, they tended to import European-made goods, including (in the case of American planters) art objects and luxury items.

Coercive labor systems spread. Because dependent economies relied on cheap production of unprocessed goods, there was a tendency to build a system of forced labor that would cost little even when the overall labor supply was precarious. In the Americas, given the population loss from disease, this led to the massive importation of African slaves. Also, for many Native Americans and **mestizos** (mehs-TEE-zohs) (people of mixed European and Native American blood), systems of estate management developed that demanded large amounts of labor. More limited examples of estate agriculture, in which peasants were forced into labor without the legal freedom to leave, arose for spice production in the Dutch East Indies and, by the 18th century, in British-dominated agricultural operations in India.

How Much World in the World Economy?

Asia, though not sponsoring the most active merchant ventures, participated strongly, and often profitably, in the world economy. The Chinese government, having renounced large-scale international trade of its own early in the 15th century, deliberately avoided involvement with international trade on someone else's terms. It did copy some firearms manufacturing from the Europeans, but at a fairly low level. Beyond this it depended on extensive government regulation, backed up by a coastal navy, to keep European activities in check. Most of the limited trade that existed was channeled through Macao. European visitors wrote scornfully of China's disdain for military advances.

A Jesuit wrote that "the military . . . is considered mean among them." The Chinese were also disparaged for adhering to tradition. One Western missionary in the 17th century described how, in his opinion, the Chinese could not be persuaded "to make use of new instruments and leave their old ones without an especial order from the Emperor to that effect. They are more fond of the most defective piece of antiquity than of the most perfect of the modern, differing much in that from us who are in love with nothing but what is new."

So China managed to avoid trying to keep up with European developments while also avoiding subservience to European merchants. Chinese manufacturing gains led to a strong export position, which is why Europeans sent a great deal of American silver to China to pay for the goods they wanted. Indeed, at the end of the 18th century, a famous British mission, appealing to the government to open the country to greater trade, was rebuffed. The imperial court, after insisting on extreme deference from the British envoy, haughtily informed him that the Chinese had no need for outside goods. European eagerness for Chinese goods—attested to by the habit adopted in the 17th century of calling fine porcelain "china"—was simply not matched by Chinese enthusiasm, but a trickle of trade continued. Westerners compensated in part by developing their own porcelain industry by the 18th century, which contributed to the early Industrial Revolution, particularly in Britain. Still, there were hopes for commercial entry to China that remained unfulfilled.

Japan, though initially attracted by Western expeditions in the 16th century, also more fully pulled back. So did Korea. The Japanese showed some openness to Christian missions, and they were fascinated by Western advances in gunnery and shipping. Artists captured the interest in exotic foreigners. Guns had particular relevance to Japan's ongoing feudal wars, for there was no disdain here for military life. Yet Japanese leaders soon worried about undue Western influence and the impact this could have on internal divisions among warring lords, as well as the threat guns posed to samurai military dominance. They encouraged a local gunmaking industry that matched existing European muskets and small cannon fairly readily, but having achieved this they cut off most contact with any world trade. Most Japanese were forbidden to travel or trade abroad, the small Christian minority was suppressed, and from the 17th until the 19th centuries Japan entered a period of almost complete isolation except for some Chinese contact and trading concessions to the small Dutch enclave near Nagasaki.

Other societies participated variously in world trade. The rulers of India's new Mughal Empire in the 16th century were interested in Western traders and even encouraged the establishment of small port enclaves. India also sold goods—not only spices but also manufactured cottons textiles and other items—in return for New World silver. Most attention, however, was riveted on internal development and land-based expansion and commerce; world trade was a sideline. The same held true for the Ottoman and Safavid empires in the Middle East through the 17th century, despite the presence of small European enclaves in key cities. Russia lay partially outside the world economic orbit until the 18th century. A largely agricultural society, Russia conducted much of its trade with nomadic peoples in central Asia, which further insulated it from west European demands.

The Expansionist Trend

The world economy was not stationary; it tended to gain ground over time, as the centerpiece of the process of proto-globalization. The process also linked to the formation of new kinds of empire. South America, the West Indies, a part of North America, and some regions in west Africa were first staked out as colonial dependencies beginning in the 16th century, and the list later expanded. Portions of southeast Asia that produced for world markets, under the dominance of the great Western trading companies, were brought into the orbit by the 17th century.

By the early 18th century, Western traders were advancing in India as the Mughal Empire began to fall apart. The British and French East India Companies staked out increasing roles in internal trade and administration. Early in the 18th century, Britain passed tariffs against the import of cotton cloth made in India as a means of protecting Britain's own cotton industry. The intent was to use India as a market for British-processed goods and a source of outright payments of gold, which the British were requiring by the late 18th century. Indian observers were aware of the shifting balance. An 18th-century account noted,

> But such is the little regard which they [the British] show to the people of this kingdom, and such their apathy and indifference for their welfare, that the people under their dominion groan everywhere, and are reduced to poverty and distress.

India maintained a complex regional economy still, with much internal manufacturing and trade; it was not forced into such complete dependency as Latin America, for example. However, what had initially been a position outside the world economy was changing, to India's disadvantage. Manufacturing began to decline.

Eastern Europe also was brought into a growing relationship with the world economy and the west European core. The growth of cities in the West created a growing market for imported grains by the 18th century. Much of this demand was met by east European growers, particularly in Prussia and Poland but also in Russia. Export grains, in turn, were produced mainly on large estates by serfs, who were subjected to prolonged periods of labor service. This relationship was similar to that which prevailed in Latin America, with one exception: outside of Poland, east European governments were much stronger than their Latin American counterparts.

Colonial Expansion

Opportunities to establish colonies were particularly inviting in the Americas, where European guns, horses, and iron weapons offered special advantages and where political disarray and the population losses provided openings in many cases (see Chapter 19).

The Americas: Loosely Controlled Colonies

Spain moved first. The Spanish colonized several West Indian islands soon after Columbus's first voyage, starting with Hispaniola and then moving into Cuba, Jamaica, and Puerto Rico. Only in 1509 did they begin settlement on the mainland, in search of gold. The first colony was established in what is now Panama, under an able but unscrupulous adventurer, **Vasco de Balboa**. Several expeditions fanned out in Central America, and then a separate expedition from Cuba launched the Spanish conquest of the Aztecs in Mexico. Another expedition headed toward the Inca realm in the Andes in 1531, where hard fighting was needed before ultimate victory. From this base several colonial expeditions spread to Colombia, other parts of the Andes, and portions of Argentina.

Expansion resulted from the efforts of a motley crew of adventurers, many of them violent and treacherous, like **Francisco Pizarro** (1478–1541), admittedly one of the more successful examples (Figure 16.5). Pizarro first came to the Americas in 1502 and settled on the island of Hispaniola. Later, he joined Balboa's colony in Panama, where he received a cattle ranch. Learning of wealth in Peru, he joined with an illiterate soldier and a priest, mounting two expeditions that failed. In 1528 he returned to Spain to gain the king's support and also his agreement that he would be governor of the new province. With these pledges and a force of about 180 men, he attacked the divided Inca Empire. Capturing Emperor Atahuallpa, he accepted a large ransom and then strangled him. Several revolts followed during Pizarro's rule from Lima, a coastal city he founded. But the Spanish king ennobled Pizarro for his success. At a dinner in 1541, Pizarro was assassinated by a group of Inca rebels.

Early colonies in the Americas typically were developed by small bands of gold-hungry Europeans, often loosely controlled by colonial administrations back home. Colonial rulers often established only limited controls over native populations at first, content to exact tribute without imposing detailed administration and sometimes leaving existing leaders in place. Gradually, more formal administration spread as agricultural settlements were established and official colonial systems took shape under control of bureaucrats sent from Spain and Portugal. Active missionary efforts, designed to Christianize the native peoples, added another layer of detailed administration throughout the Spanish holdings in North and South America.

Balboa, Vasco de (c. 1475–1519) First Spanish captain to begin settlement on the mainland of Mesoamerica in 1509; initial settlement eventually led to conquest of Aztec and Inca empires by other captains.

Pizarro, Francisco Led conquest of Inca Empire of Peru beginning in 1535; by 1540, most of Inca possessions fell to the Spanish.

Europe developed a network of overseas colonies, particularly in the Americas but also in a few parts of Africa and Asia. By the 18th century, growing European inroads in India marked a decisive change in south Asia.

Figure 16.5 Francisco Pizarro.

Western Conquerors: Tactics and Motives

In the first passage quoted here, Columbus writes to the Spanish monarchy on his way home from his 1492 expedition. In the second passage, the brother of Francisco Pizarro, the Spanish conqueror of Peru, describes in 1533 how the Inca ruler, Atahuallpa, was defeated.

Columbus's 1492 Expedition

Sir, believing that you will take pleasure in hearing of the great success which our Lord has granted me in my voyage, I write you this letter, whereby you will learn how in thirty-three days' time I reached the Indies with the fleet which the most illustrious King and Queen, our Sovereigns, gave to me, where I found very many islands thickly peopled, of all which I took possession without resistance for their Highnesses by proclamation made and with the royal standard unfurled. To the first island that I found I gave the name of *San Salvador,* in remembrance of His High Majesty, who hath marvelously brought all these things to pass; the Indians call it *Guanaham.* . . .

Espanola is a wonder. Its mountains and plains, and meadows, and fields, are so beautiful and rich for planting and sowing, and rearing cattle of all kinds, and for building towns and villages. The harbours on the coast, and the number and size and wholesomeness of the rivers, most of them bearing gold, surpass anything that would be believed by one who had not seen them. There is a great difference between the trees, fruits, and plants of this island and those of *Juana.* In this island there are many spices and extensive mines of gold and other metals. The inhabitants of this and of all the other islands I have found or gained intelligence of, both men and women, go as naked as they were born, with the exception that some of the women cover one part only with a single leaf of grass or with a piece of cotton, made for that purpose. They have neither iron, nor steel, nor arms, nor are they competent to use them, not that they are not well-formed and of handsome stature, but because they are timid to a surprising degree. . . .

Although I have taken possession of all these islands in the name of their Highnesses, and they are all more abundant in wealth than I am able to express . . . yet there was one large town in *Espanola* of which especially I took possession, situated in a locality well adapted for the working of the gold mines, and for all kinds of commerce, either with the main land on this side, or with that beyond which is the land of the great Khan, with which there is great profit. . . .

I have also established the greatest friendship with the king of that country, so much so that he took pride in calling me his brother, and treating me as such. Even should these people change their intentions towards us and become hostile, they do not know what arms are, but, as I have said, go naked, and are the most timid people in the world; so that the men I have left could, alone, destroy the whole country, and this island has no danger for them, if they only know how to conduct themselves. . . . Finally, and speaking only of what has taken place in this voyage, which has been so hasty, their Highnesses may see that I shall give them all the gold they require, if they will give me but a very little assistance; spices also, and cotton, as much as their Highnesses shall command to be shipped; and mastic, hitherto found only in Greece . . . slaves, as many of these idolators as their Highnesses shall command to be shipped. . . .

But our Redeemer hath granted this victory our illustrious King and Queen and their kingdoms, which have acquired great fame by an event of such high importance, in which all Christendom ought to rejoice, and which it ought to celebrate with great festivals and the offering of solemn thanks to the Holy Trinity with many solemn prayers, both for the great exaltation which may accrue to them in turning so many nations to our holy faith, and also for the temporal benefits which will bring great refreshment and gain, not only to Spain, but to all Christians.

Discovery and Exploration: "The New World" MAP

France, Britain, and Holland, though latecomers to the Americas, also staked out colonial settlements. French explorations along the St. Lawrence River in Canada led to small colonies around Quebec, from 1608 onward, and explorations in the Mississippi River basin. Dutch and English settlers moved into portions of the Atlantic coastal regions early in the 17th century. Also in the 17th century, all three countries seized and colonized several West Indian islands, which they soon involved in the growing slave trade.

British and French North America: Backwater Colonies

Colonies of European settlers developed in North America, where patterns differed in many respects from those in Latin America and the Caribbean. English colonies along the Atlantic received religious refugees, such as the Calvinists who fled religious tensions in Britain to settle in New England. Government grants of land to major proprietors such as William Penn led to explicit efforts to recruit settlers. New York began as a Dutch settlement but was taken over easily by an English expedition in 1664.

In Canada, the first substantial European settlements were launched by the French government under Louis XIV. The initial plan involved setting up manorial estates under great lords whose rights were carefully restricted by the state. French peasants were urged to emigrate, although it proved difficult to develop an adequate labor force. However, birth rates were high, and by 1755 **New France** had about 55,000 settlers in a peasant society that proved extremely durable as it

New France French colonies in North America; extended from St. Lawrence River along Great Lakes and down Mississippi River valley system.

Why and How Atahuallpa Was Defeated

The messengers came back to ask the Governor to send a Christian to Atahuallpa, that he intended to come at once, and that he would come unarmed. The Governor sent a Christian, and presently Atahuallpa moved, leaving the armed men behind him. He took with him about five or six thousand Indians without arms, except that under their shirts they had small darts and slings with stones.

He came in a litter, and before went three or four hundred Indians in liveries, cleaning straws from the road and singing. Then came Atahuallpa in the midst of his chiefs and principal men, the greatest among them being also borne on men's shoulders. . . . A Dominican Friar, who was with the Governor, came forward to tell him, on the part of the Governor, that he waited for him in his lodgings, and that he was sent to speak with him. The Friar then told Atahuallpa that he was a Priest, and that he was sent there to teach the things of the Faith, if they should desire to be Christians. He showed Atahuallpa a book . . . and told him that book contained the things of God. Atahuallpa asked for the book, and threw it on the ground, saying: "I will not leave this place until you have restored all that you have taken in my land. I know well who you are, and what you have come for." . . . The Friar went to the Governor and reported what was being done, and that no time was to be lost. The Governor sent to me; and I had arranged with the Captain of the artillery that, when a sign was given, he should discharge his pieces, and that, on hearing the reports, all the troops should come forth at once. This was done, and as the Indians were unarmed, they were defeated without danger to any Christian. Those who carried the litter, and the chiefs who surrounded Atahuallpa, were all killed, falling around him. The Governor came out and seized Atahuallpa, and in protecting him, he received a knife cut from a Christian in the hand. The troops continued the pursuit as far as the place where the armed Indians were stationed, who made no resistance whatever, because it was night. All were brought into town, where the Governor was quartered.

Next morning the Governor ordered us to go to the camp of Atahuallpa, where we found forty thousand pesos worth of gold and two or three pounds of silver. . . . The Governor said that he had not come to make war on the Indians, but that our Lord the Emperor, who was Lord of the whole world, had ordered him to come that he might see the land, and let Atahuallpa know the things of our Faith. . . . The Governor also told him that that land, and all other lands, belonged to the Emperor, and that he must acknowledge him as his Lord. He replied that he was content, and, observing that the Christians had collected some gold, Atahuallpa said to the Governor that they need not take such care of it, as if there was so little; for that he could give them ten thousand plates, and that he could fill the room in which he was up to a white line, which was the height of a man and a half from the floor.

QUESTIONS What were the main bases for initial European judgments about the characteristics of Native Americans? How might the native peoples have judged the Europeans? What motives does Columbus appeal to in trying to interest Spanish rulers in the new land?

These documents raise obvious problems of interpretation. They interpret interactions with another, very foreign culture from the European standpoint only. They also attribute motives to the adventurers that may or may not have been predominant. Figuring out how to gain useful, valid information from documents of this sort, which are essential in interpreting key developments in world history, is a major challenge. What parts of the accounts seem most reliable, and what criteria can be used to sort out degrees of accuracy?

---

fanned out around the fortress of Quebec. Strong organization by the Catholic Church completed this partial replica of French provincial society. Britain attacked the French strongholds (Figure 16.6) as part of a worldwide colonial struggle between the two powers. In the conflict, known as the **Seven Years War,** France lost its colony under the terms of the **Treaty of Paris,** which in 1763 settled the war. France eagerly regained its West Indian sugar islands, along with trading posts in Africa, and Britain took control of Canada and the Mississippi basin. Relations between British officials and the French Canadian community remained strained as British settlements developed in eastern Canada and in Ontario. The flight of many American loyalists after the 1776 revolution added to the English-speaking contingent in Canada.

Colonial holdings along the Atlantic and in Canada were generally of modest interest to Western colonial powers in the 17th and even the 18th centuries. The Dutch were more attached to their Asian colonies. British and French leaders valued their West Indian holdings much more than their North American colonies. The value of North American products, such as timber and furs, was not nearly as great as profits from the Caribbean or Latin America, so much less attention was given to economic regulation. As a result, some merchant and manufacturing activities emerged among the new Americans.

However, the American colonies that would become the United States had a population of a mere 3 million, far smaller than the powerful colonies in Latin America. Southern colonies that produced tobacco and sugar, and then cotton, became important. Patterns there were similar to those of Latin America, with large estates based on imported slave labor, a wealthy planter class bent

Seven Years War Fought both in continental Europe and also in overseas colonies between 1756 and 1763; resulted in Prussian seizures of land from Austria, English seizures of colonies in India and North America.

Treaty of Paris Arranged in 1763 following Seven Years War; granted New France to England in exchange for return of French sugar island in Caribbean.

Figure 16.6 British naval power allowed the light infantry to scale the French fort from the St. Lawrence River and capture Quebec in 1759. The battle was a turning point in Canadian history: the beginning of the end of French rule.

on importing luxury products from western Europe, and weak formal governments. Still, in world historical terms, the Atlantic colonies in North America were of limited value amid the larger colonial holdings staked out in the early modern centuries.

Yet European settlers did arrive. Driven by religious dissent, ambition, and other motives, Europeans, many from the British Isles, colonized the Atlantic coastal region, where native populations were quickly reduced by disease and war. The society that developed in the British colonies was far closer to west European forms than was that of Latin America. The colonies operated their own assemblies, which provided the people with political experience. Calvinist and Quaker church assemblies gave governing power to groups of elders or wider congregations. Many colonists thus had reason to share with some west Europeans a sense of the importance of representative institutions and self-government.

Colonists were also avid consumers of political theories written in Europe, such as the parliamentary ideas of John Locke. There was also wide reading and discussion of Enlightenment materials. Institutions such as the 18th-century American Philosophical Society deliberately imitated European scientific institutes, and hundreds of North Americans contributed scientific findings to the British Royal Society. The colonies remained modest in certain cultural attainments. Art was rather primitive, although many stylistic cues came from Europe. There was no question that in formal culture, North American leaders saw themselves as part of a larger Western world.

By the late 18th century, some American merchants were trading with China, their ships picking up medicinal herbs along the Pacific coast and exchanging them for Chinese artifacts and tea.

Great Britain tried to impose firmer limits on this modestly thriving local economy after the Seven Years War. It hoped to win greater tax revenues and to guarantee markets for British goods and traders, but the effort came too late and helped encourage rebellion in key colonies. Unusual among the colonies, North America developed a merchant class and some stake in manufacturing in a pattern similar to that taking shape in western Europe itself.

The spread of Western values in the Atlantic colonies and in British and French settlements in Canada was facilitated by the modest impact of Native Americans in these settled areas (Figure 16.7). The native population of this part of North America had always been less dense than in Central America or the Andes region. Because few Native American groups in these regions practiced settled agriculture, instead combining hunting with slash and burn corn growing, European colonists found it easy to displace them from large stretches of territory. The ravages of European-imported disease reduced the indigenous population greatly. Many forest peoples were pushed westward. Some abandoned agriculture, turning to a new horse-based hunting economy on the plains (the horse was brought to Mexico by the Spaniards). Many territorial wars further distracted the Native American groups. The net result of these factors was that although European colonists interacted with Native Americans, learned from them, and feared and mistreated them, the colonists did not combine with them to forge new cultural groups like those emerging in much of Latin America.

By 1700, the importation of African slaves proved to be a more important addition to the North American experience, particularly in the southern colonies. The practice of slaveholding and interactions with African culture distinguished North American life from its European counterpart. By the 18th century, 23 percent of the population of the English colonies was of African origin.

North America and Western Civilization

On balance, most white settlers intended to transplant key Western habits into their new setting. For example, family patterns were similar. American colonists were able to marry slightly earlier than ordinary western Europeans because of the greater abundance of land, and they had larger families. Still, they reproduced most features of the European-style family, including the primary emphasis on the nuclear unit. The new Americans did have unusual concern for children, if only because they depended so heavily on their work in a labor-scarce environment. European visitors commented on the child-centeredness of American families and the freedom of children to speak up. These variations, though significant, played on trends also becoming visible in Europe, such as the new emphasis on family affection.

Even when key colonies rebelled against European control, as they did in 1776, they moved in the name of Western political ideas and economic goals against the dependency the British tried to impose. They established a government that responded to the new Western political theories, implementing some key ideas for the first time.

Africa and Asia: Coastal Trading Stations

In Africa, Europeans for the most part contented themselves with small coastal fortresses, negotiating with African kings and merchants but not trying to claim large territories of their own. They sold Asian products, like Indian cotton, and European guns and decorative items in return for slaves. Generally, Europeans were deterred by climate, disease, and non-navigable rivers from trying to reach into the interior. Mostly, they dealt with West African governments and traders. There

Figure 16.7 Watercolor by John White (c. 1590) of the Native American settlement of Secoton, Virginia. White was the governor of the pioneer colony of Roanoke, in what is now North Carolina. When he returned from a desperate voyage back to England to obtain supplies, he found the settlement abandoned. Historians have never been able to determine what happened to the men, women, and children of the "Lost Colony."

Cape Colony Dutch colony established at Cape of Good Hope in 1652 initially to provide a coastal station for the Dutch seaborne empire; by 1770 settlements had expanded sufficiently to come into conflict with Bantus.

Boers Dutch settlers in Cape Colony, in southern Africa.

Calcutta Headquarters of British East India Company in Bengal in Indian subcontinent; located on Ganges; captured in 1756 during early part of Seven Years War; later became administrative center for all of Bengal.

Figure 16.8 This Indian portrait of two women in European dress illustrates the English influence in 18th-century India.

(V & A Images/Victoria and Albert Museum.)

were two important exceptions. From initial coastal settlements, Portugal sent expeditions into Angola in search of slaves. These expeditions had a more direct and more disruptive impact in this part of southwestern Africa than elsewhere along the Atlantic coast. More important still was the **Cape Colony** planted by the Dutch on the Cape of Good Hope in 1652. The intent was to form another coastal station to supply Dutch ships bound for Asia. But some Dutch farmers were sent, and these **Boers** (the Dutch word for farmers) began to fan out on large farms in a region still lightly populated by Africans. They clashed with local hunting groups, enslaving some of them. Only after 1770 did the expanding Boer settlements directly conflict with Bantu farmers, opening a long battle for control of southern Africa that raged until the late 20th century in the nation of South Africa.

European colonies in Asia were also exceptional. Spain set up an administration for the Philippines and sent active Catholic missionaries. The Dutch East India company administered portions of the main islands of present-day Indonesia and also (for a time) Taiwan, off the China coast.

Colonization in Asia entered a new phase as the British and French began to struggle for control of India, beginning in the late 17th century when the Mughal Empire weakened. Even before the Mughals faltered after the death in 1707 of their last great emperor, Aurangzeb, French and British forts dotted the east and west coasts, along with Portuguese Goa. As Mughal inefficiency increased, with a resultant surge of regional states ruled by Indians, portions of the subcontinent became an arena for the growing international rivalry between Britain and France.

The British East India Company had two advantages in this competition. Through negotiation with local princes, it had gained a station at **Calcutta**, which gave it some access to the great wealth of the Ganges valley. Furthermore, the company had enormous influence over the British government and, through Britain's superior navy, excellent communication on the ocean routes. Its French rivals, in contrast, had less political clout at home, where the government often was distracted by European land wars. The French also were more interested in missionary work than the British, for Protestants became deeply committed to colonial missions only in the 19th century. Before then, the British were content to leave Hindu customs alone and devote themselves to commercial profits.

French–British rivalry raged bitterly through the mid-18th century. Both sides recruited Indian princes and troops as allies. Outright warfare erupted in 1744 and then again during the Seven Years War. In 1756, an Indian ruler in Bengal attacked and captured the British base at Calcutta. In the aftermath of the battle, English prisoners were placed in their own jail, where humidity and overcrowding led to perhaps as many as 120 deaths before Indian officials became aware of their plight and released them. The English used this incident, which they dubbed the "black hole of Calcutta," to rally their forces. The East India Company's army recaptured Calcutta and then seized additional Indian and French territory, aided by abundant bribes to many regional princes. French power in India was destroyed, and the East India Company took over administration of the Bengal region, which stretched inland from Calcutta. Soon after this, the British also gained the island of Ceylon (Sri Lanka) from the Dutch.

The full history of British India did not begin until late in the 18th century, when the British government took a more active hand in Indian administration, supplementing the unofficial government of the East India Company (Figure 16.8). Indeed, British control of the subcontinent was incomplete. The Mughal Empire remained, although it was increasingly weak and it controlled scant territory, as did other regional kingdoms, including the Sikh state. Britain gained some new territories by force but was also content to form alliances with local princes without disturbing their internal administration.

In most colonies, European administration long remained fairly loose. Few settlers arrived, except in south Africa and the Americas. Outside the Americas, cultural impositions were slight. Missionary activity won many converts in the Philippines but not elsewhere in Asia or in Africa at this point. The main impact of colonies supplemented the more general development of the world economy: colonial administrations pressed for economic advantage for the home country by opening markets and prompting commercial production of cheap foods and raw materials. Here, of course, the consequences to colonial peoples were very real.

Impact on Western Europe

Western Europe was hugely affected by its own colonial success, not only economically but also diplomatically. Colonial rivalries and wars added to the existing hostilities between key nation-states. England and Holland early turned against Spanish success, with great effect. The Dutch and the English competed, engaging in many skirmishes in the 17th century. Then attention turned to the growing competition between the British and the French. This contest had extensive geographic scope: the Seven Years War (1756–1763), fought in Europe, India, and North America, has been called the first world war.

There were also less obvious but equally dramatic effects on European society, including daily life. For example, from the mid-17th century onward, the use of colonially produced sugar spread widely. Previously, sugar had been a costly, upper-class item. Now for the first time (salt had been the one previous exception), a basic product available to ordinary people was being traded over long distances. The spread of sugar had cultural as well as social and economic significance in giving ordinary Europeans the ability to obtain pleasurable sensations in quick doses—an interesting foreshadowing of later features of Western consumer behavior. It also promoted a growing role for dentists by the 18th century.

More broadly, the profits Europeans brought in from world trade, including the African slave trade, added wealth and capital. Many Europeans turned to manufacturing operations, as owners and workers, partly because of opportunities for export in world trade. These developments enhanced Europe's commercial character, while reducing dependence on agriculture alone. They provided additional tax revenues for growing governments and their military ambitions.

The Impact of a New World Order

The development of the world economy and European colonialism had immense impact. The range of unfree labor systems, to supply goods for world trade, became more widespread than ever before. Slavery and serfdom deeply affected Latin America and eastern Europe, while the slave trade disrupted west Africa, and millions of individual lives as well.

Yet the world economy brought benefits as well as hardships, quite apart from the profits to Europe. New foods and wider trade patterns helped some societies deal with scarcity. Individual merchants and landowners gained new wealth virtually everywhere. China prospered from the imports of silver, though rapid population growth limited gains overall. The mixture of profits and compulsion brought more and more people and regions into the world economy network.

Global Connections

The World Economy—And the World

Buoyed by its growing role in the world, western Europe unquestionably saw its economy and military power increase more rapidly than those of any other society during the early modern period. As the next chapter shows, Europe changed internally as well, often in dramatic ways. Because of these facts, it is tempting to see the early modern centuries as a European drama in which other regions either played supporting roles or watched in awe.

Yet the relationships to the world economy were in fact quite complex. They ranged from conscious isolation to controlled participation to undeniable dependency. Many societies retained vibrant political systems and internal economies. Some, although attracted to certain Western features, wanted to stand apart from the values and institutions that world economic success seemed to involve.

Even societies that had changes thrust upon them, like Latin America, were hardly passive. Pressed by missionaries, Latin Americans did not simply adopt European-style Christianity, but rather blended in traditional beliefs and practices and many distinctive artistic forms. The world was growing closer, but it was not necessarily becoming simpler.

Further Readings

Excellent discussions of Western exploration and expansion are Kenneth Pomeranz and Steven Topik, *The World that Trade Created: Society, Culture, and the World Economy, 1400 to the Present* (2006); Carlo Cipolla, *Guns, Sails, and Empires: Technological Innovation and the Early Phases of European Expansion 1400–1700* (1997); D. Boorstin, *The Discoverers* (1991); and James Tracy, ed., *The Political Economy of Merchant Empires* (1991). The resulting cultural encounters are explored in works such as Warren R. Hofstra, ed., *Cultures in Conflict: The Seven Years' War in North America* (2007); Daniel P. Barr, ed., *The Boundaries Between Us: Natives and Newcomers along the Frontiers of the Old Northwest Territory* (2006); S. Subrahmanyam, *The Portuguese Empire in Asia, 1500–1700* (1993). A vital treatment of the international results of new trading patterns of foods and disease is Alfred Crosby, *The Columbian Exchange: Biological and Cultural Consequences of 1492* (2003); see also Elinor G. Melville, *A Plague of Sheep: Environmental Consequences of the Conquest of Mexico* (1994). For a stimulating reemphasis on Asia, see Andre Gunder Frank, *ReOrient: Global Economy in the Asian Age* (1998).

On slavery and its trade, see Pamela Scully and Diana Paton, eds., *Gender and Slave Emancipation in the Atlantic World* (2005); Eric Williams, *Capitalism and Slavery* (1964); Orlando Patterson, *Slavery and Social Death: A Comparative Study* (1982); and D. B. Davis, *Slavery and Human Progress* (1984); the last two are important comparative and analytical statements in a major field of recent historical study. See also Philip D. Curtin, *Atlantic Slave Trade* (1972), and his edited volume, *Africa Remembered: Narratives by West Africans from the Era of the Slave Trade* (1967).

New world trading patterns, including Asia's role in them, are discussed in K. N. Chaundhuri, *Trade and Civilization in the Indian Ocean* (1985); Stephan Frederic Dale, *Indian Merchants and Eurasia Trade: 1600–1750* (1994); and Philip Curtin, *Cross-Cultural Trade in World History* (1984). A controversial theoretical statement about new trade relationships and their impact on politics and social structure is found in three works by Immanuel Wallerstein, the most recent of which is *Politics of the World Economy: The States, the Movements, and the Civilizations* (1984).

For discussions on where colonial North America fits in this period of world history, see Colin G. Calloway, *The Scratch of a Pen: 1763 and the Transformation of North America* (2006); William J. Eccles, *France in America*, rev. ed. (1990); and Gary Nash, *Red, White, and Black: The Peoples of Early America*, rev. ed. (2010).

On the Web

An interactive webpage on European exploration and trade can be found at http://www.learner.org/interactives/renaissance/exploration.html (click on "Read More" at end of opening file). Introductions to the lives of the world's great explorers of every region and era are offered at http://www.win.tue.nl/cs/fm/engels/discovery/. A massive on-line text retrieval system for articles on the age of discovery is located at http://www.millersville.edu/~columbus/a-c.html.

A virtual version of an exhibit mounted by the Library of Congress and other materials that look at the multicultural dimensions of the events of 1492, the life of Christopher Columbus, and the Colombian exchange his voyages initiated can be found at http://www.loc.gov/exhibits/1492/.

The complex lives and motives of the conquistadors are examined at http://www.pbs.org/opb/conquistadors/home.htm.

The global impact of the relationship between conquistador Hernán Cortés and Donna Maria, La Malinche, his female Nahuatl-speaking translator, can be studied at http://thedagger.com/archive/conquest/conquest1.html; http://www.mexconnect.com/mex_/history/malinche.html and http://thedagger.com/archive/conquest/malinche.html.

The importance of the trade in commodities such as silver and sugar in the emerging global economy is discussed at http://www.learner.org/channel/courses/worldhistory/unit_main_15.html, http://www.questia.com/PM.qst?a=o&d=97925030, http://www.cs.brown.edu/~sk/Personal/Books/Mintz-Sweetness-Power/, and http://www.zum.de/whkmla/economy/plants/sugarcane.html.

Dutch and British traders soon outstripped their Iberian competitors in the new global economy, a process glimpsed at http://www.colonialvoyage.com/, http://library.thinkquest.org/26488/en/index.html, http://www.bbc.co.uk/history/british/empire_seapower/east_india_01.shtml, http://www.colonialvoyage.com/vocd.html, and http://www.fordham.edu/halsall/mod/modsbook03.html. The latter site also contains the chief primary documentation for the early modern world system and includes a summary of Immanuel Wallerstein's World System Theory (http://www.fordham.edu/halsall/mod/wallerstein.html). The pattern of the then emerging new world order can be glimpsed through a virtual visit to the Dutch factory at Batavia (http://www.tanap.net/content/voc/organization/organization_batavia.htm). Speculation on the nature of mercantilist trade and increasing globalization is offered at http://www.umassd.edu/euro/2005papers/parker.pdf.

AP* | Test Prep

1. The main reason European conquerors and navigators were able to sail and continue to explore, and the reason the Ming Chinese fleets in the Indian Ocean were withdrawn, was

    (A) from the outset, Europeans had superior naval technologies compared to the Chinese.

    (B) Europe encountered no major military opposition, while the Chinese did when entering the East Sea and the Indian Ocean.

    (C) competing European states, desperate for wealth, lent long-term support and encouragement to overseas expeditions; the unified, wealthy and contented Ming saw less need for them.

    (D) European nations were wealthier than the Chinese and could more easily afford the great cost of the expeditions.

2. In comparison to Spain and Portugal, the northern European states and their overseas expeditions

    (A) began earlier, but conquered fewer lands.

    (B) began later, but ultimately won and held on to more and larger colonies in Asia.

    (C) had superior military technologies and commercial practices but were uninterested in acquiring colonies.

    (D) were more motivated by religion than Portugal or Spain had been.

3. British, French, and Dutch joint-stock companies engaged in exploration and colonization benefited from

    (A) copying the same business methods used successfully by the Spanish and Portuguese.

    (B) medieval guild laws which required that companies must help the government finance major military expeditions.

    (C) their governments' grant of monopolies in certain areas and many investors sharing the risks of any voyage.

    (D) governments lending investors ships and crews with the private investors paid only for trading goods.

Free-Response Question

In what ways did the voyages of Columbus redefine the interchanges among major societies and their economies in the early modern period?

4. All of following were examples of the Columbian Exchange EXCEPT

    (A) the spread of smallpox and measles to the Americas.

    (B) the spread of American crops such as corn, potatoes, peanuts and manioc to Afro-Eurasia.

    (C) the spread of Eurasian domesticated animals such as horses, cows, sheep, and chickens to the Americas.

    (D) the spread of rice from the Americas to China and other parts of Asia.

5. During the Early Modern Period in world history, rural laborers in the Americas were

    (A) wage laborers (contracted to work by hour, day or week).

    (B) unfree laborers (enslaved, indentured, subjects of labor taxes).

    (C) worked for themselves on a farm or in a family business.

    (D) mostly artisanal laborers who knew a skilled craft.

6. The new world trade network that emerged in the early modern period can best be described by which of the following statements?

    (A) The vibrant Atlantic economy replaced the Indian Ocean Basin as the most lucrative regional trade network for peoples from both hemispheres.

    (B) China continues to serve as a major center of export manufacturing.

    (C) The new world economy was based on the capitalist principle of amassing enormous profits with little governmental assistance and few regulations.

    (D) The new world economy was really an economy based in two separate hemispheres, tied together by a few trade routes across the Atlantic ocean.

7. Which of the following was the most lucrative commodity traded in the Early Modern Period?

    (A) gold

    (B) tobacco

    (C) cotton

    (D) sugar

17 The Transformation of the West, 1450–1750

The First Big Changes: Culture and Commerce, 1450–1650
The Commercial Revolution
The Scientific Revolution: The Next Phase of Change
VISUALIZING THE PAST: Versailles
Political Change

THINKING HISTORICALLY: Elites and Masses
The West by 1750
DOCUMENT: Controversies About Women
GLOBAL CONNECTIONS: Europe and the World

Throughout the early modern period, Europe's growing involvement in world trade had important impacts on internal developments—on the economy, obviously, but also on government policy and even personal taste. A case in point involved the implications of brightly-colored cotton cloth.

Cotton manufacturing had long been a specialty in India. Cheaper than silks, cotton fabrics could sport vivid dyes and designs. Indian cotton products had sold extensively in world trade during the postclassical period, reaching East Asia, the Middle East and, more tentatively, Europe. With Europe's new connections to India after 1498, availability of cottons, and consumer passion, both increased rapidly. The contrast with conventional linen and woolen fabrics, with characteristically dull colors, was marked. One European traveler to India wrote ecstatically of "cloths of the whiteness of snow, and very delicate and fine" with other fabrics "bespangled and painted with various figures." Europeans were particularly taken with floral designs, and Indian manufacturers began to target part of their production specifically for the European market. Here was one of several examples where rising levels of global trade spurred new consumer tastes, allowing new levels of personal expression through clothing. By the 17th century another observer noted that "in some things the artists of India outdo all the ingenuity of Europe" as in cotton textiles, which Europeans could not match "in their brightness and life of colour."

Portuguese traders were the first to bring cottons directly to Europe, with peddlers taking them to more northern markets. By the 17th century Danish merchants and others were traveling direct to India to seek decorative textiles for homes as well as clothing.

Royal officials in several countries worried about the impact of Indian imports on domestic production and domestic profits. There was also some chiding by moral conservatives about this kind of showy display. By the later 17th century many governments passed rules against wearing brightly colored clothing, while even more laws tried to protect European industry by banning Indian textile imports.

By this point also, however, European manufacturers themselves were beginning to wonder if they could take advantage of consumer tastes directly. In southern France, several Armenian workmen brought in new techniques in partnership with local businessmen around 1650, and Armenians also helped set up production in Amsterdam. By 1750 a factory in Switzerland, though using manual operations, employed over 1300 workers. Only by this point were European methods adequate to match the best Indian colors and designs.

By the later 18th century, dramatic new printing processes, including use of a rotary press, moved European cottons directly into the industrial revolution. By this time as well, European consumers, now seeing access to colorful cottons as a routine need, became ever more demanding of dramatic new styles each year, indulging a taste for novelty that was built into modern consumerism. What began as a deferential contact with Asia turned into an engine for European change. ■

Machiavelli, Niccolo (1469–1527) Author of *The Prince* (16th century); emphasized realistic discussions of how to seize and maintain power; one of most influential authors of Italian Renaissance.

This chapter deals with a series of big changes in Western Europe between 1450 and 1750. The specific new movements were diverse, but over the three centuries' span they added up to a novel cultural framework, for intellectuals but also many ordinary people; some key political innovations; and a more commercially-based social structure. In considering particular developments, it's important to keep the larger ultimate directions of change in mind. It's also important to remember that the developments occurred in a context of growing interaction with other parts of the world—even in areas as prosaic as new preferences for clothing.

The First Big Changes: Culture and Commerce, 1450–1650

The Italian writer Francesco Petrarch (1304–1374) once climbed Ventoux, a mountain in southern France. He wrote of his ascent, proud of his own skill and using the climb as a symbol of what he could achieve. There was a new spirit in this work, intended to be published, compared to the more religious Middle Ages. But Petrarch did not abandon religion, and in later life he talked about how he had given up poetry in favor of reading Christian texts, finding "hidden sweetness which I had once esteemed but lightly."

The Italian Renaissance

The move away from earlier European patterns began with the Renaissance, which first developed in Italy during the 14th and 15th centuries. Largely an artistic movement, the Renaissance challenged medieval intellectual values and styles. It also sketched a new, brasher spirit that may have encouraged a new Western interest in exploring strange waters or urging that old truths be reexamined.

Italy was already well launched in the development of Renaissance culture by the 15th century, based on its unusually extensive urban, commercial economy and its competitive city-state politics. Writers such as Petrarch and Boccaccio had promoted classical literary canons against medieval logic and theology, writing in Italian as well as the traditional Latin and emphasizing secular subjects such as love and pride. Painting turned to new realism and classical and human-centered themes. Religion declined as a central focus. The Italian Renaissance blossomed further in the 15th and early 16th centuries. This was a great age of Western art, as Leonardo da Vinci advanced the realistic portrayal of the human body and Michelangelo applied classical styles in painting and sculpture. In political theory, **Niccolo Machiavelli** emphasized realistic discussions of how to seize and maintain power. Like the artists, Machiavelli bolstered his realism with Greek and Roman examples.

Overall, Italian Renaissance culture stressed themes of **humanism:** a focus on humankind as the center of intellectual and artistic endeavor. Religion was not attacked, but its principles were no longer predominant. Historians have debated the reasons for this change. Italy's more urban, commercial environment was one factor, but so was the new imitation of classical Greek and Roman literature and art.

These Renaissance themes had some bearing on politics and commerce. Renaissance merchants improved their banking techniques and became more openly profit-seeking than their medieval counterparts had been. City-state leaders experimented with new political forms and functions. They justified their rule not on the basis of heredity or divine guidance but more on the basis of what they could do to advance general well-being and their city's glory. Thus, they sponsored cultural activities and tried to improve the administration of the economy. They also developed more professional armies, for wars among the city-states were common, and gave new attention to military tactics and training. They also rethought the practice of diplomacy, introducing the regular exchange of ambassadors for the first time in the West. Clearly, the Renaissance encouraged innovation, although it also produced some dependence on classical models.

The Renaissance Moves Northward

Italy began to decline as a Renaissance center by about 1500. French and Spanish monarchs invaded the peninsula, reducing political independence. At the same time, new Atlantic trade routes reduced the importance of Mediterranean ports, a huge blow to the Italian economy.

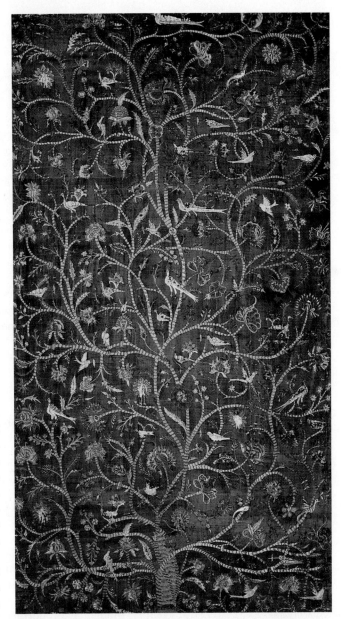

Figure 17.1 This tapestry with a Tree of Life design from India dates from the 17th century. This particular design is on silk, but it shows the colors and artistry that made Indian fabrics such a popular global commodity in the postclassical and early modern periods.

The Renaissance emphasized new styles and beliefs. Religious changes springing from the Protestant Reformation had an even wider impact.

Machiavelli's *The Prince*

DOCUMENT

humanism Focus on humankind as center of intellectual and artistic endeavor; method of study that emphasized the superiority of classical forms over medieval styles, in particular the study of ancient languages.

1300 C.E.	1450 C.E.	1500 C.E.	1550 C.E.	1650 C.E.	1750 C.E.
1300–1450 Italian Renaissance	1450–1519 Life of Leonardo da Vinci 1450–1600 Northern Renaissance 1455 First European printing press, Mainz, Germany 1469–1527 Life of Machiavelli 1475–1514 Life of Michelangelo 1490s France and Spain invade Italian city-states; beginning of Italian decline	1500–1600 Commercial revolution 1515–1547 Reign of Francis I, France 1517 Luther's 95 theses; beginning of Protestant Reformation 1534 Beginning of Church of England 1541–1564 Calvin in Geneva 1543 Copernican revolution; Copernicus's work on astronomy	1550–1649 Religious wars in France, Germany, and Britain 1555–1603 Reign of Elizabeth I, England 1564–1642 Life of Galileo 1588 English defeat the Spanish Armada 17th century Scientific Revolution 1609 Independence of Netherlands 1618–1648 Thirty Years War 1642–1649 English Civil War 1642–1727 Life of Isaac Newton 1643–1715 Reign of Louis XIV, France; absolute monarchy 1647–1648 Culmination of popular rebellions in western Europe	1670–1692 Decline of witchcraft trials 1682–1699 Habsburgs drive Turks from Hungary 1688–1690 Glorious Revolution in Britain; parliamentary monarchy; some religious toleration; political writing of John Locke 18th century Enlightenment 1712–1786 Life of Frederick the Great of Prussia, enlightened despot 1730–1850 European population boom 1733 James Kay invents flying shuttle loom 1736 Beginnings of Methodism	1756–1763 Seven Years War: France, Britain, Prussia, and Austria 1776 Adam Smith's *Wealth of Nations* 1780–1790 Reign of Joseph II, first Habsburg emperor 1792 Mary Wollstonecraft's *Vindication of the Rights of Women*

Sir Thomas More, *Utopia* (1516)

DOCUMENT

Northern Renaissance   Cultural and intellectual movement of northern Europe; began later than Italian Renaissance c. 1450; centered in France, Low Countries, England, and Germany; featured greater emphasis on religion than Italian Renaissance.

Francis I   King of France in the 16th century; regarded as Renaissance monarch; patron of arts; imposed new controls on Catholic church; ally of Ottoman sultan against Holy Roman emperor.

As Renaissance creativity faded in its Italian birthplace, it passed northward. The **Northern Renaissance**—focused in France, the Low Countries, Germany, and England—began after 1450. Renaissance styles also affected Hungary and Poland in east central Europe. Classical styles in art and architecture became the rage. Knowledge of Greek and Latin literature gained ground, although many northern humanists wrote in their own languages (English, French, and so on). Northern humanists were more religious than their Italian counterparts, trying to blend secular interests with continued Christian devotion. Renaissance writers such as Shakespeare in England and Rabelais in France mixed classical themes with an earthiness—a joy in bodily functions and human passions—that maintained elements of medieval popular culture. Renaissance literature established a new set of classics for literary traditions in the major Western languages, such as the writings of Shakespeare in England and Cervantes in Spain.

The Northern Renaissance produced some political change, providing another move toward greater state powers. As their revenues and operations expanded, Renaissance kings increased their pomp and ceremony. Kings such as **Francis I** in France became patrons of the arts, importing Italian sculptors and architects to create their classical-style palaces. By the late 16th century, many monarchs were sponsoring trading companies and colonial enterprises. Interest in military conquest was greater than in the Middle Ages. Francis I was even willing to ally with the Ottoman sultan, the key Muslim leader. His goal was to distract his main enemy, the Habsburg ruler of Austria and Spain. In fact, it was an alliance in name only, but it illustrated how power politics was beginning to abandon the feudal or religious justifications that had previously clothed it in the West.

Yet the impact of the Renaissance should not be overstated, particularly outside Italy. Renaissance kings were still confined by the political powers of feudal landlords. Ordinary people were little touched by Renaissance values; the life of most peasants and artisans went on much as before. Economic life also changed little, particularly outside the Italian commercial centers. Even in the upper classes, women sometimes encountered new limits as Renaissance leaders touted men's public bravado over women's domestic roles.

Changes in Technology and Family

More fundamental changes were brewing in Western society by 1500, beneath the glittering surface of the Renaissance. Spurred by trading contacts with Asia, workers in the West improved the quality of pulleys and pumps in mines and learned how to forge stronger iron products. Printing was introduced in the 15th century when the German **Johannes Gutenberg** introduced movable type, building on Chinese printing technology. Soon books were distributed in greater quantities in the West, which helped expand the audience for Renaissance writers and disseminated religious ideas. Literacy began to gain ground and became a fertile source of new kinds of thinking.

Family structure was also changing. A **European-style family** pattern came into being by the 15th century. This pattern involved a late marriage age and a primary emphasis on nuclear families of parents and children rather than the extended families characteristic of most agricultural civilizations. The goal was to limit family birth rates. By the 16th century, ordinary people usually did not marry until their late 20s—a marked contrast to most agricultural societies. These changes emphasized the importance of husband–wife relations. They also closely linked the family to individual property holdings, for most people could not marry until they had access to property.

Gutenberg, Johannes Introduced movable type to western Europe in 15th century; credited with greatly expanded availability of printed books and pamphlets.

European Population Density, c. 1600

European-style family Originated in 15th century among peasants and artisans of western Europe, featuring late marriage age, emphasis on the nuclear family, and a large minority who never married.

The Protestant and Catholic Reformations

In the 16th century, religious upheaval and a new commercial surge began to define the directions of change more fully. In 1517, a German monk named **Martin Luther** issued a document containing 95 theses, or propositions. He was publicly protesting claims made by a papal representative in selling indulgences, or grants of salvation, for money, but in fact his protest went deeper. Luther's reading of the Bible convinced him that only faith could gain salvation. Church sacraments were not the path, for God could not be manipulated. Luther's protest, which was rebuffed by the papacy, soon led him to challenge many Catholic beliefs, including the authority of the pope. Luther would soon argue that monasticism was wrong, that priests should marry (as he did), and that the Bible should be translated from Latin so ordinary people could have direct access to its teachings. Luther did not want to break Christian unity, but the church he wanted should be on his terms (or, as he would have argued, the terms of the true faith).

Luther picked up wide support for his views during the mid-16th century and beyond. Many Germans, in a somewhat nationalist reaction, resented the authority and taxes of the Roman pope. German princes saw an opportunity to gain more power. Their nominal leader, the Holy Roman emperor, remained Catholic. Thus, princes who turned Protestant could increase their independence and seize church lands. The Lutheran version of **Protestantism** (as the general wave of religious dissent was called) urged state control of the church as an alternative to papal authority, and this had obvious political appeal.

There were reasons for ordinary people to shift their allegiance as well. Some German peasants saw Luther's attack on authority as a sanction for their own social rebellion against landlords, although Luther specifically renounced this reading. Some townspeople were drawn to Luther's approval of work in the world. Because faith alone gained salvation, Lutheranism could sanction moneymaking and other earthly pursuits more wholeheartedly than did traditional Catholicism. Unlike Catholicism, Lutherans did not see special vocations as particularly holy; monasteries were abolished, along with some of the Christian bias against moneymaking.

Once Christian unity was breached, other Protestant groups sprang forward (see Map 17.1). In England, Henry VIII began to set up an **Anglican church,** initially to challenge papal attempts to enforce his first marriage, which had failed to produce a male heir. (Henry ultimately had six wives in sequence, executing two of them, a particularly graphic example of the treatment of women in power politics.) Henry was also attracted to some of the new doctrines, and his most durable successor, his daughter Elizabeth I, was Protestant outright.

Martin Luther, Sermon at the Castle Pleissenburg

Luther, Martin (1483–1546) German monk; initiated Protestant Reformation in 1517 by nailing 95 theses to door of Wittenberg church; emphasized primacy of faith over works stressed in Catholic church; accepted state control of church.

Protestantism General wave of religious dissent against Catholic church; generally held to have begun with Martin Luther's attack on Catholic beliefs in 1517; included many varieties of religious belief.

Anglican church Form of Protestantism set up in England after 1534; established by Henry VIII with himself as head, at least in part to obtain a divorce from his first wife; became increasingly Protestant following Henry's death.

Map 17.1 Western Europe During the Renaissance and Reformation Different Protestant denominations made inroads in much of northwestern Europe with the Reformation, but Catholicism maintained its hold on significant portions of the continent.

Calvin on
Predestination

Calvin, Jean French Protestant (16th century) who stressed doctrine of predestination; established center of his group at Swiss canton of Geneva; encouraged ideas of wider access to government, wider public education; Calvinism spread from Switzerland to northern Europe and North America.

Ignatius
Loyola, Rules
for Thinking
with the
Church

Catholic Reformation Restatement of traditional Catholic beliefs in response to Protestant Reformation (16th century); established councils that revived Catholic doctrine and refuted Protestant beliefs.

Jesuits A new religious order founded during the Catholic Reformation; active in politics, education, and missionary work; sponsored missions to South America, North American, and Asia.

Still more important were the churches inspired by **Jean Calvin,** a French theologian who established his base in the Swiss city of Geneva. Calvinism insisted on God's *predestination,* or prior determination, of those who would be saved. Calvinist ministers became moral guardians and preachers of God's word. Calvinists sought the participation of all believers in local church administration, which promoted the idea of a wider access to government. They also promoted broader popular education so that more people could read the Bible. Calvinism was accepted not only in part of Switzerland but also in portions of Germany, in France (where it produced strong minority groups), in the Netherlands, in Hungary, and in England and Scotland. By the early 17th century, Puritan exiles brought it to North America.

The Catholic church did not sit still under Protestant attack. It could not restore religious unity, but it defended southern Europe, Austria, Poland, much of Hungary, and key parts of Germany for the Catholic faith. Under a **Catholic Reformation,** a major church council revived Catholic doctrine and refuted key Protestant tenets such as the idea that priests had no special sacramental power and could marry. They also attacked popular superstitions and remnants of magical belief, which meant that Catholics and Protestants alike were trying to find new ways to shape the outlook of ordinary folk. A new religious order, the **Jesuits,** became active in politics, education, and missionary work, regaining some parts of Europe for the church. Jesuit fervor also sponsored Catholic missionary activity in Asia and the Americas.

The End of Christian Unity in the West

The Protestant and Catholic Reformations had several results in Europe during the late 16th and early 17th centuries. Most obvious was an important series of religious wars. France was a scene of bitter battles between Calvinist and Catholic forces. These disputes ended only with the granting of tolerance to Protestants through the **edict of Nantes** in 1598, although in the next century French kings progressively cut back on Protestant rights. In Germany, the **Thirty Years War** broke out in 1618, pitting German Protestants and allies such as Lutheran Sweden against the Holy Roman emperor, backed by Spain. The war was so devastating that it reduced German power and prosperity for a full century, cutting population by as much as 60 percent in some regions (Figure 17.2). It was ended only by the 1648 **Treaty of Westphalia,** which agreed to the territorial tolerance concept: Some princely states and cities chose one religion, some another. This treaty also finally settled a rebellion of the Protestant Netherlands against Spain, giving the former its full independence.

Religious fighting punctuated British history, first before the reign of Elizabeth in the 16th century, then in the **English Civil War** in the 1640s. Calvinists, Anglicans and some remaining Catholics locked on combat. There was also growing tension between the claims of parliament and some strong assertions of authority by a new line of English kings. The civil war ended in 1660 (well after King Charles I had been beheaded; Figure 17.3), but full resolution came only in 1688–1689, when limited religious toleration was granted to most Protestants, though not to Catholics.

Religious issues thus dominated European politics for almost a century. The religious wars led to a grudging and limited acceptance of the idea of religious pluralism. Christian unity could not be restored, although in most individual countries the idea of full religious liberty was still in the future. The religious wars persuaded some people that religion itself was suspect; if there was no dominant single truth, why all the cruelty and carnage? Finally, the wars affected the political balance of Europe, as Map 17.2 shows. After a period of weakness during its internal strife, France was on the upswing. The Netherlands and Britain were galvanized toward a growing international role. Spain, briefly ascendant, fell back. Internally, some kings and princes benefited from the decline of papal authority by taking a stronger role in religious affairs. This was true in many Catholic and Protestant domains. In some cases, however, Protestant dissent encouraged popular political movements and enhanced parliamentary power.

The impact of religious change went well beyond politics. Popular beliefs changed most in Protestant areas, but Catholic reform produced new impulses as well. Western people gradually became less likely to see an intimate connection between God and nature. Protestants resisted the idea of miracles or other interventions in nature's course. Religious change also promoted greater concentration on family life. Religious writers encouraged love between husband and wife. As one English Protestant put it, "When love is absent between husband and wife, it is like a bone out of joint: there is no ease, no order." This promotion of the family had ambiguous implications for women. Protestantism, abolishing religious convents, made marriage more necessary for women than before; there were fewer alternatives for women who could not marry. Fathers were also responsible for the religious training of the children. On the other hand, women's emotional role in the family improved with the new emphasis on affection.

Religious change accompanied and promoted growing literacy along with the spread of the printing press. In the town of Durham, England, around 1570, only 20 percent of all people were literate, but by 1630 the figure had climbed to 47 percent. Growing literacy opened people to additional new ideas and ways of thinking.

Figure 17.2 Hans Holbein's *The Dance of Death,* published in 1538, illustrated social upheaval resulting from the continuing plague as well as from religious conflict.

 Europe After the Treaty of Westphalia, 1648

 James I on the Divine Right of Kings

 The Ideal Wife

edict of Nantes Grant of tolerance to Protestants in France in 1598; granted only after lengthy civil war between Catholic and Protestant factions.

Thirty Years War War within the Holy Roman Empire between German Protestants and their allies (Sweden, Denmark, France) and the emperor and his ally, Spain; ended in 1648 after great destruction with Treaty of Westphalia.

Treaty of Westphalia Ended Thirty Years War in 1648; granted right to individual rulers within the Holy Roman Empire to choose their own religion—either Protestant or Catholic.

Figure 17.3 Civil war over religious issues and the relative power of king and parliament resulted in the beheading of Charles I in London in 1649. As this painting suggests, the regicide was one of the most controversial events in English history.

The Commercial Revolution

Trade and manufacturing expanded rapidly. A more commercial economy also spurred protest.

Along with religious upheaval during the 16th century, the economic structure of the West was fundamentally redefined. The level of European trade rose sharply, and many Europeans had new goods available to them. Involvement with markets and merchants increased. Here was the clearest impact of the new world economy in western Europe.

The Impact of the World Economy

English Civil War   Conflict from 1640 to 1660; featured religious disputes mixed with constitutional issues concerning the powers of the monarchy; ended with restoration of the monarchy in 1660 following execution of previous king.

A basic spur to greater commercialization was the price inflation that occurred throughout western Europe during the 16th century. The massive import of gold and silver from Spain's new colonies in Latin America forced prices up. The availability of more money, based on silver supply, generated this price rise. New wealth heightened demand for products to sell, both in the colonies and in Europe, but Western production could not keep pace, hence the price inflation. Inflation encouraged merchants to take new risks, for borrowing was cheap when money was losing value. A sum borrowed one year would be worth less, in real terms, five years later, so it made sense to take loans for new investments.

Inflation and the new colonial opportunities led to the formation of the great trading companies, often with government backing, in Spain, England, the Netherlands, and France. Governments granted regional monopolies to these giant concerns; thus, the Dutch East Indies Company long dominated trade with the islands of Indonesia. European merchants brought new profits back to Europe and developed new managerial skills and banking arrangements.

Colonial markets stimulated manufacturing. Most peasants continued to produce mainly for their own needs, but agricultural specialty areas developed in the production of wines, cheeses, wool, and the like. Some of these industries favored commercial farming and the use of paid laborers on the land. Shoemaking, pottery, metalworking, and other manufacturing specializations arose in both rural villages and the cities. Technical improvements followed in many branches of manufacture, particularly in metals and mining.

Map 17.2 Europe Under Absolute Monarchy, 1715   The rise of absolute monarchies led to consolidation of national borders as states asserted full control of areas within their boundaries. For example, a recent study shows that villages that straddled the French–Spanish border were undifferentiated before 1600, but by 1700 they showed marked national differences because of different state policies and the greater impact of belonging to one state or another.

Prosperity increased for many ordinary people as well as for the great merchants. One historian has estimated that by about 1600 the average Western peasant or artisan owned five times as many "things" as his or her counterpart in southeastern Europe. A 16th-century Englishman noted that whereas in the past a peasant and his family slept on the floor and had only a pan or two as kitchenware, by the final decades of the century a farmer might have "a fair garnish of pewter in his cupboard, three or four feather beds, so many coverlets and carpets of tapestry, a silver salt, a bowl for wine . . . and a dozen spoons." It was about this time that French peasants began to enjoy wine fairly regularly rather than simply at special occasions—the result of higher productivity and better trade and transport facilities.

Social Protest

There were victims of change as well. Growing commercialization created the beginnings of a new **proletariat** in the West—people without access to wealth-producing property. Population growth and rising food prices hit hard at the poor, and many people had to sell their small plots of land. Some proletarians became manufacturing workers, depending on orders from merchant capitalists to keep their tools busy in their cottages. Others became paid laborers on agricultural estates, where landlords were eager for a more manipulable workforce to take advantage of business opportunities in the cities. Others pressed into the cities, and a growing problem of beggars and wandering poor began to affect Western society (Map 17.3). By blaming the poor for moral failings, a new, tough attitude toward poverty took shape that has lasted to some extent to the present day.

proletariat Class of working people without access to producing property; typically manufacturing workers, paid laborers in agricultural economy, or urban poor; in Europe, product of economic changes of 16th and 17th centuries.

Map 17.3 European Population Density, c.1600 Europe experienced new levels of population concentration in some urban areas by 1600, though by Asian standards, city size remained fairly modest.

Not surprisingly, the shifts in popular economic and cultural traditions provoked important outcries. A huge wave of popular protest in western Europe developed at the end of the 16th century and extended until about 1650. Peasants and townspeople alike rose for greater protection from poverty and loss of property. The uprisings did not deflect the basic currents of change, but they revealed the massive insecurity of many workers.

The popular rebellions of the 17th century revealed social tension and new ideas of equality. Peasant songs voiced such sentiments as this: "The whole country must be overturned, for we peasants are now to be the lords, it is we who will sit in the shade." Uprisings in 1648 produced demands for a popular political voice; an English group called the Levelers gained 100,000 signatures on a petition for political rights. Elsewhere, common people praised the kings while attacking their "bad advisors" and high taxes. One English agitator said that "we should cut off all the gentlemen's heads. . . . We shall have a merrier world shortly." In France, Protestant and Catholic peasants rose together against landlords and taxes: "They seek only the ruin of the poor people for our ruin is their wealth."

An unprecedented outburst against suspected witches arose in the same decades in various parts of western Europe and also in New England. Although attacks on witches had developed before, the new scale reflected intense social and cultural upheaval. Between 60,000 and 100,000 suspected witches were accused and killed. The **witchcraft persecution** reflected new resentments

witchcraft persecution Reflected resentment against the poor, uncertainties about religious truth; resulted in death of over 100,000 Europeans between 1590 and 1650; particularly common in Protestant areas.

against the poor, who were often accused of witchcraft by communities unwilling to accept responsibility for their poverty. The hysteria also revealed new tensions about family life and the role of women, who were the most common targets of persecution. A few of the accused witches actually believed they had magical powers, but far more were accused by fearful or self-serving neighbors. The whole witchcraft experience revealed a society faced with forces of unusual complexity.

A Balance Sheet

Changes in Europe between 1450 and 1650 were untidy. Renaissance secular interests clashed with Reformation spiritual emphases. The confusion of change helped explain sharp reactions, like the witchcraft trials. Still, there were some basic directions to change. Europe was becoming more commercial; even some of the implications of the Reformation pushed toward higher valuation of commercial success. The role of families was shifting. Religion remained strong, but its expressions and its political roles became more contested. All of this finally set the stage for further change.

Scientific Revolution   Culminated in 17th century; period of empirical advances associated with the development of wider theoretical generalizations; resulted in change in traditional beliefs of Middle Ages.

Copernicus   Polish monk and astronomer (16th century); disproved Hellenistic belief that the earth was at the center of the universe.

Johannes Kepler   (December 27, 1571–November 15, 1630) Was an astronomer and mathematician who was a prominent figure in the scientific revolution.

The Scientific Revolution: The Next Phase of Change

The revolution in science, culminating in the 17th century, set the seal on the cultural reorientation of the West. Although the **Scientific Revolution** most obviously affected formal intellectual life, it also promoted changes in popular outlook. At the same time, after the political upheavals of the Reformation, a more decisive set of new government forms arose in the West, centering on the emergence of the nation-state. The functions of the state expanded. The Western nation-state was not a single form, because key variants such as absolute monarchies and parliamentary regimes emerged, but there were some common patterns beneath the surface.

A revolution in the nature and status of science occurred during the 17th century. The European state took on new forms and functions. This wave of change intensified after 1650.

Did Copernicus Copy?

This is a chapter about big changes in western Europe during the early modern period. Big changes are always complex. One key development was the rise of science in intellectual life. A key first step here was the discovery by the Polish monk **Copernicus,** in the 16th century, that the planets moved around the sun rather than the earth, as the Greeks had thought. This discovery set other scientific advances in motion, and more generally showed that new thinking could improve on tradition. Copernicus is usually taken as a quiet hero of Western science and rationalism.

 Nicolaus Copernicus: On the Revolution of the Heavenly Spheres

Copernicus based his findings on mathematics, understanding that the Greek view of earth as central raised key problems in calculating planetary motion. Historians have recently uncovered similar geometrical findings by two Arabs, al-Urdi and al-Tusi, from the 13th and 14th centuries. Did Copernicus copy, as Westerners had previously done from the Arabs, while keeping quiet because learning from Muslims was now unpopular? Or did he discover independently? It's also worth noting that scientists in other traditions, such as Chinese, Indian, and Mayan, had already realized the central position of the sun.

What is certain is that based on discoveries like that of Copernicus, science began to take on more importance in Western intellectual life than had ever been the case in the intellectual history of other societies, including classical Greece. Change may be complicated but it does occur.

Science: The New Authority

During the 16th century, scientific research quietly built on the traditions of the later Middle Ages. After Copernicus, **Johannes Kepler** (1571–1630; Figure 17.4) was another important early figure in the study of planetary motion. Unusual for a major researcher, Kepler was from a poor family; his father abandoned the family outright, and his mother was once tried for witchcraft. But Kepler made his way to university on scholarship, aiming for the Lutheran ministry but drawn to astronomy and mathematics. Using the work of Copernicus and his own observations, he resolved basic issues of planetary motion. He also worked on optics and, with the mixed interests so common in real intellectual life,

Figure 17.4 Johannes Kepler, one of the leading figures in the Scientific Revolution.

Galileo Galilei, Letter to the Grand Duchess Christina

DOCUMENT

Galileo Published Copernicus's findings (17th century); added own discoveries concerning laws of gravity and planetary motion; condemned by the Catholic church for his work.

Harvey, William English physician (17th century) who demonstrated circular movement of blood in animals, function of heart as pump.

Francis Bacon (22 January 1561–9 April 1626) Was an English philosopher, statesman, author, and scientist. He was an influential member of the scientific revolution, and is best known for work on the scientific method.

Descartes, René Established importance of skeptical review of all received wisdom (17th century); argued that human reason could then develop laws that would explain the fundamental workings of nature.

Newton, Isaac (1643–1727) English scientist; author of *Principia*; drew together astronomical and physical observations and wider theories into a neat framework of natural laws; established principles of motion; defined forces of gravity.

Deism Concept of God current during the Scientific Revolution; role of divinity was to set natural laws in motion, not to regulate once process was begun.

Locke, John (1632–1704) English philosopher who argued that people could learn everything through senses and reason and that power of government came from the people, not divine right of kings; offered possibility of revolution to overthrow tyrants.

also practiced astrology, casting horoscopes for wealthy patrons. Also around 1600, anatomical work by the Belgian Vesalius gained greater precision. These key discoveries not only advanced knowledge but also implied a new power for scientific research in its ability to test and often over-rule accepted ideas.

A series of empirical advances and wider theoretical generalizations extended the possibilities of science from the 1600s onward. New instruments such as the microscope and improved telescopes allowed gains in biology and astronomy. The Italian **Galileo** publicized Copernicus's discoveries while adding his own basic findings about the laws of gravity and planetary motion. Condemned by the Catholic Church for his innovations, Galileo proved the inadequacy of traditional ideas about the universe. He also showed the new pride in scientific achievement, writing modestly how he, "by marvelous discoveries and clear demonstrations, had enlarged a thousand times" the knowledge produced by "the wise men of bygone ages." Chemical research advanced understanding of the behavior of gasses. English physician **William Harvey** demonstrated the circular movement of the blood in animals, with the heart as the "central pumping station."

These advances in knowledge were accompanied by important statements about science and its impact. **Francis Bacon** urged the value of careful empirical research and predicted that scientific knowledge could advance steadily, producing improvements in technology as well. **René Descartes** established the importance of a skeptical review of all received wisdom, arguing that human reason could develop laws that would explain the fundamental workings of nature.

The capstone to the 17th-century Scientific Revolution came in 1687, when **Isaac Newton** published his *Principia Mathematica*. This work drew the various astronomical and physical observations and wider theories together in a neat framework of natural laws. Newton set forth the basic principles of all motion (for example, that a body in motion maintains uniform momentum unless affected by outside forces such as friction). Newton defined the forces of gravity in great mathematical detail and showed that the whole universe responded to these forces, which among other things explained the planetary orbits described by Kepler. Finally, Newton stated the basic scientific method in terms of a mixture of rational hypothesis and generalization and careful empirical observation and experiment. Here was a vision of a natural universe that could be captured in simple laws (although increasingly complex mathematics accompanied the findings). Here was a vision of a method of knowing that might do away with blind reliance on tradition or religious faith.

The Scientific Revolution was quickly popularized among educated Westerners. Here was a key step in the cultural transformation of western Europe in the early modern period. New scientific institutes were set up, often with government aid, to advance research and disseminate the findings. Lectures and easy-to-read manuals publicized the latest advances and communicated the excitement that researchers shared in almost all parts of Europe. Beliefs in witchcraft began to decline and magistrates grew increasingly reluctant to entertain witchcraft accusations in court after about 1670. There were growing signs of a new belief that people could control and calculate their environment. Insurance companies sprang up to help guard against risk. Doctors increased their attacks on popular healers, promoting a more scientific diagnosis of illness. Newsletters, an innovation by the late 17th century, began to advertise "lost and found" items, for there was no point leaving this kind of problem to customary magicians, called "cunning men," who had poked around with presumably enchanted sticks.

By the 1680s writers affected by the new science, though not themselves scientists, began to attack traditional religious ideas such as miracles, for in the universe of the Scientific Revolution there was no room for disruption of nature's laws. Some intellectuals held out a new conception of God, called **Deism**, arguing that although there might be a divinity, its role was simply to set natural laws in motion. In England, **John Locke** argued that people could learn everything they needed to know through their senses and reason; faith was irrelevant. Christian beliefs in human sinfulness crumbled in the view of these intellectuals, for they saw human nature as basically good. Finally, scientific advances created wider assumptions about the possibility of human progress. If knowledge could advance through concerted human effort, why not progress in other domains? Even literary authorities joined this parade, and the idea that past styles set timeless standards of perfection came under growing criticism.

Science had never before been central to intellectual life. Science had played important roles in other civilizations, as in China, classical Greece, Central America, and Islam. Europe's science built

Versailles

This picture shows Louis XIV's grand 17th-century palace at Versailles. It displays the sheer opulence of this absolute monarchy, in what was Europe's richest and most populous and influential nation. It also shows the renewed hold of a classical style, seen to be most prestigious for public buildings. What else does it suggest?

Architecture is sometimes thought to be the most socially and historically revealing of all the arts because it depends most heavily on public support; it is harder for architects, particularly dealing with public buildings, to be as idiosyncratic as painters or poets.

QUESTIONS What kinds of intentions on the part of Louis and his advisors does this building represent? How can Versailles be interpreted as a statement of absolute monarchy? What would the palace represent to an ordinary French person? To an aristocrat?

The palace at Versailles.

(Musee de Chateau de Versailles/Dagli Orti/ Picture Desk, Inc./Kobal Collection.)

---

in fact on continuing contacts with work in the Middle East. But while the West was not alone in developing crucial scientific ideas, it now became the leading center for scientific advance. Its key thinkers stood alone for some time in seeing science as the key to gaining and defining knowledge.

Political Change

Political change from 1600 to 1750 was complicated, even as religious strife gradually calmed. A tradition of strong monarchy developed in France and elsewhere, greatly adding to the functions of the central government. But in Britain and Holland a different emphasis emerged, providing a strong parliamentary check on royal power. Both traditions proved significant in shaping Europe's political future. More effective central governments helped Europe catch up to political forms that had been developed earlier in countries like China. At the same time, growing suggestions of what would come to be called the nation-state provided a new element in politics that would later spread to other parts of the world.

As feudalism declined in Western Europe, new political forms gained ground. Both absolute and parliamentary monarchies emerged.

Absolute Monarchies

New political currents took shape along with the rise of science, and at times the two trends connected. The feudal monarchy—the balance between king and nobles—that had defined Western politics since the late postclassical period finally came undone in the 17th century. In most countries, after the passions of religious wars finally cooled, monarchs gained new powers, curtailing the tradition of noble pressure or revolt. At the same time, more ambitious military organization, in states that defined war as a central purpose, required more careful administration and improved tax collection.

The model for this new pattern was France, now the West's largest and most powerful nation. French kings steadily built up their power in the 17th century. They stopped convening the medieval parliament and passed laws as they saw fit, although some provincial councils remained strong. They blew up the castles of dissident nobles, another sign that gunpowder was undercutting the military basis of feudalism. They appointed a growing bureaucracy drawn from the merchants and lawyers. They sent direct representatives to the outlying provinces. They professionalized the army, giving more formal training to officers, providing uniforms and support, and creating military hospitals and pensions.

Elites and Masses

What caused the end of witchcraft hysteria in the West by the later 17th century? Did wise rulers calm a frenzied populace or did ordinary people themselves change their minds? One explanation focuses on new efforts by elites, such as local magistrates, to discipline mass impulses. Authorities stopped believing in demonic disruptions of natural processes, and so forced an end to persecutions. But many ordinary people were also thinking in new ways. Without converting fully to a scientific outlook, they became open to new ideas about how to handle health problems, reducing their belief in magical remedies; they needed witches less. Potential "witches" may have become more cautious. Older women, threatened by growing community suspicion, learned to maintain a lower profile and to emphasize benign, grandmotherly qualities rather than seeking a more independent role. Without question, there was a decline both in witchcraft beliefs, once a key element in the Western mentality, and in the hysteria specifically characteristic of the 16th and 17th centuries. This decline reflected new ways of thinking about strangeness and disruption. It involved complex interactions between various segments of Western society: magistrates and villagers, scientists and priests, husbands and widows.

The transformation of Western society after 1450 raises fascinating questions about the role of elites—particularly powerful groups and creative individuals—versus the ordinary people in causing change. The growing importance of social history has called attention to ordinary people, as we have seen, but it has not answered all the questions about their actual role. This role varies by place and time, of course. Some social historians tend to see ordinary people as victims of change, pushed around by the power groups. Others tend to stress the positive historical role of ordinary people in partly shaping the context of their own lives and affecting the larger course of history.

It is easy to read the early modern transformation of western Europe as an operation created by elites, with the masses as passively watching or futilely protesting. Not only the Renaissance and Reformation but also the commercial revolution required decisive action by key leadership groups. Leading merchants spurred economic change, and they ultimately began to farm out manufacturing jobs. The resultant rise of dependent wage labor, which tore a growing minority of western Europeans away from property and so from economic control of their lives, illustrates the power disparities in Western society. Ordinary people knuckled under or protested, but they were reacting, not initiating.

> "Some historians have suggested that the rise of science opened a new gap between the ways educated upper classes and masses thought."

The rise of science rivets our attention on the activities of extraordinarily creative individuals, such as Newton, and elite institutions, such as the scientific academies. Some historians have suggested that the rise of science opened a new gap between the ways educated upper classes and masses thought.

Yet the ordinary people of western Europe were not passive, nor did they simply protest change in the name of tradition. Widespread shifts came from repeated decisions by peasants and artisans, not just from those at the top. The steady technological improvements in manufacturing thus flowed upward from practicing artisans, not downward from formal scientists. The European-style family that had taken shape by the 16th century was an innovation by ordinary people long ignored by the elite. It encouraged new parent–child relations and new tensions between young adults and the old that might spur other innovations, including a willingness to settle distant colonies in search of property. The fact that young people often had to wait to marry until their property-owning fathers died could induce many to seek new lands or new economic methods. In other words, ordinary people changed their habits too, and these changes had wide impact.

QUESTIONS Did elites gain new power over the masses in early modern Western society? Are ordinary people more conservative by nature, more suspicious of change, than groups at the top? Can you describe at least two other historical cases in which it is important to determine whether change was imposed on ordinary people from above or whether ordinary people themselves produced important innovations?

Louis XIV
Writes to
His Son
DOCUMENT

absolute monarchy Concept of government developed during rise of nation-states in western Europe during the 17th century; featured monarchs who passed laws without parliaments, appointed professionalized armies and bureaucracies, established state churches, imposed state economic policies.

Louis XIV (1638–1715) French monarch of the late 17th century who personified absolute monarchy.

So great was the power of the monarch, in fact, that the French system became known as **absolute monarchy.** Its most glorious royal proponent, King **Louis XIV,** summed up its principles succinctly: "I am the state." Louis became a major patron of the arts, giving government a cultural role beyond any previous levels in the West. His academies not only encouraged science but also worked to standardize the French language. A sumptuous palace at Versailles was used to keep nobles busy with social functions so that they could not interfere with affairs of state.

Using the new bureaucratic structure, Louis and his ministers developed additional functions for the state. They reduced internal tariffs, which acted as barriers to trade, and created new, state-run manufacturing. The reigning economic theory, mercantilism, held that governments should promote the internal economy to improve tax revenues and to limit imports from other nations, lest money be lost to enemy states. Therefore, absolute monarchs such as Louis XIV set tariffs on imported goods, tried to encourage their merchant fleets, and sought colonies to provide raw materials and a guaranteed market for manufactured goods produced at home.

The basic structure of absolute monarchy developed in other states besides France (Map 17.2). Spain tried to imitate French principles in the 18th century, which resulted in efforts to tighten control over its Latin American colonies. However, the most important spread of absolute monarchy occurred in the central European states that were gaining in importance. A series of kings in Prussia, in eastern Germany, built a strong army and bureaucracy. They promoted economic activity and began to develop a state-sponsored school system. Habsburg kings in Austria–Hungary, though still officially rulers of the Holy Roman Empire, concentrated increasingly on developing a stronger monarchy in the lands under their direct control. The power of these Habsburg rulers increased after they pushed back the last Turkish invasion threat late in the 17th century and then added the kingdom of Hungary to their domains.

Most absolute monarchs saw a strong military as a key political goal, and many hoped for territorial expansion. Louis XIV used his strong state as the basis for a series of wars from the 1680s onward. The wars yielded some new territory for France but finally attracted an opposing alliance system that blocked further advance. Prussian kings, though long cautious in exposing their proud military to the risk of major war, turned in the 18th century to a series of conflicts that won new territory.

 French Territorial Acquisitions, 1679–1714

Parliamentary Monarchies

Britain and the Netherlands, both growing commercial and colonial powers, stood apart from the trend toward absolute monarchy in the 17th century. They emphasized the role of the central state, but they also built parliamentary regimes in which the kings shared power with representatives selected by the nobility and upper urban classes. The English civil wars produced a final political settlement in 1688 and 1689 (the so-called **Glorious Revolution**) in which parliament won basic sovereignty over the king. The English parliament no longer depended on the king to convene, for regular sessions were scheduled. Its rights to approve taxation allowed it to monitor or initiate most major policies.

Furthermore, a growing body of political theory arose in the 17th century that built on these parliamentary ideas. John Locke and others argued that power came from the people, not from a divine right to royal rule. Monarchs should therefore be restrained by institutions that protected the public interest, including certain general rights to freedom and property. A right of revolution could legitimately oppose unjust rule.

Overall, western Europe developed important diversity in political forms, between absolute monarchy and a new kind of **parliamentary monarchy.** It maintained a characteristic tension between government growth and the idea that there should be some limits to state authority. This tension was expressed in new forms, but it recalled some principles that had originated in the Middle Ages.

The English Bill of Rights

Glorious Revolution   English overthrow of James II in 1688; resulted in affirmation of parliament as having basic sovereignty over the king.

parliamentary monarchy   Originated in England and Holland, 17th century, with kings partially checked by significant legislative powers in parliaments.

The Nation-State

The absolute monarchies and the parliamentary monarchies shared important characteristics as nation-states. Unlike the great empires of many other civilizations, they ruled peoples who shared a common culture and language, some important minorities apart. They could appeal to a certain loyalty that linked cultural and political bonds. This was as true of England, where the idea of special rights of Englishmen helped feed the parliamentary movement, as it was of France. Not surprisingly, ordinary people in many nation-states, even though not directly represented in government, increasingly believed that government should act for their interests. Thus, Louis XIV faced recurrent popular riots based on the assumption that when bad harvests drove up food prices, the government was obligated to help people out.

In sum, nation-states developed a growing list of functions, particularly under the banner of mercantilism, whose principles were shared by monarchists and parliamentary leaders alike. They also promoted new political values and loyalties that were very different from the political traditions of other civilizations. They kept the West politically divided and often at war.

The West by 1750

Key changes gained further ground in the 18th century. Most importantly, the Enlightenment expanded the range of intellectual innovation.

During the first half of the 18th century, several basic changes continued in Western Europe. The impact of absolutism and the parliamentary monarchies persisted, though outright political innovation was limited. Commercial changes, however, began to have even wider results, with an important expansion of manufacturing; new agricultural developments added an important element. Europe's cultural transformation, at both elite and popular levels, continued as well, with growing implications for political and social life.

Political Patterns

Many of the key changes in modern Europe drew together by the mid-18th century. Political changes were least significant. During much of the century, English politics settled into a bloated parliamentary routine in which key political groups competed for influence without major policy differences. Absolute monarchy in France changed little institutionally, but it became less effective. It could not force changes in the tax structure that would give it more solid financial footing because aristocrats refused to surrender their traditional exemptions.

The Growth of Brandenburg-Prussia   MAP

Frederick the Great   Prussian king of the 18th century; attempted to introduce Enlightenment reforms into Germany; built on military and bureaucratic foundations of his predecessors; introduced freedom of religion; increased state control of economy.

Political developments were far livelier in central Europe. In Prussia, **Frederick the Great,** building on the military and bureaucratic organization of his predecessors, introduced greater freedom of religion while expanding the economic functions of the state. His government actively encouraged better agricultural methods; for example, it promoted use of the American potato as a staple crop. It also enacted laws promoting greater commercial coordination and greater equity; harsh traditional punishments were cut back. Rulers of this sort claimed to be enlightened despots, wielding great authority but for the good of society at large.

Enlightened or not, the policies of the major Western nation-states produced recurrent warfare. France and Britain squared off in the 1740s and again in the Seven Years War (1756–1763); their conflicts focused on battles for colonial empire. Austria and Prussia also fought, with Prussia gaining new land. Wars in the 18th century were not devastating, but they demonstrated the continued linkage between statecraft and war that was characteristic of the West.

Enlightenment Thought and Popular Culture

In culture, the aftermath of the Scientific Revolution spilled over into a new movement known as the **Enlightenment,** centered particularly in France but with adherents throughout the Western world. Enlightenment thinkers continued to support scientific advance. Although there were no Newton-like breakthroughs, chemists gained new understanding of major elements, and biologists developed a vital new classification system for the natural species.

Enlightenment   Intellectual movement centered in France during the 18th century; featured scientific advance, application of scientific methods to study of human society; belief that rational laws could describe social behavior.

The Enlightenment also pioneered in applying scientific methods to the study of human society, sketching the modern social sciences. The basic idea was that rational laws could describe social as well as physical behavior and that knowledge could be used to improve policy. Thus, criminologists wrote that brutal punishments failed to deter crime, whereas a decent society would be able to rehabilitate criminals through education. Political theorists wrote about the importance of carefully planned constitutions and controls over privilege, although they disagreed about what political form was best. A new school of economists developed. In his classic book *Wealth of Nations*, Scottish philosopher **Adam Smith** set forth a number of principles of economic behavior. He argued that people act according to their self-interest but, through competition, promote general economic advance. Government should avoid regulation in favor of the operation of individual initiative and market forces. This was an important statement of economic policy and an illustration of the growing belief that general models of human behavior could be derived from rational thought.

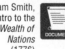

Adam Smith, Intro to the *Wealth of Nations* (1776)   DOCUMENT

Smith, Adam   Established liberal economics (*Wealth of Nations*, 1776); argued that government should avoid regulation of economy in favor of the operation of market forces.

Single individuals could sum up part of the Enlightenment's impressive range. **Denis Diderot** (duh-NEE DEE-duh-roh) (1713–1784; Figure 17.5) was a multifaceted leader of the French Enlightenment, best known for his editorial work on the *Encyclopédie* that compiled scientific and social scientific knowledge. Trained initially by the Jesuits, Diderot also wrote widely on philosophy, mathematics, and the psychology of deaf-mutes and also tried his hand at literature. An active friend of other philosophers, Diderot also traveled to foreign courts as advisor and visiting intellectual. He visited Catherine the Great of Russia in 1773–1774, for example, to thank her for generous patronage.

Denis Diderot   [duh-NEE DEE-duh-roh] (October 5, 1713–July 31, 1784) A French Enlightenment figure best known for his work on the first encyclopedia.

Controversies About Women

Changes in family structure and some shifts in the economic roles of women, as well as ambivalent Protestant ideas about women that emphasized the family context but urged affection and respect between wives and husbands, touched off new gender tensions in Western society by the 17th century. Some of these tensions showed in witchcraft trials, so disproportionately directed against women. Other tensions showed in open debate about women's relationships to men; women not content with a docile wifeliness vied with new claims of virtue and prowess by some women. Although the debate was centered in the upper class of Protestant nations such as England, it may have had wider ramifications. Some of these ramifications, though quieter during the 18th century, burst forth again in arguments about inequality and family confinement in the 19th century, when a more durable feminist movement took shape in the West. In the selections here, the antiwoman position is set forth in a 1615 pamphlet by Joseph Swetham; the favorable view implicitly urging new rights is in a 1640 pamphlet pseudonymously authored by "Mary Tattle-Well and Ioane Hit-Him-Home, spinsters."

Swetham's "Arraignment of Women"

Men, I say, may live without women, but women cannot live without men: for Venus, whose beauty was excellent fair, yet when she needed man's help, She took Vulcan, a clubfooted Smith. . . .

For women have a thousand ways to entice thee and ten thousand ways to deceive thee and all such fools as are suitors unto them: some they keep in hand with promises, and some they feed with flattery, and some they delay with dalliances, and some they please with kisses. They lay out the folds of their hair to entangle men into their love; betwixt their breasts in the vale of destruction; and in their beds there is hell, sorrow and repentance. Eagles eat not men till they are dead, but women devour them alive. . . .

It is said of men that they have that one fault, but of women it is said that they have two faults: that is to say, they can neither say well nor do well. There is a saying that goeth thus: that things far fetched and dear bought are of us most dearly beloved. The like may be said of women; although many of them are not far fetched, yet they are dear bought, yea and so dear that many a man curseth his hard pennyworths and bans his own heart. For the pleasure of the fairest woman in the world lasteth but a honeymoon; that is, while a man hath glutted his affections and reaped the first fruit, his pleasure being past, sorrow and repentance remaineth still with him.*

*Joseph Swetnam, *The Araignment of Lewde, Idle, Froward, and Unconstant Women* (London, 1615)

Tattle-Well and Hit-Him-Home's "Women's Sharp Revenge"

But it hath been the policy of all parents, even from the beginning, to curb us of that benefit by striving to keep us under and to make us men's mere Vassals even unto all posterity. How else comes it to pass that when a Father hath a numerous issue of Sons and Daughters, the sons forsooth they must be first put to the Grammar school, and after perchance sent to the University, and trained up in the Liberal Arts and Sciences, and there (if they prove not Blockheads) they may in time be book-learned? . . .

When we, whom they style by the name of weaker Vessels, though of a more delicate, fine, soft, and more pliant flesh therefore of a temper most capable of the best Impression, have not that generous and liberal Education, lest we should be made able to vindicate our own injuries, we are set only to the Needle, to prick our fingers, or else to the Wheel to spin a fair thread for our own undoing, or perchance to some more dirty and debased drudgery. If we be taught to read, they then confine us within the compass of our Mother Tongue, and that limit we are not suffered to pass; or if (which sometimes happeneth) we be brought up to Music, to singing, and to dancing, it is not for any benefit that thereby we can engross unto ourselves, but for their own particular ends, the better to please and content their licentious appetites when we come to our maturity and ripeness. And thus if we be weak by Nature, they strive to make us more weak by our Nurture; and if in degree of place low, they strive by their policy to keep us more under.

Now to show we are no such despised matter as you would seem to make us, come to our first Creation, when man was made of the mere dust of the earth. The woman had her being from the best part of his body, the Rib next to his heart, which difference even in our complexions may be easily decided. Man is of a dull, earthy, and melancholy aspect, having shallows in his face and a very forest upon his Chin, when our soft and smooth Cheeks are a true representation of a delectable garden of intermixed Roses and Lilies. . . . Man might consider that women were not created to be their slaves or vassals; for as they had not their Original out of his head (thereby to command him), so it was not out of his foot to be trod upon, but in a medium out of his side to be his fellow feeler, his equal, and companion. . . .

Thus have I truly and impartially proved that for Chastity, Charity, Constancy, Magnanimity, Valor, Wisdom, Piety, or any Grace or Virtue whatsoever, women have always been more than equal with men, and that for Luxury, Surquidant obscenity, profanity, Ebriety, Impiety, and all that may be called bad we do come far short of them.

QUESTIONS What conditions prompted a more vigorous public debate about gender in the 17th century? How did the pro-woman argument compare with more modern views about women? Did the new arguments about women's conditions suggest that these conditions were improving?

Figure 17.5 Denis Diderot, one of the key figures in the definition and dissemination of the Enlightenment.

Wollstonecraft, Mary   (1759–1797) Enlightenment feminist thinker in England; argued that new political rights should extend to women.

mass consumerism   Mass consumerism refers to the spread of deep interest in acquiring material goods and services spreading below elite levels, along with a growing economic capacity to afford some of these goods. While hints of mass consumerism can be found in several premodern societies, it developed most clearly, beginning in Western Europe, from the 18th century onward.

More generally still, the Enlightenment produced a set of basic principles about human affairs: Human beings are good, at least improvable, and they can be educated to be better; reason is the key to truth, and religions that rely on blind faith or refuse to tolerate diversity are wrong. Enlightenment thinkers attacked the Catholic Church with particular vigor, , because it seemed to support older superstitions while wielding political power. Progress was possible, even inevitable, if people could be set free. Society's goals should center on improving material and social life.

Although it was not typical of the Enlightenment's main thrust, a few thinkers applied these general principles to other areas. A handful of socialists argued that economic equality and the abolition of private property must become important goals. A few feminist thinkers, such as **Mary Wollstonecraft** (Fig 17.6) in England, argued—against the general male-centered views of most Enlightenment thinkers—that new political rights and freedoms should extend to women. Several journals written by women for women made their first appearance during this extraordinary cultural period. Madame de Beaumere took over the direction of the French *Journal des Dames* from a man, and in Germany, Marianne Ehrmann used her journal to suggest that men might be partly to blame for women's lowly position.

The popularization of new ideas encouraged further changes in the habits and beliefs of many ordinary people. Reading clubs and coffeehouses allowed many urban artisans and businessmen to discuss the latest reform ideas. Leading writers and compilations of scientific and philosophical findings, such as the *Encyclopaedia Britannica*, won a wide audience and, for a few people, a substantial fortune from the sale of books.

Other changes in popular outlook paralleled the new intellectual currents, although they had deeper sources than philosophy alone. Attitudes toward children began to shift in many social groups. Older methods of physical discipline were criticized in favor of more restrained behavior that would respect the goodness and innocence of children. Swaddling—wrapping infants in cloth so they could not move or harm themselves—began to decline as parents became interested in freer movement and greater interaction for young children. Among wealthy families, educational toys and books for children reflected the idea that childhood should be a stage for learning and growth.

Family life generally was changed by a growing sense that old hierarchies should be rethought and revised toward greater equality in the treatment of women and children in the home. Love between family members gained new respect, and an emotional bond in marriage became more widely sought. Change affected older children as well: parents grew more reluctant to force a match on a son or daughter if the emotional vibrations were not right. Here was a link not only with Enlightenment ideas of proper family relations but with novels such as Richardson's *Pamela* that poured out a sentimental view of life.

Ongoing Change in Commerce and Manufacturing

Ongoing economic change paralleled changes in popular culture and intellectual life. Commerce continued to spread. Ordinary Westerners began to buy processed products, such as refined sugar and coffee or tea obtained from Indonesia and the West Indies, for daily use. This was a sign of the growing importance of Europe's new colonies for ordinary life and of the beginnings of **mass consumerism** in Western society. The growing popularity of cotton textiles spread more widely, giving even relatively poor people the chance to express a sense of style. Theft of clothing increased in the 18th century, a clear indication of new consumer priorities. Another sign of change was the growing use of paid professional entertainment as part of popular leisure, even in rural festivals. Circuses, first introduced in France in the 1670s, began to redefine leisure to include spectatorship and a taste for the bizarre.

Agriculture began to change. Until the late 17th century, western Europe had continued to rely largely on the methods and techniques characteristic of the Middle Ages—a severe economic constraint in an agricultural society. The three-field system still meant that a full third of all farmland was left unplanted each year to restore fertility. First in the Netherlands and then elsewhere, new procedures for draining swamps added available land. Reformers touted nitrogen-fixing crops to reduce the need to leave land idle. Stockbreeding improved, and new techniques such as seed-drills and the use of scythes instead of sickles for harvesting increased productivity. Some changes spread particularly fast on large estates, but other changes affected ordinary peasants as well. Particularly vital in this category was the spread of the potato from the late 17th century onward.

A New World crop, the potato had long been shunned because it was not mentioned in the Bible and was held to be the cause of plagues. Enlightened government leaders, and the peasants' desire to win greater economic security and better nutrition, led to widespread use of this crop. In sum, the West improved its food supply and agricultural efficiency, leaving more labor available for other pursuits.

These changes, along with the steady growth of colonial trade and internal commerce, spurred increased manufacturing. Capitalism—the investment of funds in hopes of larger profits—also spread from big trading ventures to the production of goods. The 18th century witnessed a rapid spread of household production of textiles and metal products, mostly by rural workers who alternated manufacturing with some agriculture. Here was a key use of labor that was no longer needed

Figure 17.6 Portrait of feminist Mary Wollstonecraft.

for food. Hundreds of thousands of people were drawn into this domestic system, in which capitalist merchants distributed supplies and orders and workers ran the production process for pay. Although manufacturing tools were still operated by hand, the spread of domestic manufacturing spurred important technological innovations designed to improve efficiency. In 1733, John Kay in England introduced the flying shuttle, which permitted automatic crossing of threads on looms; with this, an individual weaver could do the work of two. Improvements in spinning and the mechanized printing of cotton cloth soon followed as the Western economy began to move toward a full-fledged Industrial Revolution (see Chapter 23).

Human changes accompanied and sometimes preceded technology. Around 1700, most manufacturers who made wool cloth in northern England were artisans, doing part of the work themselves. By 1720, a number of loom owners were becoming outright manufacturers with new ideas and behaviors. How were manufacturers different? They spent their time organizing production and sales rather than doing their own work. They moved work out of their homes. They stopped drinking beer with their workers. And they saw their workers as market commodities, to be treated as the conditions of trade demanded. In 1736, one such manufacturer coolly wrote that because of slumping sales, "I have turned off [dismissed] a great many of my makers, and keep turning more off weekly."

Finally, agricultural changes, commercialism, and manufacturing combined, particularly after about 1730, to produce a rapidly growing population in the West. With better food supplies, more people survived, particularly with the aid of the potato. Furthermore, new manufacturing jobs helped landless people support themselves, promoting earlier marriage and sexual relationships. Population growth, in turn, promoted further economic change, heightening competition and producing a more manipulable labor force. The West's great population revolution, which continued into the 19th century, both caused and reflected the civilization's dynamism, although it also produced great strain and confusion.

Innovation and Instability

By the 18th century, the various strands of change were increasingly intertwined in Western civilization. Stronger governments promoted agricultural improvements, which helped prod population growth. Changes in popular beliefs were fed by new economic structures; both encouraged a reevaluation of the family and the roles of children. New beliefs also raised new political challenges. Enlightenment ideas about liberty and fundamental human equality could be directed against existing regimes. New family practices might have political implications as well. Children, raised with less adult restraint and encouraged to value their individual worth through parental love and careful education, might see traditional political limitations in new ways.

There was no perfect fit, no inevitable match, in the three strands of change that had been transforming the West for two centuries or more: the commercial, the cultural, and the political. However, by 1750 all were in place. The combination had already produced an unusual version of an agricultural civilization, and it promised more upheaval in the future.

Global Connections

Europe and the World

In 1450, Europeans were convinced that their Christianity made them superior to other people. But they also understood that many societies were impressive in terms of cities and wealth and the strength of their governments. As Europe changed and prospered, participating strongly in the process of **proto-globalization,** its outlook toward the world changed as well. We saw in the previous chapter how Europeans began to use technology as a measure of society, arguing that other societies that were less interested in technological change were inferior. By the 18th century, criticisms of the superstitions of other people began to surface among Europeans proud of their science and rationalism.

The wider world could still provide a sense of wonder, but increasingly this was focused on natural phenomena and the strange animals being imported to European zoos. The Enlightenment generated the idea of a "noble savage"—a person uncorrupted by advanced civilization and urban ways. But this was largely a fiction designed to comment on Europe itself, not a source of real admiration for other peoples. Increasingly, European power and the rapid changes within Western civilization led to a sense that most other societies were backward, perhaps not even civilized. The idea had powerful impact, not only on European attitudes but also on the ways other societies perceived themselves and reacted.

Further Readings

For an overview of developments in Western society during this period, with extensive bibliographies, see Sheldon Watts, *A Social History of Western Europe, 1450–1720* (1984); Michael Anderson, *Approaches to the West European Family* (1980); and Peter N. Stearns, *Life and Society in the West: The Modern Centuries* (1988).

On more specific developments and periods, see John Man, *Gutenberg, How One Man Remade the World with Words* (2002); J. R. Hale, *The Civilization of Europe in the Renaissance* (1994); O. Chadwick, *The Reformation* (1983); Richard A. Muller, *After Calvin: Studies in the Development of a Theological Tradition* (2003); and Steven Ozment, *Protestants: The Birth of a Revolution* (1992), are fine introductions to early changes.

Later changes are sketched in Thomas Munck, *Seventeenth Century Europe: 1598–1700* (1990); and Jeremy Black, *Eighteenth*

Century Europe: 1700–1789 (1990). On England in the civil war period, see Christopher Hill, *A Nation of Change and Novelty* (1990).

Key aspects of social change in this period can be approached through Gary S. De Krey, *Restoration and Revolution in Britain: A Political History of the Era of Charles II and the Glorious Revolution* (2007); Peter Burke, *Popular Culture in Early Modern Europe* (1978); Robin Biggs, *Communities of Belief: Cultural and Social Tensions in Early Modern France* (1989); Keith Thomas, *Religion and the Decline of Magic* (1971); Lawrence Stone, *The Family, Sex and Marriage in England 1500–1800* (1977); and James Sharpe, *Instruments of Darkness: Witchcraft in Early Modern England* (1997).

On science, Matthew L. Jones, *The Good Life in the Scientific Revolution: Descartes, Pascal, Leibniz, and the Cultivation of Virtue* (2006); and Michael S. Reidy, Gary Kroll and Erik M. Conway, *Exploration and Science: Social Impact and Interaction* (2007).

On the Web

An interactive webpage addressing most aspects of the Renaissance can be found at http://www.learner.org/interactives/renaissance/. The lives and art of Leonardo da Vinci (http://www.mos.org/leonardo/), Michelangelo (http://www.michelangelo.com/buonarroti.html), and Raphael (http://www.theartgallery.com.au/ArtEducation/greatartists/Raphael/about/) were closely intertwined with the city of Florence, whose history is addressed at http://www.mega.it/eng/egui/epo/secrepu.htm. Key people and places of period, including Venice, are examined in a "secrets of the Renaissance" format at http://www.open2.net/renaissancesecrets/index.html.

Martin Luther's life and the course of the Protestant Reformation and Catholic Reformation are discussed at http://www.pbs.org/empires/martinluther/ and http://www.fordham.edu/halsall/sbook1y.html. The key texts of the Reformation and other related resources are provided at http://homepage.mac.com/shanerosenthal/reformationink/index.html. The art and literature of the Northern Renaissance is examined at http://www.artcyclopedia.com/history/northern-renaissance.html.

The Web provides insight into the role of two of the leading absolute monarchs of Europe, Frederick the Great (http://members.tripod.com/~Nevermore/king7.html) and Louis XIV (http://www.royalty.nu/Europe/France/LouisXIV.html.

Isaac Newton's life and letters can be examined at http://www.cannylink.com/historyissacnewton.htm, while links to other leading figures of the Scientific Revolution and its course and content can be explored at http://www.fordham.edu/halsall/mod/modsbook09.html and http://www.historyteacher.net/GlobalHistory-1/WebLinks/WebLinks-ScientificRevolution.htm.

The development of modern political and economic theory can be traced through the life and work of Niccolo Machiavelli (http://www.philosophypages.com/ph/macv.htm and http://www.constitution.org/mac/prince00.htm), the Medici family (http://www.pbs.org/empires/medici/medici/index.html), and Adam Smith (http://www.econlib.org/library/Enc/bios/Smith.html).

Renaissance women and their texts are addressed at http://www.yesnet.yk.ca/schools/projects/renaissance/renaissancewomen.html and http://womenshistory.miningco.com/cs/medieval/. The role of women in the arts of the Renaissance is discussed at http://www.columbia.edu/cu/sister/Renaissance.html.

AP* | Test Prep

1. The Protestant Reformation in the Holy Roman Empire was equally a religious and political revolution because it challenged all of these authorities EXCEPT

    (A) the papal position as head of the Catholic church.

    (B) the noble and aristocratic class structure within society.

    (C) the influence of the Emperor as head of the Holy Roman Empire.

    (D) the religious and economic power of monasteries.

2. The authors and artists of the Renaissance were largely influenced and supported by

    (A) the Roman Catholic church.

    (B) guilds.

    (C) everyday people.

    (D) merchants.

3. The growing commercialization of Western Europe's economy from the 16th century onward most negatively impacted the

    (A) rulers and bureaucracy.

    (B) churches and religious establishments.

    (C) merchants.

    (D) property-less rural and urban workers.

4. In Early Modern Europe, most rulers increasingly tried to

    (A) limit the power nobles had exercised before this period.

    (B) replace the Christian clergy.

    (C) restrict the power and influence of the military.

    (D) limit population growth to assure greater social stability.

5. Mercantilism characteristically

    (A) discourages colonies and overseas adventures.

    (B) encourages skilled workers to demand better pay and benefits.

    (C) allows imports and exports without tariffs and barriers.

    (D) promotes the economy by encouraging national self-sufficiency over individual gain.

6. A nation-state differs from an empire or many medieval states because it

    (A) grants rulers absolute rights to govern.

    (B) comprises a country with one dominant language and culture.

    (C) limits the power of monarchs and rulers.

    (D) has many large and different ethnic groups under a common government.

7. Which of the following statements is an example of the Enlightenment belief that rational laws of nature govern human affairs as well as physical/scientific?

    (A) All men are created equal and endowed by their Creator with certain inalienable rights; that among these are life, liberty, and the pursuit of happiness.

    (B) All who call on God in true faith, earnestly from the heart, will certainly be heard, and will receive what they have asked and desired.

    (C) I came, I saw, God conquered.

    (D) Be content with what you have; rejoice in the way things are. When you realize there is nothing lacking, the whole world belongs to you.

Free-Response Question

Analyze the effects of western European involvement in the world's economy on the changes in its political, economic, and intellectual outlooks, c. 1450–1750.

18 The Rise of Russia

Russia's Expansionist Politics Under the Tsars
Russia's First Westernization, 1690–1790
DOCUMENT: The Nature of Westernization
Themes in Early Modern Russian History

VISUALIZING THE PAST: Oppressed Peasants
THINKING HISTORICALLY: Multinational Empires
GLOBAL CONNECTIONS: Russia and the World

New rulers often face a special challenge of legitimacy: why should people accept their rule and their policies? The Russian tsars of the 15th and 16th century faced just such a challenge. They claimed the right to dominate Russia and orchestrate steady expansion of territory. How could they persuade the people that their power was legitimate? Early tsars, particularly Ivan III and Ivan IV, proved particularly inventive. First, they pointed to their family tree, noting their descent from the line of Rurik, the legendary founder of Russia. Ivan IV had huge genealogy books prepared, ignoring the claims of other descendants. The early tsars also invoked the example of the Roman Empire, speaking of Russia as the "third Rome"—after Byzantium and Rome itself. This had appeal: Rome was a much admired state from the classical past, and Byzantium added an element of Christian mission. Russia could be presented as protector of the faith. Ivan IV's genealogies were thus filled with lives of the saints and church resolutions, designed to show how God's purpose, from creation onward, had been to found a truly Christian empire and how Russia was now called to fulfill this purpose. Russia's ruler was often portrayed in religious terms, as leader of the holy church and as part of a divine mission (See Figure 18.1).

But even this was not enough. As Ivan IV campaigned in central Asia, he also invoked the heritage of the Mongols. Russia should rule in central Asia, according to this argument, because it was the long-standing property of the Rurik dynasty (which was nonsense historically but sounded good); because it was "his duty as a Christian monarch to extirpate the rule of the infidel"; and because, having defeated the Mongols, he had become a khan himself. And sure enough, at the time and thereafter, Muslim leaders often took oaths of loyalty to the tsar on the Qur'an, and the tsar styled himself, in that region, the "khan of the north." ■

Ivan III (1440–1505) Also known as Ivan the Great; prince of Duchy of Moscow; claimed descent from Rurik; responsible for freeing Russia from Mongols after 1462; took title of tsar or Caesar—equivalent of emperor.

Three lessons may be taken from all this that are important for Russian and world history alike. First, tsars claimed a lot. Second, their claims embodied significant contradictions. Were they khans, claiming arbitrary authority over the masses, or were they benevolent, gentle Christians? And third, precisely because Russian expansion touched so many different regions and traditions, the new empire would inevitably be complex and multifaceted. It came to embrace many different peoples, and its size inevitably challenged the capacity of Russia's rulers. This chapter focuses strongly on Russian expansion and tsarist power, but also on social conditions that distinguished Russia during a crucial period in the nation's development.

Russia's Expansionist Politics Under the Tsars

Russia's early modern development first emphasized territorial expansion and the strengthening of tsarist rule.

Russia's emergence as a new power in eastern Europe and central Asia initially depended on its gaining freedom from Mongol (Tatar) control. The Duchy of Moscow was the center for the liberation effort beginning in the 14th century. Local princes began to carve out greater autonomy, and the effectiveness of Mongol control began to diminish. Ironically, the Moscow princes initially gained political experience as tax collectors for the Mongols, but gradually they moved toward regional independence. Under **Ivan III**—Ivan the Great (1462–1505), who claimed succession from the Rurik dynasty and the old Kievan days—a large Russian territory emerged. Ivan organized a strong army, giving the new government a military emphasis it would long

Figure 18.1 Early Russian tsar Ivan V, 1682–1696. Ivan was actually sickly and ineffective, and soon gave way to Peter the Great. But the portrait suggests the symbolism with which the tsars were invested.

retain. By 1480, Moscow had been freed from any payment to the Mongols and Ivan had gained a vast kingdom running from the borders of the Polish Lithuanian kingdom to the Ural Mountains.

Russia's rise had some similarities to earlier Macedonian and Roman expansion: a new state, on the fringes of the "civilized world," suddenly and steadily gaining great power. The new Russian empire, important in its own right, also formed one of the novel varieties of empire introduced in the early modern period as a whole.

The Need for Revival

Mongol control never reshaped basic Russian values, for the rulers were interested in tribute, not full government. Many Russian landlords adopted Mongol styles of dress and social habits. However, most Russians remained Christians, and most local administrative issues remained in the hands of regional princes, landlords, or peasant villages. In these senses, Russia was set to resume many of its earlier patterns when full independence was achieved. On the other hand, the Mongol period had reduced the vigor of Russian cultural life, lowering the levels of literacy among the

1450 C.E.	1600 C.E.	1750 C.E.
1462 Much of Russia freed from Tatars by Ivan III (Ivan the Great) 1480 Moscow region free; Russian expansion presses south 1533–1584 Life of Ivan IV (Ivan the Terrible), first to emphasize the title of *tsar*; boyar power reduced 1552–1556 Russian expansion in central Asia, western Siberia	1604–1613 Time of Troubles 1613–1917 Romanov dynasty 1637 Russian pioneers to Pacific 1649 Law enacted making serfdom hereditary 1689–1725 Reign of Peter the Great 1700–1721 Wars with Sweden 1703 Founding of St. Petersburg	1762–1796 Reign of Catherine the Great 1773–1775 Pugachev revolt 1772, 1793, 1795 Partition of Poland 1785 Law enacted tightening landlord power over serfs

priesthood, for example. Economic life deteriorated as well: with trade down and manufacturing limited, Russia had become a purely agricultural economy dependent on peasant labor. In these senses, independence brought a challenge for revival and reform.

Ivan the Great claimed an earlier tradition of centralized rule, which went back to the Rurik dynasty and Byzantine precedents, and added to it the new sense of imperial mission. He married the niece of the last Byzantine emperor, which gave him the chance to assert control over all Orthodox churches whether in Russia or not. The idea of Russia as a third Rome explained why Ivan called himself tsar, or caesar, the "autocrat of all the Russias."

From Ivan III onward, early modern Russia was strongly shaped by military needs. Mongol counterattacks were a legitimate concern: a Tatar group sacked Moscow as late as 1571. But Russia's rulers also pressed conquests beyond defense. They seized additional territory from the Tatars in what is now Ukraine, and also in central Asia, through the 16th century, and they also began to expand in east-central Europe, which brought them face to face with other military opponents.

To recruit soldiers, the tsars began to grant hereditary territories to military nobles; this included strict controls over the peasant serfs on these lands. Harsh conditions caused many serfs to flee to border regions, with two results. First, regulations on remaining serfs tightened, to tie them to the land lest a severe labor shortage develop. This launched a pattern of constraints on serfs that was in marked contrast to trends in Western Europe at the same time, where serfdom was easing up. Peasants who fled, however, helped provide both military muscle and labor for further Russian expansion, for example into Siberia. Cossack colonies, formed from independent peasant fighting men, played a great role in Russian success.

The powers of the aristocratic landlords, called boyars, also led to conflicts with the claims of the tsars, who wanted to rule without interference. These conflicts dotted Russian history in the 16th and 17th centuries, before the boyars were finally put down. This pattern, along with the deep-seated and durable pressures on the serfs, defined key developments in Russia even beyond the early modern centuries.

The next important tsar, **Ivan IV** (1533–1584), justly called Ivan the Terrible, continued the trends of Russian expansion and consolidation of power. He placed great emphasis on promoting the tsarist autocracy, earning his nickname by killing or exiling many of the Russian *boyars*, whom he suspected of conspiracy. The tsar often flew into violent rages—during one episode he killed his son and heir—followed by deep religious repentance. His conquests were largely successful, however, and there were other key gains such as the introduction of printing into Russia.

Ivan the Terrible

Ivan IV (1530–1584) Also known as Ivan the Terrible; confirmed power of tsarist autocracy by attacking authority of boyars (aristocrats); continued policy of Russian expansion; established contacts with western European commerce and culture.

Patterns of Expansion

Russia's creation of a vast landed empire propelled it into new importance in world history, with direct impact ultimately on Europe, East Asia, and central Asia and the Middle East. Steady territorial expansion policy was motivated by a desire to push the former Mongol overlords farther back. Russia was a country of vast plains, with few natural barriers to invasion. The early tsars turned this drawback to an advantage by pushing southward toward the Caspian Sea; they also moved east into the Ural Mountains and beyond. Both Ivan III and Ivan IV recruited peasants to migrate to the newly seized lands, particularly in the south, and the efforts to flee serfdom provided another stimulus. These peasant-adventurers, or **cossacks**, were Russian pioneers, combining agriculture with daring military feats on horseback. The expansion territories long had a rough-and-ready frontier quality, only gradually settling down to more regular administration. The cossack spirit provided volunteers for further expansion, for many of the pioneers—like their American counterparts in the 19th century—chafed under detailed tsarist control and were eager to move on to new settlements. During the 16th century, the cossacks not only conquered the Caspian Sea area but also moved into western Siberia, across the Urals, beginning the gradual takeover and settlement of these vast plains, which previously had been sparsely inhabited by nomadic Asian peoples (Map 18.1).

Expansion also allowed tsars to continue to reward loyal nobles and bureaucrats by giving them estates in new territories. This practice provided new agricultural areas and sources of labor; Russia used slaves for certain kinds of production work into the 18th century. Although Russia never became as dependent on expansion for social control and economic advance as the later Roman Empire or the Ottoman Empire, it certainly had many reasons to continue the policy. Russia also created trading connections with its new Asian territories and their neighbors.

Russia's early expansion, along with that of the Ottoman Empire to the south, eliminated independent central Asia—that age-old source of nomadic cultures and periodic invasions in both the east and the west. The same expansion, though driven by the movement of Russian peasants and landlords to new areas, also added to Russia diverse new peoples, making this a multicultural empire, like that of the Mughals and Ottomans. Particularly important was the addition of a large Muslim minority, overseen by the tsarist government but not pressed to integrate with Russian culture.

cossacks Peasants recruited to migrate to newly seized lands in Russia, particularly in south; combined agriculture with military conquests; spurred additional frontier conquests and settlements.

Russia, 1462–1914

Western Contact and Romanov Policy

Along with expansion and enforcement of tsarist primacy, the early tsars added one element to their overall approach: carefully managed contacts with western Europe. The tsars realized that Russia's cultural and economic subordination to the Mongols had put them at a commercial and cultural disadvantage. Ivan III was eager to launch diplomatic missions to the leading Western states. During the reign of Ivan IV, British merchants established trading contacts with Rus-

Map 18.1 Russian Expansion Under the Early Tsars, 1462–1598   From its base in the Moscow region, Russia expanded in three directions; the move into Siberia involved pioneering new settlements, as the government encouraged Russians to push eastward. Political controls extended gradually as well.

Multinational Empires

Of all the new multinational empires created in the early modern period, Russia's was the most successful, lasting until 1991 and to an extent beyond. In contrast, India's Mughal Empire disappeared completely by the mid-19th century, and the Ottoman and Habsburg empires flickered until after World War I. All the multinational empires were reasonably tolerant of internal diversity (like the Roman and Arab empires of the past, two other multinational entities). The Russian tsar, for example, called himself "Khan of the North" to impress central Asian people and took oaths of loyalty from this region on the Qur'an. However, Russia differed from Asian empires and the Habsburgs in having a larger core of ethnic groups ready to fan out to the frontiers and establish pioneer settlements that sometimes developed into larger Russian enclaves. Russia also benefited from its willingness and ability to copy the West selectively, in contrast most obviously to the Ottoman Empire in the same period. This copying provided access to new military technologies and some new organizational forms.

Ironically, the same period that saw the creation of so many new empires also confirmed the importance of the culturally more cohesive nation-state, the dominant form in western Europe. England and France, prototypical nation-states, were not culturally homogeneous; they had important pockets of minorities who differed linguistically or religiously from the majority culture. But both maintained a clear basis for joining the political unit to the cultural one to foster loyalty. Efforts by the 17th-century French kings to purify and standardize the French language, or by English parliamentarians to claim empowerment from the "rights of freeborn Englishmen," were early signs that politics and national culture were coming together.

> "The Russian tsar, for example, called himself 'Khan of the North' to impress central Asian people and took oaths of loyalty from this region on the Qur'an."

The clash between national loyalties and multinational empires did not become serious until the 19th century, and it has continued into the 21st. In the long run, most multinational states have not been able to sustain themselves in the face of increasing demands from individual national groups. The collapse of several multinational units in the 20th century—the Ottomans in the Middle East, the Habsburgs in east central Europe, and the Russians—created new diplomatic trouble spots quite obvious in the world today, for stable nation-states have had a hard time developing in these regions.

QUESTIONS Why have nation-states been more successful, as political units, in modern world history than multinational empires have been? In what ways did the Russian Empire develop some nation-state characteristics? Amid new needs for international economic coordination in the 21st century, is it possible to build multinational organizations on some new basis?

Time of Troubles Followed death of Russian tsar Ivan IV without heir early in 17th century; boyars attempted to use vacuum of power to reestablish their authority; ended with selection of Michael Romanov as tsar in 1613.

Michael Romanov
IMAGE

Romanov dynasty Dynasty elected in 1613 at end of Time of Troubles; ruled Russia until 1917.

Alexis Romanov (1904–17 July 1918) The Russian heir to the throne at the time of the Russian revolution and the youngest member of the royal family at the time of their execution.

sia, selling manufactured products in exchange for furs and other raw materials. Soon, Western merchants established outposts in Moscow and other Russian centers. The tsars also imported Italian artists and architects to design church buildings and the magnificent royal palace in the Kremlin in Moscow. The foreign architects modified Renaissance styles to take Russian building traditions into account, producing the ornate, onion-shaped domes that became characteristic of Russian (and other east European) churches and creating a distinctive form of classicism. A tradition of looking to the West, particularly for emblems of upper-class art and status, was beginning to emerge by the 16th century, along with some reliance on Western commercial initiative (Figure 18.2).

Ivan IV died without an heir. This led to some new power claims by the boyars—the **Time of Troubles** (1604–1613), when nobles competed with each other for power—plus Swedish and Polish attacks on Russian territory. In 1613, however, an assembly of boyars chose a member of the Romanov family as tsar. This family, the **Romanov dynasty,** was to rule Russia until the great revolution of 1917. Although many individual Romanov rulers were weak, and tensions with the claims of nobles recurred, the Time of Troubles did not produce any lasting constraints on tsarist power.

The first Romanov, Michael, reestablished internal order without great difficulty. He also drove out the foreign invaders and resumed the expansionist policy of his predecessors. A successful war against Poland brought Russia part of the Ukraine, including Kiev. In the south, Russia's boundaries expanded to meet those of the Ottoman Empire. Expansion at this point was beginning to have new diplomatic implications as Russia encountered other established governments.

Alexis Romanov, Michael's successor, abolished the assemblies of nobles and gained new powers over the Russian church. He was eager to purge the church of many superstitions and errors that, in his judgment, had crept in during Mongol times. His policies resumed the Orthodox tradition of state control over the church. Dissident religious conservatives, called **Old Believers,** were exiled to Siberia or to southern Russia, where they maintained their religion and extended Russia's colonizing activities.

Measures to tightened serfdom continued, with new laws binding peasants to the land and restricting their opportunities to travel. Serf runaways were harshly punished. In 1670 a great serf revolt under Stephen Razin declared freedom from landlord control, but it was finally put down by tsarist troops.

Russia's First Westernization, 1690–1790

By the end of the 17th century Russia had become one of the great land empires, but it remained unusually agricultural by the standards of the West and the great Asian civilizations. The reign of **Peter I,** the son of Alexis and known with some justice as Peter the Great, built many new features into this framework between 1689 and 1725. In essence, Peter extended his predecessors' policies of building up tsarist control and expanding Russian territory (Map 18.2). He added a more definite interest in changing selected aspects of Russian economy and culture by imitating Western forms.

Peter's basic motives were familiar enough: he wanted to further tsarist power and enhance Russia's military strength. Early setbacks in wars with Sweden convinced him that some new departures were essential.

Peter the Great was a vigorous leader of exceptional intelligence and ruthless energy. A giant, standing 6 feet 8 inches, he was eager to move his country more fully into the Western military and cultural orbit without making it fully Western. He traveled widely in the West, incognito, seeking Western allies for a crusade against Turkish power in Europe—for which he found little enthusiasm. He also visited many Western manufacturing centers, even working as a ship's carpenter in Holland; through these activities he gained an interest in Western science and technology. He brought scores of Western artisans back with him to Russia.

Tsarist Autocracy of Peter the Great

In politics, Peter was clearly an autocrat. He put down revolts against his rule with great cruelty, in one case executing some of the ringleaders personally. He had no interest in the parliamentary features of Western centers such as Holland, seizing instead on the absolutist currents in the West at this time. Peter enhanced the power of the Russian state by using it as a reform force, trying to show that even aristocratic habits could be modified by state decree. Peter also extended an earlier policy of recruiting bureaucrats from outside aristocratic ranks and giving them noble titles to reward bureaucratic service. Here was a key means of freeing the state from exclusive dependence on aristocratic officials.

Peter imitated Western military organization, creating a specially trained fighting force that put down local militias. Furthermore, he set up a secret police to prevent dissent and to supervise the bureaucracy. Here he paralleled an earlier Chinese innovation but went well beyond the bureaucratic control impulses of Western absolutists at that time. Peter's Chancery of Secret Police survived, under different names and with changing functions, to the 1990s; it was reinstituted after 1917 by a revolutionary regime that in other respects worked to undo key features of the tsarist system.

Peter's foreign policy maintained many well established lines (see Map 18.2). He attacked the Ottoman Empire, but he won no great victories. He warred with Sweden, at the time one of the leading northern powers in Europe, and gained territory on the eastern coast of the Baltic Sea, thus reducing Sweden to second-rate military status. Russia now had a window on the sea, including a largely ice-free port. From this time onward, Russia became a major factor in European diplomatic

Figure 18.2 This icon, from the early 15th century, depicts Mary and the Christ Child. The Russian icon tradition used styles derived from Byzantine art. By the 17th century, under Western influence, they had become more naturalistic.

Peter the Great led the first westernization effort in history. Tsarist policies encouraging westernization focused only on particular aspects of Western society and left out large segments of the Russian population.

Peter the Great
IMAGE

Old Believers Russians who refused to accept the ecclesiastical reforms of Alexis Romanov (17th century); many exiled to Siberia or southern Russia, where they became part of Russian colonization.

Peter I Also known as Peter the Great; son of Alexis Romanov; ruled from 1689 to 1725; continued growth of absolutism and conquest; included more definite interest in changing selected aspects of economy and culture through imitation of western European models.

Battle of Poltava, 1709
IMAGE

Map 18.2 Russia Under Peter the Great   From 1696 to 1725, Peter the Great allowed his country only one year of peace. For the rest of this reign he radically changed the form of his government to pursue war. By the end, he had established his much-desired "Window on the West" on the southern shores of the Baltic Sea, where he founded the new city of St. Petersburg.

and military alignments. The tsar commemorated Russia's shift of interests westward by moving his capital from Moscow to a new Baltic city that he named St. Petersburg.

What Westernization Meant

Lomonosov: Panegyric to the Sovereign Emperor Peter the Great

DOCUMENT

Overall, Peter concentrated on improvements in political organization, on selected economic development, and on cultural change. He tried to streamline Russia's small bureaucracy and alter military structure by using Western organizational principles. He created a more well defined military hierarchy while developing functionally specialized bureaucratic departments. He also improved the army's weaponry and, with aid from Western advisors, created the first Russian navy. He completely eliminated the old noble councils, creating a set of advisors under his control. Peter's ministers systematized law codes to extend through the whole empire and revised the tax system, with taxes on ordinary Russian peasants increasing steadily. New training institutes were established for aspiring bureaucrats and officers—one way to bring talented non-nobles into the system.

Peter's economic efforts focused on building up metallurgical and mining industries, using Russia's extensive iron holdings to feed state-run munitions and shipbuilding facilities. Without urbanizing extensively or developing a large commercial class, Peter's reforms changed the Russian economy. Landlords were rewarded for using serf labor to staff new manufacturing operations.

The Nature of Westernization

Peter the Great and Catherine the Great were the two chief reformist rulers in Russia before 1800. In the first of the following edicts, Peter focuses on educational change; his approach reflected a real desire for innovation, Russia's autocratic tradition in government, and its hierarchical social structure. Catherine's "Instruction" borrowed heavily from Western philosophers and was hailed by one French intellectual as "the finest monument of the century." This document also showed distinctively Russian traditions and problems. However, the reforms in law and punishment were not put into practice, and the document itself was banned as subversive by Catherine's successor, as Russia's rulers began to fear the subversive qualities of Western influence after the French Revolution.

Decrees on Compulsory Education of the Russian Nobility, January 12 and February 28, 1714

Send to every *gubernia* [region] some persons from mathematical schools to teach the children of the nobility—except those of freeholders and government clerks—mathematics and geometry; as a penalty [for evasion] establish a rule that no one will be allowed to marry unless he learns these [subjects]. Inform all prelates to issue no marriage certificates to those who are ordered to go to schools. . . .

The Great Sovereign has decreed: in all *gubernias* children between the ages of ten and fifteen of the nobility, of government clerks, and of lesser officials, except those of freeholders, must be taught mathematics and some geometry. Toward that end, students should be sent from mathematical schools [as teachers], several into each *gubernia,* to prelates and to renowned monasteries to establish schools. During their instruction these teachers should be given food and financial remuneration of three altyns and two dengas per day from *gubernia* revenues set aside for that purpose by personal orders of His Imperial Majesty. No fees should be collected from students. When they have mastered the material, they should then be given certificates written in their own handwriting. When the students are released they ought to pay one ruble each for their training.

Without these certificates they should not be allowed to marry or receive marriage certificates.

From the "Instruction" of 1767

6. Russia is a European State.

7. This is clearly demonstrated by the following Observations: The Alterations which Peter the Great undertook in Russia succeeded with the greater Ease, because the Manners, which prevailed at that Time, and had been introduced amongst us by a Mixture of different Nations, and the Conquest of foreign Territories, were quite unsuitable to the Climate. Peter the First, by introducing the Manners and Customs of Europe among the European People in his Dominions, found at that Time such Means as even he himself was not sanguine enough to expect.

8. The Possessions of the Russian Empire extend upon the terrestrial Globe to 32 Degrees of Latitude, and to 165 of Longitude.

9. The Sovereign is absolute; for there is no other Authority but that which centers in his single Person, that can act with a Vigour proportionate to the Extent of such a vast Dominion.

10. The Extent of the Dominion requires an absolute Power to be vested in that Person who rules over it. It is expedient so to be, that the quick Dispatch of Affairs, sent from distant Parts, might make ample Amends for the delay occasioned by the great Distance of the Places.

11. Every other Form of Government whatsoever would not only have been prejudicial to Russia, but would even have proved its entire Ruin.

12. Another Reason is: That it is better to be subject to the Laws under one Master, than to be subservient to many.

13. What is the true End of Monarchy? Not to deprive People of their natural Liberty; but correct their Actions, in order to attain the supreme Good. . . .

272. The more happily a People live under a government, the more easily the Number of the Inhabitants increases. . . .

519. It is certain, that a high opinion of the *Glory* and *Power* of the Sovereign, would *increase* the *Strength* of his Administration; but a *good Opinion of his Love of Justice, will increase it at least as much.*

520. All this will never please those flatterers, who are daily instilling this pernicious Maxim into all the Sovereign on Earth, That their People are created for them only. But We think, and esteem it Our Glory to declare, "That We are created for Our People; and, of this Reason, We are obliged to Speak of Things just as they ought to be." For God forbid! That, after this Legislation is finished, any Nation on Earth should be more just; and, consequently, should flourish, more than Russia; otherwise the Intention of Our Laws would be totally frustrated; an Unhappiness which I do not wish to survive.

QUESTIONS In what sense did reformist measures strengthen Russian autocracy? What do the documents suggest about the motivations of leaders such as Peter and Catherine? Which westernizer maintained a closer match between their claims and appearances and Russia's real conditions?

This gave Russia the internal economic means to maintain a substantial military presence for almost two centuries.

Finally, Peter was eager to make Russia culturally respectable in Western eyes. Before Peter the Great, it was a custom in upper-class marriages for the father of the bride to pass a small whip to the groom. This symbolized the transfer of male power over women. Peter, knowing that upper-class women had greater freedom in the West, abolished this practice. He also encouraged upper-class women to wear Western-style clothing and attend public cultural events. He found support among women as a result. He also reduced a source of embarrassment among Westerners in Russia, who otherwise could easily point to uncivilized treatment of women. But, as with most of his

Figure 18.3 This contemporary Russian cartoon lampoons Peter the Great's order to his nobility to cut off their beards.

Reflections
on the
Accomplishments
of Peter the Great

CASE STUDY

Catherine the Great   German-born Russian tsarina in the 18th century; ruled after assassination of her husband; gave appearance of enlightened rule; accepted Western cultural influence; maintained nobility as service aristocracy by granting them new power over peasantry.

reforms, he made no move to change gender relations among the masses of Russian peasants.

Peter was eager to cut the Russian elite off from its traditions, to enhance state power, and to commit the elite to new identities. He required male nobles to shave off their beards (Figure 18.3) and wear Western clothes; in symbolic ceremonies he cut off the long, Mongol-type sleeves and pigtails that were characteristic of the boyars. Thus, traditional appearance was forcibly altered as part of Western-oriented change, although only the upper class was involved.

Cultural change supplemented bureaucratic training. Peter and his successors founded scientific institutes and academies along Western lines, and serious discussion of the latest scientific and technical findings became common. At the elite level, Peter built Russia into a Western cultural zone, and Western fads and fashions extended easily into the glittering new capital city. Ballet, initially encouraged in the French royal court, was imported and became a Russian specialty. The use of Christmas trees came from Germany.

This westernization effort had several features that can be compared with imitation processes in other societies later on. In the first place, the changes were selective. Peter did not try to touch the ordinary people of Russia or to involve them in the technological and intellectual aspects of westernization. In this sense Peter's reforms, which some historians see as part of a modernization program, fell well short of what modernization would later turn out to involve. New manufacturing involved serf labor that was heavily coerced, not the wage-labor spreading in the West. There was no interest in building the kind of worldwide export economy characteristic of the West. Peter wanted economic development to support military strength rather than to achieve wider commercial goals. Finally, westernization was meant to encourage the autocratic state, not to challenge it with some of the new political ideas circulating in the West. This was real change, but it did not fold Russia into Western civilization outright. Selectivity was crucial, and there was no interest in abandoning particularly Russian goals.

Furthermore, the westernization that did occur brought hostile responses. Many peasants resented the westernized airs and expenses of their landlords, some of whom no longer even knew Russian but spoke only French. Elements of the elite opposed Peter's thirst for change, arguing that Russian traditions were superior to those of the West. As one priest wrote to Tsar Alexis, "You feed the foreigners too well, instead of bidding your folk to cling to the old customs." This tension continued in Russian history from this point forward, leading to important cycles of enthusiasm and revulsion toward Western values. Here was another key component of Russian development, still vivid in the early 21st century.

Consolidation Under Catherine the Great

The death of Peter the Great in 1724 was followed by several decades of weak rule, dominated in part by power plays among army officers who guided the selection of several ineffective emperors and empresses. The weakness of tsardom in these years encouraged new grumblings about undue westernization and some new initiatives by church officials eager to gain more freedom to maneuver, but no major new policy directions were set. Russian territorial expansion continued, with several clashes with the Ottoman Empire and further exploration and settlement in Siberia. In 1761, Peter III, nephew of Peter the Great's youngest daughter, reached the throne. He was mentally unstable, but his wife, a German-born princess who changed her name to Catherine—and was later known as **Catherine the Great** (Figure 18.4)—soon took matters in hand. Catherine II (the Great) (1729–1796) is one of the fascinating women leaders of history. Born a Prussian princess, she converted to the Orthodox faith after her marriage to the heir to the Russian throne was arranged. Her married life was miserable, with frequent threats of divorce from her husband. She also disliked her son, the future Tsar Paul I. Officers of the palace guard installed her as empress in 1762. The tsar was later murdered, possibly with Catherine's consent.

Catherine actively defended the powers of the central monarch. She put down another vigorous peasant uprising, led by Emelian Pugachev, having Pugachev himself slaughtered. She used the **Pugachev rebellion** as an excuse to extend the powers of the central government in regional affairs. Catherine's reign combined genuine reform interests with her need to consolidate power as a truly Russian ruler—a combination that explains the complexities of her policies.

Like Peter the Great, Catherine was a selective westernizer, as her "instruction of 1767" (see the Document section) clearly demonstrated. She flirted with the ideas of the Enlightenment, importing several French philosophers for visits, and she established commissions to discuss new law codes and other Western-style measures, including reduction of traditionally severe punishments. Catherine also encouraged upper-class education and the arts and literature.

Catherine's policies were not always consistent with her image, however. She gave new powers to the nobility over their serfs, maintaining a trade-off that had been developing over the previous two centuries in Russia. In this trade-off, nobles served a strong central government and staffed it as bureaucrats and officers. They were in this sense a service aristocracy, not an independent force. They also accepted into their ranks newly ennobled officials chosen by the tsars. In return, however, most of the actual administration over local peasants, except for those on government-run estates, was wielded by the noble landlords. These landlords could requisition peasant labor, levy taxes in money and goods, and even impose punishments for crimes because landlord-dominated courts administered local justice. Catherine increased the harshness of punishments nobles could decree for their serfs.

Catherine patronized Western-style art and architecture encouraging leading nobles to tour the West and even send their children to be educated there. But she also tried to avoid political influence from the West. When the great French Revolution broke out in 1789, Catherine was quick to close Russia's doors to the "seditious" writings of liberals and democrats. She also censored a small but emerging band of Russian intellectuals who urged reforms along Western lines. One of the first Western-inspired radicals, a noble named Radishev, who sought abolition of serfdom and more liberal political rule, was vigorously harassed by Catherine's police, and his writings were banned.

Catherine pursued the tradition of Russian expansion with energy and success (see Map 18.3). She resumed campaigns against the Ottoman Empire, winning new territories in central Asia, including the Crimea, bordering the Black Sea. The Russian–Ottoman contest became a central diplomatic issue for both powers, and Russia became increasingly ascendant. Catherine accelerated the colonization of Russia's holdings in Siberia and encouraged further exploration, claiming the territory of Alaska in Russia's name. Russian explorers also moved down the Pacific coast of North America into what is now northern California, and tens of thousands of pioneers spread over Siberia.

Finally, Catherine pressed Russia's interests in Europe, playing power politics with Prussia and Austria, though without risking major wars. She increased Russian interference in Polish affairs. The Polish government was extremely weak, almost paralyzed by a parliamentary system that let members of the nobility veto any significant measure, and this invited interest by more powerful neighbors. Russia was able to win agreements with Austria and Prussia for the **partition of Poland.** Three partitions, in 1772, 1793, and 1795, eliminated Poland as an independent state, and Russia held the lion's share of the spoils. The basis for further Russian involvement in European affairs had obviously been created, and this would show in Russia's ultimate role in putting down

Figure 18.4 Catherine the Great in the costume of Minerva, the Roman goddess of wisdom, war, and the arts.

Catherine the Great's Constitution (1767)

Pugachev rebellion   During 1770s in reign of Catherine the Great; led by cossack Emelian Pugachev, who claimed to be legitimate tsar; eventually crushed; typical of peasant unrest during the 18th century and thereafter.

partition of Poland   Division of Polish territory among Russia, Prussia, and Austria in 1772, 1793, and 1795; eliminated Poland as independent state; part of expansion of Russian influence in eastern Europe.

The Cake of Kings—First Partition of Poland, 1773 Engraving

Map 18.3 Russia's Holdings by 1800   Expansion fluctuated from one decade to the next but persisted, bringing Russia into encounters with Europe, the Ottoman Empire, and East Asia.

the French armies of Napoleon after 1812—the first time Russian troops moved into the heartland of western Europe.

By the time of Catherine's death in 1796, Russia had passed through three centuries of extraordinary development. It had won independence and constructed a strong central state, though one that had to maintain a balance with the local political and economic interests of a powerful nobility. It had brought new elements into Russia's culture and economy, in part by borrowing from the West. And it had extended its control over the largest land empire in the world (Map 18.3). In the east it bordered China, where an 18th-century Amur River agreement set new frontiers. A tradition of careful but successful military aggrandizement had been established, along with a real pioneering spirit of settlement. It is no wonder that not long after 1800, a perceptive French observer, Alexis de Tocqueville, likened the expanded and increasingly important Russia to the new country emerging in the Western Hemisphere, the United States of America—the two giants of future world history.

Themes in Early Modern Russian History

 Russian serfdom constituted a distinctive social and economic system. Its growing burdens sparked recurrent social protest.

Because of its great estates, its local political power, and its service to the state, the Russian nobility maintained a vital position in Russian society. In Russia and in eastern Europe generally, landed nobles tended to be divided between a minority of great magnates, who lived in major cities and provided key cultural patronage, and smaller landowners, whose culture was less westernized and whose lifestyle was much less opulent.

Serfdom: The Life of East Europe's Masses

Russian Serfs

During the 17th and 18th centuries, the power of the nobility over the serfs increased steadily. Before the Mongol conquest, Russian peasants had been largely free farmers with a legal position superior to that of their medieval Western counterparts. After the expulsion of the Tatars, however, increasing numbers of Russian peasants fell into debt and had to accept servile status to the noble

Oppressed Peasants

This painting is from the early 20th century (1907), when revolutionary currents were swirling in Russia and the status of the peasantry was widely discussed. This raises obvious issues of interpretation. The subject of the painting, tax collection and the poor material conditions of 17th-century peasants, is valid for the 17th century, but the artist was also trying to score contemporary points.

QUESTIONS What aspects of the tax collector's appearance suggest that the artist was striving for an accurate rendition of the ways officials looked *before* the reforms of Peter the Great? Does this painting suggest early 20th-century rather than 17th-century sympathies in Russian culture? Given the lack of popular art from the 17th century, except religious art, does the painting provide useful material for understanding peasant conditions?

---

landowners when they could not repay. They retained access to much of the land, but not primary ownership. The Russian government actively encouraged this process from the 16th century onward. Serfdom gave the government a way to satisfy the nobility and regulate peasants when the government itself lacked the bureaucratic means to extend direct controls over the common people. As new territories were added to the empire, the system of serfdom was extended accordingly, sometimes after a period of free farming. An act of 1649 fixed the hereditary status of the serfs, so that people born to that station could not legally escape it. Laws passed during the 17th and 18th centuries tied the serfs to the land and increased the legal rights of the landlords.

Serfs on the estates of eastern Europe were also taxed, policed, and even sold by their landlords. In Russia, whole villages were sold as manufacturing labor—a process Peter the Great actively encouraged so as to spur manufacturing. Peasants were not literally slaves. They continued to use village governments to regulate many aspects of their lives, relying more heavily on community ties than their counterparts in the Western countryside. Yet most peasants were illiterate and quite poor. They paid high taxes or obligations in kind, and they owed extensive labor service to the landlords or the government—a source not only of agricultural production but also of mining and manufacturing. The labor obligation tended to increase steadily. Both the economic and the legal situation of the peasantry continued to deteriorate. Although Catherine the Great sponsored a few model villages to display her enlightenment to Western-minded friends, she turned the government of the serfs over to the landlords more completely than ever before. A law of 1785 allowed landlords to punish harshly any serfs convicted of major crimes or rebellion. By 1800, half of Russia's peasantry was enserfed to the landlords, and much of the other half owed comparable obligations to the state.

Russia was setting up a system of serfdom very close to outright slavery in that serfs could be bought and sold, gambled away, and punished by their masters. The system was a very unusual case in which a people essentially enslaved many of its own members, in contrast to most slave systems, which focused on "outsiders."

Rural conditions in many other parts of eastern Europe were similar. Nobles maintained estate agriculture in Poland, Hungary, and elsewhere.

Estate Agriculture, Trade and Dependence

In Russia, the nobility used the estate agricultural system to sustain their political power and their aristocratic status, which derived from command over land and people, not trade or commerce. This focus stifled social mobility and urbanization, which were drivers of economic growth in the

West. In between serfs and landlords, there were few layers of Russian society. Cities were small, and 95 percent of the population remained rural. The manufacturing that existed took place in the countryside, so there was no well defined artisan class. Government growth encouraged some non-noble bureaucrats and professionals. Small merchant groups existed as well, although most of Russia's European trade was handled by Westerners posted to the main Russian cities and relying on Western shipping. The nobility, concerned about potential social competition from both bureaucrats and businessmen, prevented the emergence of a substantial merchant class. The bulk of the population was increasingly composed of enserfed farmers who had little opportunity for social or economic development.

Inevitably, the intensification of estate agriculture and serf labor pursued by the nobility led to eastern Europe's growing economic subordination to the West. Coerced labor was used to produce grain surpluses purchased by Western merchants to feed the growing cities of western Europe. In return, Western merchants brought in manufactured goods, including the luxury furnishings and clothing essential to the aristocratic lifestyle. This growing dependence on Western markets and Western manufactured goods is comparable in some respects with developments in Latin America (see Chapter 19), though eastern Europe was unique in its lack of a merchant class or entrepreneurial values that could have produced more balanced economic growth.

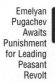

Emelyan
Pugachev
Awaits
Punishment
for Leading
Peasant
Revolt

Russia's social and economic system worked well in some respects. It produced enough revenue to support an expanding state and empire. Russia was able to trade in furs and other commodities with areas in central Asia outside its boundaries, which meant that its export economy was not totally oriented toward the more dynamic West. It underwrote the aristocratic magnates and their glittering, westernized culture. The system, along with Russia's expansion, yielded significant population growth: Russia's population doubled during the 18th century to 36 million. For an empire burdened by a harsh climate in most regions, this was no small achievement. Despite periodic famines and epidemics, there was no question that the overall economy had advanced.

Yet the system suffered from important limitations. Most agricultural methods were highly traditional, and there was little motivation among the peasantry for improvement because increased production usually was taken by the state or the landlord. Landlords debated agricultural improvements in their academies, but when it came time to increase production, they concentrated on squeezing the serfs. Manufacturing lagged behind Western standards, despite the important extension developed under Peter the Great.

Social Unrest

Russia's economic and social system led to protest. By the end of the 18th century, a small but growing number of Western-oriented aristocrats such as Radishev were criticizing the regime's backwardness, urging measures as far-reaching as the abolition of serfdom. Here were the seeds of a radical intelligentsia that, despite government repression, would grow with time. More significant still were the recurring peasant rebellions. Russian peasants for the most part were politically loyal to the tsar, but they harbored bitter resentments against their landlords, whom they accused of taking lands that were rightfully theirs. Periodic rebellions saw peasants destroy manorial records, seize land, and sometimes kill landlords and their officials.

Peasant rebellions had occurred from the 17th century onward, but the Pugachev rebellion of the 1770s was particularly strong. Pugachev (Figure 18.5), a cossack chieftain who claimed to be the legitimate tsar, promised an end to serfdom, taxation, and military conscription along with the abolition of the landed aristocracy. His forces roamed over southern Russia until they were finally defeated. Pugachev was brought to Moscow in a case and cut into quarters in a public square. The triumph of Catherine and the nobility highlighted the mutual dependence of government and the upper class but did not end protest. Radishev, finding peasants barely able to work their own plots of land and sometimes tortured to work harder, thought he saw the handwriting on the wall: "Tremble, cruel hearted landlord! On the brow of each of your peasants I see your condemnation written."

Figure 18.5 The Cossack leader Emelian Pugachev attracted supporters by appealing to the popular belief that Peter III, Catherine's husband, was still alive. Claiming to be Peter III, he led a revolt in 1773–1774 that threatened Catherine's throne. When the revolt was defeated, Pugachev was brutally executed as an example to other potential revolutionaries.

Russia and Eastern Europe

Russian history did not include the whole of eastern Europe after the 15th century. Regions west of Russia continued to form a fluctuating borderland between western European and eastern European influences. Even in the Balkans, under Ottoman control, growing trade with the West sparked some new cultural exchange by the 18th century, as Greek merchants, for example, picked up many Enlightenment ideas.

Eastern Europe, c. 1550

Areas such as present-day Poland or the Czech and Slovak regions operated more fully within the Western cultural orbit. The Polish scientist Copernicus was an early participant in fundamental discoveries in what became the Scientific Revolution. Western currents such as the Reformation also echoed in parts of east central Europe such as Hungary.

At the same time, many smaller eastern European nationalities lost political autonomy during the early modern era. Hungary, freed from the Ottomans, became part of the German-dominated Habsburg Empire. This empire also took over the Czech lands, then called Bohemia. Prussian territory pushed eastward into Polish areas.

Poland-Lithuania and Russia

The decline of Poland was particularly striking. In 1500, Poland, formed in 1386 by a union of the regional kingdoms of Poland and Lithuania, was the largest state in eastern Europe aside from Russia. Polish cultural life, linked with the West through shared Roman Catholicism, flourished in the 16th century. By 1600, however, economic and political setbacks mounted. Polish aristocrats, charged with electing the king, began deliberately choosing weak figures. As in Russia, urban centers, and thus a merchant class, were lacking. The aristocratic parliament vetoed any reform efforts until late in the 18th century, after Poland began to be partitioned by its more powerful neighbors. The eclipse of Poland highlighted Russian emergence on the European as well as the Eurasian stage.

Global Connections

Russia and the World

From a world history standpoint, Russia's emergence as a key player both in Europe and in Asia was a crucial development in the early modern period. Today, Russia spans ten time zones, and much of this territory had been acquired by the late 18th century. By this point, Russia was affecting diplomatic and military developments in Europe, in the Middle East (through its frequent battles with the Ottoman Empire), and in east Asia. It had gained a direct hold in central Asia. The spread of Russian claims to Alaska, and expeditions even to Hawaii, hinted at an even larger role. At the same time, early modern Russia did not become a major player in the process of proto-globalization. Its exports of grains and raw materials to western Europe were significant, but it deliberately did not seek a leading commercial role. This was a different kind of empire from those that Western nations were building, but it had huge impact.

Further Readings

For excellent survey coverage on this period, as well as additional bibliography, see Nicholas Riasanovsky, *History of Russia* (2005). Two excellent source collections for this vital period of Russian history are T. Riha, ed., *Readings in Russian Civilization, Vol. 2, Imperial Russia 1700–1917* (1969), and Basil Dmytryshyn, *Imperial Russia: A Sourcebook 1700–1917* (1967). On Russia's empire, see Christoph Witzenrath, *Cossacks and the Russian Empire, 1598–1725: Manipulation, Rebellion and Expansion into Siberia* (2007); John P. LeDonne, *The Grand Strategy of the Russian Empire, 1650–1831* (2004); and Williard Suderland, *Taming the Wild Field: Colonization and Empire on the Russian Steppe* (2004).

On important regimes, see P. Dukes, *The Making of Russian Absolutism: 1613–1801* (1982); J. L. I. Fennell, *Ivan the Great of Moscow* (1961); L. Hughes, *Russia in the Age of Peter the Great* (1998) and *Peter the Great and the West: New Perspectives* (2001); Isabel de Madariaga, *Ivan the Terrible: First Tsar of Russia* (2005) and *Catherine the Great: A Short History* (1990); Simon Dixon, *Catherine the Great* (2001); Simon Sebag Montefiore, *Potemkin: Catherine the Great's Imperial Partner* (2005); James Cracraft, *The Petrine Revolution in Russian Culture* (2004) and *The Revolution of Peter the Great* (2003); Paul Bushkovitch, *Peter the Great: The Struggle for Power, 1671–1725* (2001); and Inna Gorbatov, *Catherine the Great and the French Philosophers of the Enlightenment: Montesquieu, Voltaire, Rousseau, Diderot and Grim* (2006). Four good studies deal with cultural history: Richard Stites, *Serfdom Society, and the Arts in Imperial Russia: The Pleasure and the Power* (2005); H. Rogger, *National Consciousness in Eighteenth Century Russia* (1963); Marc Raeff, *Origins of the Russian*

Intelligentsia: The Eighteenth Century Nobility (1966); and Marc Raeff, ed., *Russian Intellectual History* (1986).

For economic and social history, A. Kahan, *The Knout and the Plowshare: Economic History of Russia in the 18th Century* (1985), is an important treatment. For the vital peasant question, see Jerome Blum, *Lord and Peasant in Russia from the Ninth to the Nineteenth Century* (1961); see also Richard Hellie, *Slavery in Russia, 1450–1725* (1982). For an analytical overview, see Marc Raeff, *Understanding Imperial Russia: State and Society in the Old Regime* (1984). A very revealing comparison is Peter Kolchin, *Unfree Labor: American Slavery and Russian Serfdom* (1987). A fine survey on military and diplomatic strategy is William Fuller, *Strategy and Power in Russia, 1600–1914* (1992).

On the Web

A vivid introduction to Russian history is offered at http://www.geographia.com/russia/rushis01.htm.htm with sections devoted to ancient Russia (http://www.geographia.com/russia/rushis04.htm), the Mongol impact (http://www.geographia.com/russia/rushis03.htm), and the Romanovs (http://www.geographia.com/russia/rushis04.htm). See also http://www.alexanderpalace.org/. A digital collection of maps of Russia is available at http://data.lnb.lv/nba05/kartes/Html/krievija.htm. The life and careers of Russia's early rulers, such as Ivan the Great (Ivan III) and Ivan the Terrible (Ivan IV) are examined at http://www.mnsu.edu/emuseum/history/russia/ivanthegreat.html, http://en.wikipedia.org/wiki/Ivan_III, http://www.themiddleages.net/people/ivan_the_terrible.html, http://mars.wnec.edu/~grempel/courses/russia/lectures/09ivanIV.html and http://www.mnsu.edu/emuseum/history/russia/ivantheterrible.html.

Peter the Great's maritime interests are examined at http://www.maritimeheritage.org/ports/europe/russia.html. The lives of Peter the Great and Catherine the Great are seen against the backdrop of early modern Russia at http://www.mnsu.edu/emuseum/history/russia/romanov.html and http://www.mnsu.edu/emuseum/history/russia/catherine.html. A virtual tour of their palaces at St. Petersburg is available at http://www.cityvision2000.com/city_tour/ and http://www.hermitagemuseum.org/html_En/index.html.

Peter the Great's efforts to "westernize" Russia are addressed at http://russian-ukrainian-belarus-history.suite101.com/article.cfm/peter_the_greats_reforms. The impact of later efforts to introduce "western" norms is discussed at http://www.russiansabroad.com/russian_history_28.html. See also http://www.socyberty.com/Social-Sciences/A-Comparison-of-Westernization-in-Russia-Japan-and-China.67924. A selection of Catherine the Great's letters and decrees can be found at http://www.fordham.edu/halsall/mod/18catherine.html.

Catherine the Great's efforts at westernization did not include the elimination of serfdom, but its expansion. Brief histories of Russian serfdom are offered at http://au.encarta.msn.com/encyclopedia_761567780/Serfdom.html and http://www.spartacus.schoolnet.co.uk/RUSserfs.htm. A contemporary (1891) account of the history of serfdom in Russia is offered at http://www.avalon.law.yale.edu/19th_century/koval6.asp. Prince and revolutionist Peter Koropotkin's evaluation of the Russian aristocracy and the condition of Russian serfs can be found at http://recollectionbooks.com/bleed/Encyclopedia/Kropotkin/Nobles&Serfs.htm.

Cossack life is presented at http://www.sfu.ca/archaeology/museum/russia/cossack.htm and http://en.wikipedia.org/wiki/History_of_the_Cossacks. Catherine the Great's response to the rebellion led by the cossack Emelian (Yemelyan) Pugachev, and how it illuminated the differences in the political landscape of revolutionary France and absolutist Russia, is described at http://mars.wnec.edu/~grempel/courses/russia/lectures/16catherine.html, and http://en.wikipedia.org/wiki/Yemelyan_Pugachev.

AP* | Test Prep

1. How did the early Russian tsars benefit from their expansionist policies into central Asia?

    (A) The tsars were able to reward the nobles and attain greater economic advances.

    (B) The tsars were able to extract revenge on their former Chinese overlords.

    (C) The tsars claimed personal ownership over the newly-conquered lands.

    (D) The tsars were able to challenge Britain for influence in India.

2. Which of the following symbolized Peter the Great's cultural reforms?

    (A) establishment of national awards for successful merchants

    (B) toleration of religious minorities and laws granting freedom of worship

    (C) the shaving of the nobles' beards

    (D) constructing Western-style buildings in Moscow to confirm its role as Russia's capital

3. Although early modern Russia was patriarchal, evidence that Peter the Great's westernization reforms in Russia reached out to at least noble women includes all of the following EXCEPT

    (A) the right of women to sue in court and divorce their husbands.

    (B) the encouragement of women to attend public cultural events.

    (C) the end to the marriage tradition in which a whip was handed from father to bridegroom.

    (D) decrees westernizing women's dress and manners and permitting education.

4. In order to accomplish her domestic goals, Catherine the Great

    (A) followed Enlightenment ideas and created a more democratic and representative government.

    (B) supported peasant demands for social reform and land redistribution.

    (C) abolished serfdom and slavery.

    (D) allied with the nobles and gave them absolute control over their peasants.

5. What were the social consequences of Catherine the Great's continued expansionist policies?

    (A) Serfs acquired some basic additional rights.

    (B) The non-Russian peoples were forced to convert to Orthodox Christianity or pay high taxes to keep their culture.

    (C) Landowners were given absolute power over their serfs in exchange for their government services.

    (D) Russian elites considered themselves equal to western European nobility.

6. Economically, early modern Russia was

    (A) dependent on foreign merchants for most trade with the West.

    (B) poor with few items to export and lacking in valuable raw materials.

    (C) self-sufficient enough to be uninterested in trade.

    D) one of the leaders in the international trade of manufactured goods.

7. The greatest source of social unrest in early modern Russia was due to

    (A) the opposition of the nobility to westernization.

    (B) the clergy and religious opposition to the non-Christian minorities.

    (C) rapid growth of towns and factories.

    (D) unfree conditions and grievances of the serfs.

Free-Response Question

What motivated Russian implementation of reforms inspired by western Europe? What factors limited these reforms?

19 Early Latin America

Spaniards and Portuguese: From Reconquest to Conquest
DOCUMENT: A Vision from the Vanquished
The Destruction and Transformation of Indigenous Societies
THINKING HISTORICALLY: Atlantic History
Colonial Economies and Governments
Brazil: The First Plantation Colony

Multiracial Societies
VISUALIZING THE PAST: Race or Culture? A Changing Society
The 18th-Century Reforms
GLOBAL CONNECTIONS: Latin American Civilization and the World Context

In September 1589 Captain Mancio Serra de Leguizamon lay dying in his bed in Cuzco, the ancient capital of the Incas in the highlands of Peru. His mind was still clear, but his body was failing, and he knew his time was approaching. He needed to set his affairs in order with his heirs, his king, and with God. He called a priest and a notary to his bedside to draw up his last will and testament.

Born in Castile like many young Spanish men he had been attracted to the New World by its fabled wealth and opportunities for advancement. When he was 16, he sailed for the New World in search of adventure. Sometime in 1532 he joined the 168 men under the Spanish conqueror Francisco Pizarro, who were embarked on the conquest of the Inca Empire. Mancio Serra claimed in his will that he was the first Spaniard to enter Cuzco when the Spaniards laid siege to the city in 1533. Legend has it that, in the looting that followed, he seized a great golden disk representing the sun that had hung on the walls of the principal temple of the sun in Cuzco. But that very night he fell to drinking and gambling and lost the treasure. He never got over his love of gambling.

But all was not lost with the disk of gold: for his efforts, Mancio received grants of Indian laborers and a site in the city where, using an Inca stonework foundation, he built a fine home. There were more expeditions, civil wars, an Indian mistress, a marriage to an Inca noblewoman and, later, to a Spanish woman (Figure 19.1). There were numerous children, some legitimate and some not. Mancio Serra became a respected leader in Peru, for a while mayor of Cuzco, a man of substance with many servants and slaves. But unlike most of the Spaniards involved in the conquest, on his deathbed, Mancio Serra, overcome by guilt, had sec-

ond thoughts about the justice of what he had done. Before assigning his property to his heirs, calling himself the last of the conquerors still alive and so the last who could give eye-witness testimony, in his will he addressed the king of Spain:

> We found these realms in such order that there was not a thief, nor a vicious man, nor an adulteress, nor were there prostitutes, nor were there immoral people, each being content and honest in their labor. And that their lands, forests, mines, pastures and dwellings and produce were regulated in such a manner that each person possessed his own property without any other seizing or occupying it. . . . I wish Your Catholic Majesty to understand the motive that moves me to make this statement is the peace of my conscience and because of the guilt I share. For we have destroyed by our evil behavior such a government as was enjoyed by these natives.*

Perhaps his conscience made him romanticize Inca society, but Mancio Serra went on to say that the actions and abuses of the Spaniards had ruined the inhabitants, introduced bad habits, and reduced the ancient nobility to poverty. In an earlier will he had declared that everything produced from his grant of indigenous workers, including his landed estate, should belong to them, "since it was once their own." He had seen and lived it all, it burdened his soul and his conscience, and he believed it was a matter for the royal conscience as well. "I inform Your Majesty that there is no more I can do to alleviate these injustices other than by my words, in which I beg God to pardon me." ■

*Stuart Stirling, *The Last Conquistador* (Stroud, Sutton, 1999), pp. 140–146.

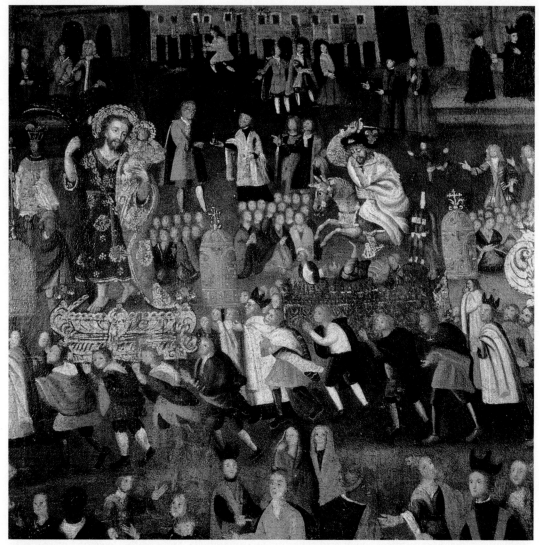

Figure 19.1 By the end of the 17th century, a society that fused Hispanic culture and indigenous elements had emerged in Spanish America.

Spain and Portugal created empires in the Americas by conquest and settlement. These lands, which became Latin America, were immediately drawn into a new world economy, providing silver, gold, new crops, and other goods. They also served as a model and as an attraction for other Europeans who eventually also created an Atlantic system based on plantations, coerced labor, and the exploitation of mineral wealth that linked Europe, West Africa, and the Americas in terms of peoples, cultures, and economies, more often by violence than by persuasion. The emerging hierarchy of world economic relationships shaped conditions in this new civilization for several centuries.

The peoples of Spain and Portugal, often collectively called Iberians because all came from the Iberian Peninsula in Europe, mixed with Native Americans and adopted aspects of their culture while introducing the religion, technologies, and many aspects of their culture to the indigenous peoples. Both groups were also influenced by the cultures of the slaves imported from Africa. The formative period for Latin American civilization extended from initial contacts in the 1490s through the 18th century, when colonial structures began to decline. New societies, created by the intrusion of the Iberians, especially the Castilians and the Portuguese, and by the incorporation or destruction of Native American cultures, arose throughout the American continents. Much of what the Iberians did in the Americas followed the patterns and examples of their European traditions. The Native Americans who survived, although they were battered and profoundly transformed, showed a vitality and resiliency that shaped later societies in many ways. What resulted drew on European and Native American precedents, but it was something new: the world's latest addition to the list of distinctive civilizations.

1450 C.E.	1500 C.E.	1600 C.E.	1750 C.E.
1492 Fall of Granada, last Muslim kingdom in Spain; expulsion of the Jews; Columbus makes landfall in the Caribbean **1493** Columbus's second expedition; beginnings of settlement in the Indies **1493–1520** Exploration and settlement in the Caribbean **1494** Treaty of Tordesillas	**1500** Cabral lands in Brazil **1519–1524** Cortés leads conquest of Mexico **1533** Cuzco, Peru, falls to Francisco Pizarro **1540–1542** Coronado explores area that is now the southwestern United States **1541** Santiago, Chile, founded **1549** Royal government established in Brazil **1580–1640** Spain and Portugal united under same rulers	**1630–1654** Dutch capture northeastern Brazil **1654** English take Jamaica **1695** Gold discovered in Brazil **1702–1713** War of the Spanish succession; Bourbon dynasty rules Spain	**1755–1776** Marquis of Pombal, prime minister of Portugal **1759** Jesuits expelled from Brazil **1756–1763** Seven Years War **1759–1788** Carlos III rules Spain; Bourbon reforms **1763** Brazilian capital moved to Rio de Janeiro **1767** Jesuits expelled from Spanish America **1781** Comunero revolt in New Granada; Tupac Amaru rebellion in Peru **1788** Conspiracy for independence in Minas Gerais, Brazil

Spaniards and Portuguese: From Reconquest to Conquest

The Spaniards and Portuguese came from societies long in contact with peoples of other faiths and cultures in which warfare and conquest were well established activities. American realities and the resistance of indigenous peoples modified these traditions, but by the 1570s, much of the Americas had been brought under Iberian control.

Christian
Reconquest of
Muslim Spain
MAP

Ferdinand of Aragon   (r. 1479–1516) Along with Isabella of Castile, monarch of largest Christian kingdoms in Iberia; marriage to Isabella created united Spain; responsible for reconquest of Granada, initiation of exploration of New World.

Isabella of Castile   (1451–1504) Along with Ferdinand of Aragon, monarch of largest Christian kingdoms in Iberia; marriage to Ferdinand created united Spain; responsible for reconquest of Granada, initiation of exploration of New World.

The peoples who inhabited the Iberian Peninsula had long lived at the frontier of Mediterranean Europe. During the Middle Ages their lands were a cultural frontier between Christianity and Islam. Conflicts created a strong tradition of military conquest and rule over peoples of other beliefs and customs. A number of Christian kingdoms emerged, such as Portugal on the Atlantic coast, Aragon in eastern Spain, and in the center of the peninsula, Castile, the largest of all. By the mid-15th century, the rulers **Ferdinand of Aragon** and his wife **Isabella of Castile** carried out a program of unification that sought to eliminate the religious and eventually the ethnic divisions in their kingdoms. With the fall in 1492 of Granada, the last Muslim kingdom, the cross triumphed throughout the peninsula. Moved by political savvy and religious fervor, Isabella ordered the Jews of her realm to convert or leave the country. As many as 200,000 people may have left, severely disrupting some aspects of the Castilian economy. It was also in 1492, with the Granada war at an end and religious unification established, that Isabella and Ferdinand were willing to support the project of a Genoese mariner named Christopher Columbus, who hoped to reach the East Indies by sailing westward around the globe.

Iberian Society and Tradition

Like many Mediterranean peoples, the Spanish and Portuguese were heavily urban, with many peasants living in small towns and villages. That pattern was also established in America, where Europeans lived in cities and towns surrounded by a rural native population. Many commoners who came to America as conquerors sought to recreate themselves as a new nobility, with native peoples as their serfs. The patriarchal family was readily adapted to Latin America, where large estates and grants of American Indian laborers provided the framework for relations based on economic dominance. The Iberian peninsula had maintained a tradition of holding slaves—part of its experience as an ethnic frontier—in contrast to most of medieval Europe, and African slaves had been imported from the trans-Sahara trade. The extension of slavery to America built on this tradition.

The political centralization of both Portugal and Castile depended on a professional bureaucracy, usually made up of men trained as lawyers and judges. This system is worthy of comparison with the systems in China and other great empires. Religion and the church served as the other pillar of Iberian politics; close links between church and state resulted from the reconquest of the Iberian Peninsula from the Muslims, and these links, including royal nomination of church officials, were also extended to the New World.

Spanish and particularly Portuguese merchants also shaped traditions that became relevant in the American colonies. Portugal had been moving down the African coast since 1415, establishing trading posts rather than outright colonies. In the Atlantic islands, however, more extensive estates were established, leading to a slave trade with Africa and a highly commercial agricultural system based on sugar. Brazil would extend this pattern, starting out as a trade factory but then shifting, as in the Atlantic islands, to plantation agriculture.

The Chronology of Conquest

The Spanish and Portuguese conquest and colonization of the Americas falls roughly into three periods during the early modern centuries. First came an era of conquest from 1492 to about 1570 (Map 19.1), during which the main lines of administration and economy were set out. The second phase was one of consolidation and maturity from 1570 to about 1700 in which the colonial institutions and societies took their definite form. Finally, during the 18th century, a period of reform and reorganization in both Spanish America and Portuguese Brazil intensified the colonial relationship and planted the seeds of dissatisfaction and revolt.

The period from 1492 to about 1570 witnessed a remarkable spurt of human destruction and creation. During roughly a century, vast areas of two continents and millions of people were brought under European control. Immigration, commerce, and exploitation of native populations linked these areas to an emerging Atlantic economy. These processes were accompanied and made possible by the conquest and destruction of many American Indian societies and the transformation of others, as well as by the introduction in some places of African slaves. Mexico and Peru, with

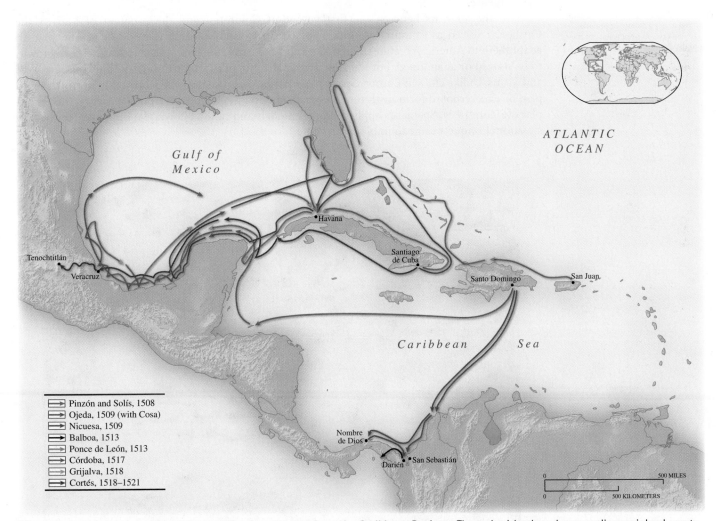

Map 19.1 Major Spanish Expeditions of Conquest in and from the Caribbean Region   The major islands and surrounding mainland coasts were explored and conquered between 1493 and c.1570. The Caribbean outposts were also the staging areas for most expeditions into the American continents, few expeditions sailed directly from Spain.

their large sedentary populations and mineral resources, attracted the Spaniards and became the focus of immigration and institution building. Other conquests radiated outward from the Peruvian and Mexican centers.

The Caribbean Crucible

Spanish and
Portuguese
Explorations,
1400–1600

Caribbean   First area of Spanish exploration and settlement; served as experimental region for nature of Spanish colonial experience; encomienda system of colonial management initiated here.

Hispaniola   First island in Caribbean settled by Spaniards; settlement founded by Columbus on second voyage to New World; Spanish base of operations for further discoveries in New World.

encomienda   Grants of Indian laborers made to Spanish conquerors and settlers in Mesoamerica and South America; basis for earliest forms of coerced labor in Spanish colonies.

encomendero   The holder of a grant of Indians who were required to pay a tribute or provide labor. The encomendero was responsible for their integration into the church.

The **Caribbean** experience served Spain as a model for its actions elsewhere in the Americas. After Columbus's first trans-Atlantic voyage in 1492, a return expedition in the next year established a colony on the island of Santo Domingo, or **Hispaniola** (Figure 19.2). From there and from Spain, expeditions carried out new explorations and conquests. Puerto Rico (1508) and Cuba (1511) fell under Spanish control, and by 1513 settlements existed in Panama and on the northern coast of South America. (Map 19.1)

In the Caribbean, the agricultural Taino people of the islands provided enough surplus labor to make their distribution to individual Spaniards feasible, and thus began what would become the encomienda, or grant of indigenous people to individual Spaniards in a kind of serfdom. The holder of an **encomienda,** an **encomendero,** was able to use the people as workers or to tax them. Gold hunting, slaving, and European diseases rapidly depopulated the islands, and within two decades little was left there to hold Spanish attention. A few strongly fortified ports, such as Havana, San Juan, and Santo Domingo, guarded Spain's commercial lifeline, but on the whole the Caribbean became a colonial backwater for the next two centuries, until sugar and slaves became the basis of its resurgence.

In the 40 years between the first voyage of Columbus and the conquest of Mexico, the Caribbean served as a testing ground. The Spaniards established Iberian-style cities but had to adapt them to American realities. Hurricanes and the native peoples' resistance caused many towns to be moved or abandoned, but the New World also provided opportunities to implant new ideas and forms. Unlike cities in Europe, Spanish American cities usually were laid out according to a grid plan or checkerboard form, with the town hall, major church, and governor's palace in the central plaza (Figure 19.3). Spaniards applied Roman models and rational town planning ideas to the new situation. Conquest came to imply settlement.

Figure 19.2 The port city of Santo Domingo was the principal Spanish settlement in the Caribbean in the 16th century.

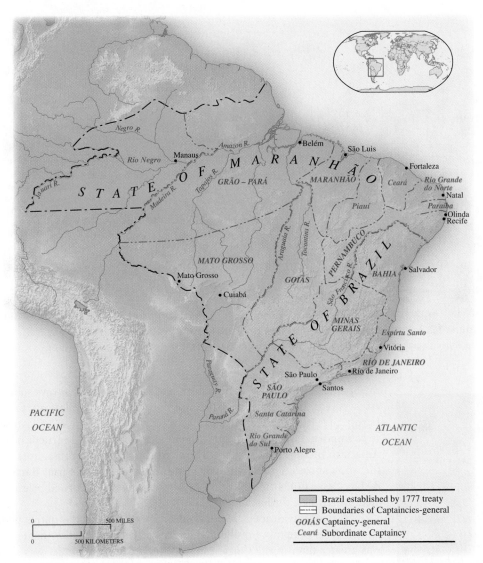

Map 19.2 Colonial Brazil The Portuguese colony was mostly limited to the coast where sugar plantations thrived until the 18th century when gold discoveries attracted settlers and prospectors to the interior. The vast Amazon region was sparsely settled, mostly along the major rivers.

To rule, Spain created administrative institutions: the governorship, the treasury office, and the royal court of appeals staffed by professional magistrates. Spanish legalism was part of the institutional transfer. Notaries accompanied new expeditions, and a body of laws was developed, based on those of Castile and augmented by American experience. The church, represented at first by individual priests and then by missionaries such as the Dominicans, participated in the enterprise. By 1530, a cathedral was being built on Hispaniola, and a university soon followed.

Rumors and hopes stimulated immigration from Castile which claimed control of the new lands but also from the other Iberian kingdoms, and by the 1510s the immigrants included larger numbers of Spanish women. Also, Spanish and Italian merchants began to import African slaves to work on the few sugar plantations that operated on the islands. The arrival of both Spanish women and African slaves marked a shift from an area of conquest to one of settlement. The gold-hunting phase had given out in the islands by the 1520s and was replaced by the establishment of ranches and sugar plantations. The adventurous, the disappointed, and the greedy repeated the pattern as expeditions spun off in new directions.

Depopulation of the Tainos led to slaving on other islands, and in 30 years or so, most of the indigenous population had died or been killed. The people of the Lesser Antilles, or "Caribs," whom

Las Casas, Bartolomé de (1484–1566) Dominican friar who supported peaceful conversion of the Native American population of the Spanish colonies; opposed forced labor and advocated Indian rights.

Figure 19.3 St. Augustine, Florida. As the oldest city in the United States (founded in 1565), it was established to guard the Spanish sea route from the Caribbean that the silver fleets traveled back to Spain.

Figure 19.4 Father Bartolomé de Las Casas. This former *conquistador* became a Dominican friar and a noted theologian who spent much of his life seeking to protect the Indians from exploitation and abuse.

the Spaniards accused of cannibalism and who were thus always subject to enslavement, held out longer because their islands were less attractive to European settlement. To meet the labor needs of the islands, African slaves were imported. As early as 1510, the mistreatment and destruction of the American Indians led to attempts by clerics and royal administrators to end the worst abuses. The activities of men such as Dominican friar **Bartolomé de Las Casas** (1484–1566; Figure 19.4), a conquistador turned priest, initiated the struggle for justice.

Expeditions leaped from island to island. Where the native peoples and cultures were more resilient, their impact on the societies that emerged was greater than in the Caribbean, but the process of contact was similar. By the time of the conquest of Mexico in the 1520s and Peru in the 1530s, all the elements of the colonial system of Latin America were in place. Even in Brazil, which the Portuguese began to exploit after 1500, a period of bartering with the Native Americans was slowly replaced by increasing royal control and development of a sugar plantation economy. There, as in the Caribbean, resistance and subsequent depopulation of the native peoples led to the importation of African laborers.

The Paths of Conquest

> No other race can be found that can penetrate through such rugged lands, such dense forests, such great mountains and deserts and cross such broad rivers as the Spaniards have done . . . solely by the valor of their persons and the forcefulness of their breed.

These words, written by Pedro Cieza de Leon, one of the conquistadors of Peru, underlined the Spaniards' pride in their accomplishments. In less than a century, a large portion of two continents and islands in an inland sea, inhabited by millions of people, was brought under Spanish control. Expeditions, usually comprising 50 to 500 men, provided the spearhead of conquest, and in their wake followed the women, missionaries, administrators, and artisans who began to form civil society.

A Vision from the Vanquished

History usually is written by the victors, so it is rare to find a detailed statement from the vanquished. In the 17th century, Guaman Poma de Ayala, an acculturated Peruvian Indian who claimed to trace his lineage to the provincial nobility of Inca times, composed a memorial outlining the history of Peru under the Incas and reporting on the current conditions under Spanish rule. Guaman Poma was a Christian and a loyal subject. He hoped that his report would reach King Philip III of Spain, who might then order an end to the worst abuses, among which were the Spanish failure to recognize the rank and status of Indian nobles. His book was not published in his lifetime and was not recovered until the 20th century.

Guaman Poma was an educated, bilingual Indian who spoke Quechua as well as Spanish and who had a profound understanding of Andean culture. His book is remarkable for its revelations of Indian life, for its detailed criticism of the abuses suffered by the Indians, and especially because Guaman Poma illustrated his memorial with a series of drawings that give his words a visual effect. The illustrations also reveal the worldview of this interesting man. The drawings and text offer a critical inside view not of the laws, but of the workings of Spain's empire in America from an Indian point of view.

Miners

At the mercury mines of Huancavelica the Indian workers are punished and ill-treated to such an extent that they die like flies and our whole race is threatened with extermination. Even the chiefs are tortured by being suspended by their feet. Conditions in the silver-mines of Potosí and Chocllococha, or at the gold-mines of Carabaya are little better. The managers and supervisors, who are Spaniards or mestizos, have virtually absolute power. There is no reason for them to fear justice, since they are never brought before the courts.

Beatings are incessant. The victims are mounted for this purpose on a llama's back, tied naked to a round pillar or put in stocks. Their hair is cut off and they are deprived of food and water during detention.

Any shortage in the labor gangs is made an excuse for punishing the chiefs as if they were common thieves or traitors instead of the nobility of the country. The work itself is so hard as to cause permanent injury to many of those who survive it. There is no remuneration for the journey to the mines and a day's labor is paid at the rate for half a day.

Proprietors

Your Majesty has granted large estates, including the right to employ Indian labor, to a number of individuals of whom some are good Christians and the remainder are very bad ones. These encomenderos, as they are termed, may boast about their high position, but in reality they are harmful both to the labor force and to the surviving Indian nobility. I therefore propose to set down the details of their life and conduct.

They exude an air of success as they go from their card games to their dinners in fine silk clothes. Their money is squandered on these luxuries, as well it may, since it costs them no work or sweat whatever. Although the Indians ultimately pay the bill, no concern is ever felt for them or even for Your Majesty or God himself.

Official posts like those of royal administrator and judge ought not to be given to big employers or mine-owners or to their obnoxious sons, because these peoples have enough to live on already. The appointments ought to go to Christian gentlemen of small means, who have rendered some service to the Crown and are educated and humane, not just greedy.

Anybody with rights over Indian labor sees to it that his own household is well supplied with servant girls and indoor and outdoor staff. When collecting dues and taxes, it is usual to impose penalties and detain Indians against their will. There is no redress since, if any complaint is made, the law always favors the employer.

The collection of tribute is delegated to stewards, who make a practice of adding something in for themselves. They too consider themselves entitled to free service and obligatory presents, and they end up as bad as their masters. All of them, and their wives as well, regard themselves as entitled to eat at the Indians' expense.

The Indians are seldom paid the few reales a day which are owed to them, but they are hired out for the porterage of wine and making rope or clothing. Little rest is possible either by day or night and they are usually unable to sleep at home.

It is impossible for servant girls, or even married women, to remain chaste. They are bound to be corrupted and prostituted because employers do not feel any scruple about threatening them with flogging, execution, or burial alive if they refuse to satisfy their master's desires.

The Spanish grandees and their wives have borrowed from the Inca the custom of having themselves conveyed in litters like the images of saints in processions. These Spaniards are absolute lords without fear of either God or retribution. In their own eyes they are judges over our people, whom they can reserve for their personal service or their pleasure, to the detriment of the community.

Great positions are achieved by favour from above, by wealth or by having relations at Court in Castile. With some notable exceptions, the beneficiaries act without consideration for those under their control. The encomenderos call themselves conquerors, but their Conquest was achieved by uttering the words: Ama mancha noca Inca, or "Have no fear. I am Inca." This false pretense was the sum total of their performance.

QUESTIONS What are the main abuses Guaman Poma complains about? What remedies does he recommend? What relationship do his views have to traditional Inca values? How might a white landlord or colonial official have answered his attacks?

The conquest was not a unified movement but rather a series of individual initiatives that usually operated with government approval. The conquest of the Americas was two pronged: one prong was directed toward Mexico; the other was aimed at South America.

We can use the well documented campaign in Mexico as an example of a conquest. In 1519 **Hernán Cortés,** an educated man with considerable ability as a leader, led an expedition of 600 men to the coast of Mexico. After hearing rumors of a great kingdom in the interior, he began to strike inland. Pitched battles were fought with towns subject to the Aztec Empire, but after gaining these victories, Cortés was able to enlist the defeated peoples' support against their overlords. With the help of the Indian allies, Cortés eventually reached the great Aztec island capital of Tenochtitlan. By a combination of deception, boldness, ruthlessness, and luck, the Aztec emperor **Moctezuma II** was captured and killed. Cortés and his followers were forced to flee the Aztec capital and retreat toward the coast, but with the help of the Aztecs' traditional enemies, they cut off and besieged Tenochtitlan. Although the Aztec confederacy put up a stiff resistance, disease, starvation, and battle brought the city down in 1521. Tenochtitlan was replaced by **Mexico City.** The Aztec poets later remembered,

> We are crushed to the ground,
> we lie in ruins.
> There is nothing but grief and suffering
> in Mexico and Tlatelolco,
> where once we saw beauty and valor.

By 1535, most of central Mexico, with its network of towns and its dense, agricultural populations, had been brought under Spanish control as the kingdom of **New Spain.** From there, the Spanish pushed their conquest southward into Central America and northward into the area of the nomadic peoples of north central Mexico.

The second trajectory of conquests led from the Caribbean outposts to the coast of northern South America and Panama. From Panama, the Spaniards followed rumors of a rich kingdom to the south. In 1532, after a false start, Francisco Pizarro led his men to the conquest of the Inca Empire, which was already weakened by a long civil war. Once again, using guile and audacity, fewer than 200 Spaniards and their native Indian allies brought down a great empire. The Inca capital of Cuzco, high in the Andes, fell in 1533, but the Spanish decided to build their major city, Lima, closer to the coast. By 1540, most of Peru was under Spanish control, although an active resistance continued in remote areas for another 30 years.

From the conquests of densely populated areas, such as Mexico and Peru, where there were surpluses of food and potential laborers, Spanish expeditions spread out in search of further riches and strange peoples. They penetrated the zones of semisedentary and nomadic peoples, who often offered stiff resistance. From 1540 to 1542, in one of the most famous expeditions, **Francisco Vázquez de Coronado,** searching for mythical cities of gold, penetrated what is now the southwestern United States as far as Kansas. At the other end of the Americas, **Pedro de Valdivia** conquered the tenacious Araucanians of central Chile and set up the city of Santiago in 1541, although the Araucanians continued to fight long after. Buenos Aires, in the southern part of the continent, founded by an expedition from Spain in 1536, was abandoned because of resistance and was not re-founded until 1580. Other expeditions penetrated the Amazon basin, and explored the tropical forests of Central and South America during these years, but there was little there to attract permanent settlement to those areas. By 1570, there were 192 Spanish cities and towns throughout the Americas, one-third of which were in Mexico and Central America.

The Conquerors

The Spanish captains led by force of will and personal power. "God in heaven the king in Spain, and me here" was the motto of one captain, and sometimes, absolute power could lead to tyranny. The crown received one-fifth of all treasure. Men signed up on a shares basis; those who brought horses or who had special skills might get double shares. Rewards were made according to the contract, and premiums were paid for special service and valor. There was a tendency for leaders to reward their friends, relatives, and men from their home province more liberally than others, so that

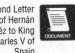

Second Letter of Hernán Cortéz to King Charles V of Spain

Cortés, Hernán Led expedition of 600 to coast of Mexico in 1519; conquistador responsible for defeat of Aztec Empire; captured Tenochtitlan.

Moctezuma II (1480–1520) Last independent Aztec emperor; killed during Hernán Cortés's conquest of Tenochtitlan.

Mexico City Capital of New Spain; built on ruins of Aztec capital of Tenochtitlan.

Excerpts from the "Account of Alva Ixtlilxochitl"

New Spain Spanish colonial possessions in Mesoamerica; included most of central Mexico; based on imperial system of Aztecs.

European Empires in Latin America, 1660

Coronado, Francisco Vázquez de (c. 1510–1554) Leader of Spanish expedition into northern frontier region of New Spain; entered what is now United States in search of mythical cities of gold.

Valdivia, Pedro de Spanish conquistador; conquered Araucanian Indians of Chile and established city of Santiago in 1541.

after each conquest there was always a group of unhappy and dissatisfied conquerors ready to organize a new expedition. As one observer put it, "if each man was given the governorship, it would not be enough."

Few of the conquerors were professional soldiers; they represented all walks of Spanish life, including a scattering of gentlemen, and sometimes even former slaves and freedmen. Some of the later expeditions included a few Spanish women such as Inés Suárez, the heroine of the conquest of Chile, but such cases were rare. In general, the conquerors were men on the make, hoping to better themselves and serve God by converting the heathen at the same time. Always on the lookout for treasure, most conquerors were satisfied by encomiendas. These adventurous men, many of humble origins, came to see themselves as a new nobility entitled to dominion over a new peasantry: the American Indians.

The reasons for Spanish success were varied. Horses, firearms, and more generally steel weapons gave them a great advantage over the stone technology of the native peoples. This technological edge, combined with effective and ruthless leadership, produced remarkable results. Epidemic disease also proved to be a silent ally of the Europeans. Finally, internal divisions and rivalries within American Indian empires, and their high levels of centralization, made the great civilizations particularly vulnerable. It is no accident that the peoples who offered the stiffest and most continuous resistance were usually the mobile, tough, nomadic tribes rather than the centralized states of sedentary peasants.

By about 1570, the age of the conquest was coming to a close. Bureaucrats, merchants, and colonists replaced the generation of the conquerors as institutions of government and economy were created. The transition was not easy. In Peru a civil war erupted in the 1540s, and in Mexico there were grumblings from the old followers of Cortés. But the establishment of viceroys in the two main colonies and the creation of law courts in the main centers signaled that Spanish America had become a colony rather than a conquest.

Conquest and Morality

Conquest involved violence, domination, and theft. The Spanish conquest of the Americas created a series of important philosophical and moral questions for Europeans. Mancio Serra was not alone in questioning the conquest. Theologians and lawyers asked: Who were the Indians? Were they fully human? Was it proper to convert them to Christianity? Could conversion by force or the conquest of their lands be justified? Driven by greed, many of the conquistadors argued that conquest was necessary to spread the gospel and that control of Indian labor was essential for Spain's rule. In 1548 Juan Gines de Sépulveda, a noted Spanish scholar, basing his arguments on Aristotle, published a book claiming that the conquest was fully justified. The Spaniards had come to free the Indians from their unjust lords and to bring the light of salvation. Most importantly, he argued, the Indians were not fully human, and some peoples "were born to serve."

In 1550 the Spanish king suspended all further conquests and convoked a special commission in Valladolid to hear arguments for and against this position. Father Bartolomé de Las Casas—former conqueror and encomendero, Dominican priest, bishop of Chiapas, untiring defender of the Indians, and critic of Spanish brutality—presented the contrary opinion against Sépulveda. Las Casas had long experience in the West Indies, and he believed that the inhabitants were rational people who, unlike the Muslims, had never done harm to Christians. Thus, the conquest of their lands was unjustified. The Indians had many admirable customs and accomplishments, he said. He argued that "the Indians are our brothers and Christ has given his life for them." Spanish rule in order to spread the Christian faith was justified, but conversion should take place only by peaceful means.

 Excerpt from Bartolomé de Las Casas in Defense of the Indians

The results of the debate were mixed. The crown had reasons to back Las Casas against the dangerous ambitions of the Spanish conquerors. Sépulveda's book was censored, but the conquests nevertheless continued. Although some of the worst abuses were moderated, in reality the great period of conquest was all over by the 1570s. It was too little, too late. Still, the Spanish government's concern with the legality and morality of its actions and the willingness of Spaniards such as Las Casas to speak out against abuses are also part of the story. The interests of many other conquerors and officials, however, ran in the opposite direction.

The Destruction and Transformation of Indigenous Societies

To varying degrees, all indigenous societies suffered the effects of European conquest. Population loss was extreme in many areas. Spain worked and taxed the native peoples often disrupting their societies.

The various American peoples responded in many different ways to the invasion of their lands and the transformation of their societies. All of them suffered a severe decline of population—a demographic catastrophe. On the main islands of the Caribbean, the indigenous population had nearly disappeared by 1540 as the result of slaving, mistreatment, and disease. In Peru a similar process brought a loss from 10 million to 1.5 million between 1530 and 1590. Elsewhere in the Americas a similar but less well documented process took place. Smallpox, influenza, and measles wreaked havoc on the American Indian population, which had developed no immunities against these diseases. In central Mexico, war, destruction, and above all disease brought the population from an estimated 25 million in 1519 to less than 2 million in 1580. That decline was matched by the rapid increase in European livestock, cattle, sheep, and horses, that flourished on newly created Spanish farms or in previously unusable lands. In a shocking way, European livestock were replacing an indigenous population on the land (Figure 19.5).

Although epidemic was the major cause of depopulation, the conquest and the weakening of indigenous societies contributed to the losses. Population declines of this size disrupted native societies in many ways. For example, in central Mexico the contraction of the indigenous populations led the Spanish to concentrate the remaining population in fewer towns, and this led in turn to the seizure of former communal farming lands by Spanish landowners. Demographic collapse made maintaining traditional social and economic structures very difficult.

Exploitation of the Indians

The Spaniards did not interfere with aspects of Native American life that served colonial goals or at least did not openly conflict with Spanish authority or religion. Thus, in Mexico and Peru, while the old religions and its priestly class were eliminated, the traditional indigenous nobility remained in place, supported by Spanish authority, as middlemen between the tax and labor demands of the new rulers and the majority of the population.

The enslavement of Indians (a term the Spaniards applied to all the native peoples of the Americas), except those taken in war, was prohibited by the mid-16th century in most of Spanish America. Instead, different forms of labor or taxation were imposed. At first, encomiendas were given to the individual conquerors of a region. The holders of these grants were able to use their dependents as workers and servants or to tax them. Whereas commoners had owed tribute or labor to the state in the Inca and Aztec empires, the new demands were arbitrary, often excessive, and usually without the reciprocal obligation and protection characteristic of the indigenous societies. In general, the encomiendas were destructive. The Spanish crown, unwilling to see a new nobility arise in the New World among the conquerors with their grants of Indian serfs, moved to end the institution in the 1540s. The crown limited the inheritability of encomiendas and prohibited the right to demand certain kinds of labor from the Indians. Although encomiendas continued to exist in marginal regions at the fringes of the empire, they were all but gone by the 1620s in the central areas of Mexico and Peru. Colonists increasingly sought grants of land rather than Indians as the basis of wealth.

Meanwhile, the colonial government increasingly extracted labor and taxes from native peoples. In many places, communities were required to send groups of laborers to work on state projects, such as church construction or road building, or in labor gangs for mining or agriculture. This forced labor, called the **mita** in Peru where it was adapted from indigenous precedents, mobilized thousands of workers for the mines and on other projects. Although they were paid a wage for this work, there were many abuses of the system by the local officials, and community labor requirements often were disruptive and destructive. By the 17th century, many Indians left their villages to avoid the labor and tax obligations, preferring instead to work for Spanish landowners or to seek

mita Labor extracted for lands assigned to the state and the religion; all communities were expected to contribute; an essential aspect of Inca imperial control.

The New Laws
of the Indies
for the Good
Treatment and
Preservation
of the Indians
(1542)

CASE STUDY

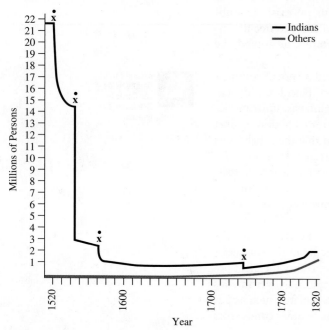

Figure 19.5 Population decline in New Spain.

employment in the cities. This process eventually led to the growth of a wage labor system in which native peoples, no longer resident in their villages, worked for wages on Spanish-owned mines and farms or in the cities.

In the wake of this disruption, Native American culture also demonstrated great resiliency in the face of Spanish institutions and forms, adapting and modifying them to indigenous ways. In Peru and Mexico, native peoples learned to use the Spanish legal system and the law courts so that litigation became a way of life. At the local level, many aspects of indigenous life remained, and Native Americans proved to be selective in their adaptation of European foods, technology, and culture.

Colonial Economies and Governments

Spanish America was an agrarian society in which perhaps 80 percent of the population lived and worked on the land. Yet in terms of America's importance to Spain, mining was the essential activity and the basis of Spain's rule in the Indies. It was precious metals that first began to fit Latin America into the developing world economy.

Although the booty of conquest provided some wealth, most of the precious metal sent across the Atlantic came from the post conquest mining industry. Gold was found in the Caribbean, Colombia, and Chile, but it was silver far more than gold that formed the basis of Spain's wealth in America.

Agriculture and mining were the basis of the Spanish colonial economy but they depended on Native Americans and Africans as laborers. Over this economy Spain built a bureaucratic empire in which the church was an essential element and a major cultural factor.

The Silver Heart of Empire

The major silver discoveries were made in Mexico and Peru between 1545 and 1565. Great silver mining towns developed. **Potosí** in upper Peru (in what is now Bolivia) was the largest mine of all, producing about 80 percent of all the Peruvian silver. In the early 17th century, more than 160,000 people lived and worked in the town and its mine. Peru's Potosí and Mexico's Zacatecas became wealthy mining centers with opulent churches and a luxurious way of life for some. As one viceroy of Peru commented, it was not silver that was sent to Spain "but the blood and sweat of Indians."

Mining labor was provided by a variety of workers. The early use of Native American slaves and encomienda workers in the 16th century gradually was replaced by a system of labor drafts. By 1572 the mining mita in Peru was providing about 13,000 workers a year to Potosí alone. Similar labor drafts were used in Mexico, but by the 17th century the mines in both places also had large numbers of wage workers willing to brave the dangers of mining in return for the good wages.

Although indigenous methods were used at first, most mining techniques were European in origin. After 1580, silver mining depended on a process of amalgamation with mercury to extract the silver from the ore-bearing rock. The Spanish discovery of a mountain of mercury at **Huancavelica** (WAHN-cah-veh-LEEK-uh) in Peru aided American silver production. Potosí and Huancavelica became the "great marriage of Peru" and the basis of silver production in South America.

According to Spanish law, all subsoil rights belonged to the crown, but the mines and the processing plants were owned by individuals, who were permitted to extract the silver in return for paying one-fifth of production to the government, which also profited from its monopoly on the mercury needed to produce the silver (Figure 19.6).

Mining stimulated many other aspects of the economy, even in areas far removed from the mines. Workers had to be fed and the mines supplied. In Mexico, where most of the mines were located beyond the area of settled preconquest populations, large Spanish-style farms developed to raise cattle, sheep, and wheat. The Peruvian mines high in the Andes were supplied from distant regions with mercury, mules, food, clothing, and even coca leaves, used to deaden hunger and make the work at high altitudes less painful. From Spain's perspective, mining was the heart of the colonial economy.

Potosí Mine located in upper Peru (modern Bolivia); largest of New World silver mines; produced 80 percent of all Peruvian silver.

Huancavelica [WAHN-cah-veh-LEEK-uh] Location of greatest deposit of mercury in South America; aided in American silver production; linked with Potosí.

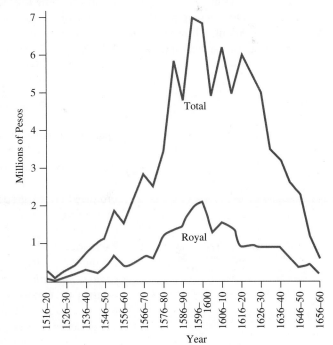

Figure 19.6 Silver production in Spanish America, 1516–1660.

An Atlantic History?

The voyages of Columbus and the subsequent Spanish and Portuguese conquest and settlement of the Americas set into motion the real beginning of a history that linked all of the lands that bordered on the Atlantic Ocean. Certainly, there had been contacts before; the Vikings had settled in Greenland, Iceland, and had reached North America by 1000 B.C.E.; the islands of the Atlantic like the Canaries and Madeira had been settled by the Spanish and Portuguese, and in the fifteenth century Europeans had ventured down the coast of West Africa and begun an active trade at the same time. But after 1492, the continuous and ever-increasing volume of contact, movement of populations, trade, and interaction between Europe, America, and Africa and their adjacent islands truly turned the Atlantic from being a barrier that impeded contact into a highway that connected disparate peoples and places into an increasingly interconnected and entwined history—for better or for worse.

The idea of conceiving of history around a maritime space like the Atlantic is not new. The great French historian Fernand Braudel had written a classic book about the commonalities and interconnections of the Mediterranean world (1959), and other scholars had used a similar approach for the lands and peoples around the Indian Ocean. The idea of Atlantic history is more recent. Increasingly since the 1970s, historians have been trying to overcome the tendency to isolate the histories of individual continents, empires, or countries in the Atlantic basin by looking at their parallels and interconnections through a lens that makes these helpful vantage points from which to see the processes of global history. It is a way of studying contacts, comparisons, and also how different regions and peoples each responded to larger global processes. The history of the Atlantic, however, is different from these other maritime approaches because unlike the Mediterranean which has a

> "Between 1492 and 1850 between ten and fifteen million Africans and over five million Europeans crossed the Atlantic to the Americas in great migratory movements."

certain climatic and geographic unity, the Atlantic world is much larger and extends over many latitudes and a vast variety of climates, environments, and cultures. Unlike the Indian Ocean where linkages had been formed by indigenous peoples long before the arrival of Europeans, in the Atlantic firm evidence of such contacts are lacking, and if they existed were intermittent, and so Atlantic history is to some extent a direct outgrowth of the rise of European overseas empires and trade even if it has become a way to understand that history of empires from a perspective that does not necessarily celebrate the imperial powers.

What are some of the themes within a history of the Atlantic world? We can start with the movement of peoples. Between 1492 and 1850 between ten and fifteen million Africans and over five million Europeans crossed the Atlantic to the Americas in great migratory movements. These peoples carried the traditions, practices, and ideas of their homes to new situations and then maintained and adapted them to a variety of conditions and circumstances. The movement of peoples thus had both demographic and cultural results. The increasing contacts between the continents also initiated biological and ecological exchanges that changed the face of the Old World and the New and transformed the lives of their inhabitants. American products like corn and the potato and tomato transformed European diets and eventually the growth of European populations, while the introduction of horses, sheep, poultry, and cattle brought from Europe changed the nature of life for millions of people in the Americas. Regions of Africa were transformed by both the introduction of new food crops like corn and manioc and by the demands of Europeans for enslaved workers. The Atlantic slave trade had many effects; in Africa, societies were transformed, political boundaries altered, and trade routes were changed by it. For example, the former great trading empires of the *sahel* like Mali lost their advantage to the coastal states that had access to the new Atlantic trade. In

Haciendas and Villages

Spanish America remained predominantly an agrarian economy, and wherever large sedentary populations lived, indigenous communal agriculture of traditional crops continued. As populations dwindled, Spanish ranches and farms began to emerge. The colonists, faced with declining indigenous populations, also found land ownership more attractive. Family-owned rural estates, which produced grains, grapes, and livestock, developed throughout the central areas of Spanish America. Most of the labor force on these estates came from Native Americans who had left the communities and from people of mixed Native American and European heritage. These rural estates, or **haciendas,** producing primarily for consumers in America, became the basis of wealth and power for the local aristocracy in many regions. Although some plantation crops, such as sugar and later cacao, were exported to Europe from Spanish America, they made up only a small fraction of the value of the exports in comparison with silver. In some regions where Native American communities continued to hold traditional farming lands, an endemic competition between haciendas and village communities emerged.

haciendas Rural estates in Spanish colonies in New World; produced agricultural products for consumers in America; basis of wealth and power for local aristocracy.

America, the African voyagers and their descendants created new cultures and new populations, creating the basis of a Black Atlantic world while in Europe the trade brought both profits and eventually provoked the moral and religious questioning of the very nature of slavery.

Not only peoples, plants, and animals, but pathogens also crossed the Atlantic highway creating new disease environments that sometimes produced disastrous consequences such as the introduction of Old World diseases to the Americas where native peoples, lacking immunities, were devastated by epidemics. The historian Alfred Crosby has pointed out that the "Columbian Exchange" of peoples, plants, animals, diseases, ideas, and technologies transformed many aspects of life on the four continents of the Atlantic world.

The creation of European empires that included settlements in the Americas and slaving bases and outposts in Africa eventually linked the various parts of the Atlantic world in a series of commercial relationships. Merchants, mariners, commodities, and currencies crossed the Atlantic continually, and despite all efforts by governments to control these exchanges within national and imperial boundaries, trade between empires and interactions such as contraband, smuggling, and piracy were also part of the Atlantic world. So too was the circulation of ideas and beliefs. We could, for example, speak of a Christian Atlantic because both Protestants and Catholics shared many common beliefs that were implanted to new settlements and colonies from Europe and because both mounted missionary activities, converting in the Americas whole populations, and in Africa, in places like the Kongo, the ruler and his court and then large sectors of the population. The challenges faced by missionaries on the far shores of the Atlantic were not as different as might first be imagined from those encountered in Europe where priests confronted with disbelief, superstition, or occult practices sometimes referred to places like southern Italy or northern Spain as the "Indies of Europe." Ideas and religions did not flow only from Europe. Africans also brought their religions which then flourished in various forms across the Atlantic as *voudon* (Haiti), *candomblé* (Brazil), or *obeah* (Jamaica). The Atlantic world became a realm of cultural creations, fusions, and adaptations.

In some ways it was the circulation of ideas that finally brought an end to the interpretative unity of Atlantic history. The circulation of the ideas of the 18th century and the emergence of local elites throughout the Atlantic world eventually led to a series of revolutions in the United States, France, Haiti and Latin America in the late eighteenth and early nineteenth centuries that resulted in the creation of independent states and the destruction or weakening of empires. Some historians believe that with the creation of the new nations of the Americas the unities and parallels of an Atlantic history began to break down. Other scholars believe that until the end of the slave trades around 1860 or perhaps the final abolition of New World slavery in 1888 that it was still possible to speak of an Atlantic history.

Like any historical approach, Atlantic history has its problems. The Atlantic communities were tied in many ways to other areas of the world. Mexican silver flowed to China in Spanish ships, the Portuguese and the Dutch carried spices from Asia to Europe, and many of the challenges of empire confronted by the Europeans in America and Africa were also met in India, China, and east Africa. An Atlantic perspective as broad as it is, may, in fact, be too narrow for an understanding of global processes. But many scholars have increasingly found the parallels, interactions, and convergences within the Atlantic world to be a useful way to study and understand a large part of world history.

QUESTIONS Is the concept of "Atlantic history" too broad or too narrow? How can matters like gender, ethnicity, or family be studied in an Atlantic perspective? Is there a date after which the concept is no longer useful, or is the concept of "Atlantic history" really the reflection of our present global way of thinking read back onto the past?

Industry and Commerce

In areas such as Ecuador, New Spain, and Peru, sheep raising led to the development of small textile sweatshops, where common cloth was produced, usually by women. America became self-sufficient for its basic foods and material goods and looked to Europe only for luxury items not locally available.

Still, from Spain's perspective and that of the larger world economy taking shape in the early modern centuries, the American "kingdoms" had a silver heart, and the whole Spanish commercial system was organized around that fact. Spain allowed only Spaniards to trade with America and imposed tight restrictions. All American trade from Spain after the mid-16th century passed through the city of Seville and, later, through the nearby port of Cadiz. A Board of Trade in Seville controlled all commerce with America, registered ships and passengers, kept charts, and collected taxes. It often worked in conjunction with a merchant guild, or **consulado,** in Seville that controlled goods shipped to America and handled much of the silver received in return. Linked to branches in Mexico City and Lima, the consulados kept tight control over the trade and were able to keep prices high in the colonies.

consulado Merchant guild of Seville; enjoyed virtual monopoly rights over goods shipped to America and handled much of the silver received in return.

Other Europeans looked on the West Indies trade with envy. To discourage foreign rivals and pirates, the Spanish eventually worked out a convoy system in which two fleets sailed annually from Spain, traded their goods for precious metals, and then met at Havana, Cuba, before returning to Spain.

The fleet system was made possible by the large, heavily armed ships, called **galleons,** that were used to carry the silver belonging to the crown. Two great galleons a year also sailed from Manila in the Philippines to Mexico loaded with Chinese silks, porcelain, and lacquer. These goods were then shipped on the convoy to Spain along with the American silver. In the Caribbean, heavily fortified ports, such as Havana and Cartagena (Colombia), provided shelter for the treasure ships, while coast guard fleets cleared the waters of potential raiders. Although cumbersome, the convoys (which continued until the 1730s) were successful. Pirates and enemies sometimes captured individual ships, and some ships were lost to storms and other disasters, but only one fleet was lost—to the Dutch in 1627.

In general, the supply of American silver to Spain was continuous and made the colonies seem worth the effort, but the reality of American treasure was more complicated. Much of the wealth flowed out of Spain to pay for Spain's European wars, its long-term debts, and the purchase of manufactured goods to be sent back to the West Indies. Probably less than half of the silver remained in Spain itself. The arrival of American treasure also contributed to a sharp rise in prices and a general inflation, first in Spain and then throughout western Europe during the 16th century. At no time did the American treasure make up more than one-fourth of Spain's state revenues; the wealth of Spain depended more on the taxes levied on its own population than it did on the exploitation of its Native American subjects. However, the seemingly endless supply of silver stimulated bankers to continue to lend money to Spain because the prospect of the great silver fleet was always enough to offset the falling credit of the Spanish rulers and the sometimes bankrupt government. As early as 1619, Sancho de Moncada wrote that "the poverty of Spain resulted from the discovery of the Indies." But there were few who could see the long-term costs of empire.

Ruling an Empire: State and Church

Spain controlled its American empire through a carefully regulated bureaucratic system. Sovereignty rested with the crown, based not on the right of conquest but on a papal grant that awarded the West Indies to Castile in return for its services in bringing those lands and peoples into the Christian community. Some Native Americans found this a curious idea, and European theologians agreed, but Spain was careful to bolster its rule in other ways. The **Treaty of Tordesillas** (1494) between Castile and Portugal clarified the spheres of influence and right of possession of the two kingdoms by drawing a hypothetical north–south line around the globe and reserving to Portugal the newly discovered lands (and their route to India) to the east of the line and to Castile all lands to the west. Thus, Brazil fell within the Portuguese sphere. Other European nations later raised their own objections to the Spanish and Portuguese claims.

The Spanish Empire became a great bureaucratic system built on a juridical core and staffed to a large extent by **letrados,** university-trained lawyers from Spain. The modern division of powers was not clearly defined in the Spanish system, so that judicial officers also exercised legislative and administrative authority. Laws were many and contradictory at times, but the **Recopilación** (1681) codified the laws into the basis for government in the colonies.

The king ruled through the **Council of the Indies** in Spain, which issued the laws and advised him. Within the West Indies, Spain created two **viceroyalties** in the 16th century, one based in Mexico City and the other in Lima. **Viceroys,** high-ranking nobles who were direct representatives of the king, wielded broad military, legislative, and, when they had legal training, judicial powers. The viceroyalties of New Spain and Peru were then subdivided into 10 judicial divisions controlled by superior courts, or **audiencias,** staffed by professional royal magistrates who helped to make law as well as apply it. At the local level, royally appointed magistrates applied the laws, collected taxes, and assigned the work required of American Indian communities. It is little wonder that they often were highly criticized for bending the law and taking advantage of the native

galleons   Large, heavily armed ships used to carry silver from New World colonies to Spain; basis for convoy system utilized by Spain for transportation of bullion.

Treaty of Tordesillas   Signed in 1494 between Castile and Portugal; clarified spheres of influence and rights of possession in New World; reserved Brazil and all newly discovered lands east of Brazil to Portugal; granted all lands west of Brazil to Spain.

letrados   University-trained lawyers from Spain in the New World; juridical core of Spanish colonial bureaucracy; exercised both legislative and administrative functions.

Recopilación   Body of laws collected in 1681 for Spanish possessions in New World; basis of law in the Indies.

Council of the Indies   Body within the Castilian government that issued all laws and advised king on all matters dealing with the Spanish colonies of the New World.

viceroyalties   Two major divisions of Spanish colonies in New World; one based in Lima; the other in Mexico City; direct representatives of the king.

viceroys   Senior government officials in Spanish America. They ruled as direct representatives of the king over the principal administrative units or viceroyalties. They were usually high ranking Spanish nobles with previous military or governmental experience. The Portuguese also used viceroys who resided in Goa for their possessions in the Indian Ocean, and then after the mid Seventeenth century for their colony in Brazil.

audiencia   Royal court of appeals established in Spanish colonies of New World; there were 10 in each viceroyalty; part of colonial administrative system; staffed by professional magistrates.

peoples under their control. Below them were many minor officials who made bureaucracy both a living and a way of life.

To some extent, the clergy formed another branch of the state apparatus, although it had other functions and goals as well. Catholic religious orders such as the Franciscans, Dominicans, and Jesuits carried out the widespread conversion of the Indians, establishing churches in the towns and villages of sedentary Indians and setting up missions in frontier areas where nomadic peoples were forced to settle.

Taking seriously the pope's admonition to Christianize the peoples of the new lands as the primary justification for Spain's rule, some of the early missionaries became ardent defenders of Indian rights and even admirers of aspects of indigenous culture. For example, Franciscan priest Fray Bernardino de Sahagún (1499–1590) became an expert in the Nahuatl language and composed a bilingual encyclopedia of Aztec culture, which was based on methods very similar to those used by modern anthropologists. Other clerics wrote histories, grammars, and studies of native language and culture. Some were like Diego de Landa, Bishop of Yucatán (1547), who admired much about the culture of the Maya but who so detested their religion that he burned all their ancient books and tortured many Maya suspected of backsliding from Christianity. The recording and analysis of Native American cultures were designed primarily to provide tools for conversion.

In the core areas of Peru and New Spain, the missionary church eventually was replaced by an institutional structure of parishes and bishoprics. Archbishops sat in the major capitals, and a complicated church hierarchy developed. Because the Spanish crown nominated the holders of all such positions, the clergy tended to be major supporters of state policy as well as a primary influence on it.

The Catholic Church profoundly influenced the cultural and intellectual life of the colonies in many ways. The construction of churches, especially the great baroque cathedrals of the capitals, stimulated the work of architects and artists, usually reflecting European models but sometimes taking up local themes and subjects. The printing presses, introduced to America in the early 16th century, always published a high percentage of religious books as well as works of history, poetry, philosophy, law, and language. Much intellectual life was organized around religion. Schools—such as those of Mexico City and Lima, founded in the 1550s—were run by the clergy, and universities were created to provide training primarily in law and theology, the foundations of state and society. Eventually, more than 70 universities flourished in Spanish America. A stunning example of colonial intellectual life was the nun **Sor Juana Inés de la Cruz** (1651–1695; Figure 19.7), author, poet, musician, and perceptive commentator on her society. Sor Juana was welcomed at the court of the viceroy in Mexico City, where her beauty and intelligence were celebrated. She eventually gave up secular concerns and her library, at the urging of her superiors, to concentrate on purely spiritual matters.

To control the morality and orthodoxy of the population, the tribunal of the Inquisition set up offices in the major capitals. Although American Indians usually were exempt from its jurisdiction, Jews, Protestants, and other religious dissenters were prosecuted and sometimes executed in an attempt to impose orthodoxy. Overall, church and state combined to create an ideological and political framework for the society of Spanish America.

Figure 19.7 Sor Juana Inés de la Cruz was a remarkable Mexican poet and writer whose talents won her recognition rarely given to women for intellectual or artistic achievements in colonial Latin America.

Sor Juana Inez de la Cruz, from *La Respuesta*

de la Cruz, Sor Juana Inés (1651–1695) Author, poet, and musician of New Spain; eventually gave up secular concerns to concentrate on spiritual matters.

Cabral, Pedro Alvares Portuguese leader of an expedition to India; blown off course in 1500 and landed in Brazil.

In Brazil the Portuguese created the first great plantation colony of the Americas, growing sugar with the use of Native American and then African slaves. In the 18th century, the discovery of gold opened up the interior of Brazil to settlement and the expansion of slavery.

Brazil: The First Plantation Colony

The first official Portuguese landfall on the South American coast took place in 1500 when **Pedro Alvares Cabral,** leader of an expedition to India, made a brief and perhaps accidental landfall on the tropical Brazilian shore. There was little at first to attract European interest except for the dyewood trees that grew in the forests, and thus the Portuguese crown paid little attention to Brazil for 30 years, preferring instead to grant licenses to merchants who agreed to exploit the dyewood. Pressure from French competitors finally moved the Portuguese crown to military action. The coast was cleared of rivals and a new system of settlement was established in 1532. Minor Portuguese nobles were given strips of land along the coast to colonize and develop. The nobles who held these **capitaincies** combined broad, seemingly feudal powers with a strong desire for commercial development. Most of them lacked the capital needed to carry out the colonization, and some had problems with the indigenous population. In a few places, towns were established, colonists were brought over, relations with the Native Americans were peaceful, and, most importantly, sugar plantations were established using first Native American, then African slaves.

In 1549 the Portuguese king sent a governor general and other officials to create a royal capital at Salvador. The first Jesuit missionaries also arrived. By 1600, indigenous resistance had been broken in many places by military action, missionary activity, or epidemic disease. A string of settlements extended along the coast, centered on port cities such as Salvador and Rio de Janeiro. These served roughly 150 sugar plantations, a number that doubled by 1630. The plantations were increasingly worked by African slaves. By 1600, the Brazilian colony had about 100,000 inhabitants: 30,000 Europeans, 15,000 black slaves, and the rest Native Americans and people of mixed origin.

> **capitaincies**   Strips of land along Brazilian coast granted to minor Portuguese nobles for development; enjoyed limited success in developing the colony.

Sugar and Slavery

During most of the next century, Brazil held its position as the world's leading sugar producer. Sugar cane had to be processed in the field. It was cut and pressed in large mills, and the juice was then heated to crystallize into sugar. This combination of agriculture and industry in the field demanded large amounts of capital for machinery and large quantities of labor for the backbreaking work (Figure 19.8). Although there were always some free workers who had skilled occupations, slaves did most of the work. During the 17th century, about 7000 slaves a year were imported from Africa. By the end of the century, Brazil had about 150,000 slaves—about half its total population.

On the basis of a single crop produced by slave labor, Brazil became the first great plantation colony and a model that later was followed by other European nations in their own Caribbean colonies. Even after the Brazilian economy became more diverse, Brazil's social hierarchy still reflected its plantation and slave origins. The white planter families became an aristocracy linked by marriage to resident merchants and to the few Portuguese bureaucrats and officials, and they dominated local institutions. At the bottom of society were the slaves, distinguished by their color and their status as property. However, a growing segment of the population was composed of people of mixed origins, the result of miscegenation between whites, Indians, and Africans who—alongside poorer whites, freed blacks, and free Indians—served as artisans, small farmers, herders, and free laborers. In many ways, society as a whole reflected the hierarchy of the plantation.

Like Spain, Portugal created a bureaucratic structure that integrated this colony within an imperial system. A governor general ruled from Salvador, but the governors in each capitaincy often acted independently and reported directly

Figure 19.8 Sugar was introduced to the Caribbean in 1493, and Brazil became the greatest producer by the next century. Sugar plantations using slave labor characterized Brazil and the Caribbean.

to the overseas council in Lisbon. The missionary orders were particularly important in Brazil, especially the Jesuits. Their extensive cattle ranches and sugar mills supported the construction of churches and schools as well as a network of missions with thousands of Native American residents.

As in Spanish America, royal officials trained in the law formed the core of the bureaucracy. Unlike the Spanish Empire, which except for the Philippines was almost exclusively American, the Portuguese Empire included colonies and outposts in Asia, Africa, and Brazil. Only gradually, in the 17th century, did Brazil become the predominant Portuguese colony. Even then, Brazil's ties to Portugal were in some ways stronger and more dependent than those between Spanish America and Spain. Unlike Spanish America, Brazil had neither universities nor printing presses. Thus, intellectual life was always an extension of Portugal, and Brazilians seeking higher education and government offices or hoping to publish their works always had to turn to the mother country. The general economic dependency of Latin America was matched by an intellectual subordination more intense in Brazil than in Spanish America.

Brazil's Age of Gold

As overseas extensions of Europe, the American colonies were particularly susceptible to changes in European politics. For 60 years (1580–1640), the Habsburg kings of Spain also ruled Portugal, a situation that promoted their cooperation and gave these rulers a truly worldwide empire. From 1630 to 1654, as part of a global struggle against Spain, the Dutch seized a portion of northeastern Brazil and controlled its sugar production. Although the Dutch were expelled from Brazil in 1654, by the 1680s the Dutch, English, and French had established their own plantation colonies in the Caribbean and were producing sugar with slave laborers. This competition, which led to a rising price for slaves and a falling world price for sugar, undercut the Brazilian sugar industry, and the colony entered into hard times. Eventually, each European nation tried to establish an integrated set of colonies that included plantations (the Caribbean, Brazil), slaving ports (Africa), and food-producing areas (New England, southern Brazil).

Although Brazil's domination of the world sugar market was lost, throughout the 17th century **Paulistas,** hardy backwoodsmen from São Paulo (an area with few sugar plantations), had been exploring the interior, capturing Indians, and searching for precious metals. These expeditions not only established Portuguese claims to much of the interior of the continent but eventually were successful in their quest for wealth. In 1695, gold strikes were made in the mountainous interior in a region that came to be called **Minas Gerais** (MEE-nuhs JEH-reyes) (General Mines), and the Brazilian colony experienced a new boom.

A great gold rush began. People deserted coastal towns and plantations to head for the gold washings, and they were soon joined by waves of about 5000 immigrants a year who came directly from Portugal. Slaves provided labor in the mines, as in the plantations. By 1775, there were over 150,000 slaves (out of a total population of 300,000 for the region) in Minas Gerais. Wild mining camps and a wide-open society eventually coalesced into a network of towns such as the administrative center of Ouro Prêto, and the government, anxious to control the newfound wealth, imposed a heavy hand to collect taxes and rein in the unruly population. Gold production reached its height between 1735 and 1760 and averaged about 3 tons a year in that period, making Brazil the greatest source of gold in the Western world.

The discovery of gold—and later of diamonds—was a mixed blessing in the long run. It opened the interior to settlement, once again with disastrous effects on the indigenous population and with the expansion of slavery. The early disruption of coastal agriculture caused by the gold strikes was overcome by government control of the slave trade, and exports of sugar and tobacco continued to be important to the colony. Mining did stimulate the opening of new areas to ranching and farming, to supply the new markets in the mining zone. **Rio de Janeiro,** the port closest to the mines, grew in size and importance. It became capital of the colony in 1763. In Minas Gerais, a distinctive society developed. The local wealth was used to sponsor the building of churches, which in turn stimulated the work of artists, architects, and composers. Like the rest of Brazil, however, the hierarchy of color and the legal distinctions of slavery marked life in the mining zones, which were populated by large numbers of slaves and free persons of color.

Paulistas   Backwoodsmen from São Paulo in Brazil; penetrated Brazilian interior in search of precious metals during 17th century.

Minas Gerais   [MEE-nuhs JEH-reyes] Region of Brazil located in mountainous interior where gold strikes were discovered in 1695; became location for gold rush.

Rio de Janeiro   Brazilian port; close to mines of Minas Gerais; importance grew with gold strikes; became colonial capital in 1763.

Finally, gold allowed Portugal to continue economic policies that were detrimental in the long run. With access to gold, Portugal could buy the manufactured goods it needed for itself and its colonies, as few industries were developed in the mother country. Much of the Brazilian gold flowed from Portugal to England to pay for manufactured goods and to compensate for a trade imbalance. After 1760, as the supply of gold began to dwindle, Portugal was again in a difficult position—it had become in some ways an economic dependency of England.

Multiracial Societies

The conquest and settlement of Latin America created the conditions for the formation of multi-ethnic societies on a large scale. The three major groups—Indians, Europeans, and Africans—had been brought together under very different conditions: the Europeans as conquerors and voluntary immigrants, the Indians as conquered peoples, and the Africans as slaves. This situation created hierarchies of masters and servants, Christians and pagans, that reflected the relationships of power and the colonial condition. In central Mexico, where an Indian nobility had existed, aspects of preconquest social organization were maintained because they served the ends of Spanish government. In theory, there was a separation between the "republic of the Spaniards," which included all non-Indians, and the "republic of the Indians," which was supposed to have its own social rankings and its own rules and laws. This separation was never a reality, however, and the "republic of the Indians" always formed the base on which all society rested. Indians paid tribute, something not required of others in society, except the mulattos in some places.

The Society of Castas

Spaniards had an idea of society drawn from their own medieval experience, but American realities soon altered that concept. The key was miscegenation. The conquest had involved the sexual exploitation of Indian women and occasional alliances formed by the giving of concubines and female servants. Marriages with indigenous women, especially of the Indian nobility, were not unknown. With few European women available, especially in frontier regions, mixed marriages and informal unions were common. The result was the growth of a large population of mixed background, the so-called mestizos. Although they were always suspected of illegitimacy, their status, especially in the early years, was higher than that of Indians. More acculturated than the Indians and able to operate in two worlds, mestizos became members of an intermediate category, not fully accepted as equals to Spaniards and yet expected to live according to the standards of Spanish society and often acting as auxiliaries to it. A similar process took place in areas such as Brazil and the Caribbean coasts, where large numbers of African slaves were imported. Slave owners exploited their female slaves or took slave women as mistresses, and then sometimes freed their mulatto children. The result was the growth of a large population of mixed background.

Throughout the Spanish Indies, European categories of noble, priest, and commoner continued, as did hierarchies based on wealth and occupation. But American realities created new distinctions in which race and place of birth also played a crucial role. This was the **sociedad de castas,** based on racial origins, in which Europeans or whites were at the top, black slaves or Native Americans were at the bottom, and the many kinds of mixes filled the intermediate categories. This accompanied the great cultural fusion in the formation of Latin America (Figure 19.9).

From the three original ethnic categories, many combinations and crosses were possible: mestizo, mulatto, and so on. By the 18th century, this segment of the population had grown rapidly, and there was much confusion

sociedad de castas   American social system based on racial origins; Europeans or whites at top, black slaves or Native Americans at bottom, mixed races in middle.

The mixture of whites, Africans, and Indians created the basis of multiracial societies in which hierarchies of color, status, and occupation all operated. By the 18th century, the castas, people of mixed origin, began to increase rapidly and had become a major segment of the population.

Castizo con Española
Español.

Español con Mora
Mulato.

7

Figure 19.9 The contact between Europeans, Africans, and Native Americans eventually produced large numbers of castas, people considered to be of mixed racial origin. By the 18th century, especially in New Spain, a genre of painting flourished that depicted a husband and wife of different racial categories and their child who would fit one of the casta designations. The purpose and public for these paintings is unclear, but they illustrate domestic relations and material culture as well as racial ideology.

Race or Culture? A Changing Society

The process of marriage or sexual contact between Spaniards, Indians, and Africans began to complicate the demographic and social structures of the American colonies. The rise of a significant number of people of mixed origin could be noted in both Peru and Mexico. These graphs point out the differences in the two areas and may imply something about the situation of the indigenous communities as well as that of the castas. We should also remember that these categories were not necessarily biological and that Indians might be classified as castas if they spoke Spanish or wore Spanish-style clothes. What seems to be precise demographic measurement may, in fact, be imprecise social definition.

QUESTION Do modern censuses that use cultural or "racial" labels face the same problems of definition that the early censuses in the colonial Americas confronted?

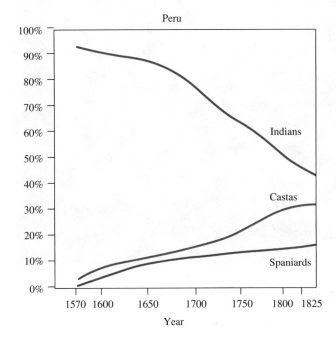

Changing ratios of ethnic categories in Mexico and Peru.

and local variation in terminology. A whole genre of painting developed simply to identify and classify the various combinations. Together, the people of mixed origins were called the castas, and they tended to be shopkeepers and small farmers. In 1650 the castas made up perhaps 5 to 10 percent of the population of Spanish America, but by 1750 they made up 35 to 40 percent (see Visualizing the Past). In Brazil, still dominated by slavery, free people of color made up about 28 percent of the population—a proportion equal to that of whites. Together, however, free and slave blacks and mulattos made up two-thirds of the inhabitants of Brazil in the late 18th century.

As the mixed population grew in Spanish America, increasing restrictions were placed on them, but their social mobility could not be halted. A successful Indian might call himself a mestizo; a mestizo who married a Spanish woman might be called white. The ranks of the castas were also swelled by former slaves who had been given or had bought their freedom and by Indians who left their communities, spoke Spanish, and lived within the orbit of the Hispanic world. Thus, physical characteristics were only one criterion of rank and status, but color and ethnicity mattered, and they created a pseudoracial hierarchy. European or white status was a great social advantage. Not every person of European background was wealthy, but most of the wealthy merchants, landowners, bureaucrats, and miners were white. As one visitor wrote, "In America, every white is a gentleman."

Originally, all whites had shared the privileged status of Spaniards regardless of the continent of their birth, but over time distinctions developed between **peninsulares,** or those actually

peninsulares People living in the New World Spanish colonies but born in Spain.

Figure 19.10 Women in colonial Latin America engaged in agriculture and manufacturing, especially in textile workshops, but social ideology still reserved the household and the kitchen as the proper sphere for women, as seen in this scene of a kitchen in a large Mexican home.

Increasing attacks on the Iberian empires by foreign rivals led to the Bourbon reforms in Spanish America and the reforms of Pombal in Brazil. These changes strengthened the two empires but also generated colonial unrest that eventually led to movements for independence.

Creoles Whites born in the New World; dominated local Latin American economies and ranked just beneath peninsulares.

amigos del país Clubs and associations dedicated to improvements and reform in Spanish colonies; flourished during the 18th century; called for material improvements rather than political reform.

born in Spain, and **Creoles,** or those born in the New World. Creoles thought of themselves as loyal American Spaniards, but with so many mestizos around, the shadow of a possible Indian ancestor and illegitimacy always made their status suspect as far as the Europeans were concerned. Still, Creoles dominated the local economies, held sway over large numbers of dependents at their haciendas and mines, and stood at the top of society, second only to the peninsulares. Increasingly, they developed a sense of identity and pride in their accomplishments, and they were sensitive to any suggestion of inferiority or to any discrimination because of their American birth. That growing sense of self-identity eventually contributed to the movements for independence in Latin America.

The hierarchy of race intersected with traditional Iberian distinctions based on gender, age, and class. The father of a family had legal authority over his children until they were 25. Women were in a subordinate position; they could not serve in government and were expected to assume the duties of motherhood and household (Figure 19.10). After marriage, women came under the authority of their husbands, but many a widow assumed the direction of her family's activities. Lower-class women often controlled small-scale commerce in towns and villages, worked in the fields, and labored at the looms of small factories. Marriages often were arranged and accompanied by the payment of a dowry, which remained the property of the woman throughout the marriage. Women also had full rights to inheritance. Some upper-class women who did not marry at a young age were placed in convents to prevent contacts or marriages with partners of unsuitable backgrounds.

The 18th-Century Reforms

No less than in the rest of Europe, the 18th century was a period of intellectual ferment in Spain and Portugal as well as in their empires. In Spain and its colonies, small clubs and associations, calling themselves **amigos del país,** or friends of the country, met in many cities to discuss and plan all kinds of reforms. Their programs were for material benefits and improvements, not political changes. In Portugal, foreign influences and ideas created a group of progressive thinkers and bureaucrats open to new ideas in economy, education, and philosophy. Much of the change that came in both empires resulted as much from the changing European economic and demographic realities as from new ideas. The expansion of population and economy in Europe, and the increased demands for American products, along with the long series of wars in the 18th century, gave the American colonies a new importance. Both the Spanish and Portuguese empires revived, but with some long-term results that eventually led to the fall of both.

The Shifting Balance of Politics and Trade

By the 18th century, it was clear that the Spanish colonial system had become outmoded and that Spain's exclusive hold on the Indies was no longer secure. To some extent the problem lay in Spain itself. Beset by foreign wars, increasing debt, declining population, and internal revolts, a weakened Spain was threatened by a powerful France and by the rising mercantile strength of England and Holland, whose Protestantism also made them natural rivals of Catholic Spain. Since the 16th century, French, Dutch, and English ship captains had combined contraband trade with raiding in the Spanish Empire, and although Spain's European rivals could not seize Mexico or Peru, the sparsely populated islands and coasts of the Caribbean became likely targets. Buccaneers, owing allegiance to no nation, raided the Caribbean ports in the late 17th century. Meanwhile, the English took Ja-

Map 19.3 Latin America around 1800 Bourbon reforms created new viceroyalties in order to improve defense, taxation, and administration. In Brazil, central control was enhanced from the new capital of Rio de Janeiro after 1763 while the northern Amazonian region was brought directly under Lisbon's control by strong governors.

maica in 1654, the French took control of western Hispaniola (Haiti) by 1697, and other islands fell to the English, French, and Dutch. Many of the islands turned to sugar production and the creation of slave and plantation colonies much like those in Brazil. These settlements were part of a general process of colonization, of which the English settlement of eastern North America and the French occupation of Canada and the Mississippi valley were also part.

Less apparent than the loss of territories, but equally important, was the failure of the Spanish mercantile and political system. The annual fleets became irregular. Silver payments from America declined, and most goods shipped to the West Indies and even the ships that carried them were non-Spanish in origin. The colonies became increasingly self-sufficient in basic commodities, and as central government became weaker, local aristocrats in the colonies exercised increasing control over the economy and government of their regions, often at the expense of the Native American and the lower-class populations. Graft and corruption were rampant in many branches of government. The empire seemed to be crumbling. What is most impressive is that Spain was able to retain its American possessions for another century.

Even with Spain in decline, the West Indies still seemed an attractive prize coveted by other powers, and the opportunity to gain them was not long in coming. A final crisis was set in motion in 1701 when the Spanish king, Charles II, died without an heir. Other European nations backed various claimants to the Spanish throne, hoping to win the prize of the Spanish monarchy and its American colonies. Philip of Anjou, a Bourbon and thus a relative of the king of France, was named successor to the Spanish throne. The **War of the Spanish Succession** (1702–1713) ensued, and the result at the Treaty of Utrecht (1713) was recognition of a branch of the Bourbon family as rulers of Spain; the price was some commercial concessions that allowed French merchants to operate in Seville and permitted England to trade slaves in Spanish America (and even to send one ship per year to trade for silver in the Americas). Spain's commercial monopoly was now being broken not just by contraband trade but by legal means as well.

The Bourbon Reforms

The new and vigorous Bourbon dynasty in Spain launched a series of reforms aimed at strengthening the state and its economy. In this age of "enlightened despotism," the Spanish Bourbon monarchs, especially **Charles III** (r. 1759–1788), were moved by economic nationalism and a desire for strong centralized government to institute economic, administrative, and military reforms in Spain and its empire. The goal of these rulers and their progressive ministers was to revive Spain within the framework of its traditional society. Their aim was to make government more effective, more powerful, and better able to direct the economy. Certain groups or institutions that opposed these measures or stood in the way might be punished or suppressed. The Jesuit order, with its special allegiance to Rome, its rumored wealth, and its missions in the New World (which controlled almost 100,000 Indians in Paraguay alone), was a prime target. The Jesuits were expelled from Spain and its empire in 1767, as they had been from the Portuguese empire in 1759. In general, however, the entrenched interests of the church and the nobility were not frontally attacked as long as they did not conflict with the authority of the crown. The reforms were aimed at material improvements and a more powerful state, not social or political upheaval. French bureaucratic models were introduced. The system of taxation was tightened. The navy was reformed, and new ships were built. The convoy fleet system was abandoned, and in 1778 new ports were opened in Spain and America for the West Indies trade, although trade still was restricted to Spaniards or to ships sailing under Spanish license.

In the West Indies, the Bourbons initiated a broad program of reform. New viceroyalties were created in New Granada (1739) and the Rio de la Plata (1778) to provide better administration and defense to the growing populations of these regions. Royal investigators were sent to the Indies. The most important of them, **José de Gálvez,** spent six years in Mexico before returning to Spain to become minister of the Indies and a chief architect of reform. His investigations, as well as reports by others, revealed the worst abuses of graft and corruption, which implicated the local magistrates and the Creole landowners and aristocracy. Gálvez moved to eliminate the Creoles from the upper bureaucracy of the colonies. New offices were created. After 1780, the *corregidores,* or local magistrates, were removed from the Indian villages, and that office was replaced by a new system of intendants, or provincial governors, based on French models. This intendancy system was introduced throughout the Indies. Such measures improved tax collection and made government more effective, but the reforms also disrupted the patterns of influence and power, especially among the Creole bureaucrats, miners, and landowners as their political power declined.

Many of the reforms in America were linked directly to defense and military matters. During the century, Spain often was allied with France, and the global struggle between England and France for world hegemony made Spain's American possessions a logical target for English attack. During the Seven Years War (1756–1763), the loss of Florida and the English seizure of Havana shocked Spain into action, particularly because when England held Havana in 1762, Cuban trade boomed. Regular Spanish troops were sent to New Spain, and militia units, led by local Creoles who

War of the Spanish Succession   Resulted from Bourbon family's succession to Spanish throne in 1701; ended by Treaty of Utrecht in 1713; resulted in recognition of Bourbons, loss of some lands, grants of commercial rights to English and French.

Charles III   Spanish enlightened monarch; ruled from 1759 to 1788; instituted fiscal, administrative, and military reforms in Spain and its empire.

Gálvez, José de   (1720–1787) Spanish minister of the West Indies and chief architect of colonial reform; moved to eliminate Creoles from upper bureaucracy of the colonies; created intendants for local government.

were given military rank, were created throughout the empire. Frontiers were expanded, and previously unoccupied or loosely controlled regions, such as California, were settled by a combination of missions and small frontier outposts. In the Rio de la Plata, foreign competitors were resisted by military means. Spain sought every means to strengthen itself and its colonies.

During the Bourbon reforms, the government took an active role in the economy. State monopolies were established for items the government considered essential, such as tobacco and gunpowder. Whole new areas of Spanish America were opened to development. Monopoly companies were granted exclusive rights to develop certain colonial areas in return for developing the economies of those regions.

The commerce of the Caribbean greatly expanded under the more liberal trading regulations. Cuba became another full-scale plantation and slave colony, exporting sugar, coffee, and tobacco and importing large numbers of Africans. Buenos Aires, on the Rio de la Plata, proved to be a great success story. Its population had grown rapidly in the 18th century, and by 1790 it had a booming economy based on ranching and the export of hides and salted beef. A newly prosperous merchant community in Buenos Aires dominated the region's trade.

The commercial changes were a double-edged sword. As Spanish and English goods became cheaper and more accessible, they undercut locally produced goods so that some regions that had specialized in producing cloth or other goods were unable to compete with the European imports. Links to international trade tightened as the diversity of Latin America's economy decreased. Later conflicts between those who favored free trade and those who wanted to limit imports and protect local industry often were as much about regional interests as about economic philosophy.

Finally, and most importantly, the major centers of the Spanish Empire also experienced rapid growth in the second half of the 18th century. Mining inspectors and experts had been sent to Peru and New Spain to suggest reforms and introduce new techniques. These improvements, as well as the discovery of new veins, allowed production to expand, especially in New Spain, where silver output reached new heights. In fact, silver production in Mexico far outstripped that of Peru, which itself saw increased production.

All in all, the Bourbon reforms must be seen from two vantage points: Spain and America. Undoubtedly, in the short run, the restructuring of government and economy revived the Spanish Empire. In the long run, the removal of Creoles from government, the creation of a militia with a Creole officer corps, the opening of commerce, and other such changes contributed to a growing sense of dissatisfaction among the elite, which only their relative well-being and the existing social tensions of the sociedad de castas kept in check.

Pombal and Brazil

The Bourbon reforms in Spain and Spanish America were paralleled in the Portuguese world during the administration of Sebastião José Carvalho e Mello, the **Marquis of Pombal** (1755–1776), Portugal's authoritarian prime minister. Pombal had lived as ambassador in England and had observed the benefits of mercantilism at firsthand. He hoped to use these same techniques, along with state intervention in the economy, to break England's hold on the Portuguese economy, especially on the flow of Brazilian gold from Portugal to England. This became crucial as the production of Brazilian gold began to decline after 1760. In another example of "enlightened despotism," Pombal brutally suppressed any group or institution that stood in the way of royal power and his programs. He developed a particular dislike for the Jesuits because of their allegiance to Rome and their semi-independent control of large areas in Brazil. Pombal expelled the Jesuits from the Portuguese Empire in 1759.

Pombal made Brazil the centerpiece of his reforms. Vigorous administrators were sent to the colony to enforce the changes. Fiscal reforms were aimed at eliminating contraband, gold smuggling, and tax evasion. Monopoly companies were formed to stimulate agriculture in older plantation zones and were given the right to import large numbers of slaves. New crops were introduced. Just as in Spanish America, new regions in Brazil began to flourish. Rio de Janeiro became the capital, and its hinterland was the scene of agricultural growth. The undeveloped Amazonian region, long dominated by Jesuit missionaries, received new attention. A monopoly company was created to develop the region's economy, and it stimulated the development of cotton plantations and the

Marquis of Pombal Prime minister of Portugal from 1755 to 1776; acted to strengthen royal authority in Brazil; expelled Jesuits; enacted fiscal reforms and established monopoly companies to stimulate the colonial economy.

export of wild cacao from the Amazonian forests. These new exports joined the traditional sugar, tobacco, and hides as Brazil's main products.

Pombal was willing to do some social tinkering as part of his project of reform. He abolished slavery in Portugal to stop the import of slaves there and to ensure a steady supply to Brazil, the economic cornerstone of the empire. Because Brazil was vast and needed to be both occupied and defended, he removed Indians from missionary control in the Amazon and encouraged whites to marry them. Immigrant couples from Portugal and the Azores were sent to colonize the Amazon basin and the plains of southern Brazil, which began to produce large quantities of wheat and cattle. Like the Bourbons in Spain, Pombal hoped to revitalize the colonies as a way of strengthening the mother country. Although new policies were instituted, little changed within the society. Brazil was just as profoundly based on slavery in the late 18th century as it had ever been: The levels of slave imports reached 20,000 a year.

Even in the long run, Pombal's policies were not fully effective. Although he reduced Portugal's trade imbalance with England during this period, Brazilian trade suffered because the demand for its products on the world market remained low. This was a classic problem for the American colonies. Their economies were so tied to the sale of their products on the European market and so controlled by policies in the metropolis that the colonies' range of action was always limited. Although Pombal's policies were not immediately successful, they provided the structure for an economic boom in the last 20 years of the 18th century that set the stage for Brazilian independence.

Reforms, Reactions, and Revolts

By the mid-18th century, the American colonies of Spain and Portugal, like the rest of the world, were experiencing rapid growth in population and productive capacity. By the end of the century, Spanish America had a population of almost 13 million. Between 1740 and 1800, the population of Mexico, the most populous area, increased from 3.5 million to almost 6 million, about half of whom were Indians. In Brazil the population reached about 2 million by the end of the century. This overall increase resulted from declining mortality rates, increasing fertility levels, increasing immigration from Europe, and the thriving slave trade. The opening of new areas to development and Europe's increasing demand for American products accompanied the population growth. The American colonies were experiencing a boom in the last years of the 18th century.

Reformist policies, tighter tax collection, and the presence of a more activist government in both Spanish America and Brazil disrupted old patterns of power and influence, raised expectations, and sometimes provoked violent colonial reactions. Urban riots, tax revolts, and Indian uprisings were not unknown before 1700, but serious and more protracted rebellions broke out after that date. In New Granada (present-day Colombia), popular complaints against the government's control of tobacco and liquor consumption, and rising prices as well as new taxes, led to the widespread **Comunero Revolt** in 1781. A royal army was defeated, the viceroy fled from Bogota, and a rebel army almost took the capital. Only tensions between the various racial and social groups, and concessions by the government, brought an end to the rebellion.

At the same time, in Peru, an even more threatening revolt erupted. A great Indian uprising took place under the leadership of Jose Gabriel Condorcanqui, known as **Tupac Amaru.** A mestizo who claimed descent from the Incas, Tupac Amaru led a rebellion against "bad government." For almost three years the whole viceroyalty was thrown into turmoil while more than 70,000 Indians, mestizos, and even a few Creoles joined in rebellion against the worst abuses of the colonial regime. Tupac Amaru was captured and brutally executed, but the rebellion smoldered until 1783. It failed mostly because the Creoles, although they had their own grievances against the government, feared that a real social upheaval might take place if they upset the political balance.

This kind of social upheaval was not present in Brazil, where a government attempt to collect back taxes in the mining region led in 1788 to a plot against Portuguese control. A few bureaucrats, intellectuals, and miners planned an uprising for independence, but their conspiracy was discovered. The plotters were arrested, and one conspirator, a militia officer nicknamed Tiradentes, was hanged.

Despite their various social bases, these movements indicated that activism by governments increased dissatisfaction in the American colonies. The new prosperity of the late 18th century

Comunero Revolt One of popular revolts against Spanish colonial rule in New Granada (Colombia) in 1781; suppressed as a result of divisions among rebels.

Amaru, Tupac (1738–1781) Mestizo leader of Indian revolt in Peru; supported by many among lower social classes; revolt eventually failed because of Creole fears of real social revolution.

contributed to a sense of self-confidence and economic interest among certain colonial classes, which made them sensitive to restrictions and control by Spain and Portugal. Different groups had different complaints, but the sharp social and ethnic divisions within the colonies acted as a barrier to cooperation for common goals and tended to undercut revolutionary movements. Only when the Spanish political system was disrupted by a crisis of legitimacy at the beginning of the 19th century did real separation and independence from the mother countries become a possibility.

Global Connections

Latin American Civilization and the World Context

In three centuries, Spain and Portugal created large colonial empires in the Americas. These American colonies provided a basis of power to their Iberian mother countries and took a vital place in the expanding world economy as suppliers of precious minerals and certain crops to the growing economy of Europe. By the 18th century, the weakened positions of Spain and Portugal within Europe allowed England and France to benefit directly from the Iberian trade with American colonies. To their American colonies, the Iberian nations transferred and imposed their language, laws, forms of government, religion, and institutions. Large numbers of immigrants, first as conquerors and later as settlers, came to the colonies. Eventually, the whole spectrum of Iberian society was recreated in the New World as men and women came to seek a better life, bringing with them their customs, ideas, religion, laws, and ways of life. By government and individual action, a certain homogeneity was created, both in Spanish America and in Brazil. That seeming unity was most apparent among the Europeanized population.

In fact, despite the apparent continuity with Spain and Portugal and homogeneity among the various colonies, there were great variations. Latin America, with its distinct environments, its various economic possibilities, and its diverse indigenous peoples, imposed new realities. In places such as Mexico and Peru, Native American cultures emerged from the shock of conquest, battered but still vibrant. Native American communities adapted to the new colonial situation. A distinctive multiethnic and multiracial society developed, drawing on Iberian precedents but also dependent on the native population, the imported Africans, and the various mixed racial categories. Argentina with few Native Americans, Cuba with its slaves and plantations, and Mexico with its large rural indigenous populations all shared the same Hispanic traditions and laws, and all had a predominantly white elite, but their social and economic realities made them very different places. Latin America developed as a composite civilization—distinct from the West but related to it—combining European and Native American culture and society or creating the racial hierarchies of slave societies in places such as Brazil.

The empires of Spain and Portugal in Latin America bear comparison with the Russian Empire that had been formed at about the same time. While Iberian expansion had been maritime and Russian expansion over land, the process of colonization and the conquest of indigenous peoples created many parallels, including the development of coerced labor. The creation of all of these empires also demonstrated the impact of gunpowder. But the cultural impact of the West was different in the Iberian and Russian empires. Whereas the Russian rulers had decided, quite selectively, what aspects of Western culture to adopt, in Latin America Western forms were often simply imposed on the populations, but not without resistance.

The American colonies of Portugal and Spain also bear comparison with those of the English, French, and Dutch who at first coveted the Iberian possessions and then created their own empires, sometimes at the expense of the Iberians, but often following their models. The empires of Portugal and Spain were global in reach, but the American colonies became part of an Atlantic system that promoted continual interchange between Africa, Europe, and America of goods, people, cultures, and ideas. This too was a pattern that other Europeans followed

From the perspective of the world economy, despite the ultimate decline in production of precious metals, Latin American products remained in great demand in Europe's markets. As Latin Americans began to seek political independence in the early 19th century, they were confronted by this basic economic fact and by their continued dependence on trade with the developing global economy. Latin America's world economic position, with its dependent and coerced labor force and outside commercial control, revealed its colonial status, but in its often bitter history of cultural clash and accommodation a new civilization had been born.

Further Readings

James Lockhart and Stuart B. Schwartz, *Early Latin America* (1983), provides an interpretation and overview. John Hemming, *Rivers of Gold* (2003) gives an excellent narrative of the early conquests while Henry Kamen, *Empire: How Spain Became a World Power* (2003) places the Americas in the context of Spain's other imperial holdings in Europe and Asia. John Elliott, *Empires of the Atlantic World* (2007) carefully compares English and Spanish colonization in the Americas. A view of Latin America within a comparative Atlantic perspective is provided by Christine Daniels and Michael V. Kennedy, eds., *Negotiated Empires: Centers and Peripheries in the Americas, 1500–1820* (2002), and in Jorge

Cañizares-Esguerra and Erik R. Seeman, eds., *The Atlantic in Global History, 1500–2000* (2007).

On the conquest period there are many excellent regional studies. James Lockhart, *Spanish Peru* (1968), is a model reconstruction of conquest society. The story of Mancio Serra is told in Stuart Stirling, *The Last Conquistador* (1999). An indigenous view of the conquest and of Spanish rule is found in Felipe Guaman Poma de Ayala, *The First New Chronicle and Good Government*, (2006) edited by David Frye. The conquest of Mexico can be seen from two different angles in Bernal Díaz del Castillo, *The Discovery and Conquest of Mexico*, trans. A. P. Maudsley (1956), and in James Lockhart's edition of the Aztec testimony gathered after the conquest by Bernardino de Sahagún, published as *We Peoples Here* (1962). Various indigenous and Spanish sources are collected in S. Schwartz, ed., *Victors and Vanquished* (2000).

The transformation of Indian societies has been studied in books such as Susan E. Ramírez, *The World Turned Upside Down* (1996) on Peru; Matthew Restall, *The Maya World* (1997), on Yucatan; Susan Kellogg, *Law and the Transformation of Aztec Culture, 1500–1700* (1995) on Mexico; or Kris Lane, *Quito, 1599* (2002) on Ecuador. Ward Stavig, *The World of Tupac Amaru* (1999), on 18th-century Peru examines the transformations of the late colonial era. Other approaches to the impact of conquest are presented in Noble David Cook, *Born to Die: Disease and New World Conquest, 1492–1650* (1998), and Carolyn Dean, *Inka Bodies and the Bodies of Christ* (1999).

The region's colonial, social, and economic history is examined in books such as Stuart Schwartz, *Sugar Plantations and the Formation of Brazilian Society* (1985); Susan Socolow, *Women in Colonial Latin America* (2000); Susan Kellogg, *Weaving the Past* (2005); and Karen Graubart, *With Our Labor and Sweat* (2007), whose focus is indigenous women of Peru. Arnold Bauer, *Goods, Power, and History* (2001), discusses material culture. Popular thought is addressed in Serge Gruzinski, *The Conquest of Mexico* and Linda Curcio-Nagy, *The Great Festivals of Colonial Mexico City* (2004).

The best introduction to the Bourbon reforms is still David Brading, *Miners and Merchants in Bourbon Mexico* (1971). David Weber, *Bárbaros: Spaniards and Their Savages in the Age of Enlightenment* (2005) examines changing policies toward Native Americans. The revolt of Tupac Amaru is analyzed in Sinclair Thomson, *We Alone Will Rule* (2002). On Brazil, James Wadsworth, *Agents of Orthodoxy* (2007) shows how Pombal's policies and the Enlightenment affected society and institutions while Kenneth Maxwell's *Pombal: Paradox of the Enlightenment* (1995) examines that statesman in an imperial context. Junia Furtado, *Xica da Silva* (2008) follows the life of one remarkable woman in Brazil in the late colonial era.

On the Web

The lives of Spanish conquistadors and their overthrow of the indigenous states in the Americas is illuminated (and lavishly il-

lustrated) at http://www.pbs.org/conquistadors/index.html and http://www.bbc.co.uk/history/british/tudors/conquistadors_01.shtml. Bartoleme De Las Casas' account of the European "devastation of the Indes" can be found at http://www.swarthmore.edu/SocSci/bdorsey1/41docs/02-las.html and http://www.healingtheland.com/resources/discovery/las_casas.html. The role of disease in the European conquest, the subsequent decimation of the indigenous population of the Americas, and the overall demographic impact of both the conquest and colonization of the region is discussed at http://www.ucalgary.ca/applied_history/tutor/migrations/three4.html, http://www.millersville.edu/~columbus/papers/orlow-e.html, and http://www.hist.umn.edu/~rmccaa/vircatas/vir6.htm (also at http://www.hist.umn.edu/~rmccaa/vita_mccaa.htm, scroll down to 1995). The larger issue of the relationship between disease, culture, and conquest in world history is addressed at http://www.uic.edu/classes/osci/osci590/8_4Disease%20Culture%20And%20Conquest.txt.htm.

The "Colombian Exchange" of plants and animals as well as diseases between the Americas and Afro-Eurasia occasioned by the European conquest of the Americas is discussed at http://www.eoearth.org/article/Columbian_exchange~_plants,_animals,_and_disease_between_the_Old_and_New_World, http://daphne.palomar.edu/scrout/colexc.htm, and http://nationalhumanitiescenter.org/tserve/nattrans/ntecoindian/essays/columbian.htm. Evidence of continuing Aztec and Inca resistance in the early years of the European conquest is analyzed at http://www.theregister.co.uk/2006/08/24/aztec_sacrifices/ and http://www.pbs.org/wgbh/nova/transcripts/3409_inca.html. Indigenous resistance to Latin America's subsequent dependent economic position is given a human face through a discussion of the rebellions of Tupac Amaru and Juan Santos Atahualpa at http://www.dickshovel.com/500.html.

The methods by which Europeans extracted wealth from Latin America by the manipulation of old or imposition of new patterns of mining, labor, and land ownership (the *mita* and *encomendero* systems) and the impact these new patterns of economic life had on both the indigenous population and the imported African slave population are collectively examined at http://www.millersville.edu/~columbus/papers/scott-m.html. The place of silver in Latin American and world history is examined at http://www.learner.org/channel/courses/worldhistory/unit_video_15-2.html, http://www-geology.ucdavis.edu/~cowen/~GEL115/115CH8.html, and http://www.unesco.org/courier/2000_03/uk/dici/txt1.htm.

Pombal's ecnomic reforms are analyzed at http://en.wikipedia.org/wiki/Sebasti%C3%A3o_de_Melo,_Marquis_of_Pombal and http://en.wikipedia.org/wiki/Bourbon_Reforms.

Some of the syncretic or composite elements of modern Latin American civilization are revealed in the "Day of the Dead" celebration, which is explored at http://www.mexonline.com/daydead.htm and http://teacherlink.ed.usu.edu/tlresources/units/Byrnes-celebrations/Day.html.

AP* | Test Prep

1. In order to administer its Latin American possessions, the Spanish crown did all of the following EXCEPT
   - (A) permitted nobles to administer lands without any royal oversight.
   - (B) retained local Indian rulers as clients provided they were loyal to Spain.
   - (C) shared some political authority with Catholic bishops and priests.
   - (D) built an elaborate bureaucracy headed by viceroys.

2. The encomieda system, the hacienda system, and the mita all had what in common?
   - (A) They were systems designed to extract forced labor from the native Americans.
   - (B) They were units of colonial administration in New Spain.
   - (C) They were royal taxes that colonists had to pay to the Spanish crown.
   - (D) They made land grants to immigrants, who worked the land and paid a percentage of their profit to Spain.

3. In reaction to the reported atrocities and harsh treatment of the Indians by the conquistadors, the Spanish crown
   - (A) ignored complaints and supported the conquerors.
   - (B) appointed the Catholic priests in the colonies to be the protectors of the Indians.
   - (C) often agreed with those who defended the Indians, but did not stop the abuses.
   - (D) created courts of inquiry and put the conquerors on trial for their crimes.

4. The dislocation of indigenous or native plants and animals around the world by European crops and domesticated animals, and the devastation of native peoples by European diseases is referred to as
   - (A) the Columbian Exchange.
   - (B) the Great Migration.
   - (C) Ecological Imperialism.
   - (D) the Great Die-Off.

5. The export of silver from the Americas led to all of these outcomes EXCEPT
   - (A) discouraging foreign rivalry and pirate activities.
   - (B) causing a sharp inflation in Western Europe.
   - (C) the acceleration in the global exchange of silver for Chinese luxuries Europeans desired.
   - (D) the increasing impoverishment and bankruptcy of Spain.

6. The existence of the society of *castas* in Latin American societies was an indication of what social factors in the colonies?
   - (A) the enduring medieval Spanish hierarchies survived and flourished in the colonies
   - (B) a growing cultural fusion in the formation of Latin America
   - (C) the decreasing importance of the native peoples and the growing importance of African slave labor
   - (D) the blending of European, African, and Native American patriarchal ideas into a syncretic blend of patriarchy

7. Which of the following best describes the results of both the Bourbon Reforms and the Pombal Reforms?
   - (A) 18th century Spanish and Portuguese colonial governments became much more responsive to the colonial peoples.
   - (B) The activist governmental policies made the creoles and the native peoples dissatisfied with their governors in Europe.
   - (C) The colonial economies became less dependent upon their European masters' economies.
   - (D) The reforms ended the use of slavery and forced labor taxes, but crippled the sugar plantation and mining economies by doing so.

Free-Response Question

How did the features unique to Iberian history influence the development of Spanish and Portuguese colonies?

To what extent were the Spanish and Portuguese able to perpetuate their own political, social, economic, and religious structures in their Latin American colonies?

20 Africa and the Africans in the Age of the Atlantic Slave Trade

Africa and the Creation of an Atlantic System

THINKING HISTORICALLY: Slavery and Human Society

African Societies, Slavery, and the Slave Trade

VISUALIZING THE PAST: The Cloth of Kings in an Atlantic Perspective

White Settlers and Africans in Southern Africa

The African Diaspora

DOCUMENT: An African's Description of the Middle Passage

GLOBAL CONNECTIONS: Africa and the African Diaspora in World Context

Sometimes a single, extraordinary life can represent the forces and patterns of a whole historical era. Born in the early 19th century, Mahommah Gardo Baquaqua was a young man from the trading town of Djougou in what is now the Benin Republic in west Africa. A Muslim, he could speak Arabic, Hausa, and a number of other languages, as was common among the trading peoples from which he came. At a young age, Baquaqua was captured and enslaved during a war with a neighboring African state; after gaining his freedom, he was enslaved again, and around 1845 he was sold into the Atlantic slave trade.

Baquaqua was taken first to northeastern Brazil and from there was purchased by a ship captain from Rio de Janeiro. After a number of voyages along the Brazilian coast, his ship eventually sailed for New York. After a failed attempt to use the American courts to gain his freedom (a strategy that many slaves attempted), Baquaqua fled to Boston with the help of local abolitionists. In that city he was befriended by antislavery Baptist missionaries. With them, he sailed for Haiti. Eventually he learned French and English and studied at a college in upstate New York in order to prepare for missionary work in his native Africa. His life was not easy. Eventually, because of racial incidents, he moved to Canada.

Although Baquaqua had left the Baptist college, he did not abandon his desire to return to Africa, and he continued to seek ways to make that voyage. In 1854, in an attempt to get the money he needed to realize his dream, he published his autobiography, *An Interesting Narrative: Biography of Mahommah G. Baquaqua.* In it he was able to provide his personal observations on his experiences. On the slave ship, he reported:

> O the loathsomeness and filth of that horrible place will never be effaced from my memory; nay as long as my memory holds her seat in this distracted brain, will I remember that. My heart, even at this day, sickens at the thought of it. Let those *humane individuals,* who are in favor of slavery, only allow themselves to take the slave's position in the noisome hold of a slave ship, just for one trip from Africa to America, and without going into the horrors of slavery further than this, if they do not come out thorough-going abolitionists, then I have no more to say in favor of abolition.

The only place worse than the hold of a slave ship, said Baquaqua, was the place to which slave owners would be condemned in the next life (Figure 20.1). We do not know whether Baquaqua finally returned to the land of his birth, but the life of this African, while singular in many aspects, represents the stories of millions of Africans in the age of the slave trade, and these make up an important part of world history. ∎

Sub-Saharan Africa, previously linked to the Muslim world in many ways, moved at its own pace even as it was pulled in new directions during the early modern centuries. Islam remained important, and eastern Africa did trade with western Asia, but the rise of Europe and of the Western-dominated world economy proved to be a powerful force in recasting the framework of African history. The strength of earlier African cultural and political traditions persisted in many places, but the impact of the West was the newest influence in Africa and in some respects an immensely powerful one. African history had its own pace, and this chapter therefore exceeds the chronological boundaries of the early modern period. The influences of Islam and the West initiated or intensified processes of religious conversion, political reorganization, and social change that persisted in some cases into the 19th century. The distinctive nature and chronology of African history should not blind us to its role in world history.

Figure 20.1 Image of African slave trade. The French artist Auguste François Biard painted this scene of the west African slave trade in 1840 in an attempt to show its cruelties. Represented here are not only the European merchants and sailors receiving the slaves but west African merchants and soldiers involved in supplying them. The painting was eventually acquired by an ardent English abolitionist.

Africa and the Creation of an Atlantic System

During the age of European maritime and commercial expansion, large areas of Africa were brought into the orbit of the expanding world economy and were influenced by the transformation that was taking place. Not all parts of Africa were influenced in the same way or at the same time. After 1450, the growing and often bitter contacts between Europeans and Africans, primarily through the slave trade, linked the destiny of Africa to the broader external trends of the emerging world economy. These contacts also resulted in a diaspora of millions of Africans to the Middle East, Europe, and especially across the Atlantic to the Americas. Not all European contact with Africa was centered on the slave trade, nor was the desire for slaves the only impulse behind European explorations, but the slave trade after 1600 overshadowed other activities until the mid-19th century. Slavery became a central feature in the links formed between the continents that bordered the Atlantic. Changing global interactions had a direct impact on certain areas of Africa, and they also made Africans an important element in the shifting balance of world civilizations. The forced movement of Africans as captive laborers and the creation of slave-based societies in the Americas were major aspects of the formation of the modern world and the growth of the economies of western Europe. This forced migration was part of the international exchange of foods, diseases, animals, and ideas that marked the era and had a profound influence on the indigenous peoples in various regions, as we saw in the case of the Americas. Moreover, in the large areas of the Americas colonized by Europeans where slavery came to be the predominant form of labor, African cultures became part of a complex mixture, contributing to the creation of new cultural forms. Although much of the analysis in this chapter emphasizes the increasing linkage between Africa and the wider world, it should be made clear at the outset that many fundamental processes of African development continued throughout this period. Almost all of Africa remained independent of outside political control, and most cultural development was autonomous as well. Although both were part of

Beginning in the 16th century the Atlantic Ocean became an "inland sea" between which the people, products and ideas of Europe, Africa, and the Americas constantly moved. Africans played an essential role in this process primarily but not exclusively through the slave trade.

1400 C.E.	1500 C.E.	1600 C.E.	1700 C.E.	1800 C.E.
1415 Portuguese capture Ceuta (Morocco); beginning of European expansion 1441 First shipment of African slaves brought directly from Africa to Portugal 1481 Portuguese fort established at El Mina (Ghana)	1562 Beginnings of English slave trade 1570 Portuguese establish colony in Angola 1591 Fall of Songhay Empire	1652 Dutch establish colony at Cape of Good Hope	1700–1717 Osei Tutu unifies the Asante kingdom 1713 English get right to import slaves to Spanish Empire 1720s Rise of the kingdom of Dahomey 1790s Abolitionist movement gains strength in England 1792 Slave uprising in Haiti	1804 Usuman Dan Fodio leads Hausa expansion 1815 Cape colony comes under formal British control 1818–1828 Shaka forges Zulu power and expansion; mfecane under way 1833 Great Britain abolishes slavery in the West Indies 1834 Boers make "Great Trek" into Natal

factories European trading fortresses and compounds with resident merchants; utilized throughout Portuguese trading empire to assure secure landing places and commerce.

Early Portuguese contacts set the patterns for contact with the African coast. The slave trade expanded to meet the demand for labor in the new American colonies, and millions were exported in an organized commerce that involved both Europeans and Africans.

Map 20.1 Portuguese Contact and Penetration of Africa
Portuguese exploration and trade in the 15th century eventually evolved into trade, conquest, and missionary activities. In West Africa regular relations were established with a number of kingdoms like Benin and Kongo; in East Africa the Portuguese created outposts in Mozambique and along the Swahili coast, and in Ethiopia missionaries sought alliance with local Christians.

a developing Atlantic system, Africa differed profoundly from Latin America in these respects during the early modern centuries.

A variety of trends affected various parts of the sub-Saharan region. Islam consolidated its position in east Africa and the Sudan. In Ethiopia the Christian kingdom of the highlands continued to hold off its Muslim rivals. In many places in Africa, as in Europe, independent states continued to form and expand, perhaps as a result of a population expansion that followed the spread of iron tools and improved agriculture. Kingdoms spread to new areas. Scholars disagree on the extent to which these long-term developments were affected by Europeans and the rise of the Atlantic slave trade. Some argue that the enlarged political scale—the growth of large kingdoms through much of the subcontinent—was the dominant theme of the period and that slavery was one of its by-products. Others see European demand as a major impulse in political expansion. In this chapter we emphasize the impact of slavery and the slave trade because our focus in a world history is not simply the geographic region of Africa but on the Africans who, like Baquaqua, and so many others, were swept into the expanding international economy. It is important to remember that before 1800 at least twice as many Africans crossed the Atlantic than did Europeans, and so they were fundamental to creation of the Atlantic system.

The Atlantic Slave Trade

Portuguese ships pushed down the west African coast and finally reached the Cape of Good Hope in 1487 (Map 20.1). Along the coast, the Portuguese established **factories**: forts and trading posts with resident merchants. The most important of these outposts was **El Mina** (1482) in the heart of the gold-producing region of the forest zone. These forts allowed the Portuguese to exercise some control with few personnel. Although the early voyagers carried out some raids, once their cannon range was exceeded the Portuguese simply were not powerful enough to enforce their will on the larger west African states. Therefore, most forts were established with the consent of local rulers, who benefited from access to European commodities and sometimes from the military support the Portuguese provided in local wars.

Africans acquired goods from the Portuguese, who sometimes provided African rulers with slaves brought from other stretches of the coast. In return, the Portuguese received ivory, pepper, animal skins, and gold. From El Mina, Accra, and other trade forts, routes led directly into the gold-producing regions of the interior, so that the Portuguese eventually traded with Mande and Soninke merchants from Mali and Songhay. Much of the

Portuguese success resulted from their ability to penetrate the existing African trade routes, to which they could also add specialized items. Portuguese and African Portuguese mulatto traders struck out into the interior to establish trade contacts and collection points.

Trade was the basis of Portuguese relations with Africans, but in the wake of commerce followed political, religious, and social relations. The small states of the Senegambian coast did not impress the Portuguese, who were particularly suspicious of Muslims, their traditional enemies. When they reached the Gold Coast (modern Ghana) and found the kingdom of Benin, they were impressed both by the power of the ruler and by the magnificence of his court. Other large African states also provoked similar responses.

Missionary efforts were made to convert the rulers of Benin, Kongo, and other African kingdoms. The Portuguese contacted the Kongo kingdom south of the Zaire River about 1484. The missionaries achieved a major success in Kongo, where members of the royal family were converted. The ruler, **Nzinga Mvemba** (NZIHNG-uh MVEHM-buh) (r. 1507–1543), with the help of Portuguese advisors and missionaries, brought the whole kingdom to Christianity. Attempts were made to "Europeanize" the kingdom. Portugal and Kongo exchanged ambassadors and dealt with each other with a certain equality in this early period, but eventually enslavement of his subjects led Nzinga Mvemba to try to end the slave trade and limit Portuguese activities. He was only partially successful because of Portugal's control of Kongo's ability to communicate with the outside world and its dominance over Kongo's trade.

These first contacts were marked by cultural preconceptions as well as by appreciation and curiosity. Africans found the newcomers strange and at first tried to fit them into their existing concepts of the spiritual and natural world. Images of Portuguese soldiers and traders began to appear in the bronzes of Benin and the carved ivory sculptures of other African peoples (Figure 20.2). The Portuguese tended to look on Africans as savages and pagans but also as capable of civilized behavior and conversion to Christianity.

Portuguese exploration continued southward toward the Cape of Good Hope and beyond in the 16th century. Early contacts were made with the Mbundu peoples south of Kongo in the 1520s, and a more permanent Portuguese settlement was established there in the 1570s with the foundation of **Luanda** on the coast. This became the basis for the Portuguese colony of Angola. As we have already seen, the Portuguese tried to dominate the existing trading system of the African ports in the Indian Ocean and Red Sea. They established an outpost on Mozambique Island and then secured bases at Kilwa, Mombasa, Sofala, and other ports that gave them access to the gold trade from Monomotapa (Mwenemutapa) in the interior. In east Africa, as on the west African coast, the number of permanent Portuguese settlers was minimal. The Portuguese effort was primarily commercial and military, although it was always accompanied by a strong missionary effort.

The patterns of contact established by the Portuguese were followed by others. In the 17th century, the Dutch, English, French, and others competed with the Portuguese and displaced them to some extent, but the system of fortified trading stations, the combination of force and diplomacy, alliances with local rulers, and the predominance of commercial relations continued as the principal pattern of European contact with Africa.

Although for a long time Portugal's major interest was in gold, pepper, and other products, a central element in this pattern was the slave trade. Slavery as an institution had been extensive in the Roman Empire but had greatly declined in most of Europe during the Middle Ages, when it was replaced by serfdom. In the Mediterranean and in Iberia, however, where there was an active military frontier between Christians and Muslims, it had remained important. Moreover, the trans-Saharan slave trade had brought small numbers of black Africans into the Mediterranean throughout the period. The Portuguese voyages now opened a direct channel to sub-Saharan Africa. The first slaves brought directly to Portugal from Africa arrived in 1441, and after that date slaves

Figure 20.2 African artists were impressed by the strangeness of Europeans and sometimes incorporated them in their own work, as can be seen in the headpiece of this beautifully carved ivory head of a Benin monarch. Europeans in turn employed African artisans to produce decorative luxury goods.
(Copyright The British Museum.)

El Mina   Most important of early Portuguese trading factories in forest zone of Africa.

Mvemba, Nzinga   [NZIHNG-uh MVEHM-buh] King of Kongo south of Zaire River from 1507 to 1543; converted to Christianity and took title Alfonso I; under Portuguese influence attempted to Christianize all of kingdom.

Luanda   Portuguese factory established in 1520s south of Kongo; became basis for Portuguese colony of Angola.

 "Voyage from Lisbon to the Island of São Thomé," by an Anonymous Portuguese Pilot, c. 1540

became a common trade item. The Portuguese and later other Europeans raided for slaves along the coast, but the numbers acquired in this way were small. After initial raids, Europeans found that trade was a much more secure and profitable way to get these human cargoes. For example, the Portuguese sent about 50 slaves per year to Portugal before 1450, when raiding was prevalent, but by 1460 some 500 slaves per year arrived in Portugal as a trade with African rulers developed. Whether the victims were acquired by raiding or by trade, the effects on them were similar. An eyewitness to the unloading of slaves in Portugal in 1444 wrote,

> But what heart could be so hard as not to be pierced with piteous feelings to see that company? For some kept their heads low and their faces bathed in tears, looking one upon another; others stood groaning very dolorously, looking up to the height of heaven, fixing their eyes upon it, crying out loudly, as if asking help of the Father of Nature.

The slave trade was given added impetus when the Portuguese and the Spanish began to develop sugar plantations on the Atlantic islands of Madeira (Portugal) and the Canaries (Spain) and off the African coast on the Portuguese-held island of São Tomé. Sugar production demanded many workers and constant labor under difficult conditions, usually in a tropical or subtropical environment. The plantation system of organization associated with sugar, in which managers were able to direct and control laborers over long periods with little restraint, was later extended to America and then to other crops. Although the system did not depend only on Africans, they became the primary plantation laborers in the Atlantic world. The slave trade grew significantly in volume and complexity after 1550 as the American plantation colonies, especially Brazil, began to develop. By 1600, the slave trade predominated over all other kinds of trade on the African coast as Africa was pulled into an Atlantic commercial system.

Trend Toward Expansion

Although debate and controversy surround many aspects of the history of slavery, it is perhaps best to start with the numbers. Estimates of the volume of the trade vary widely, and scholars still debate the figures and their implications, but the range of calculations has been narrowed by recent research and by a large quantitative data base of the slaving voyages. Between 1450 and 1850, it is estimated that about 12 million Africans were shipped across the Atlantic (Table 20.1). With a mortality rate of 10 to 20 percent on the ships, about 10 or 11 million Africans actually arrived in the Americas. How many people died in Africa as a result of the slaving wars or in the forced marches to the coast is unknown, but estimates have been as high as one-third of the total captured. The volume changed over time. In the 16th century, the numbers were small, but they increased to perhaps 16,000 per year in the 17th century. The 18th century was the great age of the Atlantic slave trade; probably more than 7 million slaves, or more than 80 percent of all those embarked, were exported between 1700 and 1800. By the latter date, about 3 million slaves lived in the Americas. Even

TABLE 20.1 Slave Exports from Africa, 1500–1900 (in thousands)				
	1500–1600 (%)	**1600–1700 (%)**	**1700–1800 (%)**	**1800–1900 (%)**	**Total**
Red Sea	200 (17)	200 (7)	200 (3)	450 (8)	1050 (6)
Trans-Sahara	550 (47)	700 (24)			
	700 (9)	1200 (22)			
	3150 (19)				
East Africa and Indian Ocean	100 (9)	100 (4)	400 (5)	442 (8)	1042 (6)
Trans-Atlantic	325 (28)	1868 (65)			
	6133 (83)	3330 (61)			
	11,656 (69)				
					16,898

Source: Adapted from Paul Lovejoy, *Transformations in Slavery: A History of Slavery in Africa* (1983).

in the 19th century, when slavery was under attack, the slave trade to some places continued. Cuba received some 700,000 slaves, and Brazil took more than 1 million in that century alone.

The high volume of the slave trade was necessary to the slave owners because, in most of the slave regimes in the Caribbean and Latin America, slave mortality was high and fertility was low (partly because more men than women were imported). Thus, over time there was usually a loss of population. The only way to maintain or expand the number of slaves was by importing more from Africa. The one exception to this pattern was the southern United States, where the slave population grew, perhaps because of the temperate climate and the fact that few worked in the most dangerous and unhealthy occupations, such as sugar growing and mining. By 1860, almost 6 million slaves worked in the Americas, about 4 million of them in the southern United States, an area that depended more on natural population growth than on the Atlantic slave trade. In terms of total population, however, slaves in British North America were never more than one-fourth of the whole population, whereas in the British and French Caribbean they made up 80 to 90 percent of the population.

The dimensions of the trade varied over time, reflecting the economic and political situation in the Americas. From 1530 to 1650, Spanish America and Brazil received the majority of African slaves, but after the English and French began to grow sugar in the Caribbean, the islands of Jamaica, Barbados, and St. Domingue (Haiti) became important terminals for the slavers. By the 18th century, Virginia and the Carolinas in North America had also become major destinations, although they never rivaled the Caribbean or Brazil (Table 20.2).

Between 1550 and 1850, Brazil alone received 3.5 to 5 million Africans, or about 42 percent of all those who reached the New World. The Caribbean islands, dedicated to sugar production, were the other major destination of Africans. The island colonies of St. Domingue and Jamaica each received more than 1 million slaves in the 18th century alone.

It should be emphasized that these figures represent only the volume in the Atlantic slave trade. The older trans-Sahara, Red Sea, and east African slave trades in the hands of Muslim traders continued throughout the period and added another 3 million people to the total of Africans exported as slaves in this period (Table 20.1). The Atlantic slave trade drew slaves from across the continent, and its concentration shifted over time. In the 16th century, the majority of slaves were exported from the Senegambia region, but by the 17th century, west central Africa (modern Zaire and Angola) was the major supplier. Also important were the areas of the Gold Coast and the Slave Coast—Dahomey and Benin—at the end of the century, when Benin alone was exporting more than 10,000 slaves per year. In the century that followed, wars for control of the interior created the large states of Asante among the Akan peoples of the Gold Coast and Dahomey among the Fon peoples. These wars were both the cause and the result of increasing slave exports from these regions.

TABLE 20.2 Estimated Slave Imports into the Americas by Importing Region, 1519–1866	
Region and Country	**Slaves**
Brazil	3,902,000
British Caribbean	2,238,200
Spanish America	1,267,800
French Caribbean	1,092,600
Guianas*	403,700
British North America	361,100
Dutch Caribbean	129,700
Danish Caribbean	73,100
	9,468,200

*Includes Dutch, French, and British colonies, namely, Berbice, Cayenne, Demerara, Essequebo, and Surinam.

Demographic Patterns

The majority of the trans-Saharan slave trade consisted of women to be used as concubines and domestic servants in north Africa and the Middle East, but the Atlantic slave trade concentrated on men. To some extent this was because planters and mine owners in the Americas were seeking workers for heavy labor and were not eager to risk buying children because of the high levels of mortality. Also, African societies that sold captives into slavery often preferred to sell the men and keep the women and children as domestic slaves or to extend existing kin groups. That was especially true by the 19th century. There were regional variations, however. Far higher proportions of women were imported to the English colonies of Jamaica and Barbados than to Brazil or Cuba

The Atlantic trade seems to have had a demographic impact on at least certain parts of west and central Africa. One estimate is that the population of about 25 million in 1850 in those regions was about one-half what it would have been had there been no slave trade. It is true that the trans-Atlantic trade carried more men than women and more women than children, but captive women and children who remained in Africa swelled the numbers of enslaved people in those societies and skewed the proportion of women to men in the African enslaving societies perhaps increasing fertility rates. Finally, as the Atlantic trade developed, new crops, such as maize and manioc introduced from the Americas provided additional food resources for the population in Africa and helped it recover from the losses to the slave trade.

Organization of the Trade

The patterns of contact and trade established by the Portuguese at first were followed by rival Europeans on the African coast. Control of the slave trade or a portion of it generally reflected the political situation in Europe. For one and a half centuries, until about 1630, the Portuguese controlled most of the coastal trade and were the major suppliers of their own colony of Brazil and the Spanish settlements in America. The growth of slave-based plantation colonies in the Caribbean and elsewhere led other Europeans to compete with the Portuguese. The Dutch became major competitors when they seized El Mina in 1637. By the 1660s, the English were eager to have their own source of slaves for their growing colonies in Barbados, Jamaica, and Virginia. The **Royal African Company** was chartered for that purpose. The French made similar arrangements in the 1660s, but not until the 18th century did France become a major carrier. Like other small European nations, even Denmark had its agents and forts on the African coast.

Each nation established merchant towns or trade forts from which a steady source of captives could be obtained. For the Europeans stationed on the coast, Africa was also a graveyard because of the tropical diseases they encountered. Fewer than 10 percent of the employees of the Royal Africa Company who went to Africa ever returned to England, and the majority died in the first year out. European mortality among the crews of slave ships was also very high because of tropical diseases such as malaria. The slave trade proved deadly to all involved, but at least some of the Europeans had a choice, whereas for the enslaved Africans there was none.

European agents for the companies often had to deal directly with local rulers, paying a tax or offering gifts. Various forms of currency were used, such as iron bars, brass rings, and cowrie shells. The Spanish developed a complicated system in which a healthy man was called an **Indies piece,** and children and women were priced at fractions of that value. Slaves were brought to the coast by a variety of means. Sometimes, as in Angola, European military campaigns produced captives for slaves, or African and mulatto agents purchased captives at interior trade centers. In Dahomey a royal monopoly was established to control the flow of slaves. Some groups used their position to tax or control the movement of slaves from the interior to the coast. Although African and European states tried to establish monopolies over the trade, private merchants often circumvented restrictions.

Clearly, both Europeans and Africans were actively involved in the slave trade. It was not always clear which side was in control. One group of English merchants on the Gold Coast complained of African insolence in 1784 because in negotiations the Africans had emphasized that "the country belongs to them." In any case, the result of this collaboration was to send millions of Africans into bondage in foreign lands.

Historians have long debated the profitability of the slave trade. Some argue that the profits were so great and constant that they were a major element in the rise of commercial capitalism and, later, the origins of the Industrial Revolution. Undoubtedly, many people profited from the trade in African slaves. A single slaving voyage might make a profit of as much as 300 percent, and merchants in the ports that specialized in fitting out ships for the slave trade, such as Liverpool, England, or Nantes, France—as well as African suppliers—derived a profit from the slave trade. But the slave trade also involved risks and costs, so that in the long run, profitability levels did not remain so high. In the late 18th century, profitability in the English slave trade probably ran from 5 to 10 percent on average, and in the French and Dutch trades it was slightly lower. The slave trade was little more profitable in the long run than most business activities of the age and by itself was not a major source of the capital needed in the Industrial Revolution.

However, it is difficult to calculate the full economic importance of slavery to the economies of Europe because it was so directly linked to the plantation and mining economies of the Americas. During some periods, a **triangular trade** existed in which slaves were carried to the Americas; sugar, tobacco, and other goods were then carried to Europe; and European products were sent to the coast of Africa to begin the triangle again. Were profits from the slave trade accumulated in Liverpool invested in the textile industry of England? And if so, how important were these invest-

Royal African Company   Chartered in 1660s to establish a monopoly over the slave trade among British merchants; supplied African slaves to colonies in Barbados, Jamaica, and Virginia.

West African Slave Fort

Indies piece   Term used within the complex exchange system established by the Spanish for African trade; referred to the value of an adult male slave.

triangular trade   Commerce linking Africa, the New World colonies, and Europe; slaves carried to America for sugar and tobacco transported to Europe.

ments for the growth of that industry? We would need to calculate the value of goods produced in Europe for exchange in the slave trade as well as the profits derived from the colonies to measure the importance of slavery to the growth of the European economies. Still, the very persistence of the slave trade indicates its viability. The slave trade surely contributed to the formation of emerging capitalism in the Atlantic world. In Africa itself, the slave trade often drew economies into dependence on trade with Europeans and suppressed the growth of other economic activities.

It is clear that by the late 18th century, the slave trade and slavery were essential aspects of the economy of the Atlantic basin, and their importance was increasing. More than 40 percent of all the slaves that crossed the Atlantic embarked during the century after 1760, and the plantation economies of Brazil, the Caribbean, and the southern United States were booming in the early 19th century. The slave trade was profitable enough to keep merchants in it, and it contributed in some way to the expanding economy of western Europe. No one in the Atlantic world, slave or free, was entirely untouched or unaffected by it. It was also the major way in which Africa was linked to the increasingly integrated economy of the world.

African Societies, Slavery, and the Slave Trade

Europeans in the age of the slave trade sometimes justified the enslavement of Africans by pointing out that slavery already existed on that continent. However, although forms of bondage were ancient in Africa, and the Muslim trans-Sahara and Red Sea trades already were well established, the Atlantic trade interacted with and transformed these earlier aspects of slavery.

African societies had developed many forms of servitude, which varied from a peasant status to something much more like chattel slavery in which people were considered things: "property with a soul," as Aristotle put it. African states usually were nonegalitarian, and because in many African societies all land was owned by the state or the ruler, the control of slaves was one of the few ways, if not the only way, in which individuals or lineages could increase their wealth and status. Slaves were used as servants, concubines, soldiers, administrators, and field workers. In some cases, as in the ancient empire of Ghana and in Kongo, there were whole villages of enslaved dependants who were required to pay tribute to the ruler. The Muslim traders of west Africa who linked the forest region to the savanna had slave porters as well as villages of slaves to supply their caravans. In many situations, these forms of servitude were fairly benign and were an extension of lineage and kinship systems. In others, however, they were exploitive economic and social relations that reinforced the hierarchies of various African societies and allowed the nobles, senior lineages, and rulers to exercise their power. Among the forest states of west Africa, such as Benin, and in the Kongo kingdom in central Africa, slavery was already an important institution before the European arrival, but the Atlantic trade opened up new opportunities for expansion and intensification of slavery in those societies.

Despite great variation in African societies and the fact that slaves sometimes attained positions of command and trust, in most cases slaves were denied choice about their lives and actions. They were placed in dependent or inferior positions, and they were often considered aliens. It is important to remember that the enslavement of women was a central feature of African slavery. Although slaves were used in many ways in African societies, domestic slavery and the extension of lineages through the addition of female members remained important in many places. Some historians believe that the excess of women led to polygyny (having more than one wife at a time) and the creation of large harems by rulers and merchants, whose power was increased by this process, and the position of women was lowered in some societies.

In the Sudanic states of the savanna, Islamic concepts of slavery had been introduced. Slavery was viewed as a legitimate fate for nonbelievers but was illegal for Muslims. Despite the complaints of legal scholars such as Ahmad Baba of Timbuktu (1556–1627) against the enslavement of Muslims, many of the Sudanic states enslaved their captives, both pagan and Muslim. In the Niger valley, slave communities produced agricultural surpluses for the rulers and nobles of Songhay, Gao, and other states. Slaves were used for gold mining and salt production and as caravan workers in the Sahara. Slavery was a widely diffused form of labor control and wealth in Africa.

The existence of slavery in Africa and the preexisting trade in people allowed Europeans to mobilize the commerce in slaves quickly by tapping existing routes and supplies. In this venture

The slave trade influenced African forms of servitude and the social and political development of African states. Newly powerful states emerged in west Africa; in the Sudan and east Africa, slavery also produced long-term effects.

"A Defense of the Slave Trade," July 1740

Slavery and Human Society

Slavery is a very old and widespread institution. It has been found at different times all over the globe, among simple societies and in the great centers of civilization. In some of these societies, it has been a marginal or secondary form of labor, whereas in others it became the predominant labor form or "mode of production" (in the jargon of Marxist analysis). The need for labor beyond the capacity of the individual or the family unit is very old, and as soon as authority, law, or custom could be established to set the conditions for coercion, the tribe, the state, the priests, or some other group or institution extracted labor by force. Coerced labor could take different forms. There are important distinctions between indentured servants, convict laborers, debt-peons, and chattel slaves.

Although most societies placed some limits on the slaveholder's authority or power, the denial of the slave's control over his or her own labor and life choices was characteristic of this form of coercion throughout history. In most societies that had a form of chattel slavery, the slave was denied a sense of belonging in the society—the idea of kinship. The honor associated with family or lineage was the antithesis of slavery. The Old Testament figure Joseph might rise to a high position at pharaoh's court, and so might a vizier of a Turkish sultan, but as slaves they were instruments of their masters' will. In fact, because they were slaves and thus unconstrained by kinship or other ties and obligations, they could be trusted in positions of command.

Because slaves became nonpersons—or, as one modern author has put it, because they suffered a "social death"—it was always

> "To paraphrase English historian Charles Boxer, no people can enslave another for 400 years without developing an attitude of superiority."

easier to enslave "others" or "outsiders": those who were different in some way. Hebrews enslaved Canaanites, Greeks enslaved "barbarians," and Muslims made slaves of nonbelievers. If the difference between slave and master was readily seen, it made enforcement of slave status that much easier. Racism as such did not cause modern slavery, but differences in culture, language, color, and other physical characteristics always facilitated enslavement. The familiarity of Europeans and Muslims with black Africans in an enslaved status contributed to the development of modern racism. To paraphrase English historian Charles Boxer, no people can enslave another for 400 years without developing an attitude of superiority.

Slavery was not only a general phenomenon that existed in many societies. Rarely questioned on any grounds, it was seen as a necessary and natural phenomenon. Slavery is accepted in the texts of ancient India, the Old Testament, and the writings of classical Greece. Aristotle specifically argued that some people were born to rule and others to serve. In Christian theology, although all people might be free in spirit in the kingdom of God, servitude was considered a necessary reality. Voices might be raised arguing for fair treatment or against the enslavement of a particular group, but the condition of servitude usually was taken as part of the natural order of the world.

In this context, the attack on slavery in Western culture that grew from the Enlightenment and the social and economic changes in western Europe and its Atlantic colonies at the end of the 18th century was a remarkable turning point in world history. Some scholars believe that slavery was an outdated labor form that was incompatible with industrial capitalism and that is why it was abolished. Others hold that it was destroyed because its immorality be-

they were aided by the rulers of certain African states, who were anxious to acquire more slaves for themselves and to supply slaves to the Europeans in exchange for aid and commodities. In the 16th-century Kongo kingdom, the ruler had an army of 20,000 slaves as part of his household, and this gave him greater power than any Kongo ruler had ever held. In general, African rulers did not enslave their own people, except for crimes or in other unusual circumstances; rather, they enslaved their neighbors. Thus, expanding, centralizing states often were the major suppliers of slaves to the Europeans as well as to societies in which slavery was an important institution.

Slaving and African Politics

As one French agent put it, "The trade in slaves is the business of kings, rich men, and prime merchants." European merchants and royal officials were able to tap existing routes, markets, and institutions, but the new and constant demand also intensified enslavement in Africa and perhaps changed the nature of slavery itself in some African societies.

In the period between 1500 and 1750, as the gunpowder empires and expanding international commerce of Europe penetrated sub-Saharan Africa, existing states and societies often were transformed. As we saw in Chapter 13, the empire of Songhay controlled a vast region of the western savanna until its defeat by a Moroccan invasion in 1591, but for the most part the many states of central and western Africa were small and fragmented. This led to a situation of instability caused

Africa, 1500–1800 MAP

came all too obvious. In any case, its demise was quick. In about a century and a half, the moral and religious underpinning of chattel slavery was cut away and its economic justifications were questioned seriously. Although slavery lingered in at least a few places well into the 20th century, few people were willing to defend the institution publicly.

Although slavery historically existed in many places, it has become intimately associated with Africa because of the scope of the Atlantic slave trade and the importance of slavery in forming the modern world system. There was nothing inevitable about Africa's becoming the primary source of slaves in the modern world. Europeans did use Native American and European indentured workers when they could, but historical precedents, maritime technology, and availability combined to make Africa the source of labor for the expanding plantation colonies of Europe.

African slavery obviously played an important role in shaping the modern world. The African slave trade was one of the first truly international trades, and it created an easy access to labor that enabled Europeans to exploit the Americas. Some have argued that it was an important, even a necessary feature in the rise of capitalism and the international division of labor. Others disagree. In this question, as in nearly every other question about modern slavery, controversies still abound.

In the context of African history, the interpretation of slavery is still changing rapidly. A recent and careful estimate of the volume involved in the Atlantic trade (10–12 million) has been questioned seriously, especially by African scholars, who see this new figure as an attempt to downplay the exploitation of Africa. Another debate centers on the impact of the trade on the population and societies within Africa. The slave trade was important to the economy of the Atlantic, but how important was this external trade in Africa itself? Reacting to the preabolitionist European self-justifications that the slave trade was no great crime because Africans had long become familiar with slavery and were selling already enslaved people, early researchers argued that African slavery often was an extension of kinship or other forms of dependency and was quite unlike the chattel slavery of western Europe. But further research has demonstrated that in many African societies, slavery was an integral part of the economy, and although specific conditions sometimes differed greatly from those in the Americas, the servile condition in Africa had much in common with chattel slavery. For example, the Sokoto caliphate in the 19th century had a proportion of slaves similar to that in Brazil and the southern United States. Slave societies did exist in Africa.

Controversy rages over the extent to which the development of African slavery resulted from the long-term impact of the slave trade and the European demand for captive labor. African societies did not live in isolation from the pressures and examples of the world economy into which they were drawn. The extent to which that contact transformed slavery in Africa is now in question. These controversies among historians reflect current concerns and a realization that the present social and political situation in Africa and in many places in the Americas continues to bear the burden of a historical past in which slavery played an essential role. In evaluating slavery, as in all other historical questions, what we think about the present shapes our inquiry and our interpretation of the past.

QUESTIONS Why did Africa become the leading source of slaves in the early modern world economy? What are some of the leading issues in interpreting African slavery? What were the roles of Africans and Europeans in the early modern slave trade?

by competition and warfare as states tried to expand at the expense of their neighbors or to consolidate power by incorporating subject provinces. The warrior or soldier emerged in this situation as an important social type in states such as the Kongo kingdom and Dahomey as well as along the Zambezi River. The endless wars promoted the importance of the military and made the sale of captives into the slave trade an extension of the politics of regions of Africa. Sometimes, as among the Muslim states of the savanna or the Lake Chad region, wars took on a religious overtone of believers against nonbelievers, but in much of west and central Africa that was not the case. Some authors see this situation as a feature of African politics; others believe it was the result of European demand for new slaves. In either case, the result was the capture and sale of millions of human beings. Although increasing centralization and hierarchy could be seen in the enslaving African societies, a contrary trend of self-sufficiency and anti-authoritarian ideas developed among the peoples who bore the brunt of the slaving attacks.

One result of the presence of Europeans on the coast was a shift in the locus of power within Africa. Just as states such as Ghana and Songhay in the savanna took advantage of their position as intermediaries between the gold of the west African forests and the trans-Saharan trade routes, the states closer to the coast or in contact with the Europeans could play a similar role. Those right on the coast tried to monopolize the trade with Europeans, but European meddling in their internal affairs and European fears of any coastal power that became too strong blocked the creation of centralized states under the shadow of European forts. Just beyond the coast it was different. With access to European goods, especially firearms, iron, horses, cloth, tobacco, and other goods, western and central African kingdoms began to redirect trade toward the coast and to expand their influence. Some historians have written of a gun and slave cycle in which increased firepower allowed these states to expand over their neighbors, producing more slaves, which they traded for more guns. The result was unending warfare and the disruption of societies as the search for slaves pushed ever farther into the interior.

Asante and Dahomey

Perhaps the effects of the slave trade on African societies are best seen in some specific cases. Several large states developed in west Africa during the slave trade era. Each represented a response to the realities of the European presence and the process of state formation long under way in Africa. Rulers in these states grew in power and often surrounded themselves with ritual authority and a luxurious court life as a way of reinforcing the position that their armies had won (Figures 20.3 and 20.4).

In the area called the Gold Coast by the Europeans, the empire of **Asante** (Ashanti) rose to prominence in the period of the slave trade. The Asante were members of the Akan people (the major group of modern Ghana) who had settled in and around Kumasi, a region of gold and kola nut production that lay between the coast and the Hausa and Mande trading centers to the north. There were at least 20 small states, based on the matrilineal clans that were common to all the Akan peoples, but those of the Oyoko clan predominated. Their cooperation and their access to firearms after 1650 initiated a period of centralization and expansion. Under the vigorous **Osei Tutu** (d. 1717), the title **asantehene** (uh-SHAHN-teh-hee-nuh) was created to designate the supreme civil and religious leader. His golden stool became the symbol of an Asante union that was created by linking the many Akan clans under the authority of the asantehene but recognizing the autonomy of subordinate areas. An all-Asante council advised the ruler, and an ideology of unity was used to overcome the traditional clan divisions. With this new structure and a series of military reforms, conquest of the area began. By 1700, the Dutch on the coast realized that a new power had emerged, and they began to deal directly with it.

With control of the gold-producing zones and a constant supply of prisoners to be sold as slaves for more firearms, Asante maintained its power until the 1820s as the dominant state of the Gold Coast. Although gold continued to be a major item of export, by the end of the 17th century, slaves made up almost two-thirds of Asante's trade.

Farther to the east, in the area of the Bight of Benin (between the Volta and Benin rivers on what the Europeans called the Slave Coast), several large states developed. The kingdom of Benin

Asante Empire   Established in Gold Coast among Akan people settled around Kumasi; dominated by Oyoko clan; many clans linked under Osei Tutu after 1650.

Tutu, Osei   (r. 1675–1717) Member of Oyoko clan of Akan peoples in Gold Coast region of Africa; responsible for creating unified Asante Empire in 1701; utilized Western firearms.

asantehene   [uh-SHAHN-teh-hee-nuh] Title taken by ruler of Asante Empire; supreme civil and religious leader; authority symbolized by golden stool.

Figure 20.3 The annual yam harvest festival was an occasion when the power and authority of the Asante ruler could be displayed. The English observers who painted this scene were impressed by the might of this west African kingdom.

Figure 20.4 The size of African cities and the power of African rulers often impressed European observers. Here the city of Loango, capital of a kingdom on the Kongo coast, is depicted as a bustling urban center. At this time it was a major port in the slave trade.

was at the height of its power when the Europeans arrived. It traced its origins to the city of Ife and to the Yoruba peoples that were its neighbors, but it had become a separate and independent kingdom with its own well developed political and artistic traditions, especially in the casting of bronze. As early as 1516, the ruler, or *oba*, limited the slave trade from Benin, and for a long time most trade with Europeans was controlled directly by the king and was in pepper, textiles, and ivory rather than slaves. Eventually, European pressure and the goals of the Benin nobility combined to generate a significant slave trade in the 18th century, but Benin never made the slave trade its primary source of revenue or state policy.

The kingdom of **Dahomey,** which developed among the Fon (or Aja) peoples, had a different response to the European presence. It began to emerge as a power in the 17th century from its center at Abomey, about 70 miles from the coast. Its kings ruled with the advice of powerful councils, but by the 1720s access to firearms allowed the rulers to create an autocratic and sometimes brutal political regime based on the slave trade. In the 1720s, under King Agaja (1708–1740), the kingdom of Dahomey moved toward the coast, seizing in 1727 the port town of Whydah, which had attracted many European traders. Although Dahomey became to some extent a subject of the powerful neighboring Yoruba state of Oyo, whose cavalry and archers made it strong, Dahomey maintained its autonomy and turned increasingly to the cycle of firearms and slaves. The trade was controlled by the royal court, whose armies (including a regiment of women) were used to raid for more captives.

As Dahomey expanded it eliminated the royal families and customs of the areas it conquered and imposed its own traditions. This resulted in the formation of a unified state, which lasted longer than some of its neighbors. Well into the 19th century, Dahomey was a slaving state, and dependence on the trade in human beings had negative effects on the society as a whole. More than 1.8 million slaves were exported from the Bight of Benin between 1640 and 1890.

This emphasis on the slave trade should not obscure the creative process within many of the African states. The growing divine authority of the rulers paralleled the rise of absolutism in Europe. It led to the development of new political forms, some of which had the power to limit the role of the king. In the Yoruba state of Oyo, for example, a governing council shared power with the ruler. In some states, a balance of offices kept central power in check. In Asante the traditional

Dahomey Kingdom developed among Fon or Aja peoples in 17th century; center at Abomey 70 miles from coast; under King Agaja expanded to control coastline and port of Whydah by 1727; accepted Western firearms and goods in return for African slaves.

Figure 20.5 Portuguese soldiers serve as the base for this ivory carving done by West African craftsmen. Objects like these demonstrated the contact of European and African cultures.

(Saltcellar: Portuguese Figures. Photo: Stan Reis. The Metropolitan Museum of Art, New York, NY, USA. Image Copyright © The Metropolitan Museum of Art/Art Resource, NY.)

Luo Nilotic people who migrated from upper Nile valley; established dynasty among existing Bantu population in lake region of central eastern Africa; center at Bunyoro.

village chiefs and officials whose authority was based on their lineage were increasingly challenged by new officials appointed by the asantehene as a state bureaucracy began to form.

The creativity of these societies was also seen in traditional arts. In many places, crafts such as bronze casting, woodcarving, and weaving flourished. Guilds of artisans developed in many societies, and their specialization produced crafts executed with great skill. In Benin and the Yoruba states, for example, remarkable and lifelike sculptures in wood and ivory continued to be produced. Often, however, the best artisans labored for the royal court, producing objects designed to honor the ruling family and reinforce the civil and religious authority of the king. This was true in architecture, weaving, and the decorative arts as well. Much of this artistic production also had a religious function or contained religious symbolism; African artists made the spiritual world visually apparent.

Europeans came to appreciate African arts and skills. In the 16th century, the Portuguese began to employ African artists from Benin, Sierra Leone, and Kongo to work local ivory into ladles, saltcellars (containers), and other decorative objects that combined African and European motifs in beautifully carved designs (Figure 20.5). Although works were commissioned by Europeans and sometimes including European religious and political symbols, African artists found ways to incorporate traditional symbols and themes from motherhood to royal power. Many of these objects ended up in the collections of nobles and kings throughout Renaissance Europe. They demonstrated the growing contact between Africa and the wider world.

East Africa and the Sudan

West Africa obviously was the region most directly influenced by the trans-Atlantic slave trade, but there and elsewhere in Africa, long-term patterns of society and economy continued and intersected with the new external influences. On the east coast of Africa, the Swahili trading cities continued their commerce in the Indian Ocean, adjusting to the military presence of the Portuguese and the Ottoman Turks. Trade to the interior continued to bring ivory, gold, and a steady supply of slaves. Many of these slaves were destined for the harems and households of Arabia and the Middle East, but a small number were carried away by the Europeans for their plantation colonies. The Portuguese and Indo-Portuguese settlers along the Zambezi River in Mozambique used slave soldiers to increase their territories, and certain groups in interior east Africa specialized in supplying ivory and slaves to the east African coast. Europeans did establish some plantation-style colonies on islands such as Mauritius in the Indian Ocean, and these depended on the east African slave trade.

On Zanzibar and other offshore islands, and later on the coast itself, Swahili, Indian, and Arabian merchants followed the European model and set up clove-producing plantations using African slave laborers. Some of the plantations were large, and by the 1860s Zanzibar had a slave population of about 100,000. The sultan of Zanzibar alone owned more than 4000 slaves in 1870. Slavery became a prominent feature of the east African coast, and the slave trade from the interior to these plantations and to the traditional slave markets of the Red Sea continued until the end of the 19th century.

Much less is known about the interior of eastern Africa. Large and small kingdoms were supported by the well watered and heavily populated region of the great lakes of the interior. Bantu speakers predominated, but many peoples inhabited the region. Linguistic and archeological evidence suggests that pastoralist peoples from the upper Nile valley with a distinctive late Iron Age technology moved southward into what is today western Kenya and Uganda, where they came into contact with Bantu speakers and with the farmers and herders who spoke another group of languages called Cushitic. The Bantu states absorbed the immigrants, even when the newcomers established ruling dynasties. Later Nilotic migrations, of people who spoke languages of the Nilotic group, especially of the **Luo** peoples, resulted in the construction of related dynasties among the states in the area of the large lakes of east central Africa. At Bunyoro, the Luo eventually established a ruling dynasty among the existing Bantu population. This kingdom exercised considerable power in the 16th and 17th centuries. Other related states formed in the region. In Buganda, near Lake Victoria, a strong monarchy ruled a heterogeneous population and dominated the region in the 16th century. These developments in the interior, as important as they were for the history of the region, were less influenced by the growing contact with the outside world than were other regions of Africa.

Across the continent in the northern savanna at the end of the 18th century, the process of Islamization, which had been important in the days of the Mali and Songhay empires, entered a new and violent stage that not only linked Islamization to the external slave trade and the growth of slavery in Africa but also produced other long-term effects in the region. After the breakup of Songhay in the 16th century, several successor states had developed. Some, such as the Bambara kingdom of Segu, were pagan. Others, such as the Hausa kingdoms in northern Nigeria, were ruled by Muslim royal families and urban aristocracies but continued to contain large numbers of animist subjects, most of whom were rural peasants. In these states the degree of Islamization was slight, and an accommodation between Muslims and animists was achieved.

Beginning in the 1770s, Muslim reform movements began to sweep the western Sudan. Religious brotherhoods advocating a purifying Sufi variant of Islam extended their influence throughout the Muslim trade networks in the Senegambia region and the western Sudan. This movement had an intense impact on the **Fulani** (Fulbe), a pastoral people who were spread across a broad area of the western Sudan.

Fulani Pastoral people of western Sudan; adopted purifying Sufi variant of Islam; under Usuman Dan Fodio in 1804, launched revolt against Hausa kingdoms; established state centered on Sokoto.

In 1804 Usuman Dan Fodio, a studious and charismatic Muslim Fulani scholar, began to preach the reformist ideology in the Hausa kingdoms. His movement became a revolution when in 1804, seeing himself as God's instrument, he preached a jihad against the Hausa kings, who, he felt, were not following the teachings of Muhammad. A great upheaval followed in which the Fulani took control of most of the Hausa states of northern Nigeria in the western Sudan. A new kingdom, based in the city of Sokoto, developed under Dan Fodio's son and brother. The Fulani expansion was driven not only by religious zeal but by political ambitions, as the attack on the well established Muslim kingdom of Bornu demonstrated. The result of this upheaval was the creation of a powerful Sokoto state under a caliph, whose authority was established over cities such as Kano and Zaria and whose rulers became emirs of provinces within the Sokoto caliphate.

By the 1840s, the effects of Islamization and the Fulani expansion were felt across much of the interior of west Africa. New political units were created, a reformist Islam that tried to eliminate pagan practices spread, and social and cultural changes took place in the wake of these changes. Literacy became more widely dispersed, and new centers of trade, such as Kano, emerged in this period. Later jihads established other new states along similar lines. All of these changes had long-term effects on the region of the western Sudan.

These upheavals, moved by religious, political, and economic motives, were affected by the external pressures on Africa. They fed into the ongoing processes of the external slave trade and the development of slavery within African societies. Large numbers of captives resulting from the wars were exported down to the coast for sale to the Europeans, while another stream of slaves crossed the Sahara to north Africa. In the western and central Sudan, the level of slave labor rose, especially in the larger towns and along the trade routes. Slave villages, supplying royal courts and merchant activities as well as a plantation system, developed to produce peanuts and other crops. Slave women spun cotton and wove cloth for sale, slave artisans worked in the towns, and slaves served the caravan traders, but most slaves did agricultural labor. By the late 19th century, regions of the savanna contained large slave populations—in some places as much as 30 to 50 percent of the whole population. From the Senegambia region of Futa Jallon, across the Niger and Senegal basins, and to the east of Lake Chad, slavery became a central feature of the Sudanic states and remained so through the 19th century.

White Settlers and Africans in Southern Africa

One area of Africa little affected by the slave trade in the early modern period was the southern end of the continent. As we saw in Chapter 8, this region was still occupied by non-Bantu hunting peoples, the San (Bushmen); by the Khoikhoi (Hottentots), who lived by hunting and sheep herding; and, after contact with the Bantu, by cattle-herding peoples. Peoples practicing farming and using iron tools were living south of the Limpopo River by the 3rd century C.E. Probably Bantu speakers, they spread southward and established their villages and cattle herds in the fertile lands along the eastern coast, where rainfall was favorable to their agricultural and pastoral way of life. The drier western regions toward the Kalahari Desert were left to the Khoikhoi (KOHWEE-kohwee) and San.

In southern Africa, a Dutch colony eventually brought Europeans into conflict with Africans, especially the southern Bantu-speaking peoples. One of these groups, the Zulu, created under Shaka a powerful chiefdom during the early 19th century in a process of expansion that affected the whole region.

Mixed farming and pastoralism spread throughout the region in a complex process that involved migration, peaceful contacts, and warfare.

By the 16th century, Bantu-speaking peoples occupied much of the eastern regions of southern Africa. They practiced agriculture and herding; worked iron and copper into tools, weapons, and adornments; and traded with their neighbors. They spoke related languages such as Tswana (TSWAH-nuh) and Sotho (SOH-toh) as well as the Nguni (uhng-GOO-nee) languages such as Zulu and Xhosa (KOH-suh). Among the Sotho, villages might have contained as many as 200 people; the Nguni lived in hamlets made up of a few extended families. Men worked as artisans and herders; women did the farming and housework and sometimes organized their labor communally.

Politically, chiefdoms of various sizes—many of them small, but a few with as many as 50,000 inhabitants—characterized the southern Bantu peoples. Chiefs held power with the support of relatives and with the acceptance of the people, but there was great variation in chiefly authority. The Bantu-speaking peoples' pattern of political organization and the splitting off of junior lineages to form new villages created a process of expansion that led to competition for land and the absorption of newly conquered groups. This situation became intense at the end of the 18th century, either because of the pressures and competition for foreign trade through the Portuguese outposts on the east African coast or because of the growth of population among the southern Bantu. In any case, the result was farther expansion southward into the path of another people who had arrived in southern Africa.

In 1652 the Dutch East India Company established a colony at the Cape of Good Hope to serve as a provisioning post for ships sailing to Asia. Large farms developed on the fertile lands around this colony. The Cape Colony depended on slave labor brought from Indonesia and Asia for a while, but it soon enslaved local Africans as well. Expansion of the colony and its labor needs led to a series of wars with the San and Khoikhoi populations, who were pushed farther to the north and west. By the 1760s, the Dutch, or Boer, farmers had crossed the Orange River in search of new lands. They saw the fertile plains and hills as theirs, and they saw the Africans as intruders and a possible source of labor. Competition and warfare resulted. By about 1800 the Cape Colony had about 17,000 settlers (or Afrikaners, as they came to be called), 26,000 slaves, and 14,000 Khoikhoi.

As the Boers were pushing northward, the southern Bantu were extending their movement to the south. Matters were also complicated by European events when Great Britain seized the Cape Colony in 1795 and then took it under formal British control in 1815. While the British government helped the settlers to clear out Africans from potential farming lands, government attempts to limit the Boer settlements and their use of African labor were unsuccessful. Meanwhile, competition for farming and grazing land led to a series of wars between the settlers and the Bantu during the early 19th century.

Great Trek Movement of Boer settlers in Cape Colony of southern Africa to escape influence of British colonial government in 1834; led to settlement of regions north of Orange River and Natal.

Various government measures, the accelerating arrival of English-speaking immigrants, and the lure of better lands caused groups of Boers to move to the north. These *voortrekkers* moved into lands occupied by the southern Nguni, eventually creating a number of autonomous Boer states. After 1834, when Britain abolished slavery and imposed restrictions on landholding, groups of Boers staged their **Great Trek** far to the north to be free of government interference. This movement eventually brought them across the Orange River and into Natal on the more fertile east coast, which the Boers believed to be only sparsely inhabited by Africans. They did not realize or care that the lack of population resulted from a great military upheaval taking place among the Bantu peoples of the region.

The Mfecane and the Zulu Rise to Power

Among the Nguni peoples, major changes had taken place. A unification process had begun in some of the northern chiefdoms, and a new military organization had emerged. In 1818 leadership fell to Shaka, a brilliant military tactician, who reformed the loose forces into regiments organized by lineage and age. Iron discipline and new tactics were introduced, including the use of a short stabbing spear to be used at close range. The army was made a permanent institution, and the regiments were housed together in separate villages. The fighting men were allowed to marry only after they had completed their service.

Shaka's own Zulu chiefdom became the center of this new military and political organization, which began to absorb or destroy its neighbors (Figure 20.6). Shaka demonstrated talent as a

Figure 20.6 This Zulu royal kraal, drawn in the 1830s, gives some idea of the power of the Zulu at the time that Shaka was forging Zulu dominance during the Mfecane.

politician, destroying the ruling families of the groups he incorporated into the growing Zulu state. He ruled with an iron hand, destroying his enemies, acquiring their cattle, and crushing any opposition. His policies brought power to the Zulu, but his erratic and cruel behavior also earned him enemies among his own people. Although he was assassinated in 1828, Shaka's reforms remained in place, and his successors built on the structure he had created. Zulu power was still growing in the 1840s, and the Zulu remained the most impressive military force in black Africa until the end of the century.

The rise of the Zulu and other Nguni chiefdoms was the beginning of the **mfecane** (uhm-feh-KAH-nee), or wars of crushing and wandering. As Zulu control expanded, a series of campaigns and forced migrations led to constant fighting as other peoples sought to survive by fleeing, emulating, or joining the Zulu. Groups spun off to the north and south, raiding the Portuguese on the coast, clashing with the Europeans to the south, and fighting with neighboring chiefdoms. New African states, such as the **Swazi,** that adapted aspects of the Zulu model emerged among the survivors. One state, **Lesotho** (luh-SOH-toh), successfully resisted the Zulu example. It combined Sotho and Nguni speakers and defended itself against Nguni armies. It eventually developed as a kingdom far less committed to military organization, one in which the people had a strong influence on their leaders.

The whole of the southern continent, from the Cape Colony to Lake Malawi, had been thrown into turmoil by raiding parties, remnants, and refugees. Superior firepower allowed the Boers to continue to hold their lands, but it was not until the Zulu Wars of the 1870s that Zulu power was crushed by Great Britain, and even then only at great cost. During that process, the basic patterns of conflict between Africans and Europeans in the largest settler colony on the continent were created. These patterns included competition between settlers and Africans for land, the expanding influence of European government control, and the desire of Europeans to use Africans as laborers.

mfecane [uhm-feh-KAH-nee] Wars of 19th century in southern Africa; created by Zulu expansion under Shaka; revolutionized political organization of southern Africa.

Swazi New African state formed on model of Zulu chiefdom; survived mfecane.

Lesotho [luh-SOH-toh] Southern African state that survived mfecane; not based on Zulu model; less emphasis on military organization, less authoritarian government.

The African Diaspora

The slave trade was the means by which the history of the Americas and Africa became linked and a principal way in which African societies were drawn into the world economy. The import into Africa of European firearms, Indian textiles, Indonesian cowrie shells, and American tobacco in return for African ivory, gold, and especially slaves demonstrated Africa's integration into the mercantile structure of the world. Africans involved in the trade learned to deal effectively with this situation. Prices of slaves rose steadily in the 18th century, and the terms of trade increasingly favored the African dealers. In many African ports, such as Whydah, Porto Novo, and Luanda, African or Afro-European communities developed that specialized in the slave trade and used this position to advantage.

Despite African resistance to enslavement, the slave trade and the horrifying Middle Passage carried millions of Africans from their original homelands. In the Americas, especially in plantation colonies, they became a large segment of the population, and African cultures were adapted to new environments and conditions.

Slave Lives

For the slaves themselves, slavery meant the destruction of their villages or their capture in war, separation from friends and family, and then the forced march to an interior trading town or to the slave pens at the coast. Conditions were deadly; perhaps as many as one-third of the captives died along the way or in the slave pens. Eventually the slaves were loaded onto the ships. Cargo sizes varied and could go as high as 700 slaves crowded into the dank, unsanitary conditions of the slave ships, but most cargoes were smaller. Overcrowding was less of a factor in mortality than the length of the voyage or the point of origin in Africa; the Bights of Benin and Biafra were particularly dangerous. The average mortality rate for slaves varied over time, but it ran at about 18 percent or so until the 18th century, when it declined somewhat. Still, losses could be catastrophic on individual ships, as on a Dutch ship in 1737, where 700 of the 716 slaves died on the voyage.

The **Middle Passage,** or slave voyage to the Americas, was traumatic. Taken from their homes, branded, confined, and shackled, the Africans faced not only the dangers of poor hygiene, dysentery, disease, and bad treatment but also the fear of being beaten or worse by the Europeans. Their situation sometimes led to suicide or resistance and mutiny on the ships. However traumatic, the Middle Passage certainly did not strip Africans of their culture, and they arrived in the Americas retaining their languages, beliefs, artistic traditions, and memories of their past.

Diagram of Slave Ship Filled for Middle Passage

Middle Passage   Slave voyage from Africa to the Americas (16th–18th centuries); generally a traumatic experience for black slaves, although it failed to strip Africans of their culture.

Africans in the Americas

The slaves carried across the Atlantic were brought mainly to the plantations and mines of the Americas. Landed estates using large amounts of labor, often coerced, became characteristic of American agriculture, at first in sugar production and later for rice, cotton, and tobacco. The plantation system already used for producing sugar on the Atlantic islands of Spain and Portugal was transferred to the New World. After attempts to use Native American laborers in places such as Brazil and Hispaniola, Africans were brought in. West Africans, coming from societies in which herding, metallurgy, and intensive agriculture were widely practiced, were sought by Europeans for the specialized tasks of making sugar. In the English colonies of Barbados and Virginia, indentured servants from England eventually were replaced by enslaved Africans when new crops, such as sugar, were introduced or when indentured servants became less available.

In any case, the plantation system of farming with a dependent or enslaved workforce characterized the production of many tropical and semitropical crops in demand in Europe, and thus the plantation became the locus of African and American life. But slaves did many other things as well, from mining to urban occupations as artisans, street vendors, and household servants. In short, there was almost no occupation that slaves did not perform, although most were agricultural laborers (Figure 20.7).

American Slave Societies

Each American slave-based society reflected the variations of its European origin and its component African cultures, but there were certain similarities and common features. Each recognized distinctions between African-born **saltwater slaves,** who were almost invariably black (by European standards)

saltwater slaves   Slaves transported from Africa; almost invariably black.

An African's Description of the Middle Passage

During the era of the slave trade, enslaved Africans by one means or another succeeded in telling their stories. These accounts, with their specific details of the injustice and inhumanities of slavery, became particularly useful in the abolitionist crusade. The autobiography of Frederick Douglass is perhaps the most famous of these accounts. The biography of Olaudah Equiano, is similarly reknown. In it Equiano states that he is an Ibo from what is today eastern Nigeria on the Niger River and he presents a personal description of enslavement in Africa and the terrors of the Middle Passage. In the story, Equiano and his sister were kidnapped in 1756 by African slave hunters and sold to British slave traders. Separated from his sister, Equiano was carried to the West Indies and later to Virginia, where he became servant to a naval officer. He traveled widely on his master's military campaigns and was later sold to a Philadelphia Quaker merchant, who eventually allowed him to buy his freedom. Later, he moved to England and became an active member in the movement to end slavery and the slave trade. His biography was published in 1789. The political uses of this kind of biography and Equiano's association with the abolitionists should caution us against accepting the account at face value. Recently questions have arisen over his place of birth which may have been the Carolinas, so that his descriptions of Africa were based on what he heard or read rather than on his personal experience, but his book was a sensation and widely read and translated. It seemed to convey the personal shock and anguish of those caught in the slave trade.

The first object which saluted my eyes when I arrived on the coast was the sea, and a slaveship, which was riding at anchor, and waiting for its cargo. These filled me with astonishment, which was soon converted into terror, which I am yet at a loss to describe, nor the then feelings of my mind. When I was carried on board I was immediately handled, and tossed up, to see if I were sound, by some of the crew; and I was now persuaded that I had got into a world of bad spirits, and that they were going to kill me. Their complexions too differing so much from ours, their long hair, and the language they spoke, which was very different from any I had ever heard, united to confirm me in this belief. Indeed, such were the horrors of my views and fears at that moment, that if ten thousand worlds had been my own, I would have freely parted with them all to have exchanged my condition with that of the meanest slave in my own country. When I looked round the ship too, and saw a large furnace or copper boiler, and a multitude of black people of every description chained together, every one of their countenances expressing dejection and sorrow, quite overpowered with horror and anguish, I fell motionless on the deck and fainted. When I recovered a little, I found some black people about me, who I believed were some of those who brought me on board, and had been receiving their pay; they talked to me in order to cheer me, but all in vain. I asked them if we were not to be eaten by those white men with horrible looks, red faces, and long hair. They told me I was not.... I now saw myself deprived of all chance of returning to my native country, or even the least glimpse of hope of gaining the shore, which I now considered as friendly; and I even wished for my former slavery, in prefer-ence to my present situation, which was filled with horrors of every kind, still heightened by my ignorance of what I was to undergo. I was not long suffered to indulge my grief; I was soon put down under decks, and there I received such a salutation in my nostrils as I had never experienced in my life; so that with the loathsomeness of the stench, and the crying together, I became so sick and low that I was not able to eat, nor had I the least desire to taste anything. I now wished for the last friend, death, to relieve me; but soon, to my grief two white men offered me eatables; and on my refusing to eat, one of them held me fast by the hands, and laid me across, I think, the windlass, and tied my feet while the other flogged me severely. I had never experienced anything of this kind before; and, although not being used to the water, I naturally feared that element the first time I saw it; yet, nevertheless, could I have got over the nettings, I would have jumped over the side; but I could not; and, besides the crew used to watch us very closely who were not chained down to the decks, lest we should leap into the water; and I have seen some of these poor African prisoners most severely cut for attempting to do so, and hourly whipped for not eating. This indeed was often the case with myself. In a little time after amongst the poor chained men, I found some of my own nation, which in a small degree gave ease to my mind. I inquired of them what was to be done with us? They gave me to understand we were to be carried to these white people's country to work for them. I then was a little revived, and thought, if it were no worse than working, my situation was not so desperate; but still I feared I should be put to death, the white people looked and acted, as I thought, in so savage a manner; for I had never seen among any people such instances of brutal cruelty; and this was not only shown to us blacks, but also to some of the whites themselves....

At last when the ship we were in had got in all her cargo, they made ready with many fearful noises, and we were all put under deck, so that we could not see how they managed the vessel. But this disappointment was the least of my sorrow. The stench of the hold while we were on the coast was so intolerably loathsome, that it was dangerous to remain there for any time, and some of us had been permitted to stay on deck for the fresh air; but now the whole ship's cargo was confined together, it became absolutely pestilential. The closeness of the place, and the heat of the climate, added to the number in the ship, which was so crowded that each had scarcely room to turn himself, almost suffocated us. This produced copious perspirations, so that the air soon became unfit for respiration, from a variety of loathsome smells, and brought on a sickness amongst the slaves, of which many died, thus falling victims to the improvident avarice, as I may call it, of their purchasers. This wretched situation was again aggravated by the galling of the chains, now become insupportable; and the filth of the necessary tubs, into which the children fell, and were almost suffocated. The shrieks of the women, and the groans of the dying, rendered the whole a scene of horror almost inconceivable.

QUESTIONS In what ways does Equiano's description contradict a previous understanding of the slave trade? What opportunities existed for the captives to resist? What effect might the experience of Africans on the slave ships have had on their perceptions of each other and of the Europeans?

Figure 20.7 Africans performed all kinds of labor in the Americas, from domestic service to mining and shipbuilding. Most worked on plantations like this sugar mill in the Caribbean.

Creole slaves American-born descendants of saltwater slaves; result of sexual exploitation of slave women or process of miscegenation.

and their American-born descendants, the **Creole slaves,** some of whom were mulattos as a result of the sexual exploitation of slave women or other forms of miscegenation. In all American slave societies, a hierarchy of status evolved in which free whites were at the top, slaves were at the bottom, and free people of color had an intermediate position. In this sense, color and "race" played a role in American slavery it had not played in Africa. Among the slaves, slaveholders also created a hierarchy based on origin and color. Creole and especially mulatto slaves were given more opportunities to acquire skilled jobs or to work as house servants rather than in the fields or mines. They were also more likely to win their freedom by manumission, the voluntary freeing of slaves.

This hierarchy was a creation of the slaveholders and did not necessarily reflect perceptions among the slaves. There is evidence that important African nobles or religious leaders, who for one reason or another were sold into slavery, continued to exercise authority within the slave community. Still, the distinctions between Creole and African slaves tended to divide that community, as did the distinctions between different African groups whose members maintained their ties and affiliations in America. Many of the slave rebellions in the Caribbean and Brazil were organized along African ethnic and political lines. In Jamaica there were several Akan-led rebellions in the 18th century, and the largest escaped slave community in 17th-century Brazil apparently was organized and led by Angolans.

Although economic factors imposed similarities, the slave-based societies also varied in their composition. In early 17th-century Lima, Peru, the capital of Spain's colony in South America, blacks outnumbered Europeans. In the 18th century, on the Caribbean islands where the indigenous population had died out or had been exterminated and where few Europeans settled, Africans and their descendants formed the vast majority. In Jamaica and St. Domingue, slaves made up more than 80 percent of the population; a large proportion of them were African born. Brazil also had large numbers of imported Africans, but its more diverse population and economy, as well as a tradition of manumitting slaves and high levels of miscegenation, meant that slaves made up only about 35 percent of the population. However, free people of color, the descendants of former slaves, made up about another one-third, so that together slaves and free colored people made up two-thirds of the total population.

North American cities such as Charleston and New Orleans also developed a large slave and free African population. But the southern colonies of British North America differed significantly

The Cloth of Kings in an Atlantic Perspective

The various artistic traditions of West Africa not only attracted the attention of European traders, but also flourished as new and powerful states were formed whose monarchs and attendant courtiers demanded objects of value for rituals and the activities of daily life. Skilled artisans produced objects of wood, ivory, iron, and pottery and textiles. Among the finest examples were the kente cloths of the Asante peoples from the region of modern-day Ghana.

With the rise of a powerful Asante state in the seventeenth century, traditional weaving techniques were turned to the making of royal and sacred cloths, often incorporating sophisticated designs, geometric patterns, and vivid colors. Usually using local cotton, trade with Europeans or across the Sahara often brought silk to Ghana which was used in the royal fabrics and new colors were introduced with the importation of dyes from Europe and India. A traditional art form was thus amplified and expanded using materials brought by the long-distance trade. Patterns and colors conveyed symbolic meanings, blue for peacefulness, silver for purity, red for sacrifice, and certain patterns were reserved for the king alone. Over time, the traditional exclusivity diminished, and the use of kente cloth was adopted as a national symbol, although historically it was usually reserved for important occasions and ritual purposes. Kente cloth has become today one of the most recognizable traditional arts of Africa and a source of pride for people of African origin in the diaspora.

QUESTIONS: In what way do artistic traditions depend on the patronage of those in power? Has this been the case in other societies in history? Kente was used to convey meanings, symbols, and proverbs. Do such things change over time? What has made kente cloth so popular today?

from the Caribbean and Brazil, by depending less on imported Africans because of natural population growth among the slaves. In North America, Creole slaves predominated, but manumission was less common, and free people of color made up less than 10 percent of the total Afro-American population. The result was that slavery in North America was less influenced by Africa. By the mid-18th century, the slave population in most places in North America was reproducing itself. By 1850, fewer than 1 percent of the slaves there were African born. The combination of natural growth and the small direct trade from Africa reduced the degree of African cultural reinforcement.

The People and Gods in Exile

Africans brought as slaves to the Americas faced a peculiar series of problems. Working conditions were exhausting, and life for most slaves often was difficult and short. Family formation was made difficult because of the general shortage of female slaves; the ratio of men to women was as much as three to one in some places. To this was added the insecurity of slave status: family members might be separated by sale or by a master's whim. Still, most slaves lived in family units, even though their marriages were not always sanctioned by the religion of their masters. Throughout the Americas, wherever Africans were brought, aspects of their language, religion, artistic sensibilities, and other cultural elements survived. To some extent, the amount of continuity depended on the intensity and volume of the slave trade from a particular area. Some slaveholders tried to mix up the slaves on their plantations so that strong African identities would be lost, but colonial dependence on slavers who consistently dealt with the same region tended to undercut such policies. In the Americas, African slaves had to adapt and to incorporate other African peoples' ideas and customs into their own lives. Moreover, the ways and customs of the masters were also imposed. Thus, what emerged as Afro-American culture reflected specific African roots adapted to a new reality. Scholars at present hotly debate the relative extent to which African identities (Yoruba, Kongo, Igbo, etc) and practices like marriage customs, political concepts, or religious beliefs continued in the New World. While some emphasize continuities, others believe that African cultures provided a framework but that emphasis should be placed on the creativity inherent in the creation of Afro-American "creole" cultures.

Religion provides a clear example an obvious example of continuity and adaptation. Slaves were converted to Catholicism by the Spaniards and the Portuguese, sometimes in Africa itself, and they showed fervent devotion as members of Black Catholic brotherhoods, some of which were organized by African origins. In North America and the British Caribbean they joined Protestant denominations. Still, African religious ideas and practices did not die out. In the English islands, **obeah** was the name given to the African religious practices, and the men and women knowledgeable in them were held in high regard within the community. In Brazilian **candomblé** (Yoruba) and Haitian **vodun** (Aja), fully developed versions of African religions flourished and continue today, despite attempts by national governments or state churches to suppress them.

The reality of the Middle Passage meant that religious ideas were easier to transfer than the institutional aspects of religion. Without religious specialists or a priestly class, aspects of African religions were changed by contact with other African peoples as well as with colonial society. In many cases, slaves held their new faith in Christianity and their African beliefs at the same time, and tried to fuse the two. For Muslim Africans this was more difficult. In 1835 in Bahia, the largest slave rebellion in Brazil was organized by Muslim Yoruba and Hausa slaves and directed against the whites and against nonbelievers.

Resistance and rebellion were other aspects of African American history. Recalcitrance, running away, and direct confrontation were present wherever slaves were held. As early as 1508, African runaways disrupted communications on Hispaniola, and in 1527, a plot to rebel was uncovered in Mexico City. Throughout the Americas, communities of runaway slaves formed. In Jamaica, Colombia, Venezuela, Haiti, and Brazil, runaway communities were persistent and sometimes large. In Brazil during the 17th century, **Palmares** (pahl-MAHR-ehs), an enormous runaway slave kingdom with five main villages and a population of perhaps 8000 to 10,000 people, resisted Portuguese and Dutch attempts to destroy it for a century. In Jamaica the runaway Maroons were able to gain some independence and a recognition of their freedom. So-called ethnic slave rebellions organized by a particular African group were common in the Caribbean and Brazil in the 18th century. In North America, where reinforcement from the slave trade was less continuous, resistance was also important, but it was based less on African origins or ethnicities.

Perhaps the most remarkable story of African American resistance is found in the forests of **Suriname,** a former Dutch plantation colony. There, large numbers of slaves ran off in the 18th century and mounted an almost perpetual war in the rain forest against the various expeditions sent to hunt them down. Those captured were brutally executed, but eventually a truce developed. Today about 50,000 Maroon descendants still live in Suriname and French Guiana. The Suriname Maroons maintained many aspects of their west African background in terms of language, kinship relations, and religious beliefs, but these were fused with new forms drawn from European and American Indian contacts. From this fusion, the Maroons created a truly Afro-American culture (Figure 20.8).

The End of the Slave Trade and the Abolition of Slavery

The end of the Atlantic slave trade and the abolition of slavery in the Atlantic world resulted from economic, political, and religious changes in Europe and its overseas American colonies and former colonies. These changes, which were manifestations of the

obeah African religious ideas and practices in the English and French Caribbean islands.

candomblé African religious ideas and practices in Brazil, particularly among the Yoruba people.

vodun African religious ideas and practices among descendants of African slaves in Haiti.

Palmares [pahl-MAHR-ehs] Kingdom of runaway slaves with a population of 8000 to 10,000 people; located in Brazil during the 17th century; leadership was

Suriname Formerly a Dutch plantation colony on the coast of South America; location of runaway slave kingdom in 18th century; able to retain independence despite attempts to crush guerrilla resistance.

Figure 20.8 African, American, or both? In Suriname, descendants of escaped slaves maintain many aspects of African culture but have adapted, modified, and transformed them in various ways. This wooden door shows the imaginative skills of African American carvers.

Enlightenment, the age of revolution, Christian revivalism, and perhaps the Industrial Revolution, were external to Africa, but once again they determined the pace and nature of change within Africa.

Like much else about the history of slavery, there is disagreement about the end of the slave trade. It is true that some African societies began to export other commodities, such as peanuts, cotton, and palm oil, which made their dependence on the slave trade less important, but the supply of slaves to European merchants was not greatly affected by this development. In general, the British plantation economies were booming in the period from 1790 to 1830, and plantations in Cuba, Brazil, and the southern United States flourished in the decades that followed. Thus, it is difficult to find a direct and simple link between economic self-interest and the movement to suppress the slave trade.

Opponents of slavery and the brutality of the trade had appeared in the mid-18th century, in relation to new intellectual movements in the West. Philosopher Jean-Jacques Rousseau in France and political economist Adam Smith in England both wrote against it. Whereas in ancient Rome during the spread of Christianity and Islam, and in 16th-century Europe, the enslavement of "barbarians" or nonbelievers was seen as positive—a way to civilize others—slavery during the European Enlightenment and bourgeois revolution came to be seen as backward and immoral. The slave trade was particularly criticized. It was the symbol of slavery's inhumanity and cruelty.

An African Pamphleteer Attacks Slavery (1787)

England, as the major maritime power of the period, was the key to the end of the slave trade. Under the leadership of religious humanitarians, such as John Wesley and **William Wilberforce,** an abolitionist movement gained strength against the merchants and the West Indies interests. After much parliamentary debate, the British slave trade was abolished in 1807. Having set out on this course, Britain tried to impose abolition of the slave trade on other countries throughout the Atlantic. Spain and Portugal were pressured to gradually suppress the trade, and the British navy was used to enforce these agreements by capturing illegal slave ships. By the 19th century, the moral and intellectual justifications that had supported the age of the slave trade had worn thin and the movement to abolish slavery was growing in the Atlantic world. In this process, the writings of ex-slaves like Baquaqua or Equiano also contributed to the change of opinion as did the resistance of slaves to their captivity like the shipboard revolt on the *Amistad* in 1839, a case heard by the Supreme Court of the United States that focused attention on the inherent legal contradictions of slavery. The full end of slavery in the Americas did not occur until 1888, when it was abolished in Brazil.

Wilberforce, William   British statesman and reformer; leader of abolitionist movement in English parliament that led to end of English slave trade in 1807.

Global Connections

Africa and the African Diaspora in World Context

Africa was drawn into the world economy in the era of the slave trade, at first slowly, but with increasing intensity after 1750. Its incorporation produced differing effects on African societies, reinforcing authority in some places, creating new states in others, and sometimes provoking social, religious, and political reactions. Although many aspects of African life followed traditional patterns, contact with the world economy forced many African societies to adjust in ways that often placed them at a disadvantage and facilitated Europe's colonization of Africa in the 19th century. Well into the 20th century, as forced labor continued in Africa under European direction, the legacy of the slave trade era proved slow to die.

Part of that legacy was the movement of millions of Africans far from their continent. Taken against their will, they and their descendants drew on the cultures and practices of Africa as they coped with slavery. Eventually, they created vibrant new cultural forms, which along with their labor and skills contributed to the growth of new societies. Africans were pulled into the developing Atlantic system of exchange of people, commodities, diseases, plants, animals, and ideas. They and their African American descendants moved between the continents not only as slaves, but also as ambassadors, soldiers, missionaries, merchants, and mariners, integral elements in a developing world economy.

Further Readings

Aside from the general books on Africa already mentioned in the Further Readings for previous chapters, some specific readings are particularly useful. Martin Hall, *The Changing Past: Farmers, Kings, and Traders in Southern Africa* (1987), discusses the use of archeological evidence in African history. D. Birmingham and Phyllis Martin, eds., *History of Central Africa,* 3 vols. (1983–98), presents extended essays on a number of regions. On the Ashanti see Ivor Wilkes, *Forests of Gold: Essays on the Akan and the*

Kingdom of Assante (1993). On southern Africa, Leonard Thompson's *A History of South Africa* (1990) presents a broad survey, while Carolyn Hamilton, *Mfecane Aftermath* (1995) looks at the long-term consequences of the Zulu expansion and Dan Wylie, *Myth of Iron: Shaka in History* (2005) is a recent interpretation of the great Zulu leader.

There are many histories of the slave trades. John Wright, *The Trans-saharan Slave Trade* (2007) and Herbert S. Klein, *The Atlantic Slave Trade* (1999), provide up-to-date and intelligent overviews. A large general history is Hugh Thomas, *The Slave Trade* (1997). Quantitative studies will depend on the CD-ROM edited by David Eltis et al. entitled *The Atlantic Slave Trade* (1998) and the updated continuation edited by David Eltis and David Richardson, *Extending the Frontiers: Essays on the New Transatlantic Slave Trade Database* (2008).

On Africa, Paul Lovejoy's *Transformations in Slavery: A History of Slavery in Africa* 2nd ed. (2000) and Patrick Manning's *Slavery and African Life* (1990) provide comprehensive overviews. Robert Harms, *The Diligent: Voyage Through the Worlds of the Slave Trade* (2002), uses one voyage to examine the whole system of the Atlantic slave trade and Marcus Rediker, *The Slave Ship* (2007) uses the ships as a basis for his analysis of the system. Joseph Miller, *Way of Death* (1989), is a detailed study of the effects of the slave trade on Angola.

John K. Thornton, *Africa and Africans in the Making of the Atlantic World* 2nd ed. (1998) is an excellent argument for the centrality of slavery in Africa. Walter Rodney's essay "Africa in Europe and the Americas," in *Cambridge History of Africa*, vol. 4, 578–622, is a succinct overview of the African diaspora. In a similar vein with a cultural emphasis is Michael Gomez, *Reversing Sail: A History of the African Diaspora* (2005), and Paul Gilroy, *Black Atlantic: Modernity and Double Consciousness* (1993) is an important statement about people of African descent in the English-speaking Atlantic world. S. Schwartz, *Tropical Babylons* (2004), examines the early association of plantations and slavery.

On the general theoretical issues of slavery, Orlando Patterson, *Slavery and Social Death* (1982), is a broad comparative sociological study. David B. Davis *Inhuman Bondage: The Rise and Fall of Slavery in the New World* (2006) takes a historical approach to the whole question and then places the abolitionist movement in context. Some of the best recent scholarship is collected in G. Heuman and J. Walvin, eds., *The Slavery Reader* (2003). Biography has also become an important genre in the field. See, for example, James Walvin, *The Trader, the Owner, the Slave* (2007). Vincent Carretta, *Equiano, the African: Biography of a Self-made Man* (2005) is a controversial reevaluation of Equiano's origins but still celebrates the power of the original autobiography, *The Interesting Narrative of the Life of Olaudah Equiano*, now in an easily accessible version edited by Robert J. Allison, 2nd ed. (2007). On the question of African continuities vs. creolization see Michael Gomez, *Diasporic Africa: A Reader* (2006), and Linda Heywood, ed. *Central Africas and Cultural Transformations in the American Diaspora* (2002) while the creolization argument is best summarized in Richard Price and Sidney Mintz, *The Birth of Afro-American Culture* (1992).

On the Web

Among the most useful of several sites exploring African history and culture is http://www-sul.stanford.edu/depts/ssrg/africa/culture .html. The starting point for Web-based examination of the African slave trade is http://www.antislavery.org/, while best Web resources for the study of the Atlantic slave trade are http://www.bbc .co.uk/worldservice/africa/features/storyofafrica/9chapter4.shtml and http://hitchcock.itc.virginia.edu/Slavery/, which contains vivid images of the trade from capture to plantation settlements. For the Arab slave trade in Africa and African slavery in the Middle East, see http://www.bbc.co.uk/worldservice/africa/features/ storyofafrica/9chapter6.shtml and http://www.fordham.edu/halsall/ med/lewis1.html. The east African slave trade is closely examined at http://www.geocities.com/CollegePark/Classroom/9912/ easterntrade.html and http://worldhistoryconnected.press.uiuc .edu/1.1/gilbert.html.

Though their present histories elide it, the states of Ashante (http://www.uiowa.edu/~africart/toc/people/Asante.html), Dahomey (http://www.zum.de/whkmla/region/westafrica/dahomeykgd.html), Oyo (http://www.ijebu.org/oyo/), Sokoto (http://www.dawodu.com/ paden1.htm and http://countrystudies.us/nigeria/9.htm), and Kongo (http://www.uiowa.edu/~africart/toc/people/Kongo.html) were closely linked to the Atlantic slave trade, while Mozambique and Kilwa (http://archaeology.about.com/od/tanzania/a/kilwa.htm, http://www.utalii.com/Off_the_normal_path/kilwa.htm, and http:// www.questia.com/library/book/the-african-slave-trade-precolonial -history1450-1850-by-basil-davidson.jsp) were centers of the east African slave trade.

Africans who encountered European settlers in southern Africa (http://www.historyworld.net/wrldhis/PlainTextHistories .asp?historyid=ad33) fared little better, though the Zulu Empire (http://www.urscene.com/Black_History_Pages/Shaka_Zulu.html), with innovative leadership provided by Shaka (http://www .carpenoctem.tv/military/shaka.html), had an imperial thrust of its own. A biography of Ibo slave Olaudah Equiano and links to the text of his albeit contested narrative of the slave life can be found at http://www.brycchancarey.com/equiano/ and http:// docsouth.unc.edu/neh/equiano1/menu.html. Quobna Ottoba Cugoano, a former African slave living in Great Britain, published a critique of slavery in 1787, extracts from which can be found at http://www.brycchancarey.com/cugoano/extract1.htm.

The history of slavery in north America is explored at http:// www.liu.edu/cwis/cwp/library/aaslavry.htm. Narratives of the lives of African slaves in the United States are collected at http://xroads .virginia.edu/~hyper/wpa/wpahome.html. The history of the slave revolt aboard the slave ship *Amistad* is presented at http://www.npg .si.edu/col/amistad/ and http://www.spartacus.schoolnet.co.uk/ USASamistad.htm. An analysis of the Amistad revolt "as fact and as film" is presented at http://historymatters.gmu.edu/d/74/. Resources for a mock re-trial of the Amistad case are offered at http:// www.wested.org/pblnet/exp_projects/amistad.html and http:// memory.loc.gov/ammem/aaohtml/exhibit/aopart1b.html. The principal slave revolts in the United States are identified at http://www .historyguy.com/slave_rebellions_usa.htm.

The lives of early British abolitionists are explored at http://www.brycchancarey.com/abolition/index.htm. For the persistence of slavery in Africa today, see http://www.oah.org/pubs/magazine/ africanamerican/rossiter.html and http://worldhistoryconnected.press.uiuc.edu/1.1/gilbert.html.

AP* Test Prep

1. The European slave trade out of Africa vastly expanded when
   (A) Europeans began to supply Muslim slave markets in the Middle East.
   (B) gold was discovered in Iberia, necessitating greater numbers of laborers.
   (C) sugar plantations were established on the Atlantic islands and in the Americas.
   (D) Spain and Portugal launched their crusades against Muslim states in Africa.

2. The large numbers and high volume of Africans in the slave trade was necessary because
   (A) most Africans escaped from slavery before arriving in the Americas.
   (B) Muslim fleets patrolled the Atlantic coast of Africa and freed the slaves.
   (C) the mortality of slaves was high and their birth rate was low.
   (D) African slaves were also needed on estates in Europe after the Black Death.

3. The largest number of enslaved Africans were sent to work in which of the following industries in the 1450-1750 era?
   (A) tobacco
   (B) sugar
   (C) gold mining
   (D) cotton

4. One of the distinguishing features of slavery in Africa was
   (A) its control by chartered companies like the Royal African Company.
   (B) its creation and development by Muslim rulers of African kingdoms.
   (C) the enslavement of women and children for domestic labor.
   (D) the high rate of emancipation for the children of slave parents.

5. What factor allowed Europeans to join in and profit from the commerce in slaves so quickly in the 16th century?
   (A) the well-established patterns of slavery in Africa prior to the arrival of European traders
   (B) Portuguese bases in the Indian Ocean
   (C) the fact that most Africans were Christian
   (D) the establishment of the colony at the Cape of Good Hope by the Dutch East Indies Company

6. With regard to the slave trade and slavery in Africa, contacts with the Europeans
   (A) decreased warfare between African states as Africans united against European slavers.
   (B) increased violence and the disruption within African societies.
   (C) led to open warfare between Europeans and Arabs for the control of the slave trade.
   (D) benefited most African states, which received high quality goods in exchange for slaves.

Free-Response Question

How did Europeans in Africa, in an era before the outright conquest of the continent, impact the African economy?

21 The Muslim Empires

The Ottomans: From Frontier Warriors to Empire Builders

DOCUMENT: An Islamic Traveler Laments the Muslims' Indifference to Europe

The Shi'a Challenge of the Safavids

THINKING HISTORICALLY: The Gunpowder Empires and the Shifting Balance of Global Power

The Mughals and the Apex of Muslim Civilization in India

VISUALIZING THE PAST: Art as a Window into the Past: Paintings and History in Mughal India

GLOBAL CONNECTIONS: Gunpowder Empires and the Restoration of the Islamic Bridge Between Civilizations

Babur (or Zahar al-Din Muhammad, who was known to his troops as "The Tiger") was the first Mughal emperor of India. Claiming descent on his mother's side from Chinggis Khan and on his father's side from the ruthless Turkish conqueror Timur, he was himself a skilled warrior and a cultured man who was known for his high spirits and love of beauty. But in April 1526, as the 44-year-old Babur led his armies into India, his future looked bleak. Though battle-hardened, his soldiers were far from their base of support and they were headed into combat with a force that outnumbered them 10 to 1. For nearly a century the Lodis had ruled an empire that stretched across north India. Babur, in contrast, had repeatedly been defeated in his attempts to win back Ferghana, the kingdom he had inherited and lost, and been driven from his ancestral home in the fabled city of Samarkand (see Map 21.1). Although in the years before his foray into India he had been able to build a small kingdom centered around Kabul in present-day Afghanistan, Babur had had little success in his attempts to recoup his earlier losses, and his plans for the conquest of Persia to the west had been foiled by the rise of the powerful Safavid dynasty in the early 1500s.

Babur decided to meet the enemy just north of the Lodi capital at Delhi, from which a succession of Muslim dynasties had dominated north India since the early 13th century. He ordered his troops to use leather strips to lash together the matchlock cannon that were positioned at the center of his army. Arrayed against them, under the command of the Lodi sultan, Ibrahim, were more than a thousand war elephants that would lead the charge to crush Babur's unimposing band of warriors. When the battle was joined at mid-morning on April 21, the roar and fire of the cannon panicked the surging elephants and they fled, trampling the Lodi soldiers marching into battle behind them. Making good use of his superior firepower—the enemy apparently had few cannons or muskets—Babur routed the massive army and went on to capture Delhi.

Babur's warriors were buoyed by their victory and the treasure seized in the capital. In the battles that followed against a Hindu alliance and an army raised by Ibrahim's brother, they effectively deployed the batteries of cannon they had arduously transported from Kabul. By the end of 1530, the Tiger was master of northern India and the founder of a new dynasty, the Mughal, which would rule varying portions of the subcontinent for nearly 300 years. ■

The Middle East MAP

Safavid dynasty Originally a Turkic nomadic group; family originated in Sufi mystic group; espoused Shi'ism; conquered territory and established kingdom in region equivalent to modern Iran; lasted until 1722.

Mughal Empire Established by Babur in India in 1526; the name is taken from the supposed Mongol descent of Babur, but there is little indication of any Mongol influence in the dynasty; became weak after rule of Aurangzeb in first decades of 18th century.

In the chapter that follows, we will see that Babur's rapid conquest of north India displayed several key themes found in the rise of each of the three major Muslim dynasties whose empires stretched from the Mediterranean to the Bay of Bengal throughout the early modern phase of global history (see Map 21.1). First, like the warrior leaders who founded the **Ottoman** and **Safavid** empires to the west, Babur and his followers were from Turkic-speaking nomadic groups in central Asia. In each of the three cases, the warrior leaders who founded these dynasties took advantage of the power vacuum left by the breakup of the Mongol empire and the devastation wrought by Timur's assaults on the Islamic heartlands of the Middle East and Muslim-ruled northern India. Babur's **Mughal Empire** was the last of the three to be established, and he drew on many of the precedents set by both the Ottomans and Safavids. But like them—and the military of all of the great Eurasian empires in the early modern era—his armies relied heavily on large cannons and, increasingly, on muskets. As we shall see, in many instances the adversaries of each of the three Muslim dynasties lacked or were less skilled at deploying these weapons, which were transforming warfare across the globe. In fact, at the Battle of Khanua, Babur copied Turkish techniques in massing his muskets and cannon to defeat yet another much larger army, led by a great Hindu warrior.

In contrast to the founders of the Ottoman and Safavid dynasties, Babur and the four Mughal rulers who succeeded him did not launch their conquests out of religious fervor. Like the Mughal monarchs, once in power, most of the Ottoman and Safavid rulers showed great tolerance for the faiths of the non-Muslim peoples who became their subjects. But as will become apparent in the accounts of the three dynasties that follow, the same tolerance was often not shown to rival Muslim sects. The Sunni–Shi'a split, which, as we have seen, arose early in the history of Islamic civilization, fueled often violent rivalries between the Ottomans and the Safavids. And sectarian identities frequently intensified ethnic divisions found in each of the great Muslim empires and across much of the Islamic world. Wars between the three empires and the constant need for their rulers to be attentive to shifting alliances and military innovations introduced by rival dynasties also go far toward explaining the inward-looking quality of much of Islamic society in this era.

The Ottomans: From Frontier Warriors to Empire Builders

For centuries before the rise of the Ottoman dynasty, Turkic-speaking peoples from central Asia played key roles in Islamic civilization as soldiers and administrators, often in the service of the Abbasid caliphs. But the collapse of the Seljuk Turkic kingdom of Rum in eastern Anatolia in Asia Minor (Map 21.2), after the invasion by the Mongols in 1243, opened the way for the Ottomans to seize power in their own right. The Mongols raided but did not directly rule Anatolia, which fell into a chaotic period of warfare between would-be successor states to the Seljuk sultans. Turkic peoples, both those fleeing the Mongols and those in search of easy booty, flooded into the region in the last decades of the 13th century. One of these peoples, called the **Ottomans** after an early leader named Osman, came to dominate the rest, and within decades they had begun to build a new empire based in Anatolia.

By the 1350s, the Ottomans had advanced from their strongholds in Asia Minor across the Bosporus straits into Europe. Thrace was quickly conquered, and by the end of the century large portions of the Balkans had been added to their rapidly expanding territories (Map 21.2). In moving into Europe in the mid-14th century, the Ottomans had bypassed rather than conquered the great city of Constantinople, long the capital of the once powerful Byzantine Empire. By the mid-15th century, the Ottomans, who had earlier alternated between alliances and warfare with the Byzantines, were strong enough to undertake the capture of the well fortified city. For seven weeks in the spring of 1453, the army of the Ottoman sultan, **Mehmed II**, "The Conqueror," which numbered well over 100,000, assaulted the triple ring of land walls that had protected the city for centuries (Figure 21.2). The outnumbered forces of the defenders repulsed attack after attack until the sultan ordered his gunners to batter a portion of the walls with their massive siege cannon. Wave after wave of Ottoman troops struck at the gaps in the defenses that had been cut by the guns, quickly overwhelmed the defenders, and raced into the city to loot and pillage for the three days that Mehmed had promised as their reward for victory.

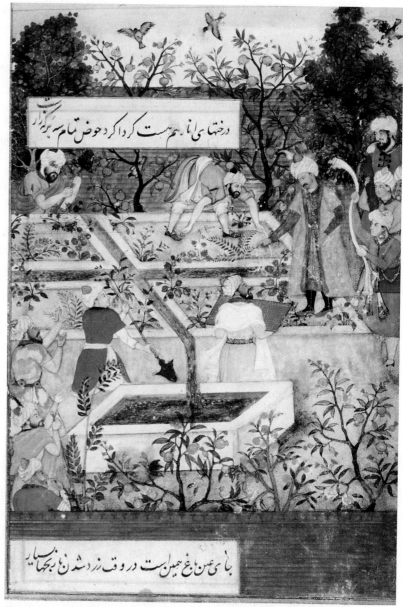

Figure 21.1 Babur superintending the planting of gardens in India. The rulers of each of the three great Muslim empires of the early modern era were lavish patrons of the arts and splendid architecture.

In the 13th and 14th centuries, the Ottomans built an empire in the eastern Mediterranean that rivaled the Abbasid imperium at its height. Though the Ottomans patterned much of their empire on the ideas and institutions of earlier Muslim civilizations, in warfare, architecture, and engineering they carried Islamic civilization to new levels of attainment.

 Mehmed II

469

1250 C.E.	1400 C.E.	1500 C.E.	1525 C.E.
1243 Mongol invasion of Asia Minor	**1402** Timur's invasion; Ottoman setbacks under Bayazid	**1501–1510** Safavid conquest of Persia (present-day Iran)	**1526** Battle of Panipat; Babur's conquest of India
1281 Founding of Ottoman dynasty	**c. 1450s** Shi'a influences enter Safavid teachings	**1507** Portuguese victory over Ottoman-Arab fleet at Diu in Indian Ocean	**1529** First Ottoman siege of Vienna
1334 Death of first Safavid Sufi master at Ardabil	**c. 1450s** Beginning of large-scale recruitment of Janissary troops	**1514** Ottoman victory over Safavids at Chaldiran	**1540** Babur's successor, Humayan, driven from India
1350s Ottoman invasion of Europe; conquest of much of the Balkans and Hungary	**1453** Ottoman capture of Constantinople	**1517** Ottoman capture of Syria and Egypt	**1540–1545** Humayan in exile at the Safavid court
		1520–1566 Rule of Suleyman the Magnificent; construction of Suleymaniye mosque in Constantinople	

The Ottoman Empire

Ottomans Turkic people who advanced from strongholds in Asia Minor during 1350s; conquered large part of Balkans; unified under Mehmed I; captured Constantinople in 1453; established empire from Balkans that included most of Arab world.

In the two centuries after the conquest of Constantinople, the armies of a succession of able Ottoman rulers extended the empire into Syria and Egypt and across north Africa, thus bringing under their rule the bulk of the Arab world (Map 21.2). The empire also spread through the Balkans into Hungary in Europe and around the Black and Red seas. The Ottomans became a formidable naval power in the Mediterranean Sea. Powerful Ottoman galley fleets made possible the capture of major island bases on Rhodes, Crete, and Cyprus. The Ottoman armies also drove the

Map 21.1 The Ottoman, Safavid, and Mughal Empires For several centuries the three great Muslim empires dominated the central trading and transit zones of Afro-Eurasia.

1550 C.E.	1650 C.E.	1700 C.E.
1556 Mughal Empire reestablished in north India 1556–1605 Reign of Akbar 1571 Battle of Lepanto 1582 Akbar's proclamation of a new religion, designed to unite Hindus and Muslims 1588–1629 Reign of Abbas I (the Great) in Persia	1657–1658 Great war of succession between sons of Shah Jahan 1658–1707 Reign of Aurangzeb 1683 Last Ottoman siege of Vienna 1680s Rajput and peasant revolts in north India 1699 Treaty of Carlowitz; Ottomans cede territories in Europe	1722 First Turkish-language printing press 1722 Fall of the Safavid dynasty 1730 Ottoman armies are defeated by Persian forces under Nadir Khan (later Nadir Shah, emperor of Persia) 1730s First Western-modeled military schools established in Constantinople 1736–1747 Reign of Nadir Shah 1739 Nadir Shah invades India from Persia, sacks Mughal capital at Delhi

Venetians and Genoese from much of the eastern Mediterranean and threatened southern Italy with invasion on several occasions. From their humble origins as frontier vassals, the Ottomans had risen to become the protectors of the Islamic heartlands and the scourge of Christian Europe. As late as 1683, Ottoman armies were able to lay siege to the capital of the Austrian Habsburg dynasty at Vienna. Even though the Ottoman Empire was in decline by this time, and the threat the assault

Mehmed II (1432–1481) Ottoman sultan called the "Conqueror"; responsible for conquest of Constantinople in 1453; destroyed what remained of Byzantine Empire.

Map 21.2 The Expansion of the Ottoman Empire Because they were a sea as well as a land power, the Ottomans were able to conquer and rule the lands of the eastern Mediterranean and Black Sea region for half a millennium.

Figure 21.2 An illuminated French manuscript from the 15th century shows the Ottoman siege of Constantinople in 1453. The Muslim capture of the great eastern bastion of Christian Europe aroused fears throughout the continent, resulting in demands for new Crusades to recapture the city. The advance of the Ottomans in the east also provided impetus to the overseas expansion of nations such as Spain and Portugal on the western coasts of Europe. Both of these Catholic maritime powers saw their efforts to build overseas empires as part of a larger campaign to outflank the Muslim powers and bring areas that they controlled into the Christian camp.

posed to Vienna was far less serious than a previous attack in the early 16th century, the Ottomans remained a major force in European politics until the late 19th century.

A State Geared to Warfare

Military leaders played a dominant role in the Ottoman state, and the economy of the empire was geared to warfare and expansion. The Turkic cavalry, chiefly responsible for the Ottomans' early conquests from the 13th to the 16th centuries, gradually developed into a warrior aristocracy. They were granted control over land and peasant producers in annexed areas for the support of their households and military retainers. From the 15th century onward, members of the warrior class also vied with religious leaders and administrators drawn from other social groups for control of the expanding Ottoman bureaucracy. As the power of the warrior aristocracy shrank at the center, they built up regional and local bases of support. These inevitably competed with the sultans and the central bureaucracy for revenue and labor control.

Janissaries Ottoman infantry divisions that dominated Ottoman armies; forcibly conscripted as boys in conquered areas of Balkans, legally slaves; translated military service into political influence, particularly after 15th century.

From the mid-15th century, the imperial armies were increasingly dominated by infantry divisions made up of troops called **Janissaries**. Most of the Janissaries had been forcibly recruited as adolescent boys in conquered areas, such as the Balkans, where the majority of the population retained its Christian faith. Sometimes the boys' parents willingly turned their sons over to the Ottoman recruiters because of the opportunities for advancement that came with service to the Ottoman sultans. Though legally slaves, the youths were given fairly extensive schooling for the time and converted to Islam. Some of them went on to serve in the palace or bureaucracy, but most became Janissaries.

Because the Janissaries controlled the artillery and firearms that became increasingly vital to Ottoman success in warfare with Christian and Muslim adversaries, they rapidly became the most powerful component in the Ottoman military machine. Their growing importance was another factor contributing to the steady decline of the role of the aristocratic cavalry. Just like the mercenary forces that had earlier served the caliphs of Baghdad, the Janissaries eventually tried to translate military service into political influence. By the late 15th century they were deeply involved in court politics; by the mid-16th century they had the power to depose sultans and decide which one of a dying ruler's sons would mount the throne.

The Sultans and Their Court

Nominally, the Ottoman rulers were absolute monarchs. But even the most powerful sultan maintained his position by playing factions in the warrior elite off each other and pitting the warriors as a whole against the Janissaries and other groups. Chief among the latter were the Islamic religious scholars and legal experts, who retained many of the administrative functions they had held under the Arab caliphs of earlier centuries. In addition to Muslim traders, commerce within the empire was in the hands of Christian and Jewish merchants, who as dhimmis, or "people of the book," were under the protection of the Ottoman rulers. Although they have often been depicted in Western writings as brutal and corrupt despots, some Ottoman sultans, especially in the early centuries of their sway, were very capable rulers. Ottoman conquest often meant effective administration and tax relief for the peoples of areas annexed to the empire.

Like the Abbasid caliphs, the Ottoman sultans grew more and more distant from their subjects as their empire increased in size and wealth. In their splendid marble palaces and pleasure gardens, surrounded by large numbers of slaves and the many wives and concubines of their harems, Ottoman rulers followed elaborate court rituals based on those of earlier Byzantine, Persian, and Arab dynasties. Day-to-day administration was carried out by a large bureaucracy headed by a grand **vizier** (*wazir* in Arabic). The vizier was the overall head of the imperial administration, and he often held more real power than the sultan. Early sultans took an active role in political decisions and often personally led their armies into battle.

vizier Ottoman equivalent of the Abbasid wazir; head of the Ottoman bureaucracy; after 5th century often more powerful than sultan.

Like earlier Muslim dynasties, however, the Ottomans suffered greatly because they inherited Islamic principles of political succession that remained vague and contested. The existence of many talented and experienced claimants to the throne meant constant danger of civil strife. The death of a sultan could, and increasingly did, lead to protracted warfare among his sons. Defeated claimants sometimes fled to the domains of Christian or Muslim rulers hostile to the Ottomans, thereby becoming rallying points for military campaigns against the son who had gained the throne.

Constantinople Restored: Link Between Asia and Europe, the Mediterranean and the Black Sea

An empire that encompassed so many and such diverse cultures from Europe, Africa, and Asia naturally varied greatly from one province to the next in its social arrangements, artistic production, and physical appearance. But the Ottomans' ancient and cosmopolitan capital at Constantinople richly combined the disparate elements of their extensive territories. Like the Byzantine Empire as a whole, Constantinople had fallen on hard times in the centuries before the Ottoman conquest in 1453. Soon after Mehmed II's armies had captured and sacked the city, however, the Ottoman ruler set about restoring its ancient glory. He had the cathedral of Saint Sophia converted into one of the grandest mosques in the Islamic world, and new mosques and palaces were built throughout the city. This construction benefited greatly from architectural advances the Ottomans derived from the Byzantine heritage. Aqueducts were built from the surrounding hills to supply the growing population with water, markets were reopened, and the city's defenses were repaired.

Each sultan who ruled in the centuries after Mehmed strove to be remembered for his efforts to beautify the capital. The most prominent additions were further mosques that represent some of the most sublime contributions of the Ottomans to Islamic and human civilization. The most spectacular of these was the Suleymaniye, pictured in Figure 21.3. As its name suggests, the mosque was built at the behest of the most successful of the sultans, Suleyman the Magnificent (r. 1520–1566). Although it smacks of hometown pride, the following description by a 17th-century Ottoman chronicler of the reaction of some Christian visitors to the mosque conveys a sense of the awe that the structure still evokes:

The Suleymaniye Mosque

> The humble writer of these lines once himself saw ten Frankish infidels skillful in geometry and architecture, who, when the door-keeper had changed their shoes for slippers, and had introduced

Figure 21.3 Built in the reign of Suleyman I in the 1550s and designed by the famous architect Sinan, the Suleymaniye mosque is among the largest domed structures in the world, and it is one of the great engineering achievements of Islamic civilization. The pencil-thin minarets flanking the great central dome are characteristic of Ottoman architecture, which was quite distinct from its Safavid and Mughal counterparts.

them into the mosque for the purpose of showing it to them, laid their finger on their mouths, and each bit his finger from astonishment when they saw the minarets; but when they beheld the dome they tossed up their hats and cried Maria! Maria! and on observing the four arches which supported the dome . . . they could not find terms to express their admiration, and the ten . . . remained a full hour looking with astonishment on those arches. [One of them said] that nowhere was so much beauty, external and internal, to be found united, and that in the whole of Frangistan [Christian Europe] there was not a single edifice which could be compared to this.

In addition to the mosques, sultans and powerful administrators built mansions, rest houses, religious schools, and hospitals throughout the city. Both public and private gardens further beautified the capital, which Ottoman writers compared to paradise itself. The city and its suburbs stretched along both sides of the Bosporus, the narrow strait between the Mediterranean and Black seas that separates Europe from Asia (Map 21.2). Its harbors and the Golden Horn, a triangular bay that formed the northern boundary of the city, were crowded with merchant ships from ports throughout the region. Constantinople's great bazaars were filled with merchants and travelers from throughout the empire and places as distant as England and Malaya. They offered all manner of commodities, from the spices of the East Indies and the ivory of Africa to slaves and forest products from Russia and fine carpets from Persia. Coffeehouses—places where men gathered to drink, smoke tobacco (introduced from America in the 17th century by English merchants), gossip, do business, and play chess—were found in all sections of the city. They were pivotal to the social life of the capital. The coffeehouses also played a major role in the cultural life of Constantinople as places where poets and scholars could congregate, read their latest works aloud, and debate about politics and the merits of each other's ideas.

Beneath the ruling classes, a sizeable portion of the population of Constantinople and other Ottoman cities belonged to the merchant and artisan classes. The Ottoman regime closely regulated commercial exchanges and handicraft production. Government inspectors were employed to ensure that standard weights and measures were used and to license the opening of new shops. They also regulated the entry of apprentice artisans into the trades and monitored the quality of the goods they produced. Like their counterparts in medieval European towns, the artisans were organized into guilds. Guild officers set craft standards, arbitrated disputes between their members, and provided financial assistance for needy members. They even arranged popular entertainments, often linked to religious festivals.

The early Ottomans had written in Persian, and Arabic remained an important language for works on law and religion throughout the empire's history. But by the 17th century, the Turkish language of the Ottoman court had become the preferred mode of expression for poets and historians as well as the language of the Ottoman bureaucracy. In writing as in the fine arts, the Ottomans' achievements have been somewhat overshadowed by those of their contemporary Persian and Indian rivals. Nonetheless, the authors, artists, and artisans of the Ottoman Empire left a considerable legacy, particularly in poetry, ceramics, carpet manufacturing, and above all in architecture.

The Problem of Ottoman Decline

Much of the literature on the Ottoman Empire concentrates on its slow decline from the champion of the Muslim world and the great adversary of Christendom to the "sick man" of Europe in the 18th and 19th centuries. This approach provides a very skewed view of Ottoman history as a whole. Traced from its origins in the late 13th century, the Ottoman state is one of the great success stories in human political history. Vigorous and expansive until the late 17th century, the Ottomans were able to ward off the powerful enemies who surrounded their domains on all sides for nearly four centuries. The dynasty endured for more than 600 years, a feat matched by no other in all human history.

Venetian Observations on the Ottoman Empire

From one perspective, the long Ottoman decline, which officials and court historians actively discussed from the mid-17th century onward, reflects the great strength of the institutions on which the empire was built. Despite internal revolts and periodic conflicts with such powerful foreign rivals as the Russian, Austrian, Spanish, and Safavid empires, the Ottomans ruled into the 20th century. Yet the empire had reached the limits of its expansive power centuries earlier, and by the late 17th century the long retreat from Russia, Europe, and the Arab lands had begun. In a sense, some contraction was inevitable. Even when it was at the height of its power, the empire was too large to be maintained, given the resource base that the sultans had at their disposal and the primitive state of transport and communications in the preindustrial era.

The Decline of the Ottomans

The Ottoman state had been built on war and steady territorial expansion. As possibilities for new conquests ran out and lands began to be lost to the Ottomans' Christian and Muslim enemies, the means of maintaining the oversized bureaucracy and army shrank. The decline in the effectiveness of the administrative system that held the empire together was signaled by the rampant growth of corruption among Ottoman officials. The corruption and incompetence of state bureaucrats prompted regional and local officials to retain more revenue for their own purposes. Poorly regulated by the central government, many local officials, who also controlled large landed estates, squeezed the peasants and the laborers who worked their lands for additional taxes and services. At times the oppressive demands of local officials and estate owners sparked rebellions. Peasant uprisings and flight resulted in the abandonment of cultivated lands and in social dislocations that further drained the resources of the empire.

From the 17th century onward, the forces that undermined the empire from below were compounded by growing problems at the center of imperial administration. The early practice of assigning the royal princes administrative or military positions, to prepare them to rule, died out. Instead, possible successors to the throne were kept like hostages in special sections of the palace, where they remained until one of them ascended the throne. The other princes and potential rivals were also, in effect, imprisoned for life in the palace. Although it might have made the reigning sultan more secure, this solution to the problem of contested succession produced monarchs far less prepared to rule than those in the formative centuries of the dynasty. The great warrior-emperors of early Ottoman history gave way, with some important exceptions, to weak and indolent rulers, addicted to drink, drugs, and the pleasures of the harem. In many instances, the later sultans were little more than pawns in the power struggles of the viziers and other powerful officials with the leaders of the increasingly influential Janissary corps. Because the imperial apparatus had been geared to strong and absolute rulers, the decline in the caliber of Ottoman emperors had devastating effects on the empire as a whole. Civil strife increased, and the discipline and leadership of the armies on which the empire depended for survival deteriorated.

Military Reverses, Iberian Expansionism, and the Ottoman Retreat

Debilitating changes within the empire were occurring at a time when challenges from without were growing rapidly. The Ottomans had made very effective use of artillery and firearms in building their empire. But their reliance on huge siege guns, and the Janissaries' determination to block all military changes that might jeopardize the power they had gained within the state, caused the Ottomans to fall farther and farther behind their European rivals in the critical art of waging war. With the widespread introduction of light field artillery into the armies of the European powers in the 17th century, Ottoman losses on the battlefield multiplied rapidly, and the threat they posed for the West began to recede.

On the sea, the Ottomans were eclipsed as early as the 16th century. The end of their dominance was presaged by their defeat by a combined Spanish and Venetian fleet at Lepanto in 1571. The great battle is depicted in the painting in Figure 21.4. Although the Ottomans had completely rebuilt their war fleet within a year after Lepanto and soon launched an assault on north Africa that preserved that area for Islam, their control of the eastern Mediterranean had been lost. Even more ominously, in the decades before Lepanto, the Ottomans and the Muslim world had been outflanked by the Portuguese seafarers who sailed down and around the coast of Africa. The failure in the early 1500s of the Ottomans and their Muslim allies in the Indian Ocean to drive the Portuguese from Asian waters proved far more harmful in the long run than Ottoman defeats in the Mediterranean.

Portuguese naval victories in the Indian Ocean revealed the decline of the Ottoman galley fleets and Mediterranean-style warships more generally. The trading goods, particularly spices, that the Portuguese carried around Africa and back to Europe enriched the Ottomans' Christian rivals. In addition, the fact that a large portion of the flow of these products was no longer transmitted to European ports through Muslim trading centers in the eastern Mediterranean meant that merchants and tax collectors in the Ottoman Empire lost critical revenues. As if this were not enough,

Figure 21.4 The clash of the galley fleets at Lepanto was one of the greatest sea battles in history. But despite devastating losses, the Ottomans managed to replace most of their fleet and go back on the offensive against their Christian adversaries within a year. Here the epic encounter is pictured in one of the many paintings devoted to it in the decades that followed. The tightly packed battle formations that both sides adopted show the importance of ramming rather than cannon fire in naval combat in the Mediterranean in this era. This pattern was reversed in the Atlantic and the other oceanic zones into which the Europeans had been expanding since the 14th century.

An Islamic Traveler Laments the Muslims' Indifference to Europe

Although most of the travelers and explorers in this era were Europeans who went to Africa, Asia, and the Americas, a few people from these lands visited Europe. One of these, Abu Taleb, was a scholar of Turkish and Persian descent whose family had settled in India. At the end of the 18th century, Abu Taleb traveled in Europe for three years and later wrote an account in Persian of his experiences there. Although his was one of the few firsthand sources of information about Europe available to Muslim scholars and leaders, Abu Taleb was deeply disturbed by the lack of interest shown by other Muslims in his observations and discoveries.

> When I reflect on the want of energy and the indolent dispositions of my countrymen, and the many erroneous customs which exist in all Mohammedan countries and among all ranks of Mussulmans, I am fearful that my exertions [in writing down his experiences in Europe] will be thrown away. The great and the rich intoxicated with pride and luxury, and puffed up with the vanity of their possessions, consider universal science as comprehended in the circle of their own scanty acquirements and limited knowledge; while the poor and common people, from the want of leisure, and overpowered by the difficulty of procuring a livelihood, have not time to attend to his personal concerns, much less to form desires for the acquirement of information of new discoveries and inventions, although such a person has been implanted by nature in every human breast, as an honour and an ornament to the species. I therefore despair of their reaping any fruit from my labours, being convinced that they will consider this book of no greater value than the volumes of tales and romances which they peruse merely to pass away their time, or are attracted thereto by the easiness of the style. It may consequently be concluded, that as they will find no pleasure in reading a work which contains a number of foreign names, treats on uncommon subjects, and alludes to other matters which cannot be understood at first glance, but require a little time for consideration, they will, under pretense of zeal for their religion, entirely abstain and refrain from perusing it.

QUESTIONS What reasons does Abu Taleb give for his fellow Muslims' indifference to his travel reports on Europe? What other factors can be added as a result of our study of long-standing Islamic attitudes toward Europe and conditions in the Ottoman Empire in this period? In what ways might the Muslims' neglect of events in Europe have hindered their efforts to cope with this expansive civilization in the centuries that followed? Were there Western counterparts to Abu Taleb in these centuries, and how were their accounts of distant lands received in Europe?

---

from the late 16th century on, large amounts of silver flowed into the Ottomans' lands from mines worked by Native American laborers in the Spanish empire in Peru and Mexico. This sudden influx of bullion into the rigid and slow-growing economy of the Ottoman Empire set off a long-term inflationary trend that further undermined the finances of the empire.

Several able sultans took measures to shore up the empire in the 17th century. The collapse of the Safavid dynasty in Persia and conflicts between the European powers at this time also gave the Ottomans hope that their earlier dominance might be restored. But their reprieve was temporary. With the scientific, technological, and commercial transformations occurring in Europe (discussed in Chapter 17), the Ottomans were falling behind their Christian rivals in most areas. But the growing gap was most critical in trade and warfare. The Ottomans inherited from their Arab, Persian, and Turkic predecessors the conviction that little of what happened in Europe was important. This belief, which is seen as a major cause of Ottoman decline by the traveler Abu Taleb quoted in the Document feature, prevented them from taking seriously the revolutionary changes that were transforming western Europe. The intense conservatism of powerful groups such as the Janissaries, and to a lesser extent the religious scholars, reinforced this fatal attitude. Through much of the 17th and 18th centuries, these groups blocked most of the Western-inspired innovations that reform-minded sultans and their advisors tried to introduce. As a result of these narrow and potentially dangerous attitudes, the isolated Ottoman imperial system proved incapable of checking the forces that were steadily destroying it.

The Shi'a Challenge of the Safavids

Like the Ottomans, the Safavid dynasty arose from the struggles of rival Turkic nomadic groups in the wake of the Mongol and Timurid invasions of the 13th and 14th centuries. Also like the Ottomans, the Safavids rose to prominence as the frontier warrior champions of a highly militant strain of Islam. But unlike the Ottomans, who became the champions of the Sunni majority of the

Abu Taleb on the West and Western Influence

In the first years of the 16th century, the Safavids founded a dynasty that conquered what is now Iran. Restoring Persia (as it was then called) as a major center of political power and cultural creativity, they also established it as one of the strongest and most enduring centers of Shi'ism within the Islamic world.

477

Muslim faithful, the Safavids espoused the Shi'a variant of Islam. As we saw in Chapter 6, in the early decades of Muslim expansion a split developed in the community of the faithful between the Sunnis, who recognized the legitimacy of the first three successors to Muhammad (Abu Bakr, Umar, and Uthman), and the Shi'a, who believed that only the fourth successor (Ali, Mohammed's cousin and son-in-law) had the right to succeed the prophet. Over time, differences in doctrine, ritual, and law were added to the disagreements over succession that originally divided the Islamic community. Divisions have also arisen within both the Shi'a and Sunni groupings, but bitter hostility and violent conflict most often have developed along Sunni–Shi'a lines. The long rivalry between the Sunni Ottomans and the Shi'a Safavids proved to be one of the most pivotal episodes in the long history of these sectarian struggles.

The Safavid dynasty had its origins in a family of Sufi mystics and religious preachers, whose shrine center was at Ardabil near the Caspian Sea (Map 21.3). In the early 14th century, one of these Sufis, **Sail al-Din**, who gave the dynasty its name, began a militant campaign to purify and reform Islam and spread Muslim teachings among the Turkic tribes of the region. In the chaos that followed the collapse of Mongol authority in the mid-14th century, Sail al-Din and other Safavid Sufi leaders gained increasing support. But as the numbers of the **Red Heads** (as the Safavids' followers were called because of their distinctive headgear) grew, and as they began in the mid-15th century to preach Shi'a doctrines, their enemies multiplied. After decades of fierce local struggles in which three successive Safavid leaders perished, a surviving Sufi commander, **Ismâ'il**, led his Turkic followers to a string of victories on the battlefield. In 1501, Ismâ'il's armies took the city of Tabriz, where he was proclaimed *shah*, or emperor.

In the next decade, Ismâ'il's followers conquered most of Persia, drove the Safavid's ancient enemies, the Ozbegs—a neighboring nomadic people of Turkic stock—back into the central Asian steppes, and advanced into what is now Iraq. The Safavid successes and the support their followers received in the Ottoman borderlands from Turkic-speaking peoples brought them into conflict with Ottoman rulers. In August 1514, at **Chaldiran** in northwest Persia, the armies of the two empires met in one of the most fateful battles in Islamic history. Chaldiran was more than a battle between the two most powerful dynasties in the Islamic world at the time. It was a clash between the

Sail al-Din   Early 14th-century Sufi mystic; began campaign to purify Islam; first member of Safavid dynasty.

Red Heads   Name given to Safavid followers because of their distinctive red headgear.

Ismâ'il   (1487–1524) Sufi commander who conquered city of Tabriz in 1501; first Safavid to be proclaimed shah or emperor.

Chaldiran   Site of battle between Safavids and Ottomans in 1514; Safavids severely defeated by Ottomans; checked western advance of Safavid Empire.

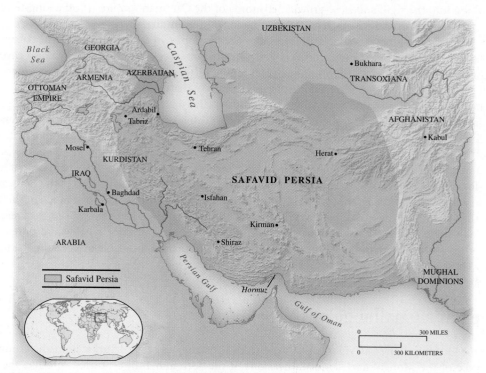

Map 21.3 The Safavid Empire   Surrounded by rival empires and nomadic peoples, Safavid Persia proved less enduring than its two Muslim rivals.

champions of the Shi'a and Sunni variants of Islam. The religious fervor with which both sides fought the battle was intensified by the long-standing Safavid persecutions of the Sunnis and the slaughter of Shi'a living in Ottoman territories by the forces of the Ottoman sultan, Selim.

The battle also demonstrated the importance of muskets and field cannon in the gunpowder age. Because his artillery was still engaged against enemies far to the east, Ismâ'il hoped to delay a decisive confrontation with the Ottoman forces under the Sultan Selim. When battle could not be avoided, Ismâ'il threw his cavalry against the cannon and massed muskets of the Ottoman forces. Despite desperate attempts to make up through clever maneuvers what he lacked in firepower, Ismâ'il's cavalry proved no match for the well armed Ottomans.

The Safavids were dealt a devastating defeat, and their victory at Chaldiran buttressed the Ottomans' efforts to build the most powerful empire in the Islamic world. But the Ottomans could not follow up the battle with conquests that would have put an end to their Safavid rivals. The latter's capital at Tabriz was too far from Ottoman supply areas to be held through the approaching winter. The withdrawal of the Ottoman armies gave the Safavids the breathing space they needed to regroup their forces and reoccupy much of the territory they had originally conquered. Nonetheless, defeat at Chaldiran put an end to Ismâ'il's dreams of further westward expansion, and most critically it checked the rapid spread of conversions to Shi'a Islam in the western borderlands that had resulted from the Safavid's recent successes in battle. The outcome at Chaldiran determined that Shi'ism would be concentrated mainly in Persia, or present-day Iran, and neighboring areas in what is today southern Iraq.

Politics and War Under the Safavid Shahs

After his defeat at Chaldiran, Ismâ'il, once a courageous warrior and a popular leader, retreated to his palace and tried to escape his troubles through drink. His seclusion, along with struggles between the factions backing each of his sons for the right to succeed him, left openings for subordinate Turkic chiefs to attempt to seize power. After years of turmoil, a new shah, Tahmasp I (r. 1534–1576), won the throne and set about restoring the power of the dynasty. The Turkic chiefs were foiled in their bid for supreme power, and the Ozbegs were again and again driven from the Safavid domains. Under Shah Abbas I (r. 1587–1629), the empire reached the height of its strength and prosperity, although the territories it controlled remained roughly equivalent to those ruled by Ismâ'il and Tahmasp I.

Under Tahmasp I and his successors, repeated efforts were made to bring the Turkic chiefs under control. They were gradually transformed into a warrior nobility comparable to that in the Ottoman domains. Like their Ottoman counterparts, the Safavid warrior nobles were assigned villages, whose peasants were required to supply them and their troops with food and labor. The most powerful of the warrior leaders occupied key posts in the imperial administration, and from the defeat at Chaldiran onward they posed a constant threat to the Safavid monarchs. To counterbalance this threat, Safavid rulers recruited Persians for positions at the court and in the rapidly expanding imperial bureaucracy. The struggle for power and influence between Turkic and Persian notables was further complicated by the practice, initiated by Ismâ'il's successor, Tahmasp I, of recruiting into the bureaucracy and army slave boys who were captured in campaigns in southern Russia. Like the Janissaries in the Ottoman Empire, many of these slaves rose to positions of power. Also like the Janissaries, the slave regiments soon became a major force in Safavid political struggles.

Of all of the Safavid shahs, Abbas I, known also as **Abbas the Great**, made the most extensive use of the youths who were captured in Russia and then educated and converted to Islam. They not only came to form the backbone of his military forces but were granted provincial governorships and high offices at court. Like the Janissaries, "slave" regiments, which were wholly dependent on Abbas's support, monopolized the firearms that had become increasingly prominent in Safavid armies. The Persians had artillery and handguns long before the arrival of the Portuguese by sea in the early 16th century. But Abbas and his successors showed little reluctance to call on the knowledgeable but infidel Europeans for assistance in their wars with the Ottomans. Of special importance were the Sherley brothers from England. They provided instruction in the casting of cannons and trained Abbas's slave infantry and a special regiment of musketeers recruited from the Iranian peasantry. By the end of his reign, Abbas had built up a standing army of nearly 40,000 troops and an elite bodyguard. These measures to strengthen his armies and his victories on the battlefield appeared to promise security for the Safavid domains for decades to come—a promise that was not fulfilled.

Abbas the Great   Safavid ruler from 1587 to 1629; extended Safavid domain to greatest extent; created slave regiments based on captured Russians, who monopolized firearms within Safavid armies; incorporated Western military technology.

The Gunpowder Empires and the Shifting Balance of Global Power

Like so many of their predecessors, each of the great Muslim dynasties of the premodern era came to power with the support of nomadic warrior peoples. Each based the military forces that won and sustained its empire on massed cavalry. But in each case, there was a significant divergence from past conditions. As the outcome of the critical battle of Chaldiran between the Ottomans and Safavids made clear, by the 16th century firearms had become a decisive element in armed conflict—the key to empire building. In military and political terms, global history had entered a new phase.

Although the Chinese had invented gunpowder and were the first to use it in war, the Mongols were the first to realize the awesome potential of the new type of weaponry based on explosive formulas. The Mongols continued to build their armies around swift cavalry and their skill as mounted archers. But siege cannons became critical to Mongol conquests once they ventured into the highly urbanized civilizations that bordered on their steppe homelands. Mongol successes against intricately walled and heavily fortified cities in China, Russia, and the Islamic heartlands impressed their sedentary and nomadic adversaries with the power of the new weaponry and contributed much to its spread throughout the Eurasian world in the late 13th and 14th centuries.

Innovation in the use of gunpowder spread quickly to many areas, especially Europe and the Muslim Middle East. By the late 15th century, muskets and field cannons, however heavy and clumsy the latter might be, were transforming warfare from Europe to China. In the Middle East, Janissary musketeers and heavy ar-

> "In feudal Europe and somewhat later in Japan . . . siege cannons reduced feudal castles to rubble."

tillery became the driving force of Ottoman expansion. The Safavids' lack of artillery was critical to their defeat at Chaldiran. In Europe, armies were increasingly built around musket and artillery regiments. Rival states vied to attract gunsmiths who could provide them with the latest weaponry or, even better, invent guns that would give them decisive advantages over their rivals. In the Atlantic and the Mediterranean, handguns and cannons were introduced into sea warfare—an innovation that proved essential to the Europeans' ability to project their power overseas from the 16th century onward.

In many areas, the new military technology contributed to broader social and political changes. In feudal Europe and somewhat later in Japan, for example, siege cannons reduced feudal castles to rubble. In so doing, they struck a mortal blow at the warrior aristocracies that had dominated these societies for centuries. But the success of the new weaponry forced a revolution in the design of fortifications and defense strategies. The defense systems that resulted, which were expensive and elaborate, spawned corps of professional officers and engineers, vast military supply industries, and urban centers enclosed by low-lying walls and star-shaped bastions. The cost of the field artillery, siege weapons, and new defense industries promoted state centralization, as the experience of the Muslim empires and the history of Europe and Japan in the gunpowder age demonstrate. Rulers with national or imperial ambitions had the firepower to level the fortresses of regional lords and thus more effectively control the populations and resources of their domains.

Although the new weaponry was vital to the rise and sustenance of nation-states and empires, some political systems were more compatible than others with efforts to exploit and improve on it. At one extreme, the Chinese scholar-gentry limited innovations in gun-

---

State and Religion

The Safavid family was originally of Turkic stock, and early shahs such as Ismâ'il wrote in Turkish, unlike their Ottoman rivals, who preferred to write in Persian. After Chaldiran, however, Persian gradually supplanted Turkish as the language of the court and bureaucracy. Persian influences were also felt in the organization of court rituals and in the more and more exalted position of the Safavid shahs. Abandoning all pretense of the egalitarian camaraderie that had marked their earlier dealings with the warrior chiefs, the Safavids took grand titles, such as *padishah,* or king of kings, often derived from those used by the ancient Persian emperors. Like the Ottoman rulers, the Safavids presided from their high thrones over opulent palace complexes crowded with servants and courtiers. The pattern of palace life was set by elaborate court rituals and social interaction governed by a refined sense of etiquette and decorum. Although the later Safavid shahs played down claims to divinity that had been set forth under Ismâ'il and his predecessors, they continued to claim descent from one of the Shi'a **imams** or successors of Ali.

Changes in the status accorded to the Safavid rulers were paralleled by shifts in the religious impulses that had been so critical to their rise to power. The militant, expansive cast of Shi'a ideology was modified as the faith became a major pillar of dynasty and empire. The early Safavids imported Arabic-speaking Shi'a religious experts. But later shahs came to rely on Persian religious scholars who entered into the service of the state and were paid by the government. **Mullahs,** who

imams According to Shi'ism, rulers who could trace descent from the successors of Ali.

mullahs Local mosque officials and prayer leaders within the Safavid Empire; agents of Safavid religious campaign to convert all of population to Shi'ism.

480

powder weaponry and its use in warfare because they feared that these changes would lead to the dominance of the military in Ming and later Qing society. After the early 1600s, the shoguns, or military leaders, of neighboring Japan virtually banned the firearms that had done so much to bring them to power. In this case, a military caste feared that the spread of firearms to the general populace would destroy what was left of the feudal order they had built centuries earlier.

The obstacles faced by nomadic peoples such as the Mongols were very different. Their sparse populations and arid lands simply did not generate the resources or sustained invention that would allow them to keep up with their sedentary neighbors in the expensive arms races that the new technology spawned. As the advantages of sedentary societies grew more pronounced in the 17th and 18th centuries, nomadic peoples found not only that they could no longer raid or conquer the agrarian cores but also that sedentary adversaries could advance into and occupy their homelands on the steppe and desert fringes.

Nomadic dynasties, such as the Ottomans, Safavids, and Mughals, who had won their empires in the early stages of the gunpowder revolution, did control the agrarian bases and skilled artisans needed to supply their armies with muskets and siege cannons. But they were confronted by internal conflicts and, perhaps more critically in the long run, formidable external rivals. To begin with, their military technology was far in advance of the transport and communication systems of their far-flung empires. This fact, and their failure to build effective imperial bureaucracies, left them at the mercy of the warrior elites who brought them to power. In each of the three empires, the regional bases of the warrior classes became increasingly independent of the ruling dynasty. This meant that the rulers were denied revenue and other resources that were vital to maintaining competitive military establishments. Their fragile and overstretched administrative systems proved difficult to reform and more and more ineffective at administering the peasant populations in their charge. Internal revolts further sapped the resources of the hard-pressed Muslim dynasties.

In each Muslim empire, decline was hastened by the rise of European rivals, who proved more adept at taking advantage of the gunpowder revolution. The smaller but highly competitive nation-states of western Europe were better able to mobilize more limited human and natural resources than their Muslim counterparts. Constant struggles for survival in the multistate European system also made the elites of Spain, England, and France more receptive to technological innovation, which became a central ingredient of political success in the gunpowder era. Emulating the more advanced states of western Europe, for example, Peter the Great forced social reforms and military innovations that transformed a weak and backward Russia into a powerful adversary of the Ottomans and the nomadic peoples of the steppes. Thus, although it began in China and was initially spread by the Mongol nomads, the gunpowder revolution eventually tipped the global balance of power in favor of the peoples of Christian Europe. This shift was an essential condition for Europe's rise to global power in the centuries that followed.

QUESTIONS What advantages would gunpowder weaponry give to those who used it over those who did not in the early modern era? Were these advantages as decisive as they were later in the industrial age? Why would the use of muskets and early field cannons take a higher level of military organization and troop discipline and training than had been needed in earlier time periods? What made the new military technology so expensive? Why did the Europeans adopt it more readily than most other peoples, and why were they so intent on improving it?

were both local mosque officials and prayer leaders, were also supervised by the state and given some support from it. All religious leaders were required to curse the first three caliphs and mention the Safavid ruler in the Friday sermon. Teaching in the mosque schools was also planned and directed by state religious officials.

Through these agents, the bulk of the Iranian population was converted to Shi'ism during the centuries of Safavid rule. Sunni Muslims, Christians, Jews, Zoroastrians, and the followers of Sufi preachers were pressured to convert to Shi'ism. Shi'a religious festivals, such as that commemorating the martyrdom of Husayn (a son of Ali) and involving public flagellation and passion plays, and pilgrimages to Shi'a shrines, such as that at Karbala in central Iraq, became the focal points of popular religion in Iran. Thus, Shi'ism not only provided ideological and institutional support for the Safavid dynasty but also came to be an integral part of Iranian identity, setting the people of the region off from most of their Arab and Turkic neighbors.

Commercial Revival, Elite Affluence and the Art of the Mosque

Although earlier rulers had built or restored mosques and religious schools and financed public works projects, Abbas I surpassed them all. After securing his political position with a string of military victories, Abbas I set about establishing his empire as a major center of international trade and Islamic culture. He had a network of roads and rest houses built, and he strove to make merchants and travelers safe within his domains. He set up workshops to manufacture the silk textiles and splendid Persian carpets that were in great demand. Abbas I encouraged Iranian merchants to trade not only with their Muslim neighbors and India and China to the east but also with the Portuguese—and later the Dutch and English—whose war and merchant ships were becoming a familiar sight in the Persian Gulf and Arabian Sea.

Although Abbas I undertook building projects throughout his empire, he devoted special attention to his capital at **Isfahan**. The splendid seat of Safavid power was laid out around a great square, which was lined with two-story shops interspersed with great mosques, government offices, and soaring arches that opened onto formal gardens. Abbas I founded several colleges and oversaw the construction of numerous public baths and rest houses. He patronized workshops where intricately detailed and brilliantly colored miniatures were produced by master painters and their apprentices.

Above all, the great mosques that Abbas I had built at Isfahan were the glory of his reign (Figure 21.5). The vividly colored ceramic tiles, which Iranian builders had begun to use centuries earlier, turned the massive domes and graceful minarets of Safavid mosques and royal tombs into creations of stunning beauty. Geometric designs, floral patterns, and verses from the Qur'an written in stylized Arabic added movement and texture to the deep blue tiles that distinguished the monumental construction of the Safavid era. Gardens and reflecting pools were built near the mosques and rest houses. By combining graceful arches, greenery, and colorful designs, Persian architects and artisans created lush, cool refuges (perhaps duplicating heaven itself, as it is described in the Qur'an) in a land that is dry, dusty, and gray-brown for much of the year.

Society and Gender Roles: Ottoman and Safavid Comparisons

Although the Ottomans and Safavids were bitter political rivals and religious adversaries, the social systems that developed under the two dynasties had much in common. Both were dominated, particularly in their earliest phases, by warrior aristocracies, which shared power with the absolutist monarchs of each empire and enjoyed prestige and luxury in the capital and on rural estates. In both cases, the warrior aristocrats gradually retreated to the estates, making life increasingly difficult for the peasants on whom they depended for the support of their grand households and many retainers. As the real power of the rulers of each empire diminished and as population increases re-

Isfahan (1592–1629) Safavid capital under Abbas the Great; planned city laid out according to shah's plan; example of Safavid architecture.

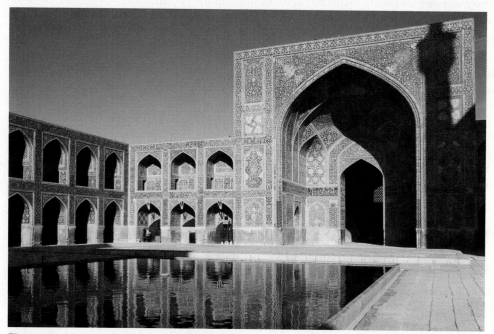

Figure 21.5 Occupying one side of the great square of the Safavid capital at Isfahan, the blue-tiled Shah Mosque was one of the architectural gems of the early modern era worldwide.

duced the uncultivated lands to which peasants might flee, the demands of the landlord class grew harsher. Foreign invasions, civil strife, and the breakdown in vital services once provided by the state added to the growing misery of the peasantry. The resulting spread of banditry, peasant uprisings, and flight from the land further drained the resources of both empires and undermined their legitimacy.

The early rulers of both the Ottoman and the Safavid empires encouraged the growth of handicraft production and trade in their realms. Both dynasties established imperial workshops where products ranging from miniature paintings and rugs to weapons and metal utensils were manufactured. The rulers of each empire lavishly patronized public works projects that provided reasonably well paid work for engineers, stonemasons, carpenters, and other sorts of artisans. Some of the more able emperors of these dynasties also pursued policies that they believed would increase both internal and international trade. In these endeavors, the Ottomans gained in the short run from the fact that large-scale traders in their empire often were from minority groups, such as Christians and Jews, who had extensive contacts with overseas traders that the bazaar merchants of the Safavid realm normally lacked. Although Safavid cooperation with Portuguese traders remedied this shortcoming to some extent, the Safavid economy remained much more constricted, less market oriented, and more technically backward than that of their Ottoman rivals.

Women in Islamic societies under Ottoman or Safavid rule faced legal and social disadvantages comparable to those we have encountered in most civilized areas so far. Within the family, women were subordinated to their fathers and husbands. They seldom had political or religious power, and they had surprisingly meager outlets for artistic or scholarly expression. Even women of nomadic Turkic and Mongol backgrounds gradually lost their independence when they settled in the towns of conquered areas. There, the dictates of increasingly patriarchal codes and restrictive practices such as seclusion and veiling were imposed on women of all classes, but most strictly on those of the elite.

However, recent evidence suggests that many women in the Islamic heartlands in this era, perhaps clinging to the memory of the lives led by their nomadic predecessors, struggled against these restrictions. Travelers to Persia in the time of Abbas I remarked on the brightly colored robes worn by women in the capital and elsewhere, and noted that many women made no effort to cover

Figure 21.6 A portrait of a Safavid notable, probably Shah Suleyman I (1667–1693), by a Persian court artist. He is surrounded by courtiers, including a European visitor bearing presents for the Persian leader. From the time of Abbas, European nations vied fiercely for influence at the Safavid court.

(Local History Museums' Collection, Durban.)

their faces in public. At both the Ottoman and Safavid courts, the wives and concubines of the rulers and royal princes continued to exert influence behind the throne and remained deeply involved in palace conspiracies. More important for ordinary women in each of these societies was the fact that many were active in trade and some in money-lending. Court records also suggest that women often could invoke provisions in Islamic law that protected their rights to inheritance, decent treatment by their spouses, and even divorce in marital situations that had become intolerable.

How typical these instances of assertion and expression were is not clear. Although some women were a good deal better off than we had once thought, perhaps as well off as or even better off than their counterparts in China and India, most women probably lived unenviable lives. Limited largely to contacts with their own families and left with little more than household chores and domestic handicrafts such as embroidery to occupy their time, the overwhelming majority of women in effect disappeared from the history of two of the great centers of Islamic civilization.

The Rapid Demise of the Safavid Empire

Given the power and splendor the Safavid Empire had achieved by the end of the reign of Abbas I, its collapse was stunningly rapid. Abbas's fears of usurpation by one of his sons, which were fed by plots on the part of several of his closest advisors, had led during his reign to the death or blinding of all who could legitimately succeed him. A grandson, who was weak and thus thought by high state officials to be easily manipulated, was placed on the throne after Abbas's death. From this point, the dynasty's fortunes declined. As was true of the Ottomans, the practice of confining the princes to the atmosphere of luxury and intrigue that permeated the court led to a sharp fall in the quality of Safavid rulers. Able shahs, such as Abbas II (r. 1642–1666), were too few to halt the decline of the imperial administration or to deal effectively with the many foreign threats to the empire. Factional disputes and rebellions shook the empire from within, and nomadic raiders and Ottoman and Mughal armies steadily reduced the territory the Safavids could tap for labor and revenue.

In March 1722, Isfahan was besieged by Afghani tribes. In October, after over 80,000 of the capital's inhabitants had died of starvation and disease, the city fell and Safavid power was ended. One of those who fought for the throne in the decade of war and destruction that followed claimed descent from the Safavid line. But a soldier-adventurer named **Nadir Khan Afshar** eventually emerged victorious from these bloody struggles. Although he began as a champion of Safavid restoration, Nadir Khan proclaimed himself shah in 1736. Despite the title, his dynasty and those that followed were short-lived. The area that had once made up the Safavid Empire was reduced for generations to a battleground for its powerful neighbors and a tempting target for nomadic raiders.

The Mughals and the Apex of Muslim Civilization in India

Despite the fact that the founder of the Mughal dynasty, **Babur**, traced his descent on one side from the Mongol khans, the Mughal in the dynasty's name was not derived from those earlier nomadic conquerors. Babur was also descended from the Turkic conqueror Timur, and most of his followers were from Turkic or mixed nomadic origins. Unlike the Ottomans and Safavids, Babur's motives for conquest and empire building had little to do with religious fervor. Originally, he directed raids into the fertile and heavily populated plains of north India only to gain booty to support his campaigns to win back his lost kingdom, Ferghana. Although India had much greater potential as a base on which to build an empire, Babur cared little for the green and well watered subcontinent. Even after he conquered India, he continued to long for the arid steppes and blue-domed mosques of his central Asian birthplace. But after decades of wars on the steppes that repeatedly ended in defeat, he was forced to give up his dream of reclaiming his homeland and to turn his full energies to the conquest of northern India. Within two years, his armies had conquered large portions of the Indus and Ganges plains and he had laid the foundations for a dynasty that would last more than 300 years.

The founder of the Mughal dynasty was a remarkable man. He was a fine military strategist and fierce fighter who went into battle alongside his troops. But Babur also cultivated a taste for the arts and music over the course of the decades when he was continually fighting for survival. He wrote one of the great histories of India, was a fine musician, and designed wonderful gardens for

Nadir Khan Afshar (1688–1747) Soldier-adventurer following fall of Safavid dynasty in 1722; proclaimed himself shah in 1736; established short-lived dynasty in reduced kingdom.

Babur Founder of Mughal dynasty in India; descended from Turkic warriors; first led invasion of India in 1526; died in 1530.

In the first centuries of Mughal rule in India, Islam reached the peak of its influence as a political and cultural force in south Asian history. Under the Mughal emperors, a blend of Hindu and Islamic civilizations produced some of the world's most sublime architecture and art.

his new capital at Delhi. But he was a better conqueror than administrator. Babur did little to reform the very ineffective Lodi bureaucracy he had taken over—a project that would have solidified the Mughals' hold on the empire he had conquered. In 1530, at the age of 48, he suddenly fell ill and died, leaving his son, **Humayan**, to inherit the newly founded kingdom.

Like his father, Humayan was a good soldier; in fact, he had won his first battle at age 18. But Babur's death was the signal for his enemies to strike from all sides. One of Humayan's brothers disputed his succession, and armies from Afghanistan and the Rajput states of western India marched on his capital (Map 21.4). By 1540, with his armies shattered, Humayan was forced to flee to Persia. There he remained in exile, an embarrassed guest at the Safavid court, for nearly a decade. Having gained a foothold at Kabul in 1545, Humayan launched a series of campaigns into India that restored Mughal rule to the northern plains by 1556. But Humayan did not live to savor his victory. Shortly after entering Delhi in triumph, he was hurrying down his library steps, his arms full of books, to answer the call to prayer. He stumbled and fell, hitting his head. He died within days.

Akbar's Religious Syncretism, Hindu Allies, and a Multi-Cultural Empire

Humayan's sudden death once again imperiled the Mughal dynasty. His son and successor, **Akbar**, was only 13 years old, and the Mughals' enemies moved quickly to take advantage of what they saw as a very favorable turn of events. Their expectations were soon dashed because Akbar proved to be one of the greatest leaders of all history. Interestingly, Akbar's reign was contemporaneous with those of several other remarkable monarchs, including Elizabeth I of England, Philip of Spain, and the Muslim rulers Suleyman the Magnificent and Abbas I. Akbar was a match for any one of these very formidable rivals.

Like his father and grandfather, Akbar was a fine military commander with great personal courage. But unlike his predecessors, Akbar also had a vision of empire and sense of mission that hinged on uniting India under his rule. A workaholic who seldom slept more than three hours a night, Akbar personally oversaw the building of the military and administrative systems that would form the backbone of the Mughal Empire for centuries. He also patronized the arts and entered into complex religious and philosophical discussions with learned scholars from throughout the Muslim, Christian, and Hindu worlds. In addition, Akbar found time to carry out social reforms and invent his own universalistic religion. Though illiterate—there had been little time for book learning when his father fought for survival in the wilderness—Akbar had an insatiable curiosity and an incredible memory. By having others read aloud to him, he became educated in many fields.

At first with the help of senior advisors, but soon on his own, Akbar routed the enemies who had hoped to capitalize on the Mughals' misfortunes. In the decades after 1560, when he took charge of the government, Akbar's armies greatly extended the empire with conquests throughout north and central India. But it was Akbar's social policies and administrative genius that made it possible to establish the foundations of a lasting dominion in the subcontinent. He pursued a policy of reconciliation and cooperation with the Hindu princes and the Hindu majority of the population of his realm. He encouraged intermarriage between the Mughal aristocracy and the families of the Hindu Rajput rulers. Akbar also abolished the much-hated *jizya,* or head tax, that earlier Muslim rulers had levied on Hindu unbelievers. He promoted Hindus to the highest ranks in the government, ended a long-standing ban on the building of new Hindu temples, and ordered Muslims to respect cows, which the Hindu majority viewed as sacred.

Despite the success of these policies in reconciling the Hindu majority to Muslim rule, Akbar viewed tolerance as merely the first stage in a longer strategy to put an end to sectarian divisions in

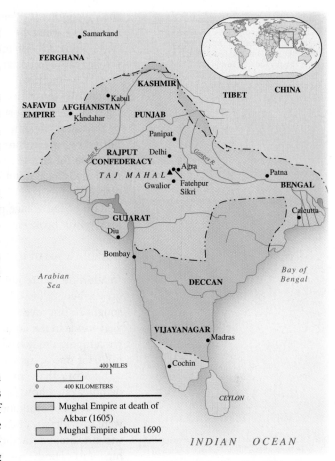

Map 21.4 The Growth of the Mughal Empire, from Akbar to Aurangzeb Though in its later phase the Mughal empire occupied much of South Asia, the cost of wars of expansion contributed in major ways to its rapid decline from the late 17th century.

 Akbar, Emperor of India

Humayan Son and successor of Babur; expelled from India in 1540, but restored Mughal rule by 1556; died shortly thereafter.

Akbar (1542–1605) Son and successor of Humayan; oversaw building of military and administrative systems that became typical of Mughal rule in India; pursued policy of cooperation with Hindu princes; attempted to create new religion to bind Muslim and Hindu populations of India.

 Akbar and the Jesuits

Din-i-Ilahi Religion initiated by Akbar in Mughal India; blended elements of the many faiths of the subcontinent; key to efforts to reconcile Hindus and Muslims in India, but failed.

the subcontinent. Blending elements of the many religions with which he was familiar, he invented a new faith, the **Din-i-Ilahi,** that he believed could be used to unite his Hindu and Muslim subjects. If the adherents of India's diverse religions could be convinced to embrace this common creed, Akbar reasoned, sectarian quarrels and even violent conflict could be brought to an end.

Like their counterparts in the Ottoman and Safavid empires, the Muslim and Hindu warrior aristocrats who formed the core of the supporters of the Mughal dynasty were granted peasant villages for their support. In turn, they were required to maintain a specified number of cavalry and to be on call if the emperor needed their services. The court and the central bureaucracy were supported by revenues drawn from the tribute paid by the military retainers and from taxes on lands set aside for the support of the imperial household. Because of a shortage of administrators, in most areas local notables, many of whom were Hindu, were left in place as long as they swore allegiance to the Mughal rulers and paid their taxes on time. These arrangements left the control and welfare of the village population largely in the hands of the military retainers of the dynasty and local power brokers.

Social Reform and Attempts to Recast Gender Relations

In addition to his administrative reforms, Akbar pushed for social changes that he believed would greatly benefit his subjects. Beyond the public works typically favored by able Muslim rulers, Akbar sought to improve the calendar, to establish living quarters for the large population of beggars and vagabonds in the large cities, and to regulate the consumption of alcohol. Whatever success the latter campaign may have had in Indian society as a whole, it apparently failed in Akbar's own household, for one of his sons was reputed to drink 20 cups of double-distilled wine per day.

sati Ritual in India of immolating surviving widows with the bodies of their deceased husbands.

More than any of Akbar's many reform efforts, those involving the position of women demonstrated how far the Mughal ruler was in advance of his time. He encouraged widow remarriage, at that point taboo for both Hindus and Muslims, and discouraged child marriages. The latter were so widespread among the upper classes that he did not try to outlaw them, and it is doubtful that his disapproval did much to curb the practice. Akbar did legally prohibit **sati**, or the burning of high-caste Hindu women on their husbands' funeral pyres (Figure 21.7). Because this custom was deeply entrenched among the Rajput princes and warrior classes that were some of his most faithful allies, this was a risky move on Akbar's part. But he was so determined to eradicate sati, particularly in cases where the widow was pressured to agree to be burned alive, that he once personally rescued a young woman despite the protestations of her angry relatives. He also tried to provide relief for

purdah Seclusion in their homes imposed on women.

women trapped in **purdah**, or seclusion in their homes, by encouraging the merchants of Delhi and other cities to set aside special market days for women only.

Mughal Splendor and Early European Contacts

Despite his many successes and the civil peace and prosperity his reign brought to much of northern India, Akbar died a lonely and discouraged man. By 1605 he had outlived most of his friends and faced revolts by sons eager to claim his throne. Above all, he died knowing that Din-i-Ilahi, the religion he had created to reconcile his Hindu and Muslim subjects, had been rejected by both.

Although neither of his successors, Jahangir (r. 1605–1627) or Shah Jahan (r. 1627–1658), added much territory to the empire Akbar had left them, in their reigns Mughal India reached the peak of its splendor. European visitors marveled at the size and opulence of the chief Mughal cities: Delhi, Agra, and Lahore. The huge Mughal armies, replete with elephant and artillery corps, dwarfed those of even the most powerful European rulers at the time. Some of the more perceptive European observers, such as François Bernier, also noted the poverty in which the lower classes in both town and countryside lived and the lack of discipline and training of most of the soldiers in the Mughal armies. Perhaps most ominously, Bernier added that in invention and the sciences, India had fallen far behind western Europe in most areas.

The English in South Asia and the Indian Ocean

Nonetheless, by the late 17th century, Mughal India had become one of the major overseas destinations for European traders. They brought products from throughout Asia, though little from Europe itself, to exchange for a variety of Indian manufactures, particularly the subcontinent's famed cotton textiles. The trade gap that the demand for Indian cotton cloth and clothing had created in the West in Roman times persisted millennia later. The importance of the Indian textile

Figure 21.7 This engraving from a late 16th-century German traveler's account of India shows a European artist's impression of an Indian widow committing sati. Not surprisingly, this practice of burning high-caste widows in some parts of India and among certain social groups on their deceased husbands' funeral pyres often was described at great length by European visitors in this era. There was some disagreement in their accounts as to whether the women went willingly into the fire, as some early authors claimed. Later inquiries in the British period revealed that some of the widows had been drugged and others tied to the funeral pyre. It is likely that many simply caved in to pressure applied by their dead spouse's relatives and at times even their own children.

trade to the West is suggested by the names we still use for different kinds of cotton cloth, from calico (after the Indian port city of Calicut) to chintz and muslin, as well as by our names for cotton clothes such as pajamas.

Because they were easily washed and inexpensive, Indian textiles first won a large market among the working and middle classes in Britain and elsewhere in Europe. In the reigns of Queen Mary and Queen Anne, fine Indian cloth came into fashion at the court as well. An incident from the reign of the Mughal emperor **Aurangzeb** (AHR-uhng-zuhb), who succeeded Shah Jahan, suggests just how fine the cloth in question was. Aurangzeb, a religious zealot, scolded his favorite daughter for appearing in his presence in garments that revealed so much of her body. The daughter protested that she had on three layers of fine cotton clothing. It is thus no wonder that even after industrialization had revolutionized cotton textile manufacture in England, European visitors to India continued to observe and write in great detail about the techniques Indian artisans used to weave and dye cotton cloth. The popularity of madras cloth today demonstrates that this interest has not died out.

Two Very Different Mughal Emperors

Aurangzeb   Mughal emperor who succeeded Shah Jajan known for his religious zealotry.

Wonders of the Early Modern World: Artistic Achievement in the Mughal Era

Both Jahangir and Shah Jahan continued Akbar's policy of tolerance toward the Hindu majority and retained most of the alliances he had forged with Hindu princes and local leaders. They made little attempt to change the administrative apparatus they had inherited from Akbar, and they fought their wars in much the same way as the founders of the dynasty had. Both mounted campaigns to crush potential enemies and in some cases to enlarge the empire. But neither was as interested in conquest and politics as in enjoying the good life. Both were fond of drink, female dancers,

Art as a Window into the Past: Paintings and History in Mughal India

In ways that were similar to China and the great Muslim empires of Asia and Africa, European states participated in the gunpowder revolution that transformed the nature of warfare and political power in the early modern era. But as the Iberians and somewhat later the Dutch, English, and French sailed out across the oceans, they were able to harness the firepower of cannons and hand guns mainly to establish their growing power on the seas.

Except in the Americas, where millennia of isolation left the indigenous peoples without metalworking and gunpowder, once the Europeans went ashore they could not hope to dominate kingdoms with far larger armies and resources than any state in Europe in the 15th and 16th centuries.

Consequently, over much of Africa and Asia, the Spanish and Portuguese and after them the northern Europeans sought for the most part to establish trading linkages, win permission to build warehouses and fortify small settlements, and pursue efforts to convert local populations from fishermen and laborers to emperors and their courtiers.

Since there were no photographs or newsreels, what we know about the interactions between Europeans and the peoples they encountered overseas in the early modern era comes mainly from different sorts of written sources. But works of art, such as the two Mughal miniatures reproduced here, can also tell us a good deal about these cross-cultural encounters.

The first depicts the Mughal armies besieging and eventually capturing the Portuguese trading post at the port of Hoogly in present day Bengal. The second is a formal painting of the Mughal emperor, Shah Jahan, receiving homage and tribute from his vassals and foreign emissaries. And there is a connection between the two paintings – the Europeans in the lower left hand corner of the imperial audience are Portuguese who have just lost their trading center at Hoogly.

QUESTIONS Study these two paintings, as well as the other artwork in this chapter that show (1) the great naval clash (p. 476) between an allied European fleet and the Ottomans at Lepanto; (2) a European emissary meeting with Shah Suleyman of Persia (p. 483); and (3) a German engraving (p. 487) of an Indian woman about to be immolated on her husband's funeral pyre. What do the placement of the Europeans in relation to the Mughal court and the Persian shah and his entourage, the postures of the Europeans and what they carry tell us about the power balance between these intruders and the rulers of the Muslim empires in this era? Contrast the battle at Lepanto in the Mediterranean with the Mughal siege of Hoogly in terms of the relative power between the two sides and discuss the factors that made for very different outcomes in the two clashes. And what can we learn about European attitudes towards the customs, dress and gender positions of ordinary people and society more broadly—in this case Hindu society in South Asia—from the German engraving of sati, or widow burning. Are paintings a reliable way to gain historical insights in the early modern era, and how do they compare to the photographs that we rely upon so heavily in the present day?

and the pleasure gardens they had laid out from Kashmir to Allahabad. Both were delighted by polo matches (a game invented by the princes of India), ox and tiger or elephant fights, and games of pachisi, which they played on life-sized boards with palace dancers as chips. Both took great pleasure in the elaborate court ceremonies that blended Indian and Persian precedents, lavish state processions, their palaces and jewel-studded wardrobes, and the scented and sweetened ices that were rushed from the cool mountains in the north to their capitals on the sweltering plains.

Jahangir and Shah Jahan are best remembered as two of the greatest patrons of the fine arts in human history. They expanded the painting workshops that had been started by the early Mughals so that thousands of exquisite miniature paintings could be produced during their reigns. Both Jahangir and Shah Jahan also devoted massive resources to building some of the most stunning architectural works of all time. The best known of these is the **Taj Mahal** (Figure 21.8), which has become a symbol for India itself. But structures such as the audience hall in the Red Fort at Delhi, Akbar's tomb at Sikandra, and the tomb of Itimad al-Dowleh at Agra rival the Taj Mahal in design and perhaps surpass it in the beauty of their detail and decoration.

At its best, Mughal architecture blends what is finest in the Persian and Hindu traditions. It fuses the Islamic genius for domes, arches, and minarets and the balance between them with the Hindu love of ornament. In place of the ceramic tiles that the Persians used to finish their mosques and tombs, Indian artisans substituted gleaming white marble, inset with semiprecious stones arranged in floral and geometric patterns. Extensive use was also made of marble reflecting pools, the most famous of which mirrors the beauty of the Taj Mahal. When these pools were inlaid with floral patterns and provided with fountains, the rippling water appeared to give life to the stone

Taj Mahal Most famous architectural achievement of Mughal India; originally built as a mausoleum for the wife of Shah Jahan, Mumtaz Mahal.

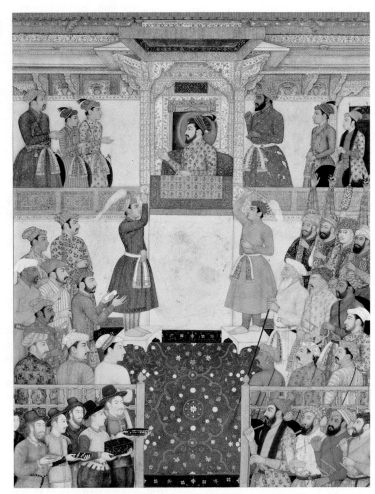

(Padshahnama: Europeans bring gifts to the Shah Jahan. The Royal Collection © 2009. Her Majesty Queen Elizabeth II.)

plant forms. Like the architects and artisans of the Ottoman Empire and Safavid Persia, those who served the Mughal rulers strove to create paradise on earth, an aspiration that was carved in marble on the audience hall of the Red Fort at Delhi. Around the ceiling of the great hall, it is written "If there is paradise on earth—It is here . . . it is here."

Court Politics and the Position of Elite and Ordinary Women

Not surprisingly, two rulers who were so absorbed in the arts and the pursuit of pleasure left most of the mundane tasks of day-to-day administration largely in the hands of subordinates. In both cases, strong-willed wives took advantage of their husbands' neglect of politics to win positions of power and influence at the Mughal court. Jahangir's wife, **Nur Jahan** (NOOR juh-HAHN), continually amassed power as he became more and more addicted to wine and opium. She packed the court with able male relatives, and her faction dominated the empire for most of the later years of Jahangir's reign. Nur Jahan was a big spender, but not only on pomp and luxury. She became a major patron of much needed charities in the major cities.

Shah Jahan's consort, **Mumtaz Mahal** (MUHM-tahz mah-HAHL), also became actively involved in court politics. But Shah Jahan was a much more engaged and able ruler than Jahangir, and thus her opportunities to amass power behind the throne were more limited. She is remembered not for her political acumen but for the love and devotion Shah Jahan bestowed upon her, a love literally enshrined in the Taj Mahal, the tomb where she is buried. Shah Jahan's plans to build a companion tomb for himself in black marble across the Jumna River were foiled by the revolt of his

Nur Jahan [NOOR juh-HAHN] (1577–1645) Wife of Jahangir; amassed power in court and created faction of male relatives who dominated Mughal empire during later years of Jahangir's reign.

Mumtaz Mahal [MUHM-tahz mah-HAHL] (1593–1631) Wife of Shah Jahan; took an active political role in Mughal court; entombed in Taj Mahal.

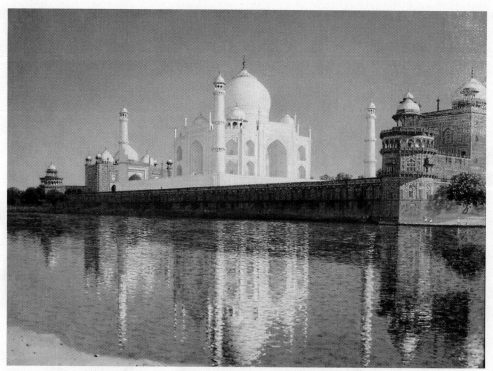

Figure 21.8 Perhaps no single building has come to symbolize Indian civilization more than the Taj Mahal. The grace and elegance of the tomb that Shah Jahan built in his wife's honor provide an enduring source of aesthetic delight. The white marble of the tomb is inlaid with flowers and geometric designs cut from semiprecious stones. The windows of the central chamber, which houses the tombs of Shah Jahan and Mumtaz Mahal, are decorated with carved marble screens, which add a sense of lightness and delicacy to the structure.

sons and by his imprisonment. He was buried next to his wife in the Taj Mahal, but her tomb is central and far larger than that of her husband.

Although the position of women at the Mughal court improved in the middle years of the dynasty's power, that of women in the rest of Indian society declined. Child marriage grew more popular, and the age limit was lowered. It was not unheard of for girls to be married at age nine. Widow remarriage among Hindus nearly died out. Seclusion was more and more strictly enforced for upper-caste women, both Hindu and Muslim. Muslim women rarely ventured forth from their homes unveiled, and those who did risked verbal and even physical abuse. The governor of one of the provinces of the Mughal Empire divorced his wife because she was seen scrambling for her life, unveiled, from a runaway elephant. Among upper-caste Hindus, the practice of sati spread despite Shah Jahan's renewed efforts to outlaw it. The dwindling scope of productive roles left to women, combined with the burden of the dowry that had to be paid to marry them off, meant that the birth of a girl was increasingly seen as an inauspicious event. At court as well as in the homes of ordinary villagers, only the birth of a son was greeted with feasting and celebrations.

The Beginnings of Imperial Decline

Aurangzeb, Shah Jahan's son and successor, seized control of an empire that was threatened by internal decay and growing dangers from external enemies. For decades, the need for essential administrative, military, and social reforms had been ignored. The Mughal bureaucracy had grown bloated and corrupt. The army was equally bloated and backward in weaponry and tactics. Peasants and urban workers had seen their productivity and living standards fall steadily. The Taj Mahal and other wonders of the Mughal artistic imagination had been paid for by the mass of the people at a very high price.

Though not the cruel bigot he is often portrayed as, Aurangzeb was not the man to restore the dynasty's declining fortunes. Courageous, honest, intelligent, and hard-working, he seemed an ideal successor to two rulers who had so badly neglected the affairs of state. But Aurangzeb was driven by

Aurangzeb,
Mughal River

two ambitions that proved disastrous to his schemes to strengthen the empire. He was determined to extend Mughal control over the whole of the Indian subcontinent, and he believed that it was his duty to purify Indian Islam and rid it of the Hindu influences he was convinced were steadily corrupting it.

The first ambition increased the number of the empire's adversaries, strained the allegiance of its vassals and allies, and greatly overextended its huge but obsolete military forces. By the time of his death in 1707, after a reign of nearly 50 years, Aurangzeb had conquered most of the subcontinent and extended Mughal control as far north as Kabul in what is now Afghanistan. But the almost endless warfare of his years in power drained the treasury and further enlarged an inefficient bureaucracy and army without gaining corresponding increases in revenues to support them.

Equally critically, the long wars occupied much of Aurangzeb's time and energies, diverting him from the administrative tasks and reforms essential to the dynasty's continued strength. While he was leading his massive armies in the south, there were peasant uprisings and revolts by Muslim and Hindu princes in the north. Perhaps even more harmful to the imperial system was the growing autonomy of local leaders, who diverted more and more revenue from the central administration into their own coffers. On the northern borders, incursions by Persian and Afghan warrior bands were increasing.

While Aurangzeb's military campaigns strained the resources of the empire, his religious policies gravely weakened the internal alliances and disrupted the social peace Akbar had so skillfully established. Aurangzeb continued to employ Hindus in the imperial service; in fact, he did not have the Muslim replacements to do without them. But non-Muslims were given far fewer posts at the upper levels of the bureaucracy, and their personal contact with the emperor was severely restricted. Aurangzeb also took measures that he and his religious advisors felt would help rid their Muslim faith and culture of the Hindu influences that had permeated it over the centuries. He forbade the building of new temples and put an end to Hindu religious festivals at court. Aurangzeb also reinstated the hated head tax on unbelievers—a measure he hoped might prod them to convert to Islam. The tax fell heavily on the Hindu poor and in some cases drove them to support sectarian movements that rose up to resist Aurangzeb.

By the end of Aurangzeb's reign, the Mughal Empire was far larger than it had been under any of the earlier emperors, but it was also more unstable. Internal rebellions, particularly those mounted by the **Marattas** in western India, put an end to effective Mughal control over large areas. The rise of new sects, such as the **Sikhs** (SEEKS), in the northwest, further strained the declining resources of an imperial system that was clearly overextended. The early leaders of the Sikhs originally tried to bridge the differences between Hindu and Muslim. But Mughal persecution of the new sect, which was seen as religiously heretical and a political threat to the dynasty, eventually transformed Sikhism into a staunchly anti-Muslim force within the subcontinent. In addition, Muslim kingdoms in central and east India continued to resist Mughal hegemony, and Islamic invaders waited at the poorly guarded passes through the Himalayas to strike and plunder once it was clear that the Mughals could no longer fend them off.

Islamic Commentators in India

Marattas Western India peoples who rebelled against Mughal control early in 18th century.

Sikhs [SEEKS] Sect in northwest India; early leaders tried to bridge differences between Hindu and Muslim, but Mughal persecution led to anti-Muslim feeling.

Global Connections

Gunpowder Empires and the Restoration of the Islamic Bridge Between Civilizations

The formation of the Ottoman, Safavid, and Mughal dynasties warrants comparison with the steadily expanding land empires of the Russian tsars and the Ming emperors, each of which also included substantial Muslim populations. And although the emerging nation-states of western Europe expanded mainly by sea, they also shared a good deal with the vast land empires of Eurasia. All were highly centralized politically and organized around absolute and hereditary rulers. Each empire's power and capacity to expand was dependent on new military technologies and modes of military organization deployed on both land and sea. In contrast to the Muslim empires, which were established by pastoral peoples, those of Russia and China expended much of their expansive energies to contain and subdue nomadic peoples. Western Europeans confronted nomadic peoples—some of whom practiced agriculture, but most of whom were primarily hunters and gatherers—in their American and south African settler colonies.

Compared with the Abbasid era, new discoveries in the sciences dropped off during this period, but the transmission of Indian and Greco-Arab learning may have accelerated in the Muslim world. Far more impressive were the influences that the artists and architects from each of these Muslim empires exerted on each other. Contravening the Muslim prohibition of the depiction of human figures, miniature painting—typically of shahs and sultans, epic sagas, social scenes, and battles—reached a level of perfection seldom equaled. And especially between Persia and India, artists, techniques, and fashions in painting were shared extensively, although regional styles could be quite distinct. Though few of the monumental buildings commissioned by Babur in India remain, all were heavily influenced by Ottoman tastes and methods of construction. In each of these fields and in every instance of emulation, borrowing, and reworking, this cross-fertilization between disparate cultures and peoples built on a tradition of exchange that had been a hallmark of Islamic civilization from its beginnings.

Changes in the position of the three great Islamic empires relative to the Russian, Chinese, and western European empires of the early modern era were gradual and complex. The Ottoman, Safavid, and Mughal empires retained active programs of overseas trade which, as we have seen, was a defining feature of early modern history worldwide. Arabs, for example, continued to interact with the peoples of the east African coast and their trade in slaves, spices, and other goods. Europeans sought luxury products both in the Middle East and in India. In fact, Indian merchants made large profits from the spices and textiles they exported and that the Europeans paid for in silver from the Americas. But the Europeans were increasingly assertive, setting up their own merchant groupings in Constantinople, for example, where they followed their laws rather than those of the Ottoman Empire.

European disdain for the slower pace of scientific and technological change in the Muslim—as well as the Chinese and Russian—empires also grew as the political and military power of the dynasties that ruled these decreased. The internal causes of decline discussed in this chapter for the early modern Muslim empires were probably sufficient to eventually undermine these great gunpowder empires. But each was also afflicted by further weaknesses that had profound significance for Islamic civilization as a whole. Captivated by their rivalries with each other and the problems of holding together their empires, none of the dynasties took the rising threat from Europe seriously. They called on Western travelers and missionaries for advice in casting cannons or military tactics, but none of the officials of the great Islamic empires systematically monitored technological advances in Europe. Eventually, the decline of the Mughals opened the door for growing political and military intervention by Europeans in the Indian subcontinent, particularly by the British and French, who formed alliances with rival princes in an increasingly decentralized society. A British empire in India was actively forming by the end of the early modern centuries.

The failure to take strong measures to meet the challenges that European overseas expansion was creating for Islamic civilization was also responsible for the weakening of the economic basis of each of the empires. Key tax revenues and merchant profits were drained off by the rise of European trading empires in Asia (see Chapters 16, 17, and 22). The Europeans' gains in ways to generate wealth and economic growth meant increasing losses for Muslim societies and political systems. These setbacks eventu-

ally proved critical to the failure of Muslim efforts to compete politically and militarily with their Christian rivals.

Further Readings

For a comparative look at this period, see William H. McNeill, *The Age of Gunpowder Empires, 1450–1800* (1989).

The most approachable exploration of the origins of the Ottoman state, see C. Kafadar, *Between Two Worlds: The Construction of the Ottoman State* (1995). G. Necipoglu, *Architecture, Ceremonial, and Power: The Topkapi Palace in the Fifteenth and Sixteenth Centuries* (1991), illuminates the potent political symbolism embedded in the Ottoman Empire's greatest artistic achievement. S. S. Blair and J. Bloom, *The Art and Architecture of Islam, 1250–1800* (1994), can be used to extend this analysis across the Muslim world. Peter F. Sugar, *Southeastern Europe Under Ottoman Rule, 1354–1804* (1977), is a fine account of life in the Christian portions of the empire. Afaf Lutfi al-Sayyid Marsot, *Women and Men in Late Eighteenth Century Egypt* (1995), explores gender roles in the age of the Ottomans.

R. M. Savory's writings, including *Iran Under the Safavids* (1980), his chapters in *The Cambridge History of Iran* (1986), and the volume that he edited on *Islamic Civilization* (1976) offer accessible discussions of the arts and society in the Turkic and Persian sectors of the Islamic heartland. The introductory sections of Nikki Keddi's *Roots of Revolution* (1981) provide a good discussion of the relationship between religion and the state in the Safavid period.

The Ikram and Ahmad books cited in Chapter 12 on expansion of Islam in India are also good resources on the Mughals. Though specialized, the works of Irfan Habib, M. Athar Ali, Richard Eaton, John F. Richards, and Douglas Streusand on the Mughal Empire are also critical, as is Muzzafar Alam's *The Crisis of the Empire in Mughal North India* (1993), one of many recent works reexamining the decline of the Mughal dynasty.

The role of women in the Islamic Gunpowder Empires is addressed in Stephen P. Blake, "Contributors to the Urban Landscape: Women Builders in Safavid Isfahan and Mughal Shahjahanabad," in Gavin Hambly, ed., *Women in the Medieval Islamic World* (1998); Ellison Banks Findly, *Nur Jahan: Empress of Mughal India* (1993); Stanley K. Freiberg, *Jahanara: Daughter of the Taj Mahal* (1999); and D. Fairchild Ruggles, ed., *Women, Patronage, and Self-Representation in Islamic Societies* (2000).

Trade between the Muslim gunpowder empires is one of the issues explored in Ashin Das Gupta and M. N. Pearson, eds., *India and the Indian Ocean, 1500–1800* (1987), and in Michael Adas, ed., *Islamic and European Expansion* (1993).

On the Web

Virtual visits to the palaces of the Ottomans (http://www.ee.bilkent .edu.tr/~history/topkapi.html and http://www.paradoxplace.com/ Insights/Topkapi/Suleiman%20Topkapi%20Ottomans.htm), the Safavids (http://www.payvand.com/news/07/nov/1118.html and http://www.persianpaintings.com/architecture-islamic/pages/ DSCN0257.htm), and the Mughals (http://www.world-heritage

-tour.org/asia/south-asia/india/agra/fatehpur-sikri/map.html, http://en.wikipedia.org/wiki/Fatehpur_Sikri, and http://www.taj-mahal.net), indicate the splendor of their empires.

Studies of the life and work of the Mughal emperor Akbar (http://www.boloji.com/history/022.htm, http://www.wsu.edu:8080/~dee/MUGHAL/AKBAR.HTM, and http://www.kamat.com/kalranga/mogul/akbar.htm) address his program of religious toleration that was promoted by his coinage (http://prabhu.50g.com/mughal/mug_akbar.html). Insight into warfare of the period and the role of Janissaries, slave troops, and slavery in gunpowder empires can be obtained at http://i-cias.com/e.o/janissaries.htm and http://www.fordham.edu/halsall/mod/1555busbecq.html. The prominent role of women in the Mughal Empire is traced through the lives of Gulbadan begum, Nur Jahan and Mumtaz Mahal at http://en.wikipedia.org/wiki/Gulbadan_Begum, http://www.boloji.com/history/029.htm, and http://www.indusundaresan.com/Mughal/mughal.aspx. The study of the role of women in the Ottoman Empire supported by resources at http://www.allaboutturkey.com/woman.htm, http://chnm.gmu.edu/wwh/lessons/lesson3/lesson3.php?s=0, and http://www.womeninworldhistory.com/toc-10.html.

AP* | Test Prep

1. Which of the following helps explain the widespread rise of the three new Muslim empires during the early modern period?
   (A) their use of gunpowder weapons
   (B) European conquests in East Asia
   (C) Japanese and Western Expansion
   (D) the introduction of new global communication technology
   (E) the decline of religious divisions

2. The Ottoman, Safavid, and Mughal empires shared all of these characteristics EXCEPT
   (A) they originated in Turkish nomadic cultures of the steppe.
   (B) they were Muslim led.
   (C) they were based on conquest and the use of military technologies.
   (D) they all ruled predominantly Muslim populations.

3. In order to supply its elite Janissaries and palace with soldiers, the Ottoman rulers
   (A) used labor taxes.
   (B) relied on Muslim noble families.
   (C) conscripted Balkan Christian boys and converted them to Islam.
   (D) imported and paid trained foreigners and mercenaries.

4. During their reign, Safavid policies in Persia
   (A) fostered a sense of Persian religious culture and social unity.
   (B) favored Turkish traditions and customs.
   (C) favored the Arabic language and Arab bureaucracies.
   (D) favored agriculture over trade and manufacturing.

5. Although the Ottomans and the Safavids were bitter political and religious rivals, which of the following is an accurate description of a similarity between them?
   (A) They took care to support the peasantry's demands against harsh landlords.
   (B) They patronized the arts and encouraged foreign and domestic trade.
   (C) They allowed women greater social and economic freedoms than did the Mughals.
   (D) They both encouraged Shi'a theology.

6. The decline of the Ottomans can be traced to all the following EXCEPT
   (A) the weakening of the Sultan's power to due to succession disputes.
   (B) the battle of Chaldiran which marked the end of Ottoman military supremacy.
   (C) the oversight of the empire hindered by poor communications and corruption.
   (D) the introduction of Latin American silver which led to crippling inflation.

7. Akbar envisioned reforming India by attempting to implement all of the following policies EXCEPT
   (A) child marriage and widowhood traditions.
   (B) the creation of a universalist religion.
   (C) reforming military and administrative training procedures.
   (D) hiring of foreign intellectuals to start new universities.

Free-Response Question

Compare the Muslim empires (Ottoman, Safavid, and Mughal) with either the Ming or the Russian empires in this period.

22 Asian Transitions in an Age of Global Change

The Asian Trading World and the Coming of the Europeans

Ming China: A Global Mission Refused

VISUALIZING THE PAST: The Great Ships of the Ming Expeditions that Crossed the Indian Ocean

DOCUMENT: Exam Questions as a Mirror of Chinese Values

THINKING HISTORICALLY: Means and Motives for Overseas Expansion: Europe and China Compared

Fending Off the West: Japan's Reunification and the First Challenge

GLOBAL CONNECTIONS: An Age of Eurasian Protoglobalization

After savoring the exhilaration that only those who have made a breakthrough discovery can know, Vasco da Gama and his Portuguese crews received a number of rude shocks on the last legs of their epic voyage to India in 1498. Da Gama's exploratory probes were conducted in sailing ships that were a good deal smaller than the Portuguese merchant vessel depicted arriving in Japan a century later in the wonderful silk screen painting (Figure 22.8) on page 514. After nearly five months at sea, his tiny flotilla of four ships made its way through the treacherous waters off the Cape of Good Hope on the southern tip of Africa and sailed into the Indian Ocean.

After rounding the cape, Da Gama's expedition followed the African coastline northward in search of other Christians and a port to take on fresh supplies (Map 22.1). To their chagrin, most of the towns they encountered were controlled by Muslim Arabs. Some of the Arabs, including those at Mombasa—the largest commercial center on the coast—became hostile once they realized that the Portuguese were Christians. Conversations with the much friendlier sultan, traders, and townspeople farther north at Malindi, however, left no doubt that Da Gama's expedition had indeed discovered a sea route from Europe to the fabled Indies.

Da Gama and his compatriots were, of course, delighted and perhaps a bit awed by what they had achieved even before they crossed to India. Their very entry into the Indian Ocean meant that they had won a momentous victory over Spain. They had bested their Iberian rivals in a contest to find a sea route to the East Indies that both nations had pursued at great expense for decades. And their triumph was all the more satisfying because they had proved correct the long-standing conviction of Portuguese navigators and mapmakers that the Indian Ocean could be reached by sailing around Africa. And that in turn confirmed the Portuguese claim that Christopher Columbus's much-touted voyage across the Atlantic had been a failure. Columbus had not reached the Indies after all. He had made landfall at islands hitherto unknown to the Europeans, and of undetermined value.

Learning that the goal of Da Gama's expedition was India, the sultan at Malindi generously offered the Portuguese captain general a pilot to guide his ships across the Arabian Sea to the lands of spices and gems. Nearly a month later, Da Gama's ships arrived at Calicut on India's Malabar coast (Map 22.1). An ancient and thriving commercial emporium controlled by a Hindu ruler whom the Portuguese at first thought might be a Christian, Calicut seemed an ideal place to conclude their long voyage from Lisbon. Da Gama and his crew scrambled ashore eager to trade for the spices, fine textiles, and other Asian products that were among the main objectives of the voyages of exploration. Delighted by the fine quality and abundance of the products from all over Asia that were available in the town's great marketplace, the Portuguese were startled to learn that the local merchants had little interest in the products they had brought to trade. In fact, their cast-iron pots, coarse cloth, and glass and coral beads elicited little more than sneers from the merchants they approached.

Da Gama and his crew faced the humbling prospect of returning home to Lisbon with little proof that they had reached Asia and begun to tap its legendary wealth. Reluctantly, they concluded that they had little choice but to use the small supply of silver bullion they had brought along for emergencies. They found that the Asian merchants were quite willing to take their precious metal. But they also realized that their meager supply of bullion would not go very far toward filling the holds of their ships with Asian treasures. ■

Figure 22.1 Vasco Da Gama's arrival in Calicut on India's Malabar coast as depicted in a 16th-century European tapestry. As the pomp and splendor captured in the scene convey, Da Gama's voyage was regarded by European contemporaries as a major turning point in world history.

Much of the enterprise that occupied the Europeans who went out to Asia in the 16th and 17th centuries, which is one of the major themes of the chapter that follows, was devoted to working out the implications of that first encounter in Calicut. The very fact of Da Gama's arrival demonstrated not only the seaworthiness of their **caravel** ships but also that the Europeans' needs and curiosity could drive them halfway around the world. Their stops at Calicut and ports on the eastern coast of Africa also confirmed reports of earlier travelers that the Portuguese had arrived in east Africa and south and southeast Asia long after their Muslim rivals. This disconcerting discovery promised resistance to Portuguese trading and empire building in Asia. It also meant major obstacles to their plans for converting the peoples of the area to Roman Catholicism. The Portuguese and the other Europeans who came after them found that their Muslim adversaries greatly outnumbered them and had long-standing and well entrenched political and economic connections from east Africa to the Philippines. As we shall see, they soon concluded that only the use of military force would allow them to break into the vast Indian Ocean trading system.

Although Da Gama's voyage marked a major turning point for western Europe, its impact on Asia was much less decisive. As was the case with the Mughal and Safavid empires (see Chapter 21), the central themes in the history of Asian civilizations in the 16th and 17th centuries often had little or nothing to do with European expansion. The development of Asian states and empires emerged from long-term processes rooted in the inner workings of these ancient civilizations and in their interactions with neighboring states and nomadic peoples. Although the European presence was felt in each of the areas considered in this chapter, the impact of Europe's global expansion was of secondary importance except in the islands of southeast Asia, which were especially vulnerable to Western sea power. Most Asian rulers, merchants, and religious leaders refused to take seriously the potential threat posed by what was, after all, a handful of strangers from across the world.

caravels Slender, long-hulled vessels utilized by Portuguese; highly maneuverable and able to sail against the wind; key to development of Portuguese trade empire in Asia.

1350 C.E.	1500 C.E.	1550 C.E.	1600 C.E.	1650 C.E.	1700 C.E.
1368 Ming dynasty comes to power in China 1368–1398 Reign of the Hongwu emperor 1390 Ming restrictions on overseas commerce 1403–1424 Reign of the Yungle emperor in China 1405–1433 Zheng He expeditions from China to southeast Asia, India, and east Africa 1498–1499 Vasco da Gama opens the sea route around Africa to Asia	1507 Portuguese defeat combined Muslim war fleet near Diu off western India 1510 Portuguese conquest of Goa in western India 1511 Portuguese conquer Malacca on the tip of Malayan peninsula 1540s Francis Xavier makes mass converts in India	1573 End of the Ashikaga shogunate 1573–1620 Reign of the Wanli emperor 1580s Jesuits arrive in China 1590 Hideyoshi unifies Japan 1592 First Japanese invasion of Korea 1597 Second Japanese invasion of Korea	1600s Dutch and British assault on Portuguese Empire in Asia; decline of Portuguese power 1603 Tokugawa shogunate established 1614 Christianity banned in Japan 1619–1620 Dutch East India Company established at Batavia on Java 1640s Japan moves into self-imposed isolation 1641 Dutch capture Malacca from Portuguese; Dutch confined to Deshima Island off Nagasaki 1644 Nomadic Manchus put an end to Ming dynasty; Manchu Qing dynasty rules China	1662–1722 Reign of the Kangxi emperor in China	1755–1757 Dutch become paramount power on Java; Qing conquest of Mongolia

The Asian Trading World and the Coming of the Europeans

In the centuries following Da Gama's voyage, most European enterprise in the Indian Ocean centered on efforts to find the most profitable ways to carry Asian products back to Europe. Some Europeans went to Asia not for personal gain but to convert others to Christianity, and these missionaries, as well as some traders, settled in coastal enclaves.

Trade Routes
to Asia

MAP

Asian sea trading network Prior to intervention of Europeans, consisted of three zones: Arab zone based on glass, carpets, and tapestries; India based on cotton textiles; China based on paper, porcelain, and silks.

As later voyages by Portuguese fleets revealed, Calicut and the ports of east Africa, which Vasco da Gama had found on the initial foray into Asia, made up only a small segment of a larger network of commercial exchange and cultural interaction. This trading system stretched thousands of miles from the Middle East and Africa along all the coasts of the massive Asian continent. Both the products exchanged in this network and the main routes followed by those who sailed it had been established for centuries—in many cases, millennia.

In general, the **Asian sea trading network** can be broken down into three main zones, each of which was focused on major centers of handicraft manufacture (Map 22.1). In the west was an Arab zone anchored on the glass, carpets, and tapestries of the Islamic heartlands at the head of the Red Sea and the Persian Gulf. India, with its superb cotton textiles, dominated the central portions of the system. China, which excelled in producing paper, porcelain, and silk textiles, formed the eastern pole. In between or on the fringes of the three great manufacturing centers were areas such as Japan, the mainland kingdoms and island states of southeast Asia, and the port cities of east Africa that fed mainly raw materials—precious metals, foods, and forest products—into the trading network.

Of the raw materials circulating in the system, the broadest demand and highest prices were paid for spices, which came mainly from Ceylon (Shri Lanka in the present day) and the islands at the eastern end of what is today the Indonesian archipelago. Long-distance trade was largely in high-priced commodities such as spices, ivory from Africa, and precious stones. But silk and cotton textiles also were traded over long distances. Bulk items, such as rice, livestock, and timber, normally were exchanged among the ports within more localized networks in each of the main trading zones.

Since ancient times, monsoon winds and the nature of the ships and navigational instruments available to sailors had dictated the main trade routes in the Asian network. Much navigation

Map 22.1 Routes and Major Products Exchanged in the Asian Trading Network, c. 1500 By the early modern era the ancient trading network that encompassed the Indian Ocean and neighboring seas from the Mediterranean to the North China sea had expanded greatly in the volume of shipping and goods traded from the Middle East to China as well as in the number of port cities engaged in local and intercontinental commerce.

was of the coasting variety that is, sailing along the shoreline and charting distances and location with reference to towns and natural landmarks. The Arabs and Chinese, who had compasses and large, well built ships, could cross large expanses of open water such as the Arabian and South China seas. But even they preferred established coastal routes rather than the largely uncharted and less predictable open seas. As the Portuguese quickly learned, there were several crucial points where segments of the trade converged or where geography funneled it into narrow areas. The mouths of the Red Sea and Persian Gulf were two of these points, as were the Straits of Malacca, which separated mainland from island southeast Asia (Map 22.1).

Two general characteristics of the trading system at the time of the Portuguese arrival were critical to European attempts to regulate and dominate it. First, there was no central control. Second, military force was usually absent from commercial exchanges within it. Although Arab sailors and merchants were found in ports throughout much of the network, they had no sense of common cause. They sailed and traded to provide for their own livelihood and to make profits for the princes or merchants who financed their expeditions. The same was true for the Chinese, southeast Asian, and Indian merchants and sailors who were concentrated in particular segments of the trading complex. Because all the peoples participating in the network had something to trade for the products they wanted from others, exchanges within the system were largely peaceful. Trading vessels were lightly armed mainly for protection against attack by pirates.

Trading Empire: The Portuguese Response to the Encounter at Calicut

The Portuguese were not prepared to abide by the informal rules that had evolved over the centuries for commercial and cultural exchanges in the great Asian trading complex. It was apparent after the trip to the market in Calicut that the Portuguese had little, other than gold and silver, to exchange with Asian peoples. In an age in which prominent economic theorists, called **mercantilists,** taught that a state's power depended heavily on the amount of precious metals a monarch had in his coffers, a steady flow of bullion to Asia was unthinkable. It was particularly objectionable because it would enrich and thus strengthen merchants and rulers from rival kingdoms and religions, including the Muslims, whose position the Portuguese had set out to undermine through their overseas enterprises (Figure 22.2). Unwilling to forgo the possibilities for profit that a sea route to Asia presented, the Portuguese resolved to take by force what they could not get through fair trade.

The decision by the Portuguese to use force to extract spices and other goods from Asia resulted largely from their realization that they could offset their lack of numbers and trading goods with their superior ships and weaponry. Except for the huge war fleets of Chinese junks, no Asian people could muster fleets able to withstand the firepower and maneuverability of the Portuguese squadrons. Their sudden appearance in Asian waters and their interjection of sea warfare into a peaceful trading system gained the European intruders an element of surprise that kept their adversaries off balance in the critical early years of empire building. The Portuguese forces were small in numbers but united at least in the early years after 1498 in their drive for wealth and religious converts. This allowed them to take advantage of the divisions that often separated their Asian competitors and the Asians' inability to combine their forces effectively in battle. Thus, when Da Gama returned on a second expedition to Asian waters in 1502, he was able to force ports on both the African and Indian coasts to submit to a Portuguese tribute regime. He also assaulted towns that re-

mercantilists Economic theorists that stressed governments' promotion of limitation of imports from other nations and internal economies in order to improve tax revenues; popular during the 17th and 18th centuries in Europe.

Portuguese Church in Southern India

Figure 22.2 In the 15th and 16th centuries, the port of Lisbon in tiny Portugal was one of the great centers of international commerce and European overseas exploration. Although aspects of the early, streamlined caravel design can be detected in the ships pictured here, additional square sails, higher fore and aft castles, and numerous cannons projecting from holes cut in the ships' sides exemplify a later stage of naval development.

fused to cooperate. When a combined Egyptian and Indian fleet was finally sent in reprisal in 1509, it was defeated off Diu on the western Indian coast. The Portuguese would not have to face so formidable an alliance of Asian sea powers again.

The Portuguese soon found that sea patrols and raids on coastal towns were not sufficient to control the trade in the items they wanted, especially spices. Thus, from 1507 onward they strove to capture towns and build fortresses at a number of strategic points on the Asian trading network (see Map 22.2). In that year they took **Ormuz** at the southern end of the Persian Gulf; in 1510 they captured **Goa** on the western Indian coast. Most critical of all, in the next year they successfully stormed Malacca on the tip of the Malayan peninsula. These ports served both as naval bases for Portuguese fleets patrolling Asian waters and as **factories,** or warehouses where spices and other products could be stored until they were shipped to Europe or elsewhere in Asia. Ships, ports, and factories became the key components of a Portuguese trading empire that was financed and officially directed by the kings of Portugal, but often actually controlled by Portuguese in Asia and their local allies.

The aim of the empire was to establish Portuguese monopoly control over key Asian products, particularly spices such as nutmeg and cinnamon (Figure 22.3). Ideally, all the spices produced were to be shipped in Portuguese vessels to Asian or European markets. There they would be sold at high prices, which the Portuguese could dictate because they controlled the supply of these goods.

Ormuz Portuguese factory or fortified trade town located at southern end of Persian Gulf; site for forcible entry into Asian sea trade network.

Goa Portuguese factory or fortified trade town located on western India coast; site for forcible entry into Asian sea trade network.

factories European trading fortresses and compounds with resident merchants; utilized throughout Portuguese trading empire to assure secure landing places and commerce.

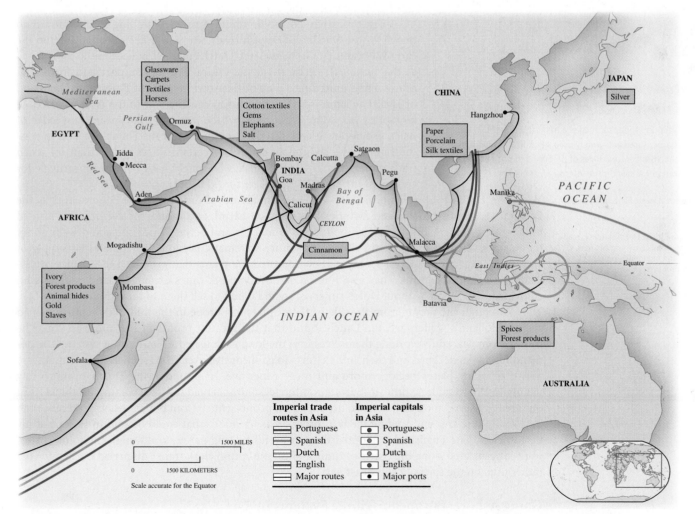

Map 22.2 The Pattern of Early European Expansion in Asia The differing routes and choice of fortified outposts adopted by successive European nations as they sought to tap directly into the Indian Ocean trading network reflect the greater information regarding centers of production that late comers, such as the Dutch and English possessed, relative to the pioneering Portuguese.

The Portuguese also sought, with little success, to impose a licensing system on all merchant ships that traded in the Indian Ocean from Ormuz to Malacca. The combination of monopoly and the licensing system, backed by force, was intended to give the Portuguese control of a sizeable portion of the Asian trading network.

Portuguese Vulnerability and the Rise of the Dutch and English Trading Empires

The plans for empire that the Portuguese drew up on paper never became reality. They managed for some decades to control some of the flow of spices, such as nutmeg and mace, which were grown in very limited areas. But a monopoly of the market in key condiments, such as pepper and cloves, eluded them. At times the Portuguese resorted to severe punishments such as cutting off the hands of the rival traders and ships' crews caught transporting spices in defiance of their monopoly. But they simply did not have the soldiers or the ships to sustain their monopolies, much less the licensing system. The resistance of Asian rivals, poor military discipline, rampant corruption among crown officials, and heavy Portuguese shipping losses caused by overloading and poor design had taken a heavy toll on the empire by the end of the 16th century.

   The overextended and declining Portuguese trading empire proved no match for the Dutch and English rivals, whose war fleets challenged it in the early 17th century. Of the two, the Dutch emerged, at least in the short term, as the victors. They captured the critical Portuguese port and fortress at Malacca and built a new port of their own in 1620 at **Batavia** on the island of Java. The latter location, which was much closer to the island sources of key spices (see Map 22.2), reflected the improved European knowledge of Asian geography. It was also the consequence of the Dutch decision to concentrate on the monopoly control of certain spices rather than on Asian trade more generally. The English, who fought hard but lost the struggle for control of the Spice Islands, were forced to fall back to India.

Figure 22.3 Although today nutmeg is a minor condiment, in the early modern era it was a treasured and widely used spice. In this manuscript illustration from the 16th century, slices of an oversized nutmeg are being weighed in preparation for sale on the international market.

Batavia   Dutch fortress located after 1620 on the island of Java.

Dutch trading empire   The Dutch system extending into Asia with fortified towns and factories, warships on patrol, and monopoly control of a limited number of products.

The **Dutch trading empire** (Map 22.2) was made up of the same basic components as the Portuguese: fortified towns and factories, warships on patrol, and monopoly control of a limited number of products. But the Dutch had more numerous and better armed ships and went about the business of monopoly control in a much more systematic fashion. To regulate the supply of cloves, nutmeg, and mace, for example, they uprooted the plants that produced these spices on islands they did not control. They also forcibly removed and at times executed island peoples who cultivated these spices without Dutch supervision and dared to sell them to their trading rivals.

   Although the profits from the sale of these spices in Europe in the mid-17th century helped sustain Holland's golden age, the Dutch found that the greatest profits in the long run could be gained from peacefully working themselves into the long-established Asian trading system. The demand for spices declined and their futile efforts to gain control over crops such as pepper that were grown in many places became more and more expensive. In response, the Dutch came to rely mainly (as they had long done in Europe) on the fees they charged for transporting products from one area in Asia to another. They also depended on profits gained from buying Asian products, such as cloth, in one area and trading them in other areas for goods that could be sold in Europe at inflated prices. The English also adopted these peaceful trading patterns, although their enterprises were concentrated along the coasts of India and on the cotton cloth trade (discussed in Chapter 17) rather than on the spices of southeast Asia.

Going Ashore: European Tribute Systems in Asia

Their ships and guns allowed the Europeans to force their way into the Asian trading network in the 16th and 17th centuries. But as they moved inland and away from the sea, their military advantages and their ability to dominate the Asian peoples rapidly disappeared. Because the vastly superior numbers of Asian armies offset the Europeans' advantage in weapons and organization for waging war on land, even small kingdoms such as those on Java and in mainland southeast Asia were able to resist European inroads into their domains. In the larger empires such as those in China, India, and Persia, and when confronted by martial cultures such as Japan's, the Europeans quickly learned their place. That they were often reduced to kowtowing or humbling themselves before the thrones of Asian potentates as demonstrated by the instructions given by a Dutch envoy about the proper behavior for a visit to the Japanese court:

> Our ministers have no other instruction to take there except to look to the wishes of that brave, superb, precise nation in order to please it in everything, and by no means to think on anything which might cause greater antipathy to us. . . . That consequently the Company's ministers frequenting the scrupulous state each year must above all go armed in modesty, humility, courtesy, and amity, always being the lesser.

In certain situations, however, the Europeans were drawn inland away from their forts, factories, and war fleets in the early centuries of their expansion into Asia. The Portuguese, and the Dutch after them, felt compelled to conquer the coastal areas of Ceylon to control the production and sale of cinnamon, which grew in the forests of the southwest portions of that island. The Dutch moved slowly inland from their base at Batavia into the highlands of western Java. They discovered that this area was ideal for growing coffee, which was in great demand in Europe by the 17th century. By the mid-18th century, the Dutch not only controlled the coffee-growing areas but were the paramount power on Java.

The Spanish, taking advantage of the fact that the Philippine Islands lay in the half of the world the pope had given them to explore and settle in 1493, invaded the islands in the 1560s. The conquest of **Luzon** and the northern islands was facilitated by the fact that the animistic inhabitants lived in small states the Spanish could subjugate one by one. The repeated failure of Spanish expeditions to conquer the southern island of **Mindanao,** which was ruled by a single kingdom whose Muslim rulers were determined to resist Christian dominance, dramatically underscores the limits of the Europeans' ability to project their power on land in this era.

In each area where the Europeans went ashore in the early centuries of expansion, they set up tribute regimes that closely resembled those the Spanish imposed on the Native American peoples of the New World (see Chapter 19). The European overlords were content to let the indigenous peoples live in their traditional settlements, controlled largely by hereditary leaders drawn from their own communities. In most areas, little attempt was made to interfere in the daily lives of the conquered peoples as long as their leaders met the tribute quotas set by the European conquerors. The tribute was paid in the form of agricultural products grown by the peasantry under forced labor systems supervised by the peasants' own elites. In some cases, the indigenous peoples continued to harvest crops they had produced for centuries, such as the bark of the cinnamon plant. In other areas new crops, such as coffee and sugar cane, were introduced. But in all cases, the demands for tribute took into account the local peasants' need to raise the crops on which they subsisted.

Luzon Northern island of Philippines; conquered by Spain during the 1560s; site of major Catholic missionary effort.

Mindanao Southern island of Philippines; a Muslim kingdom that was able to successfully resist Spanish conquest.

Spreading the Faith: The Missionary Enterprise in South and Southeast Asia

Although the Protestant Dutch and English were little interested in winning converts to Christianity during the early centuries of overseas expansion, the spread of Roman Catholicism was a fundamental part of the global mission of the Portuguese and Spanish. After the widespread conversion of Native American peoples, the meager returns from the Iberian missionary offensive in Asia were disappointing. The fact that Islam had spread over much of maritime south and southeast Asia centuries before Da Gama's arrival had much to do with the indifference or open hostility the Portuguese met when they tried to convert the peoples of these regions to Christianity. The dream of a Christian Asia joining the Iberian crusade against the Muslims was also dealt a setback by the discovery that the Hindus, whom Da Gama and some of his entourage had originally believed to be Christians, had their own sophisticated and deeply entrenched set of religious ideas and rituals.

Despite these setbacks, of all the Asian areas where European enclaves were established in the early centuries of expansion, India appeared to be one of the most promising fields for religious

Jesuits in India

St. Francis
Xavier, Jesuit
in India

DOCUMENT

Xavier, Francis Spanish Jesuit missionary; worked in India in 1540s among the outcaste and lower caste groups; made little headway among elites.

Nobili, Robert di (1577–1656) Italian Jesuit missionary; worked in India during the early 1600s; introduced strategy to convert elites first; strategy later widely adopted by Jesuits in various parts of Asia; mission eventually failed.

conversion. From the 1540s onward, Franciscan and Dominican missionaries, as well as the Jesuit **Francis Xavier,** who were willing to minister to the poor, low-caste fishers and untouchables along the southwest coast, converted tens of thousands. But the missionaries soon found that they were making little headway among high-caste groups. In fact, taboos against contact with untouchables and other low-caste groups made it nearly impossible for the missionaries to approach prospective upper-caste converts.

To overcome these obstacles, an Italian Jesuit named **Robert di Nobili** devised a different conversion strategy in the early 1600s. He learned several Indian languages, including Sanskrit, which allowed him to read the sacred texts of the Hindus. He donned the garments worn by Indian brahmans and adopted a vegetarian diet. All these measures were calculated to win over the upper-caste Hindus in south India, where he was based. Di Nobili reasoned that if he succeeded in Christianizing the high-caste Hindus, they would then bring the lower Hindu castes into the fold. But, he argued, because the ancient Hindu religion was sophisticated and deeply entrenched, Indian brahmans and other high-caste groups would listen only to those who adopted their ways. Meat eaters would be seen as defiling; those who were unfamiliar with the Hindus' sacred texts would be considered ignorant.

Despite some early successes, Di Nobili's strategy was undone by the refusal of high-caste Hindu converts to worship with low-caste groups and to give up many of their traditional beliefs and religious rituals. Rival missionary orders, particularly the Dominicans and Franciscans, denounced his approach. In assimilating to Hindu culture, they claimed, Di Nobili and his co-workers, not the Indians, were the ones who had been converted. His rivals also pointed out that the refusal of di Nobili's high-caste converts to worship with untouchable Christians defied one of the central tenets of Christianity: the equality of all believers before God. His rivals finally won the ear of the pope, and Di Nobili was forbidden to preach in India. Deprived of his energetic participation and knowledge of Indian ways, the mission in south India quickly collapsed, though he continued to translate Indian texts and eventually died in India.

Beyond socially stigmatized groups, such as the untouchables, the conversion of the general populace in Asia occurred only in isolated areas. Perhaps the greatest successes of the Christian missions occurred in the northern islands of the Philippines, which had not previously been exposed to a world religion such as Islam or Buddhism. Because the Spanish had conquered the island of Luzon and the smaller islands to the south, and then governed them as part of their vast intercontinental empire, they were able to launch a major missionary effort. The friars, as the priests and brothers who went out to convert and govern the rural populace were called, became the main channel for transmitting European influences. The friars first converted local Filipino leaders. These leaders then directed their followers to build new settlements that were centered, like those in Iberia and the New World, on town squares where the local church, the residences of the missionary fathers, and government offices were located. Beyond tending to the spiritual needs of the villagers in their congregation, the friars served as government officials.

Like the Native Americans of Spain's New World empire, most Filipinos were formally converted to Catholicism. But also like the Native Americans, the Filipinos' brand of Christianity represented a creative blend of their traditional beliefs and customs and the religion preached by the friars. Because key tenets of the Christian faith were taught in Spanish for fear that they would be corrupted if put in the local languages, it is doubtful that most of the converts had a very good grasp of Christian beliefs. Many adopted Christianity because Spanish dominance and their own leaders' conversion gave them little choice. Others embraced the new faith because they believed that the Christian God could protect them from illness or because they were taken with the notion that they would be equal to their Spanish overlords in heaven.

Almost all Filipinos clung to their traditional ways and in the process seriously compromised Christian beliefs and practices. The peoples of the islands continued public bathing, which the missionaries condemned as immodest, and refused to give up ritual drinking. They also continued to commune with deceased members of their families, often in sessions that were disguised as public recitations of the rosary. Thus, even in the Asian area where European control was the strongest and pressures for acculturation to European ways the greatest, much of the preconquest way of life and approach to the world was maintained.

Ming China: A Global Mission Refused

Zhu Yuanzhang, a military commander of peasant origins who founded the Ming dynasty, had suffered a great deal under the Mongol yoke. Both his parents and two of his brothers had died in a plague in 1344, and he and a remaining brother were reduced to begging for the land in which to bury the rest of their family. Threatened with the prospect of starvation in one of the many famines that ravaged the countryside in the later, corruption-riddled reigns of Mongol emperors, Zhu alternated between begging and living in a Buddhist monastery to survive. When the neighboring countryside rose in rebellion in the late 1340s, Zhu left the monastery to join a rebel band. His courage in combat and his natural capacity as a leader soon made him one of the more prominent of several rebel warlords attempting to overthrow the Yuan dynasty. After protracted military struggles against rival rebel claimants to the throne and the Mongol rulers themselves, Zhu's armies conquered most of China. Zhu declared himself the **Hongwu** emperor in 1368. He reigned for 30 years.

Immediately after he seized the throne, Zhu launched an effort to rid China of all traces of the "barbarian" Mongols. Mongol dress was discarded, Mongol names were dropped by those who had adopted them and were removed from buildings and court records, and Mongol palaces and administrative buildings in some areas were raided and sacked. The nomads themselves fled or were driven beyond the Great Wall, where Ming military expeditions pursued them on several occasions.

With the restoration of ethnic Chinese rule and the reunification of the country under the Ming dynasty (1368–1644), Chinese civilization enjoyed a new age of splendor. Renewed agrarian and commercial growth supported a population that was the largest of any center of civilization at the time, probably exceeding that of all western Europe.

Hongwu First Ming emperor in 1368; originally of peasant lineage; original name Zhu Yuanzhang; drove out Mongol influence; restored position of scholar-gentry.

Another Scholar-Gentry Revival

Because the Hongwu emperor, like the founder of the earlier Han dynasty, was from a peasant family and thus poorly educated, he viewed the scholar-gentry with some suspicion. But he also realized that their cooperation was essential to the full revival of Chinese civilization. Scholars well versed in the Confucian classics were again appointed to the very highest positions in the imperial government. The generous state subsidies that had supported the imperial academies in the capital and the regional colleges were fully restored. Most critically, the civil service examination system, which the Mongols had discontinued, was reinstated and greatly expanded. In the Ming era and the Qing that followed, the examinations played a greater role in determining entry into the Chinese bureaucracy than had been the case under any earlier dynasty.

In the Ming era, the examination system was routinized and made more complex than before. Prefectural, or county, exams were held in two out of three years. The exams were given in large compounds, like the one depicted in Figure 22.4, that were surrounded by walls and watchtowers from which the examiners could keep an eye on the thousands of candidates. Each candidate was assigned a small cubicle where he struggled to answer the questions, slept, and ate over the several days that it took to complete the arduous exam. Those who passed and received the lowest degree were eligible to take the next level of exams, which were given in the provincial capitals every three years. Only the most gifted and ambitious went on because the process was fiercely competitive—in some years as many as 4000 candidates competed for 150 degrees. Success at the provincial level brought a rise in status and opened the way for appointments to positions in the middle levels of the imperial bureaucracy. It also permitted particularly talented scholars to take the imperial examinations, which were given in the capital every three years. Those who passed the imperial exams were eligible for the highest posts in the realm and were the most revered of all Chinese, except members of the royal family.

Reform: Hongwu's Efforts to Root Out Abuses in Court Politics

Hongwu was mindful of his dependence on a well educated and loyal scholar-gentry for the day-to-day administration of the empire. But he sought to put clear limits on their influence and to institute reforms that would check the abuses of other factions at court. Early in his reign, Hongwu abolished the position of chief minister, which had formerly been the key link between the many ministries of the central government. The powers that had been amassed by those who occupied this office were transferred to the emperor. Hongwu also tried to impress all officials with the honesty, loyalty, and discipline he expected from them by introducing the practice of public beatings for bureaucrats found guilty of corruption or incompetence. Officials charged with misdeeds were paraded before the assembled courtiers and beaten a specified number of times on their bare

Figure 22.4 A 19th-century engraving shows the cubicles in which Chinese students and bureaucrats took the imperial civil service examinations in the capital at Beijing. Candidates were confined to the cubicles for days and completed their exams under the constant surveillance of official proctors. They brought their own food, slept in the cubicles, and were disqualified if they were found talking to others taking the exams or going outside the compound where the exams were being given.

buttocks. Many died of the wounds they received in the ordeal. Those who survived never recovered from the humiliation. To a certain extent, the humiliation was shared by all the scholar-gentry by virtue of the very fact that such degrading punishments could be meted out to any of them.

Hongwu also introduced measures to cut down on the court factionalism and never-ending conspiracies that had eroded the power of earlier dynasties. He decreed that the emperor's wives should come only from humble family origins. This was intended to put an end to the power plays of the consorts from high-ranking families, who built palace cliques that were centered on their influential aristocratic relatives. He warned against allowing eunuchs to occupy positions of independent power and sought to limit their numbers within the Forbidden City. To prevent plots against the ruler and fights over succession, Hongwu established the practice of exiling all potential rivals to the throne to estates in the provinces, and he forbade them to become involved in political affairs. On the darker side, Hongwu condoned thought control, as when he had some sections from Mencius's writings that displeased him deleted forever from the writings included on the imperial exams. Although many of these measures went far to keep peace at court under Hongwu and his strong successor, the Yungle emperor (r. 1403–1424), they were allowed to lapse under later, less capable, rulers, with devastating consequences for the Ming Empire.

A Return to Scholar-Gentry Social Dominance

Perhaps because his lowly origins and personal suffering made him sensitive to the plight of the peasantry, Hongwu introduced measures that would improve the lot of the common people. Like most strong emperors, he promoted public works projects, including dike building and the extension of irrigation systems aimed at improving the farmers' yields. To bring new lands under cultivation and encourage the growth of a peasant class that owned the lands it toiled so hard to bring into production, Hongwu decreed that unoccupied lands would become the tax-exempt property of those who cleared and cultivated them. He lowered forced labor demands on the peasantry by both the government and members of the gentry class. Hongwu also promoted silk and cotton cloth production and other handicrafts that provided supplemental income for peasant households.

Exam Questions as a Mirror of Chinese Values

The subjects and specific learning tested on the Chinese civil service exams give us insight into the behavior and attitudes expected of the literate, ruling classes of what was perhaps the best-educated preindustrial civilization. Sample questions from these exams can tell us a good deal about what sorts of knowledge were considered important and what kinds of skills were necessary for those who aspired to successful careers in the most prestigious and potentially the most lucrative field open to Chinese youths: administrative service in the imperial bureaucracy. The very fact that such a tiny portion of the Chinese male population could take the exams and very few of those successfully pass them says a lot about gender roles and elitism in Chinese society. In addition, the often decisive role of a student's calligraphy—the skill with which he was able to brush the Chinese characters—reflects the emphasis the Chinese elite placed on a refined sense of aesthetics.

Question 1: Provide the missing phrases and elaborate on the meaning of the following:

The Duke of She observed to Confucius: "Among us there was an upright man called Kung who was so upright that when his father appropriated a sheep, he bore witness against him." Confucius said . . .

[The missing phrases are, "The upright men among us are not like that. A father will screen his son and a son his father . . . yet uprightness is to be found in that."]

Question 2: Write an eight-legged essay [one consisting of eight sections] on the following:

Scrupulous in his own conduct and lenient only in his dealings with the people.

Question 3: First unscramble the following characters and then comment on the significance of this quotation from one of the classic texts:

Beginning, good, mutually, nature, basically, practice, far, near, men's

[The correct answer is, "Men's beginning nature is basically good. Nature mutually near. Practice mutually far."]

QUESTIONS Looking at the content of these questions, what can we learn about Chinese society and attitudes? For example, where do the Chinese look for models to orient their social behavior? What kinds of knowledge are important to the Chinese? Do they stress specialist skills or the sort of learning that we associate with a broad liberal arts education?

Although these measures led to some short-term improvement in the peasants' condition, they were all but offset by the growing power of rural landlord families, buttressed by alliances with relatives in the imperial bureaucracy. Gentry households with members in government service were exempted from land taxes and enjoyed special privileges, such as permission to be carried about in sedan chairs and to use fans and umbrellas. Many gentry families engaged in moneylending on the side; some even ran lucrative gambling dens. Almost all added to their estates either by buying up lands held by peasant landholders or by foreclosing on loans made to farmers in times of need in exchange for mortgages on their family plots. Peasants displaced in these ways had little choice but to become tenants of large landowners or landless laborers moving about in search of employment.

More land meant ever larger and more comfortable households for the gentry class. They justified the growing gap between their wealth and the poverty of the peasantry by contrasting their foresight and industry with the lazy and wasteful ways of the ordinary farmers. The virtues of the gentry class were celebrated in stories and popular illustrations. The latter showed members of gentry households hard at work weaving and storing grain to see them through the cold weather, while commoners who neglected these tasks wandered during the winter, cold and hungry, past the walled compounds and closed gates of gentry households.

At most levels of Chinese society, the Ming period continued the subordination of youths to elders and women to men that had been steadily intensifying in earlier periods. If anything, Neo-Confucian thinking was even more influential than under the late Song and Yuan dynasties. Some of its advocates proposed draconian measures to suppress challenges to the increasingly rigid social roles. For example, students were expected to venerate and follow the instructions of their teachers, no matter how muddle-headed or tipsy the latter might be. A terrifying lesson in proper decorum was drawn from an incident in which a student at the imperial academy dared to dispute the findings of one of his instructors. The student was beheaded, and his severed head was hung on a pole at the entrance to the academy. Not surprisingly, this rather unsubtle solution to the problem of keeping order in the classroom merely drove student protest underground. Anonymous letters critical of poorly prepared teachers continued to circulate among the student body.

Women were also driven to underground activities to ameliorate their subordination and, if they dared, expand their career opportunities. At the court, they continued, despite Hongwu's measures, to play strong roles behind the scenes. Even able rulers such as Hongwu were swayed by the advice of favorite wives or dowager mothers and aunts. On one occasion, Hongwu chided the empress Ma for daring to inquire into the condition of the common people. She replied that because he was the father of the people, she was the mother, and thus it was quite proper for her to be concerned for the welfare of her children.

Even within the palace, the plight of most women was grim. Hundreds, sometimes thousands of attractive young women were brought to the court in the hope that they would catch the emperor's fancy and become one of his concubines or perhaps even be elevated to the status of wife. Because few actually succeeded, many spent their lives in loneliness and inactivity, just waiting for the emperor to glance their way.

In society at large, women had to settle for whatever status and respect they could win within the family. As before, their success in this regard hinged largely on bearing male children and, when these children were married, moving from the status of daughter-in-law to mother-in-law. The daughters of upper-class families were often taught to read and write by their parents or brothers, and many composed poetry, painted, and played musical instruments (Figure 22.5).

For women from the nonelite classes, the main avenues for some degree of independence and self-expression remained becoming courtesans or entertainers. The former should be clearly distinguished from prostitutes because they served a very different clientele and were literate and often accomplished in painting, music, and poetry. Although courtesans often enjoyed lives of luxury, even the most successful made their living by gratifying the needs of upper-class men for uninhibited sex and convivial companionship.

An Age of Growth: Agriculture, Population, Commerce, and the Arts

The first decades of the Ming period were an age of buoyant economic growth in China that both was fed by and resulted in unprecedented contacts with other civilizations overseas. The territories controlled by the Ming emperors were never as extensive as those ruled by the Tang dynasty. But in the Ming era, the great commercial boom and population increase that had begun in the late Song were renewed and accelerated. The peopling of the Yangzi region and the areas to the south was given a great boost by the importation, through Spanish and Portuguese merchant intermediaries, of new food crops from the Americas, particularly root crops from the Andes highlands. Three plants—maize (corn), sweet potatoes, and peanuts—were especially important. Because these crops could be grown on inferior soils without irrigation, their cultivation spread quickly through the hilly and marginal areas that bordered on the irrigated rice lands of southern China. They became vital supplements to the staple rice or millet diet of the Chinese people, particularly those of the rapidly growing southern regions.

Because these plants were less susceptible to drought, they also became an important hedge against famine. The introduction of these new crops was an important factor behind the great surge

Figure 22.5 The varied diversions of the wives and concubines of Ming emperors are depicted in this scene of court life. In addition to court intrigues and maneuvers to win the emperor's favor, women of the imperial household occupied themselves with dance, music, games, and polite conversation. With eunuchs, officials, and palace guards watching them closely, the women of the palace and imperial city spent most of their lives in confined yet well appointed spaces.

(© The Trustees of the British Museum/Art Resource, NY.)

in population growth that was under way by the end of the Ming era. By 1600 the population of China had risen to as many as 150 million from 80 to 90 million in the 14th century. Two centuries later, in 1800, it had more than doubled and surpassed 300 million.

Agrarian expansion and population increase were paralleled in early Ming times by a renewal of commercial growth. The market sector of the domestic economy became ever more pervasive, and overseas trading links multiplied. Because China's advanced handicraft industries produced a wide variety of goods, from silk textiles and tea to fine ceramics and lacquerware, which were in high demand throughout Asia and in Europe, the terms of trade ran very much in China's favor. This is why China received more American silver (brought by European merchants) than any other single society in the world economy of the early modern period. In addition to the Arab and Asian traders, Europeans arrived in increasing numbers at the only two places—**Macao** and, somewhat later and more sporadically, **Canton**—where they were officially allowed to do business in Ming China. Despite state-imposed restrictions on contacts with foreigners, China contributed significantly to the process of protoglobalization that was intensifying cross-cultural contacts worldwide in the early modern era.

Not surprisingly, the merchant classes, particularly those engaged in long-distance trade, reaped the biggest profits from the economic boom. But a good portion of their gains was transferred to the state in the form of taxes and to the scholar-gentry in the form of bribes for official favors. Much of the merchants' wealth was invested in land rather than plowed back into trade or manufacturing, because land owning, not commerce, remained the surest route to social status in China.

Ming prosperity was reflected in the fine arts, which found generous patrons both at court and among the scholar-gentry class more generally. Although the monochromatic simplicity of the work of earlier dynasties was sustained by the ink brush paintings of artists such as Xu Wei, much of the Ming output was busier and more colorful. Portraits and scenes of court, city, or country life were more prominent. Nonetheless, the Chinese continued to delight in depicting individual scholars or travelers contemplating the beauty of mountains, lakes, and marshes that dwarf the human observers.

Whereas the painters of the Ming era concentrated mainly on developing established techniques and genres, major innovation was occurring in literature. Most notable in this regard was the full development of the Chinese novel, which had had its beginnings in the writings of the Yuan era. The novel form was given great impetus by the spread of literacy among the upper classes in the Ming era. This was facilitated by the growing availability of books that had resulted from the spread of woodblock printing from the 10th century onward. Ming novels such as *The Water Margin, Monkey,* and *The Golden Lotus* were recognized as classics in their own time and continue to set the standard for Chinese prose literature today.

Ming Expansion and Retreat, and the Arrival of the Europeans

The seemingly boundless energy of the Chinese in early decades of Ming rule drove them far beyond the traditional areas of expansion in central Asia and the regions south of the Yangzi. In the reign of the third Ming emperor, Yungle, they launched a series of expeditions that had no precedent in Chinese history. Between 1405 and 1433, the admiral Zheng He, one of Yungle's most trusted subordinates, led seven major expeditions overseas (See Map 22.3 and Chapter 15, p. 345). A mix of motives, including a desire

Macao One of two ports in which Europeans were permitted to trade in China during the Ming dynasty.

Canton One of two port cities in which Europeans were permitted to trade in China during the Ming dynasty.

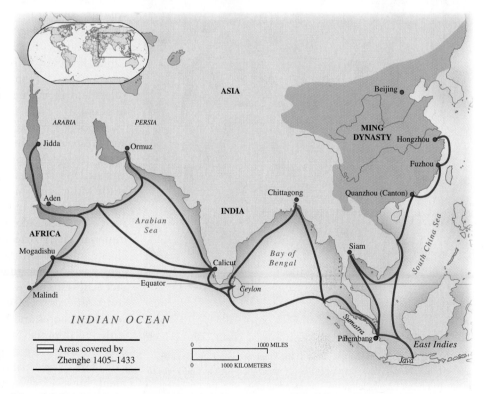

Map 22.3 Ming China and the Zheng He Expeditions, 1405–1433 The composite view of the Zheng He expeditions shown on this map indicate the great distances traveled as well as the fact that most of the voyages hugged the familiar coastlines of southern Asia and East Africa rather than risking navigation large expanses of open sea.

Ricci, Matteo [*rEEt* chEE] (1552–1610) Along with Adam Schall, Jesuit scholar in court of Ming emperors; skilled scientist; won few converts to Christianity.

Schall, Adam (1591-1666) Along with Matteo Ricci, Jesuit scholar in court of Ming emperors; skilled scientist; won few converts to Christianity.

A Ming Naval
Expedition

Matteo Ricci's
Journals

Figure 22.6 Jesuits in Chinese dress at the emperor's court. The Jesuits believed that the best way to convert a great civilization such as China was to adopt the dress, customs, language, and manners of its elite. They reasoned that once the scholar-gentry elite had been converted, they would bring the rest of China's vast population into the Christian fold.

to explore other lands and proclaim the glory of the Ming Empire to the wider world, prompted the voyages.

The early expeditions were confined largely to southeast Asian seas and kingdoms. The last three reached as far as Persia, southern Arabia, and the east coast of Africa—distances comparable to those that would be covered by the Portuguese in their early voyages around Africa. The hundreds of great ships (see the illustrations in Visualizing the Past) deployed on these expeditions exemplified the technological sophistication, wealth, and power of China in the first centuries of Ming rule.

Nonetheless, in the decades after the last of the Zheng He expeditions in 1433, China's rulers purposely abandoned the drive to extend Ming power and prestige overseas, and increasingly sought to limit and control contacts with the outside world. The shift from an emphasis on building the impressive fleets of the Zheng He voyages to repairing and joining the northern defense works to form the Great Wall as we know it today reflected these key changes in policy and decisions about geopolitical orientation.

In the centuries that followed the suspension of overseas expeditions, the Ming war fleet declined dramatically in the number and quality of its ships, and strict limits were placed on the size and number of masts with which a seagoing ship might be fitted. This return to the longstanding priority of defending against nomadic invasions eventually left China, and the Indian Ocean world as a whole, vulnerable to European incursions by sea.

While the Chinese closed themselves in, the Europeans probed ever farther across the globe and were irresistibly drawn to the most legendary of all overseas civilizations, the Middle Kingdom of China. In addition to the trading contacts noted earlier, Christian missionaries infiltrated Chinese coastal areas and tried to gain access to the court, where they hoped to curry favor with the Ming emperors. While religious orders such as the Franciscans and Dominicans toiled to win converts among the common people and made modest progress that could be counted in the tens of thousands, the Jesuits adopted the top-down strategy that Di Nobili had pursued in India (Figure 22.6). In China, however, a single person, the Ming emperor, instead of a whole caste, sat at the top of the social hierarchy, and for that reason the rulers and their chief advisors became the prime targets of the Jesuit mission.

Some Chinese scholars showed interest in Christian teachings and Western thinking more generally. But the Jesuit missionaries who made their way to Beijing clearly recognized that their scientific knowledge and technical skills were the keys to maintaining a presence at the Ming court and eventually interesting the Chinese elite in Christianity. Beginning in the 1580s, a succession of brilliant Jesuit scholars, such as **Matteo Ricci** and **Adam Schall,** spent most of their time in the imperial city, correcting faulty calendars, forging cannons, fixing clocks imported from Europe, and astounding the Chinese scholar-gentry with the accuracy of their instruments and their ability to predict eclipses. They won a few converts among the elite. However, most court officials were suspicious of these strange-looking "barbarians" with large noses and hairy faces, and they tried to limit their contacts with the imperial family. Some at the court, especially the scholar-officials who were humiliated by the foreigners' corrections to their calendars, were openly hostile to the Jesuits. Despite serious harassment, however, the later Ming emperors remained sufficiently fascinated by these very learned and able visitors that they allowed a handful to remain.

The Great Ships of the Ming Expeditions that Crossed the Indian Ocean

In the early modern era Chinese ships for canal, river and ocean transportation improved significantly and their numbers multiplied many times. By the first decades of the Ming dynasty, some of them had also increased dramatically in size (see the image below). This trend was given great impetus by the impressive series of expeditions that were led by the eunuch Zheng He through island Southeast Asia and on to coastal India and east Africa beginning in 1405. Some of the dragon ships of Zheng He's fleet exceeded four hundred feet in length, thus dwarfing the caravel Niña, one of the ships of Columbus's first voyage to the Americas (see the image below). Chinese junks in this and earlier centuries were equipped with magnetic compasses, water-tight compartments, and stern post rudders that would have allowed them to navigate the open seas rather than simply following the coastlines of the lands from which Zheng He and his crews sought to command tribute and establish direct commercial relations.

Over the course of the seven expeditions led by Zheng He, fleets of these great treasure vessels accommodated tens of thousands of sailors, merchants and soldiers. As the illustration below clearly indicates, the largest Chinese junks were far larger than the caravels, naos and other vessels that the Portuguese, Spanish, and rival Europeans deployed in their voyages of exploration and discovery from the 15th through the 17th century. They also dwarfed the ubiquitous and swift Arab dhows that plied the waters of the Indian Ocean and adjoining seas. With such vessels the Chinese became for much of the fifteenth century a dominant force in Asian seas east of the Malayan peninsula. The stout-walled Chinese ships also proved the only vessels in Asia that could stand up to the cannon carried by the first waves of Portuguese ships that sought to dominate the Indian Ocean trading network.

QUESTIONS In what ways would the dragon ships facilitate commerce both within China and overseas? What sorts of goods could ships of this size carry? Do you think that ships like these, equipped with the naval technologies described above could have crossed the Pacific Ocean to the Americas or the Atlantic and sailed to Europe? If not, why not? If so, why didn't the Chinese seek to "discover" and dominate these areas?

Ming Decline and the Chinese Predicament

By the late 1500s, the Ming retreat from overseas involvement had become just one facet of a familiar pattern of dynastic decline. The highly centralized, absolutist political structure, which had been established by Hongwu and had been run well by able successors such as Yungle, became a major liability under the mediocre or incompetent men who occupied the throne through much of the last two centuries of Ming rule. Decades of rampant official corruption, exacerbated by the growing isolation of weak rulers by the thousands of eunuchs who gradually came to dominate life within the Forbidden City, eventually eroded the foundations on which the empire was built.

Public works projects, including the critical dike works on the Yellow River, fell into disrepair, and floods, drought, and famine soon ravaged the land. Peasants in afflicted districts were reduced to eating the bark from trees or the excrement of wild geese. Some peasants sold their children into slavery to keep them from starving, and peasants in some areas resorted to cannibalism.

509

Means and Motives for Overseas Expansion: Europe and China Compared

In the early decades of the 14th century, Chinese mariners dramatically demonstrated their capacity to mount large expeditions for overseas exploration and expansion. Because their failure to sustain these initiatives left Asian waters from the Persian Gulf to the China seas open to armed European interventions a century later, the reasons for the Chinese failure to follow up on their remarkable naval achievements merits serious examination. The explanations for the Chinese refusal to commit to overseas expansion can be best understood if they are contrasted with the forces that drove the Europeans with increasing determination into the outside world. In broad terms, such a comparison underscores the fact that although both the Europeans and the Chinese had the means to expand on a global scale, only the Europeans had strong motives for doing so.

The social and economic transformations that occurred in European civilization during the late Middle Ages and the early Renaissance had brought it to a level of development that compared favorably with China in many areas (see Chapters 10 and 12). Although the Chinese empire was far larger and more populous than tiny nation-states such as Portugal, Spain, and Holland, the European kingdoms had grown more efficient at mobilizing their more limited resources. Rivalries between the states of a fragmented Europe had also fostered a greater aggressiveness and sense of competition on the part of the Europeans than the Chinese rulers could even imagine. China's armies were far larger than those of any of the European kingdoms, but European soldiers were on the whole better led, armed, and disciplined. Chinese wet rice agriculture was more productive than European farming, and the Chinese rulers had a far larger population to cultivate their fields, build their dikes and bridges, work their mines, and make tools, clothing, and weapons. But on the whole, the technological innovations of the medieval period had given the Europeans an advantage over the Chinese in the animal and machine power they could generate—a capacity that did much to make up for their deficiencies in human power.

> "Why . . . were the impressive Zheng He expeditions a dead end, whereas the more modest probes of Columbus and Da Gama were the beginning of half a millennium of European overseas expansion and global dominance?"

Despite their differences, both civilizations had the means for sustained exploration and expansion overseas, although the Chinese were ready to undertake such enterprises a few centuries earlier than the Europeans. As the voyages of Da Gama, Columbus, and Zheng He demonstrated, both civilizations had the shipbuilding and navigational skills and technology needed to tackle such ambitious undertakings. Why, then, were the impressive Zheng He expeditions a dead end, whereas the more modest probes of Columbus and Da Gama were the beginning of half a millennium of European overseas expansion and global dominance?

The full answer to this question is as complex as the societies it asks us to compare. But we can learn a good deal by looking at the groups pushing for expansion within each civilization and the needs that drove them into the outside world. There was wide-

---

Rapacious local landlords built huge estates by taking advantage of the increasingly desperate peasant population. As in earlier phases of dynastic decline, farmers who had been turned off their land and tortured for taxes, or had lost most of the crops they had grown, turned to flight, banditry, and finally open rebellion to confiscate food and avenge their exploitation by greedy landlords and corrupt officials.

True to the pattern of dynastic rise and fall, internal disorder resulted in and was intensified by foreign threats and renewed assaults by nomadic peoples from beyond the Great Wall. One of the early signs of the seriousness of imperial deterioration was the inability of Chinese bureaucrats and military forces to put an end to the epidemic of Japanese (and ethnic Chinese) pirate attacks that ravaged the southern coast in the mid-16th century. Despite an official preoccupation with the Mongols early in the Ming era and with the Manchus to the northeast of the Great Wall in later times, the dynasty was finally toppled in 1644, not by nomads but by rebels from within. By that time, the administrative apparatus had become so feeble that the last Ming emperor, **Chongzhen** (chohng-jehn), did not realize how serious the rebel advance was until enemy soldiers were scaling the walls of the Forbidden City. After watching his wife withdraw to her chambers to commit suicide, and after bungling an attempt to kill his young daughter, the ill-fated Chongzhen retreated to the imperial gardens and hanged himself rather than face capture.

Chongzhen [chohng-jehn] Last of the Ming emperors; committed suicide in 1644 in the face of a Jurchen capture of the Forbidden City at Beijing.

spread support for exploration and overseas expansion in seafaring European nations such as Portugal, Spain, Holland, and England. European rulers financed expeditions they hoped would bring home precious metals and trade goods that could be sold at great profits. Both treasure and profits could be translated into warships and armies that would strengthen these rulers in their incessant wars with European rivals and, in the case of the Iberian kingdoms, with their Muslim adversaries.

European traders looked for much the same benefits from overseas expansion. Rulers and merchants also hoped that explorers would find new lands whose climates and soils were suitable for growing crops such as sugar that were in high demand and thus would bring big profits. Leaders of rival branches of the Christian faith believed that overseas expansion would give their missionaries access to unlimited numbers of heathens to be converted or would put them in touch with the legendary lost king, Prester John, who would ally with them in their struggle with the infidel Muslims.

By contrast, the Chinese Zheng He expeditions were very much the project of a single emperor and a favored eunuch, whose Muslim family origins may go a long way toward accounting for his wanderlust. Yungle appears to have been driven by little more than curiosity and the vain desire to impress his greatness and that of his empire on peoples whom he considered inferior. Although some Chinese merchants went along for the ride, most felt little need for the voyages. They already traded on favorable terms for all the products Asia, and in some cases Europe and Africa, could offer. The merchants had the option of waiting for other peoples to come to them, or, if they were a bit more ambitious, of going out in their own ships to southeast Asia.

The scholar-gentry were actively hostile to the Zheng He expeditions. The voyages strengthened the position of the much-hated eunuchs, who vied with the scholar-gentry for the emperor's favor and the high posts that went with it. In addition, the scholar-gentry saw the voyages as a foolish waste of resources that the empire could not afford. They believed it would be better to direct the wealth and talents of the empire to building armies and fortifications to keep out the hated Mongols and other nomads. After all, the memory of foreign rule was quite fresh.

As had happened so often before in their history, the Chinese were drawn inward, fixated on internal struggles and the continuing threat from central Asia. Scholar-gentry hostility and the lack of enthusiasm for overseas voyages displayed by Yungle's successors after his death in 1424 led to their abandonment after 1430. As the Chinese retreated, the Europeans surged outward. It is difficult to exaggerate the magnitude of the consequences for both civilizations and all humankind.

QUESTIONS How might history have been changed if the Chinese had mounted a serious and sustained effort to project their power overseas in the decades before Da Gama rounded the Cape of Good Hope? Why did the Chinese fail to foresee the threat that European expansion would pose for the rest of Asia and finally for China itself? Did other civilizations have the capacity for global expansion in this era? What prevented them from launching expeditions similar to those of the Chinese and Europeans? In terms of motivation for overseas expansion, were peoples such as the Muslims, Indians, and Native Americans more like the Europeans or the Chinese?

Fending Off the West: Japan's Reunification and the First Challenge

Nobunaga, Oda (1534–1582) Japanese daimyo; first to make extensive use of firearms; in 1573 deposed last of Ashikaga shoguns; unified much of central Honshu under his command.

By the 16th century the daimyo stalemate and the pattern of recurring civil war were so entrenched in Japanese society that a succession of three remarkable military leaders was needed to restore unity and internal peace. **Oda Nobunaga,** the first of these leaders, was from a minor warrior household. But his skills as a military leader soon vaulted him into prominence in the ongoing struggles for power among the daimyo lords. As a leader, Nobunaga combined daring, a willingness to innovate, and ruthless determination—some would say cruelty. He was not afraid to launch a surprise attack against an enemy that outnumbered him ten to one, and he was one of the first of the daimyo to make extensive use of the firearms that the Japanese had begun to acquire from the Portuguese in the 1540s.

In 1573 Nobunaga deposed the last of the Ashikaga shoguns, who had long ruled in name only. By 1580 he had unified much of central Honshu under his command (Map 22.4). As his armies drove against the powerful western daimyo in 1582, Nobunaga was caught off guard by one of his vassal generals and was killed when the Kyoto temple where he had taken refuge was burned to the ground.

In the mid-16th century, the Japanese found leaders who had the military and diplomatic skills and ruthlessness needed to restore unity under a new Shogunate, the Tokugawa. By the early 1600s, with the potential threat from the Europeans looming ever larger, the Tokugawa shoguns succeeded in enveloping the islands in a state of isolation that lasted nearly two and a half centuries.

Map 22.4 Japan During the Rise of the Tokugawa Shogunate   As this map indicates, the main centers of population and political power in early modern Japan were readily accessible to the sea, which was the arena which the Europeans could best project their military prowess and exercise their commercial prerogatives.

Hideyoshi, Toyotomi   General under Nobunaga; succeeded as leading military power in central Japan; continued efforts to break power of daimyos; constructed a series of alliances that made him military master of Japan in 1590; died in 1598.

At first it appeared that Nobunaga's campaigns to restore central authority to the islands might be undone. But his ablest general, **Toyotomi Hideyoshi** (Figure 22.7), moved quickly to punish those who had betrayed Nobunaga and to renew the drive to break the power of the daimyo who had not yet submitted to him. Though the son of a peasant, Hideyoshi matched his master in military prowess but was far more skillful at diplomacy. A system of alliances and a string of victories over the last of the resisting daimyo made Hideyoshi the military master of Japan by 1590.

The ambitious overlord had much more grandiose schemes of conquest in mind. He dreamed of ruling China and even India, although he knew little about either place. Hideyoshi also threatened, among others, the Spanish in the Philippines. Apparently as the first step toward fulfilling this vision of empire building on a grand scale, Hideyoshi launched two attacks on Korea in 1592 and 1597, each of which involved nearly 150,000 soldiers. After initial successes, both campaigns stalled. The first ended in defeat; the second was still in progress when Hideyoshi died in 1598.

Ieyasu, Tokugawa   [toh-kuh-GAH-wah ee-YAH-soo] Vassal of Toyotomi Hideyoshi; succeeded him as most powerful military figure in Japan; granted title of shogun in 1603 and established Tokugawa Shogunate; established political unity in Japan.

Although Hideyoshi had tried to ensure that he would be succeeded by his son, the vassals he had appointed to carry out his wishes tried to seize power for themselves after his death. One of these vassals, **Tokugawa Ieyasu** (toh-kuh-GAH-wah ee-YAH-soo), had originally come from a minor daimyo house. But as an ally of Hideyoshi, he had been able to build up a powerful domain on the heavily populated Kanto plain. Ieyasu soon emerged triumphant from the renewed warfare that resulted from Hideyoshi's death. Rather than continue Hideyoshi's campaigns of overseas expansion, Ieyasu concentrated on consolidating power at home. In 1603 he was granted the title of shogun by the emperor, an act that formally inaugurated centuries of rule by the Tokugawa shogunate.

Edo   Tokugawa capital city; modern-day Tokyo; center of the Tokugawa Shogunate.

Under Ieyasu's direction, the remaining daimyo were reorganized. Most of the lands in central Honshu were either controlled directly by the Tokugawa family, who now ruled the land from the city of **Edo** (later Tokyo), or were held by daimyo who were closely allied with the shoguns. Although many of the outlying or vassal daimyo retained their domains, they were carefully controlled and were required to pledge their personal allegiance to the shogun. It was soon clear that the Tokugawas' victory had put an end to the civil wars and brought a semblance of political unity to the islands.

Dealing with the European Challenge

All through the decades when the three unifiers were struggling to bring the feisty daimyo under control, they also had to contend with a new force in Japanese history: the Europeans. From the time in 1543 when shipwrecked Portuguese sailors were washed up on the shore of Kyushu island, European traders and missionaries had been visiting the islands in increasing numbers. The traders brought the Japanese goods that were produced mainly in India, China, and southeast Asia and exchanged them for silver, copper, pottery, and lacquerware. Perhaps more important, European traders and the missionaries who followed them to the islands brought firearms, printing presses, and other Western devices such as clocks. The firearms, which the Japanese could themselves manufacture within years and were improving in design within a generation, revolutionized Japanese warfare and contributed much to the victories of the unifiers. Commercial contacts with the Europeans also encouraged the Japanese to venture overseas to trade in nearby Formosa and Korea and in places as distant as the Philippines and Siam.

Soon after the merchants, Christian missionaries (Figure 22.8) arrived in the islands and set to work converting the Japanese to Roman Catholicism. Beginning in the outlying ' domains, the missionaries worked their way toward the political center that was beginning to coalesce around Nobunaga and his followers by the 1570s. Seeing Christianity as a counterforce to the militant Buddhist orders that were resisting his rise to power, Nobunaga took the missionaries under his protection and encouraged them to preach their faith to his people. The Jesuits, adopting the same top-down strategy of conversion that they had followed in India and China, converted many of the daimyo and their samurai retainers. Some of the Jesuits were also convinced that they were on the verge of winning over Nobunaga, who delighted in wearing Western clothes, encouraged his artists to copy Western paintings of the Virgin Mary and scenes from the life of Christ, and permitted the missionaries to build churches in towns throughout the islands. The missionaries were persuaded that Nobunaga's conversion would bring the whole of the Japanese people into the Christian fold. Even without it, they reported converts in the hundreds of thousands by the early 1580s.

In the late 1580s, quite suddenly, the missionaries saw their carefully mounted conversion campaign collapse. Nobunaga was murdered, and his successor, Hideyoshi, though not yet openly hostile, was lukewarm toward the missionary enterprise. In part, the missionaries' fall from favor resulted from the fact that the resistance of the Buddhist sects had been crushed. More critically, Hideyoshi and his followers were alarmed by reports of converts refusing to obey their overlords' commands when they believed them to be in conflict with their newly adopted Christian beliefs. Thus, the threat that the new religion posed for the established social order was growing more apparent. That threat was compounded by signs that the Europeans might follow up their commercial and missionary overtures with military expeditions aimed at conquering the islands. The Japanese had been strongly impressed with the firearms and pugnacity of the Europeans, and they did not take threats of invasion lightly.

Japan's Self-Imposed Isolation

Growing doubts about European intentions, and fears that both merchants and missionaries might subvert the existing social order, led to official measures to restrict foreign activities in Japan, beginning in the late 1580s. First, Hideyoshi ordered the Christian missionaries to leave the islands—an

Figure 22.7 In this late 16th-century portrait, Hideyoshi (1536–1598) grasps the sword that catapulted him to power and exudes the discipline and self-confidence that made possible his campaigns to unify Japan. Although warrior skills were vital in his rise to power, he and other members of the samurai class were expected to be literate, well mannered by the conventions of the day, and attuned to the complex and refined aesthetics of rock gardens and tea ceremonies.

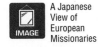

A Japanese View of European Missionaries

Figure 22.8 A number of the major forms of interaction between expansive European peoples and those of Asia are vividly illustrated in this panoramic Japanese silkscreen painting from the early 1600s. The strong impression made by the size and power of the Portuguese ship that has just arrived in harbor is evident in the artist's exaggeration of the height of its fore and aft castles. The trade goods being unloaded, mainly Chinese silks, which are also being sold in the marketplace at the right of the painting, but also exotic products such as peacocks and tiger skins, demonstrate the ways in which the Portuguese had become carriers between different areas in Asia, including Japan. The cluster of black-robed missionaries waiting to greet the arriving Portuguese sea captain (under the umbrella in the center) suggests that efforts to convert the Japanese to Christianity were in full swing, at least in this area of the kingdom.

"Closed Country Edict of 1635" and "Exclusion of the Portuguese, 1639" by Tokugawa Ieyasu

Deshima Island in Nagasaki Bay; only port open to non-Japanese after closure of the islands in the 1640s; only Chinese and Dutch ships were permitted to enter.

school of National Learning New ideology that laid emphasis on Japan's unique historical experience and the revival of indigenous culture at the expense of Chinese imports such as Confucianism; typical of Japan in 18th century.

order that was not rigorously enforced, at least at the outset. By the mid-1590s, Hideyoshi was actively persecuting Christian missionaries and converts. His successor, Ieyasu, continued this persecution and then officially banned the faith in 1614. European missionaries were driven out of the islands; those who remained underground were hunted down and killed or expelled. Japanese converts were compelled to renounce their faith; those who refused were imprisoned, tortured, and executed. By the 1630s, the persecutions, even against Christians who tried to practice their faith in secret, had become so intense that thousands of converts in the western regions joined in hard-fought but hopeless rebellions against the local daimyo and the forces of the shogun. With the suppression of these uprisings, Christianity in Japan was reduced to an underground faith of isolated communities.

Under Ieyasu and his successors, the persecution of the Christians grew into a broader campaign to isolate Japan from outside influences. In 1616 foreign traders were confined to a handful of cities; in the 1630s all Japanese ships were forbidden to trade or even sail overseas. One after another, different European nations were either officially excluded from Japan (the Spanish) or decided that trading there was no longer worth the risk (the English). By the 1640s only a limited number of Dutch and Chinese ships were allowed to carry on commerce on the small island of **Deshima** in Nagasaki Bay. The export of silver and copper was greatly restricted, and Western books were banned to prevent Christian ideas from reentering the country. Foreigners were permitted to live and travel only in very limited areas.

By the mid-17th century, Japan's retreat into almost total isolation was complete. Much of the next century was spent in consolidating the internal control of the Tokugawa shogunate by extending bureaucratic administration into the vassal daimyo domains throughout the islands. In the 18th century, a revival of Neo-Confucian philosophy, which had marked the period of the Tokugawa's rise to power, increasingly gave way to the influence of thinkers who championed the **School of National Learning.** As its name implies, the new ideology laid great emphasis on Japan's unique historical experience and the revival of indigenous culture at the expense of Chinese imports such as Confucianism. In the centuries that followed, through contacts with the small Dutch community at Deshima, members of the Japanese elite also followed developments in the West. Their avid interest in European achievements contrasted sharply with the indifference of the Chinese scholar-gentry in this period to the doings of the "hairy barbarians" from Europe.

Global Connections

An Age of Eurasian Protoglobalization

In 1700, after two centuries of European involvement in south and southeast Asia, most of the peoples of the area had been little affected by efforts to build trading empires and win Christian converts. European sailors had added several new routes to the Asian trading network. The most important of these were the link around the Cape of Good Hope between Europe and the Indian Ocean and the connection between the Philippine Islands and Mexico in the Americas. The Europeans' need for safe harbors and storage areas led to the establishment and rapid growth of trading centers such as Goa, Calicut, and Batavia. It also resulted in the gradual decline of existing indigenous commercial centers, especially the Muslim cities on the east coast of Africa and somewhat later the fortress town of Malacca. The Europeans introduced the principle of sea warfare into what had been a peaceful commercial world. But the Asian trading system as a whole survived the initial shock of this innovation, and the Europeans eventually concluded that they were better off adapting to the existing commercial arrangements rather than dismantling them.

Because exchanges had been taking place between Europe and Asia for millennia, few new inventions or diseases were spread in the early centuries of expansion. This low level of major exchanges was particularly striking compared with the catastrophic interaction between Europe and the Americas. But, as in Africa, European discoveries in the long-isolated Western Hemisphere did result in the introduction of important new food plants into India, China, Java, the Philippines, and other areas from the 1600s onward. These new foods led to substantial increases in the population in the areas affected. The import of silver was also an addition to wealth and adornment in China. Otherwise, Europeans died mainly of diseases that they contracted in Asia, such as new strains of malaria and dysentery. They spread diseases only to the more isolated parts of Asia, such as the Philippines, where the coming of the Spanish was accompanied by a devastating smallpox epidemic. The impact of European ideas, inventions, and modes of social organization was also very limited during the first centuries of expansion. Key European devices, such as clocks, were often seen as toys by Asian rulers to whom they were given as presents. But the ritual-minded Chinese emperors took these superior time-pieces very seriously, thereby providing the Jesuit missionaries who brought them to China with access to the court and ruler of the most powerful empire in an increasingly interconnected global system.

Except for clocks and guns, during the early modern period in global history, the West's surge in exploration and commercial expansion touched most of Asia only peripherally. This was particularly true of east Asia, where the political cohesion and military strength of the vast Chinese empire and the Japanese warrior-dominated states blocked all hope of European advance.

Promising missionary inroads in the 16th century were stifled by hostile Tokugawa shoguns in the early 17th century. They were also carefully contained by the Ming emperors and the nomadic Qing dynasty from the mid-1600s. Strong Chinese and Japanese rulers limited trading contacts with the aggressive Europeans and confined European merchants to a few ports—Macao and Canton in China, Deshima in Japan—that were remote from their respective capitals. In its early decades, the Ming dynasty also pursued a policy of overseas expansion that had no precedent in Chinese history. But when China again turned inward in the last centuries of the dynasty, a potentially formidable obstacle to the rise of European dominance in maritime Asia was removed. China's strong position in global trade continued, in marked contrast to Japan's greater isolation. But even China failed to keep pace with changes in European technology and merchant activity, with results that would show more clearly in the next stage of more intense global interaction.

Further Readings

The account of Da Gama's epic voyage that opens the chapter is based heavily on J. H. Parry's superb *The Discovery of the Sea* (1981). C. G. F. Simkins, *The Traditional Trade of Asia* (1968), and Anthony Reid, *Southeast Asia in the Age of Commerce, 1450–1680* (1988), provide overviews of the Asian trading network from ancient times until about the 18th century. Much more detailed accounts of specific segments of the system, as well as the impact upon it of the Dutch and Portuguese, can be found in the works of J. C. van Leur, M. A. P. Meilink-Roelofsz, K. N. Chaudhuri, Ashin Das Gupta, Sanjay Subrahmanyam, and Michael Pearson. C. R. Boxer's *The Portuguese Seaborne Empire* (1969) and *The Dutch Seaborne Empire* (1965) are still essential reading, although the latter has little on the Europeans in Asia. Boxer's *Race Relations in the Portuguese Colonial Empire, 1415–1852* (1963) provides a stimulating, if contentious, introduction to the history of European social interaction with overseas peoples in the early centuries of expansion. Important correctives to Boxer's work can be found in the more recent contributions of George Winius.

Louise Levathes, *When China Ruled the Seas: The Treasure Fleet of the Dragon Throne, 1405–33* (1994), is the most thorough account in English of China's global reach. G. B. Sansom, *The Western World and Japan* (1968), includes a wealth of information on the interaction between Europeans and, despite its title, peoples throughout Asia, and it has good sections on the missionary initiatives in both China and Japan.

The period of the Ming dynasty has been the focus of broader and more detailed studies than the dynasties that preceded it. An important early work is Charles O. Hucker, *The Censorial System of Ming China* (1966). Two essential and more recent works are Albert Chan's *The Glory and Fall of the Ming Dynasty* (1982) and Edward Dreyer's more traditional political history, *Early Ming China, 1355–1435* (1982). See also F. Mote and D. Twitchett, eds., *The Cambridge History of China: The Ming Dynasty 1368–1644,* vols. 6 and 7 (1988, 1998).

There are also wonderful insights into daily life at various levels of Chinese society in Ray Huang's very readable *1587: A Year of No Significance: The Ming Dynasty in Decline* (1981), and into the interaction between the Chinese and the Jesuits in Jonathan Spence's *The Memory Palace of Matteo Ricci* (1984). Frederic Wakeman Jr., *The Great Enterprise*, 2 vols. (1985), is essential to an understanding of the transition from Ming to Manchu rule. The early chapters of Spence's *The Search for Modern China* (1990) also provide an illuminating overview of that process.

Perhaps the best introductions to the situation in Japan in the early phase of European expansion are provided by G. B. Sansom's survey, *A History of Japan, 1615–1867* (1963) and Conrad Totman's *Politics in the Tokugawa Bakufu, 1600–1843* (1967). Numerous studies on the Europeans in Japan include those by Donald Keene, Grant Goodman, Noel Perrin, and C. R. Boxer. Intellectual trends in Japan in this era are most fully treated in H. D. Harootunian's *Toward Restoration: The Growth of Political Consciousness in Tokugawa Japan* (1970).

On the Web

The achievement of the Ming and later Qing dynasties are on view at virtual tours of their versions of the Great Wall and Forbidden City offered at http://www.chinavista.com/beijing/gugong/map.html and http://www.walkthewall.com/. A view of the Great Wall provided by satellite imagery is offered at http://www.jpl.nasa.gov/radar/sircxsar/sc-gwall.gif. An interactive 360 degree panoramic view of the Forbidden City can be found at http://www.thebeijingguide .com/forbidden_city/forbidden_city_virtual_tour.html.

Perhaps the finest of all virtual tour sites on the Web is that which provides a glimpse into the rich cultural life of the Tokugawa capital of Edo at http://www.us-japan.org/edomatsu/. This

shogunate was established after a civil war that followed the reigns of Nobunaga Oda (http://ox.compsoc.net/~gemini/simons/historyweb/oda-nobunaga.html) and Toyotomi Hideyoshi, developer of the grand Osaka Castle (http://www.osakacastle.net/castle_en/mainmenu.htm, or http://www.osakacastle.net/english/, and http://ngm.nationalgeographic.com/ngm/0312/feature5/zoomify/main.html).

Hideyoshi's death may or may not have been hastened by the great losses Japan sustained as a result of his two failed invasions of Korea (for a Korean view of these events, known as the Imjin Wars, see http://en.wikipedia.org/wiki/Imjin_War, http://en.wikipedia.org/wiki/Yi_Sunsin, and http://www.umich.edu/~urecord/9899/Feb22_99/imjin.htm). However, his passing hastened the ascension of Tokugawa Ieyasu (http://www.samurai-archives .com/ieyasu.html and http://www.japan-guide.com/e/e2128.html), whose shogunate paved the way for the construction of modern Japan.

The era of the rise and development of the Tokugawa also saw significant exchange between Asians and Christian missionaries elsewhere in Asia. An exceptional online study of these exchanges and the lives of Mateo Ricci, Adam Schall, and Robert di Nobili can be found at http://acc6.its.brooklyn.cuny.edu/~phalsall/texts/ric-jour.html, http://www.newadvent.org/cathen/13520a.htm, http://www.thefreelibrary.com/Preaching+Wisdom+to+the+Wise .+Three+Treatises-a077205106, and http://www.fordham.edu/halsall/eastasia/eastasiasbook.html#The%20Western%20Intrusion.

These exchanges were made possible by earlier developments in seagoing transportation, trade, and exploration, such as the travels of Zheng He (or Chengho) (http://chinapage.com/chengho.html) and the development of Portuguese and Dutch trading empires (http://www.colonialvoyage.com).

Web pages devoted to the activities of the Dutch East India Company (http://en.wikipedia.org/wiki/Dutch_East_India_Company, http://www.tanap.net/_resources/images/deshima .jpg, http://en.wikipedia.org/wiki/Deshima, and http://worldhistoryconnected.press.uiuc.edu/3.3/gilbert.html) provide luminous virtual tours of both Batavia and Deshima that demonstrate the still peripheral role of Europeans in Asia at this time.

AP* | Test Prep

1. When the Portuguese arrived in India in 1498, they
   (A) found they had little to offer in trade, but could get rich by forcing themselves into the existing trade network.
   (B) quickly integrated themselves on peaceful terms into the Asian trade system.
   (C) exchanged valuable European goods for Asian luxury items.
   (D) established cordial relations with Muslim merchants.

2. Which of the following characterized the Asian trading system as the first Europeans encountered it?
   (A) The Indian Ocean trade was monopolized by Hindu merchants.
   (B) The Indian Ocean trade was dominated by Muslim merchants.
   (C) The trade in slaves was the principal cargo traversing the Indian Ocean.
   (D) The Indian Ocean trade was highly militarized.

3. What circumstances prevented the Portuguese from establishing a monopoly over the Asian spice trade?
   (A) The Mughal and Ottoman navies were too strong.
   (B) French traders offered too much competition.
   (C) Portugal was a small nation and lacked the ships and manpower needed to overcome its Asian and European competition.
   (D) Access to the most profitable spices was controlled by the Chinese.

4. What Asian society witnessed the largest percentage of its population converted to Christianity?
   (A) China
   (B) India
   (C) the Philippines
   (D) Japan

5. The raw material with the broadest demand and highest price was
   (A) silk from China to the Middle East.
   (B) cottons from India to the Middle East.
   (C) bulk items, usually foodstuffs, exchanged among each of the main zones.
   (D) spices from the East Indies.

6. Following the defeat and expulsion of the Mongols from China,
   (A) Chinese manufacturing expanded further.
   (B) peasants were granted equality with the scholar-gentry and noble classes.
   (C) China converted to Buddhism.
   (D) the civil service exam system of the Mongols was ended.

7. In the 17th century, the Japanese dealt with the startling arrival of the Europeans to East Asia by
   (A) allying with the Portuguese against the other Europeans.
   (B) permitting the Jesuits to convert the Japanese to Christianity.
   (C) permitting the Europeans to establish control over Japan's foreign trade.
   (D) self-imposed isolation and forbidding most contact with Europeans.

Free-Response Question

Analyze the effects on East Asia of the intensification of European contact in the period 1450–1750.

PART IV Retrospective

A Look Back at the Early Modern Period

Contacts and Their Limits

In the context of world history, all the basic changes during the early modern period involved new levels of contacts. Merchants from many parts of the world participated in the new world economy. Their military superiority at sea allowed Europeans to reach new areas, especially along coasts and islands. Chinese merchants continued to trade in southeast Asia, encountering Europeans in the Philippines as well as through the port of Macao. The Columbian exchange was based on contacts—Asians learning of new foodstuffs, like the sweet potato, from the Americas, or Americans experiencing diseases brought by contacts with Europeans and Africans. An obvious result of new contacts was the emergence of overseas empires, but even land-based empires brought new connections. Russians, for example, came into contact with new Muslim and Jewish minorities as their conquests expanded, while the Ottoman Empire included Muslims, Jews, and Christians, not only in the general population but in the state bureaucracy as well.

On the whole, the contacts of the early modern period moved things—types of foods, germs, and goods—more than ideas. New foods from the Americas reached China, for example, which also took in massive amounts of New World silver. But the Chinese did not incorporate many new ideas or technologies from their new contacts. Small numbers of European missionaries, seen as harmless, were tolerated, and many of them took on European dress and habits. Early in the 18th century, even this tolerance declined as China began to repress Christian mis-

sionary efforts. Europeans gladly welcomed new products and wealth from other parts of the world. Indeed, many Europeans became dependent on items like sugar, one of the first great international consumer goods that involved mass taste. Europeans also eagerly imported the habit of coffee drinking, and coffee houses, initially developed in the Middle East, sprang up throughout Europe. European rulers, however, criticized coffee drinking as a foreign and dissolute habit and urged their subjects to stick to beer and wine. A new sense of superiority limited Europeans' openness to institutions and ideas from other regions than had been the case in the postclassical period. The Ottoman Empire also kept a lid on many kinds of contacts, even as it experienced growing interaction with European as well as African and Asian merchants. Despite knowledge of the printing press, for example, Ottoman rulers forbade presses in the empire until the mid-18th century, on grounds they might be used to spread subversive ideas. Ottoman rulers did import Western doctors, who actually knew no more than their local counterparts; otherwise, outside scientific developments were largely ignored.

There were exceptions to this standard rule of exchange of goods outweighing interchange of ideas. Extensive Christian conversions in the Philippines, where the Spanish occupied directly, contrasted with the experience in most of Asia, where European Christian missionaries made only limited inroads on established affiliations to Buddhism, Hinduism, or Islam. Japan reacted to the changes of the early modern era in yet another way. Initially Japan showed great interest in European firearms and some receptivity to Christianity. But at the end of the 16th century, new Japanese leaders sought to protect local traditions, including feudal military skills, and cut off both missionary activity and most gun production. For the next century and beyond, Japan remained relatively isolated from the rest of the world. India's Mughal rulers displayed considerable interest in cultural contacts with different parts of Asia as well as the West, but here too tolerance declined over time. Russia, in contrast, became an avid imitator of Western techniques and styles, though only at the elite level of society.

In Latin America outside goods—germs, animals, but also European-manufactured guns and art work—were imported extensively. Europeans also introduced new ideas, especially pressure to convert to Christianity. Native Americans combined these imports with local traditions, merging some of their own gods with the roster of Christian saints or using traditional native art in Christian celebrations. The outcome, a classic result of contact, contained the outlines of a new culture that was neither traditional nor fully Western. In some regions, imported African rituals and habits added to this mix of influences.

The point is obvious: the early modern period introduced many opportunities for new levels and types of contact. The results were, however, highly varied, with less widespread cultural exchange than might have been anticipated. Many peasant groups, in the interiors of Asia and Africa, experienced few new contacts of any sort. Even where trade and biological exchange penetrated, leaders and even ordinary people had some leeway about accepting other influences. Many people chose to stick to the tried and true; others, like the Japanese, launched a more internal pattern of cultural change. Americans, particularly those living along the coasts, were the great exception, but even here the native populations might modify unusual contacts and pressures to make them more recognizable and acceptable. The centuries of the early modern period are a somewhat transitional period. The increased number and level of contacts of the era set new patterns in motion, but people responded to those new patterns in widely varying ways.

At the same time, a few examples of striking cosmopolitanism emerged during this period—not typical, but far beyond what had been achieved by travelers in the earlier, postclassical era. A number of European missionaries became quite comfortable with Hindu or Confucian customs. Ottoman diplomats and merchants in Europe were very familiar with their surroundings, even if they imported few new ideas back home. In the later 18th century, a Muslim from India, Abu Taleb Khan, living in London, reported on his own mixed reactions to the world around him. He disliked what he saw as England's lack of religious faith, its arrogance, and its greed for money, but he very much appreciated the fairness of the English courts and (he said) the English ability to keep women in line, by force if necessary, despite women's freedom to mix in public. ■

PART

V

The Dawn of the Industrial Age, 1750–1914

Chapter 23   The Emergence of Industrial Society in the West, 1750–1914

Chapter 24   Industrialization and Imperialism: The Making of the European Global Order

Chapter 25   The Consolidation of Latin America, 1830–1920

Chapter 26   Civilizations in Crisis: The Ottoman Empire, the Islamic Heartlands, and Qing China

Chapter 27   Russia and Japan: Industrialization Outside the West

THE OVERVIEW

Maps tell a crucial story for the "long" 19th century—a period whose characteristics ran from the late 18th century to 1914. A radically new kind of technology and economy arose in a few parts of the world, in what began to be called the Industrial Revolution. The Industrial Revolution greatly increased industrial production as well as the speed and volume of transportation. Areas that industrialized early gained a huge economic lead over other parts of the world.

Industrial countries also gained power advantages over the rest of the world, thanks to new, mass-produced weaponry, steamships, and developments in communications. Western Europe led a new and unprecedented round of imperialism, taking over Africa, Oceania, and many parts of Asia. Even countries that began industrialization a bit later, like Russia and Japan, were adding to their empires by 1914.

Industrialization was not the only fundamental current in the long 19th century. Dramatic political changes in the Atlantic world competed for attention, though imperialism overshadowed liberal reform ideals in other parts of the world. Industrialization, however, was the dominant force. Its impact spread to art, as some artists sought to capture the energies of the new machines while others, even stylistic innovators, emphasized nostalgic scenes of nature as a contrast to industrial reality. Industrialization also supported a new level of global contacts, turning the proto-industrial framework of the early modern period into globalization outright.

Big Concepts

Industrialization was the dominant force in the long 19th century, but it helped spawn several more specific changes that in turn organize a series of Big Concepts. Western companies used their industrial manufacturing power, plus new systems of transportation and communication, to spread their form of capitalism on a global basis. On a global basis also, capitalists helped organize a growing segment of human labor. This was encouraged also by new patterns of global migration, reflecting population growth, new disruptions to established economies, and the changes in available global transportation. Western industrial dominance also fueled the new forms of imperialism and territorial expansion. Finally, new ideologies and political revolutions promoted reform currents of various sorts, some of them directed against the impacts of industrialization or imperialism. Industrialization and the growing globalization of capital and labor, imperialism, and the mix of new ideologies and reform currents—here were the Big Concepts that help organize a period of fundamental change.

Major World Empires, c. 1910

World Centers of Industrialization, c. 1910

TRIGGERS FOR CHANGE

By 1750 Europe's trading advantage over much of the rest of the world was increasing. Other gunpowder empires that had flourished during the Early Modern period were encountering difficulties; for example, the Ottoman Empire began to lose territory in wars with Russia. In this context, Great Britain began to introduce revolutionary new technologies, most notably the steam engine. This core innovation soon led to further inventions that increased western Europe's economic advantage over most other parts of the world.

An impressive series of inventions emerged from Britain, France, the United States, and a few other countries at this time in world history, because Europeans knew they could make money in the world economy by selling manufactured goods to other societies in return for cheap foods and raw materials (including silver and gold). Therefore businesses worked to accelerate the manufacturing process in order to increase their profits. European governments also began to create conditions designed to encourage industrial growth by improving roads and canals, developing new central banks, holding technology expositions, and limiting the rights of labor. In addition, about 1730, the population of western Europe began to grow very rapidly. This created new markets for goods and new workers who had no choice but to accept factory jobs. Finally, cultural changes encouraged invention and entrepreneurship. The rise of science and the European Enlightenment created an environment in which new discoveries seemed both possible and desirable. A rising appreciation of secular achievement encouraged businesspeople to undertake new ventures, and a growing number of western Europeans were interested in and could afford new goods.

So a combination of factors set the context for the replacement of the long-standing agricultural economy with a new industrial order. This order, in turn, would spark further changes, including the rapid growth of European imperialism.

THE BIG CHANGES

Industrialization meant new sources of power, founded initially on the use of coal. The steam engine was the crucial development. It was used to transmit power to machines that produced textiles, metal products, and other goods. Industrialization also involved new forms of work organization, particularly massing and disciplining labor within a factory system.

By 1840 the value of manufactured goods produced each year began to surpass that of agriculture, and the number of people engaged in manufacturing began to exceed the number who worked on the land. Improvements in agricultural production were vital supports to the process of industrialization.

The Industrial Revolution had two broad sets of consequences in the 19th century. First, in the indus-

1700 C.E.	1800 C.E.	1825 C.E.
1730–1850 Population boom in western Europe	1805–1849 Muhammad Ali rules Egypt	1825–1855 Repression in Russia
1770 James Watt's steam engine; beginning of Industrial Revolution	1808–1825 Latin American wars of independence	1826 New Zealand colonization begins
1776–1783 American Revolution	1815 Vienna settlement	1830, 1848 Revolutions in Europe
1786–1790 First British reforms in India	1815 British annexation of Cape Town and region of southern Africa	1835 English education in India
1788 Australian colonization begins	1822 Brazil declares independence	1838 Ottoman trade treaty with Britain
1789–1815 French Revolution and Napoleon	1823 Monroe Doctrine	1839–1841 Opium War between England and China
1789 Napoleon's invasion of Egypt		1839–1876 Reforms in Ottoman Empire
		1840 Semiautonomous government in Canada
		1846–1848 Mexican-American War
		1848 ff. Beginnings of Marxism

trial countries, the rise of the factory system changed many aspects of life. Work became more specialized and more closely supervised. The changes in work brought about by industrialization deeply affected families. Work moved out of the home, challenging traditional family life, in which all family members had participated in production. Though child labor was used early in the process of industrialization, increasingly childhood was redefined in industrial societies, away from work and toward schooling. Industrialization spurred the growth of cities. While new opportunities were involved, there was also great tension and, for a time, pockets of dreadful misery amid urban slums and machine-driven labor conditions.

Industrialization changed politics. New, middle-class groups, expanding on the basis of industrial growth, sought a political voice. As urban workers grew restive, governments had to strengthen police forces and also, gradually, to expand the right to vote among the lower classes. New nationalist loyalties involved ideological change away from primarily local and religious attachments, but they also provided identities for people whose traditional values were disrupted by industrial life and movement to the cities.

A few societies outside the West sought to industrialize early on. Egypt tried and largely failed, in the first half of the 19th century; a bit later, Japan and Russia launched industrial revolutions of their own. For most societies during the 19th century, the main effect of industrialization was to increase pressures to turn out food supplies and cheap raw materials for the industrial world, even though these societies were largely non-industrial. Western dominance in the world economy increased, and involvement in this economy became more widespread. For Latin America this meant even more such production, with newly introduced products like coffee and increased output of resources like copper. Parts of Asia that had previously profited from the world economy were now pressed into more low-cost production. All over the world, cheap manufactured goods from Western factories put hundreds of thousands of traditional manufacturing workers, many of them women, out of a job.

While industrial transformations of the world economy exerted the greatest pressure for change, they also provided the context for European imperial expansion into many new areas. When they took over in places like Africa, Europeans moved quickly to intensify low-cost production of foods, minerals, and (sometimes) simple manufactured goods.

Two other key changes accompanied this process of global economic change. First, the institution of slavery increasingly came under attack. The Atlantic slave trade was legally abolished early in the 19th century. Then slave and serf systems were progressively eliminated in the Americas, Europe, Russia, and Africa. New ideas about human rights and new confidence in "free wage labor" facilitated the change. Significant population growth provided new sources of labor to replace slaves. Immigrants poured out of Europe to the

1850 C.E.	1875 C.E.	1900 C.E.
1850–1864 Taiping Rebellion in China	1877–1878 Ottomans out of most of Balkans; Treaty of San Stefano	1901 Commonwealth of Australia
1853 Perry expedition to Edo Bay in Japan	1879–1890s Partition of west Africa	1903 Construction of Panama Canal begins
1854–1856 Crimean War	1882 British takeover of Egypt	1904–1905 Russo-Japanese War
1858 British assume control over India	1885 Formation of National Congress Party in India	1905–1906 Revolution in Russia; limited reforms
1860–1868 Civil strife in Japan	1886–1888 Slavery abolished in Cuba and Brazil	1908 Young Turk rising
1861 Emancipation of serfs in Russia	1890 Japanese constitution	1910 Japan annexes Korea
1861–1865 American Civil War	1890s Partition of east Africa	1911–1912 Revolution in China; end of empire
1863 Emancipation of slaves in U.S.	1894–1895 Sino Japanese War	1914–1918 World War I
1864–1871 German unification	1895 Cuban revolt against Spain	
1868–1912 Meiji (reform) era in Japan	1898 Formation of Marxist Social Democratic Party in Russia	
1870–1910 Acceleration of "demographic transition" in western Europe and the U.S.	1898 Spanish–American War; U.S. acquires the Philippines, Puerto Rico, and Hawaii; United States intervenes in Cuba	
1870–1910 Expansion of commercial export economy in Latin America	1898–1901 Boxer Rebellion in China	
1871–1912 High point of European imperialism		

Americas and Australia. Indenture systems brought massive numbers of Asians to Oceania, the Americas, and Africa. As slavery ended, harsh, low-paid "free" labor intensified in many places. Second, the massive economic changes brought about by the Industrial Revolution impacted the environment. In industrial societies, smoke and the steady increase of chemical and urban wastes worsened regional air and water quality. The expansion of export production in other parts of the world also affected the environment in negative ways. The introduction of crops like coffee and cotton, for example, to new parts of Africa and Latin America often caused significant soil erosion.

GLOBALIZATION

Western industrial and military power, when joined with new technologies in transportation and communication, helped generate the first full emergence of globalization after the 1850s. The telegraph, railroads and above all steam shipping greatly speeded the movement of goods and news around the world. Construction of the Suez Canal and then, early in the 20th century, the Panama Canal, cut massive amounts of time off oceanic shipping. Exchanges of bulk goods—wheat and meats from the Americas, metal ores, as well as expensive manufactured products—soared beyond any previous precedent.

Modern globalization differed from earlier proto-globalization not only because of the volume of goods exchanged and the impact of exports and imports on local economies from Hawaii to Mozambique to Honduras. Economic contacts were now enhanced by efforts as transnational political agreements. Some agreements, on international mails for example, obviously related closely to economic relationships. Other efforts, however, like the new Geneva Conventions on the treatment of military prisoners, began to globalize some ideas about human rights. New levels of cultural globalization showed particularly in the clear emergence of transnational sports interests, particularly around soccer, football and American baseball. Finally, global economic exchange began to have significant regional environmental impacts. Development of a rubber industry in Brazil, to meet needs in industrial countries, led to important levels of deforestation. The advent of globalization thus involved changes on various fronts.

Different societies participated variously in globalization, which raises important issues of comparison and continuity. New debates arose in Egypt about whether the veiling of women represented Islamic identity or an offense to global standards for women.

Many countries, even though they could not resist global involvements, deplored Western dominance, and disproportionate western benefit, from the process. Some societies, like Japan, managed to encounter globalization while preserving a sense of separate identity. The variations, and the widespread sense of resentment against too much foreign control and influence, were significant in their own right.

CONTINUITY

Industrialization's global impact did not destroy continuities from the past. In the first place, although industrialization and early globalization were indeed revolutionary, their consequences were spread out over many decades. Dramatic innovations such as department stores and ocean-going steamships should not conceal the fact that such stores controlled only about 5 percent of all retail commerce in major Western cities—the rest centered on more traditional shops, peddling, and outdoor markets.

Continuity also shows in the different ways specific groups and regions reacted to change. The need to respond to Western economic and, often, military pressure was quite real around the world. But reactions varied in part with local conditions. Japanese society adapted considerably to facilitate industrialization. The feudal system was abolished outright, while its legacy helped to shape Japanese business organizations. The absence of a comparable organizational legacy may have reduced Chinese flexibility for some time. The spread of literacy in Russia in the later 19th century—part of Russia's efforts to reform—created new opportunities for popular literature, as had occurred earlier in the West. But in contrast to Western literature, which often celebrated outlaws, Russian adventure stories always included the triumph of the state over disorder. The cultural differences illustrated by these comparisons did not necessarily persist without alteration, but they continued to influence regional patterns.

Response to change also included the "invention" of traditions. Many societies sought to compensate for disruption by appealing to apparent sources of stability that drew on traditional themes. Many Western leaders emphasized the sanctity of the family and domestic roles for women, hoping that the home would provide a "haven" amid rapid economic change. The ideas of the family as a haven and of the special domestic virtues of women were partly myths, even as both took on the status of tradition. In the 1860s the U.S. government instituted Thanksgiving as a national holiday, and many Americans assumed that this was simply an official recognition of a long-standing celebration; in fact, Thanksgiving had been only rarely and fitfully observed before this new holiday, designed to promote family and national unity, was newly established. Japanese leaders by the 1880s invented new traditions about the importance of the emperor as a divinely appointed ruler, again as a means of counterbalancing rapid change.

IMPACT ON DAILY LIFE: LEISURE

The Industrial Revolution transformed leisure. Leaders in industrial centers wanted to discourage traditional festivals, because they took too much time away from work and sometimes led to rowdiness on the part of workers. Factory rules also limited napping, chatting, wandering around, and drinking on the job. In the early decades of industrialization, leisure declined at first—replaced by long and exhausting work days—just as it had when agriculture replaced hunting and gathering.

With time, however, industrial societies introduced new kinds of leisure. Professional sports began to take shape around the middle of the 19th century. A bit later, new forms of popular theater attracted many people in the cities. The idea of vacations also spread: workers took same-day train excursions to beaches and travel companies formed to assist the middle classes in more ambitious trips. Much of the new leisure depended on professional entertainers, with the bulk of the population turning into spectators.

While the most dramatic innovations in leisure occurred in industrial societies, here too there was quick connection to the wider world—another sign of early globalization. Many mine and plantation owners sought to curb traditional forms of leisure activity in the interests of more efficient production. Although they had less success than factory owners did, they did have some impact. New forms of leisure pioneered in western Europe or the United States also caught on elsewhere. Soccer began to win interest in Latin America by the 1860s. Baseball began to spread from the United States to the rest of the Americas and Japan by the 1890s. By the 1920s, movies had won global attention as well. While most societies retained traditional, regional leisure forms, something of a global leisure culture was beginning to emerge.

SOCIETIES AND TRENDS

Chapters in this section begin with developments in the West, where industrialization and new political ideas first emerged. The West also spawned new settler societies in the United States, Canada, Australia, and New Zealand. These developments are described in Chapter 23. Chapter 24 focuses on the world economy and imperialism, tracing the effects of Western industrialization on the nonindustrial world. Chapter 25 describes the balance between new forces within Latin America. Chapter 26 describes developments in key parts of Asia as they responded to the challenges of Western power and economic change. Chapter 27 deals with two non-Western societies, Russia and Japan, that launched ambitious plans for industrialization in the late 19th century; the comparative study of the processes of industrialization in Russia, Japan, and the West sheds new light on the varied forms this process could take. ■

23 The Emergence of Industrial Society in the West, 1750–1914

The Age of Revolution

VISUALIZING THE PAST: The French Revolution in Cartoons

The Consolidation of the Industrial Order, 1850–1914

DOCUMENT: Protesting the Industrial Revolution

Cultural Transformations

Western Settler Societies

THINKING HISTORICALLY: Two Revolutions; Industrial and Atlantic

Diplomatic Tensions and World War I

GLOBAL CONNECTIONS: Industrial Europe and the World

Why did an anti-Chinese riot break out in Milwaukee in 1889 when only 16 Chinese immigrants were living in the whole state of Wisconsin? The riot occurred in March. It followed press reports that Chinese laundrymen were seducing European American girls (Figure 23.1). One paper claimed there was a sinister ring transporting girls to Chicago where they would be forced to marry Chinese men. The headlines were inflammatory: "Chinese Horrors. Twenty-two Children Are Lured into the Dens." Following accusations, police did arrest two Chinese. But court procedures were too slow for the public. Large crowds gathered, calling for lynchings, abusing Chinese effigies, and burning and looting Chinese stores. After a tense few days, most of the Chinese immigrants left town.

From a world history standpoint, this incident is not significant, but it is suggestive. First, it occurred after several decades of Chinese immigration into the United States, where initially many worked on western railways. This in turn was part of a larger movement of people from Asia to the Americas and elsewhere—a key migration theme for the period—as population growth in Asian nations combined with a deteriorating position in the world economy fuelled mass Asian emigration. Large Japanese popula-

tions, for example, emerged in places like Brazil and Hawaii. More than a million Chinese emigrated to various parts of the Americas in the decades before and after 1900, and there was massive movement from India, Japan, and the Philippines as well. This new migration from Asia to the Americas was a major departure in world history, and it would continue into the 21st century.

Second, of course, the Milwaukee incident illustrates the anxieties that contact with Asians caused among many Americans. The 1880s saw massive anti-Chinese rioting in the western United States, with more than 140 Chinese murdered and more than 10,000 forced to leave their homes and stores. In 1882 the first of several measures was passed to limit Chinese immigration, an exclusionary policy that would last until 1943. Anxiety focused both on Chinese competition with American labor and on accusations of predatory sexual behavior. It proved difficult, for several decades, for Chinese Americans to assimilate more fully into national life. And of course, as with many immigrants, some did not want to. For example, many Chinese spent considerable sums to send the bodies of their deceased relatives back to China, the only place, in their view, where ancestors could be properly accommodated. ■

Western history in the 19th century operates amid accelerating international contacts—of the sort that brought new Asian migration to the United States. Developments in the West, even more obviously, altered the global context in turn, through the effects of industrialization, political upheaval, and new social and cultural reforms.

For change was the name of the game in the 19th-century West—including the addition of important new settler societies in the United States and elsewhere substantially shaped by Western influences. In 1750 western Europe consisted almost entirely of monarchies. By 1914 many monarchies had been overthrown, and everywhere powerful legislatures, based on extensive voting systems, defined much of the political apparatus. Twice, in the first 15 years of the 19th century and again in the 1860s, western Europe was rocked by significant warfare, but much of the period was relatively peaceful, but by 1914 a new alliance system had emerged that was about to plunge not only Europe but other parts of the world into massive bloodshed. The rise of a new middle class, novel issues for women, substantial changes in science and popular culture—these were other areas in which tradition seemed to erode under the impact of industrialization and urban growth.

Figure 23.1 A Chinese laundry shop, 1855. Chinese workers began to reach the United States in the mid-19th century, part of a larger stream of Asian labor migrations to many areas in the world. The mostly uneducated and unskilled Chinese workers first came to America in response to advertising by railroad companies, who wanted cheap labor to build the Western railroads. Although the new immigrants faced resentment from American workers, both because of job competition and because of real or imagined differences in values, the Chinese managed to establish themselves in some additional types of work, especially laundries. These enterprises were attractive to the Chinese because they required little specialized skill or capital, and American men did not object to Chinese laundries, as they considered laundry to be "women's work."

The Age of Revolution

Against the backdrop of intellectual challenge, commercial growth, and population pressure, the placid politics of the 18th century were shattered by the series of revolutions that took shape in the 1770s and 1780s. This was the eve of the **age of revolution,** a period of political upheaval beginning roughly with the American Revolution in 1775 and continuing through the French Revolution of 1789 and other movements for change up to 1848. The wave of revolutions caught up many social groups with diverse motives, some eager to use revolution to promote further change and some hoping to turn back the clock and recover older values.

New ideas helped stimulate a wave of revolutions in the whole Atlantic world from the 1770s to 1848. Revolutionary patterns would gain international influence; they also interacted with the early effects of Western industrialization.

Forces of Change

Three forces were working to shatter Europe's calm by the mid-18th century. The first of the forces was cultural, for intellectual ferment was running high. Enlightenment thinkers challenged regimes that did not grant full religious freedom or that insisted on aristocratic privilege, and a few called for widespread popular voice in government. Jean-Jacques Rousseau argued for government based on a general will, and this could be interpreted as a plea for democratic voting. A gap had opened between leading intellectuals and established institutions, and this played a role in the revolutions that lay ahead. Enlightenment thinkers also encouraged economic and technological change and policies that would promote industry; manufacturers and political reformers alike could take inspiration from these ideas.

age of revolution Period of political upheaval beginning roughly with the American Revolution in 1775 and continuing through the French Revolution of 1789 and other movements for change up to 1848.

Along with cultural change, ongoing commercialization continued to stir the economy. Businesspeople, gaining new wealth, might well challenge the idea that aristocrats alone should hold the highest political offices. They certainly were growing interested in new techniques that might spur production. Commercial practices might also draw attack, from artisans or peasant villagers who preferred older economic values. This could feed revolution as well.

1700 C.E.	1820 C.E.	1840 C.E.	1860 C.E.	1880 C.E.	1900 C.E.
1730 ff. Massive population rise c. 1770 James Watt's steam engine; beginning of Industrial Revolution 1788 First convict settlement in Australia 1789 George Washington first president of the United States 1789–1799 French Revolution 1790 ff. Beginning of per capita birth rate decline (United States) 1793 First free European settlers in Australia 1793–1794 Radical phase of French Revolution 1799–1815 Reign of Napoleon 1800–1850 Romanticism in literature and art 1803 Louisiana Purchase (United States) 1810–1826 Rise of democratic suffrage in United States. 1815 Congress of Vienna ushers in a more conservative period in Europe	1820 Revolutions in Greece and Spain; rise of liberalism and nationalism 1820s ff. Industrialization in United States 1823 First legislative council in Australia 1826–1837 Active European colonization begins in New Zealand 1829 Andrew Jackson seventh president of United States 1830 Revolutions in several European countries 1832 Reform Bill of 1832 (England) 1837 Rebellion in Canada 1837–1842 U.S.–Canada border clashes 1839 New British colonial policy allows legislature and more autonomy	1840 Union act reorganizes Canada, provides elected legislature 1843–1848 First Maori War, New Zealand 1846–1848 Mexican-American War 1848 ff. Writings of Karl Marx; rise of socialism 1848–1849 Revolutions in several European countries 1850 Australia's Colonies Government Act allows legislature and more autonomy 1852 New constitution in New Zealand; elected councils 1859 Darwin's *Origin of Species* 1859–1870 Unification of Italy	1860–1870 Second Maori War 1861–1865 American Civil War 1863 Emancipation Proclamation, United States 1864–1871 German unification 1867 British North America Act unites eastern and central Canada 1870–1879 Institution of Third Republic, France 1870s ff. Rapid birth rate decline 1870s ff. Spread of compulsory education laws 1871–1914 High point of European imperialism 1879–1907 Alliance system: Germany-Austria (1879); Germany-Austria-Russia (1881); Germany-Italy-Austria (1882); France-Russia (1891); Britain-France (1904); Britain-Russia (1907)	1880s ff. High point of impressionism in art 1881–1914 Canadian Pacific Railway 1881–1889 German social insurance laws enacted 1882 United States excludes Chinese immigrants 1891–1898 Australia and New Zealand restrict Asian immigration 1893 Women's suffrage in New Zealand 1898 Spanish-American War; United States acquires Puerto Rico, Guam, Philippines 1898 United States annexes Hawaii 1899 United States acquires part of Samoa	1901 Commonwealth of Australia creates national federation 1907 New Zealand gains dominion status in British Empire 1912–1913 Balkan Wars 1914 Beginning of World War I

population revolution Huge growth in population in western Europe beginning about 1730; prelude to Industrial Revolution; population of France increased 50 percent, England and Prussia 100 percent.

A final source of disruption was occurring more quietly at all social levels. Western Europe experienced its huge population jump after about 1730. Within half a century, the population of France rose by 50 percent; that of Britain and Prussia rose 100 percent. This **population revolution** was partly the result of better border policing by the efficient nation-state governments, which reduced the movement of disease-bearing animals. More important was improved nutrition resulting from the growing use of the potato. These factors reduced the death rate, particularly for children; instead of more than 40 percent of all children dying by age 2, the figure by the 1780s was closer to 33 percent. More children surviving also meant more people living to have children of their own, so the birth rate increased as well.

Population pressure at this level always has dramatic impact. Upper-class families, faced with more surviving children, tried to tighten their grip on existing offices. In the late 18th century, it became harder for anyone who was not an aristocrat to gain a high post in the church or state. This reaction helped feed demands for change by other groups. Above all, population pressure drove many people into the working class as they lost any real chance of inheriting property, creating new motives for protest.

The population growth of the 18th century prompted a rapid expansion of domestic manufacturing in western Europe and, by 1800, in the United States. Hundreds of thousands of people became full- or part-time producers of textile and metal products, working at home but in a capitalist system in which materials, work orders, and sales depended on urban merchants. This development has been called **proto-industrialization,** and it ultimately encouraged new technologies to expand production further because of the importance of new market relationships and manufacturing volume.

Population upheaval and the spread of a propertyless class that worked for money wages had a sweeping impact on a variety of behaviors in Western society, including North America. Many villagers began to change their dress to more urban styles; this suggests an early form of new consumer interest. Premarital sex increased, and out-of-wedlock births rose to 10 percent of all births. Among groups with little or no property, parental authority began to decline because the traditional threat of denying inheritance had no meaning. Youthful independence became more marked, and although this was particularly evident in economic behavior as many young people looked for jobs on their own, the new defiance of authority might have had political implications as well.

Indeed, the spread of social tensions but also the attraction of new political ideas helped generate revolutionary political movements on both sides of the Atlantic. These Atlantic revolutions embraced independence efforts in North and later South America, a major revolution in France, and then a series of risings in various parts of western and central Europe that ran through the first half of the 19th century.

The American Revolution

When Britain's Atlantic colonies rebelled in 1775, it was primarily a war for independence rather than a full-fledged revolution. A large minority of American colonists resisted Britain's attempt to impose new taxes and trade controls on the colonies after 1763. Many settlers also resented restrictions on movement into the frontier areas. The colonists also invoked British political theory to argue that they should not be taxed without representation. The Stamp Act of 1765, imposing taxes on documents and pamphlets, particularly roused protest against British tyranny. Other grievances were involved. Crowding along the eastern seaboard led some younger men to seek new opportunities, including political office, that turned them against the older colonial leadership. Growing commerce antagonized some farmers and artisans, who looked for ways to defend the older values of greater social equality and community spirit.

With the start of the **American Revolution,** colonial rebels set up a new government, which issued the Declaration of Independence in 1776 and authorized a formal army to pursue its war. The persistence of the revolutionaries was combined with British military blunders and significant aid from the French government, designed to embarrass its key enemy. After several years of fighting, the United States won its freedom and, in 1789, set up a new constitutional structure based on Enlightenment principles, with checks and balances between the legislature and the executive branches of government, and formal guarantees of individual liberties. Voting rights, though limited, were widespread, and the new regime was for a time the most advanced in the world. Socially, the revolution accomplished less; slavery was untouched.

Crisis in France in 1789

The next step in the revolutionary spiral occurred in France. It was the **French Revolution** that most clearly set in motion the political restructuring of western Europe. Several factors combined in the 1780s in what became a classic pattern of revolutionary causation. Ideological insistence on change won increasing attention from the mid-18th century onward, as Enlightenment thinkers urged the need to limit the powers of the Catholic church, the aristocracy, and the monarchy. Social changes reinforced the ideological challenge. Some middle-class people, proud of their business or professional success, wanted a greater political role. Many peasants, pressed by population growth, wanted fuller freedom from landlords' demands.

The French government and upper classes proved incapable of reform. Aristocrats tightened their grip in response to their own population pressure, and the government proved increasingly

proto-industrialization Preliminary shift away from agricultural economy in Europe; workers become full- or part-time producers of textile and metal products, working at home but in a capitalist system in which materials, work orders, and ultimate sales depended on urban merchants; prelude to Industrial Revolution.

The Bostonians Paying the Excise Man

IMAGE

The Declaration of Independence (1776)

DOCUMENT

American Revolution Rebellion of English American colonies along Atlantic seaboard between 1775 and 1783; resulted in independence for former British colonies and eventual formation of United States of America.

French Revolution Revolution in France between 1789 and 1800; resulted in overthrow of Bourbon monarchy and old regimes; ended with establishment of French Empire under Napoleon Bonaparte; source of many liberal movements and constitutions in Europe.

Madame de Staël on the Ancien Regime

DOCUMENT

The French Revolution in Cartoons

This cartoon, titled *The Former Great Dinner of the Modern Gargantua with His Family,* appeared in 1791 or 1792, as the French Revolution was becoming more radical. It pictures the king as a latter-day Gargantua, referring to a French literary figure who was a notoriously great eater.

QUESTIONS How does the cartoon characterize the relationship between French society and economy and the monarchy? What conclusions might readers of the cartoon draw about what should happen to the monarchy? With improvements in printing and literacy, cartoons were becoming more available, and they have continued to be important into the present day. Why were they effective as a means of communicating ideas?

Oath of the Tennis Court

Declaration of the Rights of Man and the Citizen

Louis XVI (1754–1793) Bourbon monarch of France who was executed during the radical phase of the French Revolution.

Declaration of the Rights of Man and the Citizen Adopted during the liberal phase of the French Revolution (1789); stated the fundamental equality of all French citizens; later became a political source for other liberal movements.

ineffective—a key ingredient in any successful revolution. Finally, a sharp economic slump in 1787 and 1788, triggered by bad harvests, set the seal on revolution.

The French king, **Louis XVI,** called a meeting of the traditional parliament to consider tax reform for his financially pinched regime. But middle-class representatives, inspired by Enlightenment ideals, insisted on turning this assembly (which had not met for a century and a half) into a modern parliament, with voting by head (that is, each representative with a vote, rather than a single vote for each estate) and with majority representation for nonnoble property owners. The fearful king caved in after some street riots in Paris in the summer of 1789, and the revolution was under way.

Events that summer were crucial. The new assembly, with its middle-class majority, quickly turned to devising a new political regime. A stirring ***Declaration of the Rights of Man and the Citizen*** proclaimed freedom of thought. Like the American Declaration of Independence, this law enacted natural rights to "liberty, property, security, and resistance to oppression" and specifically guaranteed free expression of ideas. A popular riot stormed a political prison, the Bastille, on July 14, in what became the revolution's symbol; ironically, almost no prisoners were there. Soon after this, peasants seized manorial records and many landed estates. This triggered a general proclamation abolishing manorialism, giving peasants clear title to much land and establishing equality under the law. Although aristocrats survived for some time, the principles of aristocratic rule were undercut. The privileges of the church were also attacked, and church property was seized. A new constitution proclaimed individual rights, including freedom of religion, press, and property. A strong parliament was set up to limit the king, and about one-half the adult male population—those with property—were eligible to vote.

The French Revolution: Radical and Authoritarian Phases

By 1792 the initial push for reform began to turn more radical. Early reforms provoked massive opposition in the name of church and aristocracy, and civil war broke out in several parts of France. Monarchs in Britain, Prussia, and Austria trumpeted their opposition to the revolution, and France soon moved toward European war as well. These pressures led to a takeover by radical leaders, who wanted to press the revolution forward and to set up firmer authority in the revolution's defense. The radicals abolished the monarchy. The king was decapitated on the **guillotine,** a new device introduced, Enlightenment-fashion, to provide more humane executions, but instead it became a symbol of revolutionary bloodthirst. The radicals also executed several thousand opponents in what was named the Reign of Terror, even though by later standards it was mild.

The leader of the radical phase was Maximilien Robespierre (1758–1794), a classic example of a revolutionary ideologue. Born into a family of lawyers, he gained his law degree in 1781 and soon

guillotine Introduced as a method of humane execution; utilized to execute thousands during the most radical phase of the French Revolution known as the Reign of Terror.

was publishing Enlightenment-style political tracts. The new philosophies inspired passion in Robespierre, particularly the democratic ideas of Rousseau. Elected to all the initial revolutionary assemblies, Robespierre headed the prosecution of the king in 1792 and then took over the leadership of government. He put down many factions, sponsored the Terror, and worked to centralize the government. In 1794 he set up a civic religion, the "cult of the Supreme Being," to replace Catholicism. Personally incorruptible, Robespierre came to symbolize the single-minded revolutionary. But he shied away from significant social reforms that might have drawn urban support. He was convinced that he knew the people's will. Opposition mounted, and when he called for yet another purge of moderate leaders, he was arrested and guillotined on the same day, abandoned by the popular factions that had once spurred him on.

While in power, Robespierre and his colleagues pushed revolutionary reforms. A new constitution, never fully put into practice, proclaimed universal adult male suffrage. The radicals introduced a metric system of weights and measures, the product of the rationalizing genius of the Enlightenment. Slavery was abolished in the French colonies, though this measure was reversed after the radical regime collapsed. Robespierre and his allies also proclaimed universal military conscription, arguing that men who were free citizens owed loyalty and service to the government. And revolutionary armies began to win major success. Not only were France's enemies driven out, but the regime began to acquire new territory in the Low Countries, Italy, and Germany, spreading revolutionary gains farther in western Europe.

A new spirit of popular **nationalism** surfaced during the revolution's radical phase. Many French people felt an active loyalty to the new regime—to a state they believed they had helped create. A new symbol was a revolutionary national anthem (the world's first), with its rousing first lines, "Come, children of the nation, the day of glory has arrived." Nationalism could replace older loyalties to church or locality.

The fall of the radicals led to four years of moderate policies. Then in 1799 the final phase of the revolution was ushered in with the victory of **Napoleon Bonaparte,** a leading general who soon converted the revolutionary republic to an authoritarian empire. Napoleon reduced the parliament to a rubber stamp, and a powerful police system limited freedom of expression. However, Napoleon confirmed other liberal gains, including religious freedom, while enacting substantial equality—though for men, not women—in a series of new law codes. To train bureaucrats, Napoleon developed a centralized system of secondary schools and universities.

Driven by insatiable ambition, Napoleon devoted most of his attention to expansion abroad (Map 23.1). A series of wars brought France against all of Europe's major powers, including Russia. At its height, about 1812, the French Empire directly held or controlled as satellite kingdoms most of western Europe, and its success spurred some reform measures even in Prussia and Russia. The French Empire crumbled after this point. An attempt to invade Russia in 1812 failed miserably. French armies perished in the cold Russian winter even as they pushed deep into the empire. An alliance system organized by Britain crushed the emperor definitively in 1814 and 1815. Yet Napoleon's campaigns had done more than dominate European diplomacy for one and a half decades. They had also spread key revolutionary legislation—the idea of equality under the law and the attack on privileged institutions such as aristocracy, church, and craft guilds—throughout much of western Europe.

The revolution and Napoleon encouraged popular nationalism outside of France as well as within. French military success continued to draw great excitement at home. Elsewhere, French armies tore down local governments, as in Italy and Germany, which whetted appetites there for greater national unity. And the sheer fact of French invasion made many people more conscious of loyalty to their own nations; popular resistance to Napoleon, in parts of Spain and Germany, played a role in the final French defeat.

A Conservative Settlement and the Revolutionary Legacy

The allies who had brought the proud French emperor down met at Vienna in 1815 to reach a peace settlement that would make further revolution impossible. Diplomats at the **Congress of Vienna** did not try to punish France too sternly, on the grounds that the European balance of power should be restored. Still, a series of stronger powers was established around France, which meant gains for

Saint-Just on Democracy, Education, and Terror

nationalism   Political viewpoint with origins in western Europe; often allied with other "isms"; urged importance of national unity; valued a collective identity based on culture, race, or ethnic origin.

Madame de Rémusat on the Rise of Napoleon

The Empire of Napoleon in 1812

Napoleon's Exile to St. Helena

Bonaparte, Napoleon   Rose within the French army during the wars of the French Revolution; eventually became general; led a coup that ended the French Revolution; established French Empire under his rule; defeated and deposed in 1815.

Congress of Vienna   Meeting in the aftermath of Napoleonic Wars (1815) to restore political stability in Europe and settle diplomatic disputes.

Europe After the Congress of Vienna, 1815

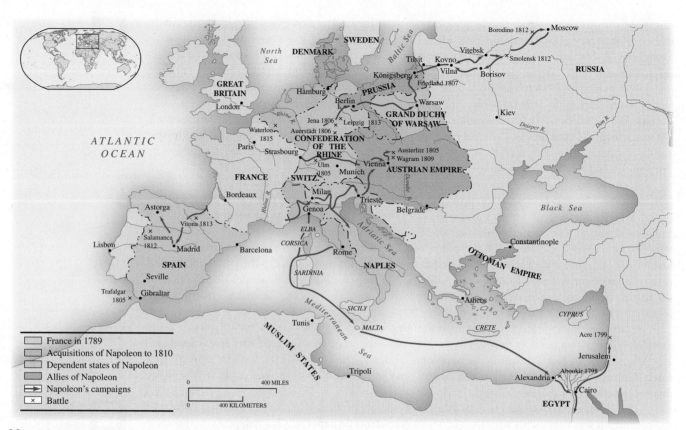

Map 23.1 Napoleon's Empire in 1812 By 1812, France dominated Europe to the borders of Russia, but Napoleon's decision to invade Russia proved disastrous, as his army was soon mired in the bitter cold and deep snows of a harsh Russian winter. Defeated in 1814, Napoleon was exiled to the island of Elba (shown above) but he escaped and returned to power. After final defeat at the Battle of Waterloo (1815), he was exiled to the remote South Atlantic island of St. Helena.

conservative Political viewpoint with origins in western Europe during the 19th century; opposed revolutionary goals; advocated restoration of monarchy and defense of church.

John Stuart Mill on Women's Rights

liberal Political viewpoint with origins in western Europe during the 19th century; stressed limited state interference in individual life, representation of propertied people in government; urged importance of constitutional rule and parliaments.

radical Political viewpoint with origins in western Europe during the 19th century; advocated broader voting rights than liberals; in some cases advocated outright democracy; urged reforms in favor of the lower classes.

Prussia within Germany and for the hitherto obscure nation of Piedmont in northern Italy. The old map was not restored, and the realignments ultimately facilitated national unifications. Britain gained new colonial territories, confirming its lead in the scramble for empire in the wider world. Russia, newly important in European affairs, maintained its hold over most of Poland.

These territorial adjustments kept Europe fairly stable for almost half a century—a major achievement, given the crisscrossed rivalries that had long characterized Western society. But the Vienna negotiators were much less successful in promoting internal peace. The idea was to promote stability by restoring monarchy in France and linking Europe's major powers in defense of churches and kings. This was a key statement of the growing movement of **conservatives** in Europe, who defined themselves in opposition to revolutionary goals.

But political movements arose to challenge conservatism. They involved concrete political agitation but also an explosion of ideals about protecting individual rights and providing some political representation. Many of the ideals would resonate in many parts of the world during the 19th and 20th centuries. **Liberals** focused primarily on issues of political structure. They looked for ways to limit state interference in individual life and urged voting rights for propertied people. Liberals touted the importance of constitutional rule and protection for freedoms of religion, press, and assembly. Largely representing the growing middle class, many liberals also sought economic reforms, including better education, which would promote industrial growth.

Radicals accepted the importance of most liberal demands, but they also wanted wider voting rights. Some advocated outright democracy. They also urged some social reforms in the interest of the lower classes. A smaller current of socialism urged an attack on private property in the name of equality and an end to capitalist exploitation of workers. Nationalists, often allied with liberalism or radicalism, urged the importance of national unity and glory.

Political protest found support among students and among urban artisans, concerned about economic changes that might displace craft skills. Revolutions broke out in several places in 1820 and again in 1830. The 1820 revolts involved a nationalist **Greek Revolution** against Ottoman rule—a key step in gradually dismantling the Ottoman Empire in the Balkans—and a rebellion in Spain. Another French Revolution of 1830 installed a different king and a somewhat more liberal monarchy. Uprisings also occurred in key states in Italy and Germany, though without durable result; the Belgian Revolution of 1830 produced a liberal regime and a newly independent nation.

Britain and the United States also participated in the process of political change, though without revolution. Key states in the United States granted universal adult male suffrage (except for slaves) and other political changes in the 1820s, leading to the election of a popular president, Andrew Jackson, in 1828. In Britain, the **Reform Bill of 1832,** a response to popular agitation, gave the parliamentary vote to most middle-class men. By the 1830s, regimes in France, Britain, Belgium, and several other countries had solid parliaments (the equivalent of Congress in the United States), some guarantees for individual rights against arbitrary state action, religious freedom not only for various Christian sects but also for Jews, and voting systems that ranged from democratic (for men) to the upper-middle class, plus aristocracy alone.

Industrialization and the Revolutions of 1848

By the 1830s and 1840s, industrialization began to add pressures to Europe's revolutionary ferment. The 1832 Reform Bill in England, for example, responded in part to growing working-class agitation, though it did not extend the vote to workers and led to further political protest. By this time France, Belgium, and Germany, as well as the United States, were fully engaged in the early stages of the Industrial Revolution, based in part on copying British models. These developments spurred some direct unrest among factory workers. They raised even more concerns among artisans, worried for the future of traditional skilled labor, and these groups provided much of the muscle that went into the final phase of the age of revolution.

Key lower-class groups turned to political protest as a means of compensating for industrial change. Artisans and workers in Britain generated a new movement to gain the vote in the 1830s and 1840s, developing a charter to spell out their demands. This **Chartist Movement** hoped that a democratic government would regulate new technologies and promote popular education.

The extraordinary wave of revolutions of 1848 and 1849 brought protest to a head. Paris was again the center. In the popular uprising that began in February 1848, the French monarchy was once again expelled, this time for good, and a democratic republic was established briefly. Urban artisans pressed for serious social reform—perhaps some version of socialism, and certainly government-supported jobs for the unemployed. Groups of women schoolteachers agitated for the vote and other rights for women. The social demands were far wider than those of the great uprising of 1789.

Revolution quickly spread to other centers. Major revolts occurred in Germany (Figure 23.2), Austria, and Hungary. Revolutionaries in these areas devised liberal constitutions to modify conservative monarchies, artisans pressed for social reforms that would restrain industrialization, and peasants sought a complete end to manorialism. Revolts in central Europe also pressed for nationalist demands: German nationalists worked for the unity of their country, and various nationalities in Austria–Hungary, including Slavic groups, sought greater autonomy. A similar liberal nationalist revolt occurred in various parts of Italy.

The revolutionary fires burned only briefly. The social demands of artisans and some factory workers were put down quickly; not only conservatives but middle-class liberals opposed these efforts. Nationalist agitation also failed for the moment, as the armies of Austria–Hungary and Prussia restored the status quo to central Europe and Italy. Democracy persisted in France, but a nephew of the great Napoleon soon replaced the liberal republic with an authoritarian empire that lasted until 1870. Peasant demands were met, and serfdom was fully abolished throughout western Europe. Many peasants, uninterested in other gains, supported conservative forces.

The substantial failure of the revolutions of 1848 drew the revolutionary era in western Europe to a close. Failure taught many liberals and working-class leaders that revolution was too risky; more gradual methods should be used instead. Improved transportation reduced the chance of food crises, the traditional trigger for revolution in Western history. Bad harvests in 1846 and 1847 had driven up food prices and helped promote insurgency in the cities, but famines of this sort did not recur in the West. Many governments also installed better riot control police.

Greek Revolution Rebellion in Greece against the Ottoman Empire in 1820; key step in gradually dismantling the Ottoman Empire in the Balkans.

Reform Bill of 1832 Legislation passed in Great Britain that extended the vote to most members of the middle class; failed to produce democracy in Britain.

Chartist movement Attempt by artisans and workers in Britain to gain the vote during the 1840s; demands for reform beyond the Reform Bill of 1832 were incorporated into a series of petitions; movement failed.

European Centers of Rebellion and Revolution, 1820–1848

Metternich on the Revolutions of 1848

Figure 23.2 The 1848 revolution in Berlin. After months of maneuvering, negotiation, and street clashes, the revolutionaries agreed on a liberal constitution that would have established a constitutional monarchy. When they offered the crown under these terms to King Friedrich Wilhelm IV, who had initially given in to the demands of the crowds, he politely declined, saying in private that he could not accept a crown "from the gutter." Friedrich Wilhelm believed he ruled by divine right—not by the consent of the governed. The great difference between the king's and the reformers' views of constitutional monarchy was indicative of the chasm that existed in mid-19th-century Europe between advocates of aristocratic and democratic government.

By 1850 an industrial class structure had come to predominate. Earlier revolutionary gains had reduced the aristocrats' legal privileges, and the rise of business had eroded their economic dominance. With industrialization, social structure came to rest less on privilege and birth and more on money. Key divisions by 1850 pitted middle-class property owners against workers of various sorts. The old alliances that had produced the revolutions were now dissolved.

The Consolidation of the Industrial Order, 1850–1914

In most respects, the 65 years after 1850 seemed calmer than the frenzied period of political upheaval and initial industrialization. Railroads and canals linked cities across Europe and spurred industrialization and urbanization (Map 23.2). City growth continued in the West; indeed, several countries, starting with Britain, passed the 50 percent mark in urbanization—the first time in human history that more than a minority of a population lived in cities. City governments began to gain ground on the pressing problems growth had created. Sanitation improved, and death rates fell below birth rates for the first time in urban history. Parks, museums, effective regulation of food and housing facilities, and more efficient police forces all added to the safety and the physical and cultural amenities of urban life. Revealingly, crime rates began to stabilize or even drop in several industrial areas, a sign of more effective social control but also of a more disciplined population.

Adjustments to Industrial Life

Family life adjusted to industrialization (Figure 23.3). Birth rates began to drop as Western society began a demographic transition to a new system that promoted fairly stable population levels through a new combination of low birth rates and low death rates. Children were now seen as a

The unification of Italy and Germany created new rivalries in western Europe. European countries developed new functions for governments, responding to industrial pressures, including socialism.

Map 23.2 Industrialization in Europe, c. 1850   By the mid-19th century, industrialization had spread across Europe, aided by the development of railroad links and canals that brought resources to the new factories and transported their finished goods to world markets.

source of emotional satisfaction and parental responsibility, not as workers contributing to a family economy. As the Document feature shows, arguments about women's special family duties gained ground.

Material conditions generally improved after 1850. By 1900 probably two-thirds of the Western population enjoyed conditions above the subsistence level. People could afford a few amenities such as newspapers and family outings, their diet and housing improved, and their health got better. The decades from 1880 to 1920 saw a real revolution in children's health, thanks in part to better hygiene during childbirth and better parental care. Infancy and death diverged for the first time in human history: Instead of one-third or more of all children dying by age 10, child death rates fell to less than 10 percent and continued to plummet. The discovery of germs by **Louis Pasteur** led by the 1880s to more conscientious sanitary regulations and procedures by doctors and other health care specialists; this reduced the deaths of women in childbirth. Women began to outlive men by a noticeable margin, but men's health also improved.

 Industrial Society and Factory Conditions

Pasteur, Louis   French scientist who discovered relationship between germs and disease in 19th century, leading to better sanitation.

In little more than a decade, between 1860 and 1873, the number of corporations in western Europe doubled. The rise of corporations, drawing on stockholder investment funds, with new laws protecting individual investors, was a major change in business and organizational life. Important labor movements took shape among industrial workers by the 1890s, with massive strike movements by miners, metalworkers, and others from the United States to Germany. The new trade union movement stressed the massed power of workers. Hosts of labor leaders sprang up amid detested work conditions and political repression. Many workers learned to bargain for better pay and shorter hours.

In the countryside, peasant protests declined. Many European peasants gained a new ability to

Figure 23.3 Respectable middle-class leisure in western Europe.

Protesting the Industrial Revolution

As machines were introduced with industrialization, attacks mounted. The process was called Luddism, after British protests between 1810 and 1820 in the name of a mythical leader called Ned Ludd. The following documents describing Luddism come from a wool manufacturing area around Vienne, in France, in 1819. The first document is a government source, the second a worker petition.

Police Report

We, king's attorney in the court of first instance at Vienne, acting on the information which we have just received, that the new cloth-shearing machine belonging to Messrs. Gentin and Odoard had just reached the bank of the Gère river near the building intended to house it when a numerous band of workers hastened toward the spot crying "*Down with the shearing machine*"; that some rifle shots were heard, and in general everything about this meeting of workers announced the will and the intent to pillage by force a piece of property, we immediately went to the place where the mayor and the police commissioner agreed to authorize us to use armed force and to state the nature of any crimes and their perpetrators, and to hear with us the declarations of any persons who had information to give us.

Having arrived near the shop of Messrs. Odoard and Gentin, on the right bank of the river, we saw in the steam, at a distance of about fifteen feet, a carriage without horses, its shafts in the air, loaded with four or five crates, one of which was obviously broken, and at three or four paces off in the water, an instrument of iron or some other metal of the same size as the crate, in terms of its length. Various calvary posts and policemen, on foot and mounted, placed at various distances on the two banks of the Gère and on the hills, regarded all the paths and roads; the windows which gave onto the river were partially closed.

Some minutes before our arrival . . . many individuals in short vests whom he did not know but whom he presumed to be workers, hurled themselves into the water and rushed the carriage, armed with wooden clubs and an iron instrument called a cloth-shearer, that they broke the first crate which fell into their hands and threw into the water one of the instruments which it contained.

Edlon Montal (Jean or Pierre) of Grenoble of Beaurepaire, who did his apprenticeship as cloth-shearer, is the man who provided half the strength to break the crates.

Jacques Ruffe, shearer for his cousin Dufieux, was on the carriage, breaking and throwing crates into the water.

The daughter of Claude Tonnerieux, butcher, threw stones at the dragoons and incited the workers with her shouts: "*Break it, smash it, be bold,* etc." Another woman, Lacroix, who has only one eye, shouted similar things. Marguerite Dupont, spinner for Mr. Frémy, called the lieutenant-colonel of dragoons a brigand.

Jacques Boullé, a glass worker, was noticed shouting among the first workers who came down the Saint-Martin bridge.

Basset, weaver, said, "*Let's get the machine*" and Rousset, an itinerant, expressed himself thus: "*We'll get Gentin* (one of the owners of the machine). *It's not the machine we ought to wreck.*"

Poster

Gentlemen, we are beside ourselves because of the inhumanity and hardness of your hearts, your scorn toward the poor workers who have helped you make your fortune. Seeing that we are abandoned by you, gentlemen, this alone has forced us to do what we don't want to do. We have no intention of attacking your fortunes, but if you don't arrange to give us work we can't avoid attacking you and the machines; so you have eight days to reflect. If at the end of these eight days you don't take your wool out of the machines in order to give work to four or five hundred people who are at your doors and whom you don't deign to look at, don't be surprised if you see a storm descend upon you and the machines—so much do we the poor workers suffer for ourselves and for our poor children.

We hope that you'll wish to spare us this effort which is otherwise inevitable.

> **QUESTIONS:** What kinds of people supported Luddism, and why? How did officials react to Luddism, and why? What effects was Luddism likely to have over the course of the industrial revolution?

---

use market conditions to their own benefit. Some, as in Holland and Denmark, developed cooperatives to market goods and purchase supplies efficiently. Many peasants specialized in new cash crops, such as dairy products. Still more widely, peasants began to send their children to school to pick up new knowledge that would improve farming operations. The traditional isolation of rural areas began to decline.

Political Trends and the Rise of New Nations

Western politics consolidated after the failed revolutions of 1848. Quite simply, issues that had dominated the Western political agenda for many decades were largely resolved within a generation. The great debates about fundamental constitutions and government structure, which had emerged in the 17th century with the rise of absolutism and new political theory and then raged during the decades of revolution, at last grew quiet.

Many Western leaders worked to reduce the need for political revolution after 1850. Liberals decided that revolution was too risky and became more willing to compromise. Key conservatives strove to develop reforms that would save elements of the old regime, including power for the landed aristocracy and the monarchy. A British conservative leader, Benjamin Disraeli, took the initiative of granting the vote to working-class men in 1867. Count Camillo di Cavour, in the Italian state of Piedmont, began even earlier to support industrial development and extend the powers of the parliament to please liberal forces. In Prussia a new prime minister, Otto von Bismarck, similarly began to work with a parliament and to extend the vote to all men (though grouping them in wealth categories that blocked complete democracy). Other Prussian reforms granted freedom to Jews, extended (without guaranteeing) rights to the press, and promoted mass education. The gap between liberal and conservative regimes narrowed in the West, although it remained significant.

The new conservatives also began to use the force of nationalism to win support for the existing social order. Previously, nationalism had been a radical force, challenging established arrangements in the name of new loyalties. Many liberals continued to defend nationalist causes. However, conservative politicians learned how to wrap themselves in the flag, often promoting an active foreign policy in the interest of promoting domestic calm. Thus, British conservatives became champions of expanding the empire, while in the United States, by the 1890s, the conservatives in the Republican Party became increasingly identified with imperialist causes.

The most important new uses of nationalism in the West occurred in Italy and Germany. After wooing liberal support, Cavour formed an alliance with France that enabled him to attack Austrian control of northern Italian provinces in 1858. The war set in motion a nationalist rebellion in other parts of the peninsula that allowed Cavour to unite most of Italy under the Piedmontese king (Map 23.3). This led to a reduction of the political power of the Catholic pope, already an opponent of liberal and nationalist ideas—an important part of the general reduction of church power in Western politics.

Following Cavour's example, Bismarck in Prussia staged a series of wars in the 1860s that expanded Prussian power in Germany. He was a classic diplomatic military strategist, a key example of an individual agent seizing on larger trends such as nationalism to produce results that were far from inevitable. For example, in 1863 Bismarck used the occasion of Danish incorporation of two heavily German provinces, Schleswig and Holstein, to justify the Prussian and Austrian defeat of Denmark. Then he maneuvered a pretext for a Prussian declaration of war against Austria. In 1866 Prussia emerged as the supreme German power. A final war, against France, led to outright German unity in 1871 (Map 23.4). The new German Empire boasted a national parliament with a lower house based on universal male suffrage and an upper house that favored conservative state governments. This kind of compromise, combined with the dizzying joy of nationalist success, won support for the new regime from most liberals and many conservatives.

Other key political issues were resolved at about the same time. The bloody **American Civil War**—the first war based extensively on industrial weaponry and transport systems, carefully watched by European military observers—was fought between 1861 and 1865. The war resolved by force the simmering dispute over sectional rights between the North and South and also brought an end to slavery in the nation. France, after its defeat by Germany in 1870, overthrew its short-lived echo of the Napoleonic Empire and established a conservative republic with votes for all men, a reduction of church power, and expansion of education, but no major social reform. Just as conservative Bismarck could be selectively radical, France proved that liberals could be very cautious.

Almost all Western nations now had parliamentary systems, usually democracies of some sort, in which religious and other freedoms were widely protected. In this system, liberal and conservative ministries could alternate without major changes of internal policy. Indeed, Italy developed a process called **trasformismo,** or transformism, in which parliamentary deputies, no matter what platforms they professed, were transformed once in Rome to a single-minded pursuit of political office and support of the status quo.

Legend:
- Kingdom of Sardinia to 1859
- To Sardinia, 1860
- Annexed to Sardinia, 1861; establishes kingdom of Italy
- To Italy, 1866
- To Italy, 1870

Map 23.3 The Unification of Italy The map shows the main separate states before unification, and when they added to the new nation.

A Letter from Otto von Bismarck (1866)

American Civil War Fought from 1861 to 1865; first application of Industrial Revolution to warfare; resulted in abolition of slavery in the United States and reunification of North and South.

trasformismo Political system in late 19th-century Italy that promoted alliance of conservatives and liberals; parliamentary deputies of all parties supported the status quo.

Prussia, 1815–1866

Annexed by Prussia, 1866

Joined Prussia in forming the North German Confederation, 1867

German Confederation, 1815–1866

Joined with Prussia to form the German Empire, 1871

Alsace-Lorraine ceded to German Empire by France, 1871

Map 23.4 **The Unification of Germany, 1815–1871** This map shows the stages of unification, under Prussian impetus, from 1866 to 1871.

social question Issues relating to repressed classes in western Europe during the Industrial Revolution, particularly workers and women; became more critical than constitutional issues after 1870.

socialism Political movement with origins in western Europe during the 19th century; urged an attack on private property in the name of equality; wanted state control of means of production, end to capitalist exploitation of the working man.

Karl Marx on the Question of Free Trade

Capitalism Challenged: *The Communist Manifesto*

Marx, Karl (1818–1883) German socialist who blasted earlier socialist movements as utopian; saw history as defined by class struggle between groups out of power and those controlling the means of production; preached necessity of social revolution to create proletarian dictatorship.

The Social Question and New Government Functions

The decline of basic constitutional disputes by the 1870s promoted the fuller development of an industrial-style state in the West. A new set of political movements emerged.

Government functions and personnel expanded rapidly throughout the Western world after 1870. All Western governments introduced civil service examinations to test applicants on the basis of talent rather than on connections or birth alone, thus unwittingly imitating Chinese innovations more than a thousand years before. With a growing bureaucracy and improved recruitment, governments began to extend their regulatory apparatus, inspecting factory safety, the health of prostitutes, hospital conditions, and even (through the introduction of passports and border controls) personal travel.

Schooling expanded, becoming generally compulsory up to age 12. Governments believed that education provided essential work skills and the basis for new levels of political loyalty. Many American states by 1900 began also to require high school education, and most Western nations expanded their public secondary school systems. Here was a huge addition to the ways in which governments and individuals interacted. The new school systems promoted literacy; by 1900, 90 to 95 percent of all adults in western Europe and the United States could read. Schools also encouraged certain social agendas. Girls were carefully taught about the importance of home and women's moral mission in domestic science programs. Schools also carefully propounded nationalism, teaching the superiority of the nation's language and history as well as attacking minority or immigrant cultures.

Governments also began to introduce wider welfare measures, replacing or supplementing traditional groups such as churches and families. Bismarck was a pioneer in this area in the 1880s as he tried to wean German workers from their attraction to socialism. His tactic failed, as socialism steadily advanced, but his measures had lasting importance. German social insurance began to provide assistance in cases of accident, illness, and old age. Some measures to aid the unemployed were soon added, initially in Britain. These early welfare programs were small and their utility limited, but they sketched a major extension of government power.

Accompanying the quiet revolution in government functions was a realignment of the political spectrum in the Western world during the late 19th century. Constitutional issues were replaced by social issues—what people of the time called the **social question**—as the key criteria for political partisanship. Socialist and feminist movements surged to the political fore, placing liberals and conservatives in a new defensive posture.

The rise of **socialism** depended above all on the power of grievances of the working class, with allies from other groups. It also reflected a redefinition of political theory by German theorist **Karl Marx.** Early socialist doctrine, from the Enlightenment through 1848, had focused on human perfectibility: set up a few exemplary communities where work and rewards would be shared, and the evils of capitalism would end. Marx's socialism, worked out between 1848 and 1860, was tough-minded, and he blasted earlier theorists as giddy utopians. Marx saw socialism as the final phase of an inexorable march of history, which could be studied dispassionately and scientifically.

History for Marx was shaped by the available means of production and who controlled those means, an obvious reflection of the looming role of technology in the industrial world forming at that time. According to Marx, class struggle always pitted a group out of power with the group controlling the means of production; hence, in the era just passed, the middle class had battled the feudal aristocracy and its hold on the land. Now the middle class had won; it dominated production and, through this, the state and the culture as well. But it had created a new class enemy, the propertyless proletariat, that would grow until revolution became inevitable. Then, after a transitional period in which proletarian dictatorship would clean up the remnants of the bourgeois social order, full freedom would be achieved. People would benefit justly and equally from their work, and the state would wither away; the historic class struggle would at last end because classes would be eliminated.

Marx's vision was a powerful one. It clearly identified capitalist evil. It told workers that their low wages were exploitive and unjust. It urged the need for violent action but also ensured that revolution was part of the inexorable tides of history. The result would be heaven on earth—ultimately, an Enlightenment-like vision of progress.

By the 1860s, when working-class activity began to revive, Marxist doctrine provided encouragement and structure. Marx himself continued to concentrate on ideological development and purity, but leaders in many countries translated his doctrine into practical political parties. Germany led the way. As Bismarck extended the vote, socialist leaders in the 1860s and 1870s were the first to understand the implications of mass electioneering. Socialist movements provided fiery speakers who courted popular votes. By the 1880s, socialists in Germany were cutting into liberal support, and by 1900, the party was the largest single political force in the nation. Socialist parties in Austria, France, and elsewhere followed a roughly similar course, everywhere emerging as a strong minority force.

The rise of socialism terrified many people in Western society, who took the revolutionary message literally. In combination with major industrial strikes and unionization, it was possible to see social issues portending outright social war. But socialism itself was not unchanging. As socialist parties gained strength, they often allied with other groups to achieve more moderate reforms. A movement called **revisionism** arose, which argued that Marx's revolutionary vision was wrong and that success could be achieved by peaceful democratic means. Many socialist leaders denounced revisionism but put their energies into building electoral victories rather than plotting violent revolution.

Socialism was not the only challenge to the existing order. By 1900 powerful **feminist movements** had arisen. These movements sought various legal and economic gains for women, such as equal access to professions and higher education as well as the right to vote. Feminism won support particularly from middle-class women, who argued that the very moral superiority granted to women in the home should be translated into political voice. Many middle-class women also chafed against the confines of their domestic roles, particularly as family size declined. In several countries, feminism combined with socialism, but in Britain, the United States, Australia, and Scandinavia, a separate feminist current arose that petitioned widely and even conducted acts of violence in order to win the vote. Several American states and Scandinavian countries extended the vote to women by 1914, in a pattern that would spread to Britain, Germany, and the whole United States after 1918.

The new feminism, like the labor movement, was no mere abstraction but the fruit of active, impassioned leadership, largely from the middle classes. Emmeline Pankhurst (1858–1928; Figure 23.4) was typical of the more radical feminist leadership both in background and tactics. Born to a reform-minded English middle-class family, she was active in women's rights issues, as was her husband. She collaborated with Richard Pankhurst, whom she had married in 1879, to work for improvements in women's property rights, and she participated in the Socialist Fabian Society. But then she turned more radical. She formed a suffrage organization in 1903 to seek the vote for women. With her daughter Christabel, she sponsored attention-getting public disturbances, including planting a bomb in St. Paul's Cathedral. Window-smashing, arson, and hunger strikes rounded out her spectacular tactical arsenal. Often arrested, she engaged in a huge strike in 1912. The suffragists' support of the war effort in 1914 gained them public sympathy. Pankhurst moved to Canada for a time, leaving the English movement to her daughter, but returned as a respected figure to run for parliament after women had gained the vote in 1928.

Figure 23.4 Emmeline Goulden Pankhurst. In her 1914 autobiography, Pankhurst recalled the early stirrings of feminism in her childhood: "The education of the English boy, then as now, was considered a much more serious matter than the education of the English boy's sister. . . . Of course [I] went to a carefully selected girls' school, but beyond the facts that the head mistress was a gentlewoman and that all the pupils were girls of my own class, nobody seemed concerned. A girl's education at that time seemed to have for its prime object the art of 'making home attractive'—presumably to migratory male relatives. It used to puzzle me to understand why I was under such a particular obligation to make home attractive to my brothers. We were on excellent terms of friendship, but it was never suggested to them as a duty that they make home attractive to me. Why not? Nobody seemed to know."

Cultural Transformations

Key developments in popular culture differentiated Western society after 1850 from the decades of initial industrialization. Better wages and the reduction of work hours gave ordinary people new opportunities. Alongside the working class grew a large white-collar labor force of secretaries,

Dramatic changes in daily life reflected the pressures and opportunities of industrialization. Cultural changes involved steady advances in sciences and increasingly defiant innovation in the arts.

revisionism Socialist movements that at least tacitly disavowed Marxist revolutionary doctrine; believed social success could be achieved gradually through political institutions.

feminist movements Sought various legal and economic gains for women, including equal access to professions and higher education; came to concentrate on right to vote; won support particularly from middle-class women; active in western Europe at the end of the 19th century; revived in light of other issues in the 1960s.

mass leisure culture An aspect of the later Industrial Revolution; based on newspapers, music halls, popular theater, vacation trips, and team sports.

clerks, and salespeople, who served the growing bureaucracies of big business and the state. These workers, some of them women, adopted many middle-class values, but they also insisted on interesting consumption and leisure outlets. The middle class itself became more open to the idea that pleasure could be legitimate.

Emphasis on Consumption and Leisure

By this point, the maturing industrial economy demanded change. Factories could now spew out goods in such quantity that popular consumption had to be encouraged simply to keep pace with production. Widespread advertising developed to promote a sense of need where none had existed before. Product crazes emerged. The bicycle fad of the 1880s, in which middle-class families flocked to purchase the new machine, was the first of many consumer fads in modern Western history. People just had to have them. Bicycles also changed previous social habits, as women needed less cumbersome garments and young couples could outpedal chaperones during courtship.

Mass leisure culture began to emerge. Popular newspapers, with bold headlines and compelling human interest stories, won millions of subscribers in the industrial West. They featured shock and entertainment more than appeals to reason or political principle. Crime, imperialist exploits, sports, and even comics became the items of the day. Popular theater soared. Comedy routines and musical revues drew thousands of patrons to music halls. After 1900 some of these entertainment themes dominated the new medium of motion pictures. Vacation trips became increasingly common, and seaside resorts grew to the level of big business.

The rise of team sports readily expressed the complexities of the late 19th-century leisure revolution. Here was another Western development that soon had international impact. Soccer, American football, and baseball surged into new prominence at both amateur and professional levels. These new sports reflected industrial life. Though based on traditional games, they were organized by means of rules and umpires. They taught the virtues of coordination and discipline and could be seen as useful preparation for work or military life. They were suitably commercial: sports equipment, based on the ability to mass-produce rubber balls, and professional teams and stadiums quickly became major businesses. But sports also expressed impulse and violence. They expressed irrational community loyalties and even, as the Olympic games were reintroduced in 1896, nationalist passions.

Overall, new leisure interests suggested a complex set of attitudes on the part of ordinary people in Western society. They demonstrated growing secularism. Religion still counted among some groups, but religious practice had declined as people increasingly looked for worldly entertainments. Many people would have agreed that progress was possible on this earth through rational planning and individual self-control. Yet mass leisure also suggested a more impulsive side to popular outlook, one bent on the display of passion or at least vicarious participation by spectators in emotional release.

Advances in Scientific Knowledge

Science and the arts took separate paths, with influential developments in each area. The size of the intellectual and artistic community in the West expanded steadily with rising prosperity and advancing educational levels. A growing audience existed for various intellectual and artistic products. The bulk of the new activity was resolutely secular. Although new churches were built as cities grew, and missionary activity reached new heights outside the Western world, the churches no longer served as centers for the most creative intellectual life. Continuing advances in science kept alive the rationalist tradition. Universities and other research establishments increasingly applied science to practical affairs, linking science and technology in the popular mind under a general aura of progress. Improvements in medical pathology and the germ theory combined science and medicine, although no breakthrough therapies resulted yet. Science was applied to agriculture through studies of seed yields and chemical fertilizers, with Germany and then the United States in the lead.

The great advance in theoretical science came in biology with the evolutionary theory of **Charles Darwin,** whose major work was published in 1859. Darwin argued that all living species

Darwin, Charles Biologist who developed theory of evolution of species (1859); argued that all living species evolved into their present form through the ability to adapt in a struggle for survival.

had evolved into their present form through the ability to adapt in a struggle for survival. Biological development could be scientifically understood as a process taking place over time, with some animal and plant species disappearing and others—the fittest in the survival struggle—evolving from earlier forms. Darwin's ideas clashed with traditional Christian beliefs that God had fashioned humankind as part of initial creation, and the resultant debate further weakened the hold of religion. Darwin also created a more complex picture of nature than Newton's simple physical laws had suggested. In this view, nature worked through random struggle, and people were seen as animals with large brains, not as supremely rational.

Developments in physics continued as well, with work on electromagnetic behavior and then, about 1900, increasing knowledge of the behavior of the atom and its major components. New theories arose, based on complex mathematics, to explain the behavior of planetary motion and the movement of electrical particles, where Newtonian laws seemed too simple. After 1900, **Albert Einstein** formalized this new work through his theory of relativity, adding time as a factor in physical measurement. Again, science seemed to be steadily advancing in its grasp of the physical universe, although it is also important to note that its complexity surpassed the understanding even of educated laypeople.

The social sciences also continued to use observation, experiment, and rationalist theorizing. Great efforts went into compiling statistical data about populations, economic patterns, and health conditions. Sheer empirical knowledge about human affairs had never been more extensive. At the level of theory, leading economists tried to explain business cycles and the causes of poverty, and social psychologists studied the behavior of crowds. Toward the end of the 19th century, Viennese physician **Sigmund Freud** began to develop his theories of the workings of the human subconscious. He argued that much behavior is determined by impulses but that emotional problems can be relieved if they are brought into the light of rational discussion.

New Directions in Artistic Expression

A second approach in Western culture developed in the 19th century. This approach emphasized artistic values and often glorified the irrational. To be sure, many novelists, such as Charles Dickens in England, bent their efforts toward realistic portrayals of human problems, trying to convey information that would inspire reform. Many painters built on the discoveries of science, using knowledge of optics and color. For example, French painter Georges Seurat was inspired by findings about how the eye processes color, applying tiny dots of paint to his canvases so that they would blend into a coherent whole in a style aptly called pointillism.

Nevertheless, the central artistic vision, beginning with **romanticism** in the first half of the century, held that emotion and impression, not reason and generalization, were the keys to the mysteries of human experience and nature. Artists portrayed intense passions, even madness, not calm reflection. Romantic novelists wanted to move readers to tears, not philosophical debate; painters sought empathy with the beauties of nature or the storm-tossed tragedy of shipwreck (Figure 23.5). Romantics and their successors after 1850 also deliberately tried to violate traditional Western artistic standards. Poetry did not have to rhyme; drama did not necessarily need plot; painting could be evocative, not literal (Figure 23.6). (For literal portrayals, painters could now argue, use a camera.) Each generation of artists proved more defiant than the last. By 1900 painters and sculptors were becoming increasingly abstract, and musical composers worked

Reactions to Darwin

DOCUMENT

Einstein, Albert Developed mathematical theories to explain the behavior of planetary motion and the movement of electrical particles; after 1900 issued theory of relativity.

Freud, Sigmund (1856–1939) Viennese physician who developed theories of the workings of the human subconscious; argued that behavior is determined by impulses.

romanticism Artistic and literary movement of the 19th century in Europe; held that emotion and impression, not reason, were the keys to the mysteries of human experience and nature; sought to portray passions, not calm reflection.

Figure 23.5 Romantic painters delighted in evocative scenes and rural nostalgia, as depicted by John Constable in *The Cornfields*.

(John Constable (1776–1837), "The Cornfield." © The National Gallery, London, Great Britain/Art Resource, NY.)

Figure 23.6 Paul Cézanne's *The Large Bathers* (1898–1905). This painting illustrates the artist's abandonment of literal pictorial realism to concentrate on what he considered fundamental. This, along with his use of nudity, alienated the "respectable" public but, by the time of his death in 1906, was beginning to win him critical acclaim. Cézanne painted slowly and was wholly absorbed in his work, spending little time with friends and family. "The landscape," he said, "becomes human, becomes a thinking, living being within me. I become one with my picture. . . . We merge in an iridescent chaos."

(Paul Cezanne, "The Large Bathers." 1906. Oil on Canvas. 6'10" x 8'2" (2.08 x 2.49 m). The W. P. Wilstach Collection. Philadelphia Museum of Art.)

The expansion of settler societies strongly influenced by European institutions and values was a leading development of the 19th century.

with atonal scales that defied long-established conventions. Some artists talked of art for art's sake, arguing essentially that art had its own purposes unrelated to the larger society around it.

At neither the formal nor the popular levels, then, did Western culture produce a clear synthesis in the 19th century. New scientific discipline and rationalism warred with impulse—even with evocations of violence. The earlier certainties of Christianity and even the Enlightenment gave way to greater debate. Some observers worried that this debate also expressed tensions between different facets of the same modern mind and that these tensions could become dangerous. Perhaps the Western world was not put together quite as neatly as the adjustments and consolidations after 1850 might suggest.

Western Settler Societies

The Industrial Revolution prompted a major expansion of the West's power in the world. Western nations could pour out far more processed goods than before, which meant that they needed new markets. They also needed new raw materials and agricultural products, which spurred the development of more commercial agriculture in places such as Africa and Latin America. The vast ships and communication networks created by industrial technology spurred the intensification of the Western-led world economy (see Chapter 24).

Industrialization also extended the West's military advantage in the wider world. Steamships could navigate previously impassable river systems, bringing Western guns inland as never before. The invention of the repeating rifle and machine gun gave small Western forces superiority over masses of local troops. These new means combined with new motives: European nations competed for new colonies as part of their nationalistic rivalry, businesspeople sought new chances for profit, and missionaries sought opportunities for conversion. Haltingly before 1860, then rapidly, Europe's empires spread through Africa, southeast Asia, and parts of China and the Middle East.

Many of the same forces, and also massive European emigration, created or expanded Western settler societies overseas in areas where indigenous populations were decimated by disease. Some settler societies maintained sizeable local populations, sometimes even a considerable majority. South Africa was a case in point, discussed in Chapter 24. But some societies filled with an overwhelming majority of immigrants, mostly of European origin, and also brought in so many institutions and beliefs from Europe that they gained a close link with Western history. Some, perhaps, were part of the West outright. The most important overseas Western nation, and the only one to become a major world force before 1914, was the United States.

All the settler societies showed massive European influence and ongoing contact. They were also shaped, however, by contacts with native peoples and frontier conditions. For the United States, particularly, many historians have long seen a pattern of exceptionalism, in which the nation must be interpreted through substantial differences from European patterns. But many trends were shared, including political and industrial revolutions, raising the question of how much the settler societies simply expanded the larger orbit of Western civilization.

Most of the older settler societies, and also Australia and New Zealand, were influenced by the results of the age of political revolution. Revolution formed the United States directly. To avoid a repetition, Britain treated other settler societies, like Canada, with greater care, facilitating the spread of parliamentary governments and liberal constitutions.

Two Revolutions: Industrial and Atlantic

During the long 19th century, two major revolutionary movements launched from Western Europe, with ramifications in other parts of the world. The industrial revolution began of course in Britain, and featured a fundamental economic and technological transformation, focused on new power sources, with huge implications for other aspects of society. The tide of political and social revolution that swept across the Atlantic, including the American revolution, the French revolution with its impacts on many other parts of Europe, the Haitian revolution, and the Latin American wars of independence, reflected new forces of nationalism and liberalism, with strong social implications of its own.

"What did they have to do with each other, and what was their combined impact in world history?"

The Atlantic revolutions were more limited in time than the industrial, ranging from the 1770s to 1849 whereas the industrial revolution, even in Western Europe alone, stretched over more than a century from the 1770s until 1900. The French revolution involved a clear sequence of events, whereas the industrial revolution was a more gradual set of processes that took some time to gain full momentum. Still, the two revolutions did overlap in time and (in some cases) place. What did they have to do with each other, and what was their combined impact in world history? Oddly, the question has not been explicitly addressed very often.

The two revolutions supported each other in several ways. Both reflected ideas drawn from the Enlightenment and dislocations caused by new population levels and the expansion of commerce. More directly, the principles of the Atlantic revolutions could be used to attack structures that also held back industrialization. Several European revolutions undid the guild system, whose restrictions on new technologies impeded factory industry; the broader movement against remnants of serfdom also could create a more mobile labor force. Revolutionary agendas often promoted education, which proved useful to industry. The rise of middle-class political interests, which resulted from several political revolutions, could also encourage economic change.

Other revolutionary principles, however, could be used to attack early industrialization in the name of greater social justice. The revolutions of 1848, in Europe, saw many factory workers appealing for the vote and for government assistance against harsh working conditions.

The revolutions also had many differing, even clashing implications, which is one reason it proves hard to discuss them in the same breath. The Atlantic revolutions appealed for popular rights against arbitrary authority: they focused on constitutions that would protect freedoms of the press or assembly. The industrial revolution created more authoritarian work environments, with factory managers and foremen trying to regulate the labor of ordinary employees. In its early stages, the industrial revolution also worked against freedom of assembly, with factory owners allying with governments to outlaw labor organizations. Even beyond these immediate tensions over authority and liberty, the revolutions moved in different directions: the Atlantic revolutions were about nationalism and political structure, the industrial revolution focused on increasing production and expanding manufacturing.

Not surprisingly, given these variations, the two revolutions hardly shared the same geography. Western Europe and the United States did, to be sure, undergo significant political change, along the lines of the Atlantic principles, while also industrializing in the same general time period. Even Germany, however, though industrializing fiercely, found it harder to assimilate the full implications of political revolution before 1914 or even, many would argue, before 1945. Even more obviously, the revolutionary currents in the Caribbean and Latin America, that created significant political change as part of the overall Atlantic movement, did not help generate industrialization, which would develop only much later and much more gradually (see Chapter 25). On the other hand, by the later 19th century the industrial revolution was spreading to other parts of the world, like Russia and Japan, that had not been deeply touched by the ideals of the Atlantic revolutions. And many parts of the world, subdued by the economic and military power of industrial Europe, saw extensive changes at the hands of Western businessmen and imperialists—but these changes bore little relationship to the glowing principles of the Atlantic revolutions.

In the long run, both revolutions would help reshape world, and not merely Western or even Atlantic history. Industrialization continues to spread even into the 21st century, along with persistent, sometimes agonizing disparities between industrial and nonindustrial economies in the global framework. Ideas derived from the Atlantic revolutions about nationalism or individual rights, have wide influence as well, though their impact is hardly uniform. Certain traditional institutions, like slavery, began to crumble even by the later 19th century under the combined impact of revolutionary ideas about human freedom and the fact that slave labor was not most suitable for industrialization.

World history requires an understanding of the workings of both the Atlantic and the industrial revolutions, over more than two centuries. It also requires recognizing that the two revolutions had complicated and extended implications, as they moved from original centers to other regions. It requires recognizing that, even today, the two movements are not entirely harmonious. Industrial societies that have also accepted elements of the political revolution let workers vote and enjoy other personal freedoms, but they also continue to regiment them strongly on the job. The changes unleashed by the long 19th century have not moved in complete unity at any point.

QUESTIONS: How were the two revolutions interacting in Europe and the United States by the mid-19th century? Which of the two revolutions has had the greater impact on ordinary people, first in the West and then worldwide? Why have some societies found it easier to accept the implications of industrialization than those of the Atlantic revolutions?

Emerging Power of the United States

The country that was to become the United States did not play a substantial role in world history in its colonial period. Its export products were far less significant than those of Latin America and the Caribbean. The American Revolution caused a stir in Europe, but the new nation emphasized internal development through the early 19th century. The Monroe Doctrine (1823) warned against European meddling in the Americas, but it was British policy and naval power that kept the hemisphere free from new colonialism. American energies were poured into elaboration of the new political system, internal commercial growth and early industrialization, and westward expansion. The Louisiana Purchase, the acquisition of Texas, and the rush to California rapidly extended the United States beyond the Mississippi River. The nation stood as a symbol of freedom to many Europeans, and it was often invoked in the revolutions of 1848, as in the earlier Latin American wars for independence. It began to receive a new stream of immigrants, particularly from Ireland and Germany, during the 1840s. Its industrialists also borrowed heavily from European investors to fund national expansion.

The crucial event for the United States in the 19th century was the Civil War. Profound differences separated the increasingly industrial North, with its growing farms, from the slaveholding South, with its export-oriented plantation economy and distinctive value system. Disputes over slaveholding led the southern states to try secession; the North opposed these actions in the interests of preserving national unity and, somewhat hesitantly, ending the slavery system. The Civil War produced an anguishing level of casualties and maimings. The North's victory brought important gains for the freed slave minority, although by the late 1870s, white politicians in the South had begun to severely constrain the political and economic rights of African Americans.

The Civil War also accelerated American industrialization. Heavy industry boomed in a push to produce for the war effort. The completion of a rail link to the Pacific opened the west to further settlement, leading to the last bitter round of wars with Native Americans. Economic expansion brought the United States into the industrial big leagues, its growth rivaling that of Germany. After the Civil War, American armaments manufacturers began to seek export markets. Other industrial producers soon followed as the United States became a major competitor worldwide. American firms, such as the Singer sewing machine company, set up branches in other countries. American agriculture, increasingly mechanized, began to pour out exports of grain and meats (the latter thanks to the development of refrigerated shipping), particularly to European markets where peasant producers could not fully compete.

American diplomacy was not particularly influential outside the Western Hemisphere, although a wave of imperialist expansion from the late 1890s onward brought American interests to the Pacific and Asia. American culture was also seen as largely parochial. Despite increasingly varied art and literature, American work had little impact abroad. Many artists and writers, such as Henry James and James McNeill Whistler, sought inspiration in European centers, sometimes becoming expatriates. Even in technology, American borrowing from Europe remained extensive, and American scientific work gained ground only in the late 19th century, partly through the imitation of German-style research universities. These developments confirmed the role of the new giant in extending many larger Western patterns.

European Settlements in Canada, Australia, and New Zealand

During the 19th century, Canada, Australia, and New Zealand filled with immigrants from Europe and established parliamentary legislatures and vigorous commercial economies that aligned them with the dynamics of Western civilization (Map 23.5). Sparse and disorganized hunting-and-gathering populations (particularly in Canada and Australia) offered little resistance. Like the United States, these new nations looked primarily to Europe for cultural styles and intellectual leadership. They also followed common Western patterns in such areas as family life, the status of women, and the extension of mass education and culture. Unlike the United States, however, these nations remained part of the British Empire, though with growing autonomy.

Canada, won by Britain in wars with France in the 18th century, had remained apart from the American Revolution. Religious differences between French Catholic settlers and British rulers and settlers troubled the area recurrently, and several uprisings occurred early in the 19th century. Determined not to lose this colony as it had lost the United States, the British began in 1839 to grant

Map 23.5 **Early 19th-Century Settlement in the United States, Canada, Australia, and New Zealand** Immigration led European settlers (and, in North America, enslaved Africans) to key areas previously populated by peoples vulnerable to imported diseases.

increasing self-rule. Canada set up its own parliament and laws but remained attached to the larger empire. Initially, this system applied primarily to the province of Ontario, but other provinces were included, creating a federal system that describes Canada to this day. French hostilities were eased somewhat by the creation of a separate province, Quebec, where the majority of French speakers was located. Massive railroad building, beginning in the 1850s, brought settlement to the western territories and a great expansion of mining and commercial agriculture in the vast plains. As in the United States, new immigrants from southern and particularly eastern Europe poured in during the last decades of the century, attracted by Canada's growing commercial development.

Britain's Australian colonies originated in 1788 when a ship deposited convicts to establish a penal settlement at Sydney. Australia's only previous inhabitants had been a hunting-and-gathering people called the aborigines, and they were in no position to resist European settlement and exploration. By 1840 Australia had 140,000 European inhabitants, engaged mainly in a prosperous sheep-raising agriculture that provided needed wool for British industries. The exportation of convicts ceased in 1853, by which time most settlers were free immigrants. The discovery of gold in 1851 spurred further pioneering, and by 1861 the population had grown to more than a million. As in Canada, major provinces were granted self-government with a multiparty parliamentary system. A unified federal nation was proclaimed on the first day of the 20th century. By this time, industrialization, a growing socialist party, and significant welfare legislation had taken shape.

Finally, New Zealand, visited by the Dutch in the 17th century and explored by the English in 1770, began to receive British attention after 1814. Here the Polynesian hunting-and-gathering people, the Maoris, were well organized politically. Missionary efforts converted many of them to Christianity between 1814 and the 1840s. The British government, fearful of French interest in the area, moved to take official control in 1840, and European immigration followed. New Zealand settlers relied heavily on agriculture (including sheep raising), selling initially to Australia's booming gold-rush population and then to Britain. Wars with the Maoris plagued the settlers during the 1860s, but after the Maori defeat, generally good relations were established, and the Maoris won some representation in parliament. As in Canada and Australia, a parliamentary system was created that allowed the new nation to rule itself as a dominion of the British Empire without interference from the mother country.

Canada, New Zealand, and Australia each had distinct national flavors and national issues. These new countries were far more dependent on the European, particularly the British, economy than was the United States. Industrialization did not overshadow commercial agriculture and mining, even in Australia, so that exchanges with Europe remained important. Nevertheless, despite their distinctive features, these countries followed the basic patterns of Western civilization, from political forms to key leisure activities. The currents of liberalism, socialism, modern art, and scientific education that described Western civilization to 1900 and beyond largely characterized these important new extensions.

It was these areas, along with the United States and part of Latin America, particularly Brazil and Argentina, that received new waves of European emigrants during the 19th century. Although Europe's population growth rate slowed after 1800, it still advanced rapidly on the basis of previous gains as more children reached adulthood and had children of their own. Europe's export of people helped explain how Western societies could take shape in such distant areas.

The spread of the Western settler societies also reflected the new power of Western industrialization. Huge areas could be settled quickly, thanks to steamships and rails, while remaining in close contact with western Europe.

Diplomatic Tensions and World War I

By the end of the 19th century, diplomatic and military tensions were escalating in Europe. Tensions reflected domestic developments, including social protest and competitive nationalisms.

The unification of Germany and its rapid industrial growth profoundly altered the power balance within Europe. Bismarck was very conscious of this, and during the 1870s and 1880s, still a skilled manipulator, he built a complex alliance system designed to protect Germany and divert European attention elsewhere. France, Germany's deepest enemy, was largely isolated. But even the French concentrated on imperialist expansion in Africa and Asia.

By 1900, however, few parts of the world were available for Western seizure. Latin America was independent but under extensive U.S. influence, so a new intrusion of colonialism was impossible. Africa was almost entirely carved up. The few final colonies taken after 1900—Morocco by France and Tripoli (Libya) by Italy—caused great diplomatic furor on the part of other colonial powers worried about the balance of forces. China and the Middle East were technically independent but were in fact crisscrossed by rivalries between the Western powers and Russia (and in China's case, Japan). No agreement was possible on further takeovers.

Yet imperialist expansion had fed the sense of rivalry between key nation-states. Britain, in particular, grew worried about Germany's overseas drive and its construction of a large navy. Economic competition between a surging Germany and a lagging Britain added fuel to the fire. France, eager to escape the Bismarck-engineered isolation, was willing to play down its traditional rivalries with Britain. The French also took the opportunity to ally with Russia, when after 1890 Germany dropped this particular alliance because of Russian–Austrian enmity.

The New Alliance System

Triple Alliance Alliance among Germany, Austria-Hungary, and Italy at the end of the 19th century; part of European alliance system and balance of power prior to World War I.

Triple Entente Alliance among Britain, Russia, and France at the outset of the 20th century; part of European alliance system and balance of power prior to World War I.

Balkan nationalism Movements to create independent nations within the Balkan possessions of the Ottoman Empire; provoked a series of crises within the European alliance system; eventually led to World War I.

By 1907 most major European nations were paired off in two alliance systems: Germany, Austria–Hungary, and Italy formed the **Triple Alliance.** Britain, Russia, and France formed the newer **Triple Entente.** Three against three seemed fair, but Germany grew increasingly concerned about facing potential enemies to the east (Russia) and west (France). These powers steadily built up their military arsenals in what turned out to be the first of several arms races in the 20th century. All powers save Britain had instituted peacetime military conscription to provide large armies and even larger trained reserves. Artillery levels and naval forces grew steadily—the addition of a new kind of battleship, the dreadnought, was a key escalation—and discussions about reducing armament levels went nowhere. Each alliance system depended on an unstable partner. Russia suffered a revolution in 1905, and its allies worried that any further diplomatic setbacks might paralyze the eastern giant. Austria–Hungary was plagued by nationality disputes, particularly by minority Slavic groups; German leaders fretted that a diplomatic setback might bring chaos. Both Austria and Russia were heavily involved in maneuverings in the Balkans, the final piece in what became a nightmare puzzle.

Small Balkan nations had won independence from the Ottoman Empire during the 19th century; as Turkish power declined, local nationalism rose, and Russian support for its Slavic neighbors paid off. But the nations were intensely hostile to one another. Furthermore, **Balkan nationalism** threatened Austria, which had a large southern Slav population. Russia and Austria nearly came to

Nationalities
Within the
Hapsburg
Empire

MAP

blows on several occasions over Balkan issues. Then, in 1912 and 1913, the Balkan nations engaged in two internal wars, which led to territorial gains for several states but satisfied no one (Map 23.6). Serbia, which bordered Austria to the south, had hoped for greater stakes. At the same time, Austria grew nervous over the gains Serbia had achieved. In 1914 a Serbian nationalist assassinated an Austrian archduke on behalf of Serbian claims. Austria vowed to punish Serbia. Russia rushed to the defense of Serbia and mobilized its troops against Austria. Germany, worried about Austria and also eager to be able to strike against France before Russia's cumbersome mobilization was complete, called up its reserves and then declared war on August 1. Britain hesitated briefly, then joined its allies. World War I had begun, and with it came a host of new problems for Western society.

Diplomacy and Society

The tensions that spiraled into major war are not easy to explain. Diplomatic maneuverings can seem quite remote from the central concerns of most people, if only because key decisions—for example, with whom to ally—are made by a specialist elite. Even as the West became more democratic, few ordinary people placed foreign affairs high on their election agendas.

Map 23.6 The Balkans After the Regional Wars, 1913 The wars pushed the Ottoman Empire almost entirely out of the Balkans, but left many small states dissatisfied.

The West had long been characterized by political divisions and rivalries. In comparison with some other civilizations, this was an inherent weakness of the Western political system. In a sense, what happened by the late 19th century was that the nation-state system got out of hand, encouraged by the absence of serious challenge from any other civilizations. The rise of Germany and new tensions in the Balkans simply complicated the growing nationalist competition.

This diplomatic escalation also had some links to the strains of Western society under the impact of industrialization. Established leaders in the West continued to worry about social protest. They tended to seek diplomatic successes to distract the people. This procedure worked nicely for a few decades when imperialist gains came easily. But then it backfired. Around 1914 German officials, fearful of the power of the socialists, wondered whether war would aid national unity. British leaders, beset by feminist dissent and labor unrest, failed to think through their own diplomatic options. Leaders also depended on military buildups for economic purposes. Modern industry, pressed to sell the soaring output of its factories, found naval purchases and army equipment a vital supplement. Mass newspapers, which fanned nationalist pride with stories of conquest and tales of the evils of rival nations, helped shape a belligerent popular culture.

Thus, just a few years after celebrating a century of material progress and peace, ordinary Europeans went to war almost gaily in 1914. Troops departed for the front convinced that war would be exciting, with quick victories. Their departure was hailed by enthusiastic civilians, who draped their trains with flowers. Four years later, almost everyone would agree that war had been unmitigated hell. However, the complexities of industrial society were such that war's advent seemed almost a welcome breath of the unexpected, a chance to get away from the disciplined stability of everyday life.

Global Connections

Industrial Europe and the World

Europe's growing power during the 19th century transformed the world. Imperialism and the redefinition of the world economy pushed European interests to every corner of the globe. The expansion of the settler societies reflected and also expanded Western influence. It was European sponsorship and power that ushered in the process of globalization.

This same power made developments in 19th-century Europe something of a global model. Some leaders, aware of Europe's political and industrial change, found the example repellent. Russian conservatives, for example, warned against the divisiveness of parliamentary politics and the exploitation of modern industry.

Europe's revolutionary heritage, however, also won admiration, partly because it contained principles that could be used to counter European power. Liberalism, radicalism, and socialism began to spread beyond the boundaries of Europe and the settler societies. They could be directed against colonial controls or the exploitation of workers in the world economy. Nationalism spread rapidly as well, from its initial base in revolutionary Europe. Europe, in sum, was a global force in the 19th century as no society had ever been before, but its message was extremely complex.

By 1914 Europe's world role promoted new anxieties within the West. Novel contacts, like Asian immigration into the United States, spurred new fears. On a wider scale, some leaders warned of competition from Asia. Ironically, growing internal tensions within the West ultimately predominated, though the results would have international effects as well.

Further Readings

On key changes see Robert B. Marks, *The Origins of the Modern World: A Global and Ecological Narrative from the Fifteenth to the Twenty-First Century* (2007); Deborah Cadbury, *Dreams of Iron and Steel: Seven Wonders of the Nineteenth Century, from the Building of the London Sewers to the Panama Canal* (2004); John Waller, *The Discovery of the Germ: Twenty Years that Transformed the Way We Think about Disease* (2002); and Nicholas Roe, ed., *Romanticism: An Oxford Guide* (2005). On Europe's Industrial Revolution: Kenneth Morgan, *The Birth of Industrial Britain: Social Change, 1750-1850* (2004); Stephen P. Rice, *Minding the Machine: Languages of Class in Early Industrial America* (2004); and Paul E. Rivard, *A New Oder of Things: How the Textile Industry Transformed New England* (2002). For a more general survey, see Peter N. Stearns, *The Industrial Revolution in World History* (2006).

For the French Revolution and political upheaval, Isser Woloch's *The New Regime: Transformations of the French Civic Order, 1789–1829* (1994) is a useful introduction. See also Nigel Aston, *The French Revolution, 1789-1804: Authority, Liberty and the Search for Stability* (2004) and Suzanne Desan, *The Family on Trial in Revolutionary France* (2004). Lynn Hunt's *Politics, Culture, and Class in the French Revolution* (1984) is an important study. Other revolutionary currents are treated in *The Crowd in History: Popular Disturbances in France and England* (1981) by George Rudé and *1848: The Revolutionary Tide in Europe* (1974) by Peter Stearns.

The impact of the Industrial Revolution on gender relations is analyzed in A. Clarke, *The Struggle for the Breeches: Gender and the Making of the British Working Class* (1995) and Harold L. Smith, *The British Women's Suffrage Campaign, 1866–1928* (2007). Major developments concerning women and the family are covered in Louise Tilly and Joan Scott, *Women, Work, and Family* (1978); and Steven Mintz and Susan Kellogg, *Domestic Revolutions: A Social History of American Family Life* (1989).

For an overview of social change, see Peter Stearns and Herrick Chapman, *European Society in Upheaval* (1991). On labor history, see Michael Hanagan, *The Logic of Solidarity* (1981); and Albert Lindemann, *History of European Socialism* (1983).

On political and cultural history, see Clive Emsley, *Napoleon: Conquest, Reform and Reorganizaiton* (2003); Gordon Craig, *Germany, 1866–1945* (1978); and Isabel V. Hull, *Absolute Destruction: Military Culture and the Practices of War in Imperial Germany* (2005). On major diplomatic developments, see D. K. Fieldhouse, *Economics and Empire, 1830–1914* (1970); and David Kaiser, *Politics and War: European Conflict from Philip II to Hitler* (1990).

The impact of these winds of change as they swept across the American sociopolitical landscape is examined in John Ferling, *Almost a Miracle: The American Victory in the War of Independence* (2007); David Armitage, *The Declaration of Independence: A Global History* (2007); Terry Bouton, *Taming Democracy: "The People," The Founders, and The Troubled Ending of the American Revolution* (2007); Robert Dahl, *How Democratic Is the American Constitution?* (2002); and S. M. Lipsett, *American Exceptionalism: A Double-Edged Sword* (1996).

On the Web

An exceptionally rich treatment of the French Revolution, from its social origins to the role of the city of Paris, can be found at http://chnm.gmu.edu/revolution/. Links to the sights, sounds, and songs of the French Revolution of 1789 are offered at http://www.andrew.cmu.edu/user/sc24/frenchrev.html, http://history.hanover.edu/modern/FRENCHRV.html and http://marseillaise.org/english/. One of the French Revolution's most lasting achievements, abolition of the feudal system in France, is recorded at http://history.hanover.edu/texts/abolfeud.htm.

The American Revolution is explored in documents, site visits, and publications at http://www.revwar.com/links/document.html. Major Websites addressing the American Revolutionary War include http://www.nps.gov/revwar/, http://revolution.h-net.msu.edu/, and http://www.pbs.org/ktca/liberty/. A glimpse into the role of women in the American Revolution, and a useful bibliography of that role is offered at http://userpages.aug.com/captbarb/femvets.html and http://www.carleton.ca/~pking/arbib/z.htm, respectively.

Many Web pages offer insight into the personalities of the age of revolution, such as Marie Antoinette (http://www2.lucidcafe.com/lucidcafe/library/95nov/antoinette.html), Napoleon (http://www.napoleon.org/en/home.asp, http://www.napoleon-series.org/, http://www.pbs.org/empires/napoleon/, http://www.pbs.org/empires/napoleon/flash/fl_home.html), and Thomas Paine (http://odur.let.rug.nl/~usa/B/tpaine/paine.htm).

Web resources that provide overviews of the Industrial Revolution include http://www.bbc.co.uk/history/british/victorians/workshop_of_the_world_01.shtml, http://www.fordham.edu/halsall/mod/modsbook14.html, and http://en.wikipedia.org/wiki/Industrial_Revolution. Key figures of that watershed in world history include James Watt (whose re-conception of the steam engine can be found at http://digilander.libero.it/calchic/index.html) and Ned Ludd, whose name became synonymous with resistance to technological change (http://www.spartacus.schoolnet.co.uk/PRluddites.htm).

The life of industrial workers in 19th-century England is examined at http://www.bbc.co.uk/history/british/victorians/workshop_of_the_world_01.shtml, http://www.fordham.edu/halsall/mod/1844engels.html, http://www.victorianweb.org/history/workers2.html, and http://www.womeninworldhistory.com/lesson7.html. Web sites illuminating the world of women and child workers include http://www.fordham.edu/halsall/mod/1842womenminers.html, http://www.fordham.edu/halsall/mod/robinson-lowell.html, and http://www.spartacus.schoolnet.co.uk/Twork.htm.

The impact of industrialization gave thrust to the writings of Karl Marx, as is illuminated in a brief essay at http://www.victorianweb .org/philosophy/phil2.htm. Two of the best sites for accessing and comparing the ideas of Marxist writers are http://www.marxists .org/index.html and http://www.anu.edu.au/polsci/marx/marx.html (which includes a very clear RealAudio file of the "Internationale" sung by an Irish folksinger).

AP* Test Prep

1. All of these were forces for change in Western Europe during the period 1750–1914 EXCEPT
   (A) the ideas of the Enlightenment.
   (B) the increasing wealth and success of the business classes.
   (C) achievement of greater religious unity
   (D) industrialization and mechanization.

2. All of these led to the outbreak of the French Revolution in 1789 EXCEPT
   (A) the inability of the French government to reform itself.
   (B) an invasion of France by Prussia and Austria.
   (C) a massive debt and need for tax reform.
   (D) a desire to limit the powers and rights of the king, nobles, and clergy.

3. The political ideology most favored by the victorious allied powers at the Congress of Vienna was
   (A) nationalism.
   (B) liberalism.
   (C) conservatism.
   (D) revolution.

4. The failures of the revolutions of 1848 taught what lesson to the liberal leaders?
   (A) They needed to embrace a more radical ideology.
   (B) They needed to get the support of the military establishment.
   (C) The needed to organize internationally.
   (D) They needed to use more gradual methods of reform.

5. What caused a noticeable increase in consumerism and leisure time in the mid-19th century?
   (A) better wages and a reduction in work hours
   (B) advances in scientific knowledge
   (C) the beginning of the Marxist movement
   (D) the emerging power of the United States in world markets

6. Which of the following is true for Italy, Germany, the U.S., Canada, and Australia in the mid-19th century?
   (A) They had industrialized, European-dependent economies.
   (B) They were highly militarized.
   (C) They had programs for eliminating their indigenous populations.
   (D) They were involved with processes of political unification.

7. All of these conditions contributed to the outbreak of World War I EXCEPT
   (A) rival systems of alliance.
   (B) international courts of justice and organizations such as the Red Cross.
   (C) increased militarization of societies.
   (D) industrial competition and the expansion of colonial empires.

Free-Response Question

What political, economic, and intellectual/cultural factors led to Europe and the U.S.'s global domination by the end of the 19th century?

24 Industrialization and Imperialism: The Making of the European Global Order

The Shift to Land Empires in Asia
THINKING HISTORICALLY: Western Education and the Rise of an African and Asian Middle Class
Industrial Rivalries and the Partition of the World, 1870–1914
Patterns of Dominance: Continuity and Change

DOCUMENT: Contrary Images: The Colonizer Versus the Colonized on the "Civilizing Mission"
VISUALIZING THE PAST: Capitalism and Colonialism
GLOBAL CONNECTIONS: A European-Dominated Early Phase of Globalization

On January 22, 1879, at the height of its century-long reign as the paramount global power, Great Britain suffered one of the most devastating defeats ever inflicted by a non-Western people on an industrialized nation. The late-Victorian painting, shown in Figure 24.1, depicts the Battle of Isandhlwana (ihs-SAND-zwah-nuh) at which more than 20,000 Zulu soldiers outmaneuvered a much smaller but overconfident British army invading their kingdom. Taking advantage of the British commander's foolhardy decision to divide his forces, the Zulus attacked the main British encampment from all directions and, in a fiercely fought battle lasting only a couple of hours, wiped out 950 European troops and nearly 850 African irregulars. Divided and caught off guard, the British could not form proper firing lines to repel the much larger and well-led Zulu *impis*—the equivalent of a division in a Western army. The flight of the African irregulars, who made up a sizeable portion of the British army, left gaps in the British force that were quickly exploited by the Zulu fighters. Soon after the main battle was joined, most of the British and mercenary African soldiers in the camp at Isandhlwana were dead or in desperate flight to a river nearby, where most were hunted down by impis positioned to block their retreat.

The well drilled Zulu impis who routed the British forces at Isandhlwana skillfully wielded the cattle-hide shields and short stabbing spears, or *assegais,* which had been the Zulus' trademark for more than half a century. In the early 1800s, warriors and weapons had provided the military power for an ambitious young leader named Shaka to forge a powerful kingdom centered on Natal in the southeastern portions of what would later become the Union of South Africa (Map 24.4). The Zulus' imposing preindustrial military organization had triumphed over all African rivals and later proved the most formidable force resisting the advance of both the Dutch-descended Boers (later called Afrikaners) and British imperial armies in southern Africa.

The British defeat was shocking in large part because it seemed implausible, given the great and ever-growing disparity between the military might of the European colonial powers and the African and Asian peoples they had come to dominate in unprecedented ways. Technological innovations and mass production made it possible for European states to supply advanced weaponry and other war materiel to sizeable naval and land forces across the globe. Set in this larger context, the aftermath of the Zulu triumph at Isandhlwana demonstrated that the British defeat was a fluke, a dramatic but short-lived exception to what had become a pervasive pattern of European (and increasingly American) political and military supremacy worldwide. Estimates of Zulu losses at Isandhlwana, for example, range from two to three times those for British units and "native" levees combined. Within hours of their utter destruction of most of the main British column, a force of some 3000 Zulu warriors was decimated in the siege of a small outpost at nearby Rorke's Drift. There a cluster of farm buildings was successfully defended by just over a hundred British soldiers, many of whom were wounded from earlier clashes.

As was the case in equally stunning massacres of the expeditionary forces of industrial powers in other colonial settings, most notably Custer's last stand in the American West, revenge for the defeat inflicted by the Zulus at Isandhlwana was massive and swift. Additional troops were drawn from throughout the far-flung British Empire and, within months, a far larger British force was advancing on the Zulu capital at Ulundi. Like the coalition of Indian tribes that had joined to destroy Custer's units of the Seventh Cavalry, the Zulu impis that had turned back the first British invasion dispersed soon after the clashes at Isandhlwana and Rorke's Drift. By late August, the Zulu ruler, Cetshwayo, had surrendered to the British and been shipped into exile at Cape Town. ■

Figure 24.1 A romantic depiction of the 1879 Battle of Isandhlwana in the Natal province of South Africa. The battle demonstrated that, despite their superior firepower, the Europeans could be defeated by well organized and determined African or Asian resistance forces.

The British advances into the heart of Cetshwayo's kingdom in the last of the wars between the Europeans and the Zulus exemplified many of the fundamental shifts in the balance of world power in the turn-of-the-century decades of the great "scramble" for overseas territories that are the focus of this chapter. In important ways imperial rivalries among the European powers did much to set the stage for World War I. Like their French, Dutch, Belgian, German, Russian, Japanese, and American competitors, the British plunged deep into Africa, the Middle East, and Asia. In contrast to the earlier centuries of overseas expansion, the European powers were driven in the late-19th century mainly by rivalries with each other, and in some instances with the Japanese and Americans, rather than fears of Muslim kingdoms in the Middle East and north Africa or powerful empires in Asia.

As we shall see, in most of the areas they claimed as colonial possessions, the Europeans established direct rule, where they had once been mainly content to subjugate and control local rulers and their retainers. The 1879 Anglo-Zulu war had been precipitated by British demands, including the right to station a resident in the Zulu kingdom and the breakup of the Zulu military machine, that would have reduced Cetshwayo to the status of a vassal. Though the British and other colonizers would continue to govern through indigenous officials in many areas, their subordinates were

1600 C.E.	1700 C.E.	1750 C.E.	1800 C.E.	1850 C.E.	1900 C.E.
1619 Dutch establish trading post at Batavia in Java 1620s Sultan of Mataram's attacks on Batavia fail 1652 First Dutch settlement in South Africa at Cape Town 1661 British port-trading center founded at Bombay 1690 Calcutta established at center of British activities in Bengal	1707 Death of Mughal emperor, Aurangzeb; beginning of imperial breakdown 1739 Nadir Shah's invasion of India from Persia 1740–1748 War of Austrian Succession; global British–French struggle for colonial dominance	1750s Civil war and division of Mataram; Dutch become the paramount power on Java 1756–1763 Seven Years War, British–French global warfare 1757 Battle of Plassey; British become dominant power in Bengal 1769–1770 Great Famine in Bengal 1775–1783 War for independence by American colonists; another British–French struggle for global preeminence 1786–1790 Cornwallis's political reforms in India 1790–1815 Wars of the French Revolution and Napoleonic era 1798 Napoleon's invasion of Egypt	1815 British annex Cape Town and surrounding area 1830 Boers begin Great Trek in South Africa 1835 Decision to give support for English education in India; English adopted as the language of Indian law courts	1850s Boer republics established in the Orange Free State and Transvaal 1853 First railway line constructed in India 1857 Calcutta, Madras, and Bombay universities founded 1857–1858 "Mutiny" or Great Rebellion in north India 1858 British parliament assumes control over India from the East India Company 1867 Diamonds discovered in Orange Free State 1869 Opening of the Suez Canal c. 1879–1890s Partition of west Africa 1879 Zulu victory over British at Isandhlwana; defeat at Rorke's Drift 1882 British invasion of Egypt 1885 Indian National Congress Party founded in India 1885 Gold discovered in the Transvaal 1890s Partition of east Africa 1898 British–French crisis over Fashoda in the Sudan 1899–1902 Anglo-Boer War in South Africa	1902 Anglo-Japanese Treaty 1904 Anglo-Russian crisis at Dogger Bank 1904–1905 First Moroccan crisis; Russo-Japanese War 1911 Second Moroccan crisis 1914 Outbreak of World War I

From the mid-18th century onward, the European powers began to build true empires in Asia similar to those they had established in the Americas beginning in the 16th century. In the first phase of the colonization process, Europeans overseas were willing to adapt their lifestyles to the climates and cultures of the lands they had gone out to rule.

increasingly recruited from new elites, both professional and commercial, who emerged from schools where the languages and customs of the imperial powers were taught to growing numbers of colonized peoples.

The Shift to Land Empires in Asia

Although we usually use the term *partition* to refer to the European division of Africa at the end of the 19th century, the Western powers had actually been carving up the globe into colonial enclaves for centuries (Map 24.1). At first this process was haphazard and often quite contrary to the interests and designs of those in charge of European enterprises overseas. For example, the directors who

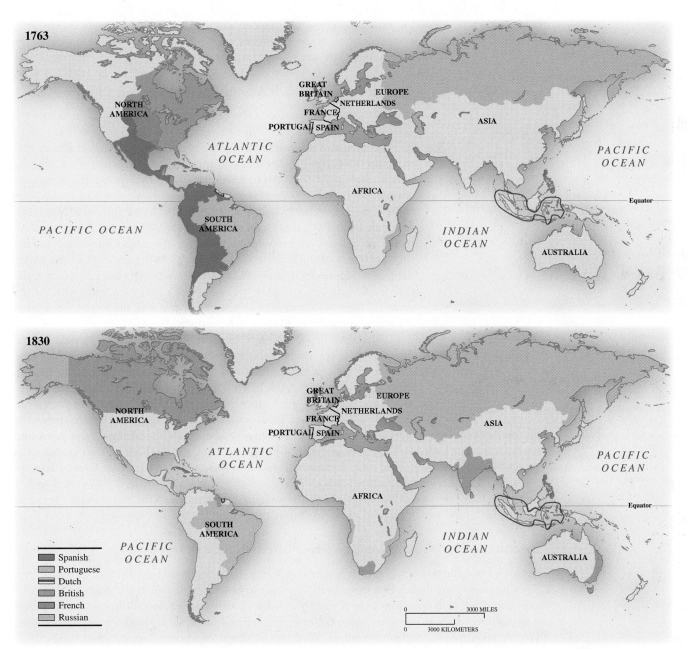

Map 24.1 European Colonial Territories, Before and After 1800   As a comparison of the two maps shows, the late 1700s marked a pivotal point of transition in both the contraction of colonial domination, particularly in the America's and it's expansion in Africa, Asia, and the Pacific.

ran the Dutch and English East India companies (which were granted monopolies of the trade between their respective countries and the East in the 17th and 18th centuries) had little interest in territorial acquisitions. In fact, they were actively opposed to involvement in the political rivalries of the Asian princes. Wars were expensive, and direct administration of African or Asian possessions was even more so. Both cut deeply into the profits gained through participation in the Asian trading system, and profits—not empires—were the chief concern of the Dutch and English directors.

   Whatever policies company directors may have instructed their agents in Africa and Asia to follow, these "men-on-the-spot" were often drawn into local power struggles. And before the Industrial Revolution produced the telegraph and other methods of rapid communication, company directors and European prime ministers had very little control over those who actually ran their trading empires. In the 18th century, a letter took months to reach Calcutta from London; the reply took many

Colonization in Africa

Map 24.2 The Stages of Dutch Expansion in Java The consolidation of Dutch power on Java, the center of its island Asian empire, accelerated dramatically from the late 17th century.

Mataram Kingdom that controlled interior regions of Java in 17th century; Dutch East India Company paid tribute to the kingdom for rights of trade at Batavia; weakness of kingdom after 1670s allowed Dutch to exert control over all of Java.

sepoys Troops that served the British East India Company; recruited from various warlike peoples of India.

British Raj British political establishment in India; developed as a result of the rivalry between France and Britain in India.

months more. Thus, commanders in the field had a great deal of leeway. They could conquer whole provinces or kingdoms before home officials even learned that their armies were on the move.

Prototype: The Dutch Advance on Java

One of the earliest empires to be built in this fashion was that pieced together in the late 17th and 18th centuries by the Dutch in Java (Map 24.2). Java was then and is now the most populous of the hundreds of islands that make up the present-day country of Indonesia. In the early years after the Dutch established their Asian headquarters at Batavia on the northwest coast of the island in 1619, it was a struggle just to survive. The Dutch were content to become the vassals of and pay tribute to the sultans of **Mataram,** who ruled most of Java. In the decades that followed, the Dutch concentrated on gaining monopoly control over the spices produced on the smaller islands of the Indonesian archipelago to the east. But in the 1670s, the Dutch repeatedly intervened in the wars between rival claimants to the throne of Mataram, and they backed the side that eventually won. As the price for their assistance, the Dutch demanded that the territories around Batavia be turned over to them to administer.

This episode was the first of a long series of Dutch interventions in the wars of succession between the princes of Mataram. Dutch armies were made up mainly of troops recruited from the island peoples of the eastern Indonesian archipelago, led by Dutch commanders. Their superior organization and discipline, even more than their firearms, made the Dutch a potent ally of whichever prince won them to his side. But the price the Javanese rulers paid was very high. Each succession dispute and Dutch intervention led to more and more land being ceded to the increasingly land-hungry Europeans. By the mid-18th century, the sultans of Mataram controlled only the south central portions of Java (Map 24.2). A failed attempt by Sultan Mangkubumi to restore Mataram's control over the Dutch in the 1750s ended with a Dutch-dictated division of the kingdom that signified Dutch control of the entire island. Java had been transformed into the core of an Asian empire that would last for 200 years.

Keystone of World Empire: The Rise of British Rule in India

In many ways, the rise of the British as a land power in India resembled the Dutch capture of Java. The directors of the British East India Company were as hostile as the Dutch financiers to territorial expansion. But British agents of the company in India repeatedly meddled in disputes and conflicts between local princes. In these interventions, the British, adopting a practice pioneered by the French, relied heavily on Indian troops, called **sepoys** (some of whom are pictured in Figure 24.2) recruited from peoples throughout the subcontinent. As had been the case in Java, Indian princes regarded the British as allies whom they could use and control to crush competitors from within India or put down usurpers who tried to seize their thrones. As had happened in Java, the European pawns gradually emerged as serious rivals to the established Indian rulers and eventually dominated the region.

Partly because the struggle for India came later, there were also important differences between the patterns of colonial conquest in India and Java as well as between the global repercussions of each. In contrast to the Dutch march inland, which resulted largely from responses to local threats and opportunities, the rise of the **British Raj** (the Sanskrit-derived name for the British political establishment in India) owed much to the fierce global rivalry between the British and the French. In the 18th century, the two powers found themselves on opposite sides in five major wars. These struggles were global in a very real sense. On land and sea, the two old adversaries not only fought in Europe but also squared off in the Caribbean, where each had valuable plantation colonies; in North America; and on the coasts and bays of the Indian Ocean. With the exception of the American War of Independence (1775–1783), these struggles ended in British victories. The British loss of the American colonies was more than offset by earlier victories in the Caribbean and especially in

India. These triumphs gradually gave the British control of the entire south Asian subcontinent.

Although the first victories of the British over the French and the Indian princes came in the south in the late 1740s, their rise as a major land power in Asia hinged on victories won in Bengal to the northeast (Map 24.3). The key battle at **Plassey** in 1757, in which fewer than 3000 British troops and Indian sepoys defeated an Indian army of nearly 50,000, is traditionally pictured as the heroic triumph of a handful of brave and disciplined Europeans over a horde of ill-trained and poorly led Asians. The battle pitted Sirāj ud-daula (sih-RAH JUHD-oh-luh), the teenage *nawab,* or ruler, of Bengal, against **Robert Clive,** the architect of the British victory in the south. The prize was control of the fertile and populous kingdom of Bengal. The real reasons for Clive's famous victory tell us a good deal about the process of empire building in Asia and Africa.

The numbers on each side and the maneuvers on the field had little to do with the outcome of a battle that in a sense was over before it began. Clive's well-paid Indian spies had given him detailed accounts of the divisions in Sirāj ud-daula's ranks in the months before the battle. With money provided by Hindu bankers who were anxious to get back at the Muslim prince for unpaid debts and for confiscating their treasure on several occasions, Clive bought off the nawab's chief general and several of his key allies. Even the nawab's leading spy was on Clive's payroll, which somewhat offset the fact that the main British spy had been bribed by Sirāj ud-daula. The backing Clive received from the Indian bankers also meant that his troops were well paid, whereas those of the nawab were not.

Thus, when the understandably nervous teenage ruler of Bengal rode into battle on June 23, 1757, his fate was already sealed. The nawab's troops under French officers and one of his Indian commanders fought well. But his major Indian allies defected to the British or remained stationary on his flanks when the two sides were locked in combat. These defections wiped out the nawab's numerical advantage, and Clive's skillful leadership and the superiority of his artillery did the rest. The British victors had once again foiled their French rivals. As the nawab had anticipated, they soon took over the direct administration of the sizeable Bengal-Bihar region. The foundations of Britain's Indian and global empire had been laid.

The Consolidation of British Rule

In the decades after Plassey, the British officials of the East India Company repeatedly went to war with Indian princes whose kingdoms bordered on the company's growing possessions (Map 24.3). These entanglements grew stronger and stronger as the Mughal Empire broke down more fully in the last decades of the century. In its ruins, regional Indian princes fought to defend or expand their territories at the expense of their neighbors. Interventions in these conflicts or assaults on war-weakened Indian kingdoms allowed the British to advance steadily inland from their three trading towns on the Indian coast: Madras, Bombay, and Calcutta. These cities became the administrative centers of the three **presidencies** that eventually made up the bulk of the territory the British ruled directly in India. In many areas, the British were content to leave defeated or allied Indian rulers on the thrones of their **princely states** and to control their kingdoms through agents stationed at the rulers' courts.

Because there was no sense of Indian national identity, it was impossible for Muslim or Hindu rulers to appeal to the defense of the homeland or the need for unity to drive out the foreigners. Indian princes continued to fear and fight with each other despite the ever growing power of the British Raj. Old grudges and hatreds ran deeper than the new threat of the British. Many

Figure 24.2 Indian soldiers, or sepoys, made up a large portion of the rank-and-file troops in the armies of British India. Commanded by European officers and armed, uniformed, and drilled according to European standards, troops such as those pictured here were recruited from the colonized peoples and became one of the mainstays of all European colonial regimes. The European colonizers preferred to recruit these soldiers from subject peoples whom they saw as particularly martial. In India, these included the Sikhs (pictured here) and Marattas, as well as Gurkhas recruited from neighboring but independent Nepal.

 MAP The Sequence of British Territorial Acquisitions in India, 1765–1856

Plassey Battle in 1757 between troops of the British East India Company and an Indian army under Sirāj ud-daula, ruler of Bengal; British victory resulted in control of northern India.

Clive, Robert (1725–1774) Architect of British victory at Plassey in 1757; established foundations of British Raj in northern India (18th century).

presidencies Three districts that made up the bulk of the directly ruled British territories in India; capitals at Madras, Calcutta, and Bombay.

princely states Domains of Indian princes allied with the British Raj; agents of East India Company were stationed at the rulers' courts to ensure compliance; made up over one-third of the British Indian Empire.

Map 24.3 The Growth of the British Empire in India, from the 1750s to 1858 In roughly a century between the late 1700s and the 1850s, the British had built an empire that encompassed virtually the entire subcontinent of South Asia.

Growth of British Control in India

ordinary Indians were eager to serve in the British regiments, which had better weapons, brighter uniforms, and higher and more regular pay than all but a handful of the armies of the Indian rulers. By the mid-19th century, Indian soldiers in the pay of the British outnumbered British officers and enlisted men in India by almost five to one.

From the first decades of the 19th century, India was clearly the pivot of the great empire being built by Britain on a global scale. Older colonies with large numbers of white settlers, such as Canada and Australia, contributed more space to the total square miles of empire the British were so fond of calculating. But India had by far the greater share of colonized peoples. Britain's largest and most powerful land forces were the armies recruited from the Indian peoples, and these were rapidly becoming the police of the entire British Indian empire. In the mid-19th century, Indian soldiers were sent to punish the Chinese and Afghans, conquer Burma and Malaya, and begin the conquest of south and east Africa. Indian ports were essential to British sea power east of the Cape of Good Hope. As the century progressed, India became the major outlet for British overseas investments and manufactured goods as well as a major source of key raw materials.

Early Colonial Society in India and Java

Although they slowly emerged as the political masters of Java and India, the Dutch and the British were at first content to leave the social systems of the peoples they ruled pretty much as they had found them. The small numbers of European traders and company officials who lived in the colonies for any length of time simply formed a new class atop the social hierarchies that already existed in Java and different parts of India. Beneath them, the aristocratic classes and often the old ruling families were preserved. They were left in charge of the day-to-day administration at all but the very highest levels. At the highest levels, the local rulers were paired with an agent of the imperial power (Figure 24.3).

To survive in the hot tropical environments of south and southeast Asia, the Dutch and English were forced to adapt to the ancient and sophisticated host cultures of their Asian colonies. After establishing themselves at Batavia, for example, the Dutch initially tried to create a little Holland in Java. They built high, close-packed houses overlooking canals, just like those they had left behind in Amsterdam and Rotterdam. But they soon discovered that the canals were splendid breeding grounds for insects and microbes that (though the Europeans did not make the connection until somewhat later) carried debilitating or lethal diseases such as malaria, dysentery, and typhoid. By the late 17th century, the prosperous merchants and officials of Batavia had begun to move away from the unhealthy center of the city to villas in the suburbs. Their large dwellings were set in gardens and separated by rice paddies and palm groves. The tall houses of the inner city gave way in the countryside to low, sprawling dwellings with many open spaces to catch the tropical breezes. Each was ringed with long porches with overhanging roofs to block the heat and glare of the sun. Similar dwellings, from which we get our term *bungalow,* came into fashion in India in the 18th century.

Europeans living in the tropical colonies also adopted, to varying degrees, the dress, the eating and work habits, and even the political symbols and styles of the Asian peoples they ruled. Some Englishmen refused to give up their tight-fitting woolen clothing, at least in public. But many (one suspects most of those who survived) took to wearing looser-fitting cotton clothing. Dutch gentlemen even donned the long skirt-like sarongs of the Javanese aristocrats. British and Dutch officials learned to appreciate the splendid cuisines of India and Java—a taste that the Dutch would never lose and the British would revive at home in the postindependence era. Englishmen smoked Indian *hookahs,* or water pipes, and delighted in performances of Indian "dancing girls." Adjusting to the heat of the colonies, both the Dutch and the English worked hard in the cool of the morning, took a long lunch break (often with a siesta), and then returned to the office for the late afternoon and early evening.

Because the Europeans who went to Asia until the mid-19th century were overwhelmingly male, Dutch and British traders and soldiers commonly had liaisons with Asian women. In some cases these involved little more than visits to the local brothel. But very often European men lived with Asian women, and sometimes they married them. Before the end of the 18th century, mixed marriages on the part of prominent traders or officers were widely accepted, particularly in Java. Examples of racial discrimination against the subject peoples on the basis of their physical appearance can certainly be found during the early decades of European overseas empire. But the frequency of liaisons that cut across racial boundaries suggests a social fluidity and a degree of interracial interaction that would be unthinkable by the last half of the 19th century, when the social distance between colonizers and colonized was consciously marked in a variety of ways.

Social Reform in the Colonies

Until the early 19th century, neither the Dutch nor the British had much desire to push for changes in the social or cultural life of their Asian subjects. The British enforced the rigid divisions of the Hindu caste system, and both the British and the Dutch made it clear that they had little interest in spreading Christianity among the Indians or the Javanese. In fact, for fear of offending Hindu and Muslim religious sentiments, the British refused to allow Christian missionaries to preach in their territories until the second decade of the 19th century.

Beginning in the 1770s, however, rampant corruption on the part of company officials forced the British parliament to enact significant reforms in the administration of the East India Company and its colonies. By that time most of those who served in India saw their brief tenure as a chance to strike it rich quickly. They made great fortunes by cheating the company and exploiting the Indian peasants and artisans. The bad manners and conspicuous consumption of these upstarts, whom their contemporaries scornfully called **nabobs,** were satirized by leading English novelists of the age.

When the misconduct of the nabobs resulted in the catastrophic Bengal famine of 1770, in which as much as one-third of the population of that once prosperous province died, their abuses could no longer be ignored. The British parliament passed several acts that restructured the company hierarchy and made it much more accountable to the British government. A succession of political reforms culminated in sweeping measures taken in the 1790s by the same **Lord Charles Cornwallis** whose surrender at Yorktown had sealed Britain's loss of the American colonies. By cleaning up the courts and reducing the power of local British administrators, Cornwallis did much to check widespread corruption. Because of his mistrust of Indians, his measures also severely limited their participation in governing the empire.

In this same period, forces were building in both India and England that caused a major shift in British policy toward social reform among the subject peoples. The Evangelical religious revival,

Figure 24.3 The close alliances that the European colonizers often struck with the "native" princes of conquered areas are graphically illustrated by this photo of the Susuhunan of Surakarta, a kingdom in central Java, standing arm-in-arm with a high Dutch official. At the upper levels of the administration, Dutch leaders were paired with Javanese rulers and aristocrats. The Dutch official always had the last say in joint decisions. But his Javanese "partner" was closely linked to subordinate administrators and often had a good deal more to say about how effectively the decision was carried out.

nabobs   Name given to British representatives of the East India Company who went briefly to India to make fortunes through graft and exploitation.

Cornwallis, Lord Charles   Reformer of the East India Company administration of India in the 1790s; reduced power of local British administrators; checked widespread corruption.

Western Education and the Rise of an African and Asian Middle Class

To varying degrees and for many of the same reasons as the British in India, all European colonizers educated the children of African and Asian elite groups in Western-language schools. The early 19th-century debate over education in India was paralleled by an equally hard-fought controversy among French officials and missionaries regarding the proper schooling for the peoples of Senegal in west Africa. The Dutch did not develop European-language schools for the sons of the Javanese elite until the mid-19th century, and many young Javanese men continued to be educated in the homes of the Dutch living in the colonies until the end of the century. Whatever their particular views on education, all colonial policymakers realized that they needed administrative assistants and postal clerks and that they could not begin to recruit enough Europeans to fill these posts. Therefore, all agreed that Western education for some segments of the colonized population was essential for the maintenance of colonial order.

One of the chief advantages of having Western-educated African and Asian subordinates—for they were always below European officials or traders—was that their salaries were much lower than what Europeans would have been paid for doing the same work. The Europeans had no trouble rationalizing this inequity. Higher pay for the Europeans was justified as compensation for the sacrifices involved in colonial service. Colonial officials also as-

> "Western education in the colonies . . . within a generation or two would produce major challenges to European colonial dominance."

sumed that European employees would be more hard-working and efficient.

Beyond the need for government functionaries and business assistants, each European colonizer stressed different objectives in designing Western-language schools for the children of upper-class families. The transmission of Western scientific learning and production techniques was a high priority for the British in India. The goal of educational policymakers, such as Macaulay, was to teach the Indians Western literature and manners and to instill in them a Western sense of morality. As Macaulay put it, the British hoped that English-language schools would turn out brown English gentlemen, who would in turn teach their countrymen the ways of the West.

The French, at least until the end of the 19th century, went even further. Because they conceived of French nationalism as a matter of culture rather than birth, it was of prime importance that Africans and other colonial students master the French language and the subtleties of French cuisine, dress, and etiquette. The French also saw the process of turning colonial subjects into black, brown, and yellow French citizens as a way to increase their stagnant population to keep up with rival nations, especially Germany and Great Britain. Both of these rivals and the United States had much higher birth rates in this period.

When the lessons had been fully absorbed and the students fully assimilated to French culture, they could become full citizens of France, no matter what their family origins or skin color. Only a tiny minority of the population of any French colony had the opportunity for the sort of schooling that would qualify them for French cit-

which had seen the spread of Methodism among the English working classes, soon spilled over into Britain's colonial domains. Evangelicals were in the vanguard of the struggle to put an end to the slave trade, and their calls for reforms in India were warmly supported by Utilitarian philosophers such as Jeremy Bentham and James Mill. These prominent British thinkers believed that there were common principles by which human societies ought to be run if decent living conditions were to be attained by people at all class levels. Mill and other Utilitarians were convinced that British society, though flawed, was far more advanced than Indian society. Thus, they pushed for the introduction of British institutions and ways of thinking in India, as well as the eradication of what they considered Indian superstitions and social abuses.

Both Utilitarians and Evangelicals agreed that Western education was the key to revitalizing an ancient but decadent Indian civilization. Both factions were contemptuous of Indian learning that was centered in *madrasas* or Islamic religious schools or Hindu *gurus* instructing individuals or small groups of students. Influential British historian Thomas Babington Macaulay put it most bluntly when he declared in the 1830s that one shelf of an English gentleman's library was worth all the writings of Asia. Consequently, the Evangelicals and the Utilitarians pushed for the introduction of English-language education for the children of the Indian elite. These officials also pushed for major reforms in Indian society and advocated a large-scale infusion of Western technology.

At the center of the reformers' campaign was the effort to put an end to sati, the ritual burning of Hindu widows on the funeral pyres of their deceased husbands (see Chapters 7 and 21). This practice, which was clearly a corruption of Hindu religious beliefs, had spread fairly widely izenship. But by the early 20th century, there were thousands of Senegalese and hundreds of Vietnamese and Tunisians who could carry French passports, vote in French elections, and even run for seats in the French parliament. Other European colonial powers adopted either the British or the French approach to education and its aims. The Dutch and the Germans followed the British pattern, whereas the Portuguese pushed assimilation for even smaller numbers of the elite classes among the peoples they colonized.

Western education in the colonies succeeded in producing clerks and railway conductors, brown Indian gentlemen, and black French citizens. It also had effects that those who shaped colonial educational policy did not intend, effects that within a generation or two would produce major challenges to European colonial dominance. The population of most colonized areas was divided into many different ethnic, religious, and language groups with separate histories and identities. Western-language schools gave the sons (and, in limited instances, the daughters) of the leading families a common language in which to communicate. The schools also spread common attitudes and ideas and gave the members of diverse groups a common body of knowledge. In all European colonial societies, Western education led to similar occupational opportunities: in government service, with Western business firms, or as professionals (e.g., lawyers, doctors, journalists). Thus, within a generation after their introduction, Western-language schools had created a new middle class in the colonies that had no counterpart in precolonial African or Asian societies.

Occupying social strata and economic niches in the middle range between the European colonizers and the old aristocracy on one hand and the peasantry and urban laborers on the other, Western-educated Africans and Asians became increasingly aware of the interests and grievances they had in common. They often found themselves at odds with the traditional rulers or the landed gentry, who, ironically, were often their fathers or grandfathers. Members of the new middle class also felt alienated from the peasantry, whose beliefs and way of life were so different from those they had learned in Western-language schools.

For more than a generation they clung to their European tutors and employers. Eventually, however, they grew increasingly resentful of their lower salaries and of European competition for scarce jobs. They were also angered by their social segregation from the Europeans, which intensified in the heightened racist atmosphere of the late 19th century. European officials and business managers often made little effort to disguise their contempt for even the most accomplished Western-educated Africans and Asians. Thus, members of the new middle class in the colonies were caught between two worlds: the traditional ways and teachings of their fathers and the modern world of their European masters. Finding that they would be fully admitted to neither world, they rejected the first and set about supplanting the Europeans and building their own versions of the second, or modern, world.

QUESTIONS Why did the Europeans continue to provide Western-language education for Africans and Asians once it was clear they were creating a class that might challenge their position of dominance? What advantages did Western-educated Africans and Asians have as future leaders of resistance to the European colonial overlords? Do you think the European colonial rule would have lasted longer if Western-language education had been denied to colonized peoples?

among upper-caste Hindu groups by the era of the Muslim invasions in the 11th and 12th centuries. In fact, the wives of proud warrior peoples, such as the Rajputs, had been encouraged to commit mass suicide rather than risk dishonoring their husbands by being captured and molested by Muslim invaders. By the early 19th century, some brahman castes and even lower-caste groups in limited areas had adopted the practice of sati.

In the 1830s, bolstered by the strong support and active cooperation of Western-educated Indian leaders, such as **Ram Mohun Roy,** the British outlawed sati. One confrontation between the British and those affected by their efforts to prevent widow burnings illustrates the confidence of the reformers in the righteousness of their cause and the sense of moral and social superiority over the Indians that the British felt in this era. A group of brahmans complained to a British official, Charles Napier, that his refusal to allow them to burn the widow of a prominent leader of their community was a violation of their social customs. Napier replied,

> The burning of widows is your custom. Prepare the funeral pyre. But my nation also has a custom. When men burn women alive, we hang them and confiscate all their property. My carpenters shall therefore erect gibbets on which to hang all concerned when the widow is consumed. Let us all act according to our national customs.

The range and magnitude of the reforms the British enacted in India in the early 19th century marked a watershed in global history. During these years, the alien British, who had become the rulers of one of the oldest centers of civilization, consciously began to transmit the ideas, inventions,

Roy, Ram Mohun Western-educated Indian leader, early 19th century; cooperated with British to outlaw sati.

modes of organization, and technology associated with western Europe's scientific and industrial revolutions to the peoples of the non-Western world. English education, social reforms, railways, and telegraph lines were only part of a larger project by which the British tried to remake Indian society along Western lines. India's crop lands were measured and registered, its forests were set aside for "scientific" management, and its people were drawn more and more into the European-dominated global market economy. British officials promoted policies that they believed would teach the Indian peasantry the merits of thrift and hard work. British educators lectured the children of India's rising middle classes on the importance of emulating their European masters in matters as diverse as being punctual, exercising their bodies, and mastering the literature and scientific learning of the West. Ironically, the very values and ideals that the British preached so earnestly to the Indians would soon be turned against colonizers by those leading India's struggle for independence from Western political domination.

Industrial Rivalries and the Partition of the World, 1870–1914

The spread of the Industrial Revolution from the British Isles resulted in ever higher levels of European and American involvement in the outside world. Beginning in the 1870s, the Europeans indulged in an orgy of overseas conquests that reduced much of the rest of the world to colonial possessions by the time of the outbreak of World War I in 1914.

Criticism of British Free Trade Policy
IMAGE

Imperialism in African (1880s)
DOCUMENT

Stanley and Kingsley in Africa
CASE STUDY

Although science and industry gave the Europeans power over the rest of the world, they also heightened economic competition and political rivalries between the European powers. In the first half of the 19th century, industrial Britain, with its seemingly insurmountable naval superiority, was left alone to dominate overseas trade and empire building. By the last decades of the century, Belgium, France, and especially Germany and the United States, were challenging Britain's industrial supremacy; they were also actively building (or in the case of France, adding to) colonial empires of their own. Many of the political leaders of these expansive nations saw colonies as essential to states that aspired to status as great powers. Colonies, particularly those in Africa and India, were also seen as insurance against raw material shortages and the loss of overseas market outlets to European or North American rivals.

Thus, the concerns of Europe's political leaders were both political and economic. The late 19th century was a period of recurring economic depressions in Europe and the United States. The leaders of the newly industrialized nations had little experience in handling the overproduction and unemployment that came with each of these economic crises. They were deeply concerned about the social unrest and, in some cases, what appeared to be stirrings of revolution that each phase of depression created. Some political theorists argued that as destinations to which unemployed workers might migrate, particularly white settlement colonies, such as Australia, and as potential markets for surplus goods, colonies could serve as safety valves to release the pressure built up in times of industrial slumps.

In the era of the scramble for colonial possessions, political leaders in Europe played a much more prominent role in decisions to annex overseas territories than they had earlier, even in the first half of the 19th century. In part, this was because of improved communications. Telegraphs and railways made it possible to transmit orders much more rapidly from the capitals of Europe to their representatives in the tropics. But more than politicians were involved in late 19th-century decisions to add to the colonial empires. The development of mass journalism and the extension of the vote to the lower middle and working classes in industrial Europe and the United States made public opinion a major factor in foreign policy. Although stalwart explorers might on their own initiative make treaties with local African or Asian potentates who assigned their lands to France or Germany, these annexations had to be ratified by the home government. In most cases, ratification meant fierce parliamentary debates, which often spilled over into press wars and popular demonstrations. Empires had become the property and pride of the nations of Europe and North America.

Unequal Combat: Colonial Wars and the Apex of European Imperialism

Industrial change not only justified the Europeans' grab for colonial possessions but made them much easier to acquire. By the late 19th century, scientific discoveries and technological innovations had catapulted the Europeans far ahead of all other peoples in the capacity to wage war. The Europeans could tap mineral resources that most peoples did not even know existed, and European chemists mixed ever more deadly explosives. Advances in metallurgy made possible the mass production of light, mobile artillery pieces that rendered suicidal the massed cavalry or infantry charges that were the mainstay of Asian and African armies. Advances in artillery were matched by great improvements in hand arms. Much more accurate and faster firing, breech-loading rifles replaced the clumsy muzzle-loading muskets of the first phase of empire building. By the 1880s, after decades of experimentation, the machine gun had become an effective battlefield weapon. Railroads gave the Europeans the mobility of the swiftest African or Asian cavalry and the ability to supply large armies in the field for extended periods of time. On the sea Europe's already formidable advantages (amply illustrated in Figure 24.4) were increased by industrial transformations. After the opening of the Suez Canal in 1869, steam power supplanted the sail, iron hulls replaced wood, and massive guns, capable of hitting enemy vessels miles away, were introduced into the fleets of the great powers.

The dazzling array of new weaponry with which the Europeans set out on their expeditions to the Indian frontiers or the African bush made the wars of colonial conquest very lopsided. This was particularly true when the Europeans encountered resistance from peoples such as those in the interior of Africa or the Pacific islands (Maps 24.4 and 24.5). These areas had been cut off from most preindustrial advances in technology, and thus their peoples were forced to fight European machine guns with spears, arrows, and leather shields. One African leader, whose followers struggled with little hope to halt the German advance into east Africa, resorted to natural imagery to account for the power of the invaders' weapons:

> On Monday we heard a shuddering like Leviathan, the voice of many cannon; we heard the roar like waves on the rocks and rumble like thunder in the rains. We heard a crashing like elephants or monsters and our hearts melted at the number of shells. We knew that we were hearing the battle of Pangani; the guns were like a hurricane in our ears.

Not even peoples with advanced preindustrial technology and sophisticated military organization, such as the Chinese and the Vietnamese, could stand against, or really comprehend, the fearful

Figure 24.4 This striking painting captures the sleek majesty of the warships that were central to British success in building a global empire. Here the *Prince of Wales* puts ashore British soldiers in Bengal in the northeast of Britain's Indian empire.

Map 24.4 The Partition of Africa Between c. 1870 and 1914 As reflected in the patchwork that partition made of the continent, no area of the globe saw more intense rivalries between the European powers than Africa in the mid and especially late-19th century.

killing devices of the Europeans. In advising the Vietnamese emperor to give in to European demands, one of his officials, who had led the fight against the French invaders, warned, "Nobody can resist them. They go where they choose. . . . Under heaven, everything is feasible to them, save only the matter of life and death."

Despite the odds against them, African and Asian peoples often fiercely resisted the imposition of colonial rule. West African leaders, such as Samory and Ahmadou Sekou, held back the European advance for decades. When rulers such as the Vietnamese emperors refused to fight, local officials organized guerrilla resistance in defense of the indigenous regime. Martial peoples such as the Zulus in South Africa had the courage and discipline to face and defeat sizeable British forces in conventional battles such as that at **Isandhlwana** in 1879 (described in the chapter opener and shown in Figure 24.1). But conventional resistance eventually ended in defeat. The guerrilla bands in Vietnam were eventually run to the ground. And, as we have seen, even at Isandhlwana, many more Zulu warriors lost their lives than the British or their African allies, and the Zulu kingdom soon fell under British control. Given European advantages in conventional battles, guerrilla resistance, sabotage, and in some cases banditry proved the most effective means of fighting the Europeans' attempts to assert political control. Religious leaders were often in the forefront of these struggles, which occurred across the globe, from the revivalist Ghost Dance religion in the late 19th-century American West to the Maji Maji uprisings in German East Africa in 1907 and the Boxer Rebellion in China in 1898. The magic potions and divine assistance they offered to protect their followers seemed to be the only way to offset the demoralizing killing power of the Europeans' weapons.

Isandhlwana Location of battle fought in 1879 between the British and Zulu armies in south Africa; resulted in defeat of British; one of few victories of African forces over western Europeans.

tropical dependencies The greater portion of the European empires consisting of Africa, Asia, and the South Pacific where small numbers of Europeans ruled large populations of non-Western peoples.

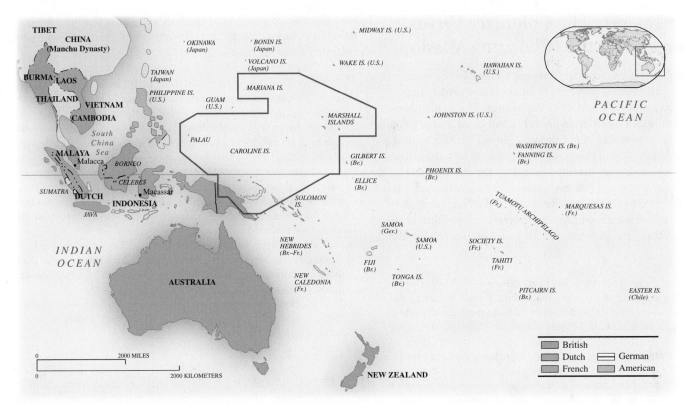

Map 24.5 The Partition of Southeast Asia and the Pacific to 1914   Though a number of industrial powers, including the United States, expanded into the islands of the Pacific over the course of the 19th century, the colonial possessions were smaller and of less economic value.

Patterns of Dominance: Continuity and Change

By the end of the 19th century, the European colonial order was made up of two different kinds of colonies. The greater portion of the European empires consisted of the so-called **tropical dependencies** in Africa, Asia, and the South Pacific. In these colonies, small numbers of Europeans ruled large populations of non-Western peoples. The tropical dependencies were a vast extension of the pattern of dominance the British, Dutch, and French had worked out earlier in India, Java, and African enclaves such as Senegal. Most of these colonies had been brought, often quite suddenly, under European rule in the late 19th and early 20th century.

Settlement colonies were the second major type of European overseas possession, but within this type there were different patterns of European occupation and indigenous response. One pattern was exhibited by colonies such as Canada and Australia, which the British labeled the **White Dominions** and are discussed in Chapter 23. These white settler colonies accounted for a good portion of the land area but only a tiny minority of the population of Britain's global empire. In these areas, as well as in some parts of Latin America, such as Chile and Argentina (see Chapter 25), descendants of European settlers made up most of the population in colonies in which small numbers of native inhabitants had been decimated by diseases and wars of conquest. These patterns of European settlement and the sharp decline of the indigenous population were also found in the portions of North America that came to form the United States, which had won its independence in the late 18th century.

In some of the areas where large numbers of Europeans had migrated, a second major variation on the settlement colony developed. Both in regions that had been colonized as early as North America, such as South Africa, and in most of the areas Europeans and Americans had begun to occupy only in 19th century, including Algeria, Kenya and Hawaii, key characteristics of tropical

The Europeans' sense of their own uniqueness and superiority, heightened by their unparalleled scientific and technological achievements, led them to seek to transform the lands and peoples they controlled. The demand for Western learning on the part of the elite and middle classes of colonized peoples in Africa and Asia rose sharply, eventually creating a counterforce to European domination.

settlement colonies   Areas, such as North America and Australia, that were both conquered by European invaders and settled by large numbers of European migrants who made the colonized areas their permanent home and dispersed and decimated the indigenous inhabitants.

White Dominions   Colonies in which European settlers made up the overwhelming majority of the population; small numbers of native inhabitants were typically reduced by disease and wars of conquest; typical of British holdings in North America and Australia with growing independence in the 19th century.

Contrary Images: The Colonizer Versus the Colonized on the "Civilizing Mission"

Each of the following passages from novels written in the colonial era expresses a different view of the reasons behind European colonization in Africa and Asia and its consequences. The first is taken from an adventure story written by John Buchan titled *Prester John,* a favorite in the pre–World War I decades among English schoolboys, many of whom would go out as young men to be administrators in the colonies. Davie, the protagonist in the story, is a "tall, square-set lad . . . renowned [for his] prowess at Rugby football." In the novel, Davie summarizes key elements of the "civilizing mission" credo by which so many European thinkers and political leaders tried to justify their colonization of most of the rest of the world.

> I knew then [after his struggle to thwart a "native" uprising in South Africa] the meaning of the white man's duty. He has to take all the risks, reck[on]ing nothing of his life or his fortunes and well content to find his reward in the fulfillment of his task. That is the difference between white and black, the gift of responsibility, the power of being in a little way a king; and so long as we know this and practise it, we will rule not in Africa alone but wherever there are dark men who live only for the day and their own bellies. Moreover the work made me pitiful and kindly. I learned much of the untold grievances of the natives and saw something of their strange, twisted reasoning.

The second passage is taken from René Maran's *Batouala,* which was first published in 1921 just after World War I. Though a French colonial official in west Africa, Maran was an African American, born in Martinique, who was highly sensitive to the plight of the colonized in Africa. Here his protagonist, a local African leader named Batouala, complains of the burdens rather than the benefits of colonial rule and mocks the self-important European agents of the vaunted civilizing mission.

> But what good does it do to talk about it? It's nothing new to us that men of white skin are more delicate than men of black skin. One example of a thousand possible. Everyone knows that the whites, saying that they are "collecting taxes," force all blacks of a marriageable age to carry voluminous packages from when the sun rises to when it sets.
>
> These trips last two, three, five days. Little matter to them the weight of these packages which are called "sandoukous." They don't sink under the burden. Rain, sun, cold? They don't suffer. So they pay no attention. And long live the worst weather, provided the whites are sheltered.
>
> Whites fret about mosquito bites. . . . They fear mason bees. They are also afraid of the "prankongo," the scorpion who lives, black and venomous, among decaying roofs, under rubble, or in the midst of debris.
>
> In a word, everything worries them. As if a man worthy of the name would worry about everything which lives, crawls, or moves around him.

QUESTIONS What sorts of roles does Davie assume that the Europeans must play in the colonies? What benefits accrue to colonized peoples from their rule? What impression does he convey of the thinking and behavior of the colonized peoples? In what ways do Batouala's views of the Europeans conflict with Davie's assumptions about himself and other colonizers? Does Batouala agree with Davie's conviction that colonial rule is beneficial for the Africans?

---

dependencies and the white settlement colonies were combined. Temperate climates and mild disease environments in these areas made it possible for tens or hundreds of thousands of Europeans to settle permanently. Despite the Europeans' arrival, large indigenous populations survived and then began to increase rapidly. As a result, in these settlement colonies, which had been brought under colonial rule for the most part in the age of industrialization, Europeans and indigenous peoples increasingly clashed over land rights, resource control, social status, and cultural differences.

Colonial Regimes and Social Hierarchies in the Tropical Dependencies

European Powers in Southeast Asia MAP

As the Europeans imposed their rule over tens of millions of additional Africans and Asians in the late 19th century, they drew heavily on precedents set in older colonies, particularly India, in establishing administrative, legal, and educational systems. As in India (or in Java and Senegal), the Europeans exploited long-standing ethnic and cultural divisions between the peoples of their new African or Asian colonies to put down resistance and maintain control. In west and east Africa in particular, they used the peoples who followed animistic religions (those that focused on nature or ancestral spirits) or who had converted to Christianity against the Muslim communities that existed in most colonies. In official reports and censuses, colonial administrators exacerbated existing ethnic differences by dividing the peoples in each colony into "tribes." The label itself, with its connotations of primitiveness and backwardness, says a great deal about general European attitudes toward the peoples of sub-Saharan Africa. In southeast Asia, the colonizers attempted to use hill-dwelling "tribal" minorities against the majority populations that lived in the lowlands. In each colonial area, favored minorities, often Christians, were recruited into the civil service and police.

As had been the case in India, Java, and Senegal, small numbers of Europeans lived mainly in the capital city and major provincial towns. From these urban centers they oversaw the administration of the African and Asian colonies, which was actually carried out at the local level mainly by hundreds or thousands of African and Asian subordinates. Some of these subordinates, normally those in positions of the greatest authority, were Western educated. But most were recruited from indigenous elite groups, including village leaders, local notables, and regional lords (Figure 24.5). In Burma, Malaya, and east Africa, thousands of Indian administrators and soldiers helped the British to rule new additions to their empire.

In contrast to Java and India, where schools were heavily state supported, Western-language education in Africa was left largely to Protestant and Catholic missionaries. As a result of deep-seated racial prejudices held by nearly all the colonizers, higher education was not promoted in Africa. As a result, college graduates were few in Africa compared with India, the Dutch East Indies, or even smaller Asian colonies such as Burma and Vietnam. This policy

Figure 24.5 The importance of co-opting African and Asian rulers and elite social groups for European building is vividly illustrated by this 1861 painting of Queen Victoria and her consort Albert presenting a Bible to an African "chief" decked out in what Victorians imagined was dress attire for such a personage.

stunted the growth of a middle class in black Africa, a consequence that European colonial officials increasingly intended. As nationalist agitation spread among the Western-educated classes in India and other Asian colonies, colonial policymakers warned against the dangers posed by college graduates. According to this argument, those with advanced educations among the colonized aspired to jobs that were beyond their capacity and were disgruntled when they could not find employment.

Changing Social Relations Among Colonizers and Colonized

In both long-held and newly acquired colonies, the growing tensions between the colonizers and the rising African and Asian middle classes reflected a larger shift in European social interaction with the colonized peoples. This shift had actually begun long before the scramble for colonies in the late 19th century. Its causes are complex, but the growing size and changing makeup of European communities in the colonies were critical factors. As more and more Europeans went to the colonies, they tended to keep to themselves on social occasions rather than mixing with the "natives." New medicines and increasingly segregated living quarters made it possible to bring to the colonies the wives and families of government officials and European military officers (but not of the rank and file until well into the 20th century). Wives and families further closed the social circle of the colonized, and European women looked disapprovingly on liaisons between European men and Asian or African women. Brothels were off limits for upper-class officials and officers, and mixed marriages or living arrangements met with more and more vocal disapproval within the constricted world of the colonial communities and back home in Europe. The growing numbers of missionaries and pastors for European congregations in the colonies obviously strengthened these taboos.

Historians of colonialism once put much of the blame on European women for the growing social gap between colonizers and colonized. But recent research has shown that male officials bore much of the responsibility. They established laws restricting or prohibiting miscegenation and other sorts of interracial liaisons. They also pushed for housing arrangements and police practices designed specifically to keep social contacts between European women and the colonized at a minimum. These measures locked European women in the colonies into an almost exclusively European world. They had many "native" servants and "native" nannies for their children. But they rarely

"The White Man's Burden" Across Two Centuries

white racial supremacy Belief in the inherent mental, moral, and cultural superiority of whites; peaked in acceptance in decades before World War I; supported by social science doctrines of social Darwinists such as Herbert Spencer.

came into contact with men or women of their own social standing from the colonized peoples. When they did, the occasions were highly public and strictly formal.

The trend toward social exclusion on the part of Europeans in the colonies and their open disdain for the culture of colonized peoples were reinforced by notions of **white racial supremacy,** which peaked in acceptance in the decades before World War I. It was widely believed that the mental and moral superiority of whites over the rest of humankind, usually divided into racial types according to the crude criterion of skin color, had been demonstrated by what were then thought to be scientific experiments. Because the non-Europeans' supposedly inferior intelligence and weak sense of morality were seen as inherent and permanent, there seemed to be little motivation for Europeans to socialize with the colonized.

There were also new reasons to fight the earlier tendency to adopt elements of the culture and lifestyle of subject peoples. As photos from the late 19th century reveal, stiff collars and ties for men and corsets and long skirts for women became obligatory for respectable colonial functionaries and their wives. The colonizers' houses were filled with the overstuffed furniture and bric-a-brac that the late Victorians loved so dearly. European social life in the colonies revolved around the infamous clubs, where the only "natives" allowed were the servants. In the heat of the summer, most of the administrators and nearly all of the colonizers' families retreated to hill stations, where the cool air and quaint architecture made it seem almost as if they were home again, or at least in a Swiss mountain resort.

Shifts in Methods of Economic Extraction

The relationship between the colonizers and the mass of the colonized remained much as it had been before. District officers, with the help of many "native" subordinates, continued to do their paternal duty to settle disputes between peasant villagers, punish criminals, and collect taxes. European planters and merchants still relied on African or Asian overseers and brokers to manage laborers and purchase crops and handicraft manufactures. But late 19th-century colonial bureaucrats and managers tried to instruct African and Asian peasants in scientific farming techniques and to compel the colonized peoples more generally to work harder and more efficiently. These efforts involved an important extension of dependant status in the Western-dominated world economy.

A wide range of incentives was devised to expand export production. Some of them benefited the colonized peoples, such as cheap consumer goods that could be purchased with cash earned by producing marketable crops or working on European plantations. In many instances, however, colonized peoples were simply forced to produce, for little or no pay, the crops or raw materials that the Europeans wanted. Head and hut taxes were imposed that could be paid only in ivory, palm nuts, or wages earned working on European estates. Under the worst of these forced-labor schemes, such as those inflicted on the peoples of the Belgian Congo in the late 19th century, villagers were flogged and killed if they failed to meet production quotas, and women and children were held hostage to ensure that the men would deliver the products demanded on time (Figure 24.6).

As increasing numbers of the colonized peoples were involved in the production of crops or minerals intended for export markets, the economies of most of Africa, India, and southeast Asia were reorganized to serve the needs of the industrializing European economies. Roads and railways were built primarily to move farm produce and raw materials from the interior of colonized areas to port centers from which they could be shipped to Europe. Benefiting from Europe's technological advances, mining sectors grew dramatically in most of the colonies. Vast areas that had previously been uncultivated or (more commonly) had been planted in food crops were converted to the production of commodities such as cocoa, palm oil, rubber, and hemp that were in great demand in the markets of Europe and, increasingly, the United States.

IN THE RUBBER COILS.

Figure 24.6 As this political cartoon of a vicious snake with Leopold II's head squeezing the life out of a defenseless African villager illustrates, an international campaign developed in the 1890s in opposition to the brutal forced-labor regime in what had become the Belgian king's personal fiefdom in the Congo after 1885. The much publicized scandal compelled the Belgian government to take over the administration of the colony in 1906.

Capitalism and Colonialism

In the century since the European powers divided up much of Africa, Asia, and the Pacific into their colonial fiefdoms, historians have often debated how much this process had to do with capitalism. They have also debated, perhaps even more intensely, over how much economic benefit the European colonial powers and the United States were able to garner from their colonies. The table shown here compares Great Britain, the premier industrialized colonial power, with Germany, Europe, the United States, and key areas of the British Empire. For each Western society and colonized area, various indices of the amount or intensity of economic interaction are indicated. A careful examination of each set of statistics and a comparison among them should enable you to answer the questions that follow on the connections between capitalism and colonialism.

QUESTIONS To which areas did the bulk of British foreign investment flow? With which areas did the British have the highest volume of trade? On which was it the most dependent for outlets for its manufactured goods? On which was it the most dependent for raw materials Do these patterns suggest that colonized areas were more or less important than independent nations; great power rivals, such as Germany and the United States; or settler colonies, such as Canada and Australia?

British Investment Abroad on the Eve of the First World War (1913)

Circa 1913	% of Total British Investment	% of Total British Imports	Main Products Exported to GB	% of Total British Exports	Main Products Imported fr. GB
Germany	0.17	8.98	Manufactures	9.82	Manufactures, Foodstuffs
Rest of Europe	5.64	27	Foodstuffs, Manufactures	30	Textiles, Machinery Manufactures
"White" Dominions (ANZAC)	24.75	10.93	Wool, Foodstuffs, Ores, Textiles	12.28	Machinery, Textiles Foodstuffs
United States of America	20.05	16.95	Manufactures, Foodstuffs	9.37	Manufactures
India (may include Ceylon)	10.07	6.30	Cotton, Jute, Narcotics, Tea, Other Comestibles	11.29	Machinery Coal, Comestibles
Egypt	1.29	0.74	Cotton	1.25	Manufactures, Textiles, Coal
West Africa	0.99		Foodstuffs, Plant Oils, Ores, Timber		Manufactures, Textiles, Machinery
South Africa	9.84	1.60	Diamonds, Gold, Wool, Other Ores	3.79	Machinery, Textiles, Consumer Products

The profits from the precious metals and minerals extracted from Africa's mines or the rubber grown in Malaya went mainly to European merchants and industrialists. The raw materials themselves were shipped to Europe to be processed and sold or used to make industrial products. The finished products were intended mainly for European consumers. The African and Asian laborers who produced these products were generally poorly paid, if they were paid at all. The laborers and colonial economies as a whole were steadily reduced to dependence on the European-dominated global market. Thus, economic dependence complemented the political subjugation and social subordination of colonized African and Asian peoples in a world order loaded in favor of the expansionist nations of western Europe.

White Settler Colonies in South Africa and the Pacific

The settlement colonies where large numbers of Europeans migrated intending to make permanent homes exhibited many of the patterns of political control and economic exploitation found in the tropical dependencies. But the presence of substantial numbers of European settlers *and* indigenous peoples considerably altered the dynamic of political and social domination in this type of colony in comparison with societies like India or the Belgian Congo, where settlers were few and overwhelmingly outnumbered by colonized peoples.

From Algeria to Argentina, settler colonies varied widely. But those settled in the 19th century, with the exception of Australia, tended to be quite different from those occupied in North and South America in the early centuries of European overseas expansion. In these early settler colonies, which included areas that eventually formed the nations of Canada, the United States, Argentina, and Chile, conquest and especially diseases transmitted unwittingly by incoming European migrants had devastating effects on the indigenous peoples, whose numbers in most of these regions were sparse to begin with. By the end of the 19th century in all of these areas, including Australia, which had been settled late but very thinly peopled when the Europeans arrived, the surviving indigenous peoples had been displaced to the margins both geographically and socially. As discussed in Chapter 23, several of these older settler societies—and particularly the United States, Canada, and Australia—imported so many people, institutions, and beliefs from Europe that they now became a part of Western history.

In most of the settler colonies established in the 19th century, the indigenous peoples were both numerous when the Europeans arrived and, in north and sub-Saharan Africa at least, largely resistant to the diseases the colonizers carried with them. Even Pacific islands, such as New Zealand and Hawaii, which had been largely isolated until their first sustained contacts with the Europeans in the late-18th century, were quite densely populated by peoples who were able over time to build up immunities to the diseases the Europeans transmitted. As a result, the history of the newer settler colonies that were formed as the result of large-scale migrations from industrializing societies has been dominated by enduring competition and varying degrees of conflict between European settlers and indigenous peoples. As these divisions were hardened by ethnic, racial, and national identities, settlers also clashed with local representatives of the European powers. In many instances the settlers sought to gain independence from meddling missionaries and transient colonial officials by force.

South Africa

South Africa   MAP

The initial Dutch colony at Cape Town was established to provide a way station where Dutch merchant ships could take on water and fresh food in the middle of their long journey from Europe to the East Indies. The small community of Dutch settlers stayed near the coast for decades after their arrival. But the Boers (or farmers), as the descendants of the Dutch immigrants in South Africa came to be called (see Chapters 16 and 20), eventually began to move into the vast interior regions of the continent. There they found a temperate climate in which they could grow the crops and raise the livestock they were accustomed to in Europe. Equally important, they encountered a disease environment they could withstand.

Like their counterparts in North America and Australia, the Boers found the areas into which they moved in this early period of colonization sparsely populated. Boer farmers and cattle ranchers enslaved the indigenous peoples, the *Khoikhoi* and the *San,* while integrating them into their large frontier homesteads. Extensive miscegenation between the Boers and Khoikhoi produced the sizeable "colored" population that exists in South Africa today. The coloreds have historically been seen as distinct from the black African majority.

The arrival of the British overlords in South Africa in the early 19th century made for major changes in the interaction between the Boers and the indigenous peoples and transformed the nature of the settlement colony in the region. The British captured Cape Town during the wars precipitated by the French Revolution in the 1790s, when Holland was overrun by France, thus making its colonies subject to British attack. The British held the colony during the Napoleonic conflicts that followed, and they annexed it permanently in 1815 as a vital sea link to their prize colony, India. Made up mainly of people of Dutch and French Protestant descent, the Boer community differed from the British newcomers in almost every way possible. The Boers spoke a different language, and they lived mostly in isolated rural homesteads that had missed the scientific, industrial, and urban revolutions that transformed British society and attitudes. Most critically, the evangelical missionaries who entered South Africa under the protection of the new British overlords were deeply committed to eradicating slavery. They made no exception for the domestic pattern of en-slavement that had developed in Boer homesteads and communities. By the 1830s, missionary pres-sure and increasing British interference in their lives drove a handful of Boers to open but futile rebellion, and many of the remaining Boers fled the Cape Colony.

In the decades of the Great Trek that followed, tens of thousands of Boers migrated in covered wagons pulled by oxen, first east across the Great Fish River and then over the mountains into the veld—the rolling grassy plains that make up much of the South African interior. In these areas, the Boers collided head-on with populous, militarily powerful, and well organized African states built by Bantu peoples such as the Zulus and the Xhosa. The ever multiplying contacts that resulted transformed the settler society in South Africa from one where the indigenous peoples were margin-alized, typical of those founded in the early centuries of expansion, into a deeply contested colonial realm akin to those established in the age of industrialization. Throughout the mid-19th century, the migrating Boers clashed again and again with Bantu peoples, who were determined to resist the seizure of the lands where they pastured their great herds of cattle and grew subsistence foods.

The British followed the Boer pioneers along the southern and eastern coast, eventually es-tablishing a second major outpost at Durban in **Natal**, (see Map 24.4). Tensions between the Boers and Britain remained high, but the imperial overlords were often drawn into frontier wars against the Bantu peoples, even though they were not always formally allied to the Boers.

In the early 1850s, the hard-liners among the Boers established two **Boer Republics** in the in-terior, named the Orange Free State and the Transvaal, which they tried to keep free of British influ-ence. For more than a decade, the Boers managed to keep the British out of their affairs. But when diamonds were discovered in the Orange Free State in 1867, British entrepreneurs, including most famously **Cecil Rhodes,** and prospectors began to move in, and tensions between the Boers and the British began to build anew. In 1880–1881, these tensions led to a brief war in which the Boers were victorious. But the tide of British immigration into the republics rose even higher after gold was discovered in the Transvaal in 1885.

Although the British had pretty much left the Boers to deal as they pleased with the African peoples who lived in the republics, British miners and financiers grew more and more resentful of Boer efforts to limit their numbers and curb their civil rights. British efforts to protect these inter-lopers and bring the feisty and independent Boers into line led to the republics' declaration of war against the British in late 1899. Boer assaults against British bases in Natal, the Cape Colony, and elsewhere initiated the **Anglo-Boer War** (1899–1902) that the British ultimately won but only at a very high cost in both lives and resources. British guilt over their brutal treatment of the Boers—men, women, and children—during the war also opened the way for the dominance of this settler minority over the black African majority that would prove to be the source of so much misery and violence in South African history through most of the 20th century.

Pacific Tragedies

The territories the Europeans, Americans, and Japanese claimed throughout the South Pacific in the 19th century were in some cases outposts of true empire and in others contested settler colonies. In both situations, however, the coming of colonial rule resulted in demographic disasters and social disruptions of a magnitude that had not been seen since the first century of European expansion into the Americas. Like the Native American peoples of the New World, the peoples of the South Pacific had long lived in isolation. This meant that, like the Native Americans, they had no immuni-ties to many of the diseases European explorers and later merchants, missionaries, and settlers car-ried to their island homes from the 1760s onward. In addition, their cultures were extremely vulnerable to the corrosive effects of outside influences, such as new religions, different sexual mores, more lethal weapons, and sudden influxes of cheap consumer goods. Thus, whatever the in-tentions of the incoming Europeans and Americans—and they were by no means always benevo-lent—their contacts with the peoples of the Pacific islands almost invariably ushered in periods of social disintegration and widespread human suffering.

Of the many cases of contact between the expansive peoples of the West and the long-isolated island cultures of the South Pacific, the confrontations in New Zealand and Hawaii are among the most informative. As we have seen, sophisticated cultures and fairly complex societies had devel-

Natal   British colony in south Africa; developed after Boer trek north from Cape Colony; major commercial outpost at Durban.

Cecil Rhodes Astride Africa

The Boer War and Queen Victoria—Dutch Caricature

Boer Republics   Transvaal and Orange Free State in southern Africa; established to assert independ-ence of Boers from British colonial government in Cape Colony in 1850s; discovery of diamonds and precious metals caused British migration into the Boer areas in 1860s.

Rhodes, Cecil   British entrepreneur in south Africa around 1900; manipulated political situation in south Africa to gain entry to resources of Boer republics; encouraged Boer War as means of de-stroying Boer independence.

Anglo-Boer War   Fought between 1899 and 1902 over the continued independence of Boer republics; resulted in British victory, but began the process of decolonization for whites in South Africa.

oped in each of these areas. In addition, at the time of the European explorers' arrivals, the two is-land groups contained some of the largest population concentrations in the whole Pacific region. Both areas were subjected to European influences carried by a variety of agents, from whalers and merchants to missionaries and colonial administrators. With the great expansion of European set-tlement after the first decades of contact, the peoples of New Zealand and Hawaii experienced a pe-riod of crisis so severe that their continued survival was in doubt. In both cases, however, the threatened peoples and cultures rebounded and found enduring solutions to the challenges from overseas. Their solutions combined accommodation to outside influences, usually represented by the large numbers of European settlers living in their midst, with revivals of traditional beliefs and practices.

New Zealand The Maori of New Zealand actually went through two periods of profound disrup-tion and danger. The first began in the 1790s, when timber merchants and whalers established small settlements on the New Zealand coast. Maori living near these settlements were afflicted with alco-holism and the spread of prostitution. In addition, they traded wood and food for European firearms, which soon revolutionized Maori warfare—in part by rendering it much more deadly—and upset the existing balance between different tribal groups. Even more devastating was the im-pact of diseases, such as smallpox, tuberculosis, and even the common cold, that ravaged Maori communities throughout the north island. By the 1840s, only 80,000 to 90,000 Maori remained of a population that had been as high as 130,000 less than a century earlier. But the Maori survived these calamities and began to adjust to the imports of the foreigners. They took up farming with European implements, and they grazed cattle purchased from European traders. They cut timber, built windmills, and traded extensively with the merchants who visited their shores. Many were converted to Christianity by the missionaries, who established their first station in 1814.

The arrival of British farmers and herders in search of land in the early 1850s, and the British decision to claim the islands as part of their global empire, again plunged the Maori into misery and despair. Backed by the military clout of the colonial government, the settlers occupied some of the most fertile areas of the north island. The warlike Maori fought back, sometimes with tempo-rary successes, but they were steadily driven back into the interior of the island. In desperation, in the 1860s and 1870s they flocked to religious prophets who promised them magical charms and su-pernatural assistance in their efforts to drive out the invaders. When the prophets also failed them, the Maori seemed for a time to face extinction. In fact, some British writers predicted that within generations the Maori would die out entirely.

The Maori displayed surprising resilience. As they built up immunities to new diseases, they also learned to use European laws and political institutions to defend themselves and preserve what was left of their ancestral lands. Because the British had in effect turned the internal administration of the islands over to the settlers' representatives, the Maori's main struggle was with the invaders who had come to stay. Western schooling and a growing ability to win British colonial officials over to their point of view eventually enabled the Maori to hold their own in their ongoing legal contests and daily exchanges with the settlers. Though New Zealand was included in the White Dominions of the British Empire, it was in fact a multiracial society in which a reasonable level of European and Maori accommodation and interaction has been achieved. Over time the Maori have also been able to preserve much of value in their precontact culture.

Hawaii The conversion of Hawaii to settler colony status followed familiar basic imperialist pat-terns but with specific twists. Hawaii did not become a colony until the United States proclaimed annexation in 1898, although an overzealous British official had briefly claimed the islands for his nation in 1843. Hawaii came under increasing Western influence from the late 18th century on-ward—politically at the hands of the British, and culturally and economically from the United States, whose westward surge quickly spilled into the Pacific Ocean.

Although very occasional contact with Spanish ships during the 16th and 17th centuries probably occurred, Hawaii was effectively opened to the West through the voyages of **Captain James Cook** from 1777 to 1779 (Figure 24.7). The Cook expedition and later British visits con-vinced a young Hawaiian prince, Kamehameha, that some imitation of Western ways could produce

Cook, Captain James Made voyages to Hawaii from 1777 to 1779 resulting in opening of islands to the West; convinced Kamehameha to establish unified kingdom in the islands.

a unified kingdom under his leadership, replacing the small and warring regional units that had previously prevailed. A series of vigorous wars, backed by British weapons and advisors, won Kamehameha his kingdom between 1794 and 1810. The new king and his successors promoted economic change, encouraging Western merchants to establish export trade in Hawaiian goods in return for increasing revenues to the royal treasury.

Hawaiian royalty began to imitate Western habits, in some cases traveling to Britain and often building Western-style palaces. Two formidable queens, Keopuolani and Liliuokalani, advanced the process of change by insisting that traditional taboos subordinating women be abandoned. In this context, vigorous missionary efforts from Protestant New England, beginning in 1819, brought extensive conversions to Christianity. As with other conversion processes, religious change had wide implications. Missionaries railed against traditional Hawaiian costumes, insisting that women cover their breasts, and a

Figure 24.7 One of the most famous, but ultimately tragic, cross-cultural encounters of the late 18th century was between Captain James Cook and the crew of the ship he commanded and the peoples of Hawaii. In this painting depicting his arrival in the islands, Cook, a renowned English explorer, is welcomed enthusiastically by the Hawaiians. When Cook was later killed due to less fortunate timing and misunderstandings with the Hawaiians, he was lamented throughout Europe as one of the great lost heroes of his age.

new garment, the muumuu, was made from homespun American nightgowns with the sleeves cut off. Backed by the Hawaiian monarchy, missionaries quickly established an extensive school system, which by 1831 served 50,000 students from a culture that had not previously developed writing.

The combination of the political and social objectives of Hawaiian rulers and the demands and imports of Western settlers produced creative political and cultural changes, though usually at the expense of previous values. Demographic and economic trends had more insidious effects. Western-imported diseases, particularly sexually transmitted diseases and tuberculosis, had the usual tragic consequences for a previously isolated people. By 1850 only about 80,000 Hawaiians remained of a prior population of about half a million. Because of the Hawaiian population decline, it was necessary to import Asian workers to staff the estates. The first Chinese contract workers had been brought in before 1800; after 1868, a larger current of Japanese arrived. Westerners began to more systematically exploit the Hawaiian economy. Whalers helped create raucous seaport towns. Western settlers from various countries (called *haoles* by the Hawaiians) experimented with potential commercial crops, soon concentrating on sugar. Many missionary families, impatient with the subsistence habits of Hawaiian commoners, turned to leasing land or buying it outright. Most settlers did not entirely forget their religious motives for migrating to the islands, but many families who came to Hawaii to do good ended by doing well.

Formal colonization came as an anticlimax. The abilities of Hawaiian monarchs declined after 1872, in one case because of disease and alcoholism. Under a weakened state, powerful planter interests pressed for special treaties with the United States that would promote their sugar exports, and the American government claimed naval rights at the Pearl Harbor base by 1887. As the last Hawaiian monarchs turned increasingly to promoting culture, writing a number of lasting Hawaiian songs but also spending money on luxurious living, American planters concluded that their economic interests required outright United States control. An annexation committee persuaded American naval officers to "protect American lives and property" by posting troops around Honolulu in 1893. The Hawaiian ruler was deposed, and an imperialist-minded U.S. Congress formally took over the islands in 1898.

As in New Zealand, Western control was combined with respect for Polynesian culture. Because Hawaiians were not enslaved and soon ceased to threaten those present, Americans in Hawaii did not apply the same degree of racism found in earlier relations with African slaves or Native Americans. Hawaii's status as a settler colony was further complicated by the arrival of many Asian immigrants. Nevertheless, Western cultural and particularly economic influence extended steadily, and the ultimate political seizure merely ratified the colonization of the islands.

Platform of the American Anti-Imperialist League

Global Connections

A European-Dominated Early Phase of Globalization

The Industrial Revolution not only gave the Europeans and North Americans the motives but also provided the means for them to become the agents of the first civilization to dominate the entire world. By the end of the 19th century, the Western industrial powers had directly colonized most of Asia and Africa, and (as we shall see in Chapter 26) indirectly controlled the remaining areas through the threat of military interventions or the manipulation of local elites. Political power made it possible for the Europeans to use their already well established position in world trade to build a global economic order oriented to their industrial societies.

In many ways the first phase of globalization in the most meaningful sense of the term occurred in the four or five decades before the outbreak of World War I in 1914. The communications and commercial networks that undergirded the European colonial order made possible an unprecedented flow of foods and minerals from Africa, Asia, and Latin America to Europe and North America. Western industrial societies provided investment capital and machines to run the mines, plantations, and processing plants in colonized areas. European dominance also made it possible to extract cheap labor and administrative services from subject populations across the globe. Western culture, especially educational norms—but also manners, fashions, literary forms, and modes of entertainment—also became the first to be extensively exported to virtually all the rest of the world. No culture was strong enough to remain untouched by the European drive for global dominance in this era. None could long resist the profound changes unleashed by European conquest and colonization.

The European colonizers assumed that it was their God-given destiny to remake the world in the image of industrial Europe. But in pushing for change within colonized societies that had ancient, deeply rooted cultures and patterns of civilized life, the Europeans often aroused resistance to specific policies and to colonial rule more generally. The colonizers were able to put down protest movements led by displaced princes and religious prophets. But much more enduring and successful challenges to their rule came, ironically, from the very leaders their social reforms and Western-language schools had done so much to nurture. These Asian and African nationalists reworked European ideas and resurrected those of their own cultures. They borrowed European organizational techniques and used the communication systems and common language the Europeans had introduced into the colonies to mobilize the resistance to colonial domination that became one of the dominant themes of global history in the 20th century.

Further Readings

An analytical and thematic overview that attempts to set forth the basic patterns in different time periods is provided by David B. Abernethy, *The Dynamics of Global Dominance: European Overseas Empires 1415–1980* (2000). Useful general histories on the different empires include Bernard Porter, *The Lion's Share: A Short History of British Imperialism 1850–1970* (1975); Raymond Betts, *Tricouleur* (1978); James J. Cooke, *The New French Imperialism, 1880–1910* (1973); and Woodruff D. Smith, *The German Colonial Empire* (1978).

The best history of centuries of British involvement in South Asia is C.A. Bayly's *The Raj: India and the British, 1600-1947* (1990). For the spread of Dutch power in Java and the "outer islands," see Merle Ricklets, *A History of Modern Indonesia* (1981).

Of the many contributions to the debate over late 19th-century imperialism, some of the most essential are those by D. C. M. Platt, Hans-Ulrich Wehler, William Appleman Williams, Jean Stengers, D. K. Fieldhouse, and Henri Brunschwig, as well as the earlier works by Lenin and J. A. Hobson. Winfried Baumgart's *Imperialism* (1982) provides a good overview of the literature and conflicting arguments. Very different perspectives on the partition of Africa can be found in Jean Suret-Canale's *French Colonialism in Tropical Africa, 1900–1945* (1971) and Ronald Robinson and John Gallagher's *Africa and the Victorians* (1961).

Most of the better studies on the impact of imperialism and social life in the colonies are specialized monographs, but Percival Spear's *The Nabobs* (1963) is a superb place to start on the latter from the European viewpoint, and the works of Frantz Fanon, Albert Memmi, and O. Mannoni provide many insights into the plight of the colonized. The impact of industrialization and other changes in Europe on European attitudes toward the colonized are treated in several works, including Philip Curtin, *The Image of Africa* (1964); William B. Cohen, *The French Encounter with Africans* (1980); and Michael Adas, *Machines as the Measure of Men* (1989). The best histories of social and cultural interactions in both colonies and the metropoles in the era of high imperialism include Frances Gouda's *Dutch Culture Overseas* (1995); Bernard S. Cohn, *Colonialism and Its Forms of Knowledge: The British in India* (1996); Alice Conklin, *A Mission to Civilize: The Republican Idea of Empire in France and West Africa* (1997). For broader comparisons Scott B. Cook, *Colonial Encounters in the Age of High Imperialism* (1996).

On the Web

The Web offers sites that illuminate the causes of late 19th century imperialism, such as at http://www.fordham.edu/halsall/mod/modsbook34.html. It also provides the means to more closely examine the trends, events, and personalities involved in imperialism by region as well as nation, such as European imperialism in Africa (http://www.fordham.edu/halsall/africa/africasbook.html), American imperialism in the Philippines and in the rest of Asia (http://smplanet.com/imperialism/toc.html), German imperialism in China and Africa (http://www.h-net.org/~german/gtext/kaiserreich/china.html, http://www.cusd.chico.k12.ca.us/~bsilva/projects/imperialism/schuller.htm, and http://www.fordham.edu/

halsall/mod/1901kaiser.html) and Japanese imperialism in Korea (http://en.wikipedia.org/wiki/Korea_under_Japanese_rule).

The onset of British imperialism in India, including studies of key personalities such as Robert Clive and events such as the Battle of Plassey receives careful treatment at http://www.sscnet.ucla.edu/southasia/History/British/EAco.html. The life of Tipu Sultan, the Indian Muslim ruler who tried to defeat the British on their own terms, is examined at http://www.kamat.com/kalranga/itihas/tippu.htm. The British defeat at the hands of the Zulus at

Isandhlwana and the Zulu wars are given fulsome treatment from a leading British historian at http://en.wikipedia.org/wiki/Anglo-Zulu_War.

Resources for the study of science, technology, medicine, racial theory, gender and the economy of imperialism are offered at http://worldhistoryconnected.press.uiuc.edu/3.1/gilbert.html. A negative answer to the question, "Does Globalization mean the end of imperialism," is offered at http://flag.blackened.net/intanark/faq/secD5.html.

AP* | Test Prep

1. Britain gained a firm footing in 18th century India by
   (A) purchasing large amounts of territory directly from the Mughal empire.
   (B) intermarriage of East India Company officials into local rulers' families.
   (C) by defeating the French and their Indian allies.
   (D) by acquiring territory Portugal and Spain.

2. The most important British colonial possession in terms of prestige and economic value in the 19th and 20th centuries was
   (A) Canada.
   (B) Australia.
   (C) New Zealand.
   (D) India.

3. All of these institutions and technologies were exported from the British Isles to India through their colonial rule EXCEPT
   (A) the telegraph and railroad.
   (B) an alphabet and an advanced literate culture.
   (C) western-style education.
   (D) social reforms including an effort to abolish *sati*.

4. European-educated colonial peoples were able to undermine the European imperial order in all of the following ways EXCEPT
   (A) producing the leaders of future independence movements.
   (B) lending mass support to efforts mounted by traditional ruling elites in the colonies against the colonizers.

   (C) emigrating to the mother countries.
   (D) seeking to promote the sciences alongside traditional religious education.

5. Generally, European leaders in the late 19th century saw colonies as
   (A) wastes of money and resources.
   (B) sources for raw materials and potential markets.
   (C) sources for slaves.
   (D) sources of new technologies.

6. The most likely reason for the success of European colonial acquisitions during the 19th century was
   (A) European advances in weaponry, tropical medicine, and steam transportation.
   (B) the conversion of local peoples to Christianity that preceded European arrival.
   (C) the lack of local resistance to the Europeans.
   (D) the European ability to improve local standards of living.

7. By 1900 India and Africa differed in that
   (A) Africa was divided among several European empires.
   (B) Indians largely abandoned their traditional religions.
   (C) a more extensive railroad network developed in Africa.
   (D) European racism did not affect attitudes to India.

Free-Response Question

Analyze the political, technological and cultural policies used by Europeans to dominate much of the globe by 1900.

25 The Consolidation of Latin America, 1830–1920

From Colonies to Nations

New Nations Confront Old and New Problems

DOCUMENT: Confronting the Hispanic Heritage:
From Independence to Consolidation

Latin American Economies and World Markets, 1820–1870

Societies in Search of Themselves

THINKING HISTORICALLY: Explaining Underdevelopment

VISUALIZING THE PAST: Images of the Spanish-American War

GLOBAL CONNECTIONS: New Latin American Nations
and the World

On a rainy morning in 1867, on the Hill of Bells just outside the Mexican city of Queretaro, the handsome, erect figure of the young Austrian Archduke Maximilian stood, flanked by his loyal generals, before a Mexican firing squad. The story of his fall is a strange one. Just three years before, he and his wife, Carlota, had been sent by Carlota's grandfather, Napoleon III, to become emperor and empress of Mexico. They had replaced Benito Juárez, a reformist Mexican leader whose government had been toppled by Napoleon as a result of its refusal to pay the debts of its predecessors. Assured by Napoleon and the Conservative party of Mexico that the Mexican people enthusiastically awaited their arrival, Maximilian and Carlota believed they would bring stability to the troubled land.

Maximilian and Carlota were both well educated and well intentioned. They had tried to bring reforms to their adopted country and had even invited Juárez and other political opponents to join in the new government—an offer that was resolutely refused. In fact, Maximilian and Carlota had been gravely misled as to the attitude of the Mexican people toward their new rulers. Their authority rested on foreign bayonets, and their very presence was seen as an insult by the majority of Mexicans, who were determined to maintain the political independence they had won after a long and bitter struggle.

Juárez and Maximilian could not have been more different in most ways. Benito Juárez, the diminutive Zapotec Indian who had risen from poverty and obscurity to become Mexico's leading liberal politician, and Maximilian von Habsburg, the foreign-backed emperor who had blood ties to every royal house in Europe, represented two different visions of what Latin America should become. Their clash not only determined the fate of Mexico but also served as an example and a warning to other foreign states with imperialist designs.

Before the execution, Carlota had traveled all over Europe, pleading her husband's case, and numerous calls for clemency had reached Juárez's desk. But for the good of his country, Juárez refused to spare Maximilian, though he confided to friends that he could not bring himself to meet the man for fear that his determination on this point would waver. Maximilian died a tragic figure; his last words were "Long live Mexico, long live independence." (Figure 25.1) Carlota spent the next 60 years in seclusion. Even more tragically, by the time of Maximilian's death, hundreds of thousands of Mexicans had perished in the civil wars that had brought him to, and finally toppled him from, the throne. ■

In the late 18th century the former colonies of Spain and Portugal were swept by the same winds of change that transformed Europe's society and economy and led to the independence of the United States. Although at present Latin America is sometimes considered part of the developing world along with many Asian and African nations, in reality its political culture was formed in the 18th century by the ideas of the Western Enlightenment. To a large degree, both Juárez and Maximilian shared these liberal ideals.

In the early 19th century, the various regions of Latin America fought for their political independence and created new nations, often based on the old colonial administrative units. But what kind of nations were these to be? The form of government, the kind of society, the role of religion, and the nature of the economy all had to be defined in each of the new countries, and deep divisions over these questions and others created bitter political struggles. Then too, there was always the shadow of foreign interference—from the old colonial powers, from new imperialist regimes, and from neighbors seeking territory or economic advantage. Latin America in the 19th century was shaped both by its internal struggles over these questions and by the dominant international forces of the day.

Figure 25.1 Emperor Maximilian was finally captured after his attempt, with French help, to reestablish a monarchy in Mexico. Well-meaning, he eventually lost the support of the conservatives. Juárez refused to spare his life, as a warning to other ambitious nations that Mexico would remain independent. Manet's painting of the execution of Maximilian, shown here flanked by his two loyal generals facing the firing squad reflected Europe's shock.

(Edouard Manet (1832–1883), "The Execution of Emperor Maximilian of Mexico, June 19, 1867." Oil on canvas. Location: Staedtische Kunsthalle, Mannheim, Germany. Art Resource, NY.)

Despite their many differences, most 19th-century Latin American leaders shared with Western political figures a firm belief in the virtues of progress, reform, representational and constitutional government, and private property rights. At the same time, Latin American leaders faced problems very different from those of Europe and the United States. The colonial heritage had left little tradition of participatory government. A highly centralized colonial state had intervened in many aspects of life and had created both dependence on central authority and resentment of it. Class and regional interests deeply divided the new nations, and wealth was very unequally distributed. Finally, the rise of European industrial capitalism created an economic situation that often placed the new nations in a weak or dependent position. These problems and tensions are the focus of our examination of Latin America in the 19th century.

From Colonies to Nations

By the late 18th century, the elites of American-born whites or Creoles (*criollos*) expressed a growing self-consciousness as they began to question the policies of Spain and Portugal. At the same time, these elites were joined by the majority of the population in resenting the increasingly heavy hand of government, as demonstrated by the new taxes and administrative reforms of the 18th century. But the shared resentment was not enough to overcome class conflicts and divisions. Early movements for independence usually failed because of the reluctance of the colonial upper classes

A combination of internal developments and the Napoleonic wars set Latin American independence movements in motion.

1800 C.E.	1820 C.E.	1840 C.E.	1860 C.E.	1880 C.E.	1900 C.E.
1792 Slave rebellion in St. Domingue (Haiti)	1821 Mexico declares independence; empire under Iturbide lasts to 1823	1846–1848 Mexican-American War	1862–1867 French intervention in Mexico	1886–1888 Cuba and Brazil abolish slavery	1903 Panamanian independence; beginning of Panama
1804 Haiti declares independence	1822 Brazil declares independence; empire established under Dom Pedro I	1847–1855 Caste War in Yucatan	1865–1870 War of the Triple Alliance (Argentina, Brazil, and Uruguay against Paraguay)	1889 Fall of Brazilian Empire; republic established	Canal (opens in 1914)
1808–1825 Spanish-American wars of independence	1823 Monroe Doctrine indicates U.S. opposition to European ambitions in the Americas	1850s Beginnings of railroad construction in Cuba, Chile, and Brazil	1868–1878 Ten-year war against Spain in Cuba	1895–1898 Cuban Spanish-American War; United States acquires Puerto Rico and Philippines	
1808 Portuguese court flees Napoleon, arrives in Brazil; French armies invade Spain	1829–1852 Juan Manuel de Roses rules Rio de la Plata	1854 Benito Juárez leads reform in Mexico	1869 First school for girls in Mexico		
1810 In Mexico, Father Hidalgo initiates rebellion against Spain	1830 Bolívar dies; Gran Colombia dissolves into separate countries of Venezuela, Colombia, and Ecuador		1876–1911 Porfirio Díaz rules Mexico		

to enlist the support of the American Indian, mestizo, and mulatto masses, who, they thought, might later prove too difficult to control. The actual movements were set in motion only when events in Europe precipitated actions in America.

Causes of Political Change

Latin American political independence was achieved as part of the general Atlantic revolution of the late 18th and early 19th centuries, and Latin American leaders were moved by the same ideas as those seeking political change elsewhere in the Atlantic world. Four external events had a particularly strong impact on political thought in Latin America. The American Revolution, from 1775 to 1783, provided a model of how colonies could break with the mother country. The French Revolution of 1789 provoked great interest in Latin America, and its slogan, "liberty, equality, and fraternity," appealed to some sectors of the population. As that revolution became increasingly radical, however, it was rejected by the Creole elites, who could not support regicide, rejection of the church's authority, and the social leveling implied by the Declaration of the Rights of Man and the Citizen.

The third external event was partially an extension of the French Revolution but had its own dynamic. Torn by internal political conflict during the turmoil in France, the whites and free people of color in St. Domingue, France's great sugar colony in the Caribbean, became divided. The slaves seized the moment in 1791 to stage a general rebellion under able leadership by **Toussaint L'Overture** (TOO-san LOO-vuhr-tyuhr). Various attempts to subdue the island were defeated, and in 1804 the independent republic of Haiti was proclaimed. For Latin American elites, Haiti was an example to be avoided. It was not accidental that neighboring Cuba and Puerto Rico, whose elites had plantations and slaves and were acutely aware of events in Haiti, were among the last of Spain's colonies to gain independence. For slaves, former slaves, and free people of color throughout the Americas, however, Haiti became a symbol of freedom and hope.

What eventually precipitated the movements for independence in Latin America was the confused Iberian political situation caused by the French Revolution and its aftermath. France invaded Portugal and Spain, and a general insurrection erupted in Spain in 1808, followed by a long guerrilla war. During the fighting, a central committee, or junta central (HOON-tuh sehn-TRAHL), ruled in the Spanish king's name in opposition to Napoleon's brother, whom Napoleon had appointed king.

L'Overture, Toussaint [TOO-san LOO-vuhr-tyuhr] (1743–1803) Leader of slave rebellion on the French sugar island of St. Domingue in 1791 that led to creation of independent republic of Haiti in 1804.

Who was the legitimate ruler? By 1810 the confusion in Spain had provoked a crisis in the colonies. In places such as Caracas, Bogotá, and Mexico, local elites, pretending to be loyal to the deposed king Ferdinand, set up juntas to rule in his name, but they ruled on their own behalf. Soon the more conservative elements of the population—royal officials and those still loyal to Spain—opposed the movements for autonomy and independence. A crisis of legitimacy reverberated throughout the American colonies.

Spanish American Independence Struggles

The independence movements divided into three major theaters of operation. In Mexico, a conspiracy among leading Creoles moved one of the plotters, the priest **Father Miguel de Hidalgo** (mee-GEHL duh hih-DAL-goh), to call for help from the American Indians and mestizos of his region in 1810. He won a number of early victories but eventually lost the support of the Creoles, who feared social rebellion more than they desired independence. Hidalgo was captured and executed, but the insurgency smoldered in various parts of the country. Eventually, after 1820 when events in Spain weakened the king and the central government, conservative Creoles in Mexico were willing to move toward independence by uniting with the remnants of the insurgent forces. **Augustín de Iturbide** (AH-guhs-tehn duh ee-tur-BEE-thay), a Creole officer at the head of an army that had been sent to eliminate the insurgents, drew up an agreement with them instead, and the combined forces of independence occupied Mexico City in September 1821. Soon thereafter, with the support of the army, Iturbide was proclaimed emperor of Mexico.

This was a conservative solution. The new nation of Mexico was born as a monarchy, and little recognition was given to the social aspirations and programs of Hidalgo and his movement. Central America was briefly attached to the Mexican Empire, which collapsed in 1824. Mexico became a republic, and the Central American states, after attempting union until 1838, split apart into independent nations.

In South America and the Caribbean, the chronology of independence was a mirror image of the conquest of the 16th century. Formerly secondary areas such as Argentina and Venezuela were among the first to opt for independence and the best able to achieve it. The old colonial center in Peru and Bolivia was among the last to break with Spain. The Caribbean islands of Cuba and Puerto Rico, fearful of slave rebellion and occupied by large Spanish garrisons, remained loyal until the end of the 19th century.

In northern South America, a movement for independence centered in Caracas had begun in 1810. After early reverses, **Simon Bolívar** (see-MOHN BOH-lee-vahr), a wealthy Creole officer, emerged as the leader of the revolt against Spain (Figure 25.2). With considerable military skill and a passion for independence, he eventually mobilized support, and between 1817 and 1822 he won a series of victories in Venezuela, Colombia, and Ecuador. Until 1830, these countries were united into a new nation called **Gran Colombia**. Political differences and regional interests led to the breakup of Gran Colombia. Bolívar became disillusioned and fearful of anarchy. "America is ungovernable," he said, and "those who have served the revolution have plowed the sea." To his credit, however, Bolívar rejected all attempts to crown him as king, and he remained until his death in 1830 firmly committed to the cause of independence and republican government.

Meanwhile, in southern South America, another movement had coalesced under **José de San Martín** in the Rio de la Plata. Buenos Aires had become a booming commercial center in the late 18th century, and its residents, called *porteños,* particularly resented Spanish trade restrictions. Pushing for freedom of trade, they opted for autonomy in 1810 but tried to keep the outlying areas, such as Paraguay, under their control. The myth of autonomy rather than independence was preserved for a while. By 1816, however, the independence of the United Provinces of the Rio de la Plata had been proclaimed, although the provinces were far from united. Upper Peru (Bolivia) remained under Spanish control, Paraguay declared independence in 1813, and the Banda Oriental (Uruguay) resisted the central authority of Buenos Aires.

In Buenos Aires, San Martín had emerged as a military commander willing to speak and act for independence. From Argentina his armies crossed the Andes to Chile to help the revolutionary forces in that colony. After winning victories there, the patriot forces looked northward. Peru was still under Spanish control. Its upper class was deeply conservative and not attracted to the

Hidalgo, Father Miguel de   [mee-GEHL duh hih-DAL-goh] Mexican priest who established independence movement among American Indians and mestizos in 1810; despite early victories, was captured and executed.

Iturbide, Augustín de   [AH-guhs-tehn duh ee-tur-BEE-thay] (1783–1824) Conservative Creole officer in Mexican army who signed agreement with insurgent forces of independence; combined forces entered Mexico City in 1821; later proclaimed emperor of Mexico until its collapse in 1824.

Bolívar, Simon   [see-MOHN BOH-lee-vahr] Creole military officer in northern South America; won series of victories in Venezuela, Colombia, and Ecuador between 1817 and 1822; military success led to creation of independent state of Gran Colombia.

Simon Bolívar on Constitutional Government

The Great Liberator—Independence Leader, Caudillo, and Future President Simon Bolívar

Gran Colombia   Independent state created in South America as a result of military successes of Simon Bolívar; existed only until 1830, at which time Colombia, Venezuela, and Ecuador became separate nations.

de San Martin, Jose   (Jose de; b. 1778–d. 1850) A leader of the struggle for independence in southern South America. Born in Argentina, he served in the Spanish army but joined in the movement for independence and led the revolutionary army that crossed the Andes and helped to liberate Chile in 1817-18, later collaborating with Simon Bolivar in the liberation of Peru. As "protector of Peru" he instituted a number of liberal reforms. For political reasons he went into exile in Europe in 1823.

Figure 25.2 Simon Bolívar (1783–1830) led the struggle for political independence in northern South America. Son of a wealthy Creole family, he became an ardent proponent of independence and a firm believer in the republican form of government. On his deathbed, Bolívar asked his closest aide to burn all of his letters and other writings. Knowing how valuable these papers would be to future historians, the aide disobeyed the order.

movements for independence. San Martín's forces entered Peru, and Creole adherence was slowly won after major victories like the battle of Ayacucho in 1824, where royalist forces were defeated (Figure 25.3). By 1825 all of Spanish South America had gained its political independence. Despite various plans to create some form of monarchy in many of the new states, all of them emerged as independent republics with representative governments. The nations of Spanish America were born of the Enlightenment and the ideas of 19th-century liberalism. The wars of independence became the foundational moments of their heroic birth.

Brazilian Independence

Although the movement for independence in Brazil was roughly contemporaneous with those in Spanish America, and many of the causes were similar, independence there was achieved by a very different process. By the end of the 18th century, Brazil had grown in population and economic importance. The growth of European demand for colonial products, such as sugar, cotton, and cacao, contributed to that growth and to the increase in slave imports to the colony. Although Brazilian planters, merchants, and miners sometimes longed for more open trade and fewer taxes, they feared that any upsetting of the political system might lead to a social revolution or a Haitian-style general slave uprising. Thus, incipient movements for independence in Minas Gerais in 1788 and Bahia in 1798 were unsuccessful. As one official said, "Men established in goods and property were unwilling to risk political change."

The Napoleonic invasions provoked an outcome in Portugal different from that in Spain. When in 1807 French troops invaded Portugal, the whole Portuguese royal family and court fled the country and, under the protection of British ships, sailed to Brazil. Rio de Janeiro became the capital of the Portuguese Empire. Brazil was raised to equal status with Portugal, and all the functions of royal government were set up in the colony. As a partial concession to England and to colonial interests, the ports of Brazil were opened to world commerce, thus satisfying one of the main desires of the Brazilian elites. Unlike Spanish America, where the Napoleonic invasions provoked a crisis of authority and led Spanish Americans to consider ruling in their own name, in Brazil the transfer of the court brought royal government closer and reinforced the colonial relationship.

Figure 25.3 The battle of Maipu in April, 1818 sealed the fate of the royalist forces in Chile. Jose de San Martin led the combined Chilean and Argentine insurgent forces and their victory led to the independence of Chile. Throughout South America between 1810 and 1825 the rebel forces were slowly mobilized into effective armies, but subsequently the new nations had to confront the personal and institutional power of the former commanders.

Until 1820, the Portuguese king, Dom **João VI** (DOHM JWUN VI), lived in Brazil and ruled his empire from there. Rio de Janeiro was transformed into an imperial city with a public library, botanical gardens, and other improvements. Printing presses began to operate in the colony for the first time, schools were created, and commerce, especially with England, boomed in the newly opened ports. The arrival of many Portuguese bureaucrats and nobles with the court created jealousy and resentment, however. Still, during this period Brazil was transformed into the seat of empire, a fact not lost on its most prominent citizens.

Matters changed drastically in 1820 when, after the defeat of Napoleon in Europe and a liberal revolution in Portugal, the king was recalled and a parliament convoked. João VI, realizing that his return was inevitable, left his young son Pedro as regent, warning him that if independence had to come, he should lead the movement. Although Brazilians were allowed representation at the Portuguese parliament, it became clear that Brazil's new status was doomed and that it would be recolonized. After demands that the prince regent also return to Europe, Pedro refused, and in September 1822 he declared Brazilian independence. He became Dom **Pedro I**, constitutional emperor of Brazil. Fighting against Portuguese troops lasted a year, but Brazil avoided the long wars of Spanish America. Brazil's independence did not upset the existing social organization based on slavery, nor did it radically change the political structure. With the brief exception of Mexico, all of the former Spanish American colonies became republics, but Brazil became a monarchy under a member of the Portuguese ruling house.

João VI [DOHM JWUN VI] Portuguese monarch who established seat of government in Brazil from 1808 to 1820 as a result of Napoleonic invasion of Iberian peninsula; made Brazil seat of empire with capital at Rio de Janeiro.

Pedro I (1798–1834) Son and successor of João VI in Brazil; aided in the declaration of Brazilian independence from Portugal in 1822; became constitutional emperor of Brazil.

New Nations Confront Old and New Problems

By 1830 the former Spanish and Portuguese colonies had become independent nations. The roughly 20 million inhabitants of these nations looked hopefully to the future. Many of the leaders of independence had shared ideals: representative government, careers open to talent, freedom of commerce and trade, the right to private property, and a belief in the individual as the basis of society. There was a general belief that the new nations should be sovereign and independent states, large enough to be economically viable and integrated by a common set of laws.

The new nations confronted difficult problems: social inequalities, political representation, the role of the church, and regionalism. These problems led to political fragmentation that allowed leaders having strong personal followings and representing various interests and their own ambitions, to rise to prominence.

On the issue of freedom of religion and the position of the church, however, there was less agreement. Roman Catholicism had been the state religion and the only one allowed by the Spanish crown. While most leaders attempted to maintain Catholicism as the official religion of the new states, some tried to end the exclusion of other faiths. The defense of the church became a rallying cry for the conservative forces.

The ideals of the early leaders of independence often were egalitarian. Bolívar had received aid from Haiti and had promised in return to abolish slavery in the areas he liberated. By 1854 slavery had been abolished everywhere except Spain's remaining colonies, Cuba and Puerto Rico, as well as in Brazil; all were places where the economy was profoundly based on it. Despite early promises, an end to American Indian tribute and taxes on people of mixed origin came much more slowly, because the new nations still needed the revenue such policies produced. Egalitarian sentiments often were tempered by fears that the mass of the population was unprepared for self-rule and democracy. Early constitutions attempted to balance order and popular representation by imposing property or literacy restrictions on voters. Invariably, voting rights were reserved for men. Although many had participated in the independence struggles, women were still disenfranchised and usually were not allowed to hold public office. The Creole elite's lack of trust of the popular classes was based on the fact that in many places the masses had not demonstrated a clear preference for the new regimes and had sometimes fought in royalist armies mobilized by traditional loyalties and regional interests.

Although some mestizos had risen to leadership roles in the wars of independence, the old color distinctions did not disappear easily. In Mexico, Guatemala, and the Andean nations, the large Indian population remained mostly outside national political life. The mass of the Latin American population—American Indians and people of mixed origins—waited to see what was to come, and they were suspicious of the new political elite, who were often drawn from the old colonial aristocracy but were also joined by a new commercial and urban bourgeoisie.

Political Fragmentation

The new Latin American nations can be grouped into regional blocks (Map 25.1). Some of the early leaders for independence had dreamed of creating a unified nation in some form, but regional rivalries, economic competition, and political divisions soon made that hope impossible. Mexico emerged as a short-lived monarchy until a republic was proclaimed in 1823, but its government remained unstable until the 1860s because of military coups, financial failures, foreign intervention, and political turmoil. Central America broke away from the Mexican monarchy and formed a union, but regional antagonisms and resentment of Guatemala, the largest nation in the region, eventually led to dissolution of the union in 1838. Spain's Caribbean colonies, Cuba and Puerto Rico, suppressed early movements for independence and remained outwardly loyal. The Dominican Republic was occupied by its neighbor Haiti, and after resisting Haiti as well as France and Spain, it finally gained independence in 1844.

In South America, the old colonial viceroyalty of New Granada became the basis for Gran Colombia, the large new state created by Bolívar that included modern Ecuador, Colombia, Panama, and Venezuela. The union, made possible to some extent by Bolívar's personal reputation and leadership, disintegrated as his own standing declined, and it ended in 1830, the year of his death. In the south, the viceroyalty of the Rio de la Plata served as the basis for a state that the peoples of Argentina hoped to lead. Other parts of the region resisted. Paraguay declared and maintained its autonomy under a series of dictators. Modern Uruguay was formed by a revolution for independence against the dominant power of its large neighbors, Argentina and Brazil. It became an independent buffer between those two nations in 1828. The Andean nations of Peru and Bolivia, with their

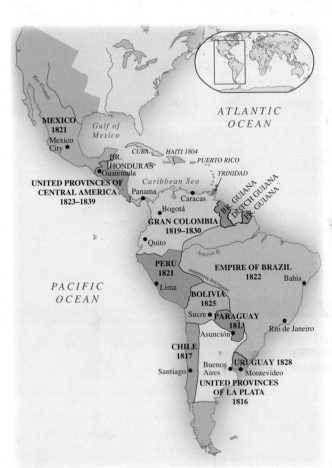

Map 25.1 Independent States of Latin America in 1830
Despite its size, traditions, language and religion provided certain unities. At independence a number of large states were formed out of coalitions, but these eventually divided because of regional differences and rivalries.

large Indian populations and conservative colonial aristocracies, flirted with union from 1829 to 1839 under the mestizo general **Andrés Santa Cruz**, but once again regional rivalries and the fears of their neighbors undermined the effort. Finally, Chile, somewhat isolated and blessed by the opening of trade in the Pacific, followed its own political course in a fairly stable fashion.

Most attempts at consolidation and union failed. Enormous geographic barriers and great distances separated nations and even regions within nations. Roads were poor and transportation rudimentary. Geography, regional interests, and political divisions were too strong to overcome. The mass of the population remained outside the political process. The problems of national integration were daunting. What is striking is not that Spanish America became 18 separate nations but that it did not separate into even more.

Caudillos, Politics, and the Church

The problems confronting the new nations were many. More than a decade of warfare in places such as Venezuela, Colombia, and Mexico had disrupted the economies and devastated wide areas. The mobilization of large armies whose loyalty to regional commanders was often based on their personal qualities, rather than their rank or politics, led to the rise of **caudillos** (kow-DEE-yuhs), independent leaders who dominated local areas by force and sometimes seized the national government itself. In times of intense division between civilian politicians, a powerful regional army commander became the arbiter of power, and thus the army sometimes made and unmade governments. Keeping the army in the barracks became a preoccupation of governments, and the amount of money spent on the military far exceeded the needs. The military had become important in the 18th century as Spain tried to shore up the defense of its empire, but it became a preserver of order.

Military commanders and regional or national caudillos usually were interested in power for their own sake, but they could represent or mobilize different groups in society. Many often defended the interests of regional elites, usually landowners, but others were populists who mobilized and claimed to speak for American Indians, peasants, and the poor and sometimes received their unquestioning support. A few, such as the conservative Rafael Carrera, who ruled Guatemala from 1839 to 1865, sincerely took the interest of the American Indian majority to heart, but other personalist leaders disregarded the normal workings of an open political system and the rule of law.

Other common issues confronted many of the new nations. Most political leaders were agreed on the republic as the basic form of government, but they could not agree on what kind of republic. A struggle often developed between **centralists**, who wanted to create strong, centralized national governments with broad powers, and **federalists**, who wanted tax and commercial policies to be set by regional governments. Other tensions developed between liberals and conservatives. Liberals stressed the rights of the individual and attacked the corporate (based on membership in a group or organization) structure of colonial society. They dreamed of a secular society and looked to the United States and France as models. Often they wanted a decentralized, or federalist, form of government. Conservatives usually believed in a strong centralized state, and they often wanted to maintain aspects of colonial society. They believed that a structure in which corporate groups (such as the American Indians), artisan guilds, or institutions (such as the church) provided the most equitable basis of social action should be recognized in law. To the conservatives, society was not based on open competition and individualism but was organic: each group was linked to the others like parts of a body whose health depended on the proper functioning of each part. Not all conservatives resisted change, and some—such as Mexican intellectual and politician Lucas Alamán—were among the most enlightened leaders in terms of economic and commercial reforms, but as a group the conservatives were skeptical of secularism and individualism and strove to keep the Catholic Iberian heritage alive.

The role of the church became a crucial issue in politics. It divided conservatives from the more secular liberals. In Mexico, for example, the church had played a major role in education, the economy, and politics. Few questioned its dogma, but liberals tried to limit its role in civil life. The church fought back with the aid of its pro-clerical supporters and with the power of the papacy, which until the 1840s refused to fill vacant positions in the hierarchy or to cooperate with the new governments.

Santa Cruz, Andrés Mestizo general who established union of independent Peru and Bolivia between 1829 and 1839.

caudillos [kow-DEE-yuhs] Independent leaders who dominated local areas by force in defiance of national policies; sometimes seized national governments to impose their concept of rule; typical throughout newly independent countries of Latin America.

centralists Latin American politicians who wished to create strong, centralized national governments with broad powers; often supported by politicians who described themselves as conservatives.

federalists Latin American politicians who wanted policies, especially fiscal and commercial regulation, to be set by regional governments rather than centralized national administrations; often supported by politicians who described themselves as liberals.

No separation of church and state

Political parties, often calling themselves Liberal or Conservative, sprang up throughout Latin America. They struggled for power and tried to impose their vision of the future on society. However, their leaders usually were drawn from the same social class of landowners and urban bourgeoisie, with little to differentiate them except their position in the church or on the question of federalism versus centralization. The general population might be mobilized by the force and personality of a particular leader such as **Juan Manuel de Rosas** in Argentina or **Antonio López de Santa Anna** in Mexico, but political ideology rarely was an issue for most of the population.

The result was political turmoil and insecurity in much of Latin America in the first 50 years after independence. Presidents came and went quickly. Written constitutions, which both liberals and conservatives thought were a positive thing, were often short-lived and were overturned with a change in government because the margin for interpretation of the constitution was slight. Great efforts were made to make constitutions precise, specific, and definitive, but this resulted in an attempt to change them each time there was a change in government. Some nations avoided the worst aspects of instability. After enacting a constitution in 1833 that gave the president broad powers, Chile established a functioning political system that allowed compromise. Brazil, with its monarchical rule, despite a period of turmoil from 1832 to 1850, was able to maintain a political system of compromise, although it was dominated by the conservatives, who were favored by the emperor. Its 1824 constitution remained in force until 1889. The issue of slavery, however, continued to gnaw at the nation's conscience, especially after 1870.

It is fair to say that in much of Latin America the basic questions of government and society remained unresolved after independence. Some observers attributed these problems to personalism, a lack of civic responsibility, and other defects in the "Latin" character. Nevertheless, the parallel experience of later emerging nations in the 20th century suggests that these problems were typical of former colonial dependencies searching for order and economic security in a world in which their options were constrained by their own potential and by external conditions.

Latin American Economies and World Markets, 1820–1870

The former colonies of Spain and Portugal now entered the world of diplomatic relations and international commerce. The new nations sought diplomatic recognition and security. In the 1820s, while Europe was undergoing the post-Napoleonic conservative reaction and monarchies were being restored, various plans to help Spain recolonize Latin America were put forward. Great Britain generally opposed those ideas, and because Great Britain was the dominant power at sea, its recognition of Latin American sovereignty was crucial. Moreover, the newly independent United States also felt an affinity and sympathy for the new nations to the south. The **Monroe Doctrine** of 1823, discussed in Chapter 23, stated clearly that any attempt by a European power to colonize in the Americas would be considered an unfriendly act by the United States. The United States at the time probably could have done little to prevent such actions, but Britain could, and its support of Latin American independence provided needed protection.

There was a price for this support. During the turmoil of the 1820s, British foreign minister Lord Canning had once said, "Spanish America is free and if we do not mismanage our affairs sadly, she is English." He was referring to the broad economic and commercial advantages that the new nations offered. British commerce had legally penetrated the area in the 18th century, and Britain had profited from illegal trade as well. Now it could afford to offer its diplomatic recognition in exchange for the freedom to trade with the new nations. Although little capital had been invested directly in Latin America before 1850, Latin American governments now turned to foreign governments and banks for loans. Meanwhile, Britain became a major consumer of Latin American products. In return Britain sold about £ 5 million worth of manufactured goods to the new nations each year, about half of which went to Brazil, where British merchants were especially strong. Although some historians argue that this was a small portion of Britain's overseas trade, it was crucial for Latin America. In some ways, Britain replaced Spain as a dominant economic force over the area in a sort of neocolonial commercial system. Although other nations, notably France and the United States, also traded with Latin America, Britain remained predominant before 1860.

Open ports and the influx of foreign goods, often of better quality and cheaper than local products, benefited the port cities that controlled customhouses and the large landowners whose

---

Rosas, Juan Manuel de Strongman leader in Buenos Aires; took power in 1831; commanded loyalty of gauchos; restored local autonomy.

Santa Anna, General Antonio López de Seized power in Mexico after collapse of empire of Mexico in 1824; after brief reign of liberals, seized power in 1835 as caudillo; defeated by Texans in war for independence in 1836; defeated by United States in Mexican-American War in 1848; unseated by liberal rebellion in 1854.

Latin American economies stagnated in the aftermath of the wars of independence. Toward mid-century, a new prosperity began as some nations found new markets for their exports that allowed liberal governments to initiate social and political changes.

Monroe Doctrine American declaration stated in 1823; established that any attempt of a European country to colonize in the Americas would be considered an unfriendly act by the United States; supported by Great Britain as a means of opening Latin American trade.

hides, sugar, and other products were exported. But these policies tended to damage local industries or regions that had specialized in producing for internal markets. Latin America became increasingly dependent on foreign markets and foreign imports and thereby reinforced the old colonial economic heritage in which land was the basis of wealth and prestige.

Mid-Century Stagnation

From about 1820 to 1850, the economy of Latin America was stagnant. Wars had destroyed many industries, roads were poor, and much money was still tied up in land. Only Cuba, with its booming sugar economy, expanded, but Cuba was still a colony of Spain. After 1850, however, this situation began to change as the expansion of the European economy created new demands for Latin American products. Coffee in Brazil, hides and beef in Argentina, and minerals and grains in Chile provided the basis of growth and allowed some Latin American governments to address social issues. For example, Peru exploited enormous **guano** (bird droppings) deposits on islands off its coast. Between 1850 and 1880, exports of this fertilizer earned Peru more than £10 million, and this income allowed the government to end American Indian tribute and to abolish slavery by compensating the owners.

Latin American cities began to grow and provide good internal markets, and the introduction of steamships and railroads began to overcome the old problems of transportation. By the 1840s, steamship lines improved communication within countries and opened up new possibilities for international commerce, and by the 1860s, railroads like the one in Figure 25.4 were being built, usually to link export-producing regions to the ports. Wealth based on large land holdings and exports continued to characterize the economies of the region, as they had in the colonial era. As the levels of exports and the governments' dependence on them increased, Latin America's vulnerability to the vagaries of the world economy increased as well.

guano   Bird droppings utilized as fertilizer; exported from Peru as a major item of trade between 1850 and 1880; income from trade permitted end to American Indian tribute and abolition of slavery.

Figure 25.4 The drive for progress made Latin American nations eager to accept foreign investment. Railroads were needed to bring export goods to seaports so that they could be carried to foreign markets. They were built principally to serve the needs of foreign capital. Railroad workers, however, often proved to be the most radical segment of the Latin American workforce.

Without detailing all the complex changes within the Latin American nations during the 19th century, we can discern a few general patterns. After the turmoil of independence, liberal reformers tried to institute a series of programs in the 1820s and 1830s intended to break the patterns of the colonial heritage and to follow the main social and economic trends of western Europe by improving primary education, promoting individualism and private property, supporting small industries, and promoting secular attitudes. These ideas often were imposed on societies and economies unprepared for drastic change, especially because the strength of opposing institutions, such as the church and the army, remained intact. By the 1840s, conservatives had returned to power in many places to slow or stop the reform measures. Some of them tried to speak for the lower classes or the American Indians, who wanted to see the paternal aspects of the old colonial state reimposed to protect them from the reforms of the liberals. In some ways, an alliance between the landowners and the peasantry emerged in opposition to the changes suggested by the middle-class, urban modernizers.

Economic Resurgence and Liberal Politics

By the last quarter of the century, as the world economy entered a phase of rapid expansion, there was a shift in attitude and possibilities in Latin America. Liberals returned to power in many places in Latin America and initiated a series of changes that began to transform their nations. The ideological basis of the new liberal surge was also changing. Based on the ideas of **positivism** of the French philosopher **Auguste Comte** (uh-GOOST KONT), who stressed observation and a scientific approach to the problems of society, Latin American politicians and intellectuals found a guiding set of principles and a justification of their quest for political stability and economic growth.

This shift was caused in large part by the general economic expansion of the second industrial revolution and the age of imperialism. The application of science to industry created new demands for Latin American products, such as copper and rubber, to accompany the increasing demand for its consumer products such as wheat, sugar, and coffee. The population of Latin America doubled to more than 43 million inhabitants in the 60 years between 1820 and 1880. After 1850, economies grew rapidly; the timing varied greatly, but the expansion of exports in places such as Colombia, Argentina, and Brazil stimulated prosperity for some and a general belief in the advantages of the liberal programs. The desire to participate in the capitalist expansion of the Western economy dominated the thinking of Latin American leaders. Foreign entrepreneurs and bankers joined hands with philosophical liberals, landowners, and urban merchants in Latin America to back the liberal programs, which now became possible because of the increased revenues generated by exports.

The leaders of the post-1860 governments were a new generation of politicians who had matured during the chaotic years of postindependence politics. Their inspiration came from England, France, and the United States. They were firm believers in progress, education, and free competition within a secular society, but they were sometimes distrustful of the mass of their own people, who seemed to represent an ancient "barbarism" in contrast to the "civilization" of progress. That distrust and their sometimes insensitive application of foreign models to a very different reality in their own countries—what one Brazilian author has called "ideas out of place"—prevented many from achieving the progress they so ardently desired.

Economic growth and progress were costly. Responding to international demand, landowners increased their holdings, often aided by the governments they controlled or influenced. Peasant lands were taken away by the government in Chile, Peru, and Bolivia; small farmers were displaced in Brazil and Costa Rica; church lands were seized in Mexico. Labor was needed. Immigrants from Europe flooded into Argentina and Brazil, and in other countries new forms of tenancy, peonage, and disguised servitude developed.

Mexico: Instability and Foreign Intervention

After the short monarchical experiment, a Mexican republic was established. Its constitution of 1824, based on the examples of France, the United States, and Spain, was a federalist document that guaranteed basic civil rights. Nevertheless, this constitution did not address the nation's continuing social problems and needs: the maldistribution of land, the status of the American Indians, the problems of education, and the situation of vast numbers of poor people among the approximately 7 million people in Mexico, the most populous of the new nations. Politics soon became a compli-

positivism French philosophy based on observation and scientific approach to problems of society; adopted by many Latin American liberals in the aftermath of independence.

Comte, Auguste [uh-GOOST KONT] French philosopher (19th century); founder of positivism, a philosophy that stressed observation and scientific approaches to the problems of society.

The Plan of Iguala
DOCUMENT

cated struggle between the conservative centralists and the liberal federalists and was made even more complicated by jockeying for advantage by commercial agents of Great Britain and the United States. For a short period from 1832 to 1835, the liberals were in control and tried to institute a series of sweeping social and economic reforms, but their attack on the church led to violent reaction and the assumption of power by General Antonio López de Santa Anna.

The mercurial Santa Anna remained until his death the maker of Mexican politics. He was a typical caudillo, a personalist, autocratic leader. But Mexico's instability resulted not only from his personality. Santa Anna was merely the symptom of deeper problems.

Mexico's instability and financial difficulties made it a target for various foreign interventions. Even more threatening to the nation, Anglo-American settlers were occupying Texas, the vast area of Mexico's northern frontier. They brought their language, customs, and religion despite restrictions on the latter. Although the Texans at first sought more autonomy as federalists within the Mexican nation, as had been done in Yucatan and other Mexican provinces, ethnic and religious differences as well as Santa Anna's attempts to suppress the Texans in 1836 led to widespread fighting and the declaration of Texan independence. Santa Anna, captured for a while by the Texans, returned to dominate Mexican politics, but the question of Texas festered and became acute when in 1845 the United States, with its eye on California and **manifest destiny**—a belief that it was destined to rule the continent from coast to coast—voted to annex Texas.

The result was war. A border dispute and the breakdown of negotiations over California led to hostilities in 1846. Santa Anna, who had been in exile, returned to lead the Mexican forces, but U.S. troops seized California, penetrated northern Mexico, and eventually occupied the Mexican capital. Mexico was forced to sign the disadvantageous **Treaty of Guadalupe-Hidalgo** (1848), in which the United States acquired about one-half of Mexico's national territory but less than 5 percent of its population. The **Mexican-American War** and the treaty left a bitter legacy of distrust of the northern neighbor, not only in Mexico but throughout the region. For Mexico there was also a serious loss of economic potential, but the heroic battle against the better-equipped Americans produced a sense of nationalism and a desire to confront the nation's serious internal problems, which also bore some responsibility for the war and the defeat.

Politics could not revert to the prewar situation. Santa Anna did return to office for a while, more unstable and despotic than ever, but now he was opposed by a new generation of liberals: intellectuals, lawyers, and some rural leaders, many of them from middle-class backgrounds, some of them mestizos and even a few American Indians. Perhaps the most prominent of them was **Benito Juárez** (beh-NEE-toh WAHR-ehz) (1806–1872), a Zapotec Indian of humble origins who had received a legal education and eventually become the governor of his state (Figure 25.5). He shared the liberal vision of a secular society based on the rule of law in which the old privileges of the church and the army would be eliminated as a way of promoting economic change and growth.

The liberal revolt, called **La Reforma,** began in 1854 and triumphed within a year. In a series of laws integrated into a new constitution in 1857, the liberals set the basis for their vision of society. Military and clerical privileges were curtailed, and church property was placed on sale. Indian communal lands also were restricted, and the government forced the sale of these lands to individuals— to the indigenous people themselves it was hoped. The goal of these programs was to create a nation of small independent farmers. However, speculators or big landowners often bought up the lands, and the result was that the peasants and American Indians lost what land they had. By 1910 about half of Mexico's rural population was landless. Good intentions had brought disastrous results.

The liberal program produced the expected conservative reaction. The church threatened to excommunicate those who upheld the new constitution. Civil war erupted, and in reaction Juárez, now president, pushed forward even more radical measures. Losing ground in the war, the conservatives turned to Europe and convinced Napoleon III of France to intervene. Attracted by possible economic advantage, dreams of empire, and a desire to please Catholics in France, Napoleon III justified French intervention by claims of a shared "Latin" culture (this was the origin of the term *Latin America*). French forces landed in 1862 and soon took the capital. At the urging of the French, **Maximilian von Habsburg**, an Austrian archduke, was convinced to take the throne of Mexico. Well intentioned but ineffective, Emperor Maximilian tried to get the support of Juárez and the liberals and even kept many of the laws of the Reforma in place, to the dismay of his conservative supporters. But Juárez absolutely rejected the idea of a foreign prince ruling Mexico. French troops and

From Monarchs to Masons: Mexico's Changing Political Arena

manifest destiny Belief of the government of the United States that it was destined to rule the continent from coast to coast; led to annexation of Texas and Mexican-American War.

Treaty of Guadalupe-Hidalgo Agreement that ended the Mexican-American War; provided for loss of Texas and California to the United States; left legacy of distrust of the United States in Latin America.

Mexican-American War Fought between Mexico and the United States from 1846 to 1848; led to devastating defeat of Mexican forces, loss of about one-half of Mexico's national territory to the United States.

Juárez, Benito [beh-NEE-toh WAHR-ehz] (1806–1872) Indian governor of state of Oaxaca in Mexico; leader of liberal rebellion against Santa Anna; liberal government defeated by French intervention under Emperor Napoleon III of France and establishment of Mexican Empire under Maximilian; restored to power in 1867 until his death in 1872.

Reforma, La The liberal rebellion of Benito Juárez against the forces of Santa Anna.

Habsburg, Maximilian von Proclaimed Emperor Maximilian of Mexico following intervention of France in 1862; ruled until overthrow and execution by liberal revolutionaries under Benito Juárez in 1867.

Figure 25.5 Benito Juárez, a Zapotec Indian from southern Mexico, rose to the presidency and began a series of sweeping reforms. His uncompromising resistance to foreign intervention and monarchy made him a symbol of Mexican sovereignty and independence. Juárez's stature as a nationalist and a man of law is portrayed in a mural by Mexican artist Diego Rivera.

(Diego Rivera's monumental work "Sunday Afternoon in Alameda Park" with Benito Juarez. © Banco de Mexico Diego Rivera & Frida Kahlo Museums Trust/Artists Rights Society (ARS), NY. D.F. Reproduction authorized by the INBA.)

the United States' preoccupation with its own Civil War allowed Emperor Maximilian and his Empress Carlota to rule. When French troops were withdrawn, the regime crumbled. It was then, in 1867, that Maximilian and his loyal generals were captured and executed (as described in the chapter opening). Maximilian's death shocked Europeans. Juárez had sent a message to Europe: "hands off Mexico."

Juárez returned to office, but his administration was increasingly autocratic—a reality that he felt was unavoidable after so long a period of instability. By his death in 1872, the force of his personality, his concern for the poor, and his nationalist position against foreign intervention had identified liberalism with nationalism in Mexico and made Juárez a symbol of the nation. By 1880 Mexico was poised on the edge of a period of strong central government and relative political stability. One of Juárez's generals, Porfirio Díaz, became president and then virtual dictator. His government witnessed rapid economic growth. Foreign companies began to invest in the exploitation of Mexican resources, and large landowners expanded their operations. Díaz, through political repression, provided a seemingly stable environment for this growth, but the seeds of revolution were also being planted.

Argentina: The Port and the Nation

Whereas Mexico and its silver had been the core of Spain's empire in America, the rolling plains, or pampas, of the Rio de la Plata in southern South America had been a colonial backwater until the 18th century, when direct trade began to stimulate its economy. The port of Buenos Aires and its merchants dominated the Rio de la Plata, but the other areas of the region had their own interests and resented the power and growth of the port city and its surrounding countryside. The United Provinces of the Rio de la Plata, which declared their independence in 1816, soon split apart, and local caudillos, able to call on the support of gauchos, dominated each region. In Buenos Aires, the liberals gained control in the 1820s and instituted a series of broad reforms in education, finance, agriculture, and immigration. These included a program of public land sales, which stimulated the growth of cattle ranches and the power of the rancher class.

As in Mexico, liberal reforms including freedom of religion produced a similar negative reaction from conservatives and the church. But the liberals' main sin was centralism, a desire to create a strong national government. Centralists (called *unitarians* in the Argentine context) provoked the reaction of the federalists, who by 1831 had taken power under Juan Manuel de Rosas, who commanded the loyalty of the gaucho employees of the ranchers.

Under Rosas, the federalist program of a weak central government and local autonomy was instituted, but Rosas's federalism favored the ranchers of the Buenos Aires province and the merchants of the great port. He campaigned against the American Indians to the south to open new lands to the cattle ranchers. Exports of hides and salted meat increased, but the revenues collected at the port were not shared with the other provinces. Although popular with the gauchos and the urban poor and remembered today as a nationalist who resisted British and French economic pressure, Rosas proved to be a despotic leader, crushing his opponents and forcing people to display his slogan: "Death to the savage, filthy unitarians." His brand of populist, authoritarian, personalist politics drove liberal opponents into exile, where they plotted his overthrow. Eventually, the liberal exiles joined forces with the caudillos jealous of the advantages Rosas's brand of federalism had given Buenos Aires province. In 1852 this coalition defeated Rosas and drove him from power.

There followed a confused decade of rival governments because the questions of federalism and the role of Buenos Aires within the nation remained unresolved. A new constitution was issued in 1853 under the influence of Juan Bautista Alberdi, an able and progressive journalist who was also a strong believer in the need to encourage immigration. This constitution incorporated the programs of the federalists but guaranteed national unity through the power of the presidency over the provincial governors. By 1862, after considerable fighting, a compromise was worked out and the new, unified nation, now called the **Argentine Republic**, entered into a period of prosperity and growth under a series of liberal presidents whose programs paralleled the Reforma in Mexico. The age of the liberals was now in full swing.

Between 1862 and 1890, able and intelligent presidents like **Domingo F. Sarmiento** (1811–1888) initiated a wide series of political reforms and economic measures designed to bring progress to Argentina. Sarmiento was an archetype of the liberal reformers of the mid-century. A great admirer of England and the United States, a firm believer in the value of education, and an ardent supporter of progress, Sarmiento had been a constant opponent of Rosas and had been driven into exile. During that time, he wrote *Facundo,* a critique of the caudillo politics of the region, in which the "barbarism" of the gauchos and their leaders was contrasted to the "civilization" of the liberal reformers. (See the Document feature in this chapter.)

Now in power, Sarmiento and the other liberal leaders were able to put their programs into practice. They were aided by several factors. Political stability made investment more attractive to foreign banks and merchants. The expansion of the Argentine economy, especially exports of beef, hides, and wool, created the basis for prosperity. Foreign trade in 1890 was five times as great as it had been in 1860. The population tripled to more than 3 million as the agricultural expansion, high wages, and opportunities for mobility attracted large numbers of European immigrants. Buenos Aires became a great, sprawling metropolis. With increased revenues, the government could initiate reforms in education, transportation, and other areas, often turning to foreign models and foreign investors. There was also an increased feeling of national unity. A long and bloody war waged by Argentina, Brazil, and Uruguay against their neighbor Paraguay from 1865 to 1870 created a sense of unity and national pride.

That sense was also heightened by the final defeat of the Indians south of Buenos Aires by 1880 as more land was opened to ranching and agriculture. At about the same time as in the United States, the railroad, the telegraph, and the repeating rifle brought an end to the Indians' resistance and opened their lands to settlement. The native peoples who were pushed far to the south, and the gauchos, whose way of life was displaced by the tide of immigrants, received little sympathy from the liberal government. By 1890, Argentina seemed to represent the achievement of a liberal program for Latin America.

The Brazilian Empire

It was sometimes said that despite its monarchical form, Brazil was the only functioning "republic" in South America in the 19th century. At first glance it seemed that Brazil avoided much of the political instability and turmoil found elsewhere in the continent and that through the mediation of the emperor a political compromise was worked out. However, problems and patterns similar to those in Spanish America lay beneath that facade. The transition to nationhood was smooth, and

Symbolism and Contested Identities in Argentina

Argentine Republic Replaced state of Buenos Aires in 1862; result of compromise between centralists and federalists.

Sarmiento, Domingo F. (1811–1888) Liberal politician and president of Argentine Republic from 1868 to 1874; author of *Facundo,* a critique of caudillo politics; increased international trade, launched internal reforms in education and transportation.

Confronting the Hispanic Heritage: From Independence to Consolidation

Simon Bolívar (1783–1830), "The Liberator," was a man of determination and perception. His campaigns for independence were defeated on several occasions, yet he did not despair. In 1815, while in exile on the island of Jamaica, he penned a letter to a newspaper that gave his evaluation of Latin America's situation and his vision for the future for its various parts. He advocated a republican form of government and rejected monarchy, but he warned against federalism and against popular democracies that might lead to dictatorships: "As long as our countrymen do not acquire the abilities and political virtues that distinguish our brothers to the north, wholly popular systems, far from working to our advantage, will, I greatly fear, bring about our downfall." Spain had left America unprepared, and in this letter Bolívar summarized many of the complaints of Latin Americans against Spanish rule and underlined the difficulty of the tasks of liberation—political, social, and economic. The famous "Letter of Jamaica" is one of the most candid writings by a leader of Latin American independence. The following excerpts suggest its tone and content.

Bolívar's "Jamaica Letter" (1815)

We are a young people. We inhabit a world apart, separated by broad seas. We are young in the ways of almost all the arts and sciences, although, in a certain manner, we are old in the ways of civilized society. I look upon the present state of America as similar to that of Rome after its fall. Each part of Rome adopted a political system conforming to its interest and situation or was led by the individual ambitions of certain chiefs, dynasties, or associations. But this important difference exists: those dispersed parts later reestablished their ancient nations, subject to the changes imposed by circumstances or extent. But we scarcely retain a vestige of what once was; we are, moreover, neither Indian nor European, but a species midway between the legitimate proprietors of this country and the Spanish usurpers. In short, although Americans by birth we derive our rights from Europe, and we have to assert these rights against the rights of the natives, and at the same time we must defend ourselves against the invaders. This places us in a most extraordinary and involved situation. . . .

The role of the inhabitants of the American hemisphere has for centuries been purely passive. Politically they were nonexistent. We are still in a position lower than slavery, and therefore it is more difficult for us to rise to the enjoyment of freedom. . . . States are slaves because of either the nature or the misuse of their constitutions; a people is therefore enslaved when the government, by its nature or its vices infringes on and usurps the rights of the citizen or subject. Applying these principles, we find that America was denied not only its freedom but even an active and effective tyranny. . . .

We have been harassed by a conduct which has not only deprived us of our rights but has kept us in a sort of permanent infancy with regard to public affairs. If we could have at least managed our domestic affairs and our internal administration, we could have acquainted ourselves with the processes and mechanics of public affairs. We should also have enjoyed a personal consideration, thereby commanding a certain unconscious respect from the people, which is so necessary to preserve amidst revolutions. That is why I say we have even been deprived of an active tyranny, since we have not been permitted to exercise its functions.

Americans today, and perhaps to a greater extent than ever before, who live within the Spanish system occupy a position in society no better than that of serfs destined to labor, or at best they have no more status than that of mere consumers. Yet even this status is surrounded with galling restrictions, such as being forbidden to grow European crops, or to store products which are royal monopolies, or to establish factories of a type the Peninsula (Spain) itself does not possess. To this add the privileges, even in articles of prime necessity, and the barriers between the American provinces, designed to prevent all exchange of trade, traffic, and understanding. In short, do you wish to know what our future held?—simply the cultivation of the fields of indigo, grain, coffee, sugar cane, cacao, and cotton; cattle raising on the broad plains, hunting wild game in the jungles; digging in the earth to mine its gold—but even these limitations could never satisfy the greed of Spain. So negative was our existence that I can find nothing comparable in any other civilized society.

By mid-century, Latin American political leaders were advocating "progress" and attempting to bring Latin America closer to the norms of life set by Europe. For liberals such as Argentine soldier, statesman, and author Domingo F. Sarmiento (1811–1888), his nation's task was to overcome the "barbarism" of rural life and implant the "civilization" of the Europeanized cities. Sarmiento saw in the bands of mounted rural workers, or *gauchos*, and their caudillo leaders an anachronistic way of life that held the nation back. His comparison of the gauchos to the Berbers of north Africa demonstrates the ancient hostility of "civilized" urban-dwellers to the nomadic way of life. In a way, Sarmiento saw the dictatorship of Juan

thus the basic foundations of Brazilian society—slavery, large landholdings, and an export economy—remained securely in place, reinforced by a new Brazilian nobility created for the new empire.

Brazilian independence had been declared in 1822, and by 1824 a liberal constitution had been issued by Dom Pedro I, the young Brazilian monarch, although not without resistance from those who wanted a republic or at least a very weak constitutional monarchy. But Dom Pedro I was an autocrat. In 1831 he was forced to abdicate in favor of his young son, Pedro (later to become Dom Pedro II), but the boy was too young to rule, and a series of regents directed the country in his name. What followed was an experiment in republican government, although the facade of monarchy was maintained.

The next decade was as tumultuous as any in Spanish America. The conflict between liberalism and conservatism was complicated by the existence of monarchist and antimonarchist factions

Manuel de Rosas as a result of the persistence of the gauchos and the manipulation of the lower classes—a sort of living example of what Bolívar had warned against. The following excerpt from Sarmiento's classic *Life in the Argentine Republic in the Days of the Tyrants, or Civilization and Barbarism* (1868) demonstrates his admiration for European culture, including that of Spain, and his desire to model his nation on it. That such a program might involve economic and cultural dependency did not concern Sarmiento and others like him.

The Search for Progress

Before 1810 two distinct, rival, and incompatible forms of society, two differing kinds of civilization existed in the Argentine Republic: one being Spanish, European, and cultivated, the other barbarous, American, and almost wholly of native growth. The revolution which occurred in the cities acted only as the cause, the impulse, which set these two distinct forms of national existence face to face, and gave occasion for a contest between them, to be ended, after lasting many years, by the absorption of one into the other.

I have pointed out the normal form of association, or want of association, of the country people, a form worse a thousand times, than that of a nomad tribe. I have described the artificial associations formed in idleness, and the sources of fame among the gauchos—bravery, daring, violence and opposition to regular law, to the civil law, that is, of the city. These phenomena of social organization existed in 1810, and still exist, modified in many points, slowly changing in others, and yet untouched in several more. These foci about which were gathered the brave, ignorant, free, and unemployed peasantry, were found by thousands through the country. The revolution of 1810 carried everywhere commotion and the sound of arms. Public life, previously wanting in this Arabo-Roman society, made its appearance in all the taverns, and the revolutionary movement finally brought about provincial, warlike associations, called montoneras [mounted gaucho guerrilla bands], legitimate offspring of the tavern and the field, hostile to the city and to the army of revolutionary patriots. As events succeed each other, we shall see the provincial montoneras headed by their chiefs; the final triumph, in Facundo Quiroga [a caudillo leader], of the country over the cities throughout the land; and by their subjugation in spirit, government, and civilization, the final formation of the central consolidated despotic government of the landed proprietor, Don Juan Manuel de Rosas, who applied the knife of the gaucho to the culture of Buenos Aires, and destroyed the work of centuries—of civilization, law, and liberty. . . .

They [revolutions for independence] were the same throughout America, and sprang from the same source, namely, the progress of European ideas. South America pursued that course because all other nations were pursuing it. Books, events, and the impulses given by these, induced South America to take part in the movement imparted to France by North American demands for liberty, and to Spain by her own and French writers. But what my object requires me to notice is that the revolution—except in its external symbolic independence of the king—was interesting and intelligible only to the Argentine cities, but foreign and unmeaning to the rural districts. Books, ideas, municipal spirit, courts, laws, statues, education, all points of contact and union existing between us and the people of Europe, were to be found in the cities, where there was a basis of organization, incomplete and comparatively evil, perhaps, for the very reason it was incomplete, and had not attained the elevation which it felt itself capable of reaching, but it entered into the revolution with enthusiasm. Outside the cities, the revolution was a problematical affair, and [in] so far [as] shaking off the king's authority was shaking off judicial authority, it was acceptable. The pastoral districts could only regard the question from this point of view. Liberty, responsibility of power, and all the questions that the revolution was to solve, were foreign to their mode of life and to their needs. But they derived this advantage from the revolution, that it tended to confer an object and an occupation upon the excess of vital force, the presence of which among them has been pointed out, and was to add a broader base of union than that to which throughout the country districts the men daily resorted.

The Argentine Revolutionary War was twofold: first, a civilized warfare of the cities against Spain; second, a war against the cities on the part of the country chieftains with the view of shaking off all political subjugation and satisfying their hatred of civilization. The cities overcame the Spaniards, and were in their turn overcome by the country districts. This is the explanation of the Argentine Revolution, the first shot of which fired in 1810, and the last is still to be heard.

QUESTIONS To what extent did the leaders of independence see their problems as a result of their Hispanic heritage? What would have been the reaction of the mass of the population to Sarmiento's idea of progress? Were the leaders naive about Latin America's possibilities for political democracy?

---

in Brazil. A series of regional revolts erupted, some of which took on aspects of social wars as people of all classes were mobilized in the fighting. The army suppressed these movements. By 1840, however, the politicians were willing to see the young Dom Pedro II begin to rule in his own name. Meanwhile, Brazil had been undergoing an economic transformation brought about by a new export crop: coffee. Coffee provided a new basis for agricultural expansion in southern Brazil. In the provinces of Rio de Janeiro and then São Paulo, coffee estates, or **fazendas**, began to spread toward the interior as new lands were opened. By 1840 coffee made up more than 40 percent of Brazil's exports, and by 1880 that figure reached 60 percent.

Along with the expansion of coffee growing came an intensification of slavery, Brazil's primary form of labor. For a variety of humanitarian and economic reasons, Great Britain pressured

fazendas Coffee estates that spread within interior of Brazil between 1840 and 1860; created major export commodity for Brazilian trade; led to intensification of slavery in Brazil.

Brazil to end the slave trade from Africa during the 19th century, but the slave trade continued on an enormous scale up to 1850. More than 1.4 million Africans were imported to Brazil in the last 50 years of the trade, and even after the trans-Atlantic slave trade ended, slavery continued. At mid-century, about one-fourth of Brazil's population was still enslaved. Although some reformers were in favor of ending slavery, a real abolitionist movement did not develop in Brazil until after 1870. Brazil did not finally abolish slavery until 1888.

As in the rest of Latin America, the years after 1850 saw considerable growth and prosperity in Brazil. Dom Pedro II proved to be an enlightened man of middle-class habits who was anxious to reign over a tranquil and progressive nation, even if that tranquility was based on slave labor. The trappings of a monarchy, a court, and noble titles kept the elite attached to the regime. Meanwhile, railroads, steamships, and the telegraph began to change communication and transportation. Foreign companies invested in these projects as well as in banking and other activities. In growing cities such as Rio de Janeiro and São Paulo, merchants, lawyers, a middle class, and an urban working class began to exert pressure on the government. Less wedded to landholding and slavery, these new groups were a catalyst for change, even though the right to vote was still very limited. Moreover, the nature of the labor force was changing.

Canudos: Millenarianism in Late-Nineteenth-Century Brazil

Inhabitants of Canudos

After 1850 a tide of immigrants, mostly from Italy and Portugal, began to reach Brazil's shores, increasingly attracted by government immigration schemes. Between 1850 and 1875, more than 300,000 immigrants arrived in Brazil; more than two-thirds of them went to work in the coffee estates of southern Brazil. Their presence lessened the dependence on slavery, and by 1870 the abolitionist movement was gaining strength. A series of laws freeing children and the aged, the sympathy of Dom Pedro II, the agitation by abolitionists (both black and white), and the efforts of the slaves (who began to resist and run away in large numbers) brought in 1888 an end to slavery in Brazil, the last nation in the Western Hemisphere to abolish it.

Support for the monarchy began to wither. The long War of the Triple Alliance against Paraguay (1865–1870) had become unpopular, and the military began to take an active role in politics. Squabbles with the church undercut support from the clergy. The planters now turned increasingly to immigrants for their laborers, and some began to modernize their operations. The ideas of positivism—the modernizing philosophy discussed above in relation to Mexico that attempted to bring about material progress by applying the scientific principles of logic and rationality to government and society—attracted many intellectuals and key members of the army. Politically, a Republican party formed in 1871 began to gather support in urban areas from a wide spectrum of the population. The Brazilian monarchy, long a defender of the planter class and its interests, could not survive the abolition of slavery. In 1889 a nearly bloodless military coup deposed the emperor and established a republic under military men strongly influenced by positivist intellectuals and Republican politicians.

But such "progress" came at certain costs in many nations in Latin America. In the harsh backlands of northeastern Brazil, for example, the change to a republic, economic hardship, and the secularization of society provoked peasant unrest. Antonio Conselheiro, a religious mystic, began to gather followers in the 1890s, especially among the dispossessed peasantry. Eventually their community, Canudos, contained thousands of followers of this messianic leader. The government feared these "fanatics" and sent four military expeditions against Canudos, Conselheiro's "New Jerusalem." The fighting was bloody, and casualties were in the thousands. Conselheiro and his followers put up a determined guerrilla defense of their town and their view of the world. The tragedy of Canudos's destruction moved journalist Euclides da Cunha to write *Rebellion in the Backlands* (*Os sertões,* 1902), an account of the events. Like Sarmiento, he saw this resistance as a struggle between civilization and barbarism. However, da Cunha maintained great sympathy for the followers of Conselheiro (Figure 25.6), and he argued that civilization could not be spread in the flash of a cannon. The book has become a classic of Latin American literature, but the problems of national

Figure 25.6 Refugees of Canudos Only women and children survived the brutal repression of the millenarian movement of Canudos in the Brazilian interior.

integration and the disruption of traditional values in the wake of modernization and change remained unresolved. In Brazil that was especially true because of the legacy of slavery and the need to integrate the ex-slaves into the nation.

Societies in Search of Themselves

The end of colonial rule opened up Latin America to direct influences from the rest of Europe. Scientific observers, travelers, and the just plain curious—often accompanied by artists—came to see and record, and while doing so introduced new ideas and fashions. Artistic and cultural missions sometimes were brought directly from Europe by Latin American governments.

The elites of the new nations adopted the tastes and fashions of Europe. The battles and triumphs of independence were celebrated in paintings, hymns, odes, and theatrical pieces in the neoclassical style in an attempt to use Greece and Rome as a model for the present. Latin Americans followed the lead of Europe, especially France. The same neoclassical tradition also was apparent in the architecture of the early 19th century.

Cultural Expression After Independence

In the 1830s, the generation that came of age after independence turned to romanticism and found the basis of a new nationality in historical images, the American Indian, and local customs. This generation often had a romantic view of liberty. They emphasized the exotic as well as the distinctive aspects of American society. In Brazil, for example, poet António Gonçalves Dias (1823–1864) used the American Indian as a symbol of Brazil and America. In Cuba, novels sympathetic to slaves began to appear by mid-century. In Argentina, writers celebrated the pampas and its open spaces. Sarmiento's critical account of the caudillos in *Facundo* described in depth the life of the gauchos, but it was José Hernández who in 1872 wrote *Martín Fierro*, a romantic epic poem about the end of the way of the gaucho. Historical themes and the writing of history became a political act because studying the past became a way of organizing the present. Many of Latin America's leading politicians were also excellent historians and the theme of their writing was the creation of the nation.

By the 1870s, a new realism emerged in the arts and literature that was more in line with the scientific approach of positivism and the modernization of the new nations. As the economies of Latin America surged forward, novelists appeared who were unafraid to deal with human frailties such as corruption, prejudice, and greed. Chilean Alberto Blest Gana and Brazilian mulatto J. Machado de Assis (1839–1908) wrote critically about the social mores of their countries during this era.

Throughout the century, the culture of the mass of the population had been little affected by the trends and tastes of the elite. Popular arts, folk music, and dance flourished in traditional settings, demonstrating a vitality and adaptability to new situations that was often lacking in the more imitative fine arts. Sometimes authors in the romantic tradition or poets such as Hernández turned to traditional themes for their subject and inspiration, and in that way they brought these traditions to the greater attention of their class and the world. For the most part, however, popular artistic expressions were not appreciated or valued by the traditional elites, the modernizing urban bourgeoisie, or the new immigrants.

Old Patterns of Gender, Class, and Race

Although significant political changes make it appealing to deal with the 19th century as an era of great change and transformation in Latin America, it is necessary to recognize the persistence of old patterns and sometimes their reinforcement. Changes took place, to be sure, but their effects were not felt equally by all classes or groups in society, nor were all groups attracted by the promises of the new political regimes and their views of progress.

For example, women gained little ground during most of the century. They had participated actively in the independence movements. Some had taken up arms or aided the insurgent forces, and some—such as Colombian Policarpa (La Pola) Salvatierra, whose final words were "Do not forget my example"—had paid for their activities on the gallows. After independence, there was almost no change in the predominant attitudes toward women's proper role. Expected to be wives and

A tension in cultural life existed between European influences and the desire to express an American reality, or between elite and folk culture. Social change came very slowly for American Indians, blacks, and women, but by the end of the century the desire for progress and economic resurgence was beginning to have social effects.

CASE STUDY

Brothers in Arms: Comparative Politics and Revolution

mothers, women could not vote, hold public office, become lawyers, or in some places testify in a court of law. Although there were a few exceptions, unmarried women younger than 25 remained under the power and authority of their fathers. Once married, they could not work, enter into contracts, or control their own estates without permission of their husbands. As in the colonial era, marriage, politics, and the creation of kinship links were essential elements in elite control of land and political power, and thus women remained a crucial resource in family strategies.

Lower-class women had more economic freedom—often controlling local marketing—and also more personal freedom than elite women under the constraints of powerful families. In legal terms, however, their situation was no better—and in material terms, much worse—than that of their elite sisters. Still, by the 1870s women were an important part of the workforce.

The one area in which the situation of women began to change significantly was public education. There had already been a movement in this direction in the colonial era. At first, the idea behind education for girls and women was that because women were responsible for educating their children, they should be educated so that the proper values could be passed to the next generation. By 1842 Mexico City required girls and boys age 7 to 15 to attend school, and in 1869 the first girls' school was created in Mexico. Liberals in Mexico wanted secular public education to prepare women for an enlightened role within the home, and similar sentiments were expressed by liberal regimes elsewhere. Public schools appeared throughout Latin America, although their impact was limited. For example, Brazil had a population of 10 million in 1873, but only about 1 million men and half that number of women were literate.

The rise of secular public education created new opportunities for women. The demand for teachers at the primary level created the need for schools in which to train teachers. Because most teachers were women, these teacher training schools gave women access to advanced education. Although the curriculum often emphasized traditional female roles, an increasing number of educated women began to emerge who were dissatisfied with the legal and social constraints on their lives. By the end of the 19th century, these women were becoming increasingly active in advocating women's rights and other political issues.

Race and Identity in Nineteenth-Century South America

CASE STUDY

In most cases, the new nations legally ended the old society of castes in which legal status and definition depended on color and ethnicity, but in reality much of that system continued. The stigma of skin color and former slave status created barriers to advancement. Indigenous peoples in Mexico, Bolivia, and Peru often continued to labor under poor conditions and to suffer the effects of government failures. There was conflict. In Yucatan, a great rebellion broke out, pitting the Maya against the central government and the whites, in 1839 and again in 1847. Despite the intentions of governments, indigenous peoples resisted changes imposed from outside their communities and were willing to defend their traditional ways. The word *Indian* was still an insult in most places in Latin America. For some mestizos and others of mixed origin, the century presented opportunities for advancement in the army, professions, and commerce, but these cases were exceptions. The former slaves throughout Latin America sought the benefits of full citizenship, but while legal equality came with abolition, their economic condition changed slowly.

In many places, expansion of the export economy perpetuated old patterns. Liberalism itself changed during the century, and once its program of secularization, rationalism, and property rights was made law, it became more restrictive. Positivists at the end of the century still hoped for economic growth, but some were willing to gain it at the expense of individual freedoms. The positivists generally were convinced of the benefits of international trade for Latin America, and large landholdings increased in many areas at the expense of small farms and Indian communal lands as a result. A small, white Creole, landed upper class controlled the economies and politics in most places, and they were sometimes joined in the political and economic functions by a stratum of urban middle-class merchants, bureaucrats, and other bourgeois types. The landed and mercantile elite tended to merge over time to create one group that, in most places, controlled the government. Meanwhile, new social forces were at work. The flood of immigration, beginning in earnest in the 1870s, to Argentina, Brazil, and a few other nations began to change the social composition of those places. Increasingly, rapid urbanization also changed these societies. Still, Latin America, though politically independent, began the 1880s as a group of predominantly agrarian nations with rigid social structures and a continuing dependency on the world market.

The Great Boom, 1880–1920

Between 1880 and 1920, Latin America, like certain areas of Asia and Africa, experienced a tremendous spurt of economic growth, stimulated by the increasing demand in industrializing Europe and the United States for raw materials, foodstuffs, and specialized tropical crops. Mexico and Argentina are two excellent examples of the effects of these changes, but not all groups shared the benefits of economic growth. By the end of the 19th century, the United States was beginning to intervene directly in Latin American affairs.

Latin America was well prepared for export-led economic expansion. The liberal ideology of individual freedoms, an open market, and limited government intervention in the operation of the economy had triumphed in many places. Whereas this ideology had been the expression of the middle class in Europe, in Latin America it was adopted not only by the small urban middle class but also by the large landowners, miners, and export merchants linked to the rural economy and the traditional patterns of wealth and land owning. In a number of countries, a political alliance was forged between the traditional aristocracy of wealth and the new urban elements. Together they controlled the presidential offices and the congresses and imposed a business-as-usual approach to government at the expense of peasants and a newly emerging working class.

The expansion of Latin American economies was led by exports. Each nation had a specialty: bananas and coffee from the nations of Central America; tobacco and sugar from Cuba; rubber and coffee from Brazil; hennequen (a fiber for making rope), copper, and silver from Mexico; wool, wheat, and beef from Argentina; copper from Chile. In this era of strong demand and good prices, these nations made high profits. This allowed them to import large quantities of foreign goods, and it provided funds for the beautification of cities and other government projects. But export-led expansion was always risky because the world market prices of Latin American commodities ultimately were determined by conditions outside the region. In that sense, these economies were particularly vulnerable and in some ways dependent.

Also, export-led expansion could result in rivalry, hostility, and even war between neighboring countries. Control of the nitrates that lay in areas between Chile, Peru, and Bolivia generated a dispute that led to the War of the Pacific (1879–1883), pitting Chile against Bolivia and Peru. Although all were unprepared for a modern war at first, eventually thousands of troops were mobilized. The Chileans occupied Lima in 1881 and then imposed a treaty on Peru. Bolivia lost Antofagasta and its access to the Pacific Ocean and became a landlocked nation. Chile increased its size by a third and benefited from an economic boom during and after the war. In Peru and Bolivia, governments fell, and a sense of national crisis set in after the defeat in the "fertilizer war."

The expansion of Latin American trade was remarkable. It increased by about 50 percent between 1870 and 1890. Argentina's trade was increasing at about 5 percent a year during this period—one of the highest rates of growth ever recorded for a national economy. "As wealthy as an Argentine" became an expression in Paris, reflecting the fortunes that wool, beef, and grain were earning for some in Argentina. In Mexico, an oligarchic dictatorship, which maintained all the outward attributes of democracy but imposed "law and order" under the dictator Porfirio Díaz, created the conditions for unrestrained profits. Mexican exports doubled between 1877 and 1900. Similar figures could be cited for Chile, Costa Rica, and Bolivia.

This rapidly expanding commerce attracted the interest of foreign investors eager for high returns on their capital. British, French, German, and North American businesses and entrepreneurs invested in mining, railroads, public utilities, and banking. More than half the foreign investments in Latin America were British, which alone were 10 times more in 1913 than they had been in 1870. But British leadership was no longer uncontested; Germany and, increasingly, the United States provided competition. The United States was particularly active in the Caribbean region and Mexico, but not until after World War I did U.S. capital predominate in the region.

Foreign investments provided Latin America with needed capital and services but tended to place key industries, transportation facilities, and services in foreign hands. Foreign investments also constrained Latin American governments in their social, commercial, and diplomatic policies.

Explaining Underdevelopment

The terms *underdeveloped* and the more benign *developing* describe a large number of nations in the world with a series of economic and social problems. Because Latin America was first among what we now call the *developing nations* to establish its independence and begin to compete in the world economy, it had to confront the reasons for its relative position and problems early and without many models to follow. The Document section of this chapter offers two visions of Latin America's early problems that are similar because both emphasize the Hispanic cultural heritage, as well as its supposed deficiencies or strengths, as a key explanation for the region's history. Such cultural explanations were popular among 19th-century intellectuals and political leaders, and they continue today, although other general theories based on economics and politics have become more popular.

> "In 19th-century Latin America ... early attempts to develop industry were faced with competition from the cheaper and better products of already industrialized nations such as England and France, so a similar path to development was impossible."

At the time of Latin American independence, the adoption of European models of economy, government, and law seemed to offer great hope. But as "progress," republican forms of government, free trade, and liberalism failed to bring about general prosperity and social harmony, Latin Americans and others began to search for alternative explanations of their continuing problems as a first step in solving them. Some critics condemned the Hispanic cultural legacy; others saw the materialism of the modern world as the major problem and called for a return to religion and idealism. By the 20th century, Marxism provided a powerful analysis of Latin America's history and present reality, although Marxists themselves could not decide whether Latin American societies were essentially feudal and needed first to become capitalist or whether they were already capitalist and were ready for socialist revolution.

Throughout these debates, Latin Americans often implicitly compared their situation with that of the United States and tried to explain the different economic positions of the two regions. At the beginning of the 19th century, both regions were still primarily agricultural, and although a few places in North America were starting small industries, the mining sector in Latin America was far stronger than that of its northern neighbor. In 1850 the population of Latin America was 33 million, the population of the United States was 23 million, and the per capita income in both regions was roughly equal. By 1940, however, Latin America's population was much larger and its economic situation was far worse than in the United States. Observers were preoccupied by why and how this disparity arose. Was there some flaw in the Latin American character, or were the explanations to be found in the economic and political differences between the two areas, and how could these differences be explained? The answers to these questions were not easy to obtain, but increasingly they were sought not in the history of individual countries but in analyses of a world economic and political system.

There had long been a Marxist critique of colonialism and imperialism, but the modern Latin American analysis of underdevelopment grew from different origins. During the 1950s, a number of European and North American scholars developed the concept of *modernization*, or *westernization*. Basing their ideas on the historical experience of western Europe, they believed that development was a matter of increasing per capita production in any society, and that as development took place, various kinds of social changes would follow. The more industrialized, urban, and modern a society became, the more social change and improvement were possible as traditional patterns and attitudes were abandoned or transformed. Technology, communication, and the distribution of material goods were the means by which the transformation would take place. Some scholars also believed that as this process occurred, there would be a natural movement toward more democratic forms of government and popular participation.

Modernization theory held out the promise that any society could move toward a brighter future by following the path taken earlier by western Europe. Its message was one of improvement through gradual rather than radical or revolutionary change, and

Mexico and Argentina: Examples of Economic Transformation

We can use these two large Latin American nations as examples of different responses within the same general pattern. In Mexico, the liberal triumph of Juárez had set the stage for economic growth and constitutional government. In 1876, Porfirio Díaz, one of Juárez's generals, was elected president, and for the next 35 years he dominated politics. Díaz suppressed regional rebellions and imposed a strong centralized government. Financed by foreign capital, the railroad system grew rapidly, providing a new way to integrate Mexican regional economies, move goods to the ports for export, and allow the movement of government troops to keep order. Industrialization began to take place. Foreign investment was encouraged in mining, transportation, and other sectors of the economy, and financial policies were changed to promote investments. For example, United States investments expanded from about 30 million pesos in 1883 to more than $1 billion by 1911.

thus it tended to be politically conservative. It also tended to disregard cultural differences, internal class conflicts, and struggles for power within nations. Moreover, sometimes it was adopted by military regimes that believed imposing order was the best way to promote the economic changes necessary for modernization.

The proponents of modernization theory had a difficult time convincing many people in the "underdeveloped" world, where the historical experience had been very different from that of western Europe. In 19th-century Latin America, for example, early attempts to develop industry were faced with competition from the cheaper and better products of already industrialized nations such as England and France, so a similar path to development was impossible. Critics argued that each nation did not operate individually but was part of a world system that kept some areas "developed" at the expense of others.

These ideas were first and most cogently expressed in Latin America. After World War II, the United Nations established an Economic Commission for Latin America (ECLA). Under the leadership of Argentine economist Raul Prebisch, the ECLA began to analyze the Latin American economies. Prebisch argued that "unequal exchange" between the developed nations at the center of the world economy and those like Latin America created structural blocks to economic growth. The ECLA suggested various policies to overcome the problems, especially the development of industries that would overcome the region's dependence on foreign imports.

From the structural analysis of the ECLA and from more traditional Marxist critiques, a new kind of explanation, usually called *dependency theory,* began to emerge in the 1960s. Rather than seeing underdevelopment or the lack of economic growth as the result of failed modernization, some scholars in Latin America began to argue that development and underdevelopment were not stages but part of the same process. They believed that the development and growth of some areas, such as western Europe and the United States, were achieved at the expense of, or because of, the underdevelopment of dependent regions such as Latin America. Agricultural economies at the periphery of the world economic system always were at a disadvantage in dealing with the industrial nations of the center, and thus they would become poorer as the industrial nations got richer. The industrial nations would continually draw products, profits, and cheap labor from the periphery. This basic economic relationship of dependency meant that external forces determined production, capital accumulation, and class relations in a dependent country. Some theorists went further and argued that Latin America and other nations of the Third World were culturally dependent in their consumption of ideas and concepts. Both modernization theory and Mickey Mouse were seen as the agents of a cultural domination that was simply an extension of economic reality. These theorists usually argued that socialism offered the only hope for breaking out of the dependency relationship.

These ideas, which dominated Latin American intellectual life, were appealing to other areas of Asia and Africa that had recently emerged from colonial control. Forms of dependency analysis became popular in many areas of the world in the 1960s and 1970s. By the 1980s, however, dependency theory was losing its appeal. As an explanation of what had happened historically in Latin America, it was useful, but as a theory that could predict what might happen elsewhere, it provided little help. Marxists argued that it overemphasized the circulation of goods (trade) rather than how things were produced and that it ignored the class conflicts they believed were the driving force of history. Moreover, with the rise of multinational corporations and globalization, capitalism itself was changing and was becoming less tied to individual countries. Thus an analysis based on trade relationships between countries became somewhat outdated.

Can development be widespread, as modernization theory argues, or is the underdevelopment of some countries inherent in the capitalist world economy, as the dependency theorists believe? The issue is still in dispute. The tilt to the left in Latin American electoral politics since 2000 is evidence of growing regional dissatisfaction in two areas—with Latin America's position in the global economy and with the misdistribution of the benefits of economic growth among the population.

QUESTIONS In what sense was 19th-century Latin America a dependent economy? Which explanation or prediction about dependency best fits world economic trends today?

The forms of liberal democracy were maintained but were subverted to keep Díaz in power and to give his development plans an open track. Behind these policies were a number of advisors who were strongly influenced by positivist ideas and who wanted to impose a scientific approach on the national economy. These **científicos** set the tone for Mexico while the government suppressed any political opposition to these policies. Díaz's Mexico projected an image of modernization led by a Europeanized elite who greatly profited from the economic growth and the imposition of order under Don Porfirio.

Growth often was bought at the expense of Mexico's large rural peasantry and its growing urban and working classes. This population was essentially native, because unlike Argentina and Brazil, Mexico had received few immigrants. They participated very little in the prosperity of export-led growth. Economic expansion at the expense of peasants and American Indian communal lands created a volatile situation.

científicos Advisors of government of Porfirio Díaz who were strongly influenced by positivist ideas; permitted Mexican government to project image of modernization.

Images of the Spanish-American War

Although the United States had fought a war with Mexico in the 1840s and commercial ties were growing in the 1880s, the real push for expansion in Latin America came in 1898 with the Spanish-American War. The U.S. motives for the war were a mixture of altruism and the desire for strategic and commercial advantages. A great deal of popular support was mobilized in the United States by the popular press, not by celebrating imperial expansion but by emphasizing the oppression suffered by people still under Spain's colonial rule. Sympathy was especially strong for the Cubans who had fought a bloody rebellion for independence from 1868 to 1878. However, the U.S. press often portrayed Latin Americans as unruly children and emphasized their "racial" difference, creating an image quite typical for the period. During the war, Teddy Roosevelt's heroic feats and the American victories stimulated national pride, but the element of altruism was always part of the mix. As in Europe, the concept of a " white man's burden" could not be separated from the drive for empire.

QUESTIONS In what way do images convey political messages more effectively than texts? When do calls for moral action justify intervention in the affairs of another country?

Among the popular political magazines of the era were *Punch* and the *Judge*. The two cover images shown here from the period of the Spanish-American War reflect popular sentiments and attitudes at the time.

Strikes and labor unrest increased, particularly among railroad workers, miners, and textile workers. In the countryside, a national police force, the Rurales, maintained order, and the army was mobilized when needed. At the regional level, political bosses linked to the Díaz regime in Mexico City delivered the votes in rigged elections.

For 35 years, Díaz reigned supreme and oversaw the transformation of the Mexican economy. His opponents were arrested or driven into exile, and the small middle class, the landowners, miners, and foreign investors celebrated the progress of Mexico. In 1910, however, a middle-class movement with limited political goals seeking electoral reform began to mushroom into a more general uprising in which the frustrations of the poor, the workers, the peasants, and nationalist intellectuals of various political persuasions erupted in a bloody 10-year civil war, the Mexican Revolution.

At the other end of the hemisphere, Argentina followed an alternative path of economic expansion. By 1880 the American Indians on the southern pampas had been conquered, and vast new tracts of land were opened to ranching. The strange relationship between Buenos Aires and the rest of the nation was resolved when Buenos Aires was made a federal district. With a rapidly expanding economy, it became "the Paris of South America," an expression that reflected the drive by wealthy Argentines to establish themselves as a modern nation. By 1914 Buenos Aires had more than 2 million inhabitants, or about one-fourth of the national population. Its political leaders, the "Generation of 1880," inherited the liberal program of Sarmiento and other liberals, and they were able to enact their programs because of the high levels of income the expanding economy generated.

Technological changes contributed to Argentine prosperity. Refrigerated ships allowed fresh beef to be sent directly to Europe, and this along with wool and wheat provided the basis of expansion. The flood of immigrants provided labor. Some were *golondrinas* (literally, "swallows"), who were able to work one harvest in Italy and then a second in Argentina because of the differences in seasons in the two hemispheres, but many immigrants elected to stay. Almost 3.5 million immigrants stayed in Argentina between 1857 and 1930, and unlike the Mexican population, by 1914 about one-third of the Argentine population was foreign born. Italians, Germans, Russians, and Jews came "hacer America"—that is, "to make America"—and remained. In a way, they really did Europeanize Argentina, as did not happen in Mexico, introducing the folkways and ideologies of the European rural and working classes. The result was a fusion of cultures that produced not only a radical workers' movement but also the distinctive music of the tango, which combined Spanish, African, and other musical elements in the cafe and red-light districts of Buenos Aires. The tango became the music of the Argentine urban working class.

As the immigrant flood increased, workers began to seek political expression. A Socialist party was formed in the 1890s and tried to elect representatives to office. Anarchists hoped to smash the political system and called for strikes and walkouts. Inspired to some extent by European ideological battles, the struggle spilled into the streets. Violent strikes and government repression characterized the decade after 1910, culminating in a series of strikes in 1918 that led to extreme repression. Development had its social costs.

The Argentine oligarchy was capable of some internal reform, however. A new party representing the emerging middle class began to organize, aided by an electoral law in 1912 that called for secret ballots, universal male suffrage, and compulsory voting. With this change, the Radical party, promising political reform and more liberal policies for workers, came to power in 1916, but faced with labor unrest it acted as repressively as its predecessors. The oligarchy made room for middle-class politicians and interests, but the problems of Argentina's expanding labor force remained unresolved, and Argentina's economy remained closely tied to the international market for its exports. On the other hand, the new political climate favored the growing calls for equality for women, and a number of feminist organizations began to emerge.

With many variations, similar patterns of economic growth, political domination by oligarchies formed by traditional aristocracies and "progressive" middle classes, and a rising tide of labor unrest or rural rebellion can be noted elsewhere in Latin America. Modernization was not welcomed by all sectors of society. Messianic religious movements in Brazil, American Indian resistance to the loss of lands in Colombia, and banditry in Mexico were all to some extent reactions to the changes being forced on the societies by national governments tied to the ideology of progress and often insensitive to its effects.

Uncle Sam Goes South

After its Civil War, the United States began to take a more direct and active interest in the politics and economies of Latin America. Commerce and investments began to expand rapidly in this period, especially in Mexico and Central America. American industry was seeking new markets and raw materials, while the growing population of the United States created a demand for Latin American products. Attempts were made to create inter-American cooperation. A major turning point came in 1898 with the outbreak of war between Spain and the United States, which began to join the nations of western Europe in the age of imperialism.

The war centered on Cuba and Puerto Rico, Spain's last colonies in the Americas. The Cuban economy had boomed in the 19th century on the basis of its exports of sugar and tobacco grown with slave labor. A 10-year civil war for independence, beginning in 1868, had failed in its main objective but had won the island some autonomy. A number of ardent Cuban nationalists, including journalist and poet José Martí, had gone into exile to continue the struggle. Fighting erupted again in 1895, and the United States joined in in 1898, declaring war on Spain and occupying Cuba, Puerto Rico, and the Philippines.

In fact, U.S. investments in Cuba had been increasing rapidly before the war, and the United States had become a major market for Cuban sugar. The **Spanish-American War** opened the door to direct U.S. involvement in the Caribbean. A U.S. government of occupation was imposed on Cuba and Puerto Rico, which had witnessed its own stirrings for independence in the 19th century. When the occupation of Cuba ended in 1902, a series of onerous conditions was imposed on independent Cuba that made it almost an American dependency—a status that was legally imposed in Puerto Rico.

For strategic, commercial, and economic reasons, Latin America, particularly the Caribbean and Mexico, began to attract American interest at the turn of the century. These considerations lay behind the drive to build a canal across Central America that would shorten the route between the Atlantic and Pacific. When Colombia proved reluctant to meet American proposals, the United States backed a Panamanian movement for independence and then signed a treaty with its representative that granted the United States extensive rights over the **Panama Canal** (Figure 25.7). President Theodore Roosevelt was a major force behind the canal, which was opened to traffic in 1914.

The Panama Canal was a remarkable engineering feat and a fitting symbol of the technological and industrial strength of the United States. North Americans were proud of these achievements and hoped to demonstrate the superiority of the "American way"—a feeling fed to some extent by racist ideas and a sense of cultural superiority. Latin Americans were wary of American power and intentions in the area. Many intellectuals cautioned against the expansionist designs of the United States and against what they saw as the materialism of American culture. Uruguayan José Enrique Rodó, in his essay *Ariel* (1900), contrasted the spirituality of Hispanic culture with the materialism of the United States. Elsewhere in Latin America, others offered similar critiques.

Latin American criticism had a variety of origins: nationalism, a Catholic defense of traditional values, and some socialist attacks on expansive capitalism. In a way, Latin America, which had achieved its political independence in the 19th century and had been part of European developments, was able to articulate the fears and the reactions of the areas that had become the colonies and semicolonies of western Europe and the United States in the age of empire.

Spanish-American War War fought between Spain and the United States beginning in 1898; centered on Cuba and Puerto Rico; permitted American intervention in Caribbean, annexation of Puerto Rico and the Philippines.

Panama Canal An aspect of American intervention in Latin America; resulted from United States support for a Panamanian independence movement in return for a grant to exclusive rights to a canal across the Panama isthmus; provided short route between Atlantic and Pacific oceans; completed 1914.

Global Connections

New Latin American Nations and the World

During the 19th century, the nations of Latin America moved from the status of colonies to that of independent nation-states. The process was sometimes exhilarating and often painful, but during the course of the century, these nations were able to create governments and begin to address many social and economic problems. These problems were inherited from the colonial era and were intensified by internal political and ideological conflicts and foreign intervention. Moreover, the Latin American nations had to revive their economies after their struggles for independence and to confront their position within the world economic system as suppliers of agricultural products and consumers of manufactured goods.

To some extent Latin America ran against the currents of global history in the 19th century. During the great age of imperi-

Figure 25.7 The drive for opening of a sea route from the Atlantic to the Pacific moved the United States to back the creation of the Panama Canal. Between 1881 and 1914 the canal, a major engineering feat, was constructed. The nation of Panama was created in the process of securing rights to the canal when the United States backed an independence movement that separated Panama from Colombia. The Panama Canal changed the nature of international maritime commerce. This image is of the Gatlin cut, which was the major excavation on the canal.

alism, Latin America cast off the previous colonial controls. Swept by the same winds of change that had transformed Europe's society and economy and led to the separation of England's North American colonies, Latin American countries struggled with the problems of nation-building while, like China and Russia, holding off colonial incursions. In this sense, and also in some efforts to define a Latin American cultural identity, Latin America became a bit more isolated in the world at large.

The heritage of the past weighed heavily on Latin America. Political and social changes were many, and pressures for these changes came from a variety of sources, such as progressive politicians, modernizing military men, a growing urban population, dissatisfied workers, and disadvantaged peasants. Still, in many ways Latin America remained remarkably unchanged. Revolts were frequent, but revolutions that changed the structure of society or the distribution of land and wealth were few, and the reforms intended to make such changes usually were unsuccessful. The elite controlled most of the economic resources, a growing but still small urban sector had emerged politically but either remained weak or had to accommodate the elite, and most of the population continued to labor on the land with little hope of improvement. Latin America had a distinctive civilization, culturally and politically sharing much of the Western tradition yet economically functioning more like areas of Asia and Africa. Latin America was the first non-Western area to face the problems of decolonization, and many aspects of its history that seemed so distinctive in the 19th century proved to be previews of what would follow: decolonization and nation-building elsewhere in the world in the 20th century.

Latin America's global connections included ongoing political and cultural ties with the West. Efforts to imitate the West accelerated in some regions, for example, with the importation of sports like soccer. Growing influence and intervention from the United States was another outside force. New immigration, from southern Europe but also now from Asia, brought additional connections. But Latin America's most significant global link continued to involve its dependent economy, drawing goods, now including machinery, from the West while exporting a growing range of foods and raw materials.

Further Readings

David Bushnell and Neil Macauley, *The Emergence of Latin America in the Nineteenth Century*, 2nd ed. (1994), provides an excellent overview that is critical of the dependency thesis. A good economic analysis is found in S. Haber, *Why Latin America Fell Behind* (1997). The movements for independence and the major leaders are described in John Chasteen, *Americanos* (2007) while Jeremy Adelman, *Sovereignty and Revolution in the Iberian Atlantic* (2006) is a broad synthetic analysis of the movements for independence. Hendrik Kraay, *Race, State, and Armed Forces in Independence Era Brazil* (2001), looks at the process of creating an army in the case of Brazil.

Catherine Davies, *South American Independence: Gender, Politics, and Text* (2006) examines the role of women while Arlene Díaz, *Female Citizens, Patriarchs, and the Law in Venezuela, 1786–1904* (2004), provides a case study of how women were affected by the new states. Kenneth Andrien and Lyman Johnson, *The Political Economy of Spanish America in the Age of Revolution, 1750–1850* (1994), presents a series of recent studies. E. Bradford Burns, *Poverty or Progress: Latin America in the Nineteenth Century* (1973), provides a challenging attack on the liberal programs and a defense of a folk political tradition. Florencia Mallon, *Peasant and Nation* (1995), suggests a peasant origin for Latin American nationalism. Eric Van Young, *The Other Rebellion* (2001), examines Mexico's independence movement. Ricardo Salvatore, Carlos Aguirre, and Gilbert Joseph, eds. *Crime and Punishment in Latin America* (2001) has essays that show the importance of law the definition of crime in the new nations. Volumes 3 to 5 of *The Cambridge History of Latin America* (1985–1986) contain fine essays on major themes and individual countries. A good essay from the collection is Robert Freeman Smith's "Latin America, the United States, and the European Powers, 1830–1930," vol. 4, 83–120. On the complex relationship between the United States and Latin America, see the essays in G. Joseph, C. Legrand, and R. Salvatore, eds., *Close Encounters of Empire* (1998). James Dunkerley, *Americana: The Americas in the World, around 1850* (2000) provides a wonderful if idiosyncratic view of that relationship.

There are many single-volume country histories and monographs on particular topics. Richard Slatta, *Gauchos and the Vanishing Frontier* (1985); José Moya, *Cousins and Strangers: Spanish Immigrants to Buenos Aires, 1850–1930* (1998); and Jeremy Adelman, *A Republic of Capital* (1999), provide a good start on Argentina. Robert Levine, *A History of Brazil* (1999) and Jeffrey Needell; *Party of Order: The Conservatives, the State, and Slavery in the Brazilian Monarchy, 1831–1871 /* (2007). Michael Meyer and William Beezley, *The Oxford History of Mexico* (2000); and Herbert Klein, *Bolivia* (1982), are good examples of national histories. There are excellent rural histories, such as B. J. Barickman, *A Bahian Counterpoint* (1998); Charles Walker, *Smoldering Ashes. Cuzco and the Creation of Republican Peru* (1999) and Charles Berquist, *Coffee and Conflict in Colombia, 1886–1910* (1978). Silvia Arrom, *The Women of Mexico City* (1985), is a fine example of the growing literature in women's history, as is Eileen J. Suárez Findlay, *Imposing Decency: The Politics of Sexuality and Race in Puerto Rico, 1870–1920* (1999). Asunción Lavrín, *Women, Feminism, and Social Change in Argentina, Chile, and Uruguay, 1890-1940* (1995) provides as detailed overview of the southern cone. On the factor of race, at the regional level of analysis Greg Grandin, *The Blood of Guatemala* (2000), discusses indigenous peoples' relation to the nation in that country.

On the Web

Simon Bolívar's views on state formation and his ambivalent attitude toward the United States are examined at http://faculty.chass .ncsu.edu/slatta/hi216/. The life and career of his co-revolutionist in the south, José de San Martín, is beautifully illustrated at http://pachami.com/English/sanmartin1E.htm and described at http://geocities.com/TimesSquare/1848/martin.html.

Bolívar and San Martín lived to see their visions compromised or betrayed, but they avoided the tragic fate of the hero of the Mexican war for independence, Father Miguel de Hidalgo, who is discussed at http://www.mexconnect.com/mex_/travel/ganderson/gadeloresh.html. Postindependence leaders such as Mexico's Santa Anna (http://www.pbs.org/weta/thewest/people/s_z/santaanna.htm and http://www.mexconnect.com/mex_/history/jtuck/jtsantaanna.html) and Argentina's Domingo Sarmiento (http://www.mexconnect.com/mex_/history/jtuck/jtsantaanna.html) faced numerous difficulties when addressing the task of nation-building.

The Monroe Doctrine (http://avalon.law.yale.edu/19th_century/monroe.asp and http://edsitement.neh.gov/lesson_images/lesson578/forMonroe.pdf) and Thomas Jefferson's comments on its "imperial" implications (http://www.mtholyoke.edu/acad/intrel/thomas.htm) are worthy of close attention. Other sites, including http://www.psci.unt.edu/ENTERLINE/MONROEDOCTRINE .PDF, stress that for all its later foreign policy implications, the Monroe Doctrine was merely a reflection of John Quincy Adams's domestic political concerns. However, discourse over the Monroe Doctrine illuminates the process by which the United States evolved from a revolutionary upstart to a world power. Jefferson rejected a seizure of Cuba on moral grounds but noted its value as a possible addition to his country. Other American leaders with fewer scruples would later seize land from their neighbors to the south, a topic addressed with some drama through primary sources and poetry at http://www.smplanet.com/imperialism/toc.html, http://www.english.uiuc.edu/maps/poets/a_f/espada/imperialism.htm, http://www.fordham.edu/halsall/mod/1913calderon .html, and http://www.fordham.edu/halsall/mod/modsbook32 .html. The concept of Manifest Destiny as applying to the American war with Mexico is explored at http://www.pbs.org/kera/usmexicanwar/prelude/manifest_destiny_overview.html. Manifest Destiny as it relates to world history beyond the Mexican conflict is discussed at http://www.let.rug.nl/usa/E/manifest/manif1.htm and http://www.pbs.org/kera/usmexicanwar/index_flash.html.

For U.S. and Latin American relations generally, see http://www.uoregon.edu/~caguirre/uslatam.html.

AP* Test Prep

1. Which group led the independence movements in most of Latin America?

   (A) American-born whites or creoles

   (B) Indians/Native Americans

   (C) Mestizos, or people of mixed Indian and European descent

   (D) Mulattos, or people of mixed African and European descent

2. Haiti's independence differed from other Latin American movements in that

   (A) it began as a slave revolt against slave owners and led to independence.

   (B) the United States supported the Haitians in their revolution with supplies.

   (C) France and Napoleon welcomed and recognized Haiti's independence.

   (D) Spain supported the movement for independence.

3. Leaders of Latin American independence revolts were generally

   (A) monarchists, who wanted monarchs to govern their states.

   (B) radicals, who wanted democratic republics and universal male suffrage.

   (C) liberals, who wanted some representative institutions but feared the masses.

   (D) conservative republicans, who favored the church and rich landowners

4. Brazil's independence differed from the rest of Latin America in that it was

   (A) the result of a successful slave rebellion.

   (B) not supported by the locally-born European population.

   (C) declared and led by the Portuguese prince in Brazil, who then named himself emperor.

   (D) extremely violent with multiple armies led by different factions.

5. Throughout Latin America, the Indian population

   (A) generally supported the new republican governments.

   (B) remained largely outside the national political life.

   (C) revolted against Europeans and later the new governments.

   (D) acquired rights in some countries but not all.

6. The fifty years following independence in most Latin American countries was marked by

   (A) political instability.

   (B) social experimentation.

   (C) religious experimentation with evangelical movements.

   (D) economic industrialization.

7. Which economic pattern continued to prevail in post-independence Latin America?

   (A) plantation economies with slave or peasant labor

   (B) dependency on foreign markets and imports

   (C) government-sponsored socialism

   (D) U.S. manipulation of tariffs and infrastructure projects

Free-Response Question

What impacts of Spanish and Portuguese rule endured in Latin America in the postcolonial period?

Civilizations in Crisis: The Ottoman Empire, the Islamic Heartlands, and Qing China

From Empire to Nation: Ottoman Retreat and the Birth of Turkey
THINKING HISTORICALLY: Western Dominance and the Decline of Civilizations
Western Intrusions and the Crisis in the Arab Islamic Heartlands
VISUALIZING THE PAST: Mapping the Decline of Civilizations

The Last Dynasty: The Rise and Fall of the Qing Empire in China
DOCUMENT: Transforming Imperial China into a Nation
GLOBAL CONNECTIONS: Muslim and Chinese Decline and a Shifting Global Balance

Hong Xiuquan was a deeply troubled young man. One of five children from a struggling peasant family living in the Guangdong region on China's southeast coast, Hong had worked hard to excel in school so that he could take the exams that would provide entry into the lower rungs of the scholar-gentry-dominated bureaucracy. Counting on Hong's demonstrated aptitude for book learning to improve the family fortunes, his parents and kinsfolk scrimped to find the money needed to send him to school and hire tutors to prepare him for the rigorous examination process.

The pressure of such life-defining testing is invariably intense, but with the fate of his family in the balance Hong found his failures deeply humiliating. Mortification was increasingly laced with anger as he tried and failed four times to pass the exams that would earn him the lowest official degree, which carried with it a modest stipend from the state and the right to wear the robes of the scholar-gentry. Perhaps to escape the shame he felt in the company of family and friends who were well aware of his failures, Hong became an avid traveler. In 1836, in Whampoa, which was close to the great port city of Canton, Hong first came into contact with Protestant missionaries from the United States. After taking up the serious study of the Bible, Hong came to believe that he was the younger son of Jesus and that God had given him a sword to rid the world of corrupt officials and other agents of the devil.

Hong was well educated in a society where few went to school. He was also a charismatic speaker, given to trances and speaking in tongues, and he was convinced that he had a divine mission. He began to preach in public and was soon baptizing hundreds, then thousands of converts to his growing band of "God worshipers." Often in very garbled renditions, Biblical teachings and Christian rituals were widely deployed by adherents to his sect, which became known as the Taipings (meaning "Great Peace"), after one of the Chinese titles Hong claimed for himself. As his following grew into the tens of thousands, Hong's preaching became more strident and openly directed against the ruling Qing dynasty. Hong charged that the Qing rulers were the source of all manner of earthly evils and responsible for China's recent defeats at the hands of the British. The Taiping revolutionary agenda was also aimed at the scholar-gentry and other fundamental aspects of the Confucian order. In rebel-controlled areas, ancestral tablets were smashed, land was seized from the local gentry, and the imperial examination system was abolished. The Taipings proclaimed that women were equal to men, adopted a Christian solar calendar, and sought to restore moral order by banning slavery, concubinage, arranged marriage, opium smoking, footbinding, judicial torture, and the worship of idols. After decisively defeating a Qing military force sent to put an end to the Taiping movement, Hong's followers launched one of the longest-lived and most deadly rebellions of the 19th century. ∎

Both Hong's personal crisis and the revolutionary movement his teachings launched were catalyzed by the disintegration—beginning in the early 1800s—of Chinese civilization, which had been one of the world's most advanced for thousands of years. At the other end of Asia, the Ottomans, the last of the rival Muslim dynasties that had ruled the Middle East and south Asia in the early modern era, had gone into decline even earlier. In both cases, the sheer size, complexity, and persisting military power of each of these empires, combined with the ongoing rivalries among the European powers, prevented them from being formally colonized like much of the rest of Asia, Africa, and the

Pacific. But, as we shall see in the chapter that follows, both dynasties and the civilizations they sought to uphold came under repeated assault during the 19th century.

The Taiping Rebellion was a violent, radical variant of a succession of movements in both China and the Middle East that sought either to reform or put an end to the existing social and political order. The Taiping Rebellion and its counterpart in the Muslim Middle East, the Mahdist upheaval that raged in the Anglo-Egyptian Sudan for most of the last two decades of the century, were dedicated to bringing down an existing social order in order to replace it with a religiously inspired utopian society. At the other end of the political spectrum, Western-educated dissidents sought to build strong nation-states patterned after those of western Europe. The disruptions that resulted from the interventions of Western industrial powers in informally dominated areas, such as China and the Ottoman Empire, often contributed to the emergence of these political movements. But growing internal divisions within the empires themselves played a far greater role in precipitating these political upheavals and determining their impact on China and the Middle East in the last half of the 19th century.

From Empire to Nation: Ottoman Retreat and the Birth of Turkey

In part, the Ottoman crisis was brought on by a succession of weak rulers within a political and social order that was centered on the sultan at the top. Inactive or inept sultans opened the way for power struggles between rival ministers, religious experts, and the commanders of the Janissary corps. Competition between elite factions further eroded effective leadership within the empire, weakening its control over the population and resources it claimed to rule. Provincial officials colluded with the local land-owning classes, the **ayan,** to cheat the sultan of a good portion of the taxes due him, and they skimmed all the revenue they could from the already impoverished peasantry in the countryside.

At the same time, the position of the artisan workers in the towns deteriorated because of competition from imported manufactures from Europe. Particularly in the 18th and early 19th centuries, this led to urban riots in which members of artisan guilds and young men's associations often took a leading role. Merchants within the empire, especially those who belonged to minority religious communities such as the Jews and Christians, grew more and more dependent on commercial dealings with their European counterparts. This pattern accelerated the influx of Western manufactured goods that was steadily undermining handicraft industries within the empire. In this way, Ottoman economic dependence on some of its most threatening European political rivals increased alarmingly.

With the Ottoman leaders embroiled in internal squabbles and their armies deprived of the resources needed to match the great advances in weaponry and training made by European rivals, the far-flung Ottoman possessions proved an irresistible temptation for their neighbors (see Visualizing

Figure 26.1 This panoramic scene painted by a Chinese witness to the Taiping rebellion shows the rebel forces besieging and burning an enemy town and a nearby estate house of a large landlord's family in central China.

Weakened by internal strife and unable to prevent European rivals from whittling away its territories, the Ottoman Empire appeared near disintegration. But in the late 18th century, able Ottoman rulers and committed reformers devised strategies that slowed the decline of the empire and the advance of the European powers.

ayan The wealthy landed elite that emerged in the early decades of Abbasid rule.

foreign trade
dependence

603

1640 C.E.	1800 C.E.	1850 C.E.	1875 C.E.	1900 C.E.
1644 Manchu nomads conquer China; Qing dynasty rules 1662–1722 Reign of Kangxi emperor in China 1722 Safavid dynasty falls in Persia 1727 First printing press set up in Ottoman Empire 1736–1799 Reign of Qianlong emperor in China 1768–1774 Disastrous Ottoman defeat in war with Russia 1789–1807 Reign of Ottoman Sultan Selim III 1793 British embassy to Qianlong emperor in China 1798 French invasion of Egypt; Napoleon defeats Egypt's Mamluk rulers	1805–1849 Reign of Muhammad Ali in Egypt 1807–1839 Reign of Ottoman Sultan Mahmud II 1826 Ottoman Janissary corps destroyed 1834 Postal system established in Ottoman Empire 1838 Ottoman treaty with British removing trade restrictions in the empire 1839–1841 Opium War in China 1839–1876 *Tanzimat* reforms in the Ottoman Empire 1839–1897 Life of Islamic thinker al-Afghani 1849–1905 Life of Egyptian reformer Muhammad Abduh	1850–1864 Taiping Rebellion in China 1854–1856 Crimean War 1856–1860 Anglo-French war against China 1866 First railway begun in Ottoman Empire 1869 Opening of the Suez Canal 1870 Ottoman legal code reformed	1876 Constitution promulgated for Ottoman Empire 1876–1908 Reign of Ottoman Sultan Abdul Hamid 1877 Treaty of San Stefano; Ottomans driven from most of the Balkans 1882 British invasion and occupation of Egypt; failed Arabi revolt in Egypt 1883 Mahdist victory over British-led Egyptian expeditionary force at Shakyan 1889 Young Turks establish the Ottoman Society for Union and Progress in Paris 1898 British-Egyptian army defeats the Mahdist army at Omdurman 1898–1901 Boxer Rebellion and 100 Days of Reform in China	1905 Fatherland Party established in Egypt 1908 Young Turks seize power in Istanbul

the Past feature, p. 614). In the early 18th century, the Austrian Habsburg dynasty was the main beneficiary of Ottoman decadence. The long-standing threat to Vienna was forever vanquished, and the Ottomans were pushed out of Hungary and the northern Balkans.

In the late 1700s the Russian Empire, strengthened by Peter the Great's forced Westernization (see Chapter 18), became the main threat to the Ottomans' survival. As military setbacks mounted and the Russians advanced across the steppes toward warm-water ports on the Black Sea, the Ottomans' weakness was underscored by their attempts to forge alliances with other Christian powers. As the Russians gobbled up poorly defended Ottoman lands in the Caucasus and Crimea, the subject Christian peoples of the Balkans grew more and more restive under Ottoman rule. In 1804 a major uprising broke out in Serbia that was repressed only after years of difficult and costly military campaigns. But military force could not quell the Greek revolt that broke out in the early 1820s, and by 1830 the Greeks had regained their independence after centuries of Ottoman rule. In 1867 Serbia also gained its freedom, and by the late 1870s the Ottomans had been driven from nearly the whole of the Balkans and thus most of the European provinces of their empire. In the decades that followed, Istanbul was repeatedly threatened by Russian armies or those of the newly independent Balkan states.

Reform and Survival

Southeast Europe and the Ottoman Empire

Despite almost two centuries of unrelieved defeats on the battlefield and steady losses of territory, the Ottoman Empire somehow managed to survive into the 20th century. Its survival resulted in part from divisions between the European powers, each of which feared that the others would gain more from the total dismemberment of the empire. In fact, the British concern to prevent the Russians from controlling Istanbul—thus gaining direct access to and threatening British naval dominance in the Mediterranean—led them to prop up the tottering Ottoman regime repeatedly in the last half of the 19th century. Ultimately, the Ottomans' survival depended on reforms from within, initiated by the sultans and their advisors at the top of the imperial system and carried out in stages over most of the 19th century. At each stage, reform initiatives increased tensions within the ruling elite. Some factions advocated far-reaching change along European lines, others argued for reforms based on precedents from the early Ottoman period, and other elite groups had a vested interest in blocking change of any sort.

These deep divisions within the Ottoman elite made reform a dangerous enterprise. Although modest innovations, including the introduction of the first printing press in 1727, had been enacted in the 18th century, Sultan **Selim III** (r. 1789–1807) believed that bolder initiatives were needed if the dynasty and empire were to survive. But his reform efforts, aimed at improving administrative efficiency and building a new army and navy, angered powerful factions within the bureaucracy. They were also seen by the Janissary corps, which had long been the dominant force in the Ottoman military (see Chapter 21), as a direct threat. Selim's modest initiatives cost him his throne—he was toppled by a Janissary revolt in 1807—and his life.

Two decades later, a more skillful sultan, **Mahmud II,** succeeded where Selim III had failed. After secretly building a small professional army with the help of European advisors, in 1826 Mahmud II ordered his agents to incite a mutiny of the Janissaries. This began when the angry Janissaries overturned the huge soup kettles in their mess area. With little thought given to planning their next move, the Janissaries poured into the streets of Istanbul, more a mob than a military force. Once on the streets, they were shocked to be confronted by the sultan's well trained new army. The confrontation ended in the slaughter of the Janissaries, their families, and the Janissaries' religious allies.

After cowing the ayan into at least formal submission to the throne, Mahmud II launched a program of much more far-reaching reforms than Selim III had attempted. Although the ulama, or religious experts, and some of Mahmud's advisors argued for self-strengthening through a return to the Ottoman and Islamic past, Mahmud II patterned his reform program on Western precedents. After all, the Western powers had made a shambles of his empire. He established a diplomatic corps on Western lines and exchanged ambassadors with the European powers (Figure 26.2). The westernization of the army was expanded from Mahmud's secret force to the whole military establishment. European military advisors, both army and navy, were imported to supervise the overhaul of Ottoman training, armament, and officers' education.

In the decades that followed, Western influences were pervasive at the upper levels of Ottoman society, particularly during the period of the **Tanzimat reforms** between 1839 and 1876. University education was reorganized on Western lines, and training in the European sciences and mathematics was introduced. State-run postal and telegraph systems were established in the 1830s, and railways were built in the 1860s. Newspapers were established in the major towns of the empire. Extensive legal reforms were enacted, and in 1876 a constitution, based heavily on European prototypes, was promulgated. These legal reforms greatly improved the position of minority religious groups, whose role in the Ottoman economy increased steadily.

Some groups were adversely affected by these changes, which opened the empire more and more to Western influences. This was especially true of the artisans, whose position was gravely weakened by an 1838 treaty with the British that removed import taxes and other barriers to foreign trade that had protected indigenous producers from competition from the West. Other social groups gained little from the Tanzimat reforms. This was particularly true of women. Proposals for women's education and an end to seclusion, polygamy, and veiling were debated in

Selim III Sultan who ruled Ottoman Empire from 1789 to 1807; aimed at improving administrative efficiency and building a new army and navy; toppled by Janissaries in 1807.

Mahmud II (1785–1839) Ottoman sultan; built a private, professional army; fomented revolution of Janissaries and crushed them with private army; destroyed power of Janissaries and their religious allies; initiated reform of Ottoman Empire on Western precedents.

Tanzimat reforms Series of reforms in Ottoman Empire between 1839 and 1876; established Western-style university, state postal system, railways, extensive legal reforms; resulted in creation of new constitution in 1876.

Reform of the State as an Imperial Project: The Hatt-i Serif of Gülhane, November 3, 1839

Figure 26.2 In the courtyard of the Topkapi Palace in Istanbul, Sultan Selim III receives dignitaries from throughout the Ottoman Empire in the midst of a splendidly attired imperial entourage.

Women and
Children
Workers in
an Ottoman
Textile Mill,
1878

Ottoman intellectual circles from the 1860s onward. But few improvements in the position of women, even among the elite classes, were won until after the last Ottoman sultan was driven from power in 1908.

Repression and Revolt

The reforms initiated by the sultans and their advisors improved the Ottomans' ability to fend off, or at least deflect, the assaults of foreign aggressors. But they increasingly threatened the dynasty responsible for them. Western-educated bureaucrats, military officers, and professionals came increasingly to view the sultanate as a major barrier to even more radical reforms and the full transformation of society. The new elites also clashed with conservative but powerful groups, such as the ulama and the ayan, who had a vested interest in preserving as much as possible of the old order.

Abdul Hamid Ottoman sultan who attempted to return to despotic absolutism during reign from 1878 to 1908; nullified constitution and restricted civil liberties; deposed in coup in 1908.

The Ottoman Sultan **Abdul Hamid** responded to the growing threat from westernized officers and civilians by attempting a return to despotic absolutism during his long reign from 1878 to 1908. He nullified the constitution and restricted civil liberties, particularly the freedom of the press. These measures deprived westernized elite groups of the power they had gained in forming imperial policies. Dissidents or even suspected troublemakers were imprisoned and sometimes tortured and killed. But the deep impact of decades of reform was demonstrated by the fact that even Abdul Hamid continued to push for westernization in certain areas. The military continued to adopt European arms and techniques, increasingly under the instruction of German advisors. In addition, railways, including the famous line that linked Berlin to Baghdad, and telegraph lines were built between the main population centers. Western-style educational institutions grew, and judicial reforms continued.

The Decline of
the Ottoman
Empire

Ottoman Society for Union and Progress Organization of political agitators in opposition to rule of Abdul Harmid; also called "Young Turks"; desired to restore 1876 constitution.

The despotism of Abdul Hamid came to an abrupt end in the nearly bloodless coup of 1908. Resistance to his authoritarian rule had led exiled Turkish intellectuals and political agitators to found the **Ottoman Society for Union and Progress** in Paris in 1889. The Young Turks (Figure 26.3), as members of the society came to be known, professed their loyalty to the Ottoman regime and were determined to restore the 1876 constitution and resume far-reaching reforms within the

Political
Oppression in
the Ottoman
Empire

growth of cities

Figure 26.3 Taken after Turkey's defeat in World War I and the successful struggles of the Turks to prevent the partition of their heartlands in Asia Minor, this photo features a group of Young Turks who had survived these challenges and grown a good deal older. The man in the business suit in the center is Mustafa Kemal, or Ataturk, who emerged as a masterful military commander in the war and went on to become the founder of modern Turkey.

empire. Clandestine printing presses operated by the Young Turks turned out tracts denouncing the regime and outlining further steps to be taken to modernize and thus save the empire. Assassinations were attempted and coups plotted, but until 1908 all were undone by a combination of divisions within the ranks of the westernized dissidents and police countermeasures.

Sympathy within the military for the 1908 coup had much to do with its success. Perhaps even more important was the fact that only a handful of the sultan's supporters were willing to die defending the regime. Although a group of officers came to power, they restored the constitution and press freedoms and promised reforms in education, administration, and even the status of women. The sultan was retained as a political figurehead and the highest religious authority in Islam.

Unfortunately, the officers soon became embroiled in factional fights that took up much of the limited time remaining before the outbreak of World War I. In addition, their hold on power was shaken when they lost a new round of wars in the Balkans and a conflict against Italy over Libya, the Ottomans' last remaining possession in north Africa. Just as the sultans had before them, however, the Young Turk officers managed to stave off the collapse of the empire by achieving last-gasp military victories and by playing the hostile European powers against each other.

Although it is difficult to know how the Young Turks would have fared if it had not been for the outbreak of World War I, their failure to resolve several critical issues did not bode well for the future. They overthrew the sultan, but they could not bring themselves to give up the empire ruled by Turks for over 600 years. The peoples most affected by their decision to salvage what was left of the empire were the Arabs of the Fertile Crescent and coastal Arabia, who still remained under Ottoman control. Arab leaders in Beirut and Damascus had initially favored the 1908 coup because they believed it would bring about the end of their long domination by the Turks. To their dismay, the Arabs discovered that the Young Turks not only meant to continue their subjugation but were determined to enforce state control to a degree unthinkable to the later Ottoman sultans. The quarrels between the leaders of the Young Turk coalition and the growing resistance in the Arab portions of what was left of the Ottoman Empire were suddenly cut short in August 1914.

Young Turks
Overthrow
Abdul Hamid
II, 1908

The
Young Turk
Revolution,
1908

Western Intrusions and the Crisis in the Arab Islamic Heartlands

By the early 1800s, the Arab peoples of the Fertile Crescent, Egypt, coastal Arabia, and north Africa had lived for centuries under Ottoman-Turkish rule. Although most Arabs resented Turkish domination, they could identify with the Ottomans as fellow Muslims, who were both ardent defenders of the faith and patrons of Islamic culture. Still, the steadily diminishing capacity of the Ottomans to defend the Arab Islamic heartlands left them at risk of conquest by the aggressive European powers. The European capture of outlying but highly developed Islamic states, from those in the Indonesian archipelago and India to Algeria in north Africa, engendered a sense of crisis among the Islamic faithful in the Middle Eastern heartlands. From the most powerful adversaries of Christendom, the Muslims had become the besieged. The Islamic world had been displaced by the West as the leading civilization in a wide range of endeavors, from scientific inquiry to monumental architecture.

The profound crisis of confidence brought on by successive reverses and the increasing strength of European rivals elicited a variety of responses in the Islamic world. Islamic thinkers debated the best way to reverse the decline and drive back the Europeans.

Muhammad Ali and the Failure of Westernization in Egypt

Although it did not establish a permanent European presence in the Islamic heartlands, Napoleon's invasion of Egypt in 1798 sent shock waves across what remained of the independent Muslim world. Significantly, Napoleon's motives for launching the expedition had little to do with designs for empire in the Middle East. Rather, he saw the Egyptian campaign as the prelude to destroying British power in India, where the French had come out on the short end of earlier wars for empire. Whatever his calculations, Napoleon managed to slip his fleet past the British blockade in the Mediterranean and put ashore his armies in July 1798 (see Visualizing the Past feature). There followed one of the most lopsided military clashes in modern history. As they advanced inland, Napoleon's forces were met by tens of thousands of cavalry bent on defending the Mamluk regime that then ruled Egypt as a vassal of the Ottoman sultans. The term *Mamluk* literally meant slave, and it suggested the Turkic origins of the regime in Egypt. Beginning as slaves who served Muslim overlords, the Mamluks had centuries earlier risen in the ranks as military commanders and seized

Western Dominance and the Decline of Civilizations

As we have seen in our examination of the forces that led to the breakup of the great civilizations in human history, each civilization has a unique history. But some general patterns have been associated with the decline of civilizations. Internal weaknesses and external pressures have acted over time to erode the institutions and break down the defenses of even the largest and most sophisticated civilizations. In the preindustrial era, slow and vulnerable communication systems were a major barrier to the long-term cohesion of the political systems that held civilizations together. Ethnic, religious, and regional differences, which were overridden by the confidence and energy of the founders of civilizations, reemerged. Self-serving corruption and the pursuit of pleasure gradually eroded the sense of purpose of the elite groups that had played a pivotal role in civilized development. The resulting deterioration in governance and military strength increased social tensions and undermined fragile preindustrial economies.

Growing social unrest from within was paralleled by increasing threats from without. A major factor in the fall of nearly every great civilization, from those of the Indus valley and Mesopotamia to Rome

> "A major factor in the fall of nearly every great civilization, from those of the Indus valley and Mesopotamia to Rome and the civilizations of Mesoamerica, was an influx of nomadic peoples, whom sedentary peoples almost invariably saw as barbarians."

and the civilizations of Mesoamerica, was an influx of nomadic peoples, whom sedentary peoples almost invariably saw as barbarians. Nomadic assaults revealed the weaknesses of the ruling elites and destroyed their military base. Their raids also disrupted the agricultural routines and smashed the public works on which all civilizations rested. Normally, the nomadic invaders stayed to rule the sedentary peoples they had conquered, as has happened repeatedly in China, Mesoamerica, and the Islamic world. Elsewhere, as occurred after the disappearance of the Indus valley civilization in India and after the fall of Rome, the vanquished civilization was largely forgotten or lay dormant for centuries. But over time, the invading peoples living in its ruins managed to restore patterns of civilized life that were quite different from, though sometimes influenced by, the civilization their incursions had helped to destroy centuries earlier.

Neighboring civilizations sometimes clashed in wars on their frontiers, but it was rare for one civilization to play a major part in the demise of another. In areas such as Mesopotamia, where civilizations were crowded together in space and time in the latter millennia B.C.E., older, long-dominant civilizations were overthrown and absorbed by upstart rivals. In most cases, however, and often in Mesopotamia, external threats to civilizations came from nomadic peoples. This was true even of Islamic civilization, which proved the most expansive before the emergence of Europe and whose rise and spread brought about

---

Murad (1790–1820) Head of the coalition of Mamluk rulers in Egypt; opposed Napoleonic invasion of Egypt and suffered devastating defeat; failure destroyed Mamluk government in Egypt and revealed vulnerability of Muslim core.

Ali, Muhammad Won power struggle in Egypt following fall of Mamluks; established mastery of all Egypt by 1811; introduced effective army based on Western tactics and supply and a variety of other reforms; by 1830s was able to challenge Ottoman government in Constantinople; died in 1848.

power in their own name. **Murad,** the head of the coalition of Mamluk households that shared power in Egypt at the time of Napoleon's arrival, dismissed the invader as a donkey boy whom he would soon drive from his lands.

Murad's contempt for the talented young French commander was symptomatic of the profound ignorance of events in Europe that was typical of the Islamic world at the time. This ignorance led to a series of crushing defeats, the most famous of which came in a battle fought beneath the pyramids of the ancient Egyptian pharaohs (see Figure 26.4). In that brief but bloody battle, the disciplined firepower of the French legions devastated the ranks of Mamluk cavalry, who were clad in medieval armor and wielded spears against the artillery Napoleon used with such devastating effect.

Because the Mamluks had long been seen as fighters of great prowess in the Islamic world, their rout was traumatic. It revealed just how vulnerable even the Muslim core areas were to European aggression and how far the Muslims had fallen behind the Europeans in the capacity to wage war. Ironically, the successful invasion of Egypt brought little advantage to Napoleon or the French. The British caught up with the French fleet and sank most of it at the Battle of Aboukir in August 1798. With his supply line cut off, Napoleon was forced to abandon his army and sneak back to Paris, where his enemies were trying to use his reverses in Egypt to put an end to his rise to power. Thus, Egypt was spared European conquest for a time. But the reprieve brought little consolation to thoughtful Muslims because the British, not Egypt's Muslim defenders, had been responsible for the French retreat.

In the chaos that followed the French invasion and eventual withdrawal in 1801, a young officer of Albanian origins named **Muhammad Ali** emerged as the effective ruler of Egypt. Deeply impressed by the weapons and discipline of the French armies, the Albanian upstart devoted his energies and the resources of the land that he had brought under his rule to building an up-to-date European-style military force. He introduced Western-style conscription among the Egyptian peasantry, hired French officers to train his troops, imported Western arms, and adopted Western tactics the collapse of several long-established civilized centers. The initial Arab explosion from Arabia that felled Sasanian Persia and captured Egypt was nomadic. But the incursions of the Arab bedouins differed from earlier and later nomadic assaults on neighboring civilizations. The Arab armies carried a new religion with them from Arabia that provided the basis for a new civilization, which incorporated the older ones they conquered. Thus, like other nomadic conquerors, the Arabs borrowed heavily from the civilizations they overran.

The emergence of western Europe as an expansive global force radically changed long-standing patterns of interaction between civilizations as well as between civilizations and nomadic peoples. From the first years of overseas exploration, the aggressive Europeans proved a threat to other civilizations. Within decades of Columbus' arrival in 1492, European military assaults had destroyed two of the great centers of civilization in the Americas: the Aztec and Inca empires. The previous isolation of the Native American societies and their consequent susceptibility to European diseases, weapons, plants, and livestock made them more vulnerable than most of the peoples the Europeans encountered overseas. Therefore, in the first centuries of Western expansion, most of the existing civilizations in Africa and Asia proved capable of standing up to the Europeans, except on the sea. With the scientific discoveries and especially the technological innovations that transformed Europe in the 17th and 18th centuries, all of this gradually changed. The unparalleled extent of the western Europeans' mastery of the natural world gave them new sources of power for resource extraction, manufacture, and war. By the end of the 18th century, this power was being translated into the economic, military, and increasingly the political domination of other civilizations.

A century later, the Europeans had either conquered most of these civilizations or reduced them to spheres they controlled indirectly and threatened to annex. The adverse effects of economic influences from the West, and Western political domination, proved highly damaging to civilizations as diverse as those of west Africa, the Islamic heartlands, and China. For several decades before World War I, it appeared that the materially advanced and expansive West would level all other civilized centers. In that era, most leading European, and some African and Asian, thinkers and political leaders believed that the rest of humankind had no alternative (except perhaps a reversion to savagery or barbarism) other than to follow the path of development pioneered by the West. All non-Western peoples became preoccupied with coping with the powerful challenges posed by the industrial West to the survival of their civilized past and the course of their future development.

QUESTIONS Can you think of instances in which one preindustrial civilization was a major factor in the collapse of another? Why do you think such an occurrence was so rare? Discuss the advantages that the Native Americans' isolation from civilizations in Europe, Africa, and Asia gave the European intruders in the 16th century. What kinds of advantages did the scientific and industrial revolutions give the Europeans over all other civilized peoples from the 18th century onward? Is the West losing these advantages today?

Figure 26.4 Napoleon's victory in the Battle of the Pyramids led to a short-lived, but transformative, French occupation of Egypt.

and modes of organization and supply. Within years he had put together the most effective fighting force in the Middle East. With it, he flouted the authority of his nominal overlord, the Ottoman sultan, by successfully invading Syria and building a modern war fleet that threatened Istanbul on a number of occasions.

Although Muhammad Ali's efforts to introduce reforms patterned after Western precedents were not confined to the military, they fell far short of a fundamental transformation of Egyptian society. To shore up his economic base, he ordered the Egyptian peasantry to increase their production of cotton, hemp, indigo, and other crops that were in growing demand in industrial Europe. Efforts to improve Egyptian harbors, particularly Alexandria, and extend irrigation works met with some success and led to modest increases in the revenues that could be devoted to the continuing modernization of the military. Attempts to reform education were ambitious, but little was actually achieved. Numerous schemes to build up an Egyptian industrial sector by setting up cotton textile factories were frustrated by the opposition of the European powers and the intense competition from imported, Western-manufactured goods.

The limited scope of Muhammad Ali's reforms ultimately checked his plans for territorial expansion and left Egypt open to inroads by the European powers. He died in 1848, embittered by the European opposition that had prevented him from mastering the Ottoman sultans and well aware that his empire beyond Egypt was crumbling. Lacking Muhammad Ali's ambition and ability, his successors were content to confine their claims to Egypt and the Sudanic lands that stretched from the banks of the upper Nile to the south. Intermarrying with Turkish families that had originally come to Egypt to govern in the name of the Ottoman sultans, Muhammad Ali's descendants provided a succession of rulers who were known as **khedives** (kuh-DEEVs) after 1867. The khedives were the formal rulers of Egypt until they were overthrown by the military coup that brought Gamel Abdul Nasser to power in 1952.

khedives [kuh-DEEVs] Descendants of Muhammad Ali in Egypt after 1867; formal rulers of Egypt despite French and English intervention until overthrown by military coup in 1952.

Bankruptcy, European Intervention, and Strategies of Resistance

Muhammad Ali's successors made a muddle of his efforts to reform and revitalize Egyptian society. While cotton production increased and the landlord class grew fat, the great majority of the peasants went hungry. The long-term consequences of these developments were equally troubling. The great expansion of cotton production at the expense of food grains and other crops rendered Egypt dependent on a single export. This meant that it was vulnerable to sharp fluctuations in demand (and thus price) on the European markets to which most of it was exported. Some further educational advances were made. But these were mainly at elite schools where French was the language of instruction.

Disraeli
Purchasing
Controlling
Interest in the
Suez Canal

Much of the revenue the khedives managed to collect, despite the resistance of the ayan, was wasted on the extravagant pastimes of the mostly idle elite connected to the palace. Most of what was left was squandered on fruitless military campaigns to assert Egyptian authority over the Sudanic peoples along the upper Nile. The increasing inability of the khedives to balance their books led in the mid-19th century to their growing indebtedness to European financiers. The latter lent money to the khedives and members of the Turkish elite because the financiers wanted continued access to Egypt's cheap cotton. By the 1850s, they had a second motive: a share in the potentially lucrative schemes to build a canal across the isthmus of Suez that would connect the Mediterranean and Red seas. The completion of the **Suez Canal** in 1869, depicted under construction in Figure 26.5, transformed Egypt into one of the most strategic places on earth. The canal soon became a vital commercial and military link between the European powers and their colonial empires in Asia and east Africa. Controlling it became one of the key objectives of their peaceful rivalries and wartime operations through the first half of the 20th century.

Suez Canal Built across Isthmus of Suez to connect Mediterranean Sea with Red Sea in 1869; financed by European investors; with increasing indebtedness of khedives, permitted intervention of British into Egyptian politics to protect their investment.

The ineptitude of the khedival regime and the Ottoman sultans, who were their nominal overlords, prompted discussion among Muslim intellectuals and political activists as to how to ward off the growing European menace. In the mid-19th century, Egypt, and particularly Cairo's ancient Muslim University of al-Azhar, became key meeting places of these thinkers from throughout the Islamic world. Some prominent Islamic scholars called for a jihad to drive the infidels from Muslim lands. They also argued that the Muslim world could be saved only by a return to the patterns of religious observance and social interaction that they believed had existed in the golden age of Muhammad.

Figure 26.5 Building a canal across the desert isthmus of Suez was a remarkable engineering feat. A massive investment in up-to-date technology was needed. By creating a water route between the Mediterranean and Red seas, the canal greatly shortened the travel time between Europe and maritime Asia as well as the east coast of Africa. Combined with the growing predominance of steamships, it helped to expand global commerce as well as tourism, which became a major middle-class activity in the late 19th century.

Other thinkers, such as **Jamal al-Din al-Afghani** (1839–1897) and his disciple **Muhammad Abduh** (1849–1905), stressed the need for Muslims to borrow scientific learning and technology from the West and to revive their earlier capacity to innovate. They argued that Islamic civilization had once taught the Europeans much in the sciences and mathematics, including such critical concepts as the Indian numerals. Thus, it was fitting that Muslims learn from the advances the Europeans had made with the help of Islamic borrowings. Those who advocated this approach also stressed the importance of the tradition of rational inquiry in Islamic history. They strongly disputed the views of religious scholars who contended that the Qur'an was the source of all truth and should be interpreted literally.

Although both religious revivalists and those who stressed the need for imports from the West agreed on the need for Muslim unity in the face of the growing European threat, they could not reconcile their very different approaches to Islamic renewal. Their differences, and the uncertainties they injected into Islamic efforts to cope with the challenges of the West, remain central problems in the Muslim world today.

The mounting debts of the khedival regime and the strategic importance of the canal gave the European powers, particularly Britain and France, a growing stake in the stability and accessibility of Egypt. French and British bankers, who had bought up a good portion of the khedives' shares in the canal, urged their governments to intervene militarily when the khedives proved unable to meet their loan payments. In the early 1880s, a major challenge to the influence of foreign interests was mounted by the supporters of a charismatic young Egyptian officer named **Ahmad Arabi.** The son of a small farmer in lower Egypt, Arabi had attended Qur'anic school and studied under the reform-minded Muhammad Abduh at al-Azhar. Though a native Egyptian, Arabi had risen in the ranks of the khedival army and had become increasingly critical of the fact that the officer corps was dominated by Turks with strong ties to the khedival regime. An attempt by the khedive to save money by disbanding Egyptian regiments and dismissing Egyptian officers sparked a revolt led by Arabi in the summer of 1882. Riots in the city of Alexandria, associated with mutinies in the Egyptian armies, drove the frightened khedive to seek British assistance. After bombarding the coastal batteries set up by Arabi's troops, the British sent ashore an expeditionary force that crushed Arabi's rebellion and secured the position of the khedive.

al-Afghani   Muslim thinker at the end of the 19th century; stressed need for adoption of Western scientific learning and technology; recognized importance of tradition of rational inquiry.

Abduh, Muhammad   Disciple of al-Afghani; Muslim thinker at end of 19th century; stressed need for adoption of Western scientific learning and technology, recognized importance of tradition of rational inquiry.

Religious and Secular Opposition Within the Middle East

Ahmad Arabi   (1841–1911) Egyptian military officer who led a revolt against Turkic dominance in the army in 1882, which forced the Khedival regime to call in British forces for support.

Khartoum [kahr-TOOM] River town that was administrative center of Egyptian authority in Sudan.

Ahmad, Muhammad Head of a Sudanic Sufi brotherhood; claimed descent from prophet Muhammad; proclaimed both Egyptians and British as infidels; launched revolt to purge Islam of impurities; took Khartoum in 1883; also known as the Mahdi.

Mahdi In Sufi belief system, a promised deliverer; also name given to Muhammad Achmad, leader of late 19th-century revolt against Egyptians and British in the Sudan.

Map 26.1 **British Egypt and the Anglo-Egyptian Sudan** Although British control over Egypt was quite secure from the time of the defeat of the Arabi revolt in 1882 until World War I, the Mahdist movement in the Sudan delayed the conquest of that vast region along the upper Nile River until 1898.

Although Egypt was not formally colonized, the British intervention began decades of dominance both by British consuls, who ruled through the puppet khedives, and by British advisors to all high-ranking Egyptian administrators. British officials controlled Egypt's finances and foreign affairs; British troops ensured that their directives were heeded by Egyptian administrators. Direct European control over the Islamic heartlands had begun.

Jihad: The Mahdist Revolt in the Sudan

As Egypt fell under British control, the invaders were drawn into the turmoil and conflict that gripped the Sudanic region to the south. Egyptian efforts to conquer and rule the Sudan, beginning in the 1820s, were resisted fiercely. The opposition forces were led by the camel- and cattle-herding nomads who occupied the vast, arid plains that stretched west and east from the upper Nile. The sedentary peoples who worked the narrow strip of fertile land along the river were more easily dominated. Thus, Egyptian authority, insofar as it existed, was concentrated in these areas and in river towns such as **Khartoum** (kahr-TOOM), which was the center of Egyptian administration in the Sudan.

Even in the riverine areas, Egyptian rule was greatly resented. The Egyptian regime was notoriously corrupt, and its taxes placed a heavy burden on the peasants compelled to pay them. The Egyptians were clearly outsiders, and the favoritism they showed some of the Sudanic tribes alienated the others. In addition, nearly all groups in the Muslim areas in the northern Sudan were angered by Egyptian attempts in the 1870s to eradicate the slave trade. The trade had long been a great source of profit for both the merchants of the Nile towns and the nomads, who attacked non-Muslim peoples, such as the Dinka in the south, to capture slaves.

By the late 1870s, Egyptian oppression and British intervention had aroused deep resentment and hostility. But a leader was needed to unite the diverse and often divided peoples of the region and to provide an ideology that would give focus and meaning to rebellion. **Muhammad Ahmed** proved to be that leader. He was the son of a boat builder, and he had been educated by the head of a local Sufi brotherhood. The fact that his family claimed descent from Muhammad and that he had the physical signs—a cleft between his teeth and a mole on his right cheek—that the local people associated with the promised deliverer, or **Mahdi,** advanced his reputation. The visions he began to experience, after he had broken with his Sufi master and established his own sectarian following, also suggested that a remarkable future was in store. What was seen to be a miraculous escape from a bungled Egyptian effort to capture and imprison Muhammad Ahmed soon led to his widespread acceptance as a divinely appointed leader of revolt against the foreign intruders.

The jihad that Muhammad Ahmed, who came to be known to his followers as the Mahdi, proclaimed against both the Egyptian heretics and British infidels was one of a number of such movements that had swept through sub-Saharan Africa since the 18th century. It represented the most extreme and violent Islamic response to what was perceived as the dilution of Islam in the African environment and the growing threat of Europe. Muhammad Ahmed promised to purge Islam of what he saw as superstitious beliefs and degrading practices that had built up over the centuries, thus returning the faith to what he claimed was its original purity. He led his followers in a violent assault on the Egyptians, whom he believed professed a corrupt version of Islam, and on the European infidels. At one point, his successors dreamed of toppling the Ottoman sultans and invading Europe.

The Mahdi's skillful use of guerrilla tactics and the confidence his followers placed in his blessings and magical charms earned his forces several stunning victories over the Egyptians. Within a few years the Mahdist forces were in control of an area corresponding roughly to the present-day nation of Sudan. At the peak of his power, the Mahdi fell ill with typhus and died. In contrast to many movements of this type, which collapsed rapidly after the death of their prophetic leaders, the Mahdists found a capable successor for Muhammad Ahmed. The **Khalifa Abdallahi** had been one of the Mahdi's most skillful military commanders. Under Abdallahi, the Mahdists built a strong, expansive state. They also sought to build a closely controlled society in which smoking, dancing, and alcoholic drink were forbidden, and theft, prostitution, and adultery were severely punished. Islamic religious and ritual practices were enforced rigorously. In addition, most foreigners were imprisoned or expelled, and the ban on slavery was lifted.

For nearly a decade, Mahdist armies attacked or threatened neighboring states on all sides, including the Egyptians to the north. But in the fall of 1896, the famous British General Kitchener was sent with an expeditionary force to put an end to one of the most serious threats to European domination in Africa. The spears and magical garments of the Mahdist forces proved no match for the machine guns and artillery of Kitchener's columns. At the battle of Omdurman in 1898, thousands of the Mahdist cavalry were slaughtered. Within a year the Mahdist state collapsed, and British power advanced yet again into the interior of Africa.

The 19th century was a time of severe reverses for the peoples of the Islamic world. By the century's end, it was clear that neither the religious revivalists, who called for a return to a purified Islam free of Western influences, nor the reformers, who argued that some borrowing from the West was essential for survival, had come up with a successful formula for dealing with the powerful challenges posed by the industrial West. Failing to find adequate responses and deeply divided, the Islamic community grew increasingly anxious over the dangers that lay ahead. Islamic civilization was by no means defeated. But its continued viability clearly was threatened by its powerful European neighbor, which had become master of the world.

The Middle East Enters the World Economy

Abdallahi, Khalifa Successor of Muhammad Achmad as leader of Mahdists in Sudan; established state in Sudan; defeated by British General Kitchener in 1598.

The Last Dynasty: The Rise and Fall of the Qing Empire in China

Although the Manchu nomads had been building an expansive state of their own north of the Great Wall for decades, their conquest of China was both unexpected and sudden. A local leader named **Nurhaci** (1559–1626) was the architect of unity among the quarrelsome Manchu tribes. He combined the cavalry of each tribe into extremely cohesive fighting units within eight **banner armies,** named after the flags that identified each. In the first decades of the 17th century, Nurhaci brought much of Manchuria, including a number of non-Manchu peoples, under his rule (see Visualizing the Past feature). Although he remained the nominal vassal of the Chinese Ming emperor, Nurhaci's forces continually harassed the Chinese who lived north of the Great Wall. During this period, the Manchu elite's adoption of Chinese ways, which had begun much earlier, was greatly accelerated. The Manchu bureaucracy was organized along Chinese lines, Chinese court ceremonies were adopted, and Chinese scholar-officials found lucrative employment in the growing barbarian state north of the Great Wall.

The weakness of the declining Ming regime, rather than the Manchus' own strength, gave the Manchus an opportunity to seize control in China. Their entry into China resulted from a bit of luck. In 1644 an official of the Ming government in charge of the northern defenses called in the Manchus to help him put down a widespread rebellion in the region near the Great Wall. Having allowed the Manchus to pass beyond the wall, the official found that they were an even greater threat than the rebels. Exploiting the political divisions and social unrest that were destroying what was left of Ming authority, the Manchus boldly advanced on the Ming capital at Beijing, which they captured within the year. It took nearly two decades before centers of Ming and rebel resistance in the south and west were destroyed by the banner armies, but the Manchus soon found themselves the masters of China.

They quickly proved that they were up to the challenge of ruling the largest empire in the world. Their armies forced submission by nomadic peoples far to the west and compelled tribute

In late-18th century China, a long period of strong rule by the Qing dynasty and a high degree of social stability gave way to rampant official corruption, severe economic dislocations, and social unrest. Over the course of the 19th century, the Western powers took advantage of these weaknesses to force open China's markets and reduce its Manchu rulers to little more than puppets.

Nurhaci (1559–1626) Architect of Manchu unity; created distinctive Manchu banner armies; controlled most of Manchuria; adopted Chinese bureaucracy and most ceremonies in Manchuria; entered China and successfully captured Ming capital at Beijing.

banner armies Eight armies of the Manchu tribes identified by separate flags; created by Nurhaci in early 17th century; utilized to defeat Ming emperor and establish Qing dynasty.

Mapping the Decline of Civilizations

Throughout much of human history, the size of the empires associated with major civilizations was usually a pretty good gauge of the extent of the political power, economic prosperity, and cultural influence they enjoyed. Civilizations on the rise were expansive and compelled even neighboring peoples who were not directly ruled to acknowledge their dominance. By contrast, civilizations in decline lost control of their borderlands to rival empires or suffered invasions—often by nomadic peoples—into the heart of the vast domains that their ruling dynasties continued to claim long after they could effectively govern them.

In the 18th and 19th centuries, two of the largest and most enduring empires in human history, the Ottoman and Qing, spiraled into decline. The plight of each of these empires is illustrated by the maps included here, which trace the advance of rival powers and the rise of internal resistance.

QUESTIONS Which of the empires would have been harder to defend? Compare the timing and nature of the external threats posed for each of the empires by rival powers and other external enemies in the late 18th and 19th centuries. Why was China affected somewhat later? Why were the Qing so much slower to respond to the outside threat compared to the Ottomans? Why were the Chinese more reluctant than the Ottomans to adopt the weapons and methods of their enemies? Which of the empires was more threatened by internal rebellions?

Map 26.2 Ottoman Empire from Late 18th Century to World War I   The vast territories of the Ottoman Empire were lost over a period of more than two centuries to external enemies and the assertion of independence by ambitious vassals.

Qing [chihng] Manchu dynasty that seized control of China in mid-17th century after decline of Ming; forced submission of nomadic peoples far to the west and compelled tribute from Vietnam and Burma to the south.

from kingdoms such as Vietnam and Burma to the south. Within decades, the Manchu regime, which had taken the dynastic name **Qing** (chihng) before its conquest of China, ruled an area larger than any previous Chinese dynasty with the exception of the Tang.

To reconcile the ethnic Chinese who made up the vast majority of their subjects, the Manchu rulers shrewdly retained much of the political system of their Ming predecessors. They added to the court calendar whatever Confucian rituals they did not already observe. They made it clear that they wanted the scholar-officials who had served the Ming to continue in office. The Manchus even pardoned many who had been instrumental in prolonging resistance to their conquest. For much of the first century of the dynasty, Chinese and Manchu officials were paired in appointments to most of the highest posts of the imperial bureaucracy, and Chinese officials predominated at the regional

Map 26.3 Qing Empire from Opium War of 1839–1841 to World War I Though much of the traditional Chinese territories remained intact, the Qing and later the government of the Republic of China lost control of regions distant from their capitals in the 19th and the first half of the 20th century.

and local levels. Manchus, who made up less than 2 percent of the population of the Qing Empire, occupied a disproportionate number of the highest political positions. But there were few limits as to how high talented ethnic Chinese could rise in the imperial bureaucracy.

Unlike the Mongol conquerors who had abolished it, the Manchus retained the examination system and had their own sons educated in the Chinese classics. The Manchu emperors styled themselves the Sons of Heaven and rooted their claims to be the legitimate rulers of China in their practice of the traditional Confucian virtues. The early Manchu rulers were generous patrons of the Chinese arts, and at least one, **Kangxi** (kohng-see) (1661–1722), was a significant Confucian scholar in his own right. Kangxi and other Manchu rulers employed thousands of scholars to compile great encyclopedias of Chinese learning.

Kangxi [kohng-see] Confucian scholar and Manchu emperor of Qing dynasty from 1661 to 1722; established high degree of Sinification among the Manchus.

Economy and Society in the Early Centuries of Qing Rule

The Manchu determination to preserve much of the Chinese political system was paralleled by an equally conservative approach to Chinese society as a whole. In the early centuries of their reign, the writings of Zhu Xi, which had been so influential in the preceding dynastic eras, continued to dominate official thinking. Thus, long-nurtured values such as respect for rank and acceptance of hierarchy—that is, old over young, male over female, scholar-bureaucrat over commoner—were emphasized in education and imperial edicts. Among the elite classes, the extended family remained the core unit of the social order, and the state grew increasingly suspicious of any forms of social organization, such as guilds and especially secret societies, that rivaled it.

The lives of women at all social levels remained centered on or wholly confined to the household. There the dominance of elder men was upheld by familial pressures and the state. Male control was enhanced by the practice of choosing brides from families slightly lower in social status than those of the grooms. Because they were a loss to their parents' household at marriage and usually needed a sizeable dowry, daughters continued to be much less desirable than sons. Despite the poor quality of the statistics relating to the practice, there are indications that the incidence of female infanticide rose in this period. In the population as a whole, males considerably outnumbered females, the reverse of the balance between the two in contemporary industrial societies.

Beyond the family compound, the world pretty much belonged to men, although women from lower-class families continued to work in the fields and sell produce in the local markets. The best a married woman could hope for was strong backing from her father and brother after she had gone to her husband's home, as well as the good luck in the first place to be chosen as the wife rather than as a second or third partner in the form of a concubine. If they bore sons and lived long enough, wives took charge of running the household. In elite families they exercised control over other women and even younger men.

Some of the strongest measures the Manchus took after conquering China were aimed at alleviating the rural distress and unrest that had become so pronounced in the last years of Ming rule. Taxes and state labor demands were lowered. Incentives such as tax-free tenure were offered to those willing to resettle lands that had been abandoned in the turmoil of the preceding decades. A sizeable chunk of the imperial budget (up to 10 percent in the early years of the dynasty) was devoted to repairing existing dikes, canals, and roadways and extending irrigation works. Peasants were encouraged to plant new crops, including those for which there was market demand, and to grow two or even three crops per year on their holdings.

Given the growing population pressure on the cultivable acreage and the near disappearance in most areas of open lands that could be settled, the regime had very little success in its efforts to control the landlord classes. After several decades of holding steady, the landlord classes found that they could add to their estates by calling in loans to peasants or simply by buying them out. With a surplus of workers, tenants had less and less bargaining power in their dealings with landlords. If they objected to the share of the crop the landlords offered, they were turned off the land and replaced by those willing to accept even less. As a result, the gap between the rural gentry and ordinary peasants and laborers increased. One could not miss the old and new rich in the rural areas, as they rode or were carried in sedan chairs, decked out in silks and furs, to make social calls on their peers. To further display their superior social standing, many men of the gentry class let their nails grow long to demonstrate that they did not have to engage in physical labor.

The sector of Chinese society over which the Qing exercised the least control was also the most dynamic. The commercial and urban expansion that had begun in the Song era gained new strength in the long peace China enjoyed during the first century and a half of Manchu rule. Regional diversification in crops such as tea was matched by the development of new ways to finance agricultural and artisan production. Until the end of the 18th century, both the state and the mercantile classes profited enormously from the great influx of silver that poured into China in payment for its exports of tea, porcelain, and silk textiles. European and other foreign traders flocked to Canton, and Chinese merchants, freed from the restrictions against overseas travel of the late Ming, found lucrative market outlets overseas. Profits from overseas trade gave rise to a wealthy new group of merchants, the **compradors,** who specialized in the import-export trade on China's south coast. In the 19th century, these merchants proved to be one of the major links between China and the outside world.

compradors Wealthy new group of Chinese merchants under the Qing dynasty; specialized in the import-export trade on China's south coast; one of the major links between China and the outside world.

Rot from Within: Bureaucratic Breakdown and Social Disintegration

By the late 18th century, it was clear that like so many Chinese dynasties of the past, the Qing was in decline. The signs of decline were pervasive and familiar. The bureaucratic foundations of the Chinese Empire were rotting from within. The exam system, which had done well in selecting able and honest bureaucrats in the early decades of the dynasty, had become riddled with cheating and favoritism. Despite formal restrictions, sons of high officials often were ensured a place in the ever-growing bureaucracy. Even more disturbing was the fact that nearly anyone with enough money could buy a post for sons or brothers. Impoverished scholars could be paid to take the exams for poorly educated or not-so-bright relatives. Examiners could be bribed to approve weak credentials or look the other way when candidates consulted cheat sheets while taking their exams. In one of the most notorious cases of cheating, a merchant's son won high honors despite the fact that he had spent the days of testing in a brothel hundreds of miles from the examination site.

Cheating had become so blatant by the early 18th century that in 1711 students who had failed the exams at Yangzhou held a public demonstration to protest bribes given to the exam officials by wealthy salt merchants. The growing influx of merchants' and poorly educated landlords' sons into the bureaucracy was particularly troubling because few of them had received the classical Confucian education that stressed the responsibilities of the educated ruling classes and their obligation to serve the people. Increasingly, the wealthy saw positions in the bureaucracy as a means of influencing local officials and judges and enhancing family fortunes. Less and less concern was expressed for the effects of bureaucratic decisions on the peasantry and urban laborers.

Over several decades, the diversion of revenue from state projects to enrich individual families devastated Chinese society. For example, funds needed to maintain the armies and fleets that defended the huge empire fell off sharply. Not surprisingly, this resulted in a noticeable drop in the training and armament of the military. Even more critical for the masses were reductions in spending on public works projects. Of these, the most vital were the great dikes that confined the Yellow River in northern China. Over the millennia, because of the silting of the river bottom and the constant repair of and additions to the dikes, the river and dikes were raised high above the densely populated farmlands through which they passed. Thus, when these great public works were neglected for lack of funds and proper official supervision of repairs, leaking dikes and the rampaging waters of the great river meant catastrophe for much of northeastern China.

Nowhere was this disaster more apparent than in the region of the Shandong peninsula (see Visualizing the Past feature). Before the mid-19th century, the Yellow River emptied into the sea south of the peninsula. By the 1850s, however, the neglected dikes had broken down over much of the area, and the river had flooded hundreds of square miles of heavily cultivated farmland. By the 1860s, the main channel of the river flowed north of the peninsula. The lands in between had been flooded and the farms wiped out. Millions of peasants were left without livestock or land to cultivate. Tens—perhaps hundreds—of thousands of peasants died of famine and disease.

As the condition of the peasantry deteriorated in many parts of the empire, further signs of dynastic decline appeared. Food shortages and landlord demands prompted mass migrations. Vagabond bands clogged the roads, and beggars crowded the city streets. Banditry, long seen by the Chinese as one of the surest signs of dynastic decline, became a major problem in many districts. As the following verse from a popular ditty of the 1860s illustrates, the government's inability to deal with the bandits was seen as a further sign of Qing weakness:

> When the bandits arrive, where are the troops?
> When the troops come, the bandits have vanished.
> Alas, when will the bandits and troops meet?

The assumption then widely held by Chinese thinkers—that the dynastic cycle would again run its course and the Manchus would be replaced by a new and vigorous dynasty—was belied by the magnitude of the problems confronting the leaders of China. The belief that China's future could be predicted from the patterns of its past ignored the fact that there were no precedents for

Map 26.4 Coastal China and Its Hinterland in the 19th Century
By the early 1800s, China's seaports and river deltas had become the main focus of European expansionist efforts. By the end of the century, China's southern coastal regions had also become seedbeds for nationalist resistance to Manchu rule and European domination.

Opium War Fought between the British and Qing China beginning in 1839; fought to protect British trade in opium; resulted in resounding British victory, opening of Hong Kong as British port of trade.

the critical changes that had occurred in China under Manchu rule. Some of these changes had their roots in the preceding Ming era (see Chapter 22), in which, for example, food crops from the Americas, such as corn and potatoes, had set in motion a population explosion. China desperately needed innovations in technology and organization that would increase its productivity to support its rapidly increasing population at a reasonable level. The corrupt and highly conservative late Manchu regime was increasingly an obstacle to, rather than a source of, these desperately needed changes.

Barbarians at the Southern Gates: The Opium War and After

Another major difference between the forces sapping the strength of the Manchus and those that had brought down earlier dynasties was the nature of the "barbarians" who threatened the empire from outside. Out of ignorance, the Manchu rulers and their Chinese administrators treated the Europeans much like the nomads and other peoples they saw as barbarians. But the Europeans presented a very different sort of challenge. They came from a civilization that was China's equal in sophistication and complexity. In fact, although European nation-states such as Great Britain were much smaller in population (in the early 19th century, England had 7 million people to China's 400 million), the scientific and industrial revolutions allowed them to compensate for their smaller numbers with better organization and superior technology. These advantages proved critical in the wars between China and Britain and the other European powers that broke out in the mid-19th century.

The issue that was responsible for the initial hostilities between China and the British did little credit to the latter. For centuries, British merchants had eagerly exported silks, fine porcelains, tea, and other products from the Chinese empire. Finding that they had little in the way of manufactured goods or raw materials that the Chinese were willing to take in exchange for these products, the British were forced to trade growing amounts of silver bullion. Unhappy about the unfavorable terms of trade in China, British merchants hit on a possible solution in the form of opium, which was grown in the hills of eastern India. Although opium was also grown in China, the Indian variety was far more potent and was soon in great demand in the Middle Kingdom. By the early 19th century an annual average of 4500 chests of opium, each weighing 133 pounds, were sold, either legally or illegally, to merchants on the south China coast. By 1839, on the eve of the **Opium War,** nearly 40,000 chests were imported by the Chinese.

Although the British had found a way to reverse the trade balance in their favor, the Chinese soon realized that the opium traffic was a major threat to their economy and social order. Within years, China's favorable trade balance with the outside world was reversed, and silver began to flow in large quantities out of the country. As sources of capital for public works and trade expansion decreased, agricultural productivity stagnated or declined, and unemployment spread, especially in the hinterlands of the coastal trading areas. Wealthy Chinese, who could best afford it, squandered increasing amounts of China's wealth to support their opium habits. Opium dens spread in the towns and villages of the empire at an alarming rate. It has been estimated that by 1838, 1 percent of China's more than 400 million people were addicted to the drug. Strung-out officials neglected their administrative responsibilities, the sons of prominent scholar-gentry families lost their ambition, and even laborers and peasants abandoned their work for the debilitating pleasures of the opium dens.

From the early 18th century Qing emperors had issued edicts forbidding the opium traffic, but little had been done to enforce them. By the beginning of the 19th century, it was clear to the court and high officials that the opium trade had to be stopped. When serious efforts were finally undertaken in the early 1820s, they only drove the opium dealers from Canton to nearby islands and other hidden locations on the coast. Finally, in the late 1830s, the emperor sent one of the most distinguished officials in the empire, **Lin Zexu** (lihn joh-shyoo), with orders to use every means available to stamp out the trade. Lin, who was famous for his incorruptibility, took his charge seriously. After being rebuffed in his attempts to win the cooperation of European merchants and naval officers in putting an end to the trade, Lin ordered the European trading areas in Canton blockaded, their warehouses searched, and all the opium confiscated and destroyed.

Not surprisingly, these actions enraged the European merchants, and they demanded military action to avenge their losses. Arguing that Lin's measures violated both the property rights of the merchants and principles of free trade, the British ordered the Chinese to stop their anti-opium campaign or risk military intervention. When Lin persisted, war broke out in late 1839. In the conflict that followed, the Chinese were routed first on the sea, where their antiquated war junks were no match for British gunboats. Then they were soundly defeated in their attempts to repel an expeditionary force the British sent ashore. With British warships and armies threatening the cities of the Yangzi River region, the Qing emperor was forced to sue for peace and send Lin into exile in a remote province of the empire.

Their victories in the Opium War and a second conflict, which erupted in the late 1850s, allowed the European powers to force China to open trade and diplomatic exchanges. After the first war, Hong Kong was established as an additional center of British commerce. European trade was also permitted at five other ports, where the Europeans were given land to build more warehouses and living quarters. By the 1890s, 90 ports of call were available to more than 300,000 European and American traders, missionaries, and diplomats. Britain, France, Germany, and Russia had won long-term leases of several ports and the surrounding territory (Figure 26.6).

Although the treaty of 1842 made no reference to the opium trade, after China's defeat the drug poured unchecked into China. By the mid-19th century, China's foreign trade and customs were overseen by British officials. They were careful to ensure that European nationals had favored access to China's markets and that no protective tariffs, such as those the Americans were using at the time to protect their young industries, were established by the Chinese. Most humiliating of all for the Chinese was the fact that they were forced to accept European ambassadors at the Qing court. Not only were ambassadors traditionally (and usually quite rightly) seen as spies, but the exchange of diplomatic missions was a concession that European nations were equal in stature to China. Given the deeply entrenched Chinese conviction that their Middle Kingdom was the civilized center of the earth and that all other peoples were barbarians, this was a very difficult concession to make. European battleships and firepower gave them little choice.

A Civilization at Risk: Rebellion and Failed Reforms

Although it was not immediately apparent, China's defeat in the Opium War contributed significantly to a building crisis that threatened not just the Qing dynasty, but Chinese civilization as a whole. Defeat and the dislocations in south China brought on by the growing commercial encroachments of the West spawned several rebellions that swept through much of south China in the 1850s and early 1860s and at one point threatened to overthrow the Qing dynasty. By far the greatest of these was the **Taiping Rebellion** led by the mentally unstable, semi-Christianized prophet **Hong Xiuquan** (hohng syoo-gwahn) (see chapter opener).

By the early 1850s, Hong's talented military commanders worked his growing numbers of followers into a formidable army that included regiments of Hakka women. Taiping fighters won a series of stunning victories against the demoralized and ill-disciplined Qing forces sent to destroy them. By the spring of 1853, they had captured a wide swath of territory in south-central China and established a capital at Nanjing, just west of Shanghai (see Visualizing the Past feature, p. 614).

With the Qing dynasty tottering on the verge of collapse, the northward drive lost its momentum, and over the next half decade it imploded. With Nanjing and a number of other prosperous cities and their hinterlands under Taiping control, the rebel leaders, including Hong, began to

Lin Zexu: Letter to Queen Victoria (1839)

Lin Zexu [lihn joh-shyoo] (1785–1850) Distinguished Chinese official charged with stamping out opium trade in southern China; ordered blockade of European trading areas in Canton and confiscation of opium; sent into exile following the Opium War.

Treaty Ports and the Boxer Rebellion in China

The Treaty of Nanjing

Taiping Rebellion Broke out in south China in the 1850s and early 1860s; led by Hong Xiuquan, a semi-Christianized prophet; sought to overthrow Qing dynasty and Confucian basis of scholar-gentry.

Nineteenth-Century China

Hong Xiuquan [hohng syoo-gwahn] (1812–1864) Leader of the Taiping rebellion; converted to specifically Chinese form of Christianity; attacked traditional Confucian teachings of Chinese elite.

Figure 26.6 In the late 19th century, the Chinese were forced to concede port and warehouse areas, such as the one in this painting, to rival imperialist powers. These areas were, in effect, colonial enclaves. They were guarded by foreign troops, flew foreign flags, and were run by Western or Japanese merchant councils.

(Illustration of Colonial Flags Flying Over a Chinese Port. Gift of Lincoln Kirstein, 1959 (JP3346). Image copyright © The Metropolitan Museum of Art/Art Resource, NY.)

plot and quarrel among themselves. As some were killed and others deserted the cause, the quality of the military commanders and the training of the God Worshipers' fighters declined precipitously. Taiping policies also alienated some of their own followers and increased the numbers of the enemies arrayed against them. None of their utopian measures to provide better lives for their followers were actually implemented, and their puritanical regulations were increasingly resented by their often hostile subjects. The ban on opium smoking and Hong's bizarre variations on Christian teachings alienated the Europeans, who threw their support behind the gravely imperiled Qing dynasty.

Of all of the rebellions that threatened to topple the Qing dynasty in the 19th century, the Taiping movement posed the most serious alternative—not only to the Qing dynasty but to Confucian civilization as a whole. The Taipings not only offered sweeping programs for social reform, land redistribution, and the liberation of women, but they also attacked the traditional Confucian elite and the learning on which its claims to authority rested. In addition to smashing ancestral tablets and shrines, the Taipings sought to develop a simplified script and mass literacy, which would have undermined some of the scholar-gentry's chief sources of power.

Their attack on the scholar-gentry was one of the main causes of the Taipings' ultimate defeat. Left no option but to rally to the Manchu regime, the provincial scholar-gentry became the focus of resistance to the Taipings. Honest and able Qing officials, such as **Zeng Guofan,** raised

Zeng Guofan Qing official who raised effective military forces against the Taiping assault on Northern China.

effective, provincially based military forces just in time to fend off the Taiping assault on northern China. Zeng and his allies in the government also carried out much needed reforms to root out corruption in the bureaucracy and revive the stagnating Chinese economy. In the late 19th century these dynamic provincial leaders were the most responsible for China's **self-strengthening movement,** which was aimed at countering the challenge from the West. They encouraged Western investment in railways and factories in the areas they governed, and they modernized their armies. Combined with the breakdown of Taiping leadership and the declining appeal of a movement that could not deliver on its promises, the gentry's efforts brought about the very bloody suppression of the Taiping Rebellion. Hong died—due to illness or suicide—before his capital at Nanjing was retaken. Nearly 100,000 of his followers perished in battle or immolated themselves in mass fires.

Despite their clearly desperate situation by the late 19th century, including a shocking loss in a war with Japan in 1894 and 1895, the Manchu rulers stubbornly resisted the far-reaching reforms that were the only hope of saving the regime and, as it turned out, Chinese civilization. Manchu rulers occasionally supported officials who pushed for extensive political and social reforms, some of which were inspired by the example of the West. But their efforts were repeatedly frustrated by the backlash of members of the imperial household and their allies among the scholar-gentry, who were determined to preserve the old order with only minor changes and to make no concessions to the West.

The last decades of the dynasty were dominated by the ultraconservative dowager empress **Cixi** (shur-shee), who became the power behind the throne. In 1898 she and her faction crushed the most serious move toward reform. Her nephew, the emperor, was imprisoned in the Forbidden City, and leading advocates for reform were executed or driven from China. On one occasion it was widely reported that Cixi defied the Westernizers by rechanneling funds that had been raised to build modern warships into the building of a huge marble boat in one of the lakes in the imperial gardens. With genuine reform blocked by Cixi and her faction, the Manchus relied on divisions among the provincial officials and among the European powers to maintain their position. Members of the Qing household also secretly backed popular outbursts aimed at expelling the foreigners from China, such as the **Boxer Rebellion** (Figure 26.7). The Boxer uprising broke out in 1898 and was put down only through the intervention of the imperialist powers in 1901. Its failure led to even greater control over China's internal affairs by the Europeans and a further devolution of power to provincial officials.

The Fall of the Qing and the Rise of a Chinese Nationalist Alternative

By the beginning of the 20th century, the days of the Manchus were numbered. With the defeat of the Taipings, resistance to the Qing came to be centered in rival secret societies such as the Triads and the Society of Elders and Brothers. These underground organizations inspired numerous local uprisings against the dynasty in the late 19th century. All of these efforts failed because of lack of coordination and sufficient resources. But some of the secret society cells became a valuable training ground that prepared the way for a new sort of resistance to the Manchus.

By the end of the 19th century, the sons of some of the scholar-gentry and especially of the merchants in the port cities were becoming more and more involved in secret society operations and other activities aimed at overthrowing the regime. Because many of these young men had received European-style educations, their resistance was aimed at more than just getting rid of the Manchus. They envisioned power passing to Western-educated, reformist leaders who would build a new, strong nation-state in China patterned after those of the West, rather than simply establishing yet another imperial dynasty. For aspiring revolutionaries such as **Sun Yat-sen,** who emerged as one of their most articulate advocates, seizing power was also seen as a way to enact desperately needed social programs to relieve the misery of the peasants and urban workers.

Although they drew heavily on the West for ideas and organizational models, the revolutionaries from the rising middle classes were deeply hostile to the involvement of the imperialist powers in Chinese affairs. They also condemned the Manchus for failing to control the foreigners. Like the

self-strengthening movement Late 19th-century movement in China to counter the challenge from the West; led by provincial leaders.

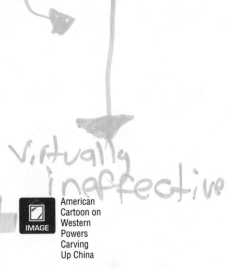

American Cartoon on Western Powers Carving Up China

Cixi [shur-shee] Ultraconservative dowager empress who dominated the last decades of the Qing dynasty; supported Boxer Rebellion in 1898 as a means of driving out Westerners.

Boxer Rebellion Popular outburst in 1898 aimed at expelling foreigners from China; failed because of intervention of armies of Western powers in China; defeat of Chinese enhanced control by Europeans and the power of provincial officials.

Sun Yat-sen Head of Revolutionary Alliance, organization that led 1911 revolt against Qing dynasty in China; briefly elected president in 1911, but yielded in favor of Yuan Shikai in 1912; created Nationalist party of China (Guomindang) in 1919; died in 1925.

Transforming Imperial China into a Nation

Faced with mounting intrusions by the Western powers into China, which the Manchu dynasty appeared powerless to resist, Chinese political leaders and intellectuals debated the ways by which China could renew itself and thus survive the challenges posed by the industrialized West. As the following passages from his journal *A People Made New* (published from 1902 to 1905) illustrate, Liang Qichao, one of the main advocates of major reforms in Chinese society, recognized the need for significant borrowing from Europe and the United States. At the same time, late 19th- and early 20th-century champions of renewal such as Liang wanted to preserve the basic features of Chinese society as they had developed over two millennia of history.

If we wish to make our nation strong, we must investigate extensively the methods followed by other nations in becoming independent. We should select their superior points and appropriate them to make up our own shortcomings. Now with regard to politics, academic learning, and techniques, our critics know how to take the superior points of others to make up for our own weakness; but they do not know that the people's virtue, the people's wisdom, and the people's vitality are the great basis of politics, academic learning, and techniques.

[Those who are for "renovation"] are worried about the situation and try hard to develop the nation and to promote well-being. But when asked about their methods, they would begin with diplomacy, training of troops, purchase of arms and manufacture of instruments; then they would proceed to commerce, mining, and railways; and finally they would come, as they did recently, to officers' training, police, and education. Are these not the most important and necessary things for modern civilized nations? Yes. But can we attain the level of modern civilization and place our nation in an invincible position by adopting a little of this and that, or taking a small step now and then? I know we cannot. . . .

Let me illustrate this by commerce. Economic competition is one of the big problems of the world today. It is the method whereby the powers attempt to conquer us. It is also the method whereby we should fight for our existence. The importance of improving our foreign trade has been recognized by all. But in order to promote foreign trade, it is necessary to protect the rights of our domestic trade and industry; and in order to protect these rights, it is necessary to issue a set of commercial laws. Commercial laws, however, cannot stand by themselves, and so it is necessary to complement them with other laws. A law which is not carried out is tantamount to no law; it is therefore necessary to define the powers of the judiciary. Bad legislation is worse than no legislation, and so it is necessary to decide where the legislative power should belong. If those who violate the law are not punished, laws will become void as soon as they are proclaimed; therefore, the duties of the judiciary must be defined. When all these are carried to the logical conclusion, it will be seen that foreign trade cannot be promoted without a constitution, a parliament, and a responsible government. . . .

What, then, is the way to effect our salvation and to achieve progress? The answer is that we must shatter at a blow the despotic and confused governmental system of some thousands of years; we must sweep away the corrupt and sycophantic learning of these thousands of years.

QUESTIONS What does Liang see as the key sources of Western strength? What does he believe China needs most to borrow from Europe and the United States? Do his recommendations strike you as specific enough to rescue China from its many predicaments? If you were the emperor's advisor, what sorts of changes would you recommend, perhaps copying the approaches tried by the leaders of other civilizations in this era?

POSSIBLE QUESTION?

Taipings, the young rebels cut off their *queues* (braided ponytails) in defiance of the Manchu order that all ethnic Chinese wear their hair in this fashion. They joined in uprisings fomented by the secret societies or plotted assassinations and acts of sabotage on their own. Attempts to coordinate an all-China rising failed on several occasions because of personal animosities or incompetence. But in late 1911, opposition to the government's reliance on the Western powers for railway loans led to secret society uprisings, student demonstrations, and mutinies on the part of imperial troops. When key provincial officials refused to put down the spreading rebellion, the Manchus had no choice but to abdicate. In February 1912, the last emperor of China, a small boy named **Puyi** (poo-yee), was deposed, and one of the more powerful provincial lords was asked to establish a republican government in China.

The revolution of 1911 toppled the Qing dynasty, but in many ways a more important turning point for Chinese civilization was reached in 1905. In that year, the civil service exams were given for the last time. Reluctantly, even the ultraconservative advisors of the empress Cixi had concluded that solutions to China's predicament could no longer be found in the Confucian learning the exams tested. In fact, the abandonment of the exams signaled the end of a pattern of civilized life the Chinese had nurtured for nearly 2500 years. The mix of philosophies and values that had come to be known as the Confucian system, the massive civil bureaucracy, rule by an educated and

Puyi [poo-yee] Last emperor of China; deposed as emperor while still a small boy in 1912.

Figure 26.7 China's peril in the aftermath of the Boxer Rebellion and the military interventions by the imperialist powers that it prompted are brilliantly captured in this contemporary cartoon showing the aggressive and mutually hostile great powers circling the carcass of the Qing Empire.

cultivated scholar-gentry elite, and even the artistic accomplishments of the old order came under increasing criticism in the early 20th century. Many of these hallmarks of the most enduring civilization that has ever existed were violently destroyed.

Global Connections

Muslim and Chinese Decline and a Shifting Global Balance

Both Chinese and Islamic civilizations were severely weakened by internal disruptions during the 18th and 19th centuries, and each was thrown into prolonged crisis by the growing challenges posed by the West. Several key differences in the interaction between each civilization and the West do much to explain why Islam, though badly shaken, survived, whereas Chinese civilization collapsed under the burden of domestic upheavals and foreign aggression. For the Muslims, who had been warring and trading with Christian Europe since the Middle Ages, the Western threat had long existed. What was new was the much greater strength of the Europeans in the ongoing contest, which resulted from their global expansion and their scientific and industrial revolutions. For China, the challenges from the West came suddenly and brutally. Within decades, the Chinese had to revise their image of their empire as the center of the world and the source of civilization itself to take into account severe defeats at the hands of peoples they once dismissed as barbarians.

The Muslims could also take comfort from the fact that, in the Judeo-Christian and Greek traditions, they shared much with the ascendant Europeans. As a result, elements of their own civilization had played critical roles in the rise of the West. This made it easier to justify Muslim borrowing from the West, which in any case could be set in a long tradition of exchanges with other civilizations. Although some Chinese technology had passed to the West, Chinese and Western leaders were largely unaware of early exchanges and deeply impressed by the profound differences between their societies. For the Chinese, borrowing from the barbarians required a painful reassessment of their place in the world—a reassessment many were unwilling to make.

In countering the thrusts from the West, the Muslims gained from the fact that they had many centers to defend; the fall of a single dynasty or regime did not mean the end of Islamic independence. The Muslims also gained from the more gradual nature of the Western advance. They had time to learn from earlier mistakes and try out different responses to the Western challenges. For the Chinese, the defense of their civilization came to be equated with the survival of the Qing dynasty, a line of thinking that the Manchus did all they could to promote. When the dynasty collapsed in the early 20th century, the Chinese lost faith in the formula for civilization they had successfully followed for more than two millennia. Again, timing was critical. The crisis in China seemed to come without warning. Within decades, the Qing went from being the arrogant controller of the barbarians to being a defeated and humbled pawn of the European powers.

When the dynasty failed and it became clear that the "barbarians" had outdone the Chinese in so many fields of civilized endeavor, the Chinese had little to fall back on. Like the Europeans, they had excelled in social and political organization and in mastery of the material world. Unlike the Hindus or the Muslims, they had no great religious tradition with which to counter the European conceit that worldly dominance could be equated with inherent superiority. In the depths of their crisis, Muslim peoples clung to the conviction that theirs was the true faith, the last and fullest of God's revelations to humankind. That faith became the basis of their resistance and their strategies for renewal, the key to the survival of Islamic civilization and its continuing efforts to meet the challenges of the West in the 20th and 21st centuries.

Both China and the Islamic lands of the Middle East and north Africa faced common challenges through the unavoidable intrusion of Western-dominated globalism. While their responses differed, both civilizations were only partially colonized (in contrast to Africa). Their situation also differed from that of Latin America, where connections to the West ran deeper amid an older pattern of economic dependency. They differed, finally, from two other societies, near neighbors, who retained fuller independence amid the same global pressures: Russia and Japan.

Further Readings

The more readable general introductions to the Ottoman decline and the origins of Turkey, include Elisabeth Özdalga, editor, *Late Ottoman Society: The Intellectual Legacy* (2005), and Caroline Finkel, *Osman's Dream: The Story of the Ottomans* (2006), and the chapter on "The Later Ottoman Empire" by Halil Inalcik in *The Cambridge History of Islam*, vol. 1 (1973). The fall of the dynasty and the development of the Turkish republic are treated in world historical perspective in Meliha Benli Altuni-sik, *Turkey: Challenges of Continuity and Change* ((2005) and Hur-I Islamo-glu-lnan, *The Ottoman Empire and the World Economy* (2004). Other recent studies on specific aspects of this process include C. V. Findley's studies of Ottoman bureaucratic reform and the development of a modern civil service in what is today Turkey; Ernest Ramsaur, *The Young Turks* (1957); Stanford Shaw, *Between Old and New* (1971); and David Kusher, *The Rise of Turkish Nationalism* (1977).

On Egypt and the Islamic heartlands in this period, see P. M. Holt, *Egypt and the Fertile Crescent, 1516–1922* (1965), or P. J. Vatikiotis, *The History of Egypt* (1985). On the Mahdist movement in the Sudan, see P. M. Holt, *The Mahdist State in the Sudan* (1958), or the fine summary by L. Carl Brown in Robert Rotberg and Ali Mazrui, eds., *Protest and Power in Black Africa* (1970). The latter also includes many informative articles on African resistance to European conquest and rule. On women and changes in the

family in the Ottoman realm, see Nermin Abadan-Unat, *Women in Turkish Society* (1981); in the Arab world, see Nawal el Saadawi, *The Hidden Face of Eve* (1980).

On the Manchu takeover in China, see Frederic Wakeman Jr., *The Great Enterprise* (1985), and Jonathan Spence and John E. Willis, eds., *Ming to Ch'ing* (1979). On Qing rule, among the most readable and useful works are Spence's *Emperor of China: Portrait of K'ang-hsi* (1974) and the relevant sections in his *The Search for Modern China* (1990); Susan Naquin and Evelyn Rawski, *Chinese Society in the 18th Century* (1987); and the essays in John Fairbank, ed., *The Cambridge History of China: Late Ch'ing 1800–1911* (1978). The early decades of Qing and Chinese decline are perceptively surveyed in F.W. Mote, *Imperial China, 900-1800* (1999). A good survey of the causes and course of the Opium War is provided in Hsin-pao Chang, *Commissioner Lin and the Opium War* (1964). The Taiping Rebellion is covered in Jen Yu-wen, *The Taiping Revolutionary Movement* (1973), and Jonathan D. Spence, *God's Chinese Son: Taiping Heavenly Kingdom of Hong Xiuquan* (1996). The rebellion heralding the last stage of Qing decline is examined in J. W. Esherick, *The Origins of the Boxer Uprising* (1987).

The first stages of the Chinese nationalist movement are examined in the essays in Mary Wright, ed., *China in Revolution: The First Phase* (1968). The early sections of Elisabeth Croll, *Feminism and Socialism in China* (1980), provide an excellent overview of the status and condition of women in the Qing era.

On the Web

Links exploring the Ming dynasty can be found at http://www.stockton.edu/~gilmorew/consorti/2feasia.htm and http://en.wikipedia.org/wiki/Ming_Dynasty. The decline of the Qing (http://library.thinkquest.org/26469/history/1900.html) was accelerated by the failure of a reform effort which climaxed in the 103 days from June 11 to September 21, 1898 (http://www-chaos.umd.edu/history/modern3.html). This failure came on top of the Opium War (http://www.wsu.edu/~dee/CHING/OPIUM.HTM and http://www.cyber.law.harvard.edu/ChinaDragon/opiumwar.html). A site at http://web.jjay.cuny.edu/~jobrien/reference/ob29.html encourages discussion of Chinese Opium Commissioner Lin Zexu's letter to Queen Victoria.

The Taiping Rebellion (http://www.chaos.umd.edu/history/modern2.html) gravely weakened 2000 years of traditional Chinese government. The Boxer Rebellion (http://www.smplanet.com/imperialism/fists.html) provided the coup de grâce.

Major General Charles "Chinese" Gordon (http://www.bbc.co.uk/history/historic_figures/gordon_general_charles.shtml), who took part in the suppression of the anti-foreign, anti-Qing Taiping Rebellion, also had to address another indigenous revolt in Egypt led by Muhammad Ahmed, the Mahdi (http://en.wikipedia.org/wiki/Muhammad_Ahmed).

Unlike the Mahdi, who sought the path of militant revivalism, Mohammad Abduh and Jamal al-din Afghani sought Western-style modernization within the context of Islam. Earlier, Muhammad Ali, ruler of Egypt, had sought the same goal through economic transformation, but even the efforts of his successors to build the Suez Canal backfired due to European control over capital flow, which ultimately led to increased European control over

Egypt (http://www.emayzine.com/lectures/egypt1798-1924.html). Much the same fate befell the Tanzimat reforms (http://www.usp.nus.edu.sg/landow/victorian/history/dora/dora9.html), the Ottoman effort that paralleled the Qing reformist experiment.

AP* Test Prep

1. The decline of the Ottoman Empire in the 19th century can be traced to all of these reasons EXCEPT
   (A) frequent defeats of the Ottoman army and foreign annexations of its land.
   (B) religious divisions within Islam.
   (C) the spread of nationalism in southeastern Europe.
   (D) restive Christian and non-Turkish populations who resented Turkish rule.

2. The groups that opposed most internal Ottoman reforms were the
   (A) university-educated students.
   (C) merchants.
   (D) peasants.
   (E) ruling religious, political, and social elites.

3. Reforms under the late Ottoman sultans and Young Turk leaders
   (A) attempted to modernize Turkey without westernizing.
   (B) sought Muslim solutions to internal problems.
   (C) emphasized westernization and copied Western models openly.
   (D) were opposed by most members of Turkish society.

4. The strategic importance of Egypt to Europeans was changed by
   (A) Napoleon's invasion in 1798.
   (B) the khedive's conquest of the Middle East and defeat of the Ottoman Empire.
   (C) building the Suez Canal.
   (D) Egypt's successful industrialization under Muhammad Ali.

5. Although they were nomadic tribesmen from beyond the Great Wall, the Manchus (Qing), when they conquered China,
   (A) tightly regulated merchant activities and overseas investments.
   (B) redistributed land to the peasants.
   (C) retained the Ming emperors as nominal leaders.
   (D) retained the Confucian gentry-scholars and much of the political system.

6. The most immediate result of the Opium War was
   (A) the collapse of the Qing dynasty and its replacement.
   (B) the beginning of a powerful reform movement to strengthen China.
   (C) Korea was ceded to Japan, and the British took Siam.
   (D) China was forced to open its ports to European trade and grant European extraterritoriality.

7. Why was the Taiping Rebellion such a serious threat to the Qing dynasty?
   (A) The rebels were allied with Western Europeans.
   (B) The rebels had a sweeping series of social, political and religious reforms.
   (C) The rebels captured the Dowager Empress Cixi and the heir.
   (D) The rebels demanded extreme westernization and an end to the scholar-gentry privileges.

Free-Response Question

Compare the Ottoman and Qing Empires under the pressure of Europeans. Consider the two empires responded.

27 Russia and Japan: Industrialization Outside the West

Russia's Reforms and Industrial Advance
DOCUMENT: Conditions for Factory Workers in Russia's Industrialization
Protest and Revolution in Russia
Japan: Transformation Without Revolution

THINKING HISTORICALLY: The Separate Paths of Japan and China
VISUALIZING THE PAST: Two Faces of Western Influence
GLOBAL CONNECTIONS: Russia and Japan in the World

Fukuzawa Yukichi (1834–1904) was one of the most ardent educational reformers in late 19th-century Japan. Very soon after Japan began to have greater contact with the West, he concluded that Japan needed to change. He began to travel to the United States and Europe as early as 1860. He was not uncritical—he did not like the outspokenness of Western women or divisive debates in parliaments. But he firmly believed that, in key respects, Western education surpassed Japanese. As he put it in his autobiography, in 1899: "When I compare the two . . . as to wealth, armament, and the greatest happiness for the greatest number, I have to put the Orient below the Occident." (Figure 27.1)

The problem in Japanese education, according to Fukuzawa, was Confucianism. The Confucian tradition, he believed, undervalued science and mathematics. It also suffered from a "lack of the idea of independence." Although independence was hard to define, Fukuzawa argued that it was essential if "mankind [was] to thrive" and if Japan was to "assert herself among the great nations of the world."

Japanese conservatives were deeply offended by this enthusiasm for Western education. Fukuzawa, a member of the elite and family friend of key conservatives, was sensitive to their criticism. In a letter to one observer, he seemed to back down. He talked of his commitment to "the teaching of filial piety and brotherly harmony." He said he worried that he was not being faithful to the memory of his own parents (who had been Confucianists). He admitted that he jumped into "Western studies" at a young age and did not know as much as he should about Confucianism. He even argued that (by the late 1870s) the traditions had reconciled: "Western and Confucian teachings have now grown into one, and no contradiction is seen."

Fukuzawa's dilemma was a common one for reformers: trying to prompt real change in a Western direction without unduly offending traditionalists and without wanting to become fully Western. Russian reformers, though different from the Japanese, faced similar problems, and handled them less successfully. Fukuzawa himself bent but did not break in his reformist zeal. In his autobiography he returned to defiance: "Again and again I had to rise up and denounce the all-important Chinese influence" even though "it was not altogether a safe road for my reckless spirit to follow." ■

This chapter deals with two important nations that defied the common pattern of growing Western domination during the 19th century. By 1914 Russia and Japan had managed to launch significant programs of industrialization and to make other changes designed to strengthen their political and social systems. Russia and Japan differed from the pattern of halting reforms characteristic of China and the Middle East in the 19th century. Theirs were the only societies outside the West to begin a wholesale process of industrialization before the 1960s. In the process, Japan pulled away from other Asian societies, while Russia ultimately enhanced its power in world affairs.

Russia and Japan did have some common characteristics, which help explain why both could maintain economic and political independence during the West's century of power. They both had prior experience of imitation: Japan from China, Russia from Byzantium and then the West. They knew that learning from outsiders could be profitable and need not destroy their native cultures. Both had improved their political effectiveness during the 17th and 18th centuries, through the Tokugawa shogunate and the tsarist empire, respectively. Both nations could use the state to sponsor changes that, in the West, had rested in part with private businesses. At the same time, change took distinctive directions in each society: Russia's road to industrialization reflected its authoritarian traditions: it was marked by political repression and harsh conditions for workers that undercut social stability. Meanwhile, Japan's long experience with cultural adaptation in the face of change helped it manage the same transition from a feudal to an industrial society while retaining a great deal of political and social cohesion. Industrialization outside the West complicated economic power relationships, but it also illustrated the growing roles of global capitalism and the new forms of integrating capital and labor.

Russia's Reforms and Industrial Advance

Russian rulers, beginning with Catherine the Great in her later years, sought ways to protect the country from the contagion of the French Revolution. The sense that Western policies might serve as models for Russia faded dramatically. Napoleon's 1812 invasion of Russia also led to a new concern with defense. Conservative intellectuals supported the move toward renewed isolation. In the eyes of these aristocratic writers, Russia knew the true meaning of community and stability. The system of serfdom provided ignorant peasants with the guidance and protection of paternalistic masters—an inaccurate social analysis but a comforting one.

Russia Before Reform

Russia was hardly changeless. To resist Napoleon's pressure early in the 19th century, the government introduced some improvements in bureaucratic training. A new tsar, Alexander I, flirted with liberal rhetoric, but at the Congress of Vienna he sponsored the **Holy Alliance** idea. In this alliance, the conservative monarchies of Russia, Prussia, and Austria would combine in defense of religion and the established order. The idea of Russia as a bastion of sanity in a Europe gone mad was appealing, although in fact the alliance itself accomplished little.

Figure 27.1 Japanese children at school. Showing children the latest in naval technology suggests the relationship between education and other aspects of Japanese development in the later 19th century.

Defending the status quo produced some important new tensions, however. Many intellectuals remained fascinated with Western progress. Some praised political freedom and educational and scientific advance. Others focused more purely on Western cultural styles. Early in the 19th century, Russia began to contribute creatively to Europe's cultural output. The poet Pushkin, for example, descended from an African slave, used romantic styles to celebrate the beauties of the Russian soul and the tragic dignity of the common people. Because of its compatibility with the use of folklore and a sense of nationalism, the romantic style took deep root in eastern Europe. Russian musical composers would soon make their contributions, again using folk themes and sonorous sentimentality within a Western stylistic context.

While Russia's ruling elite continued to welcome Western artistic styles and took great pride in Russia's growing cultural respectability, they increasingly censored intellectuals who tried to incorporate liberal or radical political values. A revolt of Western-oriented army officers in 1825—the **Decembrist uprising** (Figure 27.2)—inspired the new tsar, Nicholas I, to still more adamant conservatism. The uprising, urging reform of tsarist autocracy, showed that liberal values had spread to

Before 1861, Russia stood out among European powers by the extent of its political conservatism. The nation's reform period began in 1861 with the emancipation of the serfs. Russian leaders tried to combine change with continued tsarist autocracy.

Holy Alliance Alliance among Russia, Prussia, and Austria in defense of religion and the established order; formed at Congress of Vienna by most conservative monarchies of Europe.

Decembrist uprising Political revolt in Russia in 1825; led by middle-level army officers who advocated reforms; put down by Tsar Nickolas I.

1700 C.E.	1800 C.E.	1825 C.E.	1850 C.E.	1875 C.E.	1900 C.E.
1720 End ban on Western books in Japan	1800–1850 Growth of "Dutch Studies" in Japan	1825 Decembrist Revolt, Russia	1853 Perry expedition to Edo Bay	1875–1877 Russian–Ottoman War; Russia wins new territory	1902 Loose alliance between Japan and Britain
1762–1796 Reign of Catherine the Great	1812 Failure of Napoleon's invasion of Russia	1825–1855 Heightening of repression by Tsar Nicholas I	1854 Follow-up American and British fleet visit	1877 Final samurai rising	1904–1905 Russo-Japanese War; Japan defeats Russia
1773–1775 Pugachev Rebellion	1815 Russia reacquires Poland through Treaty of Vienna; Alexander I and the Holy Alliance	1829–1878 Serbia gains increasing autonomy in Ottoman Empire, then independence	1854–1856 Crimean War	1878 Bulgaria gains independence	1905–1906 Russian Revolution results in peasant reforms and duma (parliament)
1772–1795 Partitioning of Poland		1830–1831 Polish nationalist revolt repressed	1856 Romania gains virtual independence	1881 Anarchist assassination of Alexander II	1910 Japan annexes Korea
		1831 Greece wins independence after revolt against Ottomans	1860–1868 Civil strife in Russia	1881–1905 Growing repression and attacks on minorities in Russia	1912 Growing party strife in Russian duma
		1833, 1853 Russian–Ottoman wars	1860s–1870s Alexander II reforms	1884–1887 New Russian gains in central Asia	1912–1918 Balkan Wars
		1841–1843 Brief shogun reform effort	1861 Russian emancipation of serfs	1884–1914 Beginnings of Russian industrialization; near-completion of trans-Siberian railway (full linkage 1916)	1914 World War I begins
			1865–1879 Russian conquests in central Asia	1890 New constitution and legal code	1916–1918 Japan seizes former German holdings in Pacific and China
			1867 Mutsuhito, emperor of Japan	1892–1903 Sergei Witte, Minister of Finance	1917 Russian Revolution leads to Bolshevik victory
			1867 Russia sells Alaska to United States	1894–1895 Sino-Japanese War	
			1868–1912 Meiji period in Japan	1898 Formation of Marxist Social Democratic Party, Russia	
			1870 Ministry of Industry established in Japan		
			1870–1940 Population growth in Russia		
			1872 Universal military service established in Russia		
			1872 Education Act, Japan		

elements of the Russian elite, but its failure was more significant. Repression of political opponents stiffened, and the secret police expanded. Newspapers and schools, already confined to a small minority, were tightly supervised. What political criticism there was flourished mainly in exile in places such as Paris and London; it had little impact on Russia.

Partly because of political repression, Russia largely avoided the wave of revolutions that spread through Europe in 1830 and in 1848. In its role as Europe's conservative anchor, Russia even intervened in 1849 to help Austria put down the nationalist revolution in Hungary—a blow in favor of monarchy but also a reminder of Russia's eagerness to flex its muscles in wider European affairs.

While turning more conservative than it had been in the 18th century, Russia maintained its tradition of territorial expansion. Russia had confirmed its hold over most of Poland at the Congress of Vienna in 1815 after Napoleon briefly sponsored a separate Polish duchy. Nationalist sentiment, inspired by the growth of romantic nationalism in Poland and backed by many Polish landowners with ties to western Europe, roused recurrent Polish opposition to Russian rule. An uprising occurred in 1830 and 1831, triggered by news of the revolutions in the West and led by liberal aristocrats and loyal Catholics who chafed under the rule of an Orthodox power. Tsar Nicholas I put down this revolt with great brutality, driving many leaders into exile.

At the same time, Russia continued its pressure on the Ottoman Empire, whose weakness attracted their eager attention. A war in the 1830s led to some territorial gains. France and Britain repeatedly tried to prop up Ottoman authority in the interest of countering Russian aggression. Russia also supported many nationalist movements in the Balkans, including the Greek independence war in the 1820s; here, a desire to cut back the Turks outweighed Russia's commitment to conservatism. Overall, although no massive acquisitions marked the early 19th century, Russia continued to be a dynamic diplomatic and military force (Map 27.1).

Economic and Social Problems: The Peasant Question

Russia's economic position did not keep pace with its diplomatic aspirations. As the West industrialized and central European powers such as Prussia and Austria introduced at least the beginnings of industrialization, including some rail lines, Russia largely stood pat. This meant that it began to fall increasingly behind the West in technology and trade. Russian landlords eagerly took advantage of Western markets for grain, but they increased their exports not by improving their techniques but by tightening the labor obligations on their serfs. This was a common pattern in much of eastern Europe in the early 19th century, as Polish and Hungarian nobles also increased labor service to gain ground in the export market. In return for low-cost grain exports, Russia and other east European areas imported some Western machinery and other costly equipment as well as luxury goods for the great aristocrats to display as badges of cultured respectability. A few isolated factories that used foreign equipment were opened up in imitation of western European industrialization, but there was no significant change in overall manufacturing or transportation mechanisms. Russia remained a profoundly agricultural society based mainly on serf labor, but it was now a visibly stagnant society as well.

The widening gap between Russia and the West was driven home dramatically by a minor war in the Crimea between 1854 and 1856. Nicholas I provoked conflict with the Ottoman Empire in 1853, arguing among other things that Russia was responsible for protecting Christian interests in the Holy Land. This time, however, France and Britain were not content with diplomatic maneuverings to limit Russian gains but came directly to the sultan's aid. Britain was increasingly worried about any great power advance in the region that might threaten its hold on India, whereas France sought diplomatic glory and also represented itself as the Western champion of Christian rights. The resultant **Crimean War** was fought directly in Russia's backyard on the Black Sea, yet the Western forces won, driving the Russian armies from their entrenched positions. (Each side lost about 250,000 troops in a truly difficult struggle.) The loss was profoundly disturbing to Russian leadership, for the Western powers won this little war not because of great tactics or inspired principles but because of their industrial advantage. They had the ships to send masses of military supplies long distances, and their artillery and other weapons were vastly superior to Russia's home-produced models. This severe blow to a regime that prided itself on military vigor was a frightening portent for the future.

The Crimean War helped convince Russian leaders, including the new tsar, Alexander II, that it was time for a change. Reform was essential, not to copy the West but to allow sufficient economic adjustments for Russia to keep pace in the military arena. First and foremost, reform meant some resolution of Russia's leading social issue, the issue that most distinguished Russian society from that of the West: serfdom. Only if the status of serfs changed could Russia develop a more vigorous and mobile labor force and so be able to industrialize. Russian concern about this issue paralleled the attacks on slavery in the Americas in the same period, reflecting a desire to meet Western humanitarian standards and a need for cheap, flexible labor.

Figure 27.2 The 1825 Decembrist revolt in St. Petersburg arose when there was a disagreement over the successor to Tsar Alexander I, who had no son. While the leaders of the revolt were well educated aristocrats fighting for liberalization, many of their followers were illiterate and ill-informed subjects of the authoritarian regime. Soldiers who supported the accession of the dead tsar's liberal brother, Constantine, marched through the streets, chanting, "Constantine and Constitution." Many of these soldiers later admitted that they had assumed Constitution was the name of Constantine's wife. The revolt failed, and its leaders were executed or exiled to Siberia. Nicolas I, who became tsar, was even more repressive than his predecessor, but the courage of the Decembrists provided inspiration to future generations of reformers.
(Federal State Entity of Culture, the State Historical Museum—Moscow, Russian Federation.)

Crimean War Fought between 1854 and 1856; began as Russian attempt to attack Ottoman Empire; Russia opposed by France and Britain as well; resulted in Russian defeat in the face of Western industrial technology; led to Russian reforms under Tsar Alexander II.

Map 27.1 Russian Expansion, 1815–1914 Russia continued to push to the west, south, and east. At first, its main conflicts were with the Ottoman Empire. Later, however, conflicts in east Asia loomed larger.

So for two decades Russia returned to a policy of reform, based on Western standards and examples; serfdom had been abolished in western Europe after 1789 and in east central regions such as Prussia and Hungary in the aftermath of the revolutions of 1848. As before, however, the intention was not to duplicate Western measures fully but to protect distinctive Russian institutions, including the landed aristocracy and tightly knit peasant communities. The result was an important series of changes that, with tragic irony, created more grievances than they resolved while opening the way to further economic change.

The Reform Era and Early Industrialization

The final decision to emancipate the serfs in 1861 came at roughly the same time that the United States and Brazil decided to free slaves. Neither slavery nor rigorous serfdom suited the economic needs of a society seeking an independent position in Western-dominated world trade. While Russian reformers had specific concerns, some of them also accepted new humanitarian ideals now spreading globally, that attacked systems of unfree labor.

In some ways, the **emancipation of the serfs** was more generous than the liberation of slaves in the Americas. Although aristocrats retained part of the land, including the most fertile holdings, the serfs got most of it, in contrast to slaves, who received their freedom but nothing else. However,

emancipation of the serfs Tsar Alexander II ended rigorous serfdom in Russia in 1861; serfs obtained no political rights; required to stay in villages until they could repay aristocracy for land.

Russian emancipation was careful to preserve essential aristocratic power; the tsar was not interested in destroying the nobility, who remained his most reliable political allies and the source of most bureaucrats. Even more, emancipation was designed to retain the tight grip of the tsarist state. The serfs obtained no new political rights at a national level. They were still tied to their villages until they could pay for the land they were given. The redemption money went to the aristocrats to help preserve this class. Redemption payments added greatly to peasants' material hardship (Figure 27.3), and peasants thought that the land belonged to them with no need to pay for its return.

Emancipation did bring change; it helped create a larger urban labor force. But it did not spur a revolution in agricultural productivity because most peasants continued to use traditional methods on their small plots. And it did not bring contentment. Indeed, peasant uprisings became more common as hopes for a brighter future seemed dashed by the limits of change. Explosive rural unrest in Russia was furthered by substantial population growth as some of the factors that had earlier swelled the West's population now spread to Russia, including increased use of the potato. In sum, after 1861 Russia was a classic case of a society in the midst of rapid change where reform did not go far enough to satisfy key protest groups.

To be sure, the reform movement did not end with emancipation. Alexander II introduced a host of further measures in the 1860s and early 1870s. New law codes cut back the traditional punishments now that serfs were legally free in the eyes of the law (though subject to important transitional restrictions). The tsar created local political councils, the **zemstvoes** (ZEHMST-vohs), which had a voice in regulating roads, schools, and other regional policies. Some form of local government was essential now that the nobles no longer directly ruled the peasantry. The zemstvoes gave some Russians, particularly middle-class people such as doctors and lawyers, new political experience, and they undertook important inquiries into local problems. However, the councils had no influence on national policy; the tsar resolutely maintained his own authority and that of his extensive bureaucracy. Another important area of change was the army; the Crimean War had shown the need for reform. The officer corps was improved through promotion by merit and a new organization of essential services. Recruitment was extended, and many peasants learned new skills through their military service. Some strides also were made in providing state-sponsored basic education, although schools spread unevenly.

From the reform era onward, literacy increased rapidly in Russian society. A new market developed for popular reading matter that had some similarities to the mass reading culture developing in the West. Interestingly, Russian potboiler novels, displaying a pronounced taste for excitement and exotic adventure, also attested to distinctive values. For example, Russian "bad guys" never were glorified in the end but always were either returned to social loyalty or condemned—a clear sign of the limits to individualism. Women gained new positions in this climate of change. Some won access to higher education, and, as in the West, a minority of women mainly from the upper classes began to penetrate professions such as medicine. Even sexual habits began to change, as had occurred in the West a century earlier. Fathers' control over their children's behavior loosened a bit, particularly where nonagricultural jobs were available, and sexual activity before marriage increased.

The move toward industrialization was part of the wider process of change. State support was an industrial effort, for Russia lacked a preexisting middle class and capital. State enterprises had to make up part of the gap, in the tradition of economic activity that went back to Peter the Great.

Russia began to create an extensive railroad network in the 1870s. The establishment of the **trans-Siberian railroad,** which connected European Russia with the Pacific, was the crowning achievement of this drive when it was nearly completed by the end of the 1880s. The railroad boom directly stimulated expansion of Russia's iron and coal sectors. Railroad development also stimulated the export of grain to the West, which earned foreign currency needed to pay for advanced

Figure 27.3 This late 19th-century roadside scene depicts the poverty of a Russian peasant village. What forces produced such poor conditions, even after serfdom had been abolished?

zemstvoes [ZEHMST-vohs] Local political councils created as part of reforms of Tsar Alexander II (1860s); gave some Russians, particularly middle-class professionals, some experience in government; councils had no impact on national policy.

trans-Siberian railroad Constructed in 1870s to connect European Russia with the Pacific; completed by the end of the 1880s; brought Russia into a more active Asian role.

Conditions for Factory Workers in Russia's Industrialization

Russia passed several laws protecting workers, but enforcement was minimal. The Ministry of Finance established a factory inspectorate in the 1880s, which dutifully reported on conditions; these reports usually were ignored. The following passages deal with a number of Moscow factories in the 1880s.

In the majority of factories there are no special quarters for the workers. This applies to workers in paper, wool, and silk finishing. Skilled hand craftsmen like brocade weavers can earn good wages, and yet most of them sleep on or under their looms, for lack of anything else. Only in a few weaving factories are there special sleeping quarters, and these are provided not for the weavers, but for other workers—the winders and dyers, etc. Likewise, the velveteen cutters almost always sleep on the tables where they work. This habit is particularly unhealthy, since the work areas are always musty and the air is saturated with dye fumes—sometimes poisonous ones. Carpenters also generally sleep on their workbenches. In bastmatting factories, workers of both sexes and all ages sleep together on pieces and mats of bast which are often damp. Only the sick workers in these bast factories are allowed to sleep on the single stove. . . . Work at the mill never stops, day or night. There are two twelve-hour shifts a day, which begin at 6:00 A.M. and 6:00 P.M. The men have a half-hour for breakfast (8:30–9:00) and one hour for dinner (1:00–2:00).

The worst violations of hygienic regulations were those I saw in most of the flax-spinning mills where linen is produced. . . . Although in western Europe all the dust-producing carding and combing machines have long been covered and well ventilated, I saw only one Russian linen mill where such a machine was securely covered. Elsewhere, the spools of these machines were completely open to the air, and the scutching apparatus is inadequately ventilated. . . .

In many industrial establishments the grounds for fines and the sizes of fines are not fixed in advance. The factory rules may contain only one phrase like the following: "Those found violating company rules will be fined *at the discretion of the manager.*"

The degree of arbitrariness in the determination of fines, and thus also in the determination of the worker's wages, was unbelievably extreme in some factories. In Podolsk, for instance, in factories No. 131 and No. 135, there is a ten-ruble forfeit for leaving the factory before the expiration of one's contract. But as applied, this covers much more than voluntary breach of contract on the worker's part. This fine is exacted from every worker who for any reason has

to leave the factory. Cases are known of persons who have had to pay this fine three times. Moreover, fines are levied for so many causes that falling under a severe fine is a constant possibility for each worker. For instance, workers who for any reason came into the office in a group, instead of singly, would be fined one ruble. After a second offense, the transgressors would be dismissed—leaving behind, of course, the ten-ruble fine for breach of contract.

In factory No. 135 the workers are still treated as serfs. Wages are paid out only twice a year, even then not in full but only enough to pay the workers' taxes (other necessities are supplied by the factory store). Furthermore this money is not given to the workers directly, but is sent by mail to their village elders and village clerks. Thus the workers are without money the year around. Besides they are also paying severe fines to the factory, and these sums will be subtracted from their wages at the final year-end accounting.

Extreme regulations and regimentation are very common in our factories—regulations entangle the workers at every step and burden them with more or less severe fines which are subtracted from their often already inadequate wages. Some factory administrators have become real virtuosos at thinking up new grounds for fines. A brief description of a few of the fines in factory No. 172 is an excellent example of this variety: on October 24, 1877, an announcement was posted of new fines to be set at the discretion of the office for fourteen different cases of failure to maintain silence and cleanliness. There were also dozens of minor fines prescribed for certain individual offenses: for example, on August 4, 1883, a huge fine of five rubles was set for singing in the factory courtyard after 9:30, or at any time in any unauthorized place. On June 3, 1881, a fine was to be levied from workers who took tea and sugar, bread, or any kind of foodstuffs into the weaving building, "in order to avoid breeding any insects or vermin." On May 14, 1880, a fine was set for anyone who wrote with pencil, chalk, or anything else on the walls in the dyeing or weaving buildings.

QUESTIONS Were factory conditions worse than in western Europe during early industrialization, and if so in what ways and why? How did working conditions and management attitudes help create a revolutionary mood among Russian workers? Think also about the nature of this source. Why would a conservative government sponsor such a critical report? What do you think the results of such a report would be, in the Russian context, or indeed in any early industrial context?

Western machinery. The railroads also opened Siberia up to new development, which in turn brought Russia into a more active and contested Asian role.

By the 1880s, when Russia's railroad network had almost quintupled since 1860, modern factories were beginning to spring up in Moscow, St. Petersburg, and several Polish cities, and an urban working class was growing rapidly. Printing factories and metalworking shops expanded the skilled artisanry in the cities, and metallurgy and textile plants recruited a still newer semiskilled industrial labor force from the troubled countryside.

Under Count **Sergei Witte,** minister of finance from 1892 to 1903 and an ardent economic modernizer, the government enacted high tariffs to protect new Russian industry, improved its banking system, and encouraged Western investors to build great factories with advanced technology. As Witte put it, "The inflow of foreign capital is . . . the only way by which our industry will be

[margin handwritten note: in 20 years]

Early Russian Factory
IMAGE

Witte, Sergei Russian minister of finance from 1892 to 1903; economic modernizer responsible for high tariffs, improved banking system; encouraged Western investors to build factories in Russia.

able to supply our country quickly with abundant and cheap products." By 1900 approximately half of Russian industry was foreign owned and much of it was foreign operated, with British, German, and French industrialists taking the lead. Russia became a debtor nation as huge industrial development loans piled up. Russia had surged to fourth rank in the world in steel production and was second to the United States in the newer area of petroleum production and refining. Russian textile output was also impressive. Long-standing Russian economic lags were beginning to yield.

This industrial revolution was still in its early stages. Russia's world rank was a function more of its great size and population, along with its rich natural resources, than of thorough mechanization. Many Russian factories were not up to Western technical standards, nor was the labor force highly trained. Agriculture also remained backward, as peasants, often illiterate, had neither capital nor motives to change their ways.

Other reforms also produced ambiguous results. Russia remained a traditional peasant society in many ways. Beneath the official military reorganization, discipline and military efficiency were lax. Even more obvious was the absence of a large, self-confident middle class of the sort that had arisen earlier in the West. Businesspeople and professionals grew in numbers, but often they were dependent on state initiatives, such as zemstvo employment for doctors and economic guidance for businesspeople. They were not as assertive as their Western counterparts had been (for example, in challenging aristocratic power and values).

Protest and Revolution in Russia

Alexander II's reforms, as well as economic change and the greater population mobility it involved, encouraged minority nationalities to make demands of the great empire. Intellectuals explored the cultural traditions of Ukrainians and other groups. Nationalist beliefs initially were imported from western Europe, but here and elsewhere in eastern Europe, they encouraged divisive minority agitation that multinational states, such as Russia and Austria–Hungary, found very hard to handle. Nationalist pressures were not the main problem in Russia, but given Russia's mainstream nationalist insistence on the distinctive superiorities of a Russian tradition, they did cause concern.

Social protest was more vigorous still, and it was heightened not only by the limitations of reform but by industrialization itself. Recurrent famines provoked peasant uprisings. Peasants deeply resented redemption payments and taxes and often seized and burned the records that indicated what they owed.

Change and also the limits of change destabilized Russian society. Marxist leaders helped focus unrest.

The Road to Revolution

Along with discontent among the masses, many educated Russians, including some aristocrats, also clamored for revolutionary change. Two strands developed. Many business and professional people, though not very aggressive, began to seek a fuller political voice and new rights such as greater freedom in the schools and press; they argued for liberal reforms. At the same time, a group of radical **intelligentsia**—a Russian term for articulate intellectuals as a class—became increasingly active. As Russian universities expanded, student groups grew as well, and many were impatient with Russia's slow development and with the visible restrictions on political activity. Women students played some role in the protest current, and some specifically feminist demands (for example, toward greater professional opportunity) emerged as well.

Some intellectuals later toned down their goals as they entered the bureaucracy or business life. But many remained inspired by radical doctrines, and more than a few devoted their lives to a revolutionary cause. This kind of intellectual alienation rested on some of the principles that had roused intellectuals in the West, but it went deeper in Russia. It was the first example of a kind of intellectual radicalism, capable of motivating terrorism, which would characterize other societies caught in tense transitions during the 20th century. The Russian intelligentsia wanted political freedom and deep social reform while maintaining a Russian culture different from that of the West, which they saw as hopelessly materialistic. Their radicalism may have stemmed from the demanding task they set themselves: attacking key Russian institutions while building a new society that would not reproduce the injustices and crippling limitations of the Western world.

Many Russian radicals were **anarchists,** who sought to abolish all formal government. Although anarchism was not unknown in the West, it took on particular force in Russia in opposition

intelligentsia Russian term denoting articulate intellectuals as a class; 19th-century group bent on radical change in Russian political and social system; often wished to maintain a Russian culture distinct from that of the West.

anarchists Political groups seeking abolition of all formal government; formed in many parts of Europe and Americas in late 19th and early 20th centuries; particularly prevalent in Russia, opposing tsarist autocracy and becoming a terrorist movement responsible for assassination of Alexander II in 1881.

to tsarist autocracy. Many early anarchists in the 1860s hoped that they could triumph by winning peasant support, and a host of upper-class radicals fanned out to teach the peasantry the beauties of political activism. Failure here led many anarchists to violent methods and thus to the formation of the first large terrorist movement in the modern world. Given the lack of popular support and other political outlets, assassinations and bombings seemed the only way to attack the existing order. As anarchist leader Bakunin put it,

> We have only one plan—general destruction. We want a national revolution of the peasants. We refuse to take any part in the working out of schemes to better the conditions of life; we regard as fruitless solely theoretical work. We consider destruction to be such an enormous and difficult task that we must devote all our powers to it, and we do not wish to deceive ourselves with the dream that we will have enough strength and knowledge for creation.

Not surprisingly, the recurrent waves of terrorism merely strengthened the tsarist regime's resolve to avoid further political change in what became a vicious circle in 19th-century Russian politics. By the late 1870s, Alexander II was pulling back from his reform interest, fearing that change was getting out of hand. Censorship of newspapers and political meetings tightened; many dissidents were arrested and sent to Siberia. Alexander II was assassinated by a terrorist bomb in 1881 after a series of botched attempts. His successors, while increasing the effort to industrialize, continued to oppose further political reform. New measures of repression also were directed against minority nationalities, partly to dampen their unrest and partly to gain the support of upper-class conservatives. The Poles and other groups were supervised carefully. Russian language instruction was forced on peoples such as Ukrainians. Persecution of the large Jewish minority was stepped up, resulting in many mass attacks—called pogroms—and seizures of property. As a consequence, many Russian Jews emigrated.

By the 1890s, the currents of protest gained new force. Marxist doctrines spread from the Western socialist movement to a segment of the Russian intelligentsia, who became committed to a tightly organized proletarian revolution. One of the most active Marxist leaders was **Vladimir Ilyich Ulyanov** (VLAHD-ih-mihr IHL-lihch ool-YAH-nuhf), known as Lenin. Lenin, a man from a bureaucratic family whose brother was hanged after a trial, following his arrest by the political police, introduced important innovations in Marxist theory to make it more appropriate for Russia. He argued that because of the spread of international capitalism, a proletariat was developing worldwide in advance of industrialization. Therefore, Russia could have a proletarian revolution without going through a distinct middle-class phase. Lenin also insisted on the importance of disciplined revolutionary cells that could maintain doctrinal purity and effective action even under severe police repression. Lenin's approach animated the group of Russian Marxists known as **Bolsheviks,** or majority party (though, ironically, they were actually a minority in the Russian Marxist movement as a whole). The approach proved ideal for Russian conditions.

Working-class unrest in the cities grew with the new currents among the intelligentsia. Russian workers became far more radical than their Western counterparts. They formed unions and conducted strikes—all illegal—but many of them also had firm political goals in mind. Their radicalism stemmed partly from the absence of legal political outlets. It arose also from rural unrest—for these new workers pulled in peasant grievances against the existing order—and from the severe conditions of early industrialization, with its large factories and frequent foreign ownership. Although many workers were not linked to any particular doctrine, some became interested in Bolshevism, and they were urged on by passionate organizers.

By 1900 the contradictory currents in Russian society may have made revolution inevitable. The forces demanding change were not united, but the importance of mass protest in both countryside and city, as well as the radical intelligentsia, made it difficult to find a compromise. Furthermore, the regime remained resolutely opposed to compromise. Conservative ministers urged a vigorous policy of resistance and repression.

The Revolution of 1905

Military defeat in 1904 and 1905 finally lit this tinderbox. Russia had maintained its expansionist foreign policy through the late 19th century, in part because of tradition and in part because diplomatic success might draw the venom from internal unrest. It also wanted to match the imperialist strides of the Western great powers. A war with the Ottoman Empire in the 1870s brought substan-

Ulyanov, Vladimir Ilyich [VLAHD-ih-mihr IHL-lihch ool-YAH-nuhf] Better known as Lenin; most active Russian Marxist leader; insisted on importance of disciplined revolutionary cells; leader of Bolshevik Revolution of 1917.

Bolsheviks Literally, the majority party; the most radical branch of the Russian Marxist movement; led by V. I. Lenin and dedicated to his concept of social revolution; actually a minority in the Russian Marxist political scheme until its triumph in the 1917 revolution.

tial gains, which were then pushed back at the insistence of France and Britain. Russia also successfully aided the creation in the Balkans of new Slavic nations, such as Serbia and Bulgaria, the "little Slavic brothers" that filled nationalist hearts with pride. Some conservative writers even talked in terms of a pan-Slavic movement that would unite the Slavic people—under Russian leadership, of course. Russia participated vigorously in other Middle Eastern and central Asian areas. Russia and Britain both increased their influence in Persia and Afghanistan, reaching some uneasy truces that divided spheres of activity early in the 20th century. Russia was also active in China. The development of the trans-Siberian railroad encouraged Russia to incorporate some northern portions of Manchuria, violating the 18th-century Amur River agreement. Russia also joined Western powers in obtaining long-term leases to Chinese territory during the 1890s.

These were important gains, but they did not satisfy growing Russian ambitions, and they also brought trouble. Russia risked an overextension because its diplomatic aspirations were not backed by real increases in military power. The problem first came to a head in 1904. Increasingly powerful Japan became worried about further Russian expansion in northern China and efforts to extend influence into Korea. The **Russo-Japanese War** broke out in 1904. Against all expectations save Japan's, the Japanese won. Russia could not move its fleet quickly to the Pacific, and its military organization proved too cumbersome to oppose the more effective Japanese maneuvers (Map 27.2). Japan gained the opportunity to move into Korea as the balance of power in the Far East began to shift.

Unexpected defeat in war unleashed massive protests on the home front in the Russian Revolution of 1905 (Figure 27.4). Urban workers mounted well organized general strikes that were designed above all for political gains. Peasants led a series of insurrections, and liberal groups also agitated. After trying brutal police repression, which only infuriated the urban crowds, the tsarist regime had to change course. It wooed liberals by creating a national parliament, the **duma.** The interior minister Piotyr Stolypin (pee-UH-tuhr STOHL-yuh-pihn) introduced an important series of reforms for the peasantry. Under the **Stolypin reforms,** peasants gained greater freedom from redemption payments and village controls. They could buy and sell land more freely. The goal was to create a stratified, market-oriented peasantry in which successful farmers would move away from the peasant masses, becoming rural capitalists. Indeed, peasant unrest did die down, and a minority of aggressive entrepreneurs, called **kulaks** (KOO-laks), began to increase agricultural production and buy additional land. Yet the reform package quickly came unglued. Not only were a few new workers' rights withdrawn, triggering a new series of strikes and underground activities, but the duma was progressively stripped of power. Nicholas II, a weak man who was badly advised, could not surrender the tradition of autocratic rule, and the duma became a hollow institution, satisfying no one. Police repression also resumed, creating new opponents to the regime.

Pressed in the diplomatic arena by the Japanese advance yet eager to counter internal pressures with some foreign policy success, the Russian government turned once again to the Ottoman Empire and the Balkans. Various strategies to acquire new rights of access to the Mediterranean and to back Slavic allies in the Balkans yielded no concrete results, but they did stir the pot in this vulnerable area and helped lead to World War I. And this war, in which Russia participated to maintain its diplomatic standing and live up to the billing of Slavic protector, led to one of the great revolutions of modern times.

Russia and Eastern Europe

A number of Russian patterns were paralleled in smaller eastern European states such as Hungary (joined to Austria but autonomous after 1866), Romania, Serbia, Bulgaria, and Greece. These were new nations—unlike Russia. And emerging after long Ottoman dominance, they had no access to the diplomatic influence of their giant neighbor. Most of the new nations established parliaments,

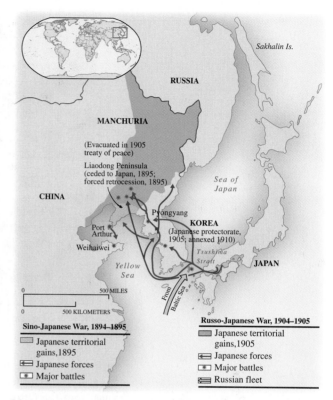

Map 27.2 The Russo-Japanese War   The Russo-Japanese war focused on disputes over Chinese territory. Japan had acquired the Liaodong peninsula after its victory over China, but Russia and others forced it out and then maneuvered for territory of their own. Japan proposed a split of Manchuria but assumed negotiations would fail, and so attacked the Russian fleet at Port Arthur, and later won over Russian armies in China as well. A Russian fleet sent from the Baltic was humiliated at Tsushima Strait, which effectively ended the war.

Russo-Japanese War   War between Japan and Russia (1904–1905) over territory in Manchuria; Japan defeated the Russians, largely because of its naval power; Japan annexed Korea in 1910 as a result of military dominance.

duma   National parliament created in Russia in the aftermath of the Revolution of 1905; progressively stripped of power during the reign of Tsar Nicholas II; failed to forestall further revolution.

Stolypin reforms   Reforms introduced by the Russian interior minister Piotyr Stolypin intended to placate the peasantry in the aftermath of the Revolution of 1905; included reduction in redemption payments, attempt to create market-oriented peasantry.

kulaks   [KOO-laks] Agricultural entrepreneurs who utilized the Stolypin and later NEP reforms to increase agricultural production and buy additional land.

Figure 27.4 Women marching in the Russian Revolution of 1905.

in imitation of Western forms, but carefully restricted voting rights and parliamentary powers. Kings—some of them new, as the Balkan nations had set up monarchies after gaining independence from the Ottoman Empire—ruled without many limits on their power. Most eastern European nations abolished serfdom either in 1848 or soon after Russia's move, but landlord power remained more extensive than in Russia, and peasant unrest followed. Most of the smaller eastern European nations industrialized much less extensively than Russia, and as agricultural exporters they remained far more dependent on Western markets.

Amid all the problems, eastern Europe enjoyed a period of glittering cultural productivity in the late 19th century, with Russia in the lead. Development of the romantic tradition and other Western styles continued. National dictionaries and histories, along with the collection of folktales and music, helped the smaller Slavic nations gain a sense of their heritage. The Russian novel enjoyed a period of unprecedented brilliance. Westernizers such as Turgenev wrote realistic novels that promoted what they saw as modern values, whereas writers such as Tolstoy and Dostoevsky tried to portray a special Russian spirit. Russian music moved from the romanticism of Tchaikovsky to more innovative, atonal styles of the early 20th century. Polish and Hungarian composers such as Chopin and Liszt also made an important mark. Russian painters began participating in modern art currents, producing important abstract work. Finally, scientific research advanced at levels of fundamental importance. A Czech scientist, Gregor Mendel, furthered the understanding of genetics, and a Russian physiologist, Ivan Pavlov, experimenting on conditioned reflexes, explained unconscious responses in human beings. Eastern Europe thus participated more fully than ever before in a cultural world it shared with the West.

Japan: Transformation Without Revolution

Western pressure forced Japan to consider reforms beginning in the 1850s. Japan was able to combine existing strengths and traditions with significant reform.

On the surface, Japan experienced little change during the first half of the 19th century, and certainly this was a quiet time compared with the earlier establishment of the Tokugawa shogunate (see Chapter 27) or the transformation introduced after the 1850s.

The Final Decades of the Shogunate

During the first half of the 19th century, the shogunate continued to combine a central bureaucracy with semifeudal alliances between the regional lords, the daimyo and the military samurai. The government repeatedly ran into financial problems. Its taxes were based on agriculture, despite the growing commercialization of the Japanese economy; this was a severe constraint. At the same time, maintaining the feudal shell was costly. The government paid stipends to the samurai in return for their loyalty. A long budget reform spurt late in the 18th century built a successful momentum for a time, but a shorter effort between 1841 and 1843 was notably unsuccessful. This weakened the shogunate by the 1850s and hampered its response to the crisis induced by Western pressure.

Japanese intellectual life and culture also developed under the Tokugawa regime. Neo-Confucianism continued to gain among the ruling elite at the expense of Buddhism. Japan gradually became more secular, particularly among the upper classes. This was an important precondition for the nation's response to the Western challenge in that it precluded a strong religious-based resistance to change. Various Confucian schools actively debated into the mid-19th century, keeping Japanese intellectual life fairly creative. Schools and academies expanded, reaching well below the upper class through commoner schools, or **terakoya**, which taught reading, writing, and the rudiments of Confucianism to ordinary people. By 1859 more than 40 percent of all men and over 15 percent of all women were literate—a far higher percentage than anywhere else in the world outside the West, including Russia, and on a par with some of the fringe areas of the West (including the American South).

Although Confucianism remained the dominant ideology, there were important rivals. Tensions between traditionalists and reformist intellectuals were emerging, as in Russia in the same decades. A national studies group praised Japanese traditions, including the office of emperor and the Shinto religion. One national studies writer expressed a typical sentiment late in the 18th century: "The 'special dispensation of our Imperial Land' means that ours is the native land of the Heaven-Shining Goddess who casts her light over all countries in the four seas. Thus our country is the source and fountainhead of all other countries, and in all matters it excels all the others." The influence of the national studies school grew somewhat in the early 19th century, and it would help inspire ultranationalist sentiment at the end of the century and beyond.

A second minority group consisted of what the Japanese called **Dutch Studies.** Although major Western works had been banned when the policy of isolation was adopted, a group of Japanese translators kept alive the knowledge of Dutch to deal with the traders at Nagasaki. The ban on Western books was ended in 1720, and thereafter a group of Japanese scholars interested in "Dutch medicine" created a new interest in Western scientific advances, based on the realization that Western anatomy texts were superior to those of the Chinese. In 1850, there were schools of Dutch Studies in all major cities, and their students urged freer exchange with the West and a rejection of Chinese medicine and culture. "Our general opinion was that we should rid our country of the influences of the Chinese altogether. Whenever we met a young student of Chinese literature, we simply felt sorry for him."

Just as Japanese culture showed an important capacity for lively debate and fruitful internal tension, so the Japanese economy continued to develop into the 19th century. Commerce expanded as big merchant companies established monopoly privileges in many centers. Manufacturing gained ground in the countryside in such consumer goods industries as soy sauce and silks, and much of this was organized by city merchants. Some of these developments were comparable to slightly earlier changes in the West and have given rise to arguments that economically Japan had a running start on industrialization once the Western challenge revealed the necessity of further economic change.

By the 1850s, however, economic growth had slowed—a situation that has prompted some scholars to stress Japan's backwardness compared with the West. Technological limitations constrained agricultural expansion and population increase. At the same time, rural riots increased in many regions from the late 18th century onward. They were not overtly political but rather, like many rural protests, aimed at wealthy peasants, merchants, and landlord controls. Although the authorities put down this unrest with little difficulty, the protests contributed to a willingness to consider change when they were joined by challenge from the outside.

The Challenge to Isolation

Some Japanese had become increasingly worried about potential outside threats. In 1791 a book was issued advocating a strong navy. Fears about the West's growing power and particularly Russia's Asian expansion fed these concerns in later decades. Fear became reality in 1853 when American

terakoya   Commoner schools founded during the Tokugawa Shogunate in Japan to teach reading, writing, and the rudiments of Confucianism; resulted in high literacy rate, approaching 40 percent, of Japanese males.

Dutch Studies   Group of Japanese scholars interested in implications of Western science and technology beginning in the 17th century; urged freer exchange with West; based studies on few Dutch texts available in Japan.

A Comic Dialogue, 1855

The Separate Paths of Japan and China

Japan's ability to change in response to new Western pressure contrasted strikingly with the sluggishness of Chinese reactions into the 20th century. The contrast draws particular attention because China and Japan had been part of the same civilization orbit for so long, which means that some of the assets Japan possessed in dealing with change were present in China as well. Indeed, Japan turned out to benefit, by the mid-19th century, from having become more like China in key respects during the Tokugawa period. The link between Chinese and Japanese traditions should not be exaggerated, of course, and earlier differences help explain the divergence that opened so clearly in the late 19th century. The east Asian world now split apart, with Japan seizing eagerly on Chinese weakness to mount a series of attacks from the 1890s to 1945, which only made China's troubles worse.

Japan and China had both chosen considerable isolation from larger world currents from about 1600 until the West forced new openings between 1830 and 1860. Japan's isolation was the more complete. Both countries lagged behind the West because of their self-containment, which was why Western industrialization caught them unprepared. China's power and wealth roused Western greed and interference first, which gave Japan some leeway.

However, China surpassed Japan in some areas that should have aided it in reacting to the Western challenge. Its leadership, devoted to Confucianism, was more thoroughly secular and bureaucratic in outlook. There was no need to brush aside otherworldly commitments or feudal distractions to deal with the West's material and organizational power. Government centralization, still an issue in Japan, had a long history in China. With a rich tradition of technological innovation and scientific discovery in its past as well, China might have appeared to be a natural to lead the Asian world in responding to the West.

However, that role fell to Japan. Several aspects of Japanese tradition gave it a flexibility that China lacked. It already knew the benefits of imitation, which China, save for its period of attraction to Buddhism, had never acknowledged. Japan's slower government growth had allowed a stronger, more autonomous merchant tradition even as both societies became more commercial in the 17th and early 18th centuries. Feudal traditions, though declining under the Tokugawa shogunate, also limited the heavy hand of government controls while stimulating a sense of military competitiveness, as in the West. In contrast, China's government probably tried to control too much by the 18th century and quashed initiative in the process.

China was also hampered by rapid population growth from the 17th century onward. This population pressure consumed great

> "Several aspects of Japanese tradition gave it a flexibility that China lacked."

energy, leaving scant capital for other economic initiatives. Japan's population stability into the 19th century pressed resources less severely. Japan's island status made the nation more sensitive to Western naval pressures.

Finally, China and Japan were on somewhat different paths when the Western challenge intruded in the mid-19th century. China was suffering one of its recurrent dynastic declines. Government became less efficient, intellectual life stagnated, and popular unrest surged. A cycle of renewal might have followed, with a new dynasty seizing more vigorous reins. But Western interference disrupted this process, complicating reform and creating various new discontents that ultimately overturned the imperial office.

In contrast, Japan maintained political and economic vigor into the 19th century. Whereas by the late 19th century China needed Western guidance simply to handle such bureaucratic affairs as tariff collection and repression of peasant rebellion, Japan suffered no such breakdown of authority, using foreign advisors far more selectively.

Once a different pattern of response was established, every decade increased the gap. Western exploitation of Chinese assets and dilution of government power made conditions more chaotic, while Japanese strength grew steadily after a very brief period of uncertainty. By the 20th century, the two nations were enemies—with Japan, for the first time, the stronger—and seemed to be in different orbits. Japan enjoyed increasing industrial success and had a conservative state that would yield after World War II to a more fully parliamentary form. China, after decades of revolution, finally won its 20th-century political solution: communism.

Yet today, at the onset of the 21st century, it is unclear whether east Asia was split as permanently as 19th- and early 20th-century developments had suggested. Japan's industrial lead remains, but China's economy is beginning to soar. Common cultural habits of group cooperation and decision making remind us that beneath different political systems, a fruitful shared heritage continues to operate. The heritage is quite different from that of the West but fully adaptable to the demands of economic change. And so Westerners begin to wonder whether a Pacific century is about to dawn.

QUESTIONS What civilization features had Japan and China shared before the 19th century? In what ways were Japanese political institutions more adaptable than Chinese institutions? Why was Russia also able to change earlier and more fundamentally than 19th-century China?

Different
Responses to
Westernization

CASE STUDY

Commodore **Matthew Perry** arrived with a squadron in Edo Bay near Tokyo and used threats of bombardment to insist that Americans be allowed to trade. The United States, increasingly an active part of the West's core economy, thus launched for Japan the same kind of pressure the Opium War had created for China: pressure from the heightened military superiority of the West and its insistence on opening markets for its burgeoning economy. In 1854 Perry returned and won the right to station an American consul in Japan; in 1856, through a formal treaty, two ports were opened to commerce. Britain, Russia, and Holland quickly won similar rights. As in China, this meant that Westerners living in Japan would be governed by their own representatives, not by Japanese law.

The bureaucrats of the shogunate saw no alternative but to open up Japan, given the superiority of Western navies. And of course, there were Japanese who had grown impatient with strict isolation; their numbers swelled as the Dutch schools began to expand. On the other hand, the daimyo, intensely conservative, were opposed to the new concessions, and their opposition forced the shogun to appeal to the emperor for support. Soon, samurai opponents of the bureaucracy were also appealing to the emperor, who began to emerge from his centuries-long confinement as a largely religious and ceremonial figure. Whereas most daimyo defended the status quo, the samurai were more divided. Some saw opportunity in change, including the possibility of unseating the shogunate. The fact was that the complex shogunate system had depended on the isolation policy; it could not survive the stresses of foreign influence and internal reactions. The result was not immediate collapse; indeed, into the late 1850s, Japanese life seemed to go on much as before.

In the 1860s, political crisis came into the open. The crisis was spiced by samurai attacks on foreigners, including one murder of a British official, matched by Western naval bombardments of feudal forts. Civil war broke out in 1866 as the samurai eagerly armed themselves with American Civil War surplus weapons, causing Japan's aristocracy to come to terms with the advantages of Western armaments. When the samurai defeated a shogunate force, many Japanese were finally shocked out of their traditional reliance on their own superiority. One author argued that the nation, compared with the West and its technology, science, and humane laws, was only half civilized.

This multifaceted crisis came to an end in 1868 when the victorious reform group proclaimed a new emperor named Mutsuhito whose region was commonly called "Meiji," or "Enlightened." In his name, key samurai leaders managed to put down the troops of the shogunate. The crisis period had been shocking enough to allow further changes in Japan's basic political structure—changes that went much deeper at the political level than those introduced by Russia from 1861 onward.

Industrial and Political Change in the Meiji State

The new Meiji government promptly set about abolishing feudalism, replacing the daimyo in 1871 with a system of nationally appointed prefects (district administrators carefully chosen from different regions; the prefect system was copied from French practice). Political power was effectively centralized, and from this base the Meiji rulers—the emperor and his close advisors, drawn from loyal segments of the aristocracy—began to expand the power of the state to effect economic and social change.

Quickly, the Japanese government sent samurai officials abroad, to western Europe and the United States, to study economic and political institutions and technology. These samurai, deeply impressed by what they saw, pulled back from their earlier anti-foreign position and gained increasing voice over other officials in the government. Their basic goal was Japan's domestic development, accompanied by a careful diplomatic policy that would avoid antagonizing the West.

Fundamental improvements in government finance soon followed. Between 1873 and 1876, the Meiji ministers introduced a real social revolution. They abolished the samurai class and the stipends this group had received. The tax on agriculture was converted to a wider tax, payable in money. The samurai were compensated by government-backed bonds, but these decreased in value, and most samurai became poor. This development sparked renewed conflict, and a final samurai uprising occurred in 1877. However, the government had introduced an army based on national conscription, and by 1878 the nation was militarily secure. Individual samurai found new opportunities in political and business areas as they adapted to change. One former samurai, Iwasaki Yataro (1834–1885), who started his career buying weapons for a feudal lord, set up the Mitsubishi Company after 1868, winning government contracts for railroad and steamship lines designed to compete with British companies in the region (Figure 27.5). Despite his overbearing personality,

Perry, Matthew American commodore who visited Edo Bay with American fleet in 1853; insisted on opening ports to American trade on threat of naval bombardment; won rights for American trade with Japan in 1854.

Figure 27.5 Born to an impoverished samurai family, the ambitious and forceful Iwasaki Yataro became one of the most powerful financiers and industrialists of late 19th-century Japan. He founded the company still known as Mitsubishi (which means Three Diamonds) in 1870 and made his fortune in shipping.

The Meiji Constitution, 1889

Diet [DEYE-iht] Japanese parliament established as part of the new constitution of 1889; part of Meiji reforms; could pass laws and approve budgets; able to advise government, but not to control it.

Iwasaki built a loyal management group, including other former samurai, and by his death had a stake in shipbuilding, mining, and banking as well as transportation. The continued existence of the samurai, reflecting Japan's lack of outright revolution, would yield diverse results in later Japanese history.

The process of political reconstruction crested in the 1880s. Many former samurai organized political parties. Meiji leaders traveled abroad to discover modern political forms. In 1884 they created a new conservative nobility, stocked by former nobles and Meiji leaders, that would operate a British-style House of Peers. Next, the bureaucracy was reorganized, insulated from political pressures, and opened to talent on the basis of civil service examinations. The bureaucracy began to expand rapidly; it grew from 29,000 officials in 1890 to 72,000 in 1908. Finally, the constitution, issued in 1889, ensured major prerogatives for the emperor along with limited powers for the lower house of the **Diet** (DEYE-iht), as the new parliament was called. Here, Germany provided the model, for the emperor commanded the military directly (served by a German-style general staff) and also directly named his ministers. Both the institution and its members' clothing were Western, as the Visualizing the Past feature shows. The Diet could pass laws, upon agreement of both houses, and could approve budgets, but failure to pass a budget would simply reinstate the budget of the previous year. Parliament could thus advise government, but it could not control it. Finally, the conservative tone of this parliamentary experiment was confirmed by high property qualifications set for voting rights. Only about 5 percent of Japanese men had enough wealth to be allowed to vote for representatives to the lower house.

Japan's political structure thus came to involve centralized imperial rule, wielded by a handful of Meiji advisors, combined with limited representative institutions copied from the West. This combination gave great power to a group of wealthy businesspeople and former nobles who influenced the emperor and also pulled strings within the parliament. Political parties arose, but a coherent system overrode their divisions into the 20th century. Japan thus followed its new policy of imitating the West, but it retained its own identity.

The Japanese political solution compared interestingly to Russian institutions after Alexander II's reforms. Both states were centralized and authoritarian, but Japan had incorporated business leaders into its governing structure, whereas Russia defended a more traditional social elite.

Japan's Industrial Revolution

Political decisions were essential after the crisis of the 1860s, but they were soon matched by other initiatives. The new army, based on the universal conscription of young men, was further improved by formal officer training and by upgrading armaments according to Western standards. With the aid of Western advisors, a modern navy was established.

Attention also focused on creating the conditions necessary for industrialization. New government banks funded growing trade and provided capital for industry. State-built railroads spread across the country, and the islands were connected by rapid steamers. New methods raised agricultural output to feed the people of the growing cities.

The new economic structure depended on the destruction of many older restrictions. Guilds and internal road tariffs were abolished to create a national market. Land reform created clear individual ownership for many farmers, which helped motivate expansion of production and the introduction of new fertilizers and equipment.

Government initiative dominated manufacturing not only in the creation of transportation networks but also in state operation of mines, shipyards, and metallurgical plants. Scarce capital and the unfamiliarity of new technology seemed to compel state direction, as occurred in Russia at the same time. Government control also helped check the many foreign advisors needed by early Japanese industry; here, Japan maintained closer supervision than its Russian neighbor. Japan established the Ministry of Industry in 1870, and it quickly became one of the key government agencies, setting overall economic policy as well as operating specific sectors. By the 1880s, model shipyards, arsenals, and factories provided experience in new technology and disciplined work systems for many Japanese. Finally, by expanding technical training and education, setting up banks and post offices, and regularizing commercial laws, the government provided a structure within

Two Faces of Western Influence

These pictures show an 1850s cartoon portraying American Commodore Matthew Perry as a greedy warlord and the first meeting of the Japanese parliament in 1890.

QUESTIONS What kinds of attitudes toward the West does the cartoon represent? What does the picture of parliament convey about attitudes toward the West? What was the model for the design of the meeting room? What do the two pictures suggest about uses of costume in a time of rapid change?

---

which Japan could develop on many fronts. Measures in this area largely copied established practices in the West, but with adaptation suitable for Japanese conditions; thus, well before any European university, Tokyo Imperial University had a faculty of agriculture.

Private enterprise quickly played a role in Japan's growing economy, particularly in the vital textile sector. Some businesspeople came from older merchant families, although some of the great houses had been ruined with the financial destruction of the samurai class. There were also newcomers, some rising from peasant ranks. Shuibuzawa Eiichi (SHOO-ih-buh-zah-wah EYE-ee-chee), for example, born a peasant, became a merchant and then an official of the Finance Ministry. He turned to banking in 1873, using other people's money to set up cotton-spinning mills and other textile operations. By the 1890s huge new industrial combines, later known as **zaibatsu** (ZEYE-baht-soo), were being formed as a result of accumulations of capital and far-flung merchant and industrial operations.

zaibatsu [ZEYE-baht-soo] Huge industrial combines created in Japan in the 1890s as part of the process of industrialization.

By 1900 the Japanese economy was fully launched in an industrial revolution. It rested on a political and social structure different from that of Russia—one that had in most respects changed more profoundly. Japan's success in organizing industrialization, including its careful management of foreign advice and models, proved to be one of the great developments of later 19th-century history.

It is important to keep these early phases of Japanese industrialization in perspective. Pre–World War I Japan was far from the West's equal. It depended on imports of Western equipment and raw materials such as coal; for industrial purposes, Japan was a resource-poor nation. Although economic growth and careful government policy allowed Japan to avoid Western domination, Japan was newly dependent on world economic conditions and was often at a disadvantage. It needed exports to pay for machine and resource imports, and these in turn took hordes of low-paid workers. Silk production grew rapidly, the bulk of it destined for Western markets. Much of this production was based on the labor of poorly paid women who worked at home or in sweatshops, not in mechanized factories. Some of these women were sold into service by farm families. Efforts at labor organization or other means of protest were met by vigorous repression.

641

Social and Diplomatic Effects of Industrialization

The Industrial Revolution and the wider extensions of manufacturing and commercial agriculture, along with political change, had significant ramifications within Japanese culture and society. These changes also helped generate a more aggressive foreign policy. Japanese society was disrupted by massive population growth. Better nutrition and new medical provisions reduced death rates, and the upheaval of the rural masses cut into traditional restraints on births. The result was steady population growth that strained Japanese resources and stability, although it also ensured a constant supply of low-cost labor. This was one of the causes of Japan's class tensions.

The Japanese government introduced a universal education system, providing primary schools for all. This education stressed science and the importance of technical subjects along with political loyalty to the nation and emperor. Elite students at the university level also took courses that emphasized science, and many Japanese students went abroad to study technical subjects in other countries.

Education also revealed Japanese insistence on distinctive values. After a heady reform period in the 1870s, when hundreds of Western teachers were imported and a Rutgers University professor brought in for high-level advice about the whole system, the emperor and conservative advisors stepped back after 1879. This was when reformers like Fukuzawa Yukichi began to tone down their rhetoric. Innovation and individualism had gone too far. A traditional moral education was essential, along with new skills, which would stress "loyalty to the Imperial House, love of country, filial piety toward parents, respect for superiors, faith in friends, charity toward inferiors and respect for oneself." The use of foreign books on morality was prohibited, and intense government inspection of textbooks was intended to promote social order.

Many Japanese copied Western fashions as part of the effort to become modern. Western-style haircuts replaced the samurai shaved head with a topknot—another example of the westernization of hair in world history. Western standards of hygiene spread, and the Japanese became enthusiastic toothbrushers and consumers of patent medicines. Japan also adopted the Western calendar and the metric system. Few Japanese converted to Christianity, however, and despite Western popular cultural fads, the Japanese managed to preserve an emphasis on their own values. What the Japanese wanted and got from the West involved practical techniques; they planned to infuse them with a distinctively Japanese spirit. As an early Japanese visitor to the American White House wrote in a self-satisfied poem that captured the national mood,

> We suffered the barbarians to look upon
> The glory of our Eastern Empire of Japan.

Western-oriented enthusiasms were not meant to destroy a distinctive Japanese spirit.

Japanese family life retained many traditional emphases. The birth rate dropped as rapid population growth forced increasing numbers of people off the land. Meanwhile, the rise of factory industry, separating work from home, made children's labor less useful. This trend, developed earlier in the West, seems inseparable from successful industrialization. There were new signs of family instability as well; the divorce rate exploded until legal changes made procedures more difficult. On the more traditional side, the Japanese were eager to maintain the inferiority of women in the home. The position of Western women offended them. Japanese government visitors to the United States were appalled by what they saw as the bossy ways of women: "The way women are treated here is like the way parents are respected in our country." Standards of Japanese courtesy also contrasted with the more open and boisterous behavior of Westerners, particularly Americans. "Obscenity is inherent in the customs of this country," noted another samurai visitor to the United States. Certain Japanese religious values were also preserved. Buddhism lost some ground, although it remained important, but Shintoism, which appealed to the new nationalist concern with Japan's distinctive mission and the religious functions of the emperor, won new interest.

Traditionalism was not the only theme in the situation of Japanese women amid industrialization. As in Russia, women were widely used in the early factory labor force—and in Japan's case, also in sweatshop silk production—because their low wages were an indispensable advantage in competitive global markets. At the same time, the government carefully provided schooling for girls, as part of its new commitment to mass education. And many upper-class women, as in Russia, had opportunities even for high education, in secondary schools or separate universities. The tension they encountered, between assumptions that women should play subservient and domestic roles and the excitement of new educational opportunities, were particularly sharp, but not entirely different from contemporary conditions in Russia or the West. Outright feminism, however, was far less common than in either western or eastern Europe. Industrialization and urbanization made literal traditionalism impossible amid rapid economic change.

Economic change, and the tensions as well as the power it generated, also produced a shift in Japanese foreign policy. This shift was partly an imitation of Western models. New imperialism also relieved some strains within Japanese society, giving displaced samurai the chance to exercise their military talents elsewhere. Even more than Western countries, which used similar arguments for imperialism, the Japanese economy also needed access to markets and raw materials. Because Japan was poor in many basic materials, including coal and oil for energy, the pressure for expansion was particularly great.

Japan's quick victory over China in the **Sino-Japanese War** for influence in Korea (1894–1895) was a first step toward expansion (Map 27.2). Japan convincingly demonstrated its new superiority over all other Asian powers. Humiliated by Western insistence that it abandon the Liaodong peninsula it had just taken from China, the Japanese planned a war with Russia as a means of striking out against the nearest European state. A 1902 alliance with Britain was an important sign of Japan's arrival as an equal nation in the Western-dominated world diplomatic system. The Japanese were also eager to dent Russia's growing strength in east Asia after the development of the trans-Siberian railroad. Disputes over Russian influence in Manchuria and Japanese influence in Korea led to the Russo-Japanese War in 1904 (Map 27.3), which Japan won handily because of its superior navy. Japan annexed Korea in 1910, entering the ranks of imperialist powers.

The Strain of Modernization

Japanese achievement had its costs, including poor living standards in the crowded cities. Many Japanese conservatives resented the passion other Japanese displayed for Western fashions. Disputes between generations, with the old clinging to traditional standards and the young more interested in Western styles, were very troubling in a society that stressed the importance of parental authority.

Some tension entered political life. Political parties in Japan's parliament clashed with the emperor's ministers over rights to determine policy. The government often had to dissolve the Diet and call for new elections, seeking a more workable parliamentary majority. Political assassinations and attempted assassinations reflected grievances, including direct action impulses in the samurai tradition.

Another kind of friction emerged in intellectual life. Many Japanese scholars copied Western philosophies and literary styles, and there was enough adaptation to prevent the emergence of a full Russian-style intelligentsia. Other intellectuals expressed a deep pessimism about the loss of identity in a changing world. The underlying theme was confusion about a Japan that was no longer traditional, but not Western either. What *was* it? Thus, some writers spoke of Japan's heading for a "nervous collapse

Sino-Japanese War War fought between Japan and Qing China between 1894 and 1895; resulted in Japanese victory; frustrated Japanese imperial aims because of Western insistence that Japan withdraw from Liaodong peninsula.

Map 27.3 Japanese Colonial Expansion to 1914 The map shows Japan's principal gains, but also the limitations that still frustrated Japanese nationalists.

from which we will not be able to recover." Others dealt with more personal conflicts such as those in the following poem:

> Do not be loved by others; do not accept their charity, do not promise anything. . . . Always wear a mask. Always be ready for a fight—be able to hit the next man on the head at any time. Don't forget that when you make friends with someone you are sooner or later certain to break with him.

As an antidote to social and cultural insecurity, Japanese leaders urged national loyalty and devotion to the emperor, and with some success. The official message promoted Japanese virtues of obedience and harmony that the West lacked. School texts thus stressed,

> Our country takes as its base the family system: the nation is but a single family, the imperial family is our main house. We the people worship the unbroken imperial line with the same feeling of respect and love that a child feels toward his parents. . . . The union of loyalty and filial piety is truly the special character of our national polity.

Japanese nationalism built on traditions of superiority, cohesion, and deference to rulers, as well as on the new tensions generated by rapid change. It became a deep force, probably in Japan more than elsewhere, that played a unique role in justifying sacrifice and struggle in a national mission to preserve independence and dignity in a hostile world. Nationalism, along with firm police repression of dissent and the sweeping changes of the early Meiji years, certainly helps explain why Japan avoided the revolutionary pressure that hit Russia, China, and other countries after 1900.

Yet Japan's very success reminds us of how unusual it was. No other society outside the Western world was yet able to match its achievements. Russia, responding to Western example in its own way, continued its growth as a world power, but amid such social disarray that further upheaval was inevitable. Most of the rest of the world faced the more immediate concern of adjusting to or resisting Western dominance; industrialization was a remote prospect. Even today, when many societies are striving for greater industrialization, the ability to emulate the Japanese pattern of rapid change seems very limited—with other parts of east Asia, interestingly enough, leading the pack.

yellow peril   Western term for perceived threat of Japanese imperialism around 1900; met by increased Western imperialism in region.

Global Connections

Russia and Japan in the World

Russia's world role, founded on its huge size and territorial expansion, had already been established in the early modern period. There were, however, new twists during the 19th century. Russian troops and diplomats periodically gained direct roles in western Europe. Russian forces entered France as part of the coalition that defeated Napoleon. A side result was the development of new restaurants in France, called bistros, based on the Russian word for *quick*. Russian armies helped put down the Hungarian revolution in 1849. Russian involvement in Middle Eastern diplomacy resulted from its steady pressure on the Ottoman Empire. By the later 19th century, Russia extended its influence in eastern Asia, seizing new territories in northern China and claiming a role elsewhere, in China and Korea alike. This set the collision course with Japan. Russia also participated somewhat more broadly in the globalization of the later 19th century, participating in international conferences and contributing to "international" styles in art.

Japan's world role was much newer, and just emerging by 1914. Long isolated, Japan had experienced only one previous attempt at assertion beyond its borders, the late-16th century invasion of Korea. Now, however, ambitions increased, fueled by economic needs, growing industrial and military strength, and population pressure. It was during the Meiji era that Japanese leaders

decided to open the wave of globalization, though without losing a distinctive identity, rather than trying to resist it. More specifically, Japan sought to be regarded as a great nation along Western imperialist lines. This brought the conflicts with China and Russia before 1914, and wider experiments thereafter. In the long run, it was Japan's striking economic success that would most clearly define its new place in the world. Initially, the unfolding of strength in the eastern Pacific region, along with the complex relationships to the West, marked Japan's dramatic entry as a force to be reckoned with.

The beginnings of serious industrialization in Russia and Japan, and the entry of Japan into world affairs, contributed important new ingredients to the global diplomatic picture by the early 20th century. These developments, along with the rise of the United States, added to the growing sense of competition between the established Western powers. Japan's surge promoted a fear in the West of a new **yellow peril** that should be opposed through greater imperialist efforts. Outright colonial acquisitions by the new powers added directly to the competitive atmosphere, particularly in the Far East.

Further Readings

Important comparative work includes Rudra Sil, *Managing "Modernity": Work, Community, and Authority in Late-Industrialized Japan and Russia* (2002) and Kaoru Sugihara, ed., *Japan, China, and the Growth of the Asian International Economy,*

1850–1949 (2005). A. Gerschenkron, *Economic Backwardness in Historical Perspective: A Book of Essays* (1962), helps define the conditions of latecomer industrialization. The best survey of Russia in this transitional period is Hans Rogger, *Russia in the Age of Modernization and Revolution, 1881–1917* (1983). See also Geoffrey Hosking, *Russia: People and Empire, 1532–1917* (1997). Russian reforms and economic change are discussed in Alexander Pulonov, *Russia in the Nineteenth Century: Autocracy, Reform and Social Change, 1814–1914* (2005); Sharon Hudgins, *The Other Side of Russia: A Slice of Life in Siberia and the Russian Far East* (2003); Patrick O'Meara, *The Decembrist Pavel Pestel: Russia's First Republican* (2003); Sidney Harcave, trans., *The Memoirs of Count Witte* (1990), includes a brief biographical sketch and his collected writings of this influential "modernizer." On social and cultural developments, see Victoria Bonnell, ed., *The Russian Worker: Life and Labor Under the Tsarist Regime* (1983); Barbara Engel, *Mothers and Daughters: Women of the Intelligentsia in Nineteenth Century Russia* (1983); and Jeffrey Brooks, *When Russia Learned to Read: Literacy and Popular Culture* (1987). On another vital area of eastern Europe, see A. Stavrianos, *The Balkans, 1815–1914* (1963).

Japan in the 19th century is viewed from a modernization perspective in R. Dore, ed., *Aspects of Social Change in Modern Japan* (1967). See also Ian Inkster, *Japanese Industrialization: Historical and Cultural Perspectives* and *The Japanese Industrial Economy: Late Development and Cultural Causation* (2001); W. W. Lockwood, *The Economic Development of Japan: Growth and Structural Change 1868–1938* (1954); J. C. Abegglen, *The Japanese Factory: Aspects of Its Social Organization*, rev. ed. (1985); Andrew Gordon, *The Evolution of Labor Relations in Japan* (1985); and Hugh Patrick, ed., *Japanese Industrialization and Its Social Consequences* (1973). E. O. Reischauer's *Japan: The Story of a Nation* (1981) remains a good general history of the period. For more closely focused works on socioeconomic change, see Masayuki Tanimoto, ed., *The Role of Tradition in Japan's Industrialization: Another Path to Industrialization* (2006); George Feifer, *Breaking Open Japan: Commodore Perry, Lord Abe, and American Imperialism in 1853* (2006); Janet Hunger, *Women and the Labour Market in Japan's Industrializing Economy: The Textile Industry before the Pacific War* (2003); S. Ericson, *The Sound of the Whistle: Railroads and the State in Meiji Japan* (1996); Peter N. Stearns, *Schools and Students in Industrial Society: Japan and the West* (1997); and E. P. Tsurumi, *Factory Girls: Women in the Thread Mills of Meiji Japan* (1990). Additional studies include R. H. Myers and M. R. Beattie, eds., *The Japanese Colonial Empire 1895–1945* (1984); W. G. Beasley, *Japanese Imperialism, 1894–1945* (1987); and P. Duus, *The Abacus and the Sword: The Japanese Penetration of Korea, 1895–1910* (1995). On Japan and Russia, see Frederic A. Sharf, et al., *A Much Recorded War: The Russo-Japanese War in History and Imagery* (2005).

On the Web

The glories of tsarist Russia are revealed in a virtual tour of the Alexander Palace at http://www.alexanderpalace.org/palace/. How-

ever, the riches of the tsars could not conceal the dismal world of the Russian peasantry, whose lot was little improved by Russian economic modernization. This world and how it was illuminated by the works of the Russian writer Nikolai Gogol are addressed at http://www.kirjasto.sci.fi/gogol.htm, http://www.spartacus.schoolnet.co.uk/RUSserfs.htm, http://www.geocities.com/Athens/Forum/4123/krimlife.htm, and http://it.stlawu.edu/~rkreuzer/ltrn101/gogol.htm. The Crimean War receives treatment at http://mars.wnec.edu/~grempel/courses/russia/lectures/19crimeanwar.html. Its most famous battle is described at http://www.nationalcenter.org/ChargeoftheLightBrigade.html and http://www.loc.gov/rr/print/coll/251_fen.html.

Russian liberalism reached its high-water mark with the abolition of serfdom, an institution whose rise and demise is described at http://avalon.law.yale.edu/19th_century/koval6. A copy of the Emancipation Manifesto ending serfdom can be found at http://en.wikisource.org/wiki/Russian_Emancipation_Manifesto_of_1861:_English_Translation. However, reaction soon set in. The failure of the Revolution of 1905, examined at http://mars.wnec.edu/~grempel/courses/russia/lectures/23rev1905.html, to achieve any significant degree of political and social reform paved the way for those favoring more radical change, such as the Bolsheviks, led by Vladimir Ilyich Ulyanov, whose life and work is examined at http://www.marxists.org/archive/lenin/ and whose voice can be heard at http://www.aha.ru/~mausoleu/speaken2.htm. Count Sergei Witte's diplomatic and economic policies are glimpsed at http://members.tripod.com/~american_almanac/witte92b.htm. Marxist intellectual Leon Trotsky's brief evaluation of Witte, found at http://www.marxists.org/archive/trotsky/works/1905/ch10.htm, is dramatically written and full of interest.

Life in Meiji Japan can be glimpsed through an exhibition of contemporary woodblock art at http://www.artgallery.sbc.edu/ukiyoe/historyofwoodblockprints.html. A virtual tour of Meiji culture and politics is offered at http://www.virtualmuseum.ca/Exhibitions/Meiji/english/html/index.html. This tour offers an examination of the Russo-Japanese War of 1905 at http://www.virtualmuseum.ca/Exhibitions/Meiji/english/html/war3.html. Meiji Restoration era industrial policy is discussed at http://www.japan-guide.com/e/e2130.html and http://kjs.nagaokaut.ac.jp/mikami/IDEAS/home.htm. Iwasaki Yataro's role in this process is illuminated at http://www.mitsubishi.com/e/history/series/yataro/index.html, http://www.mitsubishi.com/e/history/series/yataro/index.html, and http://content.cdlib.org/xtf/view?docID=ft0w1003k0&chunk.id=d0e8030&toc.id=d0e8010&brand=ucpress. A key to the process of modernization in Japan is the Constitution of the Empire of Japan (1889), which is reproduced at http://history.hanover.edu/texts/1889con.html. For further insight into this process, this document can be compared with the Constitution of Japan (1947) at http://history.hanover.edu/texts/1947con.html. An essay comparing the course of "westernization" in Russia and Japan (and China as well) can be found at http://www.socyberty.com/Social-Sciences/A-Comparison-of-Westernization-in-Russia-Japan-and-China.67924.

AP* Test Prep

1. Nineteenth-century ruling elites in Russia embraced which philosophy and ideas?

   (A) autocratic government, Orthodox religion, and extreme nationalism

   (B) liberalism, including the emancipation of serfs and British-style democracy

   (C) socialism, with land reform for peasants and protections for workers

   (D) constitutional monarchy, with an elected parliament and limitations on the ruler's Powers

2. In Russia, the supporters of westernization and radical ideas were often

   (A) land-owning elites.

   (B) the Russian Orthodox clergy.

   (C) the land-owning peasants and serfs.

   (D) intellectuals and university-educated students.

3. Russia's lag in economic development in the 19th-century was most dramatically revealed by

   (A) the French Revolution's impact on Russia.

   (B) Napoleon's invasion of Russia.

   (C) the ability to avoid revolution until after 1900.

   (D) the Crimean War.

4. The emancipation of the serfs in Russia

   (A) meant that imported slaves did most of the agricultural labor.

   (B) immediately resulted in a flood of peasant workers joining the factories or industrial workforce for high wages.

   (C) meant Russian agriculture was unable to produce export goods.

   (D) did not require the government to surrender its imperial and aristocratic power.

AP* | Test Prep

5. The unexpected defeat by the Japanese in the Russo-Japanese War led Russia to

   (A) industrialize the military.

   (B) massive protests that became the Revolution of 1905.

   (C) the emancipation of the serfs.

   (D) attack the power of the Orthodox Church.

6. Prior to the arrival of the American fleet and Commodore Perry, Japan

   (A) had not developed a literate and educated population.

   (B) was in self-imposed isolation from Europe and the U.S.

   (C) lacked a centralized, effective government.

   (D) knew little of Western developments or ideas.

7. As a way to smooth over strains within Japanese society caused by the Industrial Revolution, the government

   (A) established a social welfare and retirement system.

   (B) tolerated unions and radical groups if they worked with the government.

   (C) gave the Japanese Parliament (Diet) powers over ministers and government.

   (D) supported Japanese nationalism and devotion to the emperor.

Free-Response Question

Compare the abilities to respond to western pressure in two of the following countries: China, Japan, Russia.

PART V

Retrospective

The Dawn of the Industrial Age, 1750–1914

Contacts and Their Limits

The long 19th century was an age of new contacts. Steamships, railroads, and the telegraph provided unprecedented speed and volume for the movement of people, goods, and news. The opening of the Suez and Panama canals added greatly to the ease of global travel. Within this essentially technological framework, the unrelenting pressure of European merchants, missionaries, and imperialists caused people in almost every society in the world to have to react to the West. As east Asia discovered, it was impossible to seek isolation. The question of what to do about Western culture and Western intrusion had become an inescapable global issue by the second half of the 19th century.

By this point, it is possible to speak of the beginnings of globalization as a new, more intense, and more demanding set of global contacts than had ever existed in world history. European and American corporations began setting up operations around the world, seeking raw materials and sales outlets. Many had factories in a variety of countries. By 1900, for example, Singer Sewing Machines, an American operation, was one of the largest companies in Russia.

Political globalization emerged as well, though it lagged behind international commerce. Two driving forces emerged. First, Western reformers began to take an interest in the human rights of distant peoples with whom they shared neither religion nor race but a common humanity. The origins of global human rights movements rest in the antislavery crusade of the late 18th and early 19th centuries, and the World Anti-Slavery Society, still active today from its base in London, was the first interna-

tional organization that depended essentially on the moral pressure of world opinion. Other movements, such as the International Red Cross and conventions about the treatment of prisoners of war, followed from humanitarian concern applied internationally. Second, economic interests saw utility in new kinds of international agreements that would facilitate commercial activity. This resulted, for example, in new conventions against piracy and the establishment of international postal facilities. Building on both impulses, the 1880s saw a flurry of new international nongovernmental organizations around issues such as labor conditions and women's rights. At the end of the 19th century, an International Court, based in the Netherlands, began operations. It was designed to deal with international disputes and, ideally, to eliminate the need for war. Many of these movements had limited impact, but they showed a clear impulse to innovate in the global political arena. There was even a reformist effort to establish a blended international language, Esperanto.

Cultural globalization occurred as well. The popularity of Western sports was a case in point—for the first time popular culture spread directly from one region to the world at large. In the 1890s the Olympic Games were revived, this time as an international competition, in hopes that athletics could promote global harmony. By 1914 Hollywood was emerging as an international film capital.

While the level of international trade rose rapidly, there were limits to this first surge of globalization. It was clearly Western-dominated. The initial Olympics had athletes from North America and Australia joining European hosts—international, but hardly global. Global arrangements like the International Postal Union were truly important, but they were agreements among Western powers simply imposed on the rest of the world as part of enlightened imperialism.

Even aside from the limits of globalization, the range of contacts should not be exaggerated. Comparison is essential to determine specific reactions to the growing array of global connections. Many societies participated in global trade, willingly or under pressure, without homogenizing. Japanese leaders ventured a brief period of unalloyed enthusiasm for things Western, but they pulled back quickly. In the 1880s, for example, the Japanese set clear limits to Western influence in education, instead emphasizing Japanese values. Japan managed a massive transformation without becoming "Western." Earlier in the century the wave of Atlantic revolutions showed important connections between the Americas and much of Europe, but the rest of the world was largely untouched. On a still larger scale, Western missionaries, though hugely successful in Africa and Oceania, did not significantly impact most established centers of Islam, Hinduism, Buddhism, or Confucianism—Korea was a notable exception. Even in sub-Saharan Africa, Christian conversions were matched by new conversions to Islam.

Each region, including the West itself, continued to blend contacts with ongoing regional patterns in creative combinations. By 1914 the balance was clearly shifting toward globalization, but tremendous diversity persisted.

The spread of nationalism in fact permitted many regions to make new claims on real or imagined traditions as a reaction against too many concessions to global contacts. Nationalism was of course Western in origin. It rapidly spread to the United States, Latin America, and eastern Europe, and then to the Middle East (where it would be expressed in Arab, Turkish, and Zionist nationalisms), India, Japan, and China. Nationalism was a new political loyalty spreading, ironically, as a result of contact; it legitimized a degree of separation and a proud assertion of the validity of specific regional traditions. Nationalism could combat Western pressure, but it could also undermine non-Western regional entities such as the Ottoman Empire and, later, parts of Russia. In a world increasingly shaped by contacts, nationalism was an alternative, and largely disaggregating, force. ∎

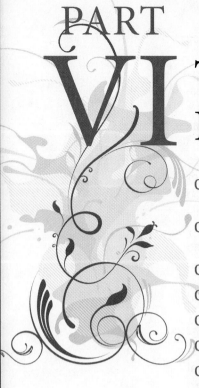

PART VI

The Newest Stage of World History: 1914–Present

Chapter 28   Descent into the Abyss: World War I and the Crisis of the European Global Order

Chapter 29   The World Between the Wars: Revolutions, Depression, and Authoritarian Responses

Chapter 30   A Second Global Conflict and the End of the European World Order

Chapter 31   Western Society and Eastern Europe in the Decades of the Cold War

Chapter 32   Latin America: Revolution and Reaction into the 21st Century

Chapter 33   Africa, the Middle East, and Asia in the Era of Independence

Chapter 34   Rebirth and Revolution: Nation-building in East Asia and the Pacific Rim

Chapter 35   The End of the Cold War and the Shape of a New Era: World History 1990–2008

Chapter 36   Globalization and Resistance: World History 1990–2008

THE OVERVIEW

These maps help tell two of the biggest stories of the 20th century. First, the great Western empires and the Ottoman, Austro-Hungarian, and part of the Russian empires had imploded by the end of the century. More new nations arose during the 20th century than during any other span in history. These massive boundary changes were related to other upheavals. The typical political system in 1914 was either monarchy or empire; by the early 21st century, almost every country had a different kind of government from what it had had a century before, and some societies had had multiple kinds of government. The typical social system in 1914 was still dominated by a landed aristocracy or an aristocratic and big business blend. By the beginning of the 21st century, the landed aristocracy had faded dramatically, displaced by revolution or the rise of industry. New nations were thus paralleled by new political systems and new social structures.

But political maps are not the only story. While the current phase of world history involves the rise of the nation-state, the late 20th and early 21st centuries saw new challenges to the nation-state. A variety of new regional combinations formed, the strongest being the European Union. And multinational corporations often possessed powers far greater than any but the largest nations.

The age of empire has passed. But its replacement is less clear. Will it be a welter of new nations, each with a stake in its separate identity, or will it be new organizations associated with globalization? A period of world history has passed. The 19th century has ended far more than chronologically. But defining the new period is an ongoing challenge. The problem is perspective: for past periods we know what the dominant trends and factors were, because we know the end of the story. For the current phase of world history, picking out the key themes amid the specific changes must be more tentative. Several clear conclusions must be mixed with several open questions.

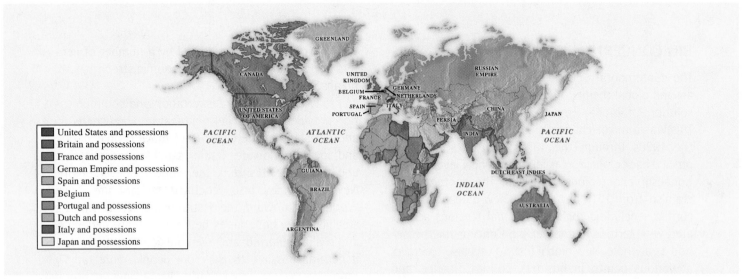

Political Map of the World in 1914

Political Map of the Present-Day World

BIG CONCEPTS

The contemporary period in world history organizes around global themes. A key concept involves the dissolution of global empires through decolonization. This was a major change, extending particularly from the 1920s through the 1970s, that in some ways pushed back global forces in favor of new levels of nationalism and regional assertion. The contemporary era also, from 1914 onward, saw new global wars and conflict—including the recent global tensions associated with terrorism, another Big Concept for the period as a whole. New global institutions also emerged, at various points, in business, politics, finance, and even culture, a third organizing concept. Finally, particularly from the late 1940s onward and increasingly fueled by new technologies and explicit policies alike, new iterations of globalization form the final Big Concept for world history's newest period.

TRIGGERS FOR CHANGE

The world of European dominance began to come crashing down with World War I, and the destruction accelerated with the worldwide economic depression and then World War II. The two world wars were, in part, European civil wars, which caused massive loss of economic, demographic, and political vitality. It became impossible to cling to exclusive economic dominance, much less to overseas empires. Add the growing strength and effectiveness of anticolonial nationalisms, and the political order of the 19th century had to crumble. Even Western military supremacy was shaken. New challenges arose. Even more pervasively, a large number of the former colonies were able to develop sufficient military arsenals to make outside intervention dauntingly expensive.

Trigger 1: The collapse of European imperial dominance and decolonization.
Question 1: What framework will replace the system?

Initially the cold war rivalry between the United States and the Soviet Union provided a political, economic, and policy framework. This ended too, and the United States emerged as sole superpower, but this was unlikely to provide a durable pattern either. Would the next phase of world history see some other dominant civilization, playing the role that the Islamic Middle East and then the West had maintained for significant stretches of world history?

Would world history be framed by a number of centers of political, military, and economic strength, with no absolute top dog?

New methods of transportation and communication provided another defining feature and ushered in another stage in the capacity to move people, goods, and ideas worldwide. Radio, satellite transmissions, and the Internet shrunk the world as never before. New technology also redefined military life. From World War I onward, the destructive power of warfare steadily grew, boundaries between military personnel and civilians blurred, and even outside of outright war it became possible to kill more people more rapidly than ever before. From World War II onward, world history was marked by purges and genocides in which millions of people could die.

Trigger 2: Massive technological innovation.
Question 2: Which aspect—military capacity or global communications networks—should be emphasized?

Tremendous population growth provided the third defining feature of the new period in world history. New public health measures, introduced beginning in the 19th century, explain most of the growth. Improvements in food supply for the most part kept pace, though some regions experienced devastating famines. In many regions, population growth was accompanied by massive urbanization, often in advance of industrial growth, and new patterns of urban poverty played their own role, not just in regional but also in world history. In 2007, half of the world's population lived in cities—a world history first.

Trigger 3: The demographic explosion.
Question 3: Will historians look back on this as a framework for disaster, inevitably leading to exhaustion of resources, battles for space, and pollution; or will the new population levels prove manageable and self-correcting, as the rapid declines in birth rates by 2000 might suggest?

How should the story of the current period of world history be written? As military technology, population pressure, and environmental crises creating a catastrophe simply waiting to happen? Or as new global linkages, restraint in the use of military technology, and successful responses to population growth leading to change but also to new opportunities?

THE BIG CHANGES

Economic, political and social changes marked the new period in world history; trends in culture were less clear, but there was new debate and conflict. Several factors spurred change. New international contacts, with the West but also communist Russia, provided examples of innovation and challenged traditional arrangements. The growth of city populations and manufacturing also put pressure on older systems. In the process, age-old arrangements, like monarchy, the dominance of landed aristocracy, and even patriarchal gender relations were newly challenged and, often, replaced.

Several shifts were quite stark. In 1914, the dominant social class in most of the world's societies was the landed aristocracy. By 2009, it was an upper middle class of educated managers and big-business owners, a huge change. In 1914, most political regimes were empires or monarchies. By 2009, monarchy, except for figure-head rulers, was quite rare, and multinational empires had largely disappeared. Concerning gender, while men and women were still unequal by the 21st century, patriarchal conventions had been seriously modified, almost everywhere, by voting rights for women, new educational access, and other legal and social changes. By the end of the 20th century, rapidly declining birth rates added another dimension to the changing lives of women.

The various core challenges to the traditions of agricultural societies did not produce uniform responses. Monarchies might be largely gone, but there was massive divergence between democratic and authoritarian replacements. Woman had new rights almost everywhere, but their economic conditions and even their gender goals varied widely. Finally, the method of innovation varied from one place to the next. Huge revolutions spurred changes in some cases, not only in social structure and politics but also (at least in principle) in women's condition. In other places, new kinds of contacts and the process of decolonization set the contexts for innovation, though with less sweeping drama.

With greater political independence and new political regimes, many parts of the world made systematic efforts to improve their position in the world economy. A few regions such as Japan and the Pacific Rim joined western Europe and the United States as advanced industrial societies at the top of the economic heap. A larger number of societies won a greater voice at the global economic table. Some,

like the oil-producing states, took advantage of their control over vital global resources. Some focused on replacing excessive reliance on the leading economic nations with local manufacturing through a process called import substitution. Others began to develop modern export sectors. Here, the biggest changes occurred from the 1970s onward. Beginning in the 1980s China became a global manufacturing powerhouse. India enhanced its exports and developed as a center for the outsourcing of services. Brazil became the world's fourth largest computer exporter. Economic change and the advance of modern manufacturing were widespread. The result was a more complex world economy than that of the 19th century. Before 1914, only about 20 percent of the world's population had been directly involved in industrialization; by 2009, the figure was passing 60 percent. Great economic inequalities persisted around the world, but the shift to more industrial economies was widespread, helping to explain other aspects of change as well.

In the cultural field, change also occurred, but here amid far greater dispute and resistance. Three cultural forces encouraged new secular loyalties. Nationalism won allegiance from most of humanity. Marxism was a persuasive belief system for many of the world's peoples during of the 20th century. From the West and Japan came an emphasis on consumer values and faith in science. The cold war brought worldwide competition between Marxism and Western consumerism. Many people changed or modified their beliefs during the 20th and 21st centuries. But the major religions retained powerful support as well. Missionary activities—Christian and Islamic—were successful in Africa and elsewhere. From the 1970s onward, a strong commitment to what many argued were fundamentalist religious values gained ground, often making use of new technology to get the message across and characterized by new levels of intolerance. The result was a real contest for cultural preferences within societies such as the Middle East, India, Russia, and the United States.

A new round of globalization occurred in the second half of the 20th century. During the middle decades of the 20th century, globalization had receded. In the 1920s and 1930s, the Soviet Union pulled out of the international economic and political system, as did Nazi Germany and authoritarian Japan. China withdrew during the early decades of the cold war. as did the United States partially, during its two decades of isolationism. The technologies promoting further contacts continued to accelerate, however, and key societies shifted position in the decades after World War II. Japan, Germany, and the United States became active global players. China reentered the global system after 1978, Russia after 1985. Not surprisingly, this second round of globalization proved even more intense than the first. Multinational corporations, for example, depended on much closer global integration than earlier international corporations. From the 1970s onward, a massive network of international nongovernmental organizations emerged, which sought to deal with an array of issues from human rights and the environment to sweatshop labor. Global cultural change, linked to consumerism, became more extensive than ever before. Population growth encouraged new forms of migration that brought people from Africa, Asia, and Latin America to industrial centers in the United States, western Europe and to some extent Japan. Many migrants now went back and forth frequently, encouraging further cultural contact between their societies of origin and their new homes.

Globalization began also to involve new kinds of environmental change. The human impact on the environment had been largely regional. Now it took on international dimensions. Multinational corporations were responsible for recurrent pollution crises, including oil spills and chemical disasters. Air pollution from industrial regions brought acid rain to forests hundreds of miles away. Most scientists became convinced by the early 21st century that air pollution and the destruction of tropical rain forests were creating global warming, which had implications for the entire planet. And while policymakers struggled to find global responses, there was a lag between economic globalization and the political will to solve the problems it created.

CONTINUITY

In the late 20th century, many people believed that change was accelerating more rapidly than at any previous point in world history. It was important, nevertheless, to recognize continuities. These fell into three related categories. While a number of regions advanced industrialization, others continued to focus on low-cost production of raw materials and foods. During much of the 20th century industrial countries intensified their control over most African exports. Parts of Latin America and southeast Asia were also still dominated by older constraints in the world economy. Even within changing societies, such as India, rural regions often maintained older economic and social forms. Worldwide, by 2005, fewer

1910 C.E.	1920 C.E.	1930 C.E.	1940 C.E.
1910–1920 Mexican Revolution	1920 Treaty of Sèvres reorganizes Middle East	1930–1945 Vargas regime in Brazil	1941 United States enters World War II
1912 African National Congress party formed in South Africa	1921 Foundation of Chinese Communist party	1931 Japan invades Manchuria	1942–1945 Holocaust
1912 Fall of Qing dynasty in China; beginning of Chinese Revolution	1927–1928 Stalin takes power in Soviet Union; initiates five-year plans and collectivization	1931–1947 Gandhi-led resistance in India	1945 Formation of United Nations
1914–1918 World War I	1929–1933 Height of Great Depression	1933 Nazis rise to power in Germany	1945 Atomic Bombs dropped on Japan
1916 Arab revolts against Ottomans		1933–1939 New Deal in United States	1945 Communists proclaim Vietnam independence
1917 United States enters World War I		1934–1940 Cárdenas reform period in Mexico	1945–1948 Soviet takeover of eastern Europe
1917 Russian Revolution		1935 German rearmament; Italy captures Ethiopia	1946 Philippine independence from the U.S.
1917 Balfour Declaration promises Jews a homeland in Palestine		1937 Army officers in power in Japan; invasion of China	1947 Peronism in Argentina
1919 Versailles peace settlement, League of Nations		1939–1945 World War II	1947 India and Pakistan gain independence
1919 Revolt in Egypt, first Pan-African Nationalist Congress, Non-violent protest in India.		1939 Nazi–Soviet Pact	1947–1949 Marshall Plan for Western Europe
			1948 Division of Korea
			1948 Israel–Palestine partition; first Arab–Israeli war
			1949 Formation of NATO
			1949 Communist victory in China

than 30 percent of the world's people had access to the Internet—this was a huge minority, of course, and an impressive sign of change; but also a reminder of ongoing limitations. Overall, many economic inequalities had worsened by the early 21st century, both within regions and among them, and most of these gaps reflected older historical patterns.

There was great resistance to change in many parts of the world. Many societies hesitated to redefine gender relation. This was one reason why, in places like Africa and the Middle East, girls continued to be less likely to receive primary education than boys. The increased influence of fundamentalist religions both reflected and encouraged resistance to many kinds of change, including in some instances the inroads of consumer culture. Even aside from outright resistance, many regions attempted to discipline change by combining it with older traditions. Early in the 21st century, in the southern Indian state of Kerala, for example, leaders attempted to organize beauty contests in which prizes would go to women with the best command of Keralan language and culture. This was an intriguing effort to use a new and popular aspect of global consumerism to revive regional tradition. The food chain McDonald's, even as it built a worldwide empire, accepted essential adjust-

ments to local customs. McDonald's provided wine and beer in its European outlets, more vegetarian fare in India, and teriyaki burgers in Japan. Globalization did not entirely override continuity or opposition in the name of continuity.

Finally, even as they responded to change, many societies retained broader orientations derived from their past. Early in the 21st century it was clear that the United States continued to be extremely suspicious of participating in international agreements that might limit its sovereignty. Hence, it rejected several pacts, including those on the environment, on punishing war criminals, and on banning land mines. China changed mightily during the 20th century, but it continued to place an unusual emphasis on order and conformity. Government attacks on a Buddhist-derived religious movement, the Falun Gong, were uncannily similar to the repression of Buddhism itself under the Tang dynasty. Russia's return to greater authoritarianism in the early 21st century reminded many observers of the strong continuities between tsarist political systems, communism, and the new leadership—all intolerant of internal opposition and critique. Thus, a key use of world history involves interpreting contemporary conditions to understand how older regional or civilizational traditions continue to shape responses to current problems. The hand of

1950 C.E.	1960 C.E.	1970 C.E.	1980 C.E.	1990 C.E.
1950–1953 Korean War	1960s Civil rights movement in United States; revival of feminism	1972, 1979 Oil crises; height of OPEC power	1980–1988 Iran–Iraq War	1990 Reunification of Germany
1955 Warsaw Pact		1973 Third Arab-Israeli War	1985 ff. Gorbachev heads Soviet Union; reforms and unrest through eastern Europe	1990–1991 Iraq invades Kuwait; Persian Gulf crisis; U.S.–Allied defeat of Iraq
1955 Bandung conference; nonaligned movement	1962 Algeria declares independence, Cuban Missile Crisis	1975 Communist victory in Vietnam		
1956 Partial end of Stalinism		1975–1998 Democratic regimes spread in Latin America	1989 Reform movement in South Africa	1992 Full economic integration of Common Market
1957 European Economic Community (Common Market)	1963–1973 U.S. military intervention in Vietnam	1976 Death of Mao; new reform pattern in China	1989 New regimes throughout eastern Europe	1994 Oslo Accords between Palestinians and Israelis; Full democracy in South Africa, Nelson Mandela President
1957 Ghana becomes first independent African nation (India only)!	1965–1968 Cultural revolution in China	1979 Iranian Revolution;	1991 Collapse of the Soviet Union	
1959 Cuban Revolution	1967 Second Arab-Israeli War; Israeli occupation of the West Bank, Gaza, the Sinai and Golan Heights			2003 U.S.–British war invasion of Iraq
	1968–1973 Student protests in West			

the past does not prevent dramatic change, but it usually colors that change.

Impact on Daily Life: Emotions and Behavior

Key developments in the 20th and 21st centuries affected people's emotions and behavior. Emotions are to some extent hardwired and not subject to historical change. Many emotional and behavioral formulations reflect individual personality or particular cultures. And some emotional and behavioral standards continued to characterize specific civilizations in the 20th century. Thus Tahitians, according to anthropologists, were slower to anger than most people. Societies around the Mediterranean maintained traditions of angry or jealous responses to offenses.

Nevertheless, three kinds of change reflected and furthered the larger currents of world history. In many societies, efforts to destroy social inequality involved attempts to reverse emotional passivity. Mao Zedong, leader of the communist upheaval in China, urged peasants to cast off their traditional reluctance to show anger. Civil rights leaders in the United States wrote childrearing manuals to show African American parents how to instill new assertiveness in their children rather than more traditional deference.

Demographic changes had emotional and behavioral implications. When families drastically lowered their birth rates, emotional attachments to individual children increased. American families in the 20th century could rarely survive the death of a child without divorce. By the 1990s Chinese educators were noting growing debates with school officials over the proper treatment of particular children by teams of parents and grandparents, now focused intensely on the fate of a single child.

The spread of global consumerism affected some behaviors. When McDonald's set up its first restaurants in Soviet Russia, it had to teach workers to smile and pretend to be cheerful, a marked contrast to the surly style that had been common among salespeople in the Soviet system. Flight attendants on international airlines received similar training in cheerfulness and service. Many consumer pitches played up emotions like romantic love and played down emotions like grief. Revealingly, when China opened up to the global economy after 1978, public expressions of romantic love increased, as did imports of foreign items that seemed to express loving care.

Emotions and behaviors hardly homogenized worldwide. Older distinctions persisted. New trends often contradicted each other. There were big differences, for example, between anger-fueled protest and the emotions suitable for consumerism. But there were some wider patterns nevertheless. A growing number of people, such as global businesspeople and immigrants who traveled back and forth between their old and new countries, learned a variety of behavioral rules depending on their setting, becoming fluent in global manners and also in the languages and habits of particular societies.

SOCIETIES AND TRENDS

The section begins with Chapter 28 on World War I, in which some of the key trends of the 19th century were brutally reversed. Chapter 29 deals with major developments between the two world wars, including the rise of anticolonialism, dramatic new regimes in Russia, Germany, China and Italy, and the global impact of economic depression. Chapter 30 describes World War II, which definitively ended the European order. Chapter 31 focuses on changes both in Western society and in eastern Europe during the cold war. Chapter 32 treats Latin America into the 21st century. Chapter 33 deals with decolonization and ensuing developments in Africa, the Middle East, and south and southeast Asia. Chapter 34 focuses on east Asia and the Pacific Rim, where complex developments and divisions had major effects on the world at large. Chapters 35 and 36 describe key changes in the transition from the 20th to the 21st century.

Taken together, the chapters in this section illustrate the larger themes of this new period in world history. But they also recognize key stages within the past century: the world wars and interwar period as a time of transition; postwar developments dominated by the cold war and decolonization; and a third phase—our current phase—in which new alignments, within a framework of accelerating global contacts, hold pride of place. ■

28 Descent into the Abyss: World War I and the Crisis of the European Global Order

The Coming of the Great War

A World at War

VISUALIZING THE PAST: Trench Warfare

Failed Peace and Global Turmoil

The Nationalist Assault on the European Colonial Order

DOCUMENT: Lessons for the Colonized from the Slaughter in the Trenches

THINKING HISTORICALLY: Women in Asian and African Nationalist Movements

GLOBAL CONNECTIONS: World War and Global Upheavals

The British overlords were staggered and even some Egyptian nationalist leaders were taken aback by the thousands of women—young and old—who joined the mass demonstrations in the spring of 1919. Spreading from Cairo to towns and villages throughout the Protectorate, the protests shook the global British imperial edifice to its very foundations. Most accounts of the demonstrations, which in many instances turned into violent clashes, stress the role of students and working-class men. The participation of women is often mentioned. But most narratives deal only with elite women—some of whom are captured in the photograph here—who marched in the streets veiled to signal their defiance of the British colonizers. Predictably, we know a good deal about the backgrounds of these elite protesters and the causes they espoused. Little attention, however, has been given to working-class women who—though they have remained largely anonymous—marched in far larger numbers alongside the students and working-class men, and who took on much more aggressive roles during the political upheavals of the early 1920s.

It is not likely that young working-class women, such as Shafika Muhammad and Hamida Khalil, gave much thought to what contemporary reporters or later historians would write about their activities during the tumultuous months from 1919 to 1922 in Egypt. They were too deeply engaged in the tense demonstrations, which held the constant threat of serious injury or even death as Egyptians became more and more aggressive in their resistance to British attempts to crush the mounting popular protest. If they had known, however, that they would be lumped together with unveiled and scantily clad prostitutes in a report on the nationalist risings by a widely read British journalist, the young women would have been outraged. For even though they too marched in the streets unveiled, it was not a reflection of their lack of modesty. In contrast to the veiled well-to-do women from prominent families who had dominated the nationalist

movement for decades, women who labored in the processing plants and farmlands of Egypt could not work effectively if restricted by veils and had never made much use of them. But unlike the prostitutes, working-class women made certain that their bodies were well covered, even if that meant wearing loose-fitting pants for some of the more dangerous revolutionary endeavors many were willing to undertake.

In important ways the grievances that sparked the popular risings all along the Nile Valley had much more to do with the lives of the working women than with the concerns of their elite counterparts. The former had always labored long hours at arduous tasks in the sweatshops or fields to earn meager wages or grow a little more food to share with their families. But the demands of the hard-pressed British rulers during World War I had proved devastating for the women and other ordinary Egyptians, who had begun to feel the effects of the global conflict within months of its outbreak in early August 1914.

The war triggered an export boom, especially in cotton, which was in great demand for uniforms, medical supplies, and many other wartime uses. For poor women like Shafika and Hamida, that meant jobs in the factories. And employment opportunities for women increased as the war dragged on, fed by the British decision to conscript Egyptian men in the tens of thousands. Most of the Egyptians worked as bearers, animal tenders, and purveyors of all sorts of services for the influx of British, Australian, and New Zealand armed forces that used Egypt as a staging area for attacks on Turkey and efforts to beat off German and Turkish threats to the Suez Canal. But the poorly paid and often dangerous jobs that became available to women like Shafika and Hamida could not begin to make up for the runaway inflation that plagued Egypt during the war years. Ordinary Egyptians were affected by sharply rising prices for all manner of household necessities, from bread to clothing to kerosene for lamps and cooking. The demands of garrisoning tens of thousands of soldiers from

Figure 28.1 In late May 1919, large numbers of veiled women joined the mass protests in Cairo and other Egyptian cities and towns that were sparked by the harsh wartime conditions that British demands had exacerbated and by the colonizers' refusal to give Egyptian leaders a hearing at the peace conference in Paris.

throughout the empire placed increasing demands on the already overstretched food supply of the Egyptian people, some of whom perished of malnutrition linked to the war. And widespread British confiscations of draft animals belonging to Egyptians enraged peasants and urban workers, both of whom depended on these animals for survival.

Although these and other abuses contributed to the buildup of social and political pressures during the war years, the British underestimated growing signs that a revolt was in the making, because they had long regarded the Egyptians as passive and pliable. Colonial officials were consequently ill-prepared to deal with the literal explosions of popular risings that occurred in the spring of 1919 in response to the British refusal to let Egyptian nationalist leaders travel to France to make the case for Egyptian independence. And none of the colonial leaders could figure out how to handle either the elite or the working-class women who displayed a great aptitude for political organization, dramatizing their causes and fearlessly confronting the police and armed forces. Working-class women even became involved in bombings and armed assaults directed against railways, telegraph stations, and government buildings during the waves of protest that swept across much of Egypt between 1919 and 1922. And, like Shafika Muhammad, who was killed by British soldiers who fired on crowds of unarmed demonstrators on March 14, 1919, some became martyrs of the national liberation movement. They were revered by ordinary Egyptians at the time (if neglected by subsequent historians), and for decades by the leaders of the nationalist movement. ■

Although far removed from the massive slaughter of young men in the trench warfare of Europe that we normally associate with World War I, the risings in Egypt and the emergence of women as a major force in resistance to continuing colonial domination underscore the importance of seeing the conflict as a truly global phenomenon with far-reaching repercussions for peoples and societies across much of Europe, the Middle East, Africa, Asia, North America, and the Pacific—especially Australia and New Zealand. The fact that the three main adversaries in the war—Great Britain, France, and Germany—were colonial powers meant that when they plunged into war, they pulled their empires into the abyss with them.

1870 C.E.	1890 C.E.	1900 C.E.	1910 C.E.	1920 C.E.
1870–1890 Cycle of economic depressions in Europe and the United States	1890 End of the Three Emperors' Alliance (Russia, Austria–Hungary, Germany) 1894 Franco-Russian alliance 1899–1901 Anglo-Boer war in South Africa	1904–1905 Japanese victory over Russia 1906 Dinshawai incident in Egypt 1909 Morley-Minto reforms in India	1910 Union of South Africa formed 1914–1918 World War I 1916 Beginning of Arab revolt against Ottoman Empire 1917 Russian Revolution 1917 United States enters World War I 1918 Treaty of Brest-Litovsk; Russia withdraws from war 1919 Treaty of Versailles; League of Nations established 1919 Gandhi leads first nonviolent protest movements in India; revolt in Egypt; Rowlatt Act in India	1922 French and British mandates set up in Middle East 1920s Pan-African Congresses in Paris 1923 Treaty of Lausanne recognizes independence of Turkey

Because the British controlled the sea approaches to Europe, they and their French allies were able to draw soldiers, laborers, raw materials, loans, and donations from their colonial possessions, and these proved critical to their ability to sustain the long war of attrition against Germany. In addition, there were major theaters of combat in the Middle East and Africa as well as clashes in China and the Pacific. The years of increasingly senseless slaughter on the Western Front made a mockery of European claims of superior rationality and a racially ingrained capacity to rule. Pressed by a shortage of trained officials, Europeans were willing to give Western-educated Africans and Indians roles in governance that would have been unimaginable without the war. When the British and French victors sought to renege on promises made to these elites and restore their prewar political prerogatives, the first wave of decolonization was set in motion in Egypt, India, Vietnam, and other colonial societies.

The Coming of the Great War

By 1914 diplomatic tensions among the major European powers had been escalating steadily for a generation. Colonial rivalries and arms races had led to the formation, beginning in the 1890s, of two increasingly hostile alliances.

Europe, 1914
MAP

Fear of Germany's growing economic and military power had driven autocratic Russia to ally first with republican France and then with the even more democratic Britain (Map 28.1). Germany's growing power also menaced its neighbor to the west, France. From the early 1890s, the arrogance and aggressive posturing of Germany's new ruler, Kaiser Wilhelm II, only magnified the threat the emerging colossus seemed to pose for the rest of Europe. The French hoped that their alliance with Russia would lead to a two-front war that would brake Germany's rising supremacy and allow France to recover the provinces of Alsace and Lorraine, which France had lost to Germany through defeat in the Franco-Prussian War of 1870. Eclipsed by Germany economically, and increasingly threatened overseas by a growing German navy, Britain joined with Russia and France to form the Triple Entente in the early 1900s.

In the same years, the Triple Entente powers increasingly confronted a counteralliance consisting of Germany, Austria–Hungary, and (nominally at least) Italy that would become known as the Central Powers. With the accession of Kaiser Wilhelm II to power, Germany had moved away from a defensive triple alliance with Russia and Austria–Hungary to a growing dependence on the latter alone. Germany had also sought to draw Italy into its coalition with promises of support for its efforts at colonial expansion. But Italian hostility to Austria–Hungary, which still controlled lands the Italians claimed as their own, kept Italy's role as one of the Central Powers tentative and liable to shift with changing international circumstances. Italian ambivalence became all too clear

Map 28.1 World War I Fronts in Europe and the Middle East   In contrast to the large swaths of territory caught up in the war on the eastern front, the area contested and the battle lines in the west were confined largely to a corner of Belgium and northernmost France.

after the outbreak of war when Italy not only refused to support Germany and Austria–Hungary but in 1915 entered the conflict on the side of the Triple Entente.

The alliance system, menacing in itself, was embittered by the atmosphere generated by imperial rivalries that were played out over most of the globe. In the decades leading up to the First World War, most of the European powers had been involved in empire-building overseas, and they came to equate the prestige of "great power" status with the possession of colonies. Their rivalries heightened nationalist sentiments in each country. But by 1900 most of the world's available territories had been colonized by one or another of the states in the two alliance systems. As a result, the scramble in the early 1900s for the few areas as yet unclaimed produced much greater tensions in the European diplomatic system. France maneuvered to annex Morocco to its north African colonies, which already included Algeria and Tunisia (Map 28.1). Germany twice threatened war if the French advance continued, only to back off when it was clear that none of the other European powers would support it. In the second of the international crises over Morocco in 1911, the Germans had to be bought off by a French concession of territory from their possessions in central Africa.

Imperialism in Asia, 1914

Africa on the Eve of World War I

Imperialist rivalries solidified the growing divisions between the two alliances and fed the jingoism (warlike nationalist sentiments that spread widely among the middle and working classes throughout Europe) that had much to do with the coming of the war. Most European leaders of both the great powers and smaller states like those in the Balkans were eager to vie for increased territories and obsessed with keeping their rivals from advancing at their country's expense (Figure 28.2).

Imperialism and the alliance system were both linked to ever more intense and costly arms races. Naval rivalry was the most apparent and fiercely contested. The Germans' decision to build a navy that could threaten Great Britain's long-standing control of the world's oceans was one of the key reasons for Britain's move for military cooperation with France and (more grudgingly) Russia. It also touched off the greatest arms race in all of history to that time. Huge new warships, such as the *Dreadnought* battleship launched in 1906 and the German ships built in response, kept the naval rivalry at fever pitch. Serious hopes for arms limitations, much less reductions, faded. Armies grew steadily in size and firepower, and they practiced massive maneuvers that national leaders were prepared to implement in the event of the outbreak of a general war. Not surprisingly, the military buildup helped pave the way to war, as some in the German military in particular pushed for a preemptive strike before army reforms in Russia made it too powerful to overcome.

Diplomatic and military competition tied foreign policy to spiraling domestic tensions. All of the major industrial nations, and those in the process of industrializing like Russia, faced growing labor unrest after 1900. Strikes, the growth of trade unions, and votes for socialist parties mounted steadily in the decade and a half before 1914. The business classes and the political elites were alarmed by these challenges to their dominance. They sought diplomatic successes and confrontations with rival powers to distract their subjects from social problems at home. British ministers and the German kaiser, for example, appealed for labor peace in the name of national unity in the face of the threat of attack by powerful rivals. Those in power also supported military buildups because they provided employment for the working classes and huge profits to industrialists who were pillars of support for each of the European regimes.

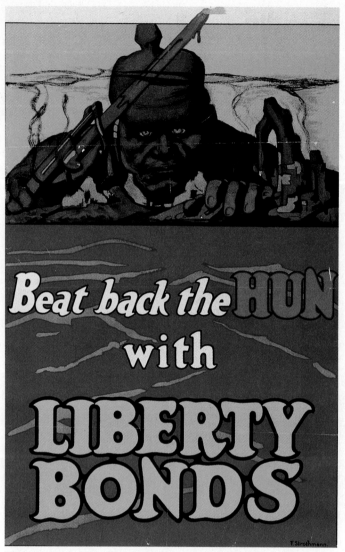

Figure 28.2 This U.S. poster drumming up financial support for the war effort epitomizes the paranoia and extreme stereotyping of adversary peoples and powers that poisoned international relations in the decades leading up to the war and drove the continuing slaughter on all fronts from 1914 to 1918.

Borijove Jevtic: The Murder of Archduke Franz Ferdinand at Sarajevo, 28 June 1914

Ferdinand, Archduke Franz (1863–1914) Heir apparent to the Austro-Hungarian throne whose assassination in Sarajevo set in motion the events that started World War I.

Sarajevo Administrative center of the Bosnian province of Austrian Empire; assassination there of Archduke Ferdinand in 1914 started World War I.

The Outbreak of the War

In the years just before 1914, decades of rivalry and mounting tensions within the European state system were increasingly centered on the Balkans, where Russia sought to back Serbia in its determined resistance to the steady advance of the Austro-Hungarian empire. The complex ethnic divisions and interstate rivalries of the Balkan area mirrored the growing crisis of Europe as a whole. It was not surprising, then, that the event that precipitated the First World War occurred in the Balkans. In July 1914 a Serbian nationalist, Gavriel Princip, assassinated the heir apparent to the Austro-Hungarian throne, **Archduke Ferdinand,** and his wife in **Sarajevo,** the administrative center of the Bosnian province of the Austrian empire. Bolstered by the infamous "blank check" promised by German leaders for reprisals against Serbia, the Austro-Hungarians drew up a list of demands that it was impossible for the Serbs to accede to without surrendering their nation's sovereignty. The ruling circles of Austria–Hungary were determined to put an end to decades of Serbian challenges to their control over portions of the Balkans, and thus they were clearly intent on forcing a war.

When the Russians vowed to support their Slavic brethren in Serbia should war break out with the Austrians, the alliance systems that had been forged in the preceding decades quickly came into play. Within months the confrontation of the two blocs had transformed what might have been a regional war among the Balkan states and their Austrian or Russian backers into the threat of a general European war. Inept diplomacy and a widespread sense of resignation to the eventual outbreak of war, which some believed would sort out the quarrels and tensions that had been building for decades, led to the mobilization of the armies of the great powers in late July 1914.

Although the leaders of most of the powers had long regarded mobilization as a way of applying diplomatic pressure, for the Germans mobilization meant war. Because they had faced the possibility of massive combat on two fronts since the 1890s, the Germans had devised an intricate plan to first attack in the west and defeat France before turning to the more backward, and thus slower to mobilize, Russians in the east. Once Russia mobilized against Germany and the German armies moved to mobilize in retaliation according to a rigid railway timetable that plotted an invasion of neutral Belgium on the way to an all-out assault on France, the alliance systems were locked into a massive war. When the British entered the conflict, officially to defend tiny Belgium, which they had long before pledged to protect, a European conflict was transformed into a global one. Britain's naval ally Japan quickly jumped into the fray. British-ruled colonial territories, from the White Dominions of Canada, Australia, and New Zealand to Britain's extensive imperial possessions in India and across Africa and southeast Asia, were brought directly into the war. After nearly a century's lapse, Europe was again consumed by a general war that rapidly spread to other parts of the world.

A World at War

Perhaps more than any other single factor, the failure of Germany's ambitious plan for a quick victory over France ensured that there would be a long war of stalemate and attrition. German political and military leaders counted on their country's superb railway system and huge armies to overwhelm the Belgians and defeat the French before they could even fully mobilize. The French obliged them by launching offensives against deeply entrenched German forces in Alsace-Lorraine that ended in the near destruction of some of France's best armies. But Belgium resisted bravely, slowing the German goliath, and the small but superbly trained British army suddenly appeared to contest the momentum of three German armies, each of which was larger than the total British forces. By the time they reached the frontiers of northern France, the German soldiers were tired and, having left the railways behind in southern Belgium, growing short of boots, food, and ammunition. Reeling from their defeats by the Germans in Alsace-Lorraine, the French forces fled toward Paris, where they regrouped, were reinforced (in part by a famous convoy of Parisian cab drivers), and prepared for the German onslaught. During a five-day battle along the Marne River in early September, the German advance was halted, then thrown back. Paris had been saved and the stage set for over three years of bloody stalemate on the **Western Front**.

To protect themselves from the withering firepower of the artillery and machine guns of the opposing armies, British and German soldiers began to dig into the ground during and after the clashes along the Marne. Soon northern and western France was crisscrossed by miles and miles of entrenchments that frustrated—with staggering levels of dead and wounded—all attempts to break the stalemate between the opposing forces until well into 1918. The almost unimaginable killing power of the industrial technology wielded by the opposing European armies favored the defensive. Devastating artillery, the withering fire of machine guns, barbed-wire barriers, and the use of poison gas turned the Western Front into a killing ground that offered no possibility of decisive victory to either side. The carnage reached unimaginable levels, with the Germans losing 850,000 troops, the French 700,000, and the British over 400,000 in the single year of 1916 on just the Western Front.

By the millions, the youths of Europe were killed, maimed, and driven insane, or they waited for the next offensive catastrophe in rat- and lice-infested trenches. Like the so-called primitive peoples the Europeans had come to dominate overseas, soldiers were exposed to rain and cold and deprived of virtually all of the material comforts that large sections of western European societies had come to regard as their birthright. A German soldier, and later novelist, captured the constant fear, the almost unendurable anxiety the soldiers experienced:

> The front is a cage in which we must await fearfully whatever may happen. We lie under the network of arching shells and live in a suspense of uncertainty. Over us chance hovers.

The Schlieffen Plan, 1905

Part of the reason that Europeans let their nations blunder into war in 1914 was that most of them expected the conflict to be brief and decisive. But after only a month, it was beginning to be clear that the world had been plunged into a conflict that was likely to go on for a good deal longer.

Bravo, Belgium— British Cartoon, WWI

The Actual German Advance, 1914

The Technology of War

Western Front   Front established in World War I; generally along line from Belgium to Switzerland; featured trench warfare and horrendous casualties for all sides in the conflict.

Trench Warfare

This World War I painting highlights soldiers in the trench fighting that dominated the conflict on the Western Front.

QUESTIONS What were the trenches like? Can the expressions and poses of the soldiers be read to suggest what war meant to them? How did life in the trenches compare with their previous lives in industrial society and with expectations in an age that had vaunted manliness and nationalism? Does the painting raise issues of bias or staging on the part of the artist, or is it a neutral piece of evidence?

 A Typical British Trench System

 Life in the Trenches During WWI

Wilfred Owen

In so many ways, the war in Europe was centered on the ongoing and senseless slaughter in the trenches. Levels of dead and wounded that would have been unimaginable before the war rose ever higher between 1915 and 1918. They were all the more tragic because neither side could break the stalemate; hundreds of thousands were killed or maimed to gain small patches of ground that were soon lost in counterattacks. Years of carnage made all too evident the lack of imagination and utter incompetence of most of the generals on both sides of the conflict. Few understood that mass assaults on mechanized defenses had become suicidal at this point in the industrial age. The aged officers in the higher commands and overmatched politicians soon demoted or dismissed those who sought to find creative ways out of the trench morass. As the years passed, as a British war poet observed:

Neither [side] had won or could win the war
The war had won and would go on winning.

The War in Eastern Europe and Italy

In the first weeks of the conflict, the Germans were alarmed by the rapidity with which the Russians were able to mount major offensives against both the Austro-Hungarians and eastern Germany. Having committed most of their forces to their own offensives against France, the German high command felt obliged to divert critical resources and manpower to check the advancing Russian armies. In late August the reorganized German forces virtually destroyed an entire Russian army (and sent a second into headlong retreat). In defeat, the Russian forces exhibited many of the weaknesses that resulted in, by far, the highest levels of casualties of any of the combatants and the ultimate and utter defeat of the tsarist armies. Aristocratic generals dispatched millions of mostly illiterate and poorly trained peasants to certain death in repeated assaults on better-armed and led German forces. Commands in critical battles were sent in uncoded format and readily picked up by their adversaries. Russian artillery, manned by upper-class personnel, usually provided little cover for massed peasant forces, which were reduced to little more than cannon and machine-gun fodder in assaults on the entrenched Germans.

Although the lines shifted over large areas in the east, they inexorably, with horrific human cost, moved east into the provinces of the Russian empire. The poor showing of the Russian commanders, including the hapless tsar **Nicholas II**, who insisted on taking control at the front, did much to spark the mutinies and peasant revolts that were critical forces in the revolutionary waves that destroyed the tsarist regime in 1917.

The Russians fared somewhat better on the Austro-Hungarian front (Map 28.1), where they faced even more inept generals and multiethnic armies whose soldiers' loyalty to the Austrian emperor was often lukewarm or nonexistent. But the Russians could not prevent the Austrians from crushing Serbia, which held out until the end of 1915. Thanks largely to timely interjections of German soldiers, the Austro-Hungarians managed, again at the cost of millions of casualties, to check repeated Russian offensives. The Austrian forces generally fought much better against the Italians, who entered the war in May 1915. Nine months earlier, Italian leaders had declined to march to war with their Central Power allies, who the Italians claimed had attacked first and thus nullified what was a defensive treaty. Having wrested British promises of substantial territorial gains, mostly at Austria–Hungary's expense, the Italians launched a series of offensives against the Austrians.

With the Austrians enjoying the high ground in the eastern Alps, the assaults all ended in disaster. Incompetent and corrupt generals, soldiers increasingly disgusted by costly campaigns that went nowhere, and venal politicians double-dealing behind the lines resulted in the near collapse of the Italian front in 1917. Although British and French reinforcements rushed from the Western Front eventually stalled the Austrian advance, Italian soldiers deserted in droves and the war plunged Italy into social and political turmoil. One of the Italian soldiers who was briefly at the front and slightly wounded, Benito Mussolini, would soon exploit this unrest to the fullest in his postwar drive to impose a fascist dictatorship on Italy.

The Home Fronts in Europe

As the war dragged on without any sign that decisive victories could be won by either side, soldiers at the fronts across Europe grew resentful of the civilians back home. Their anger was focused on political leaders who cheered them on from the safety of the sidelines far to the rear. But the soldiers were also disturbed more generally by the patriotic zeal and insensitivity of the civilian populace, which had little sense of the horrors that were endured at the front. In fact, in the soldiers' view the civilians behind the lines often had a stronger commitment and more pronounced hatred for the enemy than did the soldiers in combat. Each of the powers remained able to mobilize ever larger numbers of soldiers and military resources, despite growing food shortages and privations on the home fronts. Governments responded by rationing resources and regulating production to head off potentially crippling labor disputes.

Whole industrial sectors, such as railways, were administered directly by the state. Executive branches of the combatants' governments gradually took over the power of elected parliaments— particularly in Germany, where by late 1916 the General Staff virtually ran the country. Dissent was suppressed, often by force, and newspapers and other media outlets (as well as the letters of the soldiers) were strictly censored. Governments developed propaganda departments that grew more sophisticated and strident as the war dragged on. The British proved the most adept at propaganda. Much of this was aimed at the United States in the hope that the Americans would be drawn into the war. The British and American public were bombarded with stories of German atrocities. As the war went into its second and third years, news of severe setbacks was increasingly denied to the German people. As a consequence, most Germans were stunned by what seemed their sudden defeat in 1918. The extent of the involvement of the civilian population (in some cases as targets of bombardments and aerial assaults) and the power of governments to mobilize men and women and control the information they received about the conflict made "the Great War" truly the first total war in human history.

Nicholas II Tsar of Russia 1894–1917; forcefully suppressed political opposition and resisted constitutional government; deposed by revolution in 1917.

World War I MAP

The Eastern Front, 1915–1918 MAP

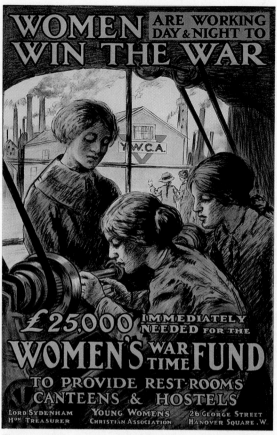

Figure 28.3 As this British recruiting poster illustrates, the drastic shortage of farm and factory workers caused by the insatiable military manpower needs of World War I generals provided abundant, but often dangerous, job opportunities for women.

The war sped up many developments already visible in industrial societies. The power of organization increased, particularly through the new interventions of governments. To maintain unified backing of the civilian population, socialists and trade union chiefs were given new recognition and allowed to serve on governing boards in charge of industrial production and negotiate improved working conditions. As their leaders became ever more drawn into the existing governmental system, some labor groups rejected their leadership and became ever more vocal critics of the war. As the war lumbered on, seemingly out of control, these trends became more pronounced, particularly in Russia and Germany. Labor protests in Moscow and St. Petersburg gave powerful momentum to the wave of discontent and mass protest that brought down the tsarist regime in February 1917 and propelled the Bolsheviks to power in October of the same year (see Chapter 34). In Germany, labor agitation, very often sparked by growing shortages of food and fuel that were intensified by the British naval blockade, also loomed as a threat to the military commanders who ran the country in the last years of the conflict. As the German front in France and Belgium collapsed in the early summer of 1918, leftist leaders and angry laborers pushed the nation to the brink of revolution in late 1918 and 1919.

As a direct consequence of the war, women's participation in the labor force increased greatly, particularly in Germany, Britain, and the United States. Defying prevailing prewar notions about the "natural" gender roles, women proved very able to work even in heavy industry, where many were engaged in the very dangerous production of munitions (Figure 28.3). Better wages and the confidence they gained from their mastery of such demanding and critical roles as factory workers and nurses at the front sparked a broader liberation for women during the war years. From the rising hemlines of their dresses and their license to smoke in public to unchaperoned dating and greatly increased political activism, many women sought to recast gender roles and images.

At war's end, the loss of many of their jobs to men returning from the front as well as government programs consciously designed to force them back into the home reversed many of the gains that women had achieved during the conflict. But in Britain, Germany, and the United States, they gained the vote, which they had struggled for in the decades before 1914. And particularly in Germany, food shortages and growing anti-war sentiment, compelled tens of thousands of women to engage in political agitation and disruptive protests to an extent almost inconceivable before the war. The visibility and influence of the career-oriented and sophisticated "new women" of the 1920s, though a small minority even in Germany and the United States, gave promise of broader advances in the decades to come.

The War Beyond Europe

Except for Austria–Hungary, all of the major powers that went to war in 1914 had colonies outside Europe. When it became clear that the war was not to be the quick, decisive clash that most had anticipated, the manpower and resources of these imperial possessions were increasingly sucked into the spreading conflict. By 1915 fighting had spread to the Middle East, west and east Africa, across most of the seas and oceans of the world, and even to China and the islands of the Pacific. Troops from Canada, Australia, New Zealand, India, and throughout much of Africa had been recruited, mainly to fight for the Triple Entente allies (Map 28.2). By 1917 the United States had entered the war, leaving only the nations of South America alone of all the continents not directly engaged in the struggle.

Britain's participation, more than that of any other power, contributed to the war's globalization. The British navy not only cut off Germany from its colonies in Africa, China, and the Pacific islands, but it hunted down German ships still on the high seas at the outbreak of war. Perhaps most critically, British naval supremacy meant that an effective blockade could be maintained that would deprive the Central Powers of supplies of food and raw materials from overseas throughout

Map 28.2 Africa During World War I Not only was Africa the site of significant combat in World War I, but from Algeria in the north to the Union of South Africa it was a recruiting ground for tens of thousands of Arab-Berber and African soldiers and bearers and other laborers.

the war. Because the British also controlled trans-Atlantic cable links, they could easily outdo the Germans in propaganda efforts to convince the neutral United States to side with them in the war. The expensive and highly touted German navy fully engaged the British grand fleet only once during the war, in 1916 off Jutland in Denmark. Though the Germans sank more ships and killed more British sailors, the high seas fleet was driven back into port and proved of little use to the larger German effort for the rest of the war.

The British entry into the war also meant that its empire and allies were drawn into the fray. Japan, which had joined Britain in a naval pact in 1902, eagerly attacked German colonies in China and the Pacific. These acquisitions, especially the seizure of the Shandong peninsula, would provide great impetus to Japan's imperialist aspirations in China in the 1930s. The islands they captured from the Germans in World War I proved components of the defense perimeter they sought to build in the Pacific during World War II.

The British Dominions—Canada, Australia, and New Zealand—quickly marshaled considerable resources to support the war effort. These areas not only supplied food and critical raw materials, but in defiance of the German U-boat fleet in the Atlantic, they swelled the initially meager ranks of Britain's armed forces. Dominion troops were a mainstay of British operations in the Middle East, including the defense of the vital Suez Canal link and the ill-fated assault at **Gallipoli**, a peninsula in Turkey south of Constantinople, in 1915. They fought valiantly on the Western Front throughout the war, at times bolstering British lines that were crumbling under massive German assaults. White settler colonials in south Africa also joined those from the Dominions in support of the British, despite bitter opposition from some segments of the Afrikaner population, which had suffered so greatly as a result of draconian British repression in the Anglo-Boer war just over a decade earlier.

Gallipoli Peninsula south of Istanbul; site of decisive 1915 Turkish victory over Australian and New Zealand forces under British command during World War I.

The British and the French also received vital support from their nonsettler colonies in Africa, India, and southeast Asia. The massive army that the British had recruited in India for over a century and a half did much of the fighting in sub-Saharan Africa and the Middle East. The French deployed tens of thousands of non-European soldiers, recruited mainly in north and west Africa, on the Western Front, where many served with distinction but with scant reward. Unlike the British, who turned mainly to women to replace the millions of farmers and factory workers who went off to war, the French relied heavily on laborers recruited in their colonies from Africa to Vietnam.

Although the Germans quickly lost most of their colonies in Africa and the Far East, superbly led African soldiers recruited and trained in German East Africa (Tanzania today) held off hundreds of thousands of British-led Indian and south African troops until two weeks after the end of hostilities in Europe. But Germany's main support outside Europe came from the Ottoman Empire (Map 28.1), which entered the war in the fall of 1915. The Young Turk leaders, who had consolidated their power in Constantinople in the decade leading up to the war (see Chapter 31), had continued the Ottoman reliance on German military advisors and financiers. After fending off the British-led campaign to capture the Gallipoli, the Turks opened up fronts in southern Russia, where they suffered severe defeats, and the Middle East, where their fortunes were more mixed, and they remained for years a threat to the British in Egypt and the Suez Canal zone.

A Turkish Officer Describes the Armenian Massacres

Armenian genocide Assault carried out by mainly Turkish military forces against Armenian population in Anatolia in 1915; over a million Armenians perished and thousands fled to Russia and the Middle East.

The Young Turk leaders sought to transfer blame for the reverses on the Russian front to the Christian Armenian minority, which was concentrated in areas that spanned the two empires in eastern Anatolia and the Caucasus. In fact, remembering earlier pogroms launched by the Turks against them, some of the Armenians living in Turkish areas had backed the Russians. But most of the minority was loyal or neutral, and poor generalship and bad planning were the main causes of the Turkish military disasters. Struggling to cover their blunders, the Young Turk leaders launched an assault in 1915 against the Armenians. The ensuing **Armenian genocide** claimed as many as a million lives and sent hundreds of thousands of Armenians in flight to Russia and the Middle East.

The last major combatant to enter the global conflagration was the United States, which declared war on Germany in the spring of 1917. The war made the United States into a major global power, culminating developments that had been underway for decades. By 1914 the United States had become an active force in international diplomacy and power politics. It had built a modest Pacific empire, centering on Hawaii and the Philippine islands, and had become increasingly forceful in its interventions in Central America and the Caribbean. The outbreak of the war was greeted with considerable ambivalence on the part of American leaders and the citizenry more generally. Distant from the battlefields, Americans disagreed over which side was in the right and whether or not they should intervene in quarrels that seemed to have little to do with them. But American businesses profited greatly from the war by selling food, raw materials, and eventually weapons, mainly (due to the British blockade) to the Entente allies. American mercantile interests, like their counterparts in Japan, also took advantage of the Europeans' need to concentrate their industrial production on the war effort by taking over new markets in Latin America and Asia. Rapidly rising exports, combined with huge loans to Britain, France, and Russia, which all needed credit to buy American goods, transformed the United States from an international debtor to the world's largest creditor and strongest economy.

Temporary Shelter for American Wounded

Despite all of the gains that the United States had accrued through neutrality, American leadership and a majority of the American public was pro-British. British successes in the propaganda war and ever growing economic ties to the Entente allies did much to explain this sentiment. But clumsy German attempts to influence American opinion and, most critically, the German need to use submarines to counter the British blockade and control sea access to Europe did much to drive the United States into the war. Following the resumption of unrestricted submarine warfare in the Atlantic, which President Woodrow Wilson had earlier warned would force military retaliation by the United States, America entered the conflict in April 1917. American warships joined with the British to create a convoy system that eventually offset an intensified German submarine campaign designed to starve the British Isles into submission.

For much of 1917, the number of American troops sent to Europe was small and largely symbolic. But by early 1918, millions of young Americans were in training and hundreds of thousands arrived in Europe each week. The growing buildup of American reinforcements, and American-produced arms and supplies, convinced the German high command that they must launch a massive strike for a quick victory, before the full manpower and resources of the United States could be brought to bear against their weary soldiers.

Endgame: The Return of Offensive Warfare

For several weeks in March and April 1918, the massive offensives launched by the Germans on the Western Front looked as if they might bring victory to the Central Powers. An entire British army had been shattered and another was in full retreat; the already demoralized French forces were also falling back toward Paris. Nearly a million German soldiers transferred from the **Eastern Front** after Russia was knocked out of the war, and new assault tactics and the deployment of storm troopers had restored the offensive and broken three long years of bloody stalemate. But just as Paris was again within the range of the great German guns, the advance slowed. Mounting casualties and sheer fatigue on the German side, counteroffensives, new weapons like tanks, and a rapidly increasing influx of fresh and enthusiastic American soldiers stalled the German drive and then began to push the German armies out of northern France. At the same time, the Austrian fronts broke down in both northeast Italy and the Balkans. The Austro-Hungarian empire fragmented along national lines, and the heir to the Habsburg throne abdicated as separate republics in Austria and Hungary sued the Entente allies for peace.

> **Eastern Front** Most mobile of the fronts established during World War I; after early successes, military defeats led to downfall of the tsarist government in Russia.

Fearing that their armies were on the verge of collapse and menaced by widespread rebellions at home, the German commanders agreed to an armistice on November 11, 1918. The generals sought to shift the blame for defeat to a civilian government that they had abruptly installed in Berlin. Made up of members of the Center and Socialist parties, Germany's new government was forced to both sue the Entente allies for peace and consent to an armistice agreement delivered by two British admirals and two French generals. Assuming that their armies were on the verge of victory just months before, the German people were stunned by the sudden reversal. Many accepted the myth that Germany had been betrayed by socialist and Jewish politicians, whose alleged "stab in the back" would become a rallying cry for **Adolf Hitler** and the Nazis' drive for power from the early 1920s.

> **Hitler, Adolf** Nazi leader of fascist Germany from 1933 to his suicide in 1945; created a strongly centralized state in Germany; eliminated all rivals; launched Germany on aggressive foreign policy leading to World War II; responsible for genocide of European Jews.

After four years of slaughter, the casualty totals were staggering (see Table 28.1). At least 10 million soldiers were dead and 20 million more wounded. The losses were, by far, the heaviest among the great powers of Europe who had been the main adversaries in the conflict. From France to Russia, virtually every European family had a death to mourn. As the fighting ended, an additional calamity struck. Hundreds of thousands of soldiers and millions of civilians died in an influenza pandemic that began in Asia and spread like wildfire around the globe. Though the direct costs of the long and widespread war and the indirect economic losses it inflicted are almost impossible to calculate with certainty, both totals reached hundreds of billions of dollars. In Belgium and northern France, northern Italy, and across east central Europe, extensive swaths of fertile farmlands and bustling cites were reduced to smoldering ruins. This devastation and a postwar economic downturn that followed the armistice dislocated economies across the globe until well into the mid-1920s and fed into the Great Depression that was to follow a decade later.

TABLE 28.1	World War I Losses		
	Dead	**Wounded**	**Prisoner**
Great Britain	947,000	2,122,000	192,000
France	1,385,000	3,044,000	446,000
Russia	1,700,000	4,950,000	500,000
Italy	460,000	947,000	530,000
United States	115,000	206,000	4,500
Germany	1,808,000	4,247,000	618,000
Austria–Hungary	1,200,000	3,620,000	200,000
Turkey	325,000	400,000	

Note: The number of known dead (round numbers) was placed at about 10 million and the wounded at about 20 million, distributed among chief combatants.

Failed Peace and Global Turmoil

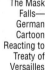 The widespread bitterness evoked by the war's unprecedented cost in lives and destruction was redoubled by the utter failure of the peace conference convened by the victorious allies in Paris.

Clemenceau, Georges   French prime minister in last years of World War I and during Versailles Conference of 1919; pushed for heavy reparations from Germans.

Lloyd George, David   Prime minister of Great Britain who headed a coalition government through much of World War I and the turbulent years that followed.

self-determination   Right of people in a region to determine whether to be independent or not.

The Mask Falls— German Cartoon Reacting to Treaty of Versailles

While the Italians and Japanese scrambled to obtain maximum advantage from their support of the Entente forces during the war, the French insisted that they had suffered the most and their losses had to be avenged. **Georges Clemenceau**, the French premier, pushed for the peace conference to brand the Germans the aggressors and thus force them to pay huge reparations to France and the other nations assaulted. He also worked to cut down the size of Germany and funnel its resources to France and the other powers.

Fearing that a reduced Germany would prove fertile ground for the spread of communist revolution, **David Lloyd George**, the British prime minister, attempted with little success to mediate between Clemenceau and Woodrow Wilson and to win enough reparations to satisfy a disgruntled electorate at home. All of the leaders of the victorious Entente powers, including Wilson, soon closed ranks against the demands welling up from peoples in colonized areas, from the Middle East to Vietnam (Figure 28.4). Dashing the expectations that he had aroused by his ringing call for the right of peoples to **self-determination**, Wilson soon made it clear that the peoples he had in mind were white ethnic groups like the Poles, not Arabs or Vietnamese. With Wilson's blessing, the British and French set about shoring up, and in fact expanding, their battered empires, while the Japanese solidified their beachhead in China and island enclaves in the western Pacific. The triumvirate of Wilson, Lloyd George, and Clemenceau, which dominated the proceedings at Versailles, also made certain that a mild antiracist clause, which was proposed by the Japanese, never made it into the final draft of the treaty.

The Peace of Paris, which was the most important of a series of treaties that emerged from the gathering at Versailles, was nothing less than the *diktat* (dictated peace, without negotiations) that German politicians across the political spectrum sought to reverse in the postwar era. The German delegation was allowed no part in drafting the treaty, and they were given no opportunity to

Figure 28.4 At the Paris peace conference of 1919, the Arabs sought a new voice. The Arab representatives included Prince Feisal, later king of Iraq, and an Iraqi general. A British delegation member, T. E. Lawrence (third from the right), was a longtime friend of the Arabs. The Arabs did not win national self-determination for their homelands, as the British had promised during the war.

amend or refuse it. The German representatives were even humiliated by being brought in by the servants' entrance for the signing and being required to stand for hours while the entire draft of the treaty was read aloud before the assembled delegates. The Germans' main allies—the Austrians—were also major targets of the treaties that emerged from the conference. The Austro-Hungarian Empire was dismembered, as nationalist groups carved out the new nations of Czechoslovakia, Hungary, and Yugoslavia. Poland was also reborn, and like Czechoslovakia, it was given substantial chunks of what had been German territory before the war. This left a somewhat fragile Germanic Austria, cut off from its traditional markets, as one of many weak countries between a smaller Germany and a massive Soviet Union to the east.

The fatal flaws of the peace process extended far beyond calculated insults to the Germans. The new Bolshevik leaders of Russia, who would be treated as pariahs for decades, were not even invited to the conference. Wartime promises to the Arabs in return for their support for the Entente in the war were forgotten, as Britain and France divided the Arab heartlands of the Middle East between themselves. China's pleas for protection from Japanese occupation of the Shandong peninsula were dismissed, and a youthful Ho Chi Minh, the future leader of Vietnam, was rudely refused an audience with Woodrow Wilson. Denied their demand that Germany be permanently partitioned, French leaders turned inward on each other and waited despondently for the next German assault they were convinced was inevitable.

Even the United States, whose President Wilson had opened the peace conference with such exuberant expectations, repudiated what had been wrought at Versailles. Despite Wilson's literally near-fatal efforts to win popular support for the treaty, the American Congress voted down the critical clauses establishing the **League of Nations** and later made a separate peace with Germany. Even as the delegates were still at work, it was clear to knowledgeable observers that Versailles was a disaster. One of the most perceptive chroniclers of the war years and their aftermath, Vera Brittain, wrote as the terms of the treaty began to be made public in the press:

> The Big Four were making a desert and calling it peace. When I thought about these negotiations . . . they did not seem to me to represent at all the kind of "victory" that the young men whom I had loved would have regarded as sufficient justification for their lost lives.

Europe and the Middle East After World War I

League of Nations International diplomatic and peace organization created in the Treaty of Versailles that ended World War I; one of the chief goals of President Woodrow Wilson of the United States in the peace negotiations; the United States was never a member.

The Nationalist Assault on the European Colonial Order

Though the European colonizers had frequently quarreled over colonial possessions in the late 19th century, during World War I they actually fought each other in the colonies for the first time. African and Asian soldiers and laborers in the hundreds of thousands served on the Western Front and in the far-flung theaters of war in Egypt, Palestine, Mesopotamia, and east Africa (Maps 28.2 and 28.3). The colonies also supplied food for the home populations of the Triple Entente powers, as well as vital raw materials such as oil, jute, and cotton. Contrary to long-standing colonial policy, the hard-pressed British even encouraged a considerable expansion of industrial production in India to supplement the output of their overextended home factories. Thus, the war years contributed to the development in India of the largest industrial sector in the colonized world.

World War I presented the subjugated peoples of Africa and Asia with the spectacle of the self-styled civilizers of humankind sending their young men by the millions to be slaughtered in the horrific and barbaric trench stalemate on the Western Front. For the first time, African and Asian soldiers were ordered by their European officers to kill other Europeans. In the process the vulnerability of the seemingly invincible Europeans and the deep divisions between them were starkly revealed. During the war years, European troops in the colonies were withdrawn to meet the need for manpower on the many war fronts. The garrisons that remained were dangerously understaffed. The need to recall administrative personnel from British and French colonies meant that colonial officials were compelled to fill their vacated posts with African and Asian administrators, many of whom enjoyed real responsibility for the first time.

To maintain the loyalty of their traditional allies among the colonized and to win the support of the Western-educated elites or new allies such as the Arabs, the British and French made many promises regarding the postwar settlement. Because these concessions often seriously compromised their prewar dominance or their plans for further colonial expansion, the leaders of the victorious

Four long years of intra-European slaughter severely disrupted the systems of colonial domination that had been expanded and refined in the century leading up to World War I. The conflict also gave great impetus to the forces of resistance that had begun to well up in the decades before the war.

Lessons for the Colonized from the Slaughter in the Trenches

The prolonged and senseless slaughter of the youth of Europe in the trench stalemate on the Western Front did much to erode the image of Europeans as superior, rational, and more civilized beings that they had worked hard to propagate among the colonized peoples in the decades before the Great War. The futility of the seemingly endless slaughter cast doubts on the Europeans' rationality and fitness to rule themselves, much less the rest of the world. The destructive uses to which their science and technology were put brought into question the Europeans' long-standing claims that these material advancements tangibly demonstrated their intellectual and organizational superiority over all other peoples. The excerpts below, taken from the writings of some of the leading thinkers and political leaders of the colonized peoples of Africa and Asia, reflect their disillusionment with the West as a result of the war and the continuing turmoil in Europe in the postwar era.

Rabindranath Tagore

Bengali poet, playwright, and novelist Rabindranath Tagore was one of the earliest non-European recipients of the Nobel Prize for literature.

> Has not this truth already come home to you now when this cruel war has driven its claws into the vitals of Europe? When her hoard of wealth is bursting into smoke and her humanity is shattered on her battlefields? You ask in amazement what she has done to deserve this? The answer is, that the West has been systematically petrifying her moral nature in order to lay a solid foundation for her gigantic abstractions of efficiency. She has been all along starving the life of the personal man into that of the professional.

Mohandas Gandhi

In the years after the First World War, Mohandas Gandhi emerged as India's leading nationalist figure.

> India's destiny lies not along the bloody way of the West, but along the bloodless way of peace that comes from a simple and godly life. India is in danger of losing her soul. . . . She must not, therefore, lazily and helplessly say, "I cannot escape the onrush from the West." She must be strong enough to resist it for her own sake and that of the world. I make bold to say that the Europeans themselves will

have to remodel their outlooks if they are not to perish under the weight of the comforts to which they are becoming slaves.

Léopold Sédar Senghor

Senegalese poet and political leader Léopold Sédar Senghor is widely regarded as one of the 20th century's finest writers in the French language.

> Lord, the snow of your Peace is your proposal to a divided world to a
>   divided Europe
> To Spain torn apart.
> And I forget
> White hands that fired the shots which brought the empires crumbling
> Hands that flogged the slaves, that flogged You [Jesus Christ]
> Chalk-white hands that buffeted You, powdered painted hands that
>   buffeted me
> Confident hands that delivered me to solitude to hatred
> White hands that felled the forest of palm trees once commanding
>   Africa, in the heart of Africa.

From *Snow upon Paris*

Aimé Césaire

West Indian poet Aimé Césaire was a founder of the négritude movement, which asserted black culture in the late 1920s.

> Heia [Praise] for those who have never invented anything
> those who never explored anything
> those who never tamed anything
> those who give themselves up to the essence of all things
> ignorant of surfaces but struck by the movement of all things.

From *Return to My Native Land*

QUESTIONS On the basis of this sample, what aspects of the West's claims to superiority would you say were called into question by the suicidal conflict of the leading powers within European civilization? What aspects of their own civilizations do these writers, both implicitly and explicitly, champion as alternatives to the ways of the West? Are these writers in danger of stereotyping both the West and their own civilizations?

---

allies repeatedly reneged on them in the years after the war. The betrayal of these pledges understandably contributed a great deal to postwar agitation against the continuance and spread of European colonial domination.

The West and the World: Changes in European Empires After World War I

For intellectuals and political leaders throughout Africa and Asia, the appalling devastation of World War I cast doubt on the claims that the Europeans had made for over a century that they were, by virtue of their racial superiority, the fittest of all peoples to rule the globe. The social and economic disruptions caused by the war in key colonies, such as Egypt, India, and the Ivory Coast, made it possible for nationalist agitators to build a mass base for their anticolonial movements for the first time. But in these and other areas of the colonized world, the war gave added impetus to movements and processes already underway, rather than initiating new responses to European global domination. Therefore, it is essential to place wartime developments in the colonies and the postwar surge in anticolonial resistance in a longer-term context that takes into account African and Asian responses that extend in some cases back to the last decades of the 19th century. Since it is impossible to relate the history of the independence struggles in all of the European colonies, key movements, such as those that developed in India, Egypt, and British and French west Africa, will be considered in some depth. These specific movements will then be related to broader patterns of African and Asian nationalist agitation and the accelerating phenomenon of decolonization worldwide.

India: The Makings of the Nationalist Challenge to the British Raj

Because India and much of southeast Asia had been colonized long before Africa, movements for independence arose in Asian colonies somewhat earlier than in their African counterparts. By the last years of the 19th century, the Western-educated minority of the colonized in India and the Philippines had been organized politically for decades. Their counterparts in Burma and the Netherlands Indies were also beginning to form associations to give voice to their political concerns. Because of India's size and the pivotal role it played in the British Empire (by far the largest of the European imperialist empires), the Indian nationalist movement pioneered patterns of nationalist challenge and European retreat that were later followed in many other colonies. Though it had been under British control for only a matter of decades, Egypt also proved an influential center of nationalist organization and resistance in the pre–World War I era (Figure 28.5).

Figure 28.5 This photograph, probably taken without the knowledge of the British authorities, shows the construction of the gallows that were used to hang the four peasants who were executed in reprisal for the attacks on British soldiers at Dinshawai in 1906. The Dinshawai incident exemplified the colonizers' tendency to overreact to any sign of overt resistance on the part of the colonized.

Local conditions elsewhere in Asia and in Africa made for important variations on the sequence of decolonization worked out in India and Egypt. But key themes—such as the lead taken by Western-educated elites, the importance of charismatic leaders in the spread of the anticolonial struggle to the peasant and urban masses, and a reliance on nonviolent forms of protest—were repeated again and again in other colonial settings.

The **National Congress party** led the Indians to independence and governed through most of the early decades of the postcolonial era. It grew out of regional associations of Western-educated Indians that were originally more like study clubs than political organizations in any meaningful sense of the term. These associations were centered in the cities of Bombay, Poona, Calcutta, and Madras (see Map 29.3). The Congress party that Indian leaders formed in 1885 had the blessing of a number of high-ranking British officials. These officials viewed it as a forum through which the opinions of educated Indians could be made known to the government, thereby heading off potential discontent and political protest.

National Congress party Grew out of regional associations of Western-educated Indians; originally centered in cities of Bombay, Poona, Calcutta, and Madras; became political party in 1885; focus of nationalist movement in India; governed through most of postcolonial period.

For most of its first decades, the Congress party served these purposes quite well. The organization had no mass base and very few ongoing staff members or full-time politicians who could sustain lobbying efforts on issues raised at its annual meetings. Some members of the Congress party voiced concern for the growing poverty of the Indian masses and the drain of wealth from the subcontinent to Great Britain. But the Congress party's debates and petitions to the government were dominated by elite-centric issues, such as the removal of barriers to Indian employment in the colonial bureaucracy and increased Indian representation in all-Indian and local legislative bodies. Most of the members of the early Congress party were firmly loyal to the British rulers and confident that once their grievances were made known to the government, they would be remedied.

Many Western-educated Indians were increasingly troubled, however, by the growing virulence of British racism. This they were convinced had much to do with their poor salaries and limited opportunities for advancement in the colonial administration. In their annual meetings, members of the Congress, who were now able to converse and write in a common English language, discovered that no matter where they came from in India, they were treated in a similar fashion. The Indians' shared grievances, their similar educational and class backgrounds, and their growing contacts through the Congress party gave rise to a sense of common Indian identity that had never before existed in a south Asian environment that was more diverse linguistically, religiously, and ethnically than the continent of Europe.

Social Foundations of a Mass Movement

By the last years of the 19th century, the Western-educated elites had begun to grope for causes that would draw a larger segment of the Indian population into their growing nationalist community. More than a century of British rule had generated in many areas of India the social and economic disruptions and the sort of discontent that produced substantial numbers of recruits for the nationalist campaigns. Indian businessmen, many of whom would become major financial backers of the Congress party, were angered by the favoritism the British rulers showed to British investors in establishing trade policies in India. Indian political leaders increasingly stressed these inequities and the more general loss to the Indian people resulting from what they termed the "drain" of Indian resources under colonial rule. Though the British rebuttal was that a price had to be paid for the peace and good government that had come with colonial rule, nationalist thinkers pointed out that the cost was too high.

Tagore, Letter on British Imperialism

A large portion of the government of India's budget went to cover the expenses of the huge army that mainly fought wars elsewhere in the British Empire. The Indian people also paid for the generous salaries and pensions of British administrators, who occupied positions that the Indians were qualified to assume. Whenever possible, as in the purchase of railway equipment or steel for public works projects, the government bought goods manufactured in Great Britain. This practice served to buttress a British economy that was fast losing ground to the United States and Germany. It also ensured that the classic colonial relationship between a manufacturing European colonizer and its raw-material-producing overseas dependencies was maintained.

In the villages of India, the shortcomings of British rule were equally apparent by the last decades of the 19th century. The needs of the British home economy had often dictated policies that pushed the Indian peasantry toward the production of cash crops such as cotton, jute, and indigo. The decline in food production that invariably resulted played a major role in the regional famines that struck repeatedly in the pre–World War I era. Radical Indian nationalists frequently charged that the British were callously indifferent to the suffering caused by food shortages and outbreaks of epidemic disease, and that they did far too little to alleviate the suffering that resulted. In many areas, landlessness and chronic poverty, already a problem before the establishment of British rule, increased markedly. In most places, British measures to control indebtedness and protect small landholders and tenants were too little and came too late.

The Rise of Militant Nationalism

Some of the issues that Indian nationalist leaders stressed in their early attempts to build a mass base had great appeal for devout Hindus. This was particularly true of campaigns for the protection of cows, which have long had a special status for the Hindu population of south Asia. But these religious-oriented causes often strongly alienated the adherents of other faiths, especially the Muslims. Not only did Muslims eat beef, and thus slaughter cattle, but they made up nearly one-fourth of the population of the Indian Empire. Some leaders, such as **B. G. Tilak**, were little concerned by this split. They believed that since Hindus made up the overwhelming majority of the Indian population, nationalism should be built on appeals to Hindu religiosity. Tilak worked to promote the restoration and revival of what he believed to be the ancient traditions of Hinduism. On this basis, he opposed women's education and raising the very low marriage age for women. Tilak turned festivals for Hindu gods into occasions for mass political demonstrations. He broke with more moderate leaders of the Congress party by demanding the boycott of British-manufactured goods. Tilak also sought to persuade Indians to refuse to serve in the colonial administration and military. Tilak demanded full independence, with no deals or delays, and threatened violent rebellion if the British failed to comply.

Tilak, B. G. (1856–1920) Believed that nationalism in India should be based on appeals to Hindu religiosity; worked to promote the restoration and revival of ancient Hindu traditions; offended Muslims and other religious groups; first populist leader in Indian nationalist movement.

Tilak's oratorical skills and religious appeal made him the first Indian nationalist leader with a genuine mass following. Nonetheless, his popularity was confined mainly to his home base in Bombay and in nearby areas in western India. At the same time, his promotion of a very reactionary sort of Hinduism offended and frightened moderate and progressive Hindus, Muslims, and followers of other religions, such as the Sikhs. When evidence was found connecting Tilak's writings to underground organizations that advocated violent revolt, the British, who had grown increasingly uneasy about his radical demands and mass appeal, arrested and imprisoned him. Six years of exile in Burma for Tilak had a dampening effect on the mass movement he had begun to build among the Hindu population.

The other major threat to the British in India before World War I came from Hindu communalists who advocated the violent overthrow of the colonial regime. But unlike Tilak and his followers, those who joined the terrorist movement favored clandestine operations over mass demonstrations. Though terrorists were active in several parts of India by the last decade of the 19th century, those in Bengal built perhaps the most extensive underground network. Considerable numbers of young Bengalis, impatient with the gradualist approach advocated by moderates in the Congress party, were attracted to underground secret societies. These were led by quasi-religious, guru-style leaders who exhorted them to build up their physiques with Western-style calisthenics and learn how to use firearms and make bombs. British officials and government buildings were the major targets of terrorist assassination plots and sabotage. On occasion the young revolutionaries also struck at European civilians and collaborators among the Indian population. But the terrorists' small numbers and limited support from the colonized populace as a whole rendered them highly vulnerable to British repressive measures. The very considerable resources the British devoted to crushing these violent threats to their rule had checked the terrorist threat by the outbreak of World War I.

Tilak's removal and the repression campaigns against the terrorists strengthened the hand of the more moderate politicians of the Congress party in the years before the war. Western-educated Indian lawyers became the dominant force in nationalist politics, and—as the careers of Gandhi, Jinnah, and Nehru demonstrate—they would provide many of the movement's key leaders throughout the struggle for independence. The approach of those who advocated a peaceful, constitutionalist route to decolonization was given added appeal by timely political concessions on the part of the British. The **Morley-Minto reforms** of 1909 provided educated Indians with considerably expanded opportunities both to vote for and serve on local and all-India legislative councils.

Morley-Minto reforms Provided educated Indians with considerably expanded opportunities to elect and serve on local and all-India legislative councils.

The Emergence of Gandhi and the Spread of the Nationalist Struggle

In the months after the outbreak of World War I, the British could take great comfort from the way in which the peoples of the empire rallied to their defense. Of the many colonies among the tropical dependencies, none played as critical a role in the British war effort as India. The Indian princes offered substantial war loans; Indian soldiers bore the brunt of the war effort in east Africa and the Middle East; and nationalist leaders, including Gandhi and Tilak, toured India selling British war bonds. But as the war dragged on and Indians died on the battlefields or went hungry at home to sustain a conflict that had little to do with them, signs of unrest spread throughout the subcontinent.

Wartime inflation had adversely affected virtually all segments of the Indian population. Indian peasants were angered at the ceilings set on the price of their market produce, despite rising costs. They were also often upset by their inability to sell what they had produced because of shipping shortages linked to the war. Indian laborers saw their already meager wages drop steadily in the face of rising prices. At the same time, their bosses grew rich from profits earned in war production. Many localities suffered from famines, which were exacerbated by wartime transport shortages that impeded relief efforts.

After the end of the war in 1918, moderate Indian politicians were frustrated by the British refusal to honor wartime promises. Hard-pressed British leaders had promised the Indians that if they continued to support the war effort, India would move steadily to self-government within the empire once the conflict was over. Indian hopes for the fulfillment of these promises were raised by the **Montagu-Chelmsford reforms** of 1919. These measures increased the powers of Indian legislators at the all-India level and placed much of the provincial administration of India under their control. But the concessions granted in the reforms were offset by the passage later in the same year of the **Rowlatt Act,** which placed severe restrictions on key Indian civil rights, such as freedom of the press. These conditions fueled local protest during and immediately after the war. At the same time, **Mohandas Gandhi** emerged as a new leader who soon forged this localized protest into a sustained all-India campaign against the policies of the colonial overlords.

Montagu-Chelmsford reforms Increased the powers of Indian legislators at the all-India level and placed much of the provincial administration of India under local ministries controlled by legislative bodies with substantial numbers of elected Indians; passed in 1919.

Rowlatt Act Placed severe restrictions on key Indian civil rights such as freedom of the press; acted to offset the concessions granted under Montagu-Chelmsford reforms of 1919.

Gandhi, Mohandas (1869–1948) Led sustained all-India campaign for independence from British Empire after World War I; stressed nonviolent but aggressive mass protest.

Gandhi on Civil Disobedience

satyagraha [suh-TYAH-grah-huh] Literally, "truth-force"; strategy of nonviolent protest developed by Mohandas Gandhi and his followers in India; later deployed throughout the colonized world and in the United States.

Gandhi

Cromer, Lord (1841–1917) British proconsul in khedival Egypt from 1883 to 1907; pushed for economic reforms that reduced but failed to eliminate the debts of the khedival regime.

Gandhi's remarkable appeal to both the masses and the Western-educated nationalist politicians was due to a combination of factors. Perhaps the most important was the strategy for protest that he had worked out a decade earlier as the leader of a successful movement of resistance to the restrictive laws imposed on the Indian migrant community in south Africa. Gandhi's stress on nonviolent but quite aggressive protest tactics endeared him both to the moderates and to more radical elements within the nationalist movement. His advocacy of peaceful boycotts, strikes, noncooperation, and mass demonstrations—which he labeled collectively **satyagraha** (suh-TYAH-grah-huh), or truth force—proved an effective way of weakening British control while limiting opportunities for violent reprisals that would allow the British to make full use of their superior military strength.

It is difficult to separate Gandhi's approach to mass protest from Gandhi as an individual and thinker. Though physically unimposing, he possessed an inner confidence and sense of moral purpose that sustained his followers and wore down his adversaries. He combined the career of a Western-educated lawyer with the attributes of a traditional Hindu ascetic and guru. The former had given him considerable exposure to the world beyond India and an astute understanding of the strengths and weaknesses of the British colonizers. These qualities and his soon legendary skill in negotiating with the British made it possible for Gandhi to build up a strong following among middle-class, Western-educated Indians, who had long been the dominant force behind the nationalist cause. But the success of Gandhi's protest tactics also hinged on the involvement of ever increasing numbers of the Indian people in anticolonial resistance. The image of a traditional mystic and guru that Gandhi projected was critical in gaining mass support from peasants and laborers alike. Many of these "ordinary" Indians would walk for miles when Gandhi was on tour. Many did so in order to honor a saint rather than listen to a political speech. Gandhi's widespread popular appeal, in turn, gave him even greater influence among nationalist politicians. The latter were very much aware of the leverage his mass following gave to them in their ongoing contests with the British overlords. Under Gandhi's leadership, nationalist protest surged in India during the 1920s and 1930s.

Egypt and the Rise of Nationalism in the Middle East

Egypt is the one country in the Afro-Asian world in which the emergence of nationalism preceded European conquest and domination (Map 28.3). Risings touched off by the mutiny of Ahmad Arabi and other Egyptian officers (see Chapter 31), which led to the British occupation in 1882, were aimed at the liberation of the Egyptian people from their alien Turkish overlords as well as the meddling Europeans. British occupation meant, in effect, double colonization for the Egyptian people by the Turkish khedives (who were left in power) and their British advisors.

In the decades following the British conquest, government policy was dominated by the strong-willed and imperious **Lord Cromer**. As high commissioner of Egypt, he pushed for much-needed economic reforms that reduced but could not eliminate the debts of the puppet khedival regime. Cromer also oversaw sweeping reforms in the bureaucracy and the construction of irrigation systems and other public works projects. But the prosperity the British congratulated themselves for having brought to Egypt by the first decade of the 20th century was enjoyed largely by tiny middle and elite classes, often at the expense of the mass of the population. The leading beneficiaries included foreign merchants, the Turco-Egyptian political elite, a small Egyptian bourgeoisie in Cairo and other towns in the Nile delta, and the ayan, or the great landlords in the rural areas.

The latter were clearly among the biggest gainers. The British had been forced to rely heavily on local, estate-owning notables in extending their control into the rural areas. As a result, the ayan, not the impoverished mass of rural cultivators and laborers, received most of the benefits of the new irrigation works, the building of railways, and the increasing orienta-

Map 28.3 The Middle East After World War I Despite promises to the Arab peoples who supported them in the war to let them decide their own postwar political fate, the victorious British and French allies divided much of the Middle East into what in effect were new colonial enclaves.

tion of Egyptian agriculture to the production of raw cotton for the export market. Unfettered by legal restrictions, the ayan greedily amassed ever larger estates by turning smallholder owners into landless tenants and laborers. As their wealth grew, the contrast between the landlords' estate houses and the thatch and mud-walled villages of the great mass of the peasantry became more and more pronounced. Bored by life in the provinces, the well heeled landed classes spent most of their time in the fashionable districts of Cairo or in resort towns such as Alexandria. Their estates were run by hired managers, who were little more than rent collectors as far as the peasants were concerned.

With the khedival regime and the great landlords closely allied to the British overlords, resistance to the occupation was left mainly to the middle class. Since the middle of the 19th century, this relatively new and small social class had been growing in numbers and influence, mainly in the towns in the Nile delta. With the memory of Arabi's revolt in 1882 still fresh, the cause of Egyptian independence was taken up mainly by the sons of the **effendi**, or the prosperous business and professional families that made up much of this new middle class. Even nationalist leaders who came from rural ayan families built their following among the urban middle classes. In contrast to India, where lawyers predominated in the nationalist leadership, in Egypt, journalists (a number of them educated in France) led the way.

In the 1890s and early 1900s, numerous newspapers in Arabic (and to a lesser extent French and English) vied to expose the mistakes of the British and the corruption of the khedival regime. Egyptian writers also attacked the British for their racist arrogance and their monopolization of well paying positions in the Egyptian bureaucracy. Like their Indian counterparts, Egyptian critics argued that these could just as well have been filled by university-educated Egyptians. In the 1890s the first nationalist party was formed. But again in contrast to India, where the Congress party dominated the nationalist movement from the outset, a variety of rival parties proliferated in Egypt. There were three main alternatives by 1907, but none could be said to speak for the great majority of the Egyptians, who were illiterate, poorly paid, and largely ignored urban laborers and rural farmers.

In the years before the outbreak of World War I in 1914, heavy-handed British repression on several occasions put down student riots or retaliated for assassination attempts against high British and Turco-Egyptian officials. Despite the failure of the nationalist parties to unite or build a mass base in the decades before the war, the extent of the hostility felt by the Egyptian masses was demonstrated by the **Dinshawai incident** in 1906 (see Figure 28.5 on p. 673). This confrontation between the British and their Egyptian subjects exemplified the racial arrogance displayed by most of the European colonizers. Though the incident at Dinshawai was seemingly a small clash resulting in only limited numbers of fatalities, the excessive British response to it did much to undermine whatever support remained for their continued presence in Egypt.

Most Egyptian villages raised large numbers of pigeons, which served as an important supplement to the meager peasant diet. Over the years, some of the British had turned the hunting of the pigeons of selected villages into a holiday pastime. A party of British officers on leave was hunting the pigeons of the village of Dinshawai in the Nile delta when they accidentally shot the wife of the prayer leader of the local mosque. The angry villagers mobbed the greatly outnumbered shooting party, which in panic fired on the villagers. Both the villagers and the British soldiers suffered casualties in the clashes that followed. In reprisal for the death of one of the officers, the British summarily hung four of the villagers. Though the actual hanging was not photographed, the building of the scaffolding was captured in a photo (Figure 28.5). The British also ordered that other villagers connected to the incident be publicly flogged or sentenced to varying terms of hard labor.

The harsh British reprisals aroused a storm of protest in the Egyptian press and among the nationalist parties. Some Egyptian leaders later recounted how the incident convinced them that cooperation with the British was totally unacceptable and fixed their resolve to agitate for an end to Egypt's occupation. Popular protests in several areas, and the emergence of ayan support for the nationalist cause, also suggested the possibility of building a mass base for anti-British agitation. More than anything else, the incident at Dinshawai had galvanized support for popular protest across the communal and social boundaries that had so long divided the peoples of Egypt.

By 1913 the British had been sufficiently intimidated by the rising tide of Egyptian nationalism to grant a constitution and representation in a parliament elected indirectly by the men of

effendi Class of prosperous business and professional urban families in khedival Egypt; as a class generally favored Egyptian independence.

Dinshawai incident Clash between British soldiers and Egyptian villagers in 1906; arose over hunting accident along Nile River where wife of prayer leader of mosque was accidentally shot by army officers hunting pigeons; led to Egyptian protest movement.

wealth and influence. World War I and the British declaration of martial law put a temporary end to nationalist agitation. But, as in India, the war unleashed forces in Egypt that could not be stopped and that would soon lead to the revival of the drive for independence with even greater strength than before.

War and Nationalist Movements in the Middle East

In the years after World War I, resistance to European colonial domination, which had been confined largely to Egypt in the prewar years, spread to much of the rest of the Middle East. Having sided with the Central Powers in the war, the Turks now shared in their defeat. The Ottoman Empire disappeared from history, as Britain and France carved up the Arab portions that had revolted against the Young Turk regime during the war. Italy and Greece attacked the Turkish rump of the empire around Constantinople and in Anatolia (Asia Minor) with the intent of sparking a partition of these areas in concert with the other Entente allies. But a skilled military commander, Mustafa Kemal, or **Ataturk**, had emerged from the Turkish officer corps during the war years. Ataturk rallied the Turkish forces and gradually drove back the Greek armies intent on colonizing the Turkish homeland.

By 1923 an independent Turkish republic had been established, but at the cost of the expulsion of tens of thousands of ethnic Greeks. As an integral part of the effort to establish a viable Turkish nation, Ataturk launched a sweeping program of reforms. Many of the often radical changes his government introduced in the 1920s and 1930s were modeled on Western precedents, including a new Latin alphabet, women's suffrage, and criticism of the veil. But in important ways his efforts to secularize and develop Turkey also represented the culmination of transformations made under the Ottomans over the preceding century (see Chapter 31).

With Turkish rule in the Arab heartlands ended by defeat in the war, Arab nationalists in Beirut, Damascus, and Baghdad turned to face the new threat presented by the victorious Entente powers, France and Britain. Betraying promises to preserve Arab independence that the British had made in 1915 and early 1916, French and British forces occupied much of the Middle East in the years after the war. **Hussein**, the sherif of Mecca, had used these promises to convince the Arabs to rise in support of Britain's war against the Turks, despite the fact that the latter were fellow Muslims. Consequently, the allies' postwar violation of these pledges humiliated and deeply angered Arabs throughout the Middle East. The occupying European powers faced stiff resistance from the Arabs in each of the **mandates** they carved out in Syria, Iraq, and Lebanon under the auspices of the League of Nations. Nationalist movements in these countries gained ground during the 1920s and 1930s. The Arabs' sense of humiliation and anger was greatly intensified by the disposition of Palestine, where British occupation was coupled with promises of a Jewish homeland.

The fact that the British had appeared to promise Palestine, for which they received a League of Nations mandate in 1922, to both the Jewish **Zionists** and the Arabs during the war greatly complicated an already confused situation. Despite repeated assurances to Hussein and other Arab leaders that they would be left in control of their own lands after the war, Lord Balfour, the British foreign secretary, promised prominent Zionist leaders in 1917 that his government would promote the establishment of a Jewish homeland in Palestine after the war. This pledge, the **Balfour Declaration**, fed existing Zionist aspirations for the Hebrew people to return to their ancient Middle Eastern lands of origin, which had been nurtured by the Jews of the diaspora for millennia. In the decades before the First World War, these dreams led to the formation of a number of organizations. Some of these were dedicated to promoting Jewish emigration to Palestine; others were committed to the eventual establishment of a Jewish state there.

These early moves were made in direct response to the persecution of the Jews of eastern Europe in the last decades of the 19th century. Particularly vicious *pogroms,* or violent assaults on the Jewish communities of Russia and Romania in the 1860s and 1870s, convinced Jewish intellectuals such as **Leon Pinsker** that assimilation of the Jews into, or even acceptance by, Christian European nations was impossible. Pinsker and other thinkers called for a return to the Holy Land. Likeminded individuals founded Zionist organizations, such as the Society for the Colonization of Israel, to promote Jewish migration to Palestine in the last decades of the 19th century. Until World War I, the numbers of Jews returning to Palestine were small—in the tens of thousands—though Zionist communities were established on lands purchased in the area.

Ataturk   Also known as Mustafa Kemal; leader of Turkish republic formed in 1923; reformed Turkish nation using Western models.

The Six Arrows of Kemalism: The Principles of the Republican People's Party (RPP), 1935

Hussein   Sherif of Mecca from 1908 to 1917; used British promise of independence to convince Arabs to support Britain against the Turks in World War I; angered by Britain's failure to keep promise; died 1931.

mandates   Governments entrusted to European nations in the Middle East in the aftermath of World War I; Britain occupied mandates in Syria, Iraq, Lebanon, and Palestine after 1922.

Zionists   Members of a movement originating in eastern Europe during the 1860s and 1870s that argued that the Jews must return to a Middle Eastern holy land; eventually identified with the settlement of Palestine.

Balfour Declaration   British minister Lord Balfour's promise of support for the establishment of Jewish settlement in Palestine issued in 1917.

Pinsker, Leon   (1821–1891) European Zionist who believed that Jewish assimilation into Christian European nations was impossible; argued for return to Middle Eastern Holy Land.

Until the late 1890s, the Zionist effort was generally opposed by Jews in Germany, France, and other parts of western Europe who enjoyed citizenship and extensive civil rights. In addition, many in these communities had grown prosperous and powerful in their adopted lands. But a major defection to the Zionists occurred in 1894. **Theodor Herzl**, an established Austrian journalist, was stunned by French mobs shouting "Death to the Jews" as they taunted the hapless army officer **Alfred Dreyfus**. Dreyfus was a French Jew who had been falsely accused of passing military secrets to the Germans. His subsequent mistreatment, including exile to the infamous penal colony on Devil's Island, became the flashpoint for years of bitter debate between the left and right in France. Soon after this incident in 1897, Herzl and a number of other prominent western European Jews joined with Jewish leaders from eastern Europe to form the **World Zionist Organization**. As Herzl made clear in his writings, the central aim of this increasingly well funded organization was to promote Jewish migration to and settlement in Palestine until a point was reached when a Zionist state could be established in the area. Herzl's nationalist ambitions, as well as his indifference to the Arabs already living in the area, were captured in the often-quoted view of one of his close associates that Palestine was "a land without people for a people [the Jews] without a land."

Lord Balfour's promises to the Zionists and the British takeover of Palestine struck the Arabs as a double betrayal of wartime assurances that Arab support for the Entente powers against the Turks would guarantee them independence after the war. This sense of betrayal was a critical source of the growing hostility the Arabs felt toward Jewish emigration to Palestine and their purchase of land in the area. Rising Arab opposition convinced many British officials, especially those who actually administered Palestine, to severely curtail the rather open-ended pledges that had been made to the Zionists during the war. This shift led in turn to Zionist mistrust of British policies and open resistance to them. It also fed the Zionists' determination to build up their own defenses against the increasingly violent Arab resistance to the Jewish presence in Palestine. But British attempts to limit Jewish emigration and settlement were not matched by efforts to encourage, through education and consultation, the emergence of strong leadership among the Arab population of Palestine. Consequently, in the critical struggles and diplomatic maneuvers of the 1930s and 1940s, the Arabs of Palestine were rarely able to speak for themselves. They were represented by Arab leaders from neighboring lands, who did not always understand Palestinian needs and desires. These non-Palestinian spokespersons also often acted more in the interests of Syrian or Lebanese Arabs than those of the Christian and Muslim Arab communities in Palestine.

Revolt in Egypt, 1919

Because Egypt was already occupied by the British when the war broke out, and it had been formally declared a protectorate in 1914, it was not included in the promises made by the British to the sherif Hussein. As a result, the anticolonial struggle in Egypt was rooted in earlier agitation and the heavy toll the war had taken on the Egyptian people, particularly the peasantry. During the war, the defense of the Suez Canal was one of the top priorities for the British. To guard against possible Muslim uprisings in response to Turkish calls for a holy war, martial law was declared soon after hostilities began. Throughout the war, large contingents of Entente and empire forces were garrisoned in Egypt. These created a heavy drain on the increasingly scarce food supplies of the area. Forced labor and confiscations by the military of the precious draft animals of the peasantry also led to widespread discontent. As the war dragged on, this unrest was further inflamed by spiraling inflation as well as by food shortages and even starvation in some areas.

By the end of the war, Egypt was ripe for revolt. Mass discontent strengthened the resolve of the educated nationalist elite to demand a hearing at Versailles, where the victorious Allies were struggling to reach a postwar settlement. When a delegation (*wafd* in Arabic) of Egyptian leaders was denied permission to travel to France to put the case for Egyptian self-determination to the peacemakers at Versailles, most Egyptian leaders resigned from the government and called for mass demonstrations. What followed shocked even the most confident British officials. Student-led riots touched off outright insurrection over much of Egypt. At one point, Cairo was cut off from the outside world, and much of the countryside was hostile territory for the occupying power. Though the British army was able, at the cost of scores of deaths, to restore control, it was clear that some hearing had to be given to Egyptian demands. The emergence of the newly formed **Wafd party** under its hard-driving leader **Sa'd Zaghlul** (SAHD ZAG-luhl) provided the nationalists

Herzl, Theodor Austrian journalist and Zionist; formed World Zionist Organization in 1897; promoted Jewish migration to Palestine and formation of a Jewish state.

Dreyfus, Alfred (1859–1935) French Jew falsely accused of passing military secrets to the Germans; his mistreatment and exile to Devil's Island provided flash-point for years of bitter debate between the left and right in France.

World Zionist Organization Founded by Theodor Herzl to promote Jewish migration to and settlement in Palestine to form a Zionist state.

Wafd party Egyptian nationalist party that emerged after an Egyptian delegation was refused a hearing at the Versailles treaty negotiations following World War I; led by Sa'd Zaghlul; negotiations eventually led to limited Egyptian independence beginning in 1922.

Zaghlul, Sa'd [SAHD ZAG-luhl] Leader of Egypt's nationalist Wafd party; their negotiations with British led to limited Egyptian independence in 1922.

Women in Asian and African Nationalist Movements

One important but often neglected dimension of the liberation struggles that Asian and African peoples waged against their colonial overlords was the emergence of a stratum of educated, articulate, and politically active women in most colonial societies. In this process, the educational opportunities provided by the European colonizers often played as vital a role as they had in the formation of male leadership in nationalist movements. Missionary girls' schools were confined in the early stages of European involvement in Africa and Asia to the daughters of low-class or marginal social groups. But by the end of the 19th century these schools had become quite respectable for women from the growing westernized business and professional classes. In fact, in many cases, some degree of Western education was essential if westernized men were to find wives with whom they could share their career concerns and intellectual pursuits.

The seemingly insurmountable barriers that separated Westernized Asian and African men from their traditional—and thus usually without formal education—wives became a stock theme in the novels and short stories of the early nationalist era. This concern was perhaps best exemplified by the works of Rabindranath Tagore. The problem was felt so acutely by the first generation of Indian nationalist leaders that many took up the task of teaching their wives English and Western philosophy and literature at home. Thus, for many upper-class Asian and African women, colonization proved a liberating force. This trend was often offset by the male-centric nature of colonial education and the domestic focus of much of the curriculum in women's schools.

Although women played a small role in the early, elitist stages of Asian and African nationalist movements, they frequently became more and more prominent as the early study clubs and political associations reached out to build a mass base. In India, women who had been exposed to Western education and European ways, such as Tagore's famous heroine in the novel *The Home and the World,* came out of seclusion and took up supporting roles, though they were still usually behind the scenes. Gandhi's campaign to supplant imported, machine-made British cloth with homespun Indian cloth, for example, owed much of whatever success it had to female spinners and weavers. As nationalist leaders moved their anticolonial campaigns into the streets, women became involved in mass demonstrations. Throughout the 1920s and 1930s, Indian women braved the *lathi*, or billy club, assaults of the Indian police, suffered the indignities of imprisonment, and launched their own newspapers and lecture campaigns to mobilize female support for the nationalist struggle.

In Egypt, the British made special note of the powerful effect that the participation of both veiled women and more westernized

> "As nationalist leaders moved their anticolonial campaigns into the streets, women became involved in mass demonstrations."

upper-class women had on mass demonstrations in 1919 and the early 1920s. These outpourings of popular support did much to give credibility to the Wafd party's demands for British withdrawal. In both India and Egypt, female nationalists addressed special appeals to British and American suffragettes to support their peoples' struggles for political and social liberation. In India in particular, their causes were advanced by feminists such as the English champion of Hinduism, Annie Besant, who became a major figure in the nationalist movement before and after World War I.

When African nationalism became a popularly supported movement in the post–World War II period, women, particularly the outspoken and fearless market women in west Africa, emerged as a major political force. In settler colonies, such as Algeria and Kenya, where violent revolt proved necessary to bring down deeply entrenched colonial regimes, women took on the dangerous tasks of messengers, bomb carriers, and guerrilla fighters. As Frantz Fanon argued decades ago, and as was later beautifully dramatized in the film *The Battle of Algiers,* this transformation was particularly painful for women who had been in seclusion right up to the time of the revolutionary upsurge. Cutting their hair and wearing lipstick and Western clothes often alienated them from their fathers and brothers, who equated such practices with prostitution.

In many cases, women's participation in struggles for the political liberation of their people was paralleled by campaigns for female rights in societies that, as we have seen, were dominated by males. Upper-class Egyptian women founded newspapers and educational associations that pushed for a higher age of marriage, educational opportunities for women, and an end to seclusion and veiling. Indian women took up many of these causes and also developed programs to improve hygiene and employment opportunities for lower-caste women. These early efforts, as well as the prominent place of women in nationalist struggles, had much to do with the granting of basic civil rights to women. These included suffrage and legal equality, which were key features of the constitutions of many newly independent Asian and African nations. The great majority of women in the new states of Africa and Asia have yet to enjoy most of these rights. Yet their inclusion in constitutions and post-independence laws provides crucial backing for the struggles for women's liberation in the nations of the postcolonial world.

QUESTIONS In what ways do you think measures to "modernize" colonial societies were oriented to males? Can you think of women who have been or are major political figures in contemporary Africa and Asia? What sorts of traditional constraints hamper the efforts of women to achieve economic and social equality and major political roles in newly independent nations?

with a focus for unified action and a mass base that far excelled any they had attracted in the pre-war decades.

When a special British commission of inquiry into the causes of the upheaval in Egypt met with widespread civil disobedience and continuing violent opposition, it recommended that the British begin negotiations for an eventual withdrawal from Egypt. Years of bargaining followed, which led to a highly qualified independence for the Egyptians. British withdrawal occurred in stages, beginning in 1922 and culminating in the British withdrawal to the Suez Canal zone in 1936. But though they pulled out of Egypt proper, the khedival regime was preserved and the British reserved the right to reoccupy Egypt should it be threatened by a foreign aggressor.

Though they had won a significant degree of political independence, the Egyptian leaders of the Wafd party, as well as its rivals in the Liberal Constitutionalist and Union parties, did little to relieve the increasing misery of the great majority of the Egyptian people. Most Egyptian politicians regarded the winning of office as an opportunity to increase their own and their families' fortunes. Many politicians from ayan households and from the professional and merchant classes used their influence and growing wealth to amass huge estates, which were worked by landless tenants and laborers. Locked in personal and interparty quarrels, as well as the ongoing contest with the khedival regime for control of the government, few political leaders had the time or inclination to push for the land reforms and public works projects that the peasantry so desperately needed.

The utter social bankruptcy of the 40 years of nationalist political dominance that preceded the military coup and social revolution led by Gamal Abdul Nasser in 1952 is suggested by some revealing statistics compiled by the United Nations in the early 1950s. By that time, nearly 70 percent of Egypt's cultivable land was owned by six percent of the population. Some 12,000 families alone controlled 37 percent of the farmland. As for the mass of the people, 98 percent of the peasants were illiterate, malnutrition was chronic among both the urban and rural population, and an estimated 95 percent of rural Egyptians suffered from eye diseases. Such was the legacy of the very unrevolutionary process of decolonization in Egypt.

The Beginnings of the Liberation Struggle in Africa

Most of Africa had come under European colonial rule only in the decades before the outbreak of World War I. Nonetheless, precolonial missionary efforts had produced small groups of Western-educated Africans in parts of west and south central Africa by the end of the 19th century. Like their counterparts in India, most Western-educated Africans were staunchly loyal to their British and French overlords during the First World War. With the backing of both Western-educated Africans and the traditional rulers, the British and especially the French were able to draw on their African possessions for manpower and raw materials throughout the war. But this reliance took its toll on their colonial domination in the long run. In addition to local rebellions in response to the forcible recruitment of African soldiers and laborers, the war effort seriously disrupted newly colonized African societies (Figure 28.6). African merchants and farmers suffered from shipping shortages and the sudden decline in demand for crops, such as cocoa. African villagers were not happy to go hungry so that their crops could feed the armies of the allies. As Lord Lugard, an influential colonial administrator, pointed out, the desperate plight of the British and French also forced them to teach tens of thousands of Africans:

> how to kill white men, around whom [they had] been taught to weave a web of sanctity of life. [They] also know how to handle bombs and Lewis guns and Maxims . . . and [they have] seen the white men budge when [they have] stood fast. Altogether [they have] acquired much knowledge that might be put to uncomfortable use someday.

The fact that the Europeans kept few of the promises of better jobs and public honors, which they had made during the war to induce young Africans to enlist in the armed forces or serve as colonial administrators, contributed a good deal to the unrest of the postwar years. This was particularly true of the French colonies, where opportunities for political organization, much less protest, were severely constricted before, during, and after the war. Major strikes and riots broke out repeatedly after the war. In the British colonies, where there was considerably more tolerance for political organization, there were also strikes and a number of outright rebellions. Throughout colonized

Figure 28.6 Soldiers, like those captured in this photograph, were extensively recruited by the French in their colonies in north and west Africa, and to a lesser extent, Vietnam to bolster their defenses on the Western Front in France and battle the Germans in colonized Africa.

Garvey, Marcus   African American political leader; had a major impact on emerging African nationalist leaders in the 1920s and 1930s.

Du Bois, W. E. B.   African American political leader; had a major impact on emerging African nationalist leaders in the 1920s and 1930s.

pan-African   Organization that brought together intellectuals and political leaders from areas of Africa and African diaspora before and after World War I.

négritude   Literary movement in Africa; attempted to combat racial stereotypes of African culture; celebrated the beauty of black skin and African physique; associated with origins of African nationalist movements.

Senghor, Léopold Sédar   (1906–2001) One of the post–World War I writers of the négritude literary movement that urged pride in African values; president of Senegal from 1960 to 1980.

Africa, protest intensified in the 1930s in response to the economic slump brought on by the Great Depression.

Though Western-educated politicians did not link up with urban workers or peasants in most African colonies until the 1940s, disenchanted members of the emerging African elite began to organize in the 1920s and 1930s. In the early stages of this process, charismatic African American political figures, such as **Marcus Garvey** and **W. E. B. Du Bois,** had a major impact on emerging African nationalist leaders. In the 1920s much effort was placed into attempts to arouse all-Africa loyalties and build **pan-African** organizations. However, the leadership of these organizations was mainly African American and West Indian, and the delegates from colonized areas in Africa faced very different challenges under different colonial overlords. Although these differences had much to do with the fact that pan-Africanism proved unworkable in Africa itself, its well attended conferences, especially the early ones in Paris, did much to arouse anticolonial sentiments among Western-educated Africans.

By the mid-1920s, nationalists from French and British colonies were pretty much going separate ways. Because of restrictions in the colonies, and because small but well educated groups of Africans were represented in the French parliament, French-speaking west Africans concentrated their organizational and ideological efforts in Paris in this period. The **négritude** literary movement nurtured by these exiles did much to combat the racial stereotyping that had so long held the Africans in psychological bondage to the Europeans. Writers such as the Senegalese poet **Léopold Sédar Senghor,** Léon Damas from French Guiana, and the West Indian Aimé Césaire celebrated the beauty of black skin and the African physique. They argued that in the precolonial era, African peoples had built societies where women were freer, old people were better cared for, and attitudes toward sex were far healthier than they had ever been in the so-called civilized West.

Except in settler colonies, such as Kenya and Rhodesia, Western-educated Africans in British territories were given greater opportunities to build political associations within Africa. In the early stages of this process, African leaders sought to nurture organizations that linked the emerging nationalists of different British colonies, such as the National Congress of British West Africa. By the late 1920s, these pan-colony associations gave way to political groupings concerned primarily with issues within individual colonies, such as Sierra Leone, the Gold Coast, or Nigeria. After the British granted some representation in colonial advisory councils to Western-educated Africans in this period, emphasis on colony-specific political mobilization became even more pronounced. Though most of these early political organizations were too loosely structured to be considered true political parties, there was a growing recognition by some leaders of the need to build a mass base. In the 1930s a new generation of leaders made much more vigorous attacks on the policies of the British. Through their newspapers and political associations, they also reached out to ordinary African villagers and the young, who had hitherto played little role in nationalist agitation. Their efforts to win a mass following would come to full fruition only after European divisions plunged humanity into a second global war.

Global Connections

World War and Global Upheavals

The First World War—or the Great War as it was called by those who lived through it and did not know a second conflict of this magnitude lay in their future—was one of several key turning points of world history in the 20th century. The long conflict, particularly the horrific and draining stalemate in the trenches, did much to undermine Europe's prewar position of global dominance. The war severely disrupted Europe's economy and bolstered already emerging rivals, especially the United States and Japan, for preeminence in world trade and finance. Over much of Europe, the hardships endured by the civilian populations on the home front reignited long-standing class tensions. In Russia, but also elsewhere in east central Europe, growing social divisions sparked full-scale revolutions. In Britain, France, Germany, and other liberal democracies in western Europe, labor parties, some socialist or communist, emerged with much greater power after the conflict. Many shared power, both in coalitions with center parties or in their own right in the 1920s and 1930s. The war saw major changes in gender roles in spheres ranging from employment and marriage to sex and fashion. It also generated growing challenges to the rigid racial hierarchies that had dominated both scientific theorizing and popular attitudes in the decades leading up to the conflict.

The victorious Entente allies, especially the British and French but also the Belgians and Japanese, managed to hold on to, and in fact enlarge, their empires. But the hardships endured by colonized peoples and the empty promises made by their desperate colonial overloads during the war gave great impetus to resistance to their empires that spread from the Middle East and India to Vietnam and China. For African and Asian intellectuals at least, the psychological advantage that racial thinking and scientific and technological superiority had given the Europeans began to dissipate. The essential cooperation of nationalist leaders like Gandhi gave them and their ideologies of liberation access to ever larger numbers of colonized peoples. In the postwar decades, mass civil disobedience campaigns in India and Egypt, and peasant risings in Vietnam and China, established the protest techniques and demands that would ultimately bring down all of the European colonial empires. The revolutionary regime in Russia, which had come to power as a direct consequence of the war, actively abetted efforts to advance the cause of decolonization around the world. Two other industrial nations whose power had been greatly enhanced by the war, the United States and Japan, sought in different ways both to supplant the European colonizers and replace them as the economic and political power centers of the 20th century.

Further Readings

James Joll, *The Origins of the First World War* (1984), offers a detailed treatment of the many and highly contested interpretations of the causes of the conflict. Fritz Fisher, *Germany's Aims in the First World War* (1967), argued that Germany's leaders purposely provoked the conflict, while Paul Kennedy, *The Rise of the Anglo-German Antagonism, 1860–1914* (1980), sees other forces at work. The impact of colonial disputes on the coming of the war is concisely and convincingly treated in L. F. C. Turner, *Origins of the First World War* (1970).

Of the many general histories of the war on land and sea, the more reliable and readable include *The World in the Crucible, 1914–1919* (1984) by Bernadotte Schmitt and Harold Vedeler, and most recently John Keegan's *The First World War* (1999). Marc Ferro's *The Great War* (1973) remains one of the most stimulating analyses of the conduct of the war. Three of the most successful attempts to understand the war from the participants' perspectives are Paul Fussell's *The Great War and Modern Memory* (1975) and John Cruickshank's *Variations on Catastrophe* (1982), which draw on literary works and memoirs, and Richard Cork's magisterial exploration of artistic images of the conflict in *A Bitter Truth: Avant-Garde Art and the Great War* (1994). Some of the better accounts by the participants include Erich Remarque, *All Quiet on the Western Front* (1929); Frederic Manning, *The Middle Parts of Fortune* (1929); Vera Brittain, *Testament of Youth* (1933); and Wilfred Owen, *Poems* (1920) reprinted as *The Collected Poems of Wilfred Owen,* (1964).

The disasters at Versailles and some of their consequences are chronicled in Ivo J. Lederer, ed., *The Versailles Settlement* (1960), Harold Nicholson's *Peace Making, 1919* (1965), Arno Mayer, *Politics and Diplomacy of Peace-Making, 1918–1919* (1967) and Charles L. Mee Jr.'s *The End of Order: Versailles, 1919* (1980).

A good general historical narrative of the impact of the war on the struggle for Indian independence can be found in Sumit

Sarkar, *Modern India, 1885–1947* (1983). A closer analysis is offered in the essays in DeWitt C. Elinwood and S. D. Pradhan, eds., *India and World War I* (1978). The war also figures importantly in the early sections of Mohandas Gandhi's autobiographical *The Story of My Experiments with Truth* (1927). Louis Fischer's *Gandhi* (1950) still yields valuable insights into the personality of one of the great nationalist leaders and the workings of nationalist politics.

P. J. Vatikiotis, *The History of Egypt* (especially the 1985 edition), has excellent sections on the war and early nationalist era in that country. Leila Ahmed, *Women and Gender in Islam* (1992), has excellent chapters on the role of women at various stages of the nationalist struggle and in the postindependence era. A comprehensive treatment of working-class women protesters in Egypt is provided by Nawal El Saadawi, *The Hidden Face of Eve* (1980). David Fromkin, *A Peace to End All Peace* (1989), provides a more recent and superb account of wartime and postwar events in the Middle East as a whole.

The early stages of the nationalist struggle, including the war years, in west Africa are well covered by Michael Crowder, *West Africa under Colonial Rule* (1982). A narrative of the history of the First World War as a whole in sub-Saharan Africa can be found in Byron Farwell, *The Great War in Africa* (1986). The continued advance of European colonialism in the Middle East and Africa in the postwar years is analyzed in *France Overseas* (1981) by Christopher Andrew and A. S. Kanya-Forstner.

On the Web

Recent interactive overviews of and resource pages on the Great War, featuring animated battle reconstructions, and the war's legacies are provided at http://www.worldwar1.com/index.html, http://www.learningcurve.gov.uk/greatwar/, http://www.bbc.co.uk/history/worldwars/wwone/, http://www.channel4.com/history/microsites/F/firstworldwar/, and http://www.geocities.com~worldwar1/default.html. Key documents of the war and useful analyses can be explored at http://wwi.lib.byu.edu/index.php/Main_Page and http://www.fordham.edu/halsall/mod/modsbook38.html. The victorious allied powers' conditional acceptance of Woodrow Wilson's "Fourteen Points" is among the many pre-war, battlefront and post-war documents and speeches digitally archived at http://www.mtholyoke.edu/acad/intrel/ww1.htm.

Links exploring the life and work of war poets such as Wilfred Owen can be found at http://www.spartacus.schoolnet.co.uk/Jgraves.htm and http://www.english.emory.edu/LostPoets/index.html.

Life in the trenches and major battles are discussed at http://www.fordham.edu/halsall/mod/1918fraser.html, http://www.firstworldwar.com/battles/vimyridge.htm, http://www.firstworldwar.com/battles/ypres1.htm, http://www.spartacus.schoolnet.co.uk/FWWpasschendaele.htm, http://www.worldwar1.com/sfsomme.htm and http://www.achtungpanzer.com/blitz.htm (**Verdun**).

The home fronts of the combatant nations, from food rationing to the impact of the related influenza epidemic, are discussed at http://www.spartacus.schoolnet.co.uk/FWWhome.htm (scroll down to "War and the Home Front"). The text of the Zimmerman Telegram that provided the proximate cause of the U.S. entry into World War I can be found at http://www.firstworldwar.com/source/zimmermann.htm. A vast collection of other major documents related to the war is offered at http://www.lib.byu.edu/~estu/wwi/ and http://www.ku.edu/~kansite/ww_one. The Great Influenza Epidemic that swept the world's post-war populations is examined at http://www.pbs.org/wgbh/amex/influenza/.

Postwar colonial issues such as Négritude is the subject of analysis at http://www.artmag.com/museums/a_allem/kultur/Africa.html and http://www.postcolonial.org/ (go to Search Tool, enter "negritude" for links on this subject), and http://www.stg.brown.edu/projects/hypertext/landow/post/poldiscourse/negritude.html. Insight into the casual brutality of imperialism that fueled postwar nationalist revolts can be derived from an account of the Dinshawai incident in Egypt http://touregypt.net/denshwaymuseum.htm and the Amritsar massacre in India at http://www.scholars.nus.edu.sg/landow/post/india/history/colonial/massacre.html and http://en.wikipedia.org/wiki/Jallianwala_Bagh_Massacre. Winston Churchill's speech on the destructive impact of that massacre on Britain's post-war imperial status is offered at http://lachlan.bluehaze.com.au/churchill/am-man.htm.

The Balfour Declaration, offered at http://www.fordham.edu/halsall/mod/balfour.html, and the McMahon-Hussein Correspondence, at http://www.mideastweb.org/mcmahon.htm, http://www.wzo.org.il/home/politic/mac.htm http://www.fordham.edu/halsall/mod/1915mcmahon.html and http://www.arab2.com/biography/conflict/McMahon-Letters-aa.htm, figured greatly in the postwar debates over Arab and Jewish homelands.

Resources for the study of South Asian independence movements can be found at http://www.yale.edu/macmillan/southasia/saim/resources.htm. Mohandas Gandhi's leadership of that movement and his key philosophical ideas such as *ahimsa*, or non-violence is explored at http://dwardmac.pitzer.edu/anarchist_archives/bright/gandhi/Gandhi.html, http://www.mkgandhi.org/articles/swaraj.htm, http://www.mkgandhi.org/nonviolence/gandhi.

Gandhi's famous Salt March, discussed at http://www.sscnet.ucla.edu/southasia/History/Gandhi/Dandi.html and http://www.algonet.se/~jviklund/gandhi/ENG.MKG.salt.html, is the subject of a film at http://harappa.com/wall/1930.html. His "Quit India" speech of 1942 is offered at http://www.ibiblio.org/pha/policy/1942/420427a.html. An audio file of one of Gandhi's speeches can be accessed at http://www.harappa.com/sounds/gandhi.html. The character of Gandhi's close associate, Jawaharlal Nehru, is offered at http://www.itihaas.com/modern/nehru-profile.html. Rabindranath Tagore, the poet laureate of the Indian independence movement, is discussed at http://www.itihaas.com/modern/tagore-profile.html. A review of the life of Muhammad Ali Jinnah, the Indian Muslim nationalist who led the campaign for the creation of the state of Pakistan and became its first president, is provided at http://www.rediff.com/news/1998/sep/10jinnah.htm. Short audio files of Jinnah delivering key speeches are available at http://harappa.com/sounds/jinnah.html.

AP* Test Prep

1. The immediate cause for the outbreak of World War I was
   (A) a naval race between Germany and Great Britain.
   (B) the assassination of Austrian Archduke Franz Ferdinand.
   (C) colonial disputes over Morocco.
   (D) the Industrial Revolution.

2. Why is the Great War referred to as the first "total war" in human history?
   (A) because of the involvement of colonial peoples
   (B) because of the numbers of men drafted into military service
   (C) because of the involvement of civilians and the power of the governments
   (D) because of the resultant labor unrest and revolutions

3. What significance did the war have on women's roles in European societies?
   (A) It challenged prewar notions of "natural" gender roles.
   (B) It contributed to women's involvement in nationalist independence movements.
   (C) It reemphasized the importance of traditional values as a sign of normalcy.
   (D) It challenged women to take even better care of their children by leaving factory jobs to men.

4. The principle of Woodrow Wilson that influenced future decolonization was
   (A) immediate independence for all colonies.
   (B) the evacuation of all occupied territories.
   (C) national self-determination.
   (D) the need for an international governing body.

5. What precipitated the attacks on Armenians in 1915?
   (A) A majority of Armenians sided with the Russians against the Ottoman Empire.
   (B) German secret agents passed incorrect information to the Ottoman government.
   (C) Ottoman leaders sought to cover up their military blunders by blaming the Armenians.
   (D) Ottoman revenge against massacres of Muslims by Armenians in the 1880s and 1890s.

6. Gandhi's style of leadership of the Indian National Congress Party
   (A) included appeals to violence against India's British rulers.
   (B) appealed only to poor Hindus.
   (C) appealed to both intellectuals and the masses throughout India.
   (D) was developed after his witnessing many acts of colonial racism in Malaya.

7. Why did Arab leaders object to the Mandate system outlined in the League of Nations Covenant?
   (A) They disliked having to obey the new Turkish president.
   (B) They objected to the policies in the Balfour Declaration.
   (C) They were opposed to the establishment of a Shi'ite state in Palestine.
   (D) They were humiliated by broken promises of independence.

Free-Response Question

In what ways did the Great War give impetus to forces of independence and resistance to European imperialism around the globe?

29 The World between the Wars: Revolutions, Depression, and Authoritarian Response

The Roaring Twenties

Revolution: The First Waves

THINKING HISTORICALLY: A Century of Revolutions

The Global Great Depression

The Authoritarian Response

VISUALIZING THE PAST: *Guernica* and the Images of War

DOCUMENT: Socialist Realism

GLOBAL CONNECTIONS: Economic Depression, Authoritarian Response, and Democratic Retreat

Russia's communist revolution in 1917 produced a regime that declared its commitment to workers. It was understandably less clear about its commitment to consumers. Department stores had spread in prerevolutionary Russia, almost exclusively for the rich. It was easy for the new communist rulers to decide to seize the stores. In their place, the government set up state department stores, headed by the chain called GUM (an acronym for State Universal Store, pronounced *goom*), with a flagship store right on Red Square in Moscow (Figure 29.1). It was also easy to proclaim that department stores were now available to all the people. GUM advertisements featured weathered peasants pondering new leather coats, and slogans trumpeted "Everything for Everybody" and "We Have Everything You Need at GUM."

There were, however, three problems. First, this was a poor society, and leaders were spending massive amounts of money on further industrialization and agricultural reform. There was not much left for abundant consumer goods. Second, communists were ambivalent about consumerism anyway. Sometimes they wanted consumerism for everybody, but sometimes they worried that consumerism was foreign, "bourgeois," and trivial. (Even in Western countries, Communist parties took some time to adjust to consumerism.) Third, the desire arose to protect workers in the stores from what the communists perceived as the demeaned status of those who "wait on" customers. The government stopped calling them clerks or salespeople, instead using the term "workers of the counter." They sought to protect these workers from the subservience Western sales clerks had to endure. Unfortunately, this led to clerks taking a surly attitude toward customers (now simply called "consumers").

The result of all this was that GUM stores became notorious for poor supplies and bad service. Customers were free to complain, and they often did, but government representatives rejected almost all the complaints with phrases like "does not correspond to reality." Communism and consumerism were both realities of the 20th century. Both movements could claim successes, but the two were not easy to combine. Russia's department stores and their poor quality goods and service became a symbol of communist inadequacy to many Western observers, particularly after World War II amid the competitive pressures of the cold war. But comparisons with Western standards could be misleading, because communist leaders were seeking different goals. Along with shoddy consumer goods came not only the huge advance in heavy industry and military production but also other, more personal gains like extensive vacation opportunities for workers. This was a different kind of industrial society, and the two decades between the wars were its seedbed. ∎

The 1920s and 1930s—the interwar period—featured several crucial developments in addition to the immediate postwar adjustments and the rise of nationalist protest against European colonialism. The 1920s featured many innovations in industrial societies, but also a combination of structural weakness and misleading illusion. The key dynamics of the interwar period revolved around a wave of major revolutions, a global economic depression, and new authoritarian regimes spearheaded by German Nazism.

Figure 29.1 The most famous link in the chain of Russian department stores known as GUM is the palatial pre-Communist era building on the right of this 1935 photograph of Red Square, Moscow.

The Roaring Twenties

The postwar challenges to western European society were immense. Massive war deaths—over 10 million Europeans had died—combined with widespread injuries and tremendous blows to morale. Property damage and economic dislocation added to the problems: because wartime governments had printed new money rather than raise taxes, an unprecedented postwar inflation occurred, wiping out savings for many groups.

In the West and Japan, consumerism and changes in women's roles gained ground, along with new political tensions. New authoritarian movements surfaced in eastern Europe and Italy.

Bouncing Back?

Superficially, however, a more buoyant attitude resumed by the middle of the decade. A new, democratic republic in Germany made some positive strides, despite the burdensome reparations payments the World War I victors had required. Artistic creativity included the **cubist movement,** led by Pablo Picasso, that rendered familiar objects in geometrical shapes, as in Figure 29.2. Writers and composers also challenged stylistic traditions. Modern design in architecture and furnishing gained ground (Figure 29.3). Important achievements in science included further work on Albert Einstein's groundbreaking theories of relativity in physics. Knowledge of atomic structure and also of genetics advanced.

cubist movement 20th-century art style; best represented by Spanish artist Pablo Picasso; rendered familiar objects as geometrical shapes.

New mass consumption items, like the radio, were important as well. Middle-class women gained new participation in popular culture, some of them going to nightclubs, smoking, and participating in dance crazes that often originated in the United States or Latin America (Figure 29.4). In several countries—Germany, Great Britain, the United States, and Turkey headed the list—women also gained the right to vote.

1910 C.E.	1920 C.E.	1930 C.E.
1917 Tsarist regime overthrown in February; Bolshevik revolution in October; Mexican constitution includes revolutionary changes	**1920–1940** Muralist movement in Mexico	**1930** U.S. Congress passes the Smoot-Hawley tariff; economic downturn in western Europe and throughout European colonial empires; rapid rise of Nazi party in Germany
1918 Armistice ends World War I in November	**1921** Albert Einstein wins the Nobel Prize; Chinese Communist party founded; Lenin's New Economic Policy begins in U.S.S.R.	**1931** Statute of Westminster gives full autonomy to British Dominions of Canada, Australia, New Zealand, South Africa, and the Irish Free State; failed rebellion against Japanese rule in Korea; poor harvests and severe economic dislocations in Japan; Japanese invasion of Manchuria
1919 Versailles conference; Peace of Paris; leftist revolution defeated in Germany; May Fourth movement in China	**1922** Mussolini and the Fascists seize power in Italy; first commercial radio station in Pittsburgh	**1932** Franklin Roosevelt begins four-term tenure as U.S. president and launches the New Deal
	1923–1924 Hyperinflation in Germany	**1932–1934** Height of forced collectivization in U.S.S.R.; genocidal famine inflicted on the Ukraine and other areas
	1923 Defeat of Japanese bill for universal suffrage; Tokyo earthquake	**1933** Adolf Hitler becomes chancellor of Germany
	1927 Charles Lindbergh's solo trans-Atlantic flight; Guomindang (Nationalists) capture north China, purge Communist party	**1934–1940** Lázaro Cárdenas president of Mexico, extensive land reform
	1927–1928 Stalin pushes the first five-year plan in the Soviet Union, collectivization begins; agricultural slump in United States	**1935** Nuremberg laws deprive Jews of German citizenship; Mussolini's armies invade Ethiopia; outbreak of civil war in Spain
	1928–1929 Skyscraper craze in New York	**1936** Popular Front government formed in France; junior army officers revolt in Japan, key political leaders assassinated
	1929 Stock market crash	**1936–1938** Height of Stalinist purges in U.S.S.R.
		1937 Full-scale Japanese invasion of China
		1938 *Kristallnacht* begins intensification of attacks on Jews in Germany; Munich agreement allows Hitler to begin destruction of Czechoslovakia
		1938 Japan's military leaders impose state control over economy and social system, Diet approves war budget
		1939 Hitler invades Poland, leading to outbreak of World War II

Aspects of the new culture, however, seemed frenzied, and certainly disturbed traditionalists. Key economic sectors—like agricultural and coal mining—did not really recover prosperity, and much of the British economy overall remained sluggish. Western Europe did not regain export markets that had been taken over by the United States or Japan. Most western European countries also faced increasing political extremism. New communist parties on the left were matched by right-wing movements, often supported by many war veterans.

Other Industrial Centers

Canada, Australia, and New Zealand gained rewards for their loyal participation in World War I. Australia, newly independent in 1901, gained particular pride in its military role. Several conferences in the 1920s confirmed the independence of the Dominions and their co-equal status with Britain (Map 29.1). The British Commonwealth of Nations was a free association of members, as British representation in the three Dominions became purely symbolic. The Dominions also registered solid export growth and population gains from immigration. Australia introduced extensive welfare measures, responding to a strong labor movement, and considerable economic planning.

Figure 29.2 Marcel Duchamp's *Nude Descending a Staircase, No. 2* (1912). Using a modified cubist style, Duchamp achieved a dramatic visual effect in an approach characteristic of Western art from the 1920s onward.

(Marcel Duchamp (American, b. France 1887–1968), "Nude Descending a Staircase, No. 2," 1912. Philadelphia Museum of Art: The Louise and Walter Arensberg Collection. 1950-134-59. © 2009 Artists Rights Society (ARS), New York/ADAGP, Paris/Succession Marcel Duchamp.)

Figure 29.3 The skyscraper, developed first in the United States, became a major expression of artistic innovation and was the result of the use of new structural materials that allowed for unprecedented heights and dramatic effects. Buildings like this one—the Wrigley Building in Chicago—combined the new technology with elements of gothic architecture that recalled the great cathedrals of the Middle Ages, earning them the nickname "Cathedrals of Commerce."

U.S. economic and popular cultural initiatives advanced rapidly during the 1920s. The economy boomed throughout much of the decade. Corporations expanded and innovated, for example adding research and development operations to their portfolios. Organization of work systems changed. Henry Ford had introduced the assembly line for automobile production in 1913, using conveyor belts to move parts past semi-skilled workers doing small, repetitive tasks as each automobile was completed. During the 1920s industrial psychologists studied how to increase output further, for example by piping in music. These production changes were widely imitated in Europe, Japan, and the Soviet Union. The United States also increased its popular cultural exports. Jazz spread from African American centers in the South to performances in Europe. Hollywood became the global film capital by 1920, and Hollywood stars, many of them foreign, became international staples.

The role of the United States worldwide had new complexities, however. The U.S. Senate rejected the Versailles treaty, refusing to enter the League of Nations. Diplomatically, the United States pursued an isolationist policy for two decades, refusing foreign alliances. Fear of communism also ran unusually high in the United States, with a "Red Scare" early in the decade heightening resistance to outside influences.

Japan entered a new phase of industrialization during the 1920s. Agricultural output improved with greater use of fertilizers and mechanical equipment. This freed labor for expanding factories. Japan rapidly augmented its heavy industrial sector, in metallurgy, shipbuilding, and electrical power, organized mainly by large industrial combines—the zaibatsu—linked to the state. Japan still depended heavily on cheap exports to the West, for it needed foreign earnings to cover the import of fuel and raw materials and to support rapid population growth. (A population of 45

Figure 29.4 The interwar decades saw the rise of a succession of dance crazes. Adults as well as young people were caught up in dancing to the new big bands.

Mussolini, Benito Italian fascist leader after World War I; created first fascist government (1922–1943) based on aggressive foreign policy and new nationalist glories.

fascism Political philosophy that became predominant in Italy and then Germany during the 1920s and 1930s; attacked weakness of democracy, corruption of capitalism; promised vigorous foreign and military programs; undertook state control of economy to reduce social friction.

Europe in the 1920s and 1930s

million in 1900 had increased to 70 million by 1940.) Politically, tensions between Japan's military leaders and the civilian government increased during the decade. Military leaders, trained separately and reporting directly to the emperor, resented political controls that periodically reduced their budgets. Liberal politicians expanded voting rights to all adult males, but there was no full agreement on the appropriate political structure. The military, suspicious of growing consumerism in Japan, regarded itself as a guardian of tradition. It also exercised considerable independence in diplomacy, particularly concerning growing Japanese involvement in China.

New Authoritarianism: The Rise of Fascism

Explicit hostility to liberal and democratic political systems emerged first on the fringes of western Europe. In 1919 a former socialist and (very briefly) former soldier, **Benito Mussolini,** formed the *fascio di combattimento,* or "union for struggle," in Italy. Italian fascists vaguely advocated a corporate state that would replace both capitalism and socialism with a new national unity. They pointed to the need for an aggressive, nationalistic foreign policy. Above all, fascists worked to seize power by any means and to build a strong state under a strong leader. They violently attacked rival political groups, seeking to promote an atmosphere of chaos.

Fascism had its roots in the late 19th century, with groups disenchanted with liberal, parliamentary systems and with social conflict. Various intellectuals, in many countries, began to urge the need for new, authoritarian leadership and devotion to nationalist values over capitalist profit-seeking and socialist class struggle.

Conditions in postwar Italy gave these impulses a huge boost. Nationalists resented the fact that Italy had gained so little new territory in World War I. Veterans often felt abandoned by civilian society, and some thirsted for new action. Labor unrest increased, which convinced some conservatives that new measures were essential against ineffective liberal leadership. The Italian parliament seemed incapable of decisive measures, as political factions jockeyed for personal advantage. In these conditions Mussolini, fascism's leading exponent, could make his mark even with a minority of direct supporters.

Amid growing political divisions and a rising threat from the working-class left, in 1922 the Italian king called on Mussolini to form a new government. Though the fascists had only limited popular support, they seemed the only hope to stem left-wing agitation and parliamentary ineptitude. Once in power, Mussolini eliminated most opposition (Figure 29.5), suspending elections outright in 1926, while seeking greater state direction of the economy and issuing strident propaganda about the glories of military conquest. This first fascist regime moved with some caution, fitting into the briefly hopeful negotiations among European states in the 1920s, but the principles it espoused suggested how far European politics had been unseated from the widespread prewar agreements on parliamentary rule.

The New Nations of East Central Europe

Authoritarian regimes also took root in east central Europe during the 1920s, though they were not explicitly fascist. New nations in this region began with Western-style parliaments, but most could not maintain them amid economic difficulties.

Most of the new nations, from the Baltic states to Yugoslavia, were consumed by nationalist excitement at independence but also harbored intense grievances about territories they had not acquired. Hence there were bitter rivalries among the small eastern European states, which weakened them both diplomatically and economically (Map 29.2). Authoritarianism arrived either through a dictator (as in Poland) or by a monarch's seizure of new power (as in Yugoslavia, the new nation expanded from Serbia). This political pattern resulted from more underlying social tensions. Most eastern European countries remained primarily agricultural, heavily dependent on sales to western Europe. They were hard hit by the collapse of agricultural prices in the 1920s and then further

Map 29.1 From Dominions to Nationhood: Formation of Canada, Australia, and New Zealand   The new states of key settler societies were an important development.

Figure 29.5 One of the most ominous acts of Mussolini's fascist regime was the burning of books and other literature deemed "subversive."

Map 29.2 Eastern Europe and the Soviet Union, 1919–1939   The Soviet Union regained some territory ceded to Germany in the 1918 peace treaty, but it lost ground to a number of east European states.

damaged by the Depression. Furthermore, most countries refused to undertake serious land reform, despite widely professed intentions. Aristocratic estate owners thus sought desperately to repress peasant movements, which brought them to support authoritarian regimes, which often had vaguely fascist trappings. Peasant land hunger and continued problems of poverty and illiteracy were simply not addressed in most cases.

A Balance Sheet

syndicalism Economic and political system based on the organization of labor; imported in Latin America from European political movements; militant force in Latin American politics.

Mexican Revolution Fought over a period of almost ten years from 1910; resulted in ouster of Porfirio Díaz from power; opposition forces led by Pancho Villa and Emiliano Zapata.

Changes in Europe, other Western societies, and Japan during the 1920s were complex. Democratic and parliamentary political forms took further root in Germany and in places like Canada and Japan. Significant industrial and social change combined with signs of creativity in culture, in sciences and the arts. On the other hand, challenges to democracy arose in Italy and in much of east central Europe, while Japanese politics became less stable. The United States tried to isolate itself from world politics. Events would soon prove that the economic foundations of the major industrial powers were shaky as well. Even in the 1920s the economy of western Europe was newly challenged by the greater vigor of the United States and Japan.

Revolution: The First Waves

Major revolutions broke out in Mexico, Russia, and China before or during World War I. All three revolutions challenged Western dominance to some degree, and all reflected concerns about world economic relationships.

A variety of social tensions affected Latin America early in the 20th century. Many countries continued to depend on a key export crop, like coffee. These crops provided profits to owners while Western demand was high, but they also depended on low wages for workers. During World War I,

European manufactured goods were diverted. Several Latin American countries expanded their industrial output, in a process called import substitution. This mainly involved light industry (Figure 29.6), and the initiative receded after the war, leading to further poverty.

These developments did stimulate some political change. In Argentina a new 1912 election law gave voice to the middle classes. Labor agitation increased, some of it under the banners of **syndicalism,** which sought to use a general strike to seize power. Major strikes occurred from 1907 onward, usually brutally repressed by the state. An atmosphere of class conflict intensified. Only in Mexico, however, was there outright revolution.

Mexico's Upheaval

Several cataclysmic events launched Latin America into the 20th century and set in motion trends that would determine much of the region's subsequent history. The first of these events was the 10-year civil war and political upheaval of the **Mexican Revolution,** caused primarily by internal forces. Eventually, the Mexican Revolution was also influenced by another major event: the outbreak of World War I. Although most Latin American nations avoided direct participation in the Great War, as World War I was called at the time, the disruption of traditional markets for Latin American exports and the elimination of European sources of goods caused a realignment of the economies of several nations in the region. They were forced to rely on themselves. A spurt of manufacturing continued the process begun after 1870, and some small steps were taken to overcome the traditional dependence on outside supply. Finally, at the end of World War I, the United States emerged as the dominant foreign power in the region, replacing Great Britain in both economic and political terms. That position created a reality that Latin Americans could not ignore and that greatly influenced the economic and political options in the region.

Figure 29.6 The growing labor force that resulted from Latin American industrialization began to change the nature of urban life and politics. Here, women in Orizaba, Mexico, are making sacks for coffee.

The regime of **Porfirio Díaz** had been in power since 1876 and seemed unshakable. During the Díaz dictatorship, tremendous economic changes had been made, and foreign concessions in mining, railroads, and other sectors of the economy had created a sense of prosperity among the Mexican elite. However, this progress had been bought at considerable expense. Foreigners controlled large sectors of the economy. The hacienda system of extensive landholdings by a small elite dominated certain regions of the country. The political system was corrupt, and any complaint was stifled. The government took repressive measures against workers, peasants, and American Indians who opposed the loss of their lands or the unbearable working conditions. Political opponents often were imprisoned or forced into exile. In short, Díaz ruled with an iron fist through an effective political machine.

Mexico nevertheless faced major issues. The economy, increasingly dependent on exports, lacked adequate investment funds. U.S. concerns owned 20 percent of the nation's territory. Growing nationalist resentment was similar to other reactions to widespread foreign control—a major spur to the revolutionary wave in general.

By 1910, moreover, Díaz was 80 years old, newly vulnerable to political opposition. **Francisco Madero,** a wealthy son of an elite family, proposed to run against Díaz. Madero believed that some moderate democratic political reforms would relieve social tensions and allow the government to continue its economic development with a minimum of popular unrest. This was more than Díaz could stand. Madero was arrested, a rigged election put Díaz back in power, and things returned to normal. When Madero was released from prison, he called for a revolt.

A general rebellion developed. In the north, small farmers, railroaders, and cowboys coalesced under the colorful former bandit and able commander **Pancho Villa.** In the southern province of Morelos, an area of old conflicts between American Indian communities and large sugar estates, a peasant-based guerrilla movement began under **Emiliano Zapata,** whose goal of land reform was expressed in his motto "Tierra y Libertad" (Land and Liberty). Díaz was driven from power by this

Díaz, Porfirio   One of Juárez's generals; elected president of Mexico in 1876; dominated Mexican politics for 35 years; imposed strong central government.

Madero, Francisco   (1873–1913) Moderate democratic reformer in Mexico; proposed moderate reforms in 1910; arrested by Porfirio Díaz; initiated revolution against Díaz when released from prison; temporarily gained power, but removed and assassinated in 1913.

Villa, Pancho   (1878–1923) Mexican revolutionary and military commander in northern Mexico during the Mexican Revolution; succeeded along with Emiliano Zapata in removing Díaz from power in 1911; also participated in campaigns that removed Madero and Huerta.

Zapata, Emiliano   Mexican revolutionary and military commander of peasant guerrilla movement after 1910 centered in Morelos; succeeded along with Pancho Villa in removing Díaz from power; also participated in campaigns that removed Madero and Huerta; demanded sweeping land reform.

 Plan de Ayala

coalition of forces, but it soon became apparent that Madero's moderate programs would not resolve Mexico's continuing social problems. Zapata rose in revolt, demanding a sweeping land reform, and Madero steadily lost control of his subordinates. In 1913, with at least the tacit agreement of the U.S. ambassador in Mexico, who wanted to forestall revolutionary changes, a military coup removed Madero from government and he was then assassinated.

General **Victoriano Huerta** sought to impose a Díaz-type dictatorship supported by the large landowners, the army, and the foreign companies, but the tide of revolution could not be stopped so easily. Villa and Zapata rose again against the government and were joined by other middle-class political opponents of Huerta's illegal rule. By 1914 Huerta was forced from power, but the victorious leaders now began to fight over the nature of the new regime and the mantle of leadership. An extended period of warfare followed, and the tides of battle shifted constantly. The railroad lines built under Díaz now moved large numbers of troops, including *soldaderas,* women who sometimes shouldered arms. Matters were also complicated by clumsy U.S. intervention, aimed at bringing order to the border regions, and by diplomatic maneuverings after the outbreak of World War I in Europe.

Villa and Zapata remained in control in their home territories, but they could not wrest the government from the control of the more moderate political leaders in Mexico City. **Alvaro Obregón,** an able general who had learned the new tactics of machine guns and trenches from the war raging in Europe and had beaten Villa's cavalry in a series of bloody battles in 1915, emerged as leader of the government.

By 1920 the civil war had ended and Mexico began to consolidate the changes that had taken place in the previous confused and bloody decade. Obregón was elected president in that year. He was followed by a series of presidents from the new "revolutionary elite" who tried to consolidate the new regime. There was much to be done. The revolution had devastated the country; 1.5 million people had died, major industries were destroyed, and ranching and farming were disrupted. But there was great hope because the revolution also promised (although it did not always deliver) real changes.

What were some of these changes? The new **Mexican Constitution of 1917** promised land reform, limited the foreign ownership of key resources, and guaranteed the rights of workers. It also placed restrictions on clerical education and church ownership of property, and promised educational reforms. The workers who had been mobilized were organized in a national confederation and were given representation in the government. The promised land reforms were slow in coming, though later, under President Lázaro Cárdenas (1934–1940), more than 40 million acres were distributed, most of it in the form of *ejidos* (eh-HEE-dos), or communal holdings. The government launched an extensive program of primary and especially rural education.

Culture and Politics in Postrevolutionary Mexico

Nationalism and *indigenism,* or the concern for the indigenous peoples and their contribution to Mexican culture, lay beneath many reforms. Having failed to integrate the American Indians into national life for a century, Mexico now attempted to "Indianize" the nation through secular schools that emphasized nationalism and a vision of the Mexican past that glorified its American Indian heritage and denounced Western capitalism. Artists such as **Diego Rivera** and **José Clemente Orozco** recaptured that past and outlined a social program for the future in stunning murals on public buildings designed to inform, convince, and entertain at the same time. The Mexican muralist movement had a wide impact on artists throughout Latin America even though, as Orozco himself stated, it sometimes created simple solutions and strange utopias by mixing a romantic image of the American Indian past with Christian symbols and communist ideology.

Novelists, such as Mariano Azuela, found in the revolution a focus for the examination of Mexican reality. Popular culture celebrated the heroes and events of the revolution in scores of ballads (*corridos*) that were sung to celebrate and inform. In literature, music, and the arts, the revolution and its themes provided a stimulus to a tremendous burst of creativity, as in the following lines of poetry:

> Gabino Barrera rose in the mountains
> his cause was noble,
> protect the poor and give them the land.
> Remember the night he was murdered

Huerta, Victoriano   Attempted to reestablish centralized dictatorship in Mexico following the removal of Madero in 1913; forced from power in 1914 by Villa and Zapata.

Obregón, Alvaro   (1880–1928) Emerged as leader of the Mexican government in 1915; elected president in 1920.

Mexican Constitution of 1917   Promised land reform, limited foreign ownership of key resources, guaranteed the rights of workers, and placed restrictions on clerical education; marked formal end of Mexican Revolution.

Rivera, Diego   (1886–1957) Mexican artist of the period after the Mexican Revolution; famous for murals painted on walls of public buildings; mixed romantic images of the Indian past with Christian symbols and Marxist ideology.

Orozco, José Clemente   (1883–1949) Mexican muralist of the period after the Mexican Revolution; like Rivera's, his work featured romantic images of the Indian past with Christian symbols and Marxist ideology.

three leagues from Tlapehuala;
22 shots rang out
leaving him time for nothing.
Gabino Barrera and his loyal steed
fell in the hail of rounds,
the face of this man of the Revolution
finally rested, his lips pressed to the ground.

The gains of the revolution were not made without opposition. Although the revolution preceded the Russian Revolution of 1917 and had no single ideological model, many of the ideas of Marxist socialism were held by leading Mexican intellectuals and a few politicians. The secularization of society and especially education met strong opposition from the Catholic Church and the clergy, especially in states where socialist rhetoric and anticlericalism were extreme. In the 1920s, a conservative peasant movement backed by the church erupted in central Mexico. These **Cristeros,** backed by conservative politicians, fought to stop the slide toward secularization. The fighting lasted for years until a compromise was reached.

Cristeros Conservative peasant movement in Mexico during the 1920s; most active in central Mexico; attempted to halt slide toward secularism; movement resulted in armed violence.

The United States intervened diplomatically and militarily during the revolution, motivated by a desire for order, fear of German influence on the new government, and economic interests. An incident provoked a short-lived U.S. seizure of Veracruz in 1914, and when Pancho Villa's forces raided across the border, the United States sent an expeditionary force into Mexico to catch him. The mission failed. For the most part, however, the war in Europe dominated U.S. foreign policy efforts until 1918. The United States was suspicious of the new government, and a serious conflict arose when U.S.-owned oil companies ran into problems with workers.

As in any revolution, the question of continuity arose when the fighting ended. The revolutionary leadership hoped to institutionalize the new regime by creating a one-party system. This organization, called the Party of the Institutionalized Revolution (PRI), developed slowly during the 1920s and 1930s into a dominant force in Mexican politics. It incorporated labor, peasant, military, and middle-class sectors and proved flexible enough to incorporate new interest groups as they developed. Although Mexico became a multiparty democracy in theory, in reality the PRI controlled politics and, by accommodation and sometimes repression, maintained its hold on national political life. Some presidents governed much like the strongmen in the 19th century had done, but the party structure and the need to incorporate various interests within the government coalition limited the worst aspects of caudillo, or personalist, rule. The presidents were strong, but the policy of limiting the presidency to one six-year term ensured some change in leadership. The question of whether a revolution could be institutionalized remained in debate. By the end of the 20th century, many Mexicans believed that little remained of the principles and programs of the revolutionaries of 1910.

Revolution in Russia: Liberalism to Communism

In March 1917, strikes and food riots broke out in Russia's capital, St. Petersburg. The outbursts were spurred by wartime misery, including painful food shortages. They also and more basically protested the conditions of early industrialization set against incomplete rural reform and an unresponsive political system. And they quickly assumed revolutionary proportions. The rioters called not just for more food and work but for a new political regime as well. The tsar's forces struck back brutally but unsuccessfully. A council of workers, called a soviet, took over the city government and arrested the tsar's ministers. Unable to rely on his own soldiers, the tsar abdicated, thus ending the long period of imperial rule.

For eight months a liberal provisional government struggled to rule the country. Russia seemed thus to launch its revolution on a basis similar to France in 1789, where a liberal period set change in motion. Like Western liberals, Russian revolutionary leaders, such as **Alexander Kerensky,** were eager to see genuine parliamentary rule, religious and other freedoms, and a host of political and legal changes. But liberalism was not deeply rooted in Russia, if only because of the small middle class, so the analogies with the first phase of the French revolution cannot be pressed too far. Furthermore, Russia's revolution took place in much more adverse circumstances, given the pressures of participation in the First World War. The initial liberal leaders were eager to maintain

Kerensky, Alexander (1881–1970) Liberal revolutionary leader during the early stages of the Russian Revolution of 1917; sought development of parliamentary rule, religious freedom.

the war effort, which linked them with democratic France and Britain. Yet the nation was desperately war weary, and prolongation drastically worsened economic conditions while public morale plummeted. Liberal leaders also held back from the massive land reforms expected by the peasantry, for in good middle-class fashion they respected existing property arrangements and did not wish to rush into social change before a legitimate new political structure could be established. Hence serious popular unrest continued, and in November (October, by the Russian calendar) a second revolution took place, which expelled liberal leadership and soon brought to power the radical, Bolshevik wing of the Social Democratic party, soon renamed the Communist party, and Lenin, their dynamic chief (Figure 29.7).

The revolution was a godsend to Lenin. This devoted revolutionary had long been writing of Russia's readiness for a communist revolt because of the power of international capitalism and its creation of a massive proletariat, even in a society that had not directly passed through middle-class rule. Lenin quickly gained a strong position among the urban workers' councils in the major cities. This corresponded to his deeply rooted belief that revolution should come not from literal mass action but from tightly organized cells whose leaders espoused a coherent plan of action.

Once the liberals were toppled, Lenin and the Bolsheviks faced several immediate problems. One, Russia's continued involvement in World War I, they handled by signing a humiliating peace treaty with Germany and giving up huge sections of western Russia in return for an end of hostilities. This treaty was soon nullified by Germany's defeat at the hands of the Western allies, but Russia was ignored at the Versailles peace conference—treated as a pariah by the fearful Western powers. Much former territory was converted into new nation-states. A revived Poland built heavily on land Russia had controlled for more than a century, and new, small Baltic states cut into even earlier acquisitions. Still, although Russia's deep grievances against the Versailles treaty would later help motivate renewed expansionism, the early end to the war was vital to Lenin's consolidation of power.

Although Lenin and the Bolsheviks had gained a majority role in the leading urban soviets, they were not the most popular revolutionary party, and this situation constituted the second problem faced at the end of 1917. The November seizure of power had led to the creation of the Council of People's Commissars, drawn from soviets across the nation and headed by Lenin, to govern the state. But a parliamentary election had already been called, and this produced a clear majority for the Social Revolutionary party, which emphasized peasant support and rural reform. Lenin, how-

Figure 29.7 Moscow workers guard the Bolshevik headquarters during the Russian Revolution of 1917.

ever, shut down the parliament, replacing it with a Bolshevik-dominated Congress of Soviets. He pressed the Social Revolutionaries to disband, arguing that "the people voted for a party which no longer existed." Russia was thus to have no Western-style, multiparty system but rather a Bolshevik monopoly in the name of the true people's will. Indeed, Communist party control of the government apparatus persisted from this point to 1989, a record for continuity much different from the fate of revolutionary groups earlier in the Western past.

Russia's revolution produced a backlash that revolutionaries in other eras would have recognized quite easily: foreign hostility and, even more important, domestic resistance. The world's leading nations—aside from Germany, now briefly irrelevant—were appalled at the communist success, which threatened principles of property and freedom they cherished deeply. As settled regimes, they also disliked the unexpected, and some were directly injured by Russia's renunciation of its heavy foreign debts. The result was an attempt at intervention, recalling the attacks on France in 1792. Britain, France, the United States, and Japan all sent troops. But this intervention, although it heightened Russian suspicion of outsiders, did relatively little damage. The Western powers, exhausted by World War I, pulled out quickly, and even Japan, though interested in lingering in Asiatic Russia, stepped back fairly soon.

Lenin Calls for Electrification of All Russia

The internal civil war, which foreign troops slightly abetted, was a more serious matter, as it raged from 1918 to 1921. Tsarist generals, religiously faithful peasants, and many minority nationalities made common cause against the communist regime. Their efforts were aided by continuing economic distress, the normal result of revolutionary disarray, but also heightened by earlier communist measures. Lenin had quickly decreed a redistribution of land to the peasantry and also launched a nationalization, or state takeover, of basic industry. Many already landed peasants resented the loss of property and incentive, and in reaction they lowered food production and the goods sent to markets. Industrial nationalization somewhat similarly disrupted manufacturing. Famine and unemployment created more economic hardship than the war had generated, which added fuel to the civil war fires. Even workers revolted in several cities, threatening the new regime's most obvious social base as well as its ideological mainstay.

Stabilization of Russia's Communist Regime

Order was restored after the revolution on several key foundations. First, the construction of the powerful new army under the leadership of Leon Trotsky recruited able generals and masses of loyal conscripts. This **Red Army** was an early beneficiary of two ongoing sources of strength for communist Russia: a willingness to use people of humble background but great ability who could rise to great heights under the new order but who had been doomed to immobility under the old system, and an ability to inspire mass loyalty in the name of an end to previous injustice and a promise of a brighter future. Next, economic disarray was reduced in 1921 when Lenin issued his **New Economic Policy,** which promised considerable freedom of action for small business owners and peasant landowners. The state continued to set basic economic policies, but its efforts were now combined with individual initiative. Under this temporary policy, food production began to recover, and the regime gained time to prepare the more durable structures of the communist system.

Red Army   Military organization constructed under leadership of Leon Trotsky, Bolshevik follower of Lenin; made use of people of humble background.

New Economic Policy   Initiated by Lenin in 1921; state continued to set basic economic policies, but efforts were now combined with individual initiative; policy allowed food production to recover.

By 1923 the Bolshevik revolution was an accomplished fact. There was a new capital: Moscow. And a new constitution set up a federal system of socialist republics. This system recognized the multinational character of the nation, which was called the **Union of Soviet Socialist Republics.** The dominance of ethnic Russians was preserved in the central state apparatus, however, and certain groups, notably Jews, were given no distinct representation. Since the separate republics were firmly controlled by the national Communist party and since basic decisions were as firmly centralized, the impact of the new nationalities policy was somewhat mixed; yet it was also true that direct nationalities' protests declined notably from the 1920s until the late 1980s.

Union of Soviet Socialist Republics   Federal system of socialist republics established in 1923 in various ethnic regions of Russia; firmly controlled by Communist party; diminished nationalities protest under Bolsheviks; dissolved 1991.

The apparatus of the central state was another mixture of appearance and reality. The **Supreme Soviet** had many of the trappings of a parliament and was elected by universal suffrage. But competition in elections was normally prohibited, which meant that the Communist party easily controlled the body, which served mainly to ratify decisions taken by the party's central executive. Parallel systems of central bureaucracy and party bureaucracy further confirmed the Communists' monopoly on power and the ability to control major decisions from the center. The

Supreme Soviet   Parliament of Union of Soviet Socialist Republics; elected by universal suffrage; actually controlled by Communist party; served to ratify party decisions.

A Century of Revolutions

Not since the late 18th and early 19th centuries had there been a succession of revolutions like those in the early decades of the 20th century. In contrast to the revolutionary movements of the earlier period, however, the early 20th-century upheavals were just the first waves of a revolutionary tide that struck with renewed fury after 1945. A number of factors account for the successive surges of revolution in the 20th century. Rural discontent was crucial, for peasants provided vital contributions to 20th-century revolutions everywhere they occurred. Peasants were newly spurred by pressures of population growth, combined with resentment against big landowners. Modern state forms tended to increase taxes on the peasantry, while making traditional protests, like banditry, more difficult.

Equally fundamentally, the rise of revolutionary movements was fed by the underlying disruptions caused by the spread of the Industrial Revolution and the Western-centered, global market system. Handicraft producers thrown out of work by an influx of machine-manufactured goods, and peasants, such as those in central Mexico who lost their land to moneylenders, frequently rallied to calls to riot and, at times, ultimately became caught up in revolutionary currents. In the colonies, unemployed Western-educated African and Asian secondary school and college graduates became deeply committed to struggles for independence that promised them dignity and decent jobs. Urban laborers, enraged by the appalling working and living conditions that were characteristic of the early stages of industrialization in countries such as Russia and China, provided key support for revolutionary parties in many countries.

Although global economic slumps did much to fire the revolutionaries' longings, world wars proved even more fertile seedbeds of revolution. Returning soldiers and neglected veterans provided the shock troops for leftist revolutionaries and fascist pretenders alike. Defeated states witnessed the rapid erosion of their power to suppress internal enemies and floundered as their armies refused to defend them or joined movements dedicated to their overthrow. In this regard, the great increase in global interconnectedness in the 20th century was critical. The economic competition and military rivalries of the industrial powers drew them into unwanted wars that they could not sustain without raw materials and manpower drawn from their colonies and other neutral states.

Another key factor that contributed to the sharp rise in the incidence of revolutions in the 20th century was the underlying intellectual climate. Notions of progress and a belief in the perfectibility of human society, which were widely held in the 19th century, deeply influenced such communist theorists as Marx, Lenin, Mao Zedong, and Ho Chi Minh. These and other revolutionary ideologues sought, in part, to overthrow existing regimes that they viewed as exploitive and oppressive. But they were also deeply committed to building radically new societies that would bring justice and a decent livelihood to previously downtrodden social groups, especially the working classes, peasantry, and urban poor. Visions of the good life in peasant communes or workers' utopias were a powerful driving force for revolutionary currents throughout the century from Mexico to China. One measure of their influence is the extent to which highly competitive capitalist societies developed social welfare programs to curb social discontent that could spiral into active protest, and perhaps even revolutionary challenges to the existing social order.

A final common ingredient of 20th-century revolutions was the need to come to terms with Western influence and often to reassert greater national autonomy. Mexico, Russia, and China all sought to reduce Western economic control and cultural influence, seeking alternative models. Many revolutions involved active anti-Western sentiment and attacks on Western investments. In Russia, Stalinism went on the attack against "decadent" Western cultural influences.

> "Visions of the good life in peasant communes or workers' utopias were a powerful driving force for revolutionary currents throughout the century from Mexico to China."

QUESTIONS What internal and external forces weakened the governments of Mexico and China in the opening decades of the 20th century and unleashed the forces of revolution? What key social groups were behind the revolutions in Mexico, China, and Russia, and why were they so important in each case? What similarities and differences can you identify among these three early revolutions in the 20th century?

Soviet political system was elaborated over time. A new constitution in the 1930s spoke glowingly of human rights. In fact, the Communists had quickly reestablished an authoritarian system, making it more efficient than its tsarist predecessor had been, complete with updated versions of political police to ensure loyalty.

Soviet Experimentation

The mid-1920s constituted a lively, experimental period in Soviet history, partly because of the jockeying for power at the top of the power pyramid. Despite the absence of Western-style political competition, a host of new groups found a voice. The Communist party, though not eager to re-

Figure 29.8 Russian children help carry the propaganda for Stalin's campaign for collectivization of agriculture. The banner reads, "Everybody to the collective farms!" These happy faces belie the tragedy resulting from the collectivization program, in which millions fell victim to slaughter or starvation.

cruit too many members lest it lose its tight organization and elite status, encouraged all sorts of subsidiary organizations. Youth movements, women's groups, and particularly organizations of workers all actively debated problems in their social environment and directions for future planning. Workers were able to influence management practices; women's leaders helped carve legal equality and new educational and work opportunities for their constituents.

One key to the creative mood of these years was the rapid spread of education promoted by the government, as well as educational and propaganda activities sponsored by various adult groups. Literacy gained ground quickly. The new educational system was also bent on reshaping popular culture away from older peasant traditions and, above all, religion, and toward beliefs in Communist political analysis and science. Access to new information, new modes of inquiry, and new values encouraged controversy.

The Soviet regime grappled with other key definitional issues in the 1920s. Rivalries among leaders at the top had to be sorted out. Lenin became ill and then died in 1924, creating an unexpected leadership gap. (St. Petersburg was renamed Leningrad in his honor, a name it retained until 1991.) A number of key lieutenants jostled for power, including the Red Army's flamboyant Trotsky and a Communist party stalwart of worker origins who had taken the name **Stalin,** meaning *steel*. After a few years of jockeying, Joseph Stalin emerged as undisputed leader of the Soviet state, his victory a triumph also for party control over other branches of government.

Stalin's accession was more than a personal bureaucratic issue, however. Stalin represented a strongly nationalist version of communism, in contrast to the more ideological and international visions of many of his rivals. At the revolution's outset Lenin had believed that the Russian rising would be merely a prelude to a sweeping communist upheaval throughout the Western industrial world. Many revolutionary leaders actively encouraged communist parties in the West and set up a **Comintern,** or Communist International office, to guide this process. But revolution did not spill over, despite a few brief risings in Hungary and Germany right after World War I. Under Stalin, the revolutionary leadership, although still committed in theory to an international movement, pulled back to concentrate on Russian developments—building "socialism in one country," as Stalin put it. Stalin in many ways represented the anti-Western strain in Russian tradition, though in new guise.

Stalin, Joseph Successor to Lenin as head of the U.S.S.R.; strongly nationalist view of communism; represented anti-Western strain of Russian tradition; crushed opposition to his rule; established series of five-year plans to replace New Economic Policy; fostered agricultural collectivization; led U.S.S.R. through World War II; furthered cold war with western Europe and the United States; died in 1953.

 Lenin, 1920, vs. Stalin, 1931
CASE STUDY

Comintern International office of communism under U.S.S.R. dominance established to encourage the formation of Communist parties in Europe and elsewhere.

collectivization Creation of large, state-run farms rather than individual holdings; allowed more efficient control over peasants, though often lowered food production; part of Stalin's economic and political planning; often adopted in other communist regimes.

Stalin also instituted a new level of police repression that ultimately led to the deaths of millions of Russian dissidents, from peasants to intellectuals. Rival leaders were killed or expelled, rival visions of the revolution downplayed. Stalin would also accelerate industrial development while attacking peasant land ownership with a new **collectivization** program (Figure 29.8).

The Russian Revolution was one of the most successful risings in human history, at least for several decades. Building on widespread if diverse popular discontent and a firm belief in centralized leadership, the Bolsheviks beat back powerful odds to create a new, though not totally unprecedented, political regime. They used features of the tsarist system but managed to propel a wholly new leadership group to power not only at the top but also at all levels of the bureaucracy and army. The tsar and his hated ministers were gone, mostly executed, but so was the overweening aristocratic class that had loomed so large in Russian history for centuries.

Toward Revolution in China

The abdication of Puyi, the Manchu boy-emperor in 1912, marked the end of a century-long losing struggle on the part of the Qing dynasty to protect Chinese civilization from foreign invaders and revolutionary threats from within, such as the massive Taiping movement (see Chapter 26). The fall of the Qing opened the way for an extended struggle over which leader or movement would be able to capture the mandate to rule the ancient society that had for millennia ordered the lives of at least one-fifth of humankind. Contenders included regional warlords; the loose alliance of students, middle-class politicians and secret societies, many of them attracted to a Western political model; and soon, Japanese intruders and a new communist movements as well. Internal divisions and foreign influences paved the way for the ultimate victory of the Chinese Communist party under Mao Zedong.

After the fall of the Qing dynasty, the best-positioned of the contenders for power were regionally based military commanders or warlords, who would dominate Chinese politics for the next three decades. Many of the warlords combined in cliques or alliances to protect their own territories and to crush neighbors and annex their lands. The most powerful of these cliques, centered in north China, was headed by the unscrupulous **Yuan Shikai** (yoo-ahn shur-geye), who hoped to seize the vacated Manchu throne and found a new dynasty. By virtue of their wealth, the merchants and bankers of coastal cities like Shanghai and Canton made up a second power center in post-Manchu China. Their involvement in politics resulted from their willingness to bankroll both favored warlords and Western-educated, middle-class politicians like Sun Yatsen.

Yuan Shikai [yoo-ahn shur-geye] Warlord in northern China after fall of Qing dynasty; hoped to seize imperial throne; president of China after 1912; resigned in the face of Japanese invasion in 1916.

Sometimes supportive of the urban civilian politicians and sometimes wary of them, university students and their teachers, as well as independent intellectuals, provided yet another factor in the complex post-Qing political equation. Though the intellectuals and students played critical roles in shaping new ideologies to rebuild Chinese civilization, they were virtually defenseless in a situation in which force was essential to those who hoped to exert political influence. Deeply divided, but very strong in some regions, secret societies represented another contender for power. Like many in the military, members of these societies envisioned the restoration of monarchical rule, but under a Chinese dynasty, not a foreign one. As if the situation were not confused enough, it was further complicated by the continuing intervention of the Western powers, eager to profit from China's divisions and weakness. Their inroads, however, were increasingly overshadowed by the entry into the contest for the control of China by the newest imperialist power, Japan. From the mid-1890s, when the Japanese had humiliated their much larger neighbor by easily defeating it in war, until 1945, when Japan's surrender ended World War II, the Japanese were a major factor in the long and bloody contest for mastery of China.

China's May Fourth Movement and the Rise of the Marxist Alternative

Sun Yatsen headed the Revolutionary Alliance, a loose coalition of anti-Qing political groups that had spearheaded the 1911 revolt. After the Qing were toppled, Sun claimed that he and the parties of the alliance were the rightful claimants to the mandate to rule all of China. But he could do little to assert civilian control in the face of warlord opposition. The Revolutionary Alliance had little power and virtually no popular support outside the urban trading centers of the coastal areas in central and south China. Even in these areas, they were at the mercy of the local warlords. The alliance formally elected Sun president at the end of 1911, set up a parliament modeled after those in Europe, and chose cabinets with great fanfare. But their decisions had little effect on warlord-dominated China.

Sun Yatsen conceded this reality when he resigned the acting presidency in favor of the northern warlord Yuan Shikai in 1912. As the most powerful of the northern clique of generals, Yuan appeared to have the best chance to unify China under a single government. He at first feigned sympathy for the democratic aims of the alliance leaders but soon revealed his true intentions. He took foreign loans to build up his military forces and buy out most of the bureaucrats in the capital at Beijing. When Sun and other leaders of the Revolutionary Alliance called for a second revolution to oust Yuan in the years after 1912, he made full use of his military power and more underhanded methods, such as assassinations, to put down their opposition. By 1915 it appeared that Yuan was well on his way to realizing his ambition of becoming China's next emperor. His schemes were foiled, however, by the continuing rivalry of other warlords, republican nationalists like Sun, and the growing influence of Japan in China. The latter increased dramatically as a result of World War I.

As England's ally according to terms of a 1902 treaty, Japan immediately entered the war on the side of the Entente, or Western allied powers. Moving much too quickly for the comfort of the British and the other Western powers, the Japanese seized German-held islands in the Pacific and occupied the Germans' concessionary areas in China. With all the great powers except the United States embroiled in war, the Japanese sought to establish a dominant hold over their giant neighbor. In early 1915, they presented Yuan's government with Twenty-One Demands, which, if accepted, would have reduced China to the status of a dependant protectorate. Though Sun and the Revolutionary Alliance lost much support by refusing to repudiate the Japanese demands, Yuan was no more decisive. He neither accepted nor rejected the demands but concentrated his energies on an effort to trump up popular enthusiasm for his accession to the throne. Disgusted by Yuan's weakness and ambition, one of his warlord rivals plotted his overthrow. Hostility to the Japanese won Yuan's rival widespread support, and in 1916, Yuan was forced to resign the presidency. His fall was the signal for a free-for-all power struggle between the remaining warlords for control of China.

As one of the victorious allies of World War I, Japan managed to solidify its hold on northern China by winning control of the former German concessions in the peace negotiations at Versailles in 1919. But the Chinese had also allied themselves to the Entente powers during the war. Enraged by what they viewed as a betrayal by the Entente powers, students and nationalist politicians organized mass demonstrations in numerous Chinese cities on May 4, 1919. The demonstrations began a prolonged period of protest against Japanese inroads. This protest soon expanded from marches and petitions to include strikes and mass boycotts of Japanese goods.

The fourth of May, 1919, the day when the resistance began, gave its name to a movement in which intellectuals and students played a leading role. Initially at least, the **May Fourth movement** was aimed at transforming China into a liberal democracy. Its program was enunciated in numerous speeches, pamphlets, novels, and newspaper articles. Confucianism was ridiculed and rejected in favor of a wholehearted acceptance of all that the Western democracies had to offer. Noted Western thinkers, such as Bertrand Russell and John Dewey, toured China, praising democracy and basking in the cheers of enthusiastic Chinese audiences. Chinese thinkers called for the liberation of women (including the abolition of footbinding), the simplification of the Chinese script in order to promote mass literacy, and the promotion of Western-style individualism. Many of these themes are captured in the literature of the period. In the novel *Family* by Ba Jin, for example, a younger brother audaciously informs his elder sibling that he will not accept the marriage partner the family has arranged for him. He clearly sees his refusal as part of a more general revolt of the youth of China against the ancient Confucian social code.

> Big Brother, I'm doing what no one in our family has ever dared do before—I'm running out on an arranged marriage. No one cares about my fate, so I've decided to walk my own road alone. I'm determined to struggle against the old forces to the end. Unless you cancel the match, I'll never come back. I'll die first.

However enthusiastically the program of the May Fourth movement was adopted by the urban youth of China, it was soon clear that mere emulation of the liberal democracies of the West

May Fourth movement Resistance to Japanese encroachments in China began on this date in 1919; spawned movement of intellectuals aimed at transforming China into a liberal democracy; rejected Confucianism.

could not provide effective solutions to China's prodigious problems. Civil liberties and democratic elections were meaningless in a China that was ruled by warlords. Gradualist solutions and parliamentary debates were folly in a nation where the great mass of the peasantry was destitute, much of them malnourished or dying of starvation. It soon became clear to many Chinese intellectuals and students, as well as to some of the nationalist politicians, that more radical solutions were needed. In the 1920s, this conviction gave rise to the communist left within the Chinese nationalist movement.

The Bolshevik victory and the programs launched to rebuild Russia prompted Chinese intellectuals to give serious attention to the works of Marx and other socialist thinkers and the potential they offered for the regeneration of China. But the careful study of the writings of Marx, Engels, Lenin, and Trotsky in the wake of the Russian Revolution also impressed a number of Chinese intellectuals with the necessity for major alterations in Marxist ideology if it was going to be of any relevance to China or other peasant societies. Marx, after all, had focused on advanced industrial societies and had regarded peasants as conservative or even reactionary. Taken literally, Marxism offered discouraging prospects for revolution in China.

The most influential of the thinkers who called for a reworking of Marxist ideology to fit China's situation was **Li Dazhao** (lee duh-JOH). Li was from peasant origins, but he had excelled in school and eventually become a college teacher. He headed the Marxist study circle that developed after the 1919 upheavals at the University of Beijing. His interpretation of Marxist philosophy placed heavy emphasis on its capacity for promoting renewal and its ability to harness the energy and vitality of a nation's youth. In contrast to Lenin, Li saw the peasants, rather than the urban workers, as the vanguard of revolutionary change. He justified this shift from the orthodox Marxist emphasis on the working classes, which made up only a tiny fraction of China's population at the time, by characterizing the whole of Chinese society as proletarian. All of China, he argued, had been exploited by the bourgeois, industrialized West. Thus, the oppressed Chinese as a whole needed to unite and rise up against their exploiters.

Li's version of Marxism, with alterations or emphasis on elements that made it suitable for China, had great appeal for the students, including the young **Mao Zedong** (mow dzuh-doong), who joined Li's study circle. They, too, were angered by what they perceived as China's betrayal by the imperialist powers. They shared Li's hostility (very much a throwback to the attitudes of the Confucian era) to merchants and commerce, which appeared to dominate the West. They, too, longed for a return to a political system, like the Confucian, in which those who governed were deeply committed to social reform and social welfare. They also believed in an authoritarian state, which they felt ought to intervene constructively in all aspects of the peoples' lives. The Marxist study club societies that developed as a result of these discoveries soon spawned a number of more broadly based, politically activist organizations.

In the summer of 1921, in an attempt to unify the growing Marxist wing of the nationalist struggle, a handful of leaders from different parts of China met in secret in the city of Shanghai. At this meeting, closely watched by the agents of the local warlord and rival political organizations, the Communist party of China was born. The party was minuscule in terms of the numbers of their supporters, and at this time it was still dogmatically fixed on a revolutionary program oriented to the small and scattered working class. But the communists at least offered a clear alternative to fill the ideological and institutional void left by the collapse of the Confucian order.

The Seizure of Power by China's Guomindang

In the years when the communist movement in China was being put together by urban students and intellectuals, the **Guomindang** (gwoh-mihn-dohng), or Nationalist party, which was to prove the communists' great rival for the mandate to rule in China, was struggling to survive in the south. Sun Yatsen, who was the acknowledged head of the nationalist struggle from the 1911 revolution until his death in early 1925, had gone into temporary exile in Japan in 1914, while warlords such as Yuan Shikai consolidated their regional power bases. After returning to China in 1919, Sun and his followers attempted to unify the diverse political organizations struggling for political influence in China by reorganizing the revolutionary movement and naming it the Nationalist party of China (the Guomindang).

Li Dazhao [lee duh-JOH] (1888–1927) Chinese intellectual who gave serious attention to Marxist philosophy; headed study circle at the University of Beijing; saw peasants as vanguard of revolutionary communism in China.

Mao Zedong [mow dzuh-doong] (1893–1976) Communist leader in revolutionary China; advocated rural reform and role of peasantry in Nationalist revolution; influenced by Li Dazhao; led Communist reaction against Guomindang purges in 1920s, culminating in Long March of 1934; seized control of all of mainland China by 1949; initiated Great Leap Forward in 1958.

Guomindang [gwoh-mihn-dohng] Chinese Nationalist party founded by Sun Yat-sen in 1919; drew support from local warlords and Chinese criminal underworld; initially forged alliance with Communists in 1924; dominated by Chiang Kai-shek after 1925.

The Nationalists began the slow process of forging alliances with key social groups and building an army of their own, which they now viewed as the only way to rid China of the warlord menace (Map 29.3). Sun strove to enunciate a nationalist ideology that gave something to everyone. It stressed the need to unify China under a strong central government, to bring the imperialist intruders under control, and to introduce social reforms that would alleviate the poverty of the peasants and the oppressive working conditions of laborers in China's cities. Unfortunately for the great majority of the Chinese people, for whom social reforms were the main concern, the Nationalist leaders concentrated on political and international issues, such as relations with the Western powers and Japan, and failed to implement most of the domestic programs they proposed, most especially land reform.

In this early stage Sun and the Nationalists built their power primarily on the support provided by urban businesspeople and merchants in coastal cities such as Canton. Sun forged an alliance with the communists that was officially proclaimed at the first Nationalist party conference in 1924. For the time being at least, the Nationalist leaders were content to let the communists serve as their major link to the peasants and the urban workers. Nationalist leaders also turned to Soviet Russia, and the Bolsheviks sent advisors and gave material assistance.

In 1924 the **Whampoa Military Academy** was founded with Soviet help and partially staffed by Russian instructors. The academy gave the Nationalists a critical military dimension to their political maneuvering. The first head of the academy was an ambitious young military officer named **Chiang Kai-shek** (jee-ahng keye-shehk). The son of a poor salt merchant, Chiang had made his career in the military and by virtue of connections with powerful figures in the Shanghai underworld. He had received some military training in Japan and managed by the early 1920s to work his way into Sun Yatsen's inner circle of advisors. Chiang was not happy with the communist alliance. But he was willing to bide his time until he had the military strength to deal with both the communists and the warlords, who remained the major obstacles to the Nationalist seizure of power.

Political tensions distracted the Nationalist leaders from the growing deterioration of the economy. The peasantry, 90 percent of the population, suffered increasing misery following a long

Whampoa Military Academy Founded in 1924; military wing of the Guomindang; first head of the academy was Chiang Kai-shek.

Chiang Kai-shek [jee-ahng keye-shehk] A military officer who succeeded Sun Yat-sen as the leader of the Guomindang or Nationalist party in China in the mid-1920s; became the most powerful leader in China in the early 1930s, but his Nationalist forces were defeated and driven from China by the Communists after World War II.

Map 29.3 China in the Era of Revolution and Civil War Political reform was constrained by the nationalist-communist dispute and by Japanese invasion.

period of government ineffectiveness and depredations by the landlords. Famine and disease stalked the countryside, while irrigation systems deteriorated. Many peasants could not even bury their deceased parents, whose bodies were left for animals to devour.

Sun gave lip service to the Nationalist party's need to deal with the peasant problem. But his abysmal ignorance of rural conditions was revealed by statements in which he denied that China had exploitive landlords and his refusal to believe that there were "serious difficulties" between the great mass of the peasantry and the landowners.

Mao and the Peasant Option

Though the son of a fairly prosperous peasant, Mao Zedong had rebelled early in his life against his father's exploitation of the tenants and laborers who worked the family fields. Receiving little assistance from his estranged father, Mao was forced to make his own way in the world. Through much of his youth and early adulthood, he struggled to educate himself in the history, philosophy, and economic theory that most other nationalist and revolutionary leaders mastered in private schools. Having moved to Beijing in the post–May Fourth era, Mao came under the influence of thinkers such as Li Dazhao (lee duh-JOH), who placed considerable emphasis on solutions to the peasant problem as one of the keys to China's survival. As the following passage from Mao's early writings reveals, almost from the outset he was committed to revolutionary solutions that depended on peasant support:

> A revolution is an insurrection, an act of violence by which one class overthrows another. A rural revolution is a revolution by which the peasantry overthrows the power of the feudal landlord class. Without using the greatest force, the peasants cannot possibly overthrow the deep-rooted authority of the landlords which has lasted for thousands of years.

The Nationalists' successful drive for national power began only after Sun Yatsen's death in 1925, which opened the way for Chiang Kai-shek and his warlord allies to seize control of the party. After winning over or eliminating the military chiefs in the Canton area, Chiang marched north with his newly created armies. His first campaign culminated in the Nationalists' seizure of the Yangzi River valley and Shanghai in early 1927. Later his forces also captured the capital at Beijing and the rest of the Yellow River basin. The refusal of most of the warlords to end their feuding meant that Chiang could defeat them or buy them out, one by one. By the late 1920s, he was the master of China in name and international standing, if not in actual fact. He was, in effect, the head of a warlord hierarchy. But most political leaders within China and in the outside world recognized him as the new president of China.

Chiang quickly turned against the communists, attacking them in various places. A brutal massacre occurred in Shanghai in 1927, with many workers gunned down or beheaded (Figure 29.9). Chiang carefully wooed support from western Europe and the United States, while lining up most police and landlord leaders at home. The offensive propelled Mao Zedong to leadership. An attack on the communist rural stronghold in south central China, supported by German advisors, caused Mao to spearhead a **Long March** of 90,000 followers in 1934, across thousands of miles to the more remote northwest. Here, in Shanxi, where some peasant communes had already been established, the new communist center took shape (Map 29.3).

While the Long March solidified Mao's leadership of Chinese communism and gave many followers a sense that they could not be defeated, it was the Japanese invasions of China in the 1930s that would begin to give communists a new advantage. Chiang had to ally with communists to fight the Japanese threat, while his own power base, along the coast, was eroded by the powerful Japanese advance. The Chinese revolution was far from over.

Long March Communist escape from Hunan province during civil war with Guomindang in 1934; center of Communist power moved to Shaanxi province; firmly established Mao Zedong as head of the Communist party in China.

Figure 29.9 The Guomindang's brutal suppression of the workers' organizations in Shanghai in 1927 was a turning point in the history of modern China. The Guomindang–Communist party alliance was shattered, and Mao Zedong's call for a peasant-based revolution became imperative as the vulnerability of the small Chinese working class was exposed.

The Global Great Depression

Coming barely a decade after the turmoil of World War I, the onset of global economic depression constituted a crucial next step in the mounting spiral of international crises. The crash of the New York stock market hit the headlines in 1929, but in fact the **Great Depression** had begun, sullenly, in many parts of the world economy even earlier. The Depression resulted from new problems in the industrial economy of Europe and the United States, combined with the long-term weakness in economies, like those of Latin America, that depended on sales of cheap exports in the international market. The result was a worldwide collapse that spared only a few economies and brought political as well as economic pressures on virtually every society.

The Great Depression was centered in the West but had global roots and impact. Western responses to the Depression varied, but none succeeded in ending the crisis.

Great Depression International economic crisis following the First World War; began with collapse of American stock market in 1929; actual causes included collapse of agricultural prices in 1920s; included collapse of banking houses in the United States and western Europe, massive unemployment; contradicted optimistic assumptions of the 19th century.

Causation

Structural problems affected many industrial societies during the 1920s, even after postwar recovery. Farmers throughout much of the Western world, including the United States, faced almost chronic overproduction of food and resulting low prices. Food production had soared in response to wartime needs; during the postwar inflation many farmers, both in western Europe and in North America, borrowed heavily to buy new equipment, overconfident that their good markets would be sustained. But rising European production combined with large imports from the Americas and New Zealand sent prices down, which lowered earnings and made debts harder to repay. One response was continued population flight from the countryside as urbanization continued. Remaining farmers were hard pressed and unable to sustain high demand for manufactured goods.

Thus although economies in France and Germany seemed to have recovered by 1925, problems continued: the fears massive postwar inflation had generated limited the capacity of governments to respond to other problems. Much of the mid-decade prosperity rested on exceedingly fragile grounds. Loans from U.S. banks to various European enterprises helped sustain demand for goods but on condition that additional loans pour in to help pay off the resultant debts.

Furthermore, most of the dependent areas in the world economy, colonies and noncolonies alike, were suffering badly. Pronounced tendencies toward overproduction developed in the smaller nations of eastern Europe, which sent agricultural goods to western Europe, as well as among tropical producers in Africa and Latin America. Here, continued efforts to win export revenue pressed local estate owners to drive up output in coffee, sugar, and rubber. As European governments and businesses organized their African colonies for more profitable exploitation, they set up large estates devoted to goods of this type. Again, production frequently exceeded demand, which drove prices and earnings down in both Africa and Latin America. This meant, in turn, that many colonies and dependant economies were unable to buy many industrial exports, which weakened demand for Western products precisely when output tended to rise amid growing U.S. and Japanese competition. Several food-exporting regions, including many of the new eastern European nations, fell into a depression, in terms of earnings and employment, by the mid-1920s, well before the full industrial catastrophe.

Governments of the leading industrial nations provided scant leadership during the emerging crisis of the 1920s. Most Western leaders had only a feeble grasp of economics. Nationalistic selfishness predominated. Western nations were more concerned about insisting on repayment of any debts owed to them or about constructing tariff barriers to protect their own industries than about facilitating balanced world economic growth. Protectionism, in particular, as practiced even by traditionally free-trade Great Britain and by the many nations in eastern Europe, simply reduced market opportunities and made a bad situation worse. By the later 1920s employment in key Western industrial sectors—coal (also beset by new competition from imported oil), iron, and textiles— began to decline, the foretaste of more general collapse.

The Debacle

The formal advent of the Depression occurred in October 1929, when the New York stock market collapsed. Stock values tumbled as investors quickly lost confidence in prices that had been pushed ridiculously high. Banks, which had depended heavily on their stock investments, rapidly echoed

Figure 29.10 This famous photograph of a tenant farmer and her children in the American South was published in the book *Let Us Now Praise Famous Men.* It exemplifies the hardship and poverty endured by many during the Great Depression.

The Great Depression: An Oral Account

the financial crisis, and many institutions failed, dragging their depositors along with them. Even before this crash, Americans had begun to call back earlier loans to Europe. Yet the European credit structure depended extensively on U.S. loans, which had fueled some industrial expansion but also less productive investments, such as German reparations payments and the construction of fancy town halls and other amenities. In Europe, as in the United States, many commercial enterprises existed on the basis not of real production power but of continued speculation. When one piece of the speculative spiral was withdrawn, the whole edifice quickly collapsed. Key bank failures in Austria and Germany followed the U.S. crisis. Throughout most of the industrial West, investment funds dried up as creditors went bankrupt or tried to cut their losses.

With investment receding, industrial production quickly began to fall, beginning with the industries that produced capital goods and extending quickly to consumer products fields. Falling production—levels dropped by as much as one-third by 1932—meant falling employment and lower wages, which in turn withdrew still more demand from the economy and led to further hardship. Unemployed and underpaid workers could not buy goods whose production might give other workers jobs. The existing weakness of some markets, such as the farm sector or the nonindustrial world, was exacerbated as demand for foods and minerals plummeted. New and appalling problems developed among workers, now out of jobs or suffering from reduced hours and reduced pay (Figure 29.10), as well as among the middle classes. The Depression, in sum, fed on itself, growing steadily worse from 1929 to 1933. Even countries initially less hard hit, such as France and Italy, saw themselves drawn into the vortex by 1931.

In itself the Great Depression was not entirely unprecedented. Previous periods had seen slumps triggered by bank failures and overspeculation, yielding several years of falling production, unemployment, and hardship. But the intensity of the Great Depression had no precedent in the brief history of industrial societies. Its duration was also unprecedented; in many countries, full recovery came only after a decade and only with the forced production schedules provoked by World War II. Unlike earlier depressions, this one came on the heels of so much other distress—the economic hardships of war, for example, and the catastrophic inflation of the 1920s—and caught most governments totally unprepared.

The Depression was more, of course, than an economic event. It reached into countless lives, creating hardship and tension that would be recalled even as the crisis itself eased. Loss of earnings, loss of work, or simply fears that loss would come devastated people at all social levels. The suicides of ruined investors in New York were paralleled by the vagrants' camps and begging that spread among displaced workers. The statistics were grim: up to one-third of all blue-collar workers in the West lost their jobs for prolonged periods. White-collar unemployment, though not quite as severe, was also unparalleled. In Germany 600,000 of 4 million white-collar workers had lost their jobs by 1931. Graduating students could not find work or had to resort to jobs they regarded as insecure or demeaning. Six million overall unemployed in Germany and 22 percent of the labor force unemployed in Britain were statistics of stark misery and despair. Families were disrupted; men felt emasculated at their inability to provide, and women and children were disgusted with authority figures whose authority was now hollow. In some cases wives and mothers found it easier to gain jobs in a low-wage economy than their husbands did, and although this development had some promise in terms of new opportunities for women, it could also be confusing for standard family roles. For many, the agony and personal disruption of the Depression were desperately prolonged, with renewed recession around 1937 and with unemployment still averaging 10 percent or more in many countries as late as 1939.

The Depression, like World War I, was an event that blatantly contradicted the optimistic assumptions of the later 19th century. To many it showed the fragility of any idea of progress, while to others it seemed to condemn the system of parliamentary democracy. Because it was a second catastrophic event within a generation, the Depression led to even more extreme results than the war had done—more bizarre experiments, more paralysis in the face of deepening despair. To be sure, there were some escapist alternatives: Hollywood movies put up a cheerful front, and in 1938 a new American comic book figure, Superman, provided an alternative to the constraints of normal life. But these were modest alternatives at best.

For most of the world outside the West, moreover, the Depression worsened an already bleak economic picture. Western markets could absorb fewer commodity imports as production fell and incomes dwindled. Hence the nations that produced foods and raw materials saw prices and earnings drop even more than before. Unemployment rose rapidly in the export sectors of the Latin American economy, creating a major political challenge not unlike that faced by the Western nations. Japan, a new industrial country, still heavily depended on export earnings for financing its imports of essential fuel and raw materials. The Japanese silk industry, an export staple, was already suffering from the advent of artificial silklike fibers produced by Western chemical giants. Now Western luxury purchases collapsed, leading to severe unemployment in Japan and a crucial political crisis. Between 1929 and 1931, the value of Japanese exports plummeted by 50 percent. Workers' real income dropped by almost one-third, and more than 3 million people were unemployed. Depression was compounded by poor harvests in several regions, leading to rural begging and near starvation. The Great Depression, though most familiar in its Western dimensions, was a truly international collapse.

Responses to the Depression in Western Europe

Western governments, already weakened, responded to the onset of the economic catastrophe counterproductively. National tariffs were raised to keep out the goods of other countries, but this merely worsened the international economy and curbed sales for everyone. Most governments tried to cut spending, reflecting the decline in revenues that accompanied falling production. They were concerned about avoiding renewed inflation, but in fact their measures further reduced economic stimulus and pushed additional workers—government employees—out of jobs. Confidence in the normal political process deteriorated. In many countries the Depression heightened political polarization. People sought solutions from radical parties or movements, both on the left and on the right. Support for communist parties increased in many countries, and in important cases the authoritarian movement on the right gained increased attention. Even in relatively stable countries, such as Britain, battles between the Conservative party and the labor movement made decisive policy difficult. Class conflict rose to new levels, in and out of politics.

In key cases, the Great Depression led to one of two effects: either a parliamentary system that became increasingly incapacitated, unable to come to grips with the new economic dilemma and too divided to take vigorous action, even in foreign policy, or the outright overturning of the parliamentary system.

France was a prime example of the first pattern. The French government reacted sluggishly to the Depression. Voters responded by moving toward the political extremes. Socialist and then communist parties expanded. Rightist movements calling for a strong leader and fervent nationalism grew, their adherents often disrupting political meetings in order to discredit the parliamentary system by making orderly debate impossible. In response liberal, socialist, and communist parties formed the **Popular Front** in 1936 to win the election. The Popular Front government, however, was unable to take strong measures of social reform because of the ongoing strength of conservative republicans hostile to change and the authoritarian right that looked to forceful leadership to contain the lower classes. The same paralysis crept into foreign policy, as Popular Front leaders, initially eager to support the new liberal regime in Spain that was attacked by conservative army leaders in the Spanish Civil War, found themselves forced to pull back. The Popular Front fell in 1938, but even before this France was close to a standstill.

There were more constructive responses. Scandinavian states, most of them directed by moderate socialist parties, increased government spending, providing new levels of social insurance against illness and unemployment. This foreshadowed the welfare state. British policy was more tentative, but new industrial sectors emerged under the leadership of innovative businesspeople. The world's first television industry, for example, took shape in southern England in the late 1930s, though it was too small to break the hold of the Depression.

Popular Front Combination of socialist and communist political parties in France; won election in 1936; unable to take strong measures of social reform because of continuing strength of conservatives; fell from power in 1938.

The New Deal

After a few years of floundering, the United States generated another set of creative responses. Initial American policies, under President Herbert Hoover, resembled those of western Europe, in seeking higher tariffs and attempting to cut spending in reaction to falling revenues. The United States also sought to accelerate war debt repayments from Europe, which also made matters worse internationally. In 1933 a new administration took over, under Franklin Roosevelt, offering a "new deal" to the American people.

New Deal President Franklin Roosevelt's precursor of the modern welfare state (1933–1939); programs to combat economic depression enacted a number of social insurance measures and used government spending to stimulate the economy; increased power of the state and the state's intervention in U.S. social and economic life.

New Deal policies, as they unfolded during the 1930s, offered more direct aid to Americans at risk, through increased unemployment benefits and other measures. Many unemployed people were given jobs on public works projects. A crucial innovation was the Social Security system, based on contributions from workers and employers and designed to provide protection in unemployment and old age. The New Deal also undertook some economic planning and stimulus, for both industry and agriculture, while installing new regulations on banking.

The New Deal ushered in a period of rapid government growth, a watershed in American history particularly as it was followed by the massive expansion of military operations in World War II. The regime did not solve the Depression, which sputtered on until wartime spending ended it in the early 1940s. It also did not install a full welfare state, holding back, for example, from plans to offer a health insurance system. But the New Deal did restore the confidence of most Americans in their political system, preempting more extremist political movements and minimizing the kind of paralysis that afflicted Britain and France in the same years.

The Authoritarian Response

European fascism expanded in response to the new crisis as Nazism took hold in Germany. New authoritarian regimes gained ground in Latin America, Japan and the Soviet Union.

German patterns differed markedly from the wavering responses of Germany's neighbors and from democratic welfare innovation as well. In Germany the impact of the Depression led directly to a new fascist regime. Germany had suffered the shock of loss in World War I, enhanced by treaty arrangements that cast primary blame for the war on the German nation, which had only recent and shaky parliamentary traditions. A number of factors, in sum, combined to make Germany a fertile breeding ground for fascism, though it took the Depression to bring this current to the fore.

The Rise of Nazism

While Germany introduced the sharpest political changes in response to the depression and to nationalist pattern, important political change also affected Japan, the Soviet Union, and later America. Western-style democracies were in substantial retreat.

Fascism in Germany, as in Italy, was a product of the war. The movement's advocates, many of them former veterans, attacked the weakness of parliamentary democracy and the corruption and class conflict of Western capitalism. They proposed a strong state ruled by a powerful leader who would revive the nation's forces through vigorous foreign and military policy. While fascists vaguely promised social reforms to alleviate class antagonisms, their attacks on trade unions as well as on socialist and communist parties pleased landlords and business groups. Although fascism won outright control only in Italy in the movement's early years, fascist parties complicated the political process in a number of other nations during the 1920s and beyond. But it was the advent of the National Socialist, or Nazi, regime in Germany under Adolf Hitler that made this new political movement a major force in world history. Here, a Western commitment to liberal, democratic political forms was challenged and reversed.

German Painting Idolizing Hitler IMAGE

In his vote-gathering campaigns, in the later 1920s and early 1930s, Hitler repeated standard fascist arguments about the need for unity and the hopeless weakness of parliamentary politics. The state should provide guidance, for it was greater than the sum of individual interests, and the leader should guide the state. Hitler promised many groups a return to more traditional ways; thus many artisans voted for him in the belief that preindustrial economic institutions, such as the guilds, would be revived. Middle-class elements, including big-business leaders, were attracted to Hitler's commitment to a firm stance against socialism and communism. Hitler also focused grievances against various currents in modern life, from big department stores to feminism, by attacking what he claimed were Jewish influences in Germany. He promised a glorious foreign policy to undo the wrongs of the Versailles treaty. Finally, Hitler represented a hope for effective action against the Depression. Although the Nazis never won a majority vote in a free election, his party did win the largest single slice in 1932, and this enabled Hitler to make arrangements with other political leaders for his rise to power legally in 1933.

Once in power, Hitler quickly set about constructing a **totalitarian state**—a new kind of government that would exercise massive, direct control over virtually all the activities of its subjects. Hitler eliminated all opposition parties; he purged the bureaucracy and military, installing loyal Nazis in many posts. His secret police, the **Gestapo,** arrested hundreds of thousands of political opponents. Trade unions were replaced by government-sponsored bodies that tried to appease low-paid workers by offering full employment and various welfare benefits. Government economic planning helped restore production levels, with particular emphasis on armaments construction. Hitler cemented his regime by continual, well staged propaganda bombardments (Figure 29.11), strident nationalism, and an incessant attack on Germany's large Jewish minority.

Hitler's hatred of Jews ran deep; he blamed them for various personal misfortunes and also for socialism and excessive capitalism—movements that in his view had weakened the German spirit. Obviously, anti-Semitism served as a catchall for a host of diverse dissatisfactions, and as such it appealed to many Germans. Anti-Semitism also played into Hitler's hands by providing a scapegoat that could rouse national passions and distract the population from other problems. Measures against Jews became more and more severe; they were forced to wear special emblems, their property was attacked and seized, and increasing numbers were sent to concentration camps. After 1940 Hitler's policy insanely turned to the literal elimination of European Jewry, as the Holocaust raged in the concentration camps of Germany and conquered territories (see Chapter 30).

Hitler's foreign and military policies were based on preparation for war. He wanted to not only recoup Germany's World War I losses but also create a land empire that would extend across much of Europe, particularly toward the east against what he saw as the inferior Slavic peoples. Progressively Hitler violated the limits on German armaments and annexed neighboring territories, provoking only weak response from the Western democracies.

The Spread of Fascism and the Spanish Civil War

Nazi triumph in Germany inevitably spurred fascism in other parts of Europe. Many east central states, already authoritarian, took on fascist trappings. Explicit fascist movements emerged in Hungary and Romania. Fascism in Austria was vindicated when Hitler proclaimed the union of Austria and Germany in 1938, quickly spreading the apparatus of the Nazi party and state.

totalitarian state   A new kind of government in the 20th century that exercised massive, direct control over virtually all the activities of its subjects; existed in Germany, Italy, and the Soviet Union.

Gestapo   Secret police in Nazi Germany, known for brutal tactics.

The Expansion of Germany in the 1930s

Figure 29.11 The adulation that the German masses felt for Adolf Hitler in the mid-1930s is evident in this rally photo. Hitler's popularity rested primarily on his promises to rebuild Germany's deeply depressed economy and restore its world power status by reversing the 1919 treaty ending World War I.

Hitler's advent galvanized the authoritarian regime of a nearby power, Italy, where a fascist state had been formed in the 1920s, led by Benito Mussolini. Like Hitler, Mussolini had promised an aggressive foreign policy and new nationalist glories, but his first decade had been rather moderate diplomatically. With Hitler in power, Mussolini began to experiment more boldly, if only to avoid being overshadowed completely.

In 1935 Mussolini attacked Ethiopia, planning to avenge Italy's failure to conquer this ancient land during the imperialist surge of the 1890s. The League of Nations condemned the action, but neither it nor the democratic powers in Europe and North America took action. Consequently, after some hard fighting, the Italians won their new colony. Here, then, was another destabilizing element in world politics.

Spanish Civil War War pitting authoritarian and military leaders in Spain against republicans and leftists between 1936 and 1939; Germany and Italy supported the royalists; the Soviet Union supported the republicans; led to victory of the royalist forces.

Fascism also spread into Spain, leading to the **Spanish Civil War.** Here, forces supporting a parliamentary republic plus social reform had feuded since 1931 with advocates of a military-backed authoritarian state. In 1936 outright civil war broke out. Spanish military forces, led by General Francisco Franco, were backed by an explicitly fascist party, the Falange (feh-LAHNJ), as well as more conventionally conservative landowners and Catholic leaders.

Republican forces included various groups, with support from peasants and workers in various parts of the country. Communists and a large anarchist movement played a crucial role. They won some support also from volunteers from the United States and western Europe, and from the Soviet Union.

Bitter fighting consumed much of Spain for three years. German and Italian forces bombed several Spanish cities, a rehearsal for the bombing of civilians in World War II. France, Britain, and the United States made vague supporting gestures to the republican forces but offered no concrete aid, fearful of provoking a wider conflict and paralyzed by internal disagreements about foreign policy. Franco's forces won in 1939. The resultant regime was not fully fascist, but it maintained authoritarian controls and catered to landlords, church, and army for the next 25 years.

Economic and Political Changes in Latin America

In the 1920s and 1930s, the limitations of liberalism became increasingly apparent in Latin America. A middle class had emerged and had begun to enter politics, but unlike its western European counterpart, it gained power only in conjunction with the traditional oligarchy or the military. In Latin America, the ideology of liberalism was not an expression of the strength of the middle class but rather a series of ideas not particularly suited to the realities of Latin America, where large segments of the population were landless, uneducated, and destitute. Increasing industrialization did not dissolve the old class boundaries, nor did public education and other classic liberal programs produce as much social mobility as had been expected.

Disillusioned by liberalism and World War I, artists and intellectuals who had looked to Europe for inspiration turned to Latin America's own populations and history for values and solutions to Latin American problems. During the 1920s intellectuals complained that Latin America was on a race to nowhere. In literature and the arts, the ideas of rationality, progress, and order associated with liberalism and the outward appearances of democracy were under attack.

Ideas of reform and social change were in the air. University students in Córdoba, Argentina, began a reform of their university system that gave the university more autonomy and students more power within it. This movement soon spread to other countries. There were other responses as well. Socialist and communist parties were formed or grew in strength in several Latin American nations in this period, especially after the Russian Revolution of 1917. The strength of these parties of the left originated in local conditions but sometimes was aided by the international communist movement. Although criticism of existing governments and of liberalism as a political and economic philosophy came from these left-leaning parties, it also came from traditional elements in society such as the Roman Catholic Church, which disliked the secularization represented by a capitalist society.

The Great Crash and Latin American Responses

The economic dependency of Latin America and the internal weaknesses of the liberal regimes were made clear by the great world financial crisis. Export sales dropped rapidly. Amid growing poverty, reform movements gained momentum. More important, however, was the rise of a conservative re-

Guernica and the Images of War

This painting, probably the most famous work of art of the 20th century, was Spanish artist Pablo Picasso's protest against the bombing of the village of Guernica during the Spanish Civil War. On April 27, 1937, German and Italian planes bombarded the city for three hours. Guernica burned for three days, and more than 1500 people were killed.

QUESTIONS What was Picasso trying to say through the painting? Why did it have such a strong impact? Picasso, a Cubist artist, was working in a nonrepresentational style of art. Can you think of other works of art, including photographs, that have helped capture the notion of modern war? Does art make a difference where war is concerned?

Pablo Picasso's *Guernica*.

(Pablo Picasso (1881–1973), "Guernica," 1937. Museo Nacional Centro de Arte Reina Sofia, Madrid, Spain. © 2010 Estate of Pablo Picasso/Artists Rights Society (ARS), New York. John Bigelow Taylor / Art Resource, NY.)

sponse, hostile to class conflict and supported by church and military leaders. A corporatist movement, aimed at curbing capitalism while avoiding Marxism, won growing attention. **Corporatism** emphasized the organic nature of society, with the state as a mediator adjusting the interests of different social groups; the ideology appealed to conservative groups and the military, in European as well as Latin American societies. Some corporatist leaders sympathized with aspects of Italian and German fascism.

New regimes, as well as a new concern with social problems, characterized much of Latin America in the 1930s. One such reforming administration was that of President **Lázaro Cárdenas** (1934–1940) in Mexico, when land reform and many of the social aspects of the revolution were initiated on a large scale. Cárdenas distributed more than 40 million acres of land and created communal farms and a credit system to support them. He expropriated foreign oil companies that refused to obey Mexican law and created a state oil monopoly. He expanded rural education programs. These measures made him broadly popular in Mexico and seemed to give substance to the promise of the revolution.

Cárdenas in Mexico was perhaps the most successful example of the new political tide that could be seen elsewhere in Latin America. In Cuba, for example, the leaders of a nationalist revolution aimed at social reform and breaking the grip of the United States took power in 1933, and although their rule soon was taken over by moderate elements, important changes and reforms did take place. To some extent, such new departures underlined both the growing force of nationalism and the desire to integrate new forces into the political process. Nowhere was this more apparent than in the populist Vargas regime of Brazil.

corporatism Political ideology that emphasized the organic nature of society and made the state a mediator, adjusting the interests of different social groups; appealed to conservative groups in European and Latin American societies and to the military.

Cárdenas, Lázaro President of Mexico from 1934 to 1940; responsible for redistribution of land, primarily to create ejidos, or communal farms; also began program of primary and rural education.

711

The Vargas Regime in Brazil

In Brazil, a contested political election in 1929, in which the state elites could not agree on the next president, resulted in a short civil war and the emergence of **Getúlio Vargas** (1872–1954) as the new president. The Brazilian economy, based on coffee exports, had collapsed in the 1929 crash. Vargas had promised liberal reforms and elimination of the worst abuses of the old system. Once in power, he launched a new kind of centralized political program, imposing federal administrators over the state governments. He held off attempted coups by the communists in 1935 and by the green-shirted fascist "Integralists" in 1937. With the support of the military, Vargas imposed a new constitution in 1937 that established the *Estado Novo* (New State), based on ideas from Mussolini's Italy. It imposed an authoritarian regime within the context of nationalism and economic reforms, limiting immigration and eliminating parties and groups that resisted national integration or opposed the government.

For a while, Vargas played off Germany and the Western powers in the hope of securing armaments and favorable trade arrangements. Despite Vargas's authoritarian sympathies, he eventually joined the Allies during World War II, supplied bases to the United States, and even sent troops to fight against the Axis powers in Italy. In return, Brazil obtained arms, financial support for industrial development, and trade advantages. Meanwhile, Vargas ran a corporatist government, allowing some room for labor negotiations under strict government supervision. Little open opposition to the government was allowed. The state organized many other aspects of the economy. Opposition to Vargas and his repressive policies was building in Brazil by 1945, but by then he was turning increasingly to the left, seeking support from organized labor and coming to terms with the Communist party leaders whom he had imprisoned.

Under criticism from both the right and the left, Vargas committed suicide in 1954. His suicide note emphasized his populist ties and blamed his death on Brazil's enemies:

> Once more the forces and interests which work against the people have organized themselves again and emerge against me. . . . I was a slave to the people, and today I am freeing myself for eternal life. But this people whose slave I was will no longer be slave to anyone. My sacrifice will remain forever in their souls and my blood will be the price of their ransom.

Much of Brazilian history since Vargas has been a struggle over his mantle of leadership. In death, Vargas became a martyr and a nationalist hero, even to those groups he had repressed and imprisoned in the 1930s.

Argentina: Populism, Perón, and the Military

Argentina was something of an anomaly. There, the middle-class Radical party, which had held power during the 1920s, fell when the economy collapsed in 1929. A military coup backed by a strange coalition of nationalists, fascists, and socialists seized power, hoping to return Argentina to the golden days of the great export boom of the 1890s. The coup failed. Argentina became more dependent as foreign investments increased and markets for Argentine products declined. However, industry was growing, and with it grew the numbers and strength of industrial workers, many of whom had migrated from the countryside. By the 1940s the workers were organized in two major labor federations. Conservative governments backed by the traditional military held power through the 1930s, but in 1943 a military group once again took control of the government.

The new military rulers were nationalists who wanted to industrialize and modernize Argentina and make it the dominant power of South America. Some were admirers of the fascist powers and their programs. Although many of them were distrustful of the workers, the man who became the dominant political force in Argentina recognized the need to create a broader basis of support for the government. Colonel **Juan D. Perón** (1895–1974) emerged as a power in the government. Using his position in the Ministry of Labor, he appealed to workers, raising their salaries, improving their benefits, and generally supporting their demands. Attempts to displace him failed, and he increasingly gained popular support, aided by his wife, Eva Duarte, known as Evita, a fascinating woman from the provincial lower classes. She became a public spokesperson for Perón among the lower classes. During World War II, Perón's admiration for the Axis powers was well known. In 1946, when the United States tried to discredit him because of his fascist sympathies, he turned the attempt into nationalist support for his presidential campaign.

Vargas, Getúlio Elected president of Brazil in 1929; launched centralized political program by imposing federal administrators over state governments; held off coups by communists in 1935 and fascists in 1937; imposed a new constitution based on Mussolini's Italy; leaned to communists after 1949; committed suicide in 1954.

Perón, Juan D. Military leader in Argentina who became dominant political figure after military coup in 1943; used position as Minister of Labor to appeal to working groups and the poor; became president in 1946; forced into exile in 1955; returned and won presidency in 1973.

As president, Perón forged an alliance among the workers, the industrialists, and the military. Like Vargas in Brazil, he learned the effectiveness of the radio, the press, and public speeches in mobilizing public support. He depended on his personal charisma and on repression of opponents to maintain his rule. The Peronist program was couched in nationalistic terms. The government nationalized the foreign-owned railroads and telephone companies, as well as the petroleum resources. The foreign debt was paid off, and for a while the Argentine economy boomed in the immediate postwar years. But by 1949 there were economic problems again. Meanwhile, Perón ruled by a combination of inducements and repression, while Evita Perón became a symbol to the *descamisados,* or the poor and downtrodden, who saw in Peronism a glimmer of hope. Her death in 1952 at age 33 caused an outpouring of national grief.

Perón's regime was a populist government with a broader base than had ever been attempted in Argentina. Nevertheless, holding the interests of the various components of the coalition together became increasingly difficult as the economy worsened. A democratic opposition developed and complained of Perón's control of the press and his violation of civil liberties. Industrialists disliked the strength of labor organizations. The military worried that Perón would arm the workers and cut back on the military's gains. The Peronist party became more radical and began a campaign against the Catholic Church. In 1955, anti-Perón military officers drove him into exile.

Argentina spent the next 20 years in the shadow of Perón. The Peronist party was banned, and a succession of military-supported civilian governments tried to resolve the nation's economic problems and its continuing political instability. But Peronism could survive even without Perón, and the mass of urban workers and the strongly Peronist unions continued to agitate for his programs, especially as austerity measures began to affect the living conditions of the working class. Perón and his new wife, Isabel, returned to Argentina in 1973, and they won the presidential election in that year— she as vice president. When Perón died the next year, however, it was clear that Argentina's problems could not be solved by the old formulas. Argentina slid once more into military dictatorship.

The Militarization of Japan

Authoritarian military rule took over in Japan even earlier than in the West. Not fascist outright, it had some clear affinities with the new regimes in Europe, including its aggressive military stance. As early as 1931, as the Depression hit Japan hard, military officials completed a conquest of the Chinese province of Manchuria, without the backing of the civilian government (Map 29.3).

As political divisions increased in response to the initial impact of the Depression, a variety of nationalist groups emerged, some advocating a return to Shintoist or Confucian principles against the more Western values of urban Japan. This was more than a political response to economic depression. As in Germany, a variety of groups used the occasion for a more sweeping protest against parliamentary forms; nationalism here seemed a counterpoise to alien Western values. Older military officers joined some bureaucrats in urging a more authoritarian state that could ignore party politics; some wanted further military expansion to protect Japan from the uncertainties of the world economy by providing secure markets and sources of raw materials.

In May 1932 a group of younger army officers attacked key government and banking officers and murdered the prime minister. They did not take over the state directly, but for the next four years moderate military leaders headed the executive branch, frustrating both the military firebrands and the political parties. Another attempted military coup in 1936 was put down by forces controlled by the established admirals and generals, but this group, including General Tojo Hideki, increasingly interfered with civilian cabinets, blocking the appointment of most liberal bureaucrats. The result, after 1936, was a series of increasingly militaristic prime ministers.

The military superseded civilian politics, particularly when renewed wars broke out between Japan and China in 1937. Japan, continuing to press the ruling Chinese government lest it gain sufficient strength to threaten Japanese gains, became involved in a skirmish with Chinese forces in the Beijing area in 1937. Fighting spread, initially quite unplanned. Most Japanese military leaders opposed more general war, arguing that the nation's only interest was to defend Manchuria and Korea. However, influential figures on the General Staff held that China's armies should be decisively defeated to prevent trouble in the future. This view prevailed, and Japanese forces quickly occupied the cities and railroads of eastern China. Several devastating bombing raids accompanied this invasion.

Japan's
Territorial
Ambition

Although Japanese voters had continued to prefer more moderate policies, their wishes were swept away by military leaders in a tide of growing nationalism. By the end of 1938 Japan controlled a substantial regional empire, including Manchuria, Korea, and Taiwan (Formosa), within which the nation sold half its exports and from which it bought more than 40 percent of all imports, particularly food and raw materials. Both the military leadership, eager to justify further modernization of Japan's weaponry and to consolidate political control, and economic leaders, interested in rich resources of other parts of Asia—such as the rubber of British Malaya or the oil of the Dutch East Indies—soon pressed for wider conquests as Japan surged into World War II (Map 29.4).

As war in Asia expanded, well before the formal outbreak of World War II, Japan also tightened its hold over its earlier empire, particularly in Korea. Efforts to suppress Korean culture were stepped up, and the Japanese military brutally put down any resistance. Japanese language and habits were forced on Korean teachers. Japanese industrialists dominated Korean resources, while peasants were required to produce rice for Japan at the expense of nutrition in Korea itself. Young men were pressed into labor groups, as the population was exhorted to join the Japanese people in "training to endure hardship."

Industrialization and Recovery

Japan's policies in the 1930s quelled the effects of the Depression for Japan even more fully than Hitler's policies were able to do for Germany. While the Depression initially hit Japan hard—half of all factories were closed by 1931, children in some areas were reduced to begging for food from passengers on passing trains, and farmers were eating tree bark—active government policies quickly responded. As a result, Japan suffered far less than many Western nations did during the Depression decade as a whole. Under the 1930s minister of finance, Korekiyo Takahashi, the government increased its spending to provide jobs, which in turn generated new demands for food and manufactured items, yielding not only the export boom but also the virtual elimination of unemployment by 1936. The same policy helped support government military purchasing, but it is not clear that this constituted an essential response.

1910: After the Wars with China and Russia   Late 1931: The Invasion of Manchuria   1937–1938: The Invasion of China

Map 29.4 The Expansion of Japan to the Outbreak of World War II   Two stages of Japan's attacks on China are clearly shown.

Indeed, Japan made a full turn toward industrialization after 1931, its economy growing much more rapidly than that of the West and rivaling the surge of the Soviet Union. Production of iron, steel, and chemicals soared. The spread of electric power was the most rapid in the world. The number of workers, mainly men, in the leading industries rose sevenfold during the 1930s. Quality of production increased as assembly-line methods were introduced, and Japanese manufacturing goods began to rival those of the West. As the level of Japanese industrial goods rose, the first Western outcry against Japanese exports was produced—even though in 1936 the Japanese controlled only 3.6 percent of world trade.

Japan also initiated a series of new industrial policies designed to stabilize the labor force and prevent social unrest. These paralleled the growing emphasis on mass patriotism and group loyalty developed by the government. Big companies began to offer lifetime contracts to a minority of skilled workers and to develop company entertainments and other activities designed to promote hard work and devotion. These distinctive Japanese policies, not part of its initial industrialization, proved to be a durable feature of Japanese society.

By 1937 Japan boasted the third largest and the newest merchant marine in the world. The nation became self-sufficient in machine tools and scientific equipment, the fruit of the growth in technical training. The basis had been set for the more significant economic expansion of the later 20th century, delayed by Japan's dash into World War II.

Stalinism in the Soviet Union

The Soviet Union was buffered from the Depression by its separate economy. Soviet leaders made much of the nation's ongoing industrial growth, even as Western economies collapsed. But the 1930s saw a tightening of the communist system under Stalin in ways that echoed authoritarian responses in other societies.

Stalin devoted himself to a double task: to make the Soviet Union a fully industrial society and to do so under full control of the state rather than through private initiative and individual ownership of producing property. He reversed the more experimental mood of the 1920s, including tolerance for small private businesses and wealthy peasant farmers. In essence, Stalin wanted modernization but with a revolutionary, noncapitalist twist. Although he was willing to borrow Western techniques and advice, importing a small number of foreign engineers, for example, he insisted on Soviet control and substantial Soviet isolation.

 Stalin Demands Rapid Industrialization of the U.S.S.R.

Economic Policies

A massive program to collectivize agriculture began in 1928. Collectivization meant the creation of large, state-run farms, rather than individual holdings as in the West. Communist party agitators pressed peasants to join in collectives. In addition to being distinctly socialistic, the collectives movement also further offered, at least in theory, the chance to mechanize agriculture most effectively, as collective farms could group scarce equipment, such as tractors and harvesters. Collectivization also allowed more efficient control over peasants, reflecting, though in radical new form, a traditional reluctance to leave peasants to their own devices. Government and party control was desirable not only for political reasons, but also because Stalin's hopes for a speedup of industrialization required that resources be taken from peasants, through taxation, in order to provide capital for industry.

The peasantry responded to collectivization with a decidedly mixed voice. Many laborers, resentful of kulak wealth, initially welcomed the opportunity to have more direct access to land. But most kulaks refused to cooperate voluntarily, often destroying livestock and other property rather than submit to collectivization. Devastating famine resulted from Stalin's insistence on pressing forward. In addition, millions of kulaks were killed or deported to Siberia during the early 1930s, in one of the most brutal oppressions of what turned out to be a brutal century in world history. Gradually, rural resistance collapsed and production began to increase once again; the decimation of the kulaks may indeed have weakened opportunities to oppose Stalin's increasingly authoritarian hold for a generation or two. But collectivization, though increasingly thorough, was not a smash success, for even those peasants who participated often seemed fairly unmotivated. Although the collective farms allowed peasants small plots of their own, as well as job security and considerable propagandizing by the omnipresent Communist party members, they created an atmosphere of factory-like discipline

Socialist Realism

One of the most fascinating features of the Soviet system was the attempt to create a distinctive art, different from the art of Western cultures (seen as decadent) and appropriate to the communist mission. This effort involved censorship and forced orthodoxy, but it also was an attempt to resolve earlier Russian problems of relating formal culture to the masses and trying to preserve a national distinctiveness amid the seductions of Western influence. The following effort to define Soviet artistic policy was written by Andrey Zhdanov in 1934, the year Stalin made him the party's spokesperson at the Congress of Soviet Writers.

There is not and never has been a literature making its basic subject-matter the life of the working class and the peasantry and their struggle for socialism. There does not exist in any country in the world a literature to defend and protect the equality of rights of the working people of all nations and the equality of rights of women. There is not, nor can there be in any bourgeois country, a literature to wage consistent war on all obscurantism, mysticism, hierarchic religious attitudes, and threats of hell-fire, as our literature does.

Only Soviet literature could become and has in fact become such an advanced, thought-imbued literature. It is one flesh and blood with our socialist construction. . . .

What can the bourgeois writer write or think of, where can he find passion, if the worker in the capitalist countries is not sure of his tomorrow, does not know whether he will have work, if the peasant does not know whether he will be working on his bit of land or thrown on the scrap heap by a capitalist crisis, if the working intellectual is out of work today and does not know whether he will have work tomorrow?

What can the bourgeois author write about, what source of inspiration can there be for him, when the world, from one day to the next, may be plunged once more into the abyss of a new imperialist war?

The present position of bourgeois literature is such that it is already incapable of producing great works. The decline and decay of bourgeois literature derives from the decline and decay of the capitalist system and are a feature and aspect characteristic of the present condition of bourgeois culture and literature. The days when bourgeois literature, reflecting the victories of the bourgeois system over feudalism, was in the heyday of capitalism capable of creating great works, have gone, never to return. Today a degeneration in subject matter, in talents, in authors and in heroes, is in progress. . . .

A riot of mysticism, religious mania, and pornography is characteristic of the decline and decay of bourgeois culture. The "celebrities" of that bourgeois literature which has sold its pen to capital are today thieves, detectives, prostitutes, pimps, and gangsters. . . .

The proletariat of the capitalist countries is already forging its army of writers and artists—revolutionary writers, the representatives of whom we are glad to be able to welcome here today at the first Soviet Writers' Congress. The number of revolutionary writers in the capitalist countries is still small but it is growing and will grow with every day's sharpening of the class struggle, with the growing strength of the world proletarian revolution.

We are firmly convinced that the few dozen foreign comrades we have welcomed here constitute the kernel, the embryo, of a mighty army of proletarian writers to be created by the world proletarian revolution in foreign countries. . . .

Comrade Stalin has called our writers "engineers of the human soul." What does this mean? What obligations does such an appellation put upon you?

It means, in the first place, that you must know life to be able to depict it truthfully in artistic creations, to depict it neither "scholastically" nor lifelessly, nor simply as "objective reality," but rather as reality in its revolutionary development. The truthfulness and historical exactitude of the artistic image must be linked with the task of ideological transformation, of the education of the working people in the spirit of socialism. This method in fiction and literary criticism is what we call the method of socialist realism.

Our Soviet literature is not afraid of being called tendentious, for in the epoch of class struggle there is not and cannot be "apolitical" literature.

And it seems to me that any and every Soviet writer may say to any dull-witted bourgeois, to any philistine or to any bourgeois writers who speak of the tendentiousness of our literature: "Yes, our Soviet literature is tendentious and we are proud of it, for our tendentiousness is to free the working people—and the whole of mankind—from the yoke of capitalist slavery."

To be an engineer of the human soul is to stand four-square on real life. And this in turn means a break with old-style romanticism, with the romanticism which depicted a nonexistent life and nonexistent heroes, drawing the reader away from the contradictions and shackles of life into an unrealizable and utopian world. Romanticism is not alien to our literature, a literature standing firmly on a materialistic basis, but ours is a romanticism of a new type, revolutionary romanticism. We say that socialist realism is the fundamental method of Soviet fiction and literary criticism, and this implies that revolutionary romanticism will appear as an integral part of any literary creation, since the whole life of our Party, of the working class and its struggle, is a fusion of the hardest, most matter-of-fact practical work, with the greatest heroism and the vastest perspectives. The strength of our Party has always lain in the fact that it has united and unites efficiency and practicality with broad vision, with an incessant forward striving and the struggle to build a communist society.

Soviet literature must be able to portray our heroes and to see our tomorrow. This will not be utopian since our tomorrow is being prepared by planned and conscious work today.

QUESTIONS How did Soviet cultural leaders analyze Western intellectual life? What were the proper tasks of an artist in Soviet society? How were these tasks expressed in socialist realism? What would the Soviet response be to Western intellectuals who claimed objectivity for their work?

and rigid planning from above that antagonized many peasants. The centralized planning process allowed few incentives for special efforts and often complicated a smooth flow of supplies and equipment, a problem also exacerbated by the Stalinist regime's priority concentration on the industrial sector. Agricultural production remained a major weakness in the Soviet economy, demanding a higher percentage of the labor force than was common under industrialization.

The collective farms did, however, allow normally adequate if minimal food supplies once the messy transition period had ended, and they did free excess workers to be channeled into the ranks of urban labor. The late 1920s and early 1930s saw a massive flow of unskilled workers into the cities, as the Soviet Union's industrialization, already launched, shifted into high gear.

If Stalin's approach to agriculture had serious flaws, his handling of industry was in most ways a stunning success. A system of **five-year plans** under the state planning commission began to set clear priorities for industrial development, including expected output levels and new facilities. The government constructed massive factories in metallurgy, mining, and electric power to make the Soviet Union an industrial country independent of Western-dominated world banking and trading patterns. There was more than a hint of Peter the Great's policies here, in updating the economy without really westernizing it, save that industrialization constituted a more massive departure than anything Peter had contemplated. The focus, as earlier, was on heavy industry, which built on the nation's great natural resources and also served to prepare for possible war with Hitler's anticommunist Germany.

five-year plans Stalin's plans to hasten industrialization of U.S.S.R.; constructed massive factories in metallurgy, mining, and electric power; led to massive state-planned industrialization at cost of availability of consumer products.

This distinctive industrialization, which slighted consumer goods production, was to remain characteristic of the Soviet version of industrial society. Further, Stalin sought to create an alternative not simply to private business ownership but also to the profit-oriented market mechanisms of the West. Thus he relied not on price competition but on formal, centralized resource allocation to distribute equipment and supplies. This led to many bottlenecks and considerable waste, as quotas for individual factories were set in Moscow, but there was no question that rapid industrial growth occurred. During the first two five-year plans, to 1937—that is, during the same period that the West was mired in the Depression—Soviet output of machinery and metal products grew 14-fold. The Soviet Union had become the world's third industrial power, behind only Germany and the United States. A long history of backwardness seemed to have ended.

Toward an Industrial Society

For all its distinctive features, the industrialization process in the Soviet Union produced many results similar to those in the West. Increasing numbers of people were crowded into cities, often cramped in inadequate housing stock. Factory discipline was strict, as communist managers sought to instill new habits in a peasant-derived workforce. Incentive procedures were introduced to motivate workers to higher production. Particularly capable workers received bonuses and also elaborate public awards for their service to society. At the same time, communist policy quickly established a network of welfare services, surpassing the West in this area and reversing decades of tsarist neglect. Workers had meeting houses and recreational programs, often including vacations on the Black Sea, as well as protection in cases of illness and old age. Soviet industrial society provided only modest standards of living at this point, but a host of collective activities compensated to some degree.

Finally, although Soviet industry was directed from the top, with no legal outlet for worker grievances—strikes were outlawed, and the sole trade union movement was controlled by the party—worker concerns were studied, and identified problems were addressed. The Soviet Union under Stalin used force and authority, but it also recognized the importance of maintaining worker support—so, informally, laborers were consulted as well.

Totalitarian Rule

Stalinism instituted new controls over intellectual life. In the arts, Stalin insisted on uplifting styles that differed from the non-representational modern art themes of the West, which he condemned as capitalist decadence. (Hitler and Stalin, bitter enemies, both viewed contemporary Western culture as dangerous.) Artists and writers who did not toe the line risked exile to Siberian prison camps, and party loyalists in groups like the Writers Union helped ferret out dissidents. **Socialist realism** was the dominant school, emphasizing heroic idealizations of workers, soldiers, and peasants

socialist realism Attempt within the U.S.S.R. to relate formal culture to the masses in order to avoid the adoption of western European cultural forms; begun under Joseph Stalin; fundamental method of Soviet fiction, art, and literary criticism.

Figure 29.12 In his 1949 painting *Creative Fellowship,* Soviet artist Shcherbakov shows the cooperation of scientists and workers in an idealized factory setting. The painting exemplifies the theories and purposes of socialist realism.

Politburo   Executive committee of the Soviet Communist party; 20 members.

(Figure 29.12). Science was also controlled. Stalin clamped down hard on free scientific inquiry, insisting for example that evolutionary biology was wrong because it contradicted Marxism. A number of scientists were ruined by government persecution.

Stalin also combined his industrialization program with a new intensification of government police procedures; he used party and state apparatus to monopolize power, even more thoroughly than Hitler's totalitarian state attempted. Real and imagined opponents of his version of communism were executed, in one of the great bloodbaths of the 20th century. During the great purge of party leaders that culminated in 1937–1938, hundreds of people were intimidated into confessing imaginary crimes against the state, and most of them were then put to death. Many thousands more were sent to Siberian labor camps. News outlets were monopolized by the state and the party, and informal meetings also risked a visit from the ubiquitous secret police, renamed the MVD in 1934. Party congresses and meetings of the executive committee, or **Politburo,** became mere rubber stamps. An atmosphere of terror spread.

Stalin's purges, which included top army officials, ironically weakened the nation's ability to respond to growing foreign policy problems, notably the rising threat of Hitler. Soviet diplomatic initiatives after the 1917 revolution had been unwontedly modest, given the nation's traditions, largely because of the intense concentration on internal development. Diplomatic relations with major nations were gradually reestablished as the fact of communist leadership was accepted, and the Soviet Union was allowed into the League of Nations. A few secret military negotiations, as with Turkey in the early 1920s, showed a flicker of interest in more active diplomacy, and of course the nations continued to encourage and often guide internal Communist party activities in many other countries.

Hitler's rise was a clear signal that more active concern was necessary. A strong Germany was inevitably a threat to Russia from the west, and Hitler was vocal about his scorn for Slavic peoples and communism, and about his desire to create a "living room" for Germany to the east. Stalin initially hoped that he could cooperate with the Western democracies in blocking the German threat. The Soviet Union thus tried to participate in a common response to German and Italian intervention during the Spanish Civil War, in 1936–1937. But France and Britain were incapable of forceful action and were in any event almost as suspicious of the Soviets as of the Nazis. So the Soviet Union, unready for war and greatly disappointed in the West, signed a historic agreement with Hitler in 1939. This pact bought some time for greater war preparation and also enabled Soviet troops to attack eastern Poland and Finland in an effort to regain territories lost in World War I. Here was the first sign of a revival of Russia's long interest in conquest, which would be intensified by the experience of World War II.

Global Connections

Economic Depression, Authoritarian Response, and Democratic Retreat

The Great Depression of the 1930s promoted a growing wave of nationalist reactions and further weakened global ties. Western European countries and the United States increased their tariffs and refused to collaborate in measures that might have alleviated economic dislocation. Their narrow policies made economic collapse even worse. Japan, badly hurt by a new U.S. tariff that cut into silk exports, increased its own nationalism; here was the context for the growing power of younger army officers pushing for overseas expansion. Japan began to think of its own new empire in east Asia that could shield it from worldwide economic trends. Nazi Germany also pulled out of the international community, seeking to make Germany as economically self-sufficient as possible. The Soviet Union still mouthed communist commitment to internationalism, but in fact Stalin concentrated on standing alone, in a nationalist and isolationist version of the great Russian

Revolution. The world was falling into pieces, and no society, certainly not the beleaguered West, seemed capable of putting it back together.

Further Readings

Sally Marks, *The Ebbing of European Ascendancy: An International History of the World: 1914–1945* (2002), is the new standard introduction to the diplomacy of the period. See also Bernard Wasserstein, *Barbarism and Colonization: A History of Europe in Our Times* (2007) and Allan Todd, *The European Dictatorships: Hitler, Stalin, Mussolini* (2002). Good overall studies of the political revolutions of the period include Eric Wolf, *Peasant Wars of the Twentieth Century* (1965); Theda Skocpol, *States and Social Revolutions* (1970); and John Dunn, *Modern Revolutions* (1972). Mark N. Katz, *Reflections on Revolutions* (1999), is an accessible survey of historical theories of revolution. See also Michael J. Gonzales, *The Mexican Revolution, 1910–1940* (2002); Thomas Kampen, *Mao Zedong, Zhou Enlai and the Evolution of the Chinese Communist Leadership* (2000); Xiaoyuan Liu, *Frontier Passages: Ethnopolitics and the Rise of Chinese Communism, 1921–1945* (2004). Two studies of the Long March that make superior use of eyewitnesses accounts are Andrew McEwen and Ed Jocelyn, *The Long March: The True Story Behind the Legendary March that Made Mao's China* and Sun Shuyun, *The Long March: The True History of Communist China's Founding Myth*, both 2006.

On the Russian Revolution, Sheila Fitzpatrick, *The Russian Revolution* (1994), is an overview with a rich bibliography. See also Ian D. Thatcher, ed., *Reinterpreting Revolutionary Russia* (2006) and S. A. Smith, *The Russian Revolution: A Very Short Introduction* (2002). Rex Wade, *The Russian Revolution, 1917* (2005), is a comprehensive social and political history of the revolution's early years. On specific social groups, see John Keep, *The Russian Revolution: A Study in Mass Mobilization* (1976); and Victoria Bonnell, *Roots of Rebellion: Workers' Politics and Organizations in St. Petersburg and Moscow, 1900–1914* (1983). Leon Trotsky's *History of the Russian Revolution*, a gripping narrative by a participant, surveys social, economic, and political dimensions of the revolution.

On fascism in Italy, see R. J. B. Bosworth, *The Italian Dictatorship: Problems and Perspectives in the Interpretation of Mussolini and Fascism* (1998) and *Mussolini's Italy: Life under the Dictatorship, 1915–1945* (2006). Philip Morgan, *Italian Fascism, 1919–1945* (1995), provides a general overview. Emilio Gentile, *The Sacralization of Politics in Fascist Italy*, trans. Keith Botsford (1996), examines popular political culture. See also Anthony L. Cardoza, *Benito Mussolini: The First Fascist* (2006).

The economic history of Latin America is summarized in the classic by Brazilian economist Celso Furtado, *Economic Development of Latin America* (1976), and in John Sheahan, *Patterns of Development in Latin America* (1987). There are many good studies of Latin American politics, but Guillermo O'Donnell's *Modernization and Bureaucratic Authoritarianism* (1973) has influenced much recent scholarship. Also useful are Alan Knight's *The Mexican Revolution*, 2 vols. (1986), and John M. Hart's *Revolutionary Mexico* (1987), which provide excellent analyses of

that event. Freidrich Katz, *The Life and Times of Pancho Villa* (1998), is an outstanding biography.

On the cultural aspects of the U.S. influence on Latin America there is Gilbert Joseph et al., eds., *Close Encounters Empire* (1998). The role of the United States is discussed in Abraham Lowenthal, *Partners in Conflict: The United States and Latin America* (1987). Lester D. Langley's *The United States and the Caribbean in the Twentieth Century* (1989) gives a clear account of the recent history of that region, and Walter La Feber's *Inevitable Revolutions* (1984) is a critical assessment of U.S. policy in Central America.

For the United States, Niall Palmer, *The Twenties in America: Politics and History* (2006); Carrie A. Meyer, *Days on the Family Farm: From the Golden Age through the Great Depression* (2007); Ronald Allen Goldberg, *America in the Twenties* (2003); and David Joseph Goldberg's *Discontented America: The United States in the 1920s* (1999) are useful introductions. Robert Cruden, *Body and Soul: The Making of American Modernism* (2000), and Lynn Dumenil and Eric Foner, *The Modern Temper: American Culture and Society in the 1920s* (1995), offer intriguing analyses of the period. Robert Stern, Gregory Gilmartin, and Thomas Mellins, *New York: 1930* (1987), examines American architecture and urbanism between the two world wars. Steve Watson, *The Harlem Renaissance* (1995), is unsurpassed as a general study of African American culture and society in the "Roaring Twenties." Paula Fass, *The Damned and the Beautiful: American Youth in the 1920's* (1977), remains the best introduction to the "Lost Generation."

Some of the best general studies on China in the early 20th century include Lucian Bianco, *The Communist Revolution in China* (1967); C. P. Fitzgerald, *Birth of Communist China* (1964); Wolfgang Franke, *A Century of Chinese Revolution, 1851–1949* (1970); and Jonathan Spence, *The Search for Modern China* (1990). For firsthand accounts of conditions in the revolutionary era, see especially Graham Peck, *Two Kinds of Time* (1950); Edgar Snow, *Red Star over China* (1938); and Theodore White and Analee Jacoby, *Thunder out of China* (1946).

On the causes and onset of the Great Depression, Amity Shlaes, *The Forgotten Man: A New History of the Great Depression* (2007) and Mary C. McComb, *Great Depression and the Middle Class: Experts, Collegiate Youth and Business Ideology, 1929–1941* (2006) are solid introductions. See also J. Galbraith, *The Great Crash: 1929* (1980), and, for a useful collection of articles, W. Lacquer and G. L. Mosse, eds., *The Great Depression* (1970). Japan's experience is covered in I. Morris, ed., *Japan, 1931–1945: Militarism, Fascism, Japanism?* (1963).

Ronald Edsforth, *The New Deal: America's Response to the Great Depression* (2000), is a readable introduction to the political history of the New Deal. For a case study of social and political change in the United States during the period, see Lizabeth Cohen, *Making a New Deal: Industrial Workers in Chicago, 1919–1939* (1990). See also William Chafe, *Women and Equality: Changing Patterns in American Culture* (1984).

Alan Bullock's *Hitler: A Study in Tyranny* (1964) remains the best introduction to the Nazi leader. The methods and manner of the rise of German fascism are explored in William S. Allen, *Nazi Seizure of Power in a Single Town, 1930–1935* (1969); Russell G. Lemmons, *Goebbels and Der Angriff: Nazi Propaganda, 1927–1933*

(1994); David Schoenbaum, *Hitler's Social Revolution: Class and Status in Nazi Germany* (1997); and Samuel W. Mitchum Jr., *Why Hitler? The Genesis of the Nazi Reich* (1996).

For a standard analysis of the Spanish Civil War, see Hugh Thomas, *The Spanish Civil War* (1977); Paul Preston, *The Spanish Civil War, 1936–1939* (1994); and Raymond Carr, *The Spanish Tragedy: The Civil War in Perspective* (1993). Peter Carroll's *The Odyssey of the Abraham Lincoln Brigade: Americans in the Spanish Civil War* (1994) deals with one of the civil war's many international aspects.

For the career of Juan Perón and Peronism, there is Frederick C. Turner, *Juan Peron and the Reshaping of Argentina* (1983). Robert M. Levine, *Getúlio Vargas: Father of the Poor* (1998), explores Brazil's corporatist state. Luis Aguilar, *Cuba 1933: Prologue to Revolution* (1972), demonstrates that, as in so many Asian and Latin American countries, the post–Second World War revolutionary movement in Cuba led by Fidel Castro was rooted in the events of the 1930s. Irwin Gellman's *Good Neighbor Diplomacy: United States Policy in Latin America, 1933–1945* (1980) and *Roosevelt and Batista: Good Neighbor Policy in Cuba, 1933–1945* (1973) address the U.S. role in shaping the regimes that were challenged by those later revolutionary movements.

On the Stalinist era, Robert Conquest's *The Great Terror: A Reassessment* (1990) and Roy Medvedev's *Let History Judge: The Origins and Consequences of Stalinism* (1989) are important studies of the period. Stephen Kotkin, *Magnetic Mountain: Stalinism as Civilization* (1995), assesses the cultural, social, and political impact of Stalin's industrialization program by looking at the experience of a planned industrial city. Sarah Davies, *Popular Opinion in Stalin's Russia: Terror, Propaganda, and Dissent, 1934–1941* (1997), offers a revealing portrayal of everyday cultural life under Stalin. Alan Bullock, *Hitler and Stalin: Parallel Lives* (1993), offers a comparative biography of the two totalitarian leaders.

Mark Selden's *The Yenan Way in Revolutionary China* (1971) provides the fullest account of the development of the communist movement after the Long March.

On the Web

The initial political program of the Russian Provisional Government is accessible on the Web at http://www.spartacus.schoolnet .co.uk/RUSprovisional.htm, http://www.dur.ac.uk/~dml0www/ provgov1.html.firstworldwar.com/source/firstprovgovt.htm, and http://www.historylearningsite.co.uk/provisional_government.htm. Some of its major political blunders are discussed at http://www .historylearningsite.co.uk/.cddc.vt.edu/marxist/archive/index.htm, http://en.wikipedia.org/wiki/Russian_Provisional_Government. The politically revealing lyrics of its national anthem can be explored at http://www.national-anthems.net/~davidk/ruf2-txt.htm. The Lenin Archive, at http://www.marxists.org/archive/lenin/, is a good place to find the works, writings, speeches, biography, and various images of the Bolshevik leader. Other useful sites for further study of Lenin and other leaders of the early communist movement are http://www2northpark.edu/history/WebChron/ EastEurope/OctRev.html and http://www.marxist.com/Russia/ rev-betrayed.html.

Benito Mussolini's vision of fascism can be glimpsed at http:// www.fordham.edu/halsall/mod/mussolini-fascism.html. Italian fascism and life in fascist Italy is explained at http://www.library .wisc.edu/libraries/dpf/Fascism/Intro.html. An internal link at this site at http://www.library.wisc.edu/libraries/dpf/Fascism/Youth.html offers a vivid look into the manner in which young fascists were indoctrinated via a magazine, a glimpse of whose front covers is alone worth a visit.

Life in the United States in the 1920s is illuminated at http:// www.users.cvip.fresno.comnet/~jsh33/roar.html and http://kclibrary .nhmccd.edu/decade20.html, and http://www.webtech.kennesaw .edu/jcheek3/roaring_twenties.htm. Other websites examine in detail the Scopes "Monkey Trial," prohibition, and Harlem in the "Jazz Age," such as those at http://www.xroads.virginia.edu/~UG97/ inherit/1925home.html, http://www.law.umkc.edu/faculty/projects/ ftrials/scopes/scopes.htm, http://www.prohibition.osu.edu, http:// www.etext.lib.virginia.edu/harlem/index.html, and http://www .42explore2.com/harlem.htm. The path that led to the winning of voting rights for women is traced at http://www.memory.loc.gov/ ammem/naw/nawshome.html, while the role of women peace activists during the Red Scare is examined at http://www.womhist .binghampton.edu/alexanderstreet.com/wilpf/intro.htm.

Sites that serve to illuminate the process of and key figures in the decline and fall of the Qing Empire include a useful biography of Yuan Shikai at http://www.wikipedia.org/wiki/Yuan_Shikai. The emergence of Republican China, including Sun Yat-sen's early political platform, is treated at http://www.chaos.umd.edu/history/ republican.html. The life of Chiang Kai-shek as seen against the background of nationalist politics is provided at http://www.wsu .edu:8001/~dee/MODCHINA/SUN.HTM. An interesting reflection on the legacy of the student-led May Fourth movement is offered at http://en.wikipedia.org/wiki/May_Fourth_Movement. An excellent introduction to the life of Chinese communist Mao Zedong is provided at http://www.asiasource.org/society/mao.cfm.

The revolution in Mexico inspired both joy and deadly reaction as detailed at http://ac.acusd.edu/History/projects/border/ page01.html.revolutions.truman.edu/mexico/ (for links, see http:// www.123exp-history.com/t/03764106010/). Insight into Mexico's best known revolutionaries is presented at various sites. Emiliano Zapata is discussed at http://www.cs.utk.edu/~miturria/project/ zapata.html, and http://www.mexconnect.com/mex_/history/ ezapata1.html. Pancho Villa receives treatment at http://ojinaga .com/villa/ and http://www.mexconnect.com/mex_/history/ panchovilla1.html. The desire of many Latin Americans for a more egalitarian society was celebrated in the works of artists such as Diego Rivera at http://www.arts~history.mx/museomural.html and http://www.diegorivera.com/index.htm.php.

The 1929 American Stock Market Crash, the Great Depression that followed and images and recollections relating to these experiences are examined at http://www.pbs.org/wgbh/amex/ crash/gallery/index.html, http://memory.loc.gov/ammem/fsowhome .html, and http://www.michigan.gov/hal/0,1607,7-160-17451_ 18670_18793-53511—,00.html.

The American Dust Bowl is discussed at http://www.pbs.org/ wgbh/amex/dustbowl/peopleevents/index.html. The Franklin Delano Roosevelt Library at http://www.fdrlibrary.marist.edu/ index.html offers a gateway to the study of America's longest serving president. His response to the Great Depression, the New Deal, is examined at what is simply one of the finest of all Internet sites, http://www.newdeal.feri.org/.

The origins and "future" of Stalinism are explored at http:// home.mira.net/~andy/bs/index.htm. Stalinism is seen through declassified documents at http://www.utoronto.ca/ceres/serap/. Stalin offers his view of Soviet industrialization at http://artsci.shu .edu/reesp/documents/Stalin—industrialization.htm. A transcript of one of Stalin's purge trials brings them alive at http://art-bin .com/art/omosc20e.html. Soviet poster art can be viewed at http://members.telering.at/pat/poster1.htm and http://www .internationalposter.com/country-primers/soviet-posters.aspx. This last collection is organized by historical period, including a section devoted to New Economic Policy Posters. Other collections of Soviet poster art include http://www.sweb.cz/posters/listy/russ6.htm, http://www.poster.s.cz/, http://www.funet.fi/pub/culture/russian/ html_pages/posters1.html, and http://www.raketa.f2s.com/pics/ index.cgi?direct=Soviet_Posters. The Museum of Socialist Realist Art, comprised of examples drawn from Russian museums, offers good links to other sources: http://www.stanford.edu/~gfreidin/ gallery/propart/propart.htm. Leon Trotsky's role as an exiled critic of Stalin's regime, offered at http://www.anu.edu.au/polsci/marx/ contemp/pamsetc/socfrombel/sfb_7.htm, can be enlivened by a virtual visit to the house in Mexico where he was assassinated by a Stalinist agent provided at http://www.mexconnect.com/mex_/ travel/jmitchell/jmtrotsky.html.

Profiles of Nazi leaders and documents illustrating the rise of German fascism are offered at http://fcit.coedu.usf.edu/holocaust/ people/perps.htm and http://www.historylearningsite.co.uk/Nazi_ leaders.htm. The origins of Hitler's anti-Semitism are revealed at http://www2.h-net.msu.edu/~german/gtext/kaiserreich/hitler1.html. Trotsky's now classic critique of fascism has been made available at http://www.workersliberty.org/node/5913. A course lesson plan that offers a very good general introduction to German National Socialism and its totalitarian state and that includes useful definitions of key terms can be found at http://www.remember.org/ guide/Facts.root.nazi.html. The nature of the totalitarian state and the relationship between politics and art can be explored at http://www.calvin.edu/academic/cas/gpa/politart.htm and http:// fcit.coedu.usf.edu/holocaust/arts/artReich.htm. The Spanish Civil War is analyzed at http://www.geocities.com/CapitolHill/9820/, while an excellent related photo file, including Robert Capra's famous "Moment of Death" photograph, can be found at http:// history.sandiego.edu/cdr2/WW2Pics/13953.jpg.

The growth course of Japanese militarism in Japan is traced at http://www.users.bigpond.com/battleforAustralia/JapWarCrimes/ Reviving_Militarism.html. The course of that growth can be traced in the career of Hideki Tojo, minister for war and foreign affairs and prime minister of imperial Japan. Tojo's life, illuminated by selections from his diary, is explored at http://www .spartacus.schoolnet.co.uk/2WWtojo.htm. The cult of State Shinto used to drive the Japanese national and martial spirit is examined at http://www.britannica.com/eb/article-9069473.

The Web provides insight into the politic of Latin American in the 1930s, offering explorations of the lives of Cuba's Fulgencio Batista (http://www.historyofcuba.com/history/batista.htm), Brazil's Getúlio Vargas (search on http://historicaltextarchive.com/), and Argentina's Juan Perón, whose followers maintain their own Web page (http://www.falange.us/peron.htm), which is devoid of critical analysis but has excellent contemporary photographs.

A guide to the global graphic art of this era, from revolution to counterrevolution and including the Spanish Civil War, is provided at http://worldhistoryconnected.press.uiuc.edu/1.2/gilbert.html.

AP* | Test Prep

1. Why did new authoritarian movements surface in parts of Europe after World War I?

   (A) Parliamentary governments seemed incapable of managing the political, social, and economic crises.

   (B) Marxist intellectuals supported fascist challenges to middle-class rule.

   (C) Authoritarian movements were led by the Catholic church.

   (D) Socialists and women's suffrage groups turned against democratic policies.

2. Which of the following statements concerning women's suffrage in the 1920s is most accurate?

   (A) Despite their service in World War I, women failed to win the vote everywhere but in the United States.

   (B) Winning the vote actually increased feminist agitation during the 1920s.

   (C) Women's suffrage was granted after World War I in Britain, Germany, and the United States.

   (D) Women gained the right to vote during the prewar period, but it was suspended indefinitely during the early years of the war.

3. The Mexican muralist movement was indicative of

   (A) the anti-Communist spirit of the Mexican Revolution.

   (B) the policy of indigenism that was incorporated into the post-revolutionary reforms.

   (C) the failure of the revolution to pay attention to Indian cultures.

   (D) the interest in attracting investment and tourism from the United States.

4. How did Stalin's view of Communism compare to that of Lenin?

   (A) Lenin was only interested in the Russian revolution and did not visualize any further revolutionary process.

   (B) Stalin concentrated on a strongly nationalist version of Communism.

   (C) Stalin contributed more fundamentally to Marxist theory.

   (D) Their views did not differ.

AP* Test Prep

5. The policies of Sun Yat-sen and Mao Zedong differed primarily in
   - (A) Sun's focus on urban and industrial interests and Mao's commitment to the peasantry.
   - (B) Sun's alliance with the Soviet Union and Mao's refusal to do so.
   - (C) Sun's alliance with the warlords and Mao's alliance with the Japanese.
   - (D) Sun's commitment to Daoism and Mao's commitment to Marxism.

6. The May the Fourth Movement
   - (A) marked the emergence of Mussolini as an important fascist leader.
   - (B) expressed the nationalist fervor of Chinese students.
   - (C) took its name from the date of the first Wafd demonstrations in Egypt.
   - (D) was opposed to the New Deal, whose first initiatives were introduced on that date in 1933.

7. Which of the following factors limited Japanese economic advance prior to World War II?
   - (A) continued dependence on relatively few export products
   - (B) low population growth
   - (C) the failure of the agricultural economy
   - (D) rapidly increasing wages in the workforce
   - (E) inability to produce the most advanced machinery

Free-Response Question

Compare the impact of the Great Depression on two of the following regions: Latin America, East Asia, Western Europe, the USSR?

30 A Second Global Conflict and the End of the European World Order

Old and New Causes of a Second World War

THINKING HISTORICALLY: Total War, Global Devastation

Unchecked Aggression and the Coming of War in Europe and the Pacific

The Conduct of a Second Global War

DOCUMENT: Japan's Defeat in a Global War

War's End and the Emergence of the Superpower Standoff

Nationalism and Decolonization in South and Southeast Asia and Africa

VISUALIZING THE PAST: National Leaders for a New Global Order

GLOBAL CONNECTIONS: Persisting Trends in a World Transformed by War

Because the Japanese forces had taken Padang on the coast of Sumatra in the Dutch East Indies so swiftly and had routed the Dutch defenders so thoroughly, Sukarno felt comfortable taking a walk through the town the morning after it had been captured. As the European global order in Asia came tumbling down in late 1941 and the first weeks of 1942, he explained to his young friend, Waworuntu, why the Japanese invaders ought to be seen as the liberators of the peoples of what was soon to be the nation of Indonesia, as well as much of the rest of southeast Asia. As he later recalled in an autobiographical account of his life related to an American reporter, Sukarno denounced the Dutch because they had long humiliated and exploited the colonized peoples of Indonesia. In addition, after posturing for centuries as a superior race, the Dutch had fled or stood by passively as the Japanese took their place as rulers of the archipelago.

In tandem with the successful Japanese sneak attack on Pearl Harbor in Hawaii, the Japanese navy and army had swept down into Malaya, Borneo, the Philippines, the Dutch East Indies (later Indonesia), and Burma (Map 30.2, p. 821). In a matter of weeks, the armed forces of the Western colonial powers—Britain, the Netherlands, and the United States, who had colonized these areas decades or in some cases centuries earlier, had been defeated. Like Sukarno and his fellow Indonesians, peoples across southeast Asia watched as bedraggled European and American soldiers, nurses, bureaucrats, and merchants were herded on long marches to prison camps; many died on the way and many more died in captivity. The Japanese intentionally staged marches, such as that depicted in Figure 30.1, to break the psychological hold "whites" had striven for centuries to establish over colonized peoples. And as they vanquished and discredited the former overlords, the Japanese sought to pass themselves off as liberators—fellow Asians whose rule would soon bring a new order and better lives to peoples so long subjected to alien rule.

Recalling this moment of profound transition decades later, Sukarno claimed that he saw through the Japanese propaganda, that he knew they were "fascists" and would be little better as rulers than the Western imperialists they had supplanted. Whether or not he had actually seen this outcome at the time, his prediction was correct. The Indonesians and other peoples now colonized by the Japanese soon came to realize that their new masters were going to be far more demanding and brutal than the Dutch, British, or Americans. The Japanese soon alienated the peasants and workers who made up the great majority of their subject peoples by introducing often brutal forced labor systems (romusha) to extract the raw materials they so desperately needed to fight the Pacific war. As the conflict began to turn against the Japanese in mid-1942, they recruited nationalist leaders like Sukarno to mobilize colonized peoples to work and fight for their self-styled Japanese "liberators." Sukarno was later branded by some among the Allied leadership as a collaborator for becoming a front man for these campaigns. But a good deal of evidence bears out his impassioned insistence after the war that he was actually working to revitalize nationalist resistance to both the Japanese and Western colonizers.

A highly charismatic speaker, Sukarno cleverly foiled the intelligence officers who shadowed him at every step as he spoke at mass rallies and to paramilitary forces being trained by the Japanese. Drawing on incidents from the *wayang* shadow puppet plays based on the great Indian epics, the *Mahabharata* and the *Ramayana,* that had for centuries been central elements of Indonesian culture, Sukarno spoke in Javanese or Indonesian, so his Japanese handlers would not understand what he said. In a spirited oratorical style that suited the shadow dramas, he mocked the Japanese pretense that they were benevolent overlords by equating them with cruel rulers or treacherous characters from the epics. ■

Figure 30.1 The victorious Japanese armies subjected the tens of thousands European and American prisoners captured in their swift conquest of Southeast Asia in 1941–42 to forced marches to remote prison camps. Many of those who survived these "death marches" perished in the harsh conditions of internment. This photograph, stolen from Japanese files by Filipinos during Japan's three-year occupation, shows Japanese soldiers standing guard over American prisoners of war just before the "death march" began.

Like many of the leaders of the decolonization movements that swept Asia and Africa after 1945, Sukarno used the power vacuum created by the weakening of the great powers on both sides during the Pacific war to arouse and organize nationalist resistance and, as the fighting wound down in 1945, to declare Indonesia's independence. Thus, as we shall see in this chapter, even more than the war between 1914 and 1918, World War II was a global conflict. The defeats suffered early in the war by the Western colonial powers doomed their empires. In part due to the success of their mobilizing efforts and agitation during the war years, Western-educated leaders like Sukarno in many cases inherited political power in the new nations that emerged from the fallen empires. Like Sukarno, many of these leaders lacked the skills and political base to deal effectively with the problems that faced their new states, which were often artificially patched together, ethnically and religiously divided, and economically disadvantaged. And many of these leaders shared Sukarno's fate, as his failures and the machinations of the superpowers locked in cold war rivalries led to his overthrow by military leaders who so often seized power in nations emerging from colonial rule.

Old and New Causes of a Second World War

The gradual militarization of Japan proceeded despite the solid majorities that moderate political parties continued to win until the end of the 1930s. And it developed in the context of a succession of regional diplomatic crises. During the later 1920s, nationalistic forces in China began to get the upper hand over the regional warlords who had dominated Chinese politics since the early 1900s. At the head of the Guomindang (or Nationalist) party, General Chiang Kai-shek in particular was

The path to World War II was paved in large part by major social and political upheavals in several of the nations that had fought in World War I. Grievances related to World War I were compounded in each case by the economic havoc, and resulting social tensions, brought on by the Great Depression.

1930 C.E.	1940 C.E.	1950 C.E.	1960 C.E.
1930s Great Depression	1941 Japanese attack Pearl Harbor; United States enters World War II	1957 Ghana established as first independent African nation	1960 Congo granted independence from Belgian rule
1931 Japan invades Manchuria	1941 German invasion of the Soviet Union	1958 Afrikaner Nationalist party declares independence of South Africa	1961 Afrikaner-dominated parliament votes for complete South African independence from Great Britain
1933 Nazis come to power in Germany	1942 Fall of Singapore to the Japanese		1962 Algeria wins independence
1935 Government of India Act	1942 Cripps mission to India; Quit India movement		
1935 Italy invades Ethiopia	1945 Atomic bomb dropped on Japan; World War II ends; United Nations established		
1936–1939 Spanish Civil War			
1936–1939 Arab uprisings in Palestine	1947 India and Pakistan gain independence, leading to wider decolonization		
1938 Germany's union (Anschluss) with Austria; Munich conference; German armies occupy the Sudetenland	1947 Cold war begins		
1939 Nazi-Soviet Pact	1948 Israel-Palestine partition, first Arab-Israeli war; beginning of apartheid legislation in South Africa		
1939 World War II begins			

able to win the support of intellectuals, students, the business classes, the rural gentry, and even members of the largely discredited Confucian elites and rival military leaders. His military successes against first the southern and later the northern warlords seemed destined to unify China under a strong central government for the first time in decades.

The success of the Guomindang worried Japan's army officers, who feared that a reunited China would move to resist the informal control the Japanese had exerted over Manchuria since their victory in the Russo-Japanese war in 1905. Fearful of curbs on their expansionist aims on the mainland and unimpeded by weak civilian governments at home, the Japanese military seized Manchuria in 1931 and proclaimed it the independent state of Manchukuo. The international crisis that resulted worked to the military's advantage because civilian politicians were reluctant to raise objections that might weaken Japan in negotiations with the United States and the other powers or undermine its armies of occupation in Manchuria and Korea, which the Japanese had declared a colony in 1910.

Rehearsals: Dictators, Militarism, and the Agony of the Spanish Civil War

In contrast to the gradual shift of power to the military in Japan, the change of regimes in Germany was more abrupt and more radical. Parliamentary government in the Weimar era had been under siege from the time its civilian leaders had agreed to the armistice in 1918, and even more so after they signed the punitive treaty at Versailles. Weimar had survived these humiliations, civil war, and the hyperinflation of the mid-1920s, but just as economic recovery appeared to be gaining real momentum, the Great Depression struck. In the social discontent and political turmoil that followed, Adolf Hitler and the **National Socialist (Nazi)** party captured a steadily rising portion of the votes and parliamentary seats in a rapid succession of elections. The Nazis promised to put the German people back to work, restore political stability, and set in motion a remilitarization program that would allow Germany to throw off the shackles of what Hitler branded the diktat of Versailles. Hitler also promised to turn back the communist bid to capture power in Germany that had grown more and more serious as the Depression deepened. The threat of the communists within was linked to that of the Soviet Union to the east. From the early 1920s, Hitler and his lieutenants had stressed the need to invade and destroy the Soviet empire, and a key part of Hitler's racist vision for the future was to reduce the Russians and other Slavic peoples to virtual slaves in the service of the Aryan master race.

As we have seen in Chapter 29, a major part of the Nazis' political agenda once in power was a systematic dismantling of the political and diplomatic system created by the Versailles settlement. Rearmament from 1935, the militarization of the Rhineland in 1936, a forced union with Austria and the seizure of areas in Czechoslovakia where German-speakers were in the majority in 1938,

National Socialist (Nazi) party   Also known as the Nazi party; led by Adolf Hitler in Germany; picked up political support during the economic chaos of the Great Depression; advocated authoritarian state under a single leader, aggressive foreign policy to reverse humiliation of the Versailles treaty; took power in Germany in 1933.

Total War, Global Devastation

War had changed radically long before the 20th century. With state centralization, war lost its ritual characteristics. It became more commonly an all-out battle, using any tactics and weapons that would aid in victory. In other words, war became less restrained than it had been among less bureaucratized peoples who often used bluff and scare more than violence.

The 20th century most clearly saw the introduction of a fundamentally new kind of war, total war, in which vast resources and emotional commitments of the belligerent nations were marshaled to support military effort. The two world wars were thus novel not only in their geographic sweep, but in their mobilization of the major combatants. The features of total war also colored other forms of struggle, helping to explain brutal guerrilla and terrorist acts by groups not powerful enough to mount total wars but nonetheless affected by their methods and passions.

Total war resulted from the impact of industrialization on military effort, reflecting both the technological innovation and the organizational capacity that accompanied the industrial economy. Key steps in the development of total war emerged in the West at the end of the 18th century. The French Revolution, building new power for the state in contact with ordinary citizens, introduced mass conscription of men, forming larger armies than had ever before been possible. New citizen involvement was reflected in incitements to nationalism and stirring military songs, including aggressive national anthems—a new idea in itself. Industrial technology was first applied to war on a large scale in the U.S. Civil War. Railroads allowed wider movement of mass armies. Mass-produced guns and artillery made a mockery of earlier cavalry charges and redefined the kind of personal bravery needed to fight in war.

However, it was World War I that fully revealed the nature of total war. Steadily more destructive technology included battleships, submarines, tanks, airplanes, poison gas (which had been banned by international agreement before the war), machine guns, and long-range artillery. Organization for war included not only massive, compulsory recruitment—the draft—but also government control of economic activity via obligatory planning and rationing. Another factor was unprecedented control of media, not only through effective censorship and the containment of dissidents but through powerful propaganda designed to incite passionate, all-out commitment to the national cause and deep, unreasoned hatred of the enemy. Vivid posters, inflammatory speeches, and outright falsehood were combined in the emotional mobilization effort. All of these features returned with a vengeance in World War II, from the new technology of bombing, rocketry, and ultimately the atomic bomb to the enhanced economic mobilization organized by government planners.

> "[O]ne measure of total war was a blurring of the distinction between military and civilians, a distinction that had often limited war's impact earlier in world history."

The people most affected by the character of total war were the troops, who directly endured—bled from and died from—the new technology. But one measure of total war was a blurring of the distinction between military and civilians, a distinction that had often limited war's impact earlier in world history. Whole civilian populations, not just those unfortunate enough to be near the front lines, were forced into certain types of work and urged to certain types of beliefs. The bombing raids, including the German rockets directed against British cities late in World War II, subjected civilians to some of the most lethal weapons available as many belligerents deliberately focused their attacks on densely populated cities. Correspondingly, psychological suffering, though less common among civilians than among frontline soldiers, could spread throughout the populations involved in war.

Total war, like any major historical development, had mixed results. Greater government economic direction often included new measures to protect workers and give them a voice on management boards. Mobilization of the labor force often produced at least temporary breakthroughs for women. Intense efforts to organize technological research often produced side effects of more general economic benefit, such as the invention of synthetic rubber and other new materials.

Still, total war was notable especially for its devastation. The idea of throwing all possible resources into a military effort made war more economically disruptive than had been the case before. The emotions unleashed in total war produced embittered veterans who might vent their anger by attacking established political values. It certainly made postwar diplomacy more difficult. One result of total war was a tendency for the victor to be inflexible in negotiations at war's end. People who fought so hard found it difficult to treat enemies generously. The results of a quest for vengeance often produced new tensions that led directly, and quickly, to further conflict. War-induced passions and disruptions could also spark new violence at home; crime rates often soared not only right after the war ended (a traditional result) but for longer periods of time. Children's toys started to reflect the most modern weaponry. Thus, much of the nature of life in the 20th and 21st centuries has been determined by the consequences of total war.

QUESTIONS How did the experience of total war affect social and political patterns after World War II? Why do many historians believe that total war made rational peacetime settlements more difficult than did earlier types of warfare?

and the occupation of the rest of the Czechoslovak republic the following year made a shambles of the agreements that had ended World War I. Hitler's successes emboldened Mussolini to embark on military adventures of his own, most infamously in Ethiopia, where Italian pilots bombed defenseless cities and highly mechanized armies made extensive use of poisonous gases against resistance forces armed with little more than rifles. The fascists stunned much of the rest of the world by routinely unleashing these weapons on a civilian population that had no means of defending itself.

Hitler and Mussolini also intervened militarily in the Spanish Civil War in the mid-1930s in the hope of establishing an allied regime. Once again, Mussolini's mechanized forces proved effective, this time against the overmatched, left-leaning armed forces of the Spanish republic. Both the Italian and German air forces used the Spanish conflict as a training ground for their bomber pilots; in the absence of enemy planes or pilots, however, their main targets were ground forces and, ominously, civilians in Spain's cities and villages. Support from Mussolini and Hitler was critical to Franco's destruction of the elected republican government and seizure of power, particularly since the Western democracies had refused to counter the Nazi and fascist interventions.

Excepting volunteer forces recruited in England, France, the United States, and other democracies, only the Soviet Union sought to provide military aid to Spain's republicans. Though valiant, these relief attempts proved futile in the face of relentless assaults by Franco's well supplied legions and both Nazi and Fascist forces. Despite the critical assistance provided by his fellow fascists, Franco refused to join them in the global war that broke out soon after he had crushed the republic and begun a dictatorial rule in Spain that would last for decades.

Unchecked Aggression and the Coming of War in Europe and the Pacific

World War II began officially on September 1, 1939, with the German invasion of Poland. But a succession of localized clashes, initiated by the Japanese seizure of Manchuria in 1931, can be seen as part of a global conflict that raged for well over a decade between 1930 and 1945. In contrast to the coming of World War I, which, as we have seen, the leaders of Europe more or less blundered into, World War II was provoked by the deliberate aggressions of Nazi Germany and a militarized and imperialist Japan. The failure of the Western democracies and the Soviet Union to respond resolutely to these challenges simply fed the militarist expansionism of what came to be called the Axis powers, in reference to the linkages, both real and imagined, between Berlin, Rome, and Tokyo.

Hitler and Mussolini discovered that Britain and France, and even more so the increasingly isolated United States, were quite willing to sacrifice small states, such as Spain and Czechoslovakia, in the false hope that fascist and especially Nazi territorial ambitions would be satisfied and thus war averted. Leaders like **Winston Churchill**, who warned that a major war was inevitable given Hitler's insatiable ambitions, were kept from power by voters who had no stomach for another world war. Rival politicians, such as Neville Chamberlain and the socialist leaders of France, also feared correctly that rearming as Churchill proposed would put an end to their ambitious schemes to build welfare states as an antidote to further economic depressions. But in the late 1930s, another round of provocative aggressions pushed the democracies into a war that none had the stomach for or was prepared at that point to fight.

The Japanese Invasion of China

Although Nazi aggressions traditionally have been stressed as the precipitants of World War II, the Japanese military actually moved first. In the second half of 1937, from their puppet state, Manchukuo, which had been carved out of Manchuria, they launched a massive invasion of China proper. Exploiting a trumped-up incident in early July that led to a fire fight between Japanese and Chinese troops, the army launched an ill-advised campaign to conquer the whole of China. Prominent naval leaders and civilian politicians had deep misgivings about this massive escalation of the war in China and were uneasy about American and British reactions to yet another major round of Japanese aggression. But they were largely cowed into silence by the threat of assassination by fanatical junior army officers and renewed appeals to patriotic solidarity in a situation where Japanese soldiers were at risk.

By the late 1930s, the leaders of the new totalitarian states acted on the lesson that international rivalries in the preceding decades seemed to offer—that blatant aggression would succeed and at little cost.

Churchill, Winston   (1874–1965) British prime minister during World War II; responsible for British resistance to German air assaults.

At first, the advancing Japanese forces met with great success, occupying most of the coastal cities, including Shanghai and, by the end of 1938, Canton as well as the hinterlands behind cities in the north. The Japanese deployed extensive aerial bombing against Guomindang forces and especially the civilian population in the coastal cities. As Chinese resistance stiffened in some areas, Japanese soldiers resorted to draconian reprisals against both the Chinese fighters and civilians. In many instances, most infamously in the capture in December 1937 of the city of Nanjing, the evacuated Guomindang capital, Japanese forces took out their frustrations on retreating Chinese troops and the civilian population (Figure 30.2). The wanton destruction and pillage, murder of innocent civilians, and rape of tens of thousands of undefended Chinese women that accompanied the Japanese occupation of the ancient city was but a prelude to the unparalleled human suffering of the world war that had now begun.

Deprived of the coastal cities and provinces that were the main centers of their power, Chiang and the Guomindang forces retreated up the Yangzi River, deep into the interior to the city of Chongqing, which became the nationalist capital for the rest of the war. Thus, long before the Japanese attacks on Pearl Harbor and Western colonies throughout southeast Asia in late 1941 that greatly expanded the war in Asia, Japan and China were engaged in a massive and deadly contest for control of all of east Asia.

The Partition of Poland and Nazi Preparations for War in the West

The Japanese had plunged into war without coordination, or even serious consultation with their likely allies, Germany and Italy. In fact the Tripartite Pact, which joined the three expansive Axis states in a loose alliance, was not signed until September 1940, when the war was well under way in both Europe and east Asia. Ironically, Nazi military advisors had contributed greatly to the training of the Guomindang officers and troops that fought to contain the Japanese invasion of China.

With a pause to consolidate his stunning gains in central Europe from 1936 to 1938, Hitler now concentrated his forces on the drive to the Slavic east, which he had long staked out as the region that would provide living space for the Germanic master race. He bought time to prepare the way for the assault on the main target, the Soviet Union, by signing a nonaggression pact with Stalin in August 1939. Military emissaries of the two dictators negotiated a division of the smaller states that separated their empires, and Stalin swallowed short-term disappointments, such as the division of Poland, to prepare the Soviet Union for the invasion that most observers were now convinced was inevitable. Within days of signing the agreement, Hitler ordered the Wehrmacht, or Nazi armies, to overrun western Poland; the Soviets then occupied the eastern half of the country, which had been promised to them in the cynical pact just concluded with the Nazis.

The brutal Nazi invasion of Poland on September 1, 1939, put an end to any lingering doubts about Hitler's contempt for treaties and repeated assurances that Germany's territorial ambitions had been satisfied by the absorption of Czechoslovakia into the Nazi Reich (Figure 30.3). Although they were helpless to assist the overmatched Poles in their futile efforts to oppose the German advance, the British and French had no choice but to declare war on Germany. But the armies of both powers simply dug in along the defensive lines that had been established in eastern France in the late 1920s. There they waited for the Nazis to turn to the west for further conquests, and prepared for another defensive war like the one they had managed to survive, at such horrific cost, between 1914 and 1918. But a second major theater of what rapidly developed into a second world war had been opened, and this conflict would prove radically different in almost all major respects from the one to which the new configuration of powers in Europe and the Pacific believed they were committing themselves.

Figure 30.2 As Chinese resistance to Japanese invasion in 1937 and 1938 stiffened, the invading armies resorted to random, mass executions to cow Chinese soldiers and civilians into submission.

Figure 30.3 Sober-faced and weeping Czechs watch the entry of the Nazi armies into Prague in the spring of 1939, as Hitler completes the takeover of the tiny democracy that was betrayed by the duplicity and cowardice of Allied leaders.

The Conduct of a Second Global War

The forces that gave rise to World War II meant that there would be more of a balance than in the Great War between a number of theaters spread across Europe, north Africa, and Asia. The largest and most costly fronts in lives lost and physical destruction resulted from the Nazi invasion of the vast expanses of the Soviet Union, and the Japanese invasion of China, and later Southeast Asia and the Pacific after the attack on the US fleet at Pearl Harbor.

The reluctance to rearm and react decisively displayed by both the Western democracies and the Soviet Union in the 1930s made possible crushing and almost unremitting victories and rapid territorial advances on the part of the main Axis powers, Germany and Japan, early in the war. But once the Nazis became bogged down in the expanses of the Russian steppes and the United States entered the war, the tide shifted steadily in favor of the Allies. Once the initial momentum of the Axis war machine was slowed, it became increasingly clear that the Anglo-American and Soviet alliance was decidedly more powerful in terms of population size, potential industrial production, technological innovation, and military capacity on land, in the seas, and in the air.

Nazi Blitzkrieg, Stalemate, and the Long Retreat

blitzkrieg German term for lightning warfare; involved rapid movement of airplanes, tanks, and mechanized troop carriers; resulted in early German victories over Belgium, Holland, and France in World War II.

As the Japanese bogged down in China and debated the necessity of tangling with the United States and the European colonial powers, the Nazi war machine captured France and the Low Countries with stunning speed, forced the British armies to beat a fast retreat to their island refuge, and then rolled over eastern Europe and drove deep into the Soviet Union (Map 30.1). Germany appeared unstoppable, and the fate of a large chunk of humanity seemed destined for a long period of tyrannical Nazi rule. From the outset, German strategy was centered on the concept of **blitzkrieg**, or "lightning war," which involved the rapid penetration of enemy territory by a combination of tanks and mechanized troop carriers, backup infantry, and supporting fighter aircraft and bombers. The effective deployment of these forces overwhelmed the Poles in 1939, and more critically routed the French and British within a matter of days in the spring of 1940, thereby accomplishing what the kaiser's armies failed to do through four long years of warfare between 1914 and 1918. German willingness to punish adversaries or civilian populations in areas that refused to yield greatly magnified the toll of death and destruction left in the wake of Hitler's armies. In early 1940, for example, the Dutch port of Rotterdam was virtually leveled by Nazi bombers, killing over 40,000 civilians.

The rapid collapse of France was, in part, a consequence of the divided and weak leadership the republic had displayed in the successive crises of the 1930s. Governments had come and gone as if contemporaries quipped that they were moving in revolving doors. Left and right quarreled and stalemated over rearming, responding to the Nazis, and allying with the British and the Soviets. When the war broke out, the citizenry of France was thoroughly demoralized, and the nation's defenses were outdated and extremely susceptible to the Wehrmacht's blitzkrieg offensives. By the summer of 1940 all of north and central France was in German hands; in the south, a Nazi puppet regime, centered on the city of **Vichy** (VEE-shee), was in charge. With the Nazi occupations of Norway and Denmark in the preceding months, Britain alone of the western democracies in Europe survived. But what remained of the British armies had been driven from the continent, while the nation's people and cities were under heavy assault by a markedly superior German air force, which strove to open the way to cross-channel invasion by the much larger and more powerful land forces of the steadily growing Nazi empire.

Remarkably, under the courageous leadership of Winston Churchill, the British people weathered what their new prime minister had aptly pronounced the nation's "darkest hour." A smaller British air force proved able to withstand the Nazi air offensive, including saturation bombing of

Vichy [VEE-shee] French collaborationist government established in 1940 in southern France following defeat of French armies by the Germans.

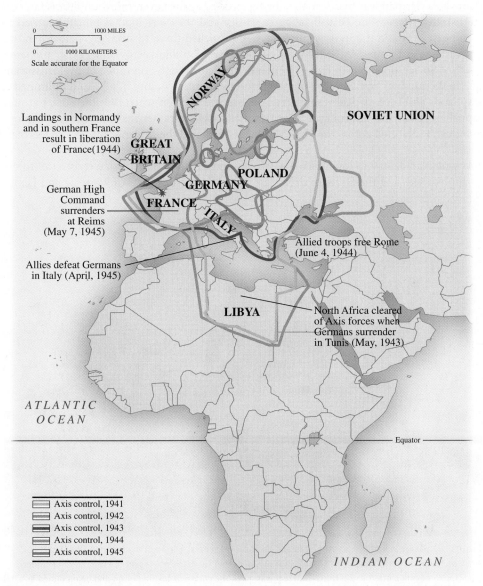

Map 30.1 World War II in Europe and the Middle East   The Nazi empire in Europe and the Middle East both rose and fell with remarkable speed but at the cost of tens of millions of lives.

Battle of Britain The 1940 Nazi air offensive including saturation bombing of London and other British cities, countered by British innovative air tactics and radar tracking of German assault aircraft.

The Nazi Empire in 1942 MAP

London and other British cities. Victory in what came to be known as the **Battle of Britain** was due to a mix of strong leadership by Churchill and a very able coalition cabinet, innovative air tactics made possible by the introduction of radar devices for tracking German assault aircraft, the bravery of Britain's royal family, and the high morale of the citizenry as a whole that the bombing raids seemed only to enhance. Unable to destroy Britain's air defenses or break the resolve of its people, Hitler and the Nazi high command had to abandon their plans for conquest of the British Isles. Without air superiority, the Germans could not prevent the Royal Navy from entering the channel and destroying the huge flotilla of landing craft that would be needed to carry the Nazi forces across the narrow but turbulent straits that had for nearly a millennium shielded Britain from outside invasion.

By mid-1941 the Germans controlled most of the continent of Europe and much of the Mediterranean. They had rescued the Italians' floundering campaign to conquer Albania and over-run Yugoslavia and Greece. They had conquered, or in the case of Sweden forced the neutralization of, the Scandinavian countries. They continued on to capture most of the islands of the Mediterranean and launched motorized offensives under the soon-to-be legendary commander Erwin Rommel (Figure 30.4) across north Africa and on to Egypt, with the goal of seizing the Suez Canal and cutting Britain off from its Asian empire. Once conquered, the hundreds of millions of peoples subjugated by Nazi aggression were compelled to provide resources, war materials, soldiers, and slave labor to a German war machine then being directed against even more ambitious targets.

Frustrated by resolute British defiance, Hitler and the Nazi high command turned to the south and east to regain the momentum that had propelled them to so many victories in the first years of the war in Europe. As Nazi forces, numbering 3.5 million, drove the poorly prepared and understaffed Soviet forces out of Finland, Poland, the Baltic states, and much of Byelorussia and the Ukraine in the summer and early fall of 1941, Hitler's grandest victory of all—and unlimited access to cheap labor and such critical resources as oil—seemed within reach. But the Soviet armies, despite appalling losses, did not collapse; they retreated eastward rather than surrender. Stalin ordered Soviet industry relocated across the Ural Mountains to shield them from capture and German aerial attacks.

As with Napoleon's invasion nearly a century and a half earlier, Russian resistance stiffened as winter approached, and the German drive east stalled on the outskirts of Moscow and Leningrad.

Figure 30.4 Erwin Rommel was the Germans' most daring general, earning the nickname "the Desert Fox" when he fought in north Africa. In 1944, when it was clear that Germany was losing the war, he came under suspicion of having plotted to kill Hitler. Rommel was given the choice of taking poison and being buried as a hero or being tried for treason. He chose poison; his death was presented to the German public as the result of war injuries.

The harsh winter caught the German forces unprepared while their Russian adversaries used terrain and weather conditions they knew well to counterattack with ferocity on a wide front. The Nazis' mass killings and harsh treatment of the Slavic peoples aroused guerrilla resistance by tens then hundreds of thousands of partisans, who fought behind German lines throughout the rest of the war. Many of the Ukrainians in particular were predisposed to back the Germans; therefore Nazi brutality proved a major obstacle to the conquest of the Soviet Union.

Renewed German offensives in the spring of 1942 again drove deep into Russia but failed a second time to capture key cities like Moscow, Leningrad, and Stalingrad, and perhaps as critically the great Baku oil fields in the southern steppes. The two sides clashed in some of the greatest battles of the entire war—in fact of all human history—including Kursk, which featured thousands of tanks deployed (and destroyed) by each of the adversaries. As another winter approached, the Germans were further away from knocking the Soviets out of the war than the year before. In fact, the failed Nazi attempt to capture Stalingrad in the bitter winter of 1942 and 1943 ended in the destruction of an entire German army and proved a decisive turning point in the war in the east.

In 1943 the Red armies went on the offensive at numerous points along the overextended, undermanned, and vulnerable German front. With staggering losses in lives and equipment, the Nazi forces, despite Hitler's rantings that they die in place, began the long retreat from the Soviet Union. By late 1944, Red armies had cleared the Soviet Union of Nazi forces and captured Poland and much of east central Europe southward into the Balkans. As the Soviet forces advanced inexorably toward Germany, it was clear that the destruction of Hitler's "thousand-year reich" was only months away. It was also apparent that the almost unimaginable sacrifices and remarkable resilience of Russian soldiers, which included many women, had contributed mightily to the destruction of the once imposing Nazi armed forces.

From Persecution to Genocide: Hitler's War Against the Jews

As the Nazi war machine bogged down in Russia, Hitler and his Nazi henchmen stepped up their vendetta against Gypsies, leftist politicians, homosexuals, and especially Jews. Jews, Polish intellectuals, and communists had been rounded up and killed in mass executions during the German offensives into eastern Europe and Russia in the early 1940s. But after a "final solution" for the "Jewish problem" was decided upon by prominent Nazi officials at the Wannsee Conference in February 1942, the regime directed its energies explicitly and systematically to genocide. The destruction, rather than the removal, of the Jewish people became the official policy of the Reich. The concentration camps that had been set up in the 1930s to incarcerate political enemies and groups branded as racially inferior—thus polluting to the Aryan people—were transformed into factories for the mass production of death.

Poland and the Death Camps

The more the war turned against Hitler and the Nazi high command, the more they pressed the genocidal campaign against the largely defenseless Jewish peoples of Europe. Vital resources were regularly diverted from the battle fronts for transportation, imprisonment, and mass murder in the camps, where the destruction of human life reached a frenetic pace in the last years of the regime. Jews and other "undesirables" were identified and arrested throughout the Nazi empire. Shipped to the camps in the east, those deemed physically fit were subjected to harsh forced labor that took a heavy toll in lives. The less fortunate, including the vast majority of the women and children, were systematically murdered, sometimes in experiments carried out by German physicians with the callous disregard for human suffering and humiliation that was a hallmark of the Nazi regime.

Emaciated Woman at Bergen-Belsen

As many as 12 million people were murdered in the genocidal orgy that has come to be known as the **Holocaust,** and which will perhaps prove to be what is remembered more than anything else about the Nazi regime. Of these, at least 6 million were Jews, and many millions of others were Slavic peoples mercilessly slaughtered on the Eastern Front. Without question, the Holocaust was by far the most costly genocide of the 20th century, which had begun with the Armenian massacres in 1915, and had the horrors of Kampuchea, Rwanda, Bosnia, and Kosovo yet to come. With the possible exceptions of the massacres in the Soviet Ukraine in the 1930s and those carried out in the 1970s by the Khmer Rouge, more than any of the other major episodes of the 20th-century genocide, the Holocaust was notable for the degree to which it was premeditated and systematic. It was carried out by the Nazi state apparatus and German functionaries, who until the very end kept precise and

The Holocaust: Memoirs from the Commandant of Auschwitz

Holocaust   Term for Hitler's genocide of European Jews during World War II; resulted in deaths of 6 million Jews.

detailed records of their noxious deeds. The Holocaust was at least passively abetted by denial on the part of the people of Germany and the occupied countries, though the Danes and Italians were notable for their resistance to Nazi demands that they turn over "their" Jews for incarceration.

The plight of the Jews of Europe was also greatly exacerbated by the refusal of the Western Allies to accept as immigrants any but the most affluent or skilled Jews fleeing Nazi atrocities, and by the failure of those same Allies to use their military assets to strike at the railway lines and killing chambers they clearly knew were in operation by the last months of the war. These responses to the Nazi horror only steeled the resolve of Zionist leaders in Palestine and elsewhere to facilitate, by negotiations with the hated Nazis if necessary, the flight of the European Jews. It also intensified their determination to establish a Jewish state in Palestine to ensure that there could never be another Holocaust.

Anglo-American Offensives, Encirclement, and the End of the 12-Year Reich

For nearly two years, the British were so absorbed in their own struggle for survival that they could provide little relief for their Soviet allies, hard-pressed by what some have seen as Hitler's foolhardy invasion of Russia. Even before the attack on Pearl Harbor in December 1941, the United States was providing substantial assistance, including military supplies, to beleaguered Britain. Franklin Roosevelt was quite openly sympathetic to the British cause and soon established a good working relationship with Churchill. American forces first entered the war in a major way in the campaigns to counter German U-boat attacks on shipping crossing the Atlantic. Then American tank divisions and infantry joined the British in reversing Rommel's gains in North Africa in 1942 and 1943. Having all but cleared Nazi forces from Africa and the Middle East, Anglo-American armies next struck across the Mediterranean at Sicily and then Italy proper. Their steady, but often costly, advance up the peninsula lasted into early 1945 but eventually toppled the fascist regime and prompted a Nazi takeover of northern Italy. Mussolini and the last of his many mistresses were captured and shot by partisans and enraged civilians, and hung upside down on a lamp post near Lake Bellagio.

With significant German forces tied down on the Eastern Front and in Italy, the allied high command, with General Dwight Eisenhower at its head, prepared landings in northern France that would carry the war into the fortress the Nazis had been building in occupied Europe ever since their defeat in the Battle of Britain in 1940. In early June, against fierce resistance, the Allies established beachheads at Normandy, from which they launched liberation campaigns into the Low Countries and the rest of France. Despite Hitler's last-ditch effort to repel the invading Allied armies in what became known as the **Battle of the Bulge** in the winter of 1944–1945, by early in 1945, the Allies had invaded Germany from the west, while the Red armies were pouring in from the east.

In late April, Russian and American troops linked up at the Elbe River, where they became caught up in spontaneous celebrations. The genuine camaraderie and mutual respect widely displayed by troops on both sides would soon be lost in high-stakes maneuvers by the political leaders in each camp to shape the postwar world order. On April 30, after haranguing his closest advisors for his betrayal by the German people, Adolf Hitler committed suicide in his Berlin bunker. Less than two weeks later, German military leaders surrendered their forces, putting an end to the war in the European and Mediterranean theaters. But the contest between the Anglo-American and Soviet allies for control of Germany had already commenced, and it would soon be extended to Europe as a whole and the rest of the world.

The Rise and Fall of the Japanese Empire in the Pacific War

Long before their attack on **Pearl Harbor** on December 7, 1941, the Japanese had been engaged in a major war on the Chinese mainland. Even after Pearl Harbor, roughly one-third of all Japanese military forces would remain bogged down in China, despite the sudden extension of the Japanese empire over much of southeast Asia and far out into the Pacific (Map 30.2). With the American Pacific fleet temporarily neutralized by the attack, Japan's combined air, sea, and army assaults quickly captured the colonial territories of the British in Hong Kong in south China as well as Malaya and Burma. They also overran the Dutch East Indies and the Philippines—despite more determined resistance—and completed the takeover of French Indochina. The Thais managed to stave off the invasion and occupation of Siam by retreating into neutrality and cooperating with the ascendant

Liberating the Concentration Camps
IMAGE

Operation Overlord, Normandy, 1944
IMAGE

Allied Victory in Europe, 1942–1945
MAP

Battle of the Bulge   Hitler's last-ditch effort to repel the invading Allied armies in the winter of 1944–1945.

Pearl Harbor   American naval base in Hawaii; attack by Japanese on this facility in December 1941 crippled American fleet in the Pacific and caused entry of United States into World War II.

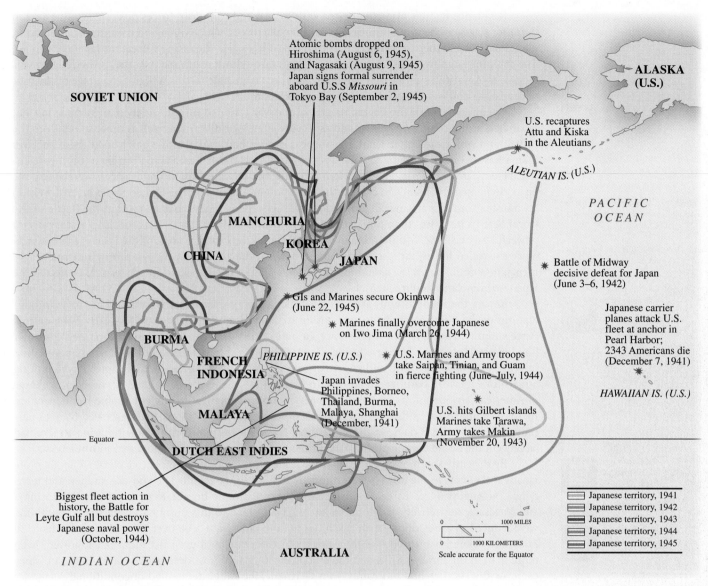

ALASKA (U.S.)

SOVIET UNION

Atomic bombs dropped on Hiroshima (August 6, 1945), and Nagasaki (August 9, 1945) Japan signs formal surrender aboard U.S.S *Missouri* in Tokyo Bay (September 2, 1945)

U.S. recaptures Attu and Kiska in the Aleutians

ALEUTIAN IS. (U.S.)

PACIFIC OCEAN

MANCHURIA

KOREA

CHINA

JAPAN

Battle of Midway decisive defeat for Japan (June 3–6, 1942)

GIs and Marines secure Okinawa (June 22, 1945)

Marines finally overcome Japanese on Iwo Jima (March 26, 1944)

Japanese carrier planes attack U.S. fleet at anchor in Pearl Harbor; 2343 Americans die (December 7, 1941)

BURMA

FRENCH INDONESIA

PHILIPPINE IS. (U.S.)

U.S. Marines and Army troops take Saipan, Tinian, and Guam in fierce fighting (June–July, 1944)

Japan invades Philippines, Borneo, Thailand, Burma, Malaya, Shanghai (December, 1941)

HAWAIIAN IS. (U.S.)

MALAYA

U.S. hits Gilbert islands Marines take Tarawa, Army takes Makin (November 20, 1943)

Equator

DUTCH EAST INDIES

Biggest fleet action in history, the Battle for Leyte Gulf all but destroys Japanese naval power (October, 1944)

INDIAN OCEAN

AUSTRALIA

0   1000 MILES
0   1000 KILOMETERS
Scale accurate for the Equator

	Japanese territory, 1941
	Japanese territory, 1942
	Japanese territory, 1943
	Japanese territory, 1944
	Japanese territory, 1945

Map 30.2 Asia and the Pacific in World War II   Although the human cost in this theatre of the war was the highest in China, the decisive battles were fought on the seas and islands of the vast Pacific Ocean.

Japanese. Although Great Britain remained a major combatant, and Australia and New Zealand provided important support, the United States soon emerged as the major counterforce to Japan's ever expanding Asian empire.

Though impressive in size and the speed with which it was formed, the Japanese empire soon proved highly vulnerable to the Allied forces committed to its destruction. The Japanese had risked alienating virtually all of the European colonial powers by their seizure of much of southeast Asia. They did so because they calculated that since the European metropoles had been overrun or were hard-pressed by the Nazis, the Europeans would not be able to reinforce their colonial enclaves. The Japanese leadership was also aware that their homeland's wartime economy was in desperate need of critical raw materials, including oil and staple foods, that could be imported from southeast Asia. But in their efforts to extract those resources, the Japanese imposed colonial regimes on the peoples of southeast Asia that were a good deal more brutally oppressive than those of any of the displaced Western colonizers. Over time, this produced growing resistance movements from Burma to the Philippines, which drew Japanese soldiers and substantial resources from the war in the Pacific against the advancing Allied forces.

Farthest Limits of Japanese Conquests

Resistance fighters also cooperated with British and American forces pushing into the area in the latter stages of the war. Southeast Asian guerrilla forces, which often had communist affiliations, played significant roles in sabotaging occupying forces and harassing retreating Japanese armies. The shipping lanes from distant colonial enclaves throughout southeast Asia also proved highly vulnerable to American submarines, which by late 1944 were able to sink a high percentage of the tons of foodstuffs and war materials shipped back to Japan.

War in the
Pacific

The main front of the Pacific theater of the war centered on the widely scattered islands that Japan had begun to occupy before, and especially after, World War I, as well as those seized from the British and Americans after Pearl Harbor. No sooner had the Japanese garrisoned these enclaves than a hastily but well prepared American advance into the central Pacific put them on the defensive. Having attacked Pearl Harbor when all of the major American aircraft carriers were at sea, the Japanese missed the chance to cripple the most potent weapons in the United States arsenal. Within six months United States naval and air forces fought the Japanese to a standoff at the **Battle of the Coral Sea**. In June, less than a month later, off **Midway Island**, they won a decisive victory over a powerful carrier force, commanded by Admiral Yamamoto, the architect of the Pearl Harbor attack. Once the Allied forces had gained the upper hand in the air and on the sea through these engagements, they could begin the assault on the double ring of Pacific island fortresses that protected the Japanese homeland (Figure 30.5).

Battle of the Coral Sea   World War II Pacific battle; United States and Japanese forces fought to a standoff.

Midway Island   World War II Pacific battle; decisive U.S. victory over powerful Japanese carrier force.

Japan in 1945

Keying their amphibious assaults on strategically vital islands, the joint air, sea, and land operations of the Allied forces had come within striking distance of Japan itself by early 1944, despite fierce and unrelenting Japanese resistance. In June of that year, the American air force began regular bomber assaults on the Japanese home islands. The high concentration of the Japanese population in urban areas and the wood and paper construction of most Japanese dwellings provided tempting targets for American bomber squadrons. In March 1945, General Curtis Le May, who was in charge of American air operations, ordered mass aerial bombardment of highly vulnerable Japanese cities. In Tokyo alone, these raids killed over 125,000 people, mostly civilians, and destroyed over 40 percent of the city within days. At the same time, Allied naval superiority and submarine attacks had largely cut the home islands off from what remained of the empire in China and southeast Asia.

An Eyewitness
to Hiroshima

By the early summer of 1945, Japanese leaders were sending out peace feelers, while the more fanatical elements in the army were promising to fight to the death. The end was sudden and terrifying. On August 6 and three days later on August 9, atomic bombs were dropped on Hiroshima and Nagasaki, respectively. In moments these cities, which to this point had been spared bombing, were reduced to ashes. Short-term casualties in both cities were well over 100,000, and deaths from radiation sickness increased this total greatly in the years, and even decades, that followed. Even more than in the European theater, the end of the long and most destructive war in human history came swiftly. As they had in dealing with Germany, the Allies demanded unconditional surrender by the Japanese. With the exception of retaining the emperor, which was finally allowed, the Japanese agreed to these terms and began to disarm. With the division of Germany that had begun some months earlier, the Allied occupation of the islands set the stage for the third main phase of the 20th century, which would be dominated by the cold war between the Soviet and American superpowers that would be waged amid the collapse of the European colonial order.

Nagasaki
Bomb
Attack—
August 1945

Figure 30.5 This artistic recreation of a scene of combat at sea, which was central to the Pacific war, shows sinking Japanese battle cruisers and a massive aircraft carrier, floundering and vulnerable to American dive bombers and fighter planes.

Japan's Defeat in a Global War

Japan's defeat in World War II brought moral and material confusion. The government was so uncertain of the intentions of the victorious Americans that it evacuated its female employees to the countryside. The following excerpt from the 1945 diary of Yoshizawa Hisako (who became a writer on home economics) reveals more popular attitudes and the mixed ingredients that composed them. The passage also suggests how the American occupation force tried to present itself and the reception it received.

August 15. As I listened to the Emperor's voice announcing the surrender, every word acquired a special meaning and His Majesty's voice penetrated my mind. Tears streamed down my cheeks. I kept on telling myself that we must not fight ourselves and work hard for our common good. Yes, I pledged myself, I must work [for Japan's recovery].

The city was quiet.

I could not detect any special expression in people's faces. Were they too tired? However, somehow they seemed brighter, and I could catch an expression showing a sign of relief. It could have been a reflection of my own feelings. But I knew I could trust what I saw . . .

The voluntary fighting unit was disbanded, and I was no longer a member of that unit. Each of us burned the insignia and other identifications.

I cannot foresee what kind of difficulty will befall me, but all I know is that I must learn to survive relying on my health and my will to live.

August 16. People do not wear expressions any different from other days. However, in place of a "good morning" or "good afternoon," people are now greeting each other with the phrase "What will become of us?"

During the morning, the city was still placed under air-raid alert.

My company announced that until everything becomes clearer, no female employees were to come to work and urged all of us to go to the countryside, adding that we should leave forwarding addresses. This measure was taken to conform to the step already taken by governmental bureaus. Are they thinking that the occupation army will do something to us girls? There are so many important questions we have to cope with, I cannot understand why governmental officials are so worried about these matters.

We did not have enough power and lost the war.

The Army continued to appeal to the people to resist the enemy to the end. This poses a lot of problems. People can show their true colors better when they are defeated than when they win. I just hope we, as a nation, can show our better side now.

Just because we have been defeated, I do not wish to see us destroying our national characteristics when we are dealing with foreign countries.

August 17. It was rumored that a number of lower echelon military officers were unhappy with the peace, and were making some secret moves. There were other rumors, and with the quiet evacuation of women and children from the cities, our fear seemed to have intensified. After all we have never experienced a defeat before. Our fear may simply be the manifestation of fear of the unknown.

Our airplanes dropped propaganda leaflets.

One of the leaflets was posted at the Kanda Station which said: "Both the Army and Navy are alive and well. We expect the nation to follow our lead." The leaflet was signed. I could understand how those military men felt. However, we already have the imperial rescript to surrender. If we are going to rebuild, we must open a new path. It is much easier to die than to live. In the long history of our nation, this defeat may become one of those insignificant happenings. However, the rebuilding after the defeat is likely to be treated as a far more important chapter in our history.

We did our best and lost, so there is nothing we have to say in our own defense. Only those people who did not do their best may now be feeling guilty, though.

Mr. C. said that everything he saw in the city was so repugnant that he wanted to retreat to the countryside. I was amazed by the narrowness of his thought process. I could say that he had a pure sense of devotion to the country, but that was only his own way of thinking. Beautiful perhaps, but it lacked firm foundation. I wish men like him would learn to broaden their perspectives.

August 18. Rationed bread distribution in the morning. I went to the distribution center with Mrs. A.

August 21. We heard that the Allied advance units will be airlifted and arrive in Japan on the 26th. And the following day, their fleet will also anchor in our harbors. The American Army will be airlifted and land in Atsugi airport.

According to someone who accompanied the Japanese delegation which went to accept surrender conditions, the Americans behaved like gentlemen. They explained to the Americans that certain conditions were unworkable in light of the present situation in Japan. The Americans immediately agreed to alter those conditions. They listened very carefully to what the Japanese delegation had to say.

An American paper, according to someone, reported that meeting as follows: "We cooked thick beefsteak expecting seven or eight Japanese would appear. But seventeen of them came, so we had to kill a turkey to prepare for them. We treated them well before they returned." . . . When I hear things like this, I immediately feel how exaggerated and inefficient our ways of doing things are. They say that Americans will tackle one item after another at a conference table, and do not waste even 30 seconds. . . .

In contrast, Japanese administration is conducted by many chairs and seals. For example when an auxiliary unit is asked to undertake a task for a governmental bureau, before anything can be done, twenty, or thirty seals of approval must be secured. So there is no concept of not wasting time. Even in war, they are too accustomed to doing things the way they have been doing and their many seals and chairs are nothing but a manifestation of their refusal to take individual responsibilities.

The fact of a defeat is a very serious matter and it is not easy to accept. However, it can bring some positive effects, if it can inculcate in our minds all the shortcomings we have had. I hope this will come true some day, and toward that end we must all endeavor. Even if we have to suffer hunger and other tribulations we must strive toward a positive goal.

QUESTIONS How did Japanese attitudes in defeat help prepare Japan for postwar redevelopment? Did defeat produce new divisions in attitudes among the Japanese? What other kinds of reactions might have been expected? How would you explain the rather calm and constructive outlook the passage suggests? Would American reactions to a Japanese victory have been similar?

War's End and the Emergence of the Superpower Standoff

The final stages of World War II quickly led to a tense worldwide half-century of confrontation between the United States and the Soviet Union, each of which headed hostile alliances anchored in nations that had been major combatants during the war.

Charter of the United Nations (excerpted) DOCUMENT

United Nations: Universal Declaration of Human Rights DOCUMENT

United Nations International organization formed in the aftermath of World War II; included all of the victorious Allies; its primary mission was to provide a forum for negotiating disputes.

World War II did not produce the sweeping peace settlements, misguided as most of them turned out to be, which had officially ended World War I. The leaders of the Allies opposed to the Axis powers met on several occasions in an attempt to build the framework for a more lasting peace free of the vindictiveness that was so prominent at the Versailles gathering. A key result of Allied discussions was agreement on establishing the **United Nations (UN)**. From the outset this new international organization was more representative of the world's peoples, in both large and small nations, than the League of Nations. The United States pledged to join, played a major role in the United Nations' planning and finance, and provided a site on the East River in Manhattan for the organization's permanent headquarters. The Soviet Union was also a charter member, along with longstanding great powers, such as Britain and France. China, represented in the first decades after 1945 by the Guomindang, was grouped with these other global powers as a permanent member of the Security Council, the steering committee for United Nations operations. In the decades after the end of the war, the vanquished Axis powers were eventually granted membership, as were the former colonies, soon after each gained independence.

With the successful establishment of the United Nations, international diplomacy and assistance moved beyond the orbit of the Western powers, who had all but monopolized them for centuries. But through their vetoes in the Security Council they retained considerable control. The United Nations' primary mission was to provide a forum for negotiating international disputes. It also took over the apparatus of more specialized international agencies, including the World Court of Justice, those concerned with human rights, and those that coordinated programs directed at specific groups and problems, ranging from labor organization and famine relief to agricultural development and women's concerns. Although UN interventions to preserve or restore peace to numerous regions have encountered much resistance by both the great powers and regional power brokers, they have repeatedly proved vital to reducing violent conflict and providing refugee relief throughout the globe. The United Nations has also sponsored initiatives, including critical international conferences, that have proved highly influential in shaping policies and programs affecting child labor, women's rights, and environmental protection.

From Hot War to Cold War

The cold war would last until the 1980s, with various points of crisis and confrontation. Direct conflict between the two superpowers did not occur, despite dire forebodings. Much of world history, however, was shaped by cold war maneuvering for over four decades.

The cold war began when the World War II allies turned, in the war's final conferences, to debate the nature of the postwar settlement. It quickly became apparent that the Soviet Union expected massive territorial gains and that Britain and the United States intended to limit these gains through their own areas of influence. Unresolved disputes then led to the full outbreak of the cold war between 1945 and 1949.

Tensions had clearly surfaced during the 1944 **Tehran Conference**, when the allies agreed on the invasion of Nazi-occupied France. The decision to focus on France rather than moving up from the Mediterranean gave the Soviet forces a free hand to move through the smaller nations of eastern Europe as they pushed the Nazi armies back. Britain negotiated separately with the Soviets to ensure Western preponderance in postwar Greece as well as equality in Hungary and Yugoslavia, with Soviet control of Romania and Bulgaria. But the United States resisted this kind of un-Wilsonian scorn for the rights of small nations.

The next settlement meeting was the **Yalta Conference** in the Soviet Crimea early in 1945. President Franklin Roosevelt of the United States was eager to press the Soviet Union for assistance against Japan and to this end promised the Soviets important territorial gains in Manchuria and the northern Japanese islands. The organization of the United Nations was confirmed. As to Europe, however, agreement was more difficult. The three powers easily arranged to divide Germany into four occupation zones (liberated France getting a chunk), which would be disarmed and purged of Nazi influence. Britain, however, resisted Soviet zeal to eliminate German industrial power, seeing a viable Germany as a potential ally in a subsequent Western–Soviet contest. Bitter dispute also raged

Tehran Conference Meeting among leaders of the United States, Britain, and the Soviet Union in 1943; agreed to the opening of a new front in France.

The Big Three at Yalta IMAGE

Yalta Conference Meeting among leaders of the United States, Britain, and the Soviet Union in 1945; agreed to Soviet entry into the Pacific war in return for possessions in Manchuria, organization of the United Nations; disputed the division of political organization in the eastern European states to be reestablished after the war.

over the smaller nations of eastern Europe. No one disagreed that they should be friendly to their Soviet neighbor, but the Western leaders also wanted them to be free and democratic. Stalin, the Soviet leader, had to make some concessions by including noncommunist leaders in what was already a Soviet-controlled government in liberated Poland—concessions that he soon violated.

The final postwar conference occurred in the Berlin suburb of **Potsdam** in July 1945. Russian forces now occupied not only most of eastern Europe but eastern Germany as well. This de facto situation prompted agreement that the Soviet Union could take over much of what had been eastern Poland, with the Poles gaining part of eastern Germany in compensation. Germany was divided pending a final peace treaty (which was not to come for more than 40 years). Austria was also divided and occupied, gaining unity and independence only in 1956, on condition of neutrality between the United States and the Soviet Union. Amid great difficulty, treaties were worked out for Germany's other allies, including Italy, but the United States and later the Soviet Union signed separate treaties with Japan.

All these maneuvers had several results. Japan was occupied by the United States and its wartime gains stripped away. Even Korea, taken earlier, was freed but was divided between U.S. and Soviet zones of occupation (the basis for the North Korea–South Korea division still in effect today). Former Asian colonies were returned to their old "masters," though often quite briefly, as new independence movements quickly challenged the control of the weakened imperialist powers. China regained most of its former territory, though here, too, stability was promptly challenged by renewed fighting between communist and nationalist forces within the nation, aided by the Soviet Union and the United States, respectively.

The effort to restore old colonial regimes applied also to the Middle East, India, and Africa. Indian and African troops had fought for Britain during the war, as in World War I, though Britain imprisoned key nationalist leaders and put independence plans on hold. African leaders had participated actively in the French resistance to its authoritarian wartime government. The Middle East and north Africa had been shaken by German invasions and Allied counterattacks. Irritability increased, and so did expectations for change. With Europe's imperial powers further weakened by their war effort, adjustments seemed inevitable, as in those parts of Asia invaded by the Japanese.

In Europe the boundaries of the Soviet Union pushed westward, with virtually all the losses after World War I erased. Independent nations created in 1918 were for the most part restored (though the former Baltic states of Latvia, Lithuania, and Estonia became Soviet provinces because they had been Russian provinces before World War I). Except for Greece and Yugoslavia, the new nations quickly fell under Soviet domination, with communist governments forced on them and Soviet troops in occupation. The nations of western Europe were free to set up or confirm democratic regimes, but most of them lived under the shadow of growing U.S. influence, manifested in continued presence of U.S. troops, substantial economic aid and coordination, and no small amount of outright policy manipulation.

The stage was set, in other words, for two of the great movements that would shape the ensuing decades in world history. The first comprised challenges by subject peoples to the tired vestiges of control by the great European empires—the movement known as "decolonization" that in a few decades would create scores of new nations in Asia, Africa, and the West Indies. The second great theme was the confrontation between the two superpowers that emerged from the war—the United States and the Soviet Union, each with new international influence and new military might. Many believed that this cold war would soon become a war in a more literal and devastating sense. That these trends constituted a peace settlement was difficult to imagine in 1945 or 1947, yet they seemed the best that could be done.

Nationalism and Decolonization in South and Southeast Asia and Africa

The Nazi rout of the French and the stunningly rapid Japanese capture of the French, Dutch, British, and U.S. colonies in southeast Asia put an end to whatever illusions the colonized peoples of Africa and Asia had left about the strength and innate superiority of their colonial overlords. Because the Japanese were non-Europeans, their early victories over the Europeans and Americans played a particularly critical role in destroying the myth of the white man's invincibility. The fall of the "impregnable" fortress at Singapore on the southern tip of Malaya and the Americans' reverses

Potsdam Conference Meeting among leaders of the United States, Britain, and the Soviet Union just before the end of World War II in 1945; Allies agreed upon Soviet domination in eastern Europe; Germany and Austria to be divided among victorious Allies.

A second global conflict between the industrial powers proved fatal to the already badly battered European colonial empires. From the Philippines to west Africa, independence was won in most of the nonsettler colonies with surprisingly little bloodshed and remarkable speed; the opposite was true in colonies with large settler communities, where liberation struggles were usually violent and prolonged.

total war Warfare of the 20th century; vast resources and emotional commitments of belligerent nations were marshaled to support military effort; resulted from impact of industrialization on the military effort reflecting technological innovation and organizational capacity.

Atlantic Charter of 1941 World War II alliance agreement between the United States and Britain; included a clause that recognized the right of all people to choose the form of government under which they live; indicated sympathy for decolonization.

Quit India movement Mass civil disobedience campaign that began in the summer of 1942 to end British control of India.

Muslim League Founded in 1906 to better support demands of Muslims for separate electorates and legislative seats in Hindu-dominated India; represented division within Indian nationalist movement.

at Pearl Harbor and in the Philippines proved to be blows from which the colonizers never quite recovered, even though they went on to eventually defeat the Japanese. The sight of tens of thousands of British, Dutch, and American troops, struggling under the supervision of the victorious Japanese to survive the "death marches" to prison camps in their former colonies, left an indelible impression on the Asian villagers who saw them pass by. The harsh regimes and heavy demands the Japanese conquerors imposed on the peoples of southeast Asia during the war further strengthened the determination to fight for self-rule and to look to their own defenses after the conflict was over.

The devastation of World War II—a **total war** fought in the cities and countryside over much of Europe—drained the resources of the European powers. This devastating warfare also sapped the will of the European populace to hold increasingly resistant African and Asian peoples in bondage. The war also greatly enhanced the power and influence of the two giants on the European periphery: the United States and the Soviet Union. In Africa and the Middle East, as well as in the Pacific, the United States approached the war as a campaign of liberation. American propagandists made no secret of Franklin Roosevelt's hostility to colonialism in their efforts to win Asian and African support for the Allied war effort. In fact, American intentions in this regard were enshrined in the **Atlantic Charter of 1941**. This pact sealed an alliance between the United States and Great Britain that the latter desperately needed to survive in its war with Nazi Germany. In it Roosevelt persuaded a reluctant Churchill to include a clause that recognized the "right of all people to choose the form of government under which they live." The Soviets were equally vocal in their condemnation of colonialism and were even more forthcoming with material support for nationalist campaigns after the war. In the cold war world of the superpowers that emerged after 1945, there was little room for the domination that the much-reduced powers of western Europe had once exercised over much of the globe.

The Winning of Independence in South and Southeast Asia

The outbreak of World War II soon put an end to the accommodation between the Indian National Congress and the British in the late 1930s. Congress leaders offered to support the Allies' war effort if the British would give them a significant share of power at the all-India level and commit themselves to Indian independence once the conflict was over. These conditions were staunchly rejected both by the viceroy in India and at home by Winston Churchill, who headed the coalition government that led Britain through the war. Labour members of the coalition government, however, indicated that they were quite willing to negotiate India's eventual independence. As tensions built between nationalist agitators and the British rulers, Sir Stafford Cripps was sent to India in early 1942 to see whether a deal could be struck with the Indian leaders. Indian divisions and British intransigence led to the collapse of Cripps's initiative and the renewal of mass civil disobedience campaigns under the guise of the **Quit India movement**, which began in the summer of 1942.

The British responded with repression and mass arrests, and for much of the remainder of the war, Gandhi, Nehru, and other major Congress politicians were imprisoned (Figure 30.6). Of the Indian nationalist parties, only the Communists—who were committed to the antifascist alliance—and, more ominously, the **Muslim League** rallied to the British cause. The League, now led by a former Congress party politician, the dour and uncompromising **Muhammad Ali Jinnah**, won much favor from the British for its wartime support. As their demands for a separate Muslim state in the subcontinent hardened, the links between the British and Jinnah and other League leaders became a key factor in the struggle for decolonization in south Asia.

Figure 30.6 In 1931 Mahatma Gandhi returned to Great Britain for the first time since his student days in 1915. Though his attempts to negotiate with British leaders came to little, he was a great hit with the British public, in part because of his sly sense of humor. When asked if he was embarrassed to meet King George V in the scant khadi-cloth apparel he wears in this photo, Gandhi quipped that the king-emperor had on enough clothes for the both of them.

World War II brought disruptions to India similar to those caused by the earlier global conflict. Inflation stirred up urban unrest, while a widespread famine in 1943 and 1944, brought on in part by wartime transport shortages, engendered much bitterness in rural India. Winston Churchill's defeat in the first postwar British election in 1945 brought a Labour government to power that was ready to deal with India's nationalist leaders. With independence in the near future tacitly conceded, the process of decolonization between 1945 and 1947 focused on what sort of state or states would be carved out of the subcontinent after the British withdrawal. Jinnah and the League had begun to build a mass following among the Muslims. In order to rally support, they played on widespread anxieties among the Muslim minority that a single Indian nation would be dominated by the Hindu majority, and that the Muslims would become the targets of increasing discrimination. It was therefore essential, they insisted, that a separate Muslim state called Pakistan be created from those areas in northwest and east India where Muslims were the most numerous.

As communal rioting spread throughout India, the British and key Congress party politicians reluctantly concluded that a bloodbath could be averted only by partition—the creation of two nations in the subcontinent: one secular, one Muslim. Thus, in the summer of 1947, the British handed power over to the leaders of the majority Congress party, who headed the new nation of India, and to Jinnah, who became the first president of Pakistan.

In part because of the haste with which the British withdrew their forces from the deeply divided subcontinent, a bloodbath occurred anyway. Vicious Hindu–Muslim and Muslim–Sikh communal rioting, in which neither women nor children were spared, took the lives of hundreds of thousands in the searing summer heat across the plains of northwest India. Whole villages were destroyed; trains were attacked and their passengers hacked to death by armed bands of rival religious adherents. These atrocities fed a massive exchange of refugee populations between Hindu, Sikh, and Muslim areas that may have totaled 10 million people. Those who fled were so terrified that they were willing to give up their land, their villages, and most of their worldly possessions. The losses of partition were compounded by the fact that there was soon no longer a Gandhi to preach tolerance and communal coexistence. On January 30, 1948, on the way to one of his regular prayer meetings, he was shot by a Hindu fanatic.

In granting independence to India, the British, in effect, removed the keystone from the arch of an empire that spanned five continents. Burma (known today as Myanmar) and Ceylon (now named Sri Lanka) won their independence peacefully in the following years. India's independence and Gandhi's civil disobedience campaigns, which had done so much to win a mass following for the nationalist cause, also inspired successful struggles for independence in Ghana, Nigeria, and other African colonies in the 1950s and 1960s.

The retreat of the most powerful of the imperial powers could not help but contribute to the weakening of lesser empires such as those of the Dutch, the French, and the Americans. In fact, the process of the transfer of power from U.S. officials to moderate, middle-class Filipino politicians was well under way before World War II broke out. The loyalty to the Americans that most Filipinos displayed during the war, as well as the stubborn guerrilla resistance they put up against the Japanese occupation, did much to bring about the rapid granting of independence to the Philippines once the war ended. The Dutch and French were less willing to follow the British example and relinquish their colonial possessions in the postwar era. From 1945 to 1949, the Dutch fought a losing war to destroy the nation of Indonesia, which nationalists in the Netherlands Indies had established when the Japanese hold over the islands broke down in mid-1945. The French struggled to retain Indochina. Communist revolutions in east Asia also emerged victorious in the postwar period. No sooner had the European colonizers suffered these losses than they were forced to deal with new threats to the last bastions of the imperial order in Africa.

The Liberation of Nonsettler Africa

World War II proved even more disruptive to the colonial order imposed on Africa than the first global conflict of the European powers. Forced labor and confiscations of crops and minerals returned, and inflation and controlled markets again cut down on African earnings. African recruits in the hundreds of thousands were drawn once more into the conflict and had even greater opportunities to use the latest European weapons to destroy Europeans. African servicemen had witnessed British and French defeats in the Middle East and southeast Asia, and they fought bravely

Indian Declaration of Independence

Nehru

Jinnah, the "Father" of Pakistan

The Tandon Family at Partition

Gandhi Speaks Against the Partition of India

Jinnah, Muhammad Ali (1876–1948) Muslim nationalist leader in India; originally a member of the National Congress party; became leader of Muslim League; traded Muslim support for British during World War II for promises of a separate Muslim state after the war; first president of Pakistan.

National Leaders for a New Global Order

Throughout Africa and Asia, struggles for decolonization and national independence often led to the emergence of leaders with exceptional mass appeal and political skills. But the personal qualities, visions of the future, and leadership styles that made for widespread loyalty to these individuals varied widely depending on the cultures and social settings from which they emerged as well as the nature of the political contests that led to the colonizers' retreat and the establishment of new nations. The following are photos of four of the most charismatic and effective leaders of independence movements in Africa and Asia. Study these photos and the background information on each of these individuals that is provided in earlier sections of this chapter and the relevant sections of Chapter 34, and answer the questions about leadership styles and images that follow.

QUESTIONS What do the dress and poses of these leaders tell us about the image each projected? Why did the style and approach each adopted win widespread popular support in each of the very different societies in which they emerged as pivotal leaders in the struggles for independence? How well do you think that each of their approaches to leadership served them in dealings with the European colonizers and contests with the rival leaders and political parties they faced in each of the societies in which they arose? What did charisma mean in each of these settings?

Mohandas Gandhi, India.

Léopold Sédar Senghor, Senegal.

Gamal Abdul Nasser, Egypt.

Kwame Nkrumah, Ghana.

only to experience renewed racial discrimination once they returned home. Many were soon among the staunchest supporters of postwar nationalist campaigns in the African colonies of the British and French. The swift and humiliating rout of the French and Belgians by Nazi armies in the spring of 1940 shattered whatever was left of the colonizers' reputation for military prowess. It also led to a bitter and, in the circumstances, embarrassing struggle between the forces of the puppet Vichy regime and those of de Gaulle's Free French, who continued fighting the Nazis mainly in France's north and west African colonies.

The wartime needs of both the British and the Free French led to major departures from long-standing colonial policies that had restricted industrial development throughout Africa. Factories were established to process urgently needed vegetable oils, foods, and minerals in western and south central Africa. These in turn contributed to a growing migration on the part of African peasants to the towns and a sharp spurt in African urban growth. The inability of many of those who moved to the towns to find employment made for a reservoir of disgruntled, idle workers that would be skillfully tapped by nationalist politicians in the postwar decades.

There were essentially two main paths to decolonization in nonsettler Africa in the postwar era. The first was pioneered by Kwame Nkrumah (KWAH-mee ehn-KROO-muh) and his followers in the British Gold Coast colony, which, as the independent nation of Ghana, launched the process of decolonization in Africa. Nkrumah epitomized the more radical sort of African leader that emerged throughout Africa after the war (see Visualizing the Past feature). Educated in African missionary schools and the United States, he had established wide contacts with nationalist leaders in both British and French West Africa and civil rights leaders in America prior to his return to the Gold Coast in the late 1940s. He returned to a land in ferment. The restrictions of government-controlled marketing boards and their favoritism for British merchants had led to widespread, but nonviolent, protest in the coastal cities. But after the police fired on a peaceful demonstration of ex-servicemen in 1948, rioting broke out in many towns.

Though both urban workers and cash crop farmers had supported the unrest, Western-educated African leaders were slow to organize these dissident groups into a sustained mass movement. Their reluctance arose in part from their fear of losing major political concessions, such as seats on colonial legislative councils, which the British had just made. Rejecting the caution urged by more established political leaders, Nkrumah resigned his position as chair of the dominant political party in the Gold Coast and established his own **Convention Peoples Party (CPP)**. Even before the formal break, he had signaled the arrival of a new style of politics by organizing mass rallies, boycotts, and strikes.

In the mid-1950s, Nkrumah's mass following, and his growing stature as a leader who would not be deterred by imprisonment or British threats, won repeated concessions from the British. Educated Africans were given more and more representation in legislative bodies, and gradually they took over administration of the colony. The British recognition of Nkrumah as the prime minister of an independent Ghana in 1957 simply concluded a transfer of power from the European colonizers to the Western-educated African elite that had been under way for nearly a decade.

The peaceful devolution of power to African nationalists led to the independence of the British nonsettler colonies in black Africa by the mid-1960s. Independence in the comparable areas of the French and Belgian empires in Africa came in a somewhat different way. Hard-pressed by costly military struggles to hold on to their colonies in Indochina and Algeria, the French took a much more conciliatory line in dealing with the many peoples they ruled in west Africa. Ongoing negotiations with such highly westernized leaders as Senegal's Léopold Sédar Senghor and the Ivory Coast's Felix Houphouât-Boigny (hoh-FOO-aht BWAHN-yay) led to reforms and political concessions.

The slow French retreat ensured that moderate African leaders, who were eager to retain French economic and cultural ties, would dominate the nationalist movements and the postindependence period in French west Africa. Between 1956 and 1960, the French colonies moved by stages toward nationhood—a process that sped up after de Gaulle's return to power in 1958. By 1960 all of France's west African colonies were free.

In the same year, the Belgians completed a much hastier retreat from their huge colonial possession in the Congo. Their virtual flight was epitomized by the fact that there was little in the way of an organized nationalist movement to pressure them into concessions of any kind. In fact, by design there were scarcely any well educated Congolese to lead resistance to Belgian rule. At independence in 1960, there were only 16 African college graduates in a Congolese population that exceeded 13 million. Though the Portuguese still clung to their impoverished and scattered colonial territories, by the mid-1960s the European colonial era had come to an end in all but the settler societies of Africa.

Convention Peoples party (CPP) Political party established by Kwame Nkrumah in opposition to British control of colonial legislature in Gold Coast.

Repression and Guerrilla War: The Struggle for the Settler Colonies

The pattern of relatively peaceful withdrawal by stages that characterized the process of decolonization in most of Asia and Africa proved unworkable in most of the settler colonies (see Map 24.1, p. 553). These included areas like Algeria, Kenya, and Southern Rhodesia, where substantial numbers of Europeans had gone intending to settle permanently in the 19th and early 20th centuries. South Africa provided few openings for nationalist agitation except that mounted by the politically and economically dominant colonists of European descent. In each case, the presence of European settler communities, varying in size from millions in South Africa and Algeria to tens of thousands in Kenya and Southern Rhodesia, blocked both the rise of indigenous nationalist movements and concessions on the part of the colonial overlords.

Because the settlers regarded the colonies to which they had emigrated as their permanent homes, they fought all attempts to turn political control over to the African majority or even to grant them civil rights. They also doggedly refused all reforms by colonial administrators that required them to give up any of the lands they had occupied, often at the expense of indigenous African peoples. Unable to make headway through nonviolent protest tactics—which were forbidden—or negotiations with British or French officials, who were fearful of angering the highly vocal settler minority, many African leaders turned to violent, revolutionary struggles to win their independence.

The first of these erupted in Kenya in the early 1950s. Impatient with the failure of the nonviolent approach adopted by **Jomo Kenyatta** and the leading nationalist party, the **Kenya African Union (KAU)**, an underground organization coalesced around a group of more radical leaders. After forming the **Land Freedom Army** in the early 1950s, the radicals mounted a campaign of terror and guerrilla warfare against the British, the settlers, and Africans who were considered collaborators. At the height of the struggle in 1954, some 200,000 rebels were in action in the capital at Nairobi and in the forest reserves of the central Kenyan highlands. The British responded with an all-out military effort to crush the guerrilla movement, which was dismissed as an explosion of African savagery and labeled the "Mau Mau" by the colonizers, not the rebels. In the process, the British, at the settlers' insistence, imprisoned Kenyatta and the KAU organizers, thus eliminating the nonviolent alternative to the guerrillas.

The rebel movement had been militarily defeated by 1956 at the cost of thousands of lives. But the British were now in a mood to negotiate with the nationalists, despite strong objections from the European settlers. Kenyatta was released from prison, and he emerged as the spokesperson for the Africans of Kenya. By 1963 a multiracial Kenya had won its independence. Under what was, in effect, Kenyatta's one-party rule, it remained until the mid-1980s one of the most stable and more prosperous of the new African states.

The struggle of the Arab and Berber peoples of Algeria for independence was longer and even more vicious than that in Kenya. Algeria had for decades been regarded by the French as an integral part of France—a department just like Provence or Brittany. The presence of more than a million European settlers in the colony only served to bolster the resolve of French politicians to retain it at all costs. But in the decade after World War II, sporadic rioting grew into sustained guerrilla resistance. By the mid-1950s, the **National Liberation Front (FLN)** had mobilized large segments of the Arab and Berber population of the colony in a full-scale revolt against French rule and settler dominance. High-ranking French army officers came to see the defeat of this movement as a way to restore a reputation that had been badly tarnished by recent defeats in Vietnam (see Chapter 34). As in Kenya, the rebels were defeated in the field. But they gradually negotiated the independence of Algeria after de Gaulle came to power in 1958. The French people had wearied of the seemingly endless war, and de Gaulle became convinced that he could not restore France to great power status as long as its resources continued to be drained by the Algerian conflict.

In contrast to Kenya, the Algerian struggle was prolonged and brutalized by a violent settler backlash. Led after 1960 by the **Secret Army Organization (OAS)**, settler violence was directed against Arabs and Berbers as well as French who favored independence for the colony. With strong support from elements in the French military, earlier resistance by the settlers had managed to topple the government in Paris in 1958, thereby putting an end to the Fourth Republic. In the early 1960s, the OAS came close to assassinating de Gaulle and overthrowing the Fifth Republic, which his accession to power had brought into existence. In the end, however, the Algerians won their independence in 1962 (Figure 30.7). After the bitter civil war, the multiracial accommodation worked out in Kenya appeared out of the question as far as the settlers of Algeria were concerned. Over 900,000 left the new nation within months after its birth. In addition, tens of thousands of harkis, or Arabs and Berbers who had sided with the French in the long war for independence, fled to France. They, and later migrants, formed the core of the substantial Algerian population now present in France.

The Persistence of White Supremacy in South Africa

In southern Africa, violent revolutions put an end to white settler dominance in the Portuguese colonies of Angola and Mozambique in 1975 and in Southern Rhodesia (now Zimbabwe) by 1980. Only in South Africa did the white minority manage to maintain its position of supremacy. Its ability to do so rested on several factors that distinguished it from other settler societies. To begin with, the white population of South Africa, roughly equally divided between the Dutch-descended Afrikaners and the more recently arrived English speakers, was a good deal larger than that of any

---

Kenyatta, Jomo (1946–1978) Leader of the nonviolent nationalist party in Kenya; organized the Kenya Africa Union (KAU); failed to win concessions because of resistance of white settlers; came to power only after suppression of the Land Freedom Army, or Mau Mau.

Kenya African Union (KAU) Leading nationalist party in Kenya; adopted nonviolent approach to ending British control in the 1950s.

Land Freedom Army Radical organization for independence in Kenya; frustrated by failure of nonviolent means, initiated campaign of terror in 1952; referred to by British as the Mau Mau.

National Liberation Front (FLN) Radical nationalist movement in Algeria; launched sustained guerilla war against France in the 1950s; success of attacks led to independence of Algeria in 1958.

Secret Army Organization (OAS) Organization of French settlers in Algeria; led guerrilla war following independence during the 1960s; assaults directed against Arabs, Berbers, and French who advocated independence.

Figure 30.7 Algerians celebrated in Oran as French barricades were torn down by members of the local Arab militia and Arab civilians just after independence was announced in July, 1962. The barricades had been erected throughout the colony to keep European residential areas off limits to the Arabs and Berbers, who made up the overwhelming majority of the population.

of the other settler societies. Though they were only a small minority in a country of 23 million black Africans and 3.5 million East Indians and coloreds (mulattos, in American parlance), by the mid-1980s, South Africa's settler-descended population had reached 4.5 million.

Unlike the settlers in Kenya and Algeria, who had the option of retreating to Europe as full citizens of France or Great Britain, the Afrikaners in particular had no European homeland to fall back upon. They had lived in South Africa as long as other Europeans had in North America, and they considered themselves quite distinct from the Dutch. Over the centuries, the Afrikaners had also built up what was for them a persuasive ideology of white racist supremacy. Though crude by European or American standards, Afrikaner racism was far more explicit and elaborate than that developed by the settlers of any other colony. Afrikaner ideology was grounded in selected biblical quotations and the celebration of their historic struggle to "tame a beautiful but hard land" in the face of opposition from both the African "savages" and the British "imperialists."

Ironically, their defeat by the British in the Boer War from 1899 to 1902 also contributed much to the capacity of the white settler minority to maintain its place of dominance in South Africa. A sense of guilt, arising especially from their treatment of Boer women and children during the war—tens of thousands of whom died of disease in what the British called concentration camps—led the victors to make major concessions to the Afrikaners in the postwar decades. The most important of these was internal political control, which included turning over the fate of the black African majority to the openly racist supremacist Afrikaners. Not surprisingly, the continued subjugation of the black Africans became a central aim of the Afrikaner political organizations that emerged in the 1930s and 1940s, culminating in the **Afrikaner National Party**. From 1948, when it emerged as the majority party in the all-white South African legislature, the National party devoted itself to winning complete independence from Britain (which came without violence in 1961). The Afrikaners also strove to complete a decades-long quest to establish white domination over the political, social, and economic life of the new nation.

A rigid system of racial segregation (which will be discussed more fully in Chapter 33), called **apartheid** by the Afrikaners, was established after 1948 through the passage of thousands of laws.

Afrikaner National Party Emerged as the majority party in the all-white South African legislature after 1948; advocated complete independence from Britain; favored a rigid system of racial segregation called apartheid.

apartheid Policy of strict racial segregation imposed in South Africa to permit the continued dominance of whites politically and economically.

Among other things, this legislation reserved the best jobs for whites and carefully defined the sorts of contacts permissible between different racial groups. The right to vote and political representation were denied to the black Africans, and ultimately to the coloreds and Indians. It was illegal for members of any of these groups to hold mass meetings or to organize political parties or labor unions. These restrictions, combined with very limited opportunities for higher education for black Africans, hampered the growth of black African political parties and their efforts to mobilize popular support for the struggle for decolonization. The Afrikaners' establishment of a vigilant and brutal police state to uphold apartheid, and their opportunistic cultivation of divisions between the diverse peoples in the black African population, also contributed to their ability to preserve a bastion of white supremacy in an otherwise liberated continent.

Conflicting Nationalisms: Arabs, Israelis, and the Palestinian Question

Haganah Zionist military force engaged in violent resistance to British presence in Palestine in the 1940s.

Along with Egypt, several Middle Eastern states, including Iraq and Syria, had technically gained independence between the world wars, though European influence remained strong. With World War II, independence became more complete, though it was not until the 1970s that governments were strong enough to shake off Western dominance of the oil fields. Egypt's 1952 revolt and independence movements in the rest of north Africa gained ground, though the struggle against France in Algeria was bitter and prolonged. Although virtually all Arab peoples who were not yet free by the end of World War II were liberated by the early 1960s, the fate of Palestine continued to present special problems. Hitler's campaign of genocide against the European Jews had provided powerful support for the Zionists' insistence that the Jews must have their own homeland, which more and more was conceived in terms of a modern national state. The brutal persecution of the Jews also won international sympathy for the Zionist cause. This was in part due to the fact that the leaders of many nations, including the United States and Great Britain, were reluctant to admit Jews fleeing the Nazi terror into their own countries. As Hitler's henchmen stepped up their race war against the Jews, the tide of Jewish immigration to Palestine rose sharply. But growing Arab resistance to Jewish settlement and land purchases in Palestine, which was often expressed in communal rioting and violent assaults on Zionist communities, led to increasing British restrictions on the entry of Jews into the colony.

A major Muslim revolt swept Palestine between 1936 and 1939. The British managed to put down this rising but only with great difficulty. It both decimated the leadership of the Palestinian Arab community and further strengthened the British resolve to stem the flow of Jewish immigrants to Palestine. Government measures to keep out Jewish refugees from Nazi oppression led in turn to violent Zionist resistance to the British presence in Palestine. The Zionist assault was spearheaded by a regular Zionist military force, the **Haganah**, and several underground terrorist organizations.

By the end of World War II, the major parties claiming Palestine were locked into a deadly stalemate. The Zionists were determined to carve out a Jewish state in the region. The Palestinian Arabs and their allies in neighboring Arab lands were equally determined to transform Palestine into a multireligious nation in which the position of the Arab majority would be ensured. Having badly bungled their mandatory responsibilities, and under attack from both sides, the British wanted more than anything else to scuttle and run. The 1937 report of a British commission of inquiry supplied a possible solution: partition. The newly created United Nations provided an international body that could give a semblance of legality to the proceedings. In 1948, with sympathy for the Jews running high because of the postwar revelations of the horrors of Hitler's Final Solution, the member states of the United Na-

Map 30.3 The Partition of Palestine After World War II The areas granted to the Palestinian people by the 1948 UN Partition were quickly occupied by the warring states of Israel and Egypt, Jordan and Syria

tions—with the United States and the Soviet Union in rare agreement—approved the partition of Palestine into Arab and Jewish countries (Map 30.3).

The Arab states that bordered the newly created nation of Israel had vehemently opposed the UN action. Soon the two sides were engaged in all-out warfare. Though heavily outnumbered, the Zionists proved better armed and much better prepared to defend themselves than almost anyone could have expected. Not only did they hold onto the tiny, patchwork state they had been given by the United Nations, but they expanded it at the Arabs' expense. The brief but bloody war that ensued created hundreds of thousands of Palestinian Arab refugees. It also sealed the persisting hostility between Arabs and Israelis that has been the all-consuming issue in the region and a major international problem to the present day. In Palestine, conflicting strains of nationalism had collided. As a result, the legacy of colonialism proved even more of a liability to social and economic development than in much of the rest of newly independent Africa and Asia.

Israel and Its Neighbors

Global Connections

Persisting Trends in a World Transformed by War

Given the fragile foundations on which it rested, the rather rapid demise of the European colonial order is not really surprising. World War II completed the process that World War I and anticolonial nationalism had begun; the end of Western imperialism came quickly. In this sense, the global framework was transformed. However, the winning of political freedom in Asia and Africa also represented less of a break with the colonial past than the appearance of many new nations on the map of the world might lead one to assume.

The decidedly nonrevolutionary, elite-to-elite transfer of power that was central to the liberation process in most colonies, even those where there were violent guerrilla movements, limited the extent of the social and economic transformation that occurred. The Western-educated African and Asian classes moved into the offices and took the jobs—and often the former homes—of the European colonizers. But social gains for the rest of the population in most new nations were minimal or nonexistent. In Algeria, Kenya, and Zimbabwe (formerly Southern Rhodesia), abandoned European lands were distributed to Arab and African peasants and laborers. But in most former colonies, especially in Asia, the big landholders that remained were indigenous, and they have held on tenaciously to their holdings. Educational reforms were carried out to include more sciences in school curricula and the history of Asia or Africa rather than Europe. But Western cultural influences have remained strong in almost all of the former colonies. Indians and many west Africans with higher educations continue to communicate in English and French.

The liberation of the colonies also did little to disrupt Western dominance of the terms of international trade or the global economic order more generally. In fact, in the negotiations that led to decolonization, Asian and African leaders often explicitly promised to protect the interests of Western merchants and businesspeople in the postindependence era. These and other limits that sustained Western influence and often dominance, even after freedom was won, greatly reduced the options open to nationalist leaders struggling to build viable and prosperous nations. Though new forces have also played important roles, the postindependence history of colonized peoples cannot be understood without a consideration of the lingering effects of the colonial interlude in their history.

Further Readings

Two of the most genuinely global histories of World War II, which also include extensive accounts of the origins of the war in both Europe and the Pacific, are Gerhard L. Weinberg, *A World at Arms: A Global History of World War II* (1994), and Peter Calvocoressi and Guy Wint, *Total War: Causes and Courses of the Second World War* (1972). For a good overview of the coming of the war in Europe from the British perspective, see Christopher Thorne, *The Approach of War 1938–1939* (1967), and from the German viewpoint, Gerhard L. Weinberg, *Germany, Hitler, and World War II* (1995). A fine analysis of the underlying patterns in the European theater can be found in Gordon Wright, *The Ordeal of Total War, 1939–1945* (1968).

From a prodigious literature on the Holocaust, some good works to begin with are Hannah Arendt's brilliant *Eichmann in Jerusalem* (1963) and Raul Hilberg's *Destruction of the European Jews* (1985). Christopher Browning's *Ordinary Men* (1992) provides a chilling account of some of those who actually carried out the killings, while Viktor Frankl's *Man's Search for Meaning* (1959) is one of the most poignant of the numerous autobiographical accounts of the concentration camps. Omer Bartov provides a thoughtful meditation on the wider meanings of the Holocaust for 20th-century history in *Murder in Our Midst* (1996).

On the causes of the Pacific war, see Michael Barnhart, *Japan Prepares for Total War* (1987), and William O'Neill, *A Democracy at War* (1993). Sukarno's reactions to the Japanese invasion of the Netherlands Indies can be found in his *Autobiography* (1965) as related to Cindy Adams, which should be balanced by John Legge's *Sukarno: A Political Biography* (1972). On the course of the war in the Pacific from differing perspectives, see Ronald Spector, *Eagle Against the Sun* (1985); Saburō Ienaga, *The Pacific War, 1931–1945* (1978); and John Dower, *War Without*

Mercy: Race and Power in the Pacific War (1986). On the end of the war and the forces that led to the cold war, see Martin Sherwin, *A World Destroyed: The Atomic Bomb and the Grand Alliance* (1975); William Craig, *The Fall of Japan* (1967); Herbert Feis, *From Trust to Terror: The Onset of the Cold War, 1945–1950* (1970); and Melvyn Leffler, *A Preponderance of Power: National Security, the Truman Administration, and the Cold War* (1992).

A thoughtful overview of the process of decolonization in the British empire as a whole can be found in the works of John Darwin. In addition to P. J. Vatikiotis's general *History of Egypt,* mentioned in Chapter 5, Jacques Berque's *Egypt: Imperialism and Revolution* (1972) and Peter Mansfield's *The British in Egypt* (1971) provide detailed accounts of the nationalist revolt and early years of quasi-independence. The struggles for decolonization in Africa are surveyed by Ali A. Mazrui and Michael Tidy in *Nationalism and New States in Africa* (1984); J. D. Hargreaves, *Decolonization in Africa* (1988); and W. R. Louis and P. Gifford, eds., *Decolonization in Africa* (1984).

From the very substantial literature on the rise of nationalism in settler societies, some of the best studies include C. Roseberg and J. Nottingham, *The Myth of "Mau Mau"* (1966), on Kenya; the writings of Terrence Ranger on Rhodesia; and Alastair Horne, *A Savage War of Peace* (1977), on Algeria. Of the many works on South Africa, the general histories of S. Throup, B. Bunting, T. D. Moodie, and Leonard Thompson provide a good introduction to the rise of Afrikaner power. The period of the partition and the first Arab-Israeli conflict have been the subject of much revisionist scholarship in recent years. Some of the best of this is included in important books by Avi Schleim, Walid Khalidi, Ilan Pappé, and Tom Segev.

On the United States in the cold war decades, see Walter Lafeber, *America, Russia, and the Cold War, 1945–2004* (2004). Ronald Powaski, *The Cold War: The United States and the Soviet Union, 1917–1991* (1998), is a reliable and readable standard political history that synthesizes the historiography of the cold war. Ellen Schrecker, *Many Are the Crimes: McCarthyism in America* (1998), has a broad social history of the political and cultural legacy of the Red Scare. T. H. Etzold and J. L. Gaddis, eds., *Containment: Documents on American Policy and Strategy, 1945–1950* (1978), provides primary source material on the political history of the early cold war.

On the Web

A superb starting point for the online study of the Second World War can be found at http://www.historywiz.com/worldwartwo .htm. The site features links to battle histories, oral histories, and exhibits, and offers an audio file of President Truman's speech announcing the use of the atomic bomb against Japan. Other useful links can be found at http://www.secondworldwar.co.uk/ and http://www.secondworldwar.co.uk/links.html which lead to sources organized by battles and by countries. Yale University provides a digital library for Second World War documents at http://www .yale.edu/lawweb/avalon/wwii/wwii.htm. Rutgers University offers records of personal experiences at http://oralhistory.rutgers.edu/

Interviews/pease_marjorie.html, which can be supplemented by other collections at http://www.eyewitnesstohistory.com/, http:// www.geocities.com/Athens/Oracle/2691/links.htm, and http://www .fsu.edu/~ww2/links.htm, which offer links to materials ranging from combat stories to prisoner of war experiences. Dramatic recreations or virtual visits to key sites of this conflict abound on the Web. These sites include the nuclear battlefield of Hiroshima (http://titan.iwu.edu/~rwilson/hiroshima/), the 1941–1944 siege of Leningrad (http://www.cityvision2000.com/history/900days.htm), and the Japanese attack on Pearl Harbor (http://execpc.com/ ~dschaaf/mainmenu.html, http://plasma.nationalgeographic.com/ pearlharbor/, and http://www.history.navy.mil/photos/events/ wwii-pac/pearlhbr/pearlhbr.htm, and http://www.pearlharbor.org/). The concept of "lightning war" or blitzkrieg is explained at http:// www.achtungpanzer.com/blitz.htm. A discussion of the use of atomic weapons against Japan via documents, scholarly debate, and simulated town meeting are explored at http://www.trumanlibrary .org/whistlestop/study_collections/bomb/large/index.php, http:// www.atomicmuseum.com/tour/decision.cfm, http://www.aldridgeshs .qld.edu.au/sose/modrespg/bomb/oops.htm, and http://oncampus .richmond.edu/academics/education/projects/webquests/wwii/.

The role of the American home front and American women in World War II is explored through photographs and interviews at http://www.pomperaug.com/socstud/stumuseum/web/ARHhome .htm, http://teacher.scholastic.com/ACTIVITIES/wwii/ahf/index.htm, http://americanhistory.si.edu/victory/, http://userpages.aug.com/ captbarb/femvets5.html, http://www.wasp-wwii.org/, and http:// www.stg.brown.edu/projects/WWII_Women/WomenInWWII.html.

The experience of internment and death camps for civilians and prisoners of war in German, Russian, and Japanese-held territories is examined at http://en.wikipedia.org/wiki/Prisoner_of_war and http://www.mansell.com/pow-index.html. The removal of the Japanese American population in America to internment camps during the war is discussed and links on the subject provided at http://www.geocities.com/Athens/8420/main.html. Many Japanese internment camps or experiences in America have their own dedicated Web site, such as that at http://www.nps.gov/manz/, http:// www.thefirstbattle.com/, and http://parentseyes.arizona.edu/ wracamps/.

Overviews and interactive digital data bases for the Holocaust are provided at http://www.remember.org, http://www .holocaust-history.org, and http://www.ushmm.org. See also the excellent teacher's guide that offers study guides, documents, and essays at http://fcit.coedu.usf.edu/holocaust/resource/document/ DocPropa.htm. A map of Nazi concentration camps is provided at http://history1900s.about.com/library/holocaust/blmap.htm. There are several Web pages devoted to those who struggled privately against the Holocaust, including Oskar Schindler (http://auschwitz .dk/Schindler2.htm), Raul Wallenberg (http://www.us-israel.org/ jsource/biography/wallenberg.html) and Chiune Sugihara (http:// www.jewishvirtuallibrary.org/jsource/Holocaust/sugihara.html, http://www.eagleman.com/sugihara/, http://www.time.com/time/ magazine/article/0,9171,404316,00.html, and http://www .independent.co.uk/news/europe/japanese-schindler-who-saved- lithuanian-jews-is-honoured-450970.html).

The struggle against those who seek to deny the genocidal nature of the Nazi regime is addressed in articles offered at http://www.holocaust-history.org/. The search for meaning in the modern European Holocaust has been pioneered by one of its victims, Simon Wiesenthal (http://www.wiesenthal.com/). Virtual visits to the Anne Frank homepages (http://www.annefrank.nl/ and http://www.annefrank.com) and other links (see http://www.coollessons.org/holocaust.htm) lend a human face to both fascist oppression and the quest for a world without hatred.

That this European Holocaust is but one of many genocides is the subject of several sites that offer comparative analyses or links to other examples from Cambodia to Rwanda. These include http://www.yale.edu/cgp/, http://www.cybercambodia.com/dachs/, http://www.hawaii.edu/powerkills/SOD.CHAP4.HTM, http://news.bbc.co.uk/1/hi/world/africa/1288230.stm, http://www.hrw.org/reports/1999/rwanda/, and http://www.webster.edu/~woolflm/holocaust.html.

The winning of India's independence, Gandhi's last years, and his assassination did not end the struggle for *satyagraha* traced at http://www.colorado.edu/conflict/peace/example/wehr7496.htm. Many others have followed this path in India and abroad (see examples and resource lists at http://www.aforcemorepowerful.org/, http://www.transnational.org/Resources_Nonviolence/2007/Galtung_Satyagraha.html, and http://www.mkgandhi.org/articles/legacy.htm). Gandhi can be seen in a short film of a visit to London and during the Salt March at http://www.historychannel.com/broadband/searchbrowse/index.jsp. Jawaharlal Nehru's life and role in the freedom movement is explored at http://www.pbs.org/wgbh/commandingheights/shared/minitextlo/prof_jawaharlalnehru.html. His "tryst with destiny speech" that inaugurated a new chapter in the history of the Indian subcontinent can be read at http://www.fordham.edu/halsall/mod/1947nehru1.html. It can be heard at http://www.harappa.com/sounds/nehru.html. A newsreel covering the birth of Pakistan can be viewed at http://harappa.com/wall/pakistan.html, while the birth pangs of Bangladesh are traced at http://www.virtualbangladesh.com/.

The generation of leaders that helped secure Africa's freedom is well represented on the Internet. For Léopold Senghor, poet of Négritude and president of Senegal, see http://web.uflib.ufl.edu/cm/africana/senghor.htm. Links to Tanzania's Julius Nyerere's life and speeches can be found at http://www.hartford-hwp.com/archives/30/index-fd.html. Jomo Kenyatta and his role in the Land Freedom Army and Mau Mau movements are listed at http://www.kenyaweb.com/history/struggle/ and http://www.ccs.neu.edu/home/feneric/maumau.html.

The African National Congress Party homepage at http://www.anc.org.za/ traces its anticolonial role from its earliest beginnings to Nelson Mandela. Apartheid in South Africa is discussed at http://www-cs-students.stanford.edu/~cale/cs201/apartheid.hist.html.

1. In 1931, the Japanese army marched into and declared the independence of which of the following states?

   (A) Korea

   (B) Vietnam

   (C) the Philippines

   (D) Manchuria

2. As a political movement, Nazism

   (A) aimed to shore up national unity by attacking socialist and communist organizations.

   (B) was not fundamentally opposed to parliamentary government.

   (C) promoted the rights of women.

   (D) was in favor of trade unions.

3. Hitler came to power in Germany

   (A) as a result of entirely legal and constitutional means.

   (B) with the support of socialists.

   (C) after a lengthy civil war between forces of conservatives and communists.

   (D) as the result of a major political assassination.

4. In order to avoid a two-front war, Hitler signed a nonaggression pact with this country in 1939.

   (A) the U.S.S.R.

   (B) Japan

   (C) Italy

   (D) France

AP* Test Prep

5. This institution was created as a result of World War II.

   (A) the League of Nations

   (B) the United Nations

   (C) the Red Cross

   (D) the Third (Communist) International

6. The Apartheid in South Africa referred to

   (A) a rigid system of racial segregation.

   (B) British efforts to prevent the spread of communism.

   (C) the idea that blacks and whites could be separate but equal.

   (D) the backwardness of the economy compared to other parts of Africa.

Free-Response Question

How did World War II impact the European colonies in Asia and Africa? Are generalizations possible?

31 Western Society and Eastern Europe in the Decades of the Cold War

After World War II: A New International Setting for the West

The Resurgence of Western Europe

THINKING HISTORICALLY: The United States and Western Europe: Convergence and Complexity

Cold War Allies: The United States, Canada, Australia, and New Zealand

Culture and Society in the West

VISUALIZING THE PAST: Women at Work in France and the United States

Eastern Europe After World War II: A Soviet Empire

Soviet Culture: Promoting New Beliefs and Institutions

DOCUMENT: A Cold War Speech

GLOBAL CONNECTIONS: The Cold War and the World

I n 1954 the United States tested a nuclear weapon in the Marshall Islands that caused radioactive fallout to shower a Japanese fishing boat, ultimately killing one crew member and hospitalizing many others. International outrage ensued. Both the United States and the Soviet Union were conducting aboveground nuclear tests, and they would soon be joined by France and Britain. All sorts of people, in all sorts of places, rallied against these tests, in a striking manifestation of what media were beginning to label "world opinion."

Church groups, from Quakers to Roman Catholics, protested the tests. Buddhist voices were also strong. Japanese leadership was crucial; given the nation's experience at the end of World War II, it was hardly surprising that 86 percent of Japanese opposed nuclear testing. Australia and New Zealand vigorously objected to the use of the Pacific for tests, while Egypt and other Middle Eastern countries resisted French use of the Sahara. In Germany, with a new pas-

sion against war, hundreds of thousands of demonstrators marched before the U.S. embassy. African and Indian voices were also strong. In the United States many women joined protest groups—there was widespread concern that testing would lead to nuclear contamination of milk that would threaten the health of children.

The governments that were doing the testing initially resisted attempts to outlaw it. Many American leaders claimed the protests were a communist plot, and it was true that Soviet groups tried to use the rallies to their advantage (Figure 31.1). But finally the great powers reconsidered. In 1958 President Dwight Eisenhower, told by a scientist that further tests would create still more awesome bombs, replied: "The new thermonuclear weapons are tremendously powerful; however they are not as powerful as is world opinion today in obliging the United States to follow certain lines of policy." A testing moratorium was declared in 1958, and an initial test ban treaty was negotiated in 1963. ■

Both western and eastern Europe had been devastated by World War II. Yet the Soviet Union emerged within a few years with a new European empire and status as a world superpower, rivaling the United States and its allies. Western Europe bounced back as well, though it did not recover its prewar world dominance. The United States, defying its earlier traditions, became very active in international affairs, maintaining a strong international presence and making massive military expenditures.

While the cold war and the rise of nuclear weapons set the framework for developments in the West and in eastern Europe, other changes may have been more important for the longer run. In the West, democratic political forms gained new vitality, along with rising consumer prosperity. In eastern Europe, dominated by the Soviet Union, the desire for economic development and cultural change vied with the wish to maintain superpower status. Both the West and the Soviet bloc emphasized industrial growth and related social and family structures, and both emphasized science. Along the cold war tensions, these parallels had important effects on the rest of the world.

Western Europe had to adjust to its loss of world dominance after the war. Western European countries lost their colonies and became secondary players in the cold war between the superpowers.

After World War II: A New International Setting for the West

World War II left western Europe in shambles. The sheer physical destruction caused problems with housing and transportation. Downed bridges and rail lines complicated food shipments, leaving many people in France and Germany ill-fed and unable to work at full efficiency. Nazi Germany's use of forced foreign labor, as well as the many boundary changes resulting from the war, generated hundreds of thousands of refugees trying to return home or find new homes. For at least two years after 1945 it was unclear that recovery would be possible—mere survival proved difficult enough. Europe's postwar weakness after three decades of strife helped trigger a crescendo of nationalist sentiment in areas the West had colonized, as well as the fuller emergence of the United States and the Soviet Union, whose size and growing industrial strength now overshadowed Europe's proud nation-states.

Europe and Its Colonies

The two larger changes provoked by the war—decolonization and the cold war—quickly intruded on the West. We have seen that colonies outside Europe, roused by the war, became increasingly restive. When the British returned to Malaya and the Dutch to Indonesia—areas from which they had been dislodged—they found a more hostile climate, with well organized nationalist resistance. It was soon clear that many colonies could be maintained only at great cost, and in the main the European nations decided that the game was not worth the candle. A few cases proved messy. France tried to defend its holdings in Vietnam against communist guerrillas, yielding only in 1954 after some major defeats. The French clung even more fiercely to Algeria, the oldest African colony and one with a large European minority. The French military joined Algerian settlers in insisting on a war to the death against nationalist forces, and bitter fighting went on for years. The tension even threatened civil war in France, until a new president, Charles de Gaulle, realized the hopelessness of the struggle and negotiated Algeria's independence in 1962.

Overall, decolonization proceeded more smoothly than this between the late 1940s and the mid-1970s, without prolonged fighting that might drain the Western nations. Kenya, Vietnam, and the Algerian morass were bitter exceptions. Western governments typically retained important cultural relations with their former colonies and sometimes provided administrative and military help as well. Both France and Belgium, for example, frequently intervened in Africa after decolonization was officially complete. Finally, Western economic interests remained strong in most former colonies—particularly in Africa, which exploited mineral and agricultural resources in a pattern of trade not radically different from that of colonial days.

The impact of decolonization on the West should not, however, be minimized. Important minorities of former settlers and officials came home embittered, though, except briefly in France, they were not a significant political force. Europe's overt power in the world was dramatically reduced. Efforts by Britain and France to attack independent Egypt in 1956, to protest Egypt's nationalization of the Suez Canal, symbolized the new state of affairs. The United States and the Soviet Union forced a quick end to hostilities, and what was once a colonial lifeline came into non-Western hands. Yet although decolonization was a powerful change in world affairs, it did not, at least in the short run, overwhelm the West, as neither economic growth nor internal political stability suffered greatly.

The Cold War

The final new ingredient of Europe's diplomatic framework, the **cold war** between the United States and the Soviet Union, had a more durable ongoing influence on politics and society within the West. The conflict took shape between 1945 and 1947. The last wartime meetings among the leaders of Britain, the United States, and the Soviet Union had rather vaguely staked out the boundaries of postwar Europe, which were certainly open to varied interpretations. By the war's end, Soviet troops firmly occupied most eastern European countries, and within three years the Soviets had installed

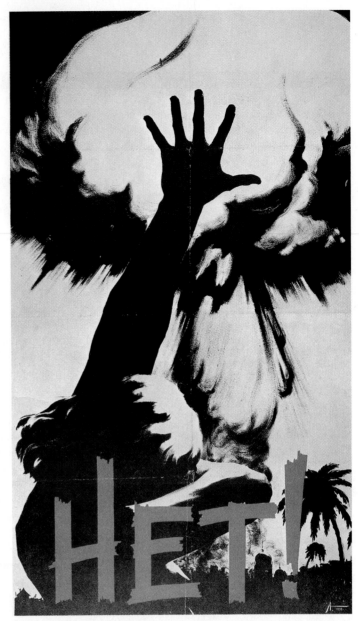

Figure 31.1 This 1958 Russian poster depicts a woman shielding her eyes from the light of a mushroom cloud and holding her hand up in a universal gesture of opposition. The lettering says "No!" The palm trees make clear that the reference is to testing in the Pacific. Why might the Soviets, who had themselves done aboveground nuclear testing, publish such a poster?

cold war The state of relations between the United States and its allies and the Soviet Union and its allies between the end of World War II and 1990; based on creation of political spheres of influence and a nuclear arms race rather than actual warfare.

 The Cold War Military Standoff

1940 C.E.	1950 C.E.	1960 C.E.
1945 End of World War II	1953 Stalin's death	1960s Civil rights and feminist movements in
1945–1948 Soviet takeover of eastern Europe;	1955 Formation of Warsaw Pact	United States
new constitutions in Italy, Germany, and	1956 Khrushchev breaks with Stalinism	1961 Berlin Wall erected
France; Labour Party victory in Britain; growth	1956 Hungarian revolt and its suppression	1962 Cuban missile crisis
of welfare states in western Europe	1957 Establishment of European Economic	1968 Czechoslovakian revolt suppressed;
1947 Marshall Plan	Community or Common Market (basis of later	Brezhnev Doctrine proclaims right to intervene
1947–1960s Cold war begins and reaches its	European Union)	in any socialist country
peak	1958 De Gaulle's Fifth Republic in France	1968–1973 Massive student protests in West
1949 Separate East and West German regimes		
established		
1949 Soviet Union develops atomic bomb;		
North Atlantic Treaty Organization established		

eastern bloc Nations favorable to the Soviet Union in eastern Europe during the cold war—particularly Poland, Czechoslovakia, Bulgaria, Romania, Hungary, and East Germany.

Truman, Harry American president from 1945 to 1952; less eager for smooth relations with the Soviet Union than Franklin Roosevelt; authorized use of atomic bomb during World War II; architect of American diplomacy that initiated the cold war.

Map 31.1 Soviet and Eastern European Boundaries by 1948 The new communist empire was joined in the Warsaw Pact, formed to respond to the West's North Atlantic Treaty Organization (itself formed in response to a perceived communist threat).

communist regimes to their liking, while excluding opposition political movements. Thus an **eastern bloc** emerged that included Poland, Czechoslovakia, Bulgaria, Romania, and Hungary. And Soviet boundaries themselves had pushed west, reversing the decisions of the post–World War I Versailles conference. The Baltic states disappeared, and Poland lost territory to Russia, gaining some former German lands as compensation. Finally, Soviet occupation of the eastern zone of Germany gave Russia a base closer toward the heart of Europe than the tsars had ever dreamed possible (Map 31.1).

Offended by the Soviet Union's heavy-handed manipulation of eastern Europe, including its zone in eastern Germany, U.S. and British policymakers tried to counter. The new American president, **Harry Truman**, was less eager for smooth relations with the Soviets than Franklin Roosevelt had been; Truman was emboldened by the U.S. development of the atomic bomb in 1945. Britain's wartime leader, Winston Churchill, had long feared communist aggression; it was he who in 1946 coined the phrase **iron curtain** to describe the division between free and repressed societies that he saw taking shape in Europe. But Britain frankly lacked the power to resist Soviet pressure, and under the Labour government it explicitly left the initiative to the United States.

The United States responded to Soviet rivalry with vigor. It criticized Soviet policies and denied Soviet applications for reconstruction loans. It bolstered regimes in Iran, Turkey, and Greece that were under Soviet pressure. Then in 1947 the United States proclaimed its **Marshall Plan**, designed to provide loans to help Western nations rebuild from the war's devastation. In Soviet eyes the Marshall Plan was a vehicle for U.S. economic dominance, and indeed there is little question that in addition to humanitarian motives the United States intended to beat back domestic communist movements in countries such as France and Italy by promoting economic growth.

The focal point of the cold war in these early years was Germany, which after the war had been divided into four zones administered by the United States, Britain, France, and the Soviet Union (Map 31.2). Soviet policy in Germany initially concentrated on seizing goods and factories as reparation. The Western Allies soon prevented Soviet intervention in their own zones and turned to some rebuilding efforts in the interests of playing a modest "German card" against growing Soviet strength in the East. That is, although the West, led by the United States, did not intend to resurrect a powerful Germany, it soon began to think in terms of constructing a viable political and economic entity. Allied collaboration started building a unified West Germany in 1946, and local political structures followed by more national ones were established through elections. When in 1947 the West moved to promote German economic recovery by creating a stable currency, the Soviet Union responded by blockading the city of Berlin, the divided

1970 C.E.	1980 C.E.	1990 C.E.	2000 C.E.
1970s Democratic regimes in Spain, Portugal, and Greece 1973, 1977 Oil crises 1979 Uprisings in Poland and their suppression; Thatcher and new conservatism in Britain; Soviet invasion of Afghanistan; significant economic recession	1981–1988 Reagan president in United States 1985–1991 Gorbachev heads Soviet Union 1989 Berlin Wall division ends; new regimes throughout eastern Europe	1992 End of economic restrictions within Common Market 1993 Division of Czechoslovakia; Clinton inauguration ends three-term Republican tenure in White House	2001 Euro currency introduced 2001 Growing concern about terrorism 2003 U.S. invasion of Iraq 2005 Expansion of European Union in eastern Europe

former capital that sat in the midst of the Soviet zone. The United States responded with a massive airlift to keep the city supplied, and the crisis finally ended in 1948, with two separate Germanies—East and West—beginning to take clear shape along a tense, heavily fortified frontier.

Cold war divisions spread from Germany to Europe more generally with the formation of two rival military alliances. The **North Atlantic Treaty Organization (NATO)** was formed in 1949, under U.S. leadership, to group most of the western European powers and Canada in a defensive alliance against possible Soviet aggression. The NATO pact soon legitimated some rearmament of West Germany in the context of resistance to communism, as well as the continued maintenance of a substantial U.S. military presence in Germany and in other member nations. In response, the Soviet Union organized the **Warsaw Pact** among its eastern European satellites. When in 1949 the Soviets developed their own nuclear capability, the world—particularly the European world—seemed indeed divided between two rival camps, each in turn dominated by its own superpower. Numerous U.S. and Soviet military units were permanently stationed in Europe on either side of the cold war divide.

The cold war had a number of implications for western Europe. It brought new influences from the United States on internal as well as foreign policy. Through the 1950s and beyond, the United States pressed for acceptance of German rearmament (though under some agreed-on limits); it lobbied for higher military expenditures in its old allies France and Britain; and it pressed for acceptance of U.S. forces and weapons systems. The Americans' wishes were not always met, but the United States had vital negotiating leverage in the economic aid it offered (and might withdraw), in the troops it stationed in Europe, and in the nuclear "umbrella" it developed (and might, in theory, also withdraw). Nuclear weapons seemed to offer the only realistic protection should the Soviet Union venture direct attack. The Soviets, for their part, influenced western Europe not only through perceived aggressive intent but also by funding and supporting substantial communist movements in France and Italy, which in turn affected but did not overwhelm the political process.

The cold war did not maintain within Europe the intensity it reached in the initial years. Centers of conflict shifted in part outside Europe as Korea, then Vietnam, and recurrently the Middle East became centers of tension. After 1958 France became more and more restless under what it viewed as Anglo-U.S. dominance of NATO, and it finally withdrew its forces from the joint NATO command, requiring also that U.S. troops leave French soil. In the 1970s Germany opened new negotiations with the Soviet Union and eastern bloc countries, wanting increased export opportunities and reduced diplomatic tension. Nevertheless, the cold war and the resultant alliance system continued to describe much of the framework of East–West relations in Europe and elsewhere in the world.

iron curtain   Phrase coined by Winston Churchill to describe the division between free and communist societies taking shape in Europe after 1946.

 Europe in the Cold War

 U.S. Test Bomb over Uninhabited Pacific Island, 1952

Map 31.2 Germany After World War II   Initial divisions of Germany and Berlin into occupied zones turned into a division between western and Soviet regimes.

Marshall Plan Program of substantial loans initiated by the United States in 1947; designed to aid Western nations in rebuilding from the war's devastation; vehicle for American economic dominance.

North Atlantic Treaty Organization (NATO) Created in 1949 under United States leadership to group most of the western European powers plus Canada in a defensive alliance against possible Soviet aggression.

Warsaw Pact Alliance organized by Soviet Union with its eastern European satellites to balance formation of NATO by Western powers in 1949.

Western Europeans introduced striking innovations in politics and the economy, sustaining a strong global role. Strides toward European unity cut through traditional enmities.

The shifting balance between the United States and Europe produced a crisscrossing of military relationships, whatever the larger implications of the shift. As western Europe abandoned military preeminence, the United States, never before a major peacetime military power, devoted growing resources to its military capacity and gave an increasing voice to its military leaders. Regardless of the political party in power, the percentage of the U.S. government budget going to the military remained stable from the 1950s to the 1980s—when it went up as a new American president put greater pressure on the Soviet Union. In contrast, some European leaders boasted that their societies had made a transition toward preeminence of civilian values and goals. Although U.S. and European values and institutions became more similar in key respects after World War II, the difference in military roles signaled ongoing distinctions within Western society.

The Resurgence of Western Europe

A new set of leaders emerged in many European countries, some from wartime resistance movements, eager to avoid the mistakes that had led to economic depression and war. Their vision was not always realized, but from 1945 onward, western Europe did move forward on three important fronts: the extension of democratic political systems, a modification of nation-state rivalries within Europe, and a commitment to rapid economic growth that reduced previous social and gender tensions.

The Spread of Liberal Democracy

In politics, defeat in war greatly discredited fascism and other rightist movements that had opposed parliamentary democracy. Several new political movements surfaced in western Europe, notably an important Christian Democratic current, which was wedded to democratic institutions and moderate social reform. Communist as well as socialist leaders largely accepted democratic procedures. Western Europe experienced a shift in the political spectrum toward fuller support for democratic constitutions and greater agreement on the need for government planning and welfare activities.

New regimes had to be constructed in Germany and Italy after the defeat of fascist and Nazi leadership. France established a new republic once occupation ended. In Germany, political reconstruction was delayed by the division of the nation by the victorious Allies. As the cold war took shape, however, France, Britain, and the United States progressively merged their zones into what became the Federal Republic of Germany (West Germany), encouraging a new constitution that would avoid the mistakes of Germany's earlier Weimar Republic by outlawing extremist political movements. Italy established a constitutional democracy. Women's voting rights spread throughout the region as well.

Western Europe's movement toward more consistent democracy continued in the 1970s, when Spain and Portugal moved from their authoritarian, semifascist constitutions (following the deaths of longtime strongmen) to democratic, parliamentary systems. Greece, increasingly linked to the West, followed the same pattern. By the 1980s western Europe had become more politically uniform than ever before in history.

The Welfare State

welfare state New activism of the western European state in economic policy and welfare issues after World War II; introduced programs to reduce the impact of economic inequality; typically included medical programs and economic planning.

The consolidation of democracy also entailed a general movement toward a **welfare state**. Resistance ideas and the shift leftward of the political spectrum helped explain the new activism of the state in economic policy and welfare issues. Wartime planning in the British government had pointed to the need for new programs to reduce the impact of economic inequality and to reward the lower classes for their loyalty (Figure 31.2). Not surprisingly, the governments that emerged at the war's end— Britain's Labour party and the Communist-Socialist–Christian Democrat coalitions in France and Italy—quickly moved to set up a new government apparatus that would play a vigorous role in economic planning and develop new social activities. By 1948 the basic nature of the modern welfare state had been established throughout western Europe, as not only the new regimes but also established reformists (as in Scandinavia) extended a variety of government programs. The United States, though somewhat more tentative in welfare measures, added to its New Deal legislation through President Lyndon Johnson's Great Society programs in the 1960s, creating medical assistance packages for the poor and the elderly. Canada enacted an even more comprehensive medical insurance plan.

Figure 31.2 This poster, published by the British Ministry of Health during the 1950s, was intended to increase public awareness of good health practices. Campaigns like these were part of a major shift in thinking about the role of government in Western societies: after World War II, most western European nations established "welfare states," intended to provide social services and economic assistance for citizens "from the cradle to the grave."

The welfare state elaborated a host of social insurance measures. Unemployment insurance was improved. Medical care was supported by state-funded insurance or, as in Britain where it became a centerpiece to the new Labour program, the basic health care system was nationalized. State-run medical facilities provided free care to the bulk of the British population from 1947 onward, although some small fees were later introduced. Family assistance was another category, not entirely new, that was now greatly expanded. All western European governments provided payments to families with several children, the amount increasing with family size. In the 1950s a French worker family with low earnings and five children could improve its income by as much as 40 percent through family aid. Governments also became more active in the housing field—a virtual necessity, given wartime destruction and postwar population growth. By the 1950s over one-fourth of the British population was housed in structures built and run by the government. The welfare state cushioned citizens against major expenses and unusual hardships, though it did not rearrange overall social structure.

The welfare state was undeniably expensive. It greatly enlarged government bureaucracies, in addition to channeling tax monies to new purposes. A new breed of bureaucrat, often called a **technocrat** because of intense training in engineering or economics and because of a devotion to the power of national planning, came to the fore in government offices. By the 1950s up to 25 percent of the gross national product of France and Holland was going to welfare purposes, and the figure tended to rise with time. As military expenses began to stabilize, welfare commitments became far and away the largest component of Western government budgets outside the United States. Here was a clear indication of the extent to which the western European state had altered its relationship to the wider society.

technocrat New type of bureaucrat; intensely trained in engineering or economics and devoted to the power of national planning; came to fore in offices of governments following World War II.

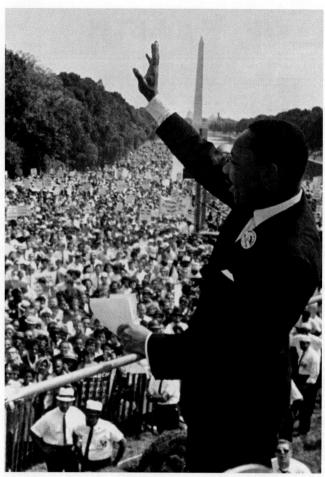

Figure 31.3 The great civil rights rally drew more than 250,000 people to Washington, D.C. in August 1963. The large numbers and high feelings expected at this rally caused much worry about civil unrest—liquor sales were suspended, thousands of troops were put on alert, police were brought in from other cities, and the public address system was set up so that government officials could shut it down if they thought it necessary—but the day was entirely peaceful.

Green movement Political parties, especially in Europe, focusing on environmental issues and control over economic growth.

European Union Flag

New Challenges to Political Stability

The Western pattern of political compromise around the mechanisms of parliamentary democracy and the welfare state were severely jolted by a series of student protests that developed in the late 1960s. Even before this, in the United States a vigorous civil rights movement had developed to protest unequal treatment of African Americans (Figure 31.3). Massive demonstrations, particularly in cities in the American South, attacked segregation and limitations on African American voting rights.

Campus unrest was a Western-wide phenomenon in the 1960s. At major American universities, campus unrest focused on the nation's growing involvement in the war against communism in North Vietnam. Young people in Europe and the United States also targeted the materialism of their societies, including the stodginess of the welfare state, seeking more idealistic goals and greater justice. Student uprisings in France in 1968 created a near revolution. By the early 1970s new rights for students and other reforms, combined with police repression, ended the most intense student protests, whereas passage of civil rights legislation in the United States ultimately reduced urban rioting and demonstrations. The flexibility of postwar Western democracy seemed triumphant. Some additional political concerns, including a new wave of feminism focusing on economic rights and dignity for women, and environmentalist movements entered the arena during the 1970s, partly as an aftermath of the student explosion. The rise of the **Green movement** in several countries in the 1970s signaled a new political tone, hostile to uncontrolled economic growth. Green parliamentary deputies in Germany even refused to wear coats and ties in their efforts to defy established political habits.

As economic growth slowed in the 1970s and the Western world faced its greatest economic recession since the immediate postwar years, other signs of political change appeared. New leadership sprang up within the British Conservative party and the U.S. Republican party, seeking to reduce the costs and coverage of the welfare state. In 1979 British Conservative leader Margaret Thatcher began the longest-running prime-ministership in 20th-century British history, working to cut welfare and housing expenses and to promote free enterprise. Neither she nor her U.S. counterpart, Ronald Reagan, fully dismantled the welfare state, but they did reduce its impact. Despite important adjustments, however, the main line of postwar government in the West persisted into the 21st century.

The Diplomatic Context

Along with the extension of democracy and the development of the welfare state, the West showed postwar vigor in addressing some traditional diplomatic problems, notably recurrent nationalistic rivalry, as well as specific manifestations, such as French–German enmity. U.S. guidance combined with innovative thinking in the new European governments.

During the war, many resistance leaders had tempered their hatred of Nazism with a plea for a reconstruction of the European spirit. The Christian Democratic movement, particularly, produced important new advocates of harmony among European nations. By 1947 U.S. leaders were also eager to spur western Europe's economic recovery, for which they judged coordination across national boundaries an essential precondition. Thus the Marshall Plan required discussion of tariffs and other development issues among recipient nations. With simultaneous U.S. insistence on the partial rearmament of West Germany and West German participation in NATO, the framework for diplomatic reform was complete.

Faced with these pressures and aware of the failure of nationalistic policies between the wars, France initiated coordination with Germany as a means of setting up a new Europe. The nations of the Low Countries and Italy were soon linked in these activities. The idea was to tie German economic activity to an international framework so that the nation's growing strength would not again threaten European peace. Institutions were established to link policies in heavy industry and later to develop atomic power. A measure to establish a united European military force proved too ambitious and collapsed under nationalist objections. But in 1958 the six western European nations (West Germany, France, Italy, Belgium, Luxembourg, and the Netherlands) set up the European Economic Community, or Common Market—later called the **European Union**—to begin to create a single economic entity across national political boundaries (Map 31.3). Tariffs were progressively reduced among the member nations, and a common tariff policy was set for the outside world. Free movement of labor and investment was encouraged. A Common Market bureaucracy was established, ultimately in Brussels, to oversee these operations. The Common Market set up a

European Union   Began as European Economic Community (or Common Market), an alliance of Germany, France, Italy, Belgium, Luxembourg, and the Netherlands, to create a single economic entity across national boundaries in 1958; later joined by Britain, Ireland, Denmark, Greece, Spain, Portugal, Sweden, Austria, Finland, and other nations for further European economic integration.

Map 31.3 The European Union   The Union, originally called the Common Market, expanded notably from its 1957 origins, particularly after the end of the cold war.

The United States and Western Europe: Convergence and Complexity

The relationship between the United States and western Europe has been important both historically and analytically for at least two centuries. Many people in the United States have tried to establish a distinctive identity while acknowledging special relationships with Europe; isolationism was one response earlier in this century. Europeans, for their part, have groped for definition of their U.S. "cousins," particularly as U.S. military and cultural influence grew in the 20th century. Were U.S. innovations to be welcomed, as stemming from a kindred society with a special flair for technology and modern mass taste, or should they be resisted as emblems of a superficial, degenerate, and essentially un-European society?

The relationship between the United States and western Europe has not been constant. Over time, and particularly since 1945, U.S. and European societies have in many important respects converged. Because of heightened imitation and shared advanced industrial economies, some earlier differences have receded.

Western Europe, for example, no longer has a very distinct peasantry. Its farmers, though smaller scale than their U.S. agribusiness counterparts, are commercialized and simply so few in numbers that they no longer set their society apart. European workers, though less likely than those in the United States to call themselves middle class, are now relatively prosperous. They have moved away from some of the political radicalism that differentiated them from their U.S. counterparts earlier in the 20th century. Europe does not have as deep-seated a racial issue as the United States inherited from slavery, but the growing influx of people from the West Indies, north Africa, and Asia has duplicated in Europe some of the same racial tensions and inner-city problems that bedevil the United States. At the other end of the social scale, trained managers and professionals now form a similar upper class in both societies, the fruit of systems of higher education that differ in particulars but resemble each other in producing something of a meritocratic elite.

A shared popular culture has certainly emerged. Although it stemmed mainly from U.S. innovations before World War II, more recently it has involved mutual borrowing. The United States, for example, embraced miniskirts and rock groups from Britain in the 1960s, and not only British but also French youth raced to buy the latest style in blue jeans.

> "The United States constituted a more traditional society, in terms of values, in the later 20th century than did western Europe."

Differences remain, some of them going back to earlier historical traditions. The United States has relied more fully on free-market capitalism than did western Europe, with the United States possessing less complete planning, fewer environmental regulations, and a more modest welfare apparatus. The difference was heightened during the 1990s. The United States proved much more religious than did western Europe. Only a minority of people in most western European countries professed religious belief by the 1990s, with less than 10 percent in most cases attending church with any regularity. In contrast the United States remains highly religious, with up to 40 percent regular church attendance, and 70 to 80 percent of its people professing religious belief. The United States made a less complete conversion to a new leisure ethic after World War II than did western Europe; European vacation time advanced toward more than a month a year, whereas the average in the United States remained two weeks or less. Europeans were franker about teenage sexuality, following the 1960 sexual revolution. They distributed birth control materials to adolescents much more commonly than did their more prudish U.S. counterparts, reducing rates of teenage pregnancy in the process.

In certain important respects, then, the United States constituted a more traditional society, in terms of values, in the later 20th century than did western Europe. Some of the variation between the two societies related to long-established distinctions (as in the degree of suspicion of government power); others emerged for the first time, sometimes surprisingly, after World War II.

The biggest distinctions between the two societies in recent decades, however, followed from their increasingly divergent world roles. Western Europe, though still highly influential in culture and trade on a global scale, concentrated increasingly on its own regional arrangements, including the European Union trading bloc, and decreasingly on military development. The United States moved in the opposite direction. Thus a traditional distinction was reversed; the United States became the more military (and some would argue militaristic) society, and many Europeans became committed to more strictly civilian goals.

QUESTIONS Why did the United States and western Europe converge in new ways during the 20th century? Do the two societies remain part of a common civilization? What are the most important issues to resolve in making this judgment?

---

court system to adjudicate disputes and prevent violations of coordination rules; it also administered a development fund to spur economic growth in such laggard regions as southern Italy and western France.

The Common Market did not move quickly toward a single government. Important national disputes limited the organization's further growth. France and Germany, for example, routinely quarreled over agricultural policy, with France seeking more payments to farmers as a matter of ob-

Contemporary Europe MAP

vious self-interest. But although the European Union did not turn into full integration, on the whole it contributed to economic growth. It even established an advisory international parliament, ultimately elected by direct vote. Further, in the 1980s firm arrangements were made to dismantle all trade and currency exchange barriers among member states in 1992, creating essentially complete economic unity. A single currency, the euro, was set up in many member countries by 2001. The European Union's success expanded its hold within western Europe. After long hesitations Britain, despite its tradition of proud island independence, decided to join, as did Ireland, Denmark, and later Greece, Spain, Portugal, Austria, Sweden, and Finland. By 2005 nine other nations, mostly in central Europe, were admitted to membership.

Nationalist tensions within Europe receded to a lower point than ever before in modern European history. After the worst scares of the cold war, focused mainly on the division between communist East and semicapitalist West, Europe became a diplomatically placid continent, enjoying one of the longest periods of substantial internal peace in its history.

Economic Expansion

After a surprisingly short, if agonizing, postwar rebuilding, striking economic growth accompanied political and diplomatic change. The welfare state and the European Union may have encouraged this growth by improving purchasing power for the masses and facilitating market expansion across national boundaries; certainly economic growth encouraged the success of new political and diplomatic systems.

There was no question that by the mid-1950s western Europe had entered a new economic phase. Agricultural production and productivity increased rapidly as peasant farmers, backed by technocrats, adopted new equipment and seeds. European agriculture was still less efficient than that of North America, which necessitated some much-resented tariff barriers by the Common Market. But food production easily met European needs, often with some to spare for export. Retooled industries poured out textiles and metallurgical products. Expensive consumer products, such as automobiles and appliances, supported rapidly growing factories. Western Europe also remained a leading center of weapons production, trailing only the United States and the Soviet Union in exports. Overall growth in gross national product surpassed the rates of any extended period since the Industrial Revolution began; it also surpassed the growth rates of the U.S. economy during the 1950s and 1960s.

By this point French, German, and Italian economies were growing between 6 percent and 11 percent annually. These growth rates depended on rapid technological change. Europe's rising food production was achieved with a steadily shrinking agricultural labor force. France's peasant population—16 percent of the labor force in the early 1950s—fell to 10 percent two decades later, but overall output was much higher than before. During the 1950s the industrial workforce grew as part of factory expansion, but by the 1960s the relative proportion of factory workers also began to drop, despite rising production. Workers in the service sector, filling functions as teachers, clerks, medical personnel, insurance and bank workers, and performers and other "leisure industry" personnel, rose rapidly in contrast. In France half of all paid workers were in the service sector by 1968, and the proportion rose steadily thereafter.

Another key change involved immigration. Many parts of the continent experienced a labor shortage and had to seek hundreds of thousands of workers from other areas—first from southern Europe, then, as this region industrialized, from Africa, the Middle East, and parts of Asia. The rise of immigrant minorities was a vital development in western Europe and also the United States, where the influx of Asian and Latin American immigrants stepped up markedly. By 2000, countries like France had Muslim minorities of up to 10 percent of the population while in the United States Latinos became the largest ethnic minority.

Unprecedented economic growth and low unemployment meant unprecedented improvements in incomes, even with the taxation necessary to sustain welfare programs. New spending money rapidly translated into huge increases in the purchase of durable consumer goods, as virtually the whole of Western civilization became an "affluent society."

Ownership of standard consumer goods like televisions and cars spread widely. Shopping malls and supermarkets migrated across the Atlantic. Advertising was not quite as ubiquitous in

Figure 31.4 In the United States, as well as in Japan and western Europe, advertisements increasingly tried to create the sense that a good life could be achieved by buying the right goods. Here, a new car was associated with a prosperous home, a loving family, and even happy pets.

Many changes in the non-European West paralleled those in Europe, including the welfare state. The United States took a distinctive role, particularly because of its new position as a military superpower.

Europe as in the United States. But promptings to buy, to smell good, to look right, to express one's personality in the latest car style began quickly to describe European life (Figure 31.4). The frenzy to find good vacation spots grew intense. Millions of Germans poured annually into Italy and Spain, seeking the sun. Britons thronged to Spanish beaches. Europeans were bent on combining efficient work with indulgent leisure.

The West's economic advance was not without some dark spots. Many immigrant workers from Turkey, north Africa, Pakistan, and the West Indies suffered very low wages and unstable employment. These immigrants, euphemistically labeled "guest workers," were often residentially segregated and victims of discrimination by employers and police.

By the 1990s slower economic growth raised new unemployment problems in western Europe. Economic inequality increased throughout the West, though particularly in the United States. Nevertheless, the West's economic vitality, a marked contrast to the interwar decades, underpinned vital social transformations and played a major role in the global economic framework as well.

Cold War Allies: The United States, Canada, Australia, and New Zealand

Developments in the so-called overseas West in many ways paralleled those in western Europe, but without the sense of grappling with prior collapse. The sheer level of innovation in domestic policy was less great, in part because the crises of the first half of the 20th century had been less severe. Crucial adjustments occurred, however, in foreign policy. The United States led the way in making the changes in its own tradition that were necessary to develop a massive peacetime military force and a global set of alliances. With the decline of European, and particularly British, international power and the emergence of the cold war context, Australia, New Zealand, and Canada tightened their links with the United States and developed new contacts with other areas of the world.

The Former Dominions

Canada forged ahead in welfare policies after World War II, establishing a greater stake in economic planning and state-run medical insurance than did the United States. At the same time, however, Canadian economic integration with the United States continued, with U.S. investments in Canadian resources and mutual exports and imports soaring steadily into the 1970s. By 1980 the Canadian government took some measures to limit further U.S. penetration, and a sense of Canadian nationalism sparked resentment of the giant to the south. In 1988, however, the two nations signed a free-trade agreement, creating a North American trading bloc at a time when European unity was increasing rapidly.

Continued emigration to Canada pointed in new directions also, with growing numbers of people arriving from various parts of Asia. Canada's most distinctive issue, however, involved growing agitation by French Canadians in Quebec for regional autonomy or even national independence. A new separatist party, founded in 1967, took control of the provincial government during the 1970s. Subsequent legislation limited the use of the English language in Quebec's public and commercial life, though referendums for full independence failed during the 1980s. A new Canadian constitution in 1982, however, granted greater voice to the provinces, both to counter French Canadian demand and also to recognize the growing economic strength of the resource-rich western provinces. Separatist tensions continue to simmer, however, into the 21st century.

From 1945 onward Australia and New Zealand moved steadily away from their traditional alignment with Great Britain and toward horizons around the Pacific. The two commonwealths joined a mutual defense pact with the United States in 1951, directed against potential communist aggression in the Pacific. Both nations cooperated with the United States in the Korean War, and Australia backed U.S. intervention in Vietnam. In 1966 the Australian prime minister declared, "Wherever the United States is resisting aggression . . . we will go a-waltzing Matilda with you." In the later 1970s and 1980s Australia and especially New Zealand began to distance themselves somewhat from U.S. foreign policy. New Zealand barred U.S. nuclear-armed vessels in 1985.

As Great Britain aligned with the European Union, Australian and New Zealand exports were increasingly directed toward other Pacific nations, notably Japan, whereas investment capital came mainly from the United States and Japan. Indeed, Australia became Japan's chief raw-materials supplier aside from oil. Asian emigration also increasingly altered the population mix, again particularly in Australia. The Australian government had to back down from a long-held whites-only immigration policy, permitting growing regional emigration, particularly from Indochina. By 1983 Asians accounted for 60 percent of the total immigrant population in Australia.

The "U.S. Century"?

Amid a host of domestic issues, the big news in U.S. history after 1945 was its assumption—in many ways, its eager assumption—of the superpower mantle, opposing the Soviet Union and serving as the world's leading defender of democratic and capitalistic values. The United States hesitated briefly after 1945, demobilizing its World War II forces rather quickly with some hope that world peace would provide some respite from further international engagement. However, Great Britain's inability to continue to police the world for the West, together with rapid Soviet successes in installing communist governments in eastern Europe, prompted a decisive U.S. stance. In 1947 President Harry Truman promised support for "free peoples who are resisting subjugation by armed minorities or by outside pressures." The doctrine was specifically directed against communist pressures on Greece and Turkey. It was soon extended into the elaboration of Marshall Plan aid to rebuild the economies of western Europe against the possibility of communist subversion in these war-torn countries.

The plunge into the cold war took a toll on the home front. The United States entered a period of intense, even frenzied concern about internal communist conspiracies, ferreting out a host of suspected spies and subjecting people in many fields to dismissal from their jobs on grounds of suspected radical sympathies.

Cold war engagement prompted other policy changes in the federal government. The Defense Department was set up in 1947 to coordinate military policy, and the Central Intelligence Agency was established to organize a worldwide information-gathering and espionage network. Military spending increased considerably, with the formation of the Strategic Air Command to stand in constant readiness in case of a Soviet bombing attack. A massive U.S. airlift thwarted Soviet pressure on the western sectors of occupied Berlin. The United States resisted the invasion of South Korea by the communist North, beginning in the 1950s; U.S. troops stationed in Japan were sent in to support the South Koreans. Under General Douglas MacArthur and backed by several allies under a hastily arranged United Nations mandate, the North Korean invasion was repulsed within a few months. The United States then authorized an invasion into North Korea, which brought a retaliatory intervention from communist China. The United States was pushed back, and more than two years of additional fighting ensued before peace was negotiated in 1953—with the new boundary line between the two Koreas relatively close to the previous line. In the meantime annual U.S. spending on the military had increased from $13.5 billion to $50 billion.

During the 1950s, under the presidency of Dwight Eisenhower, the United States settled into a policy of containment of the Soviet Union, which involved maintenance of large peacetime military forces. The United States also arranged alliances not only with western Europe, in NATO, but also with Australia and New Zealand, with several southeast Asian nations, and with several nations in the Middle East; this alliance system virtually surrounded the Soviet Union. Less novel was recurrent U.S. intervention in Central America against suspected communist movements; thus U.S. aid toppled a new Guatemalan government in 1954. The United States was unable to prevent a takeover in Cuba that propelled Cuba into the communist camp, despite a U.S.-backed invasion attempt by anticommunist Cuban rebels. Nonetheless, the United States maintained its policy of vigilance (under President John Kennedy in 1962) by forcing the Soviet Union to withdraw its missile sites on the island.

The U.S. containment policy yielded a final test that took shape during the 1960s, when intervention against communist revolutionaries in South Vietnam gradually escalated. The U.S. Air Force began bombing communist North Vietnam in 1965. Later that year American troops were sent in, reaching a total of 550,000 by 1968. By this time the United States was spending $2 billion a week on a war that never produced convincing success and gradually bogged down in horrendous bloodshed on both sides. By 1970 more bombs had been dropped on Vietnam than had been dropped by anyone, anywhere previously in the 20th century. By 1968 domestic pressure against the war, centered particularly on U.S. college campuses, began to force changes in strategy. A new U.S. president, Richard Nixon, tried to expand the war to other parts of Indochina, to increase pressure on North Vietnam. Simultaneously, peace negotiations with North Vietnam were launched, resulting finally in an agreement on a cease-fire, in 1973. By 1975, as the United States speedily withdrew, all Vietnam lay in communist hands.

Furor over the Vietnam War led to agonizing policy reassessments in the United States. Some observers judged that new directions might be forged, as the United States had discovered that its massive military might could be stalemated by fervent guerrilla tactics. Both the U.S. military and the public grew more wary of regional wars. Although the national mood sobered, decisive policy changes did not ensue. A socialist government in Chile, for example, was ousted with the aid of covert U.S. pressure even as the Vietnam conflict wound down. The socialist government was replaced by a brutal military regime.

In 1980 the United States overwhelmingly elected a new president, Ronald Reagan, who combined conservative domestic policies with a commitment to bolster military spending and make sure that the United States would "ride tall" again in world affairs. The 1980s saw no major new international involvements, but several punitive raids were conducted against suspected terrorists in the Middle East, and the small West Indian island of Grenada was invaded to topple a leftist regime. President Reagan sponsored a number of expensive new weapons systems, which helped press an afflicted Soviet economy to virtual collapse as its leaders attempted to keep pace. The next president, George Bush, continued an interventionist policy by sending U.S. troops into Panama to evict and arrest an abrasive dictator and then by spearheading a Western and moderate Arab alliance against Iraq's invasion of Kuwait, during 1990–1991. Under President Bill Clinton, the United States led participation in military action against forces in the Balkans in the 1990s.

By this point, with the cold war over, the United States emerged as "the world's only superpower." Its annual military spending outstripped that of the next twenty nations combined. This unrivaled military power enabled it to take over and expand many of the international policing functions once held by Western nations like Britain. Other Western states sometimes resented American leadership, but they generated no clear alternative and usually supported U.S. initiatives.

Culture and Society in the West

The expansion of consumer culture marked recent Western history. Dramatic changes in gender relations also defined Western society.

Political and economic changes in Western society progressively altered the contours of earlier industrial development. The West became the first example of an advanced industrial society, especially from the 1950s onward, and both the United States and western Europe shared in leading facets of change.

Social Structure

Economic growth, bringing increasing prosperity to most groups, eased some earlier social conflicts throughout the West. Workers were still propertyless, but they had substantial holdings as consumers, and their sense of social inferiority often declined as a result. Social lines were also blurred by increasing social mobility, as educational opportunities opened further and the size of the white-collar sector expanded. Much unskilled labor was left to immigrants. Economic and political change also altered conditions for western Europe's peasantry, and not only by cutting its size. Peasants became increasingly commercial, eager for improvements in standards of living, and participants, through car trips and television, in urban culture. They also became more attuned to bureaucracies, as state regulations pushed them into cooperative organizations.

Social distinctions remained. Middle-class people had more abundant leisure opportunities and a more optimistic outlook than did most workers. Signs of tension continued. Crime rates went up throughout Western society after the 1940s, though the levels were particularly high in the United States. Race riots punctuated U.S. life in the 1950s and 1960s and exploded in immigrant sections of British cities in the 1980s and Germany in the early 1990s.

The Women's Revolution

A key facet of postwar change involved women and the family, and again both western Europe and the United States participated fully in this upheaval. Although family ideals persisted in many ways—with workers, for example, urging that "a loving family is the finest thing, something to work for, to look to and to look after"—the realities of family life changed in many ways. Family leisure activities expanded. Extended-family contacts were facilitated by telephones and automobiles. More years of schooling increased the importance of peer groups for children, and the authority of parents undoubtedly declined.

The clearest innovation in family life came through the new working patterns of women. World War II brought increased factory and clerical jobs for women, as the earlier world war had done. After a few years of downward adjustment, the trends continued. From the early 1950s onward, the number of working women, particularly married women, rose steadily in western Europe, the United States, and Canada. (See Visualizing the Past feature.) Women's earlier educational gains had improved their work qualifications; the growing number of service jobs created a need for additional workers—and women, long associated with clerical jobs and paid less than men, were ideal candidates. Many women also sought entry into the labor force as a means of adding to personal or family income, to afford some of the consumer items now becoming feasible but not yet easy to buy, or as a means of personal fulfillment in a society that associated worth with work and earnings.

The growing employment of women, which by the 1970s brought the female segment of the labor force up to 44 percent of the total in most Western countries, represented particularly the employment of adult women, most of them married and many with children. Teenage employment dropped as more girls stayed in school, but long-term work commitments rose steadily. This was not, to be sure, a full stride to job equality. Women's pay lagged behind men's pay. Most women were concentrated in clerical jobs rather than spread through the occupational spectrum, despite a growing minority of middle-class women entering professional and management ranks. Clearly, however, the trends of the 19th-century Industrial Revolution, to keep women and family separate from work outside the home, had yielded to a dramatic new pattern.

Other new rights for women accompanied this shift. Where women had lacked the vote before, as in France, they now got it; of the western European nations, only Switzerland doggedly refused this concession at the national level until 1971. Gains in higher education were considerable, though again full equality remained elusive. Women constituted 23 percent of German university students in 1963, and under socialist governments in the 1970s the figure rose. Preferred subjects, however, remained different from those of men, as most women stayed out of engineering, science (except medicine), and management.

Family rights improved, at least in the judgment of most women's advocates. Access to divorce increased, which many observers viewed as particularly important to women. Abortion law eased, though more slowly in countries of Catholic background than in Britain or Scandinavia; it became increasingly easy for women to regulate their birth rate. Development of new birth control methods, such as the contraceptive pill introduced in 1960, as well as growing knowledge and acceptability of birth control, decreased unwanted pregnancies. Sex and procreation became increasingly separate considerations. Although women continued to differ from men in sexual outlook and behavior—more than twice as many French women as men, for example, hoped to link sex, marriage, and romantic love, according to 1960s polls—more women than before tended to define sex in terms of pleasure.

Women at Work in France and the United States

A statistical table of the sort presented here is essentially descriptive. What patterns are described? Is there a major change, and how can it be defined? What are the main differences between these two nations? Were they converging, becoming more similar, in 1962? In 1982? Do they end up in a similar situation with regard to women's work roles, or are they more different in 1982 than they were in 1946?

QUESTIONS From description, questions of causation arise. Statistical patterns provide a precise framework for a challenging analysis. Why were the United States and France so different in 1946? What might have caused the changes in patterns (for example, in the United States during the 1950s)? What was the role of new feminist demands in 1963? What might have caused the differences in the timing of trends in France and the United States?

Women at Work: The Female Labor Force in France and the United States

| | France | | United States | |
	Women Workers (thousands)	Percentage of Total Force	Woman Workers (thousands)	Percentage of Total Force
1946	7,880	37.90	16,840	27.83
1954	6,536	33.93	19,718	29.43
1962	6,478	33.23	24,047	32.74
1968	6,924	34.62	29,242	35.54
1975	7,675	36.48	37,553	39.34
1982	8,473	39.46	47,894	42.81

Sources: B. R. Mitchell, *International Historical Statistics: Europe, 1750–1988;* U.S. Bureau of the Census, *Historical Statistics of the United States, Colonial Times to 1970, Bicentennial Edition, Part 1;* U.S. Bureau of the Census, *Statistical Abstract of the United States: 1984.*

Predictably, of course, changes in the family, including the roles of women, brought new issues and redefined ideals of companionship. The first issue involved children. A brief increase in the Western birth rate ended in the early 1960s and a rapid decline ensued. Women working and the desire to use income for high consumer standards mitigated against children, or very many children, particularly in the middle class, where birth rates were lowest. Those children born were increasingly sent, often at an early age, to day-care centers, one of the amenities provided by the European welfare state and particularly essential where new fears about population growth began to surface. European families had few hesitations about replacing maternal care with collective care, and parents often claimed that the result was preferable for children. At the same time, however, some observers worried that Western society, and the Western family, were becoming indifferent to children in an eagerness for adult work and consumer achievements. American adults, for example, between the 1950s and 1980s, shifted their assessment of family satisfaction away from parenthood by concentrating on shared enjoyments between husbands and wives.

Family stability also opened new cracks. Pressures to readjust family roles, women working outside the family context, and growing legal freedoms for women caused men and women alike to turn more readily to divorce. In 1961, 9 percent of all British marriages ended in divorce; by 1965 the figure was 16 percent and rising. By the late 1970s, one-third of all British marriages ended in divorce, and the U.S. rate was higher still.

The development of a new surge of feminist protest, although it reflected much wider concerns than family life alone, showed the strains caused by women's new activities and continued limitations. Growing divorce produced many cases of impoverished women combining work and child care. New work roles revealed the persistent earnings gap between men and women. More generally, many women sought supporting values and organizations as they tried to define new identities less tied to the domestic roles and images of previous decades.

A **new feminism** began to take shape with the publication in 1949 of *The Second Sex* by the French intellectual Simone de Beauvoir. Echoed in the 1950s and 1960s by other works, such as *The Feminine Mystique*, by Betty Friedan of the United States (Figure 31.5), a new wave of women's rights

new feminism New wave of women's rights agitation dating from 1949; emphasized more literal equality that would play down domestic roles and qualities for women; promoted specific reforms and redefinition of what it meant to be female.

Figure 31.5 In Houston, in November 1977, the U.S. government sponsored a National Women's Conference. In order to symbolize the direct link between earlier American feminists and the women at the Conference, a torch was lit in Seneca Falls, New York—seat of the famous women's right convention of 1848—and carried 2600 miles by relay runners to Houston. In this photograph, feminist leaders accompany the torch and its three bearers on the last mile of the journey. Here, from left to right, are Susan B. Anthony II, Representative Bella Abzug, Sylvia Ortiz, Peggy Kokernot, and Michele Cearcy (the torch bearers), and Betty Friedan.

agitation rose after three decades of relative calm. The new feminism tended to emphasize a more literal equality that would play down special domestic roles and qualities; therefore, it promoted not only specific reforms but also more basic redefinitions of what it meant to be male and female.

The new feminism did not win all women, even in the middle class, which was feminism's most avid audience. It also did not cause some of the most sweeping practical changes that were taking place, as in the new work roles. But it did support the revolution in roles. From the late 1960s onward it pressed Western governments for further change, raising issues that were difficult to fit into established political contexts. The movement both articulated and promoted the gap between new expectations and ongoing inequalities in gender. And the new feminism expressed and promoted some unanswered questions about family functions. In a real sense, later 20th-century feminism seemed to respond to the same desire for individuality and work identity in women that had earlier been urged on men as part of the new mentality suitable for a commercialized economy. Family remained important in the evolving outlook of women, although some feminist leaders attacked the institution outright as hopelessly repressive. Even for many less ideological women, however, family goals were less important than they had been before.

Western Culture

Amid great innovations in politics, the economy, and social structure—including some pressing new problems—Western cultural life in many respects proceeded along established lines. A host of specific new movements arose, and a wealth of scientific data was assimilated, though basic frameworks had been set earlier, often in the more turbulent but intellectually creative decades of the early 20th century.

One key development was a shift of focus toward the United States. Greater political stability in the United States during the 1930s and 1940s, as well as Hitler's persecutions, had driven many prominent intellectuals to U.S. shores, where they often remained even as western Europe revived. As U.S. universities expanded, their greater wealth fueled more scientific research; what was called a "brain drain," based on dollar power, drew many leading European scientists to the United States even during the 1950s and 1960s. European science remained active, but the costliness of cutting-edge research produced a durable U.S. advantage. Money also mattered in art, as patronage became increasingly important, and thus New York replaced Paris as the center of international styles.

Europeans did participate in some of the leading scientific advances of the postwar years. Francis Crick, of Cambridge University in England, shared with the American James Watson key credit for the discovery of the basic structure of the genetic building block deoxyribonucleic acid (DNA), which in turn opened the way for rapid advances in genetic knowledge and industries based on artificial synthesis of genetic materials. By 2000 work on the human genome project was proceeding rapidly on both sides of the Atlantic. Europeans also participated in nuclear research, often through laboratories funded by the European Union or other inter-European agencies. European space research, slower to develop than Soviet or U.S. initiatives, nevertheless also produced noteworthy achievements by the 1970s, and again there were important commercial spin-offs in communications satellites and other activities.

Developments in the arts maintained earlier 20th-century themes quite clearly. Most artists continued to work in the "modern" modes set before World War I, which featured unconventional self-expression and a wide array of nonrepresentational techniques. The clearest change involved growing public acceptance of the modern styles. The shock that had greeted earlier innovations disappeared, and the public, even when preferring older styles displayed in museums or performed by symphony orchestras devoted to the classics, now seemed reconciled to the redefinition of artistic standards (Figure 31.6). New names were added to the roster of leading modern artists. In Paris Bernard Buffet scored important successes with gaunt, partially abstract figures. The British sculptor Henry Moore produced rounded figures and outright abstractions that conveyed some of the

Figure 31.6 In the early 1960s the struggling pop artist Andy Warhol was casting about for subject matter. A friend advised him to paint whatever he liked best in the world. He painted soup cans and became an overnight sensation. His work, which also included repeated images of celebrities such as Marilyn Monroe and Marlon Brando, is understood by critics as a statement about the "fascinated yet indifferent" experience of consumers in a society saturated by marketing images.

(Andy Warhol (1928–1987) © Copyright. "Campbell's Soup Cans" 1962. The Museum of Modern Art/Licensed by Scala-Art Resource, NY. (476.1996.1-32.vw2). © 2009 Copyright The Andy Warhol Foundation for the Visual Arts/Artists Rights Society (ARS), New York/Trademarks, Campbell Soup Company All rights reserved. Digital Image © The Museum of Modern Art/Licensed by SCALA/Art Resource, NY.)

horrors of wartime life and postwar dislocations. A new group of "pop" artists in the 1960s tried to bridge the gap between art and commercial mass culture by incorporating cans and other products, comic strips, and advertisements into paintings, prints, and collages. As also held true in the realm of fully abstract painting, U.S. artists increasingly took the lead.

Europeans retained clearer advantages in artistic films. Italian directors produced a number of gripping, realistic films in the late 1940s, portraying both urban and peasant life without frills. Italy, France, and Sweden became centers of experimental filmmaking again in the 1960s. Jean-Luc Godard and Michelangelo Antonioni portrayed the emptiness of urban life, and Swedish director Ingmar Bergman produced a series of dark psychological dramas. Individual directors in Spain, Britain, and Germany also broke new ground, as Europeans remained more comfortable than their U.S. counterparts in producing films of high artistic merit, relatively free from commercial distractions.

Fragmentation occurred in the social sciences, with no commanding figure rising to the stature of Marx or Weber in previous generations, willing to posit fundamental social dynamics or sweeping theories. Many specific fields in the social sciences turned to massive data collections and pragmatic, detailed observations; in many of these, U.S. practitioners developed a decided advantage. Economics, in particular, became something of an American specialty in the post-Keynesian decades and focused on massive quantitative studies of economic cycles and money supplies. European influence was greater in several new theoretical formulations in the humanities. French intellectuals also contributed to a redefinition of historical study, building on innovations launched between the world wars. Social history, or the focus on changes in the lives of ordinary people, became increasingly the order of the day, giving a great spur to historical research throughout western Europe and the United States.

A Lively Popular Culture

Western society displayed more vitality in its popular culture than in formal intellectual life, which reflected the results of economic and social change. As European economies struggled to recover from the war and as U.S. military forces spread certain enthusiasms more widely than before, some observers spoke of a U.S. "Coca-cola-nization" of Europe. U.S. soft drinks, blue-jean fashions, chewing gum, and other artifacts became increasingly common. U.S. films continued to wield substantial influence, although the lure of Hollywood declined somewhat. More important was the growing impact of U.S. television series. Blessed with a wide market and revenues generated from advertising, American television was quite simply "slicker" than its European counterparts, and the western drama *Bonanza*, the soap opera *Dallas*, and many other shows appeared regularly on European screens to define, for better or worse, an image of the United States.

In contrast to the interwar decades, however, European popular culture had its own power, and it even began to influence the United States. The most celebrated figures of popular culture in the 1960s were unquestionably the Beatles, from the British port city of Liverpool. Although they adopted popular music styles of the United States, including jazz and early rock, the Beatles added an authentic working-class touch in their impulsiveness and their mockery of authority. They also expressed a good-natured desire to enjoy the pleasures of life, which is a characteristic of modern Western popular culture regardless of national context. British popular music groups continued to set standards in the 1970s and had wide impact on western Europe more generally.

Other facets of popular culture displayed a new vigor. Again in Britain, youth fashions, separate from the standards of the upper class, showed an ability to innovate and sometimes to shock. Unconventional uses of color and cut, as in punk hairstyles of the later 1970s, bore some resemblance to the anti-conventional tone of modern painting and sculpture.

Sexual culture also changed in the West, building on earlier trends that linked sex to a larger pleasure-seeking mentality characteristic of growing consumerism and to a desire for personal expression. Films and television shows demonstrated increasingly relaxed standards about sexual display. In Britain, Holland, and Denmark, sex shops sold a wide array of erotic materials and products.

Like the United States, western Europe experienced important changes in sexual behavior starting around 1960, particularly among young people. Premarital sex became more common. The average age of first sexual intercourse began to go down. Expressive sexuality in western Europe was also evident in the growing number of nude bathing spots, again in interesting contrast to more hesitant initiatives in the United States. Although the association of modern popular culture with sexuality and body concern was not novel, the openness and diversity of expression unquestionably reached new levels and also demonstrated western Europe's new confidence in defining a vigorous, nontraditional mass culture of its own.

Critics of Western popular culture worried about its superficiality and its role in distracting ordinary people from ongoing problems such as social inequality. But there were no huge reactions, like those of Nazism against the cultural trends of the 1920s. Western popular culture played a major role in setting global cultural standards, enhancing the West's international influence even as its formal political dominance declined.

Eastern Europe After World War II: A Soviet Empire

Soviet Russia expanded its effective empire. Amid new challenges, the Soviet system maintained distinctive political controls.

By 1945 Soviet foreign policy had several ingredients. Desire to regain tsarist boundaries (though not carried through regarding Finland) joined with traditional interest in expansion and in playing an active role in European diplomacy. Genuine revulsion at Germany's two invasions prompted a feverish desire to set up buffer zones under Soviet control. As a result of Soviet industrialization and its World War II push westward, the nation also emerged as a world power, like the newcomer United States. Continued concentration on heavy industry and weapons development, combined with strategic alliances and links to communist movements in various parts of the world, helped maintain this status.

The Soviet Union as Superpower

Soviet participation in the late phases of the war against Japan provided an opportunity to seize some islands in the northern Pacific. The Soviet Union established a protectorate over the communist regime of North Korea, to match the U.S. protectorate in South Korea. Soviet aid to the victorious Communist party in China brought new influence in that country for a time, and in the 1970s the Soviet Union gained a new ally in communist Vietnam, which provided naval bases for the Soviet fleet. Its growing military and economic strength gave the postwar Soviet Union new leverage in the Middle East, Africa, and even parts of Latin America; alliance with the new communist regime in Cuba was a key step here, during the 1960s. The Soviet Union's superpower status was confirmed by its development of the atomic and then hydrogen bombs, from 1949 onward, and by its deployment of missiles and naval forces to match the rapid expansion of U.S. arsenals. The Soviet Union had become a world power.

The New Soviet Empire in Eastern Europe

As a superpower the Soviet Union developed increasing worldwide influence, with trade and cultural missions on all inhabited continents and military alliances with several Asian, African, and Latin American nations. But the clearest extension of the Soviet sphere developed right after World War II, in eastern Europe (Map 31.1). Here the Soviets made it plain that they intended to stay, pushing the Soviet effective sphere of influence farther to the west than ever before in history. Soviet insistence on this empire helped launch the cold war, as the Soviet Union preferred to confront the West rather than relax its grip.

The small nations of eastern Europe, mostly new or revived after World War I, had gone through a troubled period between the world wars. Other than democratic Czechoslovakia, they had failed to establish vigorous, independent economies or solid political systems. Then came the Nazi attack and ineffective Western response, as Czechoslovakia, Poland, and Yugoslavia were seized by German or Italian forces. Eastern Europe fell under Nazi control for four years. Although anti-Nazi governments formed abroad, only in Yugoslavia was a resistance movement strong enough to seriously affect postwar results.

By 1945 the dominant force in eastern Europe was the Soviet army, as it pushed the Germans back and remade the map. Through the combination of the Soviet military might and collaboration with local communist movements in the nations that remained technically independent, opposition parties were crushed and noncommunist regimes forced out by 1948. The only exceptions to this pattern were Greece, which moved toward the Western camp in diplomatic alignment and political and social systems; Albania, which formed a rigid Stalinist regime that ironically brought it into disagreement with Soviet post-Stalinist leaders; and Yugoslavia, where a communist regime formed under the resistance leader Tito quickly proclaimed its neutrality in the cold war, resisting Soviet direction and trying to form a more open-ended, responsive version of the communist economic and social system.

After what was in effect the Soviet takeover, a standard development dynamic emerged throughout most of eastern Europe by the early 1950s. The new Soviet-sponsored regimes attacked possible rivals for power, including, where relevant, the Roman Catholic Church. Mass education and propaganda outlets were quickly developed. Collectivization of agriculture ended the large estate system, without creating a property-owning peasantry. Industrialization was pushed through successive five-year plans, though with some limitation due to Soviet insistence on access to key natural resources (such as Romanian oil) on favorable terms. Finally, a Soviet and eastern European trading zone became largely separate from the larger trends of international commerce.

After the formation of NATO in western Europe, the relevant eastern European nations were enfolded in the Warsaw Pact defense alliance and a common economic planning organization. Soviet troops continued to be stationed in most eastern European states, both to confront the Western alliance and to ensure the continuation of the new regimes and their loyalty to the common cause.

Although it responded to many social problems in the smaller nations of eastern Europe, as well as to the desire of the Soviet Union to expand its influence and guard against German or more general Western attack, the new Soviet system created obvious tensions. Particularly tight controls in East Germany brought a workers' rising there in 1953, vigorously repressed by Soviet troops. Faced with a widespread exodus to West Germany, the Soviets built the **Berlin Wall** in 1961 to stem the flow. All along the new borders of eastern Europe, barbed-wire fences and armed patrols kept the people in.

Berlin Wall Built in 1961 to halt the flow of immigration from East Berlin to West Berlin; immigration was in response to lack of consumer goods and close Soviet control of economy and politics; torn down at end of cold war in 1991.

In 1956 a relaxation of Stalinism within the Soviet Union created new hopes that controls might be loosened. More liberal communist leaders arose in Hungary and Poland, with massive popular backing, seeking to create states that, although communist, would permit greater diversity and certainly more freedom from Soviet domination. In Poland the Soviets accepted a new leader more popular with the Polish people. Among other results, Poland was allowed to halt agricultural collectivization, establishing widespread peasant ownership in its place, and the Catholic Church, now the symbol of Polish independence, gained greater tolerance. But a new regime in Hungary was cruelly crushed by the Soviet army and a hard-line Stalinist leadership set up in its place (Figure 31.7).

Yet Soviet control over eastern Europe did loosen slightly overall, for the heavy-handed repression cost considerable prestige. Eastern European governments were given a freer hand in economic policy and were allowed limited room to experiment with greater cultural freedom. Several countries thus began to outstrip the prosperity of the Soviet Union itself. Contacts with the West expanded in several cases, with greater trade and tourism. Eastern Europe remained with the Soviet Union as a somewhat separate economic bloc in world trade, but there was room for limited diversity. Individual nations, such as Hungary, developed new intellectual vigor and experimented with slightly less centralized economic planning. The communist political system remained in full force, however, with its single-party dominance and strong police controls; diplomatic and military alignment with the Soviet Union remained essential.

The limits of experimentation in eastern Europe were brought home again in 1968, when a more liberal regime came to power in Czechoslovakia. Again the Soviet army responded, expelling the reformers and setting up a particularly rigid leader. A challenge came from Poland once more in the late 1970s, in the form of widespread Catholic unrest and an independent labor movement called **Solidarity**, all against the backdrop of a stagnant economy and low morale. Here response was slightly more muted, though key agitators were arrested; the Polish army took over the state, under careful Soviet supervision.

Solidarity Polish labor movement formed in 1970s under Lech Walesa; challenged U.S.S.R.-dominated government of Poland.

By the 1980s eastern Europe had been vastly transformed by several decades of communist rule. Important national diversity remained, visible both in industrial levels and in political styles. Catholic Poland thus differed from hard-line, neo-Stalinist Bulgaria or Romania. Important discontents remained as well. Yet a communist-imposed social revolution had brought considerable

Figure 31.7 As Soviet troops moved into Hungary to crush the revolt of 1956, freedom fighters in Budapest headed for the front with whatever weapons they could find. This truckload of supporters is being urged on by the crowd.

economic change and real social upheaval. The once dominant aristocracy had been abolished and the lives of ordinary people had changed greatly through new systems of mass education and industrial, urban growth. Earlier cultural ties with the West, though still greater than in the Soviet Union itself, had been lessened; Russian, not French or English, was the first foreign language learned.

The expansion of Soviet influence answered important Soviet foreign policy goals, both traditional and new. The Soviets retained a military presence deep in Europe, which among other things reduced very real anxiety about yet another German threat. Eastern European allies aided Soviet ventures in other parts of the world, providing supplies and advisors for activities in Africa, Latin America, and elsewhere. Yet the recurrent unrest in eastern Europe served as something of a check on Soviet policy as well. The need for continued military presence may have diverted Soviet leaders from emphasizing expansionist ambitions in other directions, particularly where direct commitment of troops might be involved.

Evolution of Domestic Policies

Red Square
Military
Parade

Within the Soviet Union the Stalinist system remained intact during the initial postwar years. The war encouraged growing use of nationalism as well as appeals for communist loyalty, as millions of Russians responded heroically to the new foreign threat. Elements of this mood were sustained as the cold war with the United States developed after 1947, with news media blasting the United States as an evil power and a distorted society. Many Soviets, fearful of a new war that U.S. aggressiveness seemed to them to threaten, agreed that strong government authority remained necessary. This attitude helped sustain the difficult rebuilding efforts after the war, which proceeded rapidly enough for the Soviet Union to regain its prewar industrial capacity and then proceed, during the 1950s, to impressive annual growth rates. The attitude also helped support Stalin's rigorous efforts to shield the Soviet populations from extensive contact with foreigners or foreign ideas. Strict limits on travel, outside media, or any uncensored glimpse of the outside world kept the Soviet Union unusually isolated in the mid-20th-century—its culture, like its economy, largely removed from world currents.

Stalin's political structure continued to emphasize central controls and the omnipresent party bureaucracy. Stalin himself insisted on increasing adulation, and he also grew more suspicious of possible plots against him. Moscow-based direction of the national economy, along with the steady extension of education, welfare, and police operations, expanded the bureaucracy both of the government and of the parallel Communist party. Recruitment from the ranks of peasant and worker families continued into the 1940s, as educational opportunities, including growing secondary school and university facilities, allowed talented young people to rise from below. Party membership, the ticket to bureaucratic promotion, was deliberately kept low, at about 6 percent of the population, to ensure selection of the most dedicated elements. New candidates for the party, drawn mostly from the more broadly based communist youth organizations, had to be nominated by at least three party members. Party members vowed unswerving loyalty and group consciousness.

Soviet Culture: Promoting New Beliefs and Institutions

The Soviet government was an impressive new product, not just a renewal of tsarist autocracy. It carried on a much wider array of functions than the tsars had ventured, not only in fostering industrialization but also in reaching out for the direct loyalties of individual citizens. The government and the party also maintained an active cultural agenda, and although this had been foreshadowed by the church and state links of tsarist days, it had no full precedent. The regime declared war on the Orthodox church and other religions soon after 1917, seeking to shape a secular population that would maintain a Marxist, scientific orthodoxy; limited church activities remained but under tight government regulation. Artistic and literary styles, as well as purely political writings, were carefully monitored to ensure adherence to the party line. The educational system was used not only to train and recruit technicians and bureaucrats but also to create a loyal, right-thinking citizenry. Mass ceremonies, such as May Day parades, stimulated devotion to the state and to communism.

Although the new regime did not attempt to abolish the Orthodox church outright, it greatly limited the church's outreach. Thus the church was barred from giving religious instruction to anyone under 18, and state schools vigorously preached the doctrine that religion was mere superstition. Although loyalties to the church persisted, they now seemed concentrated in a largely elderly minority. The Soviet regime also limited freedom of religion for the Jewish minority, often holding up Jews as enemies of the state in what was in fact a manipulation of traditional Russian anti-Semitism. The larger Muslim minority was given greater latitude, on condition of careful loyalty to the regime. On the whole, the traditional religious orientation of Soviet society declined in favor of a scientific outlook and Marxist explanations of history in terms of class conflict. Church attendance dwindled under government repression; by the 1950s only the elderly seemed particularly interested.

The Soviet state also continued to attack modern Western styles of art and literature, particularly when they involved abstract forms regarded as decadent, but maintained some earlier Western styles, which were appropriated as Russian. Thus Russian orchestras performed a wide variety of classical music, and the Russian ballet, though rigid and conservative by 20th-century Western norms, commanded wide attention and enforced rigid standards of excellence. In the arts, socialist realist principles spread to eastern Europe after World War II, particularly in public displays and monuments. With some political loosening and cold war thaw after 1950, however, Soviet and eastern European artists began to adopt Western styles to some extent. At the popular level, jazz and rock music bands began to emerge by the 1980s, though official suspicion persisted.

Literature in the Soviet Union remained diverse and creative, despite official controls sponsored by the communist-dominated Writers' Union. Leading authors wrote movingly of the travails of World War II, maintaining the earlier tradition of sympathy with the people, great patriotism, and concern for the Russian soul. The most imaginative Soviet artists, particularly the writers, often skirted a fine line between conveying some of the sufferings of the Russian people in the 20th century and courting official disapproval. Their freedom also depended on leadership mood; censorship eased after Stalin and then tightened again somewhat in the late 1960s and 1970s, though not to previous levels. Yet even authors critical of aspects of the Soviet regime maintained distinctive Russian values. **Aleksandr Solzhenitsyn** (sohl-zuh-NEET-suhn), for example, exiled to the United

Rapid industrialization caused significant social change in eastern Europe. Tensions increased over relationships with Western culture.

Solzhenitsyn, Aleksandr [sohl-zuh-NEET-suhn] (b. 1918) Russian author critical of the Soviet regime but also of Western materialism; published trilogy on the Siberian prison camps, *The Gulag Archipelago* (1978).

States after the publication of his trilogy on Siberian prison camps, *The Gulag Archipelago,* found the West too materialistic and individualistic for his taste. Though barred from his homeland, he continued to seek an alternative both to communist policy and to westernization, with more than a hint of a continuing belief in the durable solidarity and faith of the Russian common people and a mysterious Russian national soul.

Along with interest in the arts and a genuine diversity of expressions despite official party lines, Soviet culture continued to place great emphasis on science and social science. Scientists enjoyed great prestige and wielded considerable power. Social scientific work, heavily colored by Marxist theory, nonetheless produced important analyses of current trends and of history. Scientific research was even more heavily funded, and Soviet scientists generated a number of fundamental discoveries in physics, chemistry, and mathematics. At times scientists felt the heavy hand of official disapproval. Biologists and psychiatrists, particularly, were urged to reject Western theories that called human rationality and social progress into question, though here as in other areas controls were most stringent in the Stalinist years. Thus Freudianism was banned, and under Stalin, biologists who overemphasized genetics were jailed. Too much emphasis on the unconscious, as with Freud, or genetic determinism, contradicted the idea that the revolutionary states could control human destiny. But Soviet scientists overall enjoyed considerable freedom and great prestige. As in the West, their work was often linked with advances in technology and weaponry. After the heyday of Stalinism, scientists gained greater freedom from ideological dictates, and exchanges with Western researchers became more common in what was, at base, a common scientific culture.

Shaped by substantial state control, 20th-century Soviet culture overall proved neither traditional nor Western. Considerable ambivalence about the West remained, as Soviets continued to utilize many art forms they developed in common with the West, while instilling a comparable faith in science. Fear of cultural pollution—particularly through non-Marxist political tracts but also through modern art forms—remained lively, as Soviet leaders sought a culture that would enhance their goals of building a socialist society separate from the capitalist West (Figure 31.8).

Economy and Society

The Soviet Union became a fully industrial society between the 1920s and the 1950s. Rapid growth of manufacturing and the rise of urban populations to more than 50 percent of the total were measures of this development. Most of the rest of eastern Europe was also fully industrialized by the 1950s. Eastern European modernization, however, had a number of distinctive features. State control of virtually all economic sectors was one key element; no other industrialized society gave so little leeway to private initiative. The unusual imbalance between heavy industrial goods and consumer items was another distinctive aspect. The Soviet Union lagged in the priorities it placed on consumer goods—not only such Western staples as automobiles but also housing construction and simple items, such as bathtub plugs. Consumer-goods industries were poorly funded and did not achieve the advanced technological level that characterized the heavy-manufacturing sector.

The Soviet need to amass capital for development in a traditionally poor society helped explain the inattention to consumer goods; so did the need to create, in a society that remained poorer overall, a massive armaments industry to rival that of the United States. Soviet fears of resurgent Germany also motivated its military goals. Thus despite an occasional desire to beat the West at its own affluent-society game, communist eastern Europe did not develop the kind of consumer society that came to characterize the West. Living standards improved and extensive welfare services provided security for some groups not similarly supported in the West, but complaints about poor consumer products and long lines to obtain desired goods remained a feature of Soviet life.

Figure 31.8 Work incentives were a problem in collectivized agriculture. This 1947 poster was designed to spur Soviet farm workers to greater productivity. It proclaims, "Work hard and abundant bread will be your reward."

Soviet industrialization also caused an unusual degree of environmental damage. The drive to produce at all costs created bleak zones around factories, where waste was dumped, and in agricultural and mining areas. Up to one-quarter of all Soviet territory (and that of the eastern bloc) was environmentally degraded, often leading to severe health damages for people in the affected areas.

The communist system throughout eastern Europe also failed to resolve problems with agriculture. Capital that might have gone into farming equipment was often diverted to armaments and heavy industry. The arduous climate of northern Europe and Asia was a factor as well, dooming a number of attempts to spread grain production to Siberia, for example. But it seemed clear that the eastern European peasantry continued to find the constraints and lack of individual incentive in collectivized agriculture deterrents to maximum effort. Thus eastern Europe had to retain a larger percentage of its labor force in agriculture than was true of the industrial West, but it still encountered problems with food supply and quality.

Despite the importance of distinctive political and economic characteristics, the communist states of eastern Europe echoed a number of the themes of contemporary Western social history—simply because of the shared fact of industrial life. Work rhythms, for example, became roughly similar. Industrialization brought massive efforts to speed the pace of work and to introduce regularized supervision. The incentive systems designed to encourage able workers resembled those used in Western factories. Along with similar work habits came similar leisure activities. For decades, sports have provided excitement for the peoples of eastern Europe, as have films and television. Family vacations to the beaches of the Black Sea became cherished respites. Here, too, there were some distinctive twists, as the communist states sponsored a massive sports apparatus as part of their political program (in contrast to the Western view of sports as a combination of leisure and commercialism). East Germany, along with the Soviet Union, developed particularly extensive athletic agendas under state guidance, from training programs for talented children to substantial rewards for successful adult competitors, winning international competitions in a host of fields.

Eastern European social structure also grew closer to that of the West, despite the continued importance of the rural population and despite the impact of Marxist theory. Particularly interesting was a tendency to divide urban society along class lines—between workers and a better-educated, managerial middle class. Wealth divisions remained much less great than in the West, to be sure, but the perquisites of managers and professional people—particularly for Communist party members—set them off from the standard of living of the masses.

Finally, the Soviet family reacted to some of the same pressures of industrialization as did the Western family. Massive movements to the cities and crowded housing enhanced the nuclear family unit, as ties to a wider network of relatives loosened. The birth rate dropped. Official Soviet policy on birth rates varied for a time, but the basic pressures became similar to those in the West. Falling infant death rates, with improved diets and medical care, together with increasing periods of schooling and some increase in consumer expectations, made large families less desirable than before. Wartime dislocations contributed to birth rate decline at points as well. By the 1970s the Soviet growth rate was about the same as that of the West. As in the West, some minority groups—particularly Muslims in the southern Soviet Union—maintained higher birth rates than the majority ethnic group—in this case, ethnic Russians—a differential that caused some concern about maintaining Russian cultural dominance.

Patterns of childrearing showed some similarities to those in the West, as parents, especially in the managerial middle class, devoted great attention to promoting their children's education and ensuring good jobs for the future. At the same time children were more strictly disciplined than in the West, both at home and in school, with an emphasis on authority that had political implications as well. Soviet families never afforded the domestic idealization of women that had prevailed in the West during industrialization. Most married women worked, an essential feature of an economy struggling to industrialize and offering relatively low wages to individual workers. As had been true for peasants in the past, women performed many heavy physical tasks. They also dominated some professions, such as medicine, though these professionals remained lower in status than were their male-dominated counterparts in the West. Soviet propagandists took pride in the constructive role of women and their official equality, but there were signs that many women were suffering burdens from demanding jobs with little help from their husbands at home.

De-Stalinization

The rigid government apparatus created by Stalin and sustained after World War II by frequent arrests and exiles to forced labor camps was put to a major test after Stalin's death in 1953. The results gradually loosened, without totally reversing, Stalinist cultural isolation. Focus on one-man rule might have created immense succession problems, and indeed frequent jockeying for power did develop among aspiring candidates. Yet the system held together. Years of bureaucratic experience had given most Soviet leaders a taste for coordination and compromise, along with a reluctance to strike out in radical new directions that might cause controversy or arouse resistance from one of the key power blocs within the state. Stalin's death was followed by a ruling committee that balanced interest groups, notably the army, the police, and the party apparatus. This mechanism encouraged conservatism, as each bureaucratic sector defended its existing prerogatives, but it also ensured fundamental stability.

In 1956, however, **Nikita Khrushchev** emerged from the committee pack to gain primary power, though without seeking to match Stalin's eminence. Indeed, Khrushchev attacked Stalinism for its concentration of power and arbitrary dictatorship. In a stirring speech delivered to the Communist party congress, Khrushchev condemned Stalin for his treatment of political opponents, for his narrow interpretations of Marxist doctrine, even for his failure to adequately prepare for World War II. The implications of the de-Stalinization campaign within the Soviet Union suggested a more tolerant political climate and some decentralization of decision making. In fact, however, despite a change in tone, little concrete institutional reform occurred. Political trials became less common, and the most overt police repression eased. A few intellectuals were allowed to raise new issues, dealing, for example, with the purges and other Stalinist excesses. Outright critics of the regime were less likely to be executed and more likely to be sent to psychiatric institutions or, in the case of internationally visible figures, exiled to the West or confined to house arrest. Party control and centralized economic planning remained intact. Indeed, Khrushchev planned a major extension of state-directed initiative by opening new Siberian land to cultivation; his failure in this costly effort, combined with his antagonizing many Stalinist loyalists, led to his quiet downfall.

After the de-Stalinization furor and Khrushchev's fall from power, patterns in the Soviet Union remained stable into the 1980s, verging at times on stagnant. Economic growth continued but with no dramatic breakthroughs and with recurrent worries over sluggish productivity and especially over periodically inadequate harvests, which compelled expensive grain deals with Western nations, including the United States. A number of subsequent leadership changes occurred, but the transitions were handled smoothly.

Cold war policies eased somewhat after Stalin's death. Khrushchev vaunted the Soviet ability to outdo the West at its own industrial game, bragging on a visit to the United States that "we will bury you." The Khrushchev regime also produced one of the most intense moments of the cold war with the United States, as he probed for vulnerabilities. The Soviets installed missiles in Cuba, yielding only to a firm U.S. response in 1962 by removing their missiles but not their support of the communist regime on the island. Khrushchev had no desire for war, and overall he promoted a new policy of peaceful coexistence. He hoped to beat the West economically and actively expanded the Soviet space program; *Sputnik,* the first space satellite, was sent up in 1957, well in advance of its U.S. counterpart. Khrushchev maintained a competitive tone, but he shifted away from an exclusive military emphasis. Lowered cold war tensions with the West permitted a small influx of Western tourists by the 1960s as well as greater access to the Western media and a variety of cultural exchanges, which gave some Soviets a renewed sense of contact with a wider world and restored some of the earlier ambiguities about the nation's relationship to Western standards.

At the same time, the Soviet leadership continued a steady military buildup, adding increasingly sophisticated rocketry and bolstered by its unusually successful space program (Figure 31.9). The Soviets maintained a lead in manned space flights into the late 1980s. Both in space and in the arms race, the Soviet Union demonstrated great technical ability combined with a willingness to settle for somewhat simpler systems than those the United States attempted, which helped explain how it could maintain superpower parity even with a less prosperous overall economy. An active sports program, resulting in a growing array of victories in Olympic Games competition, also

Khrushchev, Nikita Stalin's successor as head of U.S.S.R. from 1953 to 1964; attacked Stalinism in 1956 for concentration of power and arbitrary dictatorship; failure of Siberian development program and antagonism of Stalinists led to downfall.

Nikita Khrushchev Challenges the West to Disarm and Advance World Prosperity

Figure 31.9 This Soviet postcard proclaims, "Glory! The world's first group flight in space, August, 1962," and depicts cosmonauts A. G. Nikolaev and P. R. Popovich. ("CCCP" on the cosmonauts' helmets is Cyrillic lettering meaning "U.S.S.R.") Soviet advances in science and technology both surprised and threatened the United States and western Europe.

showed the Soviet Union's new ability to compete on an international scale and its growing pride in international achievements.

The nation faced a number of new foreign policy problems, even though it maintained superpower status. From the mid-1950s onward the Soviet Union experienced a growing rift with China, a communist nation with which it shared a long border. Successful courtship of many other nations—such as Egypt, a close diplomatic friend during the 1960s—often turned sour, though these developments were often balanced by new alignments elsewhere. The rise of Muslim awareness in the 1970s was deeply troubling to the Soviet Union, with its own large Muslim minority. This prompted a 1979 invasion of Afghanistan, to promote a friendly puppet regime, which bogged down amid guerrilla warfare into the late 1980s. On balance, the Soviet Union played a normally cautious diplomatic game, almost never engaging directly in warfare but maintaining a high level of preparedness (Figure 31.10).

Problems of work motivation and discipline loomed larger in the Soviet Union than in the West by the 1980s, after the heroic period of building an industrial society under Stalinist exhortation and threat. With highly bureaucratized and centralized work plans and the absence of abundant consumer goods, many workers found little reason for great diligence. High rates of alcoholism, so severe as to cause an increase in death rates, particularly among adult males, also burdened work performance and caused great concern to Soviet leaders. More familiar were problems of youth agitation. Although Soviet statistics tended to conceal outright crime rates, it is clear that many youth became impatient with the disciplined life and eager to have greater access to Western culture, including rock music and blue jeans.

Most observers thought the Soviet Union remained firmly established in the early 1980s, thanks to careful police control, vigorous propaganda, and real, popular pride in Soviet achievements. Though even the U.S. Central Intelligence Agency failed to see major problems, however, economic conditions were in fact deteriorating rapidly, and the whole Soviet system would soon come unglued. Yet its collapse was all the more unsettling because of communism's huge success for many decades. At great cost to many people, the Soviet Union had attained world power. Many rejoiced in its fall, but many were also disoriented by it. What could and should replace a system that had dominated huge stretches of Europe and Asia for so long?

A Cold War Speech

United States President Dwight Eisenhower, a former military leader during World War II, delivered this speech in 1961, right before stepping down from office. The speech was widely noted for its focus on what journalists called the American "military-industrial complex."

Crises there will continue to be. In meeting them, whether foreign or domestic, great or small, there is a recurring temptation to feel that some spectacular and costly action could become the miraculous solution to all current difficulties. A huge increase in newer elements of our defense; development of unrealistic programs to cure every ill in agriculture; a dramatic expansion in basic and applied research—these and many other possibilities, each possibly promising in itself, may be suggested as the only way to the road we wish to travel.

But each proposal must be weighed in the light of a broader consideration: the need to maintain balance in and among national programs—balance between the private and the public economy, balance between cost and hoped for advantage—balance between the clearly necessary and the comfortably desirable; balance between our essential requirements as a nation and the duties imposed by the nation upon the individual; balance between actions of the moment and the national welfare of the future. Good judgment seeks balance and progress; lack of it eventually finds imbalance and frustration.

The record of many decades stands as proof that our people and their government have, in the main, understood these truths and have responded to them well, in the face of stress and threat. But threats, new in kind or degree, constantly arise. I mention only two.

A vital element in keeping the peace is our military establishment. Our arms must be mighty, ready for instant action, so that no potential aggressor may be tempted to risk his own destruction.

Our military organization today bears little relation to what known by any of my predecessors in peacetime, or indeed by the fighting men of World War II or Korea.

Until the latest of our world conflicts, the United States had no armaments industry. American makers of plowshares could, with time and as required, make swords as well. But now we can no longer risk emergency improvisation of national defense; we have been compelled to create a permanent armaments industry of vast proportions. Added to this, three and a half million men and women are directly engaged in the defense establishment. We annually spend on military security more than the net income of all United States corporations.

This conjunction of an immense military establishment and a large arms industry is new in the American experience. The total influence—economic, political, even spiritual—is felt in every city, every State house, every office of the Federal government. We recognize the imperative need for this development. Yet we must not fail to comprehend its grave implications. Our toil, resources, and livelihood are all involved; so is the very structure of our society.

In the councils of government, we must guard against the acquisition of unwarranted influence, whether sought or unsought, by the military industrial complex. The potential for the disastrous rise of misplaced power exists and will persist.

We must never let the weight of this combination endanger our liberties or democratic processes. We should take nothing for granted. Only an alert and knowledgeable citizenry can compel the proper meshing of the huge industrial and military machinery of defense with our peaceful methods and goals, so that security and liberty may prosper together.

Akin to, and largely responsible for the sweeping changes in our industrial-military posture, has been the technological revolution during recent decades.

In this revolution, research has become central; it also becomes more formalized, complex and costly. A steadily increasing share is conducted for, by, or at the direction of, the Federal government.

Today, the solitary inventor, tinkering in his shop, has been overshadowed by task forces of scientists in laboratories and test fields. In the same fashion, the free university, historically the fountainhead of free ideas and scientific discovery, has experienced a revolution in the conduct of research. Partly because of the huge costs involved, a government contract becomes virtually a substitute for intellectual curiosity. For every old blackboard there are now hundreds of new electronic computers.

The prospect of domination of the nation's scholars by Federal employment, project allocations, and the power of money is ever present and is gravely to be regarded. Yet, in holding scientific research and discovery in respect, as we should, we must also be alert to the equal and opposite danger that public policy could itself become the captive of a scientific-technological elite.

It is the task of statesman to mold, to balance, and to integrate these and other forces, new and old, within the principles of our democratic system—ever aiming toward the supreme goals of our free society.

QUESTIONS What kinds of changes was Eisenhower identifying, and how might they seem to clash with American or Western traditions? Were the two changes related? Did the speech have much impact on American policies since the early 1960s?

Figure 31.10 May Day in the Soviet Union was an occasion for massive military parades including troops, missiles, jets, and tanks, showcasing the country's military power, and for glorification of the State and its leaders, past and present. Enormous banners with portraits of Marx, Engels, and Lenin were stretched high over Red Square, suggesting the current leadership's connection with these giants. In this photo of the 1947 May Day parade, top Soviet leaders watch from reviewing stands in front of Lenin's tomb. Behind them is the wall of the Kremlin.

Global Connections

The Cold War and the World

The massive competition between the West and the Soviet alliance dominated many aspects of world history between 1945 and 1992. It played a key role in other major global themes, such as decolonization and nationalism. But the competition also gave other parts of the world some breathing room, as they could play one side against the other—a contrast to previous decades in which Western imperialism had dominated.

At the same time, Western and Soviet influences were not entirely contradictory. While Western consumerism and Soviet communism were quite different, both were largely secular. Both societies emphasized science. Both societies challenged key social traditions, including purely traditional roles for women. Both eagerly sold weapons on the world market. Both could stimulate hostility to new forms of outside influence and pressures to change. These factors, too, helped shape world history for a crucial half-century.

Further Readings

On post–World War II social and economic trends, see C. Kindleberger, *Europe's Postwar Growth* (1967); V. Bogdanor and R. Skidelsky, eds., *The Age of Affluence, 1951–1964* (1970); R. Dahrendorf, ed., *Europe's Economy in Crisis* (1982); and Peter Stearns and Herrick Chapman, *European Society in Upheaval* (1991). On the welfare state, see Stephen Cohen, *Modern Capitalist Planning: The French Model* (1977), and E. S. Einhorn and J. Logue, *Welfare States in Hard Times* (1982).

The Cold War dominates scholarship on the post-war world. See Wilson D. Miscamble, *From Roosevelt to Truman: Potsdam, Hiroshima, and the Cold War* (2007); Robert David Johnson, *Congress and the Cold War* (2006); Elizabeth Edwards Spalding, *The First Cold Warrior: Harry Truman, Containment, and the Remaking of Liberal Internationalism* (2006); Kenneth Osgood, *Total Cold War: Eisenhower's Secret Propaganda Battle at Home and Abroad* (2006); David Reynolds, *From World War to Cold War: Churchill, Roosevelt, and the International History of the 1940s* (2006); Yale Richmond,

Cultural Exchange & the Cold War: Raising the Iron Curtain (2003); Scott W. Palmer, *Dictorship of the Air: Aviation Culture and the Fate of Modern Russia* (2006); and Rana Mitter and Patrick Major, eds., *Across the Blocs: Cold War Cultural and Social History* (2004).

On Commonwealth nations, see Charles Doran, *Forgotten Partnership: U.S.-Canada Relations Today* (1983); Edward McWhinney, *Canada and the Constitution, 1979–1982* (1982); and Stephen Graubard, ed., *Australia: Terra Incognita?* (1985).

Postwar Soviet history is treated in Richard Barnet, *The Giants: Russia and America* (1977); A. Rubinstein, *Soviet Foreign Policy Since World War II* (1981); Alec Nove, *The Soviet Economic System* (1980); Stephen Cohen et al., eds., *The Soviet Union Since Stalin;* and Ben Eklof, *Gorbachev and the Reform Period* (1988).

On Soviet culture, Matthew Lenoe, *Closer to the Masses: Stalinist Culture, Social Revolution and Soviet Newspapers* (2004); Jeffrey Brooks, *Thank You, Comrade Stalin! Soviet Public Culture from Revolution to Cold War* (2000), is a cultural history of the communist press. James von Geldern and Richard Stites, eds., *Mass Culture in Soviet Russia: Tales, Poems, Songs, Movies, Plays, and Folklore, 1917–1953* (1995), is a valuable repository of primary cultural texts and documents.

Postwar eastern Europe is treated in F. Fetjo, *History of the People's Democracies: Eastern Europe Since Stalin* (1971) and Joseph Rothschild, *Return to Diversity: A Political History of East Central Europe Since World War II* (2000), which stands as the authoritative political history.

On women's experiences, see Barbara Engel and Christine Worobec, eds., *Russia's Women: Accommodation, Resistance, Transformation* (1990). Sabrina Ramet, ed., *Eastern Europe: Politics, Culture, and Society Since 1939* (1998), presents a cultural and social history survey through each country and includes a relevant bibliography.

On the early signs of explosion in eastern Europe, see Rose Brady, *Kapitalizm: Russia's Struggle to Free Its Economy* (1999).

James T. Patterson, *Grand Expectations: The United States, 1945–1974* (1996), offers a useful overview of the period. Trends in the postwar United States include the civil rights movement, movingly described in David J. Garrow, *Bearing the Cross: Martin Luther King Jr. and the Southern Leadership Conference, 1955–1968* (1986).

The transformation of America's cities is traced by Kenneth T. Jackson, *Crabgrass Frontier: The Suburbanization of the United States* (1985), and the growth of popular culture analyzed in R. Maltby, ed., *The Passing Parade: A History of Popular Culture in the Twentieth Century* (1989), and Lewis MacAdams, *The Birth of Cool: Beat, Bebop, and the American Avant-Garde* (2001). Arthur M. Schlesinger Jr., *A Thousand Days: John F. Kennedy in the White House* (1965); Doris Kearns, *Lyndon Johnson and the American Dream* (1976); and David Stockman, *The Triumph of Politics: Inside Story of the Reagan Revolution* (1987), offer accounts of American political aspirations during three key presidential administrations by authors closely identified with their subjects.

On the Web

Arguments in favor and opposed to the Welfare State are offered at http://en.wikipedia.org/wiki/Welfare_state. Links exploring developments in post-war America and Europe can be found at http://www.fordham.edu/halsall/mod/modsbook47.html and http://www.fordham.edu/halsall/mod/modsbook49.html. For feminism, see http://womenshistory.about.com/library/qu/blqufrie.htm and http://search.eb.com/women/articles/Friedan_Betty_Naomi_Goldstein.html and http://scriptorium.lib.duke.edu/wlm/. The origins of the Cold War and its impact on American domestic politics are illuminated at http://americanhistory.si.edu/subs/history/timeline/origins/ and http://www.spartacus.schoolnet.co.uk/USAmccarthyism.htm. For these and other postwar developments in the United States, from the civil rights movement to urbanization see http://vlib.iue.it/history/USA/ERAS/20TH/1960s.html, http://lcweb4.loc.gov/learn/collections/hay/history.html, http://memory.loc.gov/ammem/aaohtml/exhibit/aopart9.html#09a, and http://www.cnn.com/EVENTS/1997/mlk/links.html.

The life of Nikita Krushchev and his role in the de-Stalinization of the Soviet Union, as well as his own rise and fall, are addressed at http://en.wikipedia.org/wiki/Nikita_Khrushchev and http://en.wikipedia.org/wiki/History_of_the_Soviet_Union_(1953–1985). Khrushchev's famous "We will bury you" remarks at the United Nations in 1956 are analyzed at http://www.diplomacy.edu/Language/Translation/machine.htm.

Excellent overviews of the cold war in text, images, and documents are available at http://www.coldwar.org/ and http://history.sandiego.edu/gen/20th/coldwar0.html.

Soviet–American competition in Latin America during the cold war and its legacies are examined at http://web.mit.edu/cascon/cases/case_els.html, http://www.cnn.com/SPECIALS/cold.war/episodes/18/, and http://www.hartford-hwp.com/archives/47/index-ca.html. The National Security Archives site offers audio tapes of related intelligence briefings, images of Soviet missile bases in Cuba, and minute by minute chronologies of the missile crisis at http://www.gwu.edu/~nsarchiv/nsa/cuba_mis_cri/.

The 1956 uprising in Hungary is explored at http://en.wikipedia.org/wiki/Hungarian_Revolution,_1956 and http://www.rferl.org/specials/invasion1968/ and http://www.rferl.org/specials/invasion1968/. An overview of the later revolutions in Eastern Europe that heralded the end of the Soviet empire can be found at http://chnm.gmu.edu/1989/, http://www.fordham.edu/halsall/mod/modsbook50.html, http://web.archive.org/web/20021218114321/. An overview of the ill-fated Soviet invasion of Afghanistan is provided at http://www.afghanland.com/history/ussr.html. Posters made by the Afghan resistance can be viewed at http://chronicle.uchicago.edu/020124/posters.shtml.

AP* Test Prep

1. All of the following were the site of events which finally demonstrated that Europe could not retain control over its former colonies by force EXCEPT

    (A) Algeria.

    (B) Korea.

    (C) Egypt.

    (D) Vietnam.

2. What was the focal point of the Cold War in Europe immediately following World War II?

    (A) Hungary

    (B) Czechoslovakia

    (C) France

    (D) Germany

    (E) Italy

3. The growth of the Welfare State came to means all of the following EXCEPT

    (A) unemployment insurance.

    (B) state-funded medicine.

    (C) state-funded housing.

    (D) an end to the private sector.

4. Which of the following accurately reflected Western cultural shifts after the Second World War?

    (A) a shift among historians towards social history

    (B) the idealization of domestic life by feminists

    (C) the growth of a division between art and commercial mass culture

    (D) London replaced Paris as the center of international style.

5. The Women's Revolution witnessed all of the following EXCEPT

    (A) the expansion of access to education and property.

    (B) rapidly falling birthrates.

    (C) sex and procreation became separate issues.

    (D) lower divorce rates.

6. In taking primary power in 1956, Nikita Khrushchev

    (A) criticized Stalin's repressive policies.

    (B) worked to end the Cold War.

    (C) showed new tolerance for religious groups.

    (D) accepted independence movements in other East European countries.

7. Postwar Soviet society eventually fell victim to a variety of ills EXCEPT

    (A) a lack of consumer goods.

    (B) high alcoholism rates.

    (C) rising anger among workers and youths at strict government control.

    (D) AIDS.

Free-Response Question

What were the key influences on Western cultural developments in the mid-20th century?

Latin America: Revolution and Reaction into the 21st Century

Latin America After World War II

Radical Options in the 1950s

VISUALIZING THE PAST: Murals and Posters: Art and Revolution

The Search for Reform and the Military Option

DOCUMENT: The People Speak

THINKING HISTORICALLY: Human Rights in the 20th Century

Societies in Search of Change

GLOBAL CONNECTIONS: Struggling Toward the Future in a Global Economy

In the late summer of 1973, everyone in Chile knew that a coup against the government was being hatched, but no one was quite sure whether it would come from the right-wing military or from the radical left. People turned on the radio each morning to learn whether the coup had taken place during the night. The country was almost at a standstill; the currency had no international value, public transportation did not function, and soldiers armed with machine guns guarded banks and gas stations. The atmosphere was tense; a political storm was coming. Since 1964 the military forces in various Latin American countries (Brazil, 1964; Argentina, 1966; Peru, 1968) had decided to take over their governments. Latin America, like much of the world, seemed divided between the backers of radical revolutionary change and those who wished to keep the status quo or to move very slowly toward any change.

The president of Chile at the time was Salvador Allende, a socialist politician who had been elected by a plurality in 1970 and who had begun to push through a series of reforms, including land redistribution and allowing workers to take control of their factories. He was pledged to peaceful change and respect for the Chilean constitution, but his political supporters in the "Popular Unity" movement were awash with enthusiasm. For them it seemed like a new era and their motto "A People united will never be defeated" became a rallying cry for the Left all over Latin America. Such a program would have generated enthusiasms and fears at any time, but this was the era of the cold war and the nations of Latin America were pulled into the struggle between the capitalist West aligned with the United States and the communist countries aligned with the Soviet Union. The United States did its best to destabilize and undercut the Allende regime. Allende's programs and the encouragement he received from Fidel Castro provoked conservative and middle-class elements in Chile. His insistence on remaining within the limits of the constitution bothered impatient radicals who wanted a government-led socialist revolution (Figure 32.1).

On the morning of September 11, 1973, it was the military, backed by conservative and anticommunist forces, that took action and seized the presidential palace. Allende died in the palace. His wife went into exile. The military crushed any resistance and imposed a regime of authoritarian control under General Augusto Pinochet. What followed next was almost two decades of repression. About 3000 people were killed or "disappeared," more than 80,000 people were arrested for political reasons, and more than 200,000 Chileans went into exile. This was an example of the kind of "dirty war" that could be seen elsewhere in Latin America in this era; it was the internalization of the ideological and political struggles of the cold war. During this period, however, neoliberal economics also restored economic stability to the country. The country returned to democracy in 1990, but the wounds on the nation's psyche were still fresh.

In 1998 General Augusto Pinochet, the elderly former commander in chief of the Chilean army and virtual dictator of his country from 1974 to 1990, was arrested in London on charges of crimes against humanity during his years in power. Pinochet and his supporters claimed he had no personal role in the abuses and that he had saved the country from anarchy and restored economic prosperity. His opponents looked on his regime as one of brutal oppression. The arrest became an international incident, and even though Pinochet was eventually released and for "reasons of health" was not forced to stand trial, some Chileans believed that at least a message had been sent to such dictators that crimes of oppression would not be tolerated or forgotten. But many Chileans—and Latin Americans in general—remained divided over what to do about the political struggles of the past. ■

Figure 32.1 Soldiers under the command of Gen. Augusto Pinochet surround the Chilean Presidential Palace on September 11, 1973 and take cover while it is bombed in a coup against the elected President Salvador Allende. Allende apparently committed suicide rather than be taken prisoner. Once in control, Pinochet and the military remained in power rather than holding elections and returning control to the civilian legislature.

From the second half of the 20th and into the 21st century, Latin America continued to hold an intermediate position between the nations of the North Atlantic and the developing countries of Asia and Africa. Although Latin America shared many problems with these other developing areas, its earlier political independence and its often more Western social and political structures placed it in a distinct category. After 1945, and particularly from the 1970s onward, the Latin American elites led their nations into closer ties with the growing international capitalist economy over increasing objections from critics within their nations. Investments and initiative often came from Europe and the United States, and Latin American economies continued to concentrate on exports. As a result, Latin America became increasingly vulnerable to changes in the world financial system. For many Latin Americans, the economic decisions made outside the region were also reflected in a political and even cultural dependency on foreign models and influences.

Throughout the 20th century, Latin Americans grappled with the problem of finding a basis for social justice, cultural autonomy, and economic security by adopting ideologies from abroad or by developing a specifically Latin American approach. Thus, in Latin America the struggle for decolonization has been primarily one of economic disengagement and a search for political and cultural forms appropriate to Latin American realities rather than a process of political separation and independence, as in Asia and Africa.

New groups began to appear on the political stage. Although Latin America continued its 19th-century emphasis on agricultural and mineral production, an industrial sector also grew in some places. As this movement gathered strength, workers' organizations began to emerge as a political force. Industrialization was accompanied by some emigration and by explosive urban growth in many places. A growing urban middle class linked to commerce, industry, and expanding state bureaucracies also began to play a role in the political process.

 Central America Today MAP

 South America Today MAP

783

1940 C.E.	1960 C.E.	1980 C.E.	1990 C.E.	2000 C.E.
1942 Brazil joins Allies in World War II, sends troops to Europe	1961 U.S.-backed invasion of Cuba is defeated	1982 Argentina and Great Britain clash over Falkland Islands (Islas Malvinas)	1994 Brazil stabilizes economy with new currency: the *real*	2000 PRI loses presidency of Mexico; Vicente Fox elected
1944–1954 Arevalo and Arbenz reforms in Guatemala	1964 Military coup topples Brazilian government	1983 United States invades Grenada	1994 Zapatista uprising in Chiapas, Mexico	2001 Economic collapse of Argentina
1947 Juan Perón elected president of Argentina	1970–1973 Salvador Allende's socialist government in Chile; Allende overthrown and assassinated by the military in 1973	1989 Sandinistas lose election in Nicaragua	1996 Return to civilian government in Guatemala	2002 "Lula" and Workers' party win Brazilian elections
1952–1964 Bolivian revolution		1989 United States invades Panama, deposes General Noriega	1998 Colombian government initiates negotiations with FARC guerrillas but kidnappings and drug trade continue	2003 Néstor Kirchner elected president of Argentina; one wing of the Peronist party returns to power
1954 Arbenz overthrown with help from United States	1979 Sandinista revolution in Nicaragua		1998 Colonel Hugo Chávez elected president in Venezuela and new constitution approved in 1999	2005 Lula's government faces major corruption scandal
1959 Castro leads revolution in Cuba				2005 Hugo Chávez, using nationalist rhetoric, opposes U.S.-sponsored free trade policies

After World War II, the cold war helped stimulate new revolutionary agitation in Latin America, partly under Marxist inspiration and with some Soviet backing. Although Latin America had been independent of foreign rule for more than a century, the third world decolonization movement encouraged restiveness about continued economic dependency.

Figure 32.2 The populist politics of Juan Perón and his wife Evita brought new forces, especially urban workers, into Argentine politics. Their personal charisma attracted support from groups formerly excluded from politics but eventually led to opposition from the Argentine military and Perón's overthrow in 1955.

Latin America After World War II

With variations from country to country, in Latin America overall the economy and the political process were subject to a series of broad shifts. There was a pattern to these shifts, with economic expansion (accompanied by conservative regimes that, although sometimes willing to make gradual reforms, hoped to maintain a political status quo) alternating with periods of economic crisis during which attempts were made to provide social justice or to break old patterns. Thus, the political pendulum swung broadly across the region and often affected several countries at roughly the same time, indicating the relationship between international trends and the internal events in these nations.

Latin Americans have long debated the nature of their societies and the need for change. Although much of the rhetoric of Latin America stressed radical reform and revolutionary change in the 20th century, the region has remained remarkably unchanged. Revolutionaries have not been lacking since 1945, but the task of defeating the existing political and social order and creating a new one on which the majority of the population will agree is difficult, especially when this must be done within an international as well as a national context. Thus, the few revolutionary political changes that have had long-term effects stand in contrast to the general trends of the region's political history. At the same time, however, significant improvements in education, social services, the position of women, and the role of industry have taken place over the past several decades and have begun to transform many areas of Latin American life.

In 1945 several key Latin American countries were still dominated by authoritarian reformers who had responded to the impact of the Great Depression. Getulio Vargas returned to power in Brazil in 1950 with a program of populist nationalism; the state took over the petroleum industry. Juan Perón (Figure 32.2) ruled in Argentina, again with a populist platform combined with severe political repression. A military group drove Perón from power in 1955, but the popularity of Peronism, particularly among workers, continued for two decades. This encouraged severe political measures by the military dictators, including torture and execution of opponents in what was called the "dirty war." The military government involved Argentina in a war with Britain in 1982, over the Islas Malvinas, or Falkland Islands, which Britain controlled and Argentina claimed. The rulers hoped to gain nationalist support, but they lost the war and the regime was discredited.

Figure 32.3 On July 3, 2000, joyful supporters of the new Mexican president, Vicente Fox, celebrated their victory in electing an opposition candidate for the first time in more than a century.

Mexico and the PRI

From the 1940s until a historic change in the 2000 election, Mexico was controlled by the Party of the Institutionalized Revolution, or **PRI** (Figure 32.3). By the last decades of the 20th century, the stability provided by the PRI's control of politics was undercut by corruption and a lack of social improvement. Many Mexicans believed that little remained of the revolutionary principles of the 1910 revolution. Charges of corruption and repression mounted for several decades. In 1994 an armed guerrilla movement burst forth in the heavily Indian southern state of Chiapas (Figure 32.4). Calling themselves **Zapatistas** in honor of Emiliano Zapata, the peasant leader in the 1910 revolution, the movement showed how key social issues remained unresolved. The Mexican government responded with a combination of repression and negotiation (Figure 32.4).

Also in the 1990s the government joined in negotiations for the North American Free Trade Agreement (NAFTA), hoping to spur Mexican industry. Results have remained unclear, though trade with the United States has increased, and Mexico has become the second largest U.S. trade partner. Mexico is preoccupied with fears of the loss of economic control and a growing gap between a sizeable middle class and the very poor, including most of Mexico's Indians. NAFTA has also drawn Mexico into closer political and economic ties with the United States, but by 2008 the increasing flow of illegal immigration to the United States, in response to economic conditions in Mexico and opportunities in the United States, had become a contentious issue between the two countries.

In 2000 a national election ended the PRI political monopoly. Vicente Fox, leader of the conservative National Action party (PAN), became president on a platform of cleaning up corruption and improving conditions for Mexican workers in the United States. That party won again in a

PRI Party of the Institutionalized Revolution; dominant political party in Mexico; developed during the 1920s and 1930s; incorporated labor, peasant, military, and middle-class sectors; controlled other political organizations in Mexico.

Zapatistas Guerrilla movement named in honor of Emiliano Zapata; originated in 1994 in Mexico's southern state of Chiapas; government responded with a combination of repression and negotiation.

Figure 32.4 On January 1, 1994, the North American Free Trade Agreement (NAFTA) went into effect. On that day, Zapatista rebels in Chiapas, Mexico, seized control of several towns, announcing their opposition to NAFTA, seizing weapons, and freeing prisoners from jail. Although its natural resources are great, the people of Chiapas are among the poorest in Mexico. Their declaration read, in part: "We have nothing to lose, absolutely nothing, no decent roof over our heads, no land, no work, poor health, no food, no education, no right to freely and democratically choose our leaders, no independence from foreign interests, and no justice for ourselves or our children. . . . We are the descendants of those who truly built this nation, we are the millions of dispossessed, and we call upon all of our brethren to join our crusade, the only option to avoid dying of starvation!"

hotly contested election in 2006, but the peaceful settlement of the electoral dispute, despite irregularities, was a testimony to the nation's desire for democratic government.

Radical Options in the 1950s

After World War II, a surge of radical unrest in several smaller countries quickly brought cold war tensions into play. In Bolivia, Guatemala, and Cuba, revolutionaries tried to change the nature of government and society, but they had to accommodate the realities of the cold war and the interests of the United States.

The Argentine and Brazilian changes begun by Perón and Vargas were symptomatic of the continuing problems of Latin America, but their populist authoritarian solutions were only one possible response. By the 1940s, pressure for change had built up through much of Latin America. Across the political spectrum there was a desire to improve the social and economic conditions throughout the region and a general agreement that development and economic strength were the keys to a better future. How to achieve those goals remained in question. In Mexico, as we have seen, one-party rule continued, and the "revolution" became increasingly conservative and interested in economic growth rather than social justice. In a few countries, such as Venezuela and Costa Rica, reform-minded democratic parties were able to win elections in an open political system. In other places, such a solution was less likely or less attractive to those who wanted reform. Unlike the Mexican revolutionaries of 1910–1920, those seeking change in the post–World War II period could turn to

Murals and Posters: Art and Revolution

Public art for political purposes has been used since ancient Egypt, but with the development of lithography (a color printing process), the poster emerged as a major form of communication. First developed in the late 19th century as a cheap form of advertising using image and text to sell soap, wine, or chocolate or to advertise dance halls and theaters, by the 1880s posters were adapted to political purposes, and in World War I all the major combatants used them. But those opposed to governments could also use posters to convey a revolutionary message to a broad public. In Latin America, the Mexican Revolution made use of public art in great murals, but these were often expensive and took a long time to complete. The Cuban revolutionaries of the 1960s and the Nicaraguan revolutionaries of the 1980s turned to the poster as a way to convey their policies and goals to a broad public.

QUESTIONS What are the advantages of the poster over the mural, and vice versa? Is poster art really art? Why are images of the past often the subjects of revolutionary art? To whom is political art usually directed?

(David Alfaro Siqueiros. Detail from the mural, "For the Complete Safety of All Mexicans at Work." 1952–54. Art Resource, NY. © 2009 Artists Rights Society (ARS), New York/SOMAAP, Mexico City. Reproduction authorized by the Instituto Nacional de Bellas Artes and Literature.)

the well developed political philosophy of Marxian socialism as a guide. However, such models were fraught with dangers because of the context of the cold war and the ideological struggle between western Europe and the Soviet bloc.

Throughout Latin America, the failures of political democratization, economic development, and social reforms led to consideration of radical and revolutionary solutions to national problems. In some cases, the revolutions at first were successful but ultimately were unable to sustain the changes. In predominantly Indian Bolivia, where as late as 1950 90 percent of the land was owned by 6 percent of the population, a revolution erupted in 1952 in which miners, peasants, and urban middle-class groups participated. Although mines were nationalized and some land redistributed, fear of moving too far to the left brought the army back into power in 1964, and subsequent governments remained more interested in order than in reform.

Guatemala: Reform and U.S. Intervention

The first place where more radical solutions were tried was Guatemala. This predominantly Indian nation had some of the worst of the region's problems. Its population was mostly illiterate and suffered poor health conditions and high mortality rates. Land and wealth were distributed very unequally, and the whole economy depended on the highly volatile prices for its main exports of coffee and bananas. In 1944 a middle-class and labor coalition elected reformer **Juan José Arevalo** (WAHN hoh-ZAY ahr-uh-VAHL-oh) as president. Under a new constitution, he began a series of programs within the context of "spiritual socialism" that included land reform and an improvement in the rights and conditions of rural and industrial workers. These programs and Arevalo's sponsorship of an intense nationalism brought the government into direct conflict with foreign interests

Arevalo, Juan José [WAHN hoh-ZAY ahr-uh-VAHL-oh] Elected president of Guatemala in 1944; began series of socialist reforms including land reform; nationalist program directed against foreign-owned companies such as United Fruit Company.

787

United Fruit Company Most important foreign economic concern in Guatemala during the 20th century; attempted land reform aimed at United Fruit caused U.S. intervention in Guatemalan politics leading to ouster of reform government in 1954.

operating in Guatemala, especially the **United Fruit Company,** the largest and most important foreign concern there.

In 1951, after a free election, the presidency passed to Colonel Jacobo Arbenz, whose nationalist program was more radical. Arbenz announced several programs to improve or nationalize the transportation network, the hydroelectric system, and other areas of the economy. A move to expropriate unused lands on large estates in 1953 provoked opposition from the large landowners and from United Fruit, which eventually was threatened with the loss of almost half a million acres of reserve land. The U.S. government, fearing "communist" penetration of the Arbenz government and under considerable pressure from the United Fruit Company, denounced the changes and began to impose economic and diplomatic restrictions on Guatemala. At the same time, the level of nationalist rhetoric intensified, and the government increasingly received the support of the political left in Latin America and in the socialist bloc.

In 1954, with the help of the U.S. Central Intelligence Agency, a dissident military force was organized and invaded Guatemala. The Arbenz government fell, and the pro-American regime that replaced it turned back the land reform and negotiated a settlement favorable to United Fruit. The reform experiment was thus brought to a halt. By the standards of the 1960s and later, the programs of Arevalo and Arbenz seem rather mild, although Arbenz's statements and supposedly his acceptance of arms from eastern Europe undoubtedly contributed to U.S. intervention.

The reforms promised by the U.S.-supported governments were minimal. Guatemala continued to have a low standard of living, especially for its Indian population. After the coup the series of military governments failed to address the nation's social and economic problems. That failure led to continual violence and political instability. Political life continued to be controlled by a coalition of coffee planters, foreign companies, and the military. A guerrilla movement grew and provoked brutal military repression, which fell particularly hard on the rural Indian population. Guatemala's attempt at radical change, an attempt that began with an eye toward improving the conditions of the people, failed because of external intervention. The failure was a warning that change would not come without internal and foreign opposition.

The Cuban Revolution: Socialism in the Caribbean

The differences between Cuba and Guatemala underline the diversity of Latin America and the dangers of partial revolutions. The island nation had a population of about 6 million, most of whom were the descendants of Spaniards and the African slaves who had been imported to produce the sugar, tobacco, and hides that were the colony's mainstays. Cuba had a large middle class, and its literacy and health care levels were better than in most of the rest of the region. Rural areas lagged behind in these matters, however, and there the working and living conditions were poor, especially for the workers on the large sugar estates. Always in the shadow of the United States, Cuban politics and economy were rarely free of American interests. By the 1950s, about three-fourths of what Cuba imported came from the United States. American investments in the island were heavy during the 1940s and 1950s. Although the island experienced periods of prosperity, fluctuations in the world market for Cuba's main product, sugar, revealed the tenuous basis of the economy. Moreover, the disparity between the countryside and the growing middle class in Havana underlined the nation's continuing problems.

Batista, Fulgencio Dictator of Cuba from 1934 to 1944; returned to presidency in 1952; ousted from government by revolution led by Fidel Castro.

From 1934 to 1944, **Fulgencio Batista,** a strong-willed, authoritarian reformer who had risen through the lower ranks of the army, ruled Cuba. Among his reforms were a democratic constitution of 1940 that promised major changes, nationalization of natural resources, full employment, and land reform. However, Batista's programs of reform were marred by corruption, and when in 1952 he returned to the presidency, there was little left of the reformer but a great deal of the dictator. Opposition developed in various sectors of the society. Among the regime's opponents was **Fidel Castro,** a young lawyer experienced in leftist university politics who was an ardent critic of the Batista government and of the ills of Cuban society. On July 26, 1953, Castro and a few followers launched an unsuccessful attack on some military barracks. Captured, Castro faced a trial, an occasion he used to expound his revolutionary ideals, aimed mostly at a return to democracy, social justice, and the establishment of a less dependent economy.

Castro, Fidel Cuban revolutionary; overthrew dictator Fulgencio Batista in 1958; initiated series of socialist reforms; came to depend almost exclusively on Soviet Union.

Released from prison, Castro fled to exile in Mexico where, with the aid of **Ernesto "Che" Guevara** (gay-VAHR-uh), a militant Argentine revolutionary, he gathered a small military force. They landed in Cuba in 1956 and slowly began to gather strength in the mountains. By 1958 the "26th of July Movement" had found support from students, some labor organizations, and rural workers and was able to conduct operations against Batista's army. The bearded rebels, or *barbudos,* won a series of victories. The dictator, under siege and isolated by the United States (which because of his abuses of power and use of violence refused to support him any longer), fled into exile, and the rebels took Havana amid wild scenes of joy and relief (Figure 32.5).

What happened next is highly debatable, and Castro himself has offered alternative interpretations at different times. Whether Castro was already a Marxist-Leninist and had always intended to introduce a socialist regime (as he now claims) or whether the development of this program was the result of a series of pragmatic decisions is in question. Rather than simply returning to the constitution of 1940 and enacting moderate reforms, Castro launched a program of sweeping change. Foreign properties were expropriated, farms were collectivized, and a centralized socialist economy was put in place. Most of these changes were accompanied by a nationalist and anti-imperialist foreign policy. Any resistance to these changes was suppressed, and the press was stifled. Relations with the United States were broken off in 1961, and Cuba increasingly depended on the financial support and arms of the Soviet Union to maintain its revolution. With that support in place, Castro was able to survive the increasingly hostile reaction of the United States. That reaction included a disastrous U.S.-sponsored invasion by Cuban exiles in 1961 and a U.S. embargo on trade with Cuba. Increasing Cuban economic and political dependence on the Soviet Union led to a crisis in 1962, when Soviet nuclear missiles were discovered and a confrontation between the superpowers ensued. Despite these problems, to a large extent the Cuban revolution survived because of the global context. The politics of the cold war provided Cuba with a protector and a benefactor, the Soviet Union.

The results of the revolution have been mixed. The social programs were extensive. Education, health, and housing have improved greatly and rank Cuba among the world's leaders—quite unlike most other nations of the region. This is especially true in the long-neglected rural areas. A wide variety of social and educational programs have mobilized all sectors of the population. The achievements have been accompanied by severe restrictions of basic freedoms.

Attempts to diversify and strengthen the economy have been less successful. An effort to industrialize in the 1960s failed, and Cuba turned again to its ability to produce sugar. The world's falling sugar and rising petroleum prices led to disaster. Only by subsidizing Cuban sugar and supplying petroleum below the world price could the Soviet Union maintain the Cuban economy. After the breakup of the Soviet Union in the 1990s, the Cuban situation deteriorated as Castro adhered to an inflexible socialist economic policy. Increasingly isolated—along with China and North Korea, Cuba was one of the last three communist governments in the world—Cuba no longer received much-needed Soviet aid and faced an uncertain future.

Despite these problems, the Cuban revolution offered an example that proved attractive to those seeking to transform Latin American societies. Early direct attempts to spread the model of the Cuban revolution, such as Che Guevara's guerrilla operation in Bolivia, where he lost his life in 1967, were failures. But the Cuban model and the island's ability to resist the pressure of a hostile United States proved an attractive model for other nations in the Caribbean and Central America, such as Grenada and Nicaragua, that also exercised the revolutionary option. U.S. reaction to such movements has been containment or intervention.

Figure 32.5 Fidel Castro and his "barbudos" (bearded) guerillas brought down the Batista government in January 1959 to the wild acclaim of many Cubans. Castro initiated sweeping reforms in Cuba that eventually led to the creation of a socialist regime and a sharp break with the United States.

 Soviet Deputy Premier in Cuba

 Fidel Castro Defends the Revolution

Guevara, Ernesto "Che" [gay-VAHR-uh] Argentine revolutionary; aided Fidel Castro in overthrow of Fulgencio Batista regime in Cuba; died while directing guerrilla movement in Bolivia in 1967.

 The Cold War and Cuba

The People Speak

Scholarly analysis of general trends often fails to convey the way in which historical events and patterns affect the lives of people or the fact that history is made up of the collective experience of individuals. It is often very difficult to know about the lives of common people in the past or to learn about their perceptions of their lives. In recent years in Latin America, however, a growing literature of autobiographies, interpreted autobiographies (in which another writer puts the story down and edits it), and collections of interviews have provided a vision of the lives of common people. These statements, like any historical document, must be used carefully because their authors or editors sometimes have political purposes, because they reflect individual opinions, or because the events they report may be atypical. Nevertheless, these personal statements put flesh and blood on the bones of history and provide an important perspective from those whose voice in history often is lost.

A Bolivian Woman Describes Her Life

Domitilia Barrios de Chungara was a miner's wife who became active in the mine workers' political movement. Her presence at the United Nations–sponsored International Woman's Year Tribunal in 1975 moved a Brazilian journalist to organize her statements into a book about her life. This excerpt provides a picture of her everyday struggle for life.

My day begins at four in the morning, especially when my compañero is on the first shift. I prepare his breakfast. Then I have to prepare salteñas [small meat pastries] because I make about one hundred salteñas every day and I sell them on the street. I do this in order to make up for what my husband's wage doesn't cover in terms of our necessities. The night before, we prepare the dough and at four in the morning I make the salteñas while I feed the kids. The kids help me.

Then the ones that go to school in the morning have to get ready, while I wash the clothes left soaking over night.

At eight I go out to sell. The kids that go to school in the afternoon help me. We have to go to the company store and bring home the staples. And in the store there are immensely long lines and you have to wait there until eleven in order to stock up. You have to line up for meat, for vegetables, for oil. So it's just one line after another. Since everything is in a different place, that's how it has to be.

From what we earn between my husband and me, we can eat and dress. Food is very expensive: 28 pesos for a kilo of meat, 4 pesos for carrots, 6 pesos for onions. . . . Considering that my compañero earns 28 pesos a day, that's hardly enough is it?

We don't ever buy ready made clothes. We buy wool and knit. At the beginning of each year, I also spend about 2000 pesos on cloth and a pair of shoes for each of us. And the company discounts some of that each month from my husband's wage. On the pay slips that's referred to as the "bundle." And what happens is that before we finish paying the "bundle" our shoes are worn out. That's how it is.

Well, from eight to eleven in the morning I sell the salteñas. I do the shopping in the grocery store, and I also work at the Housewives Committee talking with the sisters who go there for advice.

At noon, lunch has to be ready because the rest of the kids have to go to school.

In the afternoon I have to wash clothes. There are no laundries. We use troughs and have to get the water from a pump.

The Search for Reform and the Military Option

Latin Americans continued to seek solutions to their problems using Catholic, Marxist, and capitalist doctrines. In the 1960s and 1970s nationalistic, pro-capitalist military governments created new "bureaucratic authoritarian" regimes. By the 1980s, a new wave of democratic regimes was emerging.

liberation theology Combined Catholic theology and socialist principles in effort to bring about improved conditions for the poor in Latin America in 20th century.

The revolutionary attempts of the 1950s, the durability of the Cuban revolution, and the general appeal of Marxist doctrines in developing nations underlined Latin America's tendency to undertake revolutionary change that left its economic and social structures unchanged. How could the traditional patterns of inequality and international disadvantage created by Latin America's dependence on the world consumption of its raw materials be overcome? What was the best path to the future?

For some, the answer was political stability, imposed if necessary, to promote capitalist economic growth. The one-party system of Mexico demonstrated its capacity for repression when student dissidents were brutally killed during disturbances in 1968. Mexico enjoyed some prosperity from its petroleum resources in the 1970s, but poor financial planning, corruption, and foreign debt again caused problems by the 1980s, and the PRI seemed to be losing its ability to maintain control of Mexican politics.

For others, the church, long a power in Latin America, provided a guide. Christian Democratic parties formed in Chile and Venezuela in the 1950s, hoping to bring reforms through popularly based mass parties that would preempt the radical left. The church often was divided politically, but the clergy took an increasingly engaged position and argued for social justice and human rights, often in support of government opponents. A few, such as Father Camilo Torres in Colombia, actually joined armed revolutionary groups in the 1960s.

More common was the emergence within the church hierarchy of an increased concern for social justice (Figure 32.6). By the 1970s, a **liberation theology** combined Catholic theology and so-

I've got to correct the kids' homework and prepare everything I'll need to make the next day's salteñas.

From Peasant to Revolutionary

Rigoberta Menchú, a Quiché Indian from the Guatemalan highlands, came from a peasant family that had been drawn into politics during the repression of Indian communities and human rights in the 1970s. In these excerpts, she reveals her disillusionment with the government and her realization of the ethnic division between Indians and ladinos, or mestizos, that complicates political action in Guatemala.

The CUC [Peasant Union] started growing; it spread like wildfire among the peasants in Guatemala. We began to understand that the root of all our problems was exploitation. That there were rich and poor and that the rich exploited the poor—our sweat, our labor. That's how the rich got richer and richer. The fact that we were always waiting in offices, always bowing to the authorities was part of the discrimination that we Indians suffered.

The situation got worse when the murderous generals came to power although I did not actually know who was the president at the time. I began to know them from 1974 when General Kjell Langerud came to power. He came to our region and said: "We're going to solve the land problem. The land belongs to you. You cultivate the land and I will share it out among you." We trusted him. I was at the meeting when [he] spoke. And what did he give us? My father tortured and imprisoned.

Later I had the opportunity of meeting other Indians. Achi Indians, the group that lives closest to us. And I got to know some Mam Indians too. They all told me: "The rich are bad. But not all ladinos are

bad." And I started wondering: Could it be that not all ladinos are Achi Indians, the group that lives closest to us? And I know some Mam Indians too. They all told me: "The rich are bad." . . . There were poor ladinos as well as rich ladinos, and they were exploited as well. That's when I began recognizing exploitation. I kept on going to the finca [large farm] but now I really wanted to find out, to prove if that was true and learn the details. There were poor ladinos on the finca. They worked the same, and their children's bellies were swollen like my little brother's. . . . I was just beginning to speak a little Spanish in those days and I began to talk to them. I said to one poor ladino: "You are a poor ladino, aren't you?" And he nearly hit me. He said: "What do you know about it, Indian!" I wondered: "Why is that when I say poor ladinos are like us, I'm spurned?" I didn't know then that the same system which tries to isolate us Indians also puts barriers between Indians and ladinos. . . . Soon afterwards, I was with the nuns and we went to a village in Uspantán where mostly ladinos live. The nun asked a little boy if they were poor and he said: "Yes, we're poor but we're not Indians." That stayed with me. The nun didn't notice, she went on talking. She was foreign, she wasn't Guatemalan. She asked someone else the same question and he said: "Yes, we're poor but we're not Indians." It was very painful for me to accept that an Indian was inferior to a ladino. I kept on worrying about it. It's a big barrier they've sown between us, between Indian and ladino. I didn't understand it.

QUESTIONS What was distinctive about lower-class life and outlook in late 20th-century Latin America? How had lower-class life changed since the 19th century?

---

cialist principles or used Marxist categories for understanding society in an effort to improve conditions for the poor. Liberation theologians stressed social equality as a form of personal salvation. When criticized for promoting communism in his native Brazil, Dom Helder da Camara, archbishop of Pernambuco, remarked, "The trouble with Brazil is not an excess of communist doctrine but a lack of Christian justice." The position of the Catholic Church in Latin American societies was changing, but there was no single program for this new stance or even agreement among the clergy about its validity. Still, this activist position provoked attacks against clergy such as the courageous Archbishop Oscar Romero of El Salvador, who was assassinated in 1980 for speaking out for social reform, and even against nuns involved in social programs. The church, however, played an important role in the fall of the Paraguayan dictatorship in 1988.

CASE STUDY

Liberation Theology Challenged

Out of the Barracks: Soldiers Take Power

The success of the Cuban revolution impressed and worried those who feared revolutionary change within a communist political system. The military forces in Latin America had been involved in politics since the days of the caudillos in the 19th century, and in several nations military interventions had been common. As the Latin American military became more professionalized, however, a new philosophy underlay the military's involvement in politics. The soldiers began to see themselves as above the selfish interests of political parties and as the true representatives of the nation. With technical training and organizational skills, military officers by the 1920s and 1930s believed that they were best equipped to solve their nations' problems, even if that meant sacrificing the democratic process and imposing martial law.

Figure 32.6 In September 1999, thousands of Brazilians attended a mass to celebrate the "Cry of the Excluded," a protest against the social and economic degradation of the nation's poor, who make up more than a third of the population.

Allende, Salvador President of Chile; nationalized industries and banks; sponsored peasant and worker expropriations of lands and foreign-owned factories; overthrown in 1973 by revolt of Chilean military with the support of the United States.

In the 1960s, the Latin American military establishments, made nervous by the Cuban success and the swing to leftist or populist regimes, began to intervene directly in the political process, not simply to clean out a disliked president or party, as they had done in the past, but to take over government itself. In 1964 the Brazilian military (with the support of the United States and the Brazilian middle class) overthrew the elected president after he threatened to make sweeping social reforms. In Argentina, growing polarization between the Peronists and the middle class led to a military intervention in 1966. In 1973 the Chilean military, which until then had remained for the most part out of politics, overthrew the socialist government of President **Salvador Allende,** as described in the chapter opening.

The soldiers in power imposed a new type of bureaucratic authoritarian regime. Their governments were supposed to stand above the competing demands of various sectors and establish economic stability. Now, as arbiters of politics, the soldiers believed that they would place the national interest above selfish interests by imposing dictatorships. Government was essentially a presidency, controlled by the military, in which policies were formulated and applied by a bureaucracy organized like a military chain of command. Political repression and torture were used to silence critics, and stringent measures were imposed to control inflation and strengthen the countries' economies. In Argentina, violent opposition to military rule led to a counteroffensive and the "dirty war" in which thousands of people "disappeared."

Government economic policies fell heaviest on the working class. The goal of the military in Brazil and Argentina was development. To some extent, in Brazil at least, economic improvements were achieved, although income distribution became even more unequal than it had been. Inflation was reduced, industrialization increased, and gains were made in literacy and health, but basic structural problems such as land ownership and social conditions for the poorest people remained unchanged.

There were variations within these military regimes, but all were nationalistic. The Peruvian military tried to create a popular base for its programs and to mobilize support among the peasantry. It had a real social program, including extensive land reform, and was not simply a surrogate for the conservatives in Peruvian society. In Chile and Uruguay, the military was fiercely anticommunist. In Argentina, nationalism and a desire to gain popular support in the face of a worsening economy led to a confrontation with Great Britain over the Falkland Islands (Islas Malvinas), which both nations claimed. The war stimulated pride in Argentina and its soldiers and sailors, but defeat caused a loss of the military's credibility.

The New Democratic Trends

In Argentina and elsewhere in South America, by the mid-1980s the military had begun to return government to civilian politicians. Continuing economic problems and the pressures of containing opponents wore heavily on the military leaders, who began to realize that their solutions were no more destined to success than those of civilian governments. Moreover, the populist parties, such as the Peronists and Apristas, seemed less of a threat, and the fear of Cuban-style communism had diminished. Also, the end of the cold war meant that the United States was less interested in sponsoring regimes that, though "safe," were also repressive. In Argentina, elections were held in 1983. Brazil began to restore democratic government after 1985 and in 1989 chose its first popularly elected president since the military takeover. The South American military bureaucrats and modernizers were returning to their barracks.

 Brazil's Constitution of 1988

The process of redemocratization was not easy, nor was it universal. In Peru, *Sendero Luminoso* (Shining Path), a long-sustained leftist guerrilla movement, controlled areas of the countryside and tried to disrupt national elections in 1990. In Central America, the military cast a long shadow over the government in El Salvador, but return to civilian government took place in 1992. In Nicaragua, the elections of 1990, held under threat of a U.S. embargo, removed the **Sandinista party** from control in Nicaragua. In subsequent elections the party of the Sandinistas could still muster much support, but it did not win back the presidency until 2006. The trend toward a return to electoral democracy could be seen in Guatemala as well. By 1996 civilian government had returned to Guatemala as the country struggled to overcome the history of repression and rebellion and the animosities they had created. The United States demonstrated its continuing power in the region in its invasion of Panama and the arrest of its strongman leader, Manuel Noriega.

Sandinista party   Nicaraguan socialist movement named after Augusto Sandino; successfully carried out a socialist revolution in Nicaragua during the 1980s.

Latin American governments in the last decades of the 20th century faced tremendous problems. Large foreign loans taken in the 1970s for the purpose of development had created a tremendous level of debt that threatened the economic stability of countries such as Brazil, Peru, and Mexico. In 2002 the Argentine government defaulted on its debt and faced economic crisis. High rates of inflation provoked social instability as real wages fell. Pressure from the international banking community to curb inflation by cutting government spending and reducing wages often ignored the social and political consequences of such actions. An international commerce in drugs, which produced tremendous profits, stimulated criminal activity and created powerful international cartels that could even threaten national sovereignty. In Colombia a leftist guerrilla movement controlled large areas of the country and funded itself from the drug trade. It destabilized the country and the government's legitimacy. In countries as diverse as Cuba, Panama, and Bolivia, the narcotics trade penetrated the highest government circles.

But despite the problems, the 1990s seemed to demonstrate that the democratic trends were well established. In Central America there was a return to civilian government. In Venezuela and Brazil, corruption in government led to the fall of presidents and as we have mentioned led to a major political change in Mexico in 2000. But dissatisfaction with NAFTA and continuing economic problems continued. In Brazil a leftist working-class presidential candidate, Lula (Luiz Inacio Lula da Silva), was elected in 2002, but by 2005 there had still been little change in social inequalities and major figures in his government faced charges of corruption. More radical options were also still possible. In Colombia the insurgency supported by ties to the drug trade continued to threaten the nation's stability. In neighboring Venezuela a populist military leader, Hugo Chávez, had come to power in a 1998 election. He survived a coup in 2002 and threatened to move the country toward a more independent foreign policy by rejecting Washington's economic plans and by joining forces with other opponents of U.S. policies. By 2009 he had removed restrictions on his

Human Rights in the 20th Century

In Latin America, the question of human rights became a burning issue in the 1960s and continued thereafter. The use of torture by repressive governments, the mobilization of death squads and other vigilante groups with government acquiescence, and the use of terrorism against political opponents by the state and by groups opposed to the state became all too common in the region. Latin America's record on the violation of human rights was no worse than that of some other areas of the world. However, the demonstrations by the Argentine "Mothers of the Plaza del Mayo" to focus attention on their disappeared children; the publication of prison memoirs recounting human rights violations in Brazil, Cuba, and Argentina; and films dramatizing events such as the assassination of Archbishop Oscar Romero in El Salvador have all focused attention on the problem in Latin America. Moreover, because Latin America shares in the cultural heritage of Western societies, it is difficult to make an argument that human rights there have a different meaning or importance than in Europe or North America.

"Whereas developing nations view the right to development as a human right, it is viewed as a political and economic demand in wealthier nations of the West."

The concept of human rights—that is, certain universal rights enjoyed by all people because they are justified by a moral standard that stands above the laws of any individual nation—may go back to ancient Greece. The concept of natural law and the protection of religious or ethnic minorities also moved nations in the 19th century toward a defense of human rights. To some extent, the international movement to abolish the slave trade was an early human rights movement. In modern times, however, the concept of human rights has been strongly attached to the foundation of the United Nations. In 1948 that body, with the experience of World War II in mind, issued a Universal Declaration of Human Rights and created a commission to oversee the human rights situation. The Universal Declaration, which guaranteed basic liberties and freedoms regardless of color, sex, or religion, proclaimed that it should be the "common standard for all peoples and nations." However, one critic has stated that of the 160 nations in the United Nations, only about 30 have a consistently good record on human rights.

A major problem for the international community has been enforcing the Universal Declaration. The United Nations commission did not have any specific powers of enforcement, and much debate has taken place on the power of the United Nations to intervene in the internal affairs of any nation. More recently, various regional organizations have tried to establish the norms that should govern human rights and to create institutions to enforce these norms.

One specialist has claimed that "human rights is the world's first universal ideology." The defense of human rights seems to be a cause that most people and governments can accept without hesitation, but the question is complex. Although the rights to life, liberty, security, and freedom from torture or degrading punishment are generally accepted in principle by all nations, other rights remain open to question. What is a right, and to what extent are definitions of rights determined by culture?

The question of universality versus relativism emerged quickly in the debate over human rights. What seemed to be obvious human rights in Western societies were less obvious in other parts of the world, where other priorities were held. For example, laws prohibiting child labor were enforced by most Western societies, but throughout the world perhaps 150 million children worked, often in unhealthy and exploitive conditions. They worked because of economic necessity in many cases, but in some societies such labor was considered moral and proper. Such cultural differences have led to a position of relativism, which recognizes that there are profound cultural variations in what is considered moral and just. Critics of the original Universal Declaration contend that its advocacy of the right to own property and the right to vote imposed Western political and economic values as universals. Cultural relativism had the advantage of recognizing the variety of cultures and standards in the world, but

---

continuation in office and mobilized support among other nations in Latin America. In other countries the military was sometimes troublesome, but a commitment to a more open political system in most of the region seemed firm.

The United States and Latin America: Continuing Presence

As a backdrop to the political and economic story we have traced thus far stands the continuing presence of the United States. After World War I, the United States emerged as the predominant power in the hemisphere, a position it had already begun to assume at the end of the 19th century with the Cuban–Spanish–American war and the building of the Panama Canal. European nations were displaced as the leading investors in Latin America by the United States. In South America, private investments by American companies and entrepreneurs, as well as loans from the American government, were the chief means of U.S. influence. U.S. investments rose to more than $5 billion by 1929, or more than one-third of all U.S. investments abroad.

it has also been used as a shield to deflect criticism and to excuse the continued violation of human rights.

The definition of human rights is also political. The West emphasizes the civil and political rights of the individual. The socialist nations placed social and economic justice above individual rights, although by the 1990s movements in eastern Europe and China indicated that there was pressure to modify this approach. In the developing nations, an argument for peoples' rights has emerged in which the "right to development," which calls for a major structural redistribution of the world's resources and economic opportunities, is a central concept. As Léopold Senghor of Senegal put it, "Human rights begin with breakfast"; or as a report on Ghana stated, " 'One man, one vote' is meaningless unless accompanied by the principle of 'one man, one bread.' " Whereas developing nations view the right to development as a human right, it is viewed as a political and economic demand in wealthier nations of the West.

Another dimension of human rights is the extent to which it influences national foreign policies. Governments may make statements pledging respect for human rights in their foreign policies, but considerations of national defense, security, sovereignty, war against terrorism, or other goals often move human rights concerns into a secondary position. Disputes over the role of human rights in foreign policy sometimes are posed as a conflict between "moralistic utopians" who see the world as it should be and "pragmatists" who see the world as it is. Neither approach necessarily denies the importance of human rights, but there are differences in priority and strategy. Pragmatists might argue that it is better to maintain relations with a nation violating human rights in order to be able to exercise some influence over it in the future, or that other policy considerations must be weighed along with those of human rights in establishing foreign policy. Moralists would prefer to bring pressure by isolating and condemning a nation that violates international standards.

These different approaches have been reflected in the U.S. policy shifts toward Latin America. In the 1950s, human rights considerations were secondary to opposing the spread of communism in the hemisphere, and the United States was willing to support governments that violated human rights as long as they were anticommunist allies. During the 1960s, this policy continued, but increasing and systematic abuses by military regimes in Brazil, Uruguay, Chile, Nicaragua, and elsewhere in Latin America began to elicit some changes. In 1977 President Carter initiated a new policy in which human rights considerations would be given high priority in U.S. foreign policy. The U.S. refusal to support or aid governments that violated human rights contributed to the weakening of some regimes and stimulated resistance to human rights violations in Latin America, but by the 1980s a more pragmatic approach had returned to U.S. policy. Criticism of human rights violations sometimes was made selectively, and abuses in "friendly" governments were dismissed. The extent to which human rights concerns must be balanced against issues such as security, the maintenance of peace, and nonintervention continues to preoccupy policymakers. The issue became particularly thorny in the United States in the aftermath of the terrorist attack of September 11, 2001. In 2004 the United States suspended normal legal protections and restraints against torture in the treatment of military prisoners from the wars in Iraq and Afghanistan and in dealing with potential terrorists at home. President Obama's administration was confronted with the legality of those measures and whether to prosecute those responsible.

Problems of definition still remain, and there is no universal agreement on the exact nature of human rights. Controversy on the weight of political and civil rights and social, cultural, and economic rights continues to divide richer and poorer nations. Still, the United Nations Declaration of Human Rights, to which 160 nations are signatories, provides a basic guide and an outline for the future.

QUESTIONS Why might various regimes oppose human rights, and on what basis? Is the human rights movement a Western replacement for imperialism as a way to exert international political influence? Have international human rights movements produced political change?

Cuba and Puerto Rico experienced direct U.S. involvement and almost a protectorate status. But in the Caribbean and Central America, the face of U.S. power, economic interest, and disregard for the sovereignty of weaker neighbors was most apparent. Military interventions to protect U.S.-owned properties and investments became so common that there were more than 30 before 1933 (Map 32.1). Haiti, Nicaragua, the Dominican Republic, Mexico, and Cuba all experienced direct interventions by U.S. troops. Central America was a peculiar case because the level of private investments by U.S. companies such as United Fruit was very high and the economies of these countries were so closely tied to the United States. Those who resisted the U.S. presence were treated as bandits by expeditionary forces. In Nicaragua, **Augusto Sandino** led a resistance movement against occupying troops until his assassination by the U.S.-trained Nicaraguan National Guard in 1934. His struggle against U.S. intervention made him a hero and later the figurehead of the Sandinista party, which carried out a socialist revolution in Nicaragua in the 1980s.

The grounds for these interventions were economic, political, strategic, and ideological. The direct interventions usually were followed by the creation or support of conservative governments,

Sandino, Augusto Led a guerrilla resistance movement against U.S. occupation forces in Nicaragua; assassinated by Nicaraguan National Guard in 1934; became national hero and symbol of resistance to U.S. influence in Central America.

Map 32.1 U.S. Military Interventions, 1898–2000 Moved by strategic, economic, and political considerations, the United States repeatedly intervened militarily in the Caribbean and also used its political influence to support regimes that assured "stability" and protected U.S. interests. After 1945 and especially after Castro's alliance with the Soviet Union, "Cold War" considerations also affected U.S. policy.

banana republics Term given to governments supported or created by the United States in Central America; believed to be either corrupt or subservient to U.S. interests.

often dictatorships that would be friendly to the United States. These became known as **banana republics,** a reference not only to their dependence on the export of tropical products but also to their often subservient and corrupt governments.

Foreign interventions contributed to a growing nationalist reaction. Central America with its continuing political problems became a symbol of Latin America's weakness in the face of foreign influence and interference, especially by the United States. The Nobel Prize–winning Chilean communist poet Pablo Neruda, in his poem "The United Fruit Co.," (1950) spoke of the dictators of Central America as "circus flies, wise flies, learned in tyranny" who buzzed over the graves of the people. He wrote the following eight lines with passion:

When the trumpet sounded, all was prepared in the land,
and Jehovah divided the world between Coca Cola Inc.,
Anaconda, Ford Motors, and other companies:

United Fruit Co. reserved for itself the juiciest part,
the central coast of my land,
the sweet waist of America
and baptized again its lands
as Banana Republics.

The actions of the United States changed for a time after 1937. In that year, President Franklin D. Roosevelt introduced the **Good Neighbor Policy,** which promised to deal more fairly with Latin America and to stop direct interventions. After World War II, however, the U.S. preoccupation with containment of the Soviet Union and communism as an ideology led to new strategies in Latin America. They included participation in regional organizations, the support of governments that at least expressed democratic or anticommunist principles, the covert undermining of governments considered unfriendly to U.S. interests, and when necessary, direct intervention. Underlying much of this policy was also a firm belief that economic development would eliminate the conditions that contributed to radical political solutions. Thus, U.S. programs such as the **Alliance for Progress,** begun in 1961, aimed to develop the region as an alternative to those solutions. The alliance had limited success despite good intentions and more than $10 billion in aid, but many Latin Americans perceived that it benefited the elites rather than the poor. Because of its record, Latin Americans and North Americans both began to question the assumption that development was basically a problem of capital and resources and that appropriate strategies would lead to social and economic improvement, which in turn would forestall revolution.

During the 1970s and 1980s, U.S. policy often was pragmatic, accepting Latin America as it was, which meant dealing on friendly terms with the military dictatorships. President Jimmy Carter (1977–1981) made a new initiative to deal with Latin America and to influence governments there to observe civil liberties. Most significantly, a treaty was signed with Panama that ceded to that nation eventual control of the Panama Canal. In 1979, he also received the Sandinista rebels who had overthrown the dictator of Nicaragua and offered them financial aid. But increasing violence in Central America in the 1980s and the more conservative presidencies of Ronald Reagan and George H. Bush led the United States back to policies based on strategic, economic, and defense considerations in which direct intervention or support of counterrevolutionary forces such as the Contras in Nicaragua played a part. Thus, in 1989 and 1990, the United States toppled a government in Panama that was authoritarian, defied U.S. policies, and promoted drug smuggling, replacing it with a cooperative regime backed by American troops.

After 2000 U.S. concerns with Latin America continued to focus on the issues of commerce, immigration, the drug trade, and political stability. Militarization of the campaign against drugs and increasing concern with terrorism meant that by 2003 almost 60 percent of U.S. aid to Latin America was pledged to military purposes. Globalization for Latin America did increase national economic growth, but free trade arrangements did not protect workers and well over 30 percent of the region's population still fell below the poverty line. That fact contributed to the growing tide of Latin American migration—legal and illegal—to the United States. By 2004 there were 40 million Hispanics in the United States, about 40 percent of them immigrants.

Good Neighbor Policy Established by Franklin D. Roosevelt for dealing with Latin America in 1933; intended to halt direct intervention in Latin American politics.

Alliance for Progress Begun in 1961 by the United States to develop Latin America as an alternative to radical political solutions; enjoyed only limited success; failure of development programs led to renewal of direct intervention.

Societies in Search of Change

Despite frustrated Latin American attempts at profound reform, there were great changes during the 20th century. Social and gender relations changed during the century. We have already seen how countries such as Mexico, Peru, and Bolivia sought to enfranchise their Indian populations during this century in different ways and with differing degrees of success. National ideologies and actual practice often are not the same, and discrimination on the basis of ethnicity continues. To be called "Indian" is still an insult in many places in Latin America. Although ethnic and cultural mixture characterizes many Latin American populations and makes Indian and African elements important features of national identity, relations with Indian populations often continue to be marked by exploitation and discrimination in nations as diverse as Brazil, Nicaragua, and Guatemala.

Social relations changed slowly in Latin America. Population growth, urbanization, and the migration of workers continued to challenge the region.

Slow Change in Women's Roles

The role of women has changed slowly. After World War I, women in Latin America continued to live under inequalities in the workplace and in politics. Women were denied the right to vote anywhere in Latin America until Ecuador enfranchised women in 1929 and Brazil and Cuba did the same in 1932. Throughout most of the region, those examples were not followed until the 1940s and 1950s. In some nations, the traditional associations of women with religion and the Catholic Church in Hispanic life made reformers and revolutionaries fear that women would become a conservative force in national politics. This attitude, combined with traditional male attitudes that women should be concerned only with home and family, led to a continued exclusion of women from political life. In response, women formed various associations and clubs and began to push for the vote and other issues of interest to them.

Feminist organizations, suffrage movements, and international pressures eventually combined to bring about change. In Argentina, 15 bills for female suffrage were introduced in the senate before the vote was won in 1945. Sometimes the victory was a matter of political expediency for those in power: In the Dominican Republic and some other countries, the enfranchisement of women was a strategy used by conservative groups to add more conservative voters to the electorate in an effort to hold off political change. In Argentina, recently enfranchised women became a major pillar of the Peronist regime, although that regime also suppressed female political opponents such as Victoria Ocampo, editor of the important literary magazine *Sur*.

Women eventually discovered that the ability to vote did not in itself guarantee political rights or the ability to have their specific issues heard. After achieving the vote, women tended to join the national political parties, where traditional prejudices against women in public life limited their ability to influence political programs. In Argentina, Brazil, Colombia, and Chile, for example, the integration of women into national political programs has been slow, and women have not participated in proportion to their numbers. In a few cases, however, women played a crucial role in elections (Figure 32.7).

Some of the earliest examples of mobilization of women and their integration into the national labor force of various Latin American nations came in the period just before World War I

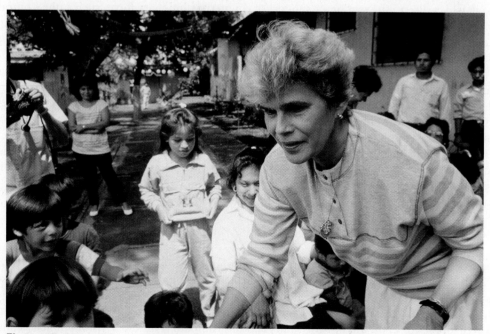

Figure 32.7 The rising participation of women in Latin American politics is marked by their election to national office. The first woman elected to the presidency of a Latin American nation, Violeta Chamorro, President of Nicaragua (1990–97) is shown here. She came to office as a candidate for peace and reconciliation after a long civil war and insurgency in her country. Subsequently, women have been elected to the presidency in Chile (Michelle Bachelet in 2006) and in Argentina (Cristina Fernández de Kirchner in 2007). The increasing participation of women in the political process has been noted throughout the region.

and continued thereafter. The classic roles of women as homemakers, mothers, and agricultural workers were expanded as women entered the industrial labor force in growing numbers. By 1911 in Argentina, for example, women made up almost 80 percent of the textile and clothing industry's workers. But women found that their salaries often were below those of comparable male workers and that their jobs, regardless of the skill levels demanded, were considered unskilled and thus less well paid. Under these conditions, women, like other workers, joined the anarchist, socialist, and other labor unions and organizations.

Labor organizations are only a small part of the story of women in the labor force. In countries such as Peru, Bolivia, and Ecuador, women working in the markets control much small-scale commerce and have become increasingly active politically. In the growing service sectors, women have also become an important part of the labor force. Shifts in attitudes about women's roles have come more slowly than political and economic changes. Even in revolutionary Cuba, where a Law of the Family guaranteed equal rights and responsibilities within the home, enforcement has been difficult.

By the mid-1990s, the position of women in Latin America was closer to that in western Europe and North America than to the other areas of the world. Women made up 9 percent of the legislators in Latin America, a percentage higher than in any other region of the world. In terms of demographic patterns, health, education, and place in the workforce, the comparative position of women reinforced Latin America's intermediate position between industrialized and developing nations.

The Movement of People

In 1950 the populations of North America (United States and Canada) and Latin America were both about 165 million, but by 1985 North America's population was 265 million, while Latin America's had grown to more than 400 million. Declining mortality and continuing high fertility were responsible for this situation.

At the beginning of the 20th century, the major trend of population movement was immigration to Latin America, but the region has long experienced internal migration and the movement of people within the hemisphere. By the 1980s, this movement had reached significant levels, fed by the flow of workers seeking jobs, the demands of capital for cheap labor, and the flight of political refugees seeking basic freedoms. During World War II, government programs to supply laborers were set up between the United States and Mexico, but these were always accompanied by extralegal migration, which fluctuated with the economy. Conditions for migrant laborers often were deplorable, although the extension of social welfare to them in the 1960s began to address some of the problems. By the 1970s, more than 750,000 illegal Mexican migrants a year were crossing the border—some more than once—as the United States continued to attract migrants.

This internationalization of the labor market was comparable in many ways with the movement of workers from poorer countries such as Turkey, Morocco, Portugal, and Spain to the stronger economies of West Germany and France. In Latin America it also reflected the fact that industrialization in the 20th century depended on highly mechanized industry that did not create enough new jobs to meet the needs of the growing population. Much of the migration has been to the United States, but there has also been movement across Latin American frontiers: Haitians migrate to work in the Dominican Republic, and Colombians illegally migrate to Venezuela. By the 1970s, about 5 million people per year were migrating in Latin America and the Caribbean.

Politics has also been a major impulse for migration. Haitians fleeing political repression and abysmal conditions have risked great dangers in small open boats to reach the United States. The Cuban revolution caused one of the great political migrations of the century. Beginning in 1959, when the Cuban middle class fled socialism, and continuing into the 1980s with the flight of Cuban workers, almost 1 million Cubans left the island. The revolutionary upheaval in Nicaragua, political violence in Central America, and poverty in Haiti have contributed to the flight of refugees. Often, it is difficult to separate political and economic factors in the movement of people from their homelands.

International migration is only part of the story. During the 20th century, there was a marked movement in Latin America from rural to urban areas (Table 32.1). Whereas in the 19th century

TABLE 32.1   Population of Capital Cities as a Percentage of Total Population in 10 Latin American Nations

Nation	Capital	1880	1930	1960	1983	2003
Argentina	Buenos Aires	12	20	32	34	33
Brazil	Rio de Janeiro	3	4	7	4*	3*
Chile	Santiago	6	13	22	37	29
Colombia	Bogotá	1	2	8	11	15
Cuba	Havana	13	15	18	20	20
Mexico	Mexico City	3	5	15	20	9
Panama	Panama City	7	16	25	20	15
Peru	Lima	3	5	19	27	30
Uruguay	Montevideo	12	28	31	40	39
Venezuela	Caracas	3	7	20	18	7

*No longer the capital city.

Sources: From J. P. Cole, *Latin America: An Economic and Social Geography* (1965), 417; and http://www.world-gazetteer.com.

Latin America was an agrarian region, by the 1980s about one-half of the population lived in cities of more than 20,000, and more than 25 of these cities had populations of more than 1 million. Some of these cities had reached enormous size. In 2009 Mexico City had more than 18 million inhabitants, São Paulo had over 18 million, and Buenos Aires had over 13 million. Latin America was by far the most urbanized area of the developing world and only slightly less urbanized than western Europe.

The problem is not simply size but rate of growth. The urban populations grew at a rate about three times that of the population as a whole, which itself has grown rapidly. Urban economies have not been able to create enough jobs for the rapidly increasing population. Often recent migrants lived in marginal neighborhoods or in shantytowns, which have become characteristic of the rapidly growing cities of Latin America. These *favelas,* to use the Brazilian term, have created awful living conditions, but over time some have become poorer neighborhoods within the cities, and community cooperation and action within them have secured basic urban services. More recently, the rate of urban growth has slowed, but the social problems in the cities remain a major challenge.

Although Latin American urbanization increased rapidly after 1940, the percentage of its people living in cities is still less than in western Europe but more than in Asia and Africa. Unlike the 19th-century European experience, the lack of employment in Latin American cities has kept rural migrants from becoming part of a laboring class with a strong identification with fellow workers. Those who do succeed in securing industrial jobs often join paternalistic labor organizations that are linked to the government. Thus, there is a separation between the chronically underemployed urban lower class and the industrial labor force. Whereas industrialization and urbanization promoted strong class solidarity in 19th-century Europe, which led to the gains of organized labor, in contemporary Latin America nationalist and populist politics have weakened the ability of the working class to operate effectively in politics.

Cultural Reflections of Despair and Hope

Latin America remains an amalgamation of cultures and peoples trying to adjust to changing world realities. Protestant denominations have made some inroads, but the vast majority of Latin Americans are still Catholic. Hispanic traditions of family, gender relations, business, and social interaction influence everyday life and help to determine responses to the modern world.

Latin American popular culture remains vibrant. It draws on African and Indian traditional crafts, images, and techniques but arranges them in new ways. Music is also part of popular culture. The Argentine tango of the turn of the century began in the music halls of lower-class working districts of Buenos Aires and became an international craze. The African-influenced Brazilian samba and the Caribbean salsa have spread widely. They are a Latin American contribution to world civilization.

The struggle for social justice, economic security, and political formulas in keeping with the cultural and social realities of their nations has provided a dynamic tension that has produced tremendous artistic achievements. Latin American poets and novelists have gained worldwide recognition. We have already noted the artistic accomplishments of the Mexican Revolution. In 1922 Brazilian artists, composers, and authors staged a Modern Art Week in São Paulo, which emphasized a search for a national artistic expression that reflected Brazilian realities.

That theme also preoccupied authors elsewhere in Latin America. The social criticism of the 1930s produced powerful realist novels, which revealed the exploitation of the poor, the peasantry, and the Indians. Whether in the heights of the Andes or in the dark streets of the growing urban slums, the plight of the common folk provided a generation of authors with themes worthy of their effort. Social and political criticism has remained a central feature of Latin American literature and art and has played an important role in the development of newer art forms such as film.

The inability to bring about social justice or to influence politics has also sometimes led Latin American artists and intellectuals to follow other paths. In the 1960s a wave of literature took place in which novels that mixed the political, the historical, the erotic, and the fantastic were produced by a generation of authors who used "magical realism" because they found the reality of Latin America too absurd to be described by the traditional forms or logic. Writers such as the Argentine Jorge Luis Borges (1899–1980) and the Colombian Gabriel García Marquez (b. 1928) won acclaim throughout the world. García Marquez's *One Hundred Years of Solitude* (1967) used the history of a family in a mythical town called Macondo as an allegory of Latin America and traced the evils that befell the family and the community as they moved from naive isolation to a maturity that included oppression, exploitation, war, revolution, and natural disaster but never subdued the spirit of its people. This literary "boom" of the 1960s has been followed by a subsequent generation of novels that has emphasized emotions and personal fulfillment and by "testimonial" books that have sometimes mixed autobiography with fiction as a way to bring the reality of Latin American life and politics to a personal level.

Global Connections

Struggling Toward the Future in a Global Economy

As Latin America entered the 21st century, it continued to search for economic growth, social justice, and political stability. No easy solutions were available. In many ways, Latin American societies remained "unrevolutionary"—unable to bring about needed changes because of deeply entrenched class interests, international conditions, or power politics. However, the struggle for change had produced some important results. The Mexican and Cuban revolutions brought profound changes in those countries and had a broad impact on the rest of the hemisphere, either as models to copy or as dangers to be avoided. Other nations, such as Bolivia, Peru, and Nicaragua, attempted their own versions of radical change with greater or lesser success. New forms of politics, sometimes populist and sometimes militarist, were tried. New political and social ideas, such as those of liberation theology, grew out of the struggle to find a just and effective formula for change. Latin American authors and artists served as a conscience for their societies and received worldwide recognition for their depiction of the sometimes bizarre reality they observed. Although tremendous problems continued to face the region, Latin America remained the most advanced part of the developing world. Levels of literacy, for example, easily surpassed those in most of Asia and in Africa.

In the age of globalization, Latin America faces new challenges. The new world economy has created opportunities for expansion, and in the 1990s Latin American economies grew considerably, but this growth has made the problems of the distribution of wealth in Latin America even more acute. Other problems also result from economic changes. The northern part of Mexico near the border with the United States has benefited from new trade opportunities while southern Mexico has gotten poorer. Then too, integration into the world economy often threatens traditional cultures. Since the 1980s, various indigenous peoples' political movements have sought to protect traditional cultures while seeking political and economic opportunities. Frustrated by continuing social problems and its disadvantages in the global economy of free trade and privatization, Latin America seemed to be moving toward the left. By 2008, Leftist presidents had been elected in Chile, Nicaragua, Ecuador, Peru and Bolivia, joining those already in power in Cuba, Venezuela, Brazil, Argentina, and Uruguay, and in Mexico, the candidate of the Left almost won. This trend revealed collective discontent and sometimes a strident rhetoric of opposition to U.S. policies, but it also demonstrated that democratic politics were functioning through much of the region. When in 2007 Venezuelan president Chávez sought by referendum to broaden his presidential powers and hold the office for life, he was defeated. He accepted the vote and later succeeded in 2008. A new political leadership was emerging. Chile elected its first woman president in 2006, and in Bolivia, Evo Morales, was the first president of Native American background to be elected. Some like Chávez and Morales joined Cuba's ailing Castro in open opposition of U.S. policies. Others like Brazil's Lula sought better trade relations. Despite the differences among these new leaders, they represent Latin American concern for the region's place in the emerging global order.

Cultural issues remain unresolved as well. Partly reflecting divisions in wealth and urbanism, Latin Americans have participated variously in global consumer currents. Middle-class Mexicans, for example, began to copy United States patterns in celebrating Halloween (previously an important traditional holiday focused on the forces of death) and Christmas. To some Mexican intellectuals, this represented a crucial abandonment of identity, and to others the new interests seemed either alien or unobtainable. The spread of new religious movements, including fundamentalist Protestantism, signaled an attempt to provide alternatives to global culture, particularly among urban slum-dwellers. About 10 percent of Latin Americans are now members of Protestant denominations. At the same time, Latin American filmmakers, artists, and popular musicians have contributed directly to global culture, often incorporating traditional elements in the process. Latin America's global position has become increasingly complex.

Further Readings

Two good introductory texts on modern Latin America, both of which present variations of the "dependency" interpretation, are E. Bradford Burns, *Latin America: A Concise Interpretive History* (1986), and Thomas E. Skidmore and Peter H. Smith, *Modern Latin America* (1989). John Charles Chasteen, *Born in Fire and Blood* (2001), and Peter Winn, *Americas: The Changing Face of Latin America and the Caribbean,* 3d. ed. (2006) gives up-to-date overviews.

A survey of the economic history of Latin America is provided by Richard Salvucci, ed., in *Latin America and the World Economy* (1996).

Charles Berquist, *Labor in Latin America* (1986) provides a good overall starting point but there are excellent case studies, such as Peter Winn, *Victims of the Chilean Miracle: Workers and Neoliberalism in the Pinochet Era, 1973–2002* (2004), while recent approaches are analyzed in Maria Lorena Cook, *The Politics of Labor Reform* (2007).

There are many good studies of Latin American politics, but Guillermo O'Donnell, *Modernization and Bureaucratic Authoritarianism* (1973), influenced a generation of scholars. The role of the United States is discussed in Peter Smith, *Talons of the Eagle: Dynamics of U.S.–Latin American Relations* (1996) and John Coatsworth, *Central America and the United States* (1994). Greg Grandin, *Empire's Workshop: Latin America, the United States and the Rise of the New Imperialism* (2006) argues that U.S. policies in Latin America were later applied in other regions. Recent scholarship has emphasized the cultural dimensions of this relationship. Frederick Pike, *The United States and Latin America: Myths and Stereotypes of Civilization and Nature* (1992), set the outlines of cultural relations. Steve Stern, *Remembering Pinochet's Chile* (2004) and his *Battling for Hearts and Minds* (2006), discusses the difficulty of national reconciliation when those rights are violated.

A few good monographs on important topics represent the high level of scholarship on Latin America. Freidrich Katz, *The Life and Times of Pancho Villa* (1998), is an outstanding biography. Florencia Mallon, *The Defense of Community in Peru's Central Highlands* (1983), looks at national change from a community perspective. The Cuban revolution and its implications are treated in Louis Perez, *On Becoming Cuban: Identity, Nationality, and Culture* (1999). David Kunzle et al. examine the role of Che Guevara in the Cuban revolution and its legacy for the wider world in *Che Guevara: Icon, Myth, and Message* (2002).

Frank McCann, *Soldiers of the Patria* (2004), on the military in Brazil, is one of the most in-depth studies of a Latin American military establishment, and Richard Gott, *Guerrilla Movements in Latin America* (1972), was a valuable book that presented analysis and documents on the movements seeking revolutionary change at that time. On some of the major themes of the 21st century, there is Juan Gonzalez, *Harvest of Empire: A History of Latinos in America* (2000); Michael Coniff, ed., *Populism in Latin America* (1999); Steve Ellner and Daniel Hellinger, *Venezuela Politics in the Chávez Era* (2003); and Carol Wise, ed., *The Post-NAFTA Political Economy: Mexico and the Western Hemisphere* (1998). Fernando-López-Alves and Diana E. Johnson, *Globalization and Uncertainty in Latin America* (2007) looks at the future economic and political challenges.

On the Web

Web resources on Latin American revolutionary movements abound, including those in Chile (http://www.hartfordhwp.com/archives/42a/130.html or http://www.soc.ucsb.edu/projects/casemethod/foran.html), Cuba (http://www.hartford-hwp.com/archives/43b/index-ab.html and http://uwacadweb.uwyo.edu/RED_FEATHER/CUBA/002durand.htm), Guatemala (http://www2.truman.edu/~marc/webpages/revsfall98/guatemala/guatemala.html, http://www.hartford-hwp.com/archives/47/index-ce.html, and http://www.gwu.edu/~nsarchiv/NSAEBB/NSAEBB4/), and Nicaragua (http://en.wikipedia.org/wiki/Nicaragua).

For the lives of revolutionary leaders, see for Cuba's Fidel Castro (http://www.cnn.com/SPECIALS/cold.war/kbank/profiles/castro/ and http://www.marxists.org/history/cuba/archive/castro/index.htm), for Mexico's Emiliano Zapata (http://www.cs.utk.edu/~miturria/project/zapata.html and http://www.mexconnect.com/mex_/history/ezapata1.html). For Mexico's women revolutionaries (http://www.ic.arizona.edu/ic/mcbride/ws200/mex-jand.htm) and for Ernesto "Che" Guevara (http://www.marxists.org/archive/guevara/index.htm, http://www.companeroche.com/, and http://www.che-lives.com/home/). To better understand why he remains an icon, see his speeches at http://www.youtube.com/watch?v=5vQfw—NYuw.

Hopes for a more egalitarian society expressed by artists such as Diego Rivera (http://www.diegorivera.com/index.php) and Jose Orozco (http://hoodmuseum.dartmouth.edu/collections/overview/Americas/Mesoamerica/murals) were dashed by the Cold War (http://www.coldwar.org and http://www.turnerlearning.com/cnn/coldwar/backyard/byrd_ttl.html) but remain alive (see http://flag.blackened.net/revolt/mexico/begindx.html and YouTube (http://www.youtube.com/watch?v=lTp1c7bUf-k).

AP* Test Prep

1. Which of the following accurately describes major revolutionary movements in 20th-century Latin America?

    (A) They freed major nations from Spanish colonial control.

    (B) The United States supported them because of its commitment to democratic political goals.

    (C) They were strongly affected by peasant issues and peasant participation.

    (D) They accelerated the pace of industrialization and consumerism.

2. In 20th-century Latin America, the military was typically

    (A) small and usually ineffective.

    (B) liberal and reform-minded.

    (C) supportive of democracy.

    (D) socially conservative, elitist and authoritarian.

3. Argentina's Perón and Brazil's Vargas regimes were

    (A) pro-European or Western.

    (B) favorably inclined toward foreign investments in national industries.

    (C) often simultaneously fascist, nationalistic, socialist, and populist.

    (D) supported by the international communist movement.

4. Throughout 20th-century Latin America, the people most often excluded from influence, or socially marginalized, were the

    (A) intellectuals, especially writers and artists.

    (B) clergy, especially Roman Catholic priests and nuns.

    (C) indigenous peoples and descendants of African slaves.

    (D) peasants and large rural landowners.

5. The Latin American country and ruler who deliberately and most directly challenged American regional hegemony during the Cold War was

    (A) Mexico's Cardenas.

    (B) Chile's Allende.

    (C) Brazil's Vargas.

    (D) Cuba's Castro.

6. Which of the following statements concerning the relations of the United States with Latin American countries is most accurate?

    (A) The United States has rarely intervened in Latin American politics.

    (B) In association with the Cold War, the United States pursued an interventionist policy to limit the spread of communism to the point of overthrowing, or lending support to rebels opposed to, democratically elected regimes which had raised its suspicions.

    (C) The United States has always refused to support authoritarian or undemocratic military regimes.

    (D) The United States-led Alliance for Progress, designed to improve economic conditions in Latin America so as to combat communism, succeeded in it is goal of benefiting the Indians, poor peasants, and small landowners of Latin America.

7. All of these are demographic trends and problems in 20th-century Latin America EXCEPT

    (A) rapid urbanization.

    (B) migration of unskilled laborers, the poor, and the politically repressed to richer countries.

    (C) millions of refugees due to wars and famines.

    (D) excessively large population growth rates.

Free-Response Question

Compare and contrast any two Latin American countries on the basis of their approach to social and economic problems in the late 20th century.

33 Africa, the Middle East, and Asia in the Era of Independence

The Challenges of Independence

DOCUMENT: Cultural Creativity in the Emerging Nations: Some Literary Samples

THINKING HISTORICALLY: Artificial Nations and the Rising Tide of Communal Strife

Post-Colonial Options for Achieving Economic Growth and Social Justice

Delayed Revolutions: Religious Revivalism and Liberation Movements in Settler Societies

VISUALIZING THE PAST: Globalization and Postcolonial Societies

GLOBAL CONNECTIONS: Postcolonial Nations in the Cold War World Order

As she had so often in the past, Indira Gandhi refused to heed those who urged her to be cautious. She had audaciously ordered the army to drive the extreme separatist Sikhs from the sacred grounds of the Golden Temple in Amritsar in northwest India. Indian troops had carried out her orders all too well. They had evicted the Sikh radicals, who demanded an independent state, which they called Khalistan. But in the process the troops had killed thousands of Sikhs inside the temple grounds and destroyed or badly damaged many revered shrines, including the library housing the Sikhs' holy scriptures. Now her advisors pleaded with her to replace her Sikh bodyguards with elite army units that had no religious or kinship ties to the aggrieved Sikh community. But Prime Minister Gandhi insisted that the Sikh units that had traditionally guarded her—and her father and British colonial rulers before him—were loyal and placed their honor as soldiers and duty to the nation above whatever sympathy they might feel for radical elements among the Sikh faithful.

So Sikh soldiers were on guard several months later as Indira Gandhi walked from her home through a beloved garden to her nearby office. As she approached the garden gate, she was challenged by two of her most trusted protectors, both Sikhs, who opened fire at close range and riddled her body with bullets. The assassination sparked anti-Sikh riots across India's capital that left thousands dead and sections of the city smoldering ruins. Her son Rajiv, who had only recently taken up a political career, was soon sworn in as her successor. But across the world's largest democracy, Indira was mourned as the lost "mother of the nation" and a relentless champion of the poor and powerless.

Few Indian politicians expected Indira Gandhi to be a forceful, dynamic prime minister with a vision of her own, when she first came to power in January, 1966. As the daughter of Jawaharlal Nehru, who was second only to Gandhi among those who fashioned the nationalist revolt and one of the most influential leaders of the early cold war decades, Indira Gandhi inherited close links to the powerful. But though she became her father's confidant and close companion, she was regarded by India's numerous time-tested and ambitious politicians as a shy young woman who was content to be her father's helpmate. Seeing her as someone they could control, several of the power brokers of the Congress party backed her as the successor to Lal Bahadur Shastri, who had become prime minister on the death of her father two years before, only to die suddenly himself of a heart attack in the first days of 1966.

Gandhi soon made it clear that she was as strong-willed as her father, and as determined to pursue her own agenda for the uplift of India's peoples and extending the nation's influence in international affairs. Perhaps even more than her famous father, she was a rousing speaker, able to energize party loyalists and supporters as well as frustrate the ambitions of rival leaders within the Congress Party and the attacks of opposition politicians. She successfully led India in war against Pakistan, and oversaw the birth of the nation of Bangladesh that had formerly made up the eastern half of the Pakistani state. Though she pursued a populist, reformist agenda in domestic politics, she maintained India's neutrality through some of the more turbulent decades of the Cold War. Her nationalization policies and moves to restrict the powers of her adversaries in the legislature were seen by many at the time as harmful to India's fledgling democracy. But in the face of a country deeply divided religiously and ethnically, in which famine and poverty remained pervasive problems, Indira Gandhi preserved the independent judiciary, multi-party competition and free elections that are the hallmarks of India to the present day. With the exception of a three-year hiatus after she had been defeated in national elections in 1977, she dominated Indian politics from 1966 until her assassination in 1984. ■

Figure 33.1 As this photograph of Indian Prime Minister Indira Gandhi on the campaign trail in 1979 strikingly reveals, she reveled in direct contact with the ordinary people of India. Seeing herself as the champion of the poor and defenseless, she refused to be isolated by the phalanxes of bodyguards commonly associated with national leaders across the globe.

The prodigious challenges faced by activist postcolonial leaders, such as Indira Gandhi, and the often very different strategies for tackling them adopted by different African and Asian leaders are the focus of this chapter. On a resource base depleted by millennia of use, Prime Minister Gandhi sought to find ways first to feed the people and then to improve the living standards of one of the poorest and most populous nations on earth. Like other leaders of developing nations, she had to find a way to balance the demands of the U.S. and Soviet superpowers while maintaining India's nonaligned status in a world threatened by nuclear conflagration. And as demonstrated by the confrontation with the Sikh separatists—only one of a number of highly inflammatory ethnoreligious divisions she had to deal with—like other leaders in the emerging nations, Indira Gandhi spent a great deal of her energy and political capital just holding the country together.

Like the majority of postcolonial heads of state in the developing world, Gandhi sought to centralize power in her own hands, and she resorted at times to preemptive strikes against her political opponents or used force to put down what she perceived as enemies of the new nation. And like so many of her counterparts in the often artificial and unstable political entities carved out of the Euro-American colonial empires, she was violently removed from power. Indira Gandhi's regime ended with her assassination by loyalists turned into implacable enemies by her violent attempt to suppress separatist forces similar to those that have threatened at one time or other to pull apart virtually all of the new nations of the developing world.

In the early decades of independence, the very existence of the nation-states that were carved out of the Western colonial empires was often challenged by internal rivalries between different social and ethnic groups. Economic growth was hampered by unprecedented rates of population increase, the structure of the international market, and the underdeveloped state of most colonial economies at the time of independence.

The Challenges of Independence

The nationalist movements that won independence for most of the peoples of Africa, the Middle East, and Asia usually involved some degree of mass mobilization. Peasants and working-class townspeople, who hitherto had little voice in politics beyond their village boundaries or local labor associations, were drawn into political contests that toppled empires and established new nations. To win the support of these groups, nationalist leaders promised jobs, civil rights, and equality once independence was won. The leaders of many nationalist movements nurtured visions of post-independence

805

1910 C.E.	1920 C.E.	1930 C.E.	1940 C.E.	1950 C.E.
1912 African National Congress party formed 1919 First Pan-African Nationalist Congress	1928 Founding of the Muslim Brotherhood in Egypt	1930s Free Officers movement develops in Egypt	1947 India and Pakistan achieve independence 1948 First Arab-Israeli War; Afrikaner Nationalist party comes to power in South Africa, bringing the beginning of apartheid 1949 Hassan al-Banna assassinated in Egypt	1951 India's first five-year plan for economic development launched 1952 Farouk and khedival regime overthrown in Egypt; Nasser and Free Officers come to power 1955 Bandung Conference; beginning of nonaligned movement 1956 Aborted British-French-Israeli intervention in Suez 1958 South Africa completely independent of Great Britain

After Empire: Africa and the Middle East — MAP

New Nations in Africa — MAP

utopias in the minds of their followers. The people were told that once the Europeans, who monopolized the best jobs, were driven away and their exploitive hold on the economy was brought to an end, there would be enough to give everyone a good life.

Unfortunately, post-independence realities in almost all of the new nations made it impossible for nationalist leaders to fulfill the expectations they had aroused among their followers and, in varying degrees, among the colonized populace at large. Even with the Europeans gone and the terms of economic exchange with more developed countries somewhat improved, there was simply not enough to go around. Thus, the socialist-inspired ideologies that nationalist leaders had often embraced and promoted were misleading. The problem was not just that goods and services were unequally distributed, leaving some people rich and the great majority poor. The problem was that there were not enough resources to take care of everybody, even if it was possible to distribute them equitably.

When utopia failed to materialize, personal rivalries and long-standing divisions between different classes and ethnic or religious groups, which had been muted by the common struggle against the alien colonizers, resurfaced or intensified. The European colonizers had established arbitrary boundaries (Maps 33.1 and 33.2), sometimes combining hostile ethnic or religious groups. In almost all the new states, these rivalries and differences became dominant features of political life. They produced political instability and often threatened the viability of the nations themselves, as with East and West Pakistan, where extreme contrasts of topography and culture led to violence and the secession of the area that became **Bangladesh.** The recurring problems of famine and starvation in parts of Africa have stemmed from human conflicts more than natural disasters (Figure 33.2). Rivalries and civil wars in many of the newly decolonized nations consumed resources that might have been devoted to economic development. They also blocked—in the name of the defense of subnational interests—measures designed to build more viable and prosperous states. Absorbed by the task of just holding their new nations together, politicians neglected problems—such as soaring population increases, uncontrolled urban growth, rural landlessness, and environmental deterioration—that soon formed as large a threat as political instability to their young nations.

Bangladesh Founded as an independent nation in 1972; formerly East Pakistan.

The Population Bomb

The nationalist leaders who led the colonized peoples of Africa and Asia to independence had firmly committed themselves to promoting rapid economic development once colonial restraints were removed. In keeping with their Western-educated backgrounds, most of these leaders saw their nations following the path of industrialization that had brought national prosperity and international power to much of western Europe and the United States. This course of development was also fostered by representatives of the Soviet bloc, who had emphasized heavy industry in their

1960 C.E.	1970 C.E.	1980 C.E.	1990 C.E.
1960 Sharpeville shootings in South Africa	1970s Peak period for OPEC cartel	1980–1988 Iran-Iraq War	1990 Nelson Mandela released from South African prison; Iraqi
1966 Nkrumah overthrown by military coup in Ghana	1971 Bangladesh revolt against West Pakistan; Indo-Pakistani War	1989 De Klerk charts path of peaceful reform in South Africa	invasion of Kuwait
1966–1970 Biafran secessionist war in Nigeria	1972 Bangladesh becomes independent nation		1991 Persian Gulf War
1967 Six-Day War between Israel and Arab nations	1973 Third Arab-Israeli War		1994 First democratic elections in South Africa
	1979 Shah of Iran overthrown; Islamic republic declared		

state-directed drives to modernize their economies and societies. Of the many barriers to the rapid economic breakthroughs postcolonial leaders hoped for, the most formidable and persistent were the spiraling population increases that often overwhelmed whatever economic advances the peoples of the new nations managed to make (Figure 33.3).

Factors making for sustained population increases in already densely populated areas of Asia and Africa had begun to take effect even before the era of high colonialism. Food crops, mostly from the New World, contributed to dramatic population growth in China, India, and Java as early as the 17th century. They also helped sustain high levels of population in areas such as the Niger delta in west Africa, despite heavy losses as a result of the slave trade. The coming of colonial rule reinforced these upward trends in a number of ways. It ended local warfare that had caused population losses and, perhaps more significantly, had indirectly promoted the spread of epidemic diseases and famine. The new railroad and steamship links established by the colonizers to foster the spread of the market economy also cut down on the regional famines that had been a major check against sustained population increase since ancient times. Large amounts of food could be shipped from areas where harvests were good to those where drought or floods threatened the local inhabitants with starvation.

With war and famine—two of the main barriers to population increase—much reduced, growth began to speed up. This was particularly true in areas such as India and Java that had been under European control for decades. Death rates declined, but birth rates remained much the same, leading to increasingly larger net increases. Improved hygiene and medical treatment played little part in this rise until the early 20th century. From that time, efforts to eradicate tropical diseases, as well as global scourges such as smallpox, and to improve sewage systems and purify drinking water have led to further population increases.

Nearly all leaders of the emerging nations headed societies in which population was increasing at unprecedented levels. This increase continued in the early years of independence. In much of Asia, it has begun to level off in recent decades. But in most of Africa, population growth continues at very high rates. In some cases, most notably south Asia, moderate growth rates have produced huge total populations because they were adding to an already large base. Population experts predicted in the 1970s that south Asia's population of more than 600 million would more than double by the year 2000. With more than 1 billion people in India alone at present, the prophecy has more than been fulfilled.

In Africa, by contrast, which began with low population levels relative to its large land area, very high birth rates and diminished mortality rates have resulted in very steep population increases in recent decades. Some population experts predict that if present growth rates continue, by the mid-21st century Nigeria will have a population equal to that of present-day China. In view of the AIDS epidemic that has spread through much of central and eastern Africa since the 1980s, some of the estimates for population increases in Africa as a whole may have to be revised downward.

Map 33.1 The Emergence of New Nations in Africa after World War II A comparison of this map with Map 24.4 on page 562 quickly reveals the pronounced overlap between the boundaries drawn by the European imperialist powers and the postcolonial nations that emerged after 1945.

Map 33.2 The Partition of South Asia: The Formation of India, Pakistan, Bangladesh, and Sri Lanka Religious fault lines largely explain the fragmentation of the South Asian empire that the British had forged in the 18th and early 19th centuries.

But recent measures of African productivity and per capita incomes suggest that even more moderate increases in population may be difficult to support at reasonable living standards. This prospect is underscored by estimates that the 400 million people of Africa are supported by a continental economy with a productive capacity equal to just 6 percent of that of the United States, or roughly equal to that of the state of Illinois.

On the face of it, the conquest of war, disease, and famine was one of the great achievements of European colonial regimes. It was certainly an accomplishment that colonial officials never tired of citing in defense of continued European dominance. But the European policy of limiting industrialization in their colonial dependencies meant that one of the key ways by which Europe had met its own population boom in the 19th and early 20th centuries was not available to the new nations. They lacked the factories to employ the exploding population that moved to the cities from the rural areas, as well as the technology to produce the necessities of life for more and more people. Unlike the Europeans and the Americans, the emerging nations found it difficult to draw food and mineral resources from the rest of the world to feed this growing population. In fact, these were the very things the colonized peoples had been set up to sell to the industrialized nations. Even in countries such as India, where impressive advances in industrialization were made in the postcolonial era, gains in productivity were swallowed up rapidly by the population explosion.

In most African and Asian countries, there has been resistance to birth control efforts aimed at controlling population growth. Some of this resistance is linked to deeply entrenched social patterns and religious beliefs. In many of these societies, procreation is seen as a sign of male virility. In addition, the capacity to bear children, preferably male children, continues to be critical to the

The Wretched of the Earth

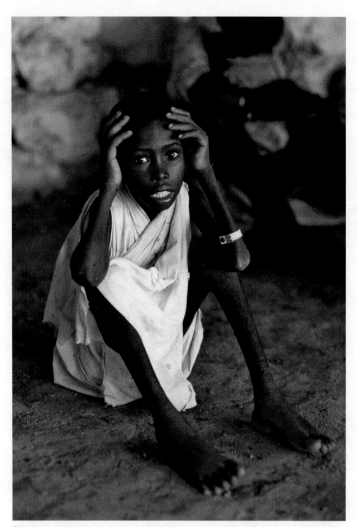

Figure 33.2 Since independence, famine has stalked much of the formerly colonized world, particularly in sub-Saharan Africa. Often, starvation has been caused by human conflicts rather than natural disasters.

social standing of women. In some cases, resistance to birth control is linked to specific cultural norms. For example, Hindus believe that a deceased man's soul cannot begin the cycle of rebirth until his eldest son has performed special ceremonies over his funeral pyre. This belief increases the already great pressure on Indian women to have children, and it encourages families to have several sons to ensure that at least one survives the father.

In Africa, children are seen as indispensable additions to the *lineage:* the extended network of relatives (and deceased ancestors) that, much more than the nuclear family, makes up the core social group over much of the subcontinent. As in India, sons are essential for continuing the patrilineal family line and performing burial and ancestral rites. The key roles played by women in agricultural production and marketing make girls highly valued in African societies. This is not true in many Asian societies, where high dowries and occupational restrictions limit their contribution to family welfare.

Before the 20th century, the high rates of stillbirths and infant mortality meant that mothers could expect to lose many of the children they conceived. Ten or 12 deaths of 15 or 16 children conceived was not unheard of. Beyond the obvious psychological scars left by these high death rates, they also fostered the conviction that it was necessary to have many children to ensure that some would outlive the parents. In societies where welfare systems and old-age pensions were meager or unknown, surviving children took on special urgency because they were the only ones who would care for parents who could no longer work for themselves. The persistence of these attitudes in recent decades, when medical advances have greatly reduced infant mortality, has been a major factor contributing to soaring population growth.

In the early decades after independence, many African and Asian leaders were deeply opposed to state measures to promote family planning and birth control. Some saw these as Western attempts to meddle in their internal affairs; others proudly declared that the socialist societies they were building would be able to take care of the additional population. As it has become increasingly clear that excessive population increase makes significant economic advances impossible, many of these leaders have begun to reassess their attitudes toward birth control. A particular cause for alarm is the fact that in many developing countries a high percentage of the population is under age 15 (as high as 40 percent in some areas) and thus dependent on others for support. But even for those who now want to promote family planning, the obstacles are staggering. In addition to the cultural and social factors just discussed, leaders often find they lack sufficient resources and the educated personnel needed to make these programs effective. High rates of illiteracy, particularly among women, must be overcome, but education is expensive. Perhaps no form of financial and technical assistance from the industrialized to the developing world will be as critical in the coming decades as that devoted to family planning.

Parasitic Cities and Endangered Ecosystems

As population increase in the rural areas of emerging nations outstripped the land and employment opportunities available to the peasantry, mass migrations to urban areas ensued. The massive movement of population from overcrowded villages to the cities was one of the most dramatic developments in the postcolonial history of most new nations. Ambitious youths and the rural poor crowded into port centers and capital cities in search of jobs and a chance to find the "good life" that the big hotels and restaurants and the neon lights of the city center appeared to offer to all comers. But because most of these cities lacked the rapidly expanding industrial sectors that had made possible the absorption of a similar migrant influx earlier in the West, they were often dead ends for migrants from the rural areas. There were few jobs, and heavy competition for them ensured that wages would remain low for most workers. The growing numbers of under-employed or unemployed migrants turned to street vending, scavenging, huckstering, begging, or petty crime to survive.

The urban poor have become a volatile factor in the political struggles of the elite. They form the crowds willing for a price to cheer on one contender or jeer down another, and ready to riot and loot in times of government crisis. In deeply divided societies, the poor, working-class, or idle youths of the urban areas often form the shock troops in communal clashes between rival ethnic and religious groups. Fear of outbursts by urban "mobs" has forced Asian, Middle Eastern, and African regimes to spend scarce resources to subsidize and thus keep low the price of bread, kerosene, and other necessities.

The sudden population influx from the rural areas to cities without sufficient jobs or the infrastructure to support them has greatly skewed urban growth in the emerging nations. Within decades Asian cities have become some of the largest in the world, and

Figure 33.3 This graph shows the growth of the world population by major global geographic areas between 1930 and 2000. It illustrates the near-stabilization of the upswing in populations of the West and the states of the former Soviet Union that began with industrialization in the 18th century. It charts the explosion that occurred in recent decades in the areas of the globe that were colonized, both formally and informally, by the industrial powers in the 19th and early 20th centuries. These increases surpass those of any other epoch in human history.

Middle Eastern and African urban areas have sprawled far beyond their modest limits in colonial times. As Figure 33.4 dramatically illustrates, the wealth of the upper- and middle-class areas, dominated by glitzy hotels and high-rises, contrasts disturbingly with the poverty of the vast slums that stretch in all directions from the city centers. Little or no planning was possible for the slum quarters that expanded as squatters erected makeshift shelters wherever open land or derelict buildings could be found. Originally, most of the slum areas lacked electricity, running water, or even the most basic sewage facilities. As shanties were gradually converted into ramshackle dwellings, many governments scrapped plans to level slum settlements and instead tried to provide them with electrical and sanitary systems. As an increasing number of development specialists have reluctantly concluded, slums often provide the only housing urban dwellers are likely to find for some time to come.

These conditions have burdened many postcolonial societies with parasitic rather than productive cities. This means that they are heavily dependent for survival on food and resources drawn from their own countryside or from abroad. In contrast to the cities of western Europe and North America, even during the decades of rapid urban expansion in the 19th century, few cities of the emerging nations have had the manufacturing base needed to generate growth in their surrounding regions or the nation as a whole. They take from the already impoverished countryside, but they are able to give little in return. Urban dependence on the countryside further stretches the already overextended resources of the rural areas.

Rural overpopulation in the decades after independence has led to soil depletion in many areas that have been worked for centuries or millennia. It has also resulted in an alarming rate of deforestation throughout Africa and Asia. Peasant villagers cut trees for fuel or clear land for farming and livestock grazing. Deforestation and overgrazing not only pose major threats to wild animal life but also upset the balance in fragile tropical ecosystems, producing further soil depletion and erosion and encouraging desertification. This environmental degradation is intensified by industrial pollution from both the developed countries and the emerging nations themselves. Although the industrial sectors in the latter are small, pollution tends to be proportionally greater than in the developed world because developing nations rarely can afford the antipollution technology introduced over the last few decades in Western Europe, Japan, and North America.

The Subordination of Women and the Nature of Feminist Struggles in the Postcolonial Era

The example of both the Western democracies and the communist republics of Eastern Europe, where women had won the right to vote in the early- and mid-20th century, encouraged the founders of many emerging nations to write female suffrage into their constitutions. The very active part women played in many nationalist struggles was perhaps even more critical to their earning the right to vote and run for political office. Women's activism also produced some semblance of equality in legal rights, education, and occupational opportunities under the laws of many new nations.

However, the equality that was proclaimed on paper often bore little resemblance to the actual rights that most women could exercise. It also had little bearing on the conditions under which they lived their daily lives. Even the rise to power of individual women such as **Indira Gandhi,** whose career and downfall were profiled in the opening section, or **Corazon Aquino,** president of the Philippines in the post-Marcos era of the late 1980s, is deceptive. In most instances, female heads of state in the emerging nations entered politics and initially won political support because they were connected to powerful men. As we have seen, Indira Gandhi was the daughter of **Jawaharlal Nehru** (juh-WAH-huhr-lahl NAY-roo), India's first prime minister. Corazon Aquino's husband was the martyred leader of the Filipino opposition to Ferdinand Marcos. **Benazir Bhutto** (BEH-nah-zeer BOO-toh), a prime minister of Pakistan, was the daughter of a domineering Pakistani prime minister who had been toppled by a military coup and executed in the late 1970s. Lacking these sorts of connections, most African, Middle Eastern, and Asian women have been at best relegated to peripheral political positions and at worst allowed no participation in the political process.

The limited gains made by women in the political sphere are paralleled by the second-class position to which most are consigned in many societies. In some respects, their handicaps are comparable to those that constrict women in the industrialized democracies and communist nations. But the obstacles to female self-fulfillment, and in many cases mere survival, in emerging nations are usually much more blatant and fundamental than the restrictions women have to contend with in developed societies. To begin with, early marriage ages for women and large families are still the norm in most African, Middle Eastern, and Asian societies. This means that women spend their youthful and middle-age years having children. There is little time to think of higher education or a career.

Figure 33.4 In the urban areas of undeveloped nations, the contrast between the wealth of the few and the poverty of the majority is revealed by the juxtaposition of the high-rise apartments of the affluent middle classes and the shantytowns of the urban poor. The city centers in emerging nations are much like those of the industrial West or Japan. But the cities as a whole often are more like collections of large villages than integrated urban units. Many of these villages are vast shantytowns with varying levels of basic services such as running water, sewer systems, and transportation networks to the city center.

The Search for Justice: Nâzim Hikmet and Nazik al-Mala'ika (20th Century)   DOCUMENT

Gandhi, Indira   Daughter of Jawaharlal Nehru (no relation to Mahatma Gandhi); installed as a figurehead prime minister by the Congress party bosses in 1966; a strong-willed and astute politician, she soon became the central figure in India politics, a position she maintained through the 1970s and passed on to her sons.

Aquino, Corazon   (b. 1933) First president of the Philippines in the post-Marcos era of late 1980s; she served from 1986 to 1992; Aquino, whose husband was assassinated by thugs in the pay of the Marcos regime, was one of the key leaders in the popular movement that toppled the dictator.

Because of the low level of sanitation in many postcolonial societies and the scarcity of food, all but elite and upper-middle-class women experience chronic anxiety about such basic issues as adequate nutrition for their children and their susceptibility to disease. The persistence of male-centric customs directly affects the health and life expectancy of women. For example, the Indian tradition that dictates that women first serve their husbands and sons and then eat what is left has obvious disadvantages. The quantity and nutritional content of the leftovers is likely to be lower than that of the original meals, and in tropical environments flies and other disease-bearing insects are more likely to have fouled the food.

The demographic consequences of these social patterns can be dramatic. In the 1970s, for example, it was estimated that as much as 20 percent of the female population of India was malnourished and that another 30 percent had a diet that was well below acceptable United Nations levels. In sharp contrast to the industrial societies of Japan, the United States, and Europe, where women outnumber (because on the average they outlive) men, in India there are only 930 females for every 1000 males.

Although the highly secular property and divorce laws many new states passed after independence have given women much greater legal protection, many of these measures are ignored in practice.

Cultural Creativity in the Emerging Nations: Some Literary Samples

Despite, or perhaps because of, political instability and chronic economic difficulties, postcolonial societies have generated a high level of artistic creativity over the past four or five decades. Nowhere has this creativity been more prominent and brilliant than in literary works for which African, Middle Eastern, and Asian writers have earned Nobel prizes and won a wide readership far beyond their own nations. The selections that follow are only a small sample of the vast and varied works of these talented writers, from poetry and drama to novels and short stories.

Many of these writers focus on the predicament of the Western-educated elites who dominate the new nations that emerged from the European colonial empires. In the following stanza from the poem "I Run Around with Them," Indonesian poet Chairil Anwar reflects on the lack of purpose and malaise he believed to be widespread among the children of these elite groups.

> I run around with them, what else can I do, now—
> Changing my face at the edge of the street, I use their eyes
> And tag along to visit the fun house:
> These are the facts as I know them
> (A new American flic at the Capitol,
> The new songs they dance to).
> We go home: there's nothing doing
> Though this kind of Death is our neighbor, our friend, now.
> Hanging around at the corner, we wait for the city bus
> That glows night to day like a gold tooth;
> Lame, deformed, negative, we
> Lean our bony asses against lamp poles
> And jaw away the years.

In the next quotation, from the novel *No Longer at Ease,* widely read Nigerian author Chinua Achebe identifies another dilemma: the pull between Western culture and the ancient civilization of one's own land.

> Nothing gave him greater pleasure than to find another Ibo-speaking student in a London bus. But when he had to speak in English with a Nigerian student from another tribe he lowered his voice. It was humiliating to have to speak to one's countryman in a foreign language, especially in the presence of the proud owners of that language. They would naturally assume that one had no language of one's own. He wished they were here today to see. Let them come to Umuofia [the protagonist's home village] now and listen to the talk of men who made a great art of conversation. Let them come and see men and women and children who knew how to live, whose joy of life had not yet been killed by those who claimed to teach other nations how to live.

Like many of the more famous novelists of the emerging nations, V. S. Naipaul is an expatriate, born in the Caribbean and now living in rural England. In his moving and controversial account of his return to his Indian ancestral home, titled *An Area of Darkness,* Naipaul confronts the problem of massive poverty and the responses of foreigners and the Indian elite to it.

> To see [India's] poverty is to make an observation of no value; a thousand newcomers to the country before you have seen and said as you. And not only newcomers. Our own sons and daughters, when they return from Europe and America, have spoken in your very words. Do not think that your anger and contempt are marks of your sensitivity. You might have seen more: the smiles on the faces of the begging children, that domestic group among the pavement sleepers waking in the cool Bombay morning, father, mother and baby in a trinity of love, so self-contained that they are as private as if walls had separated them from you; it is your gaze that violates them, your sense of outrage that outrages them. . . . It is your surprise, your anger that denies [them] humanity.

QUESTIONS Can you think of parallels in U.S. history or contemporary society to the situations and responses conveyed in these passages from recent postcolonial writings? Do they suggest that it is possible to communicate even intimate feelings across cultures, or do you find them alien, different? What other issues would you expect African, Middle Eastern, and Asian postcolonial artists to deal with in their work?

Very often, women have neither the education nor the resources to exercise their legal rights. The spread of **religious revivalism** in many cases has further eroded these rights, even though advocates of a return to tradition often argue that practices such as veiling, and stoning for women (but not men) caught in adultery, actually enhance their dignity and status. Most Asian, Middle Eastern, and African women continue to be dominated by male family members, are much more limited than men in their career opportunities, and are likely to be less well fed, educated, and healthy than men at comparable social levels.

Neocolonialism, Cold War Rivalries, and Stunted Development

The schemes of nationalist leaders aimed at building an industrial base that would support the rapidly increasing populations of their new nations soon yielded to the economic realities of the postcolonial world. Not only did most of the nations that emerged from colonialism have little in the way of an industrial base, but their means of obtaining one were meager. To buy the machines and hire or train the technical experts that were essential to get industrialization going, the new nations

Nehru, Jawaharlal [juh-WAH-huhr-lahl NAY-roo] (1889–1964) One of Gandhi's disciples; governed India after independence (1947); committed to program of social reform and economic development; preserved civil rights and democracy.

Bhutto, Benazir [BEH-nah-zeer BOO-toh] Twice prime minister of Pakistan in the 1980s and 1990s; first ran for office to avenge her father's execution by the military clique then in power.

religious revivalism An approach to religious belief and practice that stresses the literal interpretation of texts sacred to the religion in question and the application of their precepts to all aspects of social life; increasingly associated with revivalist movements in a number of world religions, including Christianity, Islam, Judaism, and Hinduism.

Artificial Nations and the Rising Tide of Communal Strife

Again and again in the postcolonial era, new states have been torn by internal strife. Often much of what we in the industrialized West know of these areas in Africa, the Middle East, and Asia is connected to the breakdown of their political systems and the human suffering that has resulted. In just the last few years, for example, international news reports have featured descriptions of famines generated by civil wars in Somalia, the Sudan, and Mozambique; by harrowing images of refugees fleeing for their lives from Rwanda, Angola, and Cambodia; by religious riots in India, and mass slaughter in Timor. Western observers are often tempted to take this instability and suffering as proof that the people of these decolonized areas are unfit to rule themselves, that they are incapable of building viable political systems.

Although these responses are understandable given the crisis-focused coverage of the emerging nations by international news agencies, they fail to take into account the daunting obstacles that have confronted African, Middle Eastern, and Asian nation-builders. They ignore the important ways in which Western colonialism contributed to the internal divisions and political weaknesses of newly independent states. They also overlook the deep, often highly disruptive social divisions within Western societies (the long history of racial conflict in the United States, for example, or the vicious civil war in the former European nation of Yugoslavia). Any analysis of the recurring political crises of Africa, the Middle East, and Asia should begin with the realization that nearly all the nations that emerged from decolonization were artificial creations. The division of Africa and Asia by the Western imperialist powers was arbitrary (see, for example, Maps 33.1 and 33.2). Some colonial boundaries cut peoples apart: the Shans of southeast Asia, the Kurds of the Middle East, the Somalis of the horn of east Africa. Some imposed boundaries that tossed together tens, sometimes hundreds, of very different and often hostile ethnic or religious groups. The roads and railways built by the colonizers, the marketing systems they established, and the educational policies they pursued all hardened the unnatural boundaries and divisions estab-

> "Any analysis of the recurring political crises of Africa, the Middle East, and Asia should begin with the realization that nearly all the nations that emerged from decolonization were artificial creations."

lished in the late 19th century. It was these artificial units, these motley combinations of peoples that defied the logic of history and cultural affinity, that African, Middle Eastern, and Asian nationalist leaders had to try to meld into nations after World War II.

The point is not that there was perfect harmony or unity among the peoples of these areas before the coming of colonial rule. As we have seen, there was a great diversity of ethnicity, languages, and religions among the peoples who built civilizations in these areas in the precolonial era. Intense competition, communal conflict, and countless wars occurred between different ethnic and religious groups. European colonization worsened these divisions while suppressing violent confrontations between different communities. In fact, European colonial regimes were built and maintained by divide-and-rule tactics. Very often the colonizers selectively recruited minority ethnic or religious groups into their armies, bureaucracies, and police forces. For example, the Tutsi minority in strife-torn Rwanda and Burundi was much favored by first the Belgians and later the French. In the colonial period, the Tutsis had greater access than the Hutu majority to missionary education, military training, and government positions. These advantages gained a disproportionate share of political power and social standing for the Tutsis after independence. But they also made them the obvious target for persecution by disgruntled Hutus. Rivalry and violent conflict between the two groups has often made a shambles of nation-building initiatives in Rwanda and Burundi over the past several decades and reached catastrophic levels in the mid-1990s. It has continued to simmer in the years since often spilling over into political struggles in neighboring states such as Congo.

The inequities of the colonial order were compounded by the increasingly frequent use of divide-and-rule policies by European officials in the last years of their rule. In addition, the colonizers' desire to scuttle and run from their colonial responsibilities when it was clear that the days of colonial rule were numbered opened the way for ethnic and religious strife. Communal violence in turn prompted the exodus of refugees that accompanied the winning of independence in many colonies, most notably in south Asia, Nigeria, the Belgian Congo, and Palestine. The Western-educated leaders who came to power in these and other newly independent states soon realized that

needed to earn capital they could invest for these ends. Some funds could be accumulated by saving a portion of the state revenues collected from the peasantry. In most cases, however, there was little left once the bureaucrats had been paid, essential public works and education had been funded, and other state expenses had been met. Thus, most emerging nations have relied on the sale of cash crops and minerals to earn the money they need to finance industrialization. As their leaders soon discovered, the structure of the world market worked against them.

The pattern of exchange promoted in the colonial era left most newly independent countries dependent on the export production of two or three food crops or industrial raw materials. The former included cocoa, palm oil, coffee, jute, and hemp. Key among the latter were minerals, such as copper, bauxite, and oil, for which there was a high demand in the industrialized economies of Eu-only a small portion of the population was committed to an overarching nationalist identity. Even among the Westernized elite classes, which had led the decolonization struggle, national loyalties were often shallow and overridden by older, subnational ethnic and religious identities. As a result, many of the new nations of Africa and southeast Asia have been threatened by secessionist movements.

The most spectacular collapse of a new state came in Pakistan, the unwieldy patchwork of a nation the British threw together at the last minute in 1947 to satisfy Jinnah's demands for majority rule in Muslim areas of the Indian subcontinent (Map 33.2). A glance at the map reveals the vulnerability of Pakistan, split into two parts: West and East Pakistan, separated by India's more than 1000 miles of hostile territory. East and West Pakistan also differed greatly in their natural environments and in the ethnic makeup of their peoples and the languages they used. They even differed in their approaches to the Islamic faith that had justified including them in the same country in the first place.

Fragile national ties were eroded rapidly by the East Pakistanis' perception that they had been in effect recolonized by West Pakistan. West Pakistanis held highly disproportionate shares of government jobs and military positions, and West Pakistan received the lion's share of state revenues although East Pakistan generated most of the new nation's foreign earnings. By the early 1970s, East and West Pakistan were locked in a bloody civil war, which ended with the creation of the nation of Bangladesh from East Pakistan in 1972.

India, which relished the chance to contribute to the breakup of Pakistan, has itself been repeatedly threatened by civil strife between different linguistic, religious, and ethnic groups. In the early 1980s, Sikh guerrillas carried on a violent campaign for separation in the north, and the Indian government was forced to intervene militarily in the violent struggle between different ethnic and religious groups in Sri Lanka (Ceylon), its neighbor to the south. In 1997 an avowedly Hindu communalist party came to power in New Delhi, in defiance of the staunch adherence to the principle of a secular state upheld by leading Indian nationalist figures in the colonial era and all of the earlier postindependence governments. The victory of the Bharatya Janata party (BJP) has intensified the anxieties of the large Muslim minority and other non-Hindu religious groups about the possibility of discrimination and even open persecution.

In Africa, where there was even less of a common historical and cultural basis on which to build nationalism than in south or southeast Asia, separatist movements have been a prominent feature of the political life of new states. Secessionist movements have raged from Morocco in the northwest to Ethiopia in the east and Angola in the south (Map 33.1). Civil wars, such as the struggle of the non-Muslim peoples of the southern Sudan against the Muslim rulers from the northern parts of that country, have also abounded. Thus far, none of the secessionist movements have succeeded, although that of the Ibo peoples of eastern Nigeria, who proclaimed an independent state of Biafra in 1967, led to three years of bloody warfare in Africa's most populous nation.

In all cases, the artificial nature of the new nations of Africa, the Middle East, and Asia has proved costly. In addition to internal divisions, boundary disputes between newly independent nations have often led to border clashes and open warfare. India and Pakistan have fought three such wars since 1947. Iraq's Saddam Hussein justified his 1990 annexation of Kuwait with the argument that the tiny but oil-rich Arab "sheikhdom" was an artificial creation of the British colonizers, who had carved Kuwait out of land that historically had been part of Iraq.

Democracy has often been one of the main victims of the tensions between rival ethnic groups within many emerging nations and threats from neighbors without. Politicians in nearly all the new states have been quick to play on communal fears as well as on ethnic and religious loyalties to win votes. As a result, freely elected legislatures have often been dominated by parties representing these special interests. Suspicions that those in power were favoring their own or allied groups has led to endless bickering and stalemates in national legislatures, which have become tempting targets for coup attempts by military strongmen. One of the more predictable reasons these usurpers have given for dictatorial rule has been the need to contain the communal tensions aroused by democratic election campaigns.

QUESTIONS How might colonial policies have been changed to reduce the tensions between different ethnic and religious communities? Why were these measures not taken? What can be done now to alleviate these divisions? Should the United Nations or industrialized nations such as the United States or Japan intervene directly to contain communal clashes or civil wars in Africa and Asia? What is to be done with the rapidly growing refugee populations created by these conflicts?

rope, North America, and increasingly Japan. Since World War II, the prices of these exports—which economists call **primary products**—have not only fluctuated widely but have declined steadily compared to the prices of most of the manufactured goods emerging nations usually buy from the industrialized world. Price fluctuations have created nightmares for planners in developing nations. Revenue estimates from the sale of coffee or copper in years when the price is high are used to plan government projects for building roads, factories, and dams. Market slumps can wipe out these critical funds, thereby retarding economic growth and throwing countries deeply into debt.

African, Middle Eastern, and Asian leaders have been quick to blame the legacy of colonialism and what they have called the **neocolonial economy**—the global economy dominated by the industrialized nations—for the limited returns yielded thus far by their development schemes. Although

primary products Food or industrial crops for which there is a high demand in industrialized economies; prices of such products tend to fluctuate widely; typically the primary exports of Third World economies.

neocolonial economy Industrialized nations' continued dominance of the world economy; ability of the industrialized nations to maintain economic colonialism without political colonialism.

there is much truth to these accusations, they do not tell the whole story. These leaders must also share the responsibility for the slow pace of economic growth in much of the developing world. The members of the educated classes that came to dominate the political and business life of newly independent nations often used their positions to enrich themselves and their relatives at the expense of their societies as a whole. Corruption has been notoriously widespread in most of the new nations. Government controls on the import of goods such as automobiles, television sets, and stereos, which are luxury items beyond the reach of most of the people, have often been lax. As a result, tax revenues and export earnings that could have fueled development have often gone to provide the good life for small minorities within emerging nations. The inability or refusal of many regimes to carry out key social reforms, such as land redistribution, which would spread the limited resources available more equitably over the population, has contributed vitally to the persistence of these patterns.

Badly strapped for investment funds and essential technology, emerging African, Middle Eastern, and Asian nations have often turned to international organizations, such as the World Bank and the International Monetary Fund, or to industrial nations for assistance. Although resources for development have been gained in this way, the price for international assistance has often been high. The industrialized nations have demanded major concessions in return for their aid. These have ranged from commitments to buy the products of, and favor investors from, the lending countries to entering into alliances and permitting military bases on the territory of the client state.

Loans from international lending agencies almost invariably have been granted only after the needy nation agreed to structural adjustments. These are regulations that determine how the money is to be invested and repaid, and they usually involve promises to make major changes in the economy of the borrowing nation. In recent years, these promises have often included a commitment to remove or reduce state subsidies on food and other essential consumer items. State subsidies were designed to keep prices for staple goods at a level that the urban and rural poor—the great majority of the people in almost all emerging nations—could afford. When carried out, subsidy reductions often have led to widespread social unrest, riots, and the collapse or near collapse of postcolonial regimes.

The leaders of the new nations of Africa, the Middle East, and Asia soon felt the need to deliver on the promises of social reform and economic well-being that had rallied support to the nationalist cause. Strategies ranged from populism to dictatorship to rejection of the West.

Post-Colonial Options for Achieving Economic Growth and Social Justice

Depending on their own skills, the talents of their advisors and lieutenants, and the resources at their disposal, leaders in the emerging nations have tackled the daunting task of development with varying degrees of success. Ways have been found to raise the living standards of a significant percentage of the population of some of the emerging nations. But these strategies have rarely benefited the majority. It may be too early to judge the outcomes of many development schemes. But so far, none has proved to be the path to the social justice and general economic development that nationalist leaders saw as the ultimate outcome of struggles for decolonization. Although some countries have done much better than others, successful overall strategies to deal with the challenges facing emerging nations have yet to be devised.

Charismatic Populists and One-Party Rule

One of the least successful responses on the part of leaders who found their dreams for national renewal frustrated has been a retreat into authoritarian rule. This approach has often been disguised by calculated, charismatic appeals for support from the disenfranchised masses. Perhaps the career of Kwame Nkrumah, the leader of Ghana's independence movement, illustrates this pattern best. There is little question that Nkrumah was genuinely committed to social reform and economic uplift for the Ghanaian people during the years of his rise to become the first prime minister of the newly independent west African nation of Ghana in 1957 (Map 33.3). After assuming power, he moved vigorously to initiate programs that would translate his

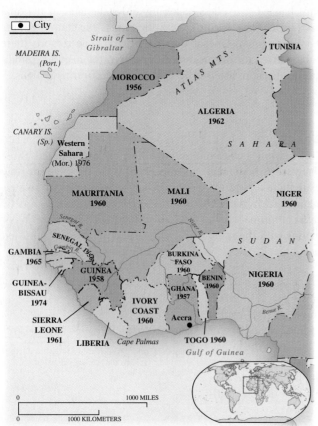

Map 33.3 The New West African Nations Ghana was one of many ethnically fragmented, new African states that came to be dominated by charismatic leaders and then military dictatorships in the Cold War era.

high aspirations for his people into reality. But his ambitious schemes for everything from universal education to industrial development soon ran into trouble.

Kwame Nkrumah

Rival political parties, some representing regional interests and ethnic groups long hostile to Nkrumah, repeatedly challenged his initiatives and tried to block the efforts to carry out his plans. His leftist leanings won support from the Soviet bloc but frightened away Western investors, who had a good deal more capital to plow into Ghana's economy. They also led to growing hostility on the part of the United States, Great Britain, and other influential noncommunist countries. Most devastatingly, soon after independence, the price of cocoa—by far Ghana's largest export crop—began to fall sharply. Tens of thousands of Ghanaian cocoa farmers were hard hit and the resources for Nkrumah's development plans suddenly dried up.

Nkrumah's response to these growing problems was increasingly dictatorial. He refused to give up or cut back on his development plans. As a result, most failed miserably because of the lack of key supplies and official mismanagement. In the early 1960s, he forcibly crushed all political opposition by banning rival parties and jailing other political leaders. He assumed dictatorial powers and ruled through functionaries in his own Convention People's Party.

Kwame Nkrumah on African Unity

Nkrumah also sought to hold on to the loyalty of the masses and mobilize their energies by highly staged "events" and the manipulation of largely invented symbols and traditions that were said to be derived from Ghana's past. Thus, he tried to justify his policies and leadership style with references to a uniquely African brand of socialism and the need to revive African traditions and African civilization. Even before independence, he had taken to wearing the traditional garb of the Ghanaian elite. The very name *Ghana,* which Nkrumah himself proposed for the new nation that emerged from the former Gold Coast colony, had been taken from an ancient African kingdom. The original Ghanaian kingdom actually was centered much farther to the north and had little to do with the peoples of the Gold Coast.

Nkrumah went about the country giving fiery speeches, dedicating monuments to the "revolution," which often consisted of giant statues of himself (Figure 33.5). He also assumed a prominent role in the nonaligned movement that was then sweeping the newly independent nations. His followers' adulation knew no bounds. Members of his captive parliament compared him to Confucius, Muhammad, Shakespeare, and Napoleon and predicted that his birthplace would serve as a "Mecca" for all of Africa's leaders. But his suppression of all opposition and his growing ties to the Communist party, coupled with the rapid deterioration of the Ghanaian economy, increased the ranks of his enemies, who waited for a chance to strike. That chance came early in 1966, when Nkrumah went off on one of his many trips, this time a peace mission to Vietnam. In his absence, he was deposed by a military coup. Nkrumah died in exile in 1972, and Ghana moved in a very different direction under its new military rulers.

Military Responses: Dictatorships and Revolutions

Given the difficulties that leaders such as Nkrumah faced after independence and the advantages the military have in crisis situations, the proliferation of coups in the emerging nations is not surprising. Armed forces have at times been divided by the religious and ethnic rivalries that have been so disruptive in new nations. But the regimentation and emphasis on discipline and in-group solidarity in military training often render soldiers more resistant than other social groups to these forces. In conditions of political breakdown and social conflict, the military possesses the monopoly—or near monopoly—of force that is often essential for restoring order. Their occupational conditioning makes soldiers not only more ready than civilian leaders to use the force at their disposal but less concerned with its destructive consequences. Military personnel also tend to have some degree of technical training, which was usually lacking in the humanities-oriented education of civilian nationalist leaders. Because most military leaders have

Figure 33.5 Many monumental statues of Kwame Nkrumah, such as this one, rose in the towns and villages of Ghana as he tried to cover the failure of his socialist-inspired development programs with dictatorial rule and self-glorification. Although Nkrumah's efforts to cover his regime's failures through self-glorifying displays and pageantry were extreme, they were not unique. The many images of the "great leader" of the moment that one finds in many developing nations are a variation on Nkrumah's tactics. These state campaigns to glorify the dictatorial figures are reminiscent of those mounted by the leaders of the communist revolutions in Russia, China, and Cuba.

been staunchly anticommunist, they have often attracted covert technical and financial assistance from Western governments.

Once in control, military leaders have banned civilian political parties and imposed military regimes of varying degrees of repression and authoritarian control. Yet the ends to which these regimes have put their dictatorial powers have differed greatly. At their worst, military regimes—such as those in Uganda (especially under Idi Amin), Myanmar (formerly Burma), and Congo—have quashed civil liberties while making little attempt to reduce social inequities or improve living standards. These regimes have existed mainly to enrich the military leaders and their allies. Military governments of this sort have been notorious for official corruption and for imprisoning, torturing, or eliminating political dissidents. Understandably uneasy about being overthrown, these regimes have diverted a high proportion of their nations' meager resources, which might have gone for economic development, into expenditures on expensive military hardware. Neither the Western democracies nor the countries of the Soviet bloc have hesitated to supply arms to these military despots.

In a few cases, military leaders have been radical in their approaches to economic and social reform. Perhaps none was more so than **Gamal Abdul Nasser** (Figure 33.6), who took power in Egypt after a military coup in 1952. As we have seen in Chapter 33, the Egyptians won their independence in the mid-1930s except for the lingering British presence in the Suez Canal zone (Map 33.4). But self-centered civilian politicians and the corrupt khedival regime had done little to improve the standard of living of the mass of the Egyptian people. As conditions worsened and Egypt's governing parties did little but rake in wealth for their elitist memberships, revolutionary forces emerged in Egyptian society.

The radical movement that succeeded in gaining power, the **Free Officers movement,** evolved from a secret organization established in the Egyptian army in the 1930s. Founded by idealistic young officers of Egyptian rather than Turco-Egyptian descent, the secret Revolutionary Command Council studied conditions in the country and prepared to seize power in the name of a genuine revolution. For many decades, it was loosely allied to the **Muslim Brotherhood,** another revolutionary alternative to the khedival regime.

Nasser, Gamal Abdul   (1918-1970) Took power in Egypt following a military coup in 1952; enacted land reforms and used state resources to reduce unemployment; ousted Britain from the Suez Canal zone in 1956.

Free Officers movement   Military nationalist movement in Egypt founded in the 1930s; often allied with the Muslim Brotherhood; led coup to seize Egyptian government from khedive in July 1952.

Muslim Brotherhood   Egyptian nationalist movement founded by Hasan al-Banna in 1928; committed to fundamentalist movement in Islam; fostered strikes and urban riots against the khedival government.

Figure 33.6 After the Free Officers seized power in the 1952 coup, a young general named Nasser emerged as the most charismatic and able of a number of rivals for power. Here cheering crowds climb toward a balcony where the new leader of Egypt has been addressing them, and Nasser is embraced by one enthusiastic supporter.

Map 33.4 The Middle East in the Cold War Era As in Africa and over much of Asia, the new states of the Middle East were very often based on the colonies established by the different European powers in the age of high imperialism.

The brotherhood was founded by Hasan al-Banna (Figure 33.7) in 1928. Al-Banna was a schoolteacher who had studied in his youth with the famous Muslim reformer Muhammad Abduh. While at Al-Azhar University in Cairo in the years after World War I, al-Banna had combined a deep interest in scientific subjects with active involvement in student demonstrations in support of Wafd demands for Egyptian independence. In this period, like many other Egyptian students, al-Banna developed contempt for the wealthy minority of Egyptians and Europeans who flourished in the midst of the appalling poverty of most of his people.

To remedy these injustices and rid Egypt of its foreign oppressors, al-Banna founded the Muslim Brotherhood in 1928. Although members of the organization were committed to a revivalist approach to Islam, the brotherhood's main focus, particularly in the early years, was on a program of social uplift and sweeping reforms. The organization became involved in a wide range of activities, from promoting trade unions and building medical clinics to educating women and pushing for land reform. By the late 1930s, the brotherhood's social service had become highly politicized. Al-Banna's followers fomented strikes and urban riots and established militant youth organizations and paramilitary assassination squads. Despite the murder of al-Banna by the khedive Farouk's assassins in 1949, the members of the brotherhood continued to expand its influence in the early 1950s among both middle-class youths and the impoverished masses.

Figure 33.7 Hasan al-Banna, founder of the Muslim Brotherhood, an opposition group in Egypt that established medical clinics and promoted unions, land reform, and women's education.

Sadat, Anwar [AHN-wahr suh-DAHT] Successor to Gamal Abdul Nasser as ruler of Egypt; acted to dismantle costly state programs; accepted peace treaty with Israel in 1973; opened Egypt to investment by Western nations.

After Egypt's humiliating defeats in the first Arab-Israeli War of 1948 and in a clash with the British over the latter's continuing occupation of the Suez Canal zone in 1952, mass anger with a discredited khedival and parliamentary regime gave the officers their chance. In July 1952, an almost bloodless military coup toppled the corrupt khedive Farouk from his jewel-encrusted throne (Figure 33.8).

The revolution had begun. The monarchy was ended, and with the installation of Nasser and the Free Officers, Egyptians ruled themselves for the first time since the 6th century B.C.E. By 1954 all political parties had been disbanded, including the Muslim Brotherhood, which had clashed with its former allies in the military and had been suppressed after an attempt on Nasser's life. Nasser was only one of several officers at the head of the Free Officers movement, and by no means was he initially the most charismatic. But after months of internal power struggles in the officer corps, he emerged as the head of a military government that was deeply committed to revolution.

Nasser and his fellow officers used the dictatorial powers they had won in the coup to force through programs that they believed would uplift the long-oppressed Egyptian masses. They were convinced that only the state had the power to carry out essential social and economic reforms, and thus they began to intervene in all aspects of Egyptian life. Land reform measures were enacted: limits were placed on how much land an individual could own, and excess lands were seized and redistributed to landless peasants. State-financed education through the college level was made available to Egyptians. The government became Egypt's main employer; by 1980, more than 30 percent of Egypt's workforce was on the state payroll. State subsidies were used to lower the price of basic food staples, such as wheat and cooking oil. State-controlled development schemes were introduced that emphasized industrial growth, modeled after the five-year plans of the Soviet Union.

To establish Egypt's economic independence, stiff restrictions were placed on foreign investment. In some cases foreign properties were seized and redistributed to Egyptian investors. Nasser also embarked on an interventionist foreign policy that stressed the struggle to destroy the newly established Israeli state, forge Arab unity, and foment socialist revolutions in neighboring lands. His greatest foreign policy coup came in 1956, when he rallied international opinion to finally oust the British and their French allies from the Suez Canal zone. Despite the setbacks suffered by Egyptian military forces, Nasser made good use of the rare combined backing of the United States and the Soviet Union to achieve his aims in the crisis.

However well intentioned, many of Nasser's initiatives misfired. Land reform efforts were frustrated by bureaucratic corruption and the clever strategies devised by the landlord class to hold on to their estates. State development schemes often lacked proper funding and failed because of mismanagement and miscalculations. Even the Aswan Dam project, the cornerstone of Nasser's development drive, was a fiasco. Egypt's continuing population boom quickly canceled out the additional cultivable lands the dam produced. The dam's interference with the flow of the Nile resulted in increasing numbers of parasites that cause blindness. It also led to a decline in the fertility of farmlands in the lower Nile delta, which were deprived of the rich silt that normally was washed down by the river. Foreign investment funds from the West, which Egypt desperately needed, soon dried up. Aid from the much poorer Soviet bloc could not begin to match what was lost, and much of this assistance was military.

In the absence of sufficient foreign investment and with Egypt's uncontrolled population rising at an alarming rate, the state simply could not afford all the ambitious schemes to which Nasser and the revolutionary officers had committed it. The gap between aspirations and means was increased in the later years of Nasser's reign (in the 1960s) by the heavy costs of his mostly failed foreign adventures, including the disastrous Six-Day War with Israel in 1967.

Although he had to move slowly at first, Nasser's successor, **Anwar Sadat** (AHN-wahr suh-DAHT), had little choice but to dismantle the massive state apparatus that had been created. He favored private rather than state initiatives. During Sadat's tenure in office, the middle class, who had been greatly restricted by Nasser, emerged again as a powerful force. After fighting the Israelis to a stalemate in 1973, Sadat also moved to end the costly confrontation with Israel as well as Egypt's support for revolutionary movements in the Arab world. He expelled the Russians and opened Egypt to aid and investment from the United States and western Europe.

Sadat's shift in direction has been continued by his successor, **Hosni Mubarak** (HOHZ-nee MOO-bahr-uhk). But neither the attempt at genuine revolution led by Nasser nor the move to capitalism and more pro-West positions under his successors has done much to check Egypt's alarming population increases and the corruption of its bloated bureaucracy. Neither path to development has had much effect on the glaring gap between the living conditions of Egypt's rich minority and its impoverished masses. No better gauge of the discontent that is bred by these inequities can be found than the proliferation of Muslim fundamentalist movements. One of these succeeded in assassinating Sadat; others have sustained campaigns aimed at overthrowing the Mubarak regime.

The Indian Alternative: Development for Some of the People

Although the approach to nation-building and economic development followed by the leaders of independent India has shared the Nasserite emphasis on socialism and state intervention, India's experience has differed from Egypt's in several significant ways. To begin with, the Indians have managed to preserve civilian rule throughout the nearly five decades since they won their independence from Great Britain. In fact, in India the military has consistently defended secular democracy against religious extremism and other would-be authoritarian trends. In addition, although India, like Egypt, has been saddled with a crushing burden of overpopulation, it came to independence with a larger industrial and scientific sector, a better communication system and bureaucratic grid, and a larger and more skilled middle class in proportion to its total population than most other emerging nations.

During the first decades of its freedom, India had the good fortune to be governed by leaders such as Jawaharlal Nehru and his allies in the Congress party, who were deeply committed to social reform and economic development as well as the preservation of civil rights and democracy. India's success at the latter has been remarkable. Despite continuous threats of secession by religious and linguistic minorities, as well as poverty, unemployment, and recurring natural disasters, India remains the world's largest functioning democracy. Except for brief periods of rule by coalitions of opposition parties, the Congress party has ruled at the center for most of the independence era. But opposition parties have controlled many state and local governments, and they remain vocal and active in the national parliament. Civil liberties, exemplified by a very outspoken press and free elections, have been upheld to an extent that sets India off from much of the rest of the emerging nations.

Nehru's approach to government and development also differed from Nasser's in his more moderate mix of state and private initiatives. Nehru and his successors pushed state intervention in some sectors but also encouraged foreign investment from countries in both of the rival blocs in the cold war. As a consequence, India has been able to build on its initial advantages in industrial infrastructure and its skilled managerial and labor endowment. Its significant capitalist sector has encouraged ambitious farmers, such as those in the Punjab in the northwest, to invest heavily in the **Green Revolution**—the introduction of improved seed strains, fertilizers, and irrigation as a means of producing higher crop yields. Industrial and agrarian growth has generated the revenue necessary for the Indian government to promote literacy and village development schemes, as well as family planning, village electrification, and other improvement projects in recent decades. Indians have also developed one of the largest and most sophisticated high-tech sectors in the postcolonial world, including its own "silicon valleys" in cities like Bangalore in southern India. From the late 1980s India also provided tens of thousands of computer and Internet experts for advanced industrial societies such as those found in the United States and Europe.

Despite its successes, India has suffered from the same gap between needs and resources that all developing nations have had to face. Whatever the government's intentions—and India has been

Figure 33.8 Growing Egyptian resistance to the British occupation of the Suez Canal zone was expressed in this effigy of a British soldier that was strung up on a Cairo street corner in January 1952. The Arabic banner that accompanies the mock hanging reminds Egyptians of the Dinshawai incident, discussed in Chapter 33, and the need to sustain resistance to British domination. Within months of this protest, mass demonstrations and a military coup freed the Egyptian people from both the British occupation and the repressive khedival regime.

Mubarak, Hosni [HOHZ-nee MOO-bahr-uhk] President of Egypt since 1981, succeeding Anwar Sadat and continuing his policies of cooperation with the West.

Green Revolution Introduction of improved seed strains, fertilizers, and irrigation as a means of producing higher yields in crops such as rice, wheat, and corn; particularly important in the densely populated countries of Asia.

hit by corruption and self-serving politicians, like most nations—there have simply not been the resources to raise the living standards of even a majority of its huge population. The middle class has grown, perhaps as rapidly as that of any postcolonial nation. Its presence is striking in the affluent neighborhoods of cities such as Mombai and Delhi and is proclaimed by the Indian film industry, the world's largest, and in many sitcoms and dramas about the lives of Indian-style yuppies. But as many as 50 percent of India's people have gained little from the development plans and economic growth that have occurred since independence.

In part, this is because population growth has offset economic gains. But social reform has been slow in most areas, both rural and urban. Groups such as the wealthy landlords, who supported the nationalist drive for independence, have continued to dominate the great mass of tenants and landless laborers, just as they did in the precolonial and colonial eras. Some development measures, most notably those associated with the Green Revolution, have greatly favored cultivators with the resources to invest in new seeds and fertilizer. They have increased the gap between rich and poor people over much of rural India. Thus, the poor have paid and will continue to pay the price for Indian gradualism.

Delayed Revolutions: Religious Revivalism and Liberation Movements in Settler Societies

As we saw in Chapter 31, not all African, Middle Eastern or Asian states were conquered and ruled outright by colonizing Western nations in the 19th century. Like Turkey and China, Iran escaped direct colonial domination. But in the late-19th and the first half of the 20th centuries, Iran was reduced to a buffer state between first the British and Russian and later the Soviet and Anglo-American great powers. Partly in response to these external threats, regional strongmen emerged to claim national leadership, such as the self-styled shahs of the Pahlavi dynasty. The second of these shahs in particular, Muhammad Reza, whose throne was rescued by covert interventions by the United States in 1953, ruled the country as an absolutist monarch with a vast secret security force repressing all serious opposition. By the late 1970s, most segments of the population had become dissatisfied with his rule and supportive of the efforts of the Ayatollah Khomeini and his supporters to carry out a religiously-based Shi'a revolution.

In South Africa, a rather different sort of popular resistance had been struggling to overthrow the minority-run apartheid regime through the same post–World War II decades. Locked out of political power and exploited and impoverished economically by the ruling, European-descended Afrikaner settlers, the black African majority and their colored and Indian allies risked prison, torture, and execution in a struggle for social justice and the right to vote and hold office. Their liberation struggle lasted decades longer than the Iranians' overthrow of the shah and arose from rather different forms of oppression. It also led to the establishment of a genuine democracy, which was ultimately denied to the Iranians, who despite periodic elections have been governed by a theocratic regime.

Iran: Religious Revivalism and the Rejection of the West

No path of development adopted by a postcolonial society has provided more fundamental challenges to the existing world order than revolutionary Iran under the direction of the **Ayatollah Ruhollah Khomeini** (EYE-uh-TOH-lah Roo-hah-luh ko-MAY-nee). In many respects, the Khomeini revolution of 1979 was a throwback to the religious fervor of such anticolonial resistance movements as that led by the Mahdi of the Sudan in the 1880s. Core motivations for the followers of both movements were provided by the emphasis on religious purification and the rejoining of religion and politics, which leaders such as the Mahdi and Khomeini have seen as central to the Islamic tradition. The call for a return to the kind of society believed to have existed in the past "golden age" of the prophet Muhammad was central to the policies pursued by both the Mahdist and Iranian regimes once they had gained power. Both movements were aimed at toppling Western-backed governments: the Mahdists' the Anglo-Egyptian presence in the Sudan, Khomeini's the autocratic Iranian shah and the Pahlavi dynasty.

Although societies like Iran and South Africa remained independent or broke free from European colonial control in the post-World War II era, the liberation of the majority of their populations was delayed. Rather, in these instances, different sorts of revolutions than those that had brought decolonization to most of Africa, Asia, and the Middle East were required.

Ayatollah Khomeini

IMAGE

Khomeini, Ayatollah Ruhollah [EYE-uh-TOH-lah Roo-hah-luh ko-MAY-nee] (1900–1989) Religious ruler of Iran following revolution of 1979 to expel the Pahlavi shah of Iran; emphasized religious purification; tried to eliminate Western influences and establish purely Islamic government.

Although they came from the Sunni and Shi'a religious traditions, respectively, both the Mahdi and Khomeini claimed to be divinely inspired deliverers. Each promised to rescue the Islamic faithful from imperialist Westerners and from corrupt and heretical leaders within the Muslim world. Both leaders promised their followers magical protection and instant paradise should they fall while waging the holy war against the heretics and infidels. Each leader sought to build a lasting state and social order on the basis of what were believed to be Islamic precedents. Thus, each revivalist movement aimed at defending and restoring what its leaders believed to be the true beliefs, traditions, and institutions of Islamic civilization. The leaders of both movements sought to spread their revolutions to surrounding areas, both Muslim and infidel, and each believed he was setting in motion forces that would eventually sweep the entire globe.

Though proclaimed as an alternative path for development that could be followed by the rest of the emerging nations, Khomeini's revolution owed its initial success in seizing power to a combination of circumstances that was unique to Iran (Map 33.4). Like China, Iran had not been formally colonized by the European powers but rather had been reduced to a sphere of informal influence, divided between Great Britain and Russia. As a result, neither the bureaucratic nor the communication infrastructures that accompanied colonial takeovers were highly developed there. Nor did a substantial Western-educated middle class emerge. Thus, the impetus for "modernization" came suddenly and was imposed from above by the Pahlavi shahs. The initiatives taken by the second shah in particular, which were supported by Iran's considerable oil wealth, wrenched Iran out of the isolation and backwardness in which most of the nation lived until the mid-20th century. The shah had fled Iran in the early 1950s after a staunch nationalist leader named Mohammed Mosaddeq rose to power. But the shah was restored by a CIA-engineered coup in 1953, designed both to counter the growing influence of the Soviet-dominated Iranian communist party and insure Anglo-American control over Iran's vast oil reserves. Once back in power, he tried to impose economic development and social change through government directives. Although advances occurred, the regime managed to alienate the great mass of the Iranian people in the process.

The shah's dictatorial and repressive regime deeply offended the emerging middle classes, whom he considered his strongest potential supporters. His flaunting of Islamic conventions and his neglect of Islamic worship and religious institutions enraged the *ayatollahs,* or religious experts. They also alienated the *mullahs,* or local prayer leaders and mosque attendants, who guided the religious and personal lives of the great majority of the Iranian population. The favoritism the shahs showed foreign investors and a handful of big Iranian entrepreneurs with personal connections to highly placed officials angered the smaller bazaar merchants, who had long maintained close links with the mullahs and other religious leaders. The shah's half-hearted land reform schemes alienated the land-owning classes without doing much to improve the condition of the rural poor. Even the urban workers, who benefited most from the boom in construction and light industrialization the shah's development efforts had stimulated, were dissatisfied. In the years before the 1979 revolution, a fall in oil prices resulted in an economic slump and widespread unemployment in urban areas such as the capital, Tehran.

Although he had treated his officers well, the shah had badly neglected the military rank-and-file, especially in the army. So when the crisis came in 1978, the shah found that few soldiers were prepared to defend his regime. His armies refused to fire on the growing crowds that demonstrated for his removal and the return of Khomeini, then in exile in Paris. Dying of cancer and disheartened by what he saw as betrayal by his people and by allies such as the United States, the shah fled without much of a fight. Khomeini's revolution triumphed over a regime that looked powerful but proved exceptionally vulnerable.

After coming to power, Khomeini, defying the predictions of most Western "experts" on Iranian affairs, followed through on his promises of radical change. Constitutional and leftist parties allied to the revolutionary movement were brutally repressed. Moderate leaders were replaced quickly by radical religious figures who were eager to obey Khomeini's every command. The "satanic" influences of the United States and western Europe were purged. At the same time, Iran also distanced itself from the atheistic communist world. Secular influences in law and government were supplanted by strict Islamic legal codes, which included such punishments as the amputation of limbs for theft and stoning for women caught in adultery. Veiling became obligatory for all women, and

 Islam and the State in the Middle East: Ayatollah Khomeini's Vision of Islamic Government

Figure 33.9 Women played a vital role in the mass demonstrations that toppled the shah of Iran and brought Ayatollah Khomeini to power in 1979. In many ways women's support for political movements in the postcolonial period was a continuation of their active participation in earlier struggles against European colonial domination. But increasingly in the postcolonial era, women have organized not only to promote political change, but to force social and economic reforms intended to improve the quality of their own lives as women.

the career prospects for women of the educated middle classes, who had been among the most favored by the shah's reforms, suddenly were limited drastically (Figure 33.9).

Khomeini's planners also drew up grand schemes for land reform, religious education, and economic development that accorded with the dictates of Islam. Most of these measures came to little because soon after the revolution, Saddam Hussein, the military leader of neighboring Iraq, sought to take advantage of the turmoil in Iran by annexing its western, oil-rich provinces. The Iran-Iraq War that resulted swallowed up Iranian energies and resources for almost the entire decade after Khomeini came to power. The struggle became a highly personal vendetta for Khomeini, who was determined to destroy Saddam Hussein and punish the Iraqis. His refusal to negotiate peace caused heavy losses and untold suffering to the Iranian people. This suffering continued long after it was clear that the Iranians' aging military equipment and handful of allies were no match for Hussein's more advanced military hardware and an Iraqi war machine bankrolled by its oil-rich Arab neighbors, who were fearful that Khomeini's revolution might spread to their own countries.

As the support of the Western powers, including the United States (despite protestations of neutrality), for the Iraqis increased, the position of the isolated Iranians became increasingly intolerable. Hundreds of thousands of poorly armed and half-trained Iranian conscripts, including tens of thousands of untrained and nearly weaponless boys, died before Khomeini finally agreed to a humiliating armistice in 1988. Peace found revolutionary Iran in shambles. Few of its development initiatives had been pursued, and shortages in food, fuel, and the other necessities of life were widespread.

Iran's decade-long absorption in the war and its continuing isolation makes it impossible to assess the potential of the religious revivalist, anti-Western option for other postcolonial nations. What had seemed at first a viable path to independent development had become mired in brutal internal repression and misguided and failed development schemes. By the 1990s, however, although control by Islamic leaders continued, more open elections began to occur in Iran, presenting new alternatives for the future. In the past decade, these trends have been reversed by the increasing hostility of the United States, which has greatly strengthened the hand of the religious hardliners and opened the way for the repression of moderate, pro-democracy forces through election reverses and political repression.

South Africa: The Apartheid State and Its Demise

South Africa was by no means the only area still under some form of colonial dominance decades after India gained its independence in 1947. Portugal, the oldest and long considered the weakest of the European colonizers, held onto Angola, Mozambique, and its other African possessions until the mid-1970s. Until 1980, Zimbabwe (formerly Southern Rhodesia) was run by white settlers, who had unilaterally declared their independence from Great Britain. Southwest Africa became fully free of South African control only in 1989, and some of the smaller islands in the West Indies and the Pacific remain under European or American rule to the present day.

By the 1970s, however, South Africa was by far the largest, most populous, richest, and most strategic area where most of the population had yet to be liberated from colonial domination. Since the 1940s, the white settlers, particularly the Dutch-descended Afrikaners, had solidified their internal control of the country under the leadership of the Nationalist party. In stages and through a series of elections in which the blacks, who made up the majority of South Africans, were not allowed to vote, the Nationalists won complete independence from Great Britain in 1960. From 1948, when the Nationalist party first came to power, the Afrikaners moved to institutionalize white supremacy and white minority rule by passing thousands of laws that, taken together, made up the system of apartheid (see Chapter 30) that dominated all aspects of South African life until the 1990s.

Apartheid was designed not only to ensure a monopoly of political power and economic dominance for the white minority, both British- and Dutch-descended, but also to impose a system of extreme segregation on all races of South Africa in all aspects of their lives. Separate and patently unequal facilities were established for different racial groups for recreation, education, housing, work, and medical care. Dating and sexual intercourse across racial lines were strictly prohibited, skilled and high-paying jobs were reserved for white workers, and nonwhites were required to carry passes that listed the parts of South Africa where they were allowed to work and live. If caught by the police without their passes or in areas where they were not permitted to travel, nonwhite South Africans were routinely given stiff jail sentences.

Spatial separation was also organized on a grander scale by the creation of numerous **homelands** within South Africa, each designated for the main ethnolinguistic or "tribal" groups within the black African population. Though touted by the Afrikaners as the ultimate solution to the racial "problem," the homelands scheme would have left the black African majority with a small portion of some of the poorest land in South Africa. Because the homelands were overpopulated and poverty-stricken, the white minority was guaranteed a ready supply of cheap black labor to work in their factories and mines and on their farms. Denied citizenship in South Africa proper, these laborers would have been forced eventually to return to the homelands, where they had left their wives and children while emigrating in search of work.

To maintain the blatantly racist and inequitable system of apartheid, the white minority had to build a police state and expend a large portion of the federal budget on a sophisticated and well trained military establishment. Because of the land's great mineral wealth, the Afrikaner nationalists were able to find the resources to fund their garrison state for decades. Until the late 1980s, the government prohibited all forms of black protest and brutally repressed even nonviolent resistance. Black organizations such as the **African National Congress** were declared illegal, and African leaders such as **Walter Sisulu** and **Nelson Mandela** were shipped off to maximum-security prisons. Other leaders, such as **Steve Biko,** one of the young organizers of the Black Consciousness movement, were murdered while in police custody.

Through spies and police informers, the regime tried to capitalize on personal and ethnic divisions within the black majority community. Favoritism was shown to some leaders and groups to keep them from uniting with others in all-out opposition to apartheid. With all avenues of constitutional negotiation and peaceful protest closed, many advocates of black majority rule in a multiracial society turned to guerrilla resistance from the 1960s onward. The South African government responded in the 1980s by declaring a state of emergency, which simply intensified the restrictions already in place in the garrison state. The government repeatedly justified its repression by labeling virtually all black protest as communist-inspired and playing on the racial fears of the white minority.

Through most of the 1970s and early 1980s, it appeared that the hardening hostility between the unyielding white minority and the frustrated black majority was building to a very violent upheaval. But from the late 1980s, countervailing forces were taking hold in South African society. An international boycott greatly weakened the South African economy. In addition, the South African army's costly and futile involvement in wars in neighboring Namibia and Angola seemed to presage never-ending struggles against black liberation movements within the country. Led by the courageous **F. W. de Klerk,** moderate Afrikaner leaders pushed for reforms that began to dismantle the system of apartheid. The release of key black political prisoners, such as the dramatic freeing of Nelson Mandela in 1990, signaled that at long last the leaders of the white majority were ready to negotiate the future of South African politics and society. Permission for peaceful mass demonstrations and ultimately the enfranchisement of all adult South Africans for the 1994 elections provided a way out of the dead end in which the nation was trapped under apartheid.

The well run and remarkably participatory 1994 elections brought to power the African National Congress party, led by Nelson Mandela, who became the first black president of South Africa. Mandela proved to be one of the most skillful and respected political leaders on the world

homelands   Under apartheid, areas in South Africa designated for ethno-linguistic groups within the black African population; such areas tend to be overpopulated and poverty-stricken.

A Liberal White Journalist on Apartheid

African National Congress   Black political organization within South Africa; pressed for end to policies of apartheid; sought open democracy leading to black majority rule; until the 1990s declared illegal in South Africa.

Sisulu, Walter   (1912–2003) Black African leader who, along with Nelson Mandela, opposed apartheid system in South Africa.

Mandela, Nelson   (b. 1918) Long-imprisoned leader of the African National Congress party; worked with the ANC leadership and F. W. de Klerk's supporters to dismantle the apartheid system from the mid-1980s onward; in 1994, became the first black prime minister of South Africa after the ANC won the first genuinely democratic elections in the country's history.

Biko, Steve   (1946–1977) An organizer of Black Consciousness movement in South Africa, in opposition to apartheid; murdered while in police custody.

de Klerk, F. W.   White South African prime minister in the late 1980s and early 1990s. Working with Nelson Mandela and the African National Congress, de Klerk helped to dismantle the apartheid system and opened the way for a democratically elected government that represented all South Africans for the first time.

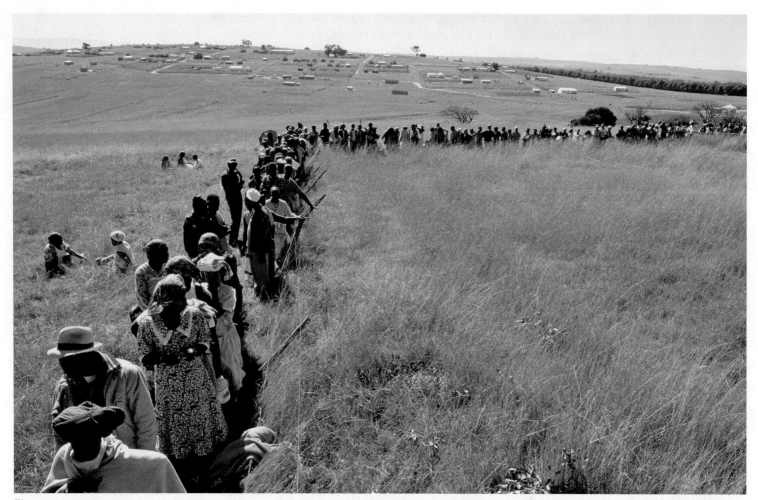

Figure 33.10 This photograph of a long line of newly enfranchised citizens waiting to vote in South Africa provides a striking contrast with the decreasing participation in elections in the United States and other older democracies in the West. For the first time, the Bantu-speaking peoples, coloreds, and Indians who make up the vast majority of South Africa's population were allowed to vote in free elections. Their determination to exercise their hard-won right to vote was demonstrated by the peoples' willingness to wait, often in stifling heat, for many hours in the long lines that stretched from polling stations throughout the country.

scene as well as a moderating force in the potentially volatile South African arena. The peaceful surrender of power by F. W. de Klerk's losing party, which was supported by most of the white minority, suggested that a pluralist democracy might well succeed in South Africa (Figure 33.10). But major obstacles remain. Bitter interethnic rivalries within the black majority community, which periodically flared into bloody battles between Zulus and Xhosas in 1990s, have yet to be fully resolved. Hard-line white supremacist organizations among the Afrikaners continue to defy the new regime. And the tasks of reforming the institutions and redistributing the wealth of South Africa in ways that will make for a just and equitable social order are formidable. Well into the 21st century, South Africa is likely to remain one of the most interesting and promising social experiments of an age in which communalism and ethnic hostility threatened to engulf much of the globe.

Globalization and Postcolonial Societies

Although many of the areas colonized by the industrialized nations of the West had participated in long-distance trade from early times, colonial rule greatly intensified their integration into the capitalist-dominated world system. Colonization also brought more remote areas that had been only marginally affected by cross-cultural trade into the world system for the first time. As we have seen in Chapter 24 and the present chapter, new market linkages not only affected the elites and trading classes of African, Middle Eastern, and Asian societies, but they also increasingly involved the peasants, who made up the great majority of the population of colonial societies, as well as smaller numbers of workers in the towns and cities.

In the postcolonial era, this process of global market integration has accelerated steadily. One key feature of advancing globalization has been the specialized production of mineral and agricultural exports for foreign consumption. Another has been the growing proportion of uprooted farmers and urban laborers in postcolonial societies employed in factories manufacturing clothing, household furnishings, audiovisual equipment, and other consumer goods for sale overseas, particularly in wealthy societies such as those in North America, western Europe, and Japan. These shifts have greatly increased trading links and economic independence between postcolonial societies and those that had formerly colonized them.

The pervasiveness of these connections in the daily lives of peoples around the globe can be readily seen in the shoes, clothing, and watches worn by the teacher and students in your class, and by the equipment and furnishings of your classrooms. Poll the class to determine where these items and other school supplies were produced. Discuss household and other personal items that were likely to have been manufactured, or at least assembled, in similar locales. Then consider the conditions under which the laborers who made these products were likely to have worked, and the international corporations that oversee and market these products.

QUESTIONS Who benefits the most from the profits made in the international marketing of goods from postcolonial societies? How does the fact they are imported in massive quantities affect the wages and working conditions of American factory laborers? What measures can be taken to improve the situation of both workers in emerging nations and those in the United States, or are the interests of the two irreconcilable?

Global Connections

Postcolonial Nations in the Cold War World Order

The years of independence for the nations that emerged from the colonial empires in Asia, the Middle East, and Africa have been filled with political and economic crises and social turmoil, and tensions between tradition and change. At the same time, it is important to put the recent history of these areas in a larger perspective. Most of the new nations that emerged from colonialism have been in existence for only a few decades. They came to independence with severe handicaps, many of which were a direct legacy of their colonial experiences. It is also important to remember that developed countries, such as the United States, took decades filled with numerous boundary disputes and outright wars to reach their current size and structure. Nearly a century after the original 13 colonies broke from Great Britain and formed the United States, a civil war, the most costly war in the nation's history, was needed to preserve the union. If one takes into account the artificial nature of the emerging nations, most have held together rather well.

What is true in politics is true of all other aspects of the postcolonial experience of the African, Middle Eastern, and Asian peoples. With much lower populations and far fewer industrial competitors, as well as the capacity to draw on the resources of much of the rest of the world, European and North American nations had to struggle to industrialize and thereby achieve a reasonable standard of living for most of their people. Even with these advantages, the human cost in terms of horrific working conditions and urban squalor was enormous, and we are still paying the high ecological price. African, Middle Eastern, and Asian countries (and, as we saw in Chapter 27, this includes Japan) have had few or none of the West's advantages. Most of the emerging nations have begun the "great ascent" to development burdened by excessive and rapidly increasing populations that overwhelm the limited resources that developing nations often must export to earn the capital to buy food and machines. The emerging nations struggle to establish a place in the world market system that is structured in favor of the established industrial powers.

Despite the cultural dominance of the West, which was one of the great legacies or burdens of the colonial era, Asian, Middle Eastern, and African thinkers and artists have achieved a great deal. If much of this achievement has depended on Western models, one should not be surprised, given the educational backgrounds and personal experiences of the emerging nations' first generations of leaders. The challenge for the coming generations will be to find genuinely African, Middle Eastern, and Asian solutions to the problems that have stunted political and economic development in the postcolonial nations. The solutions arrived at are likely to vary a great deal, given the diversity of the nations and societies involved. They are also likely to be forged from a combination of Western influences and the ancient and distinguished traditions of civilized life that have been nurtured by African, Middle Eastern, and Asian peoples for millennia.

Further Readings

Much of the prolific literature on political and economic development in the emerging nations is focused on individual countries, and it is more helpful to know several cases in some depth than to try to master them all. Robert Heilbroner's writings, starting with *The Great Ascent* (1961), still provide the most sensible introduction to challenges to the new states in the early decades of independence. Peter Worsley's *The Third World* (1964) offers a provocative, if somewhat disjointed, supplement to Heilbroner's many works. Though focused mainly on south and southeast Asia, Gunnar Myrdal's *Asian Drama,* 3 vols. (1968), is the best exploration in a single cultural area of the complexities of the challenges to development. A good overview of the history of postindependence south Asia can be found in W. N. Brown, *The United States and India, Pakistan, and Bangladesh* (1984), despite its misleadingly Western-centric title, and Ramachandra Guha's *After Gandhi* (2007). Perhaps the best account of Indian politics is contained in Paul Brass, *The Politics of India Since Independence* (1990), in the *New Cambridge History of India* series. On development policy in India, see Guha and Francine R. Frankel, *India's Political Economy, 1947–1977* (1978).

Ali Mazrui and Michael Tidy, *Nationalism and New States in Africa* (1984), provides a good survey of developments throughout Africa. Also useful are S. A. Akintoye, *Emergent African States* (1976), and H. Bretton, *Power and Politics in Africa* (1973). Frederick Cooper's *Africa Since 1940: The Past of the Present* (2002) traces the struggles for nationhood and development into the first decade of the 21st century. For the Middle East, John Waterbury's *The Egypt of Nasser and Sadat* (1983), and Tim Mitchell's *Rule of Experts* (2002) provide a detailed analyses of the politics of development.

On military coups, see Ruth First, *The Barrel of a Gun* (1971), and S. Decalo, *Coups and Army Rule in Africa* (1976). A fine analysis of the literature on the Iranian revolution is provided in Charles Kurzman's *The Unthinkable Revolution in Iran* (2004). Shaul Bakhash's *The Reign of the Ayatollahs* (1984), and R. K. Ramazani's *Revolutionary Iran* (1988) are among the more insightful of many books that have appeared about Iran since the revolution. Brian Bunting, *The Rise of the South African Reich* (1964), traces the rise of the apartheid regime in great (and polemical) detail, while Gail Gerhart, *Black Power in South Africa* (1978), is one of the better studies devoted to efforts to tear that system down. Nelson Mandela's *Long Walk to Freedom* (1994) is absolutely essential to understanding the latter processes. Among the many fine African, Middle Eastern, and Asian authors whose works are available in English, some of the best include (for Africa) Chinua Achebe, Wole Soyinka, and Ousmene Sembene; (for India) R. K. Narayan and V. S. Naipaul; (for Egypt) Nawal el Saadawi and Naguib Mahfouz; and (for Indonesia) Mochtar Lubis and P. A.

Toer. For white perspectives on the South African situation, the fictional works of Nadine Gordimer and J. M. Coetzee are superb.

On the Web

A timeline for decolonization is provided at http://smccd.net/accounts/helton/decoloni.htm and http://campus.northpark.edu/history/WebChron/World/Decolonization.html. An overview of famed African novelist Chinua Achebe's writing on imperialism and decolonization can be found at http://www.postcolonialweb.org/achebe/achebeov.html and http://www.webster.edu/~barrettb/achebe.htm.

Kwame Nkrumah's classic indictment of neocolonialism can be found at http://www.fhsu.edu/history/virtual/nkrumah.htm, while a classically neoconservative view condemning neocolonialism, but not modernization, is offered at http://www.afbis.com/analysis/neo-colonialism.html. The postcolonial burdens of African leaders are addressed at sites devoted to Léopold Senghor (http://web.uflib.ufl.edu/cm/africana/senghor.htm) and the life and speeches of Tanzania's Julius Nyerere (http://www.hartford-hwp.com/archives/30/index-fd.html). The life of Nelson Mandela is explored at http://www.pbs.org/wgbh/pages/frontline/shows/mandela/ and http://www.anc.org.za/people/mandela.html.

Gamal Abdul Nasser's cold war era experiments with Arab socialism as the best means of negotiating modernization are discussed at http://www.arab.net/egypt/et_nasser.htm and http://lexicorient.com/e.o/nasser.htm. The debate over the role of religion as a solution to the moral malaise as well as the disparity of wealth that has come to characterize the postmodern era is illuminated by the works of Hasan al-Banna of the Muslim Brotherhood (http://www.nmhschool.org/tthornton/hasan_al.php and http://en.wikipedia.org/wiki/Hassan_al_Banna) and the life of Iran's Ayatollah Ruhollah Khomeini (http://www.iranchamber.com/history/rkhomeini/ayatollah_khomeini.php and http://www.asiasource.org/society/khomeini.cfm). For further information regarding Khomeini's role as the supreme leader of the Islamic revolution in Iran, see http://www.bbc.co.uk/persian/revolution/rev_01.shtml and http://www.fordham.edu/halsall/mod/1979khom1.html. Possible moderating trends in this seedbed of the Islamic movement are analyzed at http://www.brown.edu/Departments/Anthropology/publications/IranisChanging.htm and http://www.brown.edu/Departments/Anthropology/Beeman.html.

A useful review of India's first 50 years of independence may be found at http://www.itihaas.com/independent/contrib7.html. Jawaharlal Nehru's views on Marxism, capitalism, and nonalignment are available at http://www.fordham.edu/halsall/mod/1941nehru.html. His commitment to world disarmament (http://www.indianembassy.org/policy/Disarmament/India_Disarmament.htm) failed to move the world, and as a result, India later went down the path to nuclear confrontation with Pakistan. The growing place of religion in Indian political life, which Nehru would have also opposed, is embodied in the platform of the Bharatiya Janata Party (http://www.bjp.org/). Indira Gandhi's role in postcolonial India is explored at http://www.sscnet.ucla.edu/southasia/History/Independent/Indira.html. Two views of the moderniza-

tion policies pursued by her son Rajiv are offered at http://www
.sscnet.ucla.edu/southasia/History/Independent/Rajiv.html and
http://en.wikipedia.org/wiki/Rajiv_Gandhi. Parallels between the
lives of Indira Gandhi and Benazir Bhuto of Pakistan can be explored at http://www.ajc.com/news/content/news/stories/2007/
12/27/bhuttoatlanta_1228.html and http://www.thenation.com/
doc/20080107/crossette2.

AP* Test Prep

1. The boundaries of many contemporary states, especially
   African nations,

   (A) generally conform to elements of physical geography
        such as rivers.

   (B) have been much rearranged since independence.

   (C) are representative of ethnic realities in the region or
        continent.

   (D) were set by colonial rivalries irrespective of ethnic or
        cultural realities.

2. In order to rule their colonies, Europeans frequently

   (A) established a parliamentary system and allowed their
        subjects to vote.

   (B) played various groups against each other.

   (C) tried to reduce male dominance over women.

   (D) failed to utilize traditional native elites.

   (E) encouraged land reform and industrialization.

3. The most destabilizing aspect of the 20th-century demographic transition in Africa and Asia has been the

   (A) rapid growth of the older segment of the population.

   (B) inability to expand literacy in part because of rapid
        population growth.

   (C) rise of infant and child mortality.

   (D) massive migration to cities.

4. The army has become an important institution in many nations since 1950 for all of these reasons EXCEPT:

   (A) army units are usually disciplined and their loyalty is to
        their officers rather than to religion or ethnicity.

   (B) it has a monopoly on force and power within society.

   (C) soldiers and officers are often more educated and tech-
        nically trained than the overall population.

   (D) no other indigenous institutions survived the colonial era.

5. India differs from other ex-colonial 20th-century nations
   such as Pakistan, Egypt, or Nigeria in that

   (A) its army constantly intervenes in national politics.

   (B) it has avoided overpopulation.

   (C) it preserved civilian and democratic rule since inde-
        pendence.

   (D) it has avoided sectarian religious strife.

6. Egypt's path toward independence and development

   (A) is similar to India's in that Egypt has used the state to
        bring about limited land reform and advances in edu-
        cation.

   (B) is similar to Iran's in that it has pursued the path of Is-
        lamic fundamentalism.

   (C) included the acceptance of British and French control
        of the Suez Canal.

   (D) has enabled it to overcome the forces of poverty and
        overpopulation.

7. During the last decades of the 20th century, the event that
   most determined Iranian development has been the

   (A) failure to develop an industrial sector.

   (B) Islamic revolution of the ayatollahs.

   (C) alliance with the United States.

   (D) war with Iraq.

Free-Response Question

Compare and contrast nationalism in Africa and in India in the
20th century.

34 Rebirth and Revolution: Nation-Building in East Asia and the Pacific Rim

East Asia in the Postwar Settlements

The Pacific Rim: More Japans?

VISUALIZING THE PAST: Pacific Rim Growth

THINKING HISTORICALLY: The Pacific Rim as a U.S. Policy Issue

Mao's China: Vanguard of World Revolution?

DOCUMENT: Women in the Revolutionary Struggle for Social Justice

Colonialism and Revolution in Vietnam

GLOBAL CONNECTIONS: East Asia and the Pacific Rim in the Contemporary World

Well into young adulthood, Yun Ruo seemed to be a person blessed by good fortune. Though he grew up in post-1945 China, a nation wracked by revolutionary turmoil and state repression, Yun lived a life of relative privilege and security—until the late 1960s. His father, Liu Shaoqui, had long been one of the most prominent leaders of the Communist party, and his family was firmly ensconced in the elite strata of the People's Republic. Yun was a brilliant and hard-working student who in his late teens had gained admission into the highly competitive and prestigious Beijing Aeronautics Institute. In the late 1950s, he was rewarded for his academic accomplishments by being offered the opportunity to further his technical training in the Soviet Union, which at the time was a major supporter of the struggling People's Republic of China.

In Russia, as in China, Yun went from one career achievement to the next, unaffected by the state's forcible mobilization of teachers, students, and other professionals into labor brigades for the Maoists' misguided Great Leap Forward campaign, which was launched in 1958. But when the assault on the elite social strata broadened to doctors, government officials, scientists, and technicians during the Cultural Revolution of 1967–1970, Yun found himself caught up in the persecution by the Red Guards and other political factions proclaiming their fanatical loyalty to Chairman Mao. In this more radical surge of anti-elitism in the People's Re-

public, intellectuals and party functionaries were not only sent into the countryside to labor among the peasants, but many were publicly purged, imprisoned, and killed (see Figure 34.1).

Reflecting the deep paranoia and widespread persecution of the times, Yun was branded an enemy of the revolution, ostensibly because he had fallen in love with a Russian woman while a student in the Soviet Union. Once Communist China's main backer, the Soviet Union had increasingly distanced itself from China beginning in the early 1960s, and by the end of the decade it was denounced as antirevolutionary and a threat to the People's Republic. But Yun's romantic ties were largely a pretext to use him in a campaign of vilification against his father, Liu Shaoqi.

In response to political pressures surrounding the shifting Maoist stance toward the Soviets, Yun's family forbade him to marry his Russian lover. His family confiscated the couple's love letters, which had allowed them to sustain a long-distance relationship after Yun returned to China, and the letters were passed on to government functionaries. No less a personage than Jiang Qing (Mao's wife) branded Yun a spy, and he was later convicted of treason by a "people's court." Sentenced to eight years in prison, Yun was released in 1974, when the fervor of the Cultural Revolution had begun to fade. But his experiences in prison left him mentally unbalanced, and he died several years later of a lung disease that was probably contracted during his imprisonment. ■

The turmoil and uncertainty—and finally brutality—that enveloped Yun Ruo's life were dominant motifs throughout much of east and southeast Asia during the post–World War II era. Societies across both regions had been deeply disrupted, even devastated, by the Pacific war. Most of Japan's cities were smoldering ruins; its islands were occupied and ruled by the U.S. military, and its people were threatened by starvation, disease, homelessness, and utter despair. China, Vietnam, and Korea, which had been caught up in the war to varying degrees, were embroiled in civil wars that in Korea and Vietnam would prolong wartime privations and destruction for many years. The long civil war in China was decided by the victory of the Communists in 1949 and the flight of the Guomindang to Taiwan. But persecution of the fledgling regime's perceived enemies would continue through

Figure 34.1 Mass *demonstrations*, such as the one in the photo that was staged in front of the Gate of Heavenly Peace in Beijing at the height of the Cultural Revolution in the mid-1960s, showed both the participants' adulation of Mao Zedong and their capacity to intimidate his political rivals.

much of the following decade and, as we have seen through the experience of Yun Ruo, spread to loyal supporters of the revolution and across society at large by the late 1950s and 1960s.

By the 1980s a number of non-communist nations on the **Pacific Rim,** including Japan, Korea, Singapore, Taiwan, Thailand, and Malaysia, had joined the ranks of developed nations. Their economic successes and political stability, as well as some of the challenges they have posed in recent decades for older developing societies, such as the United States, will be considered in the following chapter. By the 1980s both communist Vietnam and China had also begun to recover from foreign occupations, civil strife, and revolutionary turmoil. Since then, China in particular has emerged as a global economic power, and Vietnam has increasingly opened its tightly controlled society to the outside world. Altogether the nations of east Asia and the Pacific Rim have become major economic, and potentially political, players in the international arena of the early 21st century.

Pacific Rim Region including Japan, South Korea, Singapore, Hong Kong, Taiwan; typified by rapid growth rates, expanding exports, and industrialization; either Chinese or strongly influenced by Confucian values; considerable reliance on government planning and direction, limitations on dissent and instability.

Taiwan Island off Chinese mainland; became refuge for Nationalist Chinese regime under Chiang Kai-shek as Republic of China in 1948; successfully retained independence with aid of United States; rapidly industrialized after 1950s.

East Asia in the Postwar Settlements

The victors in World War II had some reasonably clear ideas about how east Asia was to be restructured. Korea was divided between a Russian zone of occupation in the north and an American zone in the south. The island of **Taiwan** was restored to China, which in principle was ruled by a Guomindang government headed by Chiang Kai-shek. The United States regained the Philippines and pledged to grant independence quickly, though retaining some key military bases. The European powers sought to restore control over their colonies in Vietnam, Malaya, and Indonesia. Japan was occupied by American forces bent on introducing major changes that would prevent a recurrence of military aggression.

At the end of World War II a zone of reasonably stable noncommunist states developed along the Pacific Rim. Linked to the West, these nations maintained a Neo-Confucian emphasis on the importance of conservative politics and a strong state.

1940 C.E.	1955 C.E.	1970 C.E.
1942 Japanese occupation of French Indochina	Mid–1950s Buildup of U.S. advisors in South Vietnam	1975 Communist victory in Vietnam; collapse of Republic of South Vietnam
1945 Ho Chi Minh proclaims the Republic of Vietnam	1957 "Let a Hundred Flowers Bloom" campaign in China	1976 Deaths of Zhou Enlai and Mao Zedong; purge of Gang of Four
1948 U.S.-sponsored Republic of (South) Korea established	1958–1960 "Great Leap Forward" in China	1994 Death of North Korean leader Kim Il-Sung
1949 Communist victory in China; People's Republic of China established	1960 South Korean nationalist leader Syngman Rhee forced from office by student demonstrations	
1950–1951 Purge of the landlord class in China	1963 Beginning of state family planning in China	
1950–1953 Korean War	1965–1968 Cultural Revolution in China	
1952 U.S. occupation of Japan ends	1965–1973 Direct U.S. military intervention in Vietnam	
1953 Beginning of China's first five-year plan	1968 Tet offensive in Vietnam	
1954 French defeated at Dien Bien Phu; Geneva accords, French withdrawal from Vietnam; beginning of the Sino-Soviet split		

After Empire: Independent Asia   MAP

Not surprisingly, the Pacific regions of Asia did not quickly settle into agreed-upon patterns. A little more than a decade after the war's end, not only the Philippines but also Indonesia, Malaysia, Singapore and Burma were independent, as part of the postwar tide of decolonization (Map 34.1). Taiwan was still ruled by Chiang Kai-shek, but the Chinese mainland was in the hands of a new and powerful communist regime. Chiang's nationalist regime claimed a mission to recover China, but in fact Taiwan was a separate republic. Korea remained divided but had undergone a brutal north–south conflict in which only U.S. intervention preserved South Korea's independence. Japan was one of the few Pacific regions where matters had proceeded somewhat according to plan, as the nation began to recover economically while accepting a very different political structure.

Japanese Recovery

Japan in 1945 was in shambles. Its cities were burned, its factories destroyed or idle, its people impoverished and shocked by the fact of surrender and the trauma of bombing, including the atomic devastation of Hiroshima and Nagasaki. However, like the industrial nations of the West, Japan was capable of reestablishing a vigorous economy with surprising speed. Its occupation by U.S. forces, eager to reform Japan but also eager to avoid punitive measures, provided an opportunity for a new period of selective westernization.

The American occupation government, headed by General Douglas MacArthur, worked quickly to tear down Japan's wartime political structure. (Occupation lasted until 1952, a year after Japan signed a peace treaty with most of its wartime opponents.) Japan's military forces were disbanded, the police decentralized, many officials removed, and political prisoners released. For the long run, American authorities pressed for a democratization of Japanese society by giving women the vote, encouraging labor unions, and abolishing Shintoism as a state religion. Several economic reforms were also introduced, breaking up landed estates for the benefit of small farmers—who quickly became politically conservative—and dissolving the holdings of the zaibatsu combines, (see Chapter 27, p. 739) a measure that had little lasting effect as Japanese big business regrouped quickly.

A new constitution tried to cut through older limitations by making the parliament the supreme government body. Several civil liberties were guaranteed, along with gender equality in marriage and collective bargaining rights. Military forces with "war potential" were abolished forever, making Japan a unique major nation in its limited military strength. The emperor became merely a symbolic figurehead, without political power and with no

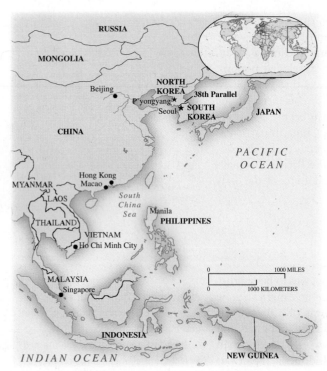

Map 34.1 The Pacific Rim Area by 1960 Geographic locations and political systems created new contacts and alignments.

claims to Shinto divinity. Even as Japan accepted many western political and legal concepts, it inserted its own values into the new constitution. Thus, a 1963 law called for special social obligations to the elderly, in obvious contrast to Western approaches: "The elders shall be loved and respected as those who have for many years contributed toward the development of society, and a wholesome and peaceful life shall be guaranteed to them."

These new constitutional measures were embraced by the Japanese people, many of whom became avid opponents of any hint of military revival. Military power and responsibility in the region were retained by the United States, which long after the occupation period kept important bases in Japan. Many of the political features of the new constitution worked smoothly—in large part because the Japanese had experienced parliamentary and political party activity for extended periods in the pre–World War II decades. Two moderate parties merged in 1955 into the new **Liberal Democratic Party,** which monopolized Japan's government into the 1990s.

Japan became a genuine multiparty democracy but with unusual emphasis on one-party control in the interests of order and elite control. It granted women the vote, but women's conditions differed markedly from men's. In education, American occupation forces insisted on reducing the nationalism in textbooks and opening secondary schools to more social groups. These changes merged with existing Japanese enthusiasm for education, heightening the emphasis on school success. Japan developed one of the most meritocratic systems in the world, with students advanced to university training on the basis of rigorous examinations. But once the occupation ended, the government reasserted some traditional components in this education package, including careful controls over textbooks. In 1966, for example, the Ministry of Education attacked "egotistic" attitudes in Japan, which were producing "a feeling of spiritual hollowness and unrest." Schools in this situation should generate ethical discipline and group consciousness, touching base with more customary goals while preparing students for their role in Japan's expanding economy. As one conservative put it in the 1980s, "You have to teach tradition [to the children] whether they like it or not."

Korea: Intervention and War

Korea's postwar adjustment period was far more troubled than Japan's. The leaders of the great Allied powers during World War II had agreed in principle that Korea should be restored as an independent state. But the United States' eagerness to obtain Soviet help against Japan resulted in Soviet occupation of the northern part of the peninsula. As the cold war intensified, American and Soviet authorities could not agree on unification of the zones, and in 1948 the United States sponsored a **Republic of Korea** in the south, matched by a Soviet-dominated **People's Democratic Republic of Korea** in the north (Map 34.1). North Korea's regime drew on an earlier Korean Communist party founded in exile in the 1900s. North Korea quickly became a communist state with a Stalinist-style emphasis on the power of the leader, Kim Il-Sung, and then his son after his death in 1994. The South Korean regime, bolstered by an ongoing American military presence, was headed by nationalist Syngman Rhee. Rhee's South Korea developed institutions that were parliamentary in form but maintained a strongly authoritarian tone.

In June 1950 North Korean forces attacked South Korea, hoping to impose unification on their own terms (Figure 34.2). The United States reacted quickly (after some confusing signals about whether South Korea was inside the U.S. "defense perimeter"). President Truman insisted on drawing another line against communist aggression, and he orchestrated United Nations sponsorship of a largely American "police action" in support of South Korean troops. In the ensuing **Korean War,** under General MacArthur's leadership, Allied forces pushed North Korea back, driving on toward the Chinese border. This action roused concern on the part of China's communist regime, which sent "volunteers" to force American troops back toward the south. The front stabilized in 1952 near the original north–south border. The stalemate dragged on until 1953, when a new American administration was able to agree to an armistice.

Korea then continued its dual pattern of development. North Korea produced an unusually isolated version of one-man communist rule as Kim concentrated his powers over the only legal political party, the military, and the government. Even Soviet liberalization in the late 1980s brought little change. South Korea and the United States concluded a mutual defense treaty in 1954; American troop levels were reduced, but the South Korean army gained more sophisticated military

The Constitution of Japan, Two Versions

Liberal Democratic party Monopolized Japanese government from its formation in 1955 into the 1990s; largely responsible for the economic reconstruction of Japan.

Republic of Korea Southern half of Korea sponsored by United States following World War II; headed by nationalist Syngman Rhee; developed parliamentary institutions but maintained authoritarian government; defended by UN forces during Korean War; underwent industrialization and economic emergence after 1950s.

People's Democratic Republic of Korea Northern half of Korea dominated by U.S.S.R.; long headed by Kim Il-Sung; attacked south in 1950 and initiated Korean War; retained independence as a communist state after the war.

Korean War Fought from 1950 to 1953; North supported by U.S.S.R. and later People's Republic of China; South supported by United States and small international United Nations force; ended in stalemate and continued division of Korea.

Figure 34.2 The internationalization of the civil conflict between the regimes of North and South Korea in the late 1940s led to the flight of hundreds of thousands of refugees from one region to another. As this photo so starkly portrays, these migrations often occurred in the harsh winter season when many of those in flight died of the cold and hunger.

equipment. The United States also poured economic aid into the country, initially to prevent starvation in a war-ravaged land. The political tenor of South Korea continued to be authoritarian. In 1961 army officers took over effective rule of the country, although sometimes a civilian government served as a front.

However, economic change began to gain ground in South Korea, ushering in a new phase of activity and international impact. Tensions between the two Koreas continued to run high, with many border clashes and sabotage, but outright warfare was avoided.

Emerging Stability in Taiwan, Hong Kong, and Singapore

Postwar adjustments in Taiwan involved yet another set of issues. As the communist revolutionary armies gained the upper hand in mainland China, between 1946 and 1948 the Guomindang (Nationalist) regime prepared to fall back on its newly reacquired island, which the communists could not threaten because they had no navy. The result was imposition over the Taiwanese majority of Chinese leadership plus a massive military force drawn from the mainland.

The authoritarian political patterns the nationalists had developed in China, centered on Chiang Kai-shek's personal control of the government, were amplified by the need to keep in check disaffected indigenous Taiwanese, who grew restive as Chinese migrants dominated political and economic life on the island. Hostility with the communist regime across the Taiwan Strait ran high. In 1955 and 1958, the communists bombarded two small islands controlled by the nationalists, Quemoy and Matsu, and wider conflict threatened as the United States backed up its ally. Tensions were defused when communist China agreed to fire on the islands only on alternate days, while

U.S. ships supplied them on the off-days, thus salvaging national honor. Finally, the United States induced Chiang to renounce any intentions of attacking the mainland, and conflict eased into mutual bombardments of propaganda leaflets. During this period, as in South Korea, the United States gave economic aid to Taiwan, ending assistance only in the 1960s, when its growing prosperity seemed assured.

Two other participants in the economic advances of the Pacific Rim were distinguished by special ties to Britain. **Hong Kong** remained a British colony after World War II; only in the 1980s was an agreement reached between Britain and China for its 1997 return to the Chinese fold. Hong Kong gained increasing autonomy from direct British rule. Its Chinese population swelled at various points after 1946 as a result of flights from communist rule.

Singapore, at first part of Malaysia (see Map 34.1), retained a large British naval base until 1971, when Britain abandoned all pretense of power in east Asia. Singapore grew into a vigorous free port, and it became an independent nation in 1965.

Overall, by the end of the 1950s a certain stability had emerged in the political situation of many smaller east Asian nations. From the 1960s onward these same areas, combining Western contacts with important traditions of group loyalty, moved from impressive economic recovery to new international influence on the basis of manufacturing and trade.

Modern
Hong Kong

Hong Kong British colony on Chinese mainland; major commercial center; agreement reached between Britain and People's Republic of China returned colony to China in 1997.

Japan, Incorporated: A Distinctive Political and Cultural Style

The chief emphasis of Japanese politics lay in conservative stability. The Liberal Democratic party held the reins of government from 1955 onward. This meant that Japan, uniquely among the democratic nations of the post-war world, had no experience with shifts in party administration until 1993. Changes in leadership, which at times were frequent, were handled through negotiations among the Liberal Democratic elite, not directly as a result of shifts in voter preference.

Clearly, this system revived many of the oligarchic features of Meiji Japan and the Japan of the 1920s. During the prosperous 1970s and 1980s, economic progress and the Liberal Democrats' willingness to consult opposition leaders about major legislation reinforced Japan's effective political unity. Only at the end of the 1980s, when several Liberal Democratic leaders were branded by corruption of various sorts, were new questions raised.

Post-War Politics and Culture

Japan's distinctive political atmosphere showed clearly in strong cooperation with business. The state set production and investment goals while actively lending public resources to encourage investment and limit imports. The government–business coordination to promote economic growth and export expansion prompted the half-admiring, half-derisory Western label "Japan, Incorporated."

The government actively campaigned to promote birth control and abortion, and population growth slowed. This was another product of the strong national tradition of state-sponsored discipline. As in politics and education, Japanese culture preserved important traditional elements, which provided aesthetic and spiritual satisfactions amid rapid economic change (Figure 34.3). Customary styles in poetry, painting, tea ceremonies, and flower arrangements continued. Each New Year's Day, for example, the emperor presided at a poetry contest, and masters of traditional arts were honored by being designated as Living National Treasures. Kabuki and Noh theater also flourished. Japanese films and novels often recalled the country's earlier history. Japanese painters and architects participated actively in the "international style" pioneered in the West, but they often infused it with earlier Japanese motifs such as stylized nature painting. City orchestras played the works of Western composers and native compositions that incorporated passages played on the Japanese flute and zither.

Cultural combinations were not always smooth. Both before and after World War II, key intellectuals used art and literature to protest change, not merely to blend Western and traditional styles. The flamboyant postwar writer Hiraoka Kimitoke (pen name Yukio Mishima, 1925–1970) was a case in point. His novels and dramas, which began to appear in 1949, dealt with controversial themes such as homosexuality while also updating versions of the Noh plays. Though a passionate nationalist, he was too sickly for military service in World War II. But he later sought to foster cults

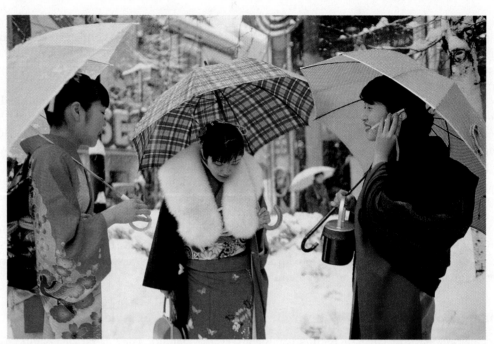

Figure 34.3 The blending of ancient Japanese culture (*kimonos*) and modern consumer goods (cellphones, backpacks, and thermoses) is evident in this photo of three young women dressed for an evening out on the town.

of body building and Samurai discipline. At first he enjoyed many Western contacts and encouragement, but he came to hate Western ways. In 1968 he formed a private army with the intent of restoring Japanese ideals. After finishing a final major novel, Mishima performed his own ritual suicide in 1970. He wrote to an American friend shortly before his death, "I came to wish to sacrifice myself for this old beautiful tradition of Japan, which is disappearing very quickly day by day."

The Economic Surge: Japan Challenges the Superpowers for Economic Supremacy

Japanese Technician Testing Equipment

Particularly after the mid-1950s, rapid economic growth made Japan's clearest mark internationally and commanded the most intense energies at home. By 1983 the total national product was equal to the combined totals of China, both Koreas, Taiwan, India, Pakistan, Australia, and Brazil. Per capita income, though still slightly behind that of the leading Western nations such as West Germany, had passed that of many countries, including Britain. Annual economic growth reached at least 10 percent regularly from the mid-1950s onward, surpassing the regular levels of every other nation during the 1960s and 1970s, as Japan became one of the top two or three economic powers in the world (Figure 34.4). Leading Japanese corporations, such as the great automobile manufacturers and electronic equipment producers, became known not simply for the volume of their international exports but for the high quality of their goods.

A host of factors fed this astounding economic performance. Active government encouragement was a major ingredient. Educational expansion played a major role as Japan began to turn out far more engineers than did more populous competitors, such as the United States. Foreign policy also played a role. Japan was able to devote almost its whole capital to investment in productive technology, for its military expenses were negligible given its reliance on United States protection.

Japan's distinctive labor policies functioned well. Workers were organized mainly in company unions that were careful not to impair their companies' productivity. Leading corporations solidified this cooperation, which spurred zealous work from most employees. Social activities, including group exercise sessions before the start of the working day, promoted and expressed group loyalty, and managers took active interest in suggestions by employees. The Japanese system also ensured lifetime employment to an important part of the labor force, a policy aided by economic growth,

Figure 34.4 Tokyo at night at the beginning of the 21st century epitomizes the resurgence of Asian economies following World War II.

low average unemployment rates, and an early retirement age. This network of policies and attitudes made Japanese labor seem both less class-conscious and less individualistic than labor forces in the advanced industrial nations of the West. It reflected older traditions of group solidarity in Japan, going back to feudal patterns.

Japanese management displayed a distinctive spirit, again as a result of adapting older traditions of leadership. There was more group consciousness, including a willingness to abide by collective decisions and less concern for quick personal profits than was characteristic of the West, particularly the United States. Few corporate bureaucrats changed firms, which meant that their efforts were concentrated on their company's success. Leisure life remained meager by Western standards, and many Japanese were reluctant to take regular vacations.

Japan's distinctiveness extended to family life, despite some features similar to the West's industrial experience. Japanese women, though increasingly well educated and experiencing an important decline in birth rates, did not follow Western patterns precisely. A feminist movement was confined to a small number of intellectuals. Within the family, women shared fewer leisure activities with their husbands, concentrating more heavily on domestic duties and intensive childrearing than was true in the West by the 1970s. In childrearing, conformity to group standards was emphasized far more than in the West or in communist China. A comparative study of nursery schools showed that Japanese teachers were bent on effacing their own authority in the interests of developing strong bonds between the children. Shame was directed toward nonconformist behaviors, a disciplinary approach the West had largely abandoned in the early 19th century. Japanese television game shows, superficially copied from those of the West, imposed elaborate, dishonoring punishment on losing contestants.

The nation had few lawyers, for it was assumed that people could make and abide by firm arrangements through mutual agreement. Psychiatrists reported far fewer problems of loneliness and individual alienation than in the West. Conversely, situations that promoted competition between individuals, such as university entrance tests, produced far higher stress levels than did analogous Western experiences. The Japanese had particular ways to relieve tension. Bouts of heavy drinking were more readily tolerated than in the West, seen as a time when normal codes of conduct could be suspended under the helpful eyes of friends. Businessmen and some politicians had recourse to traditional geisha houses for female-supplied cosseting, a normal and publicly accepted activity.

Figure 34.5 As this photo of an ultra-modern skyscraper in Hong Kong amply illustrates, some of the most innovative architecture of the age of globalization can be found in the great commercial centers along the Pacific Rim. The region also boasts one of the world's tallest buildings, a twin-tower office complex in the Malaysian capital of Kuala Lumpur.

Economic and political developments in several nations and city-states on Asia's Pacific coast echoed important elements of Japan's 20th-century history. Political authoritarianism was characteristic of most Pacific Rim states, though there were periodic bows to parliamentary forms and protests from dissidents who wanted greater freedom.

Hyundai   Example of huge industrial groups that wield great power in modern South Korea; virtually governed Korea's southeastern coast; vertical economic organization with ships, supertankers, factories, schools, and housing units.

Japanese popular culture was not static, both because of ongoing attraction to Western standards and because of rapid urbanization and economic growth. The U.S. presence after World War II brought a growing fascination with baseball, and professional teams flourished. Japanese athletes began also to excel in such sports as tennis and golf. In the mid-1980s, the government, appalled to discover that a majority of Japanese children did not use chopsticks but preferred knives and forks in order to eat more rapidly, invested money to promote chopsticks training in the schools. This was a minor development, but it indicates the ongoing tension between change, with its Western connotations, and a commitment to Japanese identity. The veneration of old age was challenged by some youthful assertiveness and by the sheer cost of supporting the rapidly growing percentage of older people, for Japan relied heavily on family support for elders.

Other issues were associated with change. By the 1960s, pollution had become a serious problem as cities and industry expanded rapidly. Traffic police, for example, sometimes wore masks to protect their lungs. The government (eager to preempt a potential opposition issue) paid increasing attention to environmental issues after 1970. The 1990s brought some new questions to Japan. Mired in political corruption, the Liberal Democrats were replaced by shaky coalition governments. A severe economic recession caused widespread unemployment. Even as Japanese methods were being touted in the West as a basis for economic and social revitalization, some of the critical patterns of postwar development were at least temporarily disrupted.

The Pacific Rim: More Japans?

South Korea was the most obvious example of the spread of new economic dynamism to other parts of the Pacific Rim (see Figure 34.5). The Korean government rested normally in the hands of a political strongman, usually from army ranks. Syngman Rhee was forced out of office by student demonstrations in 1960; a year later, a military general, Park Chung-hee, seized power. He retained his authority until his assassination in 1979 by his director of intelligence. Then another general seized power. Intense student protest, backed by wider popular support, pressed the military from power at the end of the 1980s. But a conservative politician won the ensuing general election, and it was not clear how much the political situation had changed. Opposition activity was possible in South Korea, though usually heavily circumscribed, and many leaders were jailed. There was some freedom of the press although it did not extend to publications from communist countries.

Development from the Top Down

As in postwar Japan, the South Korean government from the mid-1950s onward placed its primary emphasis on economic growth, which in this case started from a much lower base after the Korean War and previous Japanese exploitation. Huge industrial firms were created by a combination of government aid and active entrepreneurship. By the 1970s, when growth rates in Korea began to match those of Japan, Korea was competing successfully in the area of cheap consumer goods, as well as in steel and automobiles, in a variety of international markets. In steel, Korea's surge—based on the most up-to-date technology, a skilled engineering sector, and low wages—pushed past Japan's. The same held true in textiles, where Korean growth (along with that of Taiwan) erased almost one-third of the jobs held in the industry in Japan.

Huge industrial groups such as Daewoo and **Hyundai** resembled the great Japanese holding companies before and after World War II and wielded great political influence. For example,

Hyundai was the creation of entrepreneur Chung Ju Yung, a modern folk hero who walked 150 miles to Seoul, South Korea's capital, from his native village to take his first job as a day laborer at age 16. By the 1980s, when Chung was in his 60s, his firm had 135,000 employees and 42 overseas offices throughout the world. Hyundai virtually governed Korea's southeastern coast. It built ships, including petroleum supertankers; it built thousands of housing units sold to low-paid workers at below-market rates; it built schools, a technical college, and an arena for the practice of the traditional Korean martial art Tae Kwon Do. With their lives carefully provided for, Hyundai workers responded in kind, putting in six-day weeks with three vacation days per year and participating in almost worshipful ceremonies when a fleet of cars was shipped abroad or a new tanker launched (Figure 34.6).

South Korea's rapid entry into the ranks of newly industrialized countries produced a host of more general changes. The population soared. By the 1980s more than 40 million people lived in a nation about the size of the state of Indiana, producing one of the highest population densities on earth: about 1000 people per square mile. This was one reason, even amid growing prosperity, why many Koreans emigrated. The government gradually began to encourage couples to limit their birth rates. Seoul expanded to embrace 9 million people; it developed intense air pollution and a hothouse atmosphere of deals and business maneuvers. Per capita income grew despite the population increase, rising almost 10 times from the early 1950s to the early 1980s, but to a level still only one-ninth that of Japan. Huge fortunes coexisted with widespread poverty in this setting, although the poor were better off than those of less developed nations.

South Korea Enters the U.S. Auto Market

Advances in Taiwan and the City-States

The Republic of China, as the government of Taiwan came to call itself, experienced a high rate of economic development. Productivity in both agriculture and industry increased rapidly, the former spurred by land reform that benefited small commercial farmers. The government concentrated increasingly on economic gains as its involvement in plans for military action against the mainland communist regime declined. As in Japan and Korea, formal economic planning reached high levels, though allowing latitude for private business. Money was poured into education, and literacy rates and levels of technical training rose rapidly. The result was important cultural and economic change for the Taiwanese people. Traditional medical practices and ritualistic popular religion remained lively, but were expanded to allow simultaneous use of modern, Western-derived medicine and some of the urban entertainment forms popular elsewhere.

Figure 34.6 Hyundai loading dock for export to the United States.

Pacific Rim Growth

QUESTIONS The figures in the table can be used to illustrate the industrial emergence of the Pacific Rim (Japan, South Korea, Singapore, Hong Kong). Which countries most clearly have been undergoing an industrial revolution since the 1960s, and how can this be measured? How do the key Pacific Rim areas compare in growth to the neighboring "little tigers" Indonesia, Malaysia, and Thailand? Do the Philippines constitute another "little tiger"? How do Japanese patterns compare with the newer areas of the Pacific Rim, and how can this relationship be explained?

Indices of Growth and Change in the Pacific Rim: Gross National Product (GNP) 1965–1996

Per Capita GNP
East and Southeast Asia, annual growth rates (%)

	1965	1996
China	8.5	6.7
Hong Kong	7.5	5.6
Indonesia	6.7	4.6
Japan	4.5	3.6
Korea (South)	8.9	7.3
Malaysia	6.8	4.1
Philippines	3.5	0.9
Singapore	8.3	6.3
Thailand	7.3	5.0
For comparison		
All preexisting industrial countries	3.0	2.2
United States	2.4	1.4
India	4.5	2.3

Social and Economic Data

	% labor force in agriculture		% population urban	
	1965	1996	1965	1996
China	78	72	17	31
Indonesia	66	55	41	82
Japan	20	7	71	78
Korea (South)	49	18	41	82
Malaysia	54	27	34	54
Thailand	80	64	13	20

Note: Growth at 2.3 percent per year doubles the category in 30 years; 7 percent per year doubles in 10 years.
Source: Adapted from World Bank, *World Development Indicators* (Washington, D.C., 1998).

The assimilation of rapid change gave the Taiwanese government great stability despite a host of new concerns. The U.S. recognition of the People's Republic of China brought with it a steadily decreasing official commitment to Taiwan. In 1978 the United States severed diplomatic ties with the Taiwanese regime, although unofficial contacts—through the American Institute in Taiwan and the Coordination Council for North American Affairs, established by the republic in Washington—remained strong. The Taiwanese also built important regional contacts with other governments in eastern and southeastern Asia that facilitated trade. For example, Japan served as the nation's most important single trading partner, purchasing foodstuffs, manufactured textiles, chemicals, and other industrial goods.

Taiwan also developed some informal links with the communist regime in Beijing, although the latter continued to claim the island as part of its territory. The republic survived the death of Chiang Kai-shek and the accession of his son, **Chiang Ching-kuo** (jee-ahng jihn-kwoh), in 1978. The young Chiang emphasized personal authority less than his father had, and he reduced somewhat the gap between mainland-born military personnel and native Taiwanese in government ranks. However, a strong authoritarian strain continued, and political diversity was not encouraged.

Conditions in the city-state of Singapore, though less tied to great power politics, resembled those in Taiwan in many ways. Prime Minister **Lee Kuan Yew** took office in 1965, when the area first gained independence, and held power for the next three decades. The government established tight controls over its citizens, going beyond anything attempted elsewhere in the Pacific Rim. Sexual behavior and potential economic corruption, as well as more standard aspects of municipal regulation and economic planning, were scrutinized carefully. The government proclaimed the necessity of unusual discipline and restraint because such a large population crowded into a limited space. One result was unusually low reported crime rates, and another was the near impossibility of serious political protest. The dominant People's Action party suppressed opposition movements. The authoritarian political style was rendered somewhat more palatable by extraordinarily successful economic development, based on a combination of government controls and initiatives and free enterprise. Already the world's fourth largest port, Singapore saw manufacturing and banking surpass shipping as sources of revenue. Electronics, textiles, and oil refining joined shipbuilding as major sectors. By the 1980s Singapore's population enjoyed the second highest per capita income in Asia. Educational levels and health conditions improved accordingly.

Finally, Hong Kong retained its status as a major world port and branched out as a center of international banking, serving as a bridge between the communist regime in China and the wider world. Export production combined high-speed technology with low wages and long hours for the labor force, yielding highly competitive results. Textiles and clothing formed 39 percent of total exports by the 1980s, but other sectors, including heavy industry, developed impressively as well. As in other Pacific Rim nations, a prosperous middle class emerged, with links to many other parts of the world, Western and Asian alike. In 1997, after careful negotiation with the British, Hong Kong was returned to China. The communist government promised to respect the territory's free market economic system and maintain democratic political rights, although the changeover raised questions for the future.

Common Themes and New Problems

The Pacific Rim states had more in common than their rapid growth rates and expanding exports. They all stressed group loyalties against excessive individualism or protest, and in support of hard work. Confucian morality often was used, implicitly or explicitly, as part of this effort to cement group cohesion in factories and businesses. The Pacific Rim states also shared reliance on government planning and direction amid limitations on dissent and instability. Of course, they benefited greatly from the expansion of the Japanese market for factory goods, such as textiles, as well as raw materials.

The dynamism of the Pacific Rim spilled over to neighboring parts of southeast Asia by the 1980s. "Little tigers" such as Indonesia, Malaysia, and Thailand began to experience rapid economic growth, along with the pollution problems that accompanied new manufacturing and larger cities.

However, the final years of the 20th century revealed unexpected weaknesses in this dynamic region. Growth faltered, unemployment rose, and currencies from South Korea to Indonesia took a drastic hit. Many Western observers argued that this crisis could be resolved only by reducing the links between governments and major firms and introducing more free market competition. In essence, they contended that only a Western industrial model could be successful, and agencies such as the World Bank tried to insist on reforms in this direction as a condition for economic assistance. In the meantime, political pressures increased amid economic distress, and in 1998 the longtime authoritarian ruler of Indonesia was overturned in favor of pledges for future democracy. By 1999, however, economic growth rates in the region began to pick up. It was not clear that basic patterns had to be rethought.

Chiang Ching-kuo [jee-ahng jihn-kwoh] Son and successor of Chiang Kai-shek as ruler of Taiwanese government in 1978; continued authoritarian government; attempted to lessen gap between followers of his father and indigenous islanders.

Clean-Room Disc Manufacturing in Singapore

Lee Kuan Yew Ruler of Singapore from independence in 1959 through three decades; established tightly controlled authoritarian government; ruled through People's Action party to suppress political diversity.

River Market in Thailand

The Pacific Rim as a U.S. Policy Issue

Any change in the power balance between nations or larger civilizations results in a host of policy issues for all who are involved. The rise of the Pacific Rim economies posed some important questions for the West, particularly for the United States because of its military role in the Pacific as well as its world economic position. The United States had actively promoted economic growth in Japan, Korea, and Taiwan as part of its desire to discourage the spread of communism. Although American aid was not solely responsible for Pacific Rim advances, and although it tapered off by the 1960s, the United States took some satisfaction in demonstrating the vitality of noncommunist economies. The United States also was not eager to relinquish its military superiority in the region, which gave it a stake in Asian opinion.

Yet the threats posed by increasing Pacific Rim economic competition were real and growing. Japan seemed to wield a permanent balance-of-payments superiority; its exports to the United States regularly exceeded imports by the 1970s and 1980s, which contributed greatly to the United States' unfavorable overall trade balance. Japanese investment in American companies and real estate increased the United States' growing indebtedness to foreign nations. The symbolic problems were real as well. Japanese observers pointed out with some justice that Americans seemed more worried about Japanese investments than about larger British holdings in the United States, an imbalance that smacked of racism. Certainly, Americans found it harder to accept Asian competition than they did European, if only because it was less familiar. Japanese ability to gain near monopolies in key industries such as electronic recording systems as well as the growing Korean challenge in steel and automobiles meant or seemed to mean loss of jobs and perhaps a threat of more fundamental economic decline in years to come.

In the 1980s, several observers urged American imitation of the bases of Pacific Rim success: The United States should open more partnerships between government and private industry and do more economic planning, it should teach managers to commit themselves to group harmony rather than individual profit seeking, and it should build a new concord between management and labor, based on greater job security and cooperative social programs. Some firms in the United States did introduce certain Japanese management methods, including more consultation with workers, with some success.

> "Asian leaders recognized the need for some change, but they did not welcome advice that seemed to ignore successful components from the past and threatened some of the privileges of established political and business elites."

Other observers, also concerned about long-term erosion of American power on the Pacific Rim, urged a more antagonistic stance. A few wanted the United States to pull out of costly Japanese and Korean military bases so that the Pacific Rim would be forced to shoulder more of its own defense costs. Others wanted to impose tariffs on Asian goods, at least until the Pacific Rim nations made it easier for American firms to compete in Asian markets. Aggrieved American workers sometimes smashed imported cars and threatened Asian immigrants, although many American consumers continued to prefer Pacific Rim products. The options were complex, and no clear change in American policy emerged.

Pacific Rim nations also faced choices about their orientation toward the West, particularly the United States. Questions that arose earlier about what Western patterns to copy and what to avoid continued to be important, as the Japanese concern about forks and chopsticks suggests. Added were issues about how to express pride and confidence in modern achievements against what were seen as Western tendencies to belittle and patronize. In 1988 the summer Olympic games were held in South Korea, a sign of Korea's international advance and a source of great national pride. During the games, Korean nationalism flared against the U.S. athletes and television commentators, based on their real or imagined tendencies to seek out faults in Korean society. South Korea, like Japan, continued to rely on Western markets and U.S. military assistance, but there was a clear desire to put the relationship on a more fully equal footing. This desire reflected widespread public opinion, and it could have policy implications.

The Pacific Rim crisis in 1998 raised a new set of questions. American leaders urged assistance to beleaguered economies such as those of South Korea and Indonesia, but they also, with some self-satisfaction, tried to insist on introducing a more Western-style market economy. Asian leaders recognized the need for some change, but they did not welcome advice that seemed to ignore successful components from the past and threatened some of the privileges of established political and business elites.

QUESTIONS How great were the challenges posed by the Pacific Rim to the U.S. world position and well-being? What are the most likely changes in American and Pacific Rim relations over the next two decades?

Mao's China: Vanguard of World Revolution?

Just as he was convinced that he was on the verge of victory, Chiang Kai-shek's anticommunist crusade had been rudely interrupted by the Japanese invasion of the Chinese mainland (see Chapter 30). Obsessed with the communists, Chiang had done little to block the steady advance of Japanese forces in the early 1930s into Manchuria and the islands along China's coast. Even after the Japanese launched their assaults, aimed at conquering China, Chiang wanted to continue the struggle against the communists (Map 34.2).

Forced by his military commanders to concentrate on the Japanese threat, Chiang grudgingly formed a military alliance with the communists. Although he did all he could to undermine the alliance and continue the anticommunist struggle by underhanded means, for the next seven years the war against Japan took priority over the civil war in the contest for control of China.

Although it brought more suffering to the Chinese people, the Japanese invasion was enormously advantageous for the Communist party. The Japanese invaders captured much of the Chinese coast, where the cities were the centers of the business and mercantile backers of the Nationalists. Chiang's conventional military forces were pummeled by the superior air, land, and sea forces of the Japanese. The Nationalists' attempts to meet the Japanese in conventional battles led to disaster; their inability to defend the coastal provinces lowered their standing in the eyes of the Chinese people. Chiang's hasty and humiliating retreat to Chongqing (Map 34.2), in the interior of China, further eroded his reputation as the savior of the nation and rendered him more dependent than ever on his military allies, the rural landlords, and—perhaps most humiliating—foreign powers such as the United States.

The guerrilla warfare the communists waged against the Japanese armies proved far more effective than Chiang's conventional approach. With the Nationalist extermination offensives suspended, the communists used their anti-Japanese campaigns to extend their control over large areas of north China. By the end of World War II, the Nationalists controlled mainly the cities in the north; they had become (as Mao prescribed in his political writings) islands surrounded by a sea of revolutionary peasants. The communists' successes and their determination to fight the Japanese won them the support of most of China's intellectuals and many of the students who had earlier supported the Nationalists. By 1945 the balance of power within China was clearly shifting in the communists' favor. In the four-year civil war that followed, communist soldiers, who were well treated and fought for a cause, consistently routed the much-abused soldiers of the Nationalists, many of whom switched to the communist side. By 1949 it was over. Chiang and what was left of his armies fled to the island of Formosa, renamed Taiwan, and Mao proclaimed the establishment of the **People's Republic of China** in Beijing.

The Japanese invasion proved critical in the communist drive to victory. But equally important were the communists' social and economic reform programs, which eventually won the great majority of the peasantry, the students and intellectuals, and even many of the bureaucrats to their side. Whereas Chiang, whatever his intentions, was able to do little to improve the condition of the great mass of the people, Mao made uplifting the peasants the central element in his drive for power (Figure 34.7). Land reforms, access to education, and improved health care gave the peasantry a real stake in Mao's revolutionary movement and good reason to defend their soviets (or political-military bases) against both the Nationalists and the Japanese. In contrast to Chiang's armies, whose arrival meant theft, rape, and murder to China's villagers, Mao's soldiers were indoctrinated with the need to protect the peasantry and win their support. Lest they forget, harsh penalties were levied, such as execution for stealing an egg.

As guerrilla fighters, Mao's soldiers had a much better chance to survive and advance in the ranks than did the forcibly conscripted, brutally treated foot soldiers of the Nationalists. Mao and the commanders around him, such

After their victory in the long civil war against the Guomindang in 1949, Chinese communists faced the formidable task of governing a vast nation in ruins. In their pursuit of economic development and social reform, the communists sought to build on the base they had established in the "liberated" zones during their struggle for power.

People's Republic of China Communist government of mainland China; proclaimed in 1949 following military success of Mao Zedong over forces of Chiang Kai-shek and the Guomindang.

China in Civil War and Revolution

Map 34.2 China in the Years of Japanese Occupation and Civil War, 1931–1949 The Chinese political map changed radically and often in the 1930s and 1940s due to civil wars and foreign invasions.

延 安 新 春

Figure 34.7 This propaganda poster features Mao Zedong as the friend and father of the people. Soldiers, peasants, women, children, and peoples from the many regions of China are pictured here joyously rallying to Mao's vision of a strong, just, and prosperous China.

Lin Biao [lihn byoo] (1907–1971) Chinese commander under Mao; trained at Chiang Kaishek's Whampoa Academy in the 1920s.

party cadres Basis of China's communist government organization; cadre advisors were attached to military contingents at all levels.

People's Liberation Army Chinese Communist army; administered much of country under People's Republic of China.

as **Lin Biao** (lihn byoo), who had been trained at Chiang's Whampoa Academy in the 1920s, proved far more gifted—even in conventional warfare—than the often corrupt and inept Nationalist generals. Thus, although the importance of the Japanese invasion cannot be discounted, the communists won the mandate to govern China because they offered solutions to China's fundamental social and economic problems. Even more critically, they actually put their programs into action in the areas that came under their control. In a situation in which revolutionary changes appeared to be essential, the communists alone convinced the Chinese people that they had the leaders and the program that could improve their lives.

The Communists Come to Power

The communists' long struggle for control had left the party with a strong political and military organization that was rooted in the **party cadres** (thoroughly indoctrinated party members) and the **People's Liberation Army.** The continuing importance of the army was indicated by the fact that most of China was administered by military officials for five years after the communists came to power. But the army remained clearly subordinate to the party. Cadre advisors were attached to military contingents at all levels, and the central committees of the party were dominated by nonmilitary personnel.

With this strong political framework in place, the communists moved quickly to assert China's traditional preeminence in east and much of southeast Asia. Potential secessionist movements were forcibly repressed in Inner Mongolia and Tibet, although resistance in the latter has erupted periodically and continues to the present day. In the early 1950s, the Chinese intervened militarily in the conflict between North and South Korea, an intervention that was critical in forcing the United States to settle for a stalemate and a lasting division of the peninsula. Refusing to accept a similar but far more lopsided two-nation outcome of the struggle in China itself, the communist leadership has periodically threatened to invade the Nationalists' refuge on Taiwan, often touching off international incidents. China also played an increasingly important role in the liberation struggle of the Vietnamese to the south, although that did not peak until the height of American involvement in the conflict in the 1960s.

By the late 1950s, the close collaboration between the Soviet Union and China that marked the early years of Mao's rule had broken down. Border disputes, focusing on territories the Russians had seized during the period of Qing decline, and the Chinese refusal to play second fiddle to Russia, especially after Stalin was succeeded by the less imposing Khrushchev, were key causes of the split. These causes of the breakdown in collaboration worsened the differences resulting from the meager economic assistance provided by the Soviet "comrades." They also fed Mao's sense that with the passing of Stalin, he was the chief theoretician and leader of the communist world. In the early 1960s, the Chinese flexed their military and technological muscle by defeating India in a brief war that resulted from a border dispute. More startling, however, was the Chinese success in exploding the first nuclear device developed by a nonindustrial nation.

Planning for Economic Growth and Social Justice

On the domestic front, the new leaders of China moved with equal vigor, though with a good deal less success. Their first priority was to complete the social revolution in the rural areas that had been carried through to some extent in communist-controlled areas during the wars against the Japanese and Guomindang. Between 1950 and 1952, the landlord class and the large landholders, most of whom had been spared in the earlier stages of the revolution, were dispossessed and purged. Village tribunals, overseen by party cadre members, gave tenants and laborers a chance to get even for decades of oppression. Perhaps as many as three million people who were denounced as members of the exploitive landlord class were executed. At the same time, the land taken from the land-owning classes was distributed to peasants who had none or little. For a brief time at least, one of the central pledges of the communist revolutionaries was fulfilled: China became a land of peasant smallholders.

However, communist planners saw rapid industrialization, not peasant farmers, as the key to successful development. With the introduction of the first Stalinist-style five-year plan in 1953, the communist leaders turned away from the peasantry, which had brought them to power, to the urban workers as the hope for a new China. With little foreign assistance from either the West or the Soviet bloc, the state resorted to stringent measures to draw resources from the countryside to finance industrial growth. Some advances were made in industrialization, particularly in heavy industries such as steel. But the shift in direction had consequences that were increasingly unacceptable to Mao and his more radical supporters in the party. State planning and centralization were stressed, party bureaucrats greatly increased their power and influence, and an urban-based privileged class of technocrats began to develop. These changes, and the external threat to China posed by the U.S. intervention in Korea and continuing U.S.-China friction, led Mao and his followers to force a change of strategies in the mid-1950s.

Mao had long nurtured a deep hostility toward elitism, which he associated with the discredited Confucian system. He had little use for Lenin's vision of revolution from above, led by a disciplined cadre of professional political activists. He distrusted intellectuals, disliked specialization, and clung to his faith in the peasants rather than the workers as the repository of basic virtue and the driving force of the revolution. Acting to stem the trend toward an elitist, urban-industrial focus, Mao and his supporters pushed the **Mass Line** approach, beginning with the formation of agricultural cooperatives in 1955. In the following year, cooperatives became farming collectives that soon accounted for more than 90 percent of China's peasant population. The peasants had enjoyed their own holdings for less than three years. As had occurred earlier in the Soviet Union, the leaders of the revolution, who had originally given the land over to the mass of the peasants, later took it away from them through collectivization.

Mass Line Economic policy of Mao Zedong; led to formation of agricultural cooperatives in 1955; cooperatives became farming collectives in 1956.

In 1957 Mao struck at the intellectuals through what may have been a miscalculation or perhaps a clever ruse. Announcing that he wanted to "let a hundred flowers bloom," Mao encouraged professors, artists, and other intellectuals to speak out on the course of development under communist rule. His request stirred up a storm of angry protest and criticism of communist schemes. Having flushed the critics into the open (if the campaign was indeed a ruse) or having been shocked by the vehemence of the response, the party struck with demotions, prison sentences, and banishment to hard labor on the collectives. The flowers rapidly wilted in the face of this betrayal.

The Great Leap Backward

With political opposition within the party and army apparently in check (or in prison), Mao and his supporters launched the **Great Leap Forward** in 1958. The programs of the Great Leap were a further effort to revitalize the flagging revolution by restoring its mass, rural base. Rather than huge plants located in the cities, industrialization would be pushed through small-scale projects integrated into the peasant communes. Instead of the communes' surplus being siphoned off to build steel mills, industrial development would be aimed at producing tractors, cement for irrigation projects, and other manufactures needed by the peasantry. Enormous publicity was given to efforts to produce steel in "backyard" furnaces (Figure 34.8) that relied on labor rather than machine-intensive techniques. Mao preached the benefits of backwardness and the joys of mass involvement, and he looked forward to the withering away of the meddling bureaucracy. Emphasis was placed on self-reliance within the peasant communes. All aspects of the lives of their members were regulated and regimented by the commune leaders and the heads of the local labor brigades.

Great Leap Forward Economic policy of Mao Zedong introduced in 1958; proposed industrialization of small-scale projects integrated into peasant communes; led to economic disaster; ended in 1960.

Within months after it was launched, all indicators suggested that the Great Leap Forward and rapid collectivization were leading to economic disaster. Peasant resistance to collectivization, the abuses of commune leaders, and the dismal output of the backyard factories combined with drought to turn the Great Leap into a giant step backward. The worst famine of the communist era spread across China. For the first time since 1949, China had to import large amounts of grain to feed its people, and the numbers of Chinese to feed continued to grow at an alarming rate. Defiantly rejecting Western and United Nations proposals for family planning, Mao and like-thinking

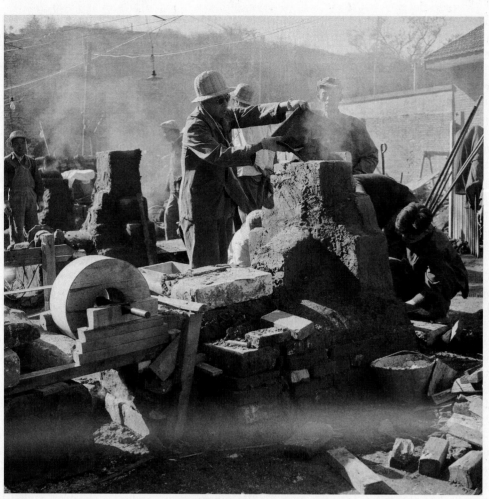

Figure 34.8 The famous backyard steel furnaces became a symbol of China's failed drive for self-sufficiency during the disastrous "Great Leap Forward" of the late 1950s.

radicals charged that socialist China could care for its people, no matter how many they were. Birth control was seen as a symptom of capitalist selfishness and inability to provide a decent living for all of the people.

Like those of India, China's birth rates were actually a good deal lower than those of many emerging nations. Also like India, however, the Chinese were adding people to a massive population base. At the time of the communist rise to power, China had approximately 550 million people. By 1965 this had risen to approximately 750 million. By the year 2000, China's population was approximately 1.3 billion.

China's One-Child Family Policy

In the face of the environmental degradation and overcrowding that this leap in population produced, even the party ideologues came around to the view that something must be done to curb the birth rate. Beginning in the mid-1960s, the government launched a nationwide family planning campaign designed to limit urban couples to two children and those in rural areas to one. By the early 1970s, these targets had been revised to two children for either urban or rural couples. By the 1980s, however, just one child per family was allowed. Although there is evidence of official excesses—undue pressure for women to have abortions, for example—these programs have greatly reduced the birth rate and have begun to slow China's overall population increase. But again, the base to which new births are added is already so large that China's population will not stabilize until well into the 21st century. By that time there will be far more people than now to educate, feed, house, and provide with productive work.

Advances made in the first decade of the new regime were lost through amateurish blunders, excesses of overzealous cadre leaders, and students' meddling. China's national productivity fell by as much as 25 percent. Population increase soon overwhelmed the stagnating productivity of the agricultural and industrial sectors. By 1960 it was clear that the Great Leap must be ended and a new course of development adopted. Mao lost his position as state chairman (although he remained the head of the party's Central Committee). The **pragmatists,** including Mao's old ally **Zhou Enlai** (joo ehn-LEYE), along with **Liu Shaoqi** (lyoh show-syee) and **Deng Xiaoping** (duhng shyoo-pihng), came to power determined to restore state direction and market incentives at the local level.

"Women Hold Up Half of the Heavens"

In Mao's struggles to renew the revolutionary fervor of the Chinese people, his wife, **Jiang Qing** (jee-AHNG chihng), played an increasingly prominent role. Mao's reliance on her was consistent with the commitment to the liberation of Chinese women he had acted upon throughout his political career. As a young man he had been deeply moved by a newspaper story about a young girl who had committed suicide rather than be forced by her family to submit to the marriage they had arranged for her with a rich but very old man. From that point onward, women's issues and women's support for the communist movement became important parts of Mao's revolutionary strategy. Here he was drawing on a well established revolutionary tradition, for women had been very active in the Taiping Rebellion of the mid-19th century, the Boxer revolt in 1900, and the 1911 revolution that had toppled the Manchu regime. One of the key causes taken up by the May Fourth intellectuals, who had a great impact on the youthful Mao Zedong, was women's rights. Their efforts put an end to footbinding. They also did much to advance campaigns to end female seclusion, win legal rights for women, and open educational and career opportunities to them.

The attempts by the Nationalists in the late 1920s and 1930s to reverse many of the gains made by women in the early revolution brought many women into the communist camp. Led by Chiang's wife, Madam Chiang Kai-shek, the Nationalist counteroffensive (like comparable movements in the fascist countries of Europe at the time) tried to return Chinese women to the home and hearth. Madam Chiang proclaimed a special Good Mother's Day and declared that for women, "virtue was more important than learning." She taught that it was immoral for a wife to criticize her husband (an ethical precept she herself ignored regularly).

The Nationalist campaign to restore Chinese women to their traditional domestic roles and dependence on men contrasted sharply with the communists' extensive employment of women to advance the revolutionary cause. Women served as teachers, nurses, spies, truck drivers, and laborers on projects ranging from growing food to building machine-gun bunkers. Although the party preferred to use them in these support roles, in moments of crisis women became soldiers on the front lines. Many won distinction for their bravery under fire. Some rose to become cadre leaders, and many were prominent in the antilandlord campaigns and agrarian reform. Their contribution to the victory of the revolutionary cause bore out Mao's early dictum that the energies and talents of women had to be harnessed to the national cause because "women hold up half of the heavens."

As was the case in many other Asian and African countries, the victory of the revolution brought women legal equality with men—in itself a revolutionary development in a society such as China's. For example, women were given the right to choose their marriage partners without familial interference. But arranged marriages persist today, especially in rural areas, and the need to have party approval for all marriages is a new form of control. Since 1949 women have also been expected to work outside the home. Their opportunities for education and professional careers have improved greatly. As in other socialist states, however, openings for employment outside the home have proved to be a burden for Chinese women. Until the late 1970s, traditional attitudes toward childrearing and home care prevailed. As a result, women were required not only to hold down a regular job but also to raise a family, cook meals, clean, and shop, all without the benefit of the modern appliances available in Western societies.

Although many women held cadre posts at the middle and lower levels of the party and bureaucracy, the upper echelons of both were overwhelmingly controlled by men. The short-lived but impressive power amassed by Jiang Qing in the early 1970s ran counter to these overall trends, but Jiang Qing got to the top because she was married to Mao. She exercised power mainly in his name and was toppled soon after his death when she tried to rule in her own right.

pragmatists   Chinese Communist politicians such as Zhou Enlai, Deng Xiaoping, and Liu Shaoqui; determined to restore state direction and market incentives at the local level; opposed Great Leap Forward.

Zhou Enlai   [joo ehn-LEYE] After Mao Zedong, the most important leader of the Communist party in China from the 1930s until his death in 1976; premier of China from 1954; notable as perhaps the most cosmopolitan and moderate of the inner circle of Communist leaders.

Liu Shaoqi   [lyoh show-syee] Chinese Communist pragmatist; with Deng Xiaoping, came to power in 1959 after Mao was replaced; determined to restore state direction and market incentives at local level; purged in 1966 as Mao returned to power.

Deng Xiaoping   [duhng shyoo-pihng] One of the more pragmatic, least ideological of the major Communist leaders of China; joined the party as a young man in the 1920s, survived the legendary Long March and persecution during the Cultural Revolution of the 1960s, and emerged as China's most influential leader in the early 1980s.

Jiang Qing   [jee-AHNG chihng] (1914–1991) Wife of Mao Zedong; one of Gang of Four; opposed pragmatists and supported Cultural Revolution of 1965; arrested and imprisoned for life in 1976.

Women in the Revolutionary Struggles for Social Justice

Even more than in the nationalist movements in colonized areas such as India and Egypt, women were drawn in large numbers into revolutionary struggles in areas such as China and Vietnam. The breakdown of the political and social systems weakened the legal and family restrictions that had subordinated women and limited their career choices. The collapse of the Confucian order also ushered in decades of severe crisis and brutal conflict in which women's survival depended on their assumption of radically new roles and their active involvement in revolutionary activities. The following quotations are taken from Vietnamese and Chinese revolutionary writings and interviews with women involved in revolutionary movements in each country. They express the women's goals, their struggle to be taken seriously in the uncharacteristic political roles they had assumed, and some of the many ways women found self-respect and redress for their grievances as a result of the changes wrought by the spread of the new social order.

> Women must first of all be masters of themselves. They must strive to become skilled workers . . . and, at the same time, they must strictly observe family planning. Another major question is the responsibility of husbands to help their wives look after children and other housework.

> We intellectuals had had little contact with the peasants and when we first walked through the village in our Chinese gowns or skirts the people would just stare at us and talk behind our backs. When the village head beat gongs to call out the women to the meeting we were holding for them, only men and old women came, but no young ones. Later we found out that the landlords and rich peasants had spread slanders among the masses saying "They are a pack of wild women. Their words are not for young brides to hear."

> Brave wives and daughters-in-law, untrammelled by the presence of their menfolk, could voice their own bitterness . . . encourage their poor sisters to do likewise, and thus eventually bring to the village-wide gatherings the strength of "half of China" as the more enlightened women, very much in earnest, like to call themselves. By "speaking pains to recall pains," the women found that they had as many if not more grievances than the men, and that given a chance to speak in public, they were as good at it as their fathers and husbands.

> In Chingtsun the work team found a woman whose husband thought her ugly and wanted to divorce her. She was very depressed until she learned that under the Draft Law [of the Communist party] she could have her own share of land. Then she cheered up immediately. "If he divorces me, never mind," she said. "I'll get my share and the children will get theirs. We can live a good life without him."

QUESTIONS On the basis of these quotations, identify the traditional roles and attitudes toward women (explored in earlier chapters on China and Vietnam) that women engaged in revolutionary movements in China and Vietnam have rejected. What do they believe is essential if women are to gain equality with men? How do the demands of the women supporting these revolutionary movements compare with those of women's rights advocates in the United States?

Mao's Last Campaign and the Fall of the Gang of Four

Having lost his position as head of state but still the most powerful and popular leader in the Communist party, Mao worked throughout the early 1960s to establish grassroots support for yet another renewal of the revolutionary struggle. He fiercely opposed the efforts of Deng Xiaoping and his pragmatist allies to scale back the communes, promote peasant production on what were in effect private plots, and push economic growth over political orthodoxy. By late 1965, Mao was convinced that his support among the students, peasants, and military was strong enough to launch what would turn out to be his last campaign, the **Cultural Revolution.** With mass student demonstrations paving the way, he launched an all-out assault on the "capitalist-roaders" in the party.

Cultural Revolution Movement initiated in 1965 by Mao Zedong to restore his dominance over pragmatists; used mobs to ridicule Mao's political rivals; campaign was called off in 1968.

Red Guard Student brigades utilized by Mao Zedong and his political allies during the Cultural Revolution to discredit Mao's political enemies.

Waving "little red books" of Mao's pronouncements on all manner of issues, the infamous **Red Guard** student brigades (Figure 34.9) publicly ridiculed and abused Mao's political rivals. Liu Shaoqi was killed, Deng Xiaoping was imprisoned, and Zhou Enlai was driven into seclusion. The aroused students and the rank and file of the People's Liberation Army were used to pull down the bureaucrats from their positions of power and privilege. College professors, plant managers, and the children of the bureaucratic elite were berated and forced to confess publicly their many crimes against "the people." Those who were not imprisoned or, more rarely, killed were forced to do manual labor on rural communes to enable them to understand the hardships endured by China's peasantry. In cities such as Shanghai, workers seized control of the factories and local bureaucracy. As Mao had hoped, the centralized state and technocratic elites that had grown steadily since the first revolution won power in 1949 were being torn apart by the rage of the people.

However satisfying for advocates of continuing revolution, such as Mao, it was soon clear that the Cultural Revolution threatened to return China to the chaos and vulnerability of the prerevolutionary era. The rank-and-file threat to the leaders of the People's Liberation Army eventually proved decisive in prompting countermeasures that forced Mao to call off the campaign by late 1968. The heads of the armed forces moved to bring the rank and file back into line; the student and worker movements were disbanded and in some cases forcibly repressed. By the early 1970s, Mao's old rivals had begun to surface again. For the next half decade, a hard-fought struggle was waged at the upper levels of the party and the army for control of the government. The reconciliation between China and the United States that was negotiated in the early 1970s suggested that, at least in foreign policy, the pragmatists were gaining the upper hand over the ideologues. Deng's growing role in policy formation from 1973 onward also represented a major setback for Jiang Qing, who led the notorious **Gang of Four** that increasingly contested power on behalf of the aging Mao.

The death in early 1976 of Zhou Enlai, who was second only to Mao in stature as a revolutionary hero and who had consistently backed the pragmatists, appeared to be a major blow to those whom the Gang of Four had marked out as "capitalist-roaders" and betrayers of the revolution. But Mao's death later in the same year cleared the way for an open clash between the rival factions. While the Gang of Four plotted to seize control of the government, the pragmatists acted in alliance with some of the more influential military leaders. The Gang of Four were arrested, and their supporters' attempts to foment popular insurrections were foiled easily. Later tried for their crimes against the people, Jiang Qing and the members of her clique were purged from the party and imprisoned for life after their death sentences were commuted.

Since the death of Mao, the pragmatists have been ascendant, and leaders such as Deng Xiaoping have opened China to Western influences and capitalist development, if not yet democratic reform. Under Deng and his allies, the farming communes were discontinued and private peasant production for the market was encouraged. Private enterprise has also been promoted in the industrial sector, and experiments have been made with such capitalist institutions as a stock exchange and foreign hotel chains.

Although it has become fashionable to dismiss the development schemes of the communist states as misguided failures, the achievements of the communist regime in China in the late 20th and early 21st centuries have been impressive. Despite severe economic setbacks, political turmoil, and a low level of foreign assistance, the communists have managed a truly revolutionary redistribution of the wealth of the country. China's very large population remains poor, but in education, health care, housing, working conditions, and the availability of food, most of it is far better off than it was in the prerevolutionary era. The Chinese have managed to provide a decent standard of living for a higher proportion of their people than perhaps any other large developing country. They have also achieved higher rates of industrial and agricultural growth than neighboring India, with its mixed state–capitalist economy and democratic polity. The Chinese have done all of this with much less foreign assistance than most developing nations have had. If the pragmatists remain in power and the champions of the market economy are right, China's growth in the 21st century should be even more impressive. But the central challenge for China's leaders will be to nurture that growth and the improved living standards without a recurrence of the economic inequities and social injustice that brought about the revolution in the first place.

Figure 34.9 Mao Zedong and his allies launched the Cultural Revolution during the mid-1960s in an effort to restore the revolutionary fervor that they felt had been eroded by the growing bureaucratization of China. In this photo a crowd of Mao's zealous young supporters rally in Beijing. The vicious assaults on anyone branded as elitist or pro-Western led to torture, imprisonment, and killings on a scale that is not yet fully understood. As the movement degenerated into mindless radicalism for its own sake, many of the gains a more moderate approach had made in the preceding decade were lost.

Gang of Four   Jiang Qing and four political allies who attempted to seize control of Communist government in China from the pragmatists; arrested and sentenced to life imprisonment in 1976 following Mao Zedong's death.

Map 34.3 Vietnam: Divisions in the Nguyen and French Periods Within decades of the unification of Vietnam under the Nguyen dynasty it was conquered piecemeal and again divided politically by French colonizers.

The Vietnamese, as well as their neighbors in Laos and Cambodia, were brought under European colonial rule in the second half of the 19th century. As in China, the collapse of the Confucian system around which the Vietnamese had organized civilized life for nearly two millennia led to violent revolution and a search for a viable social and political order that brought a communist regime to power.

Tayson Rebellion   Peasant revolution in southern Vietnam during the late 1770s; succeeded in toppling the Nguyen dynasty; subsequently unseated the Trinh dynasty of northern Vietnam.

Nguyen Anh   [nwihn ahn] (1762–1820) Last surviving member of Nguyen dynasty following Tayson Rebellion in Vietnam; with French support retook southern Vietnam; drove Tayson from northern Vietnam by 1802; proclaimed himself emperor with capital at Hue; also known as Gia Long.

Minh Mang   Second emperor of a united Vietnam; successor of Nguyen Anh; ruled from 1820 to 1841; sponsored emphasis of Confucianism; persecuted Catholics.

Colonialism and Revolution in Vietnam

French interest in Vietnam reached back as far as the 17th century. Driven from Japan by the founders of the Tokugawa shogunate, French missionaries fell back on coastal Vietnam. Vietnam attracted them both because its Confucian elite seemed similar to that of the Japanese and because the continuing wars between rival dynastic houses in the Red River valley and central Vietnam gave the missionaries ample openings for their conversion efforts (Map 34.3). From this time onward, French rulers, who considered themselves the protectors of the Catholic missions overseas, took an interest in Vietnamese affairs. As the numbers of converts grew into the tens of thousands and French merchants began to trade at Vietnamese ports, the French stake in the region increased.

By the late 18th century, French involvement had become distinctly political as a result of the power struggles that convulsed the whole region. In the south, a genuine peasant rebellion, the **Tayson Rebellion,** toppled the Nguyen dynasty in the late 1770s. In the years that followed, the Trinh dynasty, the northern rival of the Nguyen, was also dethroned. The Tayson controlled most of the country, eliminated the Trinh, and all but wiped out the Nguyen. Seeing a chance to win influence in the ruling house, the French head of the Vietnam mission, the bishop of Adran, threw his support behind the one surviving prince of the southern house, **Nguyen Anh** (nwihn ahn).

Anh had fled into the Mekong wilderness with a handful of supporters, thus escaping death at the hands of the Tayson. With the arms and advice of the French, he rallied local support for the dynasty and soon fielded a large army. After driving the Tayson from the south, Nguyen Anh launched an invasion of Tayson strongholds in the north. His task of conquest was made easier by bitter quarrels between the Tayson leaders. By 1802 the Nguyen armies had prevailed, and Nguyen Anh had proclaimed himself the Gia Long emperor of Vietnam.

Gia Long made the old Nguyen capital at Hue in central Vietnam the imperial capital of a unified Vietnam. His French missionary allies were rewarded with a special place at court, and French traders were given greater access to the port of Saigon, which was rapidly emerging as the leading city of the Mekong River valley region in the south. The Nguyen dynasty was the first in centuries to rule all of Vietnam and the first to rule a Vietnamese kingdom that included both the Red River and Mekong deltas. In fact, the Mekong region had only begun to be settled extensively by Vietnamese in the century or so before Gia Long rose to power.

Gia Long and his successors proved to be arch-traditionalists deeply committed to strengthening Confucianism in Vietnam. Their capital at Hue was intended to be a perfect miniature of the imperial palace at Beijing. The dynasty patronized Confucian schools and built its administration around scholar-bureaucrats who were well versed in Confucian learning. The second emperor, **Minh Mang** (1820–1841), prided himself on his knowledge of the Confucian classics and his mastery of the Chinese script. He even had the audacity to criticize the brushwork of the reigning Chinese emperor, who was not any more Chinese than Minh Mang but was descended from Manchu nomads. All of this proved deeply disappointing to the French missionaries, who hoped to baptize Gia Long and then carry out through the Vietnamese the sort of top-down conversion that the Jesuits had hoped for ever since their arrival in Asia.

Things actually got much worse. Gia Long's ultra-Confucian successor, Minh Mang, came to see the Catholics as a danger to the dynasty. His persecution of the Vietnamese Catholic community not only enraged the missionaries but also contributed to the growing political and military intervention of the French government in the region. Pushed both by political pressures at home and military defeats in Europe, French adventurers and soldiers exploited quarrels with the Nguyen rulers to justify the piecemeal conquest of Vietnam and neighboring Cambodia and Laos beginning in the late 1840s (Map 34.3). By the 1890s, the whole of the country was under French control, and the Nguyen dynasty had been reduced to the status of puppet princes. In the decades that followed, the French concentrated on drawing revenue and resources from Vietnam while providing very little in return.

The French determination to make Vietnam a colony that was profitable for the homeland worsened social and economic problems that were already severe under the Nguyen rulers. Most of the densely packed peasant population of the north lacked enough land for a subsistence livelihood. French taxes and the burden of obligatory purchases by each village of set amounts of government-sold opium and alcohol drove many peasants into labor in the mines. Even larger numbers left their ancestral villages and migrated to the Mekong region to work on the plantations established there by French and Chinese entrepreneurs. Other migrants chose to become tenants on the great estates that had been carved out of sparsely settled frontier regions by Vietnamese and Chinese landlords.

Migration brought little relief. Plantation workers were paid little and were treated much like slave laborers. The unchecked demands of the Mekong landlords left their tenants with scarcely enough of the crops they grew to feed, clothe, and house their families. The exploitive nature of French colonialism in Vietnam was graphically revealed by the statistics the French themselves collected. These showed a sharp drop in the food consumed by the peasantry in all parts of the colony between the early 1900s and the 1930s, a drop that occurred despite the fact that Vietnam became one of the world's major rice-exporting areas.

Vietnamese Nationalism: Bourgeois Dead Ends and Communist Survival

The failure of the Nguyen rulers after Minh Mang to rally the forces of resistance against the French did much to discredit the dynasty. But from the 1880s into the first decades of the 20th century, guerrilla warfare was waged in various parts of the country in support of the "Save the King" movement. Because this resistance was localized and small, the French were able to crush it on a piecemeal basis. In any case, French control over the puppet emperors who remained on the throne at Hue left the rebels with little cause worth fighting for. The failure of the Nguyen and the Confucian bureaucratic classes to defend Vietnam against the French did much to discredit the old order in the eyes of the new generations that came of age in the early decades of French rule. Perhaps because it was imported rather than homegrown, the Vietnamese were quicker than the Chinese to reject Confucianism once the drawbacks of its inflexibility and past-oriented leanings were clear, and they did so with a good deal less trauma. But its demise left an ideological and institutional vacuum that the Vietnamese, again like the Chinese, would struggle for decades to fill.

In the early 20th century, a new Western-educated middle class, similar to that found in other colonial settings (see Chapters 24 and 28), was formed. It was made up mainly of the children of the traditional Confucian elite and the emerging landlord class in the Mekong region. Some, taking advantage of their parents' wealth, went to French schools and emerged speaking fluent French and with a taste for French fashions and frequent holiday jaunts to Paris and the French Riviera. Many of them went to work for the French as colonial administrators, bank managers, and even labor recruiters. Others pursued independent careers as lawyers, doctors, and journalists. Many who opted for French educations and French lifestyles were soon drawn into nationalist organizations. Like their counterparts elsewhere in the colonies, the members of these organizations initially concentrated on protesting French racism and discrimination, improving their own wages, and gaining access to positions in the colonial government held by French people.

As in other colonies, nationalist newspapers and magazines proliferated. These became the focal point of an extended debate over the approach that should be taken toward winning freedom from French rule and, increasingly, what needed to be done to rebuild Vietnam as a whole. Because the French forcibly repressed all attempts to mount peaceful mass demonstrations or organize constitutional agitation, those who argued for violent resistance eventually gained the upper hand. In the early 1920s, the nationalist struggle was centered in the clandestine **Vietnamese Nationalist party** (Vietnamese Quoc Dan Dong, or VNQDD), which was committed to violent revolution against the French colonizers. Although the VNQDD made some attempt to organize urban laborers and peasant villagers, the party members were drawn overwhelmingly from the children of the landlord elite and urban professional classes. Their secret codes and elaborate rituals proved little protection against the dreaded Sûreté, or French secret police. A series of failed uprisings, culminating in a 1929 attempt to spark a general revolution with the assassination of a much-hated French official in charge of labor recruitment, decimated the party. It was particularly hard hit by the ensuing French campaign of repression, execution, and imprisonment. From that point onward, the bourgeois nationalists were never again the dominant force in the struggle for independence.

Vietnamese Nationalist party Also known as the Vietnamese Quoc Dan Dong or VNQDD; active in 1920s as revolutionary force committed to violent overthrow of French colonialism.

Frantz Fanon and Ho Chi Minh Speak Out Against Imperialism
CASE STUDY

Communist party of Vietnam   Originally a wing of nationalist movement; became primary nationalist party after decline of VNQDD in 1929; led in late 1920s by Nguyen Ai Quoc, alias Ho Chi Minh.

Ho Chi Minh   Also known as Nguyen Ai Quoc; led Vietnamese Communist party in struggle for liberation from French and U.S. dominance and to unify north and south Vietnam.

Viet Minh   Communist-dominated Vietnamese nationalist movement; operated out of base in southern China during World War II; employed guerrilla tactics similar to the Maoists in China.

Vietnamese Declaration of Independence
DOCUMENT

Giap, Vo Nguyen   [zap, vah-ah nwihn] Chief military commander of the Viet Minh; architect of the Vietnamese victory over the French at Dien Bien Phu in 1954.

Dien Bien Phu   Most significant victory of the Viet Minh over French colonial forces in 1954; gave the Viet Minh control of northern Vietnam.

The demise of the VNQDD left its major rival, the **Communist party of Vietnam,** as the main focus of nationalist resistance in Vietnam. As in China and Korea, the communist wing of the nationalist movement had developed in Vietnam during the 1920s, often at the initiative of leaders in exile. By the late 1920s, the party was dominated by the charismatic young Nguyen Ai Quoc, who would later be known as **Ho Chi Minh.** Ho had discovered Marxism while studying in France and Russia during and after World War I. Disillusioned by his failure to gain a hearing for his plea for the Vietnamese right to self-determination at the post–World War I Paris Peace Conference, Ho dedicated himself to a revolutionary struggle to drive the French from Indochina.

In the early 1930s, the Communist party still held to the rigid but unrealistic orthodox vision of a revolution based on the urban working classes. Because the workers in Vietnam made up as small a percentage of the population as they had in China, the orthodox strategy made little headway. A sudden shift in the early 1930s to a peasant emphasis, in part to take advantage of widespread but not communist-inspired peasant uprisings in central Vietnam, led to a disaster almost as great as that which had overtaken the VNQDD a year before. French repression smashed the party hierarchy and drove most of the major communist leaders into exile. But the superior underground organization of the communists and the support they received from the Comintern helped them survive the French onslaught. When the French were weakened by the Japanese invasion of Indochina in 1941, the Vietnamese communists were ready to use the colonizers' setbacks to advance the struggle for national liberation.

The War of Liberation Against the French

During World War II, operating out of bases in south China, the communist-dominated nationalist movement, known as the **Viet Minh,** established liberated areas throughout the northern Red River delta (Map 34.3). The abrupt end of Japanese rule left a vacuum in Vietnam, which only the Viet Minh was prepared to fill. Its programs for land reform and mass education had wide appeal among the hard-pressed peasants of the north, where they had been propagated during the 1930s and especially during the war. The fact that the Viet Minh actually put their reform and community-building programs into effect in the areas they controlled won them very solid support among the rural population. The Viet Minh's efforts to provide assistance to the peasants during the terrible famine of 1944 and 1945 also convinced the much-abused Vietnamese people that here at last was a political organization genuinely committed to improving their lot.

Under the leadership of general **Vo Nguyen Giap** (vah-ah nwihn zap), the Viet Minh skillfully used guerrilla tactics similar to those devised by Mao in China (See Chapter 29). These offset the advantages that first the French and then the Japanese enjoyed in conventional firepower. With a strong base of support in much of the rural north and the hill regions, where they had won the support of key non-Vietnamese "tribal" peoples, the Viet Minh forces advanced triumphantly into the Red River delta as the Japanese withdrew. By August 1945, the Viet Minh were in control of Hanoi, where Ho Chi Minh proclaimed the establishment of the independent nation of Vietnam.

Although the Viet Minh had liberated much of the north, they had very little control in the south. In that part of Vietnam a variety of communist and bourgeois nationalist parties jostled for power. The French, eager to reclaim their colonial empire and put behind them their humiliations at the hands of the Nazis, were quick to exploit this turmoil. With British assistance, the French reoccupied Saigon and much of south and central Vietnam. In March 1946, they denounced the August declaration of Vietnamese independence and moved to reassert their colonial control over the whole of Vietnam and the rest of Indochina. An unsteady truce between the French and the Viet Minh quickly broke down. Soon Vietnam was consumed by a renewal of the Viet Minh's guerrilla war for liberation, as well as bloody infighting between the different factions of the Vietnamese.

After nearly a decade of indecisive struggle, the Viet Minh had gained control of much of the Vietnamese countryside, and the French, with increasing American financial and military aid, clung to the fortified towns. In 1954 the Viet Minh decisively defeated the French by capturing the giant fortress they had built at **Dien Bien Phu** in the mountain highlands hear the Laotian border. The victory gained international recognition at a 1954 conference in Geneva for an independent state, the Democratic Republic of Vietnam, in the north. At Geneva, elections throughout Vietnam were also promised in the treaty within two years to decide who should govern a reunited north and the still politically fragmented south (Map 34.4).

The War of Liberation Against the United States

In Geneva, some hoped that free elections would eventually be held to determine who should govern a united Vietnam. However, this electoral contest never materialized. Like the rest of east Asia, Vietnam had become entangled in the cold war maneuvers of the United States and the Soviet Union. Despite very amicable cooperation between the Viet Minh and U.S. armed forces during the war against Japan, U.S. support for the French in the First Indochina War and the growing fame of Ho Chi Minh as a communist leader drove the two further and further into opposition. The anticommunist hysteria in the United States in the early 1950s fed the perception of influential American leaders that South Vietnam, like South Korea, must be protected from communist takeover.

The search for a leader to build a government in the south that the United States could prop up with economic and military assistance led to **Ngo Dinh Diem** (nyoh dihn DEE-ehm). Diem appeared to have impeccable nationalist credentials. In fact, he had gone into exile rather than give up the struggle against the French. His sojourn in the United States in the 1940s and the fact that he was Catholic also recommended him to American politicians and clergy. Unfortunately, these same attributes would alienate him from the great majority of the Vietnamese people.

With U.S. backing, Diem was installed as the president of Vietnam. He tried to legitimatize his status in the late 1950s by holding rigged elections in the south, in which the communists were not permitted to run. Diem also mounted a series of campaigns to eliminate by force all possible political rivals. Because the communists posed the biggest threat (and were of the greatest concern to Diem's American backers), the suppression campaign increasingly focused on the communist cadres that remained in the south after Vietnam had been divided at Geneva. By the mid-1950s, the **Viet Cong** (as the Diem regime dubbed the communist resistance) were threatened with extermination. In response to this threat, the communist regime in the north began to send weapons, advisors, and other resources to the southern cadres, which were reorganized as the National Liberation Front in 1960.

As guerrilla warfare spread and Diem's military responses expanded, both the United States and the North Vietnamese escalated their support for the warring parties. When Diem proved unable to stem the communist tide in the countryside, the United States authorized his generals to overthrow him and take direct charge of the war. When the Vietnamese military could make little headway, the United States stepped up its military intervention (Map 34.4).

From thousands of special advisors in the early 1950s, the U.S. commitment rose to nearly 500,000 men and women, who made up a massive force of occupation by 1968. But despite the loss of nearly 60,000 American lives and millions of Vietnamese casualties, the Americans could not defeat the communist movement. In part, their failure resulted from their very presence, which made it possible for the communists to convince the great majority of the Vietnamese people that they were fighting for their independence from yet another imperialist aggressor.

Although more explosives were dropped on tiny Vietnam, North and South, than in all of the theaters of World War II, and the United States resorted to chemical warfare against the very environment of the South Vietnamese they claimed to be trying to save, the communists would not yield. The Vietnamese emerged as the victors of the Vietnam or (from the Vietnamese perspective) Second Indochina War. In the early 1970s, U.S. diplomats negotiated an end to direct American involvement in the conflict. Without that support, the unpopular military regime in the south fell apart by 1975 (Figure 34.10). The communists united Vietnam under a single government for the first time since the late 1850s. But the nation they governed was shattered and impoverished by decades of civil war,

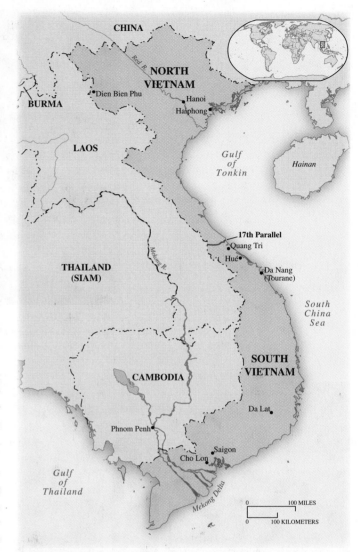

Map 34.4 North and South Vietnam   Vietnam was arbitrarily divided at the 17th parallel in 1954 due to the pressure of the great powers and over the objection of the Vietnamese Communists who had led the war of liberation against the French.

Diem, Ngo Dinh   [DEE-ehm, nyoh dihn] Political leader of South Vietnam; established as president with United States support in the 1950s; opposed Communist government of North Vietnam; overthrown by military coup approved by United

Viet Cong   Name given by Diem regime to communist guerrilla movement in southern Vietnam; reorganized with northern Vietnamese assistance as the National Liberation Front in 1958.

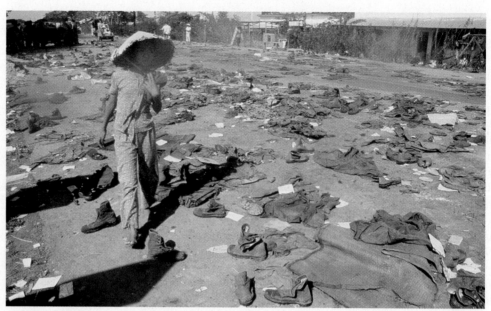

Figure 34.10 April 30, 1975. As the victorious Viet Cong entered Saigon, a photographer captured the image of a lone woman hurrying along a road strewn with uniforms abandoned by former South Vietnamese soldiers fearful of being identified as having fought on the losing side.

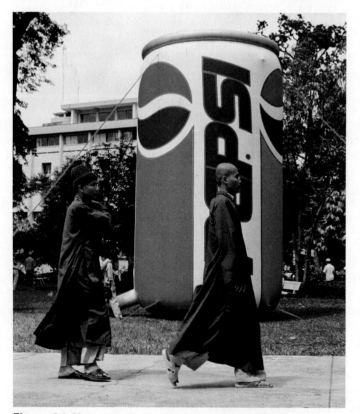

Figure 34.11 By the mid-1990s, the failed efforts of the United States to isolate Vietnam gave way to increasing economic and diplomatic contacts. One example of American corporate penetration is depicted in this street scene from Hanoi in 1993. The opening of Vietnam to foreign investment, assistance, and tourism accelerated through the 1990s. In this atmosphere it has been possible to begin to heal the deep wounds and animosities generated by decades of warfare waged by the Vietnamese people against advanced industrial nations such as Japan, France, and the United States.

revolution, and armed conflict with two major colonial powers and the most powerful nation of the second half of the 20th century.

After Victory: Salvaging Communism in an Era of Globalization

In the years since 1975 and the end of what was, for the Vietnamese, decades of wars for liberation, communist efforts to complete the revolution by rebuilding Vietnamese society have failed. In part, this failure can be linked to Vietnam's isolation from much of the rest of the international community. This isolation resulted in part from pressures applied by a vengeful United States against relief from international agencies. It was increased by border clashes with China that were linked to ancient rivalries between the two countries. Deprived of assistance from abroad and faced with a shattered economy and a devastated environment at home, Vietnam's aging revolutionary leaders pushed hard-line Marxist-Leninist (and even Stalinist) political and economic agendas. Like their Chinese counterparts, they devoted their energies to persecuting old enemies (thus setting off mass migrations from what had been South Vietnam) and imposed a dictatorial regime that left little room for popular responses to government initiatives. In contrast to the Chinese in the past decade, however, the Vietnamese leadership also tried to maintain a highly centralized command economy. The rigid system that resulted stifled growth and, if anything, left the Vietnamese people almost as impoverished as they had been after a century of colonialism and decades of civil war.

By the late 1980s, the obvious failure of these approaches and the collapse of communist regimes throughout eastern Europe prompted measures aimed at liberalizing and expanding the market sector within the Vietnamese economy. The encouraging responses of Japanese and European corporations, eager to open up Vietnamese markets, have done much to stimulate growth in the Vietnamese economy. Growing investments by their industrial rivals have placed increasing pressure on

American firms to move into the Vietnamese market (Figure 34.11). These trends have been strengthened by the genuine willingness shown by Vietnamese leaders in the past decade to work with U.S. officials to resolve questions about prisoners of war and soldiers missing in action from the Vietnam War. But, like many other postcolonial nations, Vietnam has paid a high price for its efforts at integration into the globalizing economy. Many of its workers have had to endure the sweatshop conditions widely found in foreign factories, social inequality has increased markedly, and the free education system and other public services once provided by the communist state have declined or have entirely disappeared.

Global Connections

East Asia and the Pacific Rim in the Contemporary World

In many respects, the recent histories of China and the peoples of Japan, Korea, and Vietnam, whose cultures were so profoundly affected by Chinese civilization, have been fundamentally different from those of much of the rest of Asia and Africa. Particularly in the past century, the experience of the Japanese has differed the most from those of other Asian and African peoples. The ethnically homogeneous, politically unified, and militarily adept Japanese not only were able to beat off Western imperialist advances against their island home but they have been one of the few non-Western peoples to achieve a high level of industrialization. Within decades of the forced "opening" of Japan by the United States in the 1850s, it also became the only African or Asian nation to join the ranks of the great powers. In imitation of its Western rivals, Japan embarked on its own campaign of imperialist expansion overseas. Although Korea was colonized early in the 20th century by its powerful Japanese neighbor, in the decades since World War II it has emerged as one of the leading industrial centers of the Pacific Rim. Since World War II, Taiwan and several other east Asian centers experienced rapid industrial advances, propelling the Pacific Rim to new importance in world affairs.

In contrast to industrialized Japan and to Korea in the past four decades or so, with their high standards of living and global economic power, China and Vietnam have had a good deal in common with the rest of the emerging nations. China and Vietnam suffered heavily from the assaults and exploitive terms of exchange imposed by imperialist powers, both Western and Japanese. Each has had to contend with underdevelopment, overpopulation, poverty, and environmental degradation. But unlike most of the rest of the formerly colonized peoples, the Chinese and the Vietnamese have had to deal with these awesome challenges in the midst of the collapse of the patterns of civilized life each had followed for thousands of years.

As disruptive as imperialist conquest and its effects were in the rest of the Asian and African worlds, most colonized peoples managed to preserve much of their precolonial cultures and modes of social organization. The defense and revival of traditional customs, religious beliefs, and social arrangements played a key role in their struggles for decolonization. This was not the case in China and Vietnam, where a combination of external aggression and internal upheavals discredited and destroyed the Confucian system that had long been synonymous with civilized life. With their traditional order in shambles, the peoples of China and Vietnam had no choice but to embark on full-scale revolutions that would clear away the rubble of the failed Confucian system. They needed to remove the obstacles posed by imperialist dominance and build new, viable states and societies.

In contrast to much of the rest of the colonized world, the countries of China and Vietnam derived few benefits from European domination, either informal or formal. Imperialist pressures eroded and smashed their political institutions rather than building up a bureaucratic grid and imparting political ideologies that could form the basis for nation-building. Both China and Vietnam already had the strong sense of identity, common language, and unifying polity that were among the major legacies of colonialism in other areas.

Because of economic development (in the Pacific Rim, and more recently in China and Vietnam) and the forces of revolution, east Asia has been fundamentally recast in the decades since World War II and has gained new importance in world affairs. The patterns of these transformations have varied. On the one hand, there has been a dynamic combination of industrialization and reform of the Pacific Rim in close connection to the West. On the other, the fluctuations of major revolutionary movements have been followed by the post-Maoist adoption of what one observer aptly dubbed "Market-Leninism" in China and Vietnam in recent decades. The legacy of earlier patterns in east Asia, including Confucianism, has similarly been redefined and utilized in different ways. But the themes of growing independence and self-assertion have been combined across east Asia in recent years with ongoing or new experiments in Western-style capitalism, replacing Confucianism as the state ideology and providing the philosophical basis for the new social order.

Revolution and economic change have combined to make east Asia a growing force in world affairs by the early 21st century—and of course, largely independent of Western control in contrast to the previous period of imperialism. China's size and post-revolutionary economic surge, which has come to exceed even that of the rest of the Pacific Rim nations, has prompted some observers to wonder if the twenty-first century will be the "century of east Asia." China, Japan, and South Korea have become centers of multinational corporations, along with the West. East Asian exports, including toys like Pokemon and animated films are now staples of global consumer culture. Japanese, Korean, and more recently Chinese scientific capacity in areas like super-computing have made them major global innovators, while China and Japan have come to play growing roles in space technology. China, Japan, and Korea have also become prominent participants in global athletic competitions. In various ways, including standard diplomatic and economic channels, the nations of east Asia have come to exert more influence in world affairs than ever before. Their growing predominance in all of these areas ensures that the peoples of east Asia will shape human history in the 21st century in major, perhaps transformative, ways.

Further Readings

The best account of late twentieth-century Japanese society and politics is E. O. Reischauer, *The Japanese* (1988). For recent history, see also M. Hane, *Modern Japan: A Historical Survey* (1992); William G. Beasley, *The Rise of Modern Japan* (1995); and Edward R. Beauchamp, ed., *Women and Women's Issues in Post World War II Japan* (1998).

Several novels and literary collections are accessible and useful. J. Tanizaki, *The Makioka Sisters* (1957), deals with a merchant family in the 1930s; see also H. Hibbett, ed., *Contemporary Japanese Literature: An Anthology of Fiction, Film, and Other Writing Since 1945* (1992). An important study of change, focusing on postwar rural society, is G. Bernstein, *Haruko's World: A Japanese Farm Woman and Her Community* (1983). Another complex 20th-century topic is assessed in R. Storry, *The Double Patriots: A Story of Japanese Nationalism* (1973).

On the Pacific Rim concept and its implications for the world economy, see David Aikman, *Pacific Rim: Area of Change, Area of Opportunity* (1986); Philip West et al., eds., *The Pacific Rim and the Western World: Strategic, Economic, and Cultural Perspectives* (1987); Stephen Haggard and Chung-In Moon, *Pacific Dynamics: The International Politics of Industrial Change* (1988); and Roland A. Morse et al., *Pacific Basin: Concept and Challenge* (1986). Vera Simone, *The Asian Pacific: Political and Economic Development in a Global Context* (1995), is a comparative survey of postcolonial state building and international cultural connections. Also see S. Ichimura, *The Political Economy of Japanese and Asian Development* (1998).

Excellent introductions to recent Korean history are Bruce Cumings, *The Two Koreas* (1984) and *Korea's Place in the Sun: A Modern History* (1997), and David Rees, *A Short History of Modern Korea* (1988). A variety of special topics are addressed in Marshal R. Pihl, ed., *Listening to Korea: Economic Transformation and Social Change* (1989). See also Paul Kuznet, *Economic Growth and Structure in the Republic of Korea* (1977), and Dennis McNamara, *The Colonial Origins of Korean Enterprise, 1910–1945* (1990).

For a fascinating exploration of cultural change and continuity in Taiwan regarding issues in health and medicine, see Arthur Kleinman, *Patients and Healers in the Context of Culture* (1979). On Singapore, Janet W. Salaff, *State and Family in Singapore* (1988), is an excellent study; see also R. N. Kearney, ed., *Politics and Modernization in South and Southeast Asia* (1975).

A good summary of the final stages of the civil war in China is provided in Lucien Bianco, *Origins of the Chinese Revolution, 1915–1949* (1971). Perhaps the best overview of modern Chinese history from the Qing dynasty era through the Tiananmen Square massacres can be found in Jonathan D. Spence, *The Search for Modern China* (1990). Other useful accounts of the post-1949 era include Maurice Meisner, *Mao's China and After 1984* (1984); Michael Gasster, *China's Struggle to Modernize* (1987); and Immanuel C. Y. Hsu, *China Without Mao* (1983). On the pivotal period of the Cultural Revolution, see Roderick MacFarquhar, *The Origins of the Cultural Revolution*, 2 vols. (1974, 1983), and Lowell Dittmer, *Liu Shao-ch'i and the Chinese Cultural Revolution* (1974). For a highly critical assessment of the Maoist era, it is difficult to surpass Simon Leys, *Chinese Shadows* (1977). On cultural life in the postrevolutionary era, see the essays in R. MacFarquhar, ed., *The Hundred Flowers Campaign and the Chinese Intellectuals,* and Lois Wheeler Snow, *China on Stage* (1972). Elisabeth Croll, *Feminism and Socialism in China* (1978), remains by far the best single work on the position of women in revolutionary and Maoist China.

The first war of liberation in Vietnam is covered in Ellen J. Hammer, *The Struggle for Indochina, 1940–1955* (1966). The best of many surveys of the second war, often called the American War in Vietnam, is Marilyn Young, *The Vietnam Wars, 1945–1990* (1989). Of a number of fine studies on the origins of American intervention in the area, two of the best are Patti Archimedes' *Why Vietnam?* (1980), and Lloyd Gardner's *Approaching Vietnam* (1988). On the conduct of the war, Jeffrey Race's *The War Comes to Long An* (1972); Eric Bergerud, *The Dynamics of Defeat: The Vietnam War in Hau Nghia Province* (1991); and Marc Jason Gilbert, ed., *Why the North Won the Vietnam War* (2002), are useful for the stress they place on the role of the Vietnamese in determining this conflict's course and ultimate outcome. Powerful firsthand accounts of the guerrilla war and U.S. combat include Mark Baker, *Nam* (1981); Philip Caputo, *A Rumor of War* (1977); Troung Nhu Tang, *A Viet Cong Memoir* (1985), and Bao Ninh, *The Sorrow of War* (1993).

On the Web

The career arc of leading personalities in the rise of modern Korea, such as Syngman Rhee (http://www.hartford-hwp.com/archives/55a/186.html and http://us.cnn.com/SPECIALS/cold.war/kbank/profiles/rhee/) and much of the history of postwar Japan was shaped by the Korean War (http://mcel.pacificu.edu/as/students/stanley/home.html). The nature of the Korean economy and the dominant role of large corporate entities, *chaebol,* in postwar Korea are explored at http://www.country-data.com/cgi-bin/query/r-12303.html. and http://news.bbc.co.uk/1/hi/in_depth/business/2000/review/1037276.stm, where they are compared with Japanese *keiretsu.*

The life of General Douglas Macarthur and the art and society of the occupation or "Confusion" era in Japan are the subject of a brilliant Smithsonian exhibition available online at http://

www.smithsonianeducation.org/migrations/sackler/saltfore.html. Japan's difficulty in accepting responsibility for its wartime atrocities, particularly the abuse of Korean and other Asian women by Japanese occupation troops, is discussed at http://research.unc.edu/endeavors/win97/comfort.html, http://online.sfsu.edu/~soh/cw-links.htm (a links page), and http://taiwan.yam.org.tw/womenweb/conf_women/index_e.html.

Korekiyo Takahashi's role in the building of the modern Japanese economy and his conflict with the war party led by Hideki Tojo is examined at http://www.ndl.go.jp/portrait/e/datas/122.html?c=0. Takahashi's policies in today's Japan is examined at http://www.atimes.com/Japan-econ/AB12Dh01.html. Much of the postwar recovery of east Asian economies was due to close cooperation between business and government, which recently has been criticized even in Japan, where politicians have been caught with trunks full of cash provided by leading Japanese companies. This pattern was followed by the eastern Pacific Rim's economic tigers as part of an authoritarian development strategy, most clearly expressed by Singapore's Lee Kwan Yew, who has made comparisons between himself and Machiavelli (http://unpan1.un.org/intradoc/groups/public/documents/apcity/unpan002548.pdf). However, a recent economic recession in the region, discussed in an audio file by Lee Kwan Yew himself at http://webcast.rice.edu/speeches/19981023lee.html, has forced some to question whether the east Asian model of economic growth is worthy of emulation elsewhere. A close look at the causes and lessons of the Asian economic crisis of the 1990s (and just now abating) is explored at http://www.parliament.uk/commons/lib/research/rp99/rp99-014.pdf.

The Cultural Revolution in China is examined at http://library.thinkquest.org/26469/cultural-revolution/. A virtual tour of the Cultural Revolution, including files of documents and personal reminiscences, is located at http://www.cnd.org/CR/english/. Art played a major role in the Cultural Revolution, as is borne out by two exhibitions, entitled "Rethinking Cultural Revolution Culture" and "Picturing Power: Art and Propaganda in the Great Proletarian Cultural Revolution." The first is found at http://www.sino.uni-heidelberg.de/conf/propaganda/ and the second at http://kaladarshan.arts.ohio-state.edu/exhib/poster/exhibintro.html. The story of the Red Guards as viewed through their songs can be explored at http://www.indiana.edu/~easc/resources/working_paper/noframe_10b_song.htm. Attacks by the Red Guards on teachers are discussed at http://www.cnd.org/CR/english/articles/violence.htm. The nature of the Chinese Peoples' Liberation Army is described at http://en.wikipedia.org/wiki/People's_Liberation_Army. The limits of the recent movement toward liberalization in China, and by extension in the remaining communist nations, were tested during the student occupation of Tiananmen Square in 1989. This event is explored at http://www.tsquare.tv/. The site offers film and music clips, a photo gallery, and a transcript of Deng Xiaoping's June 9, 1989, speech declaring martial law. A transcript of the Public Broadcasting Company's superb documentary on the Tiananmen Square protests in China in 1989 can be found at http://www.pbs.org/wgbh/pages/frontline/gate/. See also http://www.historywiz.com/demonstration.htm. The National Security Archives' briefing book and a wealth of documents on the 1989 Tiananmen Square student protest movement is found at http://www.gwu.edu/~nsarchiv/NSAEBB/NSAEBB16/. Still photography of the protests, their repression, and ongoing efforts at democratization in China is offered at http://www.christusrex.org/www1/sdc/tiananmen.html. A 360 degree moving image view of the square can be viewed at http://www.roundtiananmensquare.com/ and http://www.thebeijingguide.com/tiananmen_square/index.html. For a discussion of how corruption may ruin China's rise as a world power, see http://www.carnegieendowment.org/.

A balanced survey of Vietnamese history encompassing the Vietnamese past, Vietnam's struggle for independence and reunification, and the aftermath of that effort can be found at http://www.viettouch.com/hist/. The Web is particularly rich in sites documenting Vietnam's wars of national liberation, including the Emperor Bao Dai's letter of abdication of August 25, 1945 and Vietnam's Declaration of Independence of September 2, 1945 (see http://www.fordham.edu/halsall/mod/1945vietnam.html, http://www.vwip.org/doc-top.html, and http://www.vwip.org/vwiphome.html. The 1962 program of the National Liberation Front (also called the Viet Cong) is archived at http://www.fordham.edu/halsall/mod/1962vietcong1.html. There are excerpts from a host of American documents on the American War in Vietnam located at http://depts.vassar.edu/~vietnam/. A site devoted to reflecting the service of American women in Vietnam can be found at http://www.vietvet.org/women.htm. To learn about Vietnamese women who followed their female ancestors into battle, see http://worldhistoryconnected.press.uiuc.edu/4.3/gilbert.html, http://womenshistory.about.com/od/trung1/, http://www.onlinewomeninpolitics.org/vietnam/vietleads.htm, http://www.library.wisc.edu/guides/SEAsia/vnimage/women.htm, http://www.library.wisc.edu/guides/SEAsia/vnimage/rsponsib.htm, and http://worldhistoryconnected.press.uiuc.edu/4.3/gilbert.html. It is possible to view American and Vietnamese propaganda (on all sides) at http://www.library.wisc.edu/guides/SEAsia/vnimage/vnintro.htm#links, http://www.i-kirk.info/2nd14th/propag1.html, http://members.aol.com/_ht_a/firstbn6thin/VCpropaganda.html, http://www.parascope.com/articles/0497/phoenix.htm, and http://www.landscaper.net/propgand.htm. Audio feed and visual images of U.S. Secretary of Defense Robert McNamara's speech on the instability of the Republic of Vietnam, President Johnson's announcement of his decision not to run for reelection and focus on a negotiated settlement of the war, the screams of students reacting to a National Guard unit's shooting of passersby as well as antiwar demonstrators at Kent State University in May 1970, and President Nixon's announcement that he had achieved peace with honor in Vietnam can be found at http://www.historychannel.com/speeches/index.html.

The lack of economic development in the aftermath of the American War in Vietnam witnessed reconsideration by Vietnamese leaders of their post-war hard-line communist land policies and commercial regulation. This reconsideration led to a Vietnamese version of economic liberalization pursued in Russia and China known as *doi moi,* which is examined at http://www.csuchico.edu/~cheinz/syllabi/asst001/fall98/thompson/doimoi.htm and http://www.sjsu.edu/faculty/watkins/vietnam.htm.

AP* Test Prep

1. Japan's postwar government is BEST characterized as a
   - (A) communist people's democracy.
   - (B) traditional monarchy with a hereditary emperor and little popular sovereignty.
   - (C) democracy dominated by a political and economic oligarchy.
   - (D) democratic republic with an unstable party system.
   - (E) militaristic state.

2. The chief socio-cultural tension within postwar Japan has been
   - (A) a large non-Japanese ethnic minority deprived of significant rights.
   - (B) limited rights for women.
   - (C) inability to control population growth.
   - (D) defining the boundaries between tradition and Western influences.

3. Postwar Korean development has been substantially determined by
   - (A) the occupation of the country by China and the Soviet Union.
   - (B) its long term political division since the Cold War.
   - (C) the long and autocratic rule by the Korean king.
   - (D) the extreme hunger and poverty of all Korean peoples.

4. Following its defeat on mainland China, the Guomindang or Nationalist Party led by Chiang Kai-shek
   - (A) rejected support from the United States.
   - (B) fled to Taiwan and established the Republic of China.
   - (C) sought support from the U.S.S.R. for a prolonged fight with Mao's China.
   - (D) joined with the Chinese Communist Party to form the People's Republic of China.

AP* Test Prep

5. In contemporary Japan and Taiwan,
    (A) Christianity replaced the older Shinto and Confucian belief systems.
    (B) both countries maintained military alliances with China.
    (C) individualism and competitiveness were valued.
    (D) authoritarianism increasingly challenged democracy.
    (E) group consensus and collective decision making were highly valued.

6. All of the following are aspects of the Vietnamese struggle against French colonial rule EXCEPT:
    (A) many Vietnamese anti-colonialists were profoundly influenced by Western ideas.
    (B) failed uprisings weakened the non-Communist Vietnamese Nationalist Party.
    (C) the Second World War weakened the French colonial regime.
    (D) the French were able to temporarily retain their hold on Vietnam due to their victory at Dien Bien Phu.

7. With the departure of the French from Indochina
    (A) the United States threw its support to its war-time anti-Japanese ally, Ho Chi Minh.
    (B) the Vietnamese came to be governed by a pro-communist regime in the north and an anti-communist regime in the south.
    (C) Ngo Dinh Diem succeeded in building a vibrant democracy characterized by fair elections and little political repression.
    (D) the Soviet Union and China invaded Vietnam, forcing the United States to send thousands of troops to repel them.

Free-Response Question

What are the key factors in economic development in the Pacific Rim and east Asian nations?

Power, Politics, and Conflict in World History, 1990–2010

The End of the Cold War

VISUALIZING THE PAST: Symbolism in the Breakdown of the Soviet Bloc

The Spread of Democracy

DOCUMENT: Democratic Protest and Repression in China

The Great Powers and New Disputes

The United States as Sole Superpower

THINKING HISTORICALLY: Terrorism, Then and Now

GLOBAL CONNECTIONS: New Global Standards, New Divisions

A human rights activist in Guatemala put the situation this way in the mid-1980s:

> If it were not for the international assistance, primarily from Americas Watch, Amnesty International, the World Council of Churches, solidarity organizations from democratic countries, Canadian organizations, organizations of Guatemalans working in the United States, Canada or Europe, without the moral and political help of those organizations, I believe we would have been dead many years ago, the army would not have permitted our organization to develop. . . . If you don't have the contacts, if the people who are doing the killing know that nobody is going to do anything if you disappear, then you disappear. . . . It was vital to have contacts so that information could go outside (Figure 35.1).

Many Central American regimes were repressive in the 1980s and at the beginning of the 1990s. Their hostility to communism and social revolution had earned them support from a conservative president in the United States. Free elections were impossible and many resistance figures were jailed or worse. But the situation changed. Local agitation for democracy would not cease. Instead, it spread in many parts of Latin America. Movement of people between countries played a key role, bringing opportunities for new contacts and for free expression. International human rights organizations took up the cause, organizing massive peti-

tion campaigns on behalf of victims. Church groups were active. Labor organizations, from the United States and elsewhere, chimed in, as did European Common Market (European Union) and United Nations human rights groups. Despite the power of the local military and the strength of U.S. policy, there was a new international counterweight, able to publicize abuse and prevent its concealment. Activities of local "death squads" received wide media attention, as did attacks on foreign Christian missionaries. Ultimately, these pressures forced the United States to change its policies, and fledgling democratic regimes began to take shape throughout the region.

Enthusiasm for international definitions of political rights had never run higher. There was a new force in world politics. At the same time, the force had clear limits. In some areas, particularly in conflict-torn regions of Africa, ruling groups resisted international criticism and made no effective effort to stop human rights abuses. How much was the world changing?

In the last two decades of the 20th century, global history took an abrupt turn. With the remarkably sudden collapse of the Soviet Union and the communist regimes of eastern Europe, the long and tense cold war came to an end. A larger current of expanding democracy provided a context for these developments as well. At the same time, a new set of regional conflicts complicated post-cold war politics, while the emergence of the United States as sole superpower had its own pluses and minuses. By 2008 limitations on the democratic current became more visible as well, further complicating the most recent phase of world history. ■

This chapter deals with the transition to a post-cold war framework, which provided some of the leading themes in world history from the mid-1980s well into the early 21st century. Political and diplomatic changes held center stage, along with a resurgence of terrorism. The end of the cold war redefined a central issue in the new world history period that had begun to open with World War I and its aftermath: what global power balance would replace 19th century Western dominance? What political system or systems would replace the long hold of monarchies and empires? Political and diplomatic patterns were also involved however, in the renewed process of globalization, which affected an even wider range of human activities, from culture to the environment. This wider process is taken up in the chapter that follows.

Figure 35.1 During more than three decades of brutal civil conflict, 200,000 Guatemalans were killed or "disappeared" and more than a million were forced out of their homes. After a peace agreement was signed in 1996, a church commission headed by Bishop Juan José Gerardi investigated the atrocities committed during the civil war and issued a scathing report in which he found that 90 percent of the abuses had been committed by the government. Two days later, the 75-year-old bishop was bludgeoned to death. Here, throngs of mourners witness his funeral procession.

The End of the Cold War

The cold war had lasted for 30 years when its context began to shift. The Russian empire had been expanding, off and on, for 500 years, interrupted only briefly by World War I and the initial phases of the Russian Revolution before it resumed its growth, to unprecedented levels. What could cause these two firmly established patterns, the cold war and the Russian empire, to change course dramatically?

Strains within the Soviet empire forced reforms that led to its downfall.

Factors in Soviet Decline

Leadership was surely one component. After Stalin and then Khrushchev, Soviet leadership had turned conservative. Party bureaucrats, eager to protect the status quo, often advanced only mediocre people to top posts, men whose major leadership characteristic was their unwillingness to rock the boat. Many of these leaders then continued to hold power when their own aptitude declined with illness and age.

Of more general significance was the reassertion of initiative from some parts of the world surrounding the Soviet Union, despite continued pressures from the superpowers. The rise of Islamic fervor, evident in the Iranian Revolution of 1979, inevitably created anxiety in the Soviet Union with its large Muslim minority. To reduce this new threat, late in 1979 the Soviets invaded neighboring Afghanistan, hoping to set up a puppet regime that would protect Russian interests. The move drew widespread international disapproval. The war proved difficult, as Afghan guerrillas, with some backing from the United States, held their ground fiercely. Costs and casualties mounted, and the war—the first formal action the Soviets had indulged in since World War II—quickly proved unpopular at home.

At the same time, the success of western Europe's economy pushed communism into a defensive and retreating posture throughout eastern Europe. The attraction of Western institutions and consumer standards gained ground. Within the Soviet empire itself, a free trade union movement

1980 C.E.	1990 C.E.	2000 C.E.
1988 Soviet withdrawal from Afghanistan 1988–1991 Independence movements in eastern Europe and in minority states in Soviet Union 1989–1990 Collapse of Soviet Union and Warsaw Pact regimes	1990 Iraqi invasion of Kuwait 1991 Breakup of Soviet Union; Yeltsin to power in Russia; civil wars begin in Yugoslavia; Slovenia and Croatia secede; First U.S.-Iraq War, Iraq defeated 1992 North American Free Trade Agreement (NAFTA) inaugurated; Bosnia withdraws from Yugoslavia; first World Environmental Conference in Brazil 1992–1993 UN-U.S. interventions in Somalia 1994 Mass genocide in Rwanda 1994 U.S. intervention in Haiti 1995 U.S.-NATO interventions in Bosnia 1997 Second World Environmental Conference, Kyoto, Japan 1998 Serbian assault on Albanians in Kosovo 1999 U.S.-NATO war against Yugoslavia; Putin becomes president of Russia	2000 International Human Rights Conference, South Africa; Milosevic forced out as Serbian president; end of Yugoslav civil wars 2000–2002 Second Intifada in Palestine and Israel 2001 Mass demonstrations against World Trade Organization in Genoa; terrorist attacks on World Trade Center and Pentagon; U.S.–led coalition topples Taliban regime in Afghanistan 2002 India and Pakistan mobilize armies over Kashmir dispute; euro becomes common currency in much of European Union 2003 U.S. and Great Britain bring down Saddam Hussein's government in Iraq 2004–2005 Democratic regimes begin in Georgia, Ukraine; new protests begin in central Asia

resumed in Poland, linked to the Catholic Church, and while it was repressed through Soviet-mandated martial law in 1981, the stress of keeping the lid on was likely to increase.

Changes in Chinese policy entered in. China, of course, had separated itself from Soviet tutelage in the 1960s. But in 1978 the Chinese regime made a choice to participate in the world economy and to admit more market forces and competitive free enterprise in the internal economy as well. There was no relaxation of political controls, and a democratic movement was vigorously quashed in 1989. But the Chinese economy now differed dramatically from that of the Soviet Union, and change was quickly rewarded, both with international investment and with rapid growth. The Soviets now had to contend not only with China's massive population but with its superior economic performance.

Finally, U.S. diplomatic policy tightened. While President Jimmy Carter hoped to reduce tensions in the late 1970s, he was a vigorous human rights advocate, particularly eager to point out Soviet deficiencies. American conservatives heightened their own opposition to the Soviet Union. A new strategic arms limitation agreement (SALT II) was negotiated in 1979 but quickly encountered resistance in the U.S. Senate. Then came the Soviet move into Afghanistan. President Carter reacted vigorously, claiming that the move was a "stepping stone to their possible control over much of the world's oil supplies" and, even more dramatically, the "gravest threat to world peace since World War II." American participation in the 1980 Moscow Olympics was cancelled.

Then, in 1980, the new, conservative president, Ronald Reagan, who had denounced the Soviet Union as an "evil empire," announced a massive increase in U.S. defense spending. The size of domestic programs declined relative to the federal budget as a whole, and some programs were cut outright (promoting, among other things, a surge in homelessness), but conservatives accepted a growing budget deficit in favor of the new military outlays. The president also announced a "Reagan doctrine" of assisting anticommunism anywhere, and followed it up with an invasion of a small, Marxist-controlled Caribbean island, Grenada, and support for anti-Marxist military action in Central America.

These moves put new pressure on the Soviets, already stretched to the limit to maintain military and global competition with the United States, and beset with an unpopular war and new regional pressures as well. The stage was set for the events that, initially promoted for quite different reasons, undid the cold war.

The Explosion of the 1980s and 1990s

From 1985 onward the Soviet Union entered a period of intensive reform, soon matched by new political movements in eastern Europe that effectively dismantled the Soviet empire. The initial trigger for this extraordinary and unanticipated upheaval lay in the deteriorating Soviet economic performance, intensified by the costs of military rivalry with the United States. There were reasons for pride in the Soviet system, and many observers believed that public attitudes by the 1980s were shaped much less by terror than by satisfaction with the Soviet Union's world prestige and the improvements the communist regime had fostered in education and welfare. But to a degree unperceived outside the Soviet Union, the economy was grinding to a standstill. Forced industrialization had produced extensive environmental deterioration throughout eastern Europe. According to Soviet estimates, half of all agricultural land was endangered by the late 1980s; more than 20 percent of Soviet citizens lived in regions of ecological disaster. Rates and severity of respiratory and other diseases increased, impairing both morale and economic performance. Infant mortality rates also rose in several regions, sometimes nearing the highest levels in the world.

More directly, industrial production began to stagnate and even drop as a result of rigid central planning, health problems, and poor worker morale. Growing inadequacy of housing and consumer goods resulted, further lowering motivation. As economic growth stopped, the percentage of resources allocated to military production escalated, toward a third of all national income. This reduced funds available for other investments or for consumer needs. At first only privately, younger leaders began to recognize that the system was near collapse.

The Age of Reform

Yet the Soviet system was not changeless, despite its heavy bureaucratization. Problems and dissatisfactions, though controlled, could provoke response beyond renewed repression. After a succession of leaders whose age or health precluded major initiatives, the Soviet Union in 1985 brought a new, younger official to the fore. **Mikhail Gorbachev** quickly renewed some of the earlier attacks on Stalinist rigidity and replaced some of the old-line party bureaucrats (Figure 35.2). He conveyed a new, more Western style, dressing in fashionable clothes (and accompanied by his stylish wife), holding relatively open press conferences, and even allowing the Soviet media to engage in active debate and report on problems as well as successes. Gorbachev also further altered the Soviet Union's modified cold war stance. He urged a reduction in nuclear armament, and in 1987 he negotiated a new agreement with the United States that limited medium-range missiles in Europe. He ended the war in Afghanistan, bringing Soviet troops home.

Gorbachev, Mikhail U.S.S.R. premier after 1985; renewed attacks on Stalinism; urged reduction in nuclear armament; proclaimed policies of glasnost and perestroika.

Figure 35.2 Early in his first administration, President Ronald Reagan referred to the Soviet Union as the "Evil Empire" and showed little interest in cooperating in any way with Moscow. After the accession of Mikhail Gorbachev, Reagan changed his attitude, and the two men worked closely to ease tensions between the two great powers.

glasnost Policy of openness or political liberation in Soviet Union put forward by Mikhail Gorbachev in the late 1980s.

perestroika [pehr-uh-STROY-kuh] Policy of Mikhail Gorbachev calling for economic restructuring in the U.S.S.R. in the late 1980s; more leeway for private ownership and decentralized control in industry and agriculture.

Mikhail Gorbachev on the Need for Economic Reform

DOCUMENT

Internally, Gorbachev proclaimed a policy of **glasnost,** or openness, which implied new freedom to comment and criticize. He pressed particularly for a reduction in bureaucratic inefficiency and unproductive labor in the Soviet economy, encouraging more decentralized decision making and the use of some market incentives to stimulate greater output. The sweep of Gorbachev's reforms, as opposed to an undeniable new tone in Soviet public relations, remained difficult to assess. Strong limits on political freedom persisted, and it was unclear whether Gorbachev could cut through the centralized planning apparatus that controlled the main lines of the Soviet economy. There was also uncertainty about how well the new leader could balance reform and stability.

Indeed, questions about Gorbachev's prospects recalled many basic issues in Soviet history. In many ways Gorbachev's policies constituted a return to a characteristic ambivalence about the West. He reduced Soviet isolation while continuing to criticize aspects of Western political and social structure. Gorbachev clearly hoped to use some Western management techniques and was open to certain Western cultural styles without, however, intending to abandon basic control of the communist state. Western analysts wondered if the Soviet economy could improve worker motivation without embracing a Western-style consumerism or whether computers could be more widely introduced without allowing freedom for information exchange.

Gorbachev also sought to open the Soviet Union to fuller participation in the world economy, recognizing that isolation in a separate empire had restricted access to new technology and limited motivation to change. Although the new leadership did not rush to make foreign trade or investment too easy—considerable suspicion persisted—the economic initiatives brought symbolic changes, such as the opening of a McDonald's restaurant in Moscow and a whole array of new contacts between Soviet citizens and foreigners (Figure 35.3).

Gorbachev's initial policies did not quickly reform the Soviet economy, but they had immediate political effects, some of which the reform leader had almost certainly not anticipated. The keynote of the reform program was **perestroika** (pehr-uh-STROY-kuh), or economic restructuring, which Gorbachev translated into more leeway for private ownership and decentralized control in industry and agriculture. Farmers, for example, could now lease land for 50 years, with rights of inheritance, and industrial concerns were authorized to buy from either private or state operations. Foreign investment was encouraged. Gorbachev pressed for reductions in Soviet military commit-

Figure 35.3 After 14 years of negotiations between McDonald's executives and Soviet government officials, the first McDonald's restaurant opened in Moscow in 1990. Lines formed around the block to get a first taste of the famous fast food.

ments, particularly through agreements with the United States on troop reductions and limitations on nuclear weaponry, in order to free resources for consumer goods industries. He urged more self-help among the Soviets, including a reduction in drinking, arguing that he wanted to "rid public opinion of . . . faith in a 'good Tsar,' the all powerful center, the notion that someone can bring about order and organize perestroika from on high."

Politically, Gorbachev encouraged a new constitution in 1988, giving considerable power to a new parliament, the Congress of People's Deputies, and abolishing the Communist monopoly on elections. Important opposition groups developed both inside and outside the party, pressing Gorbachev between radicals who wanted a faster pace of reform and conservative hard-liners. Gorbachev himself was elected to a new, powerful presidency of the Soviet Union in 1990.

Reform amid continued economic stagnation provoked agitation among minority nationalities in the Soviet Union, from 1988 onward. Muslims and Armenian Christians rioted in the south, both against each other and against the central state. Baltic nationalist and other European minorities also stirred, some insisting on full independence, some only pressing for greater autonomy. Again, results of this diverse unrest were difficult to forecast, but some observers predicted the end of Soviet control of central Asia and the European borderlands.

Even social issues were given uncertain new twists. Gorbachev noted that Soviet efforts to establish equality between the sexes had burdened women with a combination of work and household duties. His solution—to allow women to "return to their purely womanly missions" of housework, childrearing, and "the creation of a good family atmosphere"—had a somewhat old-fashioned ring to it.

Dismantling the Soviet Empire

Gorbachev's new approach, including his desire for better relations with Western powers, prompted more definitive results outside the Soviet Union than within, as the smaller states of eastern Europe uniformly pushed for greater independence and internal reforms. Bulgaria moved for economic liberalization in 1987 but was held back by the Soviets; pressure resumed in 1989 as the party leader was ousted and free elections were arranged. Hungary changed leadership in 1988 and installed a noncommunist president. A new constitution and free elections were planned; the Communist party renamed itself Socialist. Hungary also reviewed its great 1956 rising, formally declaring it "a popular uprising . . . against an oligarchic system . . . which had humiliated the nation." Hungary moved rapidly toward a free-market economy. Poland installed a noncommunist government in 1988, and again moved quickly to dismantle the state-run economy. Prices rose rapidly as government subsidies were withdrawn. The Solidarity movement, born a decade before through a merger of noncommunist labor leaders and Catholic intellectuals, became the dominant political force. East Germany removed its communist government in 1989, expelling key leaders and moving rapidly toward unification with West Germany. The Berlin Wall was dismantled, and in 1990 noncommunists won a free election (Figure 35.4). German unification occurred in 1991, a dramatic sign of the collapse of postwar Soviet foreign policy. Czechoslovakia installed a new government in 1989, headed by a playwright, and sought to introduce free elections and a more market-driven economy.

Although mass demonstrations played a key role in several of these political upheavals, only in Romania was there outright violence, as an exceptionally authoritarian communist leader was swept out by force. As in Bulgaria, the Communist party retained considerable power, though under new leadership, and reforms moved less rapidly than in Hungary and Czechoslovakia. The same held true for Albania, where the unreconstructed Stalinist regime was dislodged and a more flexible communist leadership installed.

New divergences in the nature and extent of reform in eastern Europe were exacerbated by clashes among nationalities, as in the Soviet Union. Change and uncertainty brought older attachments to the fore. Romanians and ethnic Hungarians clashed; Bulgarians attacked a Turkish minority left over from the Ottoman period. In 1991 the Yugoslavian communist regime, though not Soviet dominated, also came under attack, and a civil war boiled up from disputes among nationalities. Minority nationality areas, notably Slovenia, Croatia, and Bosnia-Herzegovina, proclaimed independence, but the national, Serbian-dominated army applied massive force to preserve the Yugoslav nation.

Figure 35.4 Breaching the Berlin Wall in 1989: West and East Germany meet.

Amid this rapid and unexpected change, prospects for the future became unpredictable. Few of the new governments fully defined their constitutional structure, and amid innovation the range of new political parties almost compelled later consolidations. Like the Soviet Union itself, all the eastern European states suffered from sluggish production, massive pollution, and economic problems that might well lead to new political discontent.

With state controls and protection abruptly withdrawn by 1991, tensions over the first results of the introduction of the market economy in Poland brought rising unemployment and further price increases. These in turn produced growing disaffection from the Solidarity leadership. Diplomatic linkages among small states—a critical problem area between the two world wars—also had yet to be resolved.

The massive change in Soviet policy was clear. Gorbachev reversed postwar Russian imperialism, stating that "any nation has the right to decide its fate by itself." In several cases, notably Hungary, Soviet troops were rapidly withdrawn, and generally it seemed unlikely that a repressive attempt to reestablish an empire would be possible (Map 35.1). New contacts with Western nations, particularly in the European Economic Community (European Union), seemed to promise further realignment in the future.

Renewed Turmoil in the 1990s

The uncertainties of the situation within the Soviet Union were confirmed in the summer of 1991, when an attempted coup was mounted by military and police elements. Gorbachev's presidency and democratic decentralization were both threatened. Massive popular demonstrations, however, asserted the strong democratic current that had developed in the Soviet Union since 1986. The contrast with earlier Soviet history and the suppression of democracy in China two years before was striking.

In the aftermath of the attempted coup, Gorbachev's authority weakened. Leadership of the key republics, including the massive Russian Republic, became relatively stronger. The three Baltic states used the occasion to gain full independence though economic links with the Soviet Union remained. Other minority republics proclaimed independence as well, but Gorbachev struggled to win agreement on continued economic union and some other coordination. By the end of 1991 leaders of the major republics, including Russia's **Boris Yeltsin,** proclaimed the end of the Soviet Union, projecting a commonwealth of the leading republics, including the grain-rich Ukraine, in its

Statue of
Lenin Toppled
During Soviet
Collapse
IMAGE

Yeltsin, Boris Russian leader who stood up to coup attempt in 1991 that would have displaced Gorbachev; president of the Russian republic following dissolution of Soviet Union.

Map 35.1 Post–Soviet Union Russia, Eastern Europe, and Central Asia by 1991   With the collapse of the Soviet Union, the boundaries of eastern Europe and central Asia were substantially redrawn.

stead. Amid the disputes Gorbachev fell from power, doomed by his attempts to salvage a presidency that depended on some survival of a greater Soviet Union. His leadership role was taken over by Boris Yeltsin, who as president of Russia and an early renouncer of communism now emerged as the leading, though quickly beleaguered, political figure. Yeltsin soon used force to bring Russia's parliament under some control (Figure 35.5).

The former Soviet Union gave way to the loose Commonwealth of Independent States, which won tentative agreement from most of the now independent republics. But tensions immediately surfaced about economic coordination amid rapid dismantling of state controls; about control of the military, where Russia—still by far the largest unit—sought predominance, including nuclear control amid challenges from the Ukraine and from Kazakhstan (two of the other republics with nuclear weaponry on their soil); and about relationships between the European-dominated republics, including Russia, and the cluster of central Asian states. How much unity might survive in the former Soviet Union was unclear. The fate of economic reform was also uncertain. Russian leaders hesitated to convert to a full market system lest transitional disruption further antagonize the population.

By the late 1990s, the leadership of Boris Yeltsin deteriorated as the economy performed badly, individual profiteers pulled in huge fortunes, and Yeltsin's health worsened. A bitter civil war broke out with the Muslim region of Chechnya: terrorist acts by the rebels and brutal military repression seemed to feed each other. A new president, Vladimir Putin, was named in 1999, who

Break-up of the Soviet Union

Scientists Examine Russia's Economy and Environment, 1991–1993

Symbolism in the Breakdown of the Soviet Bloc

Although the majority of Latvians strongly opposed the Soviet takeover of their government in 1939, for fifty years most had been afraid to express their views. After World War II, a strong nationalist resistance movement had arisen, but was harshly suppressed. Tens of thousands of Latvians were killed and many more were imprisoned or deported to Siberia. When, in the late 1980s, Perestroika opened possibilities for change in the Soviet Union, Latvians were quick to act. They elected a new parliament that, in 1990, proclaimed its intention of beginning a transition to independence. Although Soviet hard-liners tried to crack down on Latvian independence advocates, the failed August 1991 coup in Moscow opened the door to Latvian independence. One of the first acts of the Latvians was to topple statues of Soviet leaders like this one of Lenin.

As part of the independence of the Baltic nation of Latvia, crowds toppled Soviet symbols—in this case, a giant statue of Lenin—in 1991.

QUESTIONS Imagine the toppled Lenin statue as it stood on the day it was erected. What do you think the Soviets intended to express to the Latvian people when they placed this statue? How do you think the Latvians who opposed Soviet rule might have viewed the meaning of the statue? What was the symbolism of toppling the statue? Why might it be one of the first acts of a people liberated from foreign occupation?

Figure 35.5 In the fall of 1993, the Soviet Union teetered on the brink of civil war as Boris Yeltsin's opponents, meeting in the Russian parliament building, sought to remove him from office. Mass street demonstrations led to fighting in which hundreds of people were killed and wounded. Faced with a complete breakdown of public order, the military threw its support to Yeltsin and crushed his opponents in early October. Two months later, a new constitution gave Yeltsin broad powers to carry out his reforms.

vowed to clean up corruption and install more effective government controls over separate provinces. Putin declared his commitment to democracy and a free press but also sponsored new attacks on dissident television stations and newspapers. Government repression restricted the activities of rival political parties, shaping the results of elections that returned ever-larger majorities to Putin's supporters. Many Russians seemed to agree that stronger measures were needed—why should a leader tolerate public criticism? Others longed for a return to the Soviet days of greater economic security and national glory. Reformists were able to voice their concerns, but Putin tightened his hold on the state and media, even attacking independent-minded business leaders. He also resisted appeals to compromise on the Chechnya revolt. Finishing his second term as President in 2008, Putin arranged still to serve as prime minister.

The Spread of Democracy

The end of the cold war was associated with another large trend in the world at the end of the 20th century: the spread of multiparty democracy with (reasonably) free elections (Figure 35.6). We have seen that, through much of the century, several different forms of government competed for success amid a general climate of change: communism, fascism, and other forms of authoritarianism, and democracy. But from the late 1970s onward, the tide seemed to turn toward democracy in many regions that had long been inhospitable. At the same time, several crucial societies held back, showing that the new trend had some definite limitations.

> A dramatic surge of democracy began in the 1970s, spreading further after 1989 with the fall of international communism. Important holdouts and regressions complicated the trend.

Patterns of Change

Economic and political success in western Europe, including the drawing power of the Common Market, helped propel Spain, Portugal, and Greece to democratic systems in the mid-1970s, after long periods of authoritarian control. Then the democratic wave hit Latin America, backed by U.S. and western European support. Beginning with new regimes in Argentina and Brazil, authoritarian controls were replaced by free elections (see Chapter 37). The process continued through the 1990s, when literally all Latin American countries except Cuba were in the democratic camp. Revolutionaries in Central America accepted the system in the late 1980s; Paraguay was the final authoritarian regime to yield a decade later. In 2000 Mexico elected its first president from a party other than the PRI, the party that had monopolized control since the revolution.

Democratic systems gained ground in South Korea and Taiwan in the 1980s. In the Philippines, an authoritarian ruler was cast aside, amid considerable popular pressure, in favor of an elected government. Turkey also moved more decisively toward multiparty democracy, with both secular and Islamic parties involved. By this point, of course, the democratic current captured the Soviet bloc, with democratic systems winning out in most of east central Europe and in Russia itself.

While much of Africa remained authoritarian, democratic change spread to this region by the 1990s, headed with the triumph of democracy over apartheid in South Africa. After new assertions of military control, Nigeria, the continent's most populous country, turned to democracy in 1999. At this point also, a near-revolution toppled the authoritarian system in Indonesia and replaced it with competitive elections.

Another surge occurred in 2004–2005. Largely peaceful risings in Georgia and Ukraine replaced authoritarian leaders with democratic elections (against Russian opposition). Stirrings also occurred in former Soviet republics in central Asia, although in Uzbekistan they were brutally repressed.

Spurred in part by the American invasion of Iraq, which toppled a classic authoritarian regime and led to new elections, several Arab countries experimented with greater democracy. Openly contested local elections occurred in some cases, including Saudi Arabia. Kuwait granted the

Figure 35.6 This was one of the key elections in which Russians had the chance to choose among many competing parties.

Democratic Protest and Repression in China

On June 4, 1989, Chinese troops marched on political protesters, many of them students, camped in Beijing's central Tiananmen Square. The protesters had been agitating for weeks for a more open, democratic system, as against communist one-party control. The military move caused hundreds of deaths and additional political imprisonments and exiles. It crushed the protest movement, differentiating China from the many other societies that were establishing new democracies at that time. (The imminent visit of Russia's democratizing president, Mikhail Gorbachev, was one spur to the protesters.) China continued, instead, its interesting experiment with authoritarian politics amid rapid economic change.

The following document, from a leading communist party official, Li Peng, establishes the kind of reasoning that, to the government, justified its later repression; it comes from a speech on Chinese television in mid-May. The document mixes some standard government claims about the nature of protest with some specific Chinese as well as communist traditions concerning politics and order.

Comrades, in accordance with a decision made by the Standing Committee of the CPC Central Committee, the party Central Committee and the State Council have convened a meeting here of cadres from party, government, and army organs at the central and Beijing municipal levels, calling on everyone to mobilize in this emergency and to adopt resolute and effective measures to curb turmoil in a clear-cut manner, to restore normal order in society, and to maintain stability and unity in order to ensure the triumphant implementation of our reform and open policy and the program of socialist modernization [*applause*].

The current situation in the capital is quite grim. The anarchic state is going from bad to worse. Law and discipline have been undermined. Prior to the beginning of May, the situation had begun to cool down as a result of great efforts. However, the situation has become more turbulent since the beginning of May. More and more students and other people have been involved in demonstrations. Many institutions of higher learning have come to a standstill. Traffic jams have taken place everywhere. The party and government leading organs have been affected, and public security has been rapidly deteriorating. All this has seriously disturbed and undermined the normal order of production, work, study, and everyday life of the people in the whole municipality. Some activities on the agenda for state affairs of the Sino-Soviet summit that attracted worldwide attention had to be canceled, greatly damaging China's international image and prestige.

The activities of some of the students on hunger strike at Tiananmen Square have not yet been stopped completely. Their health is seriously deteriorating and some of their lives are still in imminent danger. In fact, a handful of persons are using the hunger strikes as hostages to coerce and force the party and the government to yield to their political demands. In this regard, they have not one iota of humanity [*applause*].

The party and the government have, on one hand, taken every possible measure, to treat and rescue the fasting students. On the other hand, they have held several dialogues with representatives of the fasting students and have earnestly promised to continue to listen to their opinions in the future, in the hope that the students would stop their hunger strike immediately. But, the dialogues did not yield results as expected. The square is packed with extremely excited crowds who keep shouting demagogic slogans. Right now, representatives of the hunger striking students say that they can no longer control the situation. If we fail to promptly put an end to such a state of affairs and let it go unchecked, it will likely lead to serious consequences which none of us want to see.

The situation in Beijing is still developing, and has already affected many other cities in the country. In many places, the number

vote to women. Palestinians conducted an open election in their autonomous territory in Israel. These developments remained tentative, and key regimes, such as Egypt, continued to repress political opposition. Authoritarian systems predominated in most of the region.

Democracy and Its Limits

North and South Korea Accord, June 2000

DOCUMENT

Never before had democracy spread so widely, among so many otherwise different societies. Only China, North Korea, and parts of the Middle East and central Asia seemed to hold apart completely. In China the major democratic demonstration in Beijing in 1989 echoed the global democratic current but was brutally put down. The Chinese regimes vowed to couple rapid economic change with insistence on one-party rule, a major exception to democratic gains.

Huge questions remained about democracy's future, even in other regions. The link to economic expectations—the sense that democracy was a precondition for freer markets and economic growth that supported many Latin American conversions and also Gorbachev's reforms in Russia—was an obvious vulnerability. What if the economy did not improve?

New uncertainties emerged after 2000. The United States voiced great support for the spread of democracy, but it also allied with authoritarian regimes—in Egypt, Pakistan, and Uzbekistan, for example—that promised support against terrorism. Russia's retreat from full democracy, under President Putin, was an important development. Democratic systems struggled against poverty and social unrest of demonstrators and protestors is increasing. In some places, there have been many incidents of people breaking into local party and government organs, along with beating, smashing, looting, burning, and other undermining activities that seriously violated the law. Some trains running on major railway lines have even been intercepted, causing communications to stop. Something has happened to our trunk line, the Beijing-Guangzhou line. Today, a train from Fuzhou was intercepted. The train was unable to move out for several hours.

All these incidents demonstrate that we will have nationwide major turmoil if no quick action is taken to turn and stabilize the situation. Our nation's reforms and opening to the outside world, the cause of the modernization [program], and even the fate and future of the People's Republic of China, built by many revolutionary martyrs with their blood, are facing a serious threat [*applause*].

Our party and government have pointed out time and time again that the vast numbers of young students are kindhearted, that subjectively they do not want turmoil, and that they have fervent patriotic spirit, wishing to push forward reform, develop democracy, and overcome corruption. This is also in line with the goals which the party and government have striven to accomplish. It should be said that many of the questions and views they raise have already exerted and will continue to exert positive influence on improving the work of the party and government. However, willfully using various forms of demonstrations, boycotts of class, and even hunger strikes to make petitions have damaged social stability and will not be beneficial to solving the problems. . . .

One important reason for us to take a clear-cut stand in opposing the turmoil and exposing the political conspiracy of a handful of people is to distinguish the masses of young students from the handful of people who incited the turmoil. For almost a month, we adopted an extremely tolerant and restrained attitude in handling the student unrest. No government in the world would be so tolerant. The reason that we were so tolerant was out of our loving care for the masses of youths and students. We regard them as our own

children and the future of China. We do not want to hurt good people, particularly not the young students. However, the handful of behind-the-scenes people, who were plotting and inciting the turmoil, miscalculated and took the tolerance as weakness on the part of the party and government. They continued to cook up stories to confuse and poison the masses, in an attempt to worsen the situation. This has caused the situation in the capital and many localities across the country to become increasingly acute. Under such circumstances, the CPC, as a ruling party and a government responsible to the people, is forced to take resolute and decisive measures to put an end to the turmoil [*applause*].

Comrades, our party is a party in power and our government is a people's government. To be responsible to our sacred motherland and to all people, we must adopt firm and resolute measures to end the turmoil swiftly, to maintain the leadership of the party as well as the socialist system. We believe that our actions will surely have the support of all members of the Communist Party and the Communist Youth League, as well as workers, peasants, intellectuals, democratic parties, people in various circles, and the broad masses [*applause*]. We believe that we will certainly have the backing of the People's Liberation Army [PLA], which is entrusted by the Constitution with guarding the country and the peaceful work of the people [*applause*]. At the same time, we also hope that the broad masses will fully support the PLA, the public security cadres, and the police in their efforts to maintain order in the capital [*applause*].

QUESTIONS Why does Li Peng object to the protest movement? How does he try to persuade ordinary Chinese that the protest should cease? What arguments reflect more distinctively Chinese traditions or communist values? Why did the Chinese decide to repress political democracy?

---

in several Latin American countries, particularly in the Andes region. A new Venezuelan strongman, Hugo Chávez, recalled earlier populist authoritarians in Latin America. In 2007, however, popular vote rebuffed a Chávez effort to concentrate further power in his hands. The spread of democracy was an important development, unprecedented in world history. But the insistence of several major regions on alternative systems, and new questions about open political competition in countries like Russia, raised important questions about the extent and prospect for the democratic trend.

The Great Powers and New Disputes

The end of the cold war framework highlighted certain regional rivalries. Many of them were not new, but they became more acute as the controlling influence of U.S.-Soviet rivalry disappeared. The surge of conflicts significantly constrained the spread of democracy.

The collapse of the Soviet system created new, often bitter, regional disputes. Conflicts in other regions often led to massive bloodshed.

The Former Soviet Empire

The Soviet Union, with its totalitarian government, opposition to religion, and emphasis on class rather than ethnic conflict, had kept a lid on hosts of potential internal disputes. When it collapsed, the lid came off. Ethnic and religious clashes occurred in several of the new nations. The Chechnya

Map 35.2 The Implosion of Yugoslavia, 1991–2008 During the decade after 2000 Kosovo became autonomous with ultimate plans for nationhood and Montenegro became a separate nation.

The Former Yugoslavia

rising was a case in point within Russia itself. Armenia and Azerbaijan, now nations, conducted low-level warfare over disputed regions claimed by different ethnic groups. Disagreements between Czechs and Slovaks resulted in a split of Czechoslovakia, though in this instance the adjustment was peaceful.

The most important post-Soviet clash occurred in Yugoslavia (Map 35.2). Long-standing tensions divided different Slavic groups (Orthodox Serbs and Catholic Croats; Serbs and Muslim Bosnians) and also minority nationalities like Albanians. The communist regime had held the pieces together, particularly under Marshall Tito, who died in 1980. Amid Soviet collapse, two regions, more prosperous than the country as a whole, declared independence in 1991: Slovenia and Croatia. Serbians, eager to hold Yugoslavia together under their leadership, warred with Croatia but failed. Conflict spread to Bosnia, where Serbs attacked not only Croats but also Muslims. Brutal assaults on civilians caused massive deaths and were ultimately judged acts of genocide. After long hesitation, NATO intervened and protected a new nation in Bosnia-Herzegovina.

A second conflict developed at the end of the 1990s, over the province of Kosovo. Albanian pressure for independence was met by Serbian resistance, again with acts of genocide under the label "ethnic cleansing." Again, NATO intervention, including air attacks, ended the violence and led to a new, more democratic regime in Serbia. Only ongoing military occupation, however, protected the peace. In the process, the federated nation of Serbia and Montenegro replaced the now defunct Yugoslavia, but Montenegro declared its own independence in 2007.

Endemic Conflicts

The end of the cold war did not cause several of the most troubling regional conflicts. However, the reduction of cold war tension and controls contributed to new regional latitude (Figure 35.7). The Middle East remained a trouble spot during the 1990s. Even before the end of the cold war, Iraq and Iran had conducted a long, casualty-filled war, with the ambitions of Iraq's dictatorial leader, Saddam

Figure 35.7 Image of the road to Baghdad after bombing in the Gulf War.

Hussein, pitted against the Islamic revolutionary regime in Iran. Iraq prevailed, and then later, in 1990, invaded the small oil-rich state of Kuwait. This galvanized an international coalition of Western and moderate Arab states, which defeated Iraq in the 1991 **First U.S. Iraq War** while leaving Saddam Hussein in power. The United States maintained a large military presence in the Persian Gulf region, which drew criticism from many Arabs and Muslims.

Israeli–Palestinian tensions served as another Middle Eastern flashpoint. Israeli relations with the huge Palestinian minority deteriorated after the cold war ended, despite some promising peace moves in the mid-1990s. Though an autonomous Palestinian government was set up over two territories within Israel, tensions continued. Bitter violence between Israelis and Palestinians revived between 2001 and 2003. A wave of suicide bombings by Palestinians targeted Israeli civilians, while the Israeli government attacked Palestinian cities and refugee camps in turn. Clearly, key issues in this complex region remain to be resolved.

Tensions between India and Pakistan also escalated, with various border clashes particularly around the disputed territory of Kashmir. By 2000 both countries had conducted tests of nuclear weapons. This was the most open case of nuclear dissemination, as the limited nuclear group of the cold war began to expand. Increased Hindu nationalism within India was matched by fiercer Muslim rhetoric in Pakistan.

Ethnic and Other Conflicts: A New Surge

The upsurge of ethnic conflict in several areas constituted a striking new feature of the post–cold war scene. Ethnic rivalries were not new, of course, but several components helped explain the new and troubling outbreak. New levels of global interaction, for example, increased the potential for group identities to generate hostilities. Some groups clearly increased their investment in ethnic identity as a means of countering outside influences and global pressures.

Within Europe, a number of ethnic groups developed new opportunities for expression as the hold of the classic nation-state declined. The British government gave limited autonomy to Scottish and Welsh governments. France and Spain became more tolerant toward linguistic minorities such as the Bretons and the Catalans. During the 1990s, a number of European countries saw the rise of new political movements bent on reducing immigration in favor of protecting jobs and cultural identity for the majority national group. A National Front group in France won up to 10 percent of all votes during the mid-1990s, though it then fell back a bit. Austria generated a controversial right-wing national government rhetorically hostile to immigrants. Between 2001 and 2008, various leaders in Italy, the Netherlands and France also discussed new barriers against immigrants. Violence against immigrant groups, such as Turks in Germany, flared recurrently as well.

In the 1990s a set of far bloodier conflicts broke out in central Africa, pitting tribal groups, the Hutus and the Tutsis, against each other particularly in the nation of Rwanda (Figure 35.8). Here, too, old rivalries blended with disputes over current power; the Tutsis had long ruled, but they were outnumbered by resentful Hutus. Intervention from neighboring states like Uganda contributed to the confusion. Tremendous slaughter resulted, with hundreds of thousands killed and many more—over 2 million—driven from their homes. While outside powers, the Organization of African States, and the United Nations urged peace, there was no decisive outside intervention. Bloodshed finally ran its course, but ethnic disputes continued in central Africa, contributing to civil war in countries like Congo.

Ethnic and religious disputes were also involved in a number of other African trouble spots, including battles between government forces and various groups in Sudan, and warfare among military gangs in countries like Sierra Leone and Liberia. Violence frequently involved heavily armed children, or "boy soldiers." Sudanese conflicts resulted in over 2 million killed, and endemic warfare in the Congo (in which activities by neighboring states as well as internal ethnic struggle intensified the problems) killed almost the same number. Massive dislocations of refugees accompanied all these conflicts.

Clearly, ethnic tensions were leading not just to warfare, but to renewed acts of genocide that targeted whole populations of civilians, including women and children. Reactions from the world at

First U.S.-Iraq War 1991 war led by United States and various European and Middle Eastern allies, against Iraqi occupation of Kuwait. The war led to Iraqi withdrawal and a long confrontation with Iraq about armaments and political regime.

Israel-PLO Declaration of Principles on Interim Self-Government Arrangements, September 13, 1993

The Modern Middle East

Figure 35.8 In the last decade of the 20th century, the specter of genocide returned to a century that had seen more examples of this extreme form of violence against whole peoples than any other period in world history. Genocide infected the Balkans and, as this picture shows, the nation of Rwanda in east central Africa.

large varied. In some instances, violence seemed sufficiently menacing to major powers that some intervention occurred, though never without great hesitation. No policies emerged that offered great promise of pushing back the potential for ethnic conflict.

The United States as Sole Superpower

U.S. military power had no global rival by the 1990s, but a variety of reactions constrained American power. A new round of terrorism targeted the United States.

The decline of Russian power left the United States without a clear military competitor. Faced with economic problems, Russian leaders scaled back military expenses, which by 2001 totaled only 4 percent of American levels. Russia enjoyed some influence over neighboring states and retained a nuclear arsenal. Its role expanded in the 21st century as oil revenues fueled new prosperity. But its global military presence was greatly reduced. In contrast, U.S. military commitments remained high. By 2005 the nation was spending more on defense than the next 25 countries combined.

The United States and Other Power Centers

This level of American power obviously worried many (Figure 35.9). China increased its military arsenal, along with its growing power in the global economy. Periodic collaborations among powers like China, Russia, and Iran countered American interests, but they did not lead to permanent alignments. European countries, though allied with the United States, had their own concerns. Several nations discussed a joint military force independent of NATO, though on the whole European military outlays continued to decline.

The growth and success of the European Union (EU) sketched a potential counterweight to the United States. The new currency shared by most EU member states, the euro, surpassed the strength of the dollar. Expansion to 25 members was another key move. But an ambitious EU constitution that might provide more coordination in foreign affairs met widespread criticism in 2005 by nations concerned about their own independence of action. France and Holland voted nay, and

Figure 35.9 In this cartoon from the *Ottawa Citizen*, Uncle Sam is portrayed as a vaudeville entertainer entirely absorbed in his act who is about to lose his place in the spotlight. In the wings, China waits to go on. The "fifteen minutes" is a reference to American artist Andy Warhol's much-quoted statement, "In the future everyone will be world-famous for fifteen minutes." What feelings toward the United States does this cartoon express?

(© 2005 Cam Cardow: The Ottawa Citizen and Political Cartoons.com.)

the whole project was in doubt. The EU was a major economic force, but it was no match for American military strength. Between 1991 and 2008, American power provoked various resentments, but it was not unseated.

What was the United States to do with its world power? Americans debated how much they should try to police regional conflicts, often questioning the idea of serving as some kind of global enforcer. In 1993, for example, an American military intervention to halt civil strife in Somalia led to widespread resistance and loss of life, and the United States pulled out. At the same time, U.S. leaders clearly felt emboldened to tell other parts of the world how to organize their societies. Both business and political experts argued that the U.S. model of a free market economy should be widely adopted. U.S. leaders also worried about several medium-sized powers that had or might develop nuclear weapons or that might sponsor terrorism. Efforts to mobilize the world community against countries like Iran, Iraq, and North Korea had varying degrees of success, suggesting some limits to American influence if not its direct military strength.

The United States became increasingly suspicious of international agreements that might limit its sovereignty, particularly after George W. Bush became president in 2001. Treaties designed to protect the environment or prevent the use of land mines were rejected, despite wide international support. These gestures of independence provoked criticism in various parts of the world.

Anti-American Terrorism and Response

American interests had periodically been the targets of terrorist attacks since the 1960s. Hijacking of airplanes and other moves frequently expressed hostility to U.S. policies. But the massive attacks on the World Trade Center and the Pentagon by Islamic militants on September 11, 2001, created a new level of threat (Figure 35.10). The attacks reflected concern about specific U.S. policies in the

Terrorism, Then and Now

In the last years of the 20th century, terrorism became a major issue for the international media, the world's political and military leaders, and increasingly for civilians across the globe who became both targets and mass victims of increasingly indiscriminate violent assaults. For Americans terrorism on home soil arrived gradually as the initial, and largely failed, attempt to bomb the World Trade Center in New York City in 1993 faded from memory. By contrast, for much of the rest of the world, fear of and precautions against terrorist violence had become ongoing and a major concern as early as the late 1960s. From Basque separatists in Spain and Protestant and Catholic paramilitary units in Northern Ireland to Tamil suicide bombers in Sri Lanka and cult plotters in Japan, terrorism has become an ever-present menace in the lives of leaders and ordinary citizens alike over much of the globe.

This is particularly true in the growing conurbations where much of humanity has come to be concentrated. The well coordinated and appallingly destructive attacks of September 11, 2001, on the World Trade Center in New York and the Pentagon in Washington, D.C., brought these concerns and their vulnerability to terrorism home to Americans with mind-numbing force. Later terrorist attacks targeted commuter systems in Spain (2004) and Britain (2005).

Although current commentators often treat the late 20th-century global epidemic of terrorism as a phenomenon without historical precedent, in fact in the decades before the First World War terrorist attacks were also a major concern and were carried out by dissident groups in many areas of the globe. From the capitals and metropolitan centers of Europe (especially those of tsarist Russia) and the United States to the port cities and imperial centers of the far-flung colonial empires of the great industrial powers, assassinations and bombs killed and maimed, disoriented societies, and challenged political regimes. But in critical ways—including the nature and causes espoused by terrorist groups, the targets they favored, and the amount of damage or numbers of casualties their attacks caused—terrorism in the 1880s or the early 1900s differed significantly from its counterpart in the 1970s or 1990s. An exploration of some of these key differences can tell us a great deal not only about the transformation of terrorists' motivations and operations, but also about key contrasts in terms of the global and local contexts in which each wave of terrorism occurred.

In both time periods, the main sources of terrorist assaults were small, secret, and highly politically motivated organizations. In both the early 20th century and in the decades at its end, the main objective of the members of these organizations was to discredit, weaken, and ultimately overthrow political regimes that they be-

> "Although current commentators often treat the late-20th-century global epidemic of terrorism as a phenomenon without historical precedent, in fact in the decades before the First World War terrorist attacks were also a major concern and were carried out by dissident groups in many areas of the globe."

lieved were oppressive and supportive of exploitation at the national and international levels. Their operations were also designed to advertise the causes these extremist groups espoused and draw attention to injustices they believed could not be effectively addressed through less violent or less confrontational modes of protest. But in the pre–World War I era, most terrorists were driven either by (1) anarchist aspirations to destroy increasingly centralized states, (2) radical Marxist programs for workers to overthrow the capitalist world order, or (3) struggles for the liberation of colonized peoples, from Ireland to India. The most spectacular terrorist assault of the era was of the latter type: Bosnian Serb Gavril Princip's assassination of the Archduke Ferdinand and his wife, Sophie, which precipitated the crisis that led to the First World War.

At the turn of the 21st century, by contrast, terrorist assaults have come mainly from sectarian extremists claiming affiliation with one of the world's great religious traditions—including Christianity, Hinduism, Judaism, and Islam—or from subnationalist groups, such as the Basques in Spain or Protestant and Catholic militias in Northern Ireland. Interethnic civil wars, such as those that have raged in Lebanon, Cyprus, Bosnia, and Sri Lanka in recent decades, have also proved to be major sources of terrorist activities. Periodically, radical environmentalists and groups opposing international institutions, such as the International Monetary Fund and World Trade Organization, that promote economic globalization have also resorted to terrorist tactics.

The targets terrorists select often tell us a good deal about the differing causes they espouse. Many of the regimes that anarchists struck at in the pre–World War I period—for example, the tsarist empire or the British Raj in India—were in fact autocratic, often indifferent to the oppressive living conditions of the great majority of their subjects, and prone to respond to even peaceful protest with violent repression, including torture. Scholarly investigations of these and current causes of terrorist activities have made us aware of the frequent resort to terrorist tactics by bureaucrats, the military, and state officials who so vehemently condemn dissident violence. In fact, terrorist activities have often proved far less lethal and destructive than the violence employed by regimes in power. Though these discoveries do not justify violence, particularly that directed against innocent civilians, they help us to understand in part why terrorist groups resort to violence rather than trusting the state to carry through with reforms or to negotiate with them peacefully and in good faith.

In both time periods, terrorist acts were carried out mainly by young men. But in the decades at the turn of the 20th century, many of the operatives were middle-aged, and separatist activists in both eras have included young women. Targets differed significantly in each phase of the 20th century. In the decades before World War I, individuals—monarchs (and their spouses), government officials (including President McKinley of the United States), business tycoons, and colonial officials—were most often chosen, in part because of the propaganda value of striking at the powerful and wealthy. At times, bombs placed in public areas were used to instill mass panic and disrupt normal social life. In the case of anarchist and Marxist extremists, indiscriminate mass killings and widespread destruction in fashionable quarters of urban areas were seen as symbolic assaults on the bourgeois, capitalist global order.

At the turn of the 21st century, indiscriminate assaults on defenseless civilians have become the preferred tactic of terrorists in Ireland, Spain, Israel and the Palestinian territories, Sri Lanka, Japan, and other areas. Technological advances that allowed terrorist operatives to miniaturize bombs and automatic firearms contributed to this preference. But perhaps more critical were great advances in surveillance devices and the elaborate security measures taken to defend national and world leaders. Quite simply, it became more and more dangerous to target soldiers, police, and political leaders, and increasingly even economic magnates or religious figures. Contemporary theorists also argued that any member of a dominant society was an active agent of evil, and therefore a legitimate victim.

Technological change affected the nature of terrorist operations in other important ways. The spread of communications technologies such as the telephone and television, complex networks for delivering electric power and fuels like natural gas, and nuclear reactors and centers of scientific experimentation created a whole new range of what have often proved to be very vulnerable targets. Trains, buses, and airplanes have also become tempting objects for capture or destruction at the hands of hijackers and bombers. Finally, invention and scientific experimentation have made a whole new generation of terrorist weapons feasible, including gases like Sarin, which wreaked havoc on Tokyo's subways, toxic bacterial agents like anthrax, and miniaturized nuclear devices that, theoretically at least, can be packed in the proverbial suitcase and carried into the heart of major urban centers.

Between the 1970s and the 1990s, these shifts in science and technology greatly reduced the odds of success in operations aimed at well defended leaders, government institutions, or military organizations. This situation turned unarmed civilians going about their daily lives into ever more tempting targets for terrorists with guns or bombs. The emergence of suicide bombers, particularly in the 1990s, made this pattern even more disturbing. Terrorist organizations were confident that these attacks would serve several purposes. To begin with, they dramatically publicized the grievances that inspired armed resistance. Highly lethal attacks on civilians were also seen to destabilize target societies and deprive citizens of the sense of security required to live productive and fulfilled lives. Both outcomes, in turn, were believed to discredit targeted political regimes. The dissident groups who launched the assaults hoped they would weaken governments in power to the point where they would either make major concessions or prove vulnerable to even more ambitious attempts to overthrow them.

These expected outcomes have very rarely come to pass. In fact, indiscriminate terrorist acts have usually outraged public and world opinion, and obscured or distorted the causes that dissident groups were attempting to publicize. They have also greatly enhanced the latitude of retaliatory responses open to national governments and international agencies as well as public support for these measures. This has been true even in situations where large numbers of new civilian casualties occurred as a result. Equally critical, the terrorists' willingness to launch mass assaults on innocent civilians has tended to be equated with religious fanaticism or political radicalism that is so extreme as to preclude negotiation and even rational explanation. As a consequence, violent repression has very often been deemed the only viable response to the death and suffering visited upon innocent civilians by terrorist true believers.

These shifts in the nature and targets of terrorist assaults between the pre–World War I era and the last decades of the 20th century have in most instances greatly increased the cost in human lives and property. The magnitude of these losses has also been linked to the growing globalization of terrorist networks. This has meant a proliferation of complex linkages between dissident groups in different nations and regions, who are very often espousing radically different causes. Perhaps most sobering in this regard was the way in which the attacks on September 11, 2001, demonstrated the possibilities for well funded and organized terrorist groups to turn highly advanced civilian technologies, embodied in modern passenger planes, into appallingly lethal weapons that could be aimed at innocent and unsuspecting civilian victims. The collapse of the World Trade Towers after each had been struck by hijacked airliners also revealed the vulnerability of even the most imposing modern buildings to this sort of assault. The nearly simultaneous crash of another airliner into the Pentagon demonstrated that even the headquarters of the world's most powerful military organization was not immune to terrorist attack. These events may mark a fundamental shift in the nature of violent protest and warfare that will be played out in the century to come.

QUESTIONS What are some of the specific technologies that have shaped changes in terrorist operations over the 20th century? What sorts of systems and devices have been used by states and military organizations to counter these shifts? In what instances have terrorist organizations been successful politically? Is terrorism likely to become the dominant mode of warfare in the 21st century?

A Challenge

What kinds of measures might be taken to bring terrorism under control in the coming decades? Pick one 20th-century case where a cause that generated terrorism was ultimately resolved. What lessons does it provide for current terrorist campaigns?

Figure 35.10 At 10:05 on the morning of September 11, 2001, the south tower of the World Trade Center collapsed after having been hit by a hijacked commercial plane. The north tower, shown here in flames, collapsed less than half an hour later. This terrorist attack and the ensuing "War on Terror" changed the course of history, not just in the United States, but around the world, as terrorism became the focus of American foreign policy.

Middle East, including support for authoritarian governments, the alliance with Israel, and the stationing of troops on "sacred ground" in Saudi Arabia. The terrorists were also hostile to wider U.S. power, or as they termed it, arrogance. Their response, hijacking airliners to crash into buildings that symbolized American financial and military might, killed about 3000 people. The terrorists regarded this as justifiable action against a nation they could not hope to fight by conventional means.

The attacks clearly altered U.S. policy and focused the administration on a war against terrorism. "War on Terror" was the new catchphrase, and a number of measures were taken, including heightened screening of international visitors. The problem dominated American foreign policy. A first response involved a military attack that successfully topped the Islamic fundamentalist regime in Afghanistan that had harbored the Al Qaeda group behind the September 11 attacks. World opinion largely supported this move. The United States established new military bases near several possible centers of terrorist activity (Map 35.3).

In 2003 U.S. focus turned to Iraq, which was accused of amassing dangerous weaponry and aiding terrorists. Evidence for these charges proved largely erroneous, and world opinion turned heavily against the American move, with millions of demonstrators protesting the impending war in February 2003. But the United States, joined by several allies, including Britain, invaded and quickly conquered the country. The ensuing occupation, however, was extremely troubled, as the United States had difficulty restoring order against a variety of insurgents. In 2009, with Iraq somewhat calmer, American attention turned back to Afghanistan and also to the growing strength of radical groups in Pakistan.

Global Connections

New Global Standards, New Divisions

The end of the cold war reduced divisions in the world and dramatically lowered the danger of all-out nuclear war. The larger spread of democracy also suggested new kinds of global linkages and agreements. A few optimistic observers argued that there would be an "end of history"—that democracy and peace would predominate, ending the contentious historical processes that had defined the human experience since the dawn of civilization.

But the escalation of regional conflicts, with their tragic violence and dislocation, argued against this kind of optimism. Democracy was spreading, but not winning everywhere, and peaceful solutions to many tensions seemed impossible to achieve. The emergence of the United States as the sole superpower also caused much ambivalence. On the one hand, the disproportion of American power gave the nation true global influence. On the other hand, reactions to this power, and American uses of it, raised new disputes. The United States did not in fact have the power to reshape the world. Its policies raised new tensions with segments of Islam. The military confrontation between the United States and terrorism was far different from that of the cold war, but the deep ideological roots of the hostilities seemed distressingly familiar to some observers.

Further Readings

On recent issues in Europe, see Adrian Hyde-Price, *European Security in the Twenty-First Century: The Challenge of Multipolarity* (2007); G. W. White, *Nationalism and Territory: Constructing*

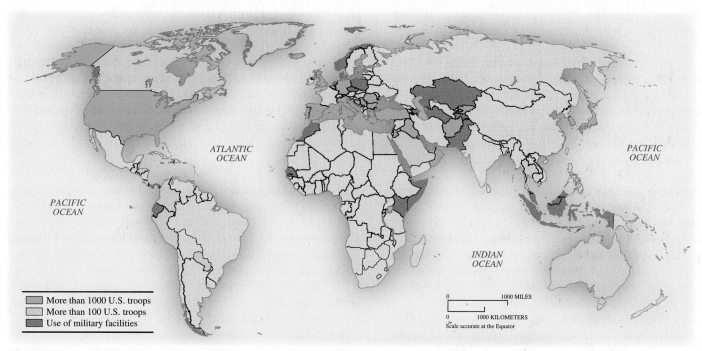

Map 35.3 Main U.S. Overseas Military Installations by 2007

Group Identity in Southeastern Europe (2000); and Andrew Valls, ed., *Ethics in International Affairs: Themes and Cases* (2000).

For the explosion of the 1980s and 1990s, David Kotz and Fred Weir, *Revolution from Above: The Demise of the Soviet System* (1997), explores the internal dissolution of the Soviet leadership. See also Alexei Yurchak, *Everything Was Forever, Until It Was No More: The Last Soviet Generation* (2006); Vladislav M. Zubok, *A Failed Empire: The Soviet Union in the Cold War from Stalin to Gorbachev* (2007); Archie Brown, *Seven Years that Changed the World: Perestroika in Perspective* (2007); Renée de Nevers, *Comrades No More: The Seeds of Political Change in Eastern Europe* (2003); and George W. Breslauer, *Gorbachev and Yeltsin as Leaders* (2002).

Mikhail Gorbachev's *Memoirs* (1995) is the central participant's reflections on the end of the Soviet Union. Raymond L. Garthoff, *The Great Transition: American-Soviet Relations at the End of the Cold War* (1994), provides the foreign policy context. Karen Dawisha and Bruce Parrott, eds., *The Consolidation of Democracy in East-Central Europe* (1997), discusses recent experiences in the direction of democratization and includes a country-by-country survey.

Nanette Funk and Magda Mueller, *Gender Politics and Post-Communism: Reflections from Eastern Europe and the Former Soviet Union* (1993), deals with women's role in the transition. Tina Rosenberg, *The Haunted Land: Facing Europe's Ghosts After Communism* (1995), is an engaging narrative that explores the legacies of repression in Germany, Poland, and the Czech Republic. Also see Paul Hockenos, *Free to Hate: The Rise of the Right in Post-Communist Eastern Europe* (1994).

For a detailed, long-term historical perspective on the successive conflicts in the Balkans, see Misha Glenny, *The Balkans: Nationalism, War, and the Great Powers, 1804–1999* (2000); and

Sabrina Ramet and Vjeran Pavlaković, eds., *Serbia Since 1989: Politics and Society under Milosović and After* (2005). On the religious dimensions of the Yugoslavian wars, see the essays in Paul Mojzes, ed., *Religion and War in Yugoslavia* (1998). On the successive conflicts of the mid-1990s more specifically, see Misha Glenny, *The Fall of Yugoslavia* (1992); Laura Silber and Allan Little, *Yugoslavia: Death of a Nation* (1995); Tim Judah, *Kosovo: War and Revenge* (2000); and Noel Malcolm, *Kosovo* (1998). From the very substantial literature that has developed on the Rwanda crisis, Gérard Prunier, *The Rwanda Crisis: History of a Genocide* (1999), is one of the most detailed accounts, and Mahmood Mamdani, *When Victims Become Killers* (2001), is an interesting analysis of the conflict's larger political and philosophical implications. Levon Chorbajian and George Shirinian, *Studies in Comparative Genocide* (1999), is a good place to begin an exploration of the darker side of 20th-century history.

Of the numerous and highly contentious writings on Islamic revivalism, Dilip Hiro, *Holy Wars: The Rise of Islamic Fundamentalism* (1989), is insightful and more balanced than most. A counterpart on Judaism is Arthur Hertzberg, *Jewish Fundamentalism* (1991). For Hinduism, see Gurdas Ahuja, *BJP and Indian Politics* (1994). For a comparative view covering Christian movements, see Richard Antoun, *Understanding Fundamentalism* (2001).

September 11, 2001, and persisting communal struggles, such as those in Northern Ireland and over Israel and Palestine, have produced a great proliferation of journalistic books and articles on terrorism in recent decades. A manageable place to begin an investigation of this highly contested and fluid category of social movement is Alexander Yonan et al., eds., *Terrorism: Theory and Practice* (1979). A historical overview with a global range for the modern period can be found in Albert Parry, *Terrorism* (2002).

George Woodcock, *Anarchism* (1970), remains the classic account of movements that were often connected to terrorism in the late 19th century.

A very substantial literature has developed on the 1991 Persian Gulf War. The essays in Ibrahim Ibrahim, ed., *The Gulf Crisis* (1992) provide a good historical introduction to the conflict. Two of the better general accounts of the war itself are Lawrence Freedman and Efraim Karsh, *The Gulf Conflict, 1990–1991* (1993); and Michael Gordon and Bernard Trainor, *The General's War* (1995). An Arab viewpoint on the conflict is provided in Mohamed Heikal, *Illusions of Triumph* (1992).

For a provocative and detailed account of U.S. interventionism since the end of the cold war, a good place to begin is David Halberstam, *War in a Time of Peace* (2001). On specific flashpoints that provoked extensive international involvement and policy debate in the United States and elsewhere, some of the best work is on Somalia, including Mark Bowden's superb recounting of the mission in crisis in *Black Hawk Down* (1990) and Jonathan Stevenson's more policy-oriented *Losing Mogadishu* (1995).

Recent work includes *Congressional Quarterly, World at Risk: A Global Issues Sourcebook* (2002); Barbara Walter and Jack Snyder, eds., *Civil Wars, Insecurity, and Intervention* (1999); and Immanuel Wallerstein, *The Decline of American Power: The U.S. in a Chaotic World* (2003).

On the Web

The role of Mikhail Gorbachev in the endgame of the Soviet Empire is explored at http://www.cs.indiana.edu/~dmiguse/Russian/mgbio.html, http://www.uea.ac.uk/his/webcours/russia/courses/gorby-ma.shtml, and http://www.mikhailgorbachev.org/. Boris Yeltzin's parallel role in that event is discussed at http://www.cs.indiana.edu/~dmiguse/Russian/bybio.html and http://en.wikipedia.org/wiki/Boris_Yeltsin. The social, political, and economic "perestroika" or restructuring of the Soviet state they favored is described at http://www.ibiblio.org/expo/soviet.exhibit/perest.html, http://www.historyguide.org/europe/perestroika.html, and http://www.econlib.org/LIBRARY/Enc/Perestroika.html.

The demise of the Berlin Wall is traced in text, video, and photographs at http://www.newseum.org/berlinwall/, http://www.appropriatesoftware.com/BerlinWall/welcome.html, and http://nhs.needham.k12.ma.us/cur/Baker_00/2001_p4/Baker_dr_bd_mh_p4/berlin_wall.htm. For the subsequent breakup of Yugoslavia, see http://news.bbc.co.uk/2/hi/europe/4997380.stm. The Web offers resources for the study of Vaclav Havel at http://www.vaclavhavel.cz/Index.php?&setln=2 or http://www.vaclavhavel.cz/ and also http://www.aril.org/capps.htm. An examination of the nature and future of NATO, and analyses of recent events and significant speeches in Europe, as well as analyses of NATO actions, can be found at http://www.nato.int/. The European quest for union is explored at http://www.eurunion.org and http://europa.eu/abc/index_en.htm.

The UN–U.S. intervention in Somalia and its troubling outcomes are considered from different vantage points at http://www.globalsecurity.org/military/world/war/somalia.htm, http://www.netnomad.com/, and http://www.flashpoints.info/countries-conflicts/Somalia-web/Somalia_briefing.htm. The genocide in Rwanda and the United Nation's slow response to ethnic conflict there and in Darfur is analyzed at http://news.bbc.co.uk/2/hi/africa/1288230.stm, http://news.bbc.co.uk/2/hi/africa/3496731.stm, http://www.eyesondarfur.org, and http://en.wikipedia.org/wiki/Darfur_conflict.

The terrorist attacks on September 11, 2001 on New York City and Washington, D.C. are recounted from many perspectives at http://911digitalarchive.org/, http://www.americanrhetoric.com/rhetoricofterrorism.htm, and http://www.9-11commission.gov/. The management of the global war against terrorism is addressed at http://www.globalissues.org/Geopolitics/WarOnTerror.asp and http://www.cnn.com/SPECIALS/2001/trade.center/.

The state of democracy in national, regional, and global contexts is analyzed at http://www.worldaudit.org/democracy.htm, http://www.meforum.org/article/216, http://news.bbc.co.uk/2/hi/africa/3586085.stm, http://www.prospect-magazine.co.uk/article_details.php?id=9836, http://www.hoover.org/publications/digest/3491911.html, and http://www.nytimes.com/2006/04/10/world/middleeast/10democracy.html. The opportunities and challenges to democracy inherent in the instability of the contemporary world are studied at http://www.secularhumanism.org/library/fi/kurtz_25_1.htm. Differing views over the prospects for democracy in the Middle East can be found at http://en.wikipedia.org/wiki/Democracy_in_the_Middle_East, http://www.islamreview.com/articles/democracy.shtml, http://yaleglobal.yale.edu/display.article?id=5622, and http://www.cato.org/pub_display.php?pub_id=332. Democracy and human rights in China are discussed at http://hrw.org/english/docs/2002/08/02/china4187.htm and http://usinfo.state.gov/eap/Archive/2006/Feb/15-436496.html. The future of democracy in rapidly growing capitalist India is examined at http://www.theglobalist.com/DBWeb/StoryId.aspx?StoryId=2987. Shortly before her assassination, Benazir Bhutto wrote about why the world needed democracy to flourish in her home country of Pakistan. That speech, which discussed how dictatorships fuels extremism the world over, can be found at http://www.csmonitor.com/2007/1210/p09s02-coop.html.

For the recent wars in the Persian Gulf and Iraq, see http://www.pbs.org/wgbh/pages/frontline/gulf/index.html. The debate over the inconclusive end of these wars and the continuing conflict in the region is discussed at http://www.pbs.org/wgbh/pages/frontline/shows/invasion/. The impact of the wars on U.S. soldiers involved in the conflict is examined at http://www.pbs.org/wgbh/pages/frontline/shows/syndrome/. For other overviews, see http://www.pbs.org/wgbh/pages/frontline/gulf/index.html and http://www.globalsecurity.org/military/ops/iraq.htm. A site offering links for the study of U.S.–Iraqi war can be found at http://www.sourcewatch.org/index.php?title=Operation_Iraqi_Freedom.

AP* Test Prep

1. All of the following resulted from Cold War tensions EXCEPT

   (A) treaties limiting greenhouse gasses.

   (B) treaties seeking to limit the size of nuclear arsenals.

   (C) construction of the Berlin Wall.

   (D) America's participation in the wars in Vietnam.

2. The Soviet leader Mikhail Gorbachev

   (A) called for the swift end of the Communist Party.

   (B) brought the Soviet war in Afghanistan to a victorious conclusion.

   (C) used force to maintain Russia's empire in Hungary and Poland.

   (D) favored the reforms called glasnost and perestroika.

3. The Persian Gulf War of 1991 erupted due to

   (A) the Iraqi invasion of Iran.

   (B) the Iraqi invasion of Kuwait.

   (C) Iranian attacks on Israel.

   (D) Syrian attacks on Saudi Arabia.

4. Which of the following contributed to the end of the Soviet Union by 1991?

   (A) United States agreement to cut its military force levels

   (B) victory of the anti-communist Liberal Party in the 1985 Soviet elections

   (C) protest movements in several east-central European countries

   (D) success of Christian missionaries in converting Russians

   (E) Successful air strikes by NATO on Russian bases

5. The spread of democracy as a global trend *from* the 1990s onward has been challenged by

   (A) the renewed spread of fascism.

   (B) China's insistence on an authoritarian regime.

   (C) India's rejection of democracy in favor of Hindu nationalism.

   (D) collapse of almost all of the long-standing democracies in sub-Saharan Africa.

6. The role of the United States as sole superpower has been weakened or challenged by all of the following EXCEPT

   (A) U.N. resolutions criticizing United States' interventions.

   (B) lack of consensus within the U.S. and its allies concerning overseas involvement.

   (C) massive reductions in U.S. military spending and support for overseas involvement.

   (D) terrorist activity.

7. Terrorism in the late 20th and early 21st centuries

   (A) is similar to earlier terrorist activities in that it targets monarchs or high-profile individuals.

   (B) is similar to earlier terrorist activities because of its anarchist ideology.

   (C) is the preferred weapon for some religious extremists and ethnic/national minorities.

   (D) led to decolonization in Asia and the Middle East.

Free-Response Question

What relationship exists between the emergence of the United States as sole superpower and the spread of democracy?

36 Globalization and Resistance

Globalization: Causes and Processes

DOCUMENT: Protests Against Globalization

Resistance and Alternatives

THINKING HISTORICALLY: How Much Historical Change?

The Global Environment

VISUALIZING THE PAST: Two Faces of Globalization

Toward the Future

GLOBAL CONNECTIONS: Civilizations and Global Forces

A recent movie about a family in Kerala (a state in southern India) makes the point inescapably. A baby girl is turned over to her "good" brother for care: he lives in the village and provides for her a simple, idyllic life. But when she enters college, she goes to the city to live with a childless aunt and uncle. They shower her with new clothes, including blue jeans, Western-style skirts, and cosmetics. She enters and wins a college beauty pageant. She gets in with a heavy-drinking, rowdy group of men and is disgraced—finally returning to the village where, in shame, she assumes the traditional costume.

By the early 21st century, Kerala had become a scene of quiet cultural struggle. Many residents worked abroad, mainly in the Persian Gulf. Television Channel V, the Indian version of MTV, piped in Japanese, Filipino, and Arab as well as Indian music, with disk jockeys—all women of Indian origin from Britain or North America—speaking English. All of this provided new levels of contact with the outside world. Growing interest in novel consumer standards formed part of this change. A word derived from lower-caste slang, *chetu*, came to mean "cool"—denoting jeans, cars, a new motorbike. But debate and opposition surfaced as well. A local Coca-Cola bottling plant, for example, was accused of contaminating the water.

Concern about beauty pageants formed part of the cultural mix. Beauty pageants had spread widely on the subcontinent after an Indian woman won the Miss Universe contest in the 1990s. Hindu nationalists, however, condemned the contests, arguing that "In India, the woman is not meant to be sold." (Figure 36.1) In Kerala, local officials attempted a compromise effort to hold a pageant in which women would be assessed for their beauty, but in traditional costume and with accompanying tests of knowledge of Keralan culture. In this case, the compromise failed because the women who wanted to be in beauty parades did not have the cultural knowledge, while those who had the knowledge shunned the beauty contest part. It was a confusing situation, with change and continuity warring for dominance and dividing the people of Kerala. ■

Global influences and local preferences interacted widely as the 21st century advanced; generating distinctive disputes but also a variety of interesting amalgams. Americans did not see beauty pageants as a global threat, for they were in fact originally an American invention. But some of them did worry, more than Indians did, about hearing too many people speaking foreign languages in the neighborhood supermarket, the result of new patterns of migration. The need to interact with new external forces, or a desire to find ways to sidestep the interaction, formed a vital part of contemporary world history, particularly as the cold war framework receded from memory.

Along with the end of the cold war and its aftermath, the larger process, called globalization, was unfolding around the world even by the first decade of the 21st century. Launched in the 19th century, globalization retreated somewhat between 1920 and 1950, but now it strongly resumed. While the new global contacts were powerful, they did not monopolize the world scene. Important alternatives were nationalism and religion. And there was explicit resistance to globalization as well. These tensions, like the uncertainties surrounding the post–cold war diplomatic and military framework, raise intriguing questions about the relationship between world history and world's future.

Figure 36.1 Indian university students in New Delhi protest India's hosting of the Indian Miss World contest by burning contestants in effigy. Like these students, some Indian conservatives see beauty pageants as decadent imports from the West that are destructive of their culture's traditional values.

Globalization: Causes and Processes

Many specific features of the decades after 1990 were shaped by the adjustments and regional tensions discussed in the previous chapter, including, of course, the resurgence of terrorism and the new status of American power. More broadly however, the end of the cold war encouraged a renewal of globalization, a much larger process that further defines the complexities of the contemporary period of world history.

What Globalization Means

Globalization as a concept developed in the 1990s. At heart, it means the intensification of contacts among all major parts of the world, such that larger influences play a growing role in human life, from trade to culture to physical well-being. Even older kinds of interchange, like migration or disease, are partially redefined. Globalization means, also, the expansion of international influences, beyond familiar aspects like commerce or formal diplomacy to include political institutions, the environment, even elements of crime.

Globalization emerged, of course, from previous patterns of inter-regional contact. We have seen how connections among Africa, Asia, and Europe increased with the intercontinental network of the post-classical period. This was a move toward later globalization, but it was not globalization in itself. The whole world was not yet involved; levels of exchange increased but still had limited impact even on economic activity. Imitation of other societies increased, but not yet around standards that could be regarded as global. The expansion of the world religions came closest here, but none achieved full global standing. The early modern period intensified connections and did bring the whole world together for the first time. Cultural impacts were limited however. International trading companies arose, but except in a few colonial settings they did not have the deep local effects that later, multinational companies would generate.

Globalization is a result of political, demographic, and cultural as well as technological changes. Economic globalization itself involves unprecedented interconnection among the world's peoples.

globalization The increasing interconnectedness of all parts of the world, particularly in communication and commerce but also in culture and politics.

 Asia, 2000
MAP

Full globalization emerged only in the later 19th century. It depended on dramatic new technologies, and also policy decisions, spearheaded by Western imperialist powers, to increase economic interdependence around the world. It was at this point that Japanese leaders made basic decisions about participation in global exchange. More widely still, for the first time, political implications of globalization began to show, for example in anti-slavery campaigns or in practical arrangements to facilitate international postal service. The beginnings of the spread of some standard sports showed a new trend in popular culture. But this first surge did not bring uniform benefits, and the middle decades of the 20th century saw many societies attempt to limit their contacts with globalization. The United States remained an active economic participant, but tried to limit political involvement through the policy of isolation in the 1920s and 1930s. Japan and Germany strove to form their own economic systems, apart from fully global exchange. Under Stalin and later Mao Zedong, Russia and China pulled away culturally and economically.

By the later 20th century, however, forces of globalization again seized center stage. Technologies were crucial: From airplanes and radio on to satellite transmission and the Internet, the speed and volume of global communication and transportation moved ahead rapidly. Policy decisions reemerged. The 1978 Chinese decision to open interchange with the wider world had huge consequences, for China and the rest of the world alike, as the force of the Chinese economy gained ground steadily. Russia's 1985 policy shift, and then the collapse of a separate communist zone (a few isolated pockets excepted), propelled global connections even more substantially.

Globalization remains a tricky process, however, in several respects. Both scholars and publics debate its meaning and impact. Even though globalization builds on previous systems of interchange, from the post-classical period onward, the process must not be seen as some inevitable force. The 20th century itself, as a new period in world history, featured bitter debates about globalization, not a steady advance of international exchange. There may be further retreats in the future.

Although globalization suggests growing uniformities around the world, it is still not a uniform process. Different regions encountered globalization differently—by 2008 only about a third of the world's population had direct access to the Internet, and globalization was a remote force for many rural regions in south Asia or sub-Saharan Africa. Different regions also see different patterns of benefit or harm. In some regions, globalization increases unemployment and economic dislocation; in many places, the process seems to promote new levels of economic inequality (a pattern visible in the two past decades in the United States, Europe, India and China). By the early 21st century several Latin American countries were questioning whether global trading patterns were bringing economic benefits to their regions, or whether separate national economic policies might make more sense. Everywhere, furthermore, globalization challenges an established sense of identity, and many people resent this challenge deeply.

World history helps identify what is new about globalization, as against earlier patterns of contact. It helps explain why some aspects of globalization bother almost every society—think, for example, of current debates over immigration in Europe and the United States, or American concern about international agreements that might limit national sovereignty. It helps explain as well why many regions, like China, seem to be willing to introduce substantial changes in order to take advantage of global connections. By the 1990s only a few nations, such as Myanmar and North Korea, remained isolated. While many states maintained concerns about some aspects of globalization, few raised systematic barriers to exchanges of goods, ideas, and people. Tentatively, growing numbers of people around the world became accustomed to global connections (Figure 36.2). The spread of English as a world language, though incomplete and often resented, was part of this connection. English served airline travel, many sports, and the early Internet as a common language. This encouraged and reflected other facets of global change.

The New Technology

A globalization guru tells the following story. In 1988 a U.S. government official traveling to Chicago was assigned a limousine with a cellular phone. He was so delighted to have this novelty that he called his wife just to brag. Nine years later, in 1997, the same official was visiting a remote village in Côte d'Ivoire, in west Africa, that was accessible only by dugout canoe. As he prepared to leave, a Côte d'Ivoire official told him he had a call from Washington and handed him a cellular

Figure 36.2 Midnight, December 31, 1999: celebration of the new millennium in Sydney, Australia. New Year's Eve 1999 was not without worry. Some experts predicted that the turn of the century would wreak havoc on the internal calendars of computers worldwide, possibly leading to massive power failures, loss of data bases by businesses and governments, and disruptions in the supply of the most basic necessities of life. In some places, panicky shoppers stripped store shelves of bottled water, canned goods, flashlights, batteries, and other emergency supplies. But "Y2K," as this potential disaster came to be called, never materialized. Thanks to fully functional telecommunications, festivities in most time zones were broadcast worldwide, making for a great global party.

phone. Cellular phones had become increasingly common. They were among the key new communication devices that, by the 1990s, had made almost constant contact with other parts of the world feasible, and for some people unavoidable. Western Europe and east Asia led in the cellular phone revolution, but people in all parts of the world participated.

During the 1980s steady improvements in miniaturization made computers increasingly efficient. By the 1990s the amount of information that could be stored on microchips increased by more than 60 percent each year. Linkages among computers improved as well, starting with halting efforts in the 1960s mainly for defense purposes. E-mail was introduced in 1972. In 1990 a British software engineer working in Switzerland, Tim Berners, developed the World Wide Web, and the true age of the Internet was born. Almost instantaneous contact by computer became possible around the world, and with it came the capacity to send vast amounts of information, from text, to videos and other imagery, to music. While the Internet was not available to everyone—by 2005 only 30 percent of the world's population had access—it did provide global contacts for some otherwise fairly remote regions. In eastern Russia, for example, international mail service was agonizingly slow, telephone access often interrupted—but a student could sit at an Internet cafe in Vladivostok and communicate easily with friends in the United States or Brazil. By 2009, further development in computer-based networking included systems like Facebook and twittering, which again could facilitate personal connections around the world.

Satellite linkages for television formed a final communications revolution, making simultaneous broadcasts possible around the world. A full quarter of the world's population now could, and sometimes did, watch the same sporting event—usually World Cup soccer or the Olympics—a phenomenon never before possible or even approachable in world history. Global technology gained new meaning.

Economic Globalization: Business Organization and Investment

Thanks in part to new technology, in part to more open political boundaries, international investment accelerated rapidly at the end of the 20th century. Stock exchanges featured holdings in Chinese utilities or Brazilian steel companies as well as the great corporations of the West and Japan. U.S. investments abroad multiplied rapidly, almost doubling in the first half of the 1970s. By the 1980s foreign operations were generating between 25 and 40 percent of all corporate profits in the United States. Japan's foreign investment rose 15-fold during the 1970s. During the 1980s Japanese car manufacturers set up factories in the United States, Europe, and other areas. German cars, French tires, German chemicals and pharmaceuticals, and Dutch petroleum all had substantial U.S. operations. At the end of the 1990s the German Volkswagen firm introduced an updated version of the automobile affectionately known as the "bug," whose initial design went back to Hitler's Germany. Its production facilities were entirely based in Mexico, but it was marketed in the United States and around the world.

Globalization in business involved rapid increases in exports and imports, the extension of business organization across political boundaries—resulting in **multinational corporations**—and division of labor on a worldwide basis (Map 36.1). Cars that were made in the United States were assembled from parts made in Japan, Korea, Mexico, and elsewhere. Japanese cars often had more American-made parts in them than Detroit products had. Firms set up operations not simply to produce closer to markets to save transportation costs; they also sought to reduce costs by looking for cheap labor and minimal environmental regulations. Computer boards were made by West Indian and African women. India developed a huge software industry, subcontracting for firms in the United States and western Europe. The linkages were dazzling.

International firms continued to seek cheap raw materials. For example, companies in Japan and the West competed for access to oil and minerals in the newly independent nations of central Asia after the collapse of the Soviet Union. China's rapid economic growth prompted active arrangements for oil supplies from Central Asia, Latin America and Africa, as well as the Middle East. International investments also followed interest rates. During the 1990s relatively attractive U.S. interest rates drew extensive investment from Europe, Japan, and the oil-rich regions in the Middle East.

multinational corporations Powerful companies, mainly from the West or Pacific Rim, with production as well as distribution operations in many different countries. Multinationals surged in the decades after World War II.

Legend:
- No parent companies
- 1–100
- 100–500
- 500–1,000
- 1,000–2,000
- 2,000–5,000
- 5,000–9,500

Map 36.1 Multinational Corporations in 2000 By the end of the twentieth century, multinational companies had become a major force for economic change and political controversy over much of the world. As Map 36.1 illustrates, these engines of globalization were especially prominent in mature industrial and more affluent societies, and much less in evidence in formerly colonized or communist countries.

While multinational corporations sometimes faced government regulation, many of them had more power, and far more resources, than the governments of most of the countries within which they operated. Thus, they could determine most aspects of labor and environmental policy. They could and did pull up stakes in one region if more attractive opportunities opened elsewhere, regardless of the impact on the workers and facilities they left behind. Early in the 21st century, for example, many multinationals pulled jobs from Mexico in favor of expansion to China or Vietnam, where wages were lower. Even clerical jobs were outsourced: telephone services for many American companies, for example, were set up in India, where wages were lower and English was widely spoken. The spread of multinationals promoted industrial skills in many previously agricultural regions and depended on improvements in communications and transportation that could bring wider changes for the people of the lands in which they hired workers (Figure 36.3).

American factories located in northern Mexico, designed to produce goods for sale back in the United States, showed the complexity of the new international economy. The owners of these factories unquestionably sought cheap labor and lax regulations. Their factories often leaked chemical waste. Wages were barely 10 percent of what U.S. workers would earn. Nonetheless these factories often paid better than their Mexican counterparts. Many workers, including large numbers of women, found the labor policies more enlightened and the foremen better behaved in the foreign firms. A key question, not yet answerable, is whether the poverty-level wages for workers in such factories will improve and whether the industrial skills they learn will make possible a widening range of opportunities.

Globalization, combined with powerful economic growth in places like China and India, increased the level of economic competition, for established industrial powers and developing societies alike. Chinese manufacturing, with low labor costs, easily beat out factories in Mexico and the United States, in a variety of product lines. The Chinese also reached out for raw materials; its needs for oil brought it into active involvements in central Asia and Africa, where its outreach easily surpassed the levels briefly obtained in the 15th century. Brazilian steel exports became internationally competitive as early as the 1970s, affecting manufacturing levels in the United States. Rising purchasing power in many societies sustained the new competition, but there were real stresses and anxieties as well.

Efforts to tally the overall economic effects of globalization are complex and contested. Some parts of Africa lost traditional manufacturing jobs to new global competition, and in these regions, unemployment rates of 30 percent or more were common. Prostitution, including new international sex trafficking in women and children, and even the sale of body organs showed the increasingly desperate poverty in some societies. Not only global competition but reductions in government services, in the name of free-market principles, contributed to new problems. In south and southeast Asia, rates of child labor rose, though the larger global patterns were different. On the other hand, new global opportunities permitted an increase in per capita income in places like China and India.

It was clear that there were winners and losers in economic globalization, both among different parts of the world and within individual societies—even within industrial societies like the United States. Gaps widened between the poor and those with higher incomes. A growing middle class developed in Latin America, India, and China, but urban slums and exploited labor expanded as well.

Figure 36.3 Change and continuity in rural India. New irrigation and electrification combine with traditional methods of tilling the soil as agricultural production rises.

Migration

Broad international patterns of migration had developed by the 1950s and 1960s, with the use of "guest workers" from Turkey and north Africa in Europe for example. Here, patterns in the 1990s built clearly on previous trends. But easier travel, along with the continued gap between slowly growing populations in the industrial countries and rapidly growing populations in Latin America, Africa, and parts of Asia, maintained high levels of exchange. A few areas, including Italy, Greece, and Japan, had almost ceased internal population growth by the 1990s, which meant that new labor needs, particularly at the lower skill levels, had to be supplied by immigration.

Japan hoped to avoid too much influx by relying on high-technology solutions, but even here worker groups were brought in from the Philippines and southeast Asia. Migration into Europe and the United States was far more extensive, producing truly multinational populations in key urban and commercial centers. By 2000 at least 25 percent of all Americans, mostly people of color, came from households where English was not the first language. Ten percent of the French population in 2003 was Muslim (Figure 36.4). Here was an important source of tension, with local populations often fearing foreigners and worried about job competition. Here also was a new opportunity, not just for new laborers but for new cultural inspiration.

Migration was hardly new in world history. But new levels of migration from distant regions had novel qualities. So did the resulting mixture of migrants and locals in the cities of North America, western Europe, or the Persian Gulf states of the Middle East. So, finally, did the new facility of traveling back and forth: many migrants, returning home to Turkey or India on vacation or permanently, brought back new styles and ideas, maintaining their own commitment to at least two different cultures.

Cultural Globalization

Thanks in part to global technologies and business organization, plus reduced political barriers, the pace of cultural exchange and contact around the world accelerated at the end of the 1990s. Much of this involved mass consumer goods, spread from the United States, western Europe, and Japan. But art shows, symphony exchanges, scientific conferences, and Internet contact increased as well. Music conductors and artists held posts literally around the world, sometimes juggling commitments among cities like Tokyo, Berlin, and Chicago within a single season. Science laboratories filled with researchers from around the world, collaborating (usually in English) with little regard for national origin.

The spread of fast-food restaurants from the United States, headed by McDonald's, formed one of the most striking international cultural influences from the 1970s onward. The company began in Illinois in 1955 and started its international career in 1967 with outlets in Canada and Puerto Rico. From then on, the company entered an average of two new nations per year and accel-

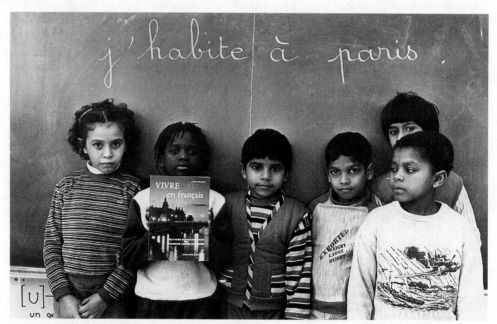

Figure 36.4 The mixtures of peoples and cultures that had become a prominent feature of world history by the end of the 20th century are wonderfully illustrated by this group of Muslim schoolchildren in a French school. By 2007, more than 10 percent of the French population was Islamic. In 2006, riots broke out in Islamic areas of French cities revealing tensions over the gap between opportunities available to immigrants and those available to the majority population.

erated the pace in the 1990s. By 1998 it was operating in 109 countries overall. The company won quick success in Japan, where it gained its largest foreign audience; "makadonaldo" first opened in Tokyo's world famous Ginza, already known for cosmopolitan department stores, in 1971. McDonald's entry into the Soviet Union in 1990 was a major sign of the ending of cold war rivalries and the growing Russian passion for international consumer goods. The restaurants won massive patronage despite (by Russian standards) very high prices. Even in gourmet-conscious France, McDonald's and other fast-food outlets were winning 26 percent of all restaurant dining by the 1990s. Not everyone who patronized McDonald's really liked the food. Many patrons in Hong Kong, for example, said they went mainly to see and be seen, and to feel part of the global world.

Cultural globalization obviously involved increasing exposure to American movies and television shows. Series like *Baywatch* won massive foreign audiences. Movie and amusement park icons like Mickey Mouse, and products and dolls derived from them, had international currency. Western beauty standards, based on the models and film stars, won wide exposure, expressed among other things in widely sought international beauty pageants. MTV spread Western images and sounds to youth audiences almost everywhere.

Holidays took on an international air. American-style Christmas trappings, including gift giving, lights, and Santa Claus, spread not only to countries of Christian background, like France, but also places like Muslim Istanbul. Northern Mexico picked up American Halloween trick-or-treating, as it displaced the more traditional Catholic observance of All Saints' Day. Muslim observance of Ramadan, the month of self-denial, began to include greeting cards and presents for children, a clear echo of new consumerism. The American jingle "happy birthday," with its implications about individualism and entertainment for children, was translated into virtually every language.

 Tradition vs. Modernity

Consumer internationalization was not just American. Japanese rock groups gained wide audience. The Pokémon toy series, derived from Japanese cultural traditions, won a frenzied audience among American children in the 1990s, who for several years could not get enough. A Japanese soap opera heroine became the most admired woman in Muslim Iran. South Korea, historically hostile to Japan, proved open to popular Japanese music groups and cartoon animation, and anime also gained popularity in the United States. European popular culture, including fashion and music groups, gained large followings around the world as well.

Dress was internationalized to an unprecedented extent. American-style blue jeans showed up almost everywhere. A major export item for Chinese manufacturing involved Western clothing pirated from famous brand names. A "Chinese market" in the cities of eastern Russia contained entirely Western-style items, mainly clothing and shoes.

The international expansion of middle-class consumerism also generated a global epidemic of obesity, particularly for children. Available foods increased along with more sedentary lives and entertainments, producing echoes in Shanghai and Bangalore of problems more obvious in Houston or Birmingham.

Cultural globalization roused extensive resistance. McDonalds became a symbol to attack by people eager to preserve local standards of food and culture; anti-McDonalds protests surged from France to South Korea. Efforts to adapt other forms of global consumer culture, like the beauty pageants, showed the interest in slowing or modifying this aspect of globalization. Some movements, at an extreme like the Taliban in Afghanistan, moved forcefully against any participation whatsoever. Contests over global culture became a standard part of life in many regions.

The penetration of cultural globalization varied—in part by wealth and urbanization, in part according to degrees of cultural tolerance (Figure 36.5). There were obvious resource limits, as in access to the Internet. Blending of global and local signals was another key development. Foreign models were often adapted to local customs. Thus foods in McDonald's in India (where the chain was not very popular in any event) included vegetarian items not found elsewhere. Comic books in Mexico, originally

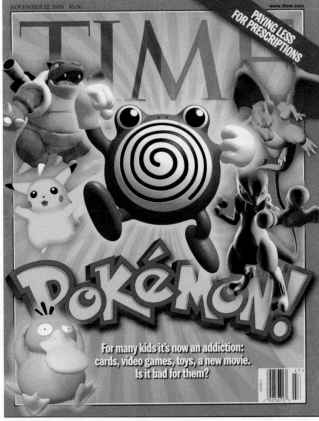

Figure 36.5 Pokémon, a children's game invented in Japan that quickly spread to become an international phenomenon and multibillion dollar industry, is often cited as an example of the globalization of culture in the early 21st century.

Protests Against Globalization

In December 1999, a series of protests rocked Seattle on the occasion of a World Trade Organization (WTO) meeting designed to discuss further international tariff cuts in the interests of promoting global trade. The following passage was written by Jeffrey St. Clair, a radical journalist who is co-editor of the political newsletter *CounterPunch*. St. Clair describes the atmosphere of the Seattle protests and some of the groups involved. The Seattle protests foreshadowed a regular sequence of popular demonstrations at the meetings of such groups as the World Bank, which continue into the 21st century, involving many of the same groups and issues.

Monday

And the revolution will be started by: sea turtles. At noon about 2000 people massed at the United Methodist Church, the HQ of the grassroots [organizations], for a march to the convention center. It was Environment Day and the Earth Island Institute had prepared more than 500 sea turtle costumes for marchers to wear. The sea turtle became the prime symbol of the WTO's threats to environmental laws when a WTO tribunal ruled that the U.S. Endangered Species Act, which requires shrimp to be caught with turtle excluder devices, was an unfair trade barrier.

But the environmentalists weren't the only ones on the street Monday morning. In the first showing of a new solidarity, labor union members from the Steelworkers and the Longshoremen showed up to join the march. In fact, Steelworker Don Kegley led the march, alongside environmentalist Ben White. (White was later clubbed in the back of the head by a young man who was apparently angry that he couldn't do his Christmas shopping. The police pulled the youth away from White, but the man wasn't arrested. White played down the incident.) The throng of sea turtles and blue-jacketed union folk took off to the rhythm of a familiar chant that would echo down the streets of Seattle for days: "The people will never be divided!"

I walked next to Brad Spann, a Longshoreman from Tacoma, who hoisted up one of my favorite signs of the entire week: "Teamsters and Turtles Together at Last!" Brad winked at me and said, "What the hell do you think old Hoffa [former Teamster leader] thinks of that?"

The march, which was too fast and courteous for my taste, was escorted by motorcycle police and ended essentially in a cage, a protest pen next to a construction site near the convention center. A large stage had been erected there hours earlier and Carl Pope, the director of the Sierra Club, was called forth to give the opening speech. The Club is the nation's most venerable environmental group. . . .

Standing near the stage I saw Brent Blackwelder, the head of Friends of the Earth. Behind his glasses and somewhat shambling manner, Blackwelder looks ever so professional. And he is by far the smartest of the environmental CEOs. But he is also the most radical politically, the most willing to challenge the tired complacency of his fellow green executives. . . .

Blackwelder's speech was a good one, strong and defiant. He excoriated the WTO as a kind of global security force for transnational corporations whose mission is "to stuff unwanted products, like genetically engineered foods, down our throats." . . .

After the speechifying most of the marchers headed back to the church. But a contingent of about 200 ended up in front of McDonald's where a group of French farmers had mustered to denounce U.S. policy on biotech foods. Their leader was José Bove, a sheep farmer from Millau in southwest France and a leader of Confederation Paysanne, a French environmental group. In August, Bove had been jailed in France for leading a raid on a McDonald's restaurant under construction in Larzac. At the time, he was already awaiting charges that he destroyed a cache of Novartis' genetically engineered corn. Bove said his raid on the Larzac McDonald's was promoted by the U.S. decision to impose a heavy tariff on Roquefort cheese in retaliation for the European Union's refusal to import American hormone-treated beef. Bove's act of defiance earned him the praise of Jacques Chirac and Friends of the Earth. Bove said he was prepared to start a militant worldwide campaign against "Frankenstein" foods. "These actions will only stop when this mad logic comes to a halt," Bove said. "I don't demand clemency but justice."

Bove showed up at the Seattle McDonald's with rounds of Roquefort cheese, which he handed out to the crowd. After listening to a rousing speech against the evils of Monsanto, and its bovine growth hormone and Roundup Ready soybeans, the crowd stormed the McDonald's breaking its windows and urging customers and workers to join the marchers on the streets. This was the first shot in the battle for Seattle.

Who were these direct action warriors on the front lines? Earth First, the Alliance for Sustainable Jobs and the Environment (the

derived from U.S. models, took on Mexican cultural images, including frequent triumphs over "gringo" supermen. A host of combinations emerged. Cultural internationalization was a real development, but it was complex and incomplete.

Institutions of Globalization

On the whole, political institutions globalized less rapidly than technology or business, or even consumer culture. Many people worried about the gap between political supervision and control and the larger globalization process. UN activity accelerated a bit in the 1990s. With the end of the cold war, more diplomatic hotspots invited intervention by multinational military forces. UN forces tried to calm or prevent disputes in a number of parts of Africa, the Balkans, and the Middle East. Growing refugee populations called for UN humanitarian intervention, often aided by other international groups. UN conferences broadened their scope, dealing for example with gender and pop-new enviro-steelworker alliance), the Ruckus Society (a direct action training center), Jobs with Justice, Rainforest Action Network, Food Not Bombs, Global Exchange, and a small contingent of Anarchists, the dreaded Black Bloc.

There was also a robust international contingent on the streets Tuesday morning: French farmers, Korean greens [environmentalists], Canadian wheat growers, Mexican environmentalists, Chinese dissidents, Ecuadorian anti-dam organizers, U'wa tribespeople from the Columbian rainforest, and British campaigners against genetically modified foods. Indeed earlier, a group of Brits had cornered two Monsanto lobbyists behind an abandoned truck carrying an ad for the *Financial Times.* They detained the corporate flacks long enough to deliver a stern warning about the threat of frankencrops to wildlife, such as the Monarch butterfly. Then a wave of tear gas wafted over them and the Monsanto men fled, covering their eyes with their neckties. . . .

As the march turned up toward the Sheraton and was beaten back by cops on horses, I teamed up with Etienne Vernet and Ronnie Cumming. Cumming is the head of one of the feistiest groups in the U.S., the PureFood Campaign, Monsanto's chief pain in the ass. Cumming hails from the oil town of Port Arthur, Texas. He went to Cambridge with another great foe of industrial agriculture, Prince Charles. Cumming was a civil rights organizer in Houston during the mid-sixties. "The energy here is incredible," Cumming said. "Black and white, labor and green, Americans, Europeans, Africans, and Asians arm in arm. It's the most hopeful I've felt since the height of the civil rights movement."

Vernet lives in Paris, where he is the leader of the radical green group EcoRopa. At that very moment the European delegates inside the convention were capitulating on a key issue: The EU, which had banned import of genetically engineered crops and hormone-treated beef, had agreed to a U.S. proposal to establish a scientific committee to evaluate the health and environmental risks of biotech foods, a sure first step toward undermining the moratorium. Still Vernet was in a jolly mood, lively and invigorated, if a little bemused by the decorous nature of the crowd. "Americans seem to have been out of practice in these things," he told me. "Everyone's so polite. The only things on fire are dumpsters filled with refuse." He pointed to a shiny black Lexus parked on Pine Street, which throngs of protesters had scrupulously avoided. In the windshield was a placard identifying it as belonging to a WTO delegate. "In Paris that car would be burning."

[David] Brower [environmental leader] was joined by David Foster, Director for District 11 of the United Steelworkers of America, one of the most articulate and unflinching labor leaders in America. Earlier this year, Brower and Foster formed an unlikely union, a coalition of radical environmentalists and Steelworkers called the Alliance for Sustainable Jobs and the Environment, which had just run an amusing ad in the *New York Times* asking, "Have You Heard the One about the Environmentalist and the Steelworker?" The groups had found they had a common enemy: Charles Hurwitz, the corporate raider. Hurwitz owned the Pacific Lumber company, the northern California timber firm that is slaughtering some of the last stands of ancient redwoods on the planet. At the same time, Hurwitz, who also controlled Kaiser Aluminum, had locked out 3000 Steelworkers at Kaiser's factories in Washington, Ohio, and Louisiana. "The companies that attack the environment most mercilessly are often also the ones that are the most anti-union," Foster told me. "More unites us than divides us."

I came away thinking that for all its promise this tenuous marriage might end badly. Brower, the master of ceremonies, isn't going to be around forever to heal the wounds and cover up the divisions. There are deep, inescapable issues that will, inevitably, pit Steelworkers, fighting for their jobs in an ever-tightening economy, against greens, defending dwindling species like sockeye salmon that are being killed off by hydrodams that power the aluminum plants that offer employment to steel workers. When asked about this potential both Brower and Foster danced around it skillfully. But it was a dance of denial. The tensions won't go away simply because the parties agree not to mention them in public. Indeed, they might even build, like a pressure cooker left unwatched. I shook the thought from my head. For this moment, the new, powerful solidarity was too seductive to let such broodings intrude for long.

From Alexander Cockburn, Jeffrey St. Clair, and Allan Sekula, *5 Days That Shook the World* (London: Verso, 2000), 16–21, 28, 29, 36–37.

QUESTIONS What were the principal groups involved in the globalization protests? Why did they feel such passion? Was this a global protest, or did different parts of the world have different issues? What were the key arguments of defenders of globalization who disapproved of this kind of protest and of its goals?

---

ulation control issues. While the results of the conferences were not always clear, a number of countries did incorporate international standards into domestic law. Women in many African countries, for example, were able to appeal to UN proclamations on gender equality as a basis for seeking new property rights in the courts. By 2001 the United Nations became increasingly active as well in encouraging assistance to stem the AIDS epidemic.

The World Health Organization also expanded its range directly. A threatened global outbreak of Severe Acute Respiratory Syndrome (SARS), after occurrences in east Asia and Canada in 2003, met with prompt controls under international guidance.

Another area of innovation involved international nongovernmental organizations (INGOs). Amnesty International, a London-based human rights agency, began in 1961. The 1970s saw a more rapid proliferation of INGOs for human rights, labor, environmental, and other issues, often with networks of local affiliates. By the 1990s Internet-based petitions against torture, labor abuses, or the death penalty became standard fare, sometimes winning significant policy responses. The range of criteria for INGOs expanded steadily as well: rape, for example, was internationally recognized as a war crime by the 1990s, a major innovation.

As more nations participated actively in international trade, the importance of organizations in this arena grew. The International Monetary Fund (IMF) and the World Bank had been founded after World War II to promote trade. Guided by the major industrial powers, these organizations offered loans and guidance to developing areas and also to regions that encountered temporary economic setbacks. Loans to Mexico and to southeast Asia during the 1990s were intended to promote recovery from recessions that threatened to affect other areas. Loans were usually accompanied by requirements for economic reform, usually through reduced government spending and the promotion of more open competition. These guidelines were not always welcomed by the regions involved. The IMF and the World Bank were widely viewed as primary promoters of the capitalist global economy.

Annual meetings of the heads of the seven leading industrial powers (four from Europe, two from North America, plus Japan) also promoted global trade and policies toward developing regions. Finally, the regional economic arrangements that had blossomed from the 1950s onward gained growing importance as globalization accelerated. The European Union headed the list, but the **North American Free Trade Agreement (NAFTA)** and other regional consortiums in Latin America and east Asia also pushed for lower tariffs and greater economic coordination.

Resistance and Alternatives

Accelerating globalization attracted a vigorous new protest movement. Meetings of the World Bank or of the industrial leaders were increasingly marked by huge demonstrations and some violence.

Protest and Economic Uncertainties

A new anti-globalization protest movement began with massive protests in Seattle in 1999, and the protests continued at key gatherings thereafter. Protesters came from various parts of the world and raised a number of issues. Many people believed that rapid global economic development was threatening the environment. Others blasted the use of cheap labor by international corporations, which was seen as damaging labor conditions even in industrial nations. Rampant consumerism was another target.

Many critics claimed that globalization was working to the benefit of rich nations and the wealthy generally, rather than the bulk of the world's population. They pointed to figures that suggested growing inequalities of wealth, with the top quarter of the world's population growing richer during the 1990s while the rest of the people increasingly suffered (Figure 36.6). This division oper-

---

World Bank-Supported Day Care Programs in Uganda

North American Free Trade Agreement (NAFTA) Agreement that created an essentially free trade zone among Mexico, Canada, and the United States, in hopes of encouraging economic growth in all three nations; after difficult negotiations, went into effect January 1, 1994.

Globalization generated direct protest at the end of the 20th century. Nationalism and religion, overlapping globalization, provided alternative sets of loyalties.

Figure 36.6 The increasing gap between rich and poor is a controversial problem in the age of globalization. Here, contemporary workers and shoppers pass a homeless person on a Hong Kong sidewalk.

How Much Historical Change?

As the cold war drew to a close, a number of analysts, primarily in the United States, looked forward to dramatic shifts in human affairs. There were two related lines of argument. The "end of history" concept emphasized the new dominance of the democratic form of government. According to this view, the contest among political and economic systems, particularly between democracy and communism, was over; democracy would now sweep over the world. With this, the need for basic questioning about political institutions would also end: democracy worked best, and it was here to stay. Further, the change in political structure also had implications for power rivalries. Some analysts contend that democracies never war on each other. Once the people control affairs of state through their votes, the selfishness and power trips that lead to war will end. Ordinary people understand the horror of war. They appreciate the common humanity they share with other democratic peoples. Just as democracy resolves internal conflicts through votes, democracies would come to resolve external conflicts through bargaining and compromise. They argue that, in the main, people do not vote for wars of aggression, at most sanctioning defense against attack.

Another argument, which might be combined with the democracy approach, focused on the spread of consumer capitalism around the world. As put forward by a U.S. journalist in a popular book called *The Lexus and the Olive Tree*, the consumer capitalism approach emphasized the benefits of a global economy. In this, every-

> "The 'end of history' concept emphasized the new dominance of the democratic form of government."

one would gain access to greater material abundance and the wonders of consumerism, and no one would wish to jeopardize prosperity by waging war. Shared interests, rather than traditional disputes over limited resources, it is alleged, would carry the day. However, history suggests that capitalism is not necessarily compatible with democracy: the drive for material wealth has often led to corruption within democratic societies, sapping the effectiveness of their institutions. The proponents of the idea that history will end in the triumph of capitalism have voiced concern that growing disparities of wealth even within the most prosperous capitalist nations might spark violent unrest that could derail the drive toward a free-market utopia.

This is a challenging kind of forecasting because it cannot easily be disproved—until the future does not correspond to the dramatic projections. The consumerism argument, particularly, has no precedent. At the same time, the predictions also could not be proved, for example, merely by pointing to some prior historical analogy. How, then, should they be assessed?

QUESTIONS Following the end of the cold war, did the world change as rapidly and fundamentally as these predictions implied? Did new systems spread as uniformly and consistently as the democracy and global consumerism arguments implied? How significant was the cold war's end in shaping global relationships?

---

ated between regions, widening the gap between affluent nations and the more populous developing areas. It also operated within regions, including the United States and parts of western Europe, where income gaps were on the rise. Bitter disagreements increasingly divided the supporters and opponents of globalization.

Nationalism and New Religious Currents

Several trends ran counter to globalization as the 21st century began. Nationalism was one. While many nations were partially bypassed by globalization—many countries were much less powerful than the multinational corporations—nationalist resistance to globalization surfaced in many ways. Many countries opposed the erosion of traditions by global cultural patterns. The French government periodically resisted the incorporation of English words into the French language. Many Chinese families began to pay for private Confucian lessons for their children, to recall key cultural traditions lest global standards and materialism sweep everything else away. Many European countries tried to regulate the number of immigrants from Africa, Asia, and the West Indies, in the interest of preserving dominance for families and workers of European background. The United States rejected a wide variety of international treaties, including a provision for regulation against war crimes, because they might interfere with national sovereignty. China and other states periodically bristled against international criticism of internal policies concerning political prisoners.

Other individual nations tried to stand out against global trends, even aside from the few regimes, like North Korea, that were almost entirely isolated. The health ministry in Indonesia, for example, worked to prevent the World Health Organization from testing for outbreaks of new diseases. Several Latin American countries periodically opposed the efforts of international economic organizations to interfere with domestic economic policies in the interest of free trade.

It was religion, however, that posed the most interesting challenge to globalization in the final decades of the 20th century. Most religious movements were not necessarily opposed to globalization, but they tended to insist on their distinctiveness, against any uniform global culture. They also bred suspicions of the consumerism and sexuality highlighted in many manifestations of globalization, including films and tourism.

As communism collapsed in eastern Europe, many people returned to previous religious beliefs, including Orthodox Christianity. Protestant fundamentalists, often from the United States, were also busy in the region. Protestant fundamentalism also spread rapidly in parts of Latin America, such as Guatemala and Brazil. In India, Hindu fundamentalism surged by the 1990s, with Hindu nationalist politicians capturing the nation's presidency. In China, an intriguing spinoff from Buddhism, the Falun Gong, won wide support, despite brutal repression by the government.

Fundamentalism also gained ground in Islam, particularly in the Middle East and nearby parts of Africa and south central Asia. The Taliban, which followed a particular version of Islamic fundamentalism, gained control of the state in Afghanistan, initially in opposition to Soviet occupation, until the party was dislodged by the American invasion after the 2001 terrorist attack. Islamic fundamentalists argued for a return to religious law, opposing more secular governments in the region as well as the lures of global consumerism. Whether Christian, Hindu, or Islamic, fundamentalists tended to urge a return to the primacy of religion and religious laws and often opposed greater freedoms for women. Frequently, fundamentalists urged government support for religious values.

Religious fundamentalism ran counter to globalization in several ways, even though many religious leaders became adept at using new global technologies such as the Internet. It tended to appeal particularly to impoverished urban groups who seemed to be left behind in the global economy. Fundamentalism also tended to increase intolerance, even in religious traditions that had historically been reasonably open. Hindu fundamentalism, for example, was more fiercely exclusive than had been true in the past, while also more eager to seek support from the state. While some advocates of globalization assumed that religious traditionalism would decline, the balance was in fact unclear as the 21st century opened.

Religious differences contributed to many regional conflicts. Catholic, Serbian Orthodox, and Muslim clashes complicated the ethnic rivalries in the former Yugoslavia. Battles between Muslims and Christians occurred in Indonesia and the Sudan, and clashes between Hindus and Muslims intensified in India during the 1990s. Judaism and Islam, and Christianity as well, generated tensions not only in Israel but also in Lebanon. Tensions between Christian fundamentalists and other groups intensified political divisions within the United States.

Religious-based terrorism was explicitly against globalization. The choice of the World Trade Center in New York as a target for the September 2001 attacks involved its symbolic role in international, and not just American, capitalism. A bloody bombing attack on a hotel in Bali, Indonesia, lashed out at Australian tourists and the consumerist lifestyle of an international resort. Reactions to terrorism, for example in generating new limitations on international travel, compounded the impact.

Most of the religious movements were not, of course, mainly terroristic, nor were they defined simply by opposition to globalization. Different strands of fundamentalism emerged: for example, many Iranian religious leaders, though eager to support religious law, regarded the Taliban in Afghanistan as crude and excessive. Many religious leaders were far more focused on local issues—like the secular regimes in the Middle East—than on global ones. Fundamentalists did, however, provide alternative identities and standards, compared to globalization. They generated debate within a large number of societies about what kind of future people should strive for.

The Global Environment

Globalization generated unfamiliar environmental problems. These problems fed resistance to globalization and also efforts at corrective reform.

Human impact on the environment was not new, but its global level was unprecedented. Industrial competition, in the context of globalization, increased the number of societies eager for economic growth regardless of environmental consequences. New technologies expanded global impact directly. Huge tankers periodically leaked massive amounts of oil into the oceans, affecting many regions. Tall smokestacks, designed to reduce local pollution in the American Midwest or the German

Ruhr, spread acidity to the forests of Canada or Scandinavia. Multinationals, seeking loose environmental controls, often spilled chemicals. Above all, the pressure to expand production, in agriculture as well as industry, steadily cut into tropical rain forests, in places like Brazil, causing regional economic damage and contributing to global warming.

A key issue was the expansion of intensive industrial development goals. The Soviet Union and its satellites, pressing production during the cold war, had already caused extensive environmental damage, particularly in regions like central Asia. By the 1990s, China's headlong industrial drive raised new concerns. China's population of over a billion people was building on a resource base that was already severely depleted and degraded—including widespread water shortages. Perpetual smoke covered large regions of the country, thanks to rapid industrial growth. The Chinese called it the "yellow dragon." Beijing planned to shut down manufacturing operations during the 2008 Olympics to provide a brief, internationally pleasant respite. The nation became the second greatest air polluter, after the United States, by 2001.

Equally alarming were reports on the ecological fallout of rapid development in southeast Asia, where multinationals based in Japan and in the newly industrialized countries of east Asia are extracting resources with abandon and where the rain forest is disappearing even more rapidly than in Brazil. Similar trends have been documented in sub-Saharan Africa, where imminent economic collapse and environmental demise are now routinely predicted.

By the end of the 20th century, the wealthy one-fifth of humanity living in the industrialized nations consumed four-fifths of all marketed goods and resources. They also produced over 70 percent of the earth's pollution. In 1998 tiny Belgium, with 9 million people, had a gross domestic product (GDP) equal to that of the 40 countries of sub-Saharan Africa, whose combined population was 450 million. It has been estimated that, at present rates of economic growth, it would take most developing nations 150 years to reach the average levels of productivity achieved in 1980 by wealthy nations like the United States, Japan, and those of western Europe. Many of these societies may not have even a fraction of this time to find sustainable solutions to dilemmas of mass poverty, overpopulation, and environmental degradation. The general issues became abundantly clear in Mexico City, where oxygen is now widely sold by peddlers in the streets. A journalist, Marc Cooper, put it this way:

> The city's poised on the abyss of a world-class bio/technic disaster . . . its infrastructure is crumbling, . . . the drinking water mixes with sewer effluent, . . . many of the scars of the 1985 killer quake won't be healed before the next tremblor strikes. [And even then] Mexico City still beats the eternally depressed, sun-baked countryside.

Environmental Issues as Global Concerns

At the turn of the 21st century, environmental issues have emerged as focal points of public debate and government policy in most human societies (Figure 36.7). After a century of unprecedented levels of mechanized warfare, scientific experimentation, and the spread of industrialization, a wide variety of complex and often interrelated environmental disruptions threaten not only humanity but all other life forms on the planet Earth (Figure 36.8).

Most scientists now agree that the greenhouse effect caused by the buildup in the atmosphere of excessive amounts of carbon dioxide and other heat-trapping gases has led to a substantial warming of the planet in recent decades. Some of the chief sources of the pollutants responsible for the atmospheric buildup are industrial wastes—including those resulting from energy production through the burning of fossil fuels like coal—and exhaust from millions of cars, trucks, and other machines run by internal combustion engines that burn petroleum. But other major sources of the greenhouse effect are both surprising and at present essential to the survival of large portions of humanity. Methane, another greenhouse gas, is introduced into the atmosphere in massive quantities as a by-product of the stew of fertilized soil and water in irrigated rice paddies, which feed a majority of the peoples of Asia, the world's most populous continent. Methane is also released by flatulent cattle, which produce milk and meat for human populations over much of the globe. Other gases have had equally alarming effects. Chlorofluorocarbons (CFCs), for example, which were once widely used in refrigeration, air conditioning, and spray cans, deplete the ozone layer, thereby removing atmospheric protection from the ultraviolet rays emanating from the sun.

Figure 36.7 In April 1986, nuclear chain reactions in the Chernobyl nuclear power plant in Ukraine (then part of the Soviet Union) leapt out of control, creating a fireball that blew the steel and concrete lid off of the reactor. Radioactive material was spewed into the open air and drifted across Europe. The area surrounding the plant, which is now closed, remains a contaminated wasteland. The Chernobyl catastrophe was unique, but it added to the larger environmental damage in many parts of the former Soviet Union.

Figure 36.8 The powerful December 2004 earthquake beneath the Indian Ocean generated *tsunami* (tidal waves) that devastated large areas of Indonesia, Sri Lanka, India, and Thailand. These waves, up to 100 feet high, killed close to 200,000 people in the Indian Ocean basin and caused deaths even as far away as South Africa. Some scientists argue that global warming and overdevelopment of the world's coastlines made the damage caused by the tsunami more severe than it otherwise would have been. Here, survivors walk amid debris from the tsunami in Banda Aceh, Sumatra, almost three weeks after the wave hit.

Two Faces of Globalization

Early in the 21st century the city of Dubai, in the United Arab Emirates, became a world commercial center, with banking, telecommunications, and other services. Many international corporations located regional offices there. The city was a beehive of construction, including work on the world's newest tallest skyscraper. Most of the buildings were in characteristic modern style, often designed by Western firms and often strikingly beautiful. This Arab center was becoming increasingly cosmopolitan, with little overt protest. But there was another face. Workers in Dubai, most of them immigrants from places like Pakistan, Palestine, and the Philippines, often had relatively low pay. Few were citizens, which limited their access to benefits such as higher education. While they wanted the work, for conditions in their host country were better than at home, they were not reaping the benefits of globalization in a way comparable to the citizens of Dubai, and their work was extremely physically challenging in a demanding climate.

QUESTIONS What does this picture say about globalization? There is an obvious side: the march of gleaming city centers in many parts of the world. A less obvious side is the people whose work built the global economy. The picture provides evidence about both sides.

If scientific predictions are correct, global warming will increasingly cause major shifts in temperatures and rainfall throughout much of the globe. Fertile and well watered areas now highly productive in foods for humans and animals may well be overwhelmed by droughts and famine. If widely accepted computer simulations are correct, coastal areas at sea level—which from Bangladesh to the Netherlands to New Jersey are among the most densely populated in the world—are likely to be inundated. As climates are drastically altered, vegetation and wildlife in many areas will be radically altered. In Asia, the recent rapid melting of glaciers in the Himalayas threatens to deprive much of India and China of water for irrigation. Temperate forests may die off in many regions and be replaced by scrub, tropical vegetation, or desert flora. Some animal species may migrate or adapt and survive, but many, unable to adjust to such rapid climatic changes, will become extinct.

Not all of the sources of global warming are the product of the Industrial Revolution and its rapid spread and intensification, which has been a major theme in 20th-century world history. Most human societies have raised cattle and sheep for millennia, and methane has been flowing from rice paddies into the atmosphere since the Neolithic revolution, which began in some areas as early as the middle of the 9th millennium B.C.E. But the intensification of industrial processes and resource demands has accelerated the greenhouse effect and global warming. The cutting and burning

The Rain
Forest

CASE STUDY

of the world's forests is one of the more notable examples. Not only does the smoke produced contribute massively to carbon dioxide buildup in the atmosphere, but the destruction of the rain forests, in particular, deprives the earth of the natural "sinks" of plant life that suck up carbon dioxide and turn it into oxygen.

The destruction of the rain forests is especially troublesome since, unlike the temperate woodlands, they cannot regenerate themselves. And in terms of evolution, the rain forests have been the source of most of the species of plant and animal life that now inhabit the earth. In this and other ways, human interventions now affect global climate and weather in the short term and will determine the fate of the planetary environment in the centuries, perhaps millennia, to come.

International discussions of environmental regulation increased from 1997 onward. A major conference in Kyoto, Japan, set limits on greenhouse gas emissions, in order to curtail global warming. It was not clear, however, whether these limits would have any effect. Many individual nations, including the United States between 2001 and 2009, opposed the limits proposed because of potential damage to national economies. Here was another area where global politics did not seem to be keeping pace with globalization. Some interest in sustainability movements and green design did gain ground in many different countries, including the United States, China and the United Arab Emirates as well as countries, like Germany and Japan, where environmental activism had an even larger pedigree.

Disease

Changes in global contacts have usually involved disease, and globalization is no exception. Rapid international travel helped spread the AIDS epidemic from 1980 onward. Southern and eastern Africa were hit most severely, but AIDS also spread to the United States and western Europe. The epidemic took on even larger proportions in places like Brazil. By the early 21st century, rates of increase in parts of Asia and in Russia began to accelerate. These were regions that had initially felt relatively safe but where global contact ultimately brought new levels of contagion. The advent of SARS in 2003 raised fears of another global contagion. This is where the response of international organizations proved particularly essential.

The problem of contagious disease remained less severe than some of the earlier epidemics associated with global contacts, though some experts warned of even greater disease problems in the future. Environmental issues, newer on the global scale, may have replaced disease as the clearest downside of international connections.

Globalization and Global Balance

As globalization processes accelerated from the mid-20th century onward, they operated initially in a framework of substantial Western dominance not unlike that of the later 19th century. To be sure, the United States now took the lead role, for example, in guiding new institutions like the International Monetary Fund designed to spur world trade and greater financial stability. By the 1960s, the growing economic and, ultimately, cultural influence of Japan was a clear innovation. Wider global participation, however, was still limited. This was symbolized in the regular meetings of heads of state called the G-8, which embraced the leading Western powers plus Japan and Russia, which sought to deal with various global issues.

By the early 21st century, however, it was clear that along with globalization itself, the world power balance was shifting. The United States remained the lead military nation, though its involvement in the wars in Iraq and Afghanistan hampered its flexibility. Economically, however, the rapid growth of countries like China, India, and Brazil cut into any claims that the West plus Japan were running the global show. Efforts to deal with environmental or health issues, similarly, had to take into account a wider range of nations in order to gain effective results.

This change in the framework for globalization was recognized in 2008, as the world's nations tried to respond to a major new financial crisis that had originated in the United States but spread quickly to virtually all regions (its speed and extent another sign of how much global interconnections had intensified). To deal with the recession a new "group of 20" was convened, representing the earlier 8, of course, but also Asia's new giants, South Africa, and leading Latin American economies such as Brazil and Mexico. Globalization's expanded cast of leaders was an important shift in its own right. It was not clear whether this additional shift would solidify or complicate the process of globalization itself.

Toward the Future

Human beings have always wanted to know what the future will hold. Various societies looked to the configurations of the stars for predictions, and astrology still has partisans in the contemporary world. Some societies generated beliefs in cycles, predicting that the future would repeat patterns already seen in the past; many Chinese scholars developed a cyclical approach. Still other societies assume that the future will differ from the past; from the Enlightenment onward, Western culture developed an additional belief in progress.

Forecasts about the future use history, but in different ways. Key issues for the future emerge from recent trends and tensions.

History suggests the futility of many efforts at forecasting. It has been estimated that well over half of the "expert" forecasts generated in the United States since World War II have been wrong. This includes predictions that by 2000 most Americans would be riding to and from work in some kind of airship, or that families would be replaced by promiscuous communes. Yet if history debunks forecasts, it also provides the basis for thinking about the future.

Projecting from Trends

The most obvious connection between history and the future involves the assessment of trends that are likely to continue at least for several decades. Thus we "know" that global population growth will slow up, because it is already slowing up. Many forecasts see stabilization by 2050, based on rapidly falling birth rates around the world. We also "know" that populations will become older; that is, the percentage of older citizens will increase. This is already happening in western Europe, the United States, and Japan and will occur elsewhere as birth rates drop. What we don't "know" of course is how societies will react to the demands of the increasing numbers of older people, or how much the environment will have deteriorated by the time global population stabilizes. Even trend-based forecasts can be thrown off by unexpected events, like wars. In the 1930s experts "knew" that the American birth rate would fall, because it was already falling, but then war and prosperity created a totally unexpected baby boom, and the experts were wrong for at least two decades. Forecasts about the rise of Chinese or Indian economic power in coming decades also build on existing trends.

Trend-based forecasting is even chancier when the trends are already fragile. The late 20th century saw a genuine global spread of democracy, though admittedly not to every region. It was possible to venture predictions about the triumph of this form of government. But by 2002 it was hard to be confident that democracies were entirely secure in parts of Latin America or even in Russia. The hold of earlier, less democratic political traditions or the sheer pressure of economic stagnation might unseat the trend.

Forecasting is also complicated when two different trends are in play. The 20th century saw a fairly steady rise in consumerism, which spread to all parts of the world. The appeal of mass media, commercialized sports, and global fashions reaches across traditional boundaries. But the last 30 years have also seen a pronounced increase in religious interest, in many if not all parts of the world. Some people participate in both trends, but overall, the priorities are different. Is one of the two trends likely to predominate? Or should we think of the future in terms of division and tension among cultural interests?

Big Changes

Some analysts have looked at the world's future in terms of stark departures from its past. They argue that trend analysis is inadequate because we are on the verge of a major shift in framework. In the 1960s a "population bomb" analysis won considerable attention. The argument was that rapid population growth was about to overwhelm all other developments, leading to resource depletion, new wars over resources, and a world far different from what we had previously known. More recently, other forecasts, of dramatic climate change and of resource exhaustion, provide another dire picture of the world's future, in which other issues, like the fate of particular political systems, fade in importance.

Another scenario for a dramatically different future that has enjoyed recurrent popularity is the vision of a postindustrial world. Some pundits argue that computer technology, genetic engineering, and other technological advances are undermining the conditions of industrial society. Information, not production, becomes the key to economic growth and to social structures. The functions of cities shift from production to entertainment. Work will become more individualized and less time consuming, creating a new premium for expressive leisure. Here too, however, critics express doubts. Many parts of the world are not yet industrial, much less postindustrial. Work does not seem to be heading toward less routine; for example, computers promote repetitive activities as much as new creativity. As is always true with intriguing predictions of massive change, the jury is still out.

The Problem of the Contemporary Period

One of the reasons prediction is particularly difficult—though also compelling—is that world history has undergone so many fundamental changes during the past century. We know, for example, that the dominance of western Europe, for centuries a staple of world history, is a thing of the past, despite the continued vitality of the region. But what will replace it? Continued United States ascendancy, with military outposts in many parts of the world? Or the rise of China or east Asia? Or perhaps no single dominant region at all? We know there's a question about the world balance that will replace Western control, but the answer is unclear.

The same applies to conditions for women. Improvements in women's education plus the decline of the birth rate add up to significant changes for women around the world. The pace of change varies with the region, to be sure. Many regions also have given new legal and political rights to women. But is there a new model for women's roles that might be applicable around the world? Continued disputes about women's work roles, significant male backlash against change, and even disputes by women themselves about the relevance of an individualistic Western model for women's lives make forecasting difficult. We can assume continued change, but it's hard to pinpoint the results.

Global Connections

Civilizations and Global Forces

A key question for the future involves the fate of individual civilizations. World history has been shaped substantially by the characteristics of key civilizations for over 5000 years, granting that not everyone has been part of a major civilization and that in some cases civilizations are not easy to define. Some observes argue that, by the 21st century, the separate characteristics of civilizations are beginning to yield to homogenizing forces. Many scientists, athletes, and businesspeople feel more commitment to their professional interests than to their region of origin—which means that global professional identities can override civilizational loyalties. The downtowns of most cities around the world look very much alike. The same products, stores, and restaurants can be found in most urban areas. Globalization may be outpacing regional labels.

Yet we have also seen that globalization can falter, as it did in the middle decades of the 20th century. Even when it accelerates, as in the 1990s, it brings efforts to reassert separate identities. Even

as it participates in the global economy, China remains distinctive, reflecting for example some of the political characteristics that were launched 3000 years ago. The Japanese easily move in global economics and culture, but with an emphasis on group identity measurably different from the personal goals emphasized in the United States. Major religions like Hinduism and Islam continue to mark their regions, and in some ways their influence seems to be on the rise.

World history has long been defined by a tension between regional features and larger connections. The specifics change, for example with shifts in technology and organizational capacity. But it may be premature to assume that some kind of global homogeneity is going to change the equation altogether.

Further Readings

For very different takes on the resurgence of globalization since 1989, see Thomas Friedman's cautious celebration in *The Lexus and the Olive Tree: Understanding Globalization* (2000), John Gray's more sober appraisal in *False Dawn* (2000), and Thomas

Frank's lively critique in *One Market Under God* (2000). See also Joseph E. Stiglitz, *Making Globalization Work* (2006); Nathan M. Jensen, *Nation-States and the Multinational Corporation: A Political Economy of Foreign Direct Investment* (2006); Dimitris Stevis and Terry Boswell, *Globalization and Labor: Democratizing Global Governance* (2008); Peter Dicken, *Global Shift: Mapping the Changing Contours of the World Economy* (2007); Guillermo de la Dehesa, *What Do We Know About Globalization?: Issues of Poverty and Income Distribution* (2007); Daniel Cohen, *Globalization and its Enemies* (2006); Nelly P. Stromquist and Karen Monkman, eds., *Globalization and Education: Integration and Contestation across Cultures* (2000); Ernest Gundling and Anita Zanchettin, *Global Diversity: Winning Customers and Engaging Employees within World Markets* (2007); and Deen K. Chatterjee, ed., *Democracy in a Global World: Human Rights and Political Participation in the 21st Century* (2008).

Differing perspectives on the cultural ramifications of the new global economic order are provided by Peter Stearns, *Consumerism in World History* (2001); Walter LaFeber, *Michael Jordan and the New Global Capitalism* (2000); and the contributions to James Watson, ed., *Golden Arches East: McDonald's in East Asia* (1998). See also Lewis Solomon, *Multinational Corporations and the Emerging World Order* (1978); Stephen Rees, *American Films Abroad* (1997); Theodore von Laue, *The World Revolution of Westernization* (1997); Peter N. Stearns, *The Industrial Revolution in World History* (1998); and Bruce Mazlish and Ralph Buultjens, eds., *Conceptualizing Global History* (1993).

J. Luccassen and L. Luccassen, eds., *Migration, Migration, History, History: Old Paradigms and New Perspectives* (1997), is a recent comparative social history—in addition to an extensive bibliography it includes chapters on conceptual issues (periodization, definitions, etc.) and several regional historical case studies. Alistair Ager, *Refugees: Perspectives on the Experience of Forced Migration* (1998), is a useful survey. See also Patrick Manning, *Migration in World History* (2002).

For genuinely global perspectives on environmental issues, see Bill McKibben, *The End of Nature* (1999 ed.); Mark Hertsgaard, *Earth Odyssey* (1998); Jennifer Clapp and Peter Dauvergen, *Paths to a Green World: The Political Economy of the Global Environment* (2005); and Ramachandra Guha, *Environmentalism: A Global History* (2000). The best accounts of environmental degradation in key regions of the world include Susanna Hecht and Alexander Cockburn, *The Fate of the Forest* (1990), about Brazil; Judith Shapiro, *Mao's War against Nature* (2001); Vaclav Smil, *The Bad Earth* (1984) and *China's Environmental Crisis* (1993); Murray Feshback and Alfred Friendly Jr., *Ecocide in the USSR* (1992); Marc Reisner, *Cadillac Desert* (1993), about the United States; and Madhav Gadgil and Ramachandra Guha, *Ecology and Equity* (1995), about India.

For a good source about the movement for sustainable development, *Ecological Literacy: Education and the Transition to a Postmodern World* by David W. Orr (1992) and Andrés R. Edwards, *The Sustainability Revolution* (2005). Several serious books (as well as many more simplistic, popularized efforts) attempt to sketch the future of the world or the West. On the concept of the postindustrial society, see Daniel Bell, *The Coming of Post-Industrial Society* (1974). For other projections, consult R. L. Heilbroner, *An Inquiry into the Human Prospect* (1974); and L. Stavrianos, *The Promise of the Coming Dark Age* (1976).

On environment and resource issues, see D. H. Meadows and D. L. Meadows, *The Limits to Growth* (1974); Al Gore, *Earth in the Balance* (1992); and L. Herbert, *Our Synthetic Environment* (1962). M. ul Haq's *The Poverty Curtain: Choices for the Third World* (1976) and L. Solomon's *Multinational Corporations and the Emerging World Order* (1978) cover economic issues, in part from a non-Western perspective. On a leading social issue, see P. Huston, *Third World Women Speak Out* (1979).

On the Web

The threat of HIV/AIDS to world civilizations is discussed at http://usinfo.state.gov/journals/itgic/0700/ijge/ijge0700.htm. This threat is also explored in regions as diverse as Afghanistan (http://www.youandaids.org/Features/AfghanistanDec04.asp and http://web.worldbank.org/WBSITE/EXTERNAL/COUNTRIES/SOUTHASIAEXT/EXTSAREGTOPHEANUT/EXTSAREGTOPHIVAIDS/0,,contentMDK:20288512~menuPK:568870~pagePK:34004173~piPK:34003707~theSitePK:496967,00.html), Africa (http://news.bbc.co.uk/1/hi/world/africa/3128973.stm), Europe (http://www.avert.org/eurosum.htm and http://www.euro.who.int/document/e87777.pdf), India (http://siteresources.worldbank.org/INTINDIA/Resources/HIV-AIDS-brief-June2005-IN.pdf, http://web.worldbank.org/WBSITE/EXTERNAL/COUNTRIES/SOUTHASIAEXT/EXTSAREGTOPHEANUT/EXTSAREGTOPHIVAIDS/0,,contentMDK:20288516~menuPK:568874~pagePK:34004173~piPK:34003707~theSitePK:496967,00.html, and http://archives.cnn.com/2000/ASIANOW/south/09/05/india.health.challenge.ap/), Laos (http://www.aegis.com/news/re/2003/RE030628.html) and Pakistan (http://www.youandaids.org/Asia%20Pacific%20at%20a%20Glance/Pakistan/index.asp). The threat posed to humanity by Severe Respiratory Distress Syndrome or SARS is examined at http://www.cdc.gov/NCIDOD/SARS/factsheet.htm.

The transcript (as well as streaming video) of a roundtable discussion on global over-population can be accessed at http://www.uncommonknowledge.org/700/726.html. To sample the views of some libertarian groups that see the idea of a growing world population as a myth or believe that controlling it is not worth the moral cost, go to http://www.cooperativeindividualism.org/sullivan-dan_on-neomalthusianism.html. This debate is explored by former World Bank leader Robert McNamara at http://www.foreignaffairs.org/19840601faessay8386/robert-s-mcnamara/time-bomb-or-myth-the-population-problem.html.

The belief that technological advance is the solution to humanity's ills has been tested by the mixed results of the Green Revolution. A variety of sites that engage in the debate over its success or failure in larger terms can be accessed at http://www.foodfirst.org/media/opeds/2000/4-greenrev.html, http://www.arches.uga.edu/~wparks/ppt/green/, and http://www.actionbioscience.org/biotech/borlaug.html. India's experience of the Green Revolution is a at http://www.indiaonestop.com/Greenrevolution.htm. Industrial agriculture is called into question at http://web.missouri.edu/ikerdj/papers/revolution.html and http://web.missouri.edu/ikerdj/papers/Ks-hrtld.htm. The nature of postindustrial society is defined and analyzed at http://www.sociology.org.uk/p1ne4.htm and http://www.worldbank.com/depweb/english/beyond/beyondco/beg_09.pdf. The new patterns of post-industrial society are examined at http://www.macalester.edu/courses/geog61/afdavis/post.htm, http://ideas.repec.org/p/cdl/issres/issr-1066.html, and http://www.randburg.com/fi/general/general_8.html. The place of women in postindustrial society is addressed at http://www.findarticles.com/p/articles/mi_m1310/is_1992_Nov/ai_13615016. A possible trend toward authoritarianism in postindustrial societies is traced at http://globalization.icaap.org/content/v3.1/04_beliaev.html and http://www.theglobalist.com/DBWeb/StoryId.aspx?StoryId=2987.

A militant view of the alleged ills of the affluent society and the growing dominance of multinational and non-state organizations in the postmodern era is presented at http://www.socialconscience.com/. A less radical view that nonetheless suggests that the twin pillars of Western civilization (the market economy and democracy) are more likely to undermine than support each other can be found at http://www.mtholyoke.edu/acad/intrel/attali.html.

The growth of Christian and Hindu religious fundamentalism in the context of increasing globalization is examined at http://www.nhc.rtp.nc.us/tserve/twenty/tkeyinfo/chr_rght.htm, http://www.religioustolerance.org/reac_ter9.htm, http://saxakali.com/southasia/newpage3.htm, and http://www.class.uidaho.edu/ngier/hindufund.htm. An indispensable discussion of recent trends in Islamic nationalism/fundamentalism is provided at http://www.csmonitor.com/2001/1004/p25s1-wosc.html. Links to virtually every aspect of recent conflicts within Islamist states and with non-Islamist nations, including the origins of the Taliban and counter-Taliban attacks on Afghanistan by much of the world community, can be found at http://www.library.vanderbilt.edu/romans/terrorism/afghanistan.html. The roots and results of the Taliban movement can currently be studied via an online version of David B. Edwards, *Before Taliban: Genealogies of the Afghan Jihad* (2002), at http://ark.cdlib.org/ark:/13030/ft3p30056w/. For the place of Hamas in Islamist efforts, see http://www.cfr.org/publication/8968/ and http://news.bbc.co.uk/2/hi/middle_east/978626.stm.

The text of, and debate over the accuracy of Samuel Huntington's argument that the world is heading toward a "clash of civilizations" can be found at http://history.club.fatih.edu.tr/103%20Huntington%20Clash%20of%20Civilizations%20full%20text.htm and http://en.wikipedia.org/wiki/Clash_of_Civilization. A critique of the essay by the late Edward Said can be found at http://www.thenation.com/doc/20011022/said. A Reading Guide with links is supplied at http://www.csmonitor.com/specials/sept11/flash_civClash.html.

Public interest sites address sites that address the Kyoto protocols and seek to address concerns over global warming include http://www.sierraclub.org/globalwarming/dangerousexperiment/, http://www.climatehotmap.org/, http://www.campaigncc.org/politics.shtml, and http://www.law.pace.edu/env/energy/globalwarming.html. The text of the Kyoto protocol on global warming that the United States has refused to sign is offered at http://www.cnn.com/SPECIALS/1997/global.warming/stories/treaty/. Another interesting site (http://www.americans-world.org/digest/global_issues/global_warming/gw2.cfm) is devoted to analyzing shifts in public opinion on the Kyoto protocols.

Former U.S. Vice-President Al Gore played a key role in the development of the accords and won an Emmy Award and an Oscar for his documentary film on global warming, *An Inconvenient Truth* in 2006. For these efforts, he was awarded the Noble Peace Prize for 2007, which he will share with Intergovernmental Panel on Climate Change, a United Nations network of scientists. That there are critics of Gore's Nobel Prize (http://nobelprize.org/nobel_prizes/peace/laureates/2007/) suggests the great depth of the continuing controversy over the subject, despite the dire consequences that may arise as a result of a slow human response to this challenge, whatever its causes.

For guides and links to sustainable development globally and on college campuses, see http://www.sustainable.org/, http://www.interfacesustainability.com/whatis.html, http://www.sciencedaily.com/news/earth_climate/sustainability/, http://www.interfacesustainability.com/whatis.html, and http://www.sciencedaily.com/news/earth_climate/sustainability/.

AP* | Test Prep

1. Globalization has been accompanied by

   (A) a decline in the use of English as the world's commercial language.

   (B) the end of isolationist policies by every nation in the world.

   (C) policies aimed at lowering tariffs.

   (D) the decline of global warming because of international environmental treaties.

2. Resistance to globalization includes all of the following EXCEPT

   (A) rising nationalism in some areas.

   (B) explicit protests against global financial institutions.

   (C) a global ban on outsourcing.

   (D) an increase in religious fundamentalism.

4. What best describes new social patterns brought by globalization?

   (A) Migration from poor to rich countries has increased.

   (B) International migration has emerged for the first time.

   (C) Gaps between rich and poor regions have closed.

   (D) Global warming is reducing world population levels.

5. What factors tend to limit cultural globalization?

   (A) regional variations in taste and values

   (B) increasing isolation of the newer nations

   (C) poor communication among world areas

   (D) inability of scientists from different regions to agree on methods and goals

   (E) United States efforts to restrict the export of pop culture

6. All of the following are characteristic of fundamentalist religious movements EXCEPT

   (A) they resist new technologies.

   (B) they appeal to those left behind by the global economy.

   (C) they are found in several major religious traditions.

   (D) they offer to purify a religion and/or return it to a perceived earlier form.

7. Environmental concerns are increasing because

   (A) developing economies like China and India agree that they should adopt the same pollution standards as those recommended by advanced industrial countries.

   (B) the United States, as world leader, has insisted on global environmental legislation.

   (C) environmental changes in one region may now have global consequences.

   (D) political disagreements have prevented even the holding of international environmental conferences.

Free-Response Question

What is the place of nationalism in today's global culture?

Credits

Literary Credits

PART I

Chapter 1 Adaptation of two maps, "Emergence and Spread of Humankind" and "Dispersal of Agriculture" from *A History of Human Community*, Third Edition by W.H. McNeil, 1990, pp. 9 & 17. Peasrson Education: Upper Saddle River, NJ.

PART II

Chapter 3 By P. Lal, original by Kalidasa, from *Great Sanskrit Plays in Modern Translation*, copyright © 1964 by New Directions Publishing Corp. Reprinted by permission of New Directions Publishing Corp.

Chapter 5 Reprinted with permission of The Free Press, a Division of Simon & Schuster, Inc., from *Chinese Civilization and Society: A Sourcebook* by Patricia Buckley Ebrey. Copyright © 1981 by The Free Press. All rights reserved.

PART III

Chapter 13 From *The Tale of Genji, Vol. I & Vol. III* by Lady Murasaki Shikibu, translated by Edward G. Seidensticker, translation copyright © 1976, copyright renewed 2004 by Edward G. Seidensticker. Used by permission of Alfred A. Knopf, a division of Random House, Inc.

Chapter 14 From *History of the Mongols: Based on Eastern and Western Accounts of the Thirteenth and Fourteenth Centuries*, by Bertold Spuler, translated by Helga and Stuart Drummond, © 1972. Published by the University of California Press.

PART IV

Chapter 18 From *Imperial Russia: A Source Book, 1700–1917* edited by Basil Dmytryshyn. Copyright Academic International Press, Gulf Breeze, Fla. Used by permission.

Chapter 20 Reprinted by permission of Waveland Press, Inc. from Philip D. Curtin, *Africa Remembered: Narratives by West Africans from the Era of the Slave Trade*. (Long Grove, IL; Waveland Press, Inc. 1967 [reissued 1997]). All rights reserved.

PART V

Chapter 24 Map adapted from *A Short History of Indonesia* by Alis Zainu'ddin, copyright © 1970. Reproduced with permission of Greenwood Publishing Group, Inc., Westport, CT.

Chapter 26 From "A People Made New (1902–1905)" by Liang Qichso from *Sources of Chinese Tradition* by William T. deBary, 1960. Reprinted with permission from Columbia University Press.

Chapter 27 Excerpts from *Readings in Russian Civilization, Vol. I*, edited by T. Riha, 1969. Reprinted by permission of The University of Chicago Press.

PART VI

Chapter 28 Senghor, Leopold Sedar. Translated by Melvin Dixon. "Snow in Paris" from The Collected Poetry. © 1991 by the Rector and Visitors of the University of Virginia. Reprinted by permission of the University of Virginia Press.

Chapter 29 Excerpts from *Readings in Russian Civilization*, vol. III, edited by T. Riha, 1969, University of Chicago Press.

Chapter 29 From *World Atlas of Revolutions* by Andrew Wheatcroft (Hamish Hamilton 1983). Text copyright © Andrew Wheatcroft, 1983. Cartography copyright © Hamish Hamilton Ltd, 1983. Reproduced by permission of Penguin Books Ltd.

Chapter 32 By Rich Clabaugh. Reproduced with permission from the December 5, 2006, issue of *The Christian Science Monitor* (www.SCMonitor.com). © 2006 The Christian Science Monitor.

Photo Credits

PART I

Chapter 1 Figure 1.1 Reeda Peel; **1.2** Douglas Mazonowicz/Art Resource, NY; **1.3** Robert Harding Picture Library; **1.4** John Swogger © Catalhoyuk Research Project; **1.5** Robert Frerck/Odyssey Productions, Inc.; **1.6** © Asian Art and Archaeology, Inc./Corbis. All Rights Reserved.

PART II

Chapter 2 Figure 2.1 © Burstein Collection/Corbis. All Rights Reserved; **2.2** Laurie Platt Winfrey/The Granger Collection, NY.

Chapter 3 Figure 3.1 © David Gurr/Eye Ubiquitous/Corbis. All Rights Reserved; **3.2** "Nataraja: Shiva as King of Dance." South India, Chola Period, 11th century. Bronze, H. 111.5 cm. © The Cleveland Museum of Art, 2001, Purchase from the J.H. Wade Fund. 1930.331; **3.3** © The Trustees of the British Museum/Art Resource, NY.

Chapter 4 Figure 4.1 Louvre, Paris/RMN/Art Resource, NY; **4.2** British Museum, London/SuperStock, Inc.; **4.3** Giraudon/Art Resource, NY; **4.4** Copyright The British Museum; **4.5** Hypothetical reconstruction of the Roman Forum in Imperial Times. Southern part. Watercolor. Soprintendenza alle Antichita, Rome, Italy/Scala/Art Resource, NY; **Visualizing the Past** © Livius.Org ; **4.6** Erich Lessing/Art Resource, NY.

Chapter 5 Figure 5.1 © Mimmo Jodice/ Corbis. All Rights Reserved; **5.2** Kunsthistorisches Museum, Vienna, Austria/Erich Lessing/Art Resource, NY.

PART III

Chapter 6 Figure 6.1 Paul Almasy/Corbis -NY; **6.2** © Corbis. All Rights Reserved; **6.3** © Jonathan Blair/Corbis. All Rights Reserved; **6.4** © Kazuyoshi Nomachi/Corbis. All Rights Reserved; **6.5** © Archive Iconografico, S.A./ Corbis. All Rights Reserved; **6.6** © British Library Board Or 2884 f17v; **6.7** Mohsin Raza/Corbis—NY; **6.8** British Library, London; **Visualizing the Past Image 1** Historical Picture Archive/Corbis-NY; **Image 2** Superstock, Inc.; **Image 3** Peter N. Stearns; **Image 4** © Sandro Vannini/Corbis All Rights Reserved; **Image 5** Erich Lessing/Art Resource, N.Y.

Chapter 7 Figure 7.1 British Library, London, UK/Art Resource, NY; **7.2** Attributed to Mir Sayyid 'Ali "Nighttime in a Palace" Folio from a Manuscript, c. 1539–1543, Opaque watercolor, gold and silver on paper; image: 28.6 x 20 cm (11 1/4 x 7 7/8 in.). Harvard Art Museum, Arthur M. Sackler Museum, Gift of John Goelet, formerly in the collection of Louis J. Cartier, 1958.76. Katya Kallsen © President and Fellows of Harvard College; **7.3** From "The Art of India" page 221. English translation copyright ©1985 by Halle Verlag GmbH, Germany; **7.4** Erich Lessing/Art Resource, NY; **7.5** The Granger Collection; **7.6** © Ric Ergenbright/Corbis. All Rights Reserved; **7.7** British Library/The Bridgeman Art Library International.

Chapter 8 Figure 8.1 The Granger Collection; **8.2** © George Steinmetz/Corbis. All Rights Reserved; **8.3** Peter Adams/Corbis -NY; **Visualizing the Past Image 1** © Sandro Vannini/Corbis. All Rights Reserved; **Image 2** © Tibor Bognar/Corbis. All Rights Reserved; **8.4** The Brooklyn Museum of Art; **8.5** National Museum of American Art, Smithsonian Institution, Washington, DC/Aldo Tutino/Art Resource, NY; **8.6** Jason Laure/Woodfin Camp & Associates, Inc.

Chapter 9 Figure 9.1 Academy of St. Petersburg, Russia/Erich Lessing/Art Resource, NY; **9.2** Dagli Orti/Picture Desk, Inc./Kobal Collection; **Visualizing the Past** Hagia Sophia, Istanbul/Erich Lessing/Art Resource, N.Y.; **9.3** © Adam Woolfitt/CORBIS. All Rights Reserved; **9.4** Erich Lessing/Art Resource, NY; **9.5** Miniatures Armeniennes, © 1960 Editions Cercle d'Art, Paris; **9.6** © Archivo Iconografico, S.A./Corbis. All Rights Reserved.

Chapter 10 Figure 10.1 Topham/The Image Works; **10.2** Sachsische Landesbibliothek; **Visualizing the Past** Giraudon/Art Resource, NY; **10.3** Coronation of Charlemagne at St. Peter's by Pope Leo III. Grandes Chroniques de France, fol. 106r. Musee Goya, Castres, France. Giraudon/Art Resource, NY; **10.4** British Library, London, UK/HIP/Art Resource, NY; **10.5** © Elio Clol/Corbis. All Rights Reserved; **10.6** Jochen Helle/Bildarchiv Monheim Fotofinder/IPNstock/Nielsen Business Media; **10.7** British Library, London, UK/Picture Desk, Inc./Kobal Collection; **10.8** Stock Montage, Inc./Historical Pictures Collection; **10.9** Musee Thomas Dobree Nantes/Dagli Orti/Picture Desk, Inc./Kobal Collection; **10.10** Bibliotheque Royale De Belgique.

Chapter 11 Figure 11.1 Sean Sprague/Mexicolore; **11.2** SEF/Art Resource, NY; **11.3** Ms. Magliabechiano: sacrificio umano azteco. Biblioteca Nazionale Firenze. Scala/Art Resource, NY; **11.4** The Granger Collection, New York; **11.5** Bodleian Library, Oxford/Picture Desk, Inc./Kobal Collection; **Visualizing the Past Image 1** © Kevin Schafer/Corbis S. All Rights Reserved; **Image 2** Peter N. Stearns; **11.6** Werner Forman/Art Resource, NY; **11.7** © Lester Lefkowitz/Corbis. All Rights Reserved.

Chapter 12 Figure 12.1 The National Palace Museum; **12.2** Handscroll "Gathering of Philosophers," unidentified artist, 16th century, China, Ming (1368–1644) or Qing dynasty (1644–1911). The Metropolitan Museum of Art, New York, NY, U.S.A. Image copyright © The Metropolitan Museum of Art/Art Resource, NY.; **12.3** © Kyodo News Service/Sakaoto Photo Research Laboratory/Corbis. All Rights Reserved; **12.4** The Granger Collection, New York; **12.5** Freer Gallery/ Picture Desk, Inc./Kobal Collection; **12.6** A detail of a silk scroll painting called "Going Up the River at the Spring Festival" which shows scenes of town and country life possibly in the old capital of Kaifeng. Song dynasty c. AD 960–1279. Ink painting on silk. Werner Forman Archive. Peking Palace Museum. Art Resource, NY.; **12.7** ©The Trustees of the British Museum/Art Resource, NY; **Visualizing the Past Image 1** G.H. Graves. Courtesy of the Library of Congress; **12.8** Ma Yuan, Chinese, 1190–1235 "Bare Willows and Distant Mountains," Chinese, Southern Song dynasty, end of 12th century. Ink and color on silk, 23.8 x 24.2 cm (9 3/8 x 9 1/2 in.) Photograph © 2010 Museum of Fine Arts, Boston. Special Chinese and Japanese Fund, 14.61.

Chapter 13 Figure 13.1 The Art Archive/Picture Desk, Inc./Kobal Collection; **13.2** Art Resource, NY; **13.3** Art Resource, NY; **13.4** Woodcut, Masahiro Murai "Illustration from Tanki Yoryaku (A Single Horseman: Summary on How to Wear Armor)," 2nd edition, Japan, 1837. The Metropolitan Museum of Art, New York, NY, U.S.A. Image copyright © The Metropolitan Museum of Art/Art Resource, NY.; **13.5** © Archivo Iconografico, S.A./ Corbis. All Rights Reserved; **13.6** Shen Zhou (Chinese 1427–1509), "Poet on a Mountain Top." Ming Dynasty (1368–1644). Album leaf mounted as a handscroll; ink and water color on paper; silk mount, image: 15 1/4" x 23 3/4" (38.73 x 60.32 cm). The Nelson-Atkins Museum of Art, Kansas City, Missouri. Purchase: Nelson Trust, 46-51/2. Photo: Robert Newcombe; **13.7** © Free Agents Limited/Corbis. All Rights Reserved; **13.8** The Bridgeman Art Library/Detroit Institute of Arts; **Visualizing the Past Image 1** Woodcut. Masahiro Murai. "Illustration from Tanki Yoryaku (A Single Horseman: Summary on How to Wear Armor), 2nd edition, Japan, 1837. The Metropolitan Museum of Art, New York, NY, U.S.A. Image copyright © The Metropolitan Museum of Art/Art Resource, NY.; **Image 2** Bodleian Library, Oxford/

Picture Desk, Inc./Kobal Collection; **Image 3** British Library, London, UK/Picture Desk, Inc./Kobal Collection; **Image 4** Handscroll "Gathering of Philosophers," unidentified artist, 16th century, China, Ming (1368–1644) or Qing dynasty (1644–1911). The Metropolitan Museum of Art, New York, NY, U.S.A. Image copyright © The Metropolitan Museum of Art/Art Resource, NY.; **13.9** John Elk III/Stock, Boston.

Chapter 14 14.1 Bibliotheque Nationale de France; **14.2** Corbis-NY; **14.3** The Granger Collection, New York; **14.4** The Mongols under their chief Hülegü conquering Baghdad in 1258. From Rashid al-Din's "Jami' al-Tawarikh" (Compendium of Chronicles). Illuminated manuscript page, 14th CE. Inv. Diez A Fol.70, image 7. Bildarchiv Preussischer/Art Resource, NY. Photo: Ruth Schacht. Oriental Division.; **14.5** The Granger Collection, New York; **14.6** The Granger Collection, New York; **14.7** Marco Polo with Kubilaj Khan in Peking, 1375. Paris, Bibliotheque Nationale, Ms. 2810.; **14.8** John Massey Steward/Peter N. Stearns.

Chapter 15 Figure 15.1 The Granger Collection, New York; **15.2** Duomo, Florence, Italy/Scala/Art Resource, NY; **15.3** The Granger Collection, New York; **15.4** The Granger Collection, New York.

PART IV

Chapter 16 Figure 16.1 The Granger Collection, New York; **16.2** The Granger Collection, New York; **16.3** The I.N. Stokes Collection of American Historical Prints, Prints Division, The New York Public Library. Stokes Cat. No B-3; **16.4** The Granger Collection, New York; **16.5** The Granger Collection, New York; **16.6** General James Wolfe's expedition against Quebec in 1759: English engraving, 1760.The Granger Collection, New York; **16.7** The Granger Collection, New York; **16.8** V & A Images/Victoria and Albert Museum.

Chapter 17 Figure 17.1 John Eskenazi Ltd, P.O Box 55621, London W9 2XA England; **17.2** Lebrecht Music & Arts Photo Library; **17.3** The Granger Collection; **17.4** Science Museum, London, Great Britain/ Art Resource, NY; **Visualizing the Past** Musee du Chateau de Versailles/Dagli Orti/ Picture Desk, Inc./Kobal Collection; **17.5** Louvre, Paris, France/Erich Lessing/Art Resource, NY; **17.6** Bildarchiv Preussischer Kulturbesitz / Art Resource, NY; **17.7** Peter N. Stearns.

Chapter 18 Figure 18.1 The Bridgeman Art Library International; **18.2** Sovfoto/Eastfoto; **18.3** Archiv fur Kunst und Geschichte, Berlin; **18.4** Hermitage/Art Resource, N.Y.; **Visualizing the Past** Sovfoto/Eastfoto; **18.5** Sovfoto/Eastfoto.

Chapter 19 Figure 19.1 Museo Pedro de Osma Lima/Mireille Vautier/Picture Desk, Inc./Kobal Collection; **19.2** The Bridgeman Art Library International; **19.3** The Granger Collection, New York; **19.4** The Granger Collection, New York; **19.7** Museo de American, Madrid, Spain/Erich Lessing/Art Resource, NY; **19.8** De Bry, America, 1565/Peter N. Stearns. **19.9** Museo Nacional del Virreinato, Tepotzotlan, Mexico/Schalkwijk/ Art Resource, N.Y.; **19.10** The Granger Collection, New York.

Chapter 20 Figure 20.1 Wilberforce House, Hull City Museums and Art Galleries, UK/The Bridgeman Art Library; **20.2** Copyright The British Museum; **20.3** © British Library Board. 146.f.17; **20.4** The Newberry Library; **20.5** Saltcellar: Portuguese Figures. 15–16th century, ivory, H x W (A&B): 7.5 x 3 in. (19.1 x 7.6 cm). Louis V. Bell and Rogers Funds, 1974 (1972.63a,b). Photo: Stan Reis. The Metropolitan Museum of Art, New York, NY, USA. Image Copyright © The Metropolitan Museum of Art/Art Resource, NY.; **20.6** Local History Museums' Collection, Durban; **20.7** Michael Holford/Michael Holford Photographs **Visualizing the Past Image 1** Dennis Michael Warren/Dennis Michael Warren; **Image 2** Cary Wolinsky/Cary Wolinsky; **Image 3** Jovonne Hope Jones; **20.8** UCLA Fowler Museum of Cultural History.

Chapter 21 Figure 21.1 Victoria and Albert Museum, London/Art Resource, NY; **21.2** Corbis-NY; **21.3** Luigi Mayer/Bridgeman Art Library International; **21.4** © National Maritime Museum Picture Library, London, England; **21.5** © Arthur Thevenart/Corbis. All Rights Reserved; **21.6** © The Trustees of the British Museum; **Visualizing the Past Image 1**

The Royal Collection © 2009, Her Majesty Queen Elizabeth II; **Image 2** Padshahnama: Europeans bring gifts to the Shah Jahan. The Royal Collection © 2009, Her Majesty Queen Elizabeth II. **21.8** Tretyakov Gallery, Moscow, Russia/Scala/Art Resource, NY.

Chapter 22 Figure 22.1 Bridgeman Art Library International; **22.2** Bridgeman Art Library International; **22.3** The nutmeg. 15th CE illuminated French manuscript page. Photo: Alfredo Dagli Orti. Biblioteca Estense, Modena, Italy.; **22.4** Peter N. Stearns. **22.5** © The Trustees of the British Museum/Art Resource, NY; **22.6** Private Collection/Giraudon/The Bridgeman Art Library International; **Visualizing the Past Image 1** Michael Boss; **Image 2** Jan Adkins; **22.7** The Granger Collection, New York; **22.8** The Granger Collection, New York.

PART V

Chapter 23 Figure 23.1 The Granger Collection, New York; **Visualizing the Past** The Bridgeman Art Library International; **23.2** ullstein bild/The Granger Collection, New York; **23.3** Mary Evans Picture Library; **23.4** The Granger Collection, New York; **23.5** John Constable (1776–1837), "The Cornfield." 1826. Oil on canvas, 143 x 122 cm. Presented by subscribers, including Wordsworth, Faraday and Sir William Beechey, 1837 (NG130). © The National Gallery, London, Great Britain/Art Resource, NY; **23.6** Paul Cezanne, "The Large Bathers." 1906. Oil on Canvas. 6′10″ x 8′2″ (2.08 x 2.49 m). The W. P. Wilstach Collection. Philadelphia Museum of Art.

Chapter 24 Figure 24.1 National Army Museum, London; **24.2** © British Library Board WD2413; **24.3** Royal Tropical Institute/APA Photo Agency/Hulton Archive/Getty Images; **24.4** © National Maritime Museum Picture Library, London, England; **24.5** The Granger Collection, New York; **24.6** Musee de l'Homme, Phototheque; **24.7** Picture Desk, Inc./Kobal Collection.

Chapter 25 Figure 25.1 Edouard Manet (1832–1883), "The Execution of Emperor Maximilian of Mexico, June 19, 1867." Oil on canvas. Location: Staedtische Kunsthalle, Mannheim, Germany. Art Resource, NY.; **25.2** Organization of American States; **25.3** Private Collection/The Bridgeman Art Library; **25.4** Peter N. Stearns. **25.5** Diego Rivera's monumental work "Sunday Afternoon in Alameda Park" with Benito Juarez. Original in Del Prado Hotel before earthquake. © Robert Frerck/Odyssey/Chicago. © Banco de Mexico Diego Rivera & Frida Kahlo Museums Trust/Artists Rights Society (ARS), NY. Av. Cinco de Mayo No. 2, Col. Centro, Del. Cuauhtemoc 06059, Mexico, D.F. Reproduction authorized by the Instituto Nacional de Bellas Artes y Literatura. **25.6** Paulo Zanettini; **Visualizing the Past Image 1** Culver Pictures, Inc..; **Image 2** Private Collection; **25.7** The Granger Collection, New York.

Chapter 26 Figure 26.1 The Granger Collection, New York; **26.2** Topkapi Palace Museum, Istanbul, Turkey/Giraudon/Art Resource, NY; **26.3** UPI/Corbis-NY; **26.4** Musee des Beaux-Arts, Lillie, France/Erich Lessing/Art Resource, N.Y.; **26.5** Art Resource/Bildarchiv Preussischer Kulturbesitz; **26.6** Illustration of Colonial Flags Flying Over a Chinese Port. The Metropolitan Museum of Art, New York, NY, U.S.A. Gift of Lincoln Kirstein, 1959 (JP3346). Image copyright © The Metropolitan Museum of Art/Art Resource, NY.; **26.7** The Granger Collection.

Chapter 27 Figure 27.1 Mary Evans Picture Library; **27.2** Federal State Entity of Culture the State Historical Museum (Moscow, Russian Federation); **27.3** Keystone-Mast Collection, UCR/California Museum of Photography, University of California, Riverside; **27.4** Sovfoto/Eastfoto; **27.5** Consulate General of Japan in New York; **Visualizing the Past Image 1** Picture Desk, Inc./Kobal Collection; **Image 2** The Granger Collection, New York.

PART VI

Chapter 28 Figure 28.1 © Bettmann/CORBIS. All Rights Reserved; **28.2** Courtesy of the Library of Congress; **Visualizing the Past** John Nash, Over the Top, oil on canvas, 79.4 x 107.3 cm, Imperial War Museum, London; **28.3** U.S. Bureau of Engraving and Printing; **28.4** Corbis-NY; **28.5** The

Granger Collection, New York; **28.6** Association des Amis de Jean-Baptiste Tournassoud.

Chapter 29 Figure 29.1 Sovfoto/Eastfoto; **29.2** Marcel Duchamp (American, b. France 1887–1968), "Nude Descending a Staircase, No. 2," 1912. Oil on canvas, 58 x 35 in. Philadelphia Museum of Art: The Louise and Walter Arensberg Collection. 1950-134-59 Photo by Graydon Wood, 1994. © 2009 Artists Rights Society (ARS), New York/ADAGP, Paris/Succession Marcel Duchamp.; **29.3** © Neil Beer/CORBIS. All Rights Reserved; **29.4** Getty Images Inc. - Hulton Archive Photos; **29.5** © Bettmann/Corbis. All Rights Reserved; **29.6** Courtesy of the Library of Congress; **29.7** Bildarchiv Preussischer Kulturbesitz/Art Resource, NY; **29.8** Sovfoto/Eastfoto; **29.9** © Bettmann/Corbis. All Rights Reserved; **29.10** Courtesy of the Library of Congress; **29.11** National Archives and Records Administration; **Visualizing the Past** Pablo Picasso (1881–1973), "Guernica," 1937. Oil on canvas, 350 x 782 cm. Museo Nacional Centro de Arte Reina Sofia, Madrid, Spain. © 2010 Estate of Pablo Picasso/Artists Rights Society (ARS), New York. John Bigelow Taylor / Art Resource, NY; **29.12** Sovfoto/Eastfoto.

Chapter 30 Figure 30.1 AP/Wide World Photos; **30.2** Ullstenbild/The Granger Collection, New York; **30.3** AP/ Wide World Photos; **30.4** Topham/The Image Works; **30.5** Getty Images Inc.—Hulton Archive Photos; **30.6** ullstein bild/The Granger Collection, New York; **Visualizing the Past Image 1** ullstein bild/The Granger Collection, New York; **Image 2** Camera Press/Globe Photos, Inc.; **Image 3** © Bettmann/Corbis. All Rights Reserved; **Image 4** © Bettmann/Corbis. All Rights Reserved; **30.7** © AP/Wide World Photos.

Chapter 31 Figure 31.1 The Granger Collection, New York; **31.2** Ministry of Information/The National Archives of the UK, INF 13/194; **31.3** AP/Wide World Photos; **31.4** The Granger Collection, New York; **31.5** Getty Images/Time Life Pictures; **31.6** Andy Warhol (1928–1987) © Copyright. "Campbell's Soup Cans" 1962, synthetic polymer paint on 32 canvases, each 20 x 16 in. (50.8 x 40.6 cm). The Museum of Modern Art/Licensed by Scala-Art Resource, NY. Gift of Irving Blum; Nelson A. Rockefeller Bequest, gift of Mr. and Mrs. William A.M. Burden, Abby Aldrich Rockefeller Fund, gift of Nina and Gordon Bunshaft in honor of Henry Moore, Lillie P. Bliss Bequest, Philip Johnson Fund, Frances Keech Bequest, gift of Mrs. Bliss Parkinson, and Florence B. Wesley Bequest (all by exchange). (476.1996.1-32.vw2). © 2009 Copyright The Andy Warhol Foundation for the Visual Arts/Artists Rights Society (ARS), New York/Trademarks, Campbell Soup Company All rights reserved. Digital Image ©The Museum of Modern Art/Licensed by SCALA/Art Resource, NY; **31.7** © Bettmann/CORBIS. All Rights Reserved; **31.8** The Granger Collection, New York; **31.9** Picture Desk, Inc./Kobal Collection; **31.10** Topham/The Image Works.

Chapter 32 Figure 32.1 AP/Wide World Photos; **32.2** © Bettmann/Corbis. All Rights Reserved; **32.3** AP/Wide World Photos; **32.4** Alyx Kellington/Getty Images, Inc.—Liaison; **Visualizing the Past Image 1** © Tim Page/Corbis. All Rights Reserved; **Image 2** David Alfaro Siqueiros. Detail from the mural, "For the Complete Safety of All Mexicans at Work." 1952–54. Hospital de la Raza, Mexico City, Mexico. National Palace, Mexico City, DF/Schalwijk/Art Resource, NY. © 2009 Artists Rights Society (ARS), New York/SOMAAP, Mexico City. Reproduction authorized by the Instituto Nacional de Bellas Artes and Literature.; **32.5** UPI/Corbis—NY; **32.6** AP/Wide World Photos; **32.7** Paolo Bosio/Getty Images, Inc.—Liaison.

Chapter 33 Figure 33.1 © Kapoor Baldev/Sygma/Corbis; **33.2** Peter Turnley/Corbis—NY; **33.4** Ilene Perlman/Stock Boston; **33.5** © Bettmann/Corbis. All Rights Reserved; **33.6** UPI/Corbis—NY; **33.7** University of California Press; **33.8** © Bettmann/Corbis. All Rights Reserved; **33.9** UPI /Corbis—NY; **33.10** © Peter Turnley/Corbis. All Rights Reserved.

Chapter 34 Figure 34.1 © Bettmann/Corbis S. All Rights Reserved; **34.2** © Bettmann/Corbis S. All Rights Reserved; **34.3** © B.S.P.I./ Corbis. All Rights Reserved; **34.4** © Bohemian Nomad Picturemakers/Corbis. All Rights Reserved; **34.5**

Walter Bibikow/Getty Images, Inc.—Taxi; **34.6** Koichi Kamoshida/Getty Images; **34.7** The Granger Collection; **34.8** Jacquet Francillon/AFP/Getty Images; **34.9** AP/Wide World Photos; **34.10** Jacques Pavlovsky/Corbis—NY; **34.11** Claro Cortes/Corbis -NY. **Chapter 35 Figure 35.1** AP/Wide World Photos; **35.2** © Bettmann/Corbis. All Rights Reserved; **35.3** © Mark Stephenson/Corbis. All Rights Reserved; **35.4** Tom Stoddart/Katz Pictures/Woodfin Camp & Associates, Inc.; **Visualizing the Past** Corbis—NY; **35.5** Anthony Suau/Getty Images, Inc.—Liaison; **35.6** Tom Sobolik/Black Star/; **35.7** © Peter Turnley/Corbis. All Rights Reserved; **35.8** © Peter Turnley/Corbis. All Rights Reserved; **35.9** © 2005 Cam Cardow: The Ottawa Citizen and Political Cartoons.com; **35.10** AP/Wide World Photos. **Chapter 36 Figure 36.1** © AP/Wide World Photos; **36.2** © Reuters New Media/Corbis. All Rights Reserved; **36.3** Corbis—NY; **36.4** Jacques Pavlovsky/Corbis—NY; **36.5** Getty Images/Time Life Pictures; **36.6** Justin Guariglia/National Geographic Image Collection; **36.7** © Igor Kostin/Corbis. All Rights Reserved; **36.8** Kimimasa Mayama/Corbis—NY; **Visualizing the Past** Agence France Presse/Getty Images.

Index

Note: Page numbers followed by *f, m,* and *t* indicate figures, maps, and tables, respectively.

A

Abbasid dynasty, 152, 154–159, 154*m*
  art in, 165*f,* 168–169
  breakdown and disorder in, 165–166
  Christian crusades and, 167, 168
  education in, 168–169
  fall of, 172
  handicraft production in, 155, 159
  Ibn Khaldun and, 168
  Islamic conversion in, 155, 163–164, 164*m*
  literature in, 169–170
  mosques in, 159
  nomadic incursions in, 166–167, 172
  religious trends in, 171
  science in, 170–171
  slaves in, 158–159
  succession disputes in, 165
  Thousand and One Nights and, 158
  trade in, 155
  urban life in, 168–169
  wealthy landed elite (ayan) in, 159
  women in, declining position of, 166
Abbas the Great, 479
Abdallahi, Khalifa (Egypt), 613
Abduh, Muhammad, 611
Abdul Hamid, 606
Abelard, Peter, 232
Absolute monarchies, 391–393
Abu Taleb, 477
Achebe, Chinua, 813
Africa
  art in, 197, 463
  Asante Empire and, 454–455, 463
  Atlantic system in, creation of, 445–446
  Christianity in, 188–189, 188*f*
  cloth in, 463
  colonial expansion in, 375–377
  colonizer *vs.* colonized, 564, 565–566
  common elements in, 186–187
  Dahomey and, 455–456
  East Africa and, 456–457
  economic extraction and, 566–567
  education and, western, 558–559
  family life in, 186–187, 192, 197, 199
  forest and plains peoples of, 197, 198, 199–202
  grassland kingdoms in, 189–195 (*See also* Sudan)
  Islam and, rise and spread of, 184–203
  kingdoms in, 200–202
  kings in, 197, 198, 199–200
  liberation of, 742–743
  middle class and, rise of, 558–559
  nationalism in
    independence era and, 806–810, 808*m*
    World War I and, 681–683, 682*f*
  partition of, 562*m*
  population growth in, 198–199
  repression and guerrilla war in, 743–744
  slave trade in, 194, 198
  slaving and politics in, 452–454
  societies in, 451–457
  South (*See* South Africa)
  states in, 185–186
  Sub-Saharan, 444
  Sudan and, 456–457
  trade in, 76, 77*m,* 187, 189–193
  tropical dependencies and, 564–565
  West African nations in, new, 816*m*
  white supremacy in, 744–746
  World War I and, 667, 668*m,* 681–683, 682*f*
  World War II and, 741–746
African Diaspora, 460–465
African National Congress, 825
Afrikaner National Party, 745
Afro-Eurasia, 155, 367
Agaja, King, 455
Age of revolution, 527
Agriculture. *See also* Irrigation
  in Africa, 109, 197, 198, 457–458, 810
  in Americas, 262
  in Aztec civilization, 250, 250*f,* 261
  in Brazil, 589–590
  in China, 23, 29, 44, 45, 506–507, 510, 618, 845, 847, 849
  chinampas for, 250
  Christianity and, 122, 189
  coffee estates (fazendas) and, 589–590
  collectivization and, 699, 771, 774*f,* 775
  cooperatives and, 845
  cossacks and, 403
  Dutch farmers and, 376
  estate, 411–412
  in Europe, 220–221, 225, 235, 397, 761
  Great Depression and, 705
  in Greco-Roman civilization, 96, 97
  in Inca civilization, 260, 261
  in India, 63, 887, 887*f*
  in Japan, 110, 689
  kulaks and, 635
  in Mali, 189, 190
  manors and, 221
  in Ming Empire, 506–507
  in Mississippian culture, 247
  in Neolithic Revolution, geography of, 12–14
  in northern Europe, 110
  in Olmec culture, 110, 111
  plantation system of, 460
  plow used in, 220–221
  in Polynesia, 112
  potato crops and, 397
  of pueblos, 263
  in Russia, 215, 411–412, 629, 631, 635
  sedentary, 16, 17, 23, 141, 262
  serfs and, 221
  slash and burn, 16, 262
  slaves used in, 369, 432–433
  in Soviet Union, collectivized, 774*f,* 775
  spread of, 2–7, 13, 14*m*
  sugar cane in Brazil and, 432–433
  of Taino people, 420
  in Tang-Song dynasties, 280, 280*f,* 283
  technological changes in, 15
  terracing, 189, 263
  three-field system of, 222, 223, 225, 397
  Vietnamese, 306

Agriculture (*cont.*)
  in western civilization, 397
  in Western Europe, medieval, 235
  wet rice, 510
Ahmad, Muhammad, 612
AIDS epidemic, 891
Aja, 455, 464
Akbar, 485–486
Akkadians, 21
Al-Afghani, Jamal al-Din, 611
Al-Aqsa Mosque, 157*f*
Al-Banna, Hassan, 820
Al-Biruni, 171
Alexander the Great, 63, 84, 86, 86*m*, 95
Alexandria, Egypt, 86
Al-Ghazali, 171
Ali, 143, 146, 149, 151
Ali, Muhammad, 607–610
Allah, 113, 141
Allende, Salvador, 792
Alliance for Progress, 797
Al-Mahdi, 163–164
Almohadis, 187
Almoravids, 187
Alphabet. *See also* Writing
  Egyptian, 21
  of Indus River peoples, 22, 25
  Latin, 214, 678
  of Olmec culture (hieroglyphic), 110
  Phoenician, 27, 85
  Slavic (Cyrillic), 214, 216
  Sumerian, 19
Al-Razi, 170–171
American Civil War, 537, 544
American Philosophical Society, 374
American Revolution, 529
Americas
  Africans in, 460
  agriculture in, 262
  Central, 110–111, 111*m*, 371, 424
  colonial expansion of, 371–372
  cultural diversity in, 263
  Middle Passage to, 460, 461
  North America, 375
  political issues in, 346–347
  slave societies in, 460–463, 462*f*
  South America, 420
Amigos del país, 436
Amistad (ship), 465
Analects, 40, 49
Anarchists, 633–634
Andes, Native American population in, 260–263, 261*t*
Anglican church, 383
Anglo-American offensives in World War II, 734
Anglo-Boer War, 569
Angola, 447
Animal husbandry, 367
Animism, 124
Anwar, Chairil, 813
Anxiety for Salvation: The Resurrection (picture), 222*f*
Apartheid, 745–746, 824–826
Aquinas, Thomas, 233, 240
Aquino, Corazon, 812
Arabian Nights, 153, 175
Arabian world, pre-Islamic, 136–161, 139*m*. *See also* Islam
  clans in, 138–140
  family in, 141
  gods in, 141–142

  marriage in, 141
  poetry in, 141
  towns in, 140–141
  trade in, 140–141, 155
Arabic numerals, 71, 167, 175
Aragon, 344
Architecture
  African, 456
  of Byzantine Empire, 207, 210
  Chinese, in Vietnam, 310*f*
  Egyptian, 20, 26
  gothic, 234
  Great Zimbabwe, 201, 201*f*
  in Greco-Roman civilization, 94
  in Hong Kong, 838*f*
  Inca, 260
  Indian, 60, 62
  Islamic, 136, 137*f*, 162, 163
  Islamic and Hindu, blended, 175*f*
  in Japan's warlord era, 301, 301*f*
  medieval, 233–234, 234*f*
  monumental, 19, 20, 85, 607
  mosque, 156, 195, 195*f*
  Mughal, 484, 488
  Ottoman, 469*f*, 473–474, 474*f*
  Persian, 84
  Renaissance, 344, 382
  skyscrapers, 689*f*, 838*f*
  Sudanic, 191
  in Tang-Song dynasties, 273*f*, 283, 284
  of Timur, 332
  Versailles palace, 391*f*
  of ziggurats, 19
Area of Darkness, An (Naipaul), 813
Arevalo, Juan José, 787
Argentina, 586–587, 594–597
Argentine Republic, 587
Ariel (Rodó), 598
Aristocracy, 90
Aristotle, 92, 232, 338
Armenian genocide, 668
Art
  in Abbasid dynasty, 165*f*, 168–169
  in Africa, 197, 197*f*, 463
  bronze portrait heads, 197, 197*f*
  Byzantine, religious, 207, 207*f*, 209*f*, 405*f*
  in China, 24, 51, 52, 284, 303, 304
  cubist movement and, 687, 689*f*
  in Egypt, 21–22
  in Greco-Roman civilization, 93–94
  icon paintings, 210
  in India, 71–72, 180*f*
  industrialization and, 520, 541–542, 542*f*
  in Japan, 293–294, 294*f*, 301–302, 301*f*
  in Korea, 304*f*
  in Ming Empire, 506–507
  modern, 636
  Mughal, 488
  Picasso's *Guernica*, 711, 711*f*
  in Polynesia, 347
  Portuguese woodcarvings, 456, 456*f*
  Renaissance, 343–344, 381, 382
  romanticism and, 541, 541*f*
  in Russia, 216–217
  in Shang era, 24
  silkscreen paintings, Japanese, 514*f*
  in Soviet Union, 716
  in Tang-Song dynasties, 283–284, 285–386, 285*f*

terra-cotta objects, 197, 197f
tomb paintings, 22, 22f, 108f
in Ukraine, 216–217
western, 689f
Artha (political and economic goals), 68
Aryan poetry, 23
Aryans, 23, 63–64
Asante Empire, 454–456, 454f, 463
Asantehene, 454
Ashikaga Shogunate, 297–298
Ashikaga Takuaji, 297
Ashoka, 65
Asia
 Christianity in, 501–502
 colonial expansion in, 375–377
 colonizer *vs.* colonized and, 564, 565–566
 East (*See* East Asia)
 economic extraction and, 566–567
 education and, western, 558–559
 expansion in, European, 500m
 middle class and, rise of, 558–559
 migrations of, during Industrial Revolution, 527f
 social reform in, 557–560
 South (*See* South Asia)
 Southeast (*See* Southeast Asia)
 trade in, 496–502, 497m
 transitions in, 494–519
 tribute systems in, European, 500–501
 tropical dependencies and, 564–565
Asian sea trading network, 496–497, 497m
Astronomy, 19
Atahuallpa, 373
Ataturk (Mustafa Kemal), 678
Athletic performances, Roman, 95
Atlantic Charter of 1941, 740
Atlantic slave trade, 446–451
Atlantic system, in Africa, 445–446
Audiencias, 430
Augustine (Saint), 117
Augustus Caesar, 87
Aurangzeb, 487
Australia, 545–546, 545m, 691m
Axum, 21m, 107, 188, 189
Ayan (wealthy landed elite), 159, 603
Ayllus, 255
Aztec civilizations, 247–254
 agriculture in, 250, 250f, 261
 clans in, 251–252, 252f
 economy of, 250
 evaluation and judgment of, by western civilizations, 258–259
 family life in, 253
 gods and goddesses and, 248–249
 human sacrifices and, 247, 249, 249f, 259
 Inca compared to, 260–261
 men in, 253
 poetry of, 249–250
 religion of, 248–250
 rise to power, 247–248
 society in, 248
 technological constraints of, overcoming, 252
 tribute system in, 250–251, 254
 women in, 253
Aztlan, 247

B
Baba, Ahmad, 451
Babur, 484
Babylonian Empire, 20, 21

Backwater colonies, expansion in, 372–375
Bacon, Francis, 390
Bactria, 65
Baghdad
 as Abbasid capital, 154, 155f
 Hulegu's capture of, 172, 324–325, 326f
 Thousand and One Nights and, 158
Baibars, 326
Bakr, Abu, 146
Bakufu, 297–298
Balboa, Vasco de, 371, 495
Balfour Declaration, 678
Balkan nationalism, 456–547, 546–547, 547m
Banana republics, 796–797
Band, 16
Bangladesh, 806
Bankruptcy, 610–612
Banks and banking, 235–236, 236f
Banner armies, 613
Bantu peoples, 200
Baquaqua, Mahommah Gardo, 444, 465
Barbados, 449
Barbarians, 80, 452
Basil II (Bulgaroktonos), 208
Batavia, 500
Batista, Fulgencio, 788
Batouala (Maran), 564
Batu, 321, 322–323, 324
Bedouins, 137–138. *See also* Nomads; Umayyads
 gender roles of, 141, 152–153
 Islamic conversion of, 145–146, 150
 Muhammad and, 142–143
 poetry of, 141
 religion of, 141–142
 Ridda Wars and, 146
Bela, King, 324
Belisarius, 207
Benedictine Rule, 122
Benedict of Nursia, 122
Benin, 199–200, 447, 451
Beowulf (medieval saga), 234
Berbers, 187, 193
Berke, 326
Berlin, revolution in, 534f
Berlin Wall, 771, 865–866, 866f
Bernard of Clairvaux, 232
Bet Giorgis (church), 188f
Bhagavad Gita (sacred hymn), 70
Bhaktic cults, 177, 178
Bharatya Janata party (BJP), 815
Bhutto, Benazir, 812, 813
Biafra, 460
Bian Liang, 267f
Biard, Auguste François, 445
Bible, 384
Bight of Benin, 454–455, 460
Biko, Steve, 825
Bishop of Yucatán, 431
Black Death, 109, 238, 239f, 321, 342
Blitzkrieg (lightning war), 730–733
Boccaccio, 381
Bodhisattvas, 119
Boers, 376, 458, 568–569
Bolívar, Simon, 577, 578f
Bolsheviks, 634
Bonaparte, Napoleon, 531, 532m, 609f
Bourbon reforms, 438–440
Boxer, Charles, 452

Boxer Rebellion, 621, 623f
Boyars, 217, 402, 404, 408
Brahma (holy essence), 69
Brahma (Krishna), 70
Brahmanism, 68. *See also* Hindus and Hinduism
Brahman priests, 68–69
Brass rings, 450
Brazil, 431–434
   Bourbon reforms in, 439–440
   coffee growing and slavery in, 589–590
   colonial, 421m
   "Cry of the Excluded," 792f
   as functioning republic, 587–591
   gold in, discovery of, 433–434
   independence struggles in, 578–579
   Pombal and, 439–440
   slavery in, 432–433, 432f
   sugar in, 432–433, 432f
   Vargas regime in, 712
Britain, 372
   consolidation of, 555–556
   Egypt and, control over, 612m
   in India, 554–555, 556m
   nationalism in, 673–674
   World War I and, 666–668, 666f, 673–674
   World War II and, 728, 730–732, 734, 741–746
Britain, Battle of, 732
British East India Company, 376–377, 554, 555
British Raj, 554
British Royal Society, 374
Bronze Age, 15
Bronze portrait heads, 197, 197f
Bubonic plague. *See* Black Death
Buchan, John, 564
Buddha, 62
   life of, 70, 71
   statues of, 70f, 273f
Buddhism, 70–71
   anti-Buddhist backlash in Tang-Song
      dynasties, 273–274
   bodhisattvas and, 119
   Chan, 272
   expansion of, 118–120
   in India, 70–71
   Mahayana and, 120, 271–272
   popularization of, 119
   pure land, 271–272
   Sutras and, 119
   women and, 120
   Zen, 272, 301
Buenos Aires, 577–578
Bulgaria, 208
Bulgaroktonos (Basil II), 208
Bulge, Battle of, 734
Bunyoro, 456
Bureaucracy
   in Byzantine Empire, 209–210
   in China, 46, 47, 89, 91, 99
   of Islamic Empire, 154
   in Persian Empire, 84
   in Tang dynasty, 270
Burial mounds, Toltec, 247
Bush, George H., 764
Bush, George W., 875
Bushi era, 298–299
Bushmen, 457
Buyids, 167

Byzantine Empire, 115–116, 205–213, 212m
   Arabs and, 207–208
   art in, religious, 207, 207f, 209f, 210, 211f
   bureaucracy in, 209–210
   Christianity in, split between, 210–213
   decline of, 212, 213
   Justinian's achievements in, 207, 208m
   politics in, 209–210
   power of, 205–210
   society in, 209–210
   women in, 209

C

Cabral, Pedro Alvares, 431
Caesar, Julius, 87
Calcutta, 376
Calicut, 495, 495f, 498–500, 498f
California, 439
Caliph, 146
Calligraphy, 51
Calpulli (clans), 251–252, 252f
Calvin, Jean, 384
Calvinism, 384
Calvinists, 372
Camel, Battle of, 149
Camels, 137, 143f
Canaanites, 452
Canada, 372–373, 544–545, 545m, 691m
Candomblé, 464
Cannibalism
   Aztecs and, 247, 249, 249f, 259
   Chinese peasants and, 509
   Spaniards and, 422
Canterbury Tales (Chaucer), 234
Canton, 507
Canudos, refugees of, 590
Cape Colony, 376, 458, 459
Cape of Good Hope, 362, 376, 446, 447
Capitaincies, 432
Capitalism, 397
Caravel ships, 495
Cárdenas, Lázaro, 711
Caribbean, 420–422, 420f, 449
Carolingians, 223–225
Cartagena, 430
Carter, Jimmy, 797
Carthage, 87
Carvalho e Mello, Sebastião José, 439
Castas society, 434–436
Caste system, 63–64, 67, 72, 74, 75
Castile, 344, 421
Castillo, Díaz del, 244
Castles, in Japan, 298–299, 300f
Castro, Fidel, 788–789
Çatal Hüyü, 16, 17f
Catherine II ("the Great"), 394, 407, 408–410, 409f
Catholicism, 210–211, 383–384, 580. *See also* Christianity
Catholic Reformation, 383–384
Caudillos, 581, 591
Causation, 365
Central African kingdoms, 200–202
Central America, 110–111, 111m, 371, 424
Centralists, 581, 587
Central Mexico, 248m
Césaire, Aimé, 672
Ceylon, 376
Cézanne, Paul, 542

Chabi, 327, 328*f*, 330
Chaldiran, 478, 480
Chamorro, Violeta, 798*f*
Chams, 309–310
Chan Buddhism, 272
Chancery of Secret Police, 405
Chan-Chan, 255, 256
Chandragupta Maurya, 65
Chang'an, 270
Charlemagne (Charles the Great), 224–225, 224*m*, 225*f*
Charles I, King, 385
Charles III, King, 438
Chartist Movement, 533
Chattel slavery, 451
Chechnya, 867, 869
Chernobyl nuclear power plant, 896*f*
Chiang Ching-kuo, 841
Chiang Kai-shek, 703
Chichimecs, 26, 247
Children
  in ancient societies, 6–7
  in China, 49, 54, 55
  in India, 67, 72
  in western civilizations, 396
Chimor, 255
Chimu kingdom, 256
China
  art in, 51, 52
  bureaucracy in, 46, 47, 89, 91, 99
  capitals in, 47*m*
  children in, 49, 54, 55
  classical, 40–59
  coastal, in 19th century, 618*m*
  complexities in, 56
  Confucianism in, 48–49, 53–54
  culture of, 24, 42, 48–52
    vs. Japan, 638
  Daoism in, 50–51
  decline in, 112–113
  democratic protest and repression in, 870–871
  early civilizations in, 23–25
  economy in, 52–55
  education in, 50
  family life in, 54–55
  gatekeepers of, 308–309
  gender and gender roles in, 54–55
  during Great Depression
    Guomindang party in, 702–704, 704*f*
    Mao's peasant option in, 704
    Marxism in, 700–702
    May Fourth movement in, 700–702
    revolution in Civil War, 700, 704*m*
  Greco-Roman civilization compared to, 89
  Han dynasty in, 42, 43*m*, 45
  India compared to, 74, 75
  legalism in, 49–50
  literature in, 51, 52
  Mandarin Chinese and, 44
  mathematics in, 52
  overview of, 40
  patterns in, 42–45
  politics in, 41–42, 46–48, 55
  Qin dynasty in, 44–45
  religion in, 48–52
  reunification and renaissance of, 266–289
  revolutionary movements in, 698
  science in, 24, 51, 52

Six Dynasties era of, 268*m*, 270, 271, 278
societies in, 52–55
Song dynasty and, 269*m*, 271–272, 274–286, 276*m*
spread of, 290–313
  to Japan, 291–302
  to Korea, 302–305
  overseas, reasons for, 510–511
  to Vietnam, 305–311
state functions in, 47–48
Sui dynasty and, 267–270, 269*m*, 278, 280
Tang dynasty and, 269–275, 269*m*, 278–286
teachings of rival schools in, 50
technology in, 54
trade in, 54
women in, 52, 53
Zhou dynasty in, 43–44, 43*m*
Chinampas, 250
Chinese River Valley, 22
Chinggis Khan, 172, 316–322, 318*f*
  career of, early, 317–318
  death of, 321–322
  Mongol Empire under, 319–325
  as Prester John, myth of, 324
  of Transcontinental Empire, 315*m*, 316–322
Choson, 302
Christ. *See* Jesus of Nazareth
Christianity. *See also* Jesus of Nazareth
  adopted by Constantine, 87
  in Africa, 188–189, 188*f*
  in Asia, 501–502
  Christian Reformation and, 385
  Copts and, 117, 148, 188–189
  Crusades and, 167, 168
  Ethiopian kingdom and, 189
  expansion of, 120–123
  New Testament of, 121
  Portuguese conversion to, 447, 553
  in Western Europe, medieval, 233
Christian Reformation, 385
Chungara, Domitilia Barrios de, 790–791
Churchill, Winston, 728
Cicero, 89, 90
Científicos, 595
City-state, 20–21
Civilizations. *See also* Western civilization
  Aztec, 247–254
  in China
    early, 23–25
    spread of, 290–313
    spread of, to Vietnam, 305–311
  Classical period, 39–129
  defining, 17–19
  early, 15–31
  in Eastern Europe, spread of, 213–215
  Greco-Roman, 84–98
  Inca, 254–261
  Mediterranean, 80–103
  river valley, 25–29
  Tigris-Euphrates, 19, 20–21
  westernization of, 608–609, 614
Civilized world, 401
Civil rights movement, 758, 758*f*
Civil service examination system, 503, 504*f*, 505
Cixi (dowager empress), 621, 622
Classical period. *See also individual civilizations*
  of Central America, 110–111, 111*m*
  changes in, 36–37

Classical period (*cont.*)
  of China, 40–59
  concepts of, 36
  continuity in, 37–38
  expansion, integration, and decline during, 104–129
  of India, 60–79
  of Japan, 110
  Kush and, developments and heritage of, 107, 109
  Mediterranean and Middle East during, 80–103
  of North Africa, 117–118
  of Northern Europe, 110
  old age in, 38–39
  overview of, 34
  of Polynesia, 112
  of South America, 110, 111*m*
  themes produced by development in, 124
  trade routes at the end of, 109*m*
  of Western Europe, 117–118
Clemenceau, Georges, 670
Clockmaking, 237
Cloth, 368, 463
Clovis, 222, 223
Coeur, Jacques, 236, 237*f*
Coffee growing in Brazil, 589–590
Cold war, 752–781
  allies, 762–764
  Armenia and Azerbaijan, disagreements between, 872
  Berlin Wall and, dismantling, 865–866, 866*f*
  Commonwealth of Independent States and, 867
  Czechs and Slovaks, disagreements between, 872
  demonstrations in 1990s and, 866–869
  Eisenhower's speech, 778
  end of, 861–869
  ethnic conflicts and, 873–874
  genocide and, 872, 873–874, 874*f*
  Gorbachev and, 863–865, 863*f*
  Middle East conflicts and, 872–873
  nationalism and, 813–816
  NATO intervention and, 755
  Soviet decline and, 861–862
  Soviet reform and, 1980s and 1990s, 862–863
  Western Europe and, post-WWII, 752–762
  World War II and, 738–739
  Yeltsin and, 866–868
Collectivization, 700
Colonialism
  capitalism and, 567
  colonizer *vs.* colonized and, 564, 565–566
  European colonial territories and, 553*m*
  in Hawaii, 570–571
  in India, 556–557
  in Java, 556–557
  in New Zealand, 570
  settlement colonies and, 563
  in South Africa, 567–569
  tropical dependencies and, 563–564
  white settler colonies in Pacific and, 567–568
Columbus, Christopher, 244, 344, 363
  expedition of, 372–373
Comintern (Communist International office), 699
Commerce, western, 381–386, 396–397
Commercialism, 341, 343, 368
Commercial Revolution, 386–389
  balance sheet of, 389
  social protest to, 387–389
  world economy and, impact of, 386–387
Communism, 854–855

Compradors (Chinese merchants), 616
Comte, Auguste, 584
Confucianism, 48–49
  social system in, 53–54
  in Song dynasty, 276–277
Confucius, 44
Congo River, 200
Congress of Vienna, 531–532
Conselheiro, Antonio, 590
Conservatism, 532
Constantine, 87
Constantinople
  Arab attack on, 207, 208
  as Byzantine capital, 205, 206
  Crusades and, 212, 213, 229–230
  Ottoman Empire and, 472*f*, 473–475
  rebuilding of, 207
  Russia and, 215, 216, 217
  transcontinental network and, 205
Consulado, 429
Consuls, 90
Consumerism, mass, 396
Contemporary period, 900
Continuity
  in Classical period, 37–38
  in early civilizations, 5–6
Convention Peoples Party (CPP), 743
Cook, Captain James, 570–571, 571*f*
Copernicus, 389
Copts, 117, 148, 188–189
Coral Sea, Battle of, 736, 736*f*
Core nations, 368
Corinthian architecture, 94
Corn, 367
Cornwallis, Lord Charles, 555
Coronado, Francisco Vázquez de, 424
Corporatism, 711
Cortés, Hernán, 424
Cossacks, 403
Cotton, 380
Council of the Indies, 430
Cowrie shells, 450
Creative Fellowship (painting), 718*f*
Creole slaves, 462
Crimean War, 629, 631
Cristeros, 695
Cromer, Lord, 676
Crusades
  in Abbasid dynasty, 167, 168
  in Western Europe, medieval, 229–230
Cruz, Juana Inés de la, 431, 431*f*
Cuba, 371, 449, 598
Cuban revolution, 788–790
Cubist movement, 687
Cultural causation, 365
Cultural Revolution, 848–849, 849*f*
Culture
  Chinese, 24, 42, 48–52, 638
  in East Africa, Swahili coast of, 196–197
  Egyptian, 21
  Greco-Roman culture in, 97
  in India, 71–72
  in Italian Renaissance, 344
  in Kievan Rus', 216–217
  in Latin America, post-WWII,
    800–801
  mass leisure, 540

in Mexico, 694–695
in Mughal Empire, 485–486
Olmec, 110
of Sinification, of elite in Korea, 303–304
in Soviet Union, 773–779
Sumerian, 21
of Toltecs, 245–247, 246*f*
western, 381–386
in Western Europe, post-WWII, 769–770
Cuneiform, 17–18
Cunning men, 390
Cushitic, 456
Cuzco, 255–259
Cyrene, Libya, 187
Cyril (missionary), 213–214
Cyrillic alphabet, 214
Cyrus the Great, 82–83
Czechoslovakia, 726–728, 729, 730*f*

D

Da Cunha, Euclides, 590
Dadu, 327
Da Gama, Vasco, 345–346, 346*f*
Dahomey, 455–456
Daimyos, 298–300
Damascus, 149–150
Dance of Death, The (Holbein), 385*f*
Dan Fodio, Usuman, 457
Dante, 343*f*
Daoism, 50–51
  expansion of, 120
  Yellow Turbans and, 112
Darwin, Charles, 540–541
Dating systems, 11*n*
Death march, 725*f*, 740
Decembrist uprising, 627–628, 629*f*
Declaration of the Rights of Man and the Citizen, 530
Deism, 390
De Klerk, F. W., 825
Demak, 180–181
Democracy, 869
  in China, protest and repression, 870–871
  conflicts and, 872–873
  in Greece, 88, 90
  in Latin America, post-WWII, 869–871
  liberal, in post-WWII Western Europe, 756
  limits of, 870
  patterns of change and, 869, 870
  United States' support of, 870
Demographic transition, 198–199
Demography, 198
Deng Xiaoping, 847
Dependency theory, 595
De San Martín, José, 577
Descartes, René, 390
Destruction of the Philosophers, The (Al-Ghazali), 338
Devi (goddess), 113
Dharma (moral path), 65, 68
Dhimmi ("people of the book"), 150, 150*f*
Dhows (sailing vessels), 155, 162
Díaz, Porfirio, 586, 593–595, 597, 693
Dictators
  in Egypt, 818–821
  in Ghana, 816–817
  in World War II, 726, 728
Diderot, Denis, 394, 396*f*
Diem, Ngo Dinh, 853

Dien Bien Phu, 852
Diet (Japanese assembly), 640, 643
Din-i-Ilahi, 486
Dinshawai incident, 673*f*, 677
Diocletian, 87
Direct democracy, 88, 90
Disease
  globalization and, 898
  spread of, 367
Disinheritance, 300
Divine Comedy (Dante), 343*f*
Divine kingship, 107–108
Divorce
  in Arabia, pre-Islamic, 141, 151, 153
  female suffrage and, 812
  in Greco-Roman civilization, 98
  Islamic law and, 484
  in Japan, 642
  in Tang and Song dynasties, 281
  in western civilization, 765, 766
Dominicans, 421
Doric architecture, 94
Dramas, Greek, 94, 95
Dreyfus, Alfred, 679
Du Bois, W. E. B., 682
Duchamp, Marcel, 689*f*
Duma, 635
Dutch advance on Java, 554, 554*m*
Dutch East India Company, 366, 458
Dutch Studies, 637
Dutch trading empire, 500
Dynasty, 43

E

Early civilizations, 15–31
  changes in, 4–5
  children in ancient societies, 6–7
  in China, early, 23–25
  concepts of, 4
  continuity in, 5–6
  defining, 17–19
  Egyptian, 21–22
  historical perspective of, 26–27
  hunters and gatherers, era of, 9–12
  Indian and Chinese River Valley, 22
  Indus Valley cities, 22–23
  Neolithic Age, 12–15
  overview of, 2
  Paleolithic developments, late, 10–12
  politics in, 20–21
  river valley, 25–29
  settled societies, 16
  spread of, 12*m*
  Tigris–Euphrates, 19, 20–21
East Africa, 456–457
East Africa, Swahili coast of, 195–197
  culture in, 196–197
  family in, 197
  trading ports in, 195–196, 196*m*
East Asia
  key centers of civilization in, 292*m*
  post-WWII settlements in, 831–832
Eastern bloc, 754
Eastern Europe, 204–219
  borderlands in, east central, 213, 214–215
  Byzantine Empire and, 205–213, 212*m*
  civilization in, spread of, 213–215

Eastern Europe (*cont.*)
  decline of, 217–218
  Kievan Rus' in, emergence of, 215–218
  post-WWII, 770–773
    domestic policies in, 772–773
    new Soviet Empire in, 770–772
    Soviet Union as superpower and, 770
  Russia and, 413, 635–636
  Slavic expansion in, 214*m*
  World War I and, 664–665
Eastern Front, 669
Eastern Orthodoxy, 210–211
Economic Commission for Latin America (ECLA), 595
Economy. *See also under* Latin America; World economy
  in Aztec civilizations, 250
  in China, 52–55
  European Global Order and, 566–567
  in India, 73
  in Japan, 637–639, 641, 643
  in Korea, 370
  maritime power and, 360–366
  in Mediterranean civilization, 95–98
  in Portugal, 362–364, 363*m*, 427, 429
  in Qing dynasty, 616
  in Russia, 412
  in Soviet Union, 774–775
  in Spain, 362–364, 363*m*, 427, 429
Ecuador, 429
Edict of Nantes, 385
Edo peoples, 199, 512
Education
  in Abbasid dynasty, 168–169
  in China, 50
  globalization and, 897
  in India, 67–68
  western, 558–559
Effendi, 677
Egypt, 21–22, 21*m*
  art of, 21–22
  British control over, 612*m*
  Christians of (Copts), 188–189
  culture of, 21
  dictatorships in, 818–821
  mathematics in, 21, 22, 25, 26
  nationalism and, in World War I, 679, 681
  sciences in, 21, 22, 25, 26
  westernization in, failure of, 607–610
  World War II and, 746
Ehrmann, Marianne, 396
Einstein, Albert, 541
Eisenhower, Dwight, 778
Elizabeth I, 383
El Mina, 446
Emancipation of the serfs, 630–631, 631*f*
Encomendero, 420
Encomienda, 420
Encyclopedia Britannica, 396
Encyclopédie (Diderot), 394
England, 368, 382
English Civil War, 385
English trading empire, 500
Enlightened despotism, 438
Enlightenment, 394, 396, 409, 452–453
Environmental concerns, 810–811
Epic age, 62–64
Equiano, Olaudah, 461, 465
Era of the Warring States, 44
Espanola, 372

Ethiopia, 107, 189, 446
Ethnocentrism, 348
Eurasian protoglobalization, 515
Europe
  Abu Taleb's travels to, 477
  family styles in, 383
  fronts, in World War I, 661*m*
  industrialization in, 535
  overseas expansion, reasons for, 510–511
  tribute systems of, in Asia, 500–501
  World War II and, 731*m*
European colonial territories, 553*m*
European Global Order
  capitalism and colonialism and, 567
  colonial wars and, 560–562
  colonizer *vs.* colonized, 564, 565–566
  dominance in, patterns of, 563–571
  economic extraction and, 566–567
  Imperialism and, 560–562
  industrial rivalries and partitioning of, 552–554, 560–562, 563*m*
  Pacific tragedies and, 569–571
  social relations in, 565–566
  South Africa and, 568–569
European Union (EU), 759, 759*m*, 874–875
Examination system, 270–271

F
Factories, 446, 499
Facundo (Sarmiento), 591
Family life
  in Africa, 186–187, 192, 197, 199
  in Arabian world, pre-Islamic, 141
  in Aztec civilizations, 253
  in China, 54–55
  European-style families, 383
  in Tang-Song dynasties, 281
  in Umayyads, 150–151
Farmers, 376
Fascism
  burning of books and, 691*f*
  rise of, 690
  spread of, 709–710
Fazendas (coffee estates), 589
Federalists, 581
Feminist movements, 539, 540
Ferdinand, Archduke Franz, 662
Ferdinand of Aragon, 418
Fertile Crescent, 147
Feudalism, 226–227, 298
Fez, 187
Firdawski, 169
First Emperor of the Han Dynasty Entering Guandang, The (Bozh), 41*f*
First U.S. Iraq War, 873
Five pillars of Islam, 145
Five-year plans, 717
Florentine Codex: The General History of the Things of New Spain (Sahagún), 253
Flying money, 279
Fon, 455
Footbinding, 282, 282*f*
Forced labor, 426
Forts, Portuguese, 446
Fox, Vicente, 785–786, 785*f*
France, 368, 372, 382. *See also* French Revolution
  peasant labor in, 223
  women in, 766
  World War II and, 727
Francis I, 382

Frederick the Great, 394
Free Officers movement, 818, 820
French East India Company, 370
French Revolution, 529–533
  in cartoons, 530
  Congress of Vienna and, 531–532
  events leading up to, 529–530
  Napoleonic Wars and, 531, 532*m*
  nationalism and, 531
  radical phase of, 530–531
Freud, Sigmund, 541
Fujiwara, 295
Fukuzawa Yukichi, 626
Fulani, 457
Fulbe, 457
Fur, 373
Futa Jallon, 457
Fuzi, Kung. *See* Confucius

G
Galileo, 390
Galleons, 430
Gallipoli, 667
Gálvez, José de, 438
Gandhi, Indira, 805, 805*f*, 812
Gandhi, Mohandas, 672, 675–676,
  740*f*, 742*f*
Gang of Four, 848–849
Garvey, Marcus, 682
Gatekeepers, 308–309
Gate of Heavenly Peace, 831*f*
Gauchos, 588–589
Gempei Wars, 297
Gender and gender roles
  of bedouins, 141, 152–153
  in China, 54–55
  of hunters and gatherers, 16
  in India, 62
  in Mughal Empire, 486
  Ottoman *vs.* Safavid, 482–484
  of Umayyads, 150–151
General Mines, 433
Geneva, 384
Gerardi, Juan José, 861*f*
Germany
  Industrial Revolution and, 537, 538*m*
  World War I and, 666–667
  after World War II, 755*m*
Ghana, 447, 451, 453, 816–817
Giap, Vo Nguyen, 852
Glasnost (openness), 864
Globalization, 134, 882–903
  balance and, 898–899
  contemporary period and, 900
  cultural, 888–889, 888*f*
  disease and, 898
  economic, 886–887, 892–893, 892*f*
  education and, 897
  environment and, 894–898, 896*f*
  full globalization and, 884
  historical change and, 892–893
  industrialization and, 524
  institutions of, 890–892
  meaning of, 883–884
  migration and, 887–888
  multinational corporations in 2000,
    886, 886*m*
  nationalism and, 827, 893–894

postcolonial societies and, 827
projecting from trends, 899
protests against, 890–891, 892–893
protoglobalization, 357, 507, 515
religion and, 893–894
resistance and alternatives, 892–894
technology and, 884–885
UN intervention and, 891–892
women and, 900
world history and, 884, 900
Glorious Revolution, 393
Goa, 499
Goats, 137
Gods and goddesses
  Aztec, 248–249
  bedouin, 141–142
  Greco-Roman, 92, 93, 94
  Hindu, 64, 68, 69
  Judaism and, 28
  Shinto, 110
  Sumerian, 19–20, 23
  of Zhou, 44, 48
Gold Coast, 447, 449, 454
Golden Horde, 322, 323, 324
Golden Pavilion, 301*f*
Good Neighbor Policy, 797
Gorbachev, Mikhail, 863–865, 863*f*
Granada, 418
Gran Colombia, 577
Grand Canal, 278, 279*f*
Great Britain, 458
Great Depression, 686–723
  Argentina and, 712–713
  causation, 705
  China and, 698, 700–704
  debacle, 705–707
  economic policies and, 715, 717
  fascism and, spread of, 709–710
  industrialization and, 714–715, 717
  Japan and, militarization of, 713–714, 715*m*
  Latin America and, 710–711
  Mexico and, 693–695
  Nazism and, rise of, 708–709
  New Deal policies and, 708
  recovery, 714–715
  Roaring Twenties and, 687–692
  Russia and, 695–700
  socialist realism and, 716, 717–718
  Soviet Union and, 715
  Vargas regime in Brazil and, 712
  Western Europe's responses to, 707
Great Leap Forward, 845–847, 846*f*
Great Sovereign, 407
Great Trek, 458
Great Wall, 44–45
Great Zimbabwe, 201–202, 201*f*
Greco-Roman civilization, 84–98
  agriculture in, 96
  architecture in, 94
  art in, 93–94
  China compared to, 89
  culture in, 97
  development of, 85–87, 85*m*, 87*m*
  fall of, impending, 98–99
  gods/goddesses in, 92, 93, 94
  philosophy in, 93–95
  politics of, 88, 90–92
  religious values in, 92

Greco-Roman civilization (*cont.*)
  science in, 93–95
  slavery in, 96, 97–98
  trade in, 96
Greece. *See also* Greco-Roman civilization
  agriculture in, 96
  Alexander the Great and, 84, 86, 86*m*, 95
  democracy in, 88, 90
  developmental stages in, 85–86, 85*m*
  dramas performed in, 94, 95
  literature in, 94, 96, 97
  mathematics in, 93
  Olympic Games, 85
Greek fire, 208
Greek Revolution, 533
Green movement, 758
Green Revolution, 821
Gregory VII, Pope, 230, 231
Griots (professional oral historians), 190, 192
Guanaham, 478
Guano, 583
Guatemala, 787–788
Gubernias, 407
Guernica (Picasso painting), 711, 711*f*
Guerrilla warfare, 743–744, 843
Guevara, Ernesto "Che," 789
Guilds, 237
Guillotine, 530
GUM (Russian department store), 686, 687*f*
Gunpowder, 439, 480–481
Guns, 368
Guomindang (Nationalist) party, 702–704, 704*f*
Gupta Empire, 66, 66*m*, 113
Gurus, 68, 69, 558
Gutenberg, Johannes, 383

H

Habsburg, Maximilian von, 574, 575*f*, 585–586
Habsburg empire, 404, 413
Hadiths (traditions of the prophet), 151
Haganah, 746
Hagia Sophia, 207, 210*f*
Haiti, 429, 437
Hajj (pilgrimage), 145, 145*f*, 184, 185*m*
Hammurabi, 20, 21
Han dynasty, 42, 43*m*, 45, 112–113
Hannibal, 87
Hanseatic League, 236
Harappa, 22–23
Harris, Marvin, 259
Harun al-Rashid, 164
Harvey, William, 390
Hausa peoples, 193
Havana, 420, 438
Hawaii, 570–571
Heian (Kyoto), 292–295
Hellenistic period, 80, 86, 86*m*, 94
Henry of Silesia, King, 324
Henry the Navigator, Prince, 346, 362*f*
Henry VIII, 383
Hercules, 92*f*
Hernández, José, 591
Hidalgo, Father Miguel de, 577
Hideyoshi, Toyotomi, 512, 513–514, 513*f*
High Middle Ages, 231
Hijra (Muhammad's migration), 143
Himalayas, 63

Himeji Castle, 300*f*
Hindus and Hinduism, 68, 69–70
  Devi and, worship of, 113
  expansion of, 118
  mathematics, 174–175
  Mughal allies of, 485–486
  in South Asia, revival of, 177, 178
Hispaniola, 420, 421, 437
Hitler, Adolf, 669, 709*f*
  Holocaust and, 733–734
  Nazi blitzkrieg and, 730–733
  Nazi invasion of Poland and, 729
  war against the Jews, 733–734
Ho Chi Minh, 852
Hojo, 297
Holbein, Hans, 385*f*
Holland, 368, 372, 405
Holocaust, 733–734
Holy Alliance, 627
Holy Roman emperors, 225
Holy Roman Empire, 393
Homelands, 825
Homo erectus, 10
Homo sapiens, 10
Homo sapiens sapiens, 10, 28
Hong Kong, 834–835
Hongwu, 503
Hong Xiuquan, 619
Horses, 367
Hottentots, 457
Huacas (holy shrines), 256
Huancavelica, 427
Huanghe. *See* Yellow River
Huari, 254, 255
Huayna Capac, 255
Huerta, Victoriano, 694
Huitzilopochtli, 249
Hulegu, 172, 173, 324–325, 326
Humane individuals, 444
Humanism, 381
Human rights, 20th century, 794–795
Human sacrifices, 247, 249, 249*f*, 259. *See also* Cannibalism
Human society, 452–453
Humayan, 485
Hundred Years War, 227, 238
Hungary, 382, 413
Huns, 45
Hunters and gatherers, 9–12, 13
  bands of, 16
  gender and gender roles in, 16
  late Paleolithic developments in, 10–12
  in North America, 263
Husayn, 149, 151
Hussein (sherif of Mecca), 678
Hyundai, 838–839, 839*f*

I

Iberian society, 418–419, 476–477
Ibn al-Athir, 325–326
Ibn al-Wardi, 342
Ibn Batuta, 190
Ibn Khaldun, 168
Ibn-Rushd, 232
Icon paintings, 210
Ideographic symbols, 24
Ideographs, 25
Ieyasu, Tokugawa, 512
Ife, 455

Ifriqiya, 187
Iguegha, 199–200
Ile-Ife, 197
Iliad (Homer), 94
Imams, 481
Inca (ruler), 255
Inca civilizations, 111, 254–261
  agriculture in, 260, 261
  architecture in, 260
  Aztecs compared to, 260–261
  cultural achievements of, 260
  evaluation and judgment of, by western civilizations, 258–259
  expansion of, 255*m*
  imperial policy of, 257–260
  irrigation in, 257, 259, 260
  political practices of, 255–256
  religion of, 255–257
  rise to power, 255
  road system in, 260
  split inheritance in, 255–256
Inca socialism, 258–259
India, 60–79
  art in, 71–72, 180*f*
  Ashoka and, 65, 65*m*
  British rule in, 554–555, 556*m*
  Buddhism in, 70–71
  caste system in, 63–64, 67, 72, 74, 75
  children in, 67, 72
  China compared to, 74, 75
  colonial society in, early, 556–557
  culture in, 71–72
  economy in, 73
  education in, 67–68
  gatekeepers in, 308–309
  gender and gender roles, 62
  geography and formative period of, 62–63
  global influence of, 73, 76
  Gupta empire in, 66, 66*m*
  Hinduism in, 68, 69–70
  independence in, 821–822
  literature in, 63, 71
  mathematics in, 71–72
  Mauryan dynasty in, 65–66
  Muslim presence in, Sultanate period and, 178, 179–180
  nationalism and, in World War I, 673–674
  numbering systems from (Arabic), 71
  overview of, 60
  patterns in, 64–66
  political institutions in, 66–67
  religion in, 67–71
  sciences in, 71–72
  societies in, 72
  suicide rituals in, 259
  temples of, 60, 61*f*, 73
  trade in, 62, 64, 65, 73
  Vedic and Epic ages of, 62–64
Indian, origin of term, 244
Indian Ocean, 368, 509
Indian River Valley, 22
Indians. *See also* Native Americans
  exploitation of, 426–427
  as slaves, 426
Indigenous societies, 426–427
Indra (god of thunder), 64
Industrialization. *See also* Industrial Revolution
  adjustments to, 534–536
  Atlantic revolutions and, 543
  consumption and, 540
  continuity and, 524–525
  in Europe, 535, 544–546, 545*m*
  globalization and, 524
  nationalism and, 813–816
  proto-industrialization and, 529
  Russian reforms in, 631–633
  triggers for change and, 522–524
  world centers of, 521
Industrial Revolution, 450, 526–549
  age of revolution and, 527
  American Civil War and, 537
  American Revolution and, 529
  art and, 541–542
  Balkan nationalism and, 546–547
  changes and, forces of, 527–529
  conservatism and, 532
  cultural transformations in, 539–542
  diplomacy and, 547
  feminist movements in, 539
  French Revolution and, 529–533
  Germany and, unification of, 537, 538*m*
  government functions and, new, 538–539
  Italy and, unification of, 537, 537*m*
  leisure transformed by, 525, 535*f*, 540
  new nations in, rise of, 536–537
  order in, consolidation of, 534–539
  political trends in, 536–537
  population revolution and, 528–529
  protesting, 532–533, 536
  Reform Bill of 1832 and, 533
  revolutions of 1848 and, 533–534
  socialism and, 538–539
  social question and, 538–539
  society and, 547
  Triple Alliance and, 546
  United States and, 544, 545*m*
  western settler societies, 542–546
  World War I and, 546–547
Indus Valley cities, 22–23
Inflation, 386
Intelligentsia, 633
Interesting Narrative: Biography of Mahommah G. Baquaqua, An (Baquaqua), 444
Intermarriage
  Akbar's encouragement of, 485
  in India, 10
  late Paleolithic, 10
  of local peoples and Muslim migrants, 176
  of Songhay peoples, 193
  of Umayyads, 150
International Monetary Fund (IMF), 816, 892
International nongovernmental organizations (INGOs), 891–892
Investiture, 231
Ionic architecture, 94
Iran, 822–824. *See also* Persia (Iran)
Iraq, 873
Iron bars, 450
Iron curtain, 754
Iroquois, 263
Irrigation
  in China, 23, 29, 45, 48, 277, 280, 283, 299, 504, 506
  in Egypt, 610, 676
  Green Revolution and, 821
  in Harappan complex, 22
  in Inca civilization, 257, 259, 260
  in India, 887*f*
  in Mesopotamia, 19
  in Native American civilizations, 263

Irrigation (*cont.*)
  in Neolithic settlements, 16
  in Sudan, 193
  in Tigris–Euphrates basin, 166
  Vietnamese, 306
Isabella of Castile, 418
Isandhlwana, 562
Isfahan, 482, 482*f*
Islam
  Abbasid dynasty and, 152, 154–159, 154*m*
  in African civilizations, 184–203
  Allah and, 113, 141
  Arabs and, 144
  five pillars, 145
  global patterns of, 173
  law, 144, 151, 152, 194
  learning and, 159
  mosques and, 156–157
  Muhammad and, 142–145
  overview of, 136–137
  Qur'an and, 143, 144, 404
  rise and spread of, 123–124, 136–161, 139*m*, 148*m* (*See also*
    Bedouins)
  in South Asia, 170*m*, 172–180
  in Southeast Asia, 170*m*, 180–182
  Umayyads and, 140, 145–153
  universal elements in, 144–145
Islamization, 457
Ismâ'il, 478
Italian Renaissance, 381
  human values and culture of, 344
  movement of, northward, 381–383
  Northern, 382
  secular directions in, 343–344
Italy. *See also* Italian Renaissance
  Industrial Revolution and, 537, 537*m*
  World War I and, 664–665
Iturbide, Augustín de, 577
Ivan IV, 400, 402
Ivan the Great (Ivan III), 400
Ivan the Terrible, 402
Ivan V, 401, 401*f*

J
Jamaica, 429, 449
Janissaries, 472
Japan
  agriculture in, 110, 689
  art in, 293–294, 294*f*, 514*f*
  in Classical period, 110
  colonial expansion of, to 1914, 643*m*
  culture of, *vs.* China, 638
  divorce in, 642
  economy of, 637–639, 641, 643
  expansion of, to outbreak of World War II, 714*m*
  gatekeepers in, 308–309
  Imperial age of, 291–296
    decline of, 295
    Heian (Kyoto) era in, 292–295
    literature in, 294–295
    Nara crisis and, 292–293
    poetry in, 295
    Taika reforms and, 291–293
    warlord era in Japan (*See* Warlord era in Japan)
    warrior elites in, 295–296
  industrialization and recovery of, 714–715
  Industrial Revolution of, 640–643
  isolation in, 513–514, 637, 639

Meiji and, 639–640
  modernization of, 643–644
  post-WWII, 832–838
    economic surge in, 836–838
    political and cultural style of, 835–836, 836*f*
    recovery of, 832–833
  Russo-Japanese War and, 635, 635*m*
  Shogunate and, 636–637
  Sino-Japanese War and, 643
  transformation of, 636–644
  world economy and, 370
  World War II and
    defeat in, 734–737
    invasion of China and, 728–729
    invasion of Pearl Harbor, 734–735
Jati, 64
Java, 554, 554*m*, 556–557
Jenne, 191, 191*f*, 193
Jerusalem, Willibald's travels to, 229
Jesuits, 384
Jesus of Nazareth, 121
  Empress Zoë and, 209, 209*f*
  Last Supper, mosaic of, 95*f*
  as Pantocrator, 105*f*
Jiang Qing, 847
Jihad (holy war), 147, 187
Jin kingdom, 278
Jinnah, Muhammad Ali, 740–741
Jinshi, 270–271
Jizya (head tax), 150
João VI, 579
John, Prester, 324
Journal des Dames, 396
Juana, 372
Juárez, Benito, 585–586, 586*f*
Judaism, 28
Judge magazine, 596
Junks, 279
Jurchens, 277–278
Justinian, 116, 207, 208*m*
Juula (Malinke merchants), 190

K
Ka'ba, 140–141, 144, 145*f*
Kabir (Muslim mystic), 177
Kaifeng, 267*f*, 279*f*
Kalidasa, 69
Kamakura regime, 297
Kamasutra (laws of love manual), 71
Kano, 457
Karakorum, 321
Karbala, 149
Karma (worldly pleasures), 68
Kautilya, 66
Kemal, Mustafa, 606*f*
Kenya, 456
Kenya African Union (KAU), 744
Kenyatta, Jomo, 744
Kepler, Johannes, 389, 389*f*
Kerensky, Alexander, 695
Khadijah, 142
Khagan, 318
Khalil, Hamida, 658
Khanates, 322, 322*m*
Khan of the North, 404
Khartoum, 612
Khedives, 610
Khitans, 275

Khmers, 305, 309–310
Khoikhoi, 457–458
Khomeini, Ayatollah Ruhollah, 822–824, 824*f*
Khrushchev, Nikita, 776
Khwarazm Empire, 314, 320, 324
Kiev, 215
Kievan Rus', 215–218
  Christianity in, 216
  culture in, 216–217
  decline of, 217
  trade patterns in, 215
Koguryo, 302
Kongo, kingdom of, 200, 429, 447, 451, 452
Korea, 302–305
  aristocratic families in, 304
  ceramics in, 304*f*
  Koryo collapse and, 304–305
  post-WWII recovery of, 833–834, 834*f*
  Sinification of elite culture in, 303–304
  spread of Chinese civilization to, 302–305
  Tang alliances and conquest of, 302–303
  Three Kingdoms Era of, 302*m*
  world economy and, 370
  Yi dynasty in, 305
Korean War, 833–834
Koryo collapse, 304–305
Kraal, 459*f*
Kremlin, 404
Krises (knives), 179
Kubilai Khan, 316, 326–330, 327*f*
Kulaks (entrepreneurs), 635
Kulikova, Battle of, 323
Kuriltai, 318
Kush, 21, 21*m*
  ancient, Muslim attempts to penetrate, 188–189
  Axum and, 188, 189
  developments and heritage of, 107, 109
  people of, 65–66

L
Lake Chad, 453, 457
Lake Malawi, 459
Lake Texcoco, 247, 248, 248*m*
Lake Titicaca, 255
Landa, Diego de, 431
Land Freedom Army, 744
Landlords, aristocratic, 402
Language
  Arabic, 162
  Hindi, 234
  Nahuatl, 247, 251
  of North America, 263
  Quechua, 255
  Sanskrit, 63, 234
  vernacular, 113, 234
  Yoruba-speaking peoples, 197
Large Bathers, The (painting), 542
Las Casas, Bartolomé de, 422, 422*f*, 425
Lateen sails, 162, 163
Latin America, 416–443, 417*f*, 437*m*. *See also* Brazil; Spain
  Argentina and, 586–587, 597
  Bourbon reforms in, 438–439
  castas society in, 434, 435
  caudillos and, 581
  church and, 430–431, 581–582
  commerce in, 429–430
  conquests and, 418–425, 419*m*
    Caribbean and, 420–422, 420*f*
    chronology of, 419–420
    conquerors and, 424–425
    Iberian society and, 418–419
    major expeditions of, 419*m*
    morality and, 425
    paths of, 422, 424
  consolidation of, 574–601
  cultural expression after independence in, 591–592
  economy in
    colonial, 427–431
    great boom, 1880-1920, 593
    resurgence of, liberal politics and, 584
    stagnation of, mid-century, 583–584
    underdevelopment of, explained, 594–595
  gender in, 591
  government of, 427–431
  haciendas of, 428
  independent states of, 580*m*
  indigenous societies in, 426–427
  industrialization and, 693
  industry in, 429–430
  multiracial societies in, 434–436
  nations of, 575–582
  politics in, 436–438, 576–577, 580–581
  post-WWII, 784–801
    Cuban revolution and, 788–790
    culture of despair and hope, 800–801
    democratic trends in, 793
    Guatemala and, reform and U.S. intervention in, 787–788
    human rights in, 20th century, 794–795
    literature in, 790–791
    Mexico and the PRI, 785–786
    movement of people and, 799–800
    population of, 800*t*
    radical and revolutionary solutions in, 786–787
    reform and military options in, 790–791
    soldiers take power in, 791–793
    U.S. military interventions in, 794–797, 796*m*
    women's roles and, 798–799, 798*f*
  race in, 591–592
  reconquest of, 418
  reforms of, 18th century, 436–441
  revolts in, 440–441
  ruling of, 430–431
  silver in, discovery of, 427, 427*f*
  social class in, 591–592
  societies in, 591–598
  Spanish American independence struggles in, 577–578
  state in, 430–431
  trade in, 436–438
  villages of, 428
  women of, 436, 436*f*
  world markets of, 582–591
Latvians, 868
Law and law codes
  in China, 46, 48, 54
  of dharma, 65, 69
  of Hammurabi, 20, 21
  in India, 66
  Islamic, 144, 151, 152, 194
  in Mesopotamia, 52
  in patriarchal societies, 52, 53
  Roman, 90, 91
  of Shi Huangdi, 46
  Twelve Tables of, 91
League of Nations, 671
League of Public Good, 238*f*
Le dynasty, 307

Lee Kuan Yew, 841
Legalism, 49–50, 421
Legitimacy, 400
Leguizamon, Mancio Serra de, 416
Lenin (Ulyanov, Vladimir Ilyich), 634
Leon, Pedro Cieza de, 422
Leone, Sierra, 456
Lepanto, 368, 476, 476*f*
Lesotho, 459
Lesser Antilles, 421–422
Letrados, 430
Let Us Now Praise Famous Men, 706*f*
Levelers, 388
Liang Qichao, 622
Liao dynasty, 275
Liberal Democratic Party, 833, 835
Liberals, 532
Liberation theology, 790–791
Li Bo (poet), 284–285
Li Dazhao, 702
Life in the Argentine Republic in the Days of the Tyrants,
     or Civilization and Barbarism (Sarmiento), 589
Lima, 371
Limpopo River, 457
Lin Biao, 844
Lin Zexu, 619
Lisbon, Portugal, 498*f*
Literature. *See also* Poetry
   in Abbasid dynasty, 169–170
   in China, 51, 52
   in emerging nations, 813
   in Greece, 94, 96
   in Imperial age of Japan, 294–295
   in India, 63, 71
   in Industrial Revolution, 541
   in Latin America, 591, 790–791
   medieval, 234
   in Rome, 114
   in Tang-Song dynasties, 283–284
   vernacular, 234
   in Vietnam, 306–307, 311
Lithuania, 413
Liu Shaoqui, 847
Li Yuan, 269
Lloyd George, David, 670
Loango, 455, 455*f*
Locke, John, 374, 390
Long March, 704
Louis XI, King, 238*f*
Louis XIV, King, 372, 391, 392
Louis XVI, King, 530
Low Countries, 227, 235, 382
Luanda, 447, 460
Luddism, 536
Luo, 456
Luther, Martin, 383
Luzon, 501
Ly Van Phúc, 290

M
Macao, 507
Macedonia, 401
Machiavelli, Niccolo, 381
Madero, Francisco, 693
Madrasas (Islamic religious schools), 558
Magellan, Ferdinand, 363
Maghrib, 187
Magi (Zoroastrian priests), 84

Magna Carta, 227
Mahabharata (epic), 63, 72
Mahayana Buddhism, 271–272
Mahdi (deliverer), 611–613
Mahdists, 822
Mahmud II, 605
Mahmud of Ghazni, 175
Maipu, Battle of, 579*f*
Maize, 450
Malacca, 180–181
Malaria, 450
Male dominance
   in patriarchal societies, 52, 53
   in Tang-Song dynasties, 281–282
Mali, 184, 190–191, 192, 446
Mamaconas (chosen women), 260*f*
Mamluks (Turkic slaves), 172, 173
Manchus society, 616
Mandarin Chinese, 44
Mandates, 678
Mandela, Nelson, 825–826
Manifest destiny, 585
Manioc, 450
Manorialism, 221–222
Mansa Musa, 184, 185*m*
Maori, 347–348
Mao Zedong, 700, 702, 704, 843–850, 844*f.*
         See also People's Republic of China
Maran, René, 564
Marathon, Battle of, 80, 81*f*
Marattas, 491
Marco Polo, 320, 328, 329*f*
Maritime power, in world economy, 360–366
Marquis of Pombal, 439
Marriage. *See also* Intermarriage
   in Arabian world, pre-Islamic, 141
   in Aztec society, 252
   child marriage in Mughal India, 384
   in European-style families, 383
   in Latin America, 435, 436
   in Manchus society, 616
   in patriarchal societies, 52, 53
   Protestantism and, 385
   of Russian nobility, 407
   in Tang and Song dynasties, 281, 282
   in western civilization, 396, 397
Marshall Plan, 754, 756
Martel, Charles, 149, 223
Martín Fierro (Hernández), 591
Marx, Karl, 538–539
Mass consumerism, 396
Mass leisure culture, 540
Mataram, 554
Mathematics
   Chinese, 52
   Egyptian, 21, 22, 25, 26
   in Greece, 93
   Hindu, 174–175
   in India, 71–72
   Islamic contribution to, 159
   Sumerian, 19
Mauritius, 456
Mauryan Empire, 65–66
Mawali (non-Arab converts to Islam), 150, 152, 155
Maya, 111
May Day parade, 773, 779*f*
May Fourth movement, 700–702
McDonald's, in Soviet Union, 864*f*

Measles, 367
Mecca, 140–141
  Islamic conversion of, 143–144
  Ka'ba in, 144, 145*f*
  pilgrimage to, 145
Medina, 138, 141, 142, 143–144, 149
Mediterranean civilization, 80–103. *See also*
    Greco-Roman civilization; Persia (Iran)
  economy in, 95–98
  overview of, 80–82
  society in, 95–98
Meenakshi Sundareswarar Temple, 61*f*
Mehmed II, 469, 471
Meiji, 639–640
Menchú, Rigoberta, 791
Mercantilism/mercantilists, 368, 498
Merchant guild, 429
Mesoamerica, postclassical, 244–265
  Aztecs in, 247–254
  cultural patterns in, 262–263
  Incas in, 254–261
  Native American populations in, 261–262,
      261–262*t*
  societies in, 263
  Toltecs in, 245–247
Mesopotamia, 19, 20*m*
Mestizos, 369, 434
Metalworking, 15, 260
Methodius (missionary), 213–214
Mexica (Aztecs), 247
Mexican Constitution of 1917, 694
Mexican Revolution, 693–694
Mexico
  culture and politics in, 694–695
  economic transformation in, 594–597
  independence and, 577
  instability and foreign intervention and, 584–586
  Maximilian von Habsburg and, 574, 575*f*, 585–586
  PRI and, 785–786
  revolution in, 693–694
Mexico City, 424
Mfecane, 458–459
Michael II, 210
Middle ages, 220–243. *See also* Western Europe
Middle East, 337
  Black Death and, 342
  China's role with, 339–334
  in Cold War era, 819*m*
  cultural changes in, 338
  fronts, in World War I, 661*m*
  international leadership, changes in, 339
  nationalism and, in World War I, 676–679, 676*m*
  new societies in, 27
  social changes in, 338
  World War II and, 731*m*, 747
Middle Kingdom, 44
Middle Passage, 460, 461
Midway Island, 736
Migrations
  to Americas, 428–429
  Asian, during Industrial Revolution, 527*f*
  globalization and, 887–888
Militant nationalism, 674–675
Millennium celebration, Sydney, Australia, 885*f*
Minamoto dynasty, 296–297
Minas Gerais, 433
Mindanao, 501
Miners, 423

Ming Empire, 331, 503
  agriculture in, 506–507
  art in, 506–507
  civil service examination system in, 503,
      504*f*, 505
  commerce of, 506–507
  decline of, 509–510
  Europeans in, arrival of, 507–508
  expansion of, 507–508
  Indian Ocean expeditions of, 509
  political reform in, 503–504
  population of, 506–507
  predicament of, 509
  retreat of, 507–508
  scholar-gentry social dominance in, 503, 504–506
  women in, 506, 506*f*
  Zheng He expeditions and, 507–508, 507*m*,
      509, 510–511
Minh Mang, Emperor, 850
Mining, 427, 449
Ministry of Rites, 270
Mira Bai, 177
Mississippi River, 372
Miss World contest protest, India, 883*f*
Mita (labor turns), 257
Moctezuma II, 248, 424
Mohenjo Daro, 22
Moldboard, 222
Mongol Empire, 172
  assaults on
    Islamic world, 319, 324–326
    Khwarazm Empire, 320
  cavalry, 315*f*, 318, 320, 323, 329
  in Chinese history, 326–332
    cultural influences, 328
    gender roles, 327
    scholar-gentry resistance, 432–433
    social policies, 328–329
  under Chinggis Khan, 319–325
  conquest of, 329–331
  cross-cultural exchange in, 320–321, 325*f*
  division of, 321–322
  global exchange network in, 325, 325*m*
  incursions in, 324
  khanates of, 322, 322*m*
  movement of, western, 317*f*, 322–326
  retreat from Europe, 324
  Russia and, 323–324, 401–402
  trade with, long distance, 320–321, 325*f*
  warriors, 318–319
Monotheism, 28
Monroe Doctrine, 582
Monsoons, 63
Montagu-Chelmsford reforms, 675
Monumental architecture, 19, 20, 85, 607
Morley-Minto reforms, 675
Moscow, 402, 404
Mosques, 156–157
  in Abbasid dynasty, 159
  Al-Aqsa Mosque, 157*f*
  architecture of, 195, 195*f*
  at Jenne, 191, 191*f*
  in Safavid Empire, 481–482
  Shah (in Isfahan, Iran), 156*f*
  Shahi (in Kush mountains, Pakistan), 175*f*
Mozambique Island, 447, 456
Mu'awiya, 149
Mubarak, Hosni, 821

Mughal Empire, 403, 404, 468, 470*m*, 484–491, 485*m*
  Akbar's religious syncretism and, 485–486
  artistic achievements of, 487–489
  culture of, 485–486
  decline of, 490–491
  European contacts with, 486–487
  gender relations in, 486
  Hindu allies of, 485–486
  political system of, 489–490
  sati, eradication of, 486, 487*f*, 490
  social reform of, 486
  women in, 489–490
Muhammad (prophet), 142–145, 457
Muhammad, Shafika, 658, 659
Muhammad of Ghur, 175
Muhammad the Great, 193
Muhammad ibn Qasim, 174
Mullahs, 480–481
Multinational corporations in 2000, 886, 886*m*
Multinational empires, 404
Multiracial societies, 434–436
Mumtaz Mahal, 489
Muqaddimah, The (Ibn Khaldun), 168
Murad, 608
Murasaki, Lady, 294, 311
Muslim Brotherhood, 818–819
Muslim League, 740
Muslims, 470*m. See also* Shi'a Muslims
  in India, Sultanate period and, 178, 179–180
  indifference to Europe, 477
  intermarriage of, 176
  Kush and, 188–189
  Mughal Empire, 468, 484–491, 485*m*
  Ottoman Empire, 468, 469–477, 470*m*
  reform movements of, 457
  revolt of, in World War II, 740–741
  Safavid Empire, 468, 477–484, 478*m*
  as slaves, 451
  in South Asia, 174–176, 174*m*, 178, 179–180
  Sunnis, 149
Mussolini, Benito, 690
Mvemba, Nzinga, 447
Mwene Mutapa, kingdom of, 201–202

N
Nabobs, 557
Nadir Khan Afshar, 484
Naipaul, V. S., 813
Nantes, edict of, 385
Napoleonic Wars, 531, 532*m*
Nara, 396–397
Nasser, Gamal Abdul, 742*f*, 818–820, 818*f*
Natal, 569
Natchez, 263
National Action party (PAN), 785
National Congress party, 673–674
Nationalism, 531, 805–829
  in Africa, 806–810, 808*m*
  Balkan, 546–547
  cold war rivalries and, 813–816
  communal conflicts and, 814–815
  cultural creativity and, 813
  environmental concerns and, 810–811
  globalization and, 827, 893–894
  industrialization and, 813–816
  neocolonialism and, 813–816
  in Pakistan, 815
  population explosion and, 806–810

  South Asia and, 807
  in Vietnam, 851–852
  women and, subordination of, 812–813
Nationalism, in World War I, 671–683
  Africa and, 681–683, 682*f*
  British and, 673–674
  Egypt and, 679, 681
  Gandhi and, 675–676
  India and, 673–674
  mass movement and, social foundations of, 674
  Middle East and, 676–679, 676*m*
  militant nationalism, rise of, 674–675
  spread of, 675–676
  women and, 680
National Liberation Front (FLN), 744
National Socialist party, 726
National Women's Conference, 767*f*
Nation-states, 393
Native Americans, 244
  in Andes, 260–263, 261*t*
  cultural diversity of, 262–263
  irrigation and, 263
  population of, 261–262, 261–262*t*
Nawab (ruler), 555
Nazism, rise of, 708–709
Négritude movement, 682
Nehru, Jawaharlal, 812, 813
Neocolonialism, 813–816
Neo-Confucians, 276–277
Neolithic Age, 12
Neolithic revolution, 12
  early agriculture in, geography of, 13
  patterns of change in, 13–14
  technological changes in, 15
Neruda, Pablo, 796
Nestorians, 148
New Deal, 708
New Economic Policy, 697
New feminism, 767–767
New France, 372–373
New Granada, 438
New Spain, 424, 426*f*, 429, 430, 431, 532*f*
New Testament of the Christian Bible, 121
Newton, Isaac, 390
New World, 416, 420
New World Order, 377
New Zealand, 691*m*
  Industrial Revolution and, 545–346, 545*m*
  Maori of, disruptions and dangers in, 570
Nezhualcoyotl, 249–250
Nguni, 458
Nguyen Anh (Gia Long), 850
Nguyen Du, 311
Nguyen dynasty, 310–311
Nicholas II, 665
Nigeria, 193, 197, 200
Nirvana, 70, 71
Nkrumah, Kwame, 742–743, 742*f*, 817–818, 817*f*
Nobili, Robert di, 502
Nobunaga, Oda, 511–512
No Longer at Ease (novel), 813
Nomads, 18. *See also* Bedouins; Chinggis Khan; Mongol Empire
  camel, 137, 138, 142
  cross-civilization contacts and exchanges and, 108–109
  decline of, 330–331
  European assessment of, 320
  postclassical, 314–335
  Timur-i-Lang and, 332

North Africa
  in Classical Period, 117–118
  Islam in, arrival of, 187–188
North America, colonial expansion in, 375
North American Free Trade Agreement (NAFTA), 785,
    786*f*, 892
North Atlantic Treaty Organization (NATO), 755, 756, 874
Northern Europe, 110
  in Classical Period, 110
  expeditions, 364–366, 366*m*
Northern Renaissance, 382
North Vietnam, 853*m*
Notre-Dame (Our Lady), 234*f*
Nubia, 188–189. *See also* Kush
Nude Descending a Staircase, No. 2 (painting), 689*f*
Numbering systems
  Arabic, 175
  Inca, 260
  Indian, 71, 159
  Phoenician, 27
  quipu, 260
  Sumerian, 18
Nurhaci (Manchu leader), 613
Nur Jahan, 489–490
Nutmeg, 500, 500*f*

O
Oases, 137, 140*f*
Oba, 200*f*
Oba, 455
Obeah, 464
Obregón, Alvaro, 694
Octavian. *See* Augustus Caesar
Oduduwa, legend of, 197, 198
Odyssey (Homer), 94
Oedipus complex, 94
Ogboni, 199
Ogedei, 321–322, 324, 326
Old Believers, 405
Old Testament, 452
Olmec culture, 110
Olympic Games, 85
Omar Khayyam, 169, 170
Oracles, 24
Order of Saint Clare, 230
Ormuz, 499
Orozco, José Clemente, 694–695
Orthodox Church, 323
Osei Tutu, 454
Ottawa Citizen, 875*f*
Ottoman Empire, 403, 405, 413, 468, 469–477, 470*m*
  Balkans and, 470, 472
  Constantinople and, 472*f*, 473–475
  decline of, 475
  expansion of, 471*m*
  gender roles in, 482–484
  Iberian expansionism in, 476–477
  from late 18th century to WWI, 614*m*
  Lepanto battle and, 476, 476*f*
  military reserves in, 476–477
  reform in, 604–606
  repression in, 606–607
  retreat of, 476–477, 603–607
  revolt of, 606–607
  Safavid Empire *vs.*, 482–484
  sultans of, 473
  survival of, 604–606
  warfare of, 472–473

Ottoman Society for Union and Progress, 606
Oyo, 199, 455

P
Pachacuti, 255
Pacific ocean regions
  tragedies in, 569–570
  white settler colonies in, 567–568
Pacific Rim
  countries in, 831
  development in, 838–839
  growth indices of, 840
  Taiwan and, 839–841
  themes and problems in, 841
  as U.S. policy issue, 842
Paekche, 302, 303
Pakistan, 175*f*, 815
Paleolithic Age, 10–12
Palestine, 746, 746*m*
Palmares, 464
Pamela (Richardson), 396
Pan-African organizations, 682
Panama, 371, 424
Panama Canal, 598, 599*f*
Pankhurst, Emmeline Goulden, 539
Parliamentary monarchy, 393
Parliaments, 227
Parthian Empire, 116–117
Partition
  of Africa, 562*m*
  of Palestine, 746, 746*m*
  of Poland, 409–410, 729
  of Southeast Asia, 563*m*
Party cadres, 844
Pasteur, Louis, 535
Patriarchal societies, 52, 53
Paul, 121
Paulistas, 433
Peace of Paris, 670–671, 670*f*
Pearl Harbor, 734–735
Peasants
  forces in warlord era in Japan,
    299–300
  labor of, in France, 223
  peasant–landlord battles, 235
  in Russia, oppressed, 411
Pedro I, 579, 588
Pedro II, 590
Peloponnesian Wars, 86
Peninsulares, 435–436
Penn, William, 372
People Made New, A (Liang Qichao), 622
People's Democratic Republic of Korea, 833
People's Liberation Army, 844
People's Republic of China, 843–850, 843*m*.
    See also China
  communism in, 844
  Cultural Revolution and, 848–849, 849*f*
  economic growth in, 844–845
  Gang of Four and, 848–849
  Great Leap Forward and, 845–847, 846*f*
  social justice in, 844–845
  women in, 847–848
Perestroika (economic restructuring), 864
Pericles, 86
Perón, Evita, 784*f*
Perón, Juan, 712–713, 784, 784*f*, 786
Perry, Matthew, 639

Persia (Iran)
  art in, 84, 84*f*
  bureaucracy in, 84
  innovations of, 83–84
  literature in, 169–170
  politics of, 83–84, 95
  Sasanian Empire of, 147
  Zoroastrianism in, 84
Persian Gulf War, 872*f*
Peru, 429
Peter I ("the Great"), 405–406, 407,
    408*f*
Petrarch, Francesco, 344, 381
Pharaoh, 20, 21
Pheidippides, 80
Philip II of Macedon, 86
Philip III, King, 423
Philip of Anjou, 438
Philippine Islands, 377
Philosophy
  Greco-Roman, 93–95
  medieval, 233
Phoenicians, 27
Phoenix Pavilion, 273*f*
Piano Carpini, Giovanni de, 320
Picasso, Pablo, 711, 711*f*
Pinochet, Augusto, 782, 783*f*
Pinsker, Leon, 678
Pizarro, Francisco, 371, 371*f*, 424
Plassey, battle at, 555
Pochteca, 250
Poetry
  Aryan, 23
  Aztec, 249–250
  bedouin, 141
  Hindu, 177
  in Imperial age of Japan, 295
  medieval, 234
  Persian, 169–170
  in Tang-Song dynasties, 284–285
  in Vietnam, 307
Poitiers, Battle of, 149
Pokémon, 889*f*
Poland, 382, 413, 729
Polis, 88
Politburo, 718
Political causation, 365
Politics
  in Byzantine Empire, 209–210
  in China, 41–42, 46–48, 55
  in Greco-Roman civilization, 88,
    90–92
  in India, 66–67
  Persian, 83–84, 95
  in Song dynasty, 275–276
  in South Asia, after spread of Islam, 174
  Sumerian, 20–21
Polygamy, 192
Polygyny, 451
Polynesia
  art in, 347
  in Classical Period, 112
  conquest of, 347
  expansion of, 347, 347*m*
  Maori achievements and, 347–348
  migration of, 347
Polytheism, 20
Poma, Guaman, 423
Pombal, 439–440

Poor Clares, 230
Pope, 121
Popular Front, 707
Population explosion, 806–810
Population revolution, 528–529
Porteños (Buenos Aires residents), 577
Porto Novo, 460
Portugal. *See also* Latin America
  art in, 456, 456*f*
  Bourbon reforms in, 439
  Calicut encounter and, 498–500, 498*f*
  Christianity and, conversion to, 447
  conquests of, 418–425
  Iberian society and, 418–419
  sugar plantations, 421*m*
  vulnerability of, 500
  world economy and, 362–364, 363*m*, 427, 429
Positivism, 584
Postclassical period
  change during, 132–134
  Chinese civilization in, spread of, 290–313
    to Japan, 291–302
    to Korea, 302–305
    reunification and renaissance of, 266–289
    Song dynasty and, 269*m*, 271–272, 274–286, 276*m*
    Tang dynasty and, 269–275, 269*m*, 278–286
    to Vietnam, 305–311
  concepts of, 132
  continuity in, 134
  in Eastern Europe: Byzantium and Orthodox Europe,
    204–219
  Islam and, rise and spread of, 136–161
    to African civilizations, 184–203
    to South and Southeast Asia, 162–183
  Islam in, rise and spread of, 136–161, 139*m*, 148*m*
  in Mesoamerica, 244–265
  nomadic challenges in, 314–335
  overview of, 130–132
  transcontinental network and, 134, 205, 337, 357
  trends and societies in, 135
  in western culture, 232–240
  in Western Europe, 220–243
  women in, 134–135
Potatoes, 394, 397
Potosi, 361*f*, 427
Potsdam Conference, 739
Pragmatists, 847
Predestination, 384
Presidencies, 555
Prester John (Buchan), 564
PRI, 785–786
Primary products, 815
Princely states, 555
Principia Mathematica (Newton), 390
Proletariat, 387
Proprietors, 423
Protestantism, 383
Protestant Reformation, 383–384
Protoglobalization, 357, 398, 507, 515
Proto-industrialization, 529
Prussia, 393, 394
Puerto Rico, 420, 598
Pugachev, Emelian, 409, 412, 412*f*
Punch magazine, 596
Punic Wars, 87
Purdah, 486
Pure land Buddhism, 271–272
Putin, Vladimir, 867–869
Puyi, Emperor, 622

Pyramids, 20, 21
Pyramids, Battle of, 609*f*

Q

Qianlong, 291*f*
Qin dynasty, 42, 44–45
Qing dynasty, 613–623
  bureaucratic breakdown of, 617–618
  Chinese Nationalist alternatives to, rise of, 621–623
  economy in, 616
  fall of, 621–623
  family life in, 616
  Opium War and, 615*m*, 618–619
  rebellion in, 619–621
  reforms in, failed, 619–621
  rise of, 613–615
  Sino-Japanese War and, 643
  social disintegration of, 617–618
Quebec, 373
Quetzalcoatl, 245–246, 249
Quipu, 260
Quit India movement, 740
Qur'an, 143, 144, 404
Quraysh, 140
Qutb-ud-din Aibak, 175

R

Radicals, 532
Rajas (kings), 175
Rajput, 113
Ramadan, 145
Ramayana, 63
Razin, Stephen, 405
Rebellion in the Backlands (da Cunha), 590
Recopilación, 430
Red Army, 697
Red Guard, 848
Red Heads, 478
Red Sea, 447, 449, 451, 456
Reformation, 413
Reform Bill of 1832, 533
Reign of Terror, 530–531. *See also* French Revolution
Reincarnation, 69
Religion. *See also specific religions*
  animism and, 124
  in China, 48–52
  distribution of, 123, 123*m*
  expansion of, 118–124
  in Greco-Roman civilization, 92
  in India, 67–71
  Judaism, 28
  monotheism, 28
  Shintoism, 110
  spread of, conversion and accommodation in, 178–179
  Sumerian, 20–21
  Zoroastrianism, 84, 117
Religious revivalism, 813
Republic of Korea, 833
Revisionism, 539, 540
Revolutions
  of 1848, 533–534
  American Revolution, 529
  French Revolution, 529–533
  Greek Revolution, 533
  Industrial Revolution, 526–549
  population revolution, 528–529
Reza, Muhammad, 822
Rhodes, Cecil, 569
Ricci, Matteo, 508

Richard the Lionhearted, 167, 230*f*
Ridda Wars, 146
Rig-Veda, 64, 68
Rio de Janeiro, 433, 590
Rio de la Plata, 438–439
Rivera, Diego, 694
River valley civilizations, 25–29
  assessment of, 28–29
  heritage of, 25, 26
  Judaism in, 28
  in Middle East, new societies in, 27
River Zab, Battle of, 153
Roaring Twenties, 687–692
  bouncing back, 687–688
  East Central Europe and, new nations of, 690–692
  fascism, rise of, 690
  industrial centers and, 688–690
Robespierre, Maximilien, 530–531
Rodó, José Enrique, 598
Roman Catholic church
  Eastern Orthodoxy and, 210–211
Romance of the Rose, The (medieval poem), 234
Romance of the West Chamber, The (musical
    drama), 329
Roman Empire, 403
Romanov, Alexis, 404, 405
Romanov, Michael, 404, 405
Romanov dynasty, 404–405
Romanov Policy, 403–405
Roman republic, 87–91
Romanticism, 541
Rome. *See also* Greco-Roman civilization
  athletic performances in, 95
  decline and fall of, 113–118
    Byzantine Empire and, 115–116
    Germanic kingdoms after invasions, 116*m*
    revival of, effort at, 115
    symptoms of decline, 114
    zones created by, 115–117, 117*m*
  literature in, 114
Rommel, Erwin, 732, 732*f*
Rosas, Juan Manuel de, 582, 587
Rowlatt Act, 675
Roy, Ram Mohun, 559
Royal African Company, 450
Rubaiyat (Omar Khayyam), 169, 170
Rural estates, 428
Rurik, 400
Russia. *See also* Soviet Union
  agriculture in, estate, 411–412
  under Catherine the Great, 408–410
  Christianity in, 216
  Constantinople and, 215, 216, 217
  dependence of, 411–412
  Eastern Europe and, 413
  economy in, 412
  estate agriculture in, 369, 411–412
  expansion of, 402–403, 403*m*, 630*m*
  factory workers in, 632
  during Great Depression
    communism in, 695–697, 698
    experimental period in, 698–700
    revolution in, 695–697
  history of, early modern, 410–413
  holdings of, by 1800, 410*m*
  Mongol Empire and, 323–324, 401–402
  peasants in, 629–630
  under Peter the Great, 406*m*
  political system of, 400–405

Russia (*cont.*)
  protest and revolution in, 633–636
    Eastern Europe and role of, 635–636
    of 1905, 634–635
    Revolution of 1905, 635, 636*f*
    Revolution of 1917, 695, 696*f*, 702, 710
    road to, 633–634
  reforms in, 627–633
    era of, 630–631
    industrialization, 631–633
    prior to, 627–629
  rise of, 400–415
  Russo-Japanese War and, 635, 635*m*
  serfdom in, 410–411
  social system of, 412
  trade with, 411–412
  tsars of, 400–405
  western contact and Romanov Policy, 403–405
  westernization of, first, 405–410
  World War II and, 732–734
Russian Orthodoxy, 211, 215

S

Sadat, Anwar, 820–821
Sa'di, 169
Safavid Empire, 468, 470*m*, 477–484, 478*m*
  arts of, 481–482
  commercial revival of, 481–482
  demise of, 484
  gender roles in, 482–484
  Ottoman Empire *vs.*, 482–484
  political system of, 479
  religion of, 480–481
  society of, 481–482
  state of, 480–481
  war and, 479
Sahagún, Bernardino de, 253, 431
Sahara, 109
Sahel grasslands, 189
Sail al-Din, 478
Saint Clare of Assisi, 230*f*
St. Clair, Jeffrey, 890
St. Lawrence River, 372, 374*f*
St. Petersburg, 406
Saladin, 167, 229, 230*f*
Saltwater slaves, 460–461
Salvador, 432
Samurai, 296
Sandhlwana, Battle of I, 551*f*
Sandinista party, 793
Sandino, Augusto, 795
San Juan, 420
Sanskrit, 63, 234
Santa Anna, General Antonio López de, 582
Santa Cruz, Andrés, 581
Santo Domingo, 420, 420*f*
São Paulo, 433, 590
Sarajevo, 662
Sarmiento, Domingo F., 587, 588–589, 591
Sasanian Empire, 141, 142, 147
Sassanid Empire, 116–117
Sati, 486, 487*f*, 490
Satyagraha, 676
Schall, Adam, 508
Schism, 211
Scholar-bureaucrats, 308, 309*f*
Scholar-gentry class, 75, 267, 270, 271*f*, 276, 285
  in Ming Empire, 503, 504–506
  in Tang-Song dynasties, 267, 270, 271*f*, 276, 285
  in Vietnam, Chinese equivalent to, 308
Scholasticism, 233
School of National Learning, 514
Science
  in Abbasid dynasty, 170–171
  in China, 24, 51, 52
  Egyptian, 21, 22, 25, 26
  in Greco-Roman civilization, 93–95
  Hindu, 174
  in India, 71–72
  Industrial Revolution and, 540–541
  Islamic contribution to, 159
  Sumerian, 19
Scientific Revolution, 389–391
Secoton, Virginia, 375*f*
Secret Army Organization (OAS), 744
Self-determination, 670
Self-strengthening movement, 621
Selim III, 605, 605*f*
Seljuk Turks, 167
Senate, 90
Seneca Falls National Women's Conference, 767*f*
Senghor, Léopold Sédar, 672, 682, 742*f*
Sepoys, 554, 555*f*
Seppuku, 296
Sépulveda, Juan Gines de, 425
Serbian Orthodoxy, 211
Serfs and serfdom, 221, 410–411
  emancipation of the, 630–631, 631*f*
Serra, Mancio, 425
Settlement colonies, 563
Seven Years War, 373, 375, 377, 438
Severe Acute Respiratory Syndrome (SARS), 891
Seville, 429
Shahi mosque (in Kush mountains, Pakistan), 175*f*
Shah mosque (in Isfahan, Iran), 156*f*
Shah-Nama (Book of Kings) (Firdawski), 169
Shah Suleyman I, 483*f*
Shaka, 458–459
Shakespeare, William, 382
Shakuntala (Kalidasa play), 69
Shang era, 24
Sharia (Islamic law), 194
Shaykhs, 138
Shcherbakov, 718*f*
Sheriffs, 226–227
Shi'a Muslims
  as Abbasid party ally, 152
  rejected by Abbasid party, 154
  in Safavid Empire, 468, 470*m*, 477–484, 478*m*
  Umayyad rule rejected by, 149
Shi Huangdi, 42, 44–45, 46
Shintoism, 110, 301
Shiva (god of destruction and reproduction), 68, 69, 69*f*
Shogunate, 636–637
Shoguns, 297
Shrivijaya, 180
Siffin, Battle of, 149
Sijilimasa, 187
Sikhs, 491
Silk Road, 57, 108
Silla, 302, 303
Silver, discovery of, 427, 427*f*
Singapore, 834–835
Sinification
  defined, 302, 303
  of elite culture in Korea, 303–304

of Khitan, 275
in Vietnam, 306
Sino-Japanese War, 643
Sirāj ud-daula, 555
Sisulu, Walter, 825
Six Dynasties era, 268*m*, 270, 271, 278
Skara Brae, 16*f*
Slash and burn agriculture, 16, 262
Slave Coast, 449, 454
Slaves and slavery, 460–465. *See also* Slave trade
  in Abbasid dynasty, 158–159
  abolition of, 464–465
  American slave societies and, 460–463, 462*f*
  in Americas, 460
  barbarians as, 452
  in Brazil, 432–433, 432*f*, 589–590
  chattel, 451
  Creole, 462
  in Greco-Roman civilization, 96, 97–98
  human society and, 452–453
  Indians as, 426
  Islamic concept of, 451
  lives of slaves, 460
  Mamluks, 172, 173
  Muslims as, 451
  people and gods in exile and, 463–465
  politics and, 452–454
  saltwater, 460–461
  Thousand and One Nights and, 158
Slave trade
  in Africa, 445*f*, 451–457
  Atlantic, 446–451
  demographical patterns in, 449–450
  end of, 464–465
  expansion of, 448–449
  exportation of, 554–555, 554*t*
  Middle Passage and, 460, 461
  organization of, 450–451
  with Portugal, 446–448, 446*m*
  trans-Saharan, 447, 449, 453
Slavs, 214*m*
Smallpox, 367, 367*f*
Smith, Adam, 394, 465
Social death, 452
Socialism, 538–539
Socialist realism, 716, 717–718
Social question, 538–539
Sociedad de castas, 434
Societies
  Aztec, 248
  in Byzantine Empire, 209–210
  in China, 52–55
  in early civilizations, 16
  Iberian, 418–419, 476–477
  in India, 72
  Indigenous, 426–427
  Manchus, 616
  medieval, 238–240
  Mediterranean, 95–98
  in Middle East, river valley civilizations and, 27
  multiracial, 434–436
  patriarchal, 52, 53
  Postclassical period, 135
  in Safavid Empire, 481–482
  slave, 460–463, 462*f*
  in Soviet Union, 774–775
  stateless, 185
  in Tang-Song dynasties, 281

Socrates, 93
Solidarity, 771
Solzhenitsyn, Aleksandr, 773–774
Song dynasty, 269*m*, 274–286, 276*m*. *See also* Tang-Song dynasties
  Confucianism in, 276–277
  decline of, 277
  founding of, 275
  Jurchens invasion of, 277–278
  politics in, 275–276
  reform and, attempts at, 277
Songhay, 193–194, 446, 453
Song of Roland, The (medieval saga), 234
Sons of Heaven, 44
Sophocles, 94
Sotho, 458
South Africa
  apartheid in, 824–826
  British overlords in, 568–569
  European Global Order and, 568–569
  mfecane in, 459
  white settler colonies in, 457–459, 567–568
  Zulu chiefdom and, 458–459
South America, 420
South Asia, 170*m*, 172–180
  accommodation patterns of, 176, 178
  challenge of, 177, 178
  conversion patterns of, 176, 178
  Hindu revival in, 177, 178
  Indian influences on, 174–175
  missionaries in, 501–502
  Muslim invasions of, 174–176, 174*m*
  Muslim presence in, 178, 179–180
  overview of, 172, 173
  political divisions and, 174
  population of, 807
  World War II and, 735–736, 739–741
Southeast Asia, 170*m*, 180–182, 181*m*
  missionaries in, 501–502
  partition of, 563*m*
  Sufi mystics and, 181–182
  trade in, 180–181
  World War II and, 735–736, 739–741
Southern Song dynasty, 276*m*, 278
South Vietnam, 853*m*
Soviet Union. *See also* Cold war; Russia
  Chechnya revolt and, 867, 869
  clashes in, ethnic and religious, 871–872
  collectivized agriculture in, 774*f*, 775
  culture in, 773–779
  de-Stalinization of, 776–777
  domestic policies in, 772–773
  economy and society in, 774–775
  during Great Depression
    artistic policy in, 716
    economic policies in, 715
    industrialization in, 714–715
    socialist realism in, 716, 717–718
    Stalinism in, 715
  Latvians opposition to, 868
  May Day in, 773, 779*f*
  new Soviet Empire in, 770–772
  Putin and, 867–869
  space program in, 776–777, 777*f*
  as superpower, 770
  Yugoslavia and, 770–771
Spain. *See also* Latin America
  an Indian's view of, 423
  Catholicism in, 580

Spain (*cont.*)
  legalism in, 421
  New, 424, 426*f*, 430, 431
  world economy and, 362–364, 363*m*, 427, 429
Spanish-American War, 596, 598
Spanish Civil War, 709–710
Speech gene, 8
Split inheritance, 255–256
Sri Lanka, 376
Stalin, Joseph, 699–700
Stalinism, 698, 699*f*, 715–718
Stateless societies, 185
Stoics, 92
Stolypin, Piotyr, 635
Stolypin reforms, 635
Stonecutting, 260
Stupas (stone shrines), 71–72
Suárez, Inés, 425
Sub-Saharan Africa, 444
Sudan, 21, 189–195, 190*m*
  city dwellers of, 191
  common elements in, 189–190
  family in, 192
  Mahdist revolt in, 612–613
  Mali, 184, 190–191, 192
  political and social life in, 194
  slave trade and, 456–457
  Songhay, 193–194
  states in, 189–190, 194
  villagers of, 191, 192–193
Suez Canal, 610, 610*f*, 667, 821
Sufi mystics, 181–182
Sugar, 432–433, 432*f*, 449
Sugar plantations, 421*m*
Suicide rituals, 259
Sui dynasty, 113, 267–270, 269*m*, 278, 280
Sultanate period, 178, 179–180
Sultans, 176, 473
Sumer, 19*m*
Sumerians, 19–21
Summas (highest works), 233
Sundiata, 190–191, 192
Sunnis Muslims, 149
Sun Yatsen, 622
Supreme Soviet, 697, 698
Suriname, 464
Sutras, 119
Swaddling, 396
Swahili coast of East Africa. *See* East Africa, Swahili coast of
Swazi, 459
Sweet potatoes, 367
Swetham, Joseph, 395
Syncretism, 34, 118
Syndicalism, 692

T

Tagore, Rabindranath, 672
Taika reforms, 291–293
Tainos, 421–422
Taiping Rebellion, 603, 603*f*, 619–622
Taipings ("Great Peace"), 602, 620–621
Taira family, 296–297
Taiwan, 831, 834–835, 839–841
Taj Mahal, 488, 490*f*
Tale of Genji, The (Lady Murasaki), 294, 295, 311
Tale of Kieu, The (Nguyen Du), 311
Tambos (weigh stations), 257
Tamerlane, 331, 332

Tang dynasty, 113, 269–275, 269*m*, 278–286. *See also* Tang-Song dynasties
  bureaucracy in, 270
  decline of, 274–275
  emergence of, 269–270
  examination system in, 270–271
  Korean alliances and conquest of, 302–303
  rebuilding, 267, 270
Tang-Song dynasties
  agrarian expansion in, 280
  agriculture in, 280, 280*f*, 283
  anti-Buddhist backlash in, 273–274
  architecture in, 273*f*, 283, 284
  art in, 279*f*, 283–284, 285–386, 285*f*
  family in, 281
  footbinding in, 282, 282*f*
  intercontinental commercial expansion of, 278–280
  inventions in, 283–284
  literature in, 283–284
  male dominance in, 281–282
  poetry in, 284–285
  prosperity in, 278
  religion in, 271–273
  rural settlements in, 280–281
  scholar-gentry class in, 267, 270, 271*f*, 276, 285
  social values in, 284
  society in, 281
  state in, 270–273
  trade in, 278–279
  urban growth in, 280
Tang Taizong, 269
Tangut tribes, 277
Tanzimat reforms, 605
Tatars/Tartars, 217–218, 323
Tayson Rebellion, 850
Technocrat, 757
Technology
  in China, 54
  and globalization, 884–885
  in Western civilization, 383
Tehran Conference, 738
Temple architecture, 94
Temple of the Sun, 256–257
Temples of India, 60, 61*f*, 73
Tenochtitlan, 244, 245*m*, 248
"Ten thousand countries," 291*f*
Teotihuacan, 111, 245
Terakoya (commoner schools), 637
Terra-cotta objects, 197, 197*f*
Terrorism
  September 11, 2001 attacks and, 875–878, 878*f*
  United States' response to, 875, 878
Theology in western culture, 232–233
Third Rome, 400, 402
Thirty Years War, 385
Thousand and One Nights, The, 158
Three estates, 227
Three-field system, 222, 223, 397
Three Kingdoms Era of Korea, 302*m*
Tigris-Euphrates civilizations, 19, 20–21
Tihuanaco, 254, 255
Tilak, B. G., 674–674
Timber, 373
Timbuktu, 191, 193, 195, 451
Time of Troubles, 404
Timurid, 330–331
Timur-i Lang, 331, 332
Tlaloc (god of rain), 248, 249

Tlaxcala, 254
Tobacco, 439–440
Tocqueville, Alexis de, 410
Tokugawa Shogunate, 302, 511, 512, 512*m*
Toltecs, 245–247
  burial mounds, 247
  culture of, 245–247, 246*f*
  heritage of, 245–246
  influence of, 246–247
Tomb art, 22, 22*f*, 108*f*
Topac Yupanqui, 255
Topiltzin, 245–246
Topkapi Palace, 605*f*
Totalitarian state, 709, 717–718
Total war, 740
Trade, 155
  in Abbasid dynasty, 155
  in Africa, 76, 77*m*, 187, 189, 190–193
  Afro-Eurasian, 155
  in Arabian world, pre-Islamic, 140–141
  Asian, 496–502, 497*m*
  in China, 54
  Dutch trading empire, 500
  English trading empire, 500
  Eurasian, 76, 77*m*
  in India, 62, 64, 65, 73
  in Kievan Rus', 215
  oases and, 140*f*
  pack animals used in, 143*f*
  Portuguese trade posts and, 446
  routes, at end of Classical Period, 109*m*
  Russian, 411–412
  in Southeast Asia, 180–181
  in Tang-Song dynasties, 278–279
  triangular, 450
  in Vietnam, 307–308
  in western culture, 235–237
  world economy and, 369–370
Transcontinental Empire, 315*m*, 316–322
Transcontinental network, 134, 205, 337, 357
Trans-Siberian railroad, 631–632
Trasformismo, 537
Treaty of Guadalupe-Hidalgo, 585
Treaty of Paris, 373
Treaty of Tordesillas, 430
Treaty of Utrecht, 438
Treaty of Westphalia, 385
Tree of Life, 381*f*
Trench warfare, in World War I, 664, 672
Triangular trade, 450
Tribute systems
  Aztec, 250–251, 254
  Chinese, 303, 339
  European, in Asia, 500–501
  Mongol, 323
  Mughal, 486
Trinh dynasty, 310
Triple Alliance, 546, 590
Triple Entente allies, 456, 610, 611*f*, 660–661,
    666, 671
Tropical dependencies, 563–564
Truman, Harry, 754
Trung sisters, 307
Tsunami, 896*f*
Tswana, 458
Tumens, 318
Tunisia, 187
Turkey, 603–607, 668

Twantinsuyu, 255, 257
Tyranny, 88

U
Uganda, 456
Ukraine, 402
Ulama (religious scholar), 171
Ulyanov, Vladimir Ilyich (Lenin), 634
Umayyads, 140, 145–153
  Arab conquests and, motives for, 146–147
  consolidation and divisions in, 146
  in Damascus, 149–150
  decline and fall of, 151, 152, 153, 154*m*
  family and gender roles in, 150–151
  Islamic converts in, 150
  succession and, 149
  Sunni-Shi'a split and, 149
  weaknesses of, 147–148
Umma (community of faithful), 144
Uncle Sam, 875*f*
Union of Soviet Socialist Republics, 697. *See also* Soviet Union
Unitarians, 587
"United Fruit Co., The" (poem), 796–797
United Fruit Company, 788
United Nations (UN), 738, 891–892
United States
  First U.S. Iraq War, 873
  Industrial Revolution and, 544, 545–546, 545*m*
  in Latin America, military interventions, 794–797, 796*m*
  Pacific Rim as policy issue for, 842
  as superpower, 874–875
  terrorism and
    response to, 875, 878
    September 11, 2001 attacks and, 875–878, 878*f*
  World War I and, 668–669
  World War II and, 738–740
Untouchables, 64
Upanishads, 63, 68
Ural Mountains, 401, 402
Urban II, Pope, 229
USSR. *See* Soviet Union
Uthman, 149

V
Vaisravana, Celestial King, 119
Valdivia, Pedro de, 424
Vargas, Getúlio, 712
Varnas, 63–64
Vassals, 226
Vedas, 63
Vedic age, 62–64
Venette, Jean de, 342
Versailles, 391
Viceroyalties, 430
Viceroys, 430
Vichy, 731
Viet Cong, 853, 854*f*
Viet Minh, 852
Vietnam
  colonialism and revolution in, 850–855
  communism in, 854–855
  divisions in Nguyen and French periods, 850*m*
  French and, war against, 852
  globalization, 854–855, 854*f*
  nationalism in, 851–852
  North Vietnam, 853*m*
  South Vietnam, 853*m*
  United States and, war against, 853–854

Vietnam, spread of Chinese civilization to, 305–311
  Chams and, 309–310
  Chinese architecture in, 310*f*
  Chinese cultural exports in, 307–308
  Chinese scholar-gentry equivalent in, 308
  Han conquest of, 305–306, 305*m*
  independence of, 307–308
  Khmers and, 305, 309–310
  Le dynasty of, 307
  literature in, 306–307, 311
  Nguyen territories in, 310–311
  poetry in, 307
  resistance against China, 306–307
  scholar-bureaucrats in, 308, 309*f*
  Sinification and conquest, 306
  Trinh family in, 310
  women in, 305, 307–308
Vietnamese Nationalist party, 852
Vikings, 220, 221, 228
Villa, Pancho, 693
Villon (poet), 234
Virgins of the Sun, 257
Vishnu (god of sacrifice), 68, 69
Vivaldis, 345
Vizier, 473
Vladimir I, 204, 205*f*, 215–216
Vodun, 464
Voortrekkers, 458

W

Wafd party, 679–681
Wang Anshi, 277–278
Warhol, Andy, 768*f*
Warlord era in Japan, 293*m*, 296–302
  architecture and, 301, 301*f*
  art and, 301–302, 301*f*
  Ashikaga Shogunate and, 297–298
  Ashikaga Takuaji and, 297
  bakufu dominance and, breakdown of, 297–298
  bushi era and, 298–299
  castles and warring houses in, 298–299
  China's influence on, declining, 297
  daimyos and, 298–300
  feudalisms and, comparing, 298
  Gempei Wars and, 297
  Kamakura regime and, 297
  peasant forces and, 299–300
  seppuku and, 296
  shoguns and, 297
  Taira and Minamoto families, feud between, 296–297
  Tokugawa shogunate and, 302
  women and, 300
War of the Spanish Succession, 438
Warring houses, in Japan, 298–299, 301*f*
Warrior elites, in Japan, 399–400
Warsaw Pact, 755, 756
Wazir (chief administrator), 154
Wealth of Nations (Smith), 394
Weaving, Portuguese, 456
Welfare state, 756–757, 757*f*
Wendi (Literary Emperor), 267
Wesley, John, 465
West Africa, 816*m*
Western civilization
  agriculture in, 397
  Black Death and, 342
  colonial expansion in, 375
  colonial patterns in, 346

  commerce, 381–385
  commercialism in, 341, 343
  Commercial Revolution during, 386–389
  culture, 381–385
  defining, 231
  dynamism in, 340–341
  during 18th century, 394–398
    commerce, 396–397
    Enlightenment, 394, 396
    innovations, 397–398
    instabilities, 397–398
    manufacturing, 396–397
    political patterns, 394
  expansion in, 345–346
  family, roles of, 383
  imitation in, 341, 343
  non-western societies evaluated and judged
    by, 258–259
  political changes during, 391–393
  populations, 341
  rise of, 340–345
  Scientific Revolution during, 389–391
  technology, 383
  transformation of, 380–399, 384*m*
  women in, controversies about, 395
Western culture, 232–240
  agricultural improvements in, 235
  architecture in, religious, 233–234
  art in, religious, 233
  banking in, 235–236, 236*f*
  Christianity and, 233
  decline of medieval society and, 238–240
  literature in, religious, 234
  peasant–landlord battles in, 235
  theology and, 232–233
  trade in, 235–237
  women in, 237–238
Western Europe
  borders in, 228*m*
  Carolingians in, 223–225
  Charlemagne in, 224–225, 224*m*, 225*f*
  church in, 222, 223
  classical, 117–118
  Crusades and, 229–230
  economic growth in, 225–226
  expansionist movements in, 228, 229–230
  colonial, 377
  feudalism in, 226–227
  in High Middle Ages, 231
  Hundred Years War and, 227, 238
  manorial system in, 221–222
  peasant labor in, 223
  population growth in, 228
  postclassical, 220–243
  Postclassical development of, 220–243
  post-WWII, 752–762
    cold war and, 753–756
    colonies of, 753
    culture of, 769–770
    diplomatic context and, 758–759, 761
    economic expansion and, 761–762
    expansion of, 759*m*
    liberal democracy in, 756
    political stability and, 758
    resurgence of, 756–762
    social structure of, 764–765
    United States and, 760
    welfare state and, 756–757

western culture and, 767–769
women's revolution and, 765–767
reconquest in, 228
religious reform in, 230, 231
Russia and, relationship between, 403–405
Vikings and, 220, 221, 228
Willibald's travels to, 229
Western Front, 663
Westernization
African middle class and, rise of, 558–559
Asian middle class and, rise of, 558–559
bankruptcy during, 610–612
civilizations during, decline of, 608–609, 614
defined, 406–408
education and, 558–559
in Egypt, failure of, 607–610
European interventions and, 610–612
faces of, 641
nature of, 407
resistance during, strategies of, 610–612
of Russia, 405–410
Whampoa Military Academy, 703
White, John, 375
White Dominions, 563
White Lotus Society, 331
White racial supremacy, 566
White supremacy, 744–746
Whydah, 455, 460
Wilberforce, William, 465
William the Conqueror, 226–227
Willibald (English monk), 229
Witchcraft persecution, 388–390, 392, 395
Witte, Sergei, 632–633
Wollstonecraft, Mary, 396, 397*f*
Women
in Abbasid dynasty, declining position of, 166
Aztec, 253
Buddhism and, 120
in Byzantine Empire, 209
in China, 52, 53
disinheritance and, 300
footbinding of, 282, 282*f*
in France, 766
as gatherers, 4, 10–11
globalization and, 900
in Latin America, 436, 436*f*, 693*f*, 798–799, 798*f*
male dominance in Tang-Song dynasties, 281–282
in Ming Empire, 506, 506*f*
in Mughal Empire, 489–490
nationalism and, 812–813
in nationalist movements, 680
in Paleolithic Age, 10–11
in patriarchal societies, 52, 53
in People's Republic of China, 847–848
Russian Revolution of 1905 and, 636*f*
sati and, 486, 487*f*, 490
in United States, 766
in Vietnam, 305, 307–308
in West, controversies about, 395
Woodcarving, Portuguese, 456
World Bank, 892
World economy, 360–379
colonial expansion of, 371–377
in Africa, 375–377
in Asia, 375–377
in backwater colonies, 372–375
of early colonies, 371–372
New World Order and, impact on, 377

in North America, 375
in western civilizations, 375
in Western Europe, 377
initiatives toward, 366–371
commercialism, 368
diseases, spread of, 367, 367*f*
expansionist trends, 370–371
food, exchange of, 367
international inequalities, 368
world trade, 369–370
maritime power in, 360–366
Northern European expeditions and, 364–366, 366*m*
in Portugal, 362–364, 363*m*
in Spain, 362–364, 363*m*
technologies of, new, 361–362
World Health Organization (WHO), 891
World Trade Center, 876, 878*f*
World Trade Organization (WTO), 890
World War I, 658–685. *See also* Nationalism, in World War I
Africa in, 667, 668*m*
Armenian genocide and, 668
Britain in, 666–668, 666*f*
brutality of, 664
Eastern Europe in, 664–665
European home fronts, 661*m*, 665–666
factors leading up to, 660–662
Germany in, 666–667
Industrial Revolution and, 546–547
Italy in, 664–665
losses, 669*t*
Middle East fronts, 661*m*
offensive warfare and, 669
outbreak of, 662–663
peace efforts, failed, 670–671
recruiting, 666, 666*f*, 668, 674, 681, 682*f*
trench warfare in, 664, 672
Triple Entente allies in, 660–661, 666, 671
Turks in, 668
United States in, 668–669
Western Front in, 663
World War II, 724–751
Africa and, 741–746
Anglo-American offensives in, 734
beginning of, 728–729
British and, 728, 730–732, 734, 741–746
causes of, 725–728
cold war and, 738–739
conduct of, 730–737
dictators and, 726, 728
Egypt and, 746
end of, 738–739
Europe and, 731*m*
French and, 727
genocide in, 733–734
global devastation and, 727
Japan and
defeat in, 734–737
invasion of China and, 728–729
invasion of Pearl Harbor, 734–735
Middle East and, 731*m*, 747
Muslim revolt and, 740–741
Nazi blitzkrieg and, 730–733
Pacific war and, 734–737
Palestine and, 746, 746*m*
Poland and, Nazi invasion of, 729
post
in East Asia, 831–832
in Eastern Europe, 770–773

World War I (*cont.*)
  in Korea, 833–834, 834*f*
  in Latin America, 784–801
  in Western Europe, 752–762
  Russia and, 732–734
  South and Southeast Asia and, 735–736,
    739–741
  superpowers and, 738–739
  United States and, 738–740
World Zionist Organization, 679
Wrigley Building, in Chicago, 689*f*
Writing. *See also* Alphabet; Literature
  calligraphy, 51
  cuneiform, 17–18, 83
  in India, 71
Wu, Empress, 272–273
Wudi, Emperor, 302
Wuzong, Emperor, 274

X

Xavier, Francis, 502
Xhosas, 458
Xuanzong, Emperor, 274–275

Y

Yalta Conference, 738–739
Yanas, 259
Yangdi emperor, 267–269
Yang Guifei, 274
Yang Jian, 267
Yangzi River basin, 270
Yaroslav, 215
Yellow peril, 644
Yellow River, 23–24

Yellow Turbans, 112
Yeltsin, Boris, 866–867
Yes and No (Abelard), 232
Yi dynasty, 305
Yoruba peoples, 197–199, 455, 464
Yuan Shikai, 700
Yugoslavia, 770–771, 872*m*

Z

Zacatecas, 427
Zaghlul, Sa'd, 679, 681
Zaibatsu, 641
Zaire River, 447
Zakat (tax or charity), 144
Zambezi River, 453, 456
Zanzibar, 456
Zapata, Emiliano, 693–694
Zapatistas, 785
Zaria, 457
Zemstvoes, 631
Zen Buddhism, 272, 301
Zeng Guofan, 620–621
Zhao Kuangyin, 275
Zheng He, 339, 507–508, 507*m*, 509, 510–511
Zhou dynasty, 43–44, 43*m*
Zhou Enlai, 847
Zhu Xi, 276
Zhu Yuanzhang, 331
Ziggurats, 19, 20
Zionists, 678–679
Zoë, Empress, 209, 209*f*
Zoroastrianism, 84, 116
Zulus, 458–459, 459*f*
Zulu Wars, 459